CROSSWORD DICTIONARY

J. A. COLEMAN

COLLINS
London and Glasgow

To Jill and Richard

British Library Cataloguing in Publication Data
Coleman, J.A.
  Crossword dictionary.
  1. Cryptic crossword puzzles. Encyclopedias.
  I. Title
  793.73′2

First published 1989
Published by William Collins Sons and Company Limited
© J.A. Coleman 1989

ISBN 0 00 434571 1

Printed in Great Britain at the Bath Press, Avon

INTRODUCTION

Why another dictionary?

There is no shortage of dictionaries for use by the crossword enthusiast so why another?

The clues in concise crosswords are usually single-part clues which require a straightforward synonym for the solution and, for this type of crossword, a general-purpose or a crossword dictionary will be adequate.

In a cryptic crossword, many of the clues will have several distinct parts, typically three. There is a direct clue (rather like the clue in the concise crossword but probably using a less common synonym); an indirect clue made up of various components (of which more later), the answer to which will give the same word as the synonym for the direct clue; and a pointer which indicates how the various components are to be manipulated to arrive at the solution. On the matter of indirect clues and pointers, ordinary dictionaries have nothing to say, and it is here that this book may be helpful. Most crossword dictionaries consist of long lists of words arranged alphabetically under the number of letters in the word; some give brief meanings, most do not, and none is very much help in the matter of indirect clues and pointers.

The compiler is looking for words to fit some particular grid and, at the outset, meanings are not important. The solver is also looking for words to fit this grid, working from the meanings given by the compiler, so, ideally, he needs to be able to look up the meaning and find the word rather than the other way round. From the point of view of the solver, a general-purpose or a typical crossword dictionary is deficient in one or more of the ways listed below.

1. It will tell you that the abbreviation NL (Latin *non licet*) means 'not permitted'; it will not tell you, if you are looking for a solution that means 'not permitted', that you need NL.
2. It will tell you that C is an abbreviation for 'about' (in the sense of approximately) but not that this C can be combined with, say, AGE to provide a solution to 'about time' (CAGE).
3. Fathead will be defined as 'dullard'; in compiler's language Fat*head* is the letter F and, once you have appreciated this, you will easily recognise cock*tail* as the letter K.
4. You can look up 'headless' and 'women' without ever learning that '*headless* women' means OMEN.
5. It will define 'legend' but will not acknowledge the fact that this is a concealed compound which can be read as 'leg end' and can therefore be translated as FOOT or TOE.
6. It will define both 'revolutionary' and 'part' without any mention of the fact that '*revolutionary* part' means TRAP.
7. In the dictionary, 'crazy' and 'idea' will have their separate meanings; to the compiler, 'crazy' indicates an anagram so these two words translate as one, i.e. AIDE.
8. A dictionary will tell you the meanings of words such as SOFTA (Moslem student), SEMMIT (Scots undershirt), SPRUIT (water-course in Africa), ALOGIA (without speech), ACINACIFORM (scimitar-shaped), ALGATE (altogether, in Spenser) but, in a crossword, you are given the words in brackets and you cannot look up the words from the meanings.
9. Dictionaries use conventional definitions; compilers think laterally so, in their language, a banker is a river, a river is a flower and a flower is a bloomer.

Introduction

In the following pages you will find many examples like those listed above.

The compiler's language consists not only of normal words used in their everyday context as most of us know it but of those same words bearing the most obscure meanings that the compiler can find, plus a very varied assortment of puns, double meanings, anagrams, hidden words, abbreviations, odd letters selected from words, part-words and so on. It would be impossible in a book of this size to list all possible variations of these factors but it is hoped that sufficient examples have been given to introduce you to the way the compiler thinks.

The construction of clues

If, in a concise crossword, a solution requires a word you have never come across, you will (unless you can make an inspired guess from letters already entered) be at a bit of a loss.

Given the same situation in a cryptic crossword, it is often possible to find the solution in the form of a word you have never met before simply by manipulating the various components of the indirect clue as indicated by the pointer given in the clue. For example, 'Eastern dancer's clumsy look in revolution' requires the word ALMAH as the solution. If you can see the indirect clues HAM (clumsy) and LA (look) and appreciate that the pointer *in revolution* indicates reversal, you may well get to ALMAH even though you have never met the word before.

The components of indirect clues are listed below together, in each case, with an example of how they are used and some typical pointers which, throughout the book, are printed in italics (see key on p. x).

Abbreviations

recognised ones, such as SS for steamship
•Direction of each [EA] street [ST](4) = EAST

briefly, contracted, initially, shortly, small

'compiler's language' forms, such as NS for North Sea
•Plant BBC boss [DG] *in* a bishopric [SE-E] (5) = SEDGE

Anagrams

letters, usually from given words, re-arranged to form another word
•Ted isn't *upsetting* a surgeon (7) = DENTIST

dozens of words implying breaking, changing, etc.

Articles

such as 'a' and 'an', printed in the clue and used as part of the solution
•She *needs* a [A] comfortable situation [BERTH] (5) = BERTHA

no pointers

– including foreign versions such as 'la', 'der', etc.
•Hidden in the *French* [LA] shelter [TENT] (6) = LATENT

names of languages or countries, *Continental, exotic, foreign, Gallic*

Cockney expressions and words

such as 'Apples and pears' (for stairs) and words from which the initial 'h' has been dropped.

Cockney, Eliza said, in Bow, in East End

•Part of City which *Cockney* is
mending [(H)EALING] (6) =
EALING

Colloquialisms or careless speech
such as 'ain't' or ''otter'   *carelessly, commonly, local*
•Alter them *commonly* [EM] at last
[END] (5) = EMEND

Compound words
which are intended to be read as two   pointers contained in the compound
separate words so that 'setback'   word itself
reads as 'set back' (i.e. written
backwards to make TES)
•Weak up*turn* [PU] leading to US city
[NY] (4) = PUNY
or concealed compounds such as   no pointers
'grimace' which can be read as two
words, 'grim' and 'ace', to mean
'grave expert'

Derived words
words derived from words given in   no pointers
the clue, as distinct from given words
•Very thin female [SHE] *beside* the
queen [ER] (5) = SHEER

Foreign words
quite often appear, frequently   name of language or country,
combined with English words   *Continental, exotic, foreign, Gallic*
•Many [D] *in* the *French* street [RU-E]
appear uncouth
(4) = RUDE

Given words
are words printed in the clue which   no pointers
are used, as printed, in the solution
•Bar [BAR] offer [TENDER] *for*
serving-man (9) = BARTENDER

Hidden words
are words forming part of given   *concealed in, embraced by,*
words   *enclosing, evidently, featuring, from,*
•Feature of *some* Fren/ch in/sults   *ingredients of, part of, seen in, some,*
(4) = CHIN   *worn by*

Homophones
words which sound the same as   *say, so to speak, they say, verbal,*
words given in the clue but which   *vocally, we hear*
have different meanings
•Suitable as supporter [PROPPER], *so*
I'm told (6) = PROPER

Numbers
particularly Roman numerals, are   *figure, many, several, some, many,*
often used to represent letters   *number*
•Kind of dignitary is 104 [CIV], I see
[IC] (5) = CIVIC

Old words
obsolete and archaic words are used in crosswords even though banned in some other word games
•Foot soldier of the *old* [YE] Gulf State [OMAN] (6) = YEOMAN

ancient, as before, former, once, one-time, stale

Part words
the clue may be so worded as to require the use of part of a given or derived word
•Youngster may pinch [NIP] *some* pepper [PER] (6) = NIPPER

bulk of, lump of, part of, piece of, share of, some

Poetic words
words used mainly by writers such as Spenser, Shakespeare, etc.
•Spenser's named member [MP] caught in trap [NE-T] (5) = NEMPT

use of writer's name, *poetically, the old poet's, the poet said*

Proper nouns
including personal names, are used, often in place of common nouns
•A girl [EVA] and a boy [DES] *make* escapes (6) = EVADES

Quotations
from literature, the Bible, the classics, history, etc., which may be direct
•'Stiffen the sinews, . . .up the blood' (*Henry V*) (6)

no pointers

or indirect
•One of the listeners requested by Antony *in* t/ear/s (3) = EAR

pointers as for any other type of clue

Rhymes
the solution is a word which rhymes with the direct clue
•Master her *rhymes* (3) = SIR

rhymes, rhyming

Selected letters
various devices are used to select letters for omission
•Man *executed* woman [(M)ADAM] (4) = ADAM

cut, headless, heartless, loveless, nearly all

or for retention for use in the solution
•Seed from these long dog *tails* (3) = EGG

beginnings, end of, finally, leaders, middles, origins, start

Singulars and plurals
'singular' words may be half of
another singular word which has two
identical parts
•Give away secrets *twice* in US prison
 [SING-SING] (4) = SING

double, twice, repeated

'plural' words may require the
repeated use of a singular word
•Being [IS] *twice* a goddess
 (4) = ISIS

Small words
insignificant given words which can
easily be overlooked
•Hat [CAP] on [ON] chicken
 (5) = CAPON

no pointers

Split words
any word can be split to allow
another word to be written inside;
some are particular favourites
•Hindrance [LET] *in*deed [DE-ED]
 blotted out (7) = DELETED
and abbreviations may be treated in
the same way
•Stays first [TOP] *in* ship [S-S]
 (5) = STOPS

*about, among, around, capturing,
carrying, catching, covered by,
embracing, holding, imprisoned by,
in, including, interrupting,
introducing, keeping, protecting,
retained by, round, surrounding,
swallowed by, without*

Stuttered words
which allow the doubling of the
stuttered letter
•Refer to a [A] *stuttering* sound
 [P'PEAL] (6) = APPEAL

stammering, stuttering

•G-general [LEE] mirth
 (4) = GLEE

repeated letter

Synonyms
straight synonyms may involve
several words with the same meaning
•Tin chimney-pot in prison
 (3) = CAN

no pointers

oblique descriptions are punning or
elaborately worded references to the
solution
•Race starter? (4) = ADAM

elaborate or unusual phraseology, use
of ?

one of a class; a general class is given,
requiring a particular example for the
solution
•Cat, *for example*, of light weight (5) =
 OUNCE or vice versa
•Private, *maybe*, but in company (7) =
 SOLDIER

*for example, for instance, maybe,
perhaps, possibly, sort of*

the particular example may be a town or county representing a general area or a country
•Man *from Glasgow* [MON] looked [EYED] wealthy (7) = MONEYED
or a phrase that implies an area or country

across the Channel, Continental, North of the Border

•Persevere through [PER] delay north of the Border [SIST] (7) = PERSIST
and the general class may be an alphabet of which any letter (character) may be the particular example

classical characters, exotic letters, foreign characters, Greek characters, Hebrew characters

opposite/negative clues require a solution which is the reverse of the word derived from the clue

apparently, on the contrary, opposite, presumably, reverse

•Information about high [HIGH] county [DOWN]? *On the contrary* (7) = LOWDOWN

Any of these components can be combined in one or more of several different ways to form the solution. The various operations that can be used to put the components together are listed below using the same notation.

Addition
parts added together to give the solution
•Member [LEG] consumed [ATE]ambassador (6) = LEGATE

across: *and, after, before, beside, given, joining, meeting, next to, taking, with*
down: *below, over, supporting, under*

Inclusion
words or parts written inside one another
•Solitary [LONE] horse [BA-Y] *on the outside?* Rot! (7) = BALONEY

see Split words

Reversal
words or parts written backwards
•Sort of water [EVIAN] *turned* green (5) = NAIVE

across: *back, overthrow, rejected, turning, reverse*
down: *climbing, going up, rising*

Substitution
one word or part substituted for another
•Old woman [BELDAM] *has change of heart* in asylum (6) = BEDLAM

change, difference, end-to-end, head-to-tail, moving, replacing, swapping

Subtraction
one word or part taken away from another
•Parent [FATHER] *loses* her [HER] lard (3) = FAT

dropping, leaving, losing, moving, omitting, no, removing, without

Combinations of these operations
include such devices as inclusions
written backwards
•lower side or *reverse* if [FI] *put in*
 piano [SOF-T] (6) = SOFFIT

The use of this dictionary.

General-purpose and specialist dictionaries are most often used as works of reference to check the existence, meaning or spelling of a particular word or to find a
synonym for it. They are useful in finding solutions to clues only when you
already have some idea of the spelling of some part of the solution.

A good standard dictionary will contain many thousands of words, some of
which will already be in your own vocabulary. No attempt has been made in this
book to deal with this wide range of words; instead, the book provides solutions
to many adjective-noun combinations such as those mentioned in 8 above which
cannot be looked up directly in other dictionaries. It also provides various lists of
physical objects (e.g. musical instruments), abstract ideas (e.g. beliefs), and so
on, all of which are dealt with in the same way as the adjective-noun combinations, allowing the word to be looked up from a general definition rather than the
other way round.

In addition, the book gives hints on the use of pointers, homophones, anagrams, etc. (see key on p. x), gives examples of how words are compiled by
adding words and abbreviations, etc., and contains an appendix devoted to personal names (see p.779). The lists of compiled words given under the heading
'hence' are not intended to be exhaustive but they should suffice to give an indi-
cation as to the line of thought involved.

While those parts of the book that contain lists will be useful for reference, the
remainder is perhaps best treated like the instruction manual that comes with an
electrical appliance or a piece of machinery which you first browse through and
then read rather more closely to get the general idea of the contents, returning to
read in detail only when some problem occurs. If you do not find the exact solution you are seeking, you may perhaps find a form of construction or a hint that
will lead you to the solution.

Some words have a number of entries, each relating to a different use and
identified by a superscripted number. When looking up a particular word, it is
worth while checking all entries; 'the *first*....T' will be found under the entry
dealing with uses of 'the' itself, whereas '*the first* ball. . ..B' is under the entry that
deals with 'the' in its normal role as an article attached to a noun.

One final point. You will note that some of the answers given in the book do
not form complete or recognisable words; do not be put off – the letters of which
these words are composed can be used with other words in, or derived from, the
clue to make up a complete solution.

KEY

anagram	<u>cat</u>
any word included or omitted	*
beginnings	IGN-
endings	-ING
examples	●
hidden word	/cat/
implied additions	(on)
implied inclusions	(in)
pointers	*out*
selected letters omitted	(a)
selected letters retained	<u>a</u>
word split for inclusion	B-ED
word used in Down clue	(D)
word written backwards – across	⟨
– down	↑

The list of words in **bold type** immediately following each head letter is of words for which that letter can be used as an abbreviation; the recognised forms are given in roman type, those in 'compiler's language' are in italics.

A

academician. accepted. ace. ack. acre. active. adult. advanced. afternoon.
aleph. alpha. alto. amateur. ampere. an. ana. ane. angström. annus. ante.
answer. are. argon. associate. atomic. atto-. Austria. *ay. aye.* before (ante).
blood group. bomb. effect. examination. film. fifty. five hundred. five
thousand. *first character.* first-class. first letter. *high class.* it. key. level.
note. one. paper. road. string. *top mark.* un. vitamin. year(annus)

a¹	AN.I.ONE.UNIT	•a poem	ANODE
dialect	HE.IT.SHE.THEY	•a poet	ANDANTE
French	UN.UNE	•a twitch	ANTIC
German	EIN	and	
Greek	ALPHA	•leave *after* a. . .	AGO
Hebrew	ALEPH	•man *behind* a. . .	AGENT
Italian	UN.UNA.UNO	•obliged to *follow* a. . .	ABOUND
Spanish	UN.UNA.UNO	**a⁴**	
a²		as a real prefix meaning 'lacking'	
as inclusion:			(*see* without²)
hence		**a⁵**	
•a *break in* the se-t	SEAT	as an artificial 'suffix':	
•be-t *about* a. . .	BEAT	hence	
•colour *including* a. . .	READ	•feature article	CHINA
	TAINT	•fish *with* a. . .	CODA
•fl-y *around* a. . .	FLAY	•one *joining*. . .	PERSONA
•me-t *round* a. . .	MEAT	•barrel *having* a. . .	TUNA
a³		**a⁶**	
as an artificial prefix:		other uses:	
hence		a *Continental*	UN.UNE
•a 2p. . .	APP-	a *deficient*	omit A
•A50	-AL	a *follower*	B
•a boat	ASS	a *for example*	VOWEL
•a book	ANT	a *French*. . .	UN.UNE
•a cereal	ACORN	hence	
•a Celt	ASCOT	•a *French* composer	UNRAVEL
•a church	ACE	•a *French* dressing	UNROBING
•a church feature	ASPIRE	•a *French* pirate	UNHOOK
•a horse	AMOUNT	•a *French* warder	UNSCREW
•a large quantity, *say*	ALLOT	•a *French* worker	UNHAND
•a learner	-AL	a *German*. . .	EIN
•a line	-ARY	a *loss*	omit A
•a meeting place	AVENUE	a *missing*. . .	omit A
•a member	AMP	a *Parisian*. . .	UN.UNE
•a mountain range	AURAL	a *Spanish*. . .	UNA.UNO
•a Northern. . .	AN	**AA**	
•a(n) opening	AGATE	AA man	AARON.ARCHIE
•a poem	AVERSE	AA gun	ARCHIE
•a poet	ANDANTE	**AAA**	DASHBOARD
•Erato, *e.g.*	AMUSE	**abandon**	
and		*abandon* a. . .	omit A

1

abandon one. . .	omit A or I
abandon *	omit *
•sen(try) *abandons* attempt	SEN
abandoned by *	omit *
•cab(le) *abandoned by* the	
French	CABLE
abandoned <u>claim</u>	MALIC
abbess/abbot/abbey	ABB
abbreviated **period**	TIM(e)
abdicated	ABD
aberration of <u>mental</u>	LAMENT
ablative	ABL
able	
able seaman	AB
	(*see also* sailor)
able-bodied seaman, *say*	
WHOLESALER	
able to be <u>used</u>	DUES.SUED
abnormal	
abnormal <u>lump</u>	PLUM
abnormal<u>ly</u> <u>low</u>	OWL
aboard	ON.(in) S-S.incl SS
abolish	
abolish a. . .	omit A
abolish *	omit *
•fa(the)r *abolishes* the. . .	FAR
about[1]	
meaning	
around	
approximately	
roughly	C.CA.CIRC.CIRCA
hence	
•about a boy	CALF.CANDY
	CANTON.CERIC
•about a girl	CANNA.CLASS
•about a member	CAMP
•about about	CARE
•about *about*	AC.ER
•about an old king	CLEAR
•about an old ship	CARGO
•about fifty	CL
•about this *Latin*. . .	CHIC
•about time	CAGE
and	
•about right	CAR.CART
•about time	CAT
•about to get up	CAROUSE
and	
•about East	CIRCE

•about the *French*. . .	CIRCLE
•about you and me	CIRCUS
about[2]	
meaning	
anent	
concerning	
in connection with	
on	
over	
regarding	
to do with	RE
hence	
•about a boy	REASON
•about now	REPRESENT
•about over	REPAST
•about some quarters	REPARTEE
and	
•I take over	IRE
•leave about. . .	GORE
•snake, one about. . .	ASPIRE
about *retirement*	ER
about[3]	
as inclusion:	
about a. . .	incl A
about a hundred	incl C
about fifty	incl L
about five	incl V
about four	incl IV
about nine	incl IX
about one	incl A or I
about right	incl R or RT
about six	incl VI
about ten	incl X
about turn	incl U
about *	incl *
•talk *about* scabies	CHITCHAT
about[4]	
other uses:	
about <u>now</u>	OWN.WON
about <u>time</u>⟨	EMIT
about turn	U
about turn at. . .⟨	TA
above	SUP(RA)
above(D)	(*see* over[2])
above ten	TENT
Abrahamville	LINCOLN
abridged	ABD
abroad	
indicates a foreign language:	

2

•*Continental* house	CASA MAISON	academician	A.ARA.PRA.RA
•*cross-channel* bridge	PONT	academy	RA.RADA
•go *abroad*	ALLER	**accept**	
•*overseas* contract	APPALTO	acceptable	OK.U
•walk *on the Continent*	MARCHER	accepted	A.U
•work *overseas*	LAVORO.TRAVAIL	*accepted by* *	incl in *
absent	AWOL	•we are *accepted by* group	SWEET
absence	(*see also* without²)	*accepting* a...	incl A
absence of approval	NOOK	*accepting* *	incl *
absent king	omit K or R	•b-at *accepting* nothing	BOAT
absent *	omit *	**accident**	HAP
•ap(pal) *absent* friend	AP	*accident* in plane	PANEL
an *absent*...	omit AN	*accidentally* spilt	SPLIT
absolutely	ABS	**accommodate**	
absolutely transparent	SHEER	*accommodated by* *	incl in *
absorb		•girl *accommodated by* a-n...	AMAIN
absorbed in *	incl in *		
•saint *absorbed in* music	ASTIR	*accommodating* a...	incl A
absorbing a...	incl A	*accommodating* *	incl *
absorbing *	incl *	•Ab-e *accommodating* us	ABUSE
•music *absorbing* saint	ASTIR	•*accommodating*	
absorbs mu/ch I li/ke	CHILI	ma/ny, ala/s	NYALA
abstainer	RECHABITE.TT	**accompany**	
abstract	ABS	accompanying page	ATTENDANT
abstract a...	omit A	*accompanied by*	incl AND
abstract *	omit *	•Henry *accompanied*	
•Greek so *abstracted*	(so)CRATES	by son	HANDS
abstract form	REMOVE	**according to:**	
absurd		art	SA
absurd idea	AIDE	law	SEC LEG
absurdly used	DUES.SUED	nature	SN
Abyssinia(n)		rule	SEC REG
baboon	GELADA	some	(*see* dialect)
capital	A.ADDIS ABABA	value	AD VAL(OREM)
coin	TALARI	**account**	AC(C).ACCT.BILL
insect	ZEBIB.ZIMB	accountant	AC.ACA.CA.FCA
king	NEGUS	accountants	CAS.SAA
language	AMHARIC.GEEZ.GIZ	**ace**	A.EXPERT.I.NOI-
measures			ONE.PRO.WINNER
—1 ounce	OKET		(*see also* expert)
—2 lbs	NATR	**achievement quotient**	AQ
—100 lbs	KANTAR	**acid test**	PH
grass	TEFF	**acknowledge**	
parliament	SHENGO	acknowledged debts	-IOUS
patriarch	ABUNA	acknowledgment	ROGER
prince	RAS	**acre**	A
academic	MA.PROF	**across**	TRANS-
academic appointment	CHAIR	across = a cross	X
		•put the man across	HEX

across the Channel = in French hence	judge's address	LORD
•bridge *across the Channel* PONT	king's address	MAJESTY
•fly *across the Channel* MOUCHE	magistrate's address HONOUR
•South *across the Channel* SUD	mayor's address	WORSHIP
(*see also* abroad)	member's address
run *across*⟨ NUR	HON(OURABLE)
act BILL.TAKE APART	pope's address HOLINESS
(*see also* indeed)	prince's address HIGHNESS
act WILDCAT	queen's address MAJESTY
act *peculiarly* CAT	vicar's address REV(EREND)
acted *strangely* CADET	**adherent** BUR(R).FAN
acting ON.(on) STAGE	**adjective** ADJ
action (*see* indeed)	**adjourned** ADJ
active A.ACT	**adjust**
active life FILE	*adjustable* seat is. . . SIESTA
actor PLAYER.TREE	*adjusted* Kit's. . . SKIT
actor's remuneration	adjustment ADJ
PART PAYMENT	*adjustment* lets us. . . TUSSLE
actors RADA	**adjutant-general** AG
actors on tour CASTAWAY	**adman** PRO
actors *on tour* CROATS	**admiral** ADM.BUTTERFLY
actuaries FA	DRAKE.HOOD
Adam	NELSON
Adam (and Eve) BELIEVE	Admiral of the Fleet AF
Adam's ale WATER	**admit¹**
Adam's first wife LILITH	admitting AM.IAM.IM
adapt	hence
adaptable sort TORS	•admitting essayist AMELIA
adaptation of recent. . . CENTRE	•admitting girl AMRITA
adapted an old. . . NODAL	•admitting one ship AMISS
adapting another's. . . SHERATON	and
add	•admitting journalists IMPRESS
add an ode ANODE	•admitting two IMPAIR
add pound *to* fee FEEL	•admitting working IMPLYING
add weight *to*	and
dreadful. . . DIRECT	•I am an attendant IMPAGE
additional	•I am out of date IMPASSE
award BAR	•I am wan IMPALE
message PS	**admit²**
postscript PPS	admitted IN
weight EXTRACT	hence
address	•*admitted* dog INCUR
indicates mode of address:	•*admitted* group INSECT.INCULT
ambassador's address	•*admitted to* hospital INWARD
EXCELLENCY	*admitted by* * incl in *
bishop's address GRACE	•men *admitted by*
dean's address VEN(ERABLE)	wrong. . . TORMENT
duke's address GRACE	*admitting* a. . . incl A
	admitting nothing incl O

admitting *	incl *
•wrong, *admitting*	
men...	TORMENT
adopt	
adopted by *	incl in *
•daughter *adopted by* Ma-e	MADE
adopting a...	incl A
adopting *	incl *
•Ma-e *adopting* daughter	MADE
adrift in the...	THINE
adult	A
adult film	X
advanced	A
advantage	VAN
advent	ADV
adverb	ADV
adverse	ANTHONY
adversely affected rats⟨	STAR
adversely affected rats	ARTS
	STAR.TARS
advertisement	AD.BILL.PLUG
	POSTER.PUFF
advice centre	CAB
advocate	ADV
advocates	BAR
aero club	AC
aeroplane	MIG
affect	
affect large...	LAGER.REGAL
affected animal	LAMINA.MANILA
affecting lots...	SLOT
affectionate boy	FONDLES
Afghan(istan)	AFG
capital	A.KABUL
clan	KHEL
coins	AFGHANI.AMANIA,PULS
greatcoat	POS(H)TEEN
language	PASHTO.PASHTU
	PUSHTO(O).PUSHTU
	TADZHIK
leader	A
people	KAFIR.NURI.PATHAN
aforesaid	DO.DITTO
Africa(n)	AFR
aardvark	ANTBEAR.EARTH HOG
	GROUND HOG
aardwolf	EARTHWOLF
Afrikaans	TAAL
Afrikaner	BOER.BOOR

	DUTCHMAN
airline	SAA
amulet	GREEGREE.GRI(S)GRI(S)
antbear	AARDVARK.EARTH HOG
	GROUND HOG
anteater	PANGOLIN
antelope	(*see* antelopes)
ape	CHIMPANZEE.GORILLA
aromatic seeds	
	GRAINS OF PARADISE
	GUINEA GRAINS
assembly	RAAD
—of elders	KGOTLA
baobab	CREAM-OF-TARTAR TREE
	MONKEY BREAD
band of warriors	IMPI
beer	POMBE
begone!	VOETSEK
beryl	HELIODOR
birds	AASVOGEL
	ADJUTANT BIRD
	BALAENICEPS.BEEFEATER
	BUPHAGA.CAPE PIGEON
	COUNCAL.GUINEA FOWL
	HAMMERHEAD.HAMMERKOP
	HONEY BIRD.HONEY GUIDE
	LARK-HEELED CUCKOO
	MARABOU(T).OSTRICH
	OXPECKER.PRINIA
	PLANTAIN-EATER
	SECRETARY BIRD.SENEGAL
	SHOEBILL.T(O)URACO
	UMBER (BIRD).UMBRETTE
	WHALE-HEAD.WHIDAH BIRD
	WHYDAH BIRD.WIDOW BIRD
blood-flower	HAEMANTHUS
bracelet (currency)	MANILLA
brandy	CAPE SMOKE.DOP
bread	KISRA.PALM PITH
bucket	EMMER
bugbear	MUMBO-JUMBO
bustard	DIKKOP.PAAUW.PAU
butter-tree	KANYA.KARITE.SHEA
camp	BOMA.LA(A)GER.LAER
Cape	
—Dutch	AFRIKAANS.TAAL
—gooseberry	GOLDENBERRY
	PHYSALIS
	STRAWBERRY TOMATO

5

—hyrax   KLIPDAS.ROCK-BADGER
—Province   CP
capital   A
carrier by wagon
   TRANSPORT-RIDER
cattle   (*see* cattle[2])
—disease   NAGANA
charm   GREEGREE
   GRI(S)GRI(S).JU-JU
chief   CAID.KAID
citadel   CASBAH.KASBA(H)
clout   LAP(PIE).LAPJE
club   KERRIE.KIERIE
   KIRI.KNOBKERRIE
coin   (KRUGER)RAND.RD
—three-penny bit   TICK(E)Y
col   NEK
coral   ZEETAK
—tree   KAFFIRBOOM
cormorant   DUIKER.DUYKER
corral   KRAAL
cotton garment   KANGA
coucal   SWAMP PHEASANT
criminal   TSOTSI
cup   BEKER
deities   (*see* gods.goddesses)
desert plant   CAMEL'S THORN
diseases   (*see* diseases)
dogs   BASENJI
   RHODESIAN RIDGEBACK
domesticated animal   CAMEL
dove   NAMAQUA
dried
—apricots   MEBOS
—fish   STINKFISH
—meat   BILTONG
drug   (CAPE) DAGGA
   (RED) DAGGA
Dutch/English   KITCHEN DUTCH
eagle   BATELEUR.BERGHAAN
ear of maize   MEALIE
earthwolf   AARDWOLF
edible
—pods   OKRA
—tuber   ELEPHANT'S-FOOT
   HOTTENTOT BREAD
enclosure   BOMA
esparto grass   (H)ALFA
expedition   SAFARI.TREK

extinct wild horse   QUAGGA
farm cart   SCOTCH CART
fetish   GREE-GREE
   GRI(S)GRI(S).JUJU
fine   MOOI
fish   BARRACOUTA.DORAS
   KABELJOU(W).PANCHAX
   POLYPTERUS.SNOEK.SNOOK
florin   SCOTCHMAN
flowers   BELLADONNA LILY
   CHINCHERINCHEE
   CHINKERINCHEE
   CINERARIA.FREESIA.NEMESIA
   NERINE.STRELITZIA
fly   BROMMER.BRUMMER.KIVU
   TSETSE
ford   DRIFT
foreigner   UITLANDER
fort   CASBAH.KASBA(H).SCHANS
fox   FENNEC.ZERDA
freedom   UHURU
frog   CAPE NIGHTINGALE
   PLATANNA
fruit   A(C)KEE.BITO.DIKA
   HOTTENTOT FIG.SHEA-NUT
   NAR(R)AS.WILD MANGO
garment   KANGA.KANZU
garden patch   ERF
gin   SQUARE-FACE
glass beads   AGGRI.AGGRY
god   MUMBO-JUMBO
gold-bearing rock   BANKET
good   MOOI
government   SERKALI
grain   DURRA.C(O)USC(O)S
   FUNDI.GUINEA CORN
grape   H(A)ANEPOOT.HONEYPOT
grass   FUNDI.GUINEA-GRASS
   MILLET.PENNISETUM
—land   VELD(T)
green rock   VERDITE
greet   WISH
ground   FLOOR
ground squirrel   MEERCAT
   MEERKAT
guitar   SANCHO.SANKO
gully   DONGA
gum resin   OLIBANUM
gun   ROER

head ornament	HEAD-RING
headman	CABOCEER
hemp	IFE.SISAL
heron/stork	HAMMERKOP
	UMBRETTE
high grassland	KAR(R)OO
hill	BERG.KOP(PIE).KOPJE
hippopotamus	RIVER HORSE
	ZEEKOE
honey badger	RATEL
hooligan	TSOTSI
horse	
—disease	NAGANA
—extinct	QUAGGA
—s'canter	TRIPPLE
Hottentot	
—fig	MESEMBRIANTHEMUM
	MESEMBRYANTHEMUM
—god	PRAYING MANTIS
hut	KRAAL.KYA.RONDAVEL
hyena	TIGER-WOLF
hyrax	DASSIE
ice-plant	MESEMBRIANTHEMUM
	MESEMBRYANTHEMUM
immature locust	VOETGANGER
Indian	GOAN
infantry soldier	VOETGANGER
insectivore	ELEPHANT SHREW
	GOLDEN MOLE
	OTTER SHREW
iris	FREESIA
it is not	AIKONA
ivory	PANGANI
jackal	DIEB
jam	KONFYT
javelin	ASSAGAI
	ASSEGAI.ASSEGAY
knife	PANGA
lake	NYANZA
languages	AFRIKAANS.BANTU
	BASUTO.BASUTU.CAFFRE
	CAPE DUTCH.HERERO
	HOTTENTOT.IBO.KABYLE
	KAFFER.KAF(F)IR.MANDINGO
	SWAHILI.TAAL.TSWANA
	TUAREG.TWI.(UNION) SHONA
	X(H)OSA.YORUBA.ZULU
	(*see also* races *below*)
leader	A

lemur	ANGWANTIBO
	(GOLDEN) POTTO
leopard	TIGER
lily of the Nile	PIG-LILY
lizard	GECKO.(I)GUANA
	MONITOR.SKINK
locust without wings	
	VOETGANGER
look out!	PAS OP
Lord's supper	NACHTMAAL
	NAGMAAL
low marshy ground	VLEI.VLY
lynx	CARACAL
mackerel	ALBACORE
magistrate	FIELD-CORNET
	LANDDROS(T)
maize	MEALIES
mango	DIKA
mantis	HOTTENTOT'S GOD
master	BAAS.BWANA
—race theory	BAASKAP
measures	
—2 acres	MORGEN
—7$^1/_2$ gallons	ANKER
—31 gallons	AUM
—3 bushels	MUID
—cloth	JACKTAN
medicinal plant	BUCHU
	BUCKU.CALUMBA
millet	DARI.D(O)URA
	D(H)URRA
mongoose	MEERCAT.MEERKAT
	SURICATE
Moslem	SENUSSI
mountain	BERG
—pass	NEK.POORT
mud hut	TEMBE
multi-coloured	BONT
music	KWELA
musical instrument	GORA(H)
	GOURA.ZANZE
national independence	UHURU
Negrito	NEGRILLO
no	AIKONA
nomadic Berber people	TUAREG
nut tree	COLA.KOLA
object of superstition	JUJU
open country	VELD(T)
open bus	MAMMY-WAGON

orchid	DISA
ostrich	STRUTHIO
oxpecker	BEEFEATER
	BUPHAGA.TICK-BIRD
palm	DOOM-PALM
	D(O)UM-PALM.PALMYRA
—civet	NANDINE
pangolin	MANIS
parliament	RAAD
partridge	FRANCOLIN
pass	NEK.POORT
—book	REFERENCE BOOK
peasant	KOPI
pedestrian	VOETGANGER
pedlar	SMOUCH.SMOUS(E)
	SMOUSER
perennial herb	LASERPICIUM
periwinkle	STROPHANTHUS
petrel	CAPE PIGEON
pioneer	VOORTREKKER
plain	VELD(T)
plants	AIZOON.GOA BEAN
	GRAPPLE-PLANT
	ROSE OF JERICHO
	WELWITSCHIA
—extract	NIGER-OIL
plateau	KA(R)ROO
pole for crossing river	
	RIVER HORSE
policeman	ASKARI
pool	VLEI.VLY
porch	STOEP
pounded maize	STAMP
preacher	PREDIKANT
precipice	KRANS.KRAN(T)Z
preserved fruit	KONFYT
prickly pear	JOINTED CACTUS
public house	CANTEEN
pygmy	NEGRITO
pyrethrum	PELLITORY
python god	ZOMBI(E)
races	BANTU.BASUTO.BASUTU
	BEJA.BERBER.BUSHMEN
	CAFFRE.GALLA.GRIQUA
	HADENDOA.HAMITE.HAUS(S)A
	HERERO.HOTTENTOT.IBO
	KABYLE.KAFFER.KAF(FIR)
	KIKUYU.KROO.KRU.MASAI
	MATABELE.MANDINGO

race theory	APARTHEID.BAASKAP
rag	LAP(PIE).LAPJE
rascal	SCHELM.SKELM
ratel	HONEY BADGER
ravine	DONGA.KLOOF
rawhide	
—boot	VELDSCHOEN
	VEL(D)SKOEN
—thong	REIM
remote area	BACKVELD(T).BUSH
resin	SANDARAC
rhinoceros	KEITLOA
ridge	RAND
rifle-shooting	
competition	WAPINS(C)HAW
	WEAPON-S(C)HAW
	WA(P)PENS(C)HAW
river	CONGO.GAMBIA
	LIMPOPO.NIGER.NILE
	ORANGE.SENEGAL.VOLTA
	ZAMBESI
—fish	POLYPTERUS
—horse	HIPPOPOTAMUS
—side plant	PALMIET
robe	KANZU
rock-badger	CAPE HYRAX
	KLIPDAS
round hut	RONDAVEL
rue	HARMALA.HARMEL
rug	CAROSSE.KAROSS
rugby player	SPRINGBOK
runner	CHEETAH.OSTRICH
scaly anteater	MANIS.PANGOLIN
secretary bird	MESSENGER
segregation of races	APARTHEID
separate development	APARTHEID
sesame	BENNE
shea-tree	KARITE
shrub	BUAZE.BUCHU.BUCKU
	BWAZI.PENTZIA.PROTEA
	SPEKBOOM.TEA-TREE
skin garment or	
rug	CAROSSE.KAROSS
skunk	ZORILLA.ZORIL(LE)
small	
—garden	ERF
—orange	NA(A)RTJE
—parrot	LOVEBIRD
—plot of ground	ERF

snake	(see snake[2])
snake-eating bird	
	SECRETARY BIRD
soldier	ASKARI
—group	IMPI
sorghum	KAFFIR-CORN
spear	ASSAGAI.ASSEGAI
	ASSEGAY
spell	GREEGREE
	GRI(S)GRI(S).JUJU.TABOO
spider	BUTTON SPIDER
	TARANTULA
spotted hyena	NANDI BEAR
spring	FONTEIN
squatter	BIWONER.BYWONER
squirrel	XERUS
stinking plant	CARRION FLOWER
stockade	BOMA
stork	MARABOU(T).SIMBIL
strawberry tomato	
	CAPE GOOSEBERRY
strata system	KAR(R)OO
taffeta	ARIDAS
tallow	ROKA
thorn	DOORN
thorny plant	WAIT-A-BIT
	WAG-'N-BIETJIE
thug	TSOTSI
tick	TAMPAN
tiger cat	BUSH-CAT.SERVAL
timber	AFRORMOSIA.AVODIRE
	CAMWOOD.EBONY.GABOON.
	IROKO.OBECHE.SAPELE.
	STINKWOOD
toad	XENOPUS
transport	KURVEY
trees	ALOE.A(C)KEE.AMBATCH
	BAOBAB.BERG-CEDAR
	BITO.BOOM.BUBINGA
	COLA.DATE PALM.FUNTUMIA
	GUMBO.KOLA.LOTE
	LOTOS.LOTUS.MOLI
	MONKEY-BREAD TREE
	MVULE.OBECHE.OKRA
	PITH-TREE.PROTEA.SHEA
	SILVER-TREE.SNEEZEWOOD
	SOUR GOURD.TARFA
	TEAK.WA(GEN)BOOM
	WILD MANGO

tribal	
—official	INDUNA
—meeting	INDABA
tribe	(see races above)
tuber	ELEPHANT'S FOOT
	HOTTENTOT BREAD.TANIA
tulip tree	SPATHODEA
turaco	LORY
uncle	OOM
unknown animal	CATOBLEPAS
verandah	STOEP
vehicle	CAPE CART
village	DORP.KRAAL
violet	SAINTPAULIA
viper	RIVER-JACK
vulture	AASVOGEL
wagon	BUCK-WAGON
—trip	TREK
watercourse	SLUIT.SPRUIT
weaverbird	OX-BIRD.QUELEA
	TAHA.WHIDAH BIRD
	WHYDAH BIRD.WIDOW BIRD
weight	OKA.ROTL
what's his name	DINGES.DINGUS
whip	(S)JAMBOK
white	
—girl	SHEILA
—rulers	SERKALI
wife purchase	LOBOLA
wild	
—cat	CHAUS.CIVET
—dog	HYENA DOG
—hog	WART HOG
—pig	RIVER HOG
wine	CONSTANTIA
witch doctor	INYANGA
	SANGOMA
woman's garment	KANGA
wooded veldt	BUSHVELD(T)
	BOSCHVELD(T)
Zulu king	CHALKA.INKOS
	(I)NKOSI
after[1]	POST
hence	
•after a time	POSTAGE
•after some hesitation	POSTER
•after the fruit	POSTDATE
•after the Italian. . .	POSTIL
•after the river. . .	POSTURE

after²
indicates one word written after
  another:
•*after* all the *old*
return⟨   ALLEY
•almost ful(l) *after*taste TASTEFUL
•not so much *after*care CARELESS
•Scot *after*guard   GUARDIAN
•space *after*ward   WARDROOM
and
•*after* he married   HEWED
•dine *after* noon   NEAT
•many *after* the. . .   THEM
after³
other uses:
after analysis it was. . .   WAIST
                         WAITS
after date   AD
after death   PM
after reform it was. . .   WAIST
                         WAITS
after retirement   (in) B-ED
                    (in) C-OT
after retreat, ogre⟨   ERGO
after tax   NET
after the style of   ALA
after the start   omit first letter
•(l)eaves *after the*
  start   EAVES
after twelve   PM
afternoon   A.IAM.PM
*after*noon   after AM
•quiet *after*noon   AMP
*after*noon   after N
•a quiet *after*noon   NAP
afternoon service   TEA-SET
afterthought   PS
again   RE
against   CON.V
hence
•against dogs   CONCURS
•against poetry   CONVERSE
•against the Church   CONCH
•against the edge   CONVERGE
and
•against drink   VALE
•against one and. . .   VIAND
•against the current   VAMPS
•against the Irish   VERSE

age
age *of backwardness*⟨   ARE.EGA
aged   AE.AET
agent   AGT.SPY
agitate
agitation of men at. . .   MEANT
agitated waters   WASTER
agitatedly paces CAPES.SPACE
agree
agree total   TALLY
agreeably sleepy   NODDING
agreement   AY.AYE.YEA
Franco-German   OUIJA
French   OUI
Italian   SI
Russian   DA
Spanish   SI
agriculture   AGR.EARTHWORK
agricultural collection   HERD
agricultural policy   CAP
aide-de-camp   ADC
ailing king is. . .   SKIING
air
air controllers   CAA
air traffic control   ATC
Air Training Corps   ATC
in the air   SK-Y
•airsick   SKILLY
airborne   (in) F-LIGHT
•a number airborne FANLIGHT
airborne policeman BLUEBOTTLE
aircraftsman   AC.LAC
airman   FO.PO
airline¹   BA.BAC.BCAL.BEA.TWA
hence
•airline fashions   BATONS
•airline girl BASAL.BALASS
•airline study   BACON
•airline toilet   BALOO
and
•airline above. . .   BACON
•airline delicacy   BACCATE
•to airline company TOBACCO
and
•airline, a *French* one   BEAUNE
•airline buildings   BEASTIES
•airline students   BE-ALL
•airline study   BEACON
and

•airline in. . .	TWAIN
•airline not known	TWANK
•airline unknown	TWAY
airline²	
airline	ISOBAR
airline dessert	PIE IN THE SKY
airline *terminal*	E
Albania(n)	AL
brigand	KLEPHT
capital	A.TIRANA
coin	GROSH.LEK.QUINT(AR)
cavalryman	SPAHI
dialect	CHAM.TOSK
flower	SEMENI
kilt	FUSTANELLA
leader	L
ruler	MPRET
soldier	ARNA(O)UT.PALIKAR
alcoholic state	DT
alderman	ALD
Alderney	GBA
aleph	A
alfresco party	OUTDO
algebra	ALG
Algeria(n)	ALG.DZ
capital	A.ALGIERS
cavalryman	SPAHEE.SPAHI
cheese	CAPRINO
citadel	CASBAH.KASBA(H)
coin	DINAR
dish	COUSCOUS(OU).
	CUSCUS.KHUSKHUS
drink	AGRAS
fort	CASBAH.KASBA(H)
governor	DEY
grass	DISS
leader	A
measure	PIK
raid	ROZZIA
ship	XEBEC(K).ZEBEC(K)
shrub	BRIAR.BRIER
soldier	GOUM.SOUAVE.SPAHI
	SPAHEE.TURCO.ZOUAVE
weight	ROTL
wine	PINARD
alien	
alien	ET
alien = foreign	
•*alien* ship	BATEAU

•*alien* soldiers	SOLDATEN
•*alien* woman	DONNA
all	
all agreed	ATONE
all dead	OLIVE
all directions	NEWS
all gone	NONE LEFT
all *gone*	omit ALL
all *in*	incl ALL
•s-ow *includes* all. . .	SALLOW
al(l) *not finished*	AL
all over the place I went	TWINE
all right	NONE LEFT.OK
all round	'ALLO
all *round*〈	LLA
all *round*	AL-L
•go al-l *round*	ALGOL
all round	incl in *
•one with wa-ter *all round*	
	WAITER
all-round achievement	HOMER
	HOME RUN
all round(er)	O.ORB.SPHERE
almost al(l)	AL
alloy	
aluminium	DURALUMIN(IUM)
bismuth, lead, tin	FUSIBLE METAL
brass	LATTEN.ORICHALC
—and manganese	
	MANGANESE BRONZE
cerium	MISCH METAL
copper and	
—arsenic	TAMBAC.TOMBAC
	TOMBAK
—manganese	MANGANIN
—nickel	CONSTANTAN
—nickel, zinc	GERMAN SILVER
	NICKEL SILVER
—tin, zinc	GUNMETAL
	SPECULUM METAL
—tin, phosphorus	
	PHOSPHOR BRONZE
—zinc	MOSAIC GOLD
	MUNTZ METAL
PINCHBECK.PRINCE'S METAL	
	WHITE BRASS
—zinc, etc.	OREIDE.OROIDE
ORMOLU.PLATINOID	
POTIN.YELLOW METAL	

gold and	
—copper, etc.	BILLON
—palladium, etc.	WHITE GOLD
—silver	ASEM.EGYP
imitation	LEAF METAL
—gold	PINCHBECK
—silver	LEAF METAL
iridium and osmium	IRIDOSMINE
	OSMIRIDIUM
iron and	
—carbon	STEEL
—nickel, carbon	INVAR
—various metals	FERRO-ALLOY
lead and	
—tin	CALIN.TERNE (METAL)
—tin, copper, etc.	PEWTER
magnesium and	
aluminium	MAGNALIUM
mercury and silver	AMALGAM
nickel	
—and steel	INVAR
—based	MONEL(L) METAL
—chrome	NICHROME
non-ferrous	TULA
pewter	BIDRI
silver and	
—copper, etc.	BILLON.VELLON
—nickel	ALFENIDE
silvery	OCCAMY
steel and	
—chromium	STAINLESS STEEL
—manganese	MANGANESE
	STEEL
tin-based	BABBIT(METAL)
	WHITE METAL
—copper, zinc, etc.	
	BRITANNIA METAL
used in dentistry	AMALGAM
yellow	SIMILOR
zinc and copper	TUTENAG
almost	
almost al(l)	AL
almost all gone	-GON.ONE
almost fal/l ove/r	LOVE
almost fully developed	ADUL(t)
almost pointless	NEEDLES(s)
almost wholly bad	BA.AD
aloft, **sailor**...(D) ↑	BA.RAT
alpha	A

Alpine Club	AC
altar	REV COUNTER
alter a trend	RANTED
alternate	ALT
*alter*nate	NEAT
alternate time intervals	TM.IE
alternating current	AC
alternative[1]	OR
hence	
•alternative energy	ORE
•alternative entrance	OR-GATE
•alternative note	ORC.ORE
•alternative piece	ORBIT
and	
•choose alternative	ELECTOR
•man *with* alternative...	MANOR
•out-of-date alternative	PASTOR
•fellow *with* alternative...	
	DONOR
alternative[2]	
alternative technology	AT
alternative to her...	OTHER
	THROE
altitude ·	ALT
alto	ALT
alumnus	OB
always	AY.AYE.EVER
hence	
•learner always...	LAY
•always *in debt*	REVERED
•always *in* the way	RAYED
amateur	A.LAY
amateur circles	LAI C.LAITY
amateur's department	DIY
ambassador	HE
amend	
amend speech	CHEEPS
amended later	ALTER
amendment of law	AWL
America(n)[1]	AM.AMER.US
hence	
•American employed	AMUSED
•American in charge	
can...	AMICABLE
•American shrub	AMBUSH
and	
•American church	AMERCE
•American in Germany	AMERIND
and	

- •American can. . . USABLE
- •American journalist USED
- •American period USAGE
- •American woman USHER

and

- •American school period TERMINUS
- •born American BUS
- •round America -OUS
- •this *Latin*-American HOCUS

and

- •American *in* acid test PUSH
- •American *in* m-e MUSE
- •American *in* Ab-e's. . . ABUSES

America(n)²

aboriginal AMERIND.ESKIMO
(RED) INDIAN
accessories FINDING
accustomed WONTED
act as paid dance partner
HOSTESS
address of welcome SALUTATORY
administrative area TOWNSHIP
admiring looks EYE SERVICE
advertising pamphlet DODGER
affair SHEBANG
against ON
agency CIA
agitated HET UP
agrimony BONESET
air control CAB
aircraft navigation system VOR
airline PAN AM.TWA
alert HEAD-UP
all
—clear COPACETIC.COPESETTIC
—right HUNKY(-DORY)
allowable RULABLE
alluvial deposits BOTTOM-LAND
almost MOST
aloe AGAVE.MAGUEY
alter BUSHEL
annoy BUG
anti-
—cartel worker TRUSTBUSTER
—communist organisation
MINUTEMEN
—fraud law BLUE-SKY LAW
antiquated FOGRAM

anything
—acquired dishonestly MAVERICK
—of little value
SMALL POTATOES
—superfluous BLITVIT
—very large S(L)OC(K)DOLAGER
Apocynum Cannabinum
INDIAN HEMP
applaud ROOT
apple BALDWIN.JONATHAN
—brandy APPLEJACK
—pie PANDOWDY
area of
—black soil BLACK BELT
—Negro population BLACK BELT
armed organisation MINUTEMEN
arrest BUST
arrogant TOPPING
art gallery MUSEUM
Artemisias SAGEBRUSH
articulated truck RIG
assistant purser MUD CLERK
astonished BUG-EYED
Astragalus LOCO(-PLANT)
LOCOWEED
asylum BUGHOUSE
at
—any rate LEASTWAYS
LEASTWISE
—odds AT OUTS
—present PRESENTLY
attend
—class AUDIT
—to TEND OUT ON
audition CATTLE CALL
autumn FALL
aware of KNOWING TO
awkward person JAY
axolotl MUD PUPPY
badger TAXEL
backwoodsman BUCKSKIN
bad whiskey TARANTULA JUICE
badge of rank SHOULDER BOARD
SHOULDER MARK
bag
—of gifts GRAB-BAG
—net FYKE
baggage for intermediate
railway station WAY-BAGGAGE

13

bait	HELLGRAM(M)ITE		BUSHTIT.CHAPARRAL COCK
baited line	TRAWL		COW (BLACK) BIRD.DICKCISSEL
bald eagle	WHITEHEADED EAGLE		FIELDLARK.GOATSUCKER
ball	FANDANGO		GRA(CK)LE.GREENLET
Baltimore oriole	FIREBIRD		GROUND ROBIN.MARSH ROBIN
	HANGBIRD.ICTERUS		MEADOWLARK.MELOPSIZA
bank			MOCKING THRUSH
—note	BILL		PURPLE FINCH.RAIL.REEDBIRD
—rate	DISCOUNT RATE		RICEBIRD.ROADRUNNER
Baptist denomination	DUNKERS		SORA.SCISSOR-TAIL
barbecue	COOKOUT		SHARPTAILED GROUSE
bargain	DICKER		SKUNK BIRD.SNOW GOOSE
barroom	EXCHANGE		SONG SPARROW.SPIRIT-DUCK
base hit	HOMER.HOME RUN		STONE CURLEW.SURFBIRD
	TATER		TATTLER.THRASHER
baseball	CHERMANY		THRESHER.TOWHEE
—field	DIAMOND		TURKEY VULTURE
bass	GROWLER		TYRANT BIRD
batter pudding	POPOVER		TYRANT FLYCATCHER
be			VEERY.VELVET SCOTER
—furiously angry	STAMP		VIREO.WAV(E)Y
—guest of	VISIT WITH		WHIPPOORWILL.WHITEWING
—school teacher	TEACH SCHOOL		WILLET.WOOD THRUSH
bear	CINNAMON BEAR.GRIZZLY		WOOD WARBLER.WREN-TIT
	KODIAK.MUSQUAW		ZOPILOTE
—berry	MANZANITA	bison	BUFFALO
beat	SHELL	black	
beaten track	TRACE	—bass	GROWLER
beating boundaries		—bird	GRA(C)KLE
	PROCESSIONING	—nurse	MAMMY
bed		—tailed deer	JUMPING DEER
—bug	CHINCH	—vulture	CARRION CROW
—quilt	COMFORTABLE	bladder campion	CAROLINA PINK
	COMFORTER		PINKROOT
bedded oyster	PLANT	blackmail	STRIKE
bee		bland	MICKEY
—hive	GUM	blindfish	AMBYLOPSIS
—line	AIR LINE	block of	
beer container	GROWLER	—buildings	SQUARE
beg	PANHANDLE	—public land	TOWNSHIP
beggar	PANHANDLER	blockhead	MUTT
	SCHNORRER	bloodroot	PUCCOON
believe	GUESS	board for cooking	PLANK
bird-eating spider	MYGALE	boat	DORY
birds	APHRIZA	bobolink	REEDBIRD
	BALTIMORE (ORIOLE)		RICEBIRD.SKUNK BIRD
	BLACKTHROATED BUNTING	boiled dumpling	DOUGHBOY
	BLUEBIRD.BOBOLINK	boiler suit	COVERALL(S)
	BOBWHITE.BUFFLEHEAD	bony pike	GARFISH

14

boo	BRONX CHEER
bookmaker's record	
of bets	HANDBOOK
boot of car	TRUNK
boring	
—old fool	FOGRAM
—person	S(C)HMO
bottle of dark glass	JUNK BOTTLE
bottom drawer	HOPE CHEST
bowfin	LAKE LAWYER
bowie knife	TOOTHPICK
bowler hat	DERBY
bowls	TEN-PINS
Boxing Association	WBA
boy	BUB(BY)
braces	SUSPENDERS
branch post office	STATION
brawl	ROUGHHOUSE
brawn	HEADCHEESE
breach in river bank	CREVASSE
bread	
—(maize)	CORN BREAD
—root	PRAIRIE TURNIP
breakdown truck	WRECKER
bribe	KICKBACK
bridesmaid	MAID OF HONOUR
brief race	BRUSH
bring up	FETCH UP
brittle	BRASH
broadcasters	ABC.CBS.RCA
broken tree	RAMPICK.RAMPIKE
brook	CREEK.RILL
brother	BUD(DY)
brownish-orange	CLAYBANK
brushwood thicket	CHAPARRAL
buckthorn	CEANOTHUS.WAHOO
buffalo	
—cattle hybrid	BEEFALO
—nut	OILNUT
building	
—earning rent to pay	
taxes	TAXPAYER
—stone	BROWNSTONE
	FIELDSTONE
bulrush	SCIRPUS.TULE
bumpkin	YAP
bungle	FLUB.MUX
bunk	HOKUM
burbot	LAKE LAWYER

burgle	BURGLARIZE
burglar	YEGG(MAN)
burning bush	WAHOO
burrowing	
—animal	(POCKET) GOPHER
—snake	GOPHER
bus charging low prices	JITNEY
bush	CHAPARRAL
	CREOSOTE PLANT
business	INC
bustle	RUSTLE
butternut	OILNUT
buzzard	REDTAIL
bye-law	ORDINANCE
cabinet	OFFICIAL FAMILY
cake	CORN CAKE.CORN-DODGER
	FRIEDCAKE.HOE-CAKE
	LOAF CAKE.SHORTCAKE
Californian	
—buckthorn bark	CASCARA
—plant	FOUR-O'CLOCK
—shrub	CHAMISE.CHAMISO
—white oak	ROBLE
call on	GAM
camp	
—follower	BUMMER
—kettle	DIXIE
camping equipment	DUFFEL
	DUFFLE
Canadian	CANUCK.KANUCK
candlefish	EULACHON.OOLAKAN
	OULACHON.OULAKAN
candyfloss	COTTON CANDY
	FLUKUM
canvasser	SALESMAN.SOLICITOR
capital	A.WASHINGTON
car	AUTO(MOBILE)
—boot	TRUNK
—bonnet	HOOD
—park	PARKING LOT
carbine	ESCOPETTE
card game	EUCHRE
cardigan	WAM(M)US.WAMPUS
caretaker	SUPERINTENDENT
cargo ship	LIBERTY SHIP
caribou	REINDEER
Carolina	
—allspice	CALYCANTHUS
—jasmine	GELSEMIUM

carriage	BUCKBOARD
	BUCKCART.BUGGY
	HERDIC.ROCKAWAY.SURREY
carry	TOTE
—on hip	HIP
—out	FILL
cast	MOLT
catapult	SLINGSHOT
cart	BUCKBOARD
	DEMOCRAT(-WAGON)
catch of fish	MESS
caterpillar	WEBWORM
catfish	HORN(ED) POUT
	MUDCAT.SILURE
cattle driver	PUNCHER
cause to fall	FALL
censorious	NEGATIVE
central reservation	PARKING
cereal	INDIAN CORN
	MAIZE.MEALIES
ceremony	EXERCISE
certainly	SURE
chairman of company	PRESIDENT
challenge	STUMP
change	
—over	TRANSFER
—suddenly	FLOP
changing cabin	CABANA
chaos	SNAFU
chaotic	SNAFU
charivari	SHIVAREE
chat	VISIT
—with	VISIT WITH
cheap	JITNEY
—cigar	LONG NINE
—hotel	FLOPHOUSE
checkerberry	PARTRIDGE-BERRY
cheer	ROOT
chemist's shop	DRUGSTORE
cheque	CHECK
cherry laurel	MOCK ORANGE
chest	
—band to support load	TUMPLINE
—of drawers	DRESSER
chevrotain	MOUSE DEER
chewink	GROUND ROBIN
child's	
—apron	TIER
—garment	PANTYWAIST

chipmunk	GROUND SQUIRREL
choice example	PEACHERINO
chopped bait	TOLL-BAIT
cicada	HARVEST FLY
cigar(ette) end	SNIPE
circular saw	BUZZ SAW
civil	
—law officer	MARSHAL
—War	WAR OF SECESSION
civilian	CITIZEN
clam	COHOG
	QUAHOG.QUAHAUG
claptrap	HOKUM
classroom	RECITATION ROOM
clearing in trees	SLASH
clever	HEAD-UP
cliff-shaped hill	BUTTE
climbing plant	CLUSIA
	GELSEMIUM
	STAR-OF-THE-NIGHT
cloakroom	CHECK(ING) ROOM
clump of trees	MOT.MOTT(E)
clumsy person	S(C)HLEMIEL
	SCHLEMIHL
coalition	FUSION
cocksfoot grass	ORCHARD-GRASS
coffin	CASKET
coin	ROCK
—unit	CENT
—cent	PENNY
—5 cents	JITNEY.NICKEL
—6¼ cents (old)	PICAYUNE
—10 cents	DIME
—12½ cents	BIT
—17 cents	PINE-TREE MONEY
—25 cents	QUARTER.TWO BITS
—50 cents	HALF-DOLLAR
—100 cents	DOLLAR
—dollar	BUCK.GREENBACK
	WHEEL
—5 dollars	ABE'S CABE.FIN
—10-dollar bill	SAWBUCK
	TENSPOT
—10 dollars	EAGLE
—20 dollars (gold)	DOUBLE
	EAGLE
—500 dollars	MONKEY
—proposed	MILL
—small	PICAYUNE

college	
—dance	PROM(ENADE)
—lecturer	INSTRUCTOR
comic strips	FUNNIES
commercial traveller	DRUMMER
	SALESMAN
commotion	RUCKUS
company	CAHOOT
	CORPORATION.OUTFIT
—chairman	PRESIDENT
—director	VICE-PRESIDENT
compass-plant	SILPHIUM
computer	ENIAC
concede	ALLOW
conclusive remark	
	S(L)OC(K)DOLAGER
conduct trial	TRY
conductor	LEADER
confectionery	CANDY
confederacy of Indian	
peoples	FIVE NATIONS
	SIX NATIONS
Confederate States	CFA
confer degree on	GRADUATE
confined to home	SHUT-IN
confounded	BLAME(D)
confused	STREAKED
—conflict	MUSS(LE)
congregation	PARISH
connecting rod	PITMAN
conscription	DRAFT
conservative Democrat	HUNKER
considerable	SMART
constituency	DISTRICT
constrain	OBLIGATE
con trick	BUNCO.BUNKO
conveyance	PROTOCOL
cook on a board	PLANK
coral snake	ELAPS
corn	MAIZE
corny	MICKEY
cotton	
—cloth	MUSLIN
—stripping machine	LINTER
cougar	PAINTER
councillor	COUNCILMAN
country	
—dance	HOEDOWN
	VIRGINIA REEL

—lout	JAKE
—music	
	STARSPANGLED BANNER
courage	GRIT.SAND
covered wagon	
	CONESTOGA (WAGON)
	PRAIRIE SCHOONER
cowardly male	PANTYWAIST
cowboy	BUCKAROO
	COWPOKE.COWPUNCHER
	WRANGLER
—hat	STETSON
	TEN-GALLON HAT
—leggings	CHAPS.SHAPS
cowcatcher	PILOT
coyote	PRAIRIE WOLF
crack shot	DEADEYE
crazy person	SCREWBALL
creature	CRITTER.CRITTUR
crib (cheating)	HORSE.TROT
critical onlooker	KIBITZER
croquet on hard court	ROQUE
cross of twigs	GOD'S EYE
crossing on different	
levels	GRADE SEPARATION
crowd	RAFT
crushed	CHAWED UP
cuckoo	COWBIRD
curtain	DRAPE
cute	CUNNING
cycad	COONTIE.COONTY
cyclist	CYCLER
dabchick	DIPPER
damnation	(TAR)NATION
damned	BLAME(D)
dance	BARN DANCE
	BUNNY HUG.JITTERBUG
dandy	DUDE
dare	STUMP
dark reddish-brown	
sandstone	BROWNSTONE
dead	
—person	DECEDENT
—tree	RAMPICK.RAMPIKE
decamp	ABSQUATULATE
	DIG OUT
decayed tree	RAMPICK.RAMPIKE
decision of council	REBOUND
decisive blow	S(L)OC(K)DOLAGER

decoration for wounds	PURPLE HEART
decoy	TOLE.TOLL
deer	CARIACOU.CARIBOU
	CARJACOU.ELK
	MOOSE.VIRGINIAN DEER
	WAPITI
—mouse	WHITE-FOOTED MOUSE
defeat	
—by narrow margin	EDGE
—totally	CHAW.UPSKUNK
defeatist	NEGATIVE
deficiency	WANTAGE
denim trousers	CHINOS
denomination	PARISH
denominational	PAROCHIAL
dentist	DOCTOR
dentures	STORE TEETH
derail	DITCH
detective	FED.G-MAN
	JACK.SHAMUS
detectives	FBI
diagram	PLAT
dinner jacket	TUXEDO
disadvantage	OUT
disaster	PROVIDENCE
discharge from military	MUSTER OUT
discompose	FAZE.PHASE
disconcert	DISCOMBOBULATE
	DISCOMBOBERATE
discounter	NOTE-SHAVER
disgruntled person	SOREHEAD
dismissal	BOUNCE
dissolute	BUM
distillery	STILL HOUSE
district	SECTION
—noted for bribes	TENDERLOIN
disturbance	ROUGHHOUSE
	RUCKUS
diving duck	BUFFLEHEAD
doctor's surgery	OFFICE
dogbane	FLYTRAP.INDIAN HEMP
dollar bill	SCRIP
dolt	CLUNK
domestication of animals	ZOOCULTURE
dosshouse	FLOPHOUSE
double plough	LISTER

doughnut	OLYCOOK.OLYKOEK
dowdy	TACKY
downright	UP-AND-DOWN
drag	SCHLEP.TUMP
drainage way	DRAW
drawback	OUT
drawer (of chest)	DRAW
drawing pin	THUMBTACK
dress up	GUSSY UP.RAG
dressing	
—table	DRESSER.LOWBOY
—gown	BATHROBE
drink	MINT JULEP
drinking	
—bar	SALOON
—fountain	SCUTTLEBUTT
—resort	DOGGERY
drive	
—cattle	PUNCH
—fast	BARREL
drought area	DUST BOWL
druggist	DOCTOR
drunk	JAGGED
drunkard	SOUSE
duck	CANVASBACK
	OLD SQUAW
dull	
—person	FLAT TIRE
—town	BOHUNK.HICKSVILLE
dung beetle	TUMBLE-BUG
	TUMBLE-DUNG
dust	
—bin	GARBAGE CAN
	(TR)ASH CAN
—coat	DUSTER
—man	GARBAGEMAN
Dutch rush	SCOURING RUSH
dwarf	
—cherry	SAND-CHERRY
—chestnut	
	CHINCAPIN.CHINKAPIN
	CHINQUAPIN
eastern	
—Indian	MOUND BUILDER
—New York	EAST SIDE
easy educational course	CAKE COURSE
eccentric	SCREWBALL
eczema	SALT-RHEUM

edible
—berry   SAL(L)AL-BERRY
—bulb   CAMAS(S)
              CAMASH.QUAMASH
—caterpillar   PUXI
—fungus   TUCKAHOE
—part of something   MEAT
educational meeting
                  CHAUTAUQUA
effeminate male   PANTYWAIST
election
—inspection   CANVASS
—with disputed result
              CONTESTED ELECTION
elk   MOOSE
elm   WAHOO
embezzle   KNOCK DOWN
encourage   ROOT
engine driver   ENGINEER
enlist   INDUCT.MUSTER IN
enroll   MUSTER IN
entertain   HOST
entrance
—fee   INITIATION FEE
—hall   HALLWAY
equinoctial storm   LINE STORM
estate agent   REALTOR
eternal   TARNAL
evangelist   RELIGIONIST
evening
—previous   OVERNIGHT
—primrose   SUN-DROPS
evergreen   LIVE OAK.MADRONA
        MADRONO.MOUNTAIN-TEA
ewer   PITCHER
excellent   COPACETIC
                        COPESETTIC
exchange courtesies at sea   GAM
exclusive social set
              THE FOUR HUNDRED
expert shot   DEADEYE
exploratory drilling   WILDCAT
expressing
—admiration   SOME POTATOES
—disgust   BLECH.BLEGH
—vexation   DOG ON IT
                        DOGGONE IT
expressway   THRUWAY
ex-serviceman   VETERAN

extinct
—grouse   HEATH HEN
—pigeon   PASSENGER PIGEON
fail   FLUB
fair   KERMESS.KERMIS(S)
false teeth   STORE TEETH
farewell address   VALEDICTORY
farm   BOWERY
—boundary fence   LINE FENCE
fast car   HOT ROD
feign death, sleep PLAY POSSUM
fellow   GUY.JACK
—lodger   ROOMMATE
fence of pales   PICKET FENCE
fight   MIX-IN
figure (foursided) with
—no parallel sides   TRAPEZIUM
—two parallel sides   TRAPEZOID
finch   CARDINAL BIRD.CHEWINK
      GROUND ROBIN.INDIGO BIRD
        PINE-FINCH.SNOWBIRD
                            TOWHEE
fine   HUNKY-DORY.SWELL
fireman's ladder   BIG STICK
firmness of resolution   SAND
first Monday in
September   LABOR DAY
fish   ALE-WIFE.BLACK BASS
    BLUEFISH.BOWFIN.CAP(E)LIN
      CISCO.CONNER.CUNNER
      DARTER.DOLLY VARDEN
      GROUPER.HORNYHEAD
    JEWFISH.LAKE HERRING
                    MENHADEN
      MISSISSIPPI STURGEON
  PIGFISH.POMPANO.ROBALO
        RONCADOR.SPECK
    SCUP(PAUG).SEA ROBIN
  SHEEPSHEAD.SHOVELHEAD
      SQUETEAGUE.SUCKER
  SURF FISH.TAUTOG.TILEFISH
      TOGUE.TUNA.TUNNY
                    WHITEBASS
—bait   TOLL-BAIT
fit out   (GRUB)STAKE
flag   OLD GLORY
            STARS AND STRIPES
—emblematic of championship
                        PENNANT

—day	TAG DAY
flat	
—bottomed boat	DORY
	MACKINAW
—railway goods wagon	GONDOLA
—region	PLAT
—sided	SLAB-SIDED
flattery	TAFFY
fliers	USAAF
flirt	CHIPPY
floor of theatre below	
galleries	PARQUET CIRCLE
flounder	LIMANDA
flow	PUT
flowers	COSMOS
	INDIAN PIPE.PENSTEMON
	RUDBECKIA.TARWEED
	TRILLIUM.WAKE-ROBIN
fly	
—catcher	KINGBIRD
	SCISSOR-TAIL
—catching thrush	SOLITAIRE
—larvae as bait	HELLGRAM(M)ITE
fodder grass	GAMA GRASS
folk concert	HOOT(E)NANNY
fool	YAP
foolish	FOOL
football	
—field	GRIDIRON
—player	SAFETY
footway	SIDEWALK
forehead band to support	
load	TUMPLINE
foreign born	HYPHENATED
forest	
—clearing	SLASH
—land	TIMBER
formal routine	EXERCISE
forward	FORTH-PUTTING
fourth- or final year college	
student	SENIOR
fox	VORCYRON
free admission	CUFFO
freeze	TAKE
fresh vegetables	TRUCK
freshwater	
—fish	ETHEOSTOMA
	GOLDEYE.LAKE LAWYER
	MOONEYE

—mussel	DEER HORN
fried	
—cake	CRULLER
—chicken	BARNYARD PIMP
friend	BUD(DY).SIDEKICK
fringe	BANG
fruit	BLUEBERRY
	CHOKEBERRY.DEEBERRY
	HUCKLEBERRY.MIN(N)EOLA
	SASKATOON
—juice and spices	SHRUB
full of	
—speed	NIP AND TUCK
—stumps	STUMPY
furnish with supplies	
	(GRUB)STAKE
furrow	LIST
garden	YARD
—flower	NEMOPHILA
—party	LAWN PARTY
gathering to	
—husk corn	HUSKING (BEE)
—raise house frame	
	RAISING-BEE
genuine	SURE-ENOUGH
German	DUTCH
get up! (horse)	HUDDUP
ghost	HAUNT
giant cactus	SAGUARO
girl	BABE.BROAD.QUAIL
give notice	DENOUNCE
glance	SLANT
glassy (surface)	GLARE
goat antelope	
	ROCKY MOUNTAIN GOAT
goatsucker	BULLBAT
gold-seeker	FORTY-NINER
good	
—condition	KELTER.KILTER
—deal more	SOME
—hand at cards	PAT
—natured	CLEVER
goods van	BOXCAR.FREIGHT CAR
gooseberry	WORCESTER-BERRY
gopher	CAMASS-RAT
gorge	BARRANCA.BARRANCO
	GULCH
gossip	S(C)HMOOZE
	SCUTTLEBUTT

got	GOTTEN
government	UNCLE SAM
—certificate to acquire	
public land	LANDSCRIP
—dockyard	NAVY YARD
—money to benefit sole	
locality	PORK BARREL
—patronage	PORK
grackle	(CROW) BLACKBIRD
gradient	GRADE
graduand giving address	
of welcome	SALUTATORIAN
grain pest	JOINTWORM
gramophone	PHONOGRAPH
grape	CATAWBA.FOX GRAPE
grasses	G(R)AMA.PASPALUM
SPIKE-GRASS.UNIOLA.XYRIS	
YELLOW-EYED GRASS	
grasshopper	KATYDID
gratuity	LAGNIAPPE
great deal	SOME
grey wolf	TIMBER WOLF
griddlecake	FLAPJACK.SLAPJACK
gromwell	PUCCOON
ground	
—cuckoo	CHAPARRAL COCK
—floor	FIRST FLOOR
—hog	MARMOT.WOODCHUCK
—squirrel	FLICKERTAIL.GOPHER
grouse	PRAIRIE CHICKEN
SAGE COCK.SAGE GROUSE	
—extinct	HEATH HEN
guard	
—(railway)	CONDUCTOR
—'s van	CABOOSE
guelder-rose	CRANBERRY TREE
—bark	CRAMP-BARK
gully	BARRANCA.BARRANCO
DRAW.GULCH	
gunman	GUNSEL
hackberry	HAGBERRY
hackee	GROUND SQUIRREL
hagberry	HACKBERRY
haggle	DICKER
hamlet	CROSSROAD
hand of welcome	GLAD HAND
handbag	POCKETBOOK.PURSE
handbill	DOGGER.THROWAWAY
handicraft article	BOONDOGGLE

hard blow	S(L)OC(K)DOLAGER
hare	JACK RABBIT
	SNOWSHOE RABBIT
harness horse	HITCH
harvest-mite larva	CHIGGER
	CHIGOE.CHIGRE.JIGGER
hat	STETSON.SUNDOWN
	TEN GALLON HAT
haul of fish	MESS
have done	BE THROUGH
headmaster	PRINCIPAL
head of	
—fire brigade	FIRE MARSHAL
—organisation	PRESIDENT
—police or fire brigade	MARSHAL
hearing of lesson	RECITATION
heat again	WARM OVER
hedge-tree	OSAGE ORANGE
height from floor to	
ceiling	STUD
helicopter	CHOPPER.HOVER
hellbender	MUD PUPPY
helping of food	ORDER
hemp agrimony	MISTFLOWER
hen	PLYMOUTH ROCK
	RHODE ISLAND RED
herd of saddle horses	REMUDA
herder	WRANGLER
herring	MENHADEN
hickory	PECAN (TREE)
highwayman	ROAD AGENT
hike	BACKPACK
hill	
—country inhabitant	HILLBILLY
—terrace	OFFSET
hippy slang	ZOWIE
hired thug	GOON
hold	HOLT
holiday	LABOR DAY
	VACATION
holloa	HOLLER
home run	HOMER.TATER
homespun	CRACKER-BARREL
hooligan	ROUGHNECK
horse	
—breaker	WRANGLER
—chestnut	BUCKEYE
—Indian	CAYUSE
—piebald	PINTO

—poor	TACKY	ineffectual person	LUNCH GUY
—race	KENTUCKY DERBY	inefficient person	SLOUCH
—riding	SADDLER	inexperienced youth	GUNSEL
—sprinter	QUARTER HORSE	infantryman	DOUGHBOY
—thin	RACKABONES	inferior	JAY.SCHLOCK
—wild	BRONC(H)O.MUSTANG	influence	DRAG
horsetail	SCOURING RUSH	inform	CUE IN
house	SHEBANG	informer	FINK
—man	INTERN(E)	innkeeper	INNHOLDER
—of Congress	CAPITOL	insects	GOLD BEETLE
—warming	INFARE		GOLDBUG.KATYDID
—with rooms to		insectivorous plants	DIONAEA
rent	ROOMING HOUSE		SARRACENIA
household effects	PLUNDER		SIDE-SADDLE FLOWER
hub of the universe	BOSTON		VENUS'S FLYTRAP
humbug	GUM	insincere work	EYE SERVICE
Hungarian	BOHUNK.HUNK(Y)	inspecting policeman	
husk	SHUCK		ROUNDSMAN
hut	SHEBANG	intelligence agency	CIA
ice-cream counter		interjection	GEE
	SODA FOUNTAIN		SON OF A GUN.ZOWIE
icy surface	GLARE	intermediate railway	
idiot	APPLEHEAD	station	WAYSTATION
ill-conditioned	TACKY	into	
illegal Mexican immigrant		—confusion	GALLEY-WEST
	WETBACK	—New England	DOWN EAST
illicit liquor shop	SPEAKEASY	—unconsciousness	GALLEY-WEST
immediately	LICKETY-SPLIT	intoxicating drink	RUM
impetuous	BRASH		TANGLEFOOT
in		invalid confined	
—collusion	IN CAHOOTS	indoors	SHUT-IN
—good order	THRIFTY	investigators	CIA.FBI
—good position	HUNKY(-DORY)	ivy	ANGELICA TREE
—less than	INSIDE OF	jaguar	(AMERICAN) TIGER
—partnership	IN CAHOOTS	jail	HOOS(E)GOW
—position of advantage		jam tart	CUPID
	IN THE CATBIRD SEAT	Japanese immigrant	ISSEI.NISEI
—proper manner	ABOUT EAST	jay	XANTH(O)URA
—the evening	EVENINGS	jubilee	SEMI-CENTENNIAL
inclination of road		jug	PITCHER
or railway	GRADE	July 4th	INDEPENDENCE DAY
inconclusive trial	MISTRIAL	jumble	WUZZLE
increase	LIFT	June 14th	FLAG DAY
Indian		jury	
—corn meal	NOCAKE	—man	VENIREMAN
—meal cake	HOE-CAKE	—writ	VENIRE (FACIAS)
—Negro	GRIFF(E)	kaput	KABLOOEY.(KER)FLOOEY
—pokeweed	ITCHWEED	Kentuckian	CORNCRACKER
(see also Red Indian)		keyless watch	STEMWINDER

kind	STRIPE
kingbird	PETCHARY
knitted jacket	WAM(M)US
lake fish	MENOMINEE
land granted to settler	HOMESTEAD
landsman	SHORESMAN
larch	HACKMATACK.TAMARACK
larder above stream	SPRINGHOUSE
large	
—estate	PLANTATION
—fish	TARPON
—quantity	SLATHER
larva of antlion	DOODLEBUG
laurel	KALMIA
lawyer	COUNSELLOR.DA.JURIST
lax in law enforcement	WIDE-OPEN
leader	A
leaf-nosed bat	MORMOPS
lean hog	LAND-SHARK
leather support-strap of carriage	THOROUGHBRACE
leave hastily	BUG OUT
leaves round maize ear	CORN HUSK.CORN SHUCK
legislature	CONGRESS
lending library	RENTAL LIBRARY
leopard	OCELOT
lesson	RECITATION
letter	
—box	MAILBOX
—for local delivery	DROP-LETTER
level	
—crossing	GRADE CROSSING
—land	BENCH
—land by river	INTERVALE
licensing law	EXCISE LAW
lift	ELEVATOR
lighter	GONDOLA
lights out	TAPS
lily	CAMAS(S).CAMASH MEDEOLA.QUAMASH
limitation of debate	CLOTURE
linden tree	BEE TREE
liquor	RUM
—law	EXCISE LAW
—shop	GROCERY

list	
—of candidates	TICKET
—or register of legal records	DOCKET
literal translation	TROT
litter bin	TRASH CAN
lizard	UTA
loaf	BUM
—around	SLOSH
lobelia	INDIAN TOBACCO
—(red)	CARDINAL FLOWER
lobster liver	TOMALLEY
local councillor	SELECTMAN
lodge of fraternal association	GRANGE
lodge(r)	ROOM(ER)
lodging house	ROOMING HOUSE
long	
—jump	BROAD JUMP
—television programme	TELETHON
look	GANDER
look out!	HEADS UP
loose jacket	VAREUSE
Lord!	LAND
lorry	RIG.TRUCK
—driver	TEAMSTER.TRUCKER
Louisiana	
—dialect	CREOLE
—settler of French descent	HABITANT
low	
—public house	GROGGERY
—sled	STONEBOAT
lower price slightly	SHADE
lowest gear	GRANDMA
lucerne	ALFALFA
luggage	
—compartment of car	TRUNK
—room	CHECK(ING) ROOM
—van	FREIGHT CAR
lumberman	RAIL-SPLITTER
—'s hook	PEAV(E)Y
lure	TOLE.TOLL
lynx	BOBCAT.CATAMOUNT
mad	LOCO(ED)
made to order	CUSTOM
mafia	COSA NOSTRA THE MOB

magnolia	CUCUMBER (TREE)
	SWEET BAY
main road	PIKE
maize	CORN
—bread	INDIAN BREAD
—drink	CORN WHISKY
—dumpling	CORN-DODGER
—exchange mart	CORN-PIT
—loaf	CORN PONE
—plantation	CORN-BRAKE
majority (relative)	PLURALITY
make	
—plan of	PLAT
—up (prescription)	FILL
—use of	IMPROVE
malicious destruction	MAYHEM
man	BO.GUY.JACK
map	PLAT
marine	LEATHERNECK
market-garden crops	TRUCK
market gardener	TRUCK FARMER
marmot	GROUNDHOG
	WOODCHUCK.PRAIRIE DOG
marsh marigold	COWSLIP
marshy creek	BAYOU.SLOUGH
marsupial	(O)POSSUM
marten	BLACKCAT.BLACKFOX
	FISHER.PEKAN
	WOODSHOCK
mass of animals on water	RAFT
match	LOCOFOCO
matter	SHEBANG
mean customer	DRAGGER
measures	
—1¼ acres	ARPENT
—1⁄16 pint	FLUID OUNCE
—6 fluid ounces	PINT
—473-551 cubic centimetres	PINT
meat closest to	
bone	TENDERLOIN
mechanic	GREASE MONKEY
medicinal root	DRAGON-ROOT
meeting of	
—delegates	CAUCUS
—voters	TOWN MEETING
melon	CANTALOUP
member of	
—Chinese criminal secret	
society	HIGHBINDER

—corporation	INCORPORATOR
—gymnastic club	TURNER
—Irish revolutionary	
organisation	FENIAN
—Ku Klux Klan	NIGHTRIDER
—lynch party	NIGHTRIDER
—People's Party	POPULIST
—secret fraternity	MOOSE
—secret party	KNOW-NOTHING
memorial tablet	MARKER
men's outfitter	HABERDASHER
mercenary soldier	HESSIAN
merge	MELD
merry-go-round	CAR(R)OUSEL
mess	JACKPOT.MUX
messenger in Congress	PAGE
Mexican	GREASER
middle	CENTER
military	
—decoration	PURPLE HEART
—headquarters	PENTAGON
—policeman	SNOWDROP
milkweed	PLEURISY ROOT
milkwort	SENEGA
mink	VISON
miscellaneous collection	RAFT
Mississippi sturgeon	
	SHOVELHEAD
mock serenade	HORNING
	SHIVAREE
mockingbird	MIMUS
mole	STAR-NOSE
money	JACK.SCRIP
	SPONDULICKS
mongrel	MUTT
monkey	MARMOSET
more than	THE RISE OF
mosquito	SKEETER
mother-in-law	MADAM
motherless calf	DOGIE.DOGY
motor junk yard	POT LOT
	IRON LOT
mottled	PINTO
mountain	
—bear	GRIZZLY
—foothill region	PIEDMONT
—mockingbird	SAGE-THRASHER
—valley	PARK
mountains	ROCKIES

mounted policeman	TROOPER
mouse	DEER MOUSE
—deer	CHEVROTAIN
move rapidly	GIGGIT
mugger of women	MOLL BUZZER
municipal	
—division of county	TOWN
—police	MP
mush	SCHMALTZ
muskrat	WATER RAT
musquash	ONDATRA
nameplate	SHINGLE
narrow, rocky valley	GULCH
national	
—Broadcasting Company	NBC
—Bureau of Standards	NBS
—emblem	BALD EAGLE
	WHITEHEADED EAGLE
—flag	OLD GLORY
	STARS AND STRIPES
—Guard	MILITIA
—holiday	INDEPENDENCE DAY
native of Illinois	SUCKER
naval	
—dockyard	NAVY YARD
—engineer	SEABEE
—petty officer	
	QUARTER-GUNNER
—quartermaster	
	PAYMASTER GENERAL
—warrant officer	SAILING
	MASTER
neck and neck	NIP AND TUCK
negative	NOPE
Negro	MOKE
—in southeast	GULLAH
—nurse	MAMMY
—patois in Louisiana	GUMBO
—song	SECULAR.SPIRITUAL
neighbouring	NEIGHBOUR
never a. . .	NARY
New York	BIG APPLE.GOTHAM
New Yorker	GOTHAMITE
	KNICKERBOCKER
news	
—agent	NEWSDEALER
—boy	NEWSHAWK.NEWSY
night	
—hawk	BULLBAT

—jar	POORWILL
—tram-car	OWL-CAR
—train	OWL-TRAIN
—watchman (remuda)	
	NIGHTHAWK
nincompoop	APPLEHEAD
Nissen hut	QUONSET HUT
non	
—conformist	MAVERICK
—venomous snake	
	GARTER SNAKE
North Carolinian	TAR-HEEL
northern sea duck	OLD SQUAW
north-south strip	RANGE
nosebleed	YARROW
not	
—Mormon	GENTILE
—one	NARY
—trade union member	
	YELLOW DOG
note down for nomination	SLATE
notecase	BILLFOLD
Nova Scotian	BLUENOSE
now	PRESENTLY
numbers betting game	POLICY
nut tree	HICKORY.PECAN
nuts	HICKORY.PECAN
	PICHURIM BEAN
	SASSAFRAS NUT
oak	QUERCITRON
obtain	
—on credit	RUN ONE'S FACE
—right of pre-emption	ENTER
occupy	IMPROVE
occurring occasionally	
	SEMI-OCCASIONAL
odd-jobman	ROUSTABOUT
of	
—certain temperament	
	COMPLECTED
—mixed nationality	
	HYPHENATED
officer	
—of lowest rank	ENSIGN
—who defines boundaries	
	PROCESSIONER
oilskin	SLICKER
old	
—Democrat	LOCOFOCO

—fashioned	FOGRAM
	SCHMALTZY
—man on a station	ROUSTABOUT
—Negro	UNCLE TOM
—New York democrat	HUNKER
—political party	WHIG
olive tree	FRINGE TREE
on the same level	AT GRADE
one	
—of Mexican descent	CHICANO
—out to be sycophantic	
	GLAD-HANDER
one who	
—carries by pack	PACKER
—conducts log rafts	
	RIVER-DRIVER
—does unskilled work	ENGINEER
—has been a JP	SQUIRE
—is nonconformist	MAVERICK
—plays dealt cards	
	STANDPATTER
—splits logs	RAIL-SPLITTER
open-air seating	BLEACHERS
opening with grille	WICKET
opossum	DIDELPHYS
optional	ELECTIVE
—subject or course	ELECTIVE
oral examination	QUIZ
ordinary	ORNERY
out	
—and-out	REGULAR
	STRAIGHT-OUT
—of date	FOGRAM.LUNCHY
—of sorts	MEAN
outwit	EUCHRE
overhead railway	EL
overshoe	ARCTIC.RUBBER
owl	WAPACUT
pack saddle	KYACK
packed in jars	CANNED
paddle steamer	STERN-WHEELER
page torn out of publication	TEAR SHEET
pair of valves or transistors	FLIP-FLOP
pal	BUD(DY).SIDEKICK
paling	PICKET FENCE
paltry	JITNEY
pancake	FLAPJACK.SLAPJACK

papa	POPPA.POPPER
paper money	SCRIP
	SHINPLASTER
parched Indian corn	PINOLE
parlour	SPARE ROOM
part of Commodity exchange floor	PIT
particular kind	STRIPE
partly damaged tree	RAMPICK
	RAMPIKE
partner	PARD(NER)
partnership	CAHOOT(S)
party given by friends exchanging gifts	SHOWER
pass over	OVERSLAUGH
passé	LUNCHY
passenger	PAX
path	TRACE
patriot	HUNDRED-PERCENTER
paved surface	PAVEMENT
pavement	PAVE.SIDEWALK
payment	COMPENSATION
penitent at religious revival rally	MOURNER
people	UNCLE SAM
perch-pike	SAUGER
peregrine falcon	DUCK-HAWK
period of slackening business	
	ROLLING ADJUSTMENT
permission to leave	OUT
personal	
—announcement	CARD
—effects	PLUNDER
perturb	FAZE.PHASE
petrol	GAS(OLENE)
	GASOLINE
Phytolacca	POKEBERRY
	POKEWEED
pickerel weed	PONTEDERIA
picket fence	RAIL FENCE
picnic	CLAMBAKE
piebald horse	PINTO
pie-plant	RHUBARB
pigsty	HOG-PEN
pigeon	GROUND PIGEON
	GROUND DOVE
	MOURNING DOVE
—berry	POKEWEED
piggin	PIPKIN

pike	PICKEREL.SAUGER
—perch	SAUGER
pinafore	TIRE
—dress	JUMPER
pine	LOBLOLLY(PINE)
pistol	DERRINGER.GAT
	IRON.ROD
pitcher plant	DARLINGTONIA
plain	HOMELY.ORNERY
plan	PLAT
plane tree	BUTTONWOOD
	SYCAMORE
plants	CHECKERBERRY
	EVENING PRIMROSE
	GODETIA.GOLDENSEAL
	JACK-IN-THE-PULPIT
	PARTRIDGE-BERRY
	PHLOX.RAGWEED.SEGO
	SNEEZEWEED.SNOW PLANT
	WINTER CLOVER
	WINTERGREEN
plant corrupt electors	COLONIZE
plateau	BARREN
play	
—cards as dealt	STAND PAT
—pizzicato	PINCH
pleaded	PLED
pliable	DOUGH-FACED
plot	PLAT
plover	KILLDEE(R)
	STONE-SNIPE
pluck	PINCH
plum that can be dried	PRUNE
pocket gopher	POUCHED RAT
pod	SHUCK
poison oak	SUMAC(H)
poisoned with locoweed	LOCOED
pokeweed	GARGET
	PIGEON-BERRY
police	
—patrol car	PROWL CAR
—station	STATION HOUSE
policeman	BULL
—on the beat	PATROLMAN
—without rank	PATROLMAN
—'s badge	SHIELD
—'s stick	NIGHT STICK
policy of corrupt public expenditure	PORK BARREL

political	
—conference	CONVENTION
—division of county	TOWN
—funds	BARREL
—party organisation	MACHINE
—party machine	ORGANISATION
—speaker	STUMP ORATOR
—wirepuller	PIPE-LAYER
pond	TANK
Pontederia	PICKERELWEED
poor	
—horse	CAYUSE.TACKY
—whisky	REDEYE
—white	CONCH.CORN-CRACKER
	LOW-DOWNER
—whites	WHITE TRASH
porch	STOOP
porgy	SCUP(PAUG)
porter	REDCAP
portion	GRIST.ORDER
postal code	ZIP CODE
postcard	MAILING CARD
	POSTAL(-CARD)
potassium bicarbonate	SALERATUS
potato pest	COLORADO BEETLE
pothole	THANK-YOU-MA'AM
pouched rat	POCKET GOPHER
poultry	PLYMOUTH ROCK
	RHODE ISLAND RED
prairie	
—chicken	GROUSE
—dog	MARMOT.WISHTONWISH
—grass	BUFFALO GRASS
—oyster	RAW EGG
—schooner	COVERED WAGON
—turnip	BREADROOT
—wolf	COYOTE
president	PREXY
	(see also president)
—of college	PREX
—'s address	WHITE HOUSE
pretend death, sleep	PLAY POSSUM
pretty girl	PEACHERINO.QUAIL
primrose	SUN-DROP
prison	BRIG
	CALABOOSE.HOOS(E)GOW
	LOG-HOUSE.PENITENTIARY

—enclosure	BULLPEN	rabbit	COTTONTAIL
—van	PATROL WAGON	racoon	COON.PROCYON
private		Radio Corporation	RCA
—detective	PINKERTON	railway	EL.L.RAILROAD.ROAD
—room on train		—buffer	BUMPER
	DRAWING ROOM	—carriage	RAIL(ROAD) CAR
probable customer	PROSPECT	—coach connection	VESTIBULE
professional killer	GUN(SEL)	—guard	CONDUCTOR
Progne	SWALLOW	—porter	REDCAP
prohibit by injunction	ENJOIN	—saloon	PARLOUR CAR
promiscuous woman	CHIPPY	—signal	TARGET
	HOOKER	—sleeper	TIE
promise of deferred acceptance of		—station	DEPOT
offer	TAKE A RAIN CHECK	—van	BOXCAR.RAILROAD CAR
promptly	IN SHORT ORDER	—worker	RAILROADER
prosecutor	DA	ramify	SPRANGLE
prosperous	THRIFTY	rapid	SA(U)LT
protection money	KICKBACK	—in a gorge	DALLE
provisions in return		rascal	SKEESICKS
for stake	GRUBSTAKE	raspberry	SALMONBERRY
public		ravine	COULEE.FLUME
—auction sale	VENDUE		GULCH.PURGATORY
—holiday	LABOR DAY	raw egg	PRAIRIE OYSTER
—lavatory	COMFORT STATION	ray	STINGAREE
—service	UTILITY	reactionary	BOURBON
pucker	POCKET	real	SURE-ENOUGH
puddle	LOBLOLLY	really	REAL
Pueblo Indian	ZUNI	rear	FETCH UP
pull	SCHLEP	rebuke	SCORE
puma	CATAMOUNT	reckless	BRASH
	PANTHER.(RED)TIGER	—youth	HOT-RODDER
pumpkin	CASHAW	recovery vehicle	WRECKER
pupil		recurring spree	PERIODICAL
—at kindergarten		red squirrel	BOOMER
	KINDERGARTENER		CHICKAREE
—'s mark	GRADE		S(E)WELLEL
puritan	BLUENOSE	redbreasted thrush	
purple medick	ALFALFA		AMERICAN ROBIN
purpose	CALCULATE	redtop (grass)	HERD('S) GRASS
put in jeopardy	JEOPARD	reedbird	BOBOLINK
quail	BOBWHITE	re-enlisted soldier	VETERAN
	COLIN.ORTYX	refuge	HOLT
quaintly pleasing	CLEVER	refuse container	(TR)ASH CAN
Quaker City	PHILADELPHIA	region	SECTION
quantity	GRIST.MESS	register	LEDGER
quickly	LICKETY-SPLIT	registrar	REGISTER
quilt	COMFORTER	reheated	WARMED-OVER
quite	REAL	reindeer	CARIBOU
—as much as	RISING	religious fervour	ROUSEMENT

Remembrance Day	
	DECORATION DAY
	MEMORIAL DAY
remove shell or husk	SHUCK
remuneration	COMPENSATION
rented farmland	MANOR
representing entire area	
	AT LARGE
reprimanded	CHAWED UP
reservation	HOLD
resident	
—in college	PARIETAL
—junior doctor	INTERN(E)
residential part of town	UP TOWN
resolute	FLAT-FOOTED
resolution	GRIT.SAND
return	ROUND TRIP
revolver	COLT.GAT.IRON.ROD
rhododendron	RHODORA
rhubarb	PIE-PLANT
ricebird	BOBOLINK
ridge or depression in	
road	THANK-YOU-MA'AM
riding horse	SADDLER
rifle	WINCHESTER
right of state to impose sovereign	
legislation	INTERPOSITION
ringplover	KILLDEE(R)
ringtail(-cat)	CACOMISTLE
	CACOMIXL
risen	RIZ
rivers	HUDSON.KILL
	MISSISSIPPI.MISSOURI
	POTOMAC.RIO GRANDE
river	
—fish	GROWLER
—mussel	NIGGER-HEAD
—side embankment	LEVEE
—sides	UPLAND
—water affected by	
tides	TIDEWATER
robbery	HEIST
rocket fuel	HYDYNE
Rocky Mountain sheep	BIGHORN
rodent	JUMPING MOUSE
	KANGAROO RAT.MARMOT
	MOUNTAIN BEAVER
	POUCHED MOUSE
	S(E)WELLEL.WOODCHUCK

rodeo performer	COWBOY
roll	BAGEL
room	SHEBANG
—attached to shop	PARLOUR
rose	RIZ
—pest	ROSE-BUG
rough country	BOONDOCKS
roundabout	CAR(R)OUSEL
routine flight	MILK RUN
rubber overshoe	GUM(SHOE)
ruffed grouse	PARTRIDGE
rumour	SCUTTLEBUTT
rural area	STICKS
rustic	HICK.RUBE
saddle	
—girth	CINCH
—horse	SADDLER
safe-breaker	YEGG(MAN)
sailor in Navy	GOB
St John's wort	ORANGE-GRASS
salal	GAULTHERIA
salamander	HELLBENDER
	MENOPOME.MUD PUPPY
saloon car	SEDAN
sand	
—bar	OVERSLAUGH
—piper/stint	SAND-PEEP
saunter	MOSEY
school	COLLEGE
	COMMON SCHOOL
	GRADE SCHOOL
	HIGH SCHOOL
—dance	PROMENADE
—imposition	PENSUM
—mistess	SCHOOL-MA'AM
scion	CION
Scout's leather cord	
	BOONDOGGLE
scrutinise	CANVASS
sea bream	PORGIE.PORGY
sea lavender	SEA ROSEMARY
seaboard	TIDEWATER
season ticket	
	COMMUTATION TICKET
seclusion	RETIRACY
second-year student	SOPHOMORE
secret organisation	
	KU KLUX (KLAN)
Secretary of State	PREMIER

sedge	CHUFA.NUT-GRASS	side (billards)	ENGLISH
	TIGER-NUT	sightseer	RUBBERNECK
seedy	TACKY	signboard	SHINGLE
seesaw	TEETER(-BOARD)	simpleton	FLATHEAD
self-appointed		sir(rah)	SIRREE
peacekeepers	LYNCH MOB	skittles	TEN-PINS
	VIGILANCE COMMITTEE	skunk	SEE-CAWK
	VIGILANTES	—bird	BOBBOLINK
self-possession	COOL	Slav	BOHUNK
sell tickets at inflated prices	SCALP	sloppy	SOZZLY
semibreve	WHOLE NOTE	slops	SOZZLE
send luggage	CHECK	slush	SPOSH
sentimentality	SCHMALTZ	small	
sergeant-fish	COBIA.CRAB-EATER	—college	FRESHWATER COLLEGE
settle	LOCATE	—lizard	FENCE-LIZARD
shadbush	SASKATOON	—loaf (maize)	CORN-DODGER
	SERVICEBERRY	—river	CREEK
shallow broken water	RIFFLE	—township	VILLAGE
sharptailed grouse		snack	LUNCH
	PRAIRIE CHICKEN	snakes	HOG-NOSE.PIT VIPER
shebeen	SPEAKEASY		RING SNAKE
shell	SHUCK	snipe	SHAD-BIRD.WILLET
shoe	TIE	snow	
—lace	(SHOE)STRING	—bird	JUNCO
shop	SHEBANG	—goose	WAV(E)Y
—assistant	(SALES) CLERK	—up	STALL
—keeper	STOREKEEPER	social	SOCIABLE
short		—blunder	BREAK
—cuts	ACROSS LOTS	—intercourse	GAM
—jacket	ROUNDABOUT	soda-fountain worker	SODA JERK
shortage	WANTAGE	sodium bicarbonate	SALERATUS
shout	ROOT	soft drink	SARSAPARILLA
show spirit	SPUNK	soil, muddy when wet	GUMBO
shrewd	HEADS-UP	soldier	DOUGHBOY.GI.SAMMY
shrubs	BUFFALO BERRY	—of both world wars	RETREAD
BUFFALO NUT.BUTTON BUSH		solicit orders	DRUM
CALICO BUSH		something	
CANDLEBERRY TREE		—done for applause	HOKUM
CORAL BERRY.FRANGIPANI		—large	SCROUGER
GREASEWOOD HAMAMELIS		—rented or hired	RENTAL
HOP TREE.HUCKLEBERRY		sound	COPACETIC.COPESETTIC
KALMIA.MOUNTAIN LAUREL		soup	BURGOO
RED JASMINE.SAL(L)AL			CHOWDER.GUMBO
SNOWBERRY SPICEBUSH		Southerner who supported	
STAFF TREE.STRAWBERRY TREE		Republican Party	SCAL(L)AWAG
SYMPHORICARPUS			SCALLYWAG
WAX MYRTLE.WINTER BERRY		Spanish-American	GREASER
WITCH-ALDER.WITCH HAZEL		—half-caste	MESTIZO
WITHE-ROD.YA(U)PON.YUPON		sparrow	SAVANNA-SPARROW

speaker of farewell address	VALEDICTORIAN
special subject	MAJOR
specialise at college	MAJOR
spectacles	CHEATERS
speculative scheme	WILDCAT
speculator	WILDCAT
speedwell	NECK-WEED
spelling competition	SPELL-DOWN
spice bush	BENJAMIN TREE
spider	BLACK WIDOW
spies	CIA
spill	LAMPLIGHTER
spindle tree	BURNING BUSH
spiny	
—fish	SCULPIN
—lizard	HORNED TOAD
Spiraea	HARDHACK
spittoon	CUSPIDOR(E)
splash	SOZZLE
spoil	MUX
sponge	BUM
sporting kit	DUFFEL.DUFFLE
spotted sandpiper	PEETWEET
sprawl	SPRANGLE
spree	BUM
sprinter (horse)	QUARTER HORSE
spruce	HEMLOCK
spy	FINK
squirrel	CHIPMUCK.CHIPMUNK
	GROUND SQUIRREL.HACKEE
	S(E)WELLEL
stag	
—beetle	HORNBUG
—party	STAG
stalk	STILL-HUNT
starchy tuber	INDIAN TURNIP
start	JUMP-OFF
state	
—governor's deputy	LIEUTENANT GOVERNOR
—militia	NATIONAL GUARD
states without slavery	FREE STATES
statesman	TEXAN
steal cattle	RUSTLE
stew	BURGOO
—of corn and beans	SUCCOTASH

stewed fruit	SAUCE
stock	
—farm	RANCH
—of a commodity	INVENTORY
stopping train	WAYTRAIN
storehouse over stream	SPRINGHOUSE
straggle	SPRANGLE
strawberry shrub	CALYCANTHUS
stray animal	MAVERICK
stream	CREEK.KILL
street	
—boy	TAD
—car	HORSECAR
—charges	STREETAGE
—ruffian	PLUG-UGLY
—vendor's barrow	PUSHCART
strip	
—occupied by railway	RIGHT OF WAY
—off	SHUCK
strong jacket	WAM(M)US
	WAMPUS
struggle	SPRANGLE
student	SOPHOMORE
stunning girl	PEACHERINO
stupid	DUMB.JAY
—fellow	BOB.BUFFLEHEAD.JAY
—man	KNUCKLE-DRAGGER
—person	APPLEHEAD
	DUMBBELL.LUNCH GUY
	MUTT.SCHMO(CK)
	SCHMUCK.SCHNOOK
—youth	GUNSEL
sturdy man	HUSKY
subdivision of county	TOWNSHIP
submarine	PIG-BOAT
sulky	STUFFY
sumac	POISON OAK
summer residence	COTTAGE
sunfish	CRAPPIE
supply	GRIST.(GRUB)STAKE
suppose	CALCULATE.GUESS
surmount	RISE
suspect	SUSPICION
swallow	PROGNE
—hole	SINK-HOLE
swamp	DISMAL.PURGATORY
	VLEI.VLY

swan	TRUMPETER
sweet	
—friedcake	CRULLER.WONDER
—popcorn	CORNBALL
—potato	YAM
—seller on train	BUTCHER
sweets	CANDIES
swerving throw in	
baseball	SCREWBALL
swift	CHIMNEY SWALLOW
swimming pool	NATATORIUM
swindler's helper	
	BUNCO-STEERER
symbol of luck	GOD'S EYE
take	
—a holiday	VACATION
—up residence	LOCATE
talk	
—bluntly	TALK TURKEY
—business	TALK TURKEY
—nonsense	BLATHER
talker of claptrap	BLATHERSKITE
tall hat	STOVEPIPE
tallboy	HIGHBOY
tap	FAUCET
teacher	SCHOOLMAN
teal	BLUE-WING
team conclave	HUDDLE
telephone	
—call box	PAY-STATION
—circuit	TRUNK
television	VIDEO
—award	EMMY
temporary school	INSTITUTE
tender	PROPOSAL
tenderfoot	GREENHORN
—in Alaska	CHE(E)CHAKO
	CHEECHALKO
	CHECHAQUO
term	SEMESTER
—of endearment	HONEY CHILE
termite	WOODLOUSE
theatre stalls	PARQUET
theatrical award	TONY
theological student	THEOLOGUE
thick soup	BURGOO
thicket of canes	CANEBRAKE
thingummy	HOOT(E)NANNY
	HOOTANANNY

think	CALCULATE.GUESS
third-year student	JUNIOR
thorn	
—apple	JIM(P)SON WEED
	JAMESTOWN WEED
—bush	MESQUITE
thorough	REGULAR
thoroughly	ALL TO PIECES
—acquainted with	NEXT TO
thousand	
—dollars	GRAND
—million	BILLION
—to fourth power	TRILLION
—to fifth power	QUADRILLION
—to sixth power	QUINTILLION
through and through	
	ALL TO PIECES
thrush	CATBIRD.VEERY
tidy up	PICK
timber	LUMBER
—wolf	GREY WOLF
timothy (grass)	HERD('S) GRASS
tiny	TEENTY
titmouse	CHICKADEE
toady	BOOTLICK
tobacco	PERIQUE
toffee	TAFFY
toll	
—for street facilities	STREETAGE
—free road	FREEWAY
top hat	PLUG-HAT
tortoise	GOPHER.TERRAPIN
tough	ROUGHNECK
towhee	GROUND ROBIN
town	BURG
townsman	COCKNEY.DUDE
track	SIGN
trade union branch	LOCAL
trader	
—with Indians	COMANCHERO
—'s jargon	CHINOOK
trading post	FORT
trail	SIGN
trailing plant	PARTRIDGE-BERRY
train with limited number of cars	
and stops	LIMITED EXPRESS
tram	STREETCAR
—car	TROLLEY (CAR)
tramp	HOBO

—light	SLUT LAMP
translation	HORSE
transport	HAUL
—agent	FREIGHTER
—of freight trailers by ship or	
barge	FISHYBACK
travel bag	GRIP(SACK)
travelling trunk	SARATOGA (TRUNK)
tread softly	CATFOOT
tree	
—allied to elm	HACKBERRY
—frog	PEEPER
—Gordonia	LOBLOLLY BAY
—Tsuga	HEMLOCK
—leathery-leaved	LOBLOLLY TREE
trees	BLACK WALNUT.CATALPA
	DOUGLAS FIR.DYER'S OAK
	FRINGE TREE.HALESIA
	HEADACHE TREE
	HONEY LOCUST.JACK PINE
	LIQUIDAMBAR.OSAGE ORANGE
	PITCHPINE.QUERCITRON
	SASSAFRAS.SEQUOIA
	SHAWNEE-WOOD.SILVER BELL
	SNOWDROP TREE
	SLIPPERY ELM
	SUGAR MAPLE.SUGAR PINE
	SWAMP CYPRESS.TAXODIUM
	TULIP TREE.WASHINGTONIA
	YELLOW-BARKED OAK
	YELLOWWOOD
trilby	FEDORA
trite	MICKEY
trounce	SHELL
trousers	HIP-HUGGERS.PANTS
trouser turn-up	CUFF
truant	HOOKEY
truck driver	TEAMSTER TRUCKER
truckling	DOUGH-FACED
truncheon	NIGHT STICK
trunk	SARATOGA
—call	TOLL CALL
tufted grouse	PHEASANT
tulip-tree	CUCUMBER TREE POPLAR
tumbleweed	WILD INDIGO

turn-out	TEAM
turtle-dove	MOURNING DOVE
twilled cotton	CHINO
tyrant flycatcher	KING-BIRD PETCHARY
ugly	HOMELY
unbranded animal	MAVERICK
uncomfortable	MEAN
underground railway	SUBWAY
undertaker	MORTICIAN
undue boldness	FORTH-PUTTING
unfounded story	MALARK(E)Y
uniform colour	OLIVE DRAB
unit trusts	MUTUAL FUNDS
United States	UNCLE SAM
university calendar	CATALOG
unlucky person	S(C)HLIMAZEL
unmade road	DIRT ROAD
unmanageable animal	OUTLAW
unsaleable item	STOREKEEPER
unsound business deal	WILDCAT
unyielding	ROCK-RIBBED
up to and including	THROUGH
upper	
—floor	LOFT
—part of river steamer	TEXAS
unskilled worker	HUNKY
usurer	NOTE-SHAVER
utterly	PLUMB
valley side	COTEAU
vegetable	
—marrow	MARROW SQUASH
—seller	SAUCEMAN
vegetables accompanying	
meat	SAUCE
vehicle	SHEBANG.SURREY
—for hire	HACK
verandah	PIAZZA PORCH.STOOP
veritably	REAL
very much	SOME
—indeed	AND HOW
vice	VISE
Virginian	TUCKAHOE
—fungus	INDIAN BREAD
—quail	PARTRIDGE
visit at sea	GAM
vote illegally by casting more	
than one vote	REPEAT

voters' meeting to nominate
candidate PRIMARY
vow VUM
vulture TURKEY BUZZARD
waiter BUS BOY.GOSSOON
waitress BUS GIRL
walk PASEAR
walking boundaries
PROCESSIONING
walnut BUTTERNUT
CARYOCAR
warbler REDSTART
warship USS
water
—cask SCUTTLEBUTT
—fall SA(U)LT
—lily SPATTER-DOCK
—leaf PAD
—proof SLICKER
—shed DIVIDE
—thrush WAGTAIL
—weed ANACHARIS.ELODEA
waxwing CEDAR-BIRD
wayfaring-tree HOBBLE-BUSH
weasel CARCAJOU
GLUTTON.WOLVERENE
WOLVERINE
wedding-gifts party SHOWER
weed SPANISH NEEDLES
weight HEFT
—25 lbs QUARTER
—100 lbs CENTAL
HUNDREDWEIGHT
—750-1200 lbs
(tobacco) HOGSHEAD
—2000 lbs SHORT TON
—2240 lbs LONG TON
well off FOREHANDED
wharf labourer ROUSTABOUT
wheat pest HESSIAN FLY
whippoorwill WISHTONWISH
whisky BOURBON.RYE
SCOTCH.TANGLEFOOT
—and soda HIGHBALL
white
—fish ROUND-FISH
—headed eagle BALD EAGLE
—hellebore INDIAN POKE
—wash SKUNK

Whitsuntide PINKSTER.PINXSTER
whopper SCROUGER
S(L)OC(K)DOLAGER
wild
—cat CATAMOUNT
—horse BRONC(H)O.MUSTANG
window
—blind SHADE
—dressing TRIM
windscreen WINDSHIELD
wine CATAWBA
wing
—making L-shape EL
—or annex of house EXTENSION
wintergreen CHECKERBERRY
GAULTHERIA
wireless news bulletin DOPE
witch
—alder FOTHERGILLA
—hazel FOTHERGILLA
HAMAMELIS
with ice cream A LA MODE
withhold support BOLT
witness-box CHAIR.STAND
witty afterthought LATTER-WIT
woman BROAD.FRAIL
women's
—academic society SORORITY
—blouse SHIRTWAIST
—blouse or bodice WAIST
—club SOROSIS
wood
—land TIMBER
—louse TERMITE
—shavings EXCELSIOR
wooden bowl or pail PIPKIN
woodpecker FLICKER.YUCKER
work LABOR
—basket CABA
—of little value BOONDOGGLE
worker using compressed
air SANDHOG
workman's railcar HANDCAR
workshop worker SHOPMAN
worm fence SNAKE FENCE
worry FAZE.PHASE
worthless man BUM
wrecking clause in
document JOKER

wrestle and throw	BULLDOG
writ issued by sheriff	
	VENIRE (FACIAS)
yarrow	NOSE BLEED
yearly step in education	GRADE
yell after a cheer	TIGER
yellowwood	GOPHER
yes	YEP
—certainly	AND HOW
yodel	WARBLE
yokel	CORNBALL.JAKE.RUBE
young	
—man	GOSSOON
—townsman	MUCKER
zero score	GOOSE-EGG
amid c/row/ds	ROW
amiss	
went *amiss*	NEWT
among	
among th/e lite/rate	ELITE
among *	incl in *
•is *among* engineers	RISE
amount	AMT
amount of metrication	LITRE
amount of metri/cat/ion	CAT
ampere	A
ampere-hour	AH
amplitude modulation	AM
amusing detour	DIVERSION
an	A.I
	(*see also* a[1])
an *Italian*. . .	UNA.UNO
an *uprising*(D)	NA
anaesthetic	NUMBER
analyse	
analysed ores	EROS.ROES.SORE
analysis of soil	OILS.SILO
anarchist	RED
ancestral tree	ELDER
ancient	ANC.FLAG.PISTOL
city	TROY.UR
times	BC
vessel	ARK
	(*see also* old[1])
and	
and *French*. . .	ET
and *German*. . .	UND
and not	NOR
ane	A.I

anent	ON.RE
	(*see also* about[5])
anew	
men hope *anew*	PHENOME
angel	BACKER.MICHAEL.RAPHAEL
	(*see also* nine)
angle	FISH.L
Anglican worship	CE
Anglo	
Anglo-French waters	SEAMER
Anglo-Saxon	AS
Angola(n)	
coin	ANGOLAR
sheep	ZUNA
angström	A
animal	
Animal Farm	RANCH.STUD
animal fur	CATNAP
animal *sound*	BRUIT
animal talk	YAK
Anitra's dance	ARTISAN
announce their. . .	THERE
annual general meeting	AGM
anonymous	AN.omit N
•*anonymous* queen	ANER
•*anonymous* ma(n)	MA
another	
another form of male. . .	LAME
	MEAL
another husband	SECOND MATE
another spell of weather	
	W(H)ETHER
another way of putting	
things	NIGHTS
another way to put. . .	TUP
answer	ANS.KEY
one answer	-IANS
ante	A
antelope	
including deer, gazelle:	
Abyssinian	MADOQUA
Alpine ibex	STEINBOCK
African	ADDAX.ADMI.ARIEL
	BISA.BLAUWBOK.BLESBOK
	BONGO.BONTEBOK.BLOUBOK
	BLUE-BUCK.BOS(SH)BO
	BOTIGO.BUBALIS.BUSHBOK
	BUSHBUCK.CAMA.CHEVROTAIN
	COBA.DAMA.DIBITAG.DIK-DIK

DUIKER.DUYKER.ELAND
GEMSBOK.GNU.GRYSBOK
GUIB.HARNESSED ANTELOPE
HARTEBEEST.IMPALA
IMPOPO.(I)NYALA.KAAMA
KLIPSPRINGER.KOB(O)
KORIN.KUDO.LECHWE
MHORR.MOHR.NAGOR
NAKONG.ORIBI.ORYX.OUREBI
OX-ANTELOPE.PALA.PALEBUCK
PALLAH.POKU.POOKOO.PUKU
PYGARG.REEBOK.REITBOK
RHEBOK.RIETBOK.SABLE
SASSABY.SPRINGBOK
SPRINGBUCK.STEENBOK
STEINBOCK.STEMBOK
STEMBUCK.SUNI.TOPI.TORA
TSESSEBE.WATERBUCK
WATERDEER. WILDEBEEST

American	CABRIE.CABRIT
	ELK.MOOSE.MULE DEER
	PRONGBUCK.PRONGHORN
	ROCKY MOUNTAIN GOAT
	WAPITI
Asian	AHU.ARIEL.AXIS
	BARKING DEER.CHITAL.DZEREN
	ELK.GAZEL(LE).HANGUL.KAKAR
	MAHA.MUNTJAC.MUNTJAK
	MUSK DEER.NAPU.RATWA
	RUSA.SAIGA.SAMBOO
	SAMBHUR.SAMB(O)UR
	SAMB(W)AR
Burmese	THAMENG.THAMIN
Chinese	MUSK DEER
	WATER DEER
East Indian	RUCERVUS
European	CHAMOIS.ELK
	IBEX.IZZARD
female	DOE.ROE
Himalayan	GORAL.SEROW
Indian	AXIS.BLACKBUCK
	CHI(N)KARA.CHIRU.CHITAL
	NILGAI.NYLG(H)AU
	RUSA.SAMBOO.SAMBHUR
	SAMB(O)UR.SAMB(W)AR
	SASIN.SEROW
Japanese	SIKA
male	BUCK.STAG
Mongolian	DZEREN.DZERON

mouse-deer	CHEVROTAIN
puff-nosed	SAIGA
Pyrenean	IBEX.IZZARD
Senegalese	NAGOR
South American	ALPACA
	GUANACO.HUANACO
	LLAMA.PACO.PUDU
striped	HARNESSED ANTELOPE
Tibetan	GOA
white-bellied	LECHWE
young	FAWN

anti

anti-aircraft	AA.ARCHIE
anti-ballistic missile	ABM
anti-tetanus serum	ATS
anticipating	(in) HOP-E
antique	(*see* old[1])
antiquarian	FAS.SAS

any

any other business	AOB
any sort	ORTS.TORS
any *sort*	NAY
anybody	ALL.ONE
anyhow I am. . .	AIM.AMI
anyway let us	LUTES
anyway	
indicates a palindrome	
•*anyway*, a flop	DUD
•father *anyway*. . .	DAD.POP
aorist	AOR

apart

apart from. . .	FORM
apart from a. . .	omit A
apart from a new. . .	omit AN
apart from the front	omit first letter
apart from the leader	omit first letter
apart from name	omit N
apart from *	omit *
•fa(the)r *apart from* the. . .	FAR
tear *apart*	RATE.TARE
apogee	APO
appalling thing	NIGHT
apparent	APP
apparent in t/he w/ay. . .	HEW
apparently	APP
apparently not	KNOT
	(*see also* appear)

appeal	SA.SOS	American	JONAGOLD
appealing	CUTE	JONATHAN.WASHINGTON RED	
appear		Canadian	MCINTOSH RED
appears in We/st End s/how		Dutch	BELLE DE BOSKOOP
	STENDS	French	ORLEANS.REINETTE
appears to be weak	WEEK	German	HOLSTEIN
appears to be <u>worse</u>	SWORE	Japanese	CRISPIN
appears to have so/me tal/l...		New Zealand	GALA
	METAL	old	LEATHER-COATS
appearance in tw/ice ni/ghtly...			POMEWATER.SWEETING
	ICENI	Swedish	KATY
* *appears in*...	incl *	**apple²**	
•it *appears in* an opening	AGITATE	apple *core*	P
(*see also* apparent)		apple *peel*	AE
apple¹	ARTHUR TURNER	apple tree	OAK
	ASHMEAD'S KERNEL	apples (and pears)	STAIRS
	BAKER'S DELICIOUS	*apportion* <u>blame</u>	MABEL
	BEAUTY OF BATH.BESS POOL	**appreciate it**	DIGIT
	BLENHEIM (ORANGE)	**apprentice**	APP.L
	BRAMLEY SEEDLING	apprentice cook	DEVIL
	CHARLES ROSS	(*see also* learner)	
CLAYGATE.PEARMAIN.COSTARD		**approval**	OK
	COX'S ORANGE (PIPPIN)	**approx(imately)**	C.CA.CIRC.SOME
	D'ARCY SPICE.DISCOVERY	(*see also* about¹)	
	DUMELOW SEEDLING	**APRE**	APIARY
	EARLY VICTORIA	**Arabia**	UAR
	EGREMONT RUSSET	**Arab(ic)¹**	AR.ARAB.UAR
	ELLISON ORANGE	hence	
	EMNETH EARLY.FORGE	•Arab adversary	ARRIVAL
	FORTUNE.GEORGE CAVE	•Arab girl	ARENA.ARGAL
	GOLDEN DELICIOUS	•Arab *on* camel	ARRIDING
	GRANNY SMITH.GRENADIER	•Arab torture	ARRACK
	JAMES GRIEVE.JONATHAN	and	
	LADY SUDELEY	•Arab *in* Maine	MARE
(LANE'S) PRINCE ALBERT		•girl *embracing* Arab	MARRY
	LAXTON'S SUPERB	•soldiers *surround* Arab	RARE
LORD BURGHLEY.LORD DERBY		**Arab(ic)²**	ALI
	LORD HINDLIP	ancient people	HIMYARITE
	LORD LAMBOURNE		SABA.SHEBA
	NEWTON WONDER	ascetic	DERVISH
	PEASGOOD NONSUCH	banker	SCHROFF
	QUEEN COX.RED ELLISON	camel	DROMEDARY
	RIBSTON PIPPIN.RUSSET	—train	CAF(F)ILA.KAFILA
	ST EDMUND'S PIPPIN	camp	D(O)UAR.DOWAR
	STURMER PIPPIN.SUNSET	capital	A.RIYADH
	TIDEMAN'S LATE ORANGE	chapter of Koran	SURA(H)
	TOM PUTT.WARNER'S KING	chief	AMEER.AMIR.CAID.EMEER
	WHITE MELROSE		EMIR.KAID.RAIS.SA(Y)ID
(WORCESTER) PEARMAIN			SAYYID.SCHIEK.SHEIK(H)

Christ's thorn	NABK.NEBBUK
	NEBE(C)K
Christian	COPT
cloak	ABA.BERNOUS(E)
	BURNOUS(E).BURNOOSE
	BOURK(H)A.BURK(H)A.CAFTAN
	(D)JIBBAH.DJELLABA.GAL(L)-
	ABEA(H).GALABIA.GAL(L)-
	ABI(Y)AH.GAL(L)ABI(Y)EH
	JUBBAH.KAFTAN.HAI(C)K
	HAIQUE.HYKE
coffee cup lacking	
handle	FINGAN.FINJAN
coins	BUCKSHA.DINAR
	QURSH.RIYAL.SAUDI
commando	FEDAYEE
courtyard	HOSH
cup-holder	ZARF.ZURF
dancing girl	ALMA(H).ALME(H)
demon	AFREET
	AFRIT.MAHOUN(D)
dervish	SANTON
desert	
—plant	CAMEL'S THORN
—rat	JERBOA
devil	SHAITAN
dish	COUSCOUS(OU)
	CUSCUS.KHUSKHUS
dog	SALUKI
domed tomb	QUBBAH
domesticated animal	CAMEL
drink	BOSA.BOZA(H)
	LEBAN.SHRAB
drug	BHANG.BENJ
	HASHEESH.HASHISH
dry river bed	WADI.WADY
dust storm	SHAITAN
encampment	D(O)UAR.DOWAR
eye shadow	KOHL
fate	KISMET
father	ABU
fort	CASBAH.KASBAH
fortified camp	ZAREBA
girl	BINT
go away!	IMSHI.IMSHY
grain	TOMAND
gum resin	FRANKINCENSE
	OLIBANUM
habit	(see cloak above)

head	
—cord	AGAL
—dress	FEZ.KAFFIYEH.KEFFIYEH
	TARBOOSH.TARB(O)USH
—man	MOCUDDUM.MOKADDAM
	MUQADDAM
hill	TEL(L)
holy	
—building (Mecca)	KAABA
—litter	MAHMAL
in the name of Allah	BISMILLAH
jinni	MARID
language	BERBER.TUAREG
leader	A
look	SHUFTI
magistrate	CADI.CAID.KADI.KAID
	SHEREEF.SHERIF
market	SOUK
measure	ARDEB.COVID(O).DEN
merchant	HOWADJI
millet grain	COUSCOUS(OU)
	CUSCUS.KHUSKHUS
mound	TEDL(L)
nomad	BEDAWIN.BEDOUIN
	SARACEN.TUAREG
ornamental holder	ZARF.ZURF
physician	HAKEEM.HAKIM
pilgrim	HADJI.HAJJI
pilgrimage	HADJ.HAJJ
poem	GAZEL.GHAZAL.GHAZEL
race	BERBER
racing camel	DELOUL.MEHARI
raider	FEDAYEEN
ravine	KHOR.WADI.WADY
reed pipe	ARGHOOL
religion	ISLAM
	MOHAMMEDANISM
religious	
—ceremony	DOSEH
—philosophy	AVERR(H)OISM
river bed	WADI.WADY
sandstorm	HABOOB
sea captain	NOCADAH
script	CUFIC.KUFIC.NES(H)KI
shawl	KAFFIYEH.KEFFIYEH
ship	BAGGALA.D(H)OW
	FELUCCA.SAIC
shirt	CAMESE.CAMIS(E)
	CAMISO.KAMIS

shrine	CAABA.KAABA
shrub	K(H)AT.NABK
	NEBBUK.NEBE(C)K
sign of glottal stop	HAMZA(H)
skull cap	CHECHIA
slave	MAMELUKE
smoking (hookah)	CHILLUM
spirit	DJINNI.GENIE
	GH(O)UL.GINNI.JINNEE
	JINNI.MARID
state of bliss	KEF
stockade	ZARE(E)BA
	ZEREBA.ZERIBA
tariff	ZABETA
tea	K(H)AT
tent village	D(O)UAR.DOWAR
thorn hedge	ZARE(E)BA
	ZEREBA.ZERIBA
title	SIDI
tree	ALHAGI
unbeliever	CAFFRE.KAFIR
verse form	G(H)AZAL.GHAZEL
water	
—pipe	CHILLUM.HOOKA(H)
—skin	KIRBEH
wheel	SAKIA.SAKI(Y)EH
weight	KELA.ROTL.ROT(T)OLO
whip	K(O)URBASH
arable land	LEA.LEY
Aramaic	SYRIAC
arbitrary rules	LURES
archaeopteryx	EARLY BIRD
archaic	ARCH
	(*see also* old[1])
archangel	GABRIEL
	MICHAEL.RAPHAEL
	RECORDING HEAD
archbishop	ABP.CANTUAR
	EBOR.LANG.LAUD
archdeacon	VEN
arched flyover	RAINBOW.VIADUCT
archer	TELL
architect	ADAM.WREN.WRIGHT
architecture	ARCH
architectural features	
apex of building	FASTIGIUM
apse	CONCHA
arc of arch	HANCE.HAUNCH
arcade over aisle	TRIFORIUM

arch	
—across interior angle	SQUINCH
—having vertical piers between	
impost and springing	
	STILTED ARCH
—over gate	PORTAL
—stone	VOUSSOIR
arched roof	VAULT
architrave	EPISTYLE
arcs and cusps	FEATHERING
arm	BRACE
astragal moulding	FUSAROL(E)
ball on pillar	BALLOON
band between flutings	FILLET
base of pillar	PATTEN
bay	
—resting on brackets	ORIEL
—window	JUT-WINDOW
beam	
—above door or window	LINTEL
—at base of opening	SILL
bedchamber (French)	ROUELLE
body of Corinthian	
capital	VASE
bottom stone of arch	SPRINGER
bracket under cornice	
	MODILLION
broad flat band	FASCIA
cap of pier	CUSHION
carved basket	CORBEIL
central stone in arch	HEADSTONE
	KEYSTONE.QUOIN
chancel	ADYTUM
chapel	
—at West end of church	GALILEE
—of prothesis	PARABEMA
—within church	SACELLUM
chevron moulding	DANCETTE
choir screen	REREDOS(SE)
	REREDORSE
church vestibule	NARTHEX
close-set columns	PYCNOSTYLE
clawlike ornament	GRIFF(E)
colonnade	PORCH
—around court or building	
	PERISTYLE
column of shaft	SCAPE.SCAPUS
combination of beams	
	TRABEATION

concave
—ceiling CUPOLA
—moulding TROCHILUS
continuous plinth PODIUM
convex
—curve of column ENTASIS
—moulding ECHINUS
—surface of arch EXTRADOS
corner
—of coping SKEW-CORBEL
    SKEW-PUT.SKEW-TABLE
—stone QUOIN
cornice above pedestal
  base SURBASE
covered
—colonnade STOA
—portico XYST(OS).XYSTUS
crescent-shaped space LUNETTE
cresting BRATTICING
    BRATTISHING
cross
—beam TRANSOM
—rib in vaulting LIERNE
crossed fillets STRAP-WORK
cupola THOLOS.THOLUS
curve at end of column
  shafts APOPHYGE
curved
—timber roof support CRUCK
—wall/ceiling junction COVE
cyma recta moulding DOUCINE
decorated
—band at top of wall FRIEZE
—with leaves FOLIATED
decoration in
—moulding LINEN-SCROLL
—panels LINENFOLD
detached support PILLAR
diagonal rib of vault OGIVE
die of a pedestal SOLIUM
dome THOLOS.THOLUS
doorway PORTAL
—enclosure PORCH
—surround ARCHITRAVE
Doric order MALE ORDER
dormer window LUCARNE
double-grooved
  ornament DIGLYPH
dripstone LABEL.LARMIER

dual-pitched roof
  MANSARD(-ROOF)
enclosed space in front of
  church PARVIS(E)
entablature TRABEATION
entrance PORTAL
—for carriage PORTE-COCHERE
entresol MEZZANINE
extension of church behind
  altar RETROCHOIR
fascia PLATBAND
female figure
—used as column CARYATID
—with basket on
  head CANEPHOR(A)
  CANEPHORE.CANEPHORUS
fillet LIST
—above architrave TAENIA
—below triglyph REGULA
—between flutes STRIA
finial CROP
five-petalled feature CINQUE-FOIL
flat
—arch PLATBAND
—fillet BANDELET
—moulding PLATBAND
—narrow moulding REGLET
—ornament PATERA
flower-bud ornament KNOSP
flower-like ornament FLEURON
four-lobed
  ornament QUATREFOIL
  QUATREFEUILLE
French Gothic style
  FLAMBOYANT
gable FASTIGIUM
—coping stone SKEW
gallery above aisle TRIFORIUM
garret SOL(L)AR.SOL(L)ER
gate PORTAL
gateway
—of Egyptian temple PYLON
—to temple PROPYLAEUM
  PROPYLON
grooved border SWAGE
grotesque ornamentation BABERY
half-round moulding ASTRAGAL
having
—1 column MONOSTYLE

—1 row of columns   PERIPTERAL
—2 columns   DISTYLE
—4 columns   TETRASTYLE
—5 columns   PENTASTYLE
—6 columns   HEXASTYLE
—8 columns   OCTASTYLE
                         OCTOSTYLE
—9 columns   ENNEASTYLE
—10 columns   DECASTYLE
—12 columns   DODECASTYLE
—many columns   POLYSTYLAR
—not more than four
   columns   PROSTYLE
head of column supporting
   arch   CHAPITER.CHAPTREL
high narrow arch   LANCET ARCH
hollow moulding   CAVETTO
                            SCOTIA
horizontal
—block   IMPOST
—division of window   TRANSOM
—member on wall   WALL-PLATE
inclined surface   SKEW-BACK
inner
—chamber of temple   CELLA
                             NAOS
—curve of arch or vault
                    INTRADOS
—fortified retreat   REDUIT
intercolumniation of
—1½ diameters   PYCNOSTYLE
—2 diameters   SYSTYLE
—2¼ diameters   EUSTYLE
—2-4 diameters
              AR(A)EOSYSTYLE
—3 diameters   DIASTYLE
—4 diameters   AR(A)EOSTYLE
internal section of dome   CUPOLA
internally splayed opening
    EMBRASURE.EMBRAZURE
intersection of vaults   GROIN
key pattern   FRET
keystone   QUOIN
lantern on dome   CUPOLA
level tablet   ABACUS
like silversmith's work
             PLATERESQUE
lintel   PLATBAND.TRANSOM
—on corbels SHOULDERED ARCH

little
—chapel   SACELLUM
—round window   OEIL-DE-BOEUF
long lintel   BRESSUMMER
         (BREAST)SUMMER
longitudinal groove   FLUTE
low
—side window   LYCHNOSCOPE
—spherical vault   CUL-DE-FOUR
                         CUPOLA
—storey between
   floors   ENTRESOL
—wall   STYLOBATE
lowest part of entablature
             ARCHITRAVE
main body of church   NAVE
male figure(s) as
   column(s)   ATLAS.ATLANTES
        PERSIAN.TELAMON
mansard roof   GAMBREL ROOF
masonary containing rubble
   EMPLECTON.EMPLECTUM
measure comprising half diameter
   of a column   MODULE
moulded border   SWAGE
moulding
—at base of column   TORUS
—at junction of shaft and
   capital   NECK-MOULDING
—base on upper part of
   pedestal   SURBASE
—on underside of
   arch   ARCHIVOLT
—round arch   ARCHITRAVE
Norman moulding   DOGTOOTH
oblique opening   SQUINT
ogee moulding   CYMA.TALON
—concave   CYMA RECTA
—convex   CYMA REVERSA
open colonnade   XYST(OS)
                       XYSTUS
opening
—for guns   EMBRASURE
             EMBRAZURE
—in parapet   CRENEL
orders CORINTHIAN.DORIC.IONIC
ornament
—bead shaped   PATERNOSTER
—like curled leaf   CROCKET

—like flower   CROCKET
—like garland   FESTOON
—like waterlily   LOTE
       LOTOS.LOTUS
—like palm-leaf   PALMETTE
—on capital   WATER-LEAF
—on mouldings
       EGG-AND-ANCHOR
       EGG-AND DART
—on pediment   ACROTER(ION)
       ACROTERIUM
—on pinnacle   CROCKET
ornamental
—channel or fluting   GLYPH
—openwork   TRACERY
outer curve of arch or
   vault   EXTRADOS
panelling at back of altar
       REREDORSE.REREDOS(SE)
part
—above columns   ENTABLATURE
—of church   TRANSEPT
—of entablature   FRIEZE
partitioning   QUARTERING
pedestal   ACROTERION
       ACROTERIUM
—base   DADO
pediment   ACROTER(ION)
       ACROTERIUM
pillar between two
   openings   TRUMEAU
plain
—face at base of wall   SOCLE
—face of plinth   SOCLE
       ZOCCO(LO)
—plinth   SOCLE
plaster
—cast in low relief   PRINT
—moulding   CORNICE
—wall coating   STUCCO
plate holding up end
   of beam   TASSEL.TORSEL
plinth at base of wall   SOCLE
       ZOCCO(LO)
pointed dome   IMPERIAL
porch   STOA
—at west of church   GALILEE
portico   PORCH.PROPYLAEUM
       PROPYLON

privy at the back of monastic
   dormitory   REREDORTER
projecting
—arch stone   CROSSETTE
—band at bottom of wall   PLINTH
—mould   HOOD-MOULD(ING)
—moulding   CORNICE
—point where arcs meet   CUSP
—part   JUTTY
—window   SHOT-WINDOW
projection   CORBEL
—of cornice   CORONA
range of columns   COLONNADE
       PORTICO
—around court or
   building   PERISTYLE
recessed space bounded by
   pediment cornices   TYMPANUM
relief   RILIEVO
rib at intersection   GROIN
roof supported by
   columns   HYPOSTYLE
rose window   CATHERINE WHEEL
       ROSACE
rosette   PATERA.ROSACE
round building   THOLOS.THOLUS
row of corbels   CORBEL-TABLE
rubble-filled
   masonry   EMPLECTON
       EMPLECTUM
sacristy DIACONICON.PARABEMA
screen at back of
   altar   REREDORSE
       REREDOS(SE)
scroll ornament   CARTOUCHE
sculpted basket   PANNIER
secondary
—beam or joist   SOLIVE
—rib   TIERCERON
semi-dome   CONCHA
sepulchral monument   CENOTAPH
shaft of column   SCAPE.TIGE
sharp-edged groove   QUIRK
shrine for standards   SACELLUM
side of
—dormer   CHEEK
—opening in wall   REVEAL
six-lobed design   SEXFOIL
skirting   DADO

slope at top of
  moulding   WEATHERING
small
—column   COLUMEL
—fillet   ANNULET.LISTEL
—gable   GABLET
—moulding   BAGUETTE.REED
—low window   MEZZANINE
soffit   INTRADOS
space between
—arch and moulding   SPANDREL
                    SPANDRIL
—bed and wall   ROUELLE
—columns INTERCOLUMNIATION
—corbels   MACHIOLATION
—lintel and arch   TYMPANUM
—pilasters   INTERPILASTER
spire   FLECHE
—formed by flying
  buttresses   CROWN
square
—block at base of column PLINTH
—block in cornice   DENTEL
                   DENTIL
—column against wall   PILASTER
—flat bracket   MUTULE
—pilaster at doorway   ANTA
—pilasters   ATTIC ORDER
space in Doric frieze   METOPE
S-shaped moulding   OGEE
stone in arch   VOUSSOIR
—central   HEADSTONE
     KEYSTONE.QUOIN
storey above aisle   TRIFORIUM
substructure of
—colonnade   STYLOBATE
—cupola or dome   THOLOBATE
sunken ceiling panel   LACUNAR
support for column   PEDESTAL
supported buttress
     HANGING BUTTRESS
tall narrow arched window
     LANCET WINDOW
temple gateway   PROPYLAEUM
                   PROPYLON
ten-column portico   DECASTYLE
three-grooved block in Doric
  frieze   TRIGLYPH
three-lobed tracery   TREFOIL

tomb   THOLOS.THOLUS
—as chapel   SACELLUM
top of
—column   CAPITAL
—entablature   CORNICE
tracery on vault   FAN TRACERY
          FAN VAULTING
triangular
—part of external wall   GABLE
—section of vaulting with
  concave sides   PENDENTIVE
—structure over porch PEDIMENT
twist in capital   HELIX
underside of arch   ARCHIVOLT
     INTRADOS.SOFFIT
uniformly coursed
  blocks   ISODOMON
             ISODOMUM
upper
—curve of arch or
  vault   EXTRADOS
—lighted storey   CLEARSTORY
          CLERESTORY
—part of pillar   IMPOST
—room   SOL(L)AR.SOL(L)ER
vertical
—part of door etc.   MONTANT
     MUNTIN.STILE
—post in roof truss   KINGPOST
     JOGGLE POST
     QUEEN-POST
vestibule of temple   PRONAOS
wall
—between two openings
     TRUMEAU
—panelling   WAINSCOT
—supporting dome or cupola
     DRUM
with flamelike tracery
     FLAMBOYANT
zigzag moulding   CHEVRON
     DANCETTE
Arctic animal   POLAR BEAR
     POLECAT
are
are, *say*   R
are (metric)   A
are not   ANT
are you and we *said*. . .   RUI-

Argentina	RA
barbecue	ASADO
capital	A.BUENOS AIRES
coin	AUSTRAL.CENTAVO.PESO
cowboy	GAUCHO
dance	TANGO
flower	PLATE
leader	A
plain	CHACO.LLANO.PAMPA
tree	TALA
weight	GRANO.QUINTAL
argentine	SILVER
argentine cast	INGOT
argonaut	JASON
aright	AR.ART
Arion's rescuer	DOLPHIN
arise	
arise, Sir...(D) ↑	RIS-
arising as an...(D) ↑	NASA
may *arise*(D) ↑	YAM
aristocratic	U
arm	
arm-lock	(HALF-)NELSON
arm-*twisting*	MAR.RAM
arms	(*see* gun²)
Armenia(n)	ARM.HAIKH
armour	MAIL
air hole in helmet	AVENTAIL(E)
breastplate	BYRNIE.CORS(E)TLET
	CUIRASS.PLACKET
—under mail	PLASTRON
buckler	PELTA.SHIELD
coat of mail	BRIGANDINE
	BRIGANTINE.HAUBERK
covering	
—arm	BRASSARD.BRASSART
	BRASSET.CORIUM
—body	BRIGANDINE
	BRIGANTINE.HAUBERK
—breast	BYRNIE.CUIRASS
	PECTORAL.PLACKET
—chin and throat	MENTONNIERE
—crotch	FA(U)LD
—elbow	COP.COUTE(R)
—face	VISOR.VIZOR
—foot	SOLARET.SOLLERET
—forearm	VAMBRACE
	VANTBRACE
—head	HELM(ET)

—hips	CULET
—horse's	
—breast	PECTORAL.POITREL
—head	CHAFFRON
	CHAMFROM.CHAMFRAIN
—joint	GUSSET
—leg	CHAUSSES.JAMB(E)
	JAMBEAU
—neck	HAUBERK
—and shoulder	GORGET
—shin	GREAVE
—shoulder	AILETTE
	PAULDRON.POULDRON
—small of back	CULET
—thigh	TACE.TASSE(T)
—throat	GORGET
—upper	
—arm	MONION.REREBRACE
—body	(PEASCOD-)CUIRASS
—leg	CUISSE
face cover	VISOR.VIZOR
for	
—horse	BARD.CHANFRAN
	CRUPPER.HARNESS
	SHANFRON
—man	BARD.HARNESS.MAIL
full suit of armour	PANOPLY
helmet	ARMET
	BASINET.BURGANET
	BURGONET.CASK.CASQUE
	MORIAN.MOR(R)ION
	SALADE.SAL(L)ET
knee-piece	GENOUILLERE
leather	
—arm-piece	CORIUM
—coat	GAMBESON
—corselet	LORICA
—doublet with steel	
strips	PLACCATE
	PLACKET
light headpiece	BASINET
mail-coat	BYRNIE
massive helmet	HEAUME
movable front of	
helmet	AVENTAIL(E)
	VENTAIL.VENTAYLE
open helmet	MOR(R)ION
padded	
—breast-shield	PLASTRON

—jacket ACTON.GAMBESON
  HA(C)QUETON.(H)AKETON
part of skirt TACE
  TASLET.TASSE(T)
plate below tasses TUILLE(TTE)
quilted coat GAMBESON
scarf over helmet LAMBREQUIN
shield BUCKLER.PELTA
—on left gauntlet GLOVE-SHIELD
shoulder-plate AILETTE
  PAULDRON
  POULDRON
skull cap CAPELINE
sleeveless coat of mail
  HABERGEON
splint armour JAZERANT
  JESSERANT
steel plates forming skirt
  LAMBOYS
suit of mail CATAPHRACT
thin metal plate LAME
visor/vizor MESAIL.MEZAIL

army[1] TA
hence
•army engineer TARE
•army man TAKEN
•army team TAXI
and
•Dad's Army PASTA
•farewell to army VALETA
•fight an army SPARTA

army[2]
chaplain HCF.OCF
dentists RADC
doctors RAMC
paymasters RAPC
teachers RAEC
technicians REME
vets RAVC

around[1]
meaning
  about, approximately, roughly,
  etc. (*see* about[4])

around[2]
around town WONT
around a... incl A
around * incl *
•run *around* one... RUIN
run *around* NUR

around[3]
around = a round O
hence
•around *following* doctor VETO
•round *in* ho-t... HOOT
•round *on* soldiers'... OMEN

arrange
arrange table BLATE.BLEAT
arranged ARR
arranged a new... WANE.WEAN
arrangement of roses SORES

arrest
arrest a... incl A
arrest * incl *
•police *arrest* king CORPS
arrested by * incl in *
•king *arrested by* police CORPS

arrive
arrive/arrival AR.ARR
arrived *finally* D

arrow-maker FLETCHER
ars RR
Arsenal's shots GUNFIRE

art
art *form* RAT.TAR
art *nouveau* RAT.TAR
artful place MUSEUM.STUDIO

article ART
English article A.AN.IT.THE
hence
•article *on* poetry AVERSE
•article *on* poetry ANODE
•article *in* church CITE
•artist *has* article... RATHE
French article LE.LA.LES.UN
  UNE
French/English articles LATHE
French/German articles UNDER
German article DAS.DER.DIE
  EIN.EINE
Italian article IL.LA.LE.UNA.UNO
Spanish article EL.LA.LAS.LO
  LOS.UNA.UNO
Spanish/Italian articles ELLA
articulated one... WON
artificial ART
artillery ART(Y).HA.HAC.RA
artist[1] ARA.PRA.RA
hence

•artist-fellow	ARAF	**Asian[1]**	E.-INE
•artist-graduate	ARABA	hence	
•artist is English	ARISE	•Asian study	EDEN
and		•Asian treaty	EPACT
•artist I exalt	PRAISING	•faint Asian. . .	DIME
•artist not known	PRANK	and	
•artist unknown	PRAY	•Asian training	INEPT
and		•fellow *with* Asian. . .	FINE
•artist ran	RASPED	•swindle Asian	CONINE
•artist *with* complaint	RAGOUT	**Asian[2]**	ASIATIC
•Cockney artist	RAINBOW	ascent	INDIAN ROPE-TRICK
and		anteater	PANGOLIN
•horse artist	COBRA	bean(-plant)	SOJA.SOY(A)
•male artist	HERA	birds	FROGMOUTH
•police artist	COPRA		MANDARIN DUCK
artist[2]	CLAUDE.ETTY.LELY	MYNA(H).PEACOCK-PHEASANT
artist, *say*	-TITION	PITTA.SIRGANG.TRAGOPAN
arty, *say*	RT	cattle	YAK.ZEBU.Z(H)O
as[1]	LIKE.QUA		(*see also* ox)
hence		chief	CHAGAN.CHAM.KHAN
•as an indication	ASSIGN	civet	PARADOXURE.ZIBET
•as below	ASUNDER	day lilies	FUNKIA
•as quiet	ASP	desert plant	CAMEL'S THORN
and		durra	GUINEA CORN
•as king	QUAKING	dwarfish negroid	NEGRITO
•as light	QUAVERY	evergreen shrub	CAMELLIA
•as unknown	QUAY	falcon	LUGGER.SHAHIN
and		felt tent	KIBITKA
•like a building	QUASHED	fibre	RAMIE
•like a caravan	QUATRAIN	fish	PANCHAX
•like a tree	QUASH	—hook money	LARI(N).LARREE
as[2]		—like sea horse	PEGASUS
as a rule	LURE	fowl	LANGSHAN
as above	US.UT SUPRA	fox	ADIVE.CORSAC.CORSAK
as arranged, Alsatians. . .		fruit	BITO.WAMPEE
	ASSAILANT	goat	JAGLA
as before	(*see* old[3])	hawk	SHIKRA
as if he would say	QD	hemp	PUA
as if some on. . .	SUMMON	horse	PRZEWALSKI'S HORSE
as much as you please	QL	—disease	SURRA
as much as you will	QV	kiang	HEMIONE
as said	UT DICT(UM)	leader	A
as said by a. . .	BUYER	legume	COWPEA
as stated, he'll. . .	HEAL.HEEL	lizard	MONITOR
as the poet said	(*see* poetic[1])	magician	SHAMAN
as you like it	AYLI	medicine man	SHAMAN
as you say, we'll. . .	WEAL.WHEEL	nut	PISTACHIO
ash dispenser	ETNA et al.	orchestra	GAMELAN
	VOLCANO	orchid	DENDROBIUM

pangolin   MANIS
paradoxure   MUSANG
partridge   SEESEE
perennial herb   LASERPICIUM
periwinkle   STRIPHANTHUS
pheasant   TRAGOPAN
piping hare   PICA
plants   GOA BEAN.HOSTA
                  LICORICE.LIQUORICE
primitive heartland
                  ANGARALAND
prince   CHAGAN.CHAM.KHAN
religion   SHAMANISM
rodent   GERBIL
sheep   ARGALI
                  (*see also* sheep)
shrubs   PATCHOULI.PATCHOULY
          SKIMMIA.TCHE.TEA
snake   KING-COBRA.SAKSAUL
                  SAXAUL
snow leopard   OUNCE
tailless hare   OCHOTONA.PICA
trees   ACLE.AILANTO.ASAK
ASOK(A).BITO.CAL(L)IATOUR
CAL(L)IATURE.DATE PALM.DIYA
LIQUIDAMBAR PAPER-MULBERRY
                  RED SANDERS
                  (RED) SANDAL(-WOOD)
          SIRIS.TREE OF HEAVEN
tusked deer   MUSK DEER
wild
—ass   DZIGGETAI.HEMIONE
          KIANG.KYANG.ONAGER
—dog   RACCOON-DOG
—goat   MARKHOR
                  SERPENT-EATER
—horse   PRZEWALSKI'S HORSE
askew it was   WAIST.WAITS
asking for tea   FORTY
asleep   OUT
asparagus *tips*   AS
aspiration(s)   H.(HH)
assassin   BOOTH.OSWALD
assemble
 a rum *assembly*   ARUM
 asesembled ratings   STARING
 assembly line   NILE
assimilate
 assimilate a rum   ARUM

assimilate a. . .   incl A
assimilate *   incl*
•companion *assimilates*
 rum   CRUMB
assimilated by *   incl in *
•rum *assimilated by*
 companion   CRUMB
assistant   ASST
associate   A
associate member   AM
associate fellow   AF
association   ASS
assort
assorted nuts   STUN.TUNS
assortment of hooks   SHOOK
assume   DON
assume a. . .   incl A
assume *   incl *
•P-a *assumes* it. . .   PITA
assumed by *   incl in *
•it *is assumed by* P-a. . . PITA
assurance company   PRU
astray in the. . .   THINE
astride
•girl *astride* a horse   JACOBEAN
astronomical unit   AU
asylum   CRANKCASE
at¹
at *first*   A
at *first*   start with AT
•male at *first*   ATMAN
at *heart*   incl AT
•h-e at *heart*. . .   HATE
at *last*   end with AT
•shape at *last*   FORMAT
at *last*   T
(a̅)t *losing* a. . .   T
at one on   -ATION
at one point   ATE
at *the* back   T
at *the* back   end with AT
•be at *the* back   BEAT
at *the* beginning   A
at *the* beginning   start with AT
•pamphlet at *the beginning*
                             ATTRACT
at *the* bottom(D)   T
at *the* end   T
at the *end*   ATE

47

at *the end*. . .	end with AT
•flourished at *the end*. . .	FLAT
at *the front*	A
at *the front*	start with AT
•tear at *the front*	ATRIP
at the middle	incl AT
•we *with* her at *the middle*	WEATHER
at *the rear*	T
at *the rear*	ATE
at *the rear*	end with AT
•about at *the rear*	CAT
at *the start*	A
at the start	start with AT
•one at *the beginning*	ATONE

at²

at cross purposes	VOTING
at first	incl -IST
•*almost* pur(r) *at* first	PURIST
at first sight	S
at *heart* s/he w/as. . .	HEW
at home	IN.(in)N-EST
at odds over. . .	ROVE
at one time	(*see* old³)
at pleasure	AD LIB(ITUM)
at sea all the. . .	LETHAL
at suit of	ATS
at the bottom of(D)	
•about *at the bottom of the* river	PORE
at the bottom of the. . .(D)	E
at the end	AD FINIT(UM)
at the heart of a/ny ala/rm system	NYALA
at the place	AD LOC(EM)
at this place	AHL
at this word	AHV
at university	UP
at work	(in) HAR-NESS
at work, boredom. . .	BEDROOM
* *at first*	start with *
•detectives ran *at first*	RANCID
* *at heart*	incl *
•sick *at heart*	SILLY
•wax is *at heart*	CERISE
* *at last*	end with *
•credit one *at last*. . .	CRONE
* *at the beginning*	start with *

•sweet, not *at the beginning*	NOTICE
* *at the end*	end with *
•quiet in *the end*	SHIN
* *at the middle*	incl *
•be *at the middle*	ABET

at³

indicates origins:

at Cardiff Arms Park = Welsh

•fervour *at Cardiff Arms Park*	HWYL

at Hampden Park = Scottish

•game *at St Andrews*	GOWF

at Longchamps = French

•horse *at Longchamps*	CHEVAL
ate *up* (D) ↑	DEF-
Athenian	TIMON
Atlantic	POND
atmosphere	ATM
atomic	A
attached	
attached to a. . .	incl A
•*attached to* a stake	ABET.BETA
•stake *attached to* a. . .	ABET.BETA
attached to *	incl *
•animal*attached to* her. . .	RATHER
attacking bat	DRACULA
attending lesson	(in) FOR-M
	INFORM
attorney	ATT
Attorney General	AG
attract	
attract game	DRAWBRIDGE
attractive	CUTE.DISHY
attractive artwork	DRAWING
attractive girl	BELLE.CUTIE.DISH
	DOLLY.PEACH.STUNNER
audio-	
audience hears a noise	ANNOYS
audible pause	PAWS
audio frequency	AF
audio-visual	AV
auditor adds	ADZE
auditors	EARS.SAA
augmentative	AUG
aunt's pain	AGONY
Australia	AUS.DOWN UNDER.OZ
Australian	AUSSIE.DIGGER.OZZIE
Aboriginal	ABO.BINGHI.MYALL

—dance CORROBOREE
—dog DINGO
—drum UBAR
—hut GUNYA(H).MIAM(IA) MIMI.WURL(E)Y
—woman GIN.LUBRA
acacia MULGA.MYALL
RASPBERRY-JAM TREE
SALLEE.SALLY.WATTLE
afternoon ARVO
agricultural worker STATION-HAND
air force RAAF
airline QUANTAS
alcoholic drink GROG
amulet CHURINGA
angry CROOK
animal gone wild SCRUBBER
animals KANGAROO.KOALA
(O)POSSUM.PLATYPUS
WALLABY.WOMBAT
anteater ECHIDNA.NUMBAT
apple COLANE
aquatic rodents HYDROMYS
arboreal marsupial KOALA
PHALANGER
area outside towns OUTSIDE COUNTRY
assembly ROLL-UP
back country OUTBACK
bag DILLY
bandit BUSHRANGER
barbecue BARBIE
be itinerant HUMP THE BLUEY
bear KOALA
beefwood FOREST-OAK
beer AMBER.FROSTY.GROG
—can TUBE
best thing or person RINGER
birds ANT-THRUSH.BELLBIRD
BITTERN.BLACK SWAN
BLOOD-BIRD.BOWERBIRD
BROLGA.BUDGERIGAR
CASSOWARY.CATBIRD
COACH-WHIP BIRD.COOEE
COOEY.COUCAL.CURRAMONG
DRONGO.EM(E)U.EMU-WREN
FANTAIL.FROGMOUTH.GALAH
HONEY-EATER

KOEL.KOOKABURRA
LARK-HEELED CUCKOO.LEIPOA
LORIKEET.LORY.LYREBIRD
MOPEHAWK.MOPOKE
MOREPORK.MOUND-BIRD
QUARRIAN.REGENT BIRD
RHIPIDURA.RIFLE(MAN) WREN
SATIN BIRD.SCRUB BIRD
SWALLOW-SHRIKE.THICKHEAD
WATTLEBIRD.WOODSWALLOW
ZEBRA PAR(R)AKEET
blanket bundle BLUEY
blind mole NOTOCYTES
boast SKITE
boiling pan BILLY(-CAN).BILLIE
boomerang KILIE.KYLEY.KYLIE
boulder GIBBER
bowerbird REGENT BIRD
SATIN BIRD
bread DAMPER
break for a smoke SMOKE-HO.SMOKO
brook CREEK
brush turkey VULTURN
buddy COBBER
bullroarer CHURINGA
TU(R)NDUN
bundle BLUEY.DRUM.SWAG
burrowing marsupial NOTORCYTES.WOMBAT
bush tramp DRUMMER
bushman's swag MATILDA
capital A.CANBERRA
—Territory ACT
carry on back HUMP
cattleman STOCKMAN
cheap unroofed seats BLEACHERS
chestnut tree CASTANOSPERMUM
child ANKLE-BITER
clergyman JOSSER
club NULLA(-NULLA)
WADDIE.WADDY
cockatoo CORELLA.GALAH
coin DOLLAR
—5 cent ZACK
—sixpence ZACK
—tossing game TWO-UP
cold beer FROSTY

collie	KELPIE.KELPY
conversation	YABBER
coucal	SWAMP PHEASANT
countryside	OUTBACK
cowboy	WADDIE.WADDY
crane	BROLGA
crayfish	YABBY
crowd	MOB
cut-off branch of river	
	BILLABONG
cyclone	WILLY-WILLY
dairy farmer	COW-COCKY
delinquent young man	BODGIE
desert pea	GLORY PEA
detective	DEMON
dewpond	GHILGAI
diarrhoea	WOG GUT
difficult situation	(FAIR) COW
dingo	WARRAGAL.WARRIGAL
dip sheep's hindquarters	CRUTCH
do	KELPIE.KELPY
drive herds for long	
distances	OVERLAND
driver of team	PUNCHER
dwarf eucalyptus	MALLEE
ear	SHELL-LIKE
edible	
—drupe	NATIVE PEACH
—grubs	WITCHETTY
effeminate man	PUNCE
egg-laying mammal	
	DUCKBILL(ED PLATYPUS)
	DUCK-MOLE
enclosed field	PADDOCK
Englishman	POM
eucalyptus	COOLABAH.GUM
IRONBARK.MALLEE.SALLEE	
SALLY.TEWART	
TOOART.TUART	
excel	RING
expert shearer	RINGER
fern	NARDOO
festive or noisy gathering	
	CORROBOREE
fibre plant	HEMP-BUSH
fish	CARANX.GROPER.JEWFISH
MORWONG.PAGROSOMUS	
PEGASUS.PIGFISH-ROCK COD	
S(CH)NAPPER.TREVALLY	

—like sea horse	PEGASUS
flashily dressed	LAIRED UP
—man	LAIR
fliers	RAAF
flock	MOB
flycatcher	WAGTAIL
fodder grass	KANGAROO GRASS
food	TUCKER
fool(ish)	DILL.DRONGO
	GALAH.NONG
football	RULES
forest	BRUSH
free immigrant	SQUAREHEAD
friarbird	LEATHERHEAD
frogmouth	MOPEHAWK.MOPOKE
	MOREPORK
fruit	NONDA
gang	PUSH
genuine	DINKUM.DINKY-DI
germ	WOG
girl	SHEILA
glory pea	(STURT'S) DESERT PEA
good	BONZER.BUDGEREE
grass	BARCOO.SPINIFEX
—tree	BLACKBOY
Greek	WERRIS CREEK
Great Britain	OLD DART
gum tree	EUCALYPTUS.KARRI
	STRINGY-BARK
	WANDOO.YARRAH
halfbeak	GARFISH
hard work	YACKER.YAKKA
	YAKKER
head-frame for cows	BAIL.BAYLE
heath-like plant	EPACRIS
hen	AUSTRALORP
herd	MOB
herdsman	STOCKMAN
hibiscus	COTTON-TREE
hold-up	BAIL-UP
honest	DINKUM.DINKY-DI
honey	
—eater	BLUE-EYE
	FRIARBIRD.WATTLEBIRD
—mouse	TARSIPES
—possum	TAIT
hooligan	LAR(R)IKIN
hornless	POLEY
horse	WALER

—jump from all four
  legs　　　　　　　　PIG-JUMP
hot places　BOOLIGAL.HAY-HELL
house on farm　　HEAD-STATION
hut　　　(*see* Aboriginal *above*)
ill　　　　　　　CRONK.CROOK
illicit　　　　　　　　　　SLY
immigrant from Britain　POM(MY)
imposter　　　　　　　BUNYIP
initiation rite　　　　　　BORA
insect　　LAAP.PERP.WITCHETTY
insignificant twerp　　　DRONGO
instrument　　　　DIDGERIDOO
interfering person　　　　　BOT
interior of station　BACKBLOCKS
jabber　　　　　　　YABBER
jackpot win　MOTSER.MOTZA
journey　　　　WALKABOUT
kangaroo　　　BOOMER.ROO
kingfisher　　　KOOKABURRA
lager　　　AMBER.FROSTY
landowners　SQUATTOCRACY
language　　　　　STRINE
large
—kangaroo　EURO.WALLAROO
—landowner　　SQUATTER
laughing jackass　　GOBURRA
　　　　　　KOOKABURRA
leader　　　　　　　　　A
learner
　COLONIAL EXPERIENCE MAN
　　JACKAROO.JACKEROO
leaves used for tea　MANUKA
liquor　　　　　NECK OIL
lizard　　　BLUE TONGUE
　GO(H)ANNA.MOLOCH
　MONITOR.PERENTIE
　　THORN-DEVIL
loafer　　　　SUNDOWNER
loop in river　ANABRANCH
lottery agency　TATTERSALLS
lout　　　　　　　LAIR
lungfish　　BARRAMUNDA
　　BURNETT SALMON
　　　ERATODUS
lyrebird　　　PHEASANT
mad　　　DILL.DRONGO
　　GALAH.NONG
magpie　　PIPING CROW

marine animal　　CUNJEVOI
marsupial　BANDICOOT.CUSCUS
　DASYURE.DENDROGALUS
　EURO.KANGAROO
　KOALA.NUMBAT
　PHALANGER.QUOKKA.TAIT
　TREE-KANGAROO.WALLABY
　WALLAROO.WOMBAT
marvellous　　　　BEAUT
mate　　　　　COBBER
mean　　　　　HUNGRY
meeting　　　　ROLL UP
miner　　　　　HATTER
mining gleaner　FOSSICKER
mix　　　　　　BOX
mixed collection　　MOB
monkey-puzzle tree
　　　BUNYA(-BUNYA)
monotreme
　DUCKBILLED PLATYPUS
monster　　　　BUNYIP
moth　　BOGONG.BUGONG
mound-bird　BRUSH TURKEY
　LEIPOA.MALLEE BIRD
　MALLEE FOWL.MALLEE HEN
　　SCRUB TURKEY
mountain　　　　RANGE
mountainous　　　RANGY
mounted
—herdsman　STOCK-RIDER
—policeman　TROOPER
Navy　　　　　RAN
nest　　　　　WURLEY
newly arrived　　YOUNG
New South Wales
　person　　CORNSTALK
New Zealand(er)　ENZED(DER)
nitwit　　　　DRONGO
no chance at all
　　BUCKLEY'S (CHANCE)
no good　　　　CROOK
north Queensland
　NEVER-NEVER LAND
nut　　QUANDONG-NUT
　　QUEENSLAND-NUT
objectionable person/thing　COW
odd-jobman in the
　outback　KNOCKABOUT
　ROUSEABOUT.ROUSTABOUT

on the move	WALKABOUT
out of season	MURKEN
owl	BOOBOOK
pack animal	PACKER
parakeet	ROSELLA
parliamentary obstruction	
	STONEWALL
parrot	COCKATOO.COCKATEEL
	COCKATIEL.CORELLA
	LORIKEET.LORY
pest	BOT
petrel	TITI
phalanger	OPOSSUM.TAGUAN
	TAIT.TARSIPES
	VULPINE OPOSSUM
pick-up truck	UTE
pigeon	BRONZE-WING
	WONGA(-WONGA)
pioneer	SANDGROPER
plan	DART
plants	CONJUVOI.BINDI-EYE
GRASS TREE.HOYA.LAPORTEA	
	LOGANIA.NETTLE TREE
	SPIGELIA.WAX FLOWER
political union	ANZUS
pond	BILLABONG
poor standard	CRONK
porcupine grass	SPINIFEX
posse	MUSTER-PARTY
potoroo	RAT KANGAROO
prejudice	DERRY
prospect	FOSSICK
Queensland hemp	SIDA
quickest sheep-shearer	RINGER
racket	RORT
rail acting as gate	SLIP-RAIL
rat kangaroo	POTOROO
ray	STINGAREE
real	DINKUM.DINKY-DI
recent immigrant	NEW CHUM
regent bird	BOWERBIRD
relative	DISTANT COUSIN
reprove	ROUSE ON
right	APPLES
river	DARLING
—effluent	BILLABONG
—flowing full	BANKER
robber of mine by	
night	NIGHT-FOSSICKER
rock hole in outback	
	GNAMMA HOLE
rodent	WATER-MOUSE
rough	LARRIKIN
round-up	MUSTER
rugby player	WALLABY
rules	FOOTBALL
running bird	EM(E)U
rural area	OUTBACK
rush bag	DILLI.DILLY(-BAG)
sailors	RAN
savage	WARRAGAL.WARRIGAL
scheme	DART
sea	
—berry	HALORAGIS
—bream	TARWHINE
—horse	SEA DRAGON
search for profit	FOSSICK
shark	MAKO
shearwater	MUTTON BIRD
shed	HUMPY
sheep	JUMBU(C)K
—dog	KELPIE.KELPY
shelter in the outback	GUNYAH
shield	HIELAMAN
shoulder	HUMP
shrub	BANKSIA.LIGNUM(-SCRUB)
PROTEA.SALT-BUSH.TEA-TREE	
	TELOPEA.WARATAH
sick	CROOK
single-storey house	COTTAGE
site for town	TOWNSHIP
slice of chocolate	
cake	LAMINGTON
slow-witted person	DRONGO
small	
—bottle	STUBBY
—farmer	COCKY
—kangaroo	WALLABY
—marsupial	HONEY MOUSE
	POUCHED MOUSE
—parrot	LORIKEET
—river	CREEK
—settlement	TOWNSHIP
spear-thrower	WOOMERA
speech	YABBER
soldier	ANZAC.DIGGER
—of both World Wars	RETREAD
something very fine	PURLER

speech STRINE
spider KATIPO.NIGHT STINGER
TARANTULA
spinifex PORCUPINE GRASS
spiv RORTER
spore case used as food NARDOO
square DINKUM.DINKY-DI
squatter JACKEROO
stampede BREAKAWAY
stampeding animal BREAKAWAY
state governor's deputy
LIEUTENANT GOVERNOR
stick used in game KIP
stingy HUNGRY
stock
—farm STATION
—man RINGER.STATION HAND
stop a horse quickly PROP
straight-haired CURLY
strike with club or
stick WADDIE.WADDY
strong tobacco NAIL-ROD
stupid DILL.DRONGO
GALAH.NONG
supplementary spouse PIRRAURU
surfer LEMONHEAD
surrender BAIL UP
swag MATILDA
sweepstake agency TATTERSALLS
take up Crown land FREE-SELECT
talk YABBER
tall thin person CORNSTALK
Tasmanian devil/wolf DASYURE
tea
—break TEA-HO
—pot BILLY(-CAN).BILLIE
—tree TI
tease CHYAK
tektite AUSTRALITE
tend TAIL
termite eater NUMBAT
thicket DEAD FINISH
MALLEE SCRUB
throwing stick BOOMERANG
WO(O)MERA.WOOMERANG
timber cart JINKER
tramp's bundle SWAG
travelling through the outback
ON THE WALLABY (TRACK)

tree snake DENDROPHIS
trees BEEFWOOD.BELAH.BELAR
BILLA.BOTTLE TREE
CASUARINA
CREAM-OF-TARTAR TREE
EUCALYPTUS.FLINDERSIA
GEEBUNG.GIDYA
HORSERADISH TREE.JARRAH
KARRI.KURRAJONG.MANUKA
MORETON BAY CHESTNUT
MULGA.PENDA.PROTEA
QUANDONG.QUEENSLAND NUT
SHE-OAK.SOUR GOURD
SPEAR-WOOD.SWAMP OAK
TOOART.TUART.TEWART
WADDYWOOD.WHITE TEAK
WOODEN PEAR
true DINKUM.DINKY-DI
tulip WARATAH
turkey VULTURN
U-turn UEY
unbranded stock CLEARSKIN
undermine another miner's
claim FOSSICK
unmanageable ROP(E)ABLE
unskilled labourer ROUSEABOUT
ROUSTABOUT
useless person GALAH
very
—angry ROP(E)ABLE
—good APPLES.BEAUT.BONZER
BOSHTA.BOSHTER.BOSKER
BUDGEREE
virus WOG
walk carrying swag HUMP
WALK MATILDA
WALTZ MATILDA
walking-stick WADDIE.WADDY
wallaby BRUSH-KANGAROO
PAD(D)YMELON
PADEMELON
wandering WALKABOUT
war club WADDIE.WADDY
wattle tree BOREE.WAIT-A-WHILE
weapon LILLIL.NULLA(-NULLA)
welsher SHICER
West Australian SANDGROPER
white man with Aboriginal
wife COMBO

wild	ROP(E)ABLE.WARRAGAL	**author**	
	WARRIGAL	author's place	WELLS
—Aboriginal	MYALL	authorisation	OK
—cat	DASYURE	Authorised Version	AV
—dog	DINGO.WARRAGAL	**autobiography**	CV
	WARRIGAL	**automatic**	
—horse	BRUMBY.WARRAGAL	automatic data processing	ADP
	WARRIGAL	automatic pilot	GEORGE
—young bull	MICK(E)(Y)	**available**	
win shearing competition		*available in* shop	HOPS.POSH
	RING THE SHED	*available in* so/me sh/ops	MESH
wool	BOTANY	**avenue**	AV(E)
work alone	HAT	**average**	AVE.AVER
wrasse	PIG-FISH	average man	MEDAL
young		**Avogadro's number**	N
—animal	JOEY	**Avonville**	BATH
—kangaroo	JOEY	**avoid**	
—pig	SLIP	*avoid* a...	omit A
zoological region	NOTOGAEA	*avoid extremes* of (h)ea(t)	EA
Austria(n)	A	*avoid* one not drinking	omit TT
capital	A.VIENNA.WIEN	*avoid* students	omit LL
coin		I'd *avoid*...	omit ID
—100 groschen	SCH.SCHILLING	**award**	CH.OBE.OM
—20 kreutzers	ZWANZIGER	**away**	-ARD.AST.OUT
—100 kreutzers	FLORIN	**awful**	
—100 heller	KRONE	*awful display of* art	TAR
—money of account	GULDEN	*awful* part	TRAP
dance	WALTZ	*awfully* tired	TRIED
flower	DANUBE	**awkward**	
leader	A	*awkward* sort	TORS
measure	FASS.MUTH	*awkwardly* I creep	PIERCE
noble	HERTZOG	**axiom**	AX
soldier	PANDUR	**ay(s).aye(s)**	A(AS).I(IS)
weight	UNZE	**azimuth**	AZ

B

a follower. *Bach*. bachelor. baron. bass. bed-bug. *bee*. Beethoven. bel. Belgium. beta. beth. billion. bishop. black. bloodgroup. *bloody*. book. born. boron. bowled. boy. Brahms. breadth. Britain. British. *inferior*. key. magnetic flux. note. *paper*. *road*. *second*. *second-class*. second letter. three hundred. three thousand. vitamin

B9	BENIGN	*back*-up⟨	PU
B10	BEATEN	*back-up* may...⟨	YAM
B-flat	BED-BUG	*back* way⟨	DR.TS.YAW
B row	BRACKET	*back way* in⟨	NI
babe	RUTH	*backfiring* guns⟨	SNUG
baby		*backing* house‿	E
baby bird	STORK	*back*bite	PIN.WANG
baby carriage	GESTATION	*back-sliding* VIPs⟨	SPIV
bachelor	B.BA.BACH	*backtracking* deer⟨	REED
bachelor of:		*backward*⟨	DRAW
Arts	AB.BA	*backward* boy DAL.NOD.NOS.YOB	
Civil Law	BCL	*back*-yard⟨	DRAY
Commerce	BCOM(M)	**bad**	
Dental Surgery	BDS	bad actor	HAM
Divinity	BD	*bad* actor	CROAT
Education	BED.EDB	bad $\overline{back}$⟨	DAB.LIVE
Engineering	BAI.BE.BENG	bad *French*	MAL
Law	BL.LLB	hence	
Letters	BL	•bad *French* relatives	MALKIN
Literature	BLITT	•bad *French* ruler	MALAGA
Medicine	BM.MB	•bad *French* sweet	MALICE
Music	BMUS	and	
Philosophy	PHB	•for bad *French*...	FORMAL
Science	BS.BSC.SCB	•neither bad *French*	NORMAL
Surgery	BCH.BS.CHB	•the *German with*	
Bach's works	S	bad *French*	DERMAL
back		bad ignition	ARSON
back again⟨	ER	bad man	CHRONICLES
back line⟨	KNAR	bad mark	SCAR
back number	EPIDURAL.REARM	bad season	OFFSPRING
back number⟨	NET.ON	bad speller	WITCH
back of lorry‿	-RY	*badly affected* by a...	BAY
back of neck‿	NAPE	*badly constructed* table	BLEAT
back of neck	K	*badly designed* town‿	WONT
back pay⟨	YAP	badly *missed*	omit ILL
back room⟨	MOOR	•badly *missed* fr(ill)y...	FRY
back seat	SADDLE	*badly* tied‿	DIET.EDIT.TIDE
back-stop⟨	POTS	**badger bait**	TEASE
back street⟨	DR.TS	**baffle**	
back stretch⟨	EMIT	*baffle* noises‿	ESSOIN
back to...⟨	OT	*baffled* by her‿	HERBY
back to front bat⟨	TAB	*bafflement of* all the...‿	LETHAL

bag
bag clasp	CATCH
bags a. . .	incl A
bags *	incl *
•m-an *bags* a duck	MOAN
bagged by *	incl in *
•duck *bagged by* m-an	MOAN
Bahamas	BS
in the Bahamas	B-S
baker	SUNBATHER
balance	BAL
balance sheet	BS

bald
bald-*headed*	B
b̄ald patch	O
•doctor *has* bald patch	VETO
bale	BL
in bales	B-LS

Balkan
guerrilla	COMITADJI.KOMITADJI
leader	B

ball   O.YORKER
hence	
•ball-boy	OLEO.OVAL
•ball-point	OE.ON.OS.OW
•ball-points	ONE(S).OWN(S)

ballet
ballets	COPPELIA.GISELLE
	LA FILLE MAL GARDEE
	LA SYLPHIDE.NUTCRACKER
	ROMEO AND JULIET
	SLEEPING BEAUTY
	SWAN LAKE
characters in:	
—Coppelia	FRANZ.SWANHILDA
—Giselle	ALBRECHT.BATHILDE
	GISELLE.HILARION
	LOYS.MYRTHA
—La Fille mal Gardée	ALAIN
	COLAS.LISE
	SIMONE.TOMAS
—La Sylphide	EFFIE.GURN
	JAMES.MADGE
—Nutcracker	CLARA
—Romeo and Juliet	
	FRIAR LAWRENCE
	JULIET.ROMEO
—Sleeping Beauty	AURORA
	CARABOSSE.LILAC

—Swan Lake	ODETTE.ODILE
	SIGFRIED VON ROTHBART
movements:	
—exercises	BATTEMENT.CAMBRE
	COUP DE PIED.DEMI PLIE
	GRAND PLIE.PENCHE.RELEVE
	ROND DE JAMBE
—leaps	GRAND JETE
	TEMPS DE POISSON
	TOURS EN L'AIR
—positions	ARABESQUE
	ATTITUDE.CROISE.EFFACE
	EN FACE.ECARTE
	PORT DE BRAS
—steps	ASSEMBLEE.GLISSADE
	JETE.PAS DE CHAT
	PAS DE BOURREE
	SISSONNES
—turns	FOUETTE.PIROUETTE

Baltic
ship	PRAM
statesman	LETT

banana
banan̄a *skin*	BA
b̄anana *split*	BAN.ANA
bananas	MAD.NUTS
band[1]	O
hence	
•band *together with*	
archdeacons	OVENS
•hat-band	CAPO
•string band	BO.CO.DO.GO
band[2]	
band *leader*	B
(b)and *without a leader*	AND
bandied about names	MANES
	MEANS
banger	TNT
bank	BK
Bank for International	
Settlements	BIS
bank rate	BR
banker	RIVER
(*see also* river)	
banking	BKG
banks of riv̄er	RR
Baptist/bapt̄is̄ed	BAP(T)
bar	SILKS
bar profits	BARGAIN

Barbados	BS	**b-bird**	BOWL
Barbados pride		**be**	
	(RED)SANDAL(-WOOD)	be keeper	HAVE.OWN
capital	B.BRIDGETOWN	be prepared	BP
in Barbados	B-S	be quick	LIVE
barbarian	HUN	Beachy *Head*	B
barbaric rite	TIER	**beady,** *say*	BD
barbarous Huns	SHUN	**bean**	(*see* pulses)
Barbary		**bear**	POOH.RUSSIAN
ape	MAGOT	bear punishment	STICK
privateer	CORSAIR	**bearing¹**	N.S.E.W
ship	SANDAL.SETTEE	hence	
	XEBEC(K)	•bearing poems	NODES
bard	WILL	•bearing wine	SHOCK
bargain crop	SNIP	•bearing flower	EASTER
baritone	BAR	•bearing one each	WIPER
bark	BK.WOOF.WOW	(*see also* directions)	
barmaid	BANJO	**bearing²**	AIR.DEMEANOUR
baron	BN	hence	
baronet	BART.BT	•bearing left	AIRPORT
baroque art	RAT.TAR	•bearing wine	AIRPORT
barrel	BL	•strong bearing	FAIR
in barrels	B-LS	**bearing³**	
barristers	BAR	meaning	
base of tree(D)	E	carrying	
basket	BKT	producing:	
basket-maker	OSIER	acorns	GLANDIFEROUS
Basque		all varieties	OMNIFEROUS
game	PELOTA	aluminium	ALUMINIFEROUS
language	EUSKERA	apples	POMIFEROUS
leader	B	arms	ARMIGEROUS
militant nationalists	ETA	balsam	BALSAMIFEROUS
region	PYRENEES	berries	BACCIFEROUS
bass note, *say*	DEEP SEA	blood	SANGUIFEROUS
bat BARBASTEL(LE).PIPISTRELLE		bones	OSSIFEROUS
bats	CRAZY.MAD	bracts	GLUMIFEROUS
bats can see	SEANCE	breasts	MAMMIFEROUS
battalion	BAT(T).BN	bristles	CHAETIFEROUS
battered crate	CATER.REACT		CHAETROPHOROUS
battery	BAT(T)		STYLIFEROUS
batting	IN	cells	CELLULIFEROUS
battle	WAR	claws	CHELIFEROUS
hence		clouds	NUBIFEROUS
•battle casualties, *say*	WARDED		NUBIGINOUS
•batle-gear	WARDRESS	coal	CARBONIFEROUS
•battle study	WARDEN	copper	CUPRIFEROUS
•wartime	WART	coral	CORALLIFEROUS
battle station	WATERLOO		CORALLIGENOUS
BBC	AUNTIE.BEEB	crosses	CRUCIFEROUS

culm (coalmine waste)		oily substance	SEBIFEROUS
	CULMIFEROUS	ovules	OVULIFEROUS
cupules	CUPULIFEROUS	partitions	SEPTIFEROUS
death	LETHIFEROUS	pearls	MARGARITIFEROUS
disease	MORBIFEROUS	pests	PESTIFEROUS
eggs	OVIFEROUS.OVIGEROUS	petrol	PETROLIFEROUS
excess hair	CHAETIFEROUS	platinum	PLATINIFEROUS
	CHAETROPHOROUS	pupa-case	PUPIGEROUS
fatty substance	SEBIFEROUS	pyrites	PYRITIFEROUS
feathers	PLUMIGEROUS	quartz	QUARTZIFEROUS
flames	FLAMMIFEROUS	salt	SALIFEROUS
flowers	FLORIFEROUS	seed	SEMINIFEROUS
forklike appendages		shade	UMBRIFEROUS
	FURCIFEROUS	silica	SILICIFEROUS
fossils	FOSSILIFEROUS	silver	ARGENTIFEROUS
fossil reptiles	REPTILIFEROUS	sleep	SOMNIFIC.SOMNIFEROUS
fruit	FERACIOUS		SOPORIFEROUS.SOPORIFIC
	FRUCTIFEROUS	small	
	FRUGIFEROUS	—glands	GLANDULIFEROUS
garnets	GARNETIFEROUS	—holes	FORAMINIFEROUS
glumes	GLUMIFEROUS	—nipples	PAPILLIFEROUS
god	DEIPAROUS	—spines	SPINULIFEROUS
gold	AURIFEROUS	spores	SPOROGENOUS
good health	SALUTIFEROUS	stars	STELLIFEROUS
granules	GRANULIFEROUS	style	STYLIFEROUS
grass stems	CULMIFEROUS	suckers	STOLONIFEROUS
guano	GUANIFEROUS	sweat	SUDORIFEROUS
hair	CRINIGEROUS.PILIFEROUS	teeth	DENTIGEROUS
honey	MELLIFEROUS	thorns	SPINIFEROUS
incense	THURIFEROUS		SPINIGEROUS
iron	FERRIFEROUS	tin	STANNIFEROUS
keratin	KERATOGENOUS	titanium	TITANIFEROUS
keys	CLAVIGEROUS	tubers	TUBERIFEROUS
lead	PLUMBIFEROUS	urine	URINIFEROUS
leaves	FRONDIFEROUS	vines	VITIFEROUS
lime	CALCIFEROUS	well being	SALUTIFEROUS
light	LUCIFEROUS	whip	FLAGELLIFEROUS
	LUMINIFEROUS		MASTIGOPHOROUS
manganese	MANGANIFEROUS	wool	LANIFEROUS
manna	MANNIFEROUS	yolk	VITELLIGENOUS
metal	METALLIFEROUS	yttrium	YTTRIFEROUS
milk	GALACTOPHOROUS	zinc	ZINCIFEROUS
	LACTIFEROUS		(see also having)
monsters	TERATOGENIC		
mucus	MUCIFEROUS	**bearing[4]**	
musk	MOSCHIFEROUS	bearing a. . .	incl A
nectar	NECTARIFEROUS	bearing *	incl *
nuts	NUCIFEROUS	•ship bearing German. . .	SHUNS
oil (as seeds)	OLEIFEROUS	borne by *	incl in *
		•German borne by ship	SHUNS

beastly

beastly fighter	GLADIATOR
	PICADOR.TOREADOR
	TORERO
beastly lot	ZOO
beastly mother	DAM.MARE
beastly overheads	ANTLERS
	HORNS

beat

beat all the...	LETHAL
beat *up*(D) ↑	MAL
beat up sorbet	STROBE
beaten silver	LIVERS.SLIVER

beau ADONIS.DANDY

beautiful blonde FAIR

because AS.COS.FOR.SINCE

become

become quiet (sh!)	GOSH
become quiet	QUITE
becomes tired	TRIED

becoming

apparently cooler	DECALESCENT
atrophied	CONTABESCENT
aware of being	
mistaken	RESIPISCENT
big	TURGESCENT
bigger	ACCRESCENT
black	NIGRESCENT
branched	DELIQUESCENT
bubbly	EFFERVESCENT
cooler	DEFERVESCENT
dark	NIGRESCENT
dry	ARESCENT
emaciated	TABESCENT
fused	COALESCENT
	CONCRESCENT
glass	VITRESCENT
green	VIRESCENT
healthy	CONVALESCENT
hidden	DELITESCENT
hot	FERVESCENT
into being	NASCENT
latent	LATESCENT
leafy	FRONDESCENT
less	DECRESCENT
light	LUMINESCENT
liquid	(COL)LIQUESCENT
lit through strong	
heat	INCANDESCENT

milk	LACTESCENT
obsolete	OBSOLESCENT
old	SENESCENT
older	ADOLESCENT
pale	PALLESCENT
quiet	QUIESCENT
reborn	RENASCENT
red	ERUBESCENT.RUFESCENT
revived	REVIVESCENT
rotten	PUTRESCENT
stone	LAPIDESCENT
swollen	(IN)TUMESCENT
	TURGESCENT
tree-like	ARBORESCENT
warm	INCALESCENT
wasted	TABESCENT
white	ALBESCENT.CANESCENT
white/red-hot	INCANDESCENT
withered	MARCESCENT
yellow	FLAVESCENT.LUTESCENT
youthful	JUVENESCENT

bed COT.GARDEN.PLOT

(*see also* between.in[3])

bed maker	GARDENER
bed makers	ROSES
bedspread	MULCH
bed*spread*	DEB
bedevilled by a...	BAY
Bedlam in the...	THINE

bee(s) B.(BB.BS)

beef consultant OMBUDSMAN

beer container DALEK.STOMACH

WALER.WHALES

Beethoven's *Third* E

beetle OVERHANG

befogged (in) M-IST

before A.AN.ANTE.BEF

ER.ERE.OR.PRE

before Christ	AC.BC
before noon	AM
before noon	in front of N
•see *before* noon	SEEN
before the day	AD
before twelve	AM
*before*hand	in front of L.LT.R.RT
•appeared *before*hand	CAMEL
•me *before*hand	MELT
•contribute *before*hand	GIVER
•he *has* one *before*hand	HEART

begin
begin *afresh*   BINGE
begin to eat   E
begin to eat   TEAT
beginning[1]
beginning   ALPHA
beginning of play   ACTI
beginning of play   P
beginning of the. . .   T
beginning of time   T
beginning[2]
meaning
  origins (of)
  reproduction (of):
alternate   HETEROGENESIS
asexual   MONOGENESIS
                       MONOGONY
blood formation
                   HAEMATOGENESIS
bones   OSTEOGENESIS
                        OSTEOGENY
by
—budding   BLASTOGENESIS
—fission   SCHIZOGENESIS
—radioactive decay RADIOGENIC
cells   CYTOGENESIS
continent formation
                     EPEIROGENESIS
disease   PATHOGENESIS
                        PATHOGENY
evolutionary development
                      PHYLOGENESIS
                        PHYLOGENY
from
—like parents   HOMOGENESIS
—living organisms   BIOGENESIS
—male and female   SYNGENESIS
—unfertilised ovum
                   PARTHENOGENESIS
gametes   GAMETOGENESIS
gods   THEOGONY
gradual development
  of parts   EPIGENESIS
heat   THERMOGENESIS
in larval state   PAEDOGENESIS
individual development
                      ONTOGENESIS
involving each body
  cell   PANGENESIS

living
—beings   ZOOGENY.ZOOGONY
—organisms   ORGANOGENESIS
many different origins
            POLYGENESIS.POLYGENY
mental processes   NOOGENESIS
                     PSYCHOGENESIS
                       PSYCHOGONY
mountains   OROGENESIS
myths   MYTHOGENESIS
outside the body   ECTOGENESIS
ovum development   OOGENESIS
                          OOGENY
phantasms PHANTASMOGENESIS
plants   PHYTOGENESIS
                        PHYTOGENY
predetermined direction of
  organisms   ORTHOGENESIS
sexual reproduction
                     GAMOGENESIS
similar origins   ISOGENY
spiritual rebirth   PALINGENESIS
                      PALINGENESIA
                       PALINGENESY
spontaneous   ABIOGENESIS
                    HETEROGENESIS
soul   PSYCHOGONY
sperm   SPERMATOGENESIS
                    SPERMATOGENY
teeth   ODONTOGENY
tissues   HISTOGENESIS
                        HISTOGENY
unlike parents   XENOGENESIS
virgin birth   PARTHENOGENESIS
be*gone*   omit BE
begotten in anger
                EARNING.NEARING
behead
beheaded (t)he (b)ad
  (a)long. . .   HEADLONG
beheaded (w)omen   OMEN
behind
behind bars   (in) C-AGE
indicates one word written after
  another:
•girl *behind* the lines   BREVE
•put directions *behind* tree ASHEN
be*holding*   B-E
•*beholding* a saint   BASTE

Belgian	BELG
airline	SABENA
capital	B.BRUSSELS
coin	BELGA.FRANC.MITE
language	FLEMISH.WALLOON
leader	B
races	FLEMISH.WALLOON
Belgium	B.BELG

belief
including
  followers
  founders
  religions:

acceptance of complete divinity of	
Christ	APOLLINARIANISM
African Christianity	DONATISM
all gods	PANTHEISM
Allah	ISLAM.MOHAMMEDANISM
	MOSLEM.MUSLIM
Alpine Christian	VALDENSIAN
	WALDENSIAN
Arab philosophy	AVERR(H)OISM
Arminian Methodism	
	WESLEYISM
Asian	SHAMANISM
attribution of soul to natural	
objects	ANIMISM
Babylonian	MANDAEAN
	MENDAITES.NASOREAN
	SABIANISM
Baptist heretic	CATABAPTIST
	PEDOBAPTIST.SE-BAPTIST
based on Gospels	
	EVANGELICALISM
Brahma	BRAHMANISM
	BRAHMINISM
Buddha	BUDDHISM
Buddhism in	
—Burma	MON
—China	CHAN.FOISM
—Japan	ZEN
—Tibet	GELUK PA.SAKYA PA
Buddhist forms	HINAYANA
	MAHAYANA.THERVADA
	VAJRAYANA
	(*see also* Buddhist)
Bulgarian Moslem	POMAK
Burmese Buddhism	MON
Calvinism	GENEVANISM

Cathar(ist)	ALBIGENSIAN
	MANICHAEAN
Catholic revival	OXFORDISM
	OXFORD MOVEMENT
	TRACTARIANISM
Children of God	SHAKERS
Chinese	CONFUCIANISM.FOISM
	TAOISM
Church of England	ANGLICANISM
denial of	
—original sin	PELAGIANISM
—predestination	ARMINIANISM
devotion to	
—bishops	EPISCOPALIANISM
—Haile Selassie	RASTA(MAN)
	RASTAFARIAN
—priests	SACERDOTALISM
Dutch Arminian	REMONSTRANT
early	
—Christian intuitive	
religion	GNOSTICISM
—heretic	CERINTHIAN
east European Christian	UNIATE
Eastern sorcery	MAG(IAN)ISM
Egyptian Christian	COPT
English monks (13th c.)	
	BETHLEHEMITES
founded by	
—Arminius	ARMIN(IAN)ISM
—Mary Baker Eddy	
	CHRISTIAN SCIENCE
—William Booth	
	SALVATION ARMY
—Buddha	BUDDHISM
—John Calvin	CALVINISM
	GENEVANISM
—Richard Cameron	
	CAMERONIAN
—Christ	CHRISTIANITY
—Erastus	ERASTIANISM
—George Fox	QUAKERISM
	SOCIETY OF FRIENDS
—Gautama	BUDDHISM
—Ron Hubbard	SCIENTOLOGY
—John Huss	HUSSITES
	MORAVIANS
—Cornelius Jansen	JANSENISM
—K'ung Fu-tse	CONFUCIANISM
—Lao-tzu	TAOISM

—Ignatius Loyola   JESUITISM
                     JESUITRY
—Martin Luther   LUTHERISM
—Mahavira   JAINISM
—Mahomet   ISLAM
          MOHAMMED(AN)ISM
—Mani(chaeus)
          MANICHAEANISM
—Melanchthon   SYNERGISM
—Menno Simons   MENNONITES
—John Maron   MARONITE
—James Morison
          MORISONIANISM
—Mo-zi   MOHISTS
—Nanak   SIKHISM
—Nestorius   NESTORIANISM
—J.H.Newman   OXFORDISM
          OXFORD MOVEMENT
          TRACTARIANISM
—E. B. Pusey   PUSEYISM
—St Maron   MARONITE
—St Vincent de Paul LAZARISM
—Sakyamuni   BUDDHISM
—William J. Seymour
          PENTECOSTAL CHURCH
—Shirazi   BABISM
—Joseph Smith   MORMONISM
—Sun Myung Moon   MOONIES
          UNIFICATION CHURCH
—Emmanuel Swedenborg
          SWEDENBORGIANISM
—Peter Waldo   VALDENSES
                     WALDENSES
                     WALDENSIANS
—John Wesley   METHODISM
—John Wycliffe   LOLLARDISM
                     LOLLARD(R)Y
—Zarathustra ZOROASTRIANISM
founded in
—America   ADVENTISTS
                     MORMONISM
—Dublin PLYMOUTH BRETHREN
                     PLYMOUTHISM
—Korea   MOONIES
          UNIFICATION CHURCH
—Pennsylvania
          JEHOVAH'S WITNESSES
Franciscan CAPUCHIN.CODELIER
                     MINORITE

French
—Gnosticism (13th c.)
          ALBIGENSIAN.CATHARIST
—Protestantism   CAMISARD
                     HUGUENOT
Genevanism   CALVINISM
German
—Judaism   ASHKENAZIM
—Protestantism   ANABAPTIST
                     LUTHER(AN)ISM
god   DEISM.THEISM
—as trinity   TRINITARIAN
—as unity   UNITARIAN
—as universe   PANTHEISM
—identified with cosmos
          COSMOTHEISM.PANTHEISM
—with one will MONOTHELETISM
—with two wills   DITHELETISM
                     (see also gods)
Hebrew   JUDAISM
—asceticism   ESSENISM
                     (see also Hebrew)
Hindu   BRAHMANISM
                     S(H)IVAISM
                     (see also Hindu)
host of heaven   SABAISM
idols   IDOLATRY
Indian   BUDDHISM.HINDUISM
                     JAINISM.SIKHISM
—Moslems   COSSAS
—Parsees   ZOROASTRIANISM
Iranian Guebres
          ZOROASTRIANISM
Islam   MOHAMMED(AN)ISM
                     (see also Moslem)
Italian
—Gnosticism (13th c.)
          ALBIGENSIAN.CATHARIST
—Unitarianism   SOCINIANISM
Japan   BUDDHISM.SHINTOISM
Japanese Buddhism   AMIDA
          AMITA.SOKA GAKKAI.ZEN
Jehovah   HEBREW.JEWISH
Jewish
—Christian   NAZARENE
—formalist   PHARISEE
—sceptic   SADDUCEE
—sect performing daily ablutions
          HEMEROBAPTISTS

Knights Templar
  (idol)　　　　　BAPHOMET
Latter Day Saints　　MORMONS
literal truth of Bible
　　　　FUNDAMENTALISM
Manichaean　　CATHAR(IST)
　　　　　　　　PATARIN(E)
many gods　　　POLYTHEISM
Maronite　　　　UNIAT(E)
Mazda　　ZOROASTRIANISM
Milanese heretic　PATARIN(E)
missionary
  Protestants　　MORAVIANS
　　　　UNITED BRETHREN
Moravians　UNITED BRETHREN
Moonies　UNIFICATION CHURCH
Mormons　LATTER DAY SAINTS
Moslem
—mysticism　SOF(I)ISM.SUF(I)ISM
—sect　　IMAMITES.ISMAILITES
　　　　KHARIJITES.SHIA(H)
　　　　WAHABEE.WAHABI
—traditional teaching　SUNNA
non-belief　　AGNOSTICISM
　　ATHEISM.HEATHENISM
　　　　　　　PAGANISM
one god　　　HENOTHEISM
　　　　　　MONOTHEISM
opposition to marriage
  of priests　　PATARIN(E)
order founded at
—Cassino　　BENEDICTINE
—Chatrousse　CARTHUSIAN
—Citeaux　　BENEDICTINE
　　BERNADINE.CISTERCIAN
—Cluny　BENEDICTINE.CLUNIAC
—Palestine　　CARMELITE
　　　　WHITE FRIARS
order founded by
—Bernard of Clairvaux
　　BERNADINE.CISTERCIAN
—Pietro da Morrone　CELESTINE
—St Augustine　AUGUSTINIAN
　　　　AUSTIN FRIARS
—St Bruno　　CARTHUSIAN
—St Dominic　BLACK FRIARS
　　　　　DOMINICANS
—St Francis of Assisi
　FRANCISCAN.GREY FRIARS

—St Francis of Paola　MINIMS
orthodox Roman Catholic
　　　　　TRIDENTINE
Oxford Movement
　　　TRACTARIANISM
Papism　ROMAN CATHOLICISM
Parsee　　ZOROASTRIAN
Persian　BABEEISM.BAB(I)ISM
　BAHAISM.IMAMISM.MAGISM
　　MAZDAISM.MASDEISM
　　PARSEEISM.PARSIISM
　　　ZOROSTRIANISM
Polish Jews　　ASHKENAZIM
Portuguese Jews　SEPHARDIM
—converted to Christianity
　　　　　MARRANO
Quakers　SOCIETY OF FRIENDS
Reformed
—Church　PROTESTANTISM
—Presbyterian Church
　　　　CAMERONIAN
rejecting jurisdiction of
  bishops　　ACEPHALITES
Roman Catholicism　PAPISM
　　　　ROMANISM
Russian Christian　UNIAT(E)
scepticism　SADDUC(EE)ISM
Scottish
—Presbyterian　CAMERONIAN
—Free Church　WEE FREES
self-baptising　SE-BAPTISTS
self-subsistence of God
　　　　AUTOTHEISM
snake worship　OPHITISM
Society of Friends　QUAKERS
　　　　　SHAKERS
Spanish Jews　SEPHARDIM
—converted to Christianity
　　　　　MARRANO
spirit worship　SHAMANISM
　　　　VOODOOISM
strange gods　ALLOTHEISM
Swedish　SWEDENBORGIANISM
Tibet　　BUDDHISM.LAMAISM
Tractarianism
　　　OXFORD MOVEMENT
Turkish Muslim　KARMATHIAN
　　　　　SALAR
two gods　　DITHEISM

Uniat(e)	MARONITE	mother *beside* herself	MAMA
Unification Church	MOONIES	soldier *beside* himself	GIGI
United Brethren	MORAVIANS	**besieged Lady**	SMITH
unity of God	ARIANISM	**besotted**	(in)LO-VE
	UNITARIANISM	**best**	WORST
universal salvation		best club	ACE
	UNIVERSALISM	best diamond	ACE
West Indies	OBEAHISM.OBEISM	best man	CHAMPION.WINNER
	OBIISM.VOODOOISM	best *possible*	BETS
	VOUDOUISM	best suit	TRUMPS
	(*see also* worship)	best time	PLUMAGE
below[1]		best type	ELITE
indicating one word written under		**beta**	B
another:		**better**	
•live (BE) *below* soldier(D)	GIBE	better half	RIB.WIFE
below[2]		better *half*	BET.TER
below seven	SIX	**between**	
below (s)even	EVEN	*between* bends	S-S
below forty	FOR.FORT	*between* ol/d and y/oung	DANDY
bemused by all. . .	BALLY	between the sheets	(in) B-ED
bend	S.U.Z		(in) C-OT
bend a knee	KNEEL	*between* us	U-S
bend a knee	KEEN	**beyond**	
bender	ELBOW.KNEE	beyond the mouth	omit first letter
bent nail	ANIL	•river *beyond the mouth*(h)UMBER
bent into shape	HEAPS.PHASE	*biased* umpire	IMPURE
benevolent Communist	KINDRED	**Bible**	AV.BIB.NT.OT.RV
Bengal		hence	
beggar	BAUL	•Bible queen	AVER
bison	GAUR	•Bible records	BIBLISTS
boat	BATEL.BAULEA(H)	•nothing *in* the Bible	NOT
capital	B	•Bible-woman	OTHER
flower	GANGES	•last word *about* the Bible	CURVE
leader	B	**biblical**	(*see* old[3])
measure	BEGA.CHATTACK	**big[1]**	OS
	COTTA(H)	hence	
tree	BOLA	•big flower	OSIRIS
Berlin division	WALL	•big sheep	OSRAM
berserk slayer	LAYERS.RELAYS	•big-time girl	OSMOSIS
berth	WATER-BED	and	
beset		•very large bird	OSTEAL
beset a	incl A	•very large vehicle	OSCAR
beset *	incl *	•very large victim	OSPREY
•runner's *besetting* sin	COSINE	**big[2]**	
beset by *	incl in *	big-bang time	REPORTAGE
•king *beset by* wo-e	WOKE.WORE	big banger	TNT
beside		Big Ben	NEVIS
father *beside* himself	PAPA	big build-up	SKYSCRAPER
man *beside* himself	TOM-TOM		TOWER

big drinker	FISH
big fight	BATTLE
big guns	RA
big landlords	BLOCK LETTERS
big letter	LARGESSE
big lie	ONER
big luminary	SUN
big man	BEN.FATAL
big noise	BOOM.VIP
big *noise*	GRATE
big sum	IMPOUNDS
big timer	BEN
Big *Top* (D)	B
bikini	ATOLL
bikini top	BRA
bikini *top*(D)	B
bill[1]	AC.AD
hence	
•Bill Hill	ACTOR
•Bill Price	ACCOST
•Bill *with* another man	ACED
	ACERIC.ACHE
	ACRON.ACTED
and	
•Bill *is in* front	FACADE
•Bill *is on* time	ADAGE
•bill it	ADIT
bill[2]	
bill of exchange	BE
bill of lading	BL
bill of parcels	BP
bill of sale	BS
bill payable	BP
bill receivable	BREC
billowing robes	BOERS.BORES
	SOBER
biochemical oxygen demand	BOD
biography	BIOG.LIFE
biology	BIOL
bird[1]	PRISON
bird-boy	RUFFIAN
bird-dog	COCKTAIL.HARRIER
bird fancier	CAT
bird food	PIE
bird-man	COCKED.COCKLES
	TERNAL.TITHE.TITLES
bird painter	WHISTLER
bird sanctuary	NEST
bird walking	CROWFOOT

bird watcher	EAGLE EYE
	GAOLER.JAILER
	SCREW.WARDER
bird's recreation	HOBBY
bird's nest	CLUTCH HOUSING
blackbird	BEAGLE.BOWL
bird[2]	AVIFAUNA.ORNIS
commonly used names	ERNE
	TERN.TIT
some alternative names and	
descriptions including group	
names:	
able to leave nest soon after	
hatching	PRAECOCES
Accentor	DUNNOCK
	HEDGE SPARROW
Accipiter	SPARROWHAWK
Alauda	(SKY)LARK
albatross	ALCATRAS
	GOONEY (BIRD)
Alpine	SNOW FINCH
Anas	GADWALL.TEAL
	WI(D)GEON
Anous	NODDY
Antarctic	PENGUIN
Anthus	PIPIT
Arctic	SNOW BUNTING
	SNOW GOOSE
Arenaria	STREPSILAS
	TURNSTONE
ariel	PETREL
	SWALLOW.TOUCAN
Astur	GOSHAWK
auk	DIVER.RAZORBILL
avocet	AVOSET
babbler	THRUSH
bald eagle	OSSIFRAGE
Baltimore oriole	HANGBIRD
bantam	DANDY-COCK
	DANDY-HEN
barn owl	MADGE.SCREECH OWL
barnacle goose	BARNACLE
	BERNICE GOOSE
bartailed godwit	SCAMEL
bat	PIPISTRELLE
bearded	
—tit(mouse)	REEDLING
	REED-PHEASANT
—vulture	LAMMERGEIER

	LAMMERGEYER
bee-eater	MEROPIDIAN
bird of	
—paradise	STANDARD-WING
—prey	RAPTOR
bittern	ARDEA.BUTTER-BUMP
	MIRE-DRUM
black	
—backed gull	SWART-BACK
—bird	AMSEL.AMZEL.MERLE
	OUSEL(COCK).OUZEL
—cap	WARBLER
—cock	BLACK GROUSE
—grouse	BLACKCOCK
	MOORCOCK.MOORFOWL
	HEATH BIRD.HEATH FOWL
—guillemot	DOVEKIE
	SEA TURTLE
—headed gull (Scottish)	
	PICKMAW
blue tit	BLUECAP.NUN
	PINCHEM.PINNOCK
	TOMTIT.YAUP
Bombycilla	WAXWING
brantail	REDSTART.RUTICULA
brent goose	BRANT GOOSE
	BRENT BARNACLE
brown owl	WOOD OWL
Bucephela	GOLDENEYE
budgerigar	SHELL-PARAKEET
	SHELL-PARROT
	ZEBRA-PAR(R)AKEET
bullfinch	MONK.SHIRLEY
bunting	CIRL.ORTOLAN
bustard	OTIS
butcherbird	SHRIKE
buzzard	PUTTOCK
Calidris	KNOT
Cape pigeon	PINTADO
Capella	GALINAGO.SNIPE
capercailzie	WOODGROUSE
carrion crow	GORCROW
carrion-eater	VULTURE
Certhia	TREE CREEPER
chaffinch	PINK.ROBINET
	SCOBBY NAPPY.SPINK
	WHEAT-BIRD
Charadrius	DOTTEREL.PLOVER
chats	SAXICOLA
chiffchaff	WARBLER
Chinese	GOLDEN PHEASANT
	SILVER PHEASANT
	SWAN-GOOSE
chough	CHEWET.SEA CROW
—group	CHATTERING
Ciconia	STORK
Circus	HARRIER
climbing	SCANSORES
coal tit	COAL-MOUSE
	COLE-MOUSE.COLE TIT
coastal bird	ROCK PIPIT
Collocalia	SWIFTLET
common -eagle	GOLDEN EAGLE
—harrier	HEN HARRIER
—kite (obs.)	GLED(E)
—lark	SKYLARK
—swan	MUTE SWAN
—wild goose	GREY
	GOOSE.GREYLAG
Coracias	ROLLER
cormorant	SEA CROW
	SEA RAVEN.URILE
—Scottish	SCART(H).SKART(H)
corncrake	CRECK.CREX
	LANDRAIL.RAIL.RALLUS
Corvus	CROW.JACKDAW
	RAVEN.ROOK
covered with down at	
birth	PRAECOCES
crane	DEMOISELLE
—genus	GRUIDAE
—group	HERD
creeper	CERTHIA
crested	
-European bird	HOOPOE
—grebe	CARGOOSE
—heron	SQUACCO
—penguin	ROCK-HOPPER
—screamer	SERIEMA
Crex	CORNCRAKE.LANDRAIL
crocodile bird	PLOVER
	TROCHILUS
crossbill	LOXIA
crow	CORVUS
cuckoo	COUCAL
curlew	TITTEREL
	(GREAT) WHAUP
Cygnus	SWAN

Cypselus	APUS.SWIFT	—blackcock	GREYHEN
dabchick	DIDAPPER.DIPCHICK	—falcon	LANNER
	DIPPER.DOBCHICK	—grouse	GORHEN.GREYHEN
	LITTLE GREBE	—moorfowl	MOORHEN
Dafilia	PINTAIL	—peregrine	FALCON-GENTIL
darcock	RALLUS.WATER RAIL		FALCON-GENTLE
darter	PLOTUS.SNAKEBIRD	—pochard	DUNBIRD
	WRYNECK	—ruff	REE(VE)
didapper	DOPPER	—sandpiper	REEVE
dipper	WATER OUZEL	—swan	PEN
diver	GAVIA	fig-pecker	BECCAFICO
diving bird	LOON	finch	BRAMBLING.BUNTING
domestic duck	INDIAN RUNNER		CIRL.CITRIL
dorbie	DUNLIN		LINNET.SPINK
dove	CULVER.PIGEON	firecrest	REGULUS
—group	FLIGHT	fledgling	QUILLER
duck	GARROT	flightless	CASSOWARY.EM(E)U
—group	BADELYNGE		KIWI.OSTRICH.PENGUIN
	BAD(D)LING		PINGUIN.RATITAE.RHEA
	SMEATH.SMEE(TH)		STRUTHIONES
dunbird	POCHARD	—pigeon (old)	SOLITAIRE
dun-diver	MERGANSER	flycatcher	MUSCICAPA
dunlin	DORBIE.OX-BIRD	forktailed gulls	XEMA
OXPECKER.PURRE.SEA MOUSE		fossil	ICTHYORNIS
	SEA PECK.STINT	Fratercula	PUFFIN
dunnock	(HEDGE-)ACCENTOR	Fregata	FRIGATE BIRD
	HEDGE SPARROW	freshwater diver	GREBE
eagle	ERNE	friarbird	FOUR-O'CLOCK
—owl	BUBO	frigate bird	ALCATRAS
Eastern dwarf goose	GOSLET		MAN-OF-WAR (BIRD)
edible nest builder	COLLOCALIA	frogmouth	PODARGUS
	SWIFTLET	fully webbed	STEGANOPOD(ES)
eider duck	SOMATERIA	fulmar	MALLEMUCK
erne	SEA EAGLE		MOLLYMAWK
European vulture		Gallicrex	KORA.WATER-COCK
	GRIFFON VULTURE	Gallinago	CAPELLA.SNIPE
fabulous	HARPY.HUMA	game bird	GROUSE.PARTRIDGE
PHOENIX.ROC.ROK.RUC		PHEASANT.QUAIL.WOODCOCK	
RUKH.SIMORG.SIMURG(H)		gannet	ALCATRAS.BOOBY
	WHISTLER		SOLAN(D)
	(*see also* monsters)	garden warbler	REELER
falcon	GERFALCON.HAWK	garganey	ANAS
PEREGRINE.SACRE.SAKER(ET)		Garrulus	JAY
STONE-HAWK.TASSEL-GENT(LE)		Gavia	DIVER
TERCEL-GENTLE.TERCEL-JERKIN		geese (group)	GAGGLE.SKEIN
Falkland Islands		giant fulmar	OSSIFRAGA
penguin	GENTOO	goatsucker	FROGMOUTH
female		MOTH-HUNTER.NIGHTHAWK	
—black grouse	HEATHHEN	godwit	SCAMEL

goldcrest
    GOLDEN-CRESTED WREN
    KINGLET.REGULUS
    ROITELET
golden
—crested wren   GOLDCREST
    KINGLET.REGULUS
    ROITELET
—eagle   AQUILA
—eye   BUCEPHELA
—oriole   LORIOT.YELLOWBIRD
    WITWALL.WOODWALE
    WOODWALL
goldfinch   GOLDSPINK.GOUDIE
    GOWDSPINK.RED-CAP
—group   CHARM.CHIRM
goosander   MERGANSER
goose   SADDLEBACK
gorcock   RED GROUSE
gorcrow   CARRION CROW
gorse-frequenting   WHINCHAT
grasshopper-warbler   REELER
great
—auk   GAREFOWL.GAIRFOWL
—black-backed gull   SADDLEBACK
—northern diver   EMBER GOOSE
—shearwater   HACKBOLT
—tit   OX-EYE
greater spotted
  woodpecker   WITWALL
    WOODWALE.WOODWALL
grebe   DIVER
green
—cormorant   SHAG
—finch   GREEN LINNET
—linnet   GREENFINCH
—woodpecker   HICKWALL
    WITWALL.WOOD-SPITE
    WOODWALE.WOODWALL
    YAFFLE
grey
—lag   GOOSE
—parrot   PSITTACUS
grosbeak   HAWFINCH.PINE-FINCH
grouse   BLACKCOCK
    BLACK GAME.CAPERCAILLIE
    CAPERCAILZIE
—female   GORHEN.GREYHEN
—male   GORCOCK

guillemot   MARROT.MURRE
    SEA HEN.WILLOCK
guinea fowl   GUINEA HEN
    PINTADO
gull   SCAURY.SEA COB
    (SEA) MAW.(SEA) MEW
    WAGGEL
—gulls   LARIDAE
—group   COLONY
haggard   HAWK
hareld   OLD WIFE
Hawaiian goose   NENE
hawfinch   GROSBEAK
hawk   BOWESS.HAGGARD
    LANNER.TARSEL.TASSEL(L)
    T(I)ERCEL(ET)
—group   CAST
—short-winged   GOSHAWK
heathcock   GROUSE
hedge sparrow   DUNNOCK
    (HEDGE-)ACCENTOR
    PINNOCK.TITLING
hen harrier   HEN-DRIVER
hen-like   GALLINACEOUS
heron   ARDEA.HERN
—group   SEDGE.SIEGE
—type   BOATBILL
hickwall   WOODPECKER
Himalayan pheasant   MONA(U)L
Himantopus   STILT(-PLOVER)
Hirundo   SWALLOW
honey buzzard   PERN(IS)
hooded
—crow   HOODIE CROW
    ROYSTON CROW
—pigeon   CAPUCHIN.JACOBIN
hoopoe   UPUPA
hummingbird   RACKET-TAIL
    COLIBRI
Iceland falcon   ICELANDER
Icterus   TROOPIAL.TROUPIAL
jacinth   PIGEON
jackdaw   JACK.KAE
ja(e)ger   SKUA
jay   GARRULUS
Jynx   WRYNECK
kestrel   STALLION.STANN(I)EL
    STAN(N)YEL
kingfisher   ALCEDO.(H)ALCYON

kinglet	FIRECREST(ED WREN)
kite	ELANET.FORKTAIL.MILVUS
	PUTTOCK
kittiwake	HACKLET.HAGLET
knot	CALIDRIS
kora	GALLICREX.WATER COCK
Lagopus	PTARMIGAN
lammergeier	OSSIFRAGE
land-rail	CORNCRAKE.RALLUS
lapwing	PE(E)WIT.PIE-WIFE
	PLOVER.TIRWIT.TEW(H)IT
—group	DESERT
—Scottish	TEUCHAT
large	
—billed bird	PELICAN
—crow	RAVEN
—duck	GOOSANDER
—gull	HERRING GULL
—running birds	STRUTHIONES
—thrush	MISSEL
largest bird	OSTRICH
Laridae	GULLS
lark	GAVILAN.LAVEROCK
—group	BEVY.EXALTATION
Limosa	GODWIT
linnet-type	REDPOLL.TWITE
little	
—auk	DOVEKIE.ICE-BIRD
	ROCH.ROTCH(E).SEA DOVE
—grebe	DABCHICK
—Scottish	WHIMBREL
long	
—tailed tit	MAG
—winged	TERN
loon	DIVER
loriot	(GOLDEN) ORIOLE
magpie	MADGE.MAG.PIE
male	
—black grouse	HEATHCOCK
—duck	DRAKE
—lanner	LANNERET
—peregrine	TERCEL-GENTLE
—red grouse	GORCOCK
—redstart	WHITECAP
—sandpiper	RUFF
—sparrowhawk	MUSKET
—swan	COB
—thrush	THROSTLE COCK
—turkey	STAG

mallards (group)	SORD.SUTE
mallemuck	FULMAR
	MOLLYMAWK
Mareca	WI(D)GEON
marsh	
—bird	BITTERN
—harrier	DUCK HAWK
	MOOR-BUZZARD
martin	MARTLET
mavis	(SONG) THRUSH
	THROSTLE
meadow pipit	ANTHUS
	TIT-LARK.TITLING
Meleagris	TURKEY
merganser	DUN-DIVER.SERULA
	SAWBILL.SMEW
merlin	ROCK HAWK
Milvus	KITE
missel (mistle) thrush	
	SCREECH THRUSH
	STORM-COCK.WOOD THRUSH
moa	DIORNIS
mollymawk	FULMAR
	MALLEMUCK
moor	
—buzzard	DUCK HAWK
—fowl	GROUSE
—hen	WATER HEN
Motacillidae	WAGTAILS
moth-hunter	GOATSUCKER
Mother Carey's chicken	
	STORM(Y) PETREL
Muscicapa	FLYCATCHER
myna	BOAT-TAIL.GRA(C)KLE
Nettapus	GOSLET
night-hawk	GOATSUCKER
nightingale	PHILOMEL(A)
	PHILOMENE.PROGNE
—group	WATCH
—type	BLUEBREAST
	BLUETHROAT
nightjar	CHURN-OWL.DORHAWK
	EVEJAR.FERN-OWL
	GOATSUCKER.SCREECH HAWK
	NIGHT HERON
northern	
—falcon	GERFALCON
	GYRFALCON
	JERFALCON

—freshwater duck	GADWALL
—grouse	WILLOW GROUSE
—sea duck	EIDER (DUCK)
	GOLDENEYE.HARELD
	OLD WIFE.OEDEMIA.SCOTER
Nucifraga	NUTCRACKER
Numida	GUINEA FOWL
nut	
—cracker	NUCIFRAGA
—hatch	SITTA
—jobber	SITTA
—pecker	SITTA
Oedemia	NORTHERN SEA
	DUCK.SCOTER
Oenanthe	WHEATEAR
oriole	LORIOT
osprey	OSSIFRAGE.PANDION
	SEA EAGLE.SEA HAWK
ossifrage	BALD EAGLE
	GIANT FULMAR
	LAMMERGEIER.OSPREY
oven-tit	WILLOW WARBLER
owl	JENNY.SCOPS.STRICK
—owls	STRIGES.STRIGIFORMES
ox	
—bird	DUNLIN.BEEFEATER
—pecker	DUNLIN.BUFFALO BIRD
oystercatcher	SEA-PIE
Pandion	OSPREY
parakeet	BUDGERIGAR
partridge	FRANCOLIN
—group	COVEY
—x quail cross	PERCOLIN
Parus	TITMOUSE
Passer	SPARROW
Pavo	PEACOCK
peacock	PAVO
—group	MUSTER
pecking birds	PICARIAE
peewit	LAPWING.PLOVER
pelican	ALCATRAS
perching birds	INSESSORES
	PASSERIFORMES
Perdix	PARTRIDGE
peregrine	FALCON.GENTLE
pern	HONEY BUZZARD
petrel	ARIEL.FULMAR.NELLY
	PINTADO.PROCELLARIA
	STORM-BIRD

Petronia	ROCK SPARROW
pheasants (group)	NYE
Philomachus	RUFF.REE(VE)
Pica	MAGPIE
Picidae	WOODPECKERS
pie	MAGPIE
pied wagtail	WATER WAGTAIL
pigeon	COLUMBA.CROPPER
	FANTAIL.HOMER.JACINTH
	POUTER.TUMBLER
	TRUMPETER.TURBIT
	WHITEHEAD
—dark-coloured	BARB
—hooded	CAPUCHIN.JACOBIN
—slaty-blue	JACINTH
—wood	CULVER.ZOO-ZOO
pink	CHAFFINCH
—footed bird	GOOSE
pinnock	BLUE TIT
	HEDGE SPARROW
pintado	CAPE PIGEON
	GUINEA FOWL
	PETREL
pintail	DAFILA.SANDGROUSE
	SMEATH.SMEE(TH)
piping crow	FLUTE-BIRD
pipit	ANTHUS.TITLARK
Plataleidae	SPOONBILL
plover	CHARADRIUS
	DOTT(E)REL.LAPWING
	PEEWIT.SURF-BIRD
—group	CONGREGATION
—like	PRATINCOLE
pochard	SCAUP DUCK.SEA DUCK
	SMEATH.SMEE(TH)
Podargus	FROGMOUTH
Podiceps	GREBE
Porphyrio	PURPLE COOT
Procellaria	PETREL
Progne	NIGHTINGALE
	SWALLOW
Psittacus	(GREY) PARROT
ptarmigan	LAGOPUS.RYPE
	WILLOW GROUSE
Pterocles	SANDGROUSE
puffin	FRATERCULA.SEA PARROT
	TOM NODDY
—Scottish	TAMMIE NORIE
Puffinus	SHEARWATER

purple coot	PORPHYRIO.SULTAN
quails (group)	BEVY
Quaker-bird	SOOTY ALBATROSS
racket-tail	HUMMINGBIRD
rafter-bird	SPOTTED FLYCATCHER
Rallus	CORNCRAKE (WATER-)RAIL
rapacious bird	KITE
razorbill	AUK.MURRE
red	
—backed sandpiper	DUNLIN
—breast	RADDOCK.ROBIN RUBECULA.RUDDOCK
—breasted merganser	HERALD (DUCK)
—cap	GOLDFINCH
—grouse	MOORCOCK.MOORFOWL
—(male)	GORCOCK
—headed duck	POCHARD POCKARD.POKER
—legged crow	CHOUGH
—shank	GAMBET.TOTANUS SANDPIPER.TATTLER
—start	BRANTAIL.RUTICILLA
—(male)	WHITECAP
reed	
—bunting	JUNCO.REED SPARROW
—pheasant	BEARDED TITMOUSE
—sparrow	REED BUNTING
—thrush	REED WARBLER
—warbler	REED THRUSH REED WREN
—wren	REED WARBLER
reedling	BEARDED TIT
reeler	GRASSHOPPER-WARBLER
Regulus	FIRECREST.GOLDCREST
Rhyncops	SKIMMER
ringdove	CUSHAT
robin	RADDOCK.REDBREAST RUBECULA.RUDDOCK
rock	
—bird	PUFFIN
—hopper	CRESTED PENGUIN
—lark	ROCK PIPIT
—pipit	ROCK LARK.SEA LARK
—sparrow	PETRONIA
roller	CANARY.CORACIAS PIGEON
rooks (group)	BUILDING
rose-coloured starling	PASTOR
rotche	DOVEKIE
ruddock	REDBREAST.ROBIN
ruffed grouse	HAZEL GROUSE
—female	HAZEL HEN
running bird	EM(E)U.OSTRICH ROADRUNNER
—birds	CURSORES
rype	PTARMIGAN
saddleback	GOOSE.GULL
sand	
—grouse	PINTAIL.PTEROCLES SYRRHAPTES
—lark	SANDPIPER
—piper	DUNLIN.GREENSHANK KNOT.SAND-LARK SANDERLING.SEA LARK SEA SNIPE.SUMMER SNIPE SURFBIRD.TAT(T)LER
—female	REE(VE)
—male	RUFF
sanderling	SANDPIPER
Saxicola	STONECHAT.WHEATEAR WHINCHAT
scaup (duck)	POCHARD
scissor-bill	SKIMMER
Scolopax	WOODCOCK
Scops	OWL
scoter	NORTHERN SEA DUCK OEDEMIA.SURF DUCK.WHILK
scraping birds	RASORES
scray(e)	TERN
screech	
—hawk	NIGHTJAR
—martin	SWIFT
—owl	BARN OWL.LICH OWL SHRIEK OWL
—thrush	MISSEL (MISTLE) THRUSH
screecher	SWIFT
sea	
—bar	TERN
—bird	TARROCK
—cob	SEAGULL
—crow	SKUA
—dotterel	TURNSTONE

—dove	ICE-BIRD.LITTLE AUK
—duck	POCHARD
—eagle	ERNE.OSPREY
—gull	SEA COB.(SEA) MAW
	(SEA) MEW
—hawk	OSPREY.SKUA
—hen	GUILLEMOT
—lark	ROCK PIPIT.SANDPIPER
—maw	GULL.SEA MEW
—mew	GULL.SEA MAW
—parrot	PUFFIN
—pie	OYSTERCATCHER
—quail	TURNSTONE
—snipe	SANDPIPER
—swallow	STORM PETREL.TERN
—turtle	BLACK GUILLEMOT
secretary bird	SERPENT-EATER
sedge	
—bird	SEDGE-WARBLER
	SEDGE-WREN
—warbler	REED SPARROW
serpent-eater	SECRETARY BIRD
serin	CANARY
shag	GREEN CORMORANT
shearwater	HACKLET.HAGLET
	PUFFINUS
shel(l)duck	TADORNA
sheldrake	BERGANDER
	BURROW-DUCK
—group	DOPPING
shell-parrot	BUDGERIGAR
shore bird	SAND-LARK
short-winged hawk	GOSHAWK
shovel(l)er	SPATULA
shrike	BUTCHERBIRD
	WOODCHAT
siskin	ABERDEVINE.TARIN
Sitta	NUTHATCH.NUTJOBBER
	NUTPECKER
skimmer	RHYNCOPS
	SCISSOR-BILL
skua	BOATSWAIN
	BONXIE.BOS(U)N.JA(E)GER
	SEA CROW.SEA HAWK
	STERCORARIUS
skylark	ALAUDA
small	
—canary	SERIN
—curlew	W(H)IMBREL

—falcon	HOBBY.KESTREL
	MERLIN
—parrot	LOVEBIRD.PAR(R)AKEET
—partridge	QUAIL
—sandpiper	DUNLIN.STINT
—seabird	MURRELET
—snipe	JACK SNIPE
smallest European	
seabird	STORM(Y) PETREL
smew	MERGANSER
	SMEATH.SMEE(TH)
snake-bird	DARTER.WRYNECK
snipe	CAPELLA.GALINAGO
	JEDCOCK.MIRE-SNIPE
—group	WALK.WISP
—type	PAINTED SNIPE
snow bunting	SNOWFLAKE
	SNOWFLECK.SNOWFLICK
solan(d)	GANNET
Somateria	EIDER DUCK
song	
—birds	OSCINES
—thrush	MAVIS.THROSTLE
sooty	
—albatross	QUAKER-BIRD
—tern	EGG-BIRD
sparrow	PASSER.PHILIP.SP(R)UG
—hawk	ACCIPITER
—like	HEDGE WARBLER
Spatula	SHOVEL(L)ER
spoonbill	PLATALEIDAE
spotted flycatcher	RAFTER-BIRD
sprug	SPARROW
spug	SPARROW
squacco	CRESTED HERON
starling	STURNUS
—group	MURMURATION
Stercorarius	SKUA
stilt(-plover)	HIMANTOPUS
stint	DUNLIN
stone	
—chat	STONECHATTER
—curlew	STONE PLOVER
	THICK-KNEE
—hawk	FALSON
stork	CICONIA
storm	
—bird	PETREL
—cock	MISSEL (MISTLE)THRUSH

—petrel	
MOTHER CAREY'S CHICKEN	
MOTHER CAREY'S GOOSE	
SEA SWALLOW	
Strepsilas	ARENARIA
	TURNSTONE
Streptopelia	TURTLEDOVE
	TURTUR
stupid	NODDY
Sturnus	STARLING
(sub)arctic grouse	PTARMIGAN
Sulidae	GANNETS
sultan	PURPLE COOT
summer	
—snipe	SANDPIPER
—teal	GARGANEY
—visitor	WHEATEAR
—warbler	YELLOWBIRD
swallow	ARIEL.HIRUNDO
	PROGNE
—like	MARTIN(ET)
—tailed	KITE
swan	CYGNUS.WHOOPER
	WHOOPING SWAN
—female	PEN
—goose	CHINA GOOSE
—group	BEVY
—male	COB
—young	CYGNET
swart-back	BLACK-BACKED GULL
swift	APUS
CYPSELUS.SCREECHER	
SCREECH MARTIN.SENEX	
swiftlet	COLLOCALIA
Sylvia	WARBLER
Syrrhaptes	SANDGROUSE
Tadorna	SHEL(L)DUCK
	SHIELDUCK
Tantalus	WOOD IBIS
tattler	WOOD-SANDPIPER
REDSHANK.SANDPIPER	
TOTANUS	
tawny owl	BROWN OWL
	GREY OWL
teal	ANAS
—group	SPRING
tern	SCRAY(E)
EGG-BIRD.SEA BAR	
SEA SWALLOW	

thick-knee	STONE CURLEW
	STONE PLOVER
throstle	MAVIS.(SONG) THRUSH
thrush	BABBLER.MAVIS
	THROSTLE.TURDUS
—disease	APHTHA
—type	FIELDFARE.REDWING
	RING OUSEL
titlark	PIPIT
titling	HEDGE SPARROW
	MEADOW PIPIT
titmouse	PARUS
Tom Noddy	PUFFIN
tomtit	BLUE TIT.PINNOCK
Totanus	REDSHANK.SANDPIPER
	TAT(T)LER
toucan	ARIEL
trained falcon	GENTLE
tree creeper	CERTHIA
Trochilus	CROCODILE BIRD
Troglodytes	WREN
tropicbird	BOATSWAIN-BIRD
troupial	ICTERUS
tumbler pigeon	ROLLER
Turdus	BLACKBIRD.FIELDFARE
	RING OUSEL.THRUSH
turkey-buzzard	GALLINAZO
turnstone	ARENARIA.STREPSILAS
	SEA DOTTEREL
turtledove	STREPTOPELIA
	TURTUR
Turtur	STREPTOPELIA
	TURTLEDOVE
twite	LINNET TYPE FINCH
umbrella	DRAGOON-BIRD
untamed hawk	HAGGARD
Upupa	HOOPOE
Uria	GUILLEMOT
variegated duck	
	HARLEQUIN DUCK
velvet-duck	VELVET SCOTER
vulture	GRIPE
wading bird	IBIS.KNOTY
	PHALAROPE
—birds	GRALLAE.GRALLATORES
wagtail	MOLLY.SEED-BIRD
	TROTTY
—group	WALK
—wagtails	MOTACILLIDAE

warbler	PEGGY.PETTICHAPS	—grouse	CAPERCAILLIE
	PETTY-CHAPS.SYLVIA		CAPERCAILZIE
water		—ibis	TANTALUS
—bird	COOT.MOORHEN	—owl	BROWN OWL
—cock	GALLICREX.KORA	—pecker	AWL-BIRD.HICKWALL
—hen	MOORHEN		WHETTLE.WITWALL
—ousel	DIPPER		WOODCHAT.WOODWALE
—rail	DARCOCK.RALLUS		WOODWALL.YAFFLE
—wagtail	PIED WAGTAIL	—peckers	PICIDAE
waterfowl (group)	PLUMP	—pigeon	CULVER.CUSHAT
wax			QUINCE(TY-COCK)
—bill	WEAVERBIRD	—sandpiper	TAT(T)LER
—wing	BOMBYCILLA.CHATTERER	—spite	GREEN WOODPECKER
weaverbird	BISHOPBIRD	—thrush	
	WAXBILL		MISSEL (MISTLE)THRUSH
web-footed	PALMIPED(E)	—wale	(GREEN) WOODPECKER
whaup (Scottish)	CURLEW	—wren	WILLOW WARBLER
wheat			WOOD WARBLER
—bird	CHAFFINCH	wren	TROGLODYTES
—ear	OENANTHE	wryneck	DARTER.JYNX
whimbrel (Scottish)			SNAKEBIRD
	LITTLE WHAUP	yaffle	GREEN WOODPECKER
white		yaup	BLUE TIT
—gerfalcon	ICELAND FALCON	yellow	
—heron	EGRET	—bunting	YELLOWHAMMER.YITE
—owl	SNOWY OWL	—hammer	
—throat	BEARDIE.PEGGY		SCRIBBLING-SCHOOLMASTER
—throated thrush	RING OUZEL		YELDRIN.YELDROCK
whooper	SWAB		YELLOW BUNTING
wi(d)geon	ANAS.MARECA		YELLOW-YITE.YOLDRING
	SMEATH.SMEE(TH)		YORLING.YOWLEY.ZIVOLA
	WHEWER	—willow warbler	
—group	COMPANY		WOOD WARBLER
wild		yellowish-green finch	SISKIN
—duck	BALDPATE.MALLARD	yite	YELLOW BUNTING
—group	PLUMP	young	BRANCHER.NESTLING
—pigeon	ROCK DOVE		PEEPER
	ROCK PIGEON	—black grouse	HEATH-POULT
willow		—goose	GOSLING.GREEN GOOSE
—grouse	PTARMIGAN	—gull	SCAURY
—warbler	OVEN-TIT	—hawk	EYAS
	WILLOW WREN	—male	EYAS-MUSKAT
	WOOD WREN	—heron	HERONSEW
—wren	WILLOW WARBLER		HER(O)NSHAW
wisp	SNIPE	—owl	(H)OWLET
witwall	WOODPECKER	—partridge	FLAPPER
wood		—wild duck	FLAPPER
—chat	SHRIKE.WOODPECKER	zebra-par(r)akeet	BUDGERIGAR
—cock	SCOLOPAX	zivola	YELLOWHAMMER

birthplace	BED.BP	**blessed**	
biscuit	GARIBALDI	blessed one	DONOR.GIVER
bishop	ABBA.ANSELM.B.BP.ODO		SAINT.TAKER
bissextile	BIS	blessed sacrament	BS
bit		Blessed Virgin (Mary)	BV(M)
bit of crest	PARTRIDGE	**blind**	
bit of luck	L.LU	*blind* dates	SATED
bit of luc/k I sh/all. . .	KISH	blind (man)	VENETIAN
bi(t) *short*	BI	*blind* mic(e)	MIC
bit out of so/me re/d. . .	MERE	**blissful state**	IGNORANCE
bits out of a/n ap/ple	NAP	*blizzard* in Ayr	RAINY
bitch	DOGMA	**blob**	O
bite		**block**	
bite out of a/n ap/ple	NAP	*block* *	incl in *
biting cold	NIPPY	•stone *blocking* river	TASTY
biting pastry	TART	*blocked by* *	incl *
bitter *end*	R	•river *blocked by* stone	TASTY
bizarre affair	RAFFIA	blockbuster	SCULPTOR
black	B.JET	blockhouse	IGLOO
hence		**blood**	
•a black deed	ABACTION	blood count	DRACULA
•a black mark	ABSTAIN	bloodgroup	A.AB.B.O
•a black tree	ABASH		FAMILY.KIN
and		blood money	ERIC
•black cat	BOUNCE	bloody	B
•black convict	JET LAG	bloody fool	BF
•black cravats	JETTIES	**bloom**	
•Black Death	BEND	bloomer	FLOWER
•black hole	BO		(*see* flower)
•blackball	BO	blooming female	IRIS.ROSE et al
•blackbird	BEAGLE.BOWL		(*see also* plants[1])
and		**blow**	ONER
•Black *has* much weight	JETTON	blower	TELEPHONE
•black Uncle	JETSAM	*blowing about* in the. . .	THINE
black[2]		*blowing up* a ship	APHIS
art	NECROMANCY	**blue**	DOWN.SAD.SPEND
	NIGROMANCY	blue boys	ROYAL
Beauty	DARK HORSE	blue film	ANGEL.MAX
	NIGHTMARE	blue jumper	ATHLETE
belt	DAN	blue water	DANUBE
lead	OTHELLO	**blunder**	
mole	JETTY	*blunder* made. . .	DAME.EDAM
salt	TAR		MEAD
stuff	COAL.OIL.TAR	*blundering* steps	PESTS
suit	C.S	*blurred* letters	SETTLER
blame	RAP	**blush**	GORED
blanket coverage	BEDSPREAD	blushing	RED
	EIDERDOWN	**board**	BD
blend of teas	SATE.SEAT	board meeting	DINNER PARTY

Board of
—Control BC
—Education BE
—Trade BOT
boarded by a... incl A
boarded by * incl *
•bri-g *boarded by* number...
BRING
boarding * incl in *
•number *boarding* bri-g BRING
boards BDS
boasting AM.IAM.IM
(*see also* declaring)
boat TUB
boat builder ARKWRIGHT.NOAH
SHIPWRIGHT
boat propeller GONDOLIER
OARSMAN
boatman JEROME.KERN
bob S
body odour BO
bogged down (in) FE-N.(in) MAR-SH
Bohemia(n) BOH
dance REDOWA
boil FURUNCLE
boiled over ROVE
boiling *point* B
boiling point BP
boiling swede SEWED.WEEDS
boisterous gale GAEL
Bolivia(n) BOL
capital B.LA PAZ
coins
—unit CENTAVO
—100 centavos DOLLAR
language AYMARA.QUECHA
leader B
measure CELEMIN.LEAGUE
ruminant VICUNA
weight LIBRA
bond SPY
bond lover SCRIPOPHILE
Bond's boss M
bondsman ERNIE
bone T
bonehead CONDYLE.SKULL
bone*head* B
bone*shaking* EBON
book¹ B.BK.LIB.TOME.VOL

Book *I* B
book cover COPYRIGHT
book matches NOVELTIES
bookmaker AMOS.EZRA.JOB.et al
AUTHOR(ESS).EDITOR
books BB.NT.OT
Books *I & III* BO
booksellers BA
book-store RESERVE
book²
indicates character in novel etc.:
•*booked* as thief
(ARTFUL) DODGER
•*booked* captain... AHAB
HORNBLOWER.NEMO
•*booked* Finn HUCKLEBERRY
•*booked* traveller GULLIVER
Booth, *say* ASSASSIN
boots WELLER
border
border dispute HEDGEROW
border poet SIDEBURNS
borders of Hungary HY
borders of the... TE
boring holes DRY CELLS
born B.N.NAT.NE.NEE
hence
•born a monarch BAKING
•born *and* bred BRAISED
•born at her... BATHER
and
•born in New York NINNY
•born right on... NATRON
•born at hospital NEATH
•born dead, *say* NEEDED
born fool GOD'S APE
borne (*see* bearing³)
Borneo (*see* East Indies)
borough BOR
botany BOT
both
both directions indicates a
palindrome
•flat *in both directions* LEVEL
both ends of the TE
both sides LR.RL
hence
•copper *on* both sides CURL
•girl *in* both sides LEVER.REVEL

both sides indicates an inclusion	
•river *on both sides of* road	TARDY
both ways indicates a palindrome	
•look *both ways*	PEEP
both ways indicates reversal	
•played *both ways*	STRAD
bother	
a bit of *bother*	BAIT
bother about...	U-BOAT
bothering to write a...	WAITER
bottle	BOT.NERVE
bottle fruit	GOURD
bottle-*opener*	B
bottle-party	PINTADO
bottled	(in) VI-AL
bottled spirit	GENIE
bottling premises	CHATEAU
bottom	
bottom of all the big...(D)	LEG
bottom of foot	SOLE
bottom of foot(D)	T
mug, *bottom up*	GUM
bought	BT.BOT
bounce	
bouncer	BALL
bouncing babe	ABBE
bound	BD
bounds of possibility	PY
boundary	
boundaries of Surrey	SY
boundaries of the...	TE
boundary dispute	HEDGEROW
boundary trees	LIMES
bow	
bow of liner	L
bows	FIDDLESTICKS
bows of ship	SH
Bowman's (h)ouse	OUSE
bowl	
bowled	B
bowler	DRAKE
bowling	ON.TOM
box	
boxed	(in) CR-ATE
boxed in by *	incl in *
•is *boxed in by* r-ing	RISING
boxer	ALI.CLAY.PUG(ILIST)
boxers	ABA.WBA.WBC
boxer's diary	SCRAPBOOK

boxer's supporter	DOG-LEG
boxing a...	incl A
boxing belt	CROSS.HOOK.LEFT
	RIGHT.SWING.UPPERCUT
Boxing Day duo	TURTLE DOVES
Boxing Club	ABA
boxing *	incl *
•r-ing-*boxing* is...	RISING
boy	B.LAD
affectionate boy	FONDLES
boy *and* girl	ANNEAL.BENGAL
	DIJON.LEONORA.PATELLA
	PATINA.REGINA
boy *and* a girl	LENA
boyfriend	REGALLY
	(*see also* friend)
boy-worker	PAGEANT
boys	AL.DES.DON
	ED.LES.RON.TED
	(*see also* Appendix)
brace of peacock	STRUT
brain	
brain treatment	ECG
brain *treatment*	BAIRN
branch	BR
branch office	BO
brandy	
brandy and soda	BANDS
in brandy and soda	B-S
brass	
brass animal	RHINO
brass band	MONEY-BELT
brave	INDIAN.REDSKIN
brave wife	SQUAW
brave opponent	PALEFACE
Brazil(ian)[1]	BR.BRA.NUT
hence	
•Brazilian drunk	BROILED
•Brazilian *wears* spectacles *at*	
church	BROOCH
•Brazilian *with* different...	
	BROTHER
Brazilian[2]	
ant	TUCANDERA
armadillo	TATOU.TATU
birds	CARACARA.GUAN.KAMICHI
biting insects	MOTUCA
	MUTUCA.PIUM
capital	B.BRASILIA

cocoa	GUARANA
coffee	BAHIA
coins	
—old	LEMPIRA.REIS
—unit	CENTAVO
—100 centavos	CRUIZERO
	CRUSADO
—1000 cruizeros	CONTO
dance	BATUQUE.BOSSA NOVA
	CARIOCA.MAXIXE.SAMBA
drink	ASSAI
drug	JABORANDI.PAREIRA
fish	PERAI.PIABA.PIRAL
	PIRAN(H)A.PIRAYA
flowers	GLOXINIA.TREE-LILY
	VELLOZIA
flycatcher	YETAPA
grass	PARA-GRASS
—land	CAMPO
half-caste	MAMELUCO
leader	B
log canoe	MONTARIA
macaw	ARARA.MARACAN
monkey	SAI
negro	MINA
nut	COQUILLA.PARA-NUT
	SAPUCAIA
open forest	CAATINGA
opossum	SARIGUE
palm	(see palm)
parrot	ARA
piassava	PARA GRASS
plain	CAMPO.SAVANNAH
plant	IPECAC(UANHA).PIPI
pods used in tanning	PIPI
river	AMAZON
rodent	CAPIBARA.CAPYBARA
rubber	CAUCHO.(H)ULE.PARA
—tree	MANGABEIRA.SERINGA
sirenian	MANATEE.MANATI
snake	BOMA
stork	JABIRU
timber	EMBUIA.KINGWOOD
	MAHOGANY.ROSEWOOD
trade language	LINGOA GERAL
trees	ANDA.APA.ARAROBA
	BARBATIMEO.BRAUNA.DALI
	GOMAVEL.GUARABUA
	HERCULES CLUB.LECYTHIS

	MACERANDUBA.MANGABEIRA
	MASSARANDUBA
	MASSERANDUBA
	MUSTAIBA.PARANA PINE
	PRICKLY ASH.SAPUCAIA.TINGUY
	TOOTHACHE TREE.WALLABA
	XANTHOXYLUM
waterlily	VICTORIA
weight	LIBRA.ARROBA
breached wall of...	FALLOW
breadth	B
break¹	HOL.WE
break²	
break down result	ULSTER
break into a...	-ATION
break out of Broadmoor	
	BOARDROOM
break plate	PETAL
break up town	WONT
break down	WOND
breakdown of law	AWL
breaking rules	LURES
break*out*	BAKER.BRAKE
break*out*	TOU
break*out* last	SLAT
breakthrough in art	TRAIN
broken down van I...	IVAN.VAIN
broken leg	GEL.-GLE
broken romance	SERIAL
broken romance	CREMONA
broken statue	BUST
broken up by a	BAY
brokenly I moan...	NAOMI
break³	
break end off shove(l)	SHOVE
break ends off (s)hove(l)	HOVE
break ends off bran(ch)	BRAN
break head off (f)lower	LOWER
break tip off (s)pear	PEAR
break of day	D
break⁴	
break into *	incl in *
•all *break into* sh-op	SHALLOP
break open *	incl *
•English master	
breaks open cr-ate	CREMATE
breaks *	incl in *
•war *breaks* flier	BEWARE
broken by a...	incl A

broken by *	incl *
•flier *broken by* war	BEWARE
broken into by a. . .	incl A
broken into by *	incl *
•sh-op *broken into by* all	SHALLOP
breather	GILL.LUNG
breathing space	PORE
breeding	(*see* rearing)
Breton dialect	ARMORIC
brewing <u>ales</u>	SALE.SEAL
brick carrier	HOD.STRETCHER
bridge	BR.DENTURE.SPAN
opponents	NE.NW.SE.SW
partners	EW.NS
players	E.N.S.W
Bridgend	G
bridle path, *say*	AISLE
brief	
brief attire	LAW SUIT
brief farewell	SOLON(g)
brief reply	ANS
brig	BR
brigade	BDE
brigade-major	BM
bright	
bright boy	RAY
bright land	WEST
brightly coloured	(in) R-ED.RED
brilliant champion	STARCH
brimstone	S.SULPHUR
bring	
bring back new⟨	WEN
bring in a	incl A
bring in *	incl *
•pun-t *brings in* girl	PUNDIT
•Bill *brought in* the	
French. . .	LACE
bring round a. . .	incl A
bring round *	incl *
•king *brought round*	
the. . .	LEATHER
bring up boy(D) ↑	YOB
brought about by	
<u>a new</u>. . .	WANE.WEAN
brought forward	BF
brought round <u>his pal</u>	PHIALS
brought together	ATI
brought up <u>a lot</u>. . .(D) ↑	TOLA
Britain	B.BR.GB

British¹	BR
hence	
•British and *French*	BRET
•British fish	BRANGLE.BRIDE
•British landlord	BROWNER
•British philosopher	BRAYER
•British service women	BRATS
•British state	BRAVER
•British tree	BRASH
British²	
Academy	BA
Airways	BA
America	BA
Association	BA
capital	B.LONDON
Columbia	BC
company	BL
country music	
	GOD SAVE THE QUEEN
	NATIONAL ANTHEM
Empire Medal	BEM
flower	THAMES.SEVERN
Home Stores	BHS
Honduras	BH
Institute of	
—Management	BIM
—Radiology	BIR
leader	B
Legion	BL
Library	BL
Medical Journal	BMJ
Museum	BM
—Library	BML
Optical Association	BOA
Oxygen Company	BOC
Pharmacopoeia	BP
Pharmaceutical Codex	BPC
Petroleum	BP
Printing Corporation	BPC
Rail	BR
	(*see also* transport)
Red Cross Society	BRCS
Road Services	BRS
Shipbuilders	BS
Standards (Institution)	BS(I)
Steel (Corporation)	BS(C)
Sugar Corporation	BSC
Summer Time	BST
Thermal Unit	BT(H)U

United Provident Association
                BUPA

broadcast
 broad*cast*   BOARD
 <u>broadcast</u> race   RELAY
 broadcast <u>race</u>   ACER
 broadcaster   SOWER
 broadcasting organisation
            AUNTIE.BEEB
Broadmoor   CRANK CASE
broken   (*see* break)
bronchitic
 bronchitic, *say*   COFFER
 bronchitic lungs ANCIENT LIGHTS
brother   BILLY.BR.BRO
brought   (*see* bring)
brown[1]   BR.TAN
 hence
 •brown and. . .   BRAND
 •brown insect   BRANT
 •Brown drunk   BROILED
 and
 •Brown *has* little weight
            TANGRAM
 •brown man   TANGENT
 •brown potassium   TANK
brown[2]
 brown bread   TOAST
 brown schoolboy   TOM
Browning
 words found in the works of:
 amount required   EXIGENT
 argue about   DISCEPT
 dandruff   FURFAIR
 dispute   DISCEPT
 frighten off AROINT.AROYNT
 greatest astrologer
       ARCH-GENETHLIAC
 horse's mane   ENCOLURE
 instrument of torture GADGE
 lucerne   LUZERN
 pompous language AMPOLLOSITY
 spat upon   BESPATE
brush   BASIL.SAGE
buckled <u>post</u>   POTS.SPOT
        STOP.TOPS
Buddhist
 absolute blessedness NIBBANA
        NIRVANA

canon of scriptures TRIPITAKA
Chinese sect   CHAN
circle   MANDALA
collected discourses SUTRA
column   LAT
compassion   KARUNA
concentration   SAMADHI
cross   SWASTIKA
demon   MARA
design symbolising the
 universe   MANDALA
disciple   CHELA
discipline   VINAYA
enlightenment BODHI.NIBBANA
        NIRVANA
ethical conduct   SHILA
evil spirit   MARA
faith   SHRADDHA
fate   KARMA
fertility spirit YAKSHA.YAKSHI
forms HINAYANA.MAHAYANA
     RUPA.THERVADA
     VAJRAYANA
function   YUNG
future Buddha BODHISATTVA
gateway   TORAN(A)
giving   DANA
holy day   UPOSATHA
impermanence   ANICCA
inevitable consequence KARMA
Japanese sect AMIDA.AMITA
    SOKA GAKKAI.ZEN
law   DHARMA
—of effect   KARMA
leader   B
liberation NIBBANA.NIRVANA
means   UPAYA
meditation   BHAVANA
metaphysics ABHIDHARMA
method   UPAYA
mind   CHITTA
monastery LAMASERY.VIHARA
monk AR(A)HAT.BO.BONZE
    LAMA.TALAPOIN
mound   STUPA.TOPE
nativity   JATAKA
'no-self' doctrine   ANATTA
novice   CHELA
perfection SIDDHA.SIDDHI

pillar   LAT
precinct   VIHARA
priest   BONZE.LAMA.PONGYI
reality   TATHATA
reincarnated person   TULKA
relic   STUPA
religious
—book   PITAKA
—painting   TANKA
sacred
—language   PALI
—mountain   OMEI
—tree   BO.BODHI.PEEPUL
—verse   MANTRA
scripture   SUTRA.SUTTA
                                   (TI)PITAKA
seed   BIJA
shrine   DAGABA.DAGO(U)BA
D(H)AGOBA.STUPA.TOPE
spiritual leader   DALAI LAMA
                            PANCHEN LAMA
sudden enlightenment   SATORI
teaching   SHASTRAS
temple   SANGHA.TERA.VIHARA
three bodies of Buddha   TRIKAYA
throne   ASANA
Tibetan sect   GELUK PA
                                   SAKYA PA
title   MAHATMA
unsatisfactoriness   DUKKHA
wisdom   PRAJNA
world   LOKA
Buenos Aires   BA
build
builder   JACK.JERRY
builders of Kew longed. . .
                            KNOWLEDGE
building   BDG
building Ma used   MEDUSA
built of stone   ONSET.TONES
Bulgaria(n)   BG.BULG
capital   B.SOFIA
coins   LEV.LEY.STOTINKA
head of church   EXARCH
king   CZAR.TSAR.TZAR
leader   B
measure   KRINE.LEKHA
                                   OKA.OKE
Muslim   POMAK

national assembly   SOBRANJE
                                 SOBRANYE
revolutionary   COMITAJI
                                 KOMITAJI
weight   OKA.OKE.TOVAR
bulk
bulk of grain   GRA.RAIN
bulk*head*   B
bull*head*   B
bully   COWER.FLASHMAN
                                   HECTOR
bully beef   WARFARE
bum-boat   TRAMP
bumpy lane   ELAN.LEAN
bundle
bundle of papers   SAPPER
bundle was tied   WAISTED
bundled up in rags   GRAINS
                                   RASING
buoyant actress   MAE WEST
Burlington House   RA
Burma   BUR
Burmese
borderer   SHAN
Buddhist priest   PONGYI
capital   B.RANGOON
civet   LINSANG
coin   KYAT.PYA
devil   NAT
flower   IRRAWADDY
garment   TAMEIN
girl   MINA
governor   WOON.WUN
guerrilla   CHINDIT
hill-dweller   LAI
knife   DA(H).DHAR.DOUT.DOW
language   KAREN.SHAN
leader   B
measure   BYEE.DAIN.DHA
                 PALGAT.TENG.LAN
robber   DACOIT.DAKOIT
robbery   DACOITAGE.DACOITI
                                  DACOITY
shrimp   NAPEE
timber   IRONWOOD.TEAK
tree   IRONWOOD.PADAUK
              PADOUK.PYENGADU
tribe   CHIN.KACHIN.KAREN(NI)
                 LAI.MON.SHAN

violin	TURR
weight	KAIT.KYAT.MAT
	TICUL.VIS(S)
burn *both ends*	BN
Burns	
words found in the works of:	
angle formed by side and bottom	
of dish	LAGGEN.LAGGIN
beast kept outside	OUTLER
bonny	BONIE
determine	LAW
dwarf	(K)NURL
fate	FALL
fine linen	SEVENTEEN-HUNDER
hoop at bottom of barrel	
	LAGGEN-GIRD
hot embers	AIZLE.EASLE
person	
—of admirable character	ACE
—out of office	OUTLER
(*see also* Scottish)	
burst	
burst into. . .	-TION
burst into *	incl in *
•he *bursts into* mas-s	MASHES
bursting vein	VINE
Burundi	RU
capital	BUJUMBURA
language	KIRUNDI
leader	B
bury	
bury a. . .	incl A
bury *	incl *
•*bury* saint in ha-y	HASTY
burying *	incl in *
•ha-y *burying* saint	HASTY
bus	(*see* transport)
bushel	BU.BUS(H)
bushman	TOPIARIST
bushwhacker	TOPIARIST
business	ADO.BIZ.CO.FIRM
hence	
•business about	ADORE
•business exercise	ADOPT
•business *with* the Navy	ADORN
and	
•business woman	COW
•businessman	COGENT
•Brown on business. . .	BRONCO

and	
•a loud business	AFFIRM
•in business *with*	
a line. . .	INFIRMARY
•study business	CONFIRM
bust	
bust bust	BUTS.STUB
bust *bust*	BUTS.STUB
bust in marble	RAMBLE
busted gut	TUG
busybody	ANT
but *once*	SED
butcher	
butcher's complaint	BEEF
butcher's (hook)	LOOK.SEE
butler	JEEVES.RAB.RHET
butter	GOAT.RAM
butterfly	
black and scarlet	RED ADMIRAL
black-spotted	FRITILLARY
black with white	
spots	DINGY SKIPPER
	GRIZZLED SKIPPER
	WHITE ADMIRAL
blue	ADONIS.CHALKHILL BLUE
	COMMON BLUE
	HOLLY BLUE.LARGE BLUE
	LONG-TAILED BLUE
	SMALL BLUE
	SHORT-TAILED BLUE
brown	ARGUS.GATEKEEPER
	GRAYLING.HEATH
	LULWORTH SKIPPER
	MEADOW BROWN
dark brown	ARGUS.RINGLET
chocolate-brown with yellow	
edges	CAMBERWELL BEAUTY
copper	LARGE COPPER
	SMALL COPPER
groupings	LYCAENIDAE
	NYMPHALIDAE
	PAPILIO.PIERIDAE
	RHOPALOCERA.SATYRIDAE
	THECLA.VANESSA
marbled	MARBLED WHITE
multi-coloured	SWALLOWTAIL
	TORTOISESHELL
purple	PURPLE EMPEROR
purplish-blue	MAZARINE BLUE

reddish-brown with purple	
eyespots	PEACOCK
tawny-orange	
	CHEQUERED SKIPPER
ESSEX SKIPPER.LARGE SKIPPER	
	PAINTED LADY
	SILVER-SPOTTED SKIPPER
	SMALL SKIPPER
various colours	HAIRSTREAK
white	BATH WHITE
	BLACK-VEINED WHITE
	CABBAGE(-WHITE)
	GREEN-VEINED WHITE
LARGE WHITE.SMALL WHITE	
	WOOD WHITE
white-marked	COMMA
	POLYGONIA
white with orange-tipped	
wings	ORANGE-TIP
yellow	BRIMSTONE
	CLOUDED YELLOW

buy

buy *sound*...	BY
buyer's option	BO

buzzer　　　　　　　　　　　　BEE.FLY

by　　　　　　　　　　　　　　　PER

by accident spilt...	SPLIT
by all accounts might...	MITE
by arrangement I went...	TWINE
by ear, Handel...	HANDLE
by *half*	B.Y
by means...	MANES.NAMES
by name	SC

by no means al(l)	AL
by using miracles	RECLAIMS
by-passed by *	incl in *
•city *by-passed by* r-ing	RELYING
by-passing a...	incl A
by-passing *	incl *
•r-ing *by-passing* city	RELYING
by proxy	PP
by *returning*⟨	REP
by the sound of her...	OFFER
by *the sound of it*	BUY
by the way	incl RD or ST
hence	
•the man, *by* the way	HERD
•a Red, *by* the way	STARED
•the *French, by* the way	LAST
	LEST
by the way	incl N.S.E.W
by *turning over*⟨	REP
by turning over	ROVE
by word of mouth passed	PAST
by-pass	COLOSTOMY
	ILEOSTOMY

Byzantine

•*Byzantine* art is	STAIR
capital	B.CONSTANTINOPLE
gold coin	BEZANT.BYZANT
	SOLIDUS
governor	CATAPAN
guard	PROTOSPATHARIUS
head of guard	ACOLOUTHOS
	AKOL(O)UTHOS
leader	B

C

about. approximately. cape. caput. carbon. Catholic. caught. credi. cee.
Celsius. cent. centi. centigrade. centime. *century*. chapter. Charles. circa.
club. clef. cold. colony. complex numbers. computer language.
Conservative. contralto. copyright. coulomb. Cuba. cubic. electrical
capacitance. hundred. hundred thousand. key. *lot. many.* note. *number.*
roughly. san. *sea. see.* speed of light. spring. tap. vitamin

cab	(*see* transport)	pearl plant	HAWORTHIA
cabinet maker	ADAM	Peruvian old man	ESPOSTOA
	CHIPPENDALE.EBENISTE	pincushion cactus	MAMMILLARIA
	HEPPLEWHITE.SHERATON	rat's tail cactus	APOROCACTUS
	KINGWOOD.ROSEWOOD	silver torch cactus	
	SATINWOOD		CLEISTOCACTUS
cacti		star window plant	HAWORTHIA
some species of cacti and		string of beads	SENECIO
succulents:		sugar almond plant	
bishop's cap	ASTROPHYTUM		PACHYPHYTUM
brain cactus		sunset cactus	LOBIVIA
	ECHINOFOSSULOCACTUS	tiger's jaws	FORCARIA
bunny ears	OPUNTIA	Tom Thumb cactus	PARODIA
burro's tail	SEDUM	Turkish temple	EUPHORBIA
candle plant	KLEINIA	velvet leaf	KALANCHOE
Cape hart's tongue	GASTERIA	wart plant	HAWORTHIA
chain cactus	RHIPSALIS	**Caesar**	
Christmas cactus	ZYGOCACTUS	Caesar's = Latin (Roman)	
cinnamon cactus	OPUNTIA	•*Caesar's* cloak	TOGA
column cactus	CEREUS	**cage**	
Easter cactus	SCHLUMBERGERA	*caged in* *	incl in *
fish-hook cactus	FEROCACTUS	•cat *caged* in pen	SCATTY
ghost plant	GRAPTOPETALUM	*caging* a...	incl A
goat's horn	ASTROPHYTUM	*caging* *	incl *
golden		•pen *caging* a cat	SCATTY
—barrel	ECHINOCACTUS	cagey, *say*	KG
—lily	LOBIVIA	**cake**	
hen and chickens	SEMPERVIVUM	cake burner	ALFRED
houseleek	SEMPERVIVUM	Cakesville	ECCLES
jelly bean plant	SEDUM	*calamitous* drop	PROD
leaf cactus	PERESKIA	**Caledonian** = Scottish	
living stones	LITHOPS		(*see* Scottish)
Mexican sunball	REBUTIA	**calf**	CF.NEW JERSEY
milk bush	EUPHORBIA	**Californian city**	LA
mistletoe cactus	RHIPSALIS	**call**	
old man		call-boy	RINGED
—cactus	CEPHALOCEREUS	call round	RING
—of the Andes	OREOCEREUS	*call* to prayer	NEIL
orchid cactus	EPIPHYLLUM	call *up*(D) ↑	BUD
panda plant	KALANCHOE	*called* cops	COPSE
peanut cactus	CHAMAECEREUS	*called in* a...	incl A

called in *	incl *	—race	ALGONIN
•L-en *called in* doctor	LEMON		ALGONQUIN.MICMAC
calling for. . .	FORE.FOUR	jay	WHISKY-JACK.WHISKY-JOHN
calorie	CAL	leader	C
Cambodia(n)	KA	logging-camp store	WAN(I)GAN
capital	C.PHNOM PENH		WANGUN
coin	RIEL	marsh	MUSKEG
language	KHMER	mounted police	MOUNTIES.RCMP
leader	C	national	
people	KHMER	—emblem	MAPLE LEAF
Cambridge university	HARVARD	—Railway	CNR
came	(*see* come)	navy	RCN
camouflaged <u>tanks</u>	STANK	old-timer	SOURDOUGH
camp		Pacific Railway	CPR
camping	(in) T-ENT.INTENT	pay office	WAN(I)GAN.WANGUN
camping holiday	INTENT	police force	MOUNTIES.RCMP
can	-ABLE.MAY.TIN	pondweed	WATER-THYME
can be heard coughing	COFFIN	porcupine	URSON
can be <u>leased</u>	SEALED	provinces	(*see* provinces)
can become <u>angry</u>	RANGY	ravine	COULEE
canned	(in) TI-N.(in) CA-N	rice	INDIAN RICE
can't keep a. . .	omit A	river	FRASER.NELSON
can't keep quiet	omit P		ST LAWRENCE
can't keep *	omit *	Royal Academy	CRA
•fat(her) *can't keep* her	FAT	ruminant	MUSK-OX.MUSK-STEER
can't spell too *well*	TO.TWO	sailors	RCN
can't spell too well	TOWEL	sledge	TRAIN
Canada	CDN	soldiers	CEF
Canadian		swamp	MUSKEG
Air Force	RCAF	tenderfoot	CHE(E)CHAKO
alewife (fish)	GASPEREAU		CHEECHALKO.CHECHAQUO
bird	SHARP-TAILED GROUSE	timber	LUMBER
bog	MUSKEG	travel by dog-sled	MUSH
Canadian	CANUCK.KANUCK	waterweed	ELODEA
—of French descent	HABITANT	weatherproof garment	PARKA
capital	C.OTTOWA		PARKEE.PARKI
coin	CENT.DOLLAR	**cancel**	
cut grain	SWATHE	cancelled	incl O
dog	NEWFOUNDLAND	hence	
dried skin	PARFLECHE	•*cancelled* match	OWED
fliers	RCAF	•*cancelled* race	ORAN
freeze	TAKE	•*cancelled* soldiers'. . .	OMEN
halfcaste	METIS	**candela**	CD
hare	SNOW-SHOE RABBIT	**candlepower**	CP
houseboat for loggers		**canine**	
	WAN(I)GAN.WANGUN	canine letter	R
Indian		canine racer	LAPDOG
—language	ALGONKIN	**canon**	CAN
	ALGONQUIN.MICMAC	**canto**	CAN

canvas	PAINTING
canvas support	EASEL
canvassed area	CAMP SITE
capability	BROWN
cape	C.HORN
Capek's play	RUR
capital	AI.CAP
capital authority	GLC
Capital Gains Tax	CGT
capital issue	BEARD.HAIR
capital letters	TOPAZ
capital loss in (S)pain	PAIN
capital of Spain	S
capital punishment	FINE
capital punishment for	
(s)entry	ENTRY
Capital Transfer Tax	CTT
capital type	BERLINER
LONDONER.NEW YORKER	
PARISIAN.ROMAN	
raise capital(D) ↑	-IA
capless **(m)ale**(D)	ALE
capricious mood	DOOM
capsize	
capsized ship	HIPS.PISH
capsized vessel⟨	TOP
captain	CID.OLD MAN.SKIP(PER)
captivate	
captivate a. . .	incl A
captivate *	incl *
•ma-n *captivates* one. . .	MAIN
captivated by gent/le har/mony	
LEHAR	
captivated by *	incl in *
•one *captivated by* ma-n	MAIN
captive	
captive	incl in *
•no-ted *captive* bird	NOMINATED
captive	(in) C-AGE.(in) GA-OL
capture	
captured by *	incl in *
•queen *captured by* PM	PERM
captures a. . .	incl A
captures *	incl *
•PM *captures* queen	PERM
car	GT.MINI.RR.VW
car club	AA.RAC
car driver	AUTO-PILOT
car indicator	AUTO-CUE

car lifter	JACK
car-test	MOT
(c)ar *won't start*	AR
(*see also* transport)	
carat	CAR.CT
card	A.ACE.J.K.Q
CHARACTER.DENRY MACHIN	
card games BANK CRAPS.BEZIQUE	
BLIND HOOKEY.BRAG.CASINO	
CATCH-THE-TEN.CRIB(BAGE)	
GRAB.HEARTS.KALABRIAS	
KLABBERJASS.KLOB(IOSH)	
LANTERLOO.LONG WHIST.LOO	
MATRIMONY.NAP(OLEON)	
NEWMARKET.NODDY	
OLD FOURS.ONE-AND-THIRTY	
PAM.PITCH	
(PROGRESSIVE) WHIST	
RUFF (AND HONOURS)	
SANCHO-PEDRO.SETBACK	
SHORT WHIST.SLAM	
SOLO WHIST.SPECULATION	
SPOIL-FIVE.TRUMP	
American EUCHRE.FARO	
PINOCHLE.POKER	
bridge AUCTION.CHICAGO.CLUB	
CONTRACT.FOUR DEAL	
children's game MUGGINS	
OLD MAID.SNAP	
SNIP-SNAP-SNORUM	
faro variants BUCKING THE TIGER	
(CHINESE) FAN-TAN.FAROBANK	
JEWISH FARO.MONTE (BANK)	
PUT AND TAKE.RED DOG.SKIN	
STUSS.ZIGINETTE	
for	
—32 cards PICQUET	
—40 cards COON CAN.MONTE	
OMBRE.QUADRILLE	
SEVEN AND A HALF	
ZIGINETTE	
—45 cards FARMER	
—48 cards CRAP CARDS	
fortune-telling TAROK.TAROT	
French BACCARAT.BOUILLOTTE	
CHEMIN DE FER.ECARTE	
QUINZE.ROUGE-ET-NOIR	
TRENTE-ET-QUARANTE	
VINGT-ET-UN	

like
—bezique PINOC(H)LE
—nap PUT(T)
Mexican THREE-CARD MONTE
old BINOCHLE.BRISCAN
BRUSQUEMBILLE
CINQ CENTS.FIVE HUNDRED
FLAKERNOBLE.LANSQUENET
MARIAGE.NODDY
PRIMERO.REVERSIS
—(Scottish) PENNEECH
PENNEECK
patience KLONDIKE.KLONDYKE
SOLITAIRE
pinochle variants AEROPLANE
AUCTION.CUTTHROAT.CHECK
CONTRACT.FIREHOUSE
HARTFORD.NEW ENGLAND
(RADIO) PARTNERSHIP
TURN-UP
poker DRAW.STUD
—variants ACEY-DEUCY
ALBEMARLE.ANACONDA
BASEBALL.BASKETBALL.BEAT IT
BEAT YOUR NEIGHBOUR
BLAZER.BLIND ANTE
BLIND OPENERS.BLUFF.BULL
CANADIAN.CINCINNATI
CONFUSION
CRAZY.CRISS CROSS
DOUBLE BARTER.DOUBLE UP
DR PEPPER.ENGLISH.FAIRVIEW
FIVE BETS.FIVE-CARD
FIVES AND TENS.FLIP
FOLLOW MARY
FOLLOW THE KING
FOLLOW THE QUEEN.FOOTBALL
FOUR FORTY-FOUR.FREEZE-OUT
HEINZ.HIGH-LOW.HOLD 'EM
JACKPOT.KANAKEE
KLONDIKE (BOB).LAINO
LAME BRAIN (PETE)
LEG.LOWBALL.MISTIGRIS
MONTEREY.NEW YORK
NIGHT BASEBALL.NO LOOKIE
NO PEEKIE.OMAHA
PASS THE GARBAGE
PIG (IN A POKE).PROGRESSIVE
PUT AND TAKE.ROCKLEIGH

ROLL 'EM.ROLL OVER
ROUND THE WORLD.RUM
SCREW YOUR NEIGHBOUR
SCREWY LOUIE.SHIFTING SANDS
SHOWDOWN.SKARNEY.SKEETS
SPANISH.SPIT IN THE OCEAN
ST LOUIS.STORMY WEATHER
THREE FORTY-FIVE.TIGER
TURN-UP.TWIN BEDS.TWO-LEG
WHISKY.WILD WIDOW
WOOLWORTH
pontoon VINGT-ET-UN
—variants ACE-DEUCE-JACK
ACE LOW.BACCARAT (BANQUE)
BANGO.BANKER AND BROKER
BLACKJACK.CHEMIN-DE-FER
CHEMMY.FARMER.FIFTEEN
HORSE RACE.PONTOON
QUINCE.SEVEN-AND-A-HALF
SHIMMY.SLOGGER.THIRTY-FIVE
TWENTY-ONE.VANJOHN
VINGT-ET-UN.YOU CALL 'EM
rummy GIN
—variants BANKERS.BLOCK
BOAT HOUSE.CALOOCHI
CANASTA.CAPTAINS
CAROUSEL.CINCINNATI
COMBINATION.CONTINENTAL
COON CAN.DIZZY.ELIMINATION
FORTUNE.FREEZE OUT.GIN
JAVA.JERSEY GIN.INDIAN CRAPS
KALOOKI.KNOCK.LIVERPOOL
MICHIGAN.MISSISSIPPI
OKLAHOMA.OLD-FASHIONED
PAN.PARTNERSHIP.PERSIAN
PIF-PAF.PROGRESSIVE
QUEEN CITY.RAMINO
ROUND ROBIN
ROUND-THE-CORNER.SKARNEY
SKIP.STANDARD HOLLYWOOD
SUPER GIN.TONK.TURN-UP
Russian VINT
single-handed PATIENCE
SOLITAIRE
Spanish COON CAN
three-handed
CUT-THROAT (BRIDGE)
GLEEK.OMBRE.SKAT.TRED(D)ILLE
Venetian BASSET

cards	HAND.TALON
cardinal	CARD.RED.WOLSEY
cardinal points	NEWS
cardiograph	TICKER TAPE
care	
care of	CO
careless bonds	CASUALTIES
careless (h)ost	OST
carelessly done	NODE
rank *carelessness*	KNAR.NARK
career people	RACE
cargo boats	MN
Caribbean Islands	WI
carpenter	
carpenter's mate	WALRUS
carpentry	CARP
carpet	REPRIMAND
carriage	
agricultural	WAG(G)ON
American	BUCKBOARD
	SURREY.ROCKAWAY
coach	FOUR-IN-HAND
closed	BROUGHAM
—covered	JINGLE
	(HANSOM-)CAB
—military	TUMBREL.TUMBRIL
—US	HERDIC
decrepit chaise	SHANDRYDAN
dung-cart	TUMBREL.TUMBRIL
fast stagecoach	FLY
four-horse	FOUR-IN-HAND
four-wheeled	CLARENCE
	COUPE.GROWLER
	PHAETON.WAG(G)ON
—folding hood	LANDAU
	VICTORIA
—US	HERDIC.SURREY
French	FIACRE
gig	DENNET.TILBURY
high-wheeled	SPIDER
hired coach	HACKNEY-CARRIAGE
Indian	TONGA
light	
—cart	SHANDRY(DAN)
—gig	(TIM-)WHISK(E)Y
mail-coach	POST
one	
—horse	FLY
—person	SULKY

—seater	STANHOPE
open carriage	WAGONETTE
passenger coach	STAGECOACH
Russian	DROS(H)KY
shaky vehicle	SHANDRYDAN
Spanish, covered	TARTANA
small landau	LANDAULET(TE)
tip-cart	TUMBREL.TUMBRIL
three-wheeled pedal-car	TRISHAW
—for hire	PEDICAB
two-wheeled	BUGGY.CABRIOLET
	DENNET.DOG-CART.GIG
	GOVERNESS CAR(T).SCURRY
with facing seats	VIS-A-VIS
carriage paid	CP
carrier	BARKIS.BR.RY.RLY
carry	
carried by (D)	
•mother carried by boy	DAMSON
carried by mo/st ar/tists	STAR
carried by *	incl in *
•log *carried by* ship	SLOGS
carried out a test	TASTE
carries a. . .	incl A
carries *	incl *
•ship *carries* log	SLOGS
carries(D)	
•boy *carries* mother	DAMSON
	(*see also* bearing[3])
Cartesian *formula*	ASCERTAIN
cartoon-fish	STRIPLING
carved up meat	MATE.TAME.TEAM
case	
cased in a. . .	incl A
cased in *	incl *
•gold *cased in* iron	FORE
casing in *	incl in *
•iron *casing in* gold	FORE
cases	CA
cash	BRASS.READY.RHINO.TIN
cash against documents	CAD
cash collapse	BRASSFOUNDER
cash on delivery	COD
	MATERNITY GRANT
cash with order	CWO
casseroled lamb	BALM
cast	
cast a net	NEAT
cast about ten. . .⟨	NET

cast about ten	ENT.NET	*catching* a...	incl A
c(as)t as *not wanted*	CT	*catching* the one-five	incl IV
cast *spell*	ACTS.CATS.SCAT	*catching* *	incl *
*cast*away	YAW	•ma-n *catching* one...	MAIN
casting director	PLASTERER	*caught* a...	incl A
castle	R(OOK)	*caught* *	incl *
casual		•ma-n *caught* one	MAIN
casual remark	MARKER	*caught by* *	incl in *
casual worker	TEMP	•one *caught by* ma-n	MAIN
hence		caught *in*	incl C
•worker is *French*	TEMPEST	*caught in* m/an t/rap	ANT
•worker, the *French*...	TEMPLE	caught *out*	omit C
•worker *with* ring	TEMPO	**catechism**	CAT
casualty ward	DRAW	**cathedral**	ELY
cat¹	FELIX.OUNCE.MOG	**cathode**	
	REX.TOM	cathode-ray oscillograph	CRO
catbird	TOMTIT	cathode-ray tube	CRT
catcall	MEW.MIAU.MIAOW	**Catholic**	RC
cat-o'-nine-tails	BACKMARKER	**cattle¹**	KINE.NEAT
cat²		cattle complaint	BEEF
curly-coated	REX	cattle plague	RINDERPEST
female domestic cat	TABBY		STEPPE MURRAIN
in *Reynard the Fox*	TIBERT	cattle stealing	ABIGEAT
Samuel Johnson's cat	HODGE		RUSTLING
long-haired	TANGORA	cattle thief	ABACTOR
	BALINESE.BIRMAN	**cattle²**	
	MAIN COON.PERSIAN	African	AFRICANDER.ANKOLE
	RAGDOLL.TURKISH		BAHEMI.BAPEDI.BASHI
Norwegian	SKOGCATT		BORAN.DRAKENSBERGER
old	GIB.GRIMALKIN		KIGEZI.KURI.LANDIM.N'DAMA
Sancho Panza's cat	BAVIECA		NGUNI.WATUSI
she-cat	TIB(CAT)		WHITE FULANI
short-haired	ABYSSINIAN	American	BUFFALO
	BOMBAY.BURMESE		BRAHMAN.BRANGUS
DEVON REX.EGYPTIAN.EXOTIC			HOLSTEIN-FRIESIAN
HAVANA.JAPANESE BOBTAIL			SANTA GERTRUDIS
KORAT.MANX.RUSSIAN BLUE			TEXAS LONGHORN
	SIAMESE.SINGAPURA	Australian	DROUGHTMASTER
	SNOWSHOE.SOMALI		MURRAY GREY
	SPHYNX.TONKINESE		TASMANIAN GREY
	WIREHAIR	Austrian	PINZGAU(E)R
tailless	MANX	Belgian	BELGIAN BLUE
theatre cat	GUS.PUSS-IN-BOOTS	Canadian	HOLSTEIN-FRIESIAN
yellow and black			RED AND WHITE FRIESIAN
	TORTOISE-SHELL	Channel Islands	JERSEY
catalogue	CAT		GUERNSEY
catch		Danish	DANISH RED
catch cold	incl C	dehorned	MUL(L)EY
catch *up*(D) ↑	BAN.TEN	diseases	(*see* cattle diseases)

English	BRITISH WHITE.DEVON
	GLOUCESTER.HEREFORD
	LINCOLN RED.LONGHORN
	RED AND WHITE FRIESIAN
	SHORTHORN.SOUTH DEVON
	SUSSEX.(WILD) WHITE PARK
Egyptian	BALADI.DAMIETTA
	MARYUTI
	SAIDI
female	COW.HEIFER.OX
Finnish	FINNCATTLE
	FINNISH AYRSHIRE
French	AUBRAC
	BLONDE D'AQUITAINE
	CHAROL(L)AIS
	GASCONNE.LIMOUSIN
	MAINE ANJOU.NORMANDY
	PIE ROUGE DE L'EST.SALERS
	SIMMENTAL.TARENTAISE
German	ANGELN.FLECKVIEH
	GERMAN RED PIED
	GERMAN YELLOW
	HOLSTEIN
heavy breed	FRI(E)SIAN
Hebrides	KYLOE
heifer (Scottish)	QUEY
hornless	REDPOLL
Indian	GIR.KANKREJ.KHILLARI
	RED SINDHI.THARPARKAR
Irish	DEXTER
	IRISH MOILED.KERRY
Italian	CHIANINA.MARCHIGIANA
	PIE(D)MONTESE.ROMAGNOLA
male	BULL.STEER.OX
Netherlandish	DUTCH FRIESIAN
	GRONINGEN
	MEUSE-RHINE-IJSSEL
Norwegian	
	BLACKSIDED TRONDHEIM
	TELEMARK
old breed	BLUE ALBION
Portuguese	BARROSA.GALEGA
	MIRANDA
Russian	ALA TAU.KHOL MOGOR
	KOSTROMA.RED STEPPE
Scottish	ABERDEEN ANGUS
	AYRSHIRE
	(BELTED) GALLOWAY
	HIGHLAND CATTLE.LUING

	SHETLAND.WEST HIGHLAND
	(see also Scottish)
short-horned	DURHAM
Spanish	
	ANDALUSIAN FIGHTING BULL
	GALICIAN BLOND
Swiss	BROWN SWISS
	SIMMENTAL
Texan	LONGHORN
Welsh	WELSH BLACK
west country	DEVON
West Indian	JAMAICA HOPE
white-faced	HAWKEY.HAWKIE
	HEREFORD
young	CALF.HEIFER.STIRK
cattle diseases	ANTHRAX
	BLACK QUARTER
	BLACKWATER.BLUE TONGUE
	BRUCELLOSIS.REDWATER
actinobacillosis	WOODY-TONGUE
actinomycosis	LUMPY JAW
bacterial	ANTHRAX.JOINT-ILL
	LEPTOSPIROSIS.NAVEL-ILL
	PLEURO-PNEUMONIA
	SALMONELLOSIS
	TUBERCULOSIS
cattle plague	RINDERPEST
	STEPPE MURRAIN
contagious abortion	
	BRUCELLOSIS
deficiency disease	ACETONAEMIA
	HYPOMAGNESAEMIA.KETOSIS
eye disease	
	KERATOCONJUNCTIVITIS
	NEW FOREST EYE
foot disease	FOOT AND MOUTH
	FOUL IN THE FOOT.LAMINITIS
fungal	ACTINOMYCOSIS
	RINGWORM
gas in the stomach	BLOAT
grass staggers	
	HYPOMAGNESAEMIA.TETANY
husk	LUNGWORM
hypocalcaemia	MILK FEVER
hypomagnesaemia	
	GRASS STAGGERS.TETANY
intestinal	JOHNES DISEASE
lumpy jaw	ACTINOMYCOSIS
milk fever	HYPOCALCAEMIA

parasitic	HUSK
	LIVER FLUKE.LUNGWORM
	ROUNDWORM.TAPEWORM
	WARBLE-FLY
rinderpest	CATTLE PLAGUE
	STEPPE MURRAIN
steppe murrain	CATTLE PLAGUE
	RINDERPEST
tetany	GRASS STAGGERS
	HYPOMAGNESAEMIA
udder disease	MASTITIS
viral	EBL
	ENZOOTIC BOVINE LEUCOSIS
	IBR
woody tongue	
	ACTINOBACILLOSIS
caught¹	C.CT
hence	
•caught a married...	CAWED
•caught an anthropoid	CANAPE
•caught at church	CATCH
•caught bird	CRAVEN.CROOK
•caught *by* leg	CLIMB
•caught fish	CLING
•caught man	CALF.CHAL.CLEW
•caught *with* nothing on	COON
•caught *with* stolen goods	CLOOT
caught²	(*see* catch)
cauliflower *head pickled*	AULIC
cause alarm	MALAR
cave	
cave, *say*	KV
caveman	SPELEOLOGIST
cavity	O
cavorting like...	KIEL
cavy, *say*	KV
cayenne, *say*	KN
c-current	CAMPS
Celebes wild hog	BABIR(O)USA
	DEER HOG.HORNED HOG
celebrate	SING
celebrated	CEL
celebration	DO
celebrity	LION.STAR.VIP
Celtic	
alphabet	OG(H)AM
festival	BELTANE
harp	CLAIRSCHACH.CLARSACH
high steward	MORMAOR

noble	TOISECH
sword	CLAYMORE
censor	CATO.EDIT
cent	C.CT
centi-	
centilitre	CL
centime	C.CT
centimetre	CM
centipede	CLIMBS
central	CEN
central character in Tosca	S
Central European Time	CET.MEZ
central heating	CH
central heating	T
central nervous system	CNS
central processing unit	CPU
Central Standard Time	CST
central Wales	ALE.L
Central African Republic	CAR.RCA
capital	BANGUI.C
Central American	
agave	SISAL
ant	KELEP
bird	MOTMOT.SAWBILL
capitals	CA
coin	COLON
lapwing	TERU-TERO
leaders	CA
measure	VARA
race	AZTEC.CARIB.MAYA
rubber (tree)	(H)ULE
tree	AMATE.EBO(E),S(A)OUARI
	(*see also* South America)
centre	
centre-*half*	CEN.TRE
centre-half	AL
centre of gravity	CG
centre of gravity	V
centre of Paris	R
centre of *	incl in *
•the *centre of* scared...	
	FEATHERED
centrepiece	K.KING.Q.QU.QUEEN
*centre*piece	E
centrepiece of decorations	RAT
self-centred	EL
soft-centred	OF
century	C.CEN
cerebro-spinal fluid	CSF

certain	SURE	*change* <u>coins</u>	SCION
certain amount of beer	PINT	*change ends of* *	
certain amount of <u>beer</u>	BEE	•*change ends* of lever	REVEL
certain amount of bee/r I se/nt		*change* <u>gear</u>	RAGE
	RISE	*change-over*	ROVE
certainly	YES	*change-over of* <u>duties</u>	SUITED
Certificated Master	CM	*changeable* <u>weather</u>	WREATHE
Ceylon(ese)	SRI LANKA(N)	*changed* <u>diet</u>	EDIT.TIDE.TIED
aboriginal race	VEDDA	changes	PEAL
Buddhist shrine	DAGOBA	*changing character* of	
capital	C.COLOMBO	weather	HEATHER
form of marriage	BEENAH	changing place	CREWE.JUNCTION
grass	CITRONELLA	**channel**	WAY
language	PALI.SINGHALESE	**Channel Islands**	CI
	TAMIL	coin	DOUBLE
leader	C	*chaotic* mess <u>on. . .</u>	MESONS
lemur	LORIS	**chaplain**	CF.CHAP.HCF
milkweed	COW-PLANT		OCF.REV(D)
palm	CORYPHA.TALIPAT.TALIPOT	**chaps**	(*see* man.two²)
—leaf book	OCA	**chapter(s)**	C.(CC).CAP.CH.CHAP
people	CINGALESE.SINHALA	Chapter I	CHI
	SIN(G)HALESE.TAMIL	Chapters I & III	CA
pig-rat	BANDICOOT	**character**	
spice	CINNAMON	*characters in* <u>play</u>	PALY
timber	CALAMANDER	<u>all the</u> *characters*	LETHAL
	COROMANDEL	character's size	(*see* type)
chain-letters	MAIL	Greek characters	(*see* Greek)
chairman	ADAM.CHIPPENDALE	Hebrew characters	(*see* Hebrew)
	HEPPLEWHITE	**charge**	-ION
	PROFESSOR.SHERATON	charged *up*(D) ↑	EVIL
Chaldean bible	TARGUM	**charitable group**	KIND
chaldron	CH	Charles II	H
champion	ACE.CH	**charmer**	MUSIC
champion boxer	SPARKING	**cheap**	ID.IP
	TOP DOG	cheap floor	KNOCKDOWN
chance	HAP	cheap transport	
change			PENNY-FARTHING
change into	BECOME	**cheat**	CON
change <u>into</u>	-TION	**check**	REIN
change of <u>heart</u>	EARTH.HATER	hence	
	RATHE	•check certain	REINSURE
change of heart	HEARS	•check condition	REINSTATE
change of heart		•check garment	REINVEST
	change middle letters	check mate	TEST MATCH
•*change of heart* for Tory	TROY		TRIAL MARRIAGE
•leper has *change of heart*	LEVER	checked *out*	SE-EN
change of <u>scene</u>	CENSE.-SENCE	•five checked *out*	SEVEN
change of scene	SCONE	**cheek**	LIP.NECK
change sides	RAT	**cheer***leader*	C

cheese

Ayrshire	DUNLOP
(cheesemaker)	RENNET
container	ROLL
Danish	TYBO
Dorset	BLUE VINNEY
Dutch	EDAM.GOUDA
English	BEAMERDALE.BOTTON
	CHESHIRE.COTHERSTONE
	DERBY.DOUBLE GLOUCESTER
	LANCASHIRE.LEICESTER
	LYMESWOLD.STILTON
	WENSLEYDALE
French	BANON.BOURSIN.BRIE
	CAMEMBERT.CANTAL
	COULOMMIERS
	ERVY.ROQUEFORT
from ewe's milk	EWE-CHEESE
	FETA.ROQUEFORT
Greek	FETA.KEFALOTYRIS
Irish	CASHEL BLUE
Italian	BEL PAESE
	GORGONZOLA.MOZZARELLA
	PARMESAN.PECORINO
	RICOTTA.ROBIOLA.STRACCHINO
	TALEGGIO.TARTUFELLE
mediocre	MOUSETRAP
soft	COTTAGE.CREAM
	LYMESWOLD
Somerset	CHEDDAR
Swiss	EMMENT(H)AL(ER)
	GRUYERE.SAPSAGO
Welsh	CAERPHILLY
	LLANBOIDY.MERLIN
	PENCAR(R)EG

chemical   NITRE

Chemical Society	CS
chemist	MPS
chemists	CS

chest expander   MEDAL

chewing up <u>bone</u>   EBON

chi   X

chief	CH.CID
chief accountant	MAJORCA
chief manufacturer	KINGMAKER
chief mason	MASTER BUILDER

child   BRAT.CH

Child Guidance Officer   JUNIOR COUNSEL

childless	SP
children	SEED

Chile(an)   RCH

capital	SANTIAGO
coin	CONDOR.DOBLON
flower	SCHIZANTHUS
fruit	LUCAMA
saltpetre	CALICHE
palm	COQUITO
shrub	MAQUI
tree	ALERCE

chiming = rhyming

•*chiming* bell	CELL.DELL.FELL
	HELL.SELL.TELL.WELL.YELL
•*chiming* sound	BOUND.FOUND.
	HOUND.MOUND
	POUND.ROUND
•*chiming* merrily	VERILY

chimney

Scottish	LUM
chimney-pot	CAN

china[1]   PORCELAIN.POTTERY

	SERVICE
American	REDWARE
Austrian	VIENNA
Belgian	TOURNAI
black background	FAMILLE NOIR
brown terracotta	RUSTIC-WARE
Chinese	BLANC-DE-CHINE
	CANTON.CELADON.CHUN.HAN
	JU(AN).KO.MING.NANKEEN
	QING.SUNG.TING.YUAN
coarse ware	SAXON STONE
	SEMI-PORCELAIN
	STONE CHINA
cream Wedgwood	
	QUEEN'S WARE
Danish	COPENHAGEN
Dutch	DELF(T)
earthenware	FIGULINE
English	AYNSLEY.BOW
	BRISTOL.CHELSEA.COALPORT
	COPELAND.CROUCHWARE
	(CROWN) DERBY.DOULTON
	LIVERPOOL.LOWESTOFT
	MOORCROFT.MINTON
	ROCKINGHAM.SPODE
	STAFFORDSHIRE.SWANSEA
	WEDGWOOD.WORCESTER

enamelled
—earthenware   MAJOLICA
—terracotta   DELLA-ROBBIA
felspar porcelain   PARIAN
fine pottery   PEBBLEWARE
French   CHANTILLY.LIMOGES
    MARSEILLES.PARIS.SEVRES
German   ANSBACH.DRESDEN
    FRANKFURT.MEISSEN
green pattern   FAMILLE VERTE
hard porcelain   JASPERWARE
Italian   CAPODIMONTE.FAENZA
    MAIOLICA.NAPLES.PESARO
Japanese   ARITA.HAMADA
    IMARI.KAKIEMON
    SATSUMA.SHOJI
matt-surfaced stoneware
    JASPERWARE
pink pattern   FAMILLE ROSE
refined earthenware
    CREAMWARE
Swiss   ZURICH
white earthenware
    IRONSTONE CHINA
    PORCELAIN
with calcium phosphate
    BONE CHINA
yellow background
    FAMILLE JAUNE

china²
china (plate)   MATE.PAL
China³   CATHAY.CH.CHIN
    MIDDLE KINGDOM
area (Far East)   FARE
river   PLATE
Chinese   CHIN.SERIC.SINAEAN
    SINIC.SINO
abacus   S(H)WANPAN
aborigines   LOLOS.MAIOTSE
    MANS.MANZU
    YAO(-MIN)
agricultural worker with medical
  training   BAREFOOT DOCTOR
arch   PAILOU
assembly   HUI
association   TONG
bamboo stick   WHANGEE
bean   ADZUKI.MUNG
best quality   FIRST CHOP

birds   SILVER PHEASANT
    SWAN-GOOSE
boat   JUNK.SAMPAN.SANPAN
    TONGKANG
—population   TANK(I)A
brand   CHOP
Buddha   FO(H)
Buddhist
—paradise   CHINGTU
—priest   BONZE
—sect   CHAN
business   PIDGIN
cabbage   BOKCHOY.PAKCHOI
cane   WHANGEE
capital   C.PEKING
carriage   JINRICKISHA
    (JIN)RICKSHA(W)
chestnut   LING
Chinaman CATAIAN.CAT(H)AYAN
    CHINK.CHOW
club   ONG
coat   MANDARIN
coins
—small   CASH.CHIAO.FEN
—unit   CHIAO
—10 chiao   YUAN
—silver bar   LIANG.SYCEE.TAEL
condiment   NAPEE
cooking pan   WOK
crab   MITTEN-CRAB
criminal society   TRIAD
cyclone   TYPHOON
dark principle   YIN
— deities   (*see* gods.goddesses)
department   FOO
dialect   CANTONESE.HAKKA
    MANDARIN.PEKIN(G)ESE.WU
dish   CHOP-SUEY.CHOW-MEIN
    WONTON
dog CHOW-CHOW.PEKIN(G)ESE
    SHIH TZU
dress CHEONG-SAM.SAMFOO
    SAMFU
drink   KAOLIANG.MAO-TAI
drug   GINSENG
duck   MANDARIN
—eggs in brine   PIDAN
dynasty   HAN.MING.SUNG
    TANG.YIN.YUAN

eating utensils	CHOPSTICKS
fabulous	
—animal	KYLIN
—bird	FUM.FUNG
factory	HONG
feminine principle	YIN
fibre	CHINA-JUTE
fish	CARP.GOLDFISH
	PARADISE-FISH.TREPANG
foreign commercial house	HONG
fruit	CUMQUAT.KUMQUAT
	LEECHEE.LITCHI.LYCHEE
	LONGAN.LOQUAT.WAMPEE
game	FAN-TAN.MAH-JONG(G)
	PUTZI
ginger	CURCCUMA.ZEDOARY
grass	RAMEE.RAMI(E).WHANGEE
grotesque figure	MAGOT
guild	HUI.TONG
herb	GINSENG
hen	BRAHMA.LANGSHAN
houseboat	TANKA-BOAT
idol	JOSS
incense	JOSS-STICK
instrument	KIN
jacket	MAKWA
jade	YU(-STONE)
jargon	PIDGIN ENGLISH
jigsaw	TANGRAM
jute	ABUTILON
labourer	COOLIE.COOLY
lacquered screen	
	COROMANDEL SCREEN
language	KUO-YO.MANCHOO
	MANCHU.MANDARIN
leader	C
light principle	YANG
liquor	KAOLIANG
magnolia	YULAN
mandarin's house	YAMEN
	YAMUN
martial art	KUNG-FU
masculine principle	YANG
measures	
—1 inch	TSUN
—foot	CHIH
—12 feet	CHANG
—1/3 mile	LI
—15 gallons	PARAH

military governor	TUCHUN
mixed condiment	CHOW-CHOW
mouth organ	SANG
National People's Party	
	KUOMINTANG
negative principle	YIN
no good	NO CHOP
obeisance	COTTOW.KOWTOW
office	YAMEN.YAMUN
official	MANDARIN.TAO-TAI
	TAOYAN
oil	TUNG
old military race	MANCHOO
	MANCHU
orange	TAEL
overseer	HOPPO
pagoda	TAA
pheasant	TRAGOPAN
philosophy	CONFUCIANISM
pickled eggs	PIDAN
pillory	CANG(UE)
poor quality	NO CHOP
porcelain	MING
positive principle	YANG
prefecture	FU
promptly	CHOP-CHOP
prostration	KO(W)TOW
puzzle	TANGRAM
quickly	CHOP-CHOP
raspberry	WINE-BERRY
rebel	TAIPING
reed instrument	CHENG
religion	CONFUCIANISM
	BUDDHISM.TAOISM
resident official	AMBAN
rice spirit	SAMSHOO.SAMSHU
river	YANGTZE KIANG
rodent	JUMPING-MOUSE
ruler	MANCHOO.MANCHU
	YAO(U).YAU
sauce	SOY
seal (impression)	CHOP
secret society	BOXER.HOEY
	TONG.TRIAD
ship	JUNK.SAMPAN.SANPAN
shop	TOKO
silkworm	AILANTHUS.SINA
	TASAR.TUSSAH
silver	PAKFONG.PAKTONG

sleeping platform	KANG	*chopping* logs	SLOG
sorghum	KAOLIANG	**chorus girl**	SHOWPIECE
statuette of seated figure		**Christ**	CHR.X.XT
	MANDARIN	**Christian**	CHR.XN
steamed dumplings	DIM SUM	Christian endeavour	CE
sugar cane	SWEET SORGHUM	Christian era	AD
takeaway	SHANGHAI	Christian service	CS
tax	LIKIN	**Christmas**	XM(AS)
tip	CUMSHAW	Christmas girl	CAROL
temple	PAGOD(A)	Christmas period	DEC
toy	TANGRAM	Christmas present drawer	
trade go-between			REINDEER
	COMPRADOR(E)	**church**	CE.CH.RC
transit duty	LIKIN	hence	
trees	GINGKO.GINKGO.LITCHEE	•a church	ACE
	LITCHI.LONGAN.LOQUAT	•a church gallery	ACETATE
MAIDENHAIR-TREE.PAULOWNIA		and	
	TUNG-TREE.VARNISH-TREE	•American church	AMERCE
tuber	KUDZOO.KUDZU	•Italian church	ROMANCE
umbrella	TEE	•many in church	MINCE
unarmed martial art	KUNG-FU	•mother church	MACE
vehicle	JINRICKISHA	•when at church. . .	WHENCE
	(JIN)RICKSHA(W)	and	
warehouse	HONG	•hurried *in* church	CRANE
water jar	KANG	•man *in* church	CHIME
wax insect	TELA	and	
weights		•church keys	CEDE
—1 ounce	LIANG.TAEL	•Church Street	CEST
—1 lb	CATTY.CHIEN.KIN	and	
—133 lbs	PECUL.PICUL	•a church	ACH
	PIKUL.TAN	•church militant	CHARMED
wormwood	MOXA		CHARMING
yellow dye	WONGSHY	•church music (writer)	
yoke	CANG(UE)		CHAIR(MAN)
chips	OLD MASTER	•church painter	CHARTIST
choice	OR	•church vessel	CHURN
hence		•church-woman	CHALICE
•choice cut	ORLOP	•church-worker	CHANT
•choice of directions	NORE.NORN	and	
	SORE.SORN.WORE.WORN	•church *on* the hill	TORCH
•make choice *with* pin	ORPIN	•Egyptian church	ETCH
choose	OPT	•German chuch	HUNCH
hence		•in church	INCH
•choose one hundred	OPTIC	•low church	MOOCH
•choose one mother	OPTIMUM	•mother church	MACH
•choose particle	OPTION	•which church?	THATCH
chop		and	
chopped spice	CLOVE	•a church	ARC
chopped spice	EPICS	•spies surround church	CIRCA

churl	CARL
churn	
churning a pint	PAINT
churning up earth	RATHE
CID member	YARD-ARM
cigarette-end	E
cinema director	USHERETTE
cipher	O
ciphered signal	ALIGNS
circle[1]	DISC.O.RING
hence	
•circle above...	DISCOVER
•circle America	DISCUS
•circle drops	DISCLOSES
and	
•Circle line	-ORY
•circle of friends	OPALS
•lady's circle	HERO
•race *in* circles	OTTO
and	
•a race *in* a circle	RATTING
•circle permitted	RINGLET
•lady's circle	HERRING
circles	DISCO.RING-DIAL
circuit	O
circular letter	O
circular objects	DISCO
	RING-DIAL
circle[2]	
arty *circles*	TRAY
circle a...	incl A
circle *	incl *
•rodent *circles* it	CAVITY
circle *around*...	CLERIC
* *circled by*...	incl in *
•it is *circled by* rodent	CAVITY
circling plane	PANEL
circuit of town	WONT
circulating in the...	THINE
circumvent	
circumvent a...	incl A
circumvent *	incl *
•writing *circumvents* end...	
	MENDS
circumvented by *	incl in *
•end *circumvented by* writing...	
	MENDS
citation	CIT
citizen	CIT

city[1]	EC.ELY
city girl	ADELAIDE.ALICE
	FLORENCE.NANCY.VICTORIA
city judge	TRIER
city (old)	TROY.UR
city road	ANCHORAGE
c(it)y *with no centre*	CY
	(*see also* town)
city[2]	
Abrahamville	LINCOLN
Buenos Aires	BA
Cakesville	ECCLES
city of	
—angels	LOS ANGELES
—bells	BRUGES
—bridges	BRUGES
—canals	VENICE
—kings	LIMA
—masts	LONDON
—monuments	BALTIMORE
—one hundred towers	PAVIA
—palaces	ROME
—saints	SALT LAKE CITY
—seven hills	ROME
—plains	SODOM.GOMORRAH
—prophet	MEDINA
—the West	GLASGOW
—violet crown	ATHENS
—three kings	COLOGNE
—victory	CAIRO
eternal city	ROME
granite city	ABERDEEN
holy city	JERUSALEM.MEDINA
	MECCA.ROME
Los Angeles	LA
New York	BIG APPLE.GOTHAM
	NY
Quaker City	PHILADELPHIA
second city	BIRMINGHAM
Venice of the north	LENINGRAD
Witchville	SALEM
Wyeville	ROSS
civil	
civil defence	ARP.CD
civil engineer	CE
civil servant	(in)C-S
civil service	CS
civilian	CIV
—dress	MUFTI

cladding
cladding a... incl A
cladding * incl *
•i-vy *cladding* for gold... IVORY
clad with * incl in *
•gold *clad with* i-vy IVORY
claiming AM-.IAM.IM-
hence
•claiming *French* father AMPERE
•claiming lamb AMELIA
•claiming our... AMOUR
•claiming to be essayist AMELIA
and
•claiming *to have* vehicle IAMBUS
•two claiming... PRIAM
and
•claiming goodness IMPIETY
     IMPIOUSNESS
     IMPURITY
•claiming some... IMPART
•claiming two... IMPAIR
class CL
classic
Classic races DERBY.GUINEAS
    OAKS.ST LEGER
classic trees OAKS
Classics (examination) GREATS
classic(al) = Greek or Roman
god DEUS
man VIR
musician ORPHEUS
place LOCUS
power VIS
skill ARS
 (*see also* Greek.Latin.Roman)
classified papers SAPPER
classy U
clause CL
clay ALI
clay-pigeon FLYING SAUCER
clean
clean *out* LANCE
cleaner hair CHARLOCK
clear RID
clear *out* CLARE
clear out drawers REWARDS
clear photograph
    TRANSPARENCY
clearance granted DRAGNET

clearer run BALDERDASH
clearing snow OWNS
cleric BD.DD
clerical error SPOONERISM
clerk
Clerk of the Peace CP
Clerk to the Signet CS
climb
climber AMPELOPSIS.IVY
climbing party(D) ↑ OD
climbing(D) ↑ tor ROT
clinch
clinch a... incl A
clinch * incl *
•*clinch* deal *in* fog MISDEALT
clinched by * incl in *
•deal *clinched in* fog MISDEALT
cling
cling to a... incl A
cling to money incl L
cling to * incl *
•bo-y *clings to* ship BOSSY
clip
clip from fil/m or n/egative MORN
clip win(g) WIN
cloak
cloaked in * incl in *
•hollow *cloaked in* m-ist MOIST
cloaking a... incl A
cloaking * incl *
•m-ist *cloaking* hollow MOIST
clock *up*(D) ↑ REMIT
close
close book K
closing of mill L
closing remark K
cloth worker SERGEANT
clothe
clothed by * incl in *
•man *clothed in* re-d REMAND
clothing a... incl A
clothing workers SHIFT
clothing * incl *
•re-d *clothing* man REMAND
clouds
anvil-like CUMULONIMBUS
cauliflower-like CUMULUS
cirro-cumulus WOOL-PACK
cirrus GOAT'S-HAIR

cloud nine	EUPHORIA
deep	CUMULONIMBUS
delicate cirrus	CUMULO-CIRRUS
discharging showers	NIMBUS
globular masses	
	STRATOCUMULUS
high	CIRRUS
—detached	CIRRUS
—sheet	CIRROSTRATUS
—thin layer	CIRROSTRATUS
—transparent veil	
	CIRROCUMULUS
horizontal sheet	STRATUS
long streaks	MARES'-TAILS
low	
—rain	NIMBOSTRATUS
—rounded masses	
	STRATOCUMULUS
mackerel sky	CIRROCUMULUS
middle	
—grey cloud layer	STRATUS
—grey sheet	ALTOSTRATUS
—rain cloud	NIMBOSTRATUS
rounded heaps	CUMULUS
small flakes or ripples	
	CIRROCUMULUS
thin streaks	MACKEREL SKY
club	C.IRON.RAC.WOOD
club-house	VILLA
club magazine	ARSENAL
clubman	GOLFER.PICKWICK
clucking female	HEN.LAYER
clumsy	
clumsily treads	TRADES
clumsy oafs	SOFA
clutch	
clutch housing	BIRD'S NEST
clutching a...	incl A
clutching *	incl *
•Ra-y *clutching* £50	RALLY
clutched by *	incl in *
•£50 *clutched by* Ra-y	RALLY
CO₂	SECOND-IN-COMMAND
coaches	TRAIN
coalescence of a mass	AMASS
coal-hole	MINE.PIT
coarse actors	BROADCAST
coating	
coating a...	incl A

coating *	incl *
•frost *coating* tree	RIMFIRE
coated by *	incl in *
•tree coated by frost	RIMFIRE
cobbler's *last*	R
cocaine	CRACK.SNOW
cock	
cock an ear(D) ↑	GUL.RAE
cocked a snook	NOOKS
cocked up great...	GRATE
cocked up an...(D) ↑	NA
Cockney¹	omit H
hence	
•*Cockney* girl	(h)ER
•*Cockney* woodman	(h)EWER
•*East Ender's* (h)aunt	AUNT
•*Eliza* getting better	(h)EALING
•fireplace *in Bow*	(h)EARTH
•hirsute *Bowman*	(h)AIRY
Cockney²	
rhyming slang:	
Adam and Eve	BELIEVE
almond rocks	SOCKS
apple pie	SKY
apples (and pears)	STAIRS
April showers	FLOWERS
army and navy	GRAVY
army rocks	SOCKS
artful dodger	LODGER
bacon and eggs	LEGS
Baden Powell	TROWEL
bag of fruit	SUIT
baker's dozen	COUSIN
ball of chalk	WALK
Band of Hope	SOAP
Barnaby Rudge	JUDGE
bath bun	SON
blue moon	SPOON
Bo-Peep	SLEEP
butcher's (hook)	LOOK
Cain and Abel	TABLE
carving knife	WIFE
China (plate)	MATE
cut and carried	MARRIED
currant bun	SUN
Dicky Bird	WORD
Dicky Dirt	SHIRT
dinky-doo	TWENTY-TWO
Dutch	WIFE

four by two	JEW
frog and toad	ROAD
ham and eggs	LEGS
Jack (Jones)	ALONE
Joanna	PIANO
Mickey Mouse	HOUSE
mince pies	EYES
Mutt and Jeff	DEAF
Ned Kelly	BELLY
old Dutch	WIFE
on one's Tod (Sloan)	ALONE
penny bun	SON.SUN
pig's ear	BEER
plates/platters (of meat)	FEET
pride and joy	BOY
Rosie/Rosy Lea/Lee	TEA
skin and blister	SISTER
sky rocket	POCKET
trouble (and strife)	WIFE
tit for tat (titfer)	HAT
tit willow	PILLOW
Tod (Sloan)	ALONE
cocktail[1]	
cock*tail*	K
cocktail of <u>gin</u>	-ING
cocktail[2]	(*see* drink)
code	
<u>code</u>-*breaking*	CO-ED
code <u>words</u>	SWORD
codex	COD
codicil	PS
coffee time	ELEVENTH HOUR
cogitate	GOG
coiled <u>rope</u>	PORE
coin[1]	
coin a <u>phrase</u>	SHAPER.SHERPA
counterfeit coin	SLIP.STUMER
coin[2]	
small	DUMP.MAWPUS
	MOPUS.STIVER
—old silver	SILVERING
half-farthing	GROAT
2 groats	FARTHING
farthing (old)	STICA.STYCA
½d	HA(LF)PENNY.MAG(PIE)
	MAIK.MAIL(E).MAKE
—old	OB(OLUM).OBOLUS
	PORTCULLIS
penny	COPPER.D.P

—old silver	STERLING
1½d	DANDIPRAT.DANDYPRAT
	THREE-HALFPENNY
3d	JOEY.THREEPENNY BIT
4d	GROAT.JOE(Y)
—silver	FOURPENNY
6d	TANNER.TILBURY.TIZZY
—old	TESTER(N).TESTON
	TESTRIL(L)
12d	SHILLING
shilling	DEANER.BOB.S
—old	TESTON.TESTER(N)
	TESTRIL(L)
1/6d-2/- (old)	GILDER
2 shillings	FLORIN
florin (gold)	FLORENCE
2/6d	HALF-CROWN
	SWORD-DOLLAR
5 shillings	CROWN
crown	THICKUN
6/8d	HALF-MARK.NOBLE
10 shillings	HALF-SOVEREIGN
—old	PISTOLET.RIAL.RYAL
10/6d	HALF-GUINEA
half-guinea	SMELT
13/4d (old)	MARK
15 shillings (gold)	SPUR-RIAL
	SPUR-R(O)YAL
20 shillings	POUND
—old	BROAD(-PIECE)
100p	POUND
pound	IL.L.NICKER.QUID
	SMACKER.SOVEREIGN
—old	CAROLUS.FLORENCE
	JACOBUS
sovereign	THICKUN
21 shillings	GEORDIE.GUINEA
5 pounds	FIVER.VL
10 pounds	TENNER.XL
25 pounds	PONY
100 pounds	TON
500 pounds	MONKEY
100,000 pounds	PLUM
old gold	ANGEL.BRITANNIA
	ROSE NOBLE.RUDDOCK
	SCEATT.SPADE GUINEA
	SPANKER.YELLOW BOY
old silver	SCEATT
	THREE FARTHINGS

produced under siege	
	SIEGE-PIECE
proposed	MIL(L)
cold	C
hence	
•cold earth	CLOAM
•cold meat	CHAM
•cold on. . .	CON-
cold-blooded poisoner	ADDER
	ASP.SNAKE
cold-hearted	OL
collapsed arch	CHAR
colleague	COLL
collect	
collected poems	MOPES
collection	ANA
collector	COLL
college	COLL.ETON.POLY
hence	
•college that is. . .	COLLIE
•railway college	BRETON
•college training	POLYPE
college girl	CLARE
	MAGDALEN(E)
college window	ORIEL
colliery area	MINEFIELD
collision of heads	HADES.SHADE
colloquially	COLL
colloquially cannot	CANT
Colombia	CO
colonel	COL
colony	C
Colonial Office	CO
colonist	ANT
colour	
colour bar	LIPSTICK
colour blind	SHADE
colour *up*(D) ↑	DER
coloured	(in) R-ED
coloured man	TANGENT
coloured people	ORANGEMEN
colour*less*	omit RED
•cove(red) colour*less*	COVE
column	COL
columnist	NELSON
combine	
combination of pills	SPILL
combined ops	SOP
combining pairs	PARIS

come	
came down	RAINED
came *to* nothing	CAMEO
come to a *conclusion*	end with A
•he *comes to* a *conclusion*	MANA
comes from N/ew E/ngland	EWE
comes from Spain	PAINS
* *comes off*. . .	omit *
•motor *comes off* (car)ousel	
	OUSEL
comes through *	incl in *
•heat *comes through* opening of	
shed. . .	SHEATH
comes out of past	PATS.TAPS
comes out of th/e ra/in	ERA
comes out of court on. . .	
	CROUTON
comes to terms in. . .	MINSTER
comes to grief in race	ACER.ACRE
	CARE
comes to grief on court	CROUTON
comes to light *in* s/ear/ch	EAR
comes to surface	
•sub *comes to* surface(D) ↑	BUS
coming *to* river	ADVENTURE
come*back*⟨	EMOC
comeback dance	GIG
comeback made. . .	EDAM
comedown	HAIL.RAIN
	SLEET.SNOW
comedy	COM
comic	
comic acts	CATS.SCAT
comic figure	FUND
command	
command sequence	ORDER
commander	CBE.CDR.CINC
	CO.COM.OC
commanding officer	CO.OC
commemorative meal	REPAST
commencement of her. . .	H
commerce	COM
commercial	AD
commissioner	COM
committee	COM
common	COM
common metre	CM
common pleas	CP
commonly (h)as. . .	AS

commonly is not. . .	AINT
commons	FARE.HC.HOUSE
Commonwealth (Relations) Office	
	C(R)O
commotion	TODO
commotion in street	INTEREST
commune	COM
communication system	GRAPEVINE
communion	HC
communist	COM.RED.TROT
hence	
•anarchist deed	REDACT
•communist-*backed*. . .⟨	DER
•Communist study	REDDEN
•Russian food	REDDISH
•tender Communist	KINDRED
and	
•communist *has* hard. . .	TROTH
•one *in* communist. . .	TAROT
•turn *in* communist. . .	TROUI
Communist Party	CP
community	
Community Service Order	CSO
Community Service Volunteer	
	CSV
companion	CB.CH
company	CO.FIRM.TWO
hence	
•company doctor	COMB
•company uniform	COHABIT
•company work	COOP
and	
•company cost	FIRM PRICE
•company employed. . .	
	FIRM HAND
•company position	FIRM STANCE
company board	GANGPLANK
compare	CF.CP
comparatively cold	COLDER
comparatively cold (cold as)	
	CHARITY
	ICE
(*see also* proverbially)	
compere	MC
compiled list	SLIT
complaint	(*see* diseases)
complete	
complete meal	THOROUGHFARE
completed twice	OVERDONE

complex	
complex design	SIGNED
complex number	C
complicated affair	RAFFIA
component	
components in mo/tors o/r. . .	
	TORSO
components of cars	ARCS.SCAR
compose	
compose poetry	SING
compose some popul/ar son/gs	
	ARSON
composed of nuts	FOUNTS
composed of nuts	STUN
composer	ARNE.GILBERT
composer's girl, *say*	MISHANDLE
composition complies. . .	
	POLEMICS
compound	
compound of tin he. . .	THINE
compounded lots. . .	SLOT
comprehensive case	SCHOOL-BAG
comprises all the. . .	LETHAL
computer	
aided design	CAD
aided typesetting	CAT
assisted instruction	CAI
assisted learning	CAL
club	BCS
firm	BIG BLUE.IBM
integrated	
—business	CIB
—manufacturing	CIM
language	
—recorder	CLR
—translator	CLT
languages	ADA.ALGOL.BASIC.C
	COBOL.FOCUS.FORTH
	FORTRAN.LISP.LOGO.LUCID
	MODUL.PASCAL.PISTOL
	POWERHOUSE.PROLOG
	SIMULA.SMART.SNOBOL
	UNIX.ZENIX
managed instruction	CMI
oriented language	COL
output microfilm	COM
scanner	CAT.CT
computer terms	
add-on parts	PERIPHERALS

breakdown	CRASH
broadcast information	CEEFAX
	ORACLE.PRESTEL
	TELETEXT
continuous repetition	RECURSION
correct errors	DEBUG
disc operating system	DOS
(erasable) programmable read	
only memory	(E)PROM
error(s)	BUG.VIRUS
garbage in, garbage out	GIGO
heart of the computer	
	MICRO-PROCESSOR
holding area	BUFFER
Industry Standard Architecture	
	ISA
input/output system	BIOS
large computer	MAINFRAME
light-emitting diode	LED
liquid-crystal diode	LCD
load program(me)	BOOT(STRAP)
	REBOOT
machinery	HARDWARE
medium-sized computer	
	MINI-(COMPUTER)
micro-channel architecture	MCA
micro-processing unit	MPU
modulator-demodulator	MODEM
move blocks of data	DUMP
moving screen display	
	SCROLLING
numbering system	BINARY
	OCTAL.HEXADECIMAL
pictorial information	GRAPHICS
portable computer	LAPTOP
printed output	HARD COPY
processor	CPU
program(me) diagram	
	FLOWCHART
program(me)s	SOFTWARE
random access memory	RAM
read only memory	ROM
screen	MONITOR.VDU
—display	SOFT COPY
—drawing instrument	LIGHT PEN
	MOUSE
section of program(me)	
	(SUB)ROUTINE
slot-in circuit board	CARD

small computer	
	MICRO(-COMPUTER)
	PC.PERSONAL COMPUTER
storage device	FLOPPY DISC
	HARD DISC.MAGNETIC DISC
	WINCHESTER DRIVE
Transient Program Area	TPA
unerasable memory	FIRMWARE
visual display unit	VDU
what you see is what you get	
	WYSIWYG
write once, read many	WORM
(see also measure)	

conceal

conceal head	omit first letter
concealed by *	incl in *
•it is *concealed by* m-e	MITE
concealed in <u>Dorset</u>	STORED
concealed in <u>h</u>/er go/wn	ERGO
concealing a...	incl A
concealing *	incl *
•m-e *concealing* it	MITE
concern	CO
concerning	ON.RE
(see also about[2])	

conclude

concluding remar<u>k</u>	K
conclusion	CON
conclusion he *came to*	E
conclusion o<u>f</u> play	Y
conclusions the panel	
had made after...	ELDER
conclusive proof	F
final *conclusion*	L

concoct

concoction of <u>ices</u>	SICE
concocted <u>recipe</u>	PIERCE
concubine	SULTANA
condition	IF
conditioned to heat	HOT TEA
(see also diseases)	
conference	PEAR

confess

confessing	AM-.IAM.IM-
hence	
•*confessing* aims	AMENDS
•*confessing* I can	AMIABLE
•*confessing* to being	
right wing	AMATORY

and	
•confessing age	IMAGE
•confessing weight	IMPOUND
•confessing before jury	IMPANEL
confessor	EDWARD
confidante	GATE POST
confidential hint	INTIMATE
confine	
confined by *	incl in *
•winner *confined* by two. . .	
	PACER
confined to bed (in) B-ED.(in) CO-T	
confining a. . .	incl A
confining *	incl *
•two *confining* winner	PACER
conflict	
conflict of wills	SWILL
conflicting ways	SWAY.YAWS
conflicting ways	EW.NS.SN.WE
conforming	INSTEP
confound devil	LIVED
confront	C
confuse	
confused ideas	AIDES.SADIE
confusing item	EMIT.MITE.TIME
confusion no greater. . .	
	GENERATOR
Congo	RCB
congregation	INCE.(in) C-E
	INCH.(in) C-H
conjure up devil	LIVED
connected with	
indicates addition	
•mother is *connected with*	
church	MACE
conquered *by Caesar*	VICI
conscientious objector	CO
conservationists	GREENS.NT
Conservative	BLUE.C.CON
	TORY.U
hence	
•conservative dress	BLUEGOWN
•Conservative whip	CLASH
•Conservative state	CONGA
•six hundred Conservative. . .	
	VICTORY
considerable	TIDY
conspirator	CADE.OATES
Constable's house	ART GALLERY

constellation	
Archer	SAGITTARIUS
Argo's stern	PUPPIS
Arrow	SAGITTA
Balance	LIBRA
Bear	URSA
Berenice's Hair	COMA BERENICE
Big Dipper	GREAT BEAR
Bird of Paradise	APUS
Bull	TAURUS
Centaur	CENTAURUS
Charioteer	AURIGA
Charles's wain	GREAT BEAR
	PLOUGH.URSA MAJOR
Colt	EQUULEUS
Crab	CANCER
Crane	GRUS
Cross	CRUX
Crow	CORVUS
Cynosure	URSA MINOR
Dolphin	DELPHINUS
Dragon	DRACO
Eagle	AQUILA
Easel	PICTOR
Fishes	PISCES
Fly	MUSCA
Flying Fish	VOLANS
four stars	SOUTHERN
	CROSS.URSA (MAJOR)
Giraffe	CAMELOPARDALIS
Goat	CAPRICORNUS
Graving-tool	CAELUM
Great Bear	CHARLES'S WAIN
	PLOUGH
Greater Dog	CANIS MAJOR
Hare	LEPUS
Herdsman	BOOTES
Hunting Dog	CANES VENATICI
Hunter	ORION
Indian	INDUS
Keel	CARINA
Lesser	
—Bear	LESSER WAIN
	URSA MINOR.WAG(G)ON
—Dog	CANIS MINOR
—Lion	LEO MINOR
Level	NORMA
Lion	LEO
Lizard	LACERTA

Lyre	LYRA
Milky Way	VIA LACTEA
Net	RETICULUM
Northern Crown	
	CORONA BOREALIS
others	
—northern	ANDROMEDA
	CAMELOPARDALIS
	CASSIOPEIA.CEPHEUS.CETUS
—southern	APUS.ARA.ARGO
	ASTRINUS.CENTAURUS
	COLUMBA.OCTANS
	PHOENIX.SOUTHERN FISH
Ox-driver	BOOTES
Peacock	PAVO
Plough	CHARLES'S WAIN
	GREAT BEAR
	URSA MAJOR
Pump	ANTILLA
Ram	ARIES
Rule	NORMA
Sail	VELA
Scales	LIBRA
Scorpion	SCORPIO.SCORPIUS
Serpent	SERPENS
—holder	OPHIUCHUS
Seven Stars	ORION
Southern Crown	
	CORONA AUSTRALIS
Swordfish	DORADO
Table	MENSA
Telescope	TELESCOPIUM
Triangle	TRIANGULUM
Twins	GEMINI
Veil	VELA
Virgin	VIRGO
Wag(g)on	LESSER BEAR
	LESSER WAIN
	URSA MINOR
Wag(g)oner	AURIGA
Water-monster	HYDRA
Winged Horse	PEGASUS
Wolf	LUPUS

constitute

constituent of *	incl in *
•new *constituent of* ba-d. . .	BAND
constitute <u>my</u> bases. . .	EMBASSY
construct a <u>redoubt</u>	OBDURATE
construe <u>a line</u>	ALIEN.ANILE

consulting room

	INSPECTION CHAMBER

consume

consumed by *	incl in *
•six *consumed* by o-ne	OVINE
consumed <u>peas</u>	APES.APSE
consuming a. . .	incl A
consuming interest	EATING
consuming *	incl *
•o-ne *consuming* six	OVINE

contagious disease   CD

contain

contained in *	incl in *
•one *contained in* tin	CANON
contained in <u>soup</u>	OPUS
containing a. . .	incl A
containing *	incl *
•tin *containing* one. . .	CANON
containing some th/in k/ind	INK
contents o/f a t/in	FAT
contents of <u>crate</u>	RAT
contents of <u>crate</u>	REACT
contaminate <u>pure soil</u>	PERILOUS

contemporary   AD

contemptible fellow   CAD.TWERP

contents   (*see* contain)

continent   ASIA.EUR

Continental	M
continental = in French	
	(*see* abroad. French)
continental art	ES
continental articles	UNDER

contort

contorted <u>face</u>	CAFE
contortions of <u>animal</u>	LAMINA

contract

boys *contracted*	TIMED
contract debts	INCURIOUS
contract cannot. . .	CANT
contract illness	FLU
contract manager	
	BRIDGEMASTER
contract written. . .	WRIT
contracted le(g)	LE
contractor's word for finished	OER
I have *contracted*. . .	-IVE
	(*see also* short)

contradict

contradiction of all. . .	SOME

contradiction of young. . .	OLD
contradictions	E-E.N-S.S-N.W-E
contribute	
contributing to t/he ed/itor's. . .	
	HEED
contribution t/o a f/und	OAF
contrived a plot	PLATO
control	REIN
control animal	STEER
controversy	
controversial remark	MARKER
controversy in Dail	DIAL.LAID
convenience	CON
converse	
adults converse	CHILDREN
converse of all. . .	SOME
converse of old. . .	YOUNG
converse quietly	LOUDLY
conversation	CON
conversing aloud	ALLOWED
convert	
conversion of sinner	INNERS
convert lire	LIER.RILE
converted infidel	INFIELD
convertible coins	ICONS.SONIC
convey delight	TRANSPORT
convolute	
convoluted ideas	AIDES
convolutions of dance	CANED
convulse	
convulsion of face	CAFE
convulsive leap	PALE.PEAL.PLEA
cook	
cooked meal	LAME
cooking pots	SPOT.STOP.TOPS
cook's weapon	MACE
co-ordinated with his. . .	WHITISH
copper	CU.D.P.PC
hence	
•copper coin	CUD.CUP
•copper colour	CURED
•copper embargo	CUBAN
•copper ring	CURING
and	
•copper *and* unknown. . .	DANDY
•copper I dropped	DISHED
•copper I threw	DICAST
and	
•copper *and* a. . .	PANDA

•copper fields	PLEAS
•copper I valued	PIRATED
and	
•coppers	CUD.CUP
coppers	PENNY-FARTHING
Coptic	COP(T)
bishop	ABBA
dialect	SAHIDIC
copy	
copy soldier	GIGI
	(*see also* double)
copy some. . .	SUM
*copy*right	RITE.WRIGHT
copyright	APER.C
cor	BLIMEY.FRENCH HORN
corn	EARS
corn cracker	(WIND)MILL
corner	L
Cornwall	SW
coroner	COR
corporal	CPL.NYM
corporation	BEEB.CO.INC.TUM
correct	OK.TICK
correct fare	FEAR
correct marks	TICKS
corrected angle	GLEAN
correction of skid	KIDS
corresponding member	CM
corrupt	
corrupt dealer	LEADER
corrupted all the. . .	LETHAL
corruption of leader	DEALER
corseted in cali/co st/uff	COST
cost	
cost, insurance, freight	CIF
costs nothing	omit O
Costa Rica(n)	CR
capital	C.SAN JOSE
coin	COLON
leaders	CR
measure (11 bushels)	FANEGA
co-tangent	COT
could	
could be Easter	FEAST
could be feast	EASTER
could be worse	SWORE
could become easy	AYES.YEAS
could go into Leith	LITHE
coulomb	C

council
Council of
—Engineering Institutions CEI
—Europe CE
—Industrial Design CID
council *leader* C
councillor CR
counter GEIGER.GM
counter-*revolutionary* TROUNCE
counter-strike BUFFET
counterfeit note DUDE
country
country accent LANDGRAVE
country air NATIONAL ANTHEM
country bar LANDRAIL
country dishes CHINA
country man JOHN BULL
 UNCLE SAM
country music
 NATIONAL ANTHEM
country town CHINAWARE
country ways LANES
country woman BRITANNIA
county AVON.CO.DOWN.SOM
county alderman CA
county council CC
couple PAIR.PR.TWAIN
couple of boys REGAL.ROYAL
couple of days WE
couple of fellows CHAPMAN
couple of people EVADES
 SALTED
couple of times TT
 (*see also* man.two[2])
couplet TT
course N.S.E.W
course fee REFRESHER
court CT
court action SUITCASE
court martial CM
Court of Session CS
courtly animal KANGAROO
courtly lord LUD
courtesan SULTANA
cover
covered by * incl in *
•one *covered by* British. . . BONER
covering a. . . incl A
covering * incl *

•British *covering* one. . . BONER
cover-*up*(D) ↑ DIL.POT
covers lar/ge ar/ea GEAR
cow LOWER
cow-girl IO
 (*see also* cattle)
cowardly show CAVALCADE
crack ACE.DAB.EXPERT.PRO
hence
•crack dossier PROFILE
•crack king ACER
•crack rear, almost DABSTER
crack-*up*(D) ↑ BAD
cracked vase SAVE
cracking code in. . . COINED
crackshot SURE-FIRE
cradle song ROCK MUSIC
craft SS
craft of wickerwork CORACLE
crafty director RUDDER
crafty operator BOATMAN
 PUNTER
crafty seer SERE
cramped by a c/rowd y/ou. . .
 ROWDY
crank case ASYLUM.BROADMOOR
crash
crashed car ARC
crashing bore EBOR.ROBE
craze (*see* love[3])
Crazy Horse SHORE
create
create anew WANE.WEAN
creation HAT
creation of life FILE
credit[1] CR
hence
•credit cut CREDITED
•credit due CROWED.CROWING
•credit state CRAVER
credit[2]
credit notes -IOUS
creditor CR
creed -ISM
 (*see also* belief)
crew BOASTED.FOUR.EIGHT
cricket
cricket club BAT.CC
cricket side LEG.OFF.ON.XI

cricket spectator	OVERSEER	•French cross-country runner	
criminal	CROOK		LOIRE
criminal error	CLUE	•German cross-country runner	
criminal procrastinator	THIEF		RHINE
criminal pursuit	MANHUNT	**crowd**	THREE
Criminal (Records) Office	C(R)O	**crown**	CR
cripple		crown commission	MAJORITY
cripple master	RE-MAST.STREAM	crown jewels	TIARA
crippled man is. . .	MAINS	*crowned*(D) indicates one word	
crippling trade	RATED	written below another	
crook	CRIMINAL.CROSIER	•man *crowned with* gold	ORAL
	CROZIER	**crude**	
crook is not an	NATIONS	*crude form of* words	SWORD
crooked leg	GEL	*crude* ore	ROE
cross¹	IO.TAU.TEN.X	*crudely* made. . .	DAME.EDAM
hence		*crudely made* table	BLEAT
•cross *in* right. . .	RIOT	*crumbling* ruins Ed. . .	INSURED
•dog crosses. . .	CURIOS	*crunched* under a. . .	UNREAD
•five cross fifty. . .	VIOL	**crush**	
hence		crushed fabric	WORSTED
•cross ten. . .	TAUTEN	*crushed* orange	ONAGER
•cross to grand. . .	TAUTOG	**cry**	
•cross *with* cross	TAUTEN	*cry* aloud	ALLOWED
hence		*cry* 'Foul!'	FOWL
•cross a town	TENACITY	cry of delight	OLE
•cross-bones	TENTS	cry of triumph	IO
•cross legs	TEN-PINS	*crying* 'Fore!'	FOR.FOUR
•crossover	TENON	*cryptic* clue	LUCE
•cross the river	TENURE	**Cuba(n)**	C
and		capital	C.HAVANA
•cross-beam	X-RAY	castle	MORRO
•monkey-cross	APEX	coin	PESO
cross²		dance	CONGO.DANZA.DANZON
cross a	incl A		GUARACHA.HABANERA
cross river	incl R		R(H)UMBA
cross street	incl RD or ST	drum	BONGO
cross *	incl *	knife	MACHETE
•saint *crosses* friend	SPALT	leader	C
crossed by *	incl *	measure	TAREA
•friend *crossed by* saint	SPALT	rattle	MARACA
cross-channel = French		secret police	PORRA
	(*see* abroad)	squall	BAYAMO
	(*see also* French)	tobacco field	VEGA
cross-country runner	RIVER	tree	CULLA.CUYA
hence		weight	LIBRA.TERCIO
•cross-country runner			(*see also* West Indies)
changes line	NILE	**cube root**	SUGAR BEET
•former English cross-country		**cubic**	CU.CUB
runner	EXE	cubic feet per minute	CUMIN

cubic feet per second	CUSEC
cuckold	ACTAEON
cue, *say*	Q
cultivate	
cultivated dwarf	BONZAI
cultivating soil	OILS.SILO
(*see also* rearing)	
cup	
cup-bearer	GANYMEDE
(*see* trophy)	
cure my pet	EMPTY
curie	CI
curious rite	TIER.TIRE
curly	
curly beard BARED.BREAD.DEBAR	
curly *head*	C
current¹	AC.DC.TIDE
hence	
•current price	ACCOST
•current tax	ACCESS
•current usage	ACCUSTOM
current²	
current cost accounting	CCA
current purchasing power	CPP
current recession	EBB(-TIDE)
current stoppage	DAM
current success	WINNOW
current (this month)	CUR(T)
current unit	A.AMP.COULOMB
	KWH(R).VOLT
curtailed tri(p)	TRI-
curtain	
curtain material	BAMBOO.IRON
curtains	DEATH
custom	
customer	(in) SHO-P
customs	HMC
customs assigned number	CAN
cut¹	
cut *	incl in *
•king *cuts* corners	ANGLERS
cut *back*⟨	EXA-.POL.TUC.WAS
cut by a...	incl A
cut by *	incl *
•corners *cut by* king	ANGLERS
cut cloth	CLOT.LOTH
cut-down ship	RAZEE
cut down (s)hip	HIP
cut down tree	FELL

cut down tree	TRE-.REE
cut finger	FRINGE
cut key	CUTE
cut later...	GASHOLDER
cut off part...	ART.PAR
cut-price	COS(t)
cut production	CROP
cu(t) *short*	CU
cut short greeting	AV(e)
cut t/he len/gth...	HELEN
cut *up**(D) ↑	POL.TUC.WAS
cut up steak	SKATE.STAKE
	TAKES
cut out a...	omit A
cut out *	omit *
•le(ad)er *cuts out* notice	LEER
cut out odd bits of (t)w(e)e(d)	WE
cuts face	CHOPS
cut*back*⟨	EXA-.POL.TUC.WAS
cutdown ship	RAZEE
cut²	
into:	
abdominal wall	LAPAROTOMY
animals	ZOOTOMY
artery	ARTERIOTOMY
beard	POGONOTOMY
bladder	CYSTOTOMY
bodies of animals	ZOOTOMY
bone	OSTEOTOMY
bowel	ENTERO(S)TOMY
brain	ENCEPHALOTOMY
	LEUCOTOMY
	LOBOTOMY
colon	COLOTOMY
ear-drum	MYINGOTOMY
for fistula	SYRINGOTOMY
front of brain	LEUCOTOMY
	LEUKOTOMY
	LOBOTOMY
gall bladder	
	CHOLECYSTO(S)TOMY
head	CEPHALOTOMY
—of foetus	CRANIOTOMY
human anatomy	
	ANTHROPOTOMY
intestine	ENTERO(S)TOMY
into	
—two parts	BISECTION
	DICHOTOMY

—three parts	TRISECTION
	TRICHOTOMY
—four parts	QUADRISECTION
	TETRACHOTOMY
kidney	NEPHROTOMY
larynx	LARYNGOTOMY
living animal	VIVISECTION
lobe of organ	LOBOTOMY
lung tissue	PNEUMONECTOMY
ovary	OOPHORECTOMY
	OVARIOTOMY
perin(a)eum	EPISIOTOMY
pharynx	PHARYNGOTOMY
plant	PHYTOTOMY
pubic junction	SYMPHYSEOTOMY
	SYMPHESIOTOMY
(reflex separation)	AUTOTOMY
solids	STEREOTOMY
spine	CORDOTOMY
stomach	GASTROTOMY
tendon	TENOTOMY
thorax	THORACOTOMY
to	
—cure squinting	STRABOTOMY
—make opening	SYRINGOTOMY
—remove stones	LITHOTOMY
tonsils	TOLSIL(L)OTOMY
trachea	TRACHEO(S)TOMY
tumour	ONCOTOMY
uterus	
	HYSTEROTOMY.UTEROTOMY
vein	
	PHLEBOTOMY.VENESECTION
womb	
	HYSTEROTOMY.UTEROTOMY
cut³	
out:	
appendix	APPEND(IC)ECTOMY
bone of middle ear	
	STAPEDECTOMY
bony plate	LAMINECTOMY
bowel	ENTERECTOMY
breast	MASTECTOMY
cerebral cortex	TOPECTOMY
duodenum	DUODENECTOMY
Fallopian tubes	SALPINGECTOMY
gall bladder	CHOLECYSTECTOMY
gland	ADENECTOMY
gums	GINGIVECTOMY
iris	IRIDECTOMY
kidney	NEPHRECTOMY
lobe (of lung)	LOBECTOMY
liver	HEPATECTOMY
lump in breast	LUMPECTOMY
	TYLECTOMY
ovaries	OOPHORECTOMY
(specimen)	BIOPSY
spleen	SPLENECTOMY
(sterilising)	VASECTOMY
stomach	GASTRECTOMY
sympathetic nerve	
	SYMPATHECTOMY
tonsils	TONSIL(L)ECTOMY
uterus	HYSTERECTOMY
	UTERECTOMY
womb	HYSTERECTOMY
	UTERECTOMY
cutie, *say*	QT
cycles per second	CPS.CS.HERTZ
cyclists	CTC
cyclopaedia	CYC(LO)
Cymric	CYM
Cyprus	CY
scent	CHYPRE
Czechoslovakia(n)	CS
capital	C.PRAGUE
coin	HALER.HELLER.KORUNA
gymnastic club	SOKOL
leader	C
measure	LATRO

D

damn. *date*. *daughter*. day. deal. deci. *Dee*. degree. dele. delete. delta.
Democrat. denarius. deserted. deuterium. Deutsch. diameter. diamond.
died. differential operator. doctor. duke. electrical flux. five hundred. four.
four thousand. Germany. *lot*. mark. key. *many*. note. notice. *number*. old
penny. penny. Schubert's works. string. vitamin

dad	
Dad's Army	HG.PASTA
Dad's double	PAPA
dagger	
daggers drawn	OBELI
	(*see* knife)
Dahomey	DY
in Dahomey	D-Y
Dai's = Welsh	
•*Dai's* violin	CRWTH
daily	CHAR
	(NEWS)PAPER.TIMES
daily job	PAPERWORK
damaged <u>pear</u>	PARE.RAPE.REAP
damp	
damp course	SOUP
damp-proof course	DPC
damp-proof membrane	DPM
dance[1]	
Alpine	GAVOTTE
American	BARN DANCE
	(BE)BOP.BLACK BOTTOM
	BOSTON (REEL).BREAK DANCE
	BUNNY-HUG.CAKEWALK
	CHARLESTON.JITTERBUG
	JIVE.LINDY HOP.PAUL JONES
	ROCK 'N ROLL.TWIST
	TURKEY TROT
Argentinian	TANGO
Basque	BOURREE
Bohemian	POLKA.REDOWA
Brazilian	BATUQUE
	BOSSA NOVA.CARIOCA
	MAXIXE.SAMBA
changing partners	PAUL JONES
college	HOP.PROM
country	ALTHEA.AURESCA
	BARN DANCE.COTILL(I)ON
	ECOSSAISE.GAVOTTE
	HAY.HEY.REEL.MORRIS(-DANCE)
	(SIR) ROGER DE COVERLEY
	ROUNDEL

Cuban	HABANERA.R(H)UMBA
folkdance	SQUARE-DANCE
for two persons	PAS DE DEUX
fourth movement of	
quadrille	TRENISE
French	BOURREE.CANCAN
	CHACONNE.CORANTO
	COURANTE.FARANDOLE
	GAVOTTE.GIGUE
—old	BRAN(S)LE.BRANTLE
	BRAWL
frolicsome	CAPER
gavotte	CIBELL
German	ALLEMANDE
	ALMAIN.LANDLER
gliding	COURANT(E)
	PALAIS GLIDE.WALTZ
Greek	PROMAIKA.SIKINNIS
Hawaiian	HULA(-HULA)
Hebrew	HORA
hornpipe	MATELOTE
Hungarian	CSARDAS.CZARDAS
in duple time	TWO-STEP
in ring	ROUND
Irish	FADING.PLANXTY.REEL
	RINKAFADDA
Italian	BERGAMASK
	BERGOMASK.GIGA
	RIGOLETTO.SALTARELLO
	TARANTELLA.VOLTA
leaping	ALLEMANDE.ALMAIN
like	
—minuet	PASPY.PASSEPEID
—polka	SCHOTTISCHE
lively	CORANTO.GALLIARD
	GALOP(ADE).GIG(UE).JIG
	RIGADOON.STOMP
—Shakespeare	CANARY
	UPSPRING
march	ONE-STEP
Maytime	MORISCO.MORISK
	MORRIS(-DANCE)

Mexican	RASPA
Moorish	MORESCO
movement in quadrille	
	PANTALON.PASTOURELLE
Neapolitan	TARANTELLA
Negro	WALK-AROUND
Norwegian	HALLING
obsolete (slow)	DUMP
old	BRAWL.CINQUE-PACE
	GAILLARD.GALLIARD
HAY-DE-GUISE.HAY-DE-GUY(ES)	
HEY-DE-GUISE.HEY-DE-GUY(ES)	
HUY-DE-GUY.LAVOLT(A)	
	LOURE.MINUET
PASSY-MEASURE.PAVIN	
	SINK-A-PACE.VOLTA
on sanded floor	SAND-DANCE
orgiastic	SIKINNIS
Peruvian	CUECA
Polish	CRACOVIENNE.MAZURKA
	POLONAISE.VARSOVIENNE
Polynesian	HULA(-HULA).SIVA
Portuguese	FADO
Provencal	TAMBOURIN
public	RIDOTTO
quadrilles	LANCERS
quick	GALLOPADE.FOX-TROT
—pavan(e)	PASSAMEZZO
	PASSE-MEASURE
	PASSY-MEASURE
—movement of csardas	FRIS(KA)
—step	PAS REDOUBLE
ragtime	TURKEY-TROT
ring-dance	RO(U)NDEL
	ROUNDELAY.ROUNDLE
reel	CIRCASSIAN CIRCLE
	EIGHTSOME
Roman	TRIPUDIUM
round dance	ROUNDABOUT
Russian	GOPAK.KOLO.ZIGANKA
sailor's	HORNPIPE
Scottish	ECOSSAISE
EIGHTSOME.GAY GORDONS	
	HIGHLAND FLING
HOOLACHAN.HULLACHAN	
	PETRONELLA.REEL
STRATHSPEY.SWORD-DANCE	
Serbian	KOLO
shivering	SHIMMY(-SHAKE)

shuffling	FOX-TROT
Sicilian	SICILIANA.SICILIANO
	SICILIENNE
skipping	SALTARELLO
—slow	CHACONNE
(HESITATION-)WALTZ	
	MINUET.PAVANE
—waltz	VALETA.VELETA
solo	VARIATION
Spanish	BOLERO.CACHUCHA
	FANDANGO.FARRUCA
	FLAMENCO.JOTA
PASO DOBLE.PASSACAGLIA	
PAVAN(E).PAVEN.PAVIN	
SALTARELLO.SARABAND(E)	
SEGUIDILLA.ZAPATEADO	
square	DOS-A-DOS.DOSI-DO
	HOE-DOWN.QUADRILLE
stately	MINUET.PAVANE
Venetian	FORLANA.FURLANA
waltz	BOSTON.VALETA.VELETA
West Indian	BEGUINE
	CHA-CHA(-CHA)
	LIMBO.MAMBO
with fans	FAN-DANCE
with quick movements	
	LAVOLT(A)

dance²

(d)ance *not started*	-ANCE
dancing <u>bear</u>	BARE.BRAE
dancing <u>girl</u>	ALMA.ALME(H)
GEISHA.ISADORA DUNCAN	
	NAUTCH.PAVLOVA
	SALOME
dandy	ADONIS.BEAU
Dane	HAMLET
dangerous man	DAN
Danish	DAN
capital	COPENHAGEN.D
characters	DAN.D
cheese	TYBO
coin	KR.KRONE.ORE
fiord	ISE.LIM
hero	HOLGER.OGIER
hors d'oeuvres	SMOR(RE)BROD
invader	JUTE
leader	D
measure	ALEN.ESER.LANDMILL
	MORGEN.RODE.TOMME

national flag	DANNEBROG	dead-centre	CEMETERY
order	DANNEBROG		CREMATORIUM
parliament	RIGSDAG		FUNERAL PARLOUR
—Lower House	FOLKETING	dead end	CEMETERY.GRAVE
—Upper House	LANDST(H)ING		TOMB
sandwiches	SMOR(RE)BROD	dead *end*	D
sea monster	KRAKEN	dead*head*	D
weight	ESER.KVINT.PUND	dead language	OBIT(UARY)
	QUINT.TONDE	dead on arrival	DOA
	(*see also* Denmark)	dead reckoning	DR
dark		dead right	LATER
dark blue	OXONIAN	*dealt with* evil...	LIVE.VILE
dark horse	BLACK BEAUTY	**dean**	INGE
	NIGHTMARE	Dean of Faculty	DF
Dark Lady	NEGRESS	**dear**	
darling girl	GRACE	dear *French*..	CHER(E)
dart *back*	PIN.TRAD	dear money	SWEETBREAD
dashing		**debt**	IOU
dashing about	U-BOAT	debtor	DR
dashing about town	WONT	debtor's documents	-IOUS
data		debts	-IOUS
processing	ADP.DP.EDP	*decapitated* (k)ing	-ING
transfer	DT	*decayed* leaf	FLEA
date	D	**deceased**	D.DEC
date of birth	DOB	**decentralise**	CORE
dative	DAT	**decider**	ARBITRATOR.JUDGE
daughter	D.DAU		JUMP-OFF.PLAY-OFF
hence			REFEREE.TIE-BREAK
•daughter is hard...	DISH	**deci-**	
•daughters-*in*-law	RUDDLE	decigramme	DG
•grand-daughter	GD	decilitre	DL
David's work	PSALMS	decimal *system*	CLAIMED
dawn (sun-*up*)(D) ↑	NUS		MEDICAL
day(s)	D(DD)	decimally	INTENS-
day-long	DL	decimetre	DM
day-*trip*	-ADY	*decimated* by a...	BAY
days after date	DD	*decipher* signal	ALIGNS
days after sight	DS	**declare¹**	AM-.IAM.IM-
day's date	DD	hence	
daybreak	DAWN.SHORT LEAVE	•declaring our...	AMOUR
day*break*	-ADY	•declaring rightist views	
day*break*	D		AMATORY
daze		•declaring the result	AMEND
days, *say*	DAYS	and	
dazed reaction	CREATION	•declaring agreement	IMPACT
in a daze he was...	HAWSE	•declaring some...	IMPART
d-duster	DRAG	•declaring wine	IMPORT
dead	D.OBIT	**declare²**	
dead *beat*	EDDA	declare perfect	UTTER

declaration	DEC	definition	DEF
declaration of war	WORE	*deflect* blade	BALED
declare scent...	SENT	*deformed* feet	FETE
declension	DEC	**defrost**	TAKE OFFICE
decoded German...	MANGER	*degradable* type A...	PEATY
decorate[1]		**degree**	BA.D.DEG.MA
indicates use of abbreviation		*degree of* f/reed/om	REED
such as	OBE	*degree of* hop(e)	HOP
•company *has* decoration	COMBE	degree student	MAL
•decorated queen	OMER	**delegate**	DEL
•decorated unknown...	OBEY	delete	D
•King decorated...	ROBE	delete score	SCRATCH
•King *with* no decoration	ROOM	**delightful drawing**	FETCHING
decorate[2]		*delinquent* kids	SKID
decoration of room	MOOR	**delirium tremens**	DT(S)
decorated plate	PLEAT	**deliver**	
decreasing *(ret)urns*	URNS	deliver *up*(D) ↑	REVILED
Dee	D	deliveries	OVER
Dee's predecessor	C	delivery	BALL
deep[1]	MAIN.SEA	deliveryman	BOWLER
hence			GYNAECOLOGIST
•deep breath	SEA BREEZE		LIBERATOR.SPEAKER
•deep pink	SEA-ROSE	**delta**	D
•deep tone	SEARING	**delusion(s)**	DT(S)
deep[2]		*demented* Greek in...	REEKING
deep blue	LOW	**Democrat**	D
deep consideration		*demolished* barn	BRAN
	OCEANOGRAPHY	*demonstrated*	SATIN
deer	(*see* antelope)	**Denmark**	DK
defeat		hence	
defeat champion	BEST	•a name *in* Denmark	DANK
defeat party	THRASH	•smuggle *into* Denmark	DRUNK
defect		•we *in* Denmark	DUSK
defect of nut	FOUNT	(*see also* Danish)	
defective hearing	MISTRIAL	**dentist**	BDS.DDS.DRILLER
defective tap	APT.PAT		FILLER.LDS.MDS.STOPPER
defend		dentist's chair	DRILLING SITE
defendant	DEF.DFT	dentist's surgery	DRAWING ROOM
defender	BACK		FILLING STATION
Defender of the Faith	DF	dentists	BDA
deficient		**deny**	
deficient of a...	omit A	*denial of* her...	HIS
deficient of *	omit *	*denying* right...	LEFT
•left *deficient of* part...	DEED	**depart**	
defile		departed saint	LATEST
defile art	RAT.TAR	departure	DEP
defiling chapel	PLEACH	*departure of* *	omit *
defilement of virgin	RIVING	•*departure of* king *from*	
definitely was...	SAW	par(k)	PAR

departure platform	BIER	description	(*see* write³)
* *departing*	omit *	**desert**	
•King *departing from* No(r)way		desert	RAT
	NO-WAY	hence	
department	DEPT.DPT	•desert in the East	RATINE
Department of		•desert man	RATHE
—Economic Affairs	DEA	•desert tribe	RAT RACE
—Education and Science	DES	desert fighter	RAT
—Employment		desert holiday	LEAVE
(and Productivity)	DE.DEP	deserted	D
—Health and Social Security		*deserted by* *	omit *
	DHSS	•pa(la)ce *deserted by* the	
—the Environment	DOE	*French*	PACE
—Trade (and Industry)	DOT.DTI	deserter	RAT
depict		* *deserting*	omit *
depicted in orange	ONAGER	•princess *deserting* (di)vine...	
depicting a last...	ATLAS		VINE
depleted (s)tor(e)	TOR	**design**	
deploy		Design Council	CID
deploy tanks	STANK	*designed* tables	STABLE
deployed in *	incl in *	designer	DIOR
•engineers *deployed* in		**desire merely...**	WANTONLY
fort-s	FORTRESS	**desperate**	
deployment of guns	SNUG	*Desperate* Dan	AND
depose		*desperate* shriek	HIKERS.SHRIKE
depose leader	omit first letter	*desperately* tired	TRIED
•*depose leader* of (S)cots	COTS	**dessert**	FOOL
deposed	DEP	**destroy**	
depression	COL	*destroyed* castle	CLEATS
deprive		*destructive* blow Seb...	WOBBLES
deprive of a...	omit A	*desultorily* read...	DARE.DEAR
deprive of leader	omit first letter	**detached**	
•(p)arty *deprived of leader*	ARTY	*detached* retina	RETAIN
deprive of love	omit O	detached territory	ISLAND
deprive of money	omit L	**detail**	
deprived of *	omit *	*detailed* ca(t)	CA
•(tot)ally *deprived of* drink	ALLY	*detailed* drawin(g)	DRAW-IN
deputy	DEP	**detective**	BLOODHOUND
deputy head	D		BUSY.DET.TEC
deputy-lieutenant	DL	detectives	BUSIES.CID.YARD
deranged or insane	IN REASON	**Deutsch**	D
deregulating more...	OMER.ROME	*devastated* realm	LAMER
derelict chapel	PLEACH	**develop**	
derive		*developed* a new...	WANE.WEAN
derivation	DER	*development of* site	TIES
derived	DER	*device* may be...	BEAMY
derived from one Red's...		**devil**	ABADDON.APOLLYON
	ENDORSE	BELIAL.CLOOT(IE).DAVY-JONES	
derived from o/ur ge/nes	URGE	(OLD) SCRATCH.RAGMAN	

devilish control	POSSESSION	ant	EMMET
devilish skill	IMPART	anything withered	SCRUMP
devious men are...	MEANER		SKRIMP.SKRUMP
devised name	MANE.MEAN	apart from	OUTSIDE OF
Devon	SW	approaching	TOWARD
devoted to her...	THROE	apt	TOWARD
devour		arduous contest	PINGLE
devoured by *	incl in *	area mined	SET
•one *devoured by* men	MEAN	arouse	YERK
	MIEN	arrogant	COBBY
devouring a...	incl A	as	
devouring *	incl *	—if about	LIKE
•men *devouring* one...	MEAN	—it were	LIKE
	MIEN	—much as	WHAT
devout	PI	ass	DICK(E)Y
dial	O	assertion	THREAP.THREEP
dialect	DIAL	astride STRIDE-WAYS.STRIDLING	
dialect terms		at	
indicated by		—hand	TOWARD
according to some		—least LEASTWAYS.LEASTWISE	
in some parts		attention	GAUM.GORM
locally		autumn	HARVEST
regional		awkward	UNGAIN
some say:		—girl	MAUTHER.MAWTHER
abide	WON	awn-removing device	
about	AWAY		HUMMELLER
accusation	THREAP.THREEP	baker's peel	PALE
ache	WORK	bar in chimney	RANDLE-BALK
active	WIMBLE	RANDLE-PERCH.RANDLE-TREE	
adit	STULM	RANNEL-TREE.RANNLE-TREE	
advancing swiftly	RAKING	RANTLE-TREE	
affected		bark	WAFF
—with fear	EERIE.EERY	barter	COPE
—with illness	WAMBLY	basket	WISKET
afternoon snack	FOUR(SES)	batter	DIALECT
aftertaste	TWANG	be	
agitate	WHEMMLE	—dishevelled	SLATTER
	WHOMBLE.WHOMMLE	—off work	PLAY
	WHUMMLE	—over-refined	MIMMICK
agitated	HET UP	MINNICK.MINNOCK	
alert	SPRACK.SPRAG	—painful	WORK
all	A	—peevish	NATTER
allow to be believed	LET ON	—sparing	STINT
almost	MOST	—twisted or warped	WIND
along	ALONGST	bear offspring	YEAN
amount carried on one trip RAKE		bearer of coffin UNDERBEARER	
anemone	ENEMY	beat	JO(U)LE.JOLL.JOWL
angry word	MISWORD		POLT.YERK
annual holiday	WAKE	—violently WHITHER.WUTHER	

because	CAUSE
bed	
—of fireclay	THILL
—time	DOWN-LYING
beetle	CLOCK
behave in artificial	
manner	MIMMICK
	MINNICK.MINNOCK
belch	YESK.YEX
belly	WAME
—band of cart-horse	WANTY
bellyful	WAMEFUL
bend	TREND
beneath	NEATH
benumb	SCRAM
besmirch	SLUR
best	WALE
bewitch	BESPEAK.WISH
big man	COB
bilberry	WINE-BERRY
bind	YERK
bindweed	WITH(Y)WIND
birch	BIRK
biscuit	PARKIN
bite	SNACK
blame	WITE.WYTE
blanket	WHITTLE
blast	WHITHER.WUTHER
bleat	WHICKER
blink	WAPPER
blinking	WAPPER-EYED
blow	DA(U)D.SCAT.WHITHER
	WUTHER
blustering	BLUFF
bodily build	SET
boggy	SPEWY
bogland	SPEW.SPUE
bogle	BOGGARD.BOGGART
	BOGGLE
boisterous	RANDIE.RANDY
booby	PATCH
botch	BODGE.MUX
bottle (with ears)	COSTREL
bounce	BANG
bound	MERE
boundary	MERE
—ridge	LINCH(ET).LYNCHET
—stone	MERESTONE
branch	GRAIN.SHROUD

brawl	FRATCH
brawling	FRATCH(ET)Y
bread soaked in gravy	BREVIS
breadth of choice	WALE
breastbone	HEART-SPOON
breccia	BROCKRAM
brisk	COBBY.KEDGE
	KEDGY.KIDGE.YARE
brood	TEAM
broil	BRU(I)LZE
broth	BREVIS
brushwood	RICE
bugbear	BOGGARD
	BOGGART.BOGGLE
bullroarer	HUMBUZZ
bumblebee	DUMBLEDORE
bump	JO(U)LE.JOLL.JOWL
bunch	BOB
bundle of hay	WAP
burn	SCALD
burning ember	GLEED
burrow	BURY
burst	BRAST
buss	SMOUCH
bustle about	WHEW
buttermilk	KIRN-MILK.WHIG
cairn	RAISE
candle snuffer	SNASTE
capsize	WHEMMLE.WHOMBLE
	WHOMMLE.WHUMMLE
careful	EYEFUL
carp	YERK
carrier	TRANTER
cart with last harvest load	
	HOCKCART
cartload	FOTHER.SEAM
catch with bird-line	TEAGLE
catfish	WOOF
cattle	
—dung	TATH
—shed	SHIPPEN.SHIPPON
caught	CATCHED.CATCHT
caul	KELL
cause to bend	STEEP
causing illness	WAMBLY
celebration drink	BEVERAGE
chaffinch	SPINK
chain	TEAM
change clothes	SHIFT

changeable	WANKLE	comfortable	CANNY
chap	SPRAY.SPREATHE	commotion	FRAISE
	SPREETHE	comrade	BUTTY
	SPREAZE.SPREEZE	conceal	HEAL.HEEL.HELE
chapped	SPRAID.SPRAYED	conceited	CONCEITY
charm	COMETHER	confoundedly	GALLOWS.MORTAL
chat	COSHER	confuse	MOIDER.MOITHER
chatter	MAG	confused sound	WHOOBUB
cheat	MUMP	confusion	DUDDER.WHEMMLE
cheerful	CADGY		WHOMBLE.WHOMMLE
cheese scoop	PALE		WHUMMLE
chide	BAN	conical hill	PAP
children	CHILDER	connecting ridge	HALSE.HAUSE
chimney	CHIMLEY.CHUMLEY		HAWSE
chitterlings	CHIDLINGS	consort	MAKE.SORT
	CHITLINGS	conspire	COLLOGUE
choice	WALE	contemptible	CRUDDY
choose/choosing	WALE	contend vigorously with	PINGLE
chubby	CHUFF.FUBSY	contract miners	
chum	BUTTY	BUTTY-COLLIER(S).BUTTY-GANG	
churn	KIRN	contrary	CONTRAIR
circus tumbler		convenient	GAIN
	JERRY-COME-TUMBLE	coolness	COOLTH
clamp	HOG	corn	
clean out (ditch)	FAY.FEY	—marigold	GOLD
clear	REMBLE	—spurrey	YARR
climbing plant	WITH(Y)WIND	cough	HOAST
clip	DOD	courageous	WIGHT
clog	CLAM	cover	HEAL.HEEL.HELE
closed handful	NIEVEFUL	—with dish	
clot	LOPPER		WHEMMLE.WHOMBLE
clover	SUCKLING		WHOMMLE.WHUMMLE
club foot	POLTFOOT	—with soil	HELE IN
clump	TUMP	cow	
clumsy	GAUMLESS.GORMLESS	—dung	SHARN
	UNHEPPEN	—dung and coal cake	
—person	LERRUP		SHARNY PEAT
cluster	BOB	—house	SHIPPEN.SHIPPON
coal box	DAN	—'s yield	MESS
coarse grass	TATH	crane fly	JENNY-SPINNER
coax	CARN(E)Y	creature	WIGHT
cockchafer	BUZZARD-CLOCK	creek	WICK
	DUMBLEDORE	crest of hill	KNOLL
	HUMBUZZ	crisp	CRUMPY
coddle	COSHER	croak	CRAKE
collapse	SCAT	crook	CROMB.CROME
comb	KEMB	cross	FRANZY
combed	KEMPT	crouch	DARE
comely	GAINLY.LIKELY.TIDY	crow	CRAKE

crowberry	CRAKEBERRY
crowd	MONG
crumbly	NESH
crybaby	MARDY
crystal-gaze	SCRY
cunning	VARMENT.VARMINT
—mischief	PAWK
cur	TYKE
curd	CRUD
curdle	LOPPER.RUN.WHIG
	(Y)EARN
currant cake	SINGING-HINNY
customer	CHAPMAN
cut the hair of	DOD
dace	GRAINING
dally	PINGLE
damaged piece of cloth	FENT
damnably	GALLOWS
dampness	CLAM
dangerous	NO'CANNY
dash	DAD.DAUD
dashing	VARMENT.VARMINT
daze	GALLY
deaf	DUNNY
decent	GRADELY.GRAITHLY
decoy	TOLE.TOLL
defective mentally	WANTING
defile	HALSE.HAUSE.HAWSE
defilement	MOIL
deformed person	URCHIN
degree	GRE(E)CE
	GRECIAN.GRE(E)SE
	GREESING.GRESSING
	GRI(E)CE.GRISE.GRIZE
demure	MIM(-MOU'D)
depression in breast	
	HEART-SPOON
destructive	VENGEABLE
devour	SCOFF.SKOFF
die	SWELT
dig	GRAFT
diminutive person	NIFF-NAFF
dirt	CROCK
disease of	
—horse's hoof	FRUSH
—sheep	DUNT
disgusting	MAWKISH
dismayed	DARE
dispense with	WANT

dispute	THREAP.THREEP
dissolute	OUTWARD
distinctive flavour	TACK
ditch	GRAFT
division of county	WARD
do	
—anything briskly	LILT
—without	WANT
dog	TYKE
doorpost	DURN
doze	DARE
drain	SEW
drainage canal	EA(U)
draining shaft	STULM
dram	TIFT
draw tight (stitches)	YERK
dress up	BUCK
drink	TIFT
—money	BEVERAGE
drinker	BIRLER
drop dung	TATH
drudge	MOIL
dwell	WON
earliest	RATHEST
early	
—fruit or vegetables	HASTINGS
—ripe (variety)	RATH(E)RIPE
earwig	FORIT-TAIL.FORKY-TAIL
easily handled	YARE
eat sparingly	PINGLE
eerie	UNKED.UNKET.UNKID
egg	COCKNEY
either	OUTHER
elaborate flowerbed	KNOT
embankment	STAITH(E)
embrace	HALSE.HAUSE.HAWSE
enclose	TINE
enclosed hollow part	WAME
end	SHANK
—of season	BACK END
endearment	PIGSN(E)Y.PIGSNIE
endure	ABEAR
engage in with energy	YERK
ensnare	SNARL
equal	MAKE
escort	SET
eve	E'EN.EVEN
every way	A'GATE
everybody	A'BODY

everywhere	A'WHERE
ewe	YOW(E)
excavation	GRAFT
exceedingly	MAIN
except	NOBBUT.ONLY
	OUTSIDE OF.WITHOUT
exchange	COPE.TOLSEL.TOLSEY
	TOLZEY
excite repulsion	UG
exert oneself	PINGLE
exit	OUTGATE
—expert	SLY
express yearning	YAMMER
expression of	
—commendation	FAIR
—courtesy	FAIR
extremely	MORTAL
eye	WINKER
fade away	WALLOW
faggot	KNITCH
failure to comprehend	ANAN
fair	PLAYING
fairy	PISKY
faith	FAIX
falsehood	LEASING
fantastical	CONCEITED
farm	WICK
farthing	FARDEN.FARDING
fascinated	DARE
fast	
—horse	GANGER
—pace	RAKER
favourable	TOWARD
feeble	WEARISH
feeling of sickness	WAMBLE
ferrule	VERREL
fertile	BATTLE
festival	PLAYING
fibre	VIVER
film	KELL
finch	SPINK
fine	GRADELY.GRAITHLY
—(Oxford)	SCONCE
fireside shelf	STOCK
fish	
—pond	VIVER
—trap	WEEL
fist	NEIF.NEIVE.NIEF.NIEVE
fit	GRADELY.GRAITHLY

—of perversity	GEE
flap	FLACKER
flared	FLEW.FLUE
flat	FLEW.FLUE
—basket	TRUG
flattery	CARN(E)Y
flexible rod	WATTLE
flight of steps	GRE(E)CE.GRECIAN
	GRE(E)SE.GREESING.GRESSING
	GRI(E)CE.GRISE.GRIZE
floor	PLANCH
—of coal seam	THILL
flounder about	TOLTER
fluffy	PLUFFY
flutter	FLACKER
fly wide (hawk)	RAKE
fodder	FOTHER
follow scent (dog)	RAKE
fool	MUMCHANCE
foolish person	GUMP
foot rot	HALT
forget	MISREMEMBER
fork	GRAIN
form a single file	RAKE
forward	FORRAD
fowl	BIDDY
framework for corn stack	HOVEL
freckle	FERN(I)TIC(K)LE
	FAIRNITIC(K)LE.FERNYTIC(K)LE
friendly	CADGY
frog of horse's hoof	FRUSH
frolic	GAMMOCK
frolicsome	CADGY
fuddle	FUZZLE
fuel	ELDIN(G)
full cloth or yarn	WALK
fumes	SMEECH
fun	GAMMOCK.GIG
fungus for tinder	SPUNK
fuss	WORK
fusty	FROWSY.FROWZY
gable	GAVEL
gang	RAKE
gap	SHARD.SHERD
garfish	HORNBEAK
gasp	CHINK
gather fallen fruit	SCRUMP
	SKRIMP.SKRUMP
geld	LIB

get
—by begging   MUMP
—over   OVERGET
—together with exertion
     SCAMBLE
getting on   TOWARD
ghost   GYTRASH
gin and treacle   MAHOGANY
gird   YERK
girl   GAL
give birth prematurely   WARP
glean   LEASE
glimpse   WHIFF
gluey substance   LIME
go
—about idly   SAMP
—about noisily   CLUTTER
—astray   MISGO
—easy   CA'CANNY
—courting   WENCH
—short   STINT
goad   BROD
goat   GATE
goblin   BOGGARD.BOGGART
     BOGGLE
good
—condition   KELTER.KILTER
—number   THR(E)AVE
—even   GOD-DEN
—for-nothing   DONNAT.DONNOT
gooseberry   GOOSEGOG
     WINE-BERRY
graceful   GAINLY
grandfather   GRANFER
grass   HAVER
grating in river   HECK
grease on side of candle
     WINDING-SHEET
great deal   MORT
greater spotted woodpecker
     WITWALL
green woodpecker   HICKWALL
     WITWALL
greyhound   GREW(HOUND)
grilse   PEAL.PEEL
grimace   MUMP
ground ivy   GILL
grumble   CHUNNER.CHUNTER
hairnet   KELL

halter for hanging   WIDDY
hamper   PED
hand   DADDLE
handle   HANDFAST.STALE
     STEAL(E).STEEL.STEIL.STELE
—on scythe shaft   NIB
handy   GEMMY.JEMMY
hanging clock
     WAG-AT-THE-WALL
     WAG-BY-THE-WALL
hangman's rope   WIDDY
happy chance   MERCY
harangue   SPEECH
harass   PINGLE
hard
—blow   POLT
—work   LOUSTER
hardened cutting edge   FIRE-EDGE
harmless   CANNY
harsh expression   MISWORD
harvest
—home   HAWKEY.HOCKEY
     HORKEY
—supper   HAWKEY
     HOCKEY.HORKEY
have a mind to   MIND
hawker   TRANTER
he   A
head-pad   WASE
heap   TASS
heap (waste)   BING
heart of decayed tree   DADDOCK
hearty kiss   SMOUCH
heated   HET
heed   GAUM.GORM
help in need   BEETMISTER
helter-skelter   LIKE HEY-GO-MAD
hiccup   YESK.YEX
hidden   DE(A)RN
hide   HEAL.HEEL.HELE
hillcrest   KNAP
hillock   KNAP.TOFT.TUMP
him   UN
hither and thither
     HITHER AND YON(D)
hobgoblin   BULLBEGGAR
hoist   TEAGLE
hold   HOLT
hollo   HOLLER

hollow enclosed section	WAME
homeward	UP ALONG
honey	HINNY
honeysuckle	SUCKLING
hook	CROMB.CROME
hop about	LILT
horizontal mine prop	STULL
horse	KEFFEL
—block	JOSS-BLOCK
—'s bellyband	WANTY
hot coal	GLEED
hubbub	WHOOBUB
hummocky	TUMPY
hunchback	URCHIN
hurdle	WATTLE
hurdy-gurdy	HUMSTRUM
hurt	NOY
husband	MASTER
hussy	HUZZY
I	A.CHE
—am	CHAM
—have	CHAVE
—will	CHILL
idler	DONNAT.DONNOT
ill	QUEER
—natured person	PATCH
—tempered	STINGY
imbecile	INNOCENT
impending	TOWARD
improve	BEET.BETE
in	
—good condition or order	TIDY
—good spirits	PEART.PIERT
—order to	FOR TO
—poor health	INDIFFERENT
—the way in front	TOWARD
inclined	LIKE
inconvenient	UNGAIN
indict	TROUNCE
indirect	UNGAIN
infect(ion)	SMIT
infectious	SMITTLE
inflate	BLAST
information	WITTING
infuse	MASH
inner door	HECK
innocent	CANNY
insipid	MAWKISH
insist	THREAP.THREEP

interjection of	
—excitement	HEY-GO-MAD
—surprise	LAWK(S)
inward	TOWARD
iris	GLADDON
it	A
itch(ing)	EWK.(Y)EUK.YOUK
	YUCK.YUKE
jack (bowls)	KITTY
jail	KITTY
jaw	CHAFT
join	PIECEN
journey	RAKE
jumping pole	QUANT
keep from one year to next	
	OVERYEAR
keep scratching	SCRATTLE
kick	PUNCH.WINCE.YERK
kid	YEANLING
kindle	TIND
kiss	SMOUCH
knock	CON.JO(U)LE.JOLL
	JOWL.SCAT
knowledge	WITTING
known	BEKNOWN
labour	MOIL
ladder	STY
lamb	YEANLING
lame	GAMMY.MAIN
lament	YAMMER
lane between	
—houses	ENTRY
—walls or hedges	TWITTEN
lapwing	TEW(H)IT
larder	SPENCE
large beetle	CLOCKER
lark about	GAMMOCK
lash out with	YERK
last	YESTERN
late autumn	BACK END
latter part	SHANK
lay eggs prematurely	WARP
lean part of loin of pork	GRISKIN
leap(ed)	LEP
lease	SET
leash	TRASH
leave undisturbed	LET-A-BE
ledge	LINCH(ET).LYNCHET
leg	PESTLE

Lent boat races	TORPIDS
let	SET
letter Z	IZZARD.IZZET
level a measure of grain	STRIKE
lie	LIG
lie	LIG(GE).LIGGEN
lies/lying	LEASING
lift	TEAGLE
light cart	SHANDRY(DAN)
lightly cooked (eggs)	RARE
likely	LIKE
linger about	HANKER
liquid filth	ADDLE
litter	TEAM
little	LEET.LITE.WHEEN
—pig	GRICE
—things	FEWTRILS
lively	COBBY.KEDGE.KEDGY
	KIDGE.PEART.PIERT
load	FOTHER.RAKE
loaf	MICHE
loathe	UG
loathly	LAIDLY
loathsome	MAWKISH
loft	TALLAT.TALLET.TALLOT
lonely	UNKED.UNKET.UNKID
long	SIDE
lop(pings)	SHROUD
lore	LARE
lounge about	HAWM
lout	LOBLOLLY
low	
—hill	HOW.LAW
—stool	CRICKET
—whisper	PIG'S-WHISPER
lower part of door	HECK
lump	DAD.DAUD.GOB.LUNCH
lunch	TIFT
lure	TOLE.TOLL
lurk	DARE
madam	MISTRESS
maggot(y)	MAWK(ISH)
maim	MAIN
maimed	GAMMY
maintain resolutely	THREAP
	THREEP
make	
—a cheerless roaring	WHITHER
	WUTHER
—a mess of	BOSS
—a mound around	TUMP
—outcry	YAMMER
—progress by exertion	
	THRUTCH
—ready	TEEL
—tea	WET
mall	MELL
man	MUN
manageable	YARE
manner of doing	GATE
manure	TATH
marble	MARL
marbled	MARLED.MARLY.MIRLY
mark off	MERE.SMIT
maslin	MONGCORN
	MUNGCORN
match	SPUNK
mate	MAKE
maudlin	MAWKISH
maul	MELL
may (past tense)	MOUGHT
mean	FOOTY
mediator	STICKLER
mend	BEET.BETE
mentally	
—normal	WISE
—sub-normal	WANTING
mess	MUX
mild bang	PLUFF
militiaman	LUMP
milk strainer	SYE
mine	WHEAL
mining lease	SET
mischievous	GALLOWS
missel (mistle) thrush	THROSTLE
	-COCK
misshapen egg	COCKNEY
mixture	MONG
moderately warm	LUKE
mole	WANT
mop	MALKIN.MAWKIN
mope	MUMP
more forward	FORRADER
most convenient	EFTEST
mouch	MICHE
mouldboard	PLAT
mouldy	FOUGHTY
mouthful	GOB

move	QUATCH.QUETCH.QUITCH
—diagonally	CATER(CORNER)
—tremulously	WAPPER
—unsteadily	WAMBLE
—with a jerk	YERK
mow	TASS
mowing	MATH
much	MORT.MICKLE
	MUCKLE
mud	SLAKE
—flat	SLAKE
mumble	MUMP
munch	MUMP
murderer	MURTHERER
musical instrument	HUMSTRUM
must	MAN.M(A)UN
musty	FOUGHTY
mutter	CHUNNER.CHUNTER
	MUMP
nag (horse)	KEFFEL
nail	BROD
nape of neck	NODDLE.SC(R)UFF
	SCUFT
natty	VARMENT.VARMINT
near	GAIN
neat	GEMMY.JEMMY
neck	HALSE.HAUSE.HAWSE
neigh	WHICKER
neighbour	BOR
network	KELL
never a. . .	NARY
newt	ASK(ER)
next	NEIST
nighest	NEIST
nightjar	EVEJAR
nimble	WAN(D)LE.WANNEL
	WIGHT.WIMBLE
nipple	PAP
noise	CLUTTER
nonsense	FADDLE
normal mentally	WISE
not	
—dangerous	CANNY
—one	NARY
—to be depended upon	WANKLE
—well	INDIFFERENT
notable man	COB
notice	GAUM.GORM.MIND
nourishing	BATTLE

now for	HEY FOR
nozzle	TEWEL
oats	HAVER
occasion	WHET
odd piece of cloth	FENT
of	ON
—good omen	CANNY
—stone	STONERN
off we go	HEY FOR
offensive	FROWSY.FROWZY
on	
—account	LONG
—account of	ALONG
—hand	TOWARD
—the near or left side	TOWARD
—one	UN
—who picks	PIKER
—who thrives	WELL-DOER
only	NOBBUT
ooze	SEW
open shed	LINHAY.LINNY
osier	
—pike trap	KIPE
—rope	WIDDY
otter's den	HOLT
out-and-out	FAIR.TEETOTAL
outing	OUT
outlet	OUTGATE
overcoat	JAMES.JEMMY
overcome	MOIDER.MOITHER
overnice person	QUIDDLE(R)
overthrow	WHEMMLE.WHOMBLE
	WHOMMLE.WHUMMLE
overturn	WHEMMLE.WHOMBLE
	WHOMMLE.WHUMBLE
overweight woman	
	HORSE-GODMOTHER
oyster spawn	CUL(T)CH
packhorse load	SEAM
pamper	COSHER
pannier	PED
pantry	SPENCE
paralyse	SCRAM
parlour	KEEPING-ROOM
part of	
—leg of beef	MUSCLE
—spinning machine	HECK
parting gift	FOY
partition	TRAVIS.TREVIS(S)

partner	BUTTY
pass	HALSE.HAUSE.HAWSE
pasture	LEASE.LEAZE.LEASOW(E)
path	GATE
pawky	CANNY
pay heed to	GAUM.GORM
pedlar woodturner	BODGER
peel	PILL
peevish	FRANZY
peony	PINY
perch	PERK
period of work	YOLE
person	WIGHT
pet name (cow, etc.)	MOG(GY)
petticoat	COAT
petulant child	MARDY
phosphorescence (sea)	BRIMING
physiognomy	VISNOMIE
	VISNOMY
pick	PIKE.WALE
pile (waste)	BING
pilfer	MICHE
pilferer	PIKER
pit of stomach	HEART-SPOON
pitch	PICK
place in pickle	PUT DOWN
plantain	WAYBREAD
play	LAKE.LAIK
—the beggar	MUMP
—truant	MICHE
pleaded	PLED
pleasing	LIKELY
pliant	WAN(D)LE.WANNEL
plough	
—chain	TEAM
—handle	STILT
plump	TIDY
plunder	SCOFF.SKOFF
poke	PEG.POACH.POTE.PROKE
pole	PERCH
poll	DOD
pollard	DOD
pond	POUND
porridge stick	THIBLE.THIVEL
post	STOOP.STOUP
postman	POST
potato	TATER
pot-bellied	KEDGE.KEDGY.KIDGE
pour in a stream	HUSH

powder puff	PLUFF
praise	ROOSE
pre-breakfast snack	MORNING
prepared	YARE
preserve	PUT DOWN
press	THRUTCH
press eagerly	THREAP.THREEP
pretend	LET ON
preternatural	NO'CANNY
pretty drunk	FAIRISH
prick	BROD
prim	MIM(-MOU'D)
prize	GREE
probable	LIKE
proceed	RAKE
profitable work	THRIFT
prominent lower jaw	
	WAPPER-JAW
promiscuous girl	GAMMERSTANG
promptly	YARELY
prong	GRAIN
pronounce	TONGUE
proper(ly)	GRADELY.GRAITHLY
prostrate	FELL
protuberance	KNAP
protuberant section	WAME
public fountain	PANT
puddle	PANT
puff	PLUFF
puffed up	PLUFFY
pull	
—by the ears	SOOLE.SOWL(E)
—quickly or brusquely	WAP
punch	POUNCE
punt mooring pole	RIPECK
	RY(E)PECK
punting pole	QUANT
puny	WEARY.SCRAM
puppet	PUPPY
purge	WORK
quake	WAMBLE
quantity	FOTHER
quarrel	FRATCH
	OUTFALL.WHID
quarrelling	FRATCH(ET)Y
quick	YARE
quickly	YARELY
quill	TWILL
quilt	TWILT

quitch	QUICK(EN)
quite	FAIR
rack	BAN
—and manger	HECK AND MANGER
—for fodder	HECK
ragged robin	WILD-WILLIAMS
rail	BAN
raised path	CLAPPER
ramify	SPRANGLE
range widely	RAKE
rapid	STICKLE
rat	RATTON.ROTTAN.ROTTEN
raven	CRAKE
readiest	EFTEST
readily	GRADELY.GRAITHLY
ready	YARE
—to learn	TOWARD
rebuke	THREAP.THREEP
recked	RECKAN
reckless gamble	RAKER
recover from	OVERGET
red	
—apple	QUAR(R)ENDER
	QUARANTINE.QUARENDEN
	QUARRINGTON
—currant	WINE-BERRY
reed thicket	REED-RAND
	REED-ROND
refuge	HOLT
regard	GAUM.GORM
relieve	BEET.BETE
remind	REMEMBER
remnant	FENT
remove	REMBLE
—sprouts from	SPROUT
—stalk from	STRIG
—to a distance	FAR
rend	RENT
reproach	WITE.WYTE
respectable	SPONSIBLE
responsible	SPONSIBLE
restrain	STINT
restraining grip	HANK
restraint	TRASH
rick in barn	GOAF
ricked	RECKAN
ridge of land	STITCH
riot	WHOOBUB
rise	PLUFF
—with a jerk	YERK
river	EA(U)
roam	RAKE
rolling	
—in the belly	WAMBLE
—movement	WAMBLE
roofing slab	SLAT
rootlet	VIVER
rope	WIDDY
—for securing hay	WANTY
rough	ROW
—bridge	CLAPPER
—mannered man	TYKE
roughen	SPRAY.SPREATHE
	SPREETHE.SPREAZE.SPREEZE
roughened	SPRAID.SPRAYED
rouse	YERK
rowing-bench	THOFT
rubbish	CUL(T)CH
rump	NATCH
rung	SPELL
running water	EA(U)
rush	FEEZE.PHE(E)SE.PHEEZE
—basket	JUNKET
—of water	HUSH
sad	WO(E)
saddler	WHITTAW(ER)
sandwich	BUTTY
saucy	PEART.PIERT
scare	GALLY.SKEAR.SKEER
scarecrow	BOGGARD.BOGGART
	BOGGLE
	GALLYBAGGER.GALLYBEGGAR
	MALKIN.MAWKIN
	GALLICROW.GALLYCROW
scatter	SCAMBLE
school	SCUL(L).SCULLE
scolding	HEARING
scorch	SCALD.SCRAT
scratch	SCRAWM
screech	SHRITCH
scrimmage	ROUGE
scuttle	SCRATTLE
sea	
—bird of several species	
	TARROCK
—fog	HAAR
—weed	ORE.WARE

second		sick	QUEER
—boat or crew	TORPID	sickly	MAWKISH
—year salmon	SPROD	sieve	SYE
secondary rainbow	WATER-GALL	sigh	SITHE
secret	DE(A)RN	sightly	EYEFUL
sedge	SEG	simpleton	GABY.ZANY
separate	SLEAVE	sip	TIFT
set	TILL	sit	SET
—dogs on	SLATE	sitting-room	KEEPING-ROOM
—on	SLATE	skewer	SKIVER
sewer	(COMMON-)SHORE	skilful	CANNY
shaft	STALE.STEAL(E).STEEL	skilfully	YARELY
	STEIL.STELE	skilled in magic	WISE
—of vehicle	LIMBER	skirt	COAT
shake	DIDDER	skirting board	WASHBOARD
shall	SAL	skulk	MICHE
shallot	SCALLION	slap	TWANK
shallow	FLEET.FLEW.FLUE	slate	SLAT
shamble	SCAMBLE	slater	HELLIER
shank	STALE.STEAL(E)	slice of meat	COLLOP
	STEEL.STEIL.STELE	slime	SLAKE
shape surface of mould	STRIKE	slimy substance	LIME
shapely	GAINLY.TIDY	slink	MICHE
sharp	VARMENT.VARMINT	slip	SLIVE
—flavour	TWANG	slipped	SLIVED.SLIVEN.SLOVE
she	A	slippery	GLIDDER
sheaf of corn upended	GAIT	slop about	SLATTER
shed	SHADE	sloppy	SOZZLY
ship's doctor's medicine		slops	SOZZLE
	LOBLOLLY	slovenly woman	BESOM
shirt	SHIFT	slow	LATE
shock of corn	STITCH	slumber	SLOOM
shoes	SHOON	slush	LOPPER
shoot	CHIT.PLUFF	slut	DRAZEL
short		sly	CANNY
—and thick	PUNCH	smack	SMOUCH.TACK.TWANG
—piece of cloth	FENT	small	
—rope	WANTY	—branch	RICE
—twang	TWANK	—gate	HATCH
shot	PLUFF	—landholder	STATESMAN
shove	THRUTCH	—potato	CHAT
shovel	SHOOL	smart	GEMMY.JEMMY.SPIFF(Y)
shrewd	CANNY	smear	CLAM.SLUR
shriek	SHRITCH	smoke	SMEECH
shrink	DARE	smooth	STRIKE
shrivel up	SCRUMP.SKRIMP	smut	CROCK
	SKRUMP	snack	BEVER.BUTTY
shrunk	WEARISH	snail	DODMAN
shut	SHET.TINE	snap	SNACK

snare	GRIN	—'s nest	CAGE
—for fish	WEEL	stain	SMIT
snigger	WHICKER	stale liquor	TIFT
soak through	SIPE	stalk	STALE.STRIG
soft	NESH	stall	TRAVIS.TREVIS(S)
—and brittle	FROUGHY.FROWY	stare	DARE
—sandstone	HASSOCK	statesman	ESTATESMAN
soldier	SO(D)GER	steal	MAG
something	SUMMAT	steep	STICKLE
somewhat	SUMMAT	—narrow valley	GRIFF(E)
sorry	WO(E)	step	GRE(E)CE.GRECIAN
sound of rushing water	HUSH		GRE(E)SE.GREESING.GRESSING
sour			GRI(E)CE.GRISE.GRIZE
—liquor	TIFT	stern	STARN
—milk	WHIG	stir	CLUTTER.QUATCH
southernwood	LAD'S LOVE		QUETCH.QUITCH
sown	SAWN	—up	POACH
spade	PICK	stone vessel	STEAN.STEEN
sparing with cash	CANNY	store vegetables in clamp	HOG
spark	SPUNK	stout	COBBY.STUGGY
sparrow	SPUG	straddle	STRODDLE
speckled	SPRECKLED	straggle	SPRANGLE
spell	SCAT	straggler	STRAG
spike	BROD	straight	GAIN
spill	SHED.SLATTER	straightforward	JANNOCK
—about	SWATTER	strain	SYE
spirited person	SPUNK	strange	UNKED.UNKET.UNKID
spit	YESK.YEX	stray	STRAG
splash	FLOUSE.FLOUSH	street	GATE
	SLATTER.SOZZLE	stretch	STREEK.STREAK
—about	SWATTER	—of work	YOKE
splayed	FLEW.FLUE	strickle	STRIKE
splinter	SPELL	stride	STROAM
spoil	MUX	strike	FRAP.YERK
spoilt child	MARDY	striking woman	BOBBY-DAZZLER
sponge	MUMP	string	RAKE
sport	GIG.LAKE.LAIK	strip	UNSTRIP
spot	MOIL	strive	PINGLE
spotted	GAY	stroke	JO(U)LE.JOLL.JOWL
sprawl	SCAMBLE.SPRANGLE	strong	WIGHT
sprightly	SPRACK.SPRAG	strop	STRAP
springtime	WARE	struggle	SPRANGLE
sprout	CHIT	stubble field	AR(R)ISH
spruce	SPIFF(Y)	stubborn reiteration	THREAP
squat	FUBSY		THREEP
squatter	SWATTER	stuffy	FROWSY.FROWZY
squeamish	MAWKISH	stupefy	MOIDER.MOITHER
squeeze	SCRUZE	stupid	GAUMLESS.GORMLESS
squirrel	SKUG	substandard asparagus	SPRUE

suggestion	TWANG
sulk	MUMP
superiority	GREE
supple	SOUPLE.WAN(D)LE
	WANNEL
surly	BLUFF
surveyor of boundaries	
	MERESMAN
suspect	SUSPICION
sweetmeats	SPICE
swell	BLAST.PLIM
swift	WIGHT
taint	SMIT
tainted	FOUGHTY
talon	TALENT
tap	TIT
tare	TINE
tattle	TITTLE
tease	MAG
tender	NESH
tepid	LUKE
terrace	LINCH(ET).LYNCHET
territorial subdivision	
	WAPENTAKE
test cheese	PALE
than	AS.NOR.
that	YON
—same	THICK.THILK
thatcher	HELLIER
the	T
—one	TONE
—same	THILK
—same	THICK
—thing you know of	YON
they	A
thick	
—gruel	LOBLOLLY
—slice	LUNCH
thickset	STUGGY
—man	PUNCH
thin	
—liquor	TIFT
—mud	SLUR
third finger of left hand	RINGMAN
thirty	THRETTY
this	THILK
those	YON
thou shalt	THOUS
thrash	PAY

throat	HALSE.HAUSE.HAWSE
throb	QUOP
throw	YERK
—against	DAD.DAUD
—briskly	WAP
—into chaos	WHEMMLE
	WHOMBLE
	WHOMMLE.WHUMMLE
—violently	WHITHER.WUTHER
thrust	PEG.POACH.POTE
	THRUTCH.YERK
thump	DAD.DAUD
tidy up	FETTLE
tiler	HELLIER
till next year	OVERYEAR
time	WHET
timorous	EERIE.EERY
titter	WHICKER
to	
—an extent	LIKE
—bankruptcy	SCAT
toil	MOIL
tolerate	ABEAR
toll	JO(U)LE.JOLL.JOWL
—booth	TOLSEL.TOLSEY.TOLZEY
totter	DADDLE
touchdown in football	ROUGE
towed barge	BUTTY
town	WICK
track	RAKE
trap	GRIN
treat with setterwort root	
	SETTER
tremble	WHITHER.WUTHER
trick	PAWK
trifle	FADDLE.NIFF-NAFF.PINGLE
	QUIDDLE
trifles	FEWTRILS
trifling	FADDLE
trivet	BRANDISAF
trouble	NOY.WORK
trouser braces	GALLUSES
tub	DAN
tug	PUG
tun	COWL
turmoil	MOIL
turn	
—around	WAMBLE
—of string	WAP

—over and over	WAMBLE
—upside down	WAMBLE
	WHEMMLE.WHOMBLE
	WHOMMLE.WHUMMLE
turnip	TURMIT
tuyere	TEWEL
twelvemonth	TOWMON(D)
	TOWMONT
twig	WATTLE
twigs	RICE
twinge	TWANG
twist	WAMBLE
two	
—dozen	THR(E)AVE
—handled mug	SCONCE
—stooks of sheaves	THR(E)AVE
uncomfortable	
	UNKED.UNKET.UNKID
uncouth	UNKED.UNKET.UNKID
undefiled	UNFILED
underclay	THILL
underhand throw	HAUNCH
underlip	FIPPLE.JIB
underneath	UNNEATH
undersized person	SCRUMP
	SKRIMP.SKRUMP
understanding	GAUM.GORM
unexpected shower	SKIT
unkempt	FROWSY.FROWZY
unless	WITHOUT
unpleasant	UNGAIN
unploughed strip	LINCH(ET)
	LYNCHET
unprepossessing	UNLIKELY
unreliable	WANKLE
unskilled	UNGAIN
unstable	WANKLE
unsteady	WAMBLY.WANKLE
—movement	WAMBLE
until	WHILE
unwind	REAVE.REEVE
unyielding	STOUT
up the road	UP ALONG
uproar	WHOOBUB
urge	THREAP.THREEP
vagrant	STRAG.WALKER
vegetable store	HOG
vein of ore	RAKE
veritable	FAIR

vermin	VARMENT.VARMINT
very	GRADELY.GRAITHLY.RIGHT
—much	PURELY
—small	TIDDLEY.TIDD(L)Y
vexation	NOY
victory	GREE
vigorous	SPRACK.SPRAG
village	WICK
villainous	GALLOWS
visit for purpose of begging	MUMP
voice	STEVEN
wail	YAMMER
wait for	WAIT ON
walk	TRAVEL
—unsteadily	DADDLE
wander	
—idly about	STROAM
—in mind	MOIDER.MOITHER
wanton	CADGY
warrant	WARN
wassail	SWIG
watch-hill	TOOT
water	
—channel to mill	LEAT.LEET
—course	RHINE
watery-looking sky	WATER-GALL
wave	WAFFLE
way	GATE
wearisome trip	JAUNCE
	JAUNSE
well	
—disposed	TOWARD
—nigh	WELLY
wet	WEET
wharf	STAITH(E)
whatsoever	WHATSOMEVER
wheedle	CARN(E)Y
wheedling	COMETHER
whey	WHIG
which	WHILK
whine	YAMMER
whisper	TITTLE
wholemeal bread	
	RAVEL(LED) BREAD
wholeness	HALENESS
whooping cough	CHINCOUGH
whore's baby	WOSBIRD
wick	SNASTE
wicked	WICK

widow	WIDDY	—sow	(Y)ELT
widower	WIDOW-MAN	Yorkshireman	TYKE
wield	WELD.WIND	yours	YOURN
wife	WOMAN	**dialling system**	STD
wild		**diamond**	ICE.ROCK
—orchid	PIONY	diamond case	ICEBOX
—vetch	TINE	diamond ring	ENGAGED SIGNAL
will	WULL	**diameter**	D
willow basket	WILL(E)Y	**diarist**	EVELYN.PEPYS
willowing machine	WILL(E)Y	**Dickensian dance**	TWIST
wind	REAVE.REEVE	**dicky**	ILL
wisp of hay, straw etc.	WASE	*Dicky*, Sue *and* Sam	ASSUME
withered	WEARISH	dictionary	OED
without a mate	MAKELESS	**did it**	FEC(IT).FF
witless	GAUMLESS.GORMLESS	**die**	
woman	PIECE OF GOODS	die *off*	IDE.-IED
—'s headdress	KELL	die *out*	IDE.-IED
womb	WAME	died	D.OB(IT)
wood	TIMBER	died without children	OSP
—pigeon	ZOO-ZOO	**differ**	
—louse	SLATER	*differ* from anil	FORMALIN
—pecker	WITWALL	*differing* points	PINTOS
woollen shawl	WHITTLE	**different**	
word incorrectly	MISWORD	*difference* in the...	THINE
work		different *conclusion*	T
—done over one period	YOKING	*different role* for actress	RECASTS
—hard	MOIDER.MOITHER	*different spell of* witch	WHICH
—ineffectually	PINGLE	different ways	!N.S.E.W
—mate	BUTTY	•*in* different ways, girl...	ENSUES
worry	FRAB.PINGLE.WORRIT	*different* ways	SWAY.YAWS
worse	WAR(RE).WAUR	*differential* gear	RAGE
worst	WA(U)RST	*differently constructed* steel...	
wrap	HAP		LEETS.STELE
wreck	WRACK	**difficult**	
wrest	WRAST	*difficult* time	EMIT.MITE
wrestle	WRAXLE	difficulty	ADO.ER.NET
wretched	WO(E)	*difficulty* in art	TRAIN
wriggle	WAMBLE.WIND	*digested* meal	LAME.MALE
wrinkle	FRUMPLE	**dilute**	DI
writhe	WIND	*diluted* sp(i)rit	SPRIT
yellow		*dim*wit	TWI-
—flower	GOLLAN(D).GOWLAND	**dime**	IOC
—hammer	YITE	**diminish**	
yonder	YON	*diminish* th(e)...	TH
young		*diminish* the girt(h)	GIRT
—ewe	THEAVE	*diminish* t/he len/gth	HELEN
—oak	FLITTERN	*diminishing* asset	ASS.SET
—pig	SLIP	*diminution of*	
—sea trout	PEAL.PEEL	—interest	INT

—height	H
—power	P
diminutive	
footballer	HALF
girl	DI.G
man	CHAPLET
mother	MA.MUM.MINIMUM
Senator	SEN
sister	SIS
(*see also* small[2])	
dine *out*	ENID.NIDE
diploma	DIP
Diploma	
—in Industrial Health	DIH
—in Public Health	DPH
—in Ophthalmic Medicine and Surgery	DOMS
—in Psychological Medicine	DPM
—of Art	DA
—of the Imperial College	DIC
diplomat	CD
diplomatic retreat	CONSULATE.EMBASSY
diplomats	CD.FO.UN
Dirac's constant	H
direct	
direct current	DC
directions	E.N.S.W
•in all directions	NEWS
(*see also* way)	
director	DIR
Director of Public Prosecutions	DPP
directors	BOARD
directors of astronomy	STARBOARD
dirty	
dirty dogs	GODS
dirty old man	DOM
disabled (income group)	DIG
disadvantage (draw*back*⟨ ⟩	WARD
disagree with **all. . .**	PART.SOME
disappear	
disappearance of a. . .	omit A
disappearance of *	omit *
•*disappearance of* shilling from pur(s)e	PURE
disapprove	BOO
disarmers	CND

disarray in team	INMATE
disaster	
disaster in the. . .	THINE
disastrous fire	RIFE
disc	O
disc jockey	DJ
discard	
discard a. . .	omit A
discard reserves	SCRAP-BOOKS
discard *	omit *
•Wh(it)e, N.*discards* it	WHEN
discoloured figures	LIVID
discontinued	DIS
discord results. . .	LUSTRES
discount	
•*50% discount on* tic(ket)	TIC
discourage man	DETERGENT
discover	
dis*covered by* *	incl DIS
•dis*covered by* an Old English. . .	ANODE
discovered in Sou/th Eir/e	THEIR
discovered in *	incl in *
•one *discovered in* m-y. . .	MONEY
dis*covering*. . .	incl in DI-S
•dis*covering* me. . .	DIMES
diseases	
including	
complaints	
conditions	
disorders	
illnesses:	
abnormal	
—childhood development	AUTISM
—contraction of pupil	MYOSIS
—elation	EUPHORIA
—enlargement	HYPERTROPHY
—growth of spleen	SPLENOMEGALY
—redness of skin	ROSACEA
	RUBOR
—reduction of blood sugar content	HYPOGLYC(A)EMIA
—sensation	PARAESTHESIA
—sound from lungs	RALE
	RHONCHUS
—thickness of skin	PACHYDERMIA

abnormally	
—high arches	PES CAVUS
—high body temperature	
	HYPERPYREXIA
—high blood pressure	
	HYPERTENSION
—low intestines	VISCEROPTOSIS
—swollen veins	VARICOSE VEINS
—tortuous vein	VARIX
abscess	BOIL.EMPYEMA
—round tonsil	QUINSY
absorption of rays	
	RADIATION SICKNESS
actinomycosis	WOODEN-TONGUE
	WOODY-TONGUE
actinobacillosis	
	WOODEN-TONGUE
	WOODY-TONGUE
air in pleural cavity	
	PNEUMOTHORAX
alastrim	SMALLPOX
	VARIOLA MINOR
allergy	HAY FEVER
alopecia	FOX-EVIL
alternating	
—laughter and tears	
	DACRYGELOSIS
—muscular spasm	CLONIC SPASM
amaurosis	BLINDNESS
amnesia	FUGUE
anthrax	SANG
WOOLSORTER'S DISEASE	
anxiety about health	
	HYPOCHONDRIA
apoplexy	STROKE
asbestos in lungs	ASBESTOSIS
back-arching spasm	
	OPISTHOTONOS
back pain	LUMBAGO.SCIATICA
bacterial	
—disease	LEPTOSPIROSIS
—infection	SEPSIS.SEPTICAEMIA
Banti's disease	SPLENIC ANAEMIA
bean poisoning	FAVISM
bejel	YAWS
bilharzia	SCHISTOSOMA
	SCHISTOSOMIASIS
birthmark	MOLE
Black Death	BUBONIC PLAGUE

blackhead	COMEDO
bleeding	HAEMORRHAGE
—disease	THAEMOPHILIA
—into pleural cavity	
	HAEMOTHORAX
—into tissues	HAEMATOMA
—into urine	HAEMATURIA
—nose	EPITAXIS
—under skin	PURPURA
blind spot	SCOTOMA
blindness	AMAUROSIS
blister	VESICLE
blockage of artery	EMBOLISM
blood	
—diseases	LEUCOCYTHAEMIA
	LEOCOCYTOPENIA
	LEUCOCYTOSIS
	LEUC(H)AEMIA.LEUKAEMIA
	POLYCYTHAEMIA.PY(A)EMIA
	THALASSAEMIA
—poisoning	SEPTICAEMIA
	SUPRAEMIA.TOXAEMIA
—spitting	HAEMOPTYSIS
blueness from lack of oxygen	
	CYANOSIS
boba	BUBA.BUTTON SCURVY
	FRAMBOESIA
VERRUGA PERUVIANA.YAWS	
bodily wasting	MARASMUS
boil	ABSCESS.FURUNCLE
—on eyelid	HORDEOLUM.STYE
bone	
—and cartilage erosion	
	OSTEO-ARTHRITIS
—disease	OSTEOPOROSIS
—injury	FRACTURE
—marrow disease	
	OSTEOMYELITIS
Bornholm disease	DEVIL'S GRIP
	PLEURODYNIA
botulism	FOOD POISONING
	SAUSAGE-POISONING
bow-leggedness	VALGUS
bowel disease	CONSTIPATION
	DIARRHOEA.DYSENTERY
	STEATORRHEA
brain	
—disorder	DELIRIUM (TREMENS)
	ENCEPHALOPATHY

—fever   PHRENESIS.PHRENITIS
breakdown of
—immune system   AIDS
—red blood cells   HAEMOLYSIS
Bright's disease   NEPHRITIS
bronchial diseases   ASTHMA
                           BRONCHITIS
brucellosis   MALTA FEVER
bruise   ECCHYMOSIS
buba   BOBA.BUTTON SCURVY
                         FRAMBOESIA
             VERRUGA PERUVIANA
                               YAWS
bubonic plague   BLACK DEATH
build-up of fat on buttocks
                        STEATOPYGIA
button scurvy   BOBA.BUBA
                         FRAMBOESIA
     VERRUGA PERUVIANA.YAWS
calenture   SHIP FEVER
cancer   CARCINOMA
                (see tumour below)
caused by
—breathing oxygen-deficient air
          MOUNTAIN-SICKNESS
—flies or larvae   MYIASIS
—fungus   MYCOSIS
—mould   ASPERGILLOSIS
—tea-drinking   THEISM
cerebrospinal fever   MENINGITIS
cessation of breathing   APNOEA
chemical disorder of joint   GOUT
chest pain   ANGINA
chickenpox   VARICELLA
chilblain   PERNIO
chlorine poisoning   FLUOROSIS
chlorosis   GREEN SICKNESS
cholesterol deposits   XANTHOMA
chorea   ST VITUS'S DANCE
cirrhosis of liver   WHISKY-LIVER
clergyman's knee   BURSITIS
clot blocking artery   EMBOLUS
clotting in blood vessel
                        THROMBOSIS
clubfoot   KYLLOSIS.TALIPES
coal dust in lungs ANTHRACOSIS
cold sore   HERPES (SIMPLEX)
colour blindness
               MONOCHROMASY

comedo   BLACKHEAD
common cold   CORYZA
compression sickness   BENDS
compulsive pulling out of
  hair   TRICHOTILLOMANIA
congestion of blood HYPERAEMIA
conjunctivitis   PINK-EYE
connective tissue disease
          RHEUMATOID ARTHRITIS
constipation   STENOSIS
constriction of blood vessels,
   pores, etc.   STENOSIS
consumption TB.TUBERCULOSIS
contagious disease   ZYMOSIS
contraction of pupil   MIOSIS
                            MYOSIS
convulsions   EPILEPSY.FIT
                        PAROXYSM
—at end of pregnancyECLAMPSIA
corn on foot   HELOMA
cotton workers' disease
                        BYSSINOSIS
cowpox   VACCINIA
Crohn's disease   ENTERITIS
crop of boils   FURUNCULOSIS
curvature of spine   KYPHOSIS
cyst in gland under tongue
                            RANULA
cystic fibrosis MUCOVISCIDOSIS
dandruff   FURFUR
death of part   NECROSIS
decay   GANGRENE
defect of
—fibrin in blood   HYPINOSIS
—red blood cells
                    OLIGOCYTHAEMIA
defective
—acid-alkali balance   ACIDOSIS
                          ALKALOSIS
—bone growth
    OSTEOCHONDROSIS.RICKETS
—interpretation of writing
                          PARALEXIA
—reasoning   PARALOGIA
deficiency disease   BERI-BERI
                 PELLAGRA.SCURVY
deficiency of
—blood   ISCH(A)EMIA
                         OLIGAEMIA

—blood-clotting   HAEMOPHILIA
—carbon dioxide   ACAPNIA
—cartilage   ACHONDROPLASIA
—enzyme   PHENYLKETONURIA
—essential food   MALNUTRITION
                        STARVATION
—haemoglobin   ANAEMIA
—hydrochloric acid
                     ACHLORHYDRIA
—insulin   DIABETES
—iron   SIDEROPENIA
—oxygen   ANOXIA
—sugar in blood
                   HYPOGLYCAEMIA
—thyroid hormone   CRETINISM
—vitamin B   ANAEMIA
           BERI-BERI.PELLAGRA
—vitamin C   SCURVY
—vitamin D   OSTEOMALACIA
                        RICKETS
—white blood cells
              AGRANULOCYTOSIS
deformation of
—arms and legs   PHOCOMELIA
—ear   CAULIFLOWER EAR
—fingers
    DUPUYTREN'S CONTRACTURE
—foetus   TERATOMA
—foot   CLUB FOOT.TALIPES
—head   HYDROCEPHALY
                   MICROCEPHALY
—hip (splayed hip) COXA VULGA
—joints   OSTEOARTHRITIS
                OSTEOARTHROSIS
—knee (knock-knee)
                  GENU VALGUM
—neck muscle   TORTICOLLIS
                        WRYNECK
—toe joint   HALLUX VALGUS
degeneration of kidney
                      NEPHROSIS
delirium   PHRENESIS.PHRENITIS
delusion
—man as beast   ZOANTHROPY
—seeing animals   ZOOSCOPY
—seeing self as another
              APPERSONATION
dementia praecox
            SCHIZOPHRENIA

deposit of melanin   MELANOSIS
depression   MELANCHOLIA
                  MELANCHOLY
deranged nutrition   TROPHESY
               TROPHONEUROSIS
dermatitis   ECZEMA
destruction of kidneys
            ADDISON'S DISEASE
devil's grip BORNHOLM DISEASE
diarrhoea   LIENTERY
               WEANING-BRASH
dilatation of
—arteries   TELANGIECTASIS
—blood vessels HAEMORRHOIDS
                          PILES
—pupil   MYDRIASIS
dilated bronchi BRONCHIECTASIS
difficulty in
—breathing   DYSPNOEA
—focusing on near objects
                    PRESBYOPIA
—swallowing   DYSPHAGIA
dimness of sight   CALIGO
discharge
—from ear   OTORRHOEA
—from glands   SEBORRHOEA
—of pus   PYORRHOEA
disintegration of blood cells LYSIS
dislocation of joint   LUXATION
disordered
—cell growth   CANCER
                      CARCINOMA
—hearing   PARACUSIS
—speech   PARARTHRIA
displacement of
—eye   PROTOPSIS
—organ   PROLAPSE
—parts   ECTOPIA.ECTOPY
disseminated sclerosis   DS
             MULTIPLE SCLEROSIS
distension of intestines
                     METEORISM
dizziness SCOTODINIA.SCOTOMA
double vision   DIPLOPIA
Down's syndrome   MONGOLISM
dracontiasis
        GUINEA-WORM DISEASE
drooping of upper eyelid   PTOSIS
dropsy   (O)EDEMA.HYDROPSY

—in chest   HYDROTHORAX
—of abdomen   ASCITES
—of the brain   HYDROCEPHALUS
dryness of
—conjunctiva   XEROMA
                 XEROPHTHALMIA.XEROSIS
—hair   XERASIA
—mouth   XEROSTOMIA
—skin ICTHYOSIS.XERODERM(I)A
dullness of sight   AMBLYOPIA
dust in lungs   PNEUMOCONIOSIS
                 PNEUMO(NO)KONIOSIS
—from
  —asbestos   ASBESTOSIS
                          MESOTHELIOMA
  —carbon   ANTHRACOSIS
  —cotton   BYSSINOSIS
  —fungus   FARMER'S LUNG
  —iron   SIDEROSIS
  —silica   SILICOSIS
dustman's shoulder   BURSITIS
dwarfism   ATELEIOSIS
dyslexia   WORD BLINDNESS
dyspepsia   INDIGESTION
ear
—ache   OTALGIA.OTALGY
—disorder   CHOLESTEATOMA
                 OTOSCLEROSIS.TINNITUS
early insanity   HEBEPHRENIA
East Coast fever   TICK FEVER
ecchymosis   BRUISE
eczema   DERMATITIS
elephantiasis   BARBADOS LEG
encephalitis lethargica
                          SLEEPY SICKNESS
enlargement of
—baby's head   HYDROCEPHALIS
—bone   EXOSTOSIS
—kidney   HYDRONEPHROSIS
—prostate   PROSTATISM
—spleen   SPLENOMEGALY
—thyroid   GOITRE
enteric fever   GASTRIC FEVER
                                 TYPHOID
epidemic disease   ZYMOSIS
epilepsy   FALLING SICKNESS
                 PETIT MAL.PYKNOLEPSY
eruption on
—nose   ROSE-DROP

—palms or soles   POMPHOLYX
eruptive disease   POX
—of skin   SHEEP-POX
erysipelas   ROSE
                      ST ANTHONY'S FIRE
excess of
—body fat   ADIPOSITY.OBESITY
—calcium   HYPERCALC(A)EMIA
—gas in stomach   FLATULENCE
—red blood cells
                          POLYCYTHAEMIA
—salt in blood
                          HYPERNATRAEMIA
—sugar in blood   DIABETES
—urea in blood   URAEMIA
—water in tissue   (HY)DROPSY
                                 OEDEMA
—white blood cells
                          MONONUCLEOSIS
excessive
—activity of
  —adrenal gland
                          HYPERADRENALISM
  —sebaceous gland
                              SEBORRHOEA
  —thyroid gland
                          THYROTOXICOSIS
—bleeding   HAEMOPHILIA
—deposit of fat in
  arteries   ATHEROMA
—discharge from nose
                              RHINORRHOEA
—excitement   HYPERSTHENIA
—fibrin in blood   HYPERINOSIS
—flow of
  —mucus   CATARRH
  —saliva   PTYALISM
—growth   ACROMEGALY
                               GIGANTISM
—growth of
  —fat   LIPOMATOSIS
  —papillae   PAPILLOMA
  —tissue   HYPERPLASIA
                              HYPERTROPHY
—nose-bleeding   RHINORRHAGIA
—number of
  —breasts   POLYMASTIA
                 POLYMASTISM.POLYMASTY
  —chromosomes   POLYSOMY

—overgrowth　　　　　GIGANTISM
—secretion of mucus
　　　　　　　　BLENNORRHOEA
—sensitivity to
　—pain　　　　HYPERALGESIA
　—stimuli　HYPERAESTHESIA
—sweating　　　　　　HIDROSIS
　　　　　　HYPER(H)IDROSIS
—temperature　HYPERPYREXIA
—thirst　　　　　POLYDIPSIA
—vitamins　HYPERVITAMINOSIS
—vomiting　　HYPEREMESIS
expansion of blood
　vessels　VASODILATATION
eye diseases　　　　CATARACT
　　CYCLOPLEGIA.DIPLOPIA
　　GLAUCOMA.PANNUS
　　　　　　　TRACHOMA
failure of
—brain growth　ANENCEPHALY
—blood circulation　　SHOCK
—heart to empty itself ASYSTOLE
failure to
—assimilate
　—fats, etc.　　　SPRUE
　　COELIAC DISEASE
　—food　MALABSORPTION
—co-ordinate movements
　　　　　　　　ATAXIA
—secrete
　—milk　　　AGALACTIA
　—urine　　　　ANURIA
faint　　　　　　SYNCOPE
false
—joint　PSEUDARTHROSIS
—pregnancy　PSEUDOCYESIS
fatty
—degeneration　STEATOSIS
—tumour　　　STEATOMA
faulty
—alignment of
　—eyes　　　　SQUINT
　　STRABISM(US)
　—teeth　MALOCCLUSION
—healing of fracture　MALUNIO
fever　　PLAGUE.PYREXIA
—recurring
　—daily　　QUOTIDIAN
　—every three days　TERTIAN

fit　CONVULSION.EPILEPSY
　PAROXYSM.SEIZURE
fixed delusions　PARANOIA
flat foot　　PES PLANUS
flatulent distension TYMPANITES
flea-borne　PLAGUE.TYPHUS
floating kidney　NEPHROPTOSIS
fluid in knee joint
　WATER ON THE KNEE
food-poisoning　BOTULISM
　LISTERIOSIS.PTOMAINE
　SALMONELLOSIS
framboesia　BOBA.BUBA
　BUTTON SCURVY.MORULA
　VERRUGA PERUVIANA.YAWS
freckle　　　　LENTIGO
from
—animals　　ZOONOSIS
—cattle　ACTINOMYCOSIS
　BRUCELLOSIS.COWPOX
　UNDULANT FEVER
—dogs　LEPTOSPIROSIS
　TOXOCARIASIS
—farm animals　ANTHRAX
　LEPTOSPIROSIS
—goats　MALTA FEVER
—rabbits　RABBIT-FEVER
　TULAR(A)EMIA
—rats　LEPTOSPIROSIS
　RAT(BITE)-FEVER
—sheep　Q-FEVER
frozen shoulder　BURSITIS
functional disorder　NEUROSIS
fungal
—disease　ATHLETE'S FOOT
　ASPERGILLOSIS
　BLASTOMYCOSIS
　CRYPTOCOCCOSIS
　FARMER'S LUNG
　FAVUS.TORULOSIS
—growth　MYCOSIS
furfur　DANDRUFF.SCURF
furuncle　　　BOIL
fusion of bones　ANCHYLOSIS
　ANKYLOSIS
galactose in blood
　GALACTOSAEMIA
gangrene　THANATOSIS
gaol fever　　TYPHUS

genital ulceration   CHANCROID
German measles   ROSEOLA
                                RUBELLA.RUBEOLA
giddiness   VERTIGO
glanders   FARCY
glandular
—condition   ADENOSIS
—fever   MONONUCLEOSIS
glaucoma   WALL-EYE
goitre   STRUMA
gout   PODAGRA
—in all joints   HAMARTHRITIS
gripes   TORMINA
growth
—disorder   ACROMEGALY
—of fibrous tissue   FIBROSIS
Guinea-worm disease
                                DRACONTIASIS
hair disease   TRICHOSIS
hard
—swelling   SCIRRHUS
—tumour   SCLERIASIS
hardening of   SCLEROSIS
—arteries   ARTERIOSCLEROSIS
                                ATHEROSCLEROSIS
—skin   CALLOSITY.ICTHYOSIS
—tissue   SCLERIASIS
haemorrhoids   PILES
headache   MIGRAINE
heart
—burn   CARDIALGY.CARDIALGIA
                PYROSIS.WATER-BRASH
—diseases   ANGINA PECTORIS
                CORONARY THROMBOSIS
                                ENDOCARDITIS
—disorder   TACHYCARDIA
                                TOBACCO-HEART
hepatitis   FAVISM
hereditary
—diseases   CHOREA MAJOR
                                CYSTIC FIBROSIS
                                HAEMOPHILIA
                HUNTINGTON'S CHOREA
—tendency to disease   DIATHESIS
hernia   RUPTURE
—of bladder   CYSTOCELE
herpes   COLD SORE.DARTRE
                                SHINGLES.ZOSTER
hiccuping   SINGULTUS

high blood pressure HYPERPIESIA
                                HYPERTENSION
hip-gout   SCIATICA
hives   NETTLE RASH.URTICARIA
Hodgkin's disease
                                LYMPHADENOMA
hordeolum   STYE
hospital gangrene PHAGED(A)ENA
housemaid's knee   BURSITIS
hunchback   GIBBUS
hydatid disease   TAPEWORM
hydrocephalus
                WATER ON THE BRAIN
hydrophobia   LYSSA.RABIES
                ST HUBERT'S DISEASE
hydropsy   DROPSY.OEDEMA
hysterical
—mania   HYSTEROMANIA
—trance   CAPTALEPSY
icterus   JAUNDICE
immersion foot   TRENCH FOOT
imperfect development of organ
    or part   APLASIA
inability to
—distinguish certain
    colours   COLOUR BLINDNESS
—perform intended motion
                                PARAPHRAXIA
                                PARAPHRAXIS
—swallow   HYDROPHOBIA
indigestion   DYSPEPSIA
infantile paralysis POLIOMYELITIS
infection
—after childbirth   MILK-FEVER
                PUERPERAL MANIA
—at childbirth PUERPERAL FEVER
—by micro-organisms
                                TOXOPLASMOS
—following disease   SEQUELA
—of fifth cranial nerve
                                TIC DOLOUREUX
—of nervous system   TORULOSIS
infectious
—disease   ZYMOTIC
—mononucleosis
                GLANDULAR FEVER
infestation with
—lice   PEDICULOSIS
—parasites   PARASITOSIS

inflamed sore	FELON.MORMAL
inflammation of	
—all joints	PANARTHRITIS
—appendix	APPENDICITIS
—artery	ARTERITIS
—bladder	CYSTITIS
—blind-gut	TYPHLITIS
—blood vessels in brain	
	CHOROIDITIS
—bone	OSTEITIS
	OSTEO-MYELITIS
—brain	ENCEPHALITIS
	MENINGITIS
	PHRENESIS.PHRENITIS
	PANOPHTHALMITIS
—breast	CYSTIC DISEASE
	MASTITIS
—bronchi	BRONCH(IOL)ITIS
—bursae	BURSITIS
—cerebrum	CEREBRITIS
—colon	COLITIS
—cornea	CERATITIS.KERATITIS
—diverticula	DIVERTICULITIS
—duodenum	DUODENITIS
—ear	CONCHITIS.OTITIS
—ear membrane	TYMPANITIS
—elbow joint	BURSITIS
	TENNIS ELBOW
—eye	CONJUNCTIVITIS
	OPHTHALMIA
	OPHTHALMITIS
—eyeball	SCLER(OT)ITIS
—eyelids	BLEPHARITIS
—Fallopian tubes	SALPINGITIS
—fibrous tissue	BURSITIS
	FIBROSITIS
—follicles	ACNE
—gall bladder	CHOLECYSTITIS
—glands	ADENITIS
—gums	GINGIVITIS
—head of optic nerve	PAPILLITIS
—heart	CARDITIS
—heart sac	PERICARDITIS
—heart valve	VALVULITIS
—inner ear	LABYRINTHITIS
—intestines	CROHN'S DISEASE
	ENTERITIS
	ILEITIS
—iris	IRITIS.UVEITIS

—joints	
	(RHEUMATOID) ARTHRITIS
—kidneys	BRIGHT'S DISEASE
	(PYELO)NEPHRITIS.PYELITIS
—knee joint	BURSITIS
	HOUSEMAID'S KNEE
—larynx	CROUP.LARYNGITIS
—lens of eye	CRYSTALLITIS
—lining of	
—artery	ENDARTERITIS
—heart	ENDOCARDITIS
—nose	RHINITIS
—stomach	GASTRO-ENTERITIS
—liver	HEPATITIS
—lymphatic glands	
	LYMPHANGITIS
—lungs	(LOBAR) PNEUMONIA
—marrow	MYELITIS
—mastoid process	MASTOIDITIS
—mouth and throat	THRUSH
—mucous membrane of	
—eyelids	TRACHOMA
—mouth	STOMATITIS
—nose	CATARRH.RHINITIS
—muscle	FIBROSITIS.MYOSITIS
—nail	ONYCHITIS
—nerves	(POLY)NEURITIS
—neurosis	HYSTERIA
—nose and throat	
	RHINOPHARYNGITIS
—ovary	OOPHORITIS.OVARITIS
—pancreas	PANCREATITIS
—parotid gland	PAROT(ID)ITIS
—part of lung	
	LOBULAR PNEUMONIA
—pelvis of kidney	PYELITIS
—peritoneum	PERITONITIS
—of liver	PERIHEPATITIS
—pharynx	PHARYNGITIS
—pleura	EMPYEMA
	PLEURITIS.PLEURISY
—prostate	PROSTATITIS
—rectum	PROCTITIS
—retina	RETINITIS
—sinus	SINU(S)ITIS
—skin	DERMATITIS.INTERTRIGO
—spinal cord	(POLIO)MYELITIS
—spine	RACHITIS.SPONDYLITIS
—spleen	SPLENITIS

—stomach GASTRITIS
—and intestines
     GASTRO-ENTERITIS
—subcutaneous CELLULITIS
—tendon sheath SYNOVITIS
—throat ANGINA
—tongue GLOSSITIS
—tonsils ANTIADITIS
     TONSILLITIS
—thyroid gland STRUMITIS
     THYROIDITIS
—tongue GLOSSITIS
—tonsils TONSIL(L)ITIS
—trachea TRACH(E)ITIS
—ureter URETERITIS
—urethra URETHRITIS
—uterus HYSTERITIS
—uvula STAPHYLITIS.UVULITIS
—vein (THROMBO)PHLEBITIS
—vertebra SPONDYLITIS
—whole eye PANOPHTHALMIA
—womb UTERITIS
inflammatory disease of
  the face ERYSIPELAS
influenza GRIPPE
ingrowing toenail
     ONYCHOCRYPTOSIS
intermittent fever
     RELAPSING FEVER
intestinal diseases COLITIS
     CHOLERA.DIARRHOEA
     DIVERTICULITIS
     DUODENAL ULCER
     DYSENTERY.MEGACOLON
intolerance of light
     PHOTOPHOBIA
irregularity of heartbeat
     ARRHYTHMIA
     EXTRASYSTOLE
itch PRURITIS.PSORA.SCABIES
itching PRURITIS
jail fever TYPHUS
jet lag TIME-ZONE DISEASE
joint
—disorder GOUT
     RHEUMATIC FEVER
     RHEUMATISM
—injury FRACTURE.SPRAIN
kala-azar DUMDUM FEVER

     LEISHMANIASIS
     LEISHMANIOSIS
kidney diseases
     ADDISON'S DISEASE
     BRIGHT'S DISEASE
     NEPHRITIS.NEPHROSIS
king's evil SCROFULA
     TUBERCULOSIS
knock-knees VALGUS
kyllosis CLUB-FOOT
lack of
—food MALNUTRITION
     STARVATION
—hydrochloric acid in stomach
     ACHLORHYDRIA
large boil CARBUNCLE
laryngitis HIVES
lateral spinal curvature
     SCOLIOSIS
lead poisoning MOLYBDOSIS
     PLUMBISM.SATURNISM
leakage of fluid EXTRAVASATION
     EXUDATION
leprosy LEONTIASIS
lice-borne disease
     RELAPSING FEVER
     TRENCH-FEVER.TYPHUS
like
—typhoid PARATYPHOID
—typhus TYPHOID
limited vision TUNNEL VISION
limping CLAUDICATION
Little's disease CEREBRAL PALSY
     SPASTIC PARALYSIS
liver disease CIRRHOSIS
lockjaw TETANUS
long-sightedness
     HYPER(METR)OPIA
looseness of bowels DIARRH(O)EA
loss of
—ability to
—focus eyes PREBYOPIA
—manipulate objects APRAXIA
—all sensation ANAESTHESIA
—appetite ANOREXIA (NERVOSA)
     ANOREXY
—hair ALOPECIA.MADROSIS
     PSILOSIS
—hearing DEAFNESS

	PREBYACUSIS
—memory	AMNESIA
—movement in joint	ANKYLOSIS
—muscle control	PALSY
—power of	
—motion	PARALYSIS
—writing	AGRAPHIA
—sense of pain	ANALGESIA
—skin pigment	VITILIGO
—speech	ALALIA.APHEMIA
	DUMBNESS
—taste	AGEUSIA
—vision	BLINDNESS.AMBYLOPIA
—voice	APHONIA.APHONY
—weight	CACHEXIA
low blood pressure	
	HYPOTENSION
lung diseases	ANTHRACOSIS
	ASBESTOSIS
	BRONCHIECTASIS
	BRONCH(IOL)ITIS
	(BRONCHO)PNEUMONIA
	BYSSINOSIS.EMPHYSEMA
	FARMER'S LUNG
	MESOTHELIOMA
	MINER'S PHTHISIS.PLEURISY
	PNEUMONCONIOSIS
	PNEUMOTHORAX
	SILICOSIS.SIDEROSIS
lupus	TOUCH-ME-NOT
lymph node disease	
	HODGKIN'S DISEASE
	LYMPHANGITIS
lymphoid tumour	LYMPHOMA
lyssa	HYDROPHOBIA.RABIES
malaria	MARSH-FEVER
	PALUDISM
Maltese fever	BRUCELLOSIS
matchmakers' disease	
	PHOSSY-JAW
measles	MORBILLI
melanin in blood	MELANAEMIA
memory disorder	PARAMNESIA
meningitis	
	CEREBRO-SPINAL FEVER
mental	
—derangement	PSYCHOPATHY
—disorder	
	ALZHEIMER'S DISEASE

	AMENTIA.AUTISM.DEMENTIA
	FOLIE A DEUX.HEBEPHRENIA
	IDIOCY.IMBECILITY
	MANIA.MONGOLISM.PARANOIA
	PHOBIA.PSYCHASTHENIA
	(PSYCHO)NEUROSIS
	PSYCHOSIS.SCHIZOPHRENIA
metabolic	
—defect in excretion of	
pigment	PORPHYRIA
—disorder	PHENYLKETONURIA
mild smallpox	ALASTRIM
miner's	
—anaemia	ANCHYLOSTOMIASIS
	ANKYLOSTOMIASIS
—elbow	BURSITIS
—lung	PNEUMOCONIOSIS
moniliasis	THRUSH
morbid	
—adhesion	SYNECHIA
—contraction	STENOSIS
—state of blood	CACHAEMIA
morbilli	MEASLES
mortification	GANGRENE
morula	YAWS
mosquito-borne	FILARIASIS
	MALARIA.YELLOW FEVER
mouth	
—gangrene	NOMA
—infection	APHTHA.CANDIDA
	MONILIASIS.THRUSH
	TRENCH MOUTH
	VINCENT'S DISEASE
multiple sclerosis	DS
	DISSEMINATED SCLEROSIS
mumps	PAROT(ID)ITIS
muscle	
—deterioration	
	MUSCULAR DYSTROPHY
—disease	MYASTHENIA
—pain	FIBROSITIS.MYALGIA
—spasm	CRAMP.OPISTHOTONOS
—tumour	MYOMA
muscular	
—atrophy	MYOPATHY
—distrophy	MYOPATHY
—inflammation	MYOSITIS
—rheumatism	FIBROSITIS
—tension	MYOTONIA

myopia	MOUSE-SIGHT
narrowing of	
—blood vessels	
	BUERGER'S DISEASE
	STENOSIS
	VASOCONSTRICTION
—organ	STENOSIS.STRICTURE
neoplasm	TUMOUR
nephritis	BRIGHT'S DISEASE
nerve pain	NEURALGIA
nervous	
—activity	NEUROSIS
—debility	NEURASTHENIA
—system disorder	
	DISSEMINATED SCLEROSIS
	EPILEPSY.LOCOMOTOR ATAXY
	MULTIPLE SCLEROSIS
	NEUROPATHY.NEUROSIS
nettle rash	HIVES.URTICARIA
neuralgia	
—in face	FACE-ACHE
	TIC DOULOUREUX
—of chest-wall	PLEURODYNIA
neuralgic ache in rectum	
	PROCTALGIA
neuritis of sciatic nerve	SCIATICA
night blindness	NYCTALOPIA
nosebleed	EPITAXIS
numbness of legs	NIGHT-PALSY
obstruction of intestine	
	ILEAC PASSION
	ILIAC PASSION.ILEUS
oedema	(HY)DROPSY
one-eyed vision	MONOBLEPSIS
opacity of	
—cornea	LEUCOMA.ONYX
—lens	CATARACT
open sore	ULCER
ornithosis	PSITTACOSIS
over-	
—activity of thyroid	
	THYROTOXICOSIS
	HYPERTHYROIDISM
—excitability	HYPOMANIA
—growth	AGROMEGALY
—of a part	HYPERPLASIA
—of skin of nose	RHINOPHYMA
—heating	HYPERTHERMIA
—nourishment	HYPERTROPHY

pain in	
—joint	ARTHRALGIA
—kidneys	NEPHRALGIA
	NEPHRALGY
—sciatic nerve	SCIATICA
—tongue	GLOSSODYNIA
—upper stomach	CARDIALGIA
	CARDIALGY
painful physical illness	PASSION
palsy	PARALYSIS
paludism	MALARIA
papilloma	WART
paralysis	PALSY
—agitans	PARKINSONISM
—partial	PARESIS
paralysis of	
—all limbs	QUADRIPLEGIA
—both arms or both legs	
	DIPLEGIA
—eye muscles	
	OPHTHALMOPLEGIA
—facial nerve	BELL'S PALSY
—legs	LATHYRISM
—lower body	PARAPLEGIA
—one part	MONOPLEGIA
—part	PARESIS
—pupil	CYCLOPLEGIA
parasitic diseases	BILHARZIA(SIS)
	BILHARSIOSIS
	CHAGASS DISEASE.KALA
	AZAR.LEISHMANIASIS
	LEISHMANIOSIS
	SHISTOSOMIASIS
	SLEEPING SICKNESS
	STRONGYLOSIS.TOXOCARIASIS
	TOXOPLASMOSIS
	TRICHINIASIS.TRICHINOSIS
	TRICHOMONIASIS
	TRYPANOSOMIASIS
paronychia	WHITLOW
parotid gland infection	MUMPS
parot(id)itis	MUMPS
parrot-disease	PSITTACOSIS
partial	
—dislocation	SUBLUXATION
—paralysis	PARESIS
pathological softening	MALACIA
pellagra	MAIDISM
pernio	CHILBLAIN

Perthes' disease	
	OSTEOCHONDROSIS
pertussis	WHOOPING-COUGH
perverted appetite	MALACIA
pes planus	FLAT FOOT
petit mal	EPILEPSY
piles	HAEMORRHOIDS
pimple	LENTIGO
pink	
—eye	CONJUNCTIVITIS
—rash	ROSEOLA
pleurisy with pneumonia	
	PLEURO-PNEUMONIA
pleurodynia	
	BORNHOLM DISEASE
plumbism	LEAD-POISONING
poisoning by	
—acetone	KETOSIS
—beans	FAVISM
—ergot	ERGOTISM.RAPHANIA
—ketone	KETOSIS
—lead	PLUMBISM
poliomyelitis	
	INFANTILE PARALYSIS
porous structure of bones	
	OSTEOPOROSIS
postnatal disease	MILK-LEG
	WHITE-LEG
premature	
—ageing	PROGERIA
—greying	POLIOSIS
—senility	ALZHEIMER'S DISEASE
presence of diverticula	
	DIVERTICULOSIS
prickly heat	MILIARIA.SUDAMEN
primary disease	IDIOPATHY
protusion of	
—eyeballs	EXOPHTHALMIA
	EXOPHTHALMOS
—meninges	MENINGOCELE
—organ	HERNIA
—spinal cord	MYELOCELE
prunella	QUINSY.SORE THROAT
pruritis	ITCH
psittacosis	ORNITHOSIS
psora	ITCH.SCABIES
psychosis	MANIA
—with delusions	SCHIZOPHRENIA
putrefaction	SEPSIS

putrid fever	TYPHUS
pyrexia	FEVER
pyrosis	HEARTBURN
	WATER-BRASH
quartan fever	MALARIA
quinsy	ANGINA.CYNANCHE
	PRUNELLA
rabbit fever	TULAR(A)EMIA
rabies	HYDROPHOBIA.LYSSA
rachitis	RICKETS
rapid heart beat	TACHYCARDIA
rat(bite) fever	SODUKU
	TULAR(A)EMIA
ravenous appetite	LIMOSIS
redness of skin	ERYTHEMA
resembling typhoid	
	PARATYPHOID
respiratory	ASTHMA.FLU
	INFLUENZA.PLEURISY
	PNEUMONIA
retention of	
—urine	HYDRONEPHROSIS
	STRANGURY
—waste in blood	UR(A)EMIA
rheumatism in lumbar	
region	LUMBAGO
rickets	RACHITIS
ringing in one or both	
ears	TINNITUS
ringworm	TINEA
	TRICHOPHYTOSIS
Rock fever	UNDULANT FEVER
rose	ERYSIPELAS
—rash	ROSEOLA
roseola	GERMAN MEASLES
	ROSE-RASH
rubella	GERMAN MEASLES
rubeola	(GERMAN) MEASLES
rupture	HERNIA.RHEXIS
sagging of organ	PTOSIS
St Hubert's disease	
	HYDROPHOBIA
St Vitus's dance	CHOREA (MINOR)
sang	ANTHRAX
sausage-poisoning	BOTULISM
scabies	ITCH.PSORA
scalp disease	PORRIGO
scaly scalp	DANDRUFF
scarlatina	SCARLET FEVER

scarlet fever	SCARLATINA
schistosomiasis	BILHARZIA
schizophrenia	
	DEMENTIA PRAECOX
sciatica	HIP-GOUT
scrofula	KING'S EVIL.STRUMA
	TUBERCULOSIS
scurf	FURFUR
sebaceous cyst	WEN
seizure	EPILEPSY.STROKE
sensation without physical	
origin	HALLUCINATION
septic finger	FELON
severe	
—anaemia	CHLOROSIS
—anxiety neurosis	SHELL SHOCK
—depression	MELANCHOLIA
—schizophrenia	CATATONIA
shaking	TREMOR
—of brain	CONCUSSION
—palsy	PARKINSONISM
	PARKINSON'S DISEASE
shell shock	WAR NEUROSIS
shingles	HERPES.ZOSTER
ship fever	CALENTURE.TYPHUS
shivering	AGUE.RIGOR
short-sightedness	MYOPIA
	PRESBYOPIA
	PRESBYOPY
singleminded madness	
	MONOMANIA
skin	
—disease	ACNE.DERMATITIS
	DERMATOSIS.ECZEMA
	ELEPHANTIASIS.ERYSIPELAS
	EXANTHEM(A).HERPES
	ICTHYOSIS.IMPETIGO
	INTERTRIGO.ITCH
	LEPROSY.MYXOEDEMA
	PEMPHIGUS.PITYRIASIS
	PSORA.PSORIASIS
	SCABIES.SERPIGO
—fungal	ATHLETE'S FOOT
	TINEA
—eruption	EXANTHEM(A)
	PRURIGO
—ulcer	RUPIA
sleeping sickness	
	TRYPANOSOMIASIS

sleepy sickness	
	ENCEPHALITIS LETHARGICA
small abscess	PUSTULE
smallpox	ALASTRIM.VARIOLA
soduku	RAT(BITE) FEVER
softening	MALACIA
—of bones	OSTEOMALACIA
	RICKETS
sore throat	PRUNELLA
spasm	TIC
—of jaw muscles	TRISMUS
—of muscle fibre	FIBRILLATION
—of muscles	TETANY
spasmodic eye movement	
	NYSTAGMUS
speech disturbance	PARALALIA
spine curvature	
—backwards	KYPHOSIS
—forward	LORDOSIS
—sideways	SCOLIOSIS
spinal cord disease	
	POLIOMYELITIS
	SPINA BIFIDA.SYRINGOMELIA
spine disease	RACHISCHISIS
	RACHITIS.SPONDYLITIS
	SPONDYLOSIS
spleen disease	
	HODGKIN'S DISEASE
splenic anaemia	BANTI'S DISEASE
spongy bone of ear	
	OTOSCLEROSIS
spontaneous bruising	PURPURA
squint	STRABISM(US)
stagnation of bile	CHOLESTASIS
stiff neck	MENINGISMUS
stomach	
—disease	GASTRIC ULCER
	GASTRITIS.PEPTIC ULCER
—pain	COLIC
stone	
—(gallstone)	CALCULUS
—in kidney	NEPHROLITHIASIS
—(small stones)	GRAVEL
streptococcal infection	
	RHEUMATIC FEVER
stroke	APOPLEXY.SEIZURE
struma	GOITRE.SCROFULA
strychnine poisoning	
	STRYCH(NI)NISM

stye	HORDEOLUM	tormina	GRIPES
subnormal body temperature		torn skin beside nail	AGNAIL
	HYPOTHERMIA		HANGNAIL
sugar in urine	GLUCOSURIA	torticollis	WRYNECK
	GLYCOSURIA	touch-me-not	LUPUS
summer flu	LYME DISEASE	transmitted by	
superfluous mass of bone		—birds	ORNITHOSIS
	EXOSTOSIS		PSITTACOSIS
suppurative tonsillitis	QUINSY	—cattle	ACTINOBACILLOSIS
sweat blister	SUDAMEN		ACTINOMYCOSIS.ANTHRAX
swelling	TUMOUR.TYMPANY		BRUCELLOSIS
—in nose	RHINOSCLEROMA		FOOT AND MOUTH DISEASE
—made up of blood, etc.			KERATOCONJUNCTIVITIS
	HAEMATOMA		LEPTOSPIROSIS.MALTA FEVER
—of joints	GOUT		RINGWORM.SALMONELLOSIS
—of thyroid	GOITRE		TUBERCULOSIS
swollen lymphatic gland			UNDULANT FEVER
	FARCY-BUD	—cats	TOXOPLASMOSIS
—in groin	BUBO	—dogs	TOXOCARIASIS
syncope	FAINT	—flies	KALA-AZAR
syphilis	POX		SANDFLY FEVER
tabes dorsalis			SLEEPING SICKNESS
	LOCOMOTOR ATAXY		TRYPANOSOMIASIS
talipes	CLUB FOOT	—lice	INTERMITTENT FEVER
tapeworm	HYDATID DISEASE		RELAPSING FEVER.TYPHUS
tea-drunkenness	THEISM	—mites	ACARIASIS.ITCH
teething rash	RED-GUM		SCABIES.SCRUB-TYPHUS
temporary blindness with		—mosquitoes	MALARIA
migraine	TEICHOPSIA		YELLOW FEVER.YELLOW JACK
tetanic spasm of jaw muscles		—rats	TULAR(A)EMIA
	TRISMUS	—rat fleas	PLAGUE
tetanus	LOCK-JAW	—ticks	LYME DISEASE
thanatosis	GANGRENE		INTERMITTENT FEVER
thickening of skin			RELAPSING FEVER
	ELEPHANTIASIS	trembling	TREMOR
thin concave fingernails		trench	
	KOILONYCHIA	—fever	TYPHUS
throat disease	CYNANCHE	—foot	IMMERSION FOOT
DIPHTHERIA.LARYNGITIS		—mouth	VINCENT'S ANGINA
	PHARYNGITIS	trichophytosis	RINGWORM
thrush	APHTHA.CANDIDA	trismus	LOCK JAW
	MONILIASIS	tropical	
thyroid deficiency	MYXOEDEMA	—complication of malaria	
tick			BLACKWATER FEVER
—borne disease		—deficiency of	
RELAPSING FEVER.TYPHUS		—protein	KWASHIORKOR
—fever	EAST COAST FEVER	—vitamin B	
time-zone disease	JET LAG		BERIBERI.PELLAGRA
tinea	RINGWORM	—dengue	BREAKBONE FEVER

—fly-borne	SLEEPING SICKNESS
	TRYPANOSOMIASIS
—fungal	MADURA FOOT
	MADUROMYCOSIS
—mouth infection	NOMA
—mosquito-borne	MALARIA
	YELLOW FEVER
	YELLOWJACK
—parasitic	BILHARZIA(SIS)
	BILHARZIOSIS.DELHI BOIL
DUMDUM FEVER.FRAMBOESIA	
GUINEA WORM.HOOKWORM	
	KALA-AZAR.LOA
	ORIENTAL SORE.YAWS
—rodent-borne	LASSA FEVER
—skin diseases	BOBA.BUBA
	BUTTON SCURVY
	FRAMBOESIA.LEPROSY
PINTA.VERRUGA PERUVIANA	
	YAWS
—undernourishment	
	KWASHIORKOR
trypanosomiasis	
	SLEEPING SICKNESS
tuberculosis of	
—lungs	CONSUMPTION
	PHTHISIS
—lymph nodes	KING'S EVIL
	SCROFULA
—skin	LUPUS (VULGARIS)
—vertebrae	POTT'S DISEASE
tuberculous lesion	
	TUBERCULOMA
tular(a)emia	RABBIT FEVER
tumour	
—connected with teeth	
	ODONTOMA
—jelly-like	MYXOMA
—yellow	XANTHOMA
tumour of	
—blood vessels	AGIOMA.NAEVIS
—bone	OSTEO(CLASTO)MA
	SARCOMA
—connective tissue	SARCOMA
—of brain	GLIOMA
—fat	LIPOMA
—gums	EPULIS
—kidney	NEPHROBASTOMA
—lungs	MESOTHELIOMA

—lymph glands	LYMPHOMA
—membrane	CARCINOMA
—muscle	MYOMA.SARCOMA
—nerve tissue	NEUROMA
—papilla	PAPILLOMA
—pigmented skin	MELANOMA
—uterus	FIBROID
tumour on	
—eyelid	STY(E)
—mucous membrane	POLYP(US)
—skin	RODENT ULCER
turning in of eyelashes	TRICHIASIS
twisted intestine	VOLVULUS
typhoid fever	ENTERIC FEVER
	GASTRIC FEVER
typhus	GAOL FEVER.JAIL FEVER
PUTRID FEVER.SHIP FEVER	
	TRENCH FEVER
typist's cramp	TENOSYNOVITIS
ulceration	PHAGED(A)ENA
unconsciousness	COMA
undulant fever	BRUCELLOSIS
	MALTA FEVER
MEDITERRANEAN FEVER	
	NEAPOLITAN FEVER
	ROCK FEVER
uniform muscular	
spasm	TONIC SPASM
unpigmented skin	LEUKODERMA
	VITILIGO
unremembered automatic	
behaviour	FUGUE
urinary organ infection	UROSIS
urticaria	NETTLE RASH.HIVES
vaccinia	COWPOX
varicella	CHICKENPOX
	WATERPOX
variola	SMALLPOX
verruca	PAPILLOMA.WART
verruga Peruviana	BOBA.BUBA
	BUTTON SCURVY
	FRAMBOESIA.YAWS
vertigo	GIDDINESS
vesicle	BLISTER
Vincent's angina	TRENCH MOUTH
viral disease	VIROSIS
wall-eye	GLAUCOMA
war neurosis	SHELL SHOCK
wart	PAPILLOMA.VERRUCA

wasting
—away   ATROPHY.MARASMUS
—diseases   HECTIC FEVER
                PHTHISIS.TABES
—of muscle tissue   DYSTROPHY
water
—borne diseases   CHOLERA
    LEGIONNAIRES' DISEASE
                     TYPHOID
—brash   HEARTBURN.PYROSIS
—on the brain HYDROCEPHALUS
—pox   VARICELLA
weak physical condition
         CACHEXIA.CACHEXY
Weil's disease   LEPTOSPIROSIS
whisky-liver   CIRRHOSIS
white
—leg   PHLEGMASIA
—patches
   —on skin   LEUKODERMA
   —on membrane   LEUKOPLAKIS
whitlow   PANARITIUM
                PARONYCHIA
whooping cough   PERTUSSIS
Wilm's tumour
        NEPHROBLASTOMA
wolf-madness   LYCANTHROPY
wooden-tongue
      ACTINOBACILLOSIS
woody-tongue
      ACTINOBACILLOSIS
woolsorter's disease   ANTHRAX
word
—blindness   DYSLEXIA
—substitution   PARAPHASIA
wound   TRAUMA
writer's cramp
      SCRIVENER'S PALSY
wryneck   TORTICOLLIS
yaws   BEJEL.BOBA.BUBA
     BUTTON SCURVY
     FRAMBOESIA.MORULA
     VERRUGA PERUVIANA
yellow
—fever   VOMITO.YELLOW JACK
—tumour   XANTHOMA
yellowing   JAUNDICE
zoster   HERPES.SHINGLES
     (*see also* without[2])

disfigure
disfigure a large...   LAAGER
disfiguring icon   COIN
disfiguration of Roman...
                 MANOR
     NORMA.RAMON
disguise
disguised as priest   PIASTRES
disguised by *   incl in *
•a king *disguised by* man   LEARN
disguising a...   incl A
disguising *   incl *
•man *disguising* a king   LEARN
disguising m/any how/itzers
               ANYHOW
dish out gruel   LUGER
disheartened b(o)y   BY
dishevelled robes   BORES.SOBER
dishonest tendency   BENT
disintegrate
disintegrating meteor   REMOTE
disintegrations per minute   DPM
dislike   THING
dislocated elbow   BELOW.BOWEL
dismantle   UNDRESS
dismembered cats   SCAT
dismiss
dismissed   OFF.OUT
dismissing a   omit A
dismissing *   omit *
•co(lone)l *dismissed* single... COL
disorder
disorder I cannot...   CONTAIN
disorder of bowels   ELBOWS
disorderly trainer   TERRAIN
           (*see also* disease)
disorganised army   MARY.MYRA
disorient
disorientation of brain   BAIRN
disoriented by all...   BALLY
dispatch
dispatched a...   omit A
dispatched *   omit *
•board *dispatched* nothing   BARD
dispense
dispense with a...   omit A
dispense with *   omit *
•pa(ye)r *dispenses with* the *old*...
               PAR

disperse
dispersed much...   CHUM
dispersing a mob   BOMA.MOAB
dispersion of gas   SAG
displace
displace a...   omit A
displace *   omit *
•(k)night *displace* king   NIGHT
displace silent...   ENLIST.LISTEN
displaced by a...   BAY
displaced person   DP
displacement of ship   TONNAGE
displacement of ship   HIPS.PISH
display
display of art   RAT.TAR
displayed in Ta/te g/allery   TEG
displaying wares   SWEAR.WEARS
displaying wa/res in/side...RESIN
dispose
dispose of a...   omit A
dispose of leader   omit first letter
dispose of money   omit L
dispose of *   omit *
•moth(er) *disposed of* queen
    MOTH
disposed to rent   ROTTEN
disposition of latest...   FALSETTO
waste *disposal*   SWEAT
    TAWSE
dispossess   EXORCISE
disrupt
disrupted lives   EVILS
disrupting life   FILE.LIEF
disruption entails...   SALIENT
disseminated sclerosis   DS
dissipate
dissipate boredom   BEDROOM
dissipated Poles   LOPES.SLOPE
dissipating asset   SEATS
dissipation of gas   SAG
dissolve
dissolve into tears   RATES.STARE
    TARES
dissolution of later...
    ALTER.RATEL
dissolving a gel   GALE.GAEL
distil
distillation of oils   SILO.SOIL
distilled scent   CENTS

distillers   DCL
distilling gin   -ING
Distinguished
Conduct Medal   DCM
Flying
—Cross   DFC
—Medal   DFM
Service
—Cross   DSC
—Medal   DSM
—Order   DSO
distort
distorted faces   CAFES
distorting views   WIVES
distortion of arch   CHAR
distract
distracted all the...   LETHAL
distractedly paces   SPACE
distraction of a...   OAF
distraught as one is...   ANOESIS
distress
distressed wives   VIEWS
distressing   HAIRCUT(TING)
distressing news I...   SINEW
distribute
distribute alms   SLAM
distributed alms on...   SALMON
distribution of rice   ERIC
District
Attorney   DA
Commissioner   DC
of Columbia   DC
Officer Commanding   DOC
disturb
disturbed sleep   PEELS
disturbing reports   PORTERS
recent *disturbance*   CENTRE
ditch   HAHA
ditch digger   OFFA
divers   SOME.SUNDRY
diverse ways   SWAY.YAWS
divert
diversion into Turin   NUTRITION
diverted stream   MASTER
divide   DIV
a *divided*...   incl A
•a *divided* group   SEAT
divided by a...   incl A
•group *divided* by a...   SEAT

divided by * incl *	
•Hull, say, *divided by* ten	
PORTENT	
dividing * incl in *	
•ten *dividing* Hull, say PORTENT	
divination SORTILEGE	
by/from/with:	
arrows BELINOMANCY	
ashes SPODOMANCY	
TEPHROMANCY	
atmospheric conditions	
AEROMANCY	
augury AURUSPICY	
bible readings BIBLIOMANCY	
birds ORNITHOMANCY	
ORNITHOSCOPY	
books BIBLIOMANCY	
divine inspiration THEOMANCY	
dreams ONEIROMANCY	
ONEIROSCOPY	
dropping of food scraps by	
birds TRIPUDIUM	
feast spread over	
sacrifical victims CRITHOMANCY	
fingernails ONYCHOMANCY	
finger rings DACTYLIOMANCY	
fire PYROMANCY	
flames LAMPADOMANCY	
flights of birds ORNITHOMANCY	
hands CH(E)IROMANCY	
images on earth GEOMANCY	
inspection of liver HEPATOSCOPY	
knots in umbilical cord	
OMPHALOMANCY	
lot CIEROMANCY	
mirrors CATOPTROMANCY	
movements of	
—axe AXINOMANCY	
—mice MYOMANCY	
numbers NUMEROLOGY	
objects used in sacrifice	
HEIROMANCY	
observation of animals	
ZOOMANCY	
oracles THEOMANCY	
plants BOTANOMANCY	
playing cards CARTOMANCY	
rods RHABDOMANCY	
sieve and shears COSCINOMANCY	

smoke CAPNOMANCY	
soles of feet PEDOMANCY	
spirits of the dead NECROMANCY	
NIGROMANCY	
splits in burning shoulder	
blades OMOPLATOSCOPY	
stomach sounds GASTROMANCY	
stones LITHOMANCY	
transparent bodies	
CRYSTALLOMANCY	
walking in spirals	
and fainting GYROMANCY	
water HYDROMANCY	
wine OENOMANCY	
divine DD	
divine substance SENSE	
divorced DIV	
dizzy city SWIMMING BATH	
do	
do a *turn* OD	
do badly SWINDLE	
do *fully* DITTO	
do gooder S.ST	
do in HOUSE PARTY	
do *wrong* OD	
do you know JUNO	
doesn't go REMAINS	
STAYS.STOPS	
doesn't get a... omit A	
doesn't get on omit ON	
doesn't get * omit *	
•B(ill)y *doesn't get* ill BY	
doesn't include a... omit A	
doesn't include * omit *	
•fa(the)r *doesn't include*	
the... FAR	
doesn't make amen(ds) AMEN	
doesn't start (p)lay LAY	
doing the rounds	
near the... EARTHEN	
don't begin (t)o... O	
don't change it STET	
don't finish son(g) SON	
don't open (t)he... HE	
don't stand SIT	
don't start (t)o... O	
don't stop GOON	
don't take a... omit A	
don't take * omit *	

•so(me) *don't take* me. . .	SO
don't tear off. . .	RIPON

docked

docked animal	DO(g)
docked wages	PA(y)

doctor¹   BM.DR.GP.LEECH
                MD.MO.WHO

hence

•dr copying	DRAPING
•dr not well	DRILL
•dr with one. . .	DRONE
•dr works	DROPS

and

•Dr Hill	MOTOR
•dr on unknown. . .	MOONY
•dr with your *old*. . .	MOTHY

doctor²

of

Canon and Civil Law	JUD.UJD
Civil Law	DCL.JCD
Dental Surgery	DDS
Divinity	DD
Education	DED
Engineering	DENG.DING
Law	LLD
Letters	DLIT(T).LHD.LITD
Literature	DLIT.LITD
Medicine	MD
Music	DMUS
Philosophy	DPH.PHD
Science	DSC.SCD
Theology	DTH.THD

doctor³

Doctor <u>Cameron</u>	CREMONA
	ROMANCE
doctored <u>wines</u>	SINEW.SWINE
doctors	BMA
doctors' dance	MEDICINE BALL
doctor's paper-knife	LANCET

doctrine	-ISM
document	MS
doddering <u>old men</u>	DOLMEN

dodge

dodge <u>past</u>	PATS.TAPS
dodged <u>issues</u>	SUISSE
dodging <u>rain</u>	IRAN.RANI

doesn't	(*see* do)
dog¹	BARKER.CUR.MUTT
hence	

•dogbasket	CURBED
•dogfish	CURLING
•dog trial	CURTEST
•dogged, *say*	KURD
•rear of dog	CURTAIL

and

•dog on. . .	MUTTON

dog²

dogfight	BLENHEIM
dogfood	CHOW
Dog star	SIRIUS
dogged policeman	HANDLER

dog(s)³

African	BASENJI
	RHODESIAN RIDGEBACK
Alsatian	GERMAN SHEEPDOG
Arab	SALUKI
Australian	KELPIE.KELPY
—wild	DINGO
badgerhound	BASSET(HOUND)
	DACHSHUND
Belgian	BOUVIER DE FLANDRES
	LAEKENOIS.MALINOIS
	TURVUEREN
bloodhound	LIME-HOUND
	LYAM-HOUND
	LYME-HOUND.SLEUTH-HOUND
boarhound	GERMAN MASTIFF
	GREAT DANE
bulldog	
—x mastiff	BULL MASTIFF
—x terrier	BOSTON TERRIER
	BULL TERRIER
butterfly dog	PAPILLON
Canadian	NEWFOUNDLAND
cartoon	LADY.PLUTO.TRAMP
Chinese	CHOW-CHOW
	PEKIN(G)ESE
	SHAR PEI.SHIHTZU
coach-dog	CARRIAGE-DOG
	DALMATIAN
coarse-haired terrier	GRIFF
cross-bred	CUR.MONGREL.MUTT
	POOCH.TYKE.WOLF-DOG
	YELLOW-DOG
curly-tailed	TRENDLE-TAIL(ED)
	TRINDLE-TAIL(ED)
	TRUNDLE-TAIL(ED)
Dalmatian	LESSER DANE

Dutch	KEESHOND.SCHIPPERKE
Eskimo	HUSKY
	MALAMUTE.MALEMUTE
extinct	TALBOT
female	BITCH
film star	LASSIE
Finnish	LAIKA.SPITZ
French	BRIARD.CHIEN
German	AFFENPINSCHER
	ALSATIAN.BOXER
	DACHSHUND
	DOBERMAN(N) (PINSCHER)
	ROTTWEILER.SCHNAUZER
	TECKEL.WEIMARANER
greyhound	LONG-TAIL
—hybrid	LURCHER
—x spaniel	WHIPPET
—x terrier	WHIPPET
gun dog	BRITTANY
	CHESAPEAKE BAY.CLUMBER
	COCKER.FIELD SPANIEL
	LABRADOR.POINTER
	MUNSTERLANDER
	RETRIEVER.SETTER.SPINNONE
	SPRINGER.WEIMARANER
heavy-jawed dog	JOWLER
hunting dog	AFGHAN.ALAN(D)
	ALANT.BASSET.BEAGLE
	BRACH.BRA(T)CHET.COURSER
	DACHSHUND.DEERHOUND
	GREYHOUND.HARRIER
	IBIZAN.IRISH WOLF HOUND
	OTTER HOUND
	PHAROAH HOUND
	POINTER.RETRIEVER
	RHODESIAN RIDGEBACK.SALUKI
	SETTER.SLOUGHI.SPITZ
hunting by scent	RACHE.RATCH
Indian (wild)	DHOLE
Irish	IRISH TERRIER
Italian	NEAPOLITAN MASTIFF
	SPINONE.VOLPINO
Japanese	AKITA.CHIN
large	GREAT DANE
	NEWFOUNDLAND
	ST BERNARD
long	
—bodied	BEDLINGTON (TERRIER)
	BLENHEIM.DACHSHUND

—eared	BASSET.BEAGLE
	BLOODHOUND.SPANIEL
loose-skinned	SHAR PEI
Mexican	CHIHUAHUA
mountain dog	ESTRELA
	PYRENEAN.ST BERNARD
Isaac Newton's dog	DIAMOND
Norwegian	ELKHOUND
Nottinghamshire	
	CLUMBER (SPANIEL)
old	LYM.SHOUGH.SHOWGHE
otter-hunting	OTTER HOUND
performing tricks	TUMBLER
Persian	SALUKI
pet	LAPDOG.TOY DOG.POODLE
Pomeranian	SPITZ
Punch's dog	TOBY
racing dog	GREYHOUND
	WHIPPET
rough-coated greyhound	
	DEERHOUND
Russian	BORZOI.WOLFHOUND
	SAMOYED(E)
Scottish	CAIRN (TERRIER)
	DANDIE DINMONT.MESSAN
	SCOTCH TERRIER.SCOTTIE
	SKYE TERRIER
shaggy dog	ICELAND DOG
	OLD ENGLISH SHEEPDOG
	SHOCK.SHOUGH
sheepdog	COLLIE.COLLY
	MAREMMA
short	
—eared	ALAN(D).ALANT
—legged	BEAGLE
	DACHSHUND.SEALYHAM
silky-haired	MALTESE
small hunting	JACK RUSSELL
	KENNET
snub-nosed	BULLDOG.PUG
Spitz	POMERANIAN
spotted	DALMATIAN
staghound	BUCKHOUND
	DEERHOUND
stray on race-course	DERBY DOG
Swedish	VALLHUND
tailless	SCHIPPERKE
terriers	AUSTRALIAN.AIREDALE
	BORDER.BOSTON.BULL

	CAIRN.DANDY DINMONT	**don't**	(see do)
	GLEN OF IMAAL.IRISH	**doodlebug**	VI
	LAKELAND.KERRY BLUE	**door catch**	WICKET
	NORFOLK.NORWICH.SCOTTISH	**dope**	ASS
	SEALYHAM.SKYE.SMOOTH FOX	**Doric**	DOR
	STAFFORDSHIRE BULL.WELSH	**double**[1]	BI-.DI-.KA
	WEST HIGHLAND.WIRE FOX	hence	
Tibetan	LHASA APSO.SHIH TZU	•double carriageway	BIRD
	TIBETAN MASTIFF	•Doubleday	BID
	TIBETAN SPANIEL	•double the *French*	BILE
toy	AFFENPINSCHER	and	
	AUSTRALIAN SILKY TERRIER	•Doubleday	DID
	BICHON FRISE	•double double	DIKA
	BRUSSELS GRIFFON	•double poem	DIODE
	CHIHUAHUA	**double**[2]	
	ITALIAN GREYHOUND	act	DODO
	JAPANESE CHIN	carriageway	MIMI
	KING CHARLES'S SPANIEL	chant	SING-SING
	LOWCHEN.MALTESE	dose of sulphur	SS
	MINIATURE PINSCHER	feature	CHIN-CHIN
	PAPILLON.PEKIN(G)ESE	life	ISIS
	POMERANIAN.POODLE.PUG	lot of food	CHOW-CHOW
	YORKSHIRE TERRIER	meat ration	CHOP-CHOP
tracker	BLOODHOUND	note	MIMI
Turkish	ANATOLIAN	rations	CHOW-CHOW
watchdog	BULLDOG.MASTIFF	share of profits	DIVI-DIVI
	HOUSE DOG	your money	LL
Welsh	CORGI	**double**[3]	
wild		double cross	TWENTY
—Australian	DINGO		TWO TIMES
—Indian	DHOLE.PARIAH	double-*header*	D
	PI(E)-DOG.PYE-DOG	double vision	DOPPELGANGER
wretched	CUR.HUNT-COUNTER		LOOK-SEE
young	CUB.PUP(PY)	*doublet*	TT
	SLEEVE-DOG.WHELP	**doubly**	
young hound(s)	ENTRY	deep	SEA BASS
dollar	DOL.S	good	BONBON
dollar area	BUCKS	loud	FF
dollar pieces	CENTS.DIMES	quiet	HUSH-HUSH.PP
	NICKELS	**doubt**	ER.UM
domestic boiler	(TEA-)KETTLE	doubter	THOMAS
dominant bird	TOPKNOT	*doubtful* result	LUSTRE
donkey	ASS.NED	**dove**	(see pigeon)
don		**down**	
don *	incl in *	down-hearted	incl LOW
•king *dons* ha-t	HART	•s-ing down*heart*edly	SLOWING
—*donned by* *	incl *	down-*hearted*	OW
•ha-t *donned by* king	HART	downfall	HAIL.RAIN.SLEET.SNOW
dons	SCR-	down-market bird	EIDER(DUCK)

drachma	DR	**drink¹**	
draft	DFT	*drink* *	incl *
drag		•wa-g *drinks* gin	WAGING
drag *back*⟨	GUL.WARD	drink pop	HOCK
drag-race	ACRE.ACER.CARE	drink time	PORTERAGE
drag swag	HAUL	drink wine	SUPPORT
drag *up*(D) ↑	GUL.WARD	drink *up*	STIRRUP-CUP
dragging a log	GAOL.GOAL	drink *up*(D) ↑	EMIL.PIN.PUS
dram	DR	*drunk by* *	incl in *
dramatist	SHAKESPEARE.SHAW	•gin *drunk by* wa-g	WAGING
	TERENCE.WILDE	*drunk on* gin	-ING
drastic step	PETS	drunken nap	TIDDLYWINKS
draw	TIE.X	drunken sailor	HIGHJACK
draw from t/he r/anks	HER	*drunken* sots	TOSS
draw game	TIEPOLO	**drink²**	
draw in a. . .	incl A	acid drink	SOUR
draw in *	incl *	African	POMBE.SKOKIAAN
•sh-ow *draws in* everybody		aguardiente	BRANDY
	SHALLOW	alcoholic, sweetened	LIQUEUR
drawn in by *	incl in *	ale	TIPPER
•everybody *drawn in by*		—and honey	BRAGGET
sh-ow	SHALLOW	—cheap	TWOPENNY.FOUR-ALE
draw *out*	WARD	—heated and spiced	PURL
drawback⟨	EIT.WARD	—new (Scottish)	SWATS
drawback part. . .⟨	TRAP	—strong	MOROCCO
drawer	ARTIST		NAPPY.NOG.OCTOBER
	DR.MAGNET	—with nutmeg	MACE ALE
drawer *overturned*⟨	RD.REWARD	—with pulped apples, etc.	
drawing	(*see* write³)		LAMB'S-WOOL
drawing material	TOBACCO	—with roasted apples, etc.	
dreadful rage	GEAR		WASSAIL
dreamer	JOSEPH	aniseed liqueur	OUZO
dress	DON	aperitif	CAMPARI.CINZANO
dress business	SHIFTWORK		DUBONNET.MARTINI
dressed by *	incl in *		OUZO.PASTIS.PERNOD
•fish *dressed by* ma-n	MAIDEN		RICARD.SHERRY.SUZE
dressed up in gown	OWNING		VERMOUTH
dressed up in *	incl in *	bad	
•king *dressed up in* robe	GROWN	—beer	SWIPES
dressing a. . .	incl A	—liquor	ROTGUT
dressing *	incl *	—whisky (American)	
•ma-n *dressing* a fish	MAIDEN		TARANTULA JUICE
dressmaker	NEEDLE	beer	BITTER.MILD.WALLOP
	SATIN.SILK.etc.	—and gin	DOG'S NOSE
drifting ship	HIPS.PISH	—and ginger-beer	
drilling			SHANDY(GAFF)
drilling rig	BRACE	—and ground ivy	GILL ALE
drilling site	DENTIST'S CHAIR		GILL BEER
	PARADE GROUND	—and lemonade	SHANDY(GAFF)

—Australian	AMBER.FROSTY GROG
—cheap	FOUR-ALE
—Egyptian	BO(U)SA.ZYTHUM
—German	BOCK.LAGER PILS(E)NER
—Russian	KWASS.QUASS
bingo	BRANDY
bitters	ANGOSTURA FERNET BRANCA KHOOSH.ORANGE.PEACH UNDERBERG
blue ruin	GIN
brandy	AQUA VITAE.BINGO EAU DE VIE
—and water	BRANDY PAWNEE MAHOGANY
—and soda	PEG
—distilled from	
—wine	FINE CHAMPAGNE
—fruit juices (American)	MOBBIE.MOBBY
—grape pomace	MARC
—French	ARMAGNAC COGNAC.FINE
—Italian	GRAPPA
—Mediterranean	ROSOLIO
—obsolete	NANTZ
—Portuguese	AGUARDIENTE
—South African	CAPE SMOKE
—Spanish	AGUARDIENTE
Brazilian	ASSAI
champagne	SILLERY.THE WIDOW VEUVE CLIQUOT
—Indian	SIM(P)KIN
cider from sweet apples	SCRUMPY
cocktail	
—brandy/cointreau	SIDECAR
—brandy/crème de cacao	ALEXANDER
—brandy/ginger-ale	HORSE'S NECK
—champagne/Guinness	BLACK VELVET
—gin/Dubonnet	DUBONNET
—gin/cointreau	WHITE LADY
—gin/lemon or lime	GIN FIZZ GIN SOUR.TOM COLLINS
—gin/vermouth	MARTINI

—gin/vermouth/fruit juice	BRONX
—gin/white of egg	PINK LADY
—rum/calvados	KICKER
—rum/lime	DAQUIRI
—rye/vermouth	MANHATTAN
—sherry/vermouth	BAMBOO
—vodka/orange juice	SCREWDRIVER
—vodka/tomato juice	BLOODY MARY
—whisky/vermouth	ROB ROY
—whisky/lemon juice	WHISKY SOUR
coffee and whiskey	IRISH COFFEE
cognac	BRANDY.FINE
cordial	PERSICO(T)
—after coffee	POUSSE-CAFE
—from anise	ANISETTE
—from raisins	ROSO(G)LIO
—from sundew juice	ROSA-SOLIS
curdled cream	SILLABUB SYLLABUB
demerara	RUM
distilled from wine	BRANDY
dry sherry	AMONTILLADO FINO.MANZANILLA
East Indian	NIPA
eastern	ARAK.ARRACK
effervescent	SHERBET
extra strong porter	STOUT
fermented	
—grape juice	WINE
—palm juice	TODDY
—palm sap	NIPA.SURA
—rice	RICE BEER
fizzy	GINGER ALE.GINGER BEER LEMONADE.SODA WATER
for toasts	WASSAIL
fortified wine	PORT
from	
—agave (Mexican)	TEQUIL(L)A
—anise	PERNOD
—apples	CALVADOS.CIDER POMAGNE
—aromatic herbs	HERB BEER HERB TEA
—barley	PTISAN.TISANE
—cacao seeds	COCOA
—Coffea seeds	COFFEE

—dandelions, sassafras ROOT BEER
—dough and sugar (American) HOO(T)CH
—fruit RATAFIA
—fruit-refuse MARC(-BRANDY)
—herbs BITTERS
—honey (Welsh) METHEGLIN
—mint PEPPERMINT
—orchis SALOOP
—pears PERRY
—sassafras SALOOP
—walnuts NOCINO
fruit juice CRUSH.LEMONADE
LIMEADE.ORANGEADE
SHERBET.SQUASH
—and vinegar (American) SHRUB
fruit syrup ROB.SUCCADE
geneva GIN
gin BLUE RUIN.MAX
MOTHER'S RUIN
OLD TOM.TWANKAY
—and treacle MAHOGANY
—and vermouth GIN AND IT
—and water GIN SLING
—Dutch HOLLANDS
SCHNAP(P)S.SCHIEDAM
—effervescent GIN FIZZ
—with angostura PINK GIN
grain and juniper berries
GENEVA GIN.HOLLANDS
grape juice with
brandy, etc. GEROPIGA
Greek spirit OUZO.RAKEE.RAKI
—wine RETSINA.RESINATA
Holland gin SCHNAP(P)S
Hollands GIN.SCHIEDAM
honey and
—mulberry juice MORAT
—water HYDROMEL.MEAD
hot
—drink NEGUS.RUMFUSTIAN
—rum and eggs TOM-AND-JERRY
Indian
—champagne SIM(P)KIN
—spirit SOMA
intoxicating liquor BOOSE
BOOZE.BOUSE
—American TANGLEFOOT

Irish GUINNESS
—illicit whiskey POT(H)EEN
Italian
—brandy GRAPPA
—liqueur NOCINO
—vermouth IT
lemon juice with spirits SHRUB
lettuce juice THRIDACE
light beer LAGER.PILS(E)NER
TABLE BEER
liqueur
—after dinner POUSSE-CAFE
—from
—aniseed
—(French) ANISETTE
—(German) GOLDWASSER
—(Greek) OUZO
—apples CALVADOS
—apricots APRICOT BRANDY
—brandy ARMAGNAC
COGNAC
—caraway KUMMEL
—cherries CHERRY BOUNCE
CHERRY BRANDY
KIRSCH(WASSER)
MARASCHINO
—France ANISETTE
—herbs BENEDICTINE
CHARTREUSE
—Holland ADVOCAAT
—Italy STREGA
—Jamaica TIA MARIA
—nut kernels NOYAU
—orange peel CURACAO
CURACOA
—oranges COINTREAU
GRAND MARNIER
—peaches PEACH BRANDY
—peppermint
CREME DE MENTHE
—plums MIRABELLE
PRUNELLE.SLIVOVITZ
—Scotland DRAMBUIE
—sloes SLOE GIN
—tangerines
—(French) MANDARINE
—(South African)
VAN DER HUM
—walnuts NOCINO

—West Indies
CREME DE CACAO
—made at Fécamp BENEDICTINE
—with rum, lime juice, etc.
RUM-SHRUB
liquor GOOD STUFF.MALT.TIPPLE
—Scottish SKINK.STRUNT
Madeira LONDON PARTICULAR
Malay rum TAFIA
malt liquor JOHN BARLEYCORN
STINGO
Martinique spirit
EAU DE CREOLES
max GIN
medicated ale SCURVY-GRASS
medicinal PTISAN.TISANE
mediocre beer (Scottish)
SWANK(E)Y
Mediterranean spirit RAKEE
RAKI.ROSOLIO
Mexican PEYOTE.TEQUIL(L)A
milk with spirits MILK-PUNCH
mineral water EVIAN.SELTZER
VICHY (WATER)
mixed drink TWIST
mixture added to weak
beer STUM
molasses and water SWITCHEL
mother's ruin GIN
muscatel MUSCAT.MUSCADINE
negus RUMFUSTIAN
new
—ale (Scottish) SWATS
—wine STUM
Norwich strong ale NOG
of the gods NECTAR
Old Tom GIN
Paraguay tea MATE
Persian BOSA.SHIRAZ
Philippines rice beer PANGASI
plum brandy QUETSCH
SLIVOVITZ.SLIVOVIC(A)
SLIVOVITZ
Portuguese brandy
AGUARDIENTE
posset made with sack
SACK-POSSET
quince juice and sugar QUIDDANY
raisin wine BASTARD

Red Indian whiskey HOO(T)CH
red wine and methylated
spirit RED BIDDY
revived wine STUM
rice spirit (China) SAMSHOO
SAMSHU
rum DEMERARA.GROG
NELSON'S BLOOD
—and water GROG
—(Malayan) TAF(F)IA
—punch RUMBO
Russian
—beer KWASS.QUASS
—spirit VODKA
Scandinavian spirit AKVAVIT
AQUAVIT
Scottish ATHOLL BROSE
HEATHER ALE
—sour, stale or thin liquor TIFT
—spiced, hot PLOTTIE.PLOTTY
—whisky GLENLIVET.MALT
SCOTCH
sherry with lemon, etc.
SHERRY-COBBLER
sherry-type MADEIRA
small beer SWIPES
soft LEMONADE.LIMEADE
ORANGEADE
—American COCA-COLA
PEPSI-COLA.SARSAPARILLA
sour liquor TIFF
South American spirit ASSAI
CHICHA.DEMERARA
MATE.YERBA
Spanish
—fortified wine SHERRY
—liquor AGUARDIENTE
—wine ALICANT.MALAGA
PETER-SEE-ME
RIOJA.TARRAGONA
Shakespearean BASTARD
SHERRIS-SACK
spiced
—sherry, etc. NEGUS
—sweetened wine PIMENT
—wine HIPPOCRAS.SANGAREE
SANGRIA
spicy wine MUSCADEL
MUSCATEL

spirit
—cocktail   SWIZZLE
—from
  —aniseed   ABSINTHE
  —asclepiad   SOMA
  —blue plums   SLIVOVITZ
  —golden plums   MIRABELLE
  —pears   EAU DE VIE
  —purple plums   QUETSCH
  —raspberries   EAU DE VIE
  —rice   SAMSHOO.SAMSHU
  —rye   RYE WHISKY
  —sugar cane   RUM
  —sweet potatoes   MOBBIE
                                MOBBY
—Italian   GRAPPA
—Greek   OUZO.RAKI
—Mediterranean   RAKI
—Russian   VODKA
—Scandinavian   AKVAVIT
         AQUAVIT.SCHNAP(P)S
—sour or stale   TIFF
—with water, spice, etc.   PUNCH
—with hot water, sugar   TODDY
stale liquor   TIFF
strong
—ale   MOROCCO.NAPPY
                       OCTOBER
—(Norwich)   NOG
—beer   MARCH BEER
—liquor   HOGAN.HOGEN
—(Shakespeare)   TICKLE-BRAIN
stum   MUST
sugar and water (Sikh)   AMRIT
sugar/water/spices   GINGER WINE
sweet wine   BARSAC.MALVESIE
       MALVOISIE.MALMSEY
       MALVASIA.SAUTERNES
sweetened
—gin   OLD TOM
—spirits (American)   SLING
—spruce shoots   SPRUCE BEER
—wine (W.Indies)   SANGAREE
syrup from
—almonds, sugar, etc.   ORGEAT
—aniseed   ANISETTE
—apples   POMME
—bananas   BANANE
—blackcurrants   CASSIS

—cherries   CERISE
—gooseberries   GROSEILLE
—grapes   RAISIN
—lemons   CITRON
—mint   MENTHE
—pineapple   ANANAS
—plums   PRUNE
—pomegranates   GRENADINE
—prunes   PRUNE
—pure sugar   GOMME
—raspberries   FRAMBOISE
—strawberries   FRAISE
tea   (see tea)
thin liquor   GROG.TIFF
treacle-beer   SWITCHEL
Turkish   AIRAN.BOZA.MASTIC(H)
unfermented
—grape juice   MUST.STUM
—malt and hops   WORT
vinegar and honey   OXYMEL
Welsh spiced mead   METHEGLIN
West Indian
—spirit   MOBBIE.MOBBY
—sweetened wine   SANGAREE
Westmorland ale   MOROCCO
wheatmalt beer   MUM
whisky   AQUA VITAE.AULD KIRK
       GOOD STUFF.HOO(T)CH
MOUNTAIN-DEW.THE CRATUR
           USQUEBAUGH
—American   BOURBON.RYE
          TANGLEFOOT
—poor   REDEYE
—and lemon, etc.
         WHISK(E)Y SOUR
—and soda   HIGHBALL
      STENGAH.STINGER
—from maize   BOURBON
—with hot water, etc.
        WHISKY TODDY
white wine etc.   FUSTIAN
—with wormwood   VERMOUTH
wine
—and juniper berries
           GENEVRETTE
—Caroline   SCUPPERNONG
—French   ANJOU.BARSAC
    BEAUJOLAIS.BEAUNE
    BORDEAUX.BURGUNDY

CHABLIS.CHAMBERTIN	
CHAMPAGNE	
CHATEAUNEUF-DU-PAPE	
CHENAS.CHINON.FLEURIE	
GIGONDAS.GRAVES	
HERMITAGE.JULIENAS.LIRAC	
MACON.MARGAUX.MEDOC	
MERSAULT.MUSCADET	
NUIT ST GEORGES	
POMEROL.POMMARD	
POUILLY-FUISSE	
POUILLY-FUME.ST EMILION	
ST ESTEPHE.ST JULIEN	
SANCERRE.SAUTERNES	
TAVEL.VOLNAY.VOUVRAY	

—German   AUSLESE.BADEN
    HOCK.EISWEIN.KABINETT
    LIEBFRAUMILCH
    JOHANNISBERGER.MOSEL(LE)
    MARCOBRUNNER.NIERSTEINER
    RIESLING.RHEIN WINE
    RHINE(WINE).RUDESHEIMER
    SPATLESE.STEINBERGER

—Greek   KOUTAKIS.METAXIS
    RETSINA

—Hungarian   TOKAY

—Italian   ASTI (SPUMANTE)
    BARBERA.BARDOLINI
    BAROLA.CHIANTI
    FALERNIAN.FRASCATI
    FRIULI.LACHRYMA CHRISTI
    LAMBRUSCO.ORVIETO.SOAVE
    TRENTINO.VALPOLICELLA

—Portuguese   BUCELLAS.DAO
    DOURO.LISBON
    MADEIRA.MATEUS ROSE
    PORT.SANTOS.VINHO VERDE

—Sicilian   MARSALA
    CONSTANTIA

—Spanish   ALICANT(E)JEREZ
    MALAGA.PETER-SEE-ME
    RIOJA.SACK.SHERRY
    TARRAGONA.TORO
    VALENCIA.XERES

—sparkling   ASTI SPUMANTE
    CHAMPAGNE.FRIZZANTE
    MOUSSEC.POMAGNE
    SEKT.VALPOLICELLA

—with lemon, etc.   COBBLER

—with spirit, eggs, etc.   EGG-FLIP
wood alcohol   WOOD SPIRIT
wood spirit   WOOD ALCOHOL

drive   DR
drivers   AA.RAC
driving <u>rain</u>   IRAN.RANI

drop
drop a...   omit A
drop *   omit *
•ski(p) and *drop* coin   SKI
drop a point   omit N.S.E.W
drop dead   omit D
drop end of plan(k)   PLAN
drop litter   FARROW.WHELP
drop money   omit L
drop of water   W
drop off   SLEEP
drop off a...   omit A
drop quietly *off*   omit P
drop off *   omit *
drop out *   omit *
drop*head*   D
*drop*head   omit first letter
•*drop*head (c)ar my...   ARMY
dropped letter   H
•(h)as *dropped* letter   AS
dropping a...   omit A
dropping in   omit IN
•pa(in)ter *dropping* in   PATER
dropping in *   incl *
•*dropping* students *in* river   TALLY
dropping out   omit OUT
•nearly *dropping* out   AB
dropping *   omit *
•(p)arty *dropping* leader   ARTY
dropping zone   PARASITE

drown
drowned in *   incl in *
•learner *drowned in* river   CLAM
drowning a...   incl A
drowning *   incl *
•river *drowning* learner   CLAM

drug^1
drug dispenser   CHEMIST
drug supplier   POPPY.PUSHER

drug(s)^2 ACID.GRASS.LSD.POT
    SMACK.SNOW.SPEED
aloes and canella bark
    HICKERY-PICKERY

HIERA-PICRA.HIGRY-PIGRY
alpha blocker   TOLAZOLINE
amphetamine   METHEDRINE
anabolic steroids   ANAPOLON
ANAVAR.CYPIONATE
DECA DURABOLIN
DIANABOL.NOLVADEX
PARABOLON
STANAZOLOL
anaesthetic   COCAINE
BENZOCAINE.ETHYL CHLORIDE
CHLOROFORM.EUCAIN(E)
EVIPAN.HALOTHANE
LAUGHING GAS.LIGNOCAINE
NITROUS OXIDE.PROCAINE
STOVAINE.THIOPENTONE
analgesic   AMIDOPYRINE
PAIN KILLER.PETHIDINE
antibiotic   AMPICILLIN
CEPHALORIDINE
CHLORAMPHENICOL
ERYTHROMYCIN
GRAMICIDIN.GRISEOFULVIN
MITURAMYCIN.NYSTATIN
POLYMIXIN.STREPTOMYCIN
TETRACYCLINE.VIOMYCIN
antiseptic   MANDELIC ACID
arrow poison   CURARE.CURARI
bactericide   TERRAMYCIN
barbitone   VERONAL
barbiturate   SECONAL
beta blocker ATENOLOL.INDERAL
bhang   INDIAN HEMP
body-building
(ANABOLIC) STEROID
Brazilian   JABORANDI.PAREIRA
cannabis   BHANG.DAGGA
(INDIAN) HEMP
MARIJUANA.POT
causing
—dilation of pupil   MYDRIATIC
—flow of urine   DIURETIC
—vomiting   EMETIC
coramine   NIKETHAMIDE
dagga   BHANG.HASH
(INDIAN) HEMP.LOVE-DRUG
MARIJUANA.POT
diuretic   ACETOZOLAMIDE
MERSALYL

emetic APOMORPHINE.EMETINE
expectorant   APOMORPHINE
for
—contracting pupil   MIOTIC
PILOCARPINE
—reducing fever   ANTIPYRETIC
—stimulating
—brain   NIKETHAMIDE
—breathing   LOBELINE
PICROTOXIN
—central nervous system
BEMEGRIDE
—heart   DIGITALIS
—nervous system   ATROPINE
CAFFEINE.STRYCHNINE
—treating
—abnormal cell growth
VINBLASTINE.VINCRISTINE
—allergies ANTIHISTAMINE
—angina   AMYL NITRATE
BETA BLOCKER
—asthma   EPHEDRINE
—bacterial infections
ANTITOXIN
SULPHONAMIDE.SULPHONE
—blood clotting
ANTI-COAGULANT
COUMARIN.HEPARIN
PHENIDIONE
—diabetes   TOLBUTAMIDE
—dysentery
SULPHAGUANIDINE
—epilepsy   PHENYTOIN
PRIMIDONE
—fast heartbeat   PRACTOLOL
PROPANOLOL
—fragile blood vessels   RUTIN
—goitre   THIOURACIL
—gout   ALLOPURINOL
CHINCHOPHEN.COLCHININE
PROBENECID
—heart disease   DIGITALIS
SQUILL
—high blood pressure
BETA BLOCKER
GUANETHEDINE
RESERPINE
—irregular heartbeat
QUINIDINE

—leprosy   DAPSONE
—malaria   ATABRIN.ATEBRIN
          CHLOROQUINE
    MEPACRINE.PALUDRINE
           PRIMAQUINE
        PYRIMETHAMINE
    QUINACRINE.QUININE
—meningitis SULPHAPYRIDINE
—nasal congestion
          AMPHETAMINE
—nausea   CYCLIZINE
—nervous tension
           NEUROLEPTIC
—peptic ulcers   BANTHINE
—pneumonia SULPHAPYRIDINE
—poliomyelitis SALK VACCINE
—protozoa   TRYPANOCIDE
—psoriasis   CHRYSAROBIN
           DITHRANOL
—rashes   ANTIHISTAMINE
—skin infections
   METHOTREXATE.NEOMYCIN
—sleeping sickness
         PENTAMIDINE
       TRYPARSAMIDE
—staphylococci
       SULPHATHIAZOLE
—stomach disorders   ANTACID
—travel sickness   CYCLIZINE
      DIMENHYDRINATE
         HYOSCINE
—tuberculosis   ISONIAZID(E)
    PAS.STREPTOMYCIN
—worms   PIPERAZINE
    QUASSIA.VERMIFUGE
from
—belladonna   ATROPINE
     HYOSC(YAM)INE
       SCOPOLAMINE
—cinchona   QUIN(ID)INE
—coal tar   SAFFRANIN(E)
—coca leaves   COCAINE
—coffee   CAFFEINE
—datura   STRAMONIUM
—ergot   LSD.LYSERGIC ACID
—foxgloves   DIGITALIS
—fungus   ERGOMETRINE
       ERGOTAMINE
—henbane   HYOSC(YAM)INE

—jaborandi   PILOCARPINE
—lobelia   LOBELINE
—morphine   HEROIN
—mould   PATULIN
—mushrooms   PSILOCYBIN
—nux vomica   STRYCHNINE
—opium   CODEINE.LAUDANUM
    MORPHIA.NARCOTINE
—orchis   SALEP.SALOP
—periwinkle   VINBLASTINE
        VINCRISTINE
—poppies   OPIUM.PAPAVERINE
          RHOEADINE
—rauwolfia   RESERPINE
—strophanthus   OUABAIN
           WABAIN
—tea   THEINE.THEOPHYLLINE
—thorn apple   STRAMONIUM
—toads   BUFOTENIN
—tobacco   NICOTINE
ganglion blocker
       MECAMYLAMINE
grass   MARIJUANA
hallucinatory   BUFOTENIN
       CANNABIS.LSD
LYSERGIC ACID.MESCALIN(E)
          PSILOCYBIN
grief palliative   NEPENTHE
hash(ish)   HASHEESH
       INDIAN HEMP
heart stimulant   CORAMINE
        NIKETHAMIDE
       NORADRENALIN
hemp   BHANG.MARIHUANA
      MARIJUANA.POT
hypnotic   BARBITURATE
        PARALDEHYDE
PHENOBARBITONE.TERONAL
imaginary   SOMA
laxative   LIQUORICE.SENNA
liquefies blood, etc.   VARIDASE
local anaesthetic   COCAINE
         STOVAINE
lysergic acid   LSD
marijuana   BHANG.CANNABIS
    DAGGA.GRASS.HASH
   INDIAN HEMP.POT.TEA
Mexican   JALAP.MESCALIN(E)
mixture of drugs   CRACK

SPEED-BALL
muscle relaxant
    CURARINE.SOMA
narcotic   MANDRAGORA
    MANDRAKE.OPIATE
—antidote   NALOXONE
opium   HOP
painkiller   ANALGESIC.ASPIRIN
    CODEINE.PANADOL
PARACETAMOL.PENTAZOCINE
PETHIDINE.PHENACETIN
PHENAZONE
PHENYLBUTAZONE.SOMA
pot   BHANG.CANNABIS.DAGGA
    HASH.INDIAN HEMP
    MARIJUANA.TEA
reducing
—heart rate   BETA BLOCKER
—temperature   ANTIPYRETIC
relaxant   MEPROBAMATE
    MILTOWN
santonin   WORM-SEED
sedative   CODEINE
MEPROBAMATE.MILTOWN
NEMBUTAL.PHENOBARBITONE
TETRONAL.DESERPIDINE
THALIDOMIDE
strengthening   ROBORANT
sulphonamide   PRONTOSIL
synthetic stimulant
    AMPHETAMINE
BENZEDRINE.EPHEDRINE
METHADONE.PENTAZOCINE
PETHIDINE
tincture of opium   LAUDANUM
    PAREGORIC
tonic   ROBORANT
tranquiliser   CHLORPROMAZINE
DIAZEPAM.HALOPERIDOL
LARGACTIL.LIBRIUM
MEPROBAMATE
PHENOTHIAZINE.RESERPINE
VALIUM
truth drug   HYOSCINE
    SCOPOLAMINE
universal antidote
    MITHRIDATICUM
vegetable   ANDROMEDOTOXIN
    BOTANICAL

worm-seed   SANTONICA
    SANTONIN
drummer   DR
drunk   (in) AL-E.OILED
drunken counsel   OILED SILK
dry   SEC.TT
dry *up*(D) ↑   CES
dual carriageway   MIMI
dubious <u>fate</u>   FEAT
duck[1]   O
hence
•duck feathers   OPINIONS
•duck-house   OCELLAR.OPEN
•duck liver   OLIVER
•duck's eggs   OO
•portion of duck   ORATION
and
•duck *in* the mud   MOIRE
•duck *in* the road   SOT
•eat meal *including* duck   SOUP
and
•duck *on* her. . .   HERO
•father duck   DADO
•leg of duck   LIMBO
•shoot at duck   POTATO
duck *eaten*. . .   incl O
duck-*keeping*   incl O
duck[2]
domestic   AYLESBURY.BARBARY
CAMPBELL.INDIAN RUNNER
MUSCOVY.PEKIN
PERUVIAN.ROUEN
WELSH HARLEQUIN
WHALESBURY
wild   BLACK.EIDER
FERRUGINOUS.GADWALL
GARGANEY.GOLDENEYE
GOOSANDER.HARLEQUIN
LONG-TAILED MALLARD
MANDARIN.MERGANSER
PINTAIL.POCHARD
RING-NECKED.RUDDY
SCAUP.SCOTER.SHELDUCK
SMEW.SHOVELER.TEAL
TUFTED.WIGEON
due *for conversion*   EDU.-UDE
<u>duff</u> <u>part</u>   RAPT.TRAP
duke   FIST
duke's protector

	KNUCKLE-DUSTER
dull film	TARNISH
duly performed	DP
dunder_head_	D
duplicate	
duplicate essays	GOGO
duplicate _French_ words	MOT-MOT
duplicate keys	AA.BB.CC
	DD.EE.FF.GG
duplicate sounds	HUM-HUM
duplicate tests	MOT-MOT
	(_see also_ two³)
duplicating your...	YORE
Durham area	NE
during	
during he/r ear/ly...	REAR
during Prohibition	(in) DO-NT
during race	(in) T-T
during *	incl in *
•fiddle _during_ pla-y	PLAGUEY
	(_see also_ in²)
Dutch	DU
advocate	PENSIONARY
airline	KLM
bargain	KOOP
capital	D.THE HAGUE
car	DAF
cheese	EDAM.GOUDA
chief magistrate	BURGEMEESTER
	BURGOMASTER
coins	DOIT.FLORIN
—½ farthing	DODKIN.DOIT(KIN)
—penny	STIVER
—florin	GLD.GULDEN.GUILDER
—gold	RIDER
—obsolete	RIX-DOLLAR
—silver	STOOTER
county	AMT
cupboard	KAS
dog	KEESHOND.SCHIPPERKE
donkey	EZEL
drink	AKVAVIT.ACQUAVIT
	ADVOCAAT.HOLLANDS
	SCHIEDAM.SCHNAP(P)S
fair	KERMESS.KERMIS
	KIRMESS
flower	TULIP
game	KORFBALL
half-caste	GRIQUA

head of state	STAD(T)HOLDER
horse	SCHIMMEL
housewife	FROW.WROUW
legal adviser	PENSIONARY
lock/weir	SASSE
knife	SNEE
lace	LANGET
leader	D
magistrate	AMMAN.AMTMAN
	SCHEPEN
man	MYNHEER
meal	MAAL
measures	
—length	DUIM.VOET
—2 acres	MORGEN
—8½ gallons	ANKER
—30-35 gallons	AAM
—(old)	LEAGUER
mister	(MYN)HEER
municipal officer	SCHOUT
my lord	MYNHEER
news agency	ANETA
night	NACHT
path	PAD
pottery	DELFT
president	GRAND PENSIONARY
privateer	CAPER
provincial governor	
	STAD(T)HOLDER
reclaimed land	POLDER
river	MAAS
sea	MEER
ship	BEZANT.BILANDER
	BYLANDER.BUSS
	GAL(L)IOT.HOOKER
	HOWKER.HOY.KOFF.PINKIE
	PINKY.SCHUIT.SCHUYT
sir	MYNHEER
States General	HOGEN-MOGEN
uncle	EME.OOM
vagrant	LANDLOOPER
viceroy	STAD(T)HOLDER
village	DORP
wife/woman	FROW.VROUW
dwarf	DOC
dye	
blue	DYER'S WOAD
coal-tar	SAFRANIN(E)
blackish	NIGROSINE

fuchsia	MAGENTA
magenta	PARAROSANILINE
orange	AN(N)ATTA
	AN(N)ATTO.ARNOTTO
purple	LITMUS.MAUVE
	ORCEIN.TURNSOLE
purple or violet	CUDBEAR
red	PARA-RED

red or purple	CORKIR.KORKIR
red or violet	ARCHIL.ORCHEL(LA)
	ORCHIL(LA).ORSEILLE
reddish-orange	HENNA
yellow	PICRIC ACID
dynamo(meter)	DYN
dyne	DYN

E

Asian. boat. bridge player. east. eastern. Edward. eight. eight thousand.
electron charge. Elizabeth. energy. England. English. epsilon. eta.
European. exa-. five. five thousand. food additive. key. logarithm base. *low-
grade*. natural base. note. *Orient*. *Oriental*. note. Spain. two hundred and
fifty. two hundred and fifty thousand. string. universal set. vitamin.

each		*out* East	omit E
each side of. . . indicates inclusion:		*out* East	SATE.SEAT
•*put* on *each side of* one	ONION	**east²**	E
•ways *on each side of* pond		East Africa	EA
	SPONDEE	East Central	EC
each way indicates a palindrome		East *French*	EST
•look *each way*	PEEP	East *German*	OST
each year	PA	east-north-east	ENE
ear, nose and throat	ENT	east *of Berlin*	OST
early		east *of Paris*	EST
early morning	IAM	east-south-east	ESE
early bird	ARCHAEOPTERYX.EVE	**eastern¹**	E
early birds	BI	hence	
early examples of Roman art form		•Eastern agent	ESPY
to...	RAFT	•Eastern country	ESTATE
early flier	ICARUS.WRIGHT	•Eastern property	EQUALITY
early landfall	ARARAT	•Eastern ruler	EKING
early letters	ATOC	•Eastern traveller	EMIGRANT
early riser	SUN	and	
early sign	S	•in the East	-INE
early sign of spring	S	**eastern²**	
early stage	BUD	acacia	BABLAH.BABUL
early stage	S	banker	SHROFF
early stages of his life	HL	bedcover	PALAMPORE
early transport	PRAM		PALEMPORE
	PERAMBULATOR	bird	ANT-THRUSH
	PUSHCHAIR	bishop	ABBA
early warning system	DEW	—'s vestment	SAKKOS
earn	NET		OMOPHORION
earth		bosun	SERANG
earth-*moving*	HATER.HEART	camel-hair fabric	ABA
	RATHE	chewing nut	BETEL(NUT)
earth *shattering*	HATER.HEART	chieftain	AMEER.EMEER.EMIR
	RATHE	coasting vessel	GRAB
ease	EE.ES	coin	CASH
easily won	NOW.OWN	cymbal	ZEL
east¹	E	dervish	SANTON
hence		disease	BERI-BERI
•East River	-ER	dish	PILAFF.PIL(L)AU
•h-ard *out* East	HEARD		PILAW.PILOW
•in the East	-INE	dress	CHEONG-SAM
East River	GANGES	drink	ARAK.ARRACK

dulcimer	SANTIR.SANT(O)UR
dwarf goose	GOSLET
European Time	EET
eye-shadow	KOHL
folk dance	KOLO
fruit	SEBESTEN
gift	BA(C)KSHEESH.BA(C)KSHISH
	BAKHSHISH.BUCKSHISH
gold bar	TAEL
governor	MUDIR
—'s province	MUDIRIA.MUDIRIEH
guitar	TAMBOURA
gum	GALBANUM
guide	DRAGOMAN
headdress	TURBAN
inn	(CARAVAN)SERAI
	CARAVANSARY
	CHO(UL)TRY.KHAN
interpreter	DRAGOMAN
leader	E
magician	MAGE.MAGUS.ZENDIK
market	BAZA(A)R.SOUK
mendicant	FAKIR
money-changer/lender	SHROFF
musical instrument	PANDORA
	PANDORE.PANDURA
newcomer	GRIFFIN.GRIFFON
novice	GRIFFIN.GRIFFON
order of monks	ACOEMETI
ownerless dog	PARIAH
palm	PALMYRA
paymaster	BUCKSHEE.BUKSHI
pheasant	ARGUS
—plane tree	CHENAR.CHINAR
porter	MAM(M)AL
printed muslin	PERSIENNE
punishment	BASTINADE
	BASTINADO
sailor	LASCAR
saint	SANTON
salutation	SALAAM
ship	JUNK
shrub	BITTER-KING
silk-satin	ATLAS
skirt	SARONG
slipper	BABOOSH.BAB(O)UCHE
Standard Time	EST
tabor	TIMBREL
tambourine	TIMBREL

temple	PAGOD(A)
tip	BA(C)KSHEESH.BA(C)KSHISH
	BAKHSHISH.BUCKSHISH
title	AG(H)A.ALI.RAS
tree	LEBBEK.SEBESTEN
unbeliever	ZENDIK
vase	POTICHE
waterwheel	SAKIA.SAKI(Y)EH
weight	ROTL
whip	K(O)URBASH
	(*see also* Orient)
East Indian	EI
ape	ORANG(UTAN)
aromatic	
—gum	BENZOIN
	GUM BENJAMIN
	JEW'S FRANKINCENSE
—root	GALINGALE
aubergine	EGGPLANT
berry	CUBEB
birds	CASSOWARY
	JAVA SPARROW
	KORA.PADDY-BIRD.RICE-BIRD
	TAILOR-BIRD.WATER-COCK
breadfruit tree	JA(C)K (TREE)
brinjal	EGG-PLANT
civet	BINTURONG.LINSANG
	RASSE
climbing shrub	CUBEB
	GAMBI(E)R
cloth	HUMHUM
coin	BONK.DUIT
condiment	CHUTNEY
currency	Y.YEN
drink	NIPA
drug	ZERUMBET
dyeing process	BATIK
edible fat	KOKUM BUTTER
eggplant	AUBERGINE.BRINJAL
fern	BAROMETZ
fish	ANABAS.POMFRET
flying squirrel	TAGUAN
fruit	CARAMBOLA.MANGO
	MARKING-NUT
	ROSE-APPLE.TAMPOE
gamboge tree	TAMANU
ginger	CASSUMUNAR
ground pigeon	GOURA
gum resin	TACAMAHAC

hat	MITRE	eat turkey	GOBBLE
hibiscus	ROSELLE.ROZELLE	*eat* *	incl *
insectivore	SQUIRREL-SHREW	•man *eats* roll	TROLLED
	TREE-SHREW	*eaten by* *	incl in A
leaders	EI	roll *eaten by* man	TROLLED
lemur	LORIS	*eating away part of* (c)oast	OAST
mat	TAT	eating fish	FINISHING SCHOOL
measures		*eating into* *	incl in *
—dry	GANTANG	•the *French eat into* foo-d	FOOLED

eat[2]

including
  eater of
  eating:

—yard	GUZ	all things	OMNIVOROUS
—30-35 gallons	AAM		PANTOPHAGY
native of New Guinea	BOONG	animals	ZOOPHAGOUS
orange dye	KAMALA.KAMELA	ants	MYRMECOPHAGOUS
	KAMILA	bacteria	BACTERIOPHAGOUS
palm	AT(T)AP.NIPA	bees	APIVOROUS
parrot	LORY	berries	BACCIVOROUS
plant yielding arrowroot	PIA	blood	SANGU(IN)IVOROUS
resting-frame	DUTCH WIFE	bones	OSSIVOROUS
spice	NUTMEG	books (avid reader)	BIBLIOPHAGE
squirrel-shrew	PENTAIL	carrion	NECROPHAGOUS
timber	BLOODWOOD	children	P(A)EDOPHAGOUS
	BRAZIL(-WOOD).JELUTONG	dead bodies	NECROPHAGOUS
trees	ABROMA.AGALLOCH	decaying matter	SAPROPHAGOUS
	AGILA.BILIAN		SAPROZOIC
	B(I)LIMBI(NG).CARAMBOLA	dung	COPROPHAGOUS
	CUCUMBER-TREE		SCATOPHAGOUS
	EAGLEWOOD.EMBLIC(A)	earth	GEOPHAGY
	GARJAN.GURJUN.JELUTONG	family or tribe	ENDOPHAGY
	KAMALA.KAMELA.KAMILA	fish	ICTHYOPHAGOUS
	KUMBUK.KOKUM		PISCIVOROUS
	MANGO.NUX VOMICA	flesh	CARNIVOROUS
	PONTIANAC.PONTIANAK		CREOPHAGOUS
	POON.ROSE-APPLE		SARCOPHAGOUS
	SANDAL(-WOOD).SAP(P)AN	—of strangers	EXOPHAGY
	TAMANU.UPAS.SACK-TREE	frogs	RANIVOROUS
	SUNDARI.SUNDER.SUNDRA	fruit	FRUGIVOROUS
	SUNDRI	fungus	MYCOPHAGOUS
—lizard	DRAGON-LIZARD	god	THEOPHAGY
—shrew	BANGSRING.BANXRING	grain	GRANIVOROUS
tribe	D(A)YAK.IBAN	grass	GRAMINIVOROUS
upas tree	SACK-TREE		HERBIVOROUS
weasel-cat	DELUNDUNG	honey	MELIPHAGOUS
weight (3½ cwts)	BAHAR		MELLIVOROUS
wild		horses	EQUIVOROUS
—hog	BABIR(O)USSA		HIPPOPHAGY
—ox	(*see* ox)		
weapon	TOMBOC		

eat[1]

eat a...	incl A

insects	ENTOMOPHAGOUS	
	INSECTIVOROUS	
leaves	PHYLLOPHAGOUS	
lotus eaters	LOTOPHAGI	
man (cannibal)		
	ANTHROPOPHAGOUS	
many different things		
	POLYPHAGIA.POLYPHAGY	
nails	ONYCHOPHAGY	
nuts	NUCIVOROUS	
nutmegs	MYRISTICIVOROUS	
one kind of		
food	MONOPHAGOUS	
oysters	OSTREOPHAGOUS	
plants	PHYTOPHAGOUS	
poisons	TOXI(CO)PHAGOUS	
raw flesh	OMOPHAGIA	
roots	RADICIVOROUS	
	RHIZOPHAGOUS	
seeds	GRANIVOROUS	
self	AUTOPHAGOUS	
snakes	OPHIOPHAGOUS	
stone	LITHOPHAGOUS	
thistles	CARDOPHAGOUS	
toadstools	MYCOPHAGOUS	
wood	LIGNIVOROUS	
	XYLOPHAGOUS	
wool	MALLOPHAGOUS	
worms	VERMIVOROUS	
eau de Cologne	RHINE	
ebb		
ebb-tide	WATERFALL	
ebbing sea⟨	DEM	
ebbing tide⟨	EDIT	
eccentric	CARD	
eccentric teacher	CHEATER	
eccentric woman	NUTMEG	
eccentric's instrument		
	CARDSHARP	
ecclesiastical member	CHARM	
	(*see also* church)	
echo of guns	SNUG	
economy		
economical bowl	MAIDEN	
economist	MILL.SMITH	
ecstatic	SENT	
Ecuador	EC	
capital	E.QUITO	
coin	SUCRE	

leader		E
eddy		NELSON
edge		
edged by *		incl in *
•feature *edged by* silver		ACHING
edging a. . .		incl A
edging *		incl *
•silver *edging to* feature		ACHING
edges of <u>table</u>		TE
edit		
edited		ED.EDIT
edited <u>indent</u>	INTEND.TINNED
editing <u>text or</u>. . .		EXTORT
edition		ED.EDIT
edition of <u>a last</u>		ATLAS
editor		ED
editor <u>wrote</u>		TOWER
educate		
educated man		MA
educational		
—establishment		ETON.U
—journal		TES
—supplement		TES
educationally subnormal		ESN
EEC		TWELVE
EEC, *say*		EASY
e-emperor		EKING
effort		
effort*less*		omit TRY
•effort*less* indus(try)		INDUS
egg		O.OVAL.SPUR
egghead		E
egg-topping(D) ↑		E
ego-*trip*		GEO-
Egypt		ET
hence		
•Egypt *almost* alon(e)		ETALON
•Egypt *and* her. . .		ETHER
•Egypt *joins with* North America	
		ETNA
and		
•archdeacon *in* Egypt		EVENT
•father *in* Egypt		EPOPT
•I study *in* Egypt		EIDENT
the record is in Egypt		ELOGIST
and		
•charge Egypt. . .		BILLET
•draw Egypt. . .		PULLET
•odds in Egypt		SPINET

Egyptian

beer	BO(U)SA.ZYTHUM
beetle	SCARAB
boat	BARIS
boulevard along Nile	CORNICHE
capital	CAIRO.E
catfish	DOCMAC
characters	ET
Christian	COPT
coin	MILLIEME
—100 milliemes	PIASTRE
—100 piastres	POUND
commander	SIRDAR
cotton	MACO.PIMO.SAK(EL)
cross	ANKH.TAU
crown	ATEF.PSCHENT
dancing girl	ALMA(H).ALME(H)
deities	(*see* gods.goddesses)
double	KA
department	NOME
fish	OXYRHYNCUS.SAIDE
floating vegetation	SUDD
funeral effigy	USHABTI
granite	STENITE
guard	GHAF(F)IR
hat	FEZ
holy rattle	SISTRUM
jar	CANOPIC
king	PHARAOH
leader	E
life symbol	ANKH
lizard	ADDA.WORRAL.WORREL
measures	
—7¹/₂ miles	SCHENE
—100 square feet	AROURA
—209 square yards	QIRAT
—1 acre	FEDDAN
—¹/₂ bushel	KELA
—5 bushels	ARDEB
melon	ABDALAVI
military officer	BIMBASHI
	BINBASHI
mongoose	ICHNEUMON
month	AHET.APAP
National Party	WAFD
peasant(s)	FELLAH(IN)
picture-writing	HIEROGLYPHICS
pike	MORMYRUS
potsherd for writing on	

	OSTRACON.OSTRAKON
precious alloy	ASEM
province	NOME
region of the dead	AMENTI
religious ceremony	DOSEH
river	NILE
royal crown	PSCHENT
ruler	PHARAOH
ruling class	MAMELUKE
secret chamber	SERDAB
serpent emblem	URAEUS
ship	DAHABI(Y)EH
	DAHABBIYEH.DAHABEEAH
soldier-slave	MAMELUKE
soda	TRONA
soul	BA.KA.SAHJ
sultan	MAMELUKE.SOLDAN
tambourine	RIKK
temporary blockage	SUDD
tomb	MASTABA
underground chamber	SERDAB
viceroy	KHEDIVE
—'s wife	KHEDIVA
water lily	LOTE.LOTOS.LOTUS
water-raising mechanism	
	SHADOOF.SHADUF
weight	
—variable	ROTL
—¹/₃ ounce	K(H)AT
—1 ounce	ORIEH
—3 lbs	OKA
—99 lbs	CANTAR.KANTAR
	QUANTAR
white slave	MAMELUKE
wire rattle	SISTRUM

eight

Biblical texts	OCTAPLA
Christmas presents	MILKMAIDS
cleft	OCTAFID
combining form	OCT-
figure of...	SKATING
fold	OCTAPLOID.OCTOPLOID
	OCTUPL(ICAT)E
groups	EIGHTSOME.OCTAD
	OCTAVE.OCTET(T).OCTETTE
	OCTONARY.OCTUOR.OGDOAD
having eight	
—angles	OCTAGONAL
—arms	OCTOPOD

—columns	OCTOSTYLE
—eyes	OCTONOCULAR
—faces	OCTOHEDRAL
—feet	OCTONARIAN.OCTOPOD
—leaves per sheet	OCTAVO
—petals	OCTOPETALOUS
—pistils	OCTOGYNIAN
	OCTOGYNOUS
—rows	OCTASTICHOUS
	OCTOSTICHOUS
—segments	OCTOFID
—sepals	OCTOSEPALOUS
—sides	OCTAGONAL
—stamens	OCTANDRIAN
	OCTRANDROUS
—styles	OCTOGYNIAN
	OCTOGYNOUS
—times normal number of chromosomes	OCTAPLOID
—tones	OCTACHORD
—year intervals	OCTENNIAL
hundred	O.OMEGA
hundred thousand	O.OMEGA
hundredth year	OCTINGEN(TEN)ARY
	OCTOCENTENARY
iron	NIBLICK
nil	EIGHTY
notes	OCTAVE
one over the...	DRUNK.NINE
parts in eights	OCTAMEROUS
pieces of...	COINS
rowers	CREW
yearly	OCTENNIAL
eighteen	MAJORITY.MANAGE
holes	GOLF COURSE
in team	AUSTRALIAN RULES
leaves per sheet	EIGHTEENMO
	OCTODECIMO
eighth	
note	QUAVER
part of circle	OCTANT
eighty	P.PI.R
eighty-eight	PIANO
thousand	P.PI.R
years old	OCTOGENARIAN
	OCTOGENARY
either way	
indicates a palindrome:	

•blow *either way*	TOOT
el(s)	L.(LL.LS)
elastic	
elastic rope	PORE
elasticated edges	SEDGE
elbow bender	BICEPS
elected	IN
electoral system	PR
electric	
electrical	
—capacity	C
—charge	Q
—current	AC.DC.I
—fence	RADIO RECEIVER
—unit	AH.AMP.VOLT
electricity	AC
hence	
•electricity *in* iron	FACE
•electricity money	ACCENTS
•price of electricity	ACCOSTS
	(*see also* current)
electro-	
cardiogram	ECG
convulsive therapy	ECT
encephalogram	ECG
magnetic unit	EMU
motive force	EMF
plated	EP
static unit	ESU
electron	
electron volt	EV
electronic data processing	EDP
elegant	
elegant beasts	NEAT
elegant cape	NEATNESS
elements	
ancient	EARTH.AIR
	FIRE.WATER
modern (alternative or unconfirmed names in brackets):	
actinium	AC
alabamine	(*see* astatine *below*)
alucinium	(*see* beryllium *below*)
aluminium	AL
americum	AM
antimony (regulus)	SB.STIBIUM
argon	A
arsenic	AS

astatine (alabamine)	AT	iron	FE
barium	BA	kalium	(*see* potassium *below*)
berkelium	BK	krypton	KR
beryllium (alucinium,		kurchatovium	
glucinium)	BE		(*see* rutherfordium *below*)
bismuth	BI	lanthanum	LA
boron	B	lawrencium	LR.LW
bromine	BR	lead	PB
cadmium	CD	lithium	LI
caesium	CS	lutetium (cassiopium)	LU
calcium	CA	magnesium	MG
californium	CF	manganese	MN
carbon	C	masurium	
cassiopium	(*see* lutetium *below*)		(*see* technetium *below*)
cerium	CE	mendelevium	MD.MV
chlorine	CL	mercury	AZOTH.HG
chromium	CR	molybdenum	MO
cobalt	CO	neodymium	ND
columbium (niobium)	CB	neon	NE
copper	CU.D.P	neoytterbium	
crypton	(*see* krypton *below*)		(*see* ytterbium *below*)
curium	CM	neptunium	NP
deuterium (diplogen)	D	nickel	NI
didymium (spurious element)		niobium	(*see* columbium *above*)
dysprosium	DY	nitrogen	AZOTE.N
einsteinium	ES	nobelium	NO
erbium	ER	osmium	OS
europium	EU	oxygen	O
fermium	FM	palladium	PD
florentium		phosphorus	P
	(*see* promethium *below*)	platinum	PT
fluorine	F	plutonium	PU
francium (virginium)	FR	polonium	PO
gadolinium	GD	potassium (kalium)	K
gallium	GA	praseodymium	PR
germanium	GE	promethium (florentinium,	
glucin(i)um (beryllium)	GL	illinium)	PM
gold	AU.BULL.OR	pro(to)tactinium	PA
hafnium	HF	radium	RA
hahnium	HA	radon	RN
helium	HE	regulus (antimony)	SB.STIBIUM
helvetium	(*see* astatine *above*)	rhenium	RE
holmium	HO	rhodium	RH
hydrogen (protium, deuterium,		rubidium	RB
tritium)	H	ruthenium	RU
illinium	(*see* promethium *below*)	rutherfordium (kurchatovium)	RF
indium	IN	samarium	SM
iodine	I	scandium	SC
iridium	IR	selenium	SE

silicon	SI
silver	AG.ARGENTUM
sodium	NA
strontium	SR
sulphur	S
tantalum	TA
technetium (masurium)	TC
tellurium	TE
terbium	TB
thallium	TL
thorium	TH
thulium	TM
tin	SN
titanium	TI
tritium	T.WOLFRAM
tungsten	W
uranium	U
vanadium	V
virginium	(*see* francium *above*)
wolfram	W
xenon	XE
ytterbium (neoytterbium)	YB
yttrium	Y
zinc	ZN
zirconium	ZR
elevated land	UP COUNTRY
eleven	LEGS.O.SIDE.TEAM.XI
Christmas presents	PIPERS
having eleven	
—leaves	HENDECAPHYLLOUS
—notes	HENDECACHORD
—pistils	HENDECAGYNIAN
	HENDECAGYNOUS
—stamens	HENDECANDROUS
—styles	HENDECAGYNIAN
	HENDECAGYNOUS
—syllables	HENDECASYLLABIC
hundred	MC
thousand	O
elevens(es)	SNACK
eleventh hour	COFFEE TIME
eliminate	
eliminate a...	omit A
eliminate about...	omit C.CA.RE
eliminate *	omit *
•pur(g)e *eliminates* 1000	PURE
•(p)urge *eliminates* leader	URGE
Eliza's (h)at	AT
ell(s)	L.(LL.LS)

em(s)	M.(MM.MS)
emancipated worker	FREE HAND
embark on journey	J
embarrassed	RED
embarrassed <u>all the</u>...	LETHAL
embarrassing <u>remark</u>	MARKER
embed	
embedded in so/lid o/nyx	LIDO
embedded in *	incl in *
•queen *embedded in*	
stones	ROCKERS
embedding a...	incl A
embedding *	incl *
•stones *embedding*	
queen..	ROCKERS
embody	
embodied in *	incl in *
•old *embodied in*	
attempt...	TRAGEDY
embody a...	incl A
embodying *	incl *
•attempt *embodying*	
old...	TRAGEDY
embrace	
embraced by *	incl in *
•you, *say, embraced by* boy	BUOY
embraced in stron/g ar/ms	GAR
embracing a...	incl A
embracing *	incl *
•boy *embracing* you, *say*	BUOY
embroidered yarn	TALL STORY
embroil	
embroiling a...	incl A
embroiling *	incl *
•row *embroiling* a king	TARIFF
embroiled in *	incl in *
•a king *embroiled in* row	TARIFF
emend	
emendation of <u>line</u>	NILE
emended <u>phrase</u>	SHAPER
emending <u>verses</u>	SERVES
eminent pupil	BIG APPLE
empire	
emperor	EMP.NERO.OTTO
empire state	NY
empire woman	DBE
employ	
employ a...	incl A
employ *	incl *

•student *employed in* b-and	BLAND
employed in m/unit/ions	UNIT

empty¹

empty	incl O
hence	
•*empty* container	-TION
•*empty* bed	COOT
•*empty* ship	SOS
empty-*headed*	start with O
hence	
•empty-*headed* boy	ODES
•empty-*headed* girl	OKAY
•empty-*headed* teacher is. . .	OSIRIS
empty-*headed*	E
hence	
•empty-*headed* boy	EVICTOR
•empty-*headed* girl	EROSE
•empty-*headed* agent	ESPY

empty²

indicates omission of middle:

•*empty* h(ous)e	HE
•*empty* b(a)r	BR

en

en route	(in) R-D.(in) S-T
en voyage	(in) S-S

en(s)   N.(NN.NS)

encage

encaged	(in) C-AGE
encaged by *	incl in *
•owl *encaged by* B-ing	BOWLING
encaged in ste/el m/esh	ELM
encaging a. . .	incl A
encaging *	incl *
•B-ing *encaging* owl	BOWLING

encase

encased in *	incl in *
•gold *encased in* iron	FORE
encasing a. . .	incl A
encasing *	incl *
•iron *encasing* gold	FORE

encipher signal   ALIGNS

encircle

encircle a. . .	incl A
encircle *	incl *
•water *encircles* rat	DERATE
encircled by *	incl in *
•rat *encircled by* water	DERATE

enclose

enclosed in t/he al/tar	HEAL
enclosed in *	incl in *
•auditor *enclosed in* sh-ed	SHEARED
enclosing a. . .	incl A
enclosing *	incl *
•sh-ed *enclosing* auditor	SHEARED
enclosure in wi/de cor/ral	DECOR
large *enclosure*	BI-G

encompass

encompass a. . .	incl A
encompass *	incl *
•pla-n *encompassing* one. . .	PLAIN
encompassed by *	incl in *
•one *encompassed by* pla-n	PLAIN
encompassed in Engli/sh ed/ition	SHED

end

end of	
—crossing	PASSOVER
—crossing	G
—go	TURNOVER
—go	O
—cake	ROLLOVER
—cake	E
—draw	PULLOVER
—draw	W
—filming	TAKEOVER
—filming	G
—June	E
—music	CODA
—music	C
—race	TAPE
—race	E
—season	N
—season	(sum)MER.(win)TER
—the. . .	E
—the road	ED
—the world	D
end off	
•*end off* th(e) ree(d)	THREE
end-to-end lever	REVEL
endless bel(t)	BEL
endless (f)light	LIGHT
endless talk	DISCUS(s)
ends of May and April	MYAL

energy   E

figures   VIM

engage

engaged in war	RAW
engaged in w̄/ar t/o. . .	ART
engaged in *	incl in *
•chief *engaged in* de-ed	DECIDED
engagement ring	WARRING
(*see also* battle)	
engaging a. . .	incl A
engaging *	incl *
•de-ed *engaging* the	
chief. . .	DECIDED

engine

engine driver	STEAM
engineer	ENG
engineer(s)	CE.RE.REME
hence	
•engineers *almost* well off	CERIC
•engineer *gets* wage increase	
	CERISE
•engineer learners *have* nothing	
	CELLO
and	
•engineer designs	REDRAWS
•engineer *with a* vehicle	REBUS
•engineer's gallery	RESTATE
•engineer's teach. . .	RESTRAIN
and	
•engineer's graduated scale	
	REMEDIAL
•engineer's unknown quantity	
	REMEX
engineman	STEPHENSON.WATT

England/English[1] E.ENG

hence

•English clergyman	ERECTOR
•English country	ELAND.ESTATE
•English flower	EASTER
•English landowner	ESQUIRE
and	
•English nation	ENGRACE
•English period	ENGAGE
•English waterfall	ENGRAIN
•English went mad	ENGRAVED
and	
•England's *opening pair*	EN

England/English[2]

as a

—foreign language	EFL
—second language	ESL

capital	E.LONDON
Chamber Orchestra	ECO
Church Union	ECU
country music	
	NATIONAL ANTHEM
Dialect Society	EDS
Golf Union	EGU
language teaching	ELT
leader	E
national emblem	ROSE
patron saint	GEORGE
river	THAMES
Speaking Union	ESU
vale	FAREWELL.GOODBYE

engrave (*see also* write[3])

engraver	ENG
	FUNERAL DIRECTOR
	UNDERTAKER
engravers	RE
engraving	ENG

engulf

engulfed by *	incl in *
•one *engulfed by* wa-ve	WAIVE
engulfed in re/bell/ion	BELL
engulfing a. . .	incl A
engulfing *	incl *
•wa-ve *engulfing* one. . .	WAIVE

Enigma *Variation* GAMINE

enjoying hot weather (in) SU-N

enrol(l)

enrol a. . .	incl A
enrol student(s)	incl L(L)
enrol *	incl *
•I *enrol in* par-ty	PARITY

ensconce

ensconced in *	incl in *
•Premier *has* queen *ensconced*	
in. . .	PERM

enshrine

enshrine a. . .	incl A
enshrine *	incl *
•church *enshrines* a saint	CASTE
enshrined by *	incl in *
•a saint *enshrined by*	
church	CASTE
enshrined by wor/ship/pers	SHIP

ensign ENS

ensnare

ensnare a. . .	incl A

ensnare *	incl *
•rustic *ensnares*	
learner	PLEASANT
ensnared by *	incl in *
•learner *ensnared by*	
rustic	PLEASANT
ensnared in pl/ot her s/ister…	
	OTHERS
entangle	
entangle a…	incl A
entangle *	incl *
•re-ed-*entangled* fin	REFINED
entangled in *	incl in *
•fin *entangled in* re-ed	REFINED
entangled <u>nets</u>	STEN
enter	
entered by *	incl in *
•the river *entered by*	
stream	THRILLER
•animals had *entered*	SHADOWS
entered in da/ta b/ank	TAB
entrance to tunnel	T
Entry of the G̲ladiators	G
I *enter*	incl I
no *entry*	N
⁎ *enters*	incl *
•stream *enters* the river	THRILLER
enthrall	
enthralls a…	incl A
enthralls *	incl *
•state *enthralled* me	CAMEL
enthralled by *	incl in *
•see me *enthralled by* state	CAMEL
enthralled by cine/ma st/ars	MAST
entomology	ENT
enunciated **clause**	CLAWS
environmentalist	GREEN
envy, *say*	NV
enzyme	
breaking down	
—acetyl choline	
	CHOLINE ESTERASE
—adrenaline	
	MONOAMINE OXIDASE
—asparagine	ASPARAGINASE
—bacterial cells	LYSOZYME
—casein	EREPSIN
—cellulose	CYTASE
—fats	LIPASE

—fibrin	FIBRINOLYSIN
—gelatine	EREPSIN
—glucose	GLUCOKINASE
—hydrogen peroxide	CATALASE
—lactose	LACTASE
—proteins	EREPSIN
	PROTEASE.TRYPSIN
—urea	UREASE
digestive	(CHYMO)TRYPSIN
	PAPAIN.PEPSIN
	RENNIN
found in	
—animal secretions	LYSOZYME
—egg-white	LYSOZYME
—liver and kidneys	URICASE
—pancreas	
	CHYMOTRYPSINOGEN
	TRYPSIN.RIBO-NUCLEASE
—pancreatic juices	DIASTASE
—papaya tree	PAPAIN
—plants	LYSOZYME
—saliva	PTYALIN
—small intestine	EREPSIN
—stomach	PEPSIN
inactive	PROENZYME
inverts cane sugar	INVERTASE
producing	
—fructose	INULASE
—grape sugar	MALTASE
—luminosity	LUCIFERASE
—starch from sugar	DIASTASE
—sugar from starch	PTYALIN
promoting	
—alcoholic fermentation	ZYMASE
—oxidation	OXYDASE
epistle	EP
epsilon	E
equal	
equal contest	MATCH
Equal Opportunities	
Commission	EOC
equal *returns*	LEVEL
equestrian appendage	RIDER
erect	
are *erected*(D) ↑	ERA
erect bat(D) ↑	TAB
erected dam(D) ↑	MAD
erection of part(D) ↑	TRAP
was *erected*(D) ↑	SAW

ergo	SO
erratic drive	DIVER
error	
error in the. . .	THINE
errors excepted	EE
errors and omissions	
excepted	EOE
erupt	
erupt in a. . .	AIN.INA
erupting like. . .	KIEL
eruption of Etna	NATE.NEAT
escape	
escaped a. . .	omit A
escaped deer	REED.REDE
escaped from Ber/lin g/aol	LING
escaped king	omit R
escaped queen	omit ER
one *escaped*	omit A.I
I *escaped*	omit I
escudo	ESC
Eskimo	HUSKY.IN(N)UIT
boat	OOMIA(C)K.UMIAK
	KAIAK.KAYAK
boot	MUCLUC.MUCKLUCK
	MUCKLUK
clover	ALSIKE
conjurer	ANGEKKOK
dog	HUSKY.MALAMUTE
	MALEMUTE
fur coat	ANARAK
	ANORAK
house	IGLOO
language	HUSKY
leader	E
especially	ESP
esquire	ESQ
essay	
essay, *say*	SA
essayist	ELIA.LAMB
Essen, *say*	SN
essential in bre/ad mix/ture	ADMIX
Essex, *say*	SX
establish	
established	EST
established church	EC.CE
* *established*	incl *
•one *established in* pos-t	POSIT
estate agent's brochure	
	SEMI-CIRCULAR

estimated	
estimated time of arrival	ETA
estimated time of departure	ETD
eta	E
etchers	RE
Ethiopia(n)	(*see* Abyssinian)
etymology	ETY
Europe(an)	E.EUR
agreement	JA.OUI.OUIJA.SI
articles	ELLA.LATHE.UNDER
Broadcasting Union	EBU
capital	BERLIN.E.PARIS.ROME
cherry	GEAN
city	ESSEN
clover	ALSIKE
Council	CE.EC
deer	ELK
Defence Community	EDC
Development Fund	EDF
dormouse	LEROT.LOIR
dwarf-cherry	GROUND-CHERRY
Economic	
—Commission	ECE
—Community	EEC
extinct horse	TARPAN
fish (Danube)	ZINGEL
hawk	FALLER
kite	GLE(A)D.GLEDE
leader	E
lily	GREEN DRAGON
Monetary Agreement	EMA
Payments Union	EPU
perennial herb	LASERPICIUM
plain	STEPPE
plant	GOLD-THREAD
Productivity Agreement	EPA
rabbit	CON(E)Y.LEPORID
rodent	ERD.LEMMING
shrub	DAPHNE.SPURGE-LAUREL
squirrel	SISEL
timber	SATIN-WOOD
	ZANTE(-WOOD)
vulture	GALLINAZO
	GRIFFON VULTURE.
LAMMERGEIER.LAMMERGEYER	
wheat	SPELT
wildcat	CATAMOUNT
wine measure	ANKER
Evangelical Union	EU

even
  even characters abandon
  p(l)a(y)   PA
  even characters in p<u>la</u>y   LY
  eve(n) *less*   EVE
  even number   FLATTEN
evening
  evening sun   RED SETTER
  evening work   IRONING
           PLANING.PRESSING
eventually   (in) EN-D
ever   AY.AYE.ER.EER
  ever-*changing*   REVE
  ever*more*   EVERT.LEVER.NEVER
every
  every other day   EOD
  every other part of Spain   SPA.IN
  everyone   ALL.EACH
  everyone *up*⟨ north(D) ↑   LLAN-
evict
  evict a   omit A
  evict people   omit MEN
  evict *   omit *
  •*evict* girl *from* sor(di)d   SORD
  evident in hi/s ap/proach   SAP
evil boy   VICEROY
evolve
  evolution   (*see* beginning[2])
  evolution of <u>man</u> is...   MAINS
  evolve <u>a new</u>...   WANE.WEAN
  evolving from <u>past</u>...   PATS.TAPS
ewe(s)   U.(US.UU)
ex   X
     (*see also* old[3].out of[1].without[1])
  ex-captain   MAJOR
  ex-works   incl OP
  •*ex-works* sl-ed   SLOPED
exact time   DEAD MARCH
examine
  examination   A-LEVEL.CSE.GCE
           GCSE.O-LEVEL
           ORAL.TEST.VIVA
  examined   EX
example   EX
  excavated from de/ep ic/e   EPIC
excel
  excel, *say*   XL
  excellency   HE
  excellent   AI.VG

  excellent character   CAPITAL
  excellent disguise   SUPERVISOR
  excellent eyesight   SUPERVISION
  excellent ruler   SOVEREIGN
except
  except a...   omit A
  except *   omit *
  •*except* the fa(the)r   FAR
  exception   EX(C)
  exceptional <u>talent</u>   LATENT
excessive
  excessive love   MANIA
           (*see also* love[3])
  excessive *rise*(D) ↑   OOT.REVO
  exchange <u>rate</u>   TARE.TEAR
excise
  excise a   omit A
  excise one...   omit A.I
  excise some t(um)ours   TOURS
  excise *   omit *
  •fa(the)r *excised* the...   FAR
  excited <u>boys</u>   YOBS
exclude
  exclude outsiders
           omit first and last letters
  •(b)oar(d) *excludes outsiders*   OAR
  excluded by a...   incl A
  excluded by *   incl *
  •Ma-e *excluded by*
     king   MAKE.MARE
  excluding a...   omit A
  excluding *   omit *
  •king *excluding*
  Ma-e   MAKE.MARE
  excruciating <u>pains</u>   SPAIN
  excursion <u>by bus</u>   BUSBY
excursus   EX
Exe   X
execute
  executed (k)ing   -ING
  executioner   TOPPER
  executive   EX
  executive officer   HANGMAN
  executor   EXR.EXOR
exemplified   EG
exempt
  exempt at the end   omit last letter
  •mat(e) *exempt at the end*   MAT
  exempt at the start   omit first letter

•(m)ate *exempt at the start*	ATE
exercise	PE.PT
exercise <u>dogs</u>	GODS
exercise sequence	TRAIN
exercising <u>men at</u>. . .	MEANT
exhaust pipe	DRAIN
exhibit	
exhibited by *	incl in *
•spectacles *exhibited by*	
musician	BOOM
exhibiting a. . .	incl A
exhibiting *	incl *
•musician *exhibiting*	
spectacles	BOOM
existing state	ASIS
Exodus	EX
exorcise	DISPOSSESS
exorcise a. . .	omit A
exorcise alien. . .	omit ET
exorcise one. . .	omit A.I
exotic	
exotic = foreign (language):	
•*exotic* flower	FLEUR
•*exotic* friend	KAMERAD
•*exotic* garden	GIARDINO
•*exotic* girl	SENORITA
exotic	ALIEN.ET
exotic <u>trees</u>	STEER
expectant mother	
LADY-IN-WAITING	
expel	
expel a. . .	omit A
expel *	omit *
•(l)over *expels* student. . .	OVER
expert[1]	ABLE.ACE.DAB.PRO
hence	
•expert sound	ACETONE
•expert *with* twitch	ACETIC
and	
•British expert	BRACE
•friend and expert	PALACE
•quiet expert	PACE
•stern expert	GRIMACE
and	
•fifty experts	LACES
•many experts	MACES
and	
•expert lost blood	DABBLED
•expert worker	DAB HAND
and	
•expert in good shape	PROFIT
•expert remedy	PROCURE
•expert examination	PROTEST
(*see also* professional)	
expert[2]	
expert oarsman	
MASTER-STROKE	
expert's knowledge	ONIONS
explode	
exploding <u>mine</u>	MIEN
explosion of <u>rage</u>	GEAR
explosive	HE.TNT
explosive finale	KO
explosive <u>rate</u>	TARE.TEAR
exponential	EXP
export	EX(P)
expose some l/aye/rs	AYE
express condition	STATE
extend	
extended play	EP
extension	EXT
exterior	
exterior of <u>cabin</u>	CAN
* *exterior*	incl in *
•animal has re-d *exterior*	REAPED
external	
external *	incl in *
•university's *external* entrance	
AUDIT	
externally	EXT
extinct	EXT
extra	BYE.EXT.WIDE
extra-sensory perception	ESP
extra-terrestrial	ET
extra thought	PS
extract	
extract a. . .	omit A
extract a/n oun/ce	NOUN
extract *	omit *
•*extract* lubricant *from* b(oil)ed..	
BED	
extract of <u>roe</u>	ORE
extraordinary <u>caper</u>	PACER
extreme	
extreme characters	AZ
extreme characters in <u>play</u>	PY
extreme *left*	L
extreme left	L.T

extreme *right*	E	**eye**	
extrem**e**ly light	VERY	eye(s), *say*	I.(II.IS)
extremely light	LT	eyeball	ORB
extremes	N-S	eye*less*	omit I
extremes of fanaticism	FM	eye-*opener*	E
extremists in Paris	PS	eye-*opener*	start with I
extremities of endurance	EE	•member has eye-*opener*	IMP
extremity	TOE	eyesore	STYE
		Ezra	EZ

F

clef. Fahrenheit. farad. farthing. fathom. fellow. female. feminine. femto-.
filly. *fine*. fluorine. folio. following. foot. force. forte. forty. France.
frequency. Friday. hole. key. loud. *noisy*. note. vitamin

fabric

American cloth   LEATHER CLOTH
Angora goat's hair   ANGORA
  MOHAIR
artificial silk   (CUPRAMMONIUM)
  RAYON
blue   MAZARINE.PERSE
  WATCHET
brocade   BALDACHIN(O)
  BALDAQUIN.BAUDEKIN
buff-coloured cotton   NANKEEN
  NANKIN
camel hair   BAR(R)ACAN
  CAMELINE.CAMELOT
  CAMLET
canvas   BINCA.BURLAP
cashmere   CIRCASSIAN
  CIRCASSIENNE
checked   GINGHAM.MADRAS
  TARTAN
closely woven
—cotton   PERCALE
—rayon   FAILLE
—silk   FAILLE.SATIN
—wool   WORSTED
cloth of gold   GOLD CLOTH
—Indian   SONERI
—or silver   LUPPA
coarse   BAFT.GRASSCLOTH
—canvas   BURLAP
—cotton   CALICO.CANVAS
  DENIM.FROCKING.HUCKABACK
  JEAN.MEXICAN.OSNABURG
—East Indian   HUMHUM
—hemp and jute   HOPSACKING
—hemp   CANVAS
—homespun   HODDEN.RUSSET
—linen   DOWLAS.DRABBET
  HARDEN.HARN.HOLLAND
  HUCKABACK.LOCKRAM
—and wool   LINSEY-WOOLSEY
—muslin   MUSLINET
—silk   DUPION
—silk and mohair   GROGRAM

—wool   KELT.RUG
—twilled cotton   DENIM
  FUSTIAN.MOLESKIN
corded   REP(P).REPS
  GROSGRAIN
—18th c.   PADUASOY
—silk and wool or cotton
  BENGALINE
—cotton and wool
  RUSSEL(-CORD)
—ribbed muslin   CORTELINE
—wool or cotton   MOREEN
cotton   CAMBRIC.GINGHAM
  LAWN.POPLIN
—and mohair   SICILIAN
—and rayon   BARATHEA
—and wool   DOMETT.LUSTRE
  WOOLSEY.WINCEY.WINSEY
—and worsted   ORLEANS
—crinkled   SEERSUCKER
—imitation
 —flannel   FLANNELETTE
 —velvet   VELVETEEN
—muslin   JACONET.NAINSOOK
—white   CAMBRIC.DIMITY
—with deep nap   LAMBSKIN
—raised nap   WINCEYETTE
—with silk pile   VELVERET
—with woven pattern   DIAPER
crinkled linen or cotton
  SEERSUCKER
durable   DURANCE
—silk   FLORENCE.FLORENTINE
—wool   SEMPITERNUM
elastic   STOCKINET(TE)
  STOCKINGETTE
embossed   CLOQUE
  MATEL(L)ASSE
embroidered
—damask   DAMASSIN
—silk (Indian)   KINOB.TASH
fawn silk   TASAR.TUSSER
  TUSSORE.TUSSAH
  TUSSEH

fine	SINDON		LUTESTRING.(SILK) SATIN
—cotton	BATISTE.CAMBRIC		TAFFETA(S).TAFFETY
	LAWN.MADRAS.MUSLIN	—wool	CALAMANCO
	ORGANDIE.PONGEE	goat's hair	ANGORA
—lace	MIGNONETTE		CASHMERE.CILICE
—linen	BYSSUS.CAMBRIC.		KASHMIR.MOHAIR
	LAWN.SENDAL		THIBET
—with cotton or wool	BATISTE	—underfleece	PASH(I)M
—silk	PONGEE.TULLE		PASHMINA
—and wool	EOLIENNE	grass cloth	RAMIE
—transparent	CHIFFON	green	BAIZE.KENDAL GREEN
—wool	CASSIMERE		LINCOLN GREEN
	KERSEYMERE	grey	DRAB.WIGAN
—white linen or cotton	CAMBRIC	—wool	OXFORD MIXTURE
—wool	BATISTE.BROADCLOTH	haircloth	CILICE
	FOULE.	hemp and jute	HOPSACKING
	PUKE.WORCESTER	—sailcloth	RAVEN('S)-DUCK
	WORSTED	homespun wool	HODDEN
—and cotton	MERINO	—black and white	HODDEN GREY
—worsted	CUBICA	horsehair and linen	CRINOLINE
firm nylon or silk		imitation	
	BO(U)LTING CLOTH	—cotton	POPLINETTE
forester's cloth	KENDAL GREEN	—leather	DURANT
from			LEATHER CLOTH
—bark fibre	BARK CLOTH		LEATHERETTE
	PAPER CLOTH	inferior	MOCKADO.SHODDY
—flax or lint	LINEN	jute	BUCKRAM.HOPSACKING
—outer coat of sheep,		knitted	JERSEY
goats, etc.	WOOL	—cotton	BALBRIGGAN
—llama	VICUNA	—wool	TRICOT
—pineapple-leaf fibre		knotted into mesh	NET
	PINA (CLOTH)	lace	COLBERTINE.TROLL(E)Y
—recycled rags	MONG(E)	leather	CORDOVAN.CORDWAIN
	MUNGO.SHODDY		MAROQUIN.MOROCCO
—woody shrub fibre		—cloth	AMERICAN CLOTH
	GRASS CLOTH.RAMIE	light	
gauze		—cotton	JEANETTE
—silk-like	TIFFANY	—silk, etc.	CRAPE.CREPE
—wool	BAREGE		CREPE DE CHINE.CREPON
glazed		—or mixed fibres	GRENADINE
—cotton	AMERICAN CLOTH	—wool	BAREGE.CASHMERE
	CHINTZ.CIRE		CIRCASSIAN.CIRCASSIENNE
—worsted	TAMIN(E)		KASHMIR
—wool	TAMMY	—and cotton	DELAINE
glossy		linen	
—cotton	PERCALINE.SATIN	—and wool, cotton, etc.	WINCEY
	JEAN		WINSEY
—or linen	SATEEN	—crinkled	SEERSUCKER
—silk	LUSTRINE.LUSTRING	—patterned	DIAPER

loosely woven   CHEESECLOTH
lustrous   CRYSTALLINE.SATEEN
mohair and cotton   ALEPINE
mosquito net   MARQUISETTE
moth fibre   SILK
muslin   JACONET.MOUSSELINE
    NAINSOOK.ORGANDIE
orange-coloured   NACARET
ornamental   TAPESTRY
patterned cotton or
  linen   DIAPER
pile with
—three loops   THREE-PILE
—uncut loops   TERRY
point lace   NEEDLEPOINT
printed
—cotton   CHINTZ.CRETONNE
—East Indian   BAT(T)IK
—muslin or cambric   PERSIENNE
rabbit's hair   ANGORA
rayon
—heavy   SHARKSKIN
—shaded   JASPE
ribbed   TRICOT
—cotton   CORDUROY
  —and wool   RUSSEL
—silk   SICILIENNE
—wool   DROGUET
  —Indian   SATARA
rich piled   PLUSH
rough wool   TWEED
satin
—soft   CHARMEUSE
—wool   CALAMANCO
—with mat finish   SLIPPER SATIN
semi-transparent   VOILE
shaded   JASPE
silk   TOBINE
  —and cotton   LAMPAS
  —and wool   BARATHEA
  CRYSTALLINE
  —or hair   FAR(R)ANDINE
  FERRANDINE
  —and worsted   CHALLI(S)
  SHALLI
—brocade   BALDACHIN(O)
  BALDAQUIN.BAUDEKIN
  BAWDKIN
—crepe   CREPE DE CHINE

  CREPON
—Ghanaian   KENTE CLOTH
—heavy   SAMITE
—muslin   MOUSSELINE DE SOIE
—Philippine   HUSI
—Shakespearean   SAY
—soft   SURAH
—stiffish   ARMOZEEN.ARMOZINE
  TAFFETA
—twilled   SURAH
—undyed   PONGEE
—voile   NINON
—wild   SHANTUNG.TUSSER
—with cotton and wool
  TOILINETTE
—with short pile   VELVET
soft napped   VELVET PILE
stiff   PIQUE
stiffened   FOUNDATION MUSLIN
  FOUNDATION NET
stiffening   PETERSHAM.WIGAN
striped   DIMITY.DO(O)REA
  DORIA.GALATEA.GINGHAM
  MADRAS.SUSI
strong
—coarse linen   CRASH
—cotton (mattress)   COUTIL(LE)
synthetic   ACRYLIC.COURTELLE
  NYLON.POLYESTER
  RAYON
taffeta   ARMOZEEN.ARMOZINE
—with pile   TUFTAFFETY
  TUFF-TAFFETA.TUFT-TAFFETA
thin
—cotton   LENO.MUSLIN
—satin   SATINET(TE)
—silk   GEORGETTE.SARCENET
  SARS(E)NET.SENDAL.TULLE
transparent   GAUZE.TIFFANY
—black   CYPRESS.CYPRUS
—silk   OIL-SILK.ORGANZA
trimming   GALLOON.GIMP
  ORRIS
twilled   WHIPCORD
—cotton   CHINO.DENIM
  DRILL(ING).FUSTIAN
  JANE.JEAN.MARCELLA
—and silk   SATIN SHEETING
—and wool   GABARDINE

	GABERDINE
—and worsted	BOMBASINE
	BOMBAZINE
—linen DRILL(ING).MARCELLA	
—silk and worsted	BOMBASINE
	BOMBAZINE
—wool	PLAIDING
—worsted SERGE.SHARKSKIN	
—and cotton	GAMBROON
twisted warp	LENO
unbleached cotton	BALBRIGGAN
undyed wool	BEIGE
untwilled silk	FOULARD
unwoven	FELT
upholsterer's silk	TABARET
velvety	CHENILLE
—corded wool	VELOUTINE
	VELOUR(S)
wall-covering	TAPESTRY
watered	
—ribbon	PAD
—silk	MOIRE
waterproof	MACKINTOSH
	OILSKIN
—linen or hemp TARPAULIN(G)	
waxed	WAX CLOTH
Welsh	FRAIZE
white	
—cotton	CALICO.DIMITY
—wool	BLANKET
with	
—looped yarn	BOUCLE
—metal threads	LAME
—woolly surface	NAP
wool BEAVER.CHEVIOT	
DRAP DE BERRY.JAEGER	
LAMBSKIN.MARQUISETTE	
PAISLEY.SAGATHY	
WORCESTER	
—and cotton LINSEY-WOOLSEY	
—and goat's hair	C(H)AMLET
CAMELOT.MOHAIR	
—and silk ALEPINE.ARRASENE	
—coloured THIBET.TIBET CLOTH	
—dark grey OXFORD MIXTURE	
—dyed red	STAMMEL
—like serge	SAY
—Middle Ages	BURNET
—printed	THIBET

—resembling satin	SATEEN
—roughly woven	HOPSACK
—smooth	FOULE
—soft FLANNEL.NUN'S VEILING	
	ZIBEL(L)INE
—speckled HEATHER MIXTURE	
—thick	WADMA(A)L
WADMOL(L).TWEED	
—thin	TAMISE.ZEPHYR
worsted	
—and cotton PAR(R)AMATTA	
—ribbon	CADDIS
—soft	BARATHEA
—thin BUNTING.ZEPHYR	
woven JACQUARD.TEXTILE	
—and felted wool	DRUGGET
—hemp	WEBBING
—like brocade	BROCHE
—with diagonal lines	TWILL

fabulous

bird	ROC
hare	LOSER
place	ELDORADO
supporter	UNICORN
tortoise	WINNER

facade of respectability   R

face

face pain	PANACHE
face *up*(D) ↑	LAID
face wall	PLASTER.RENDER
faces of the old woman	TOW

fact   (*see* indeed)

facts	DATA.GEN

Faculty of Actuaries	FA
fag-*end*	G
Fahrenheit	F

fail

failed	CAMEO
failing test	SETT
fails to finish	omit last letter
•sh(e) *fails to finish*	SH
•a girl *fails to finish*	ALAS(s)
fails to start	omit first letter
•(b)us *fails to start*	US
failure	(*see* without[2])
failure of arch	CHAR

faint

faint point	WANE
faint *sound*	FEINT

fair

fair game	HOOPLA.SKITTLES
fair location	PLEASURE GROUND
fair punishment	FINE
fair *shares*	FA.IR

fairy PERI

fairy king	OBERON
fairy queen	MAB.TITANIA

faith (*see* belief)

fall HAIL.RAIN.SLEET.SNOW

fall *for a Frenchman*	AUTOMNE
fall *for American...*	AUTUMN
fall from *	omit from *
•he *falls from* t(he)...	T
•he *falls from* (he)avens	AVENS
fall in *	incl in *
•rat *falling in* river	DERATE
* *falls off*	omit *
•nose *falls off* (p)lane	LANE
fallen angel	ANGLE
falling over step	PEST.PETS
falling star	ARTS.RATS.TARS
fell *back*	DENNIS

false

false start	TARTS
false *start*	F
falsely said...	DAIS
falsify report	PORTER

Falstaff's tipple SACK

faltering steps PESTS

familiar FAM

indicates colloquial, diminutive, slang:

familiar face	MUG
familiarity with Philip	PIP
familiarly eccentric	LOOPY

family FAM

Family Income Supplement	FIS
Family Planning Association	FPA

famous day VE

fancy

fancy food shop	DELI
fancy heel	IDEALIST
fancy I can...	CAIN
fanciful ideas	AIDES.SADIE

fanlight BLOW-TORCH

fantastic

... fantastic scene I	NIECES
Fantasy in B	BIN.NIB

far

far *away*	FRA.RAF
far-*flung*	FRA.RAF
far *off*	FRA.RAF

farad F

farewell BV.SUCCEED.VALE

farm

farm butter	GOAT.RAM
farm victims	MIC(E)
farmer	GILES.YEOMAN
farmer's punch	HAYMAKER
farming	(on) LAND
•fish*farming*	GARLAND
farming policy	CAP

farthing F.Q

fashion¹ ALA.RAGE.TON

hence

•fashion *in* South Dakota	SALAD
•fashion lines	ALARY
•note fashion	BALA.GALA

and

•current *in* fashion	RAMPAGE

and

•fashion *in* Home Counties	STONE
•fashion notes	TONDO.TONGA
•South American fashion	SAT ON

fashion²

fashion = foreign language:

•a *Greek fashion*	ALPHA
•leader *in Italian fashion*	DUCE
•new *French fashion*	NOUVEAU
•older *Spanish fashion*	MAYOR
•sweet *American fashion*	CANDY
•the *German fashion*	DAS.DER DIE

fashion³

fashion city	BRISTOL
fashion models	FORMS.MAKES SHAPES
fashion models	SELDOM
fashion shop	BOUTIQUE
fashion shop	HOPS.POSH
fashion that is...	CUTIE
fashionable	HIP.IN.POSH

hence

•fashionable curve	HIPS
•kin(g)s *almost* fashionable ...	KINSHIP
•woman *with* fashionable ...	WHIP

and
•fashionable dress   INHABIT
•fashionable group INSECT.INSET
•fashionable sound   INTONE
                          INVOICE

fast
fast car   GT.ROD
fast mover   CLAPPER

fasten
fastened gates   STAGE
fastened in *   incl in *
•four *fastened in* str-ing STRIVING
fastening in a...   incl A
fastening in *   incl *
•str-ing *fastening in* four STRIVING

fat
fat boy   LARDED
fat-*headed*   F
fāt monarch   LARDER

Fates
Greek   MOIRA.MOIRAI
—spins thread of life   CLOTHO
—controls thread of life LACHESIS
—cuts thread of life   ATROPOS
Norse   NORNA.NORNS
—past   URD
—present   VERDANDE
—future   SKULD
Roman   PARCAE.DECUMA
           MORTA.NONA

father ABBA.DAD.FR.PA.POP
          THAMES.TIME
hence
•father *has* cut   DADDOCK
•father *with* a...   DADA
•father *with* nothing   DADO
and
•father at church   FRATCH
•father should...   FRAUGHT
•father *with* East German FROST
and
•father-figure   PAD.PAL.PAM
•Father Thomas   PATHOS
•father's wise   PASSAGE
and
•father above   POPOVER
•father I would, *say* POP-EYED
•father is hot   POPISH
father*less*   omit PA

•father*less* (Pa)than   THAN
fathom   F.FTH.FTHM
fattening food   BLOATER
fault
fault*less* ser(vice)   SER
faulty sign   SING
favour
favoured   IN
favourite man PETAL.PETTED
fear   PHOBIA
fear of
all things   PANTOPHOBIA
animals   ZOOPHOBIA
being
—alone   MONOPHOBIA
—buried alive TAPHEPHOBIA
           TAPHOPHOBIA
—looked at SCOPOPHOBIA
books   BIBLIOPHOBIA
cats   AIL(O)UROPHOBIA
confined spaces
     CLAUSTROPHOBIA
corpses   NECROPHOBIA
crossing streets DROMOPHOBIA
crowds   DEMOPHOBIA
         OCHLOPHOBIA
death   NECROPHOBIA
      THANATOPHOBIA
disease   NOSOPHOBIA
        PATHOPHOBIA
draughts   AEROPHOBIA
drawing attention to
 oneself   AUTOPHOBY
English   ANGLOPHOBIA
falling from height
      BATHOPHOBIA
familiar places NOSTOPHOBIA
foreigners and foreign
 things
        XENOPHOBIA
French   GALLOPHOBIA
Germans GERMANOPHOBIA
God   THEOPHOBIA
groundless fears PANOPHOBIA
heights   ACROPHOBIA
light   PHOTOPHOBIA
men   ANDROPHOBIA
motorway madness
      AMAXOPHOBIA

negroes	NEGROPHOBIA
new things	NEOPHOBIA
night	NYCTOPHOBIA
poisons	TOXI(CO)PHOBIA
pollution	MYSOPHOBIA
pope	PAPAPHOBIA
punishment	RHABDOPHOBIA
rain	OMBROMOPHOBIA
Russians	RUSSOPHOBIA
sitting down	CATHISOPHOBIA
sun	HELIOPHOBIA
symmetry	SYMMETROPHOBIA
thirteen	TRISKAIDECAPHOBIA
	TRISKAIDEKAPHOBIA
thunder and lightning	
	ASTRA(PO)PHOBIA
venereal disease	SYPHILOPHOBIA
water	AQUAPHOBIA
	HYDROPHOBIA
work	ERGOPHOBIA

fearful rage   GEAR
feature
feature a...   incl A
feature editor
    COSMETIC SURGEON
feature of t/he be/st   HEBE
feature *   incl *
•*feature* article *in* story LIANE
featuring *   incl in *
•story *featuring* article   LIANE
featuring remarka/ble st/unt
                      BLEST
February   FEB
fed *up*(D) ↑   DEF
feed*back*⟨   DEEF
feel sad   BELOW
feet   FT
feet *up*(D) ↑   DRAY
FEG, *say*   EFFIGY
fell   (*see also* fall)
fell sergeant   DEATH
fellow COVE.DON.F.GENT.MAN
hence
•a *French* fellow *with*
  king   UNCOVER
•fellow Russian   COVERED
•gangster fellow   ALCOVE
and
•fellow *at* tea, *say*   DONT

•fellow dined   DONATE
•fellow *with* a Conservative
                DONATORY
and
•fellow *has* a cow   FLOWER
•fellow is not...   FAINT
•fellow *with* spectacular
  fish   FOOLING
and
•brown fellow   TANGENT
•fellow the *French*...   GENTLE
•fellow *with* Scottish boy GENTIAN
and
•fellow is *back* on MANSION
•fellow-man   MANAL.MANED
•the *French* fellow   LEMAN
Fellow of the
Antiquarian Society   FAS
British Academy   FBA
Institute of Chartered
  Accountants   FCA
Historical Society   FHS
Institute of Journalists FIJ
Royal Society FRS.JRS.RSS
Society of
—Antiquaries   SAS
—Arts   FAS
female   F.HEN.HER.SHE
female adviser   EGERIA
female bookmaker AUTHORESS
                      RUTH
female cat   ANNOUNCE
feminine   F.FEM
hence
•feminine appearance FLOOK
•feminine limbs   FARMS
•feminine usefulness FUTILITY
fence
fenced in by *   incl in *
•cow *fenced by* saints SCOWS
fencing in a...   incl A
fencing in *   incl *
•saints *fencing in* a cow SCOWS
fermenting cask   SACK
fern
some alternative names:
Adiantum   MAIDENHAIR FERN
Asplenium   BIRD'S NEST FERN
               SPLEENWORT

	WALL-RUE	fertile crescent	GROWING
Athyrium	LADY FERN	fertiliser	NITRE.STAMEN
bird's-nest fern	ASPLENIUM	*festering* sore	EROS.ORES
Boston Fern	NEPHROLEPSIS		ROES.ROSE
bracken	PTERIDIUM.TARA	**fewer clothes**	LESSON
button fern	PELLAEA	**f-fish**	FLING
Christmas fern	POLYSTICHUM	*fickle* friend	FINDER
Cyathea	TREEFERN	**fiddle**	AMATI.CREMONA
Dryopteris	MALE FERN		STRAD(IVARIUS)
feather fern	NEPHROLEPSIS	*fiddled* a lot	TOLA
filmy fern	BRISTLE FERN	fiddler	NERO
fishtail fern	CYRTOMIUM	fiddlesticks	BOWS
green-brake fern	PELLAEA	*fiddling* takings	SKATING
hare's-foot fern	PHLEBODIUM	**field**	
hart's-tongue fern	PHYLLITIS	field-dressing	FERTILISER
holly fern	CYRTROMIUM		NITRE.POTASH
	POLYSTICHUM	field-effect transistor	FET
lace fern	NEPHROLEPSIS	field-marshal	FM
lady fern	ATHYRIUM	field officer	FO
maidenhair fern	ADIANTUM	**fiery**	
male fern	DRYOPTERIS	fiery mount	ETNA.VOLCANO
Nephrolepsis	BOSTON FERN	fiery revolutionary	IXION
	FEATHER FERN.LACE FERN	**fifteen**	RU TEAM
	SWORD FERN	**fifth**	
Osmunda	ROYAL FERN	anniversary	QUINQUENNIAL
peacock fern	SELAGINELLA	of November	M
Phyllitis	HART'S-TONGUE FERN	**fifty**	A.L.N.NU.V
Polystichum	CHRISTMAS FERN	hence	
	HOLLY FERN	·50-50	LL
Pteris	RIBBON FERN	·50 copies	LIMITATIONS
	SILVER LACE FERN	·50 experts	LACES
rabbit's-foot fern	DAVALLIA	·50 I know	LIKEN
ribbon fern	PTERIS	·50 I know, *say*	LINO
rose maidenhair	ADIANTUM	·50 in cage, *say*	LINKAGE
royal fern	OSMUNDA	·50 in store	LINSTOCK
rustyback	CETERACH	·50 or 500	LORD
silver-lace fern	PTERIS	fifty per cent of people	PEO.PLE
spleenwort	ASPLENIUM	fifty-fifty	EVENS.LL
stag's-horn fern	PLATYCERIUM	fifty-one	LI
sword fern	NEPHROLEPSIS	hence	
table fern	PTERIS	·51 can...	LIABLE
tara(fern)	BRACKEN	·51 directions	LINES
Thelypteris		·51 doctors	LIMBS
	LEMON-SCENTED FERN	·51 extremely...	LIVERY
water fern	AZOLLA	·51 iron ships	LIFEBOATS
tree fern	CYATHEA	·51 pounds	LIQUIDS
trembling fern	PTERIS	·51 ran	LISPED
ferryman	CHARON	·51 support...	LIBRA
fertile		·51 swindle	LISTING

fifty-nine	LIX
Fifties	LL
States	US.USA
thousand	L.N.NU.V
years old	QUINQUAGENARIAN

fight

fight*back*⟨	RAW
fighter	GI.MAN.SOLDIER
fighting (in)	AC-TION.INACTION
fighting figure	MARS
fighting situation	BATTLEFIELD
	(BOXING) RING
fighting woman	ATS

figure C.CL.D.FIG.L.M.

figure-*hugging*	incl number
•figure-*hugging* p-ants	PLANTS
figure of eight	OCTAGON
figure *out*	omit number
•(c)an figure *out*	AN
•figure *out* c(l)ues	CUES
figure *out*	CON-E.F-IVE.N-INE
	ON-E.TE-N
figures (in Rome)	C.D.L.M
	CI.CL.DI.LI.MI.MM
hence	
•cut a figure	SLICED
•figure eight, *say*	CATE.DATE
	LATE.MATE
•figure on	CON.DON.LION.MON
•figure out	CLOUT.LOUT
figures *out*	incl in numbers
•girl figures *out*	MADAM
•man figures *out*	CALL
figure*head*	F
figuratively	FIG
	(*see also* shape)

file WILDLIFE

filial claim MESON

fill

fill the gap in *	incl in *
•always *fill the gap*	
in r-ed...	REVERED
fill the gap with *	incl *
•*fill gap in* bo-rder	
with a...	BOARDER
filled with a...	incl A
filled with *	incl *
•a *French* bed *filled with*	
men	ALIMENT

filling	incl in *
•men *filling* a *French*	
bed	ALIMENT
	(*see also* full)

film A.ET.PG.U.X

dull film	TARNISH
film distributor	AEROSOL
	SPRAY(-GUN)
film girl	GIGI
filming	(on) SET
•scholars *filming*	BASSET
old film	PATINA

final

final examination	ENDPAPER
final letter	OMEGA.Z
final message	OBIT.RIP
final venue	TWICKENHAM
final word	AMEN.OMEGA
finalists at Wimbledon	ON
finally	(in) EN-D
finally arrived	D
finally failing	omit last letter
•hear(t) *finally failing*	HEAR
finally left	end with L
•Al *finally left*	ALL
finally left	omit last letter
•the(y) *finally left*	THE
finally *lost*	omit last letter
•Franc(e) *finally lost*	FRANC

finance

finance company	BRASS BAND
financial liability	-IOUS
Financial Times	FT

find

find a log, *ruin*...	LOURING
find a log, *ruin*...	GAOL.GAOL
find another way to drive...	DIVER
find another way to say so	SEW
	SOW
finding *a synonym*	LOCATING
finds it in ver/y ear/ly...	YEAR
	(*see also* found)

fine AI.F.OK.SCOT

fine *form*	FEIN
fine man	MAGISTRATE
finesse by Dan	BANDY
fingered fabric	FELT

finish

finish at Epsom	M

finish cross	ENDANGERED
finish game	MATE
finish game_	E
finish off	F
finish *off*	omit last letter
•finish *off* boo(k)	BOO
finish work	RETIRE
finish work_	K
mat *finish*_	T
all *finished*	L
finishing touch_	H
Finland	SF
Finnish	
author	TWAIN
capital	F.HELSINKI
coin	MARK.MARK(K)A
	MKK.PENNI
dialect	KAREL
dog	LAIKA
epic	KALEVALA
instrument	KANTELE
language	SUOMI
leader	F
measure	KANNOR.TUNNA
underworld	TUONELA
fire	
fire hydrant	FH
fire plug	FP
fire rifle	SACK
fire-ship	LIGHTER
fireman	GUNNER
firemen	GUNNERS.RA
firm¹	CO.FAST
hence	
•firm friend	COPAL
•firm supporter	COBRA
•firm's a...	COCOA
firm-*hearted*	incl CO
firm²	
firm control	HOUSEHOLD
firm ruler(MANAGING) DIRECTOR	
firm undertaking	
FUNERAL CONTRACTORS	
first¹	A.-IST.NOI
hence	
•first man	AGENT
•first team	ASIDE
•girl first	GALA
and	

•fat man first	FATALIST
•first *after* many...	LIST.MIST
•first the *French*	ISTLE
and	
•first *back*⟨	-ION
•first directions	NOISE
•first *to return*⟨	-ION
first²	
first born	B
first character in Hamlet	H
first half of game_	GA
first man	M
first mate_	M
first mother	M
first of all	A
first of April	A
first of the...	T
first prize	P
first round	R
first service	S
first showings of play in Neath	PIN
first sightings of West Indies	WI
first sign of Spring_	S
first slice	S
first slice of cake_	C
first to win	W
first to win_	TWIN
(*see also* monarchs)	
first³	
first and foremost	A
first chance	OPENING
first character	A.ADAM.ALPHA
first class	A.ACE.AI.CRACK.PRO
	SMASHING
hence	
•first-class degrees	ADD
•first-class fellow	AIDES
•first-class fish	AILING
first gear	FIG-LEAF.LAYETTE
first in, first out	FIFO
first item in sale	LOTI
first lady	EVE
first letter	A.ALPHA
first man	ADAM
first man	start with MAN
•first man *has* appointment	
	MANDATE
first mate	ADAM.EVE
first mother	EVE

first mover   WHITE
first murderer   CAIN
first nine characters
  returned⟨   IOTA
first offender   EVE
first person   ADAM.I.ME
first place   EDEN
first prize   GOLD.PALM
first question   QI
first reading book   ABC.ABCEE
                              ABSEY.PRIMER
first slip   (ORIGINAL) SIN
first to be struck   PENNY BLACK
first victim   ABEL
first wife   EVE

fish[1]   ANGLE.SWIMMER
some commonly used
  names: CARP.COD.EEL
                           GAR.ID.IDE.-LING
hence
•fish *with* alien. . .   CARPET
•fish-stream   CO-DRIVER
•k-ing *without* fish   KEELING
•fish study   GARDEN
•fish *in* Kent, perhaps   SIDE
•sunfish   SIDE.SLING
•two fish   CODLING

fish[2]
some alternative names:
ablet   BLEAK
Acipenser   STURGEON
accompanies sharks, etc.
                               PILOT FISH
Anableps   FOUR-EYED FISH
angelfish   ANGELSHARK
              MONKFISH.POMACANTHUS
angler   BRIABOT.DEVILFISH
          FISHING-FROG.FROGFISH
                             GOOSE-EGG
archerfish   DARTER
Argonaut   NAUTILUS
Balistes   FILEFISH
ballan wrasse   SEA SWINE
barracouta   SNOEK.SNOOK
basking shark   SAILFISH.SUNFISH
bass   ROCCUS.SEA DACE
                             SEA PERCH
bellows fish   SNIPEFISH
Belone   GARFISH.SEA PIKE

bergylt   NORWAY HADDOCK
                               ROSEFISH
bib   BLAIN.(WHITING-)POUT
black goby   ROCKFISH
blain   BIB.(WHITING-)POUT
bleak   ABLET.BLAY.BLEY
blenny   EEL-POUT.GREENBONE
                                SHANNY
blind fish   AMBYLOPSIS
                              CAVEFISH
blueback salmon   SOCKEYE
bluefish   SNAPPER
blue roach   AZURINE
Bombay duck   BUMMALO
bony
—fish   ANABLEPS
                           COFFER-FISH
—pike   LEPIDOSTEUS
                          GROUNDLING
bounce   MORGAY
                   SPOTTED DOGFISH
braise   PORGY.SEA BREAM
brill   TURBOT
bristle-headed   HOGFISH
Brosmius   TORSK
bull trout   SALMON TROUT
                             SEA TROUT
bullhead   MILLER'S THUMB
bummalo   BOMBAY DUCK
burbot   EELPOUT.LOTA
burrowing fish   MUDFISH
butterfish   GUNNEL
Californian trout
                     RAINBOW TROUT
carp   CYPRINUS.ROUND FISH
—type   BARBEL.BREAM
cartilaginous   CHIMAERA
catfish   SEA CAT.SILURE
                             WOLFFISH
char   RED-BELLY.SAIBLING
                             TORGOCH
Chinese fish   CARP.GOLDFISH
chub   CHAVENDER.CHEVEN
                              CHEVIN
climbing fish   ANABAS.GOURAMI
coalfish   BLECK.COLEY.DORSE
       GLISSAUN.SAITH(E).SILLOCK
—(Scottish)   STENLOCK
cobia   SERGEANT FISH.SNOOK

Cobitidae	LOACH	electric	RAY.TORPEDO
cod	GADIDAE	—eel	GYMNOTUS
—family	DORSE	elleck	RED GURNET
	GADUS MORHUA	Esox	PIKE
	HADDOCK.TORSK	European carp	ID(E)
—like	HAKE.ROCKLING	father lasher	SCORPION FISH
—small	CODLING		SEA SCORPION.HARDHEAD
coffer-fish	OSTRACION	filefish	OLD WIFE
coho(e)	PACIFIC SALMON	finnock	HERLING.HIRLING
	SILVER SALMON	flatfish	BRILL.BUTT.FLOUNDER
coley	COALFISH		HALIBUT.HOLIBUT.PLAICE
conger	SEA EEL		PSETTA.(DOVER) SOLE
corkwing	GOLDSINNY.WRASSE		LEMON SOLE.TURBOT
craig-fluke	WITCH	—fishes	HETEROSOMATA
cramp-fish	ELECTRIC RAY	flounder	FLUKE
	TORPEDO	flying	PILOTFISH.SEA BAT
crayfish	CRAWFISH	fox shark	SEA FOX.THRESHER
	SPINY LOBSTER	found in lakes	LAKER
cross-fish	ASTERIAS	freshwater	
cross-mouthed	PLAGIOSTOME	—carp	GUDGEON.ROACH
cured cod	DUNFISH	—fishes	LEUCISCUS
cusk	TORSK	garfish	GREENBONE
cuttlefish	SEA SLEEVE.SEPIA		MACKEREL-GUIDE.SNOOK
cyclostome	ROUND-MOUTH	garpike	GARFISH.NEEDLEFISH
dab	LIMANDA.LEMON DAB	giant ray	DEVILFISH
dace	DARE.DART.GRAINING	globefish	DIODON.PUFFER
dealfish	RIBBONFISH		SEA PORCUPINE
	TRACHYPTERUS		SEA HEDGEHOG
demoiselle	WRASSE		TAMBOR
devilfish/devilray	MANTA	goatfish	RED MULLET
Diodon	GLOBEFISH	goby	DRAGONET.GOBIO
	SEA PORCUPINE		MUDSKIPPER
dogfish	GREYFISH.HOUNDFISH	golden id	ORFE
	MORGAY.NURSE	goldfish with double fins	FANTAIL
	ROUSETTE.SEADOG	goldsinny	CORKWING.WRASSE
	SEAHOUND	goramy	GO(U)RAMI
dog salmon	KETA	grayling	THYMALLUS.UMBER
dolphin	CORYPHAENA.DORADO	gudgeon	GOBIO.GOBY.WAPPER
dorado	DOLPHIN	gunnel	BUTTERFISH
	GOLDEN SALMON	guppy	MILLIONS
dory	DOREE.JOHN DORY	gurnard/gurnet	ELLECK.GURNET
dragonet	CALLIONYMIDAE.GOBY		HARDHEAD.SEA COCK
(drum)fish	SCIAENIDAE		SEA ROBIN.TUBFISH
eagle ray	SEA EAGLE	Gymnotus	ELECTRIC EEL
eel	ANGUILLA.CONGER.GRIG	haddock (Scottish)	HADDIE
	MORAY.MURRAY	hagfish	MYXINE
	MURR(E)Y.MURAENA	hake	SEA PIKE.WHITING
—electric	GYMNOTUS	hammerhead shark	SPHYRNA
—young	ELVER	herring	CLUPEA.ELOPS

—American	ALE-WIFE
—like	PILCHARD
—Mediterranean	ANCHOVY
—type	RABBITFISH.SHAD
—young	SILD
Hippocampus	SEA HORSE
hornyhead	JERKER
horse mackerel	BOARFISH
	SAUREL.SCAD.SKIPJACK
humpback salmon	DOG SALMON
inflating	BOTTLEFISH
Irish trout	GILLAROO
Japanese	CARP.GOLDFISH
jellyfish	ACALEPH(A).ACALEPHE
	ARVEL.CNIDA.MEDUSA
	QUARL.SEA BLUBBER
	SEA JELLY.SEA NETTLE
—fishes	SCYPHOMEDUSAE
jewfish	TARPON.TARPUM
kelt	LIGGER
keta	DOG SALMON
king of herrings	RABBITFISH
	SHAD
kingfish	OPAH
	SUNFISH
Labrus	WRASSE
Lake Bala	GWINIAD.GWYNIAD
lamprey	CYCLOSTOME.HAG
	NINE-EYES.ROUND-MOUTH
	SAND-PRIDE
Lampris	KINGFISH.OPAH
	SUNFISH
large	
—mouthed	PELICAN FISH
—ray	MANTA
launce	SAND EEL
lemon dab	SMEAR DAB
lesser spotted dogfish	BOUNCE
ling	MOLVA
lizard fish	SAURUS
loach	COBITIDAE
Loch Lomond and Loch Eck	POWAN
Loligo	CUTTLEFISH.SQUID
long-tailed shark	FOX SHARK
Lough Neagh	POLLAN
luce	GED.PIKE
lumpfish	LUMPSUCKER.SEA OWL
lungfish	MUDFISH
—fishes	DIPNOI
Lutjanidae	SNAPPERS
mackerel	CARANX.SCOMBER
—S. African	ALBACORE
maigre	BAR.MEAGRE.SCIAENA
Malayan	GORAMY.GO(U)RAMI
male fish ready to breed	MILTER
manta	DEVILFISH.DEVILRAY
marine	
—perch	SEA BASS
—stickleback	SEA ADDER
Mediterranean	MEAGRE.MAIGRE
Megalops	TARPON
menhaden	HARDHEAD
	MOSSBUNKER
miller's	
—dog	PENNY-DOG.TOPE
—thumb	BULLHEAD
millions	GUPPY
minnow	BANNY.PINK.TIDDLER
Molidae	KINGFISH.OPAH
	SUNFISH
monkfish	ANGELFISH(SHARK)
moray	MURAENA
mossbunker	MENHADEN
mud	
—fish	BOWFIN.LUNGFISH
—minnow	UMBRA
—skipper	GOBY
Mugilidae	MULLET
mullet	MUGIL.MULLUS
	MYXUS
Mullus	MULLET
nautilus	ARGONAUT
needlefish	GARPIKE.PIPEFISH
oarfish	RIBBONFISH
octopus	DEVILFISH
old wife	FILEFISH
opah	KINGFISH.LAMPRIS
ornamental	BLACKMOOR.CARP
	GOLDFISH.KOI.MOLIDAE
	ORFE.RUDD.SHUBUNKIN
	SUNFISH
Ostracion	COFFER-FISH
oxyrhync(h)us	SACRED FISH
Pacific salmon	KETA
parrotfish	PARROT WRASSE
	SCARUS
pelican fish	EURYPHARYNX

penny-dog	MILLER'S DOG.TOPE
perch	BLACK FISH.BLACK RUFF
	PERCA.ZINGEL
—pike	SANDER.ZANDER
percoid	PERCH
phosphorescent shrimps	KRILL
pike	ESOX.GED.LUCE
—perch	FOGASH
—young	JACK
pilot fish	RUDDERFISH
pink	MINNOW.SAMLET
pipefish	NEEDLEFISH.SEA ADDER
—fishes	LOPHOBRANCH
piranha	SERRASALMO
plaice	PLEURONECTES
pleuronectides	PLAICE
pogge	SEA POACHER
pollack	COALFISH.LYTHE
	POLLOCK
pope	RUFFE
porbeagle	MACKEREL SHARK
porgy	BRAISE.SCUP.SEA BREAM
pout	BIB.BLAIN.WHITING POUT
prehistoric	COELACANTH
prickleback	STICKLEBACK
Prussian carp	GIBEL
rabbitfish	KING OF THE HERRINGS
rainbow trout	
	CALIFORNIAN TROUT
ray	SAWFISH.SKATE
	THORNBACK.TORPEDO
razor-fish	SOLEN
red	
—belly	CHAR
—eye	RUDD
—mullet	GOATFISH.SURMULLET
ribbonfish	BANDFISH.DEALFISH
	OARFISH.TRACHYPTERUS
river	
—fish	CHUB.DACE.LOACH
	TENCH.TROUT
—lamprey	LAMPERN
roach	RUTILUS
robalo	SEA PIKE.SNOEK.SNOOK
rock	
—perch	SCORPION FISH
—turbot	WOLFFISH
rockling	MACKEREL MIDGE
	SEA LOACH.WHISTLEFISH

roker	RAY.THORNBACK
rosefish	BERGYLT
	NORWAY HADDOCK
rudd	RED-EYE
rudderfish	PILOT FISH
ruffe	POPE
Russian	GOLOMYNKA
sacred fish	OXYRHYNC(H)US
sail	
—fish	BASKING SHARK
	SPIKEFISH.SWORDFISH
—fluke	WHIFF
Salmon	SALMON.TROUT
salmon	
—at one year	BLUECAP
—at two years	SPROD
—at three years	MORT
—blueback	NERKA.SOCKEYE
—dog salmon	KETA
—female after spawning	KELT
	SHEDDER
—fry	ALEVIN
—grilse	PEAL.PEEL
—king salmon	QUINNAT
—large Pacific	KING SALMON
	QUINNAT
—male after spawning	KIPPER
—old female	BAGGIT.BLACKFISH
—N. Pacific	ONCORHYNCHUS
—Pacific	BLUEBACK.COHO(E)
	HUMP.KETA.NERKA
	SOCKEYE
—sockeye	BLUEBACK.NERKA
—S. American	GOLDEN SALMON
—silver	COHO(E)
—spent	KELT.LIGGER
—trout	BULL TROUT.SEA TROUT
—type	SMELT
—young	GRILSE.PAR(R).PINK.
	SAMLET.SEWEN.SEWIN
	SKEGGER.SMOLT.SPROD
samlet	PINK
sand	
—eel	GRIG.LANT.(SAND) LAUNCE
—launce	SAND EEL
—pride	LAMPREY
—sole	LEMON SOLE
—sucker	DAB
sander	PERCH-PIKE.ZANDER

sardine-type	SARDEL(LE)
saurel	HORSE MACKEREL
	SCAD.SKIPJACK
saury	SKIPPER
scad	CARANX
	HORSE MACKEREL.SAUREL
scaldfish	MEGRIM
scaleless	EEL
scar(us)	PARROT FISH
	PARROT WRASSE
Sciaena	MAIGRE
Scomber	MACKEREL
scorpion fish	ROCK PERCH
	SEA SCORPION.ZEBRA FISH
sculpin	DRAGONET
Scyphomedusae	JELLYFISH
Scyphozoa	JELLYFISH
sea	
—adder	PIPEFISH
—ape	THRESHER SHARK
—bass	ROCK COD.SEA PERCH
—blubber	JELLYFISH
—bream	BRAISE.BRAIZE
	GILTHEAD.PORGIE.PORGY
	SAR(GO).SARGUS.SPARIDAE
—cat	CATFISH
—cock	GURNARD.GURNET
—dace	BASS
—devil	DEVILFISH
—dog	DOGFISH
—dragon	DRAGONET
—eagle	EAGLE-RAY
—eel	CONGER
—fox	FOX SHARK.THRESHER
—hedgehog	GLOBEFISH
—horse	HIPPOCAMPUS
—type	LOPHO BRANCH
	PIPEFISH
—hound	DOGFISH
—jelly	JELLYFISH
—lawyer	SHARK
—loach	ROCKLING
—nettle	JELLYFISH
—owl	LUMPSUCKER
—perch	COMBER.GAPER
	SEA BASS.SERRAN
—pike	BELONE.HAKE.ROBALO
—poacher	POGGE
—porcupine	DIODON.GLOBEFISH

—robin	GURNARD
— scorpion	FATHER-LASHER
	SCORPAENA
	SCORPION FISH
—sleeve	CUTTLEFISH
—snail	SNAILFISH
—surgeon	DOCTOR
	SURGEON FISH
—swine	BALLAN WRASSE
—trout	BULL TROUT
	SALMON TROUT
—urchin	CROSS-FISH
—young	PEAL.PEEL
—wife	WRASSE
—wolf	WOLFFISH
selacian	DOGFISH.RAY
	SHARK.SKATE
sephen	STINGRAY
sepia	CUTTLEFISH
Serrasalmo	PIRANHA
shad	ALLIS.ALLICE.ALOSA
	KING OF THE HERRINGS
	TWAITE
Shagreen ray	DUN COW
shanny	BLENNY
shark	ANGELFISH.BEAGLE
	CESTRACION.GATA
	HAMMERFISH.HAMMERHEAD
	MONKFISH.MORGAY
	NURSE.PENNY-DOG
	PORBEAGLE.SAWFISH
	SEA FOX.SEA LAWYER
	SELACHIAN.THRESHER.TOPE
sharks	ELASMOBRANCH
	SPHYRNA
sharp-beaked	SAURY
sheat(h)fish	CATFISH.SILURUS
shrimp	MYSIS
Silurus	SHEAT(H)FISH
silver salmon	COHO
silver-white goldfish	SILVERFISH
skate	RAY
skates	ELASMOBRANCH
skipjack	BLUEFISH.TUNA
	HORSE MACKEREL.SAUREL
skipper	SAURY
sleeve-fish	SQUID
small	BITTERLING.CLIONE.FRY
	KRILL.MINNOW.NEKTON

	SPRATS.SHRIMPS
	STICKLEBACK.TIDDLER
	WHITEBAIT
—bright tropical	ANGELFISH
	BUTTERFLY FISH
—cod	CODLING.DORSE
—herring type	SPRAT
—sea-fish	WHITING
—shark	DOGFISH
—sole	SLIP.SOLENETTE
—sturgeon	STERLET
—turbot-type	TOP-KNOT
smear-dab	SMOOTH DAB
smelt	OSMERIDAE
—scottish	SPARLING.SPIRLING
smoked herring	BLOATER
	BUCKLING.KIPPER
snailfish	SEA SNAIL
snake mackerel	ESCOLAR
snapper	BLUEFISH.GRUNTER
snappers	LUCJANIDAE
snipefish	BELLOWS FISH
	TRUMPET FISH
snook	COBIA.BARRACOUTA
	GARFISH.ROBALO
	SNOEK
sockeye	BLUEBACK SALMON
sole	MEGRIM
Solen	RAZOR-FISH
Sparidae	SEA BREAM
sparling	SMELT
spearfish	SWORDFISH
	TETRAPTURUS
Sphyrna	HAMMERHEAD SHARK
spike-fish	SAILFISH
spirling	SMELT
spotted dogfish	BOUNCE
	MORGAY
sprat	BRISLING.CLUPEA
	GARVIE.GARVOCK
squid	LOLIGO.SLEEVE-FISH
star	
—fish	ASTEROIDEA
	FIVE-FINGER SEAPAD
—gazers	URANOSCOPUS
stenlock	COALFISH
stickleback	FLUTEMOUTH
	PRICKLEBACK.TIDDLER
sting	
—fish	STINGBULL
	TRACHINUS.WEEVER
—ray	EAGLE-RAY
	SEPHEN.TRYGON
sturgeon	ACIPENSER.BELUGA
	HUSO.OSSETER
suckerfish	LAMPREY.REMORA
sunfish	BASKING SHARK.OPAH
swine-fish	WOLFFISH
swordfish	GLADUS
	(H)ISTIOPHORUS.MARLIN
	SAILFISH.SPEARFISH
	XIPHIAS
Syngnathidae	PIPEFISH
tarpon	ELOPS.MEGALOPS
tench	TINCA
Tetrapturus	SPEARFISH
thornback	RAY.ROKER
thresher	FOX SHARK.SEA FOX
	SEA APE.THRASHER
Thymallus	GRAYLING
tiddler	MINNOW.STICKLEBACK
tiger shark	DEMOISELLE
Tinca	TENCH
tope	MILLER'S DOG.PENNY-DOG
torgoch	CHAR
torpedo	(ELECTRIC) RAY
torsk	BROSMIUS.CUSK
Trachinus	STINGBULL
	STINGFISH.WEEVER
Trachypterus	RIBBONFISH
triggerfish	PUFFER
Trigla	GURNARD.GURNET
trout	FINNOCK
—Irish	GILLAROO
—little	TROUTLET.TROUTLING
—young	WHITLING
trumpet-fish	BELLOWS FISH
	SNIPEFISH
Trygon	STINGRAY
tubfish	GURNARD
tuna	TUNNY
tunny	ALBACORE.BONETTO
	BONITO.TUNA
turbot	BRET.BRILL.PSETTA
—type	SAIL-FLUKE.WHIFF
twaite	SHAD
umber	GRAYLING
Umbra	MUD MINNOW

Uranoscopus	STARGAZER
viviparous blenny	EEL-POUT
	GREENBONE
weaver/weever	STINGBULL
	STINGFISH.TRACHINUS
whiff	SAIL-FLUKE
whistle-fish	ROCKLING
white fish	COREGONUS
—Lake District	VENDACE
	VENDIS(S)
—N. Irish	POLLAN
—Scottish	VENDACE.VENDIS(S)
whiting	MERLING
—pout	BIB.POUTING
witch	CRAIG-FLUKE
with	
—gills in tufts	LOPHOBRANCH
—long under-jaw	HALF-BEAK
—lungs and gills	LUNGFISH
—whiplike tail	HAIRTAIL
	STINGRAY
wolffish	CATFISH.ROCK TURBOT
	SEA WOLF.SWINEFISH
wrasse	BALLAN.COMBER
	CROWGER.DEMOISELLE
	GOLDFINNY.GOLDSINNY
	JULIS.LABRUS.ROCKFISH
	SEA-WIFE
Xiphias	SWORDFISH
young	
—coalfish	GREYFISH
—Scottish	PODLEY
—eel	ELVER
—fish	BRIT
—herring	BRIT.SILD
—pike	PICKEREL
—pilchard	SARDINE
—sea trout	FINNAC(K).FINNOCK
	HERLING.HIRLING
	PHINNACK.SEWEN
	SEWIN
—sprat	BRIT
—trout	WHITLING
zander	PIKE-PERCH.SANDER

fish³

fish cleaner	CHAR
fish club	ANGLE IRON
fish-house	BLEAK
fish-plate	SCALE

fish-woman	SALMONELLA
fisherman	PEDRO.PETER
fishing (industry)	NETWORK
fishing rod	PIKESTAFF
five¹	CINQUE.V
hence	
•5 x 50	VIOL
•5 drinks	VALES
•5 I lease	VIRENT
•5 in debt	VOWING
•5 *in* low island	CAVY
•5 *with* no instrument	VOLUTE
•5 *with* one *German...*	VEIN

five²

arrangement of five things	QUINCUNX
Articles	DOCTRINES
books of Old Testament	PENTATEUCH
bunch of fives	FIST
Christmas presents	GOLD RINGS
Cinque Ports	DOVER.HASTINGS
	HYTHE.ROMNEY
	SANDWICH
cities	PENTAPOLIS
combining forms	PENT(A)-
	QUINQU(E)-
daily interval	SEXTAN
days	PENTAD
event contest	PENTATHLON
exercises	PENTATHLON
fold	PENTAPLOID.QUINARY
	QUINQUEFARIOUS
	QUINTUPL(ICAT)E
groups	PENTAD.QUIN.QUINT
	QUINTET(T).QUINTETTE
	QUINTETTO.QUINTUPLET
having five	
—angles	PENTANGULAR
—atoms	PENTATOMIC
—banks of oars	QUINQUEREME
—digits or fingers	PENTADACTYL(E)
	PENTADACTYLIC
	PENTADACTYLOUS
—electrodes	PENTODE
—faces	PENTAHEDRAL
—leaflets	QUINATE
	QUINQUEFOLIATE

—lines (poem) PENTASTICHOUS
—members PENTAMEROUS
—metrical feet PENTAMETER
—musical notes
     PENTATONIC (SCALE)
—parts, petals, sepals, etc.
     PENTAMEROUS
     QUINQUEPARTITE
     QUINTUPLE
—pistils PENTAGYNIAN
     PENTAGYNOUS
—players, voices QUINTET(TE)
—rays PENTACT(INAL)
—rings PENTACYCLIC
—rulers PENTARCHY
—sets of chromosomes
     PENTAPLOID
—sides PENTAGONAL
—stamens PENTANDRIAN
     PENTANDROUS
—toes PENTADACTYL(E)
     PENTADACTYLIC
     PENTADACTYLOUS
—valencies PENTAVALENT
hundred A.D
hence
•500 in time DINT
•500 is. . . DIS-
•501 DI
—years old QUINQUAGENARIAN
hundredth anniversary
     QUINCENTENARY
     QUINGENTENARY
in government PENTARCHY
in Magnet (comic) FAMOUS
iron MASHIE
kings PENTARCHY
Nations AMERICAN INDIANS
nil FIFTY
one of five at birth QUINTUPLET
Pentateuch GENESIS.EXODUS
     LEVITICUS.NUMBERS
     DEUTERONOMY
Points DOCTRINES
pound note FIVER
senses HEARING.SIGHT
     SMELL.TASTE.TOUCH
star FIRST CLASS
states PENTARCHY

thousand A.V
Towns BURSLEM.HANLEY
     LONGTON.POTTERIES
     STOKE.TUNSTALL
tricks NAP
Ws WHO.WHAT.WHERE
     WHEN.WHY
years LUSTRUM.PENTAD
     QUINQUENNIUM
year-prison sentence HANDFUL

fix
fix *up* (D) ↑ TES
fixed up a new. . . WANE.WEAN
fixing tiles STILE

flag
flag IRIS.LIS
flag officer ENSIGN
flailing arms MARS.RAMS
flak AA
flaky stuff SNOW
flaming redhead MATCH.VESTA
flashing character ROBOT

flat
flat UNNATURAL
Flat 10 FLATTEN
flat *opposite* HILLY.SHARP
     UNEVEN
flat-finding agency SPIRIT LEVEL

flaw
flaw in glass SLAGS
flawed sense ESSEN

fleet RN
Flemish boat BOYER

flex
flexible friend FINDER
flexing arms MARS.RAMS
flickering lamps PALMS
flight (*see* fly)
fling stone NOTES.ONSET.TONES
floating voter TROVE

flood
flood of tears RATES.STARE
     TARES
flood survivor HAM.JAPHET
     NOAH

florin FN

flounder
flounder in sea in. . . ASININE
floundering in sea ANISE

flourished	FL.FLOREAT
flow	
flow	WILDFOWL
flow *over* ⟨	NUR
flow through *	incl in *
•river *flows through*	
Sp-ain	SPRAIN
flowing ale	LEA
flowing through	
wa/ter m/eadow	TERM
flower[1]	ROSE
flower-bird	POPPYCOCK
flower girl	DAISY.ROSE.etc.
flower spray	ROSE
	WATERING CAN
flower sprinkler	WATERING CAN
flowers	LEI
flowery item	PETAL.SEPAL
flower[2]	RIVER
hence	
•flower experiment	INDUSTRY
•flower for each. . .	CAMPER
•that *French* flower	CELADON
blue and white flower	NILE
blue flower	DANUBE
flower of France	RHONE.SEINE
flower seen in Ireland	SHANNON
German flower	RHINE
	(*see also* river)
flower[3]	(*see* plant[1])
fluctuating beat is not. . .	
	OBSTINATE
fluid	FL
hence	
•fluid *has* unknown. . .	FLY
•fluid measure	FLINCH
•fluid style	FLAIR
flushed	RED
flustered and red	DANDER
fluttering lids	SLID
fly	
fliers	RAF
flight	HEGIRA.HEJ(I)RA.HIJRA(H)
flight of swan I. . .	SWAIN.WAINS
flight member	RISER.STAIR
	TREAD
flight unit	STAIR
flighty sort	TORS
fly-by-night	BAT.MOTH

flying animal	BULLDOG.CAMEL
fl-ying *around* a. . .	FLAYING
flying around a. . .	incl A
•b-ird *flying around* a. . .	BAIRD
flying around China	CHAIN
flying around E.isle ⟨	ELSIE
flying around *	incl *
•ti-t *flying around* pole	TINT
flying ants	STAN.TANS
flying fish	PILOT
flying officer	ENSIGN.FO
flying out airman	MARINA
flying saucer	CLAY PIGEON
flying *start*	F
flying up on an(D) ↑ . . .	NANO-
flyover	HIGH ROAD
focus	
focus of *	incl in *
•learner is *focus of*	
mu-ch. . .	MULCH
fogey	SQUARE
folding arms	MARS.RAMS
folio(s)	F.(FF).FO.FOL
follow	
follow my *leader*	first letter M
followers of ABC	DE
followers *of* CND	DOE
following(s)	F.(FF).SQ.SEQ
	.SEQUENS
following his *leader*	first letter H
food	
Food and Agriculture	
Organisation	FAO
food container	STOMACH
	TUM(MY)
food crusher	MOLAR.TOOTH
food processor	STOMACH
	TUM(MY)
fool	FESTE
fool about	NITRE
fool *around*	AS-S
foolish boy	YOB
foolishly I went. . .	TWINE
foolscap	FC(A)P
foot	DANCE.F.FT
foot fault	BUNION.CORN
	HAMMER TOE
foot-pound-second	FPS
football	FA.RU

Football Association	FA
football club	AFA.FA
football clubhouse	VILLA
football club incentives	SPURS
football match	RUB OUT
footman	PEDESTRIAN
footnote	PS

for — PER.PRO

for and against	PROV-
for and on behalf of	PP
for each	PER
for example	EG.VG
for example, it...	PRONOUN
for example, Jeeves	SERVANT
for instance, servant	JEEVES
for instance, hire	HIGHER
for one, Constable	PAINTER
for starters have egg mayonnaise	HEM

forbidden *to speak* — BAND

force — F.G

forced	FZ
forced into...	-TION
forced into action	CATION

forecast

indicates anagram in front:

•so I *forecast*, weight	ISOGRAM

forego

forego a .	omit A
forego money	omit L
forego *	omit *
•mot(her) *foregoes* her ...	MOT

forehead

*fore*head	F
*fore*head	H

foreign[1]

indicates use of other languages:

•*foreign* castle	SCHLOSS
•*foreign* character	ALPHA
•*foreign* man	HOMBRE
•*foreign* town	VILLE
•*foreign* wine	VINO

foreign[2]

Foreign (and Commonweath) Office	F(C)O
foreign goddess	ALIENATE

foremost

foremost authority	A
foremost character in party	P
foremost in any good English...	AGE

forester — AOF

forge

forged coin	ICON
forger's shop	SMITHY
forging note	TONE

forget

forget a...	omit A
forget money	omit L
forget *	omit *
•(To)by *forgets* to...	BY

form

Form One	EON
form a line	ANILE
form of stapler	PLASTER
form round a...	incl a
form round *	incl *
•r-ing *forms round* a king	RAKING
form union	WED
formation of planes	PANELS

formal

formal body	STIFF
formal *introduction*	F
formally attired	(in) TA-ILS

former — EX

(*see also* old[3].old[4])

former painter	OLD ROPE
former pupil	FP.OB.OG
formerly	NEE

formula

formula for Cartesian...	ASCERTAIN
formulate his new...	WHINES
formulation of shape	HEAPS PHASE

fort — FT

forte — F

forte-piano	FP
fortissimo	FF

fortune-telling — (*see* divination)

forty[1] — F.M.MU.XL

forty, *say*	EXCEL.FOR TEA.FORTE
Forties	ROARING.SEA AREA
forty-five	DISC.EP.RECORD
Forty-five	JACOBITE REBELLION
forty-nine	IL
forty-niner	GOLD-SEEKER PROSPECTOR

—days	QUADRAGESIMA
	QUARANTINE
—in book	THIEVES
—thousand	F.M.MU
—winks	NAP
—year-old	QUADRAGENARIAN

forward

forward part of ship BOW.FOCSLE
FORECASTLE.PROW
forward part of ship   S

forzando/forzato   FZ

found

found in S/anti/ago   ANTI-
found in *   incl in *
•we are *found in* building SHEWED
found out <u>why</u> it. . .   WITHY
found vessel   LAUNCH
(*see also* find)

found abroad

indicates use of foreign word:
•coin *found in Spain*   PESETA
•flower *found in France*   FLEUR
•girl *found in Italy*   RAGAZZA
•I *found in Germany*. . .   ICH
•man *found abroad*   HOMME
HOMBRE.HUOMO.MANN

foundation of <u>house</u> (D)   E

four   IV

aces etc.	QUATORZE
based	QUATERNARY
books	JOHN

branches of mathematics
QUADRIVIUM
Christmas presents
CALLING BIRDS
cleft in four   QUADRIFID
QUADRIPARTITE
combining form   QUADR(I)-
QUADRU-.TETR(A)-

dramas	TETRALOGY
estates	CLERGY.COMMONS
	LORDS.PRESS
event contest	TETRATHLON
feet	ELL
fold	QUADRIFARIOUS

QUADRIFORM.QUADRUPLEX
QUADRUPL(ICAT)E

foot	ORGAN PIPE
fortresses	QUADRILATERAL

freedoms	FEAR.SPEECH
	WANT.WORSHIP
gills	PINT
groups	QUAD.QUARTET(T)

QUARTETTE.QUARTETTO
QUATERNION.QUATERNITY
TETRAD

having four

—angles	QUADRANGULAR
	TETRAGONAL
—columns	TETRASTYLE

—compartments
QUADRILOCULAR

—ethyl groups	TETRAETHYL
—electrodes	TETRODE
—faces	TETRAHEDRAL
— feet	QUADRUPED(AL)
	TETRAPODOUS
—fingers	TETRADACTYLOUS
—forms	QUADRIFORM
	TETRAMORPHIC
—gills	TETRABRANCHIATE
—hands	QUADRUMANOUS
—languages	TESSARAGLOT
—leaflets	QUADRIFOLIATE
—leaves per sheet	QUARTO
—letters	QUADRILITERAL
	TETRAGRAM
—like parts	QUADRIGEMINAL
	QUADRIGEMINATE
	QUADRIGEMINOUS

QUADRIPARTITE.TETRAMERAL
TETRAMEROUS

—petals/leaflets	QUATREFOIL
—pistils	TETRAGYNIAN
	TETRAGYNOUS
—rays	TETRACT(INAL)
	TETRACTINE
—rings	TETRACYCLIC
—rows	QUADRIFARIOUS
—rulers	TETRACH

—sets of chromosomes
TETRAPLOID

—stamens	TETRADYNAMOUS
	TETRANDRIAN
	TETRANDROUS
—syllables	QUADRISYLLABLE
	TETRASYLLABLE
—terms	QUADRINOMIAL

—toes	TETRADACTYLOUS
—valencies	QUADRIVALENT
	TETRAVALENT
—variables	QUATERNARY
—wheels	QUADRIROTAL
—wings	TETRAPTERAN
	TETRAPTEROUS
hundredth anniversary	
	QUADRICENTENNIAL
	QUADRIGENARY
	QUATERCENTENARY
in-hand	COACH.FINGERS
	NECKTIE
letter word	QUADRILITERAL
	TETRAGRAM
line poem	QUATRAIN
men	QUADRUMVIRATE
nil	FORTY
of <u>hearts</u>	HEAR
of the best	ACES
one of four	QUADRUPLET
pence	GROAT
poster	BED
times a day	QID
towns	TETRAPOLIS
years	QUADRENNIUM
fourteen	
fourteen at piquet	QUATORZE
fourteen-line poem	QUATORZAIN
	SONNET
fourteen lbs	STONE
fourth	D.QUARTER
fourth dimension	TIME
fourth man	SETH
fourth of December	DE.CE.MB.ER
fourth of Jul<u>y</u>	Y
fourth part	QUARTER
fourth part of circle	QUADRANT
fourth power of a million	
	QUADRILLION
fox	TOD
fracas <u>she saw</u>	WASHES
fracture	
fracture <u>hip</u>	PHI
fracturing <u>arm</u>	MAR.RAM
fragment	FR
fragmented <u>bone</u>	EBON
fragments of <u>petals</u>	PEAL
fragments of <u>petals</u>	STAPLE

frail <u>prince</u>	PINCER
frame	
framed by *	incl in *
•aim *framed by* manuscript	
	MENDS
framing a...	incl A
framing *	incl *
•manuscript *framing* aim	MENDS
franc	FR
France	FR.RF
Franco-German agreement	OUIJA
frankincense	THUS
frantic	
frantic <u>leap</u>	PALE.PEAL
frantically <u>stare</u>	RATES.TARES
	TEARS
frayed <u>nerves</u>	SEVERN
free[1]	RID
hence	
•free movement	RIDDANCE
•free *return*, for example ⟨	RIDGE
•free-*standing*(D) ↑	DIR
•free study	RIDDEN
free *admission*	incl RID
•free *admission to* Geological	
Society	GRIDS
free[2]	
alongside ship	FAS
of charge	FOC
on board	FOB
on rail	FOR
free[3]	
free a...	omit A
free *	omit *
•*free* her from fat(her)'s...	FATS
<u>free</u> *movement*	REEF
Free Presbyterian	FP
free publication	RELEASE
free-range eggs	LAID OUT
free <u>slaves</u>	SALVES
free-style <u>event seen</u>...	
	SEVENTEEN
free transfer for <u>player</u>	REPLAY
free <u>vote</u>	VETO
free<u>dom</u>	MOD
free<u>ly</u> <u>as her</u>...	HARES.HEARS
	SHARE
insect-*free*	omit FLY
•(f)air(ly) insect-*free*	AIR

freezing

freezing point	FP
freezing point	F

French¹

hence	
•a French help	AFRAID
•French caper	FRANTIC
•French crew	FREIGHT
French fort	STRONG
Frenchman	M.RENE
French manger	EAT
Frenchmen	MM

French²

French friend	AMI(E)
hence	
•*French* friend can	AMIABLE
•*French* friend with 500. . .	AMID
•*French* friend *in* the Louvre	
initially	TAMIL
-leader	E
—traffic jam	RUEFUL

French³

ability to do the right thing	
SAVOIR-FAIRE	
above	SUR
abridgment	ABREGE
absent-minded	DISTRAIT(E)
accomplished fact	FAIT ACCOMPLI
according to	A LA
across	A TRAVERS
actor in farces	FARCEUR
administrative chief of	
department	PREFECT
adventurer	
CHEVALIER D'INDUSTRIE	
advice	CONSEIL
aeroplane	AVION
affectedly stylish	CHI(-)CHI
after	APRES
again	ENCORE
against the grain	A REBOURS
agent	COMMIS
agreed	D'ACCORD
agreement	OUI
air	ALLURE
alas	HELAS
all	TOUT(E)
—at once	TOUT A COUP
—right	BIEN ENTENDU

	TRES BIEN
—the rage (to be)	FAIRE FUREUR
—the same	TOUT DE MEME
—the world	TOUT LE MONDE
—things considered	
	MALGRE TOUT
—together	EN MASSE
aloud	A HAUTE VOIX
already	DEJA
—seen	DEJA VU
amazing event	COUP DE FOUDRE
andiron	CHENET
angel	ANGE
annual income	RENTE
annulment of higher court	
decision	CASSATION
anonymous	ANONYME
anthem	MARSEILLAISE
applause	ECLAT.VIVE
apple brandy liquor	CALVADOS
apprentice chef	COMMIS
appropriate(ly)	APROPOS
approval	OUI
April fool	POISSON D'AVRIL
arch	ESPIEGLE
aristocrat	GRAND SEIGNEUR
arm(s)	BRAS
armchair	FAUTEUIL
arrogance	HAUTEUR
arrow	FLECHE
art	
—of acquiring publicity	
	RECLAME
—of make-up	MAQUILLAGE
artful	RUSE
article	LE.LA.LES
—from journal	TIRAGE A PART
—of artistic worth	OBJET D'ART
—collector of objets d'art	
	GRAND AMATEUR
—made of esparto	SPARTERIE
artistic	
—quarter of Paris	LEFT BANK
—skill	CHIC
as	
—a body	EN BLOC
—a friend	EN AMI
—a spectacle	EN SPECTACLE
—a whole	EN BLOC

—it should be	COMME IL FAUT	barracks	CASERN(E)
—part of a set	EN SUITE	base coin	BILLON
ash-blond	CENDRE	bashfulness	MAUVAISE HONTE
assistant	ADJOINT	basic fact, premise	DONNEE
associate	CONFRERE	basis	FOND
assumed name	NOM DE GUERRE	bath	BAIN
	NOM DE PLUME	be born	NAITRE
at		beach	PLAGE
—all costs	A TOUTE FORCE	bean	FEVE.HARICOT
—any cost	A TOUT PRIX	bearing	TENUE
—any risk	A TOUTE HAZARD	beautiful	BEAU.BELLE
—bottom	AU FOND	bed	LIT
—ease	SANS GENE	before	AVANT
—full speed	VENTRE A TERRE	—this	CI-DEVANT
—great cost	A GRANDS FRAIS	behaviour (good)	TENUE
—home	CHEZ.EN FAMILLE	behind	DERRIERE.EN ARRIERE
—once	TOUT DE SUITE	below	SOUS
—one's ease	EN PANTOUFLES	belt	CEINTURE
—random	A LA VOLEE	besides	AU RESTE
	TORT ET A TRAVERS	betrothal	FIANCAILLES
—room temperature	CHAMBRE(E)	betrothed person	FIANCE(E)
—the forefront	AVANT GARDE	betting system	PARI-MUTUEL
—the worst	AU PIS ALLER	between	ENTRE
attitudiniser	POSEUR	—ourselves	ENTRE NOUS
audacious	RISQUE	bewilderment	EGAREMENT
aunt	TANTE	beyond	SUR
avenue	ALLEE	—comparison	PAR EXCELLENCE
awkwardness	GAUCHERIE	bittersweet	AIGRE-DOUX
baby's entire set of clothes, etc.		blackmail	CHANTAGE
	LAYETTE	blandishments	AGREMENTS
background of design	FOND	bleach	EAU DE JAVEL(LE)
back-to-back	DOS-A-DOS	blind alley	CUL-DE-SAC
backwards	A REBOURS	blow	COUP
bad	MAL.MAUVAIS(E)	blue	BLEU
—form	MAUVAIS TON	—ribbon	CORDON BLEU
—moment	MAUVAIS MOMENT	—stocking	BAS BLEU
—taste	MAUVAIS GOUT		FEMME SAVANTE
badly groomed	MAL SOIGNE(E)	blues (the)	CAFARD
bagpipe	CORNEMUSE.LOURE	blunder	BEVUE.FAUX PAS
	MUSETTE.SORDELINE	boarding-school	PENSIONNAT
bailiff	HUISSIER	boat	BATEAU
ballet		boiled leather	CUIR-BOUILLI
—company	CORPS DE BALLET	bonfire	FEU DE JOIE
—dancer	DANSEUSE	bookseller	LIBRAIRE
—leap	JETE	bookshop/book-trade	LIBRAIRIE
—master	MAITRE	bored	ENNUYE
—step	FOUETTE	boredom	ENNUI
bar	BRASSERIE	—period of	LONGUEUR
barley	ORGE	boring instrument	AIGUILLE

born	NE(E)	—January, rain	PLUVIOSE
bosom friend	AMI DE COEUR	—February, wind	VENTOSE
box at theatre	LOGE	—March, seed	GERMINAL
boxing with use of feet	SAVATE	—April, blossom	FLOREAL
boyish	GAMIN	—May, pasture	PRAIRIAL
—girl	GAMINE	—June, harvest	MESSIDOR
brand	MARQUE	—July, heat	THERMIDOR
brandy	ARMAGNAC.COGNAC	—August, fruit	FRUCTIDOR
	FINE	—September, vintage	
bread	PAIN		VENDEMIAIRE
—crumbs	PANURE	—October, fog	BRUMAIRE
—roll	PETIT PAIN	—November, sleet	FRIMAIRE
breakfast	(PETIT) DEJEUNER	—December, snow	NIVOSE
breeches	CULOTTES	called	DIT
bridgehead	TETE-DE-PONT	calling	METIER
brilliance	ECLAT	calmness	SANG-FROID
brother	FRERE	candour	FRANCHISE
brotherhood	CONFRERIE	cape	MANTILLE
brown	BRUN	capital	F.PARIS
—sugar	CASSONADE	*capitalist*	PARISIEN(NE)
brute	BETE	caprice	BOUTADE
buckler	RONDACHE	captivated	EPRIS(E)
business	METIER	card games	BACCARAT
—man	HOMME D'AFFAIRES		BOUILLOTTE
butcher's shop	CHARCUTERIE	CHEMIN DE FER.OMBRE	
butler	SOMMELIER	carelessly dressed	DESHABILLE
butterfly	PAPILLON	carriage	CAROCHE.FIACRE
buttocks	DERRIERE.LE CUL		VOITURE
button	BOUTON	—with facing seats	VIS-A-VIS
—hole	BOUTONNIERE	carried away	ENLEVE
by	PAR	carthorse	PERCHERON
—air(mail)	PAR AVION	case	ETUI
—all means	A TOUTE FORCE	cask	TONNEAU
—force of arms	A MAIN ARMEE	cassock	SOUTANE
—halves	A DEMI.A MOITIE	castle	CHATEAU
—stealth	A LA DEROBEE	—governor	CHATELAIN(E)
—the way	APROPOS DE BOTTES	—in Spain	
	EN PASSANT	CHATEAU EN ESPAGNE	
cab	FIACRE	casual	DEGAGE
cabaret performer		cattle	CHAROL(L)AIS.LIMOUSIN
	CHANSONNIER(E)	cause	RAISON
cabbage	CHOU	cavalier	CHEVALIER
cabinet-maker	EBENISTE	cavalryman	CHASSEUR
cable-car	TELEFERIQUE	ceiling	PLAFOND
café	BISTRO	celebrating holiday	EN FETE
—with music	CAFE CHANTANT	censer	CASSOLETTE
	CAFE CONCERT	certainly	BIEN ENTENDU
cake	GATEAU.MILLEFEUILLE	chambermaid	FILLE DE CHAMBRE
calendar (Revolution)		characters	FR.RF

charmingly ugly	BELLE LAIDE	—wearer	SABOTIER
	JOLIE LAIDE	close-fitting sleeveless garment	
charm	AGREMEN(T)S		JUPON
chattering	BAVARDAGE	closure	CLOTURE
cheap	A BON MARCHE	clumsy(-iness)	GAUCHE(RIE)
cheap(ly)	BON MARCHE	coach (opera)	REPETITEUR
cheeses	BRIE.FROMAGE	coarseness	GROSSIERETE
	ROQUEFORT	coffee	CAFE
—sauce	FONDUE	—filtered	CAFE FILTRE
chestnut	MARRON	—house	CAFE
chewed	MACHE	—with milk	CAFE AU LAIT
chic	CHICHI	—without milk	CAFE NOIR
chicken	POULE(T)	coins	
chief		—unit	FRANC
—magistrate (Swiss)	AVOYER	—farthing (old)	LIARD
—prize	GRAND PRIX	—halfpenny (old)	SOL
child	ENFANT	—5 centimes	SOU
—of his times		—10 centimes	DECIME
	ENFANT DE SON SIECLE	—100 centimes	FRANC
—of the house		—franc (old)	LIVRE
	ENFANT DE LA MAISON	—20 sols	LIVRE
chin	MENTON	—5 francs	ECU.SCUTE
china	SEVRES	—20 franc piece	LOUIS(D'OR)
Chinese-style art or		—20 francs (old)	NAPOLEON
objects	CHINOISERIE	—old copper	DENIER
chocolate and cream cake	ECLAIR	—old gold	ANGELOT
choice	RECHERCHE		LOUIS(D')OR
choose	CHOISIR.VOULOIR	—old silver	CARDECU(E).DENIER
chop	COTELETTE		ECU.SCUTE
choreographer		colleague	CONFRERE
	MAITRE DE BALLET	collision	RENCONTRE
churchmen	GENS D'EGLISE	come	
cinema enthusiast	CINEAST(E)	—in	ENTREZ
circle	CERCLE.COTERIE	—on	ALLONS
circus	CIRQUE	comet tail	CHEVELURE
civil		comic opera	OPERA BOUFFE
—officer assisting mayor	ADJOINT	committed to a particular	
—servant	FONCTIONNAIRE	theory	ENGAGE
claret glass	MOUSSELINE	commons	TIERS ETAT
clash of foes	RENCONTRE	communication trench	BOYAU
classical period of France		communist	ROUGE
(17th c.)	GRAND SIECLE	company	CIE.COMPAGNIE.SA
clear soup	CONSOMME	competition	CONCOURS
	JULIENNE	—parade of cars	
clearing up	ECLAIRCISSEMENT		CONCOURS D'ELEGANCE
cleric's coif	CALOTTE	complete reversal of	
clerk of the court	GREFFIER	opinion, etc.	VOLTE-FACE
cloak	MANTEAU	composure	SANG-FROID
clog	SABOT	compromised	BRULE

conciliator	PRUD'HOMME
concrete	BETON
confectioner	CONFISEUR
confectionery	CONFISERIE
confused	DESORIENTE
connection	ET
conscription	LEVEE-EN-MASSE
contemptuously	DE HAUT EN BAS
contest	CONCOURS
contradiction	DEMENTI
control by state	DIRIGISM(E)
conventional art	POMPIER
convict	FORCAT
cook	CHEF (DE CUISINE)
cooked	
—and served in greaseproof	
paper	EN PAPILLOTE
—with brown sugar	BRULE
cookery	CUISINE
cooking	
—utensils	BATTERIE DE CUISINE
—of highest standard	
	CORDON BLEU
—vessel	BAIN MARIE
coolness	APLOMB.FRAICHEUR
	SANG-FROID
coquetry	AGACERIE
corded silk fabric	GROSGRAIN
corked	BOUCHE
Corpus Christi	FETE-DIEU
correctly	COMME IL FAUT
cosmetics	MAQUILLAGE
council	CONSEIL
—of state	CONSEIL D'ETAT
country	PAYS
—house	BASTIDE.CHATEAU
—music	MARSEILLAISE
courtly love	AMOUR COURTOIS
covered	
—walk	BERCEAU
—with breadcrumbs or	
cheese	AU GRATIN
cradle	BERCEAU
—song	BERCEUSE
cream	CREME
—bun	CHOU
creative evolutionary force in	
organisms	ELAN VITAL
credulous	NAIF (NAIVE)

crescent-shaped roll	CROISSANT
crest of helmet	CIMIER
crime of passion	
	CRIME PASSIONEL
criminal	APACHE
—identification system	
	BERTILLONAGE
—investigation department	
	SURETE
critical commentary	CRITIQUE
cross-stitching	GROS POINT
crow	CORBEAU
cry from the heart	CRI DE COEUR
cunning	NARQUOIS
cupboard	ARMOIRE
curling	FRISURE
current events	ACTUALITES
curtain	RIDEAU
—raiser	LEVER DE RIDEAU
custom-built	HORS DE SERIE
customs	
—house	DOUANE
—officer	DOUANIER
cutlet	COTELETTE
dainty	FRIAND(E)
dais	HAUT PAS
daisy	MARGUERITE
damned soul	AME DAMNEE
dances	BOURREE.BRAN(S)LE
	BRANTLE.CAN-CAN
CARMAGNOLE.CHACONNE	
CORANTO.COURANTE	
	GAVOTTE
—for two	PAS DE DEUX
—of death	DANSE MACABRE
—step	CHASSE-CROISE
	CHASSEE
dandy	BEAU
dangerously attractive	
woman	FEMME FATALE
dark red	SANG DE BOEUF
dash	ELAN
daughter	FILLE
Dauphin	MONSEIGNEUR
day	JOUR
—dreamer	REVEUR.REVEUSE
—school	EXTERNAT
—'s march	ETAPE
dazzling	FOUDROYANT

dead	MORT(E)
deadlock	IMPASSE
deal (cards)	DONNE
dear	CHER(E).CHOU.
death	MORT
debauchee	ROUE
decadent	FIN DE SIECLE
decision	PARTI
decorative trimming	
	PASS(E)MENT
decorum	BIENSEANCE
decree	ARRET
deliberate	VOULU
delicate	FRIAND(E)
delicatessen	CHARCUTERIE
denial	DEMENTI
department	ISERE.MEUSE.MIDI
	OISE.SEINE
—administrative chief	PREFECT
—of Military Intelligence	
	DEUXIEME BUREAU
depressed	ACCABLE
depression	CAFARD
—about the state of the	
world	MAL DU SIECLE
deputy	COMMIS
deranged person	DETRAQUE
desk	BONHEUR DU JOUR
despatch	DEPECHE
dessert	COUPE
detective	AGENT.POLICIER
—novel	ROMAN POLICIER
developed	EVOLUE
dialect	LANGUEDOC.PATOIS
	PROVENCAL.WALLOON
diary	JOURNAL (PARTICULIER)
difficult	DIFFICILE
difficulty without	
solution	IMPASSE
diplomatic	DEMARCHE
—agent	CHARGE D'AFFAIRES
—corps	CORPS DIPLOMATIQUE
—staff	CORPS DIPLOMATIQUE
disabled	HORS DE COMBAT
discomfort	MALAISE
discordant din or	
music	CHARIVARI
dish	
—between main courses	ENTREE

—cloth	TORCHON
—from cream with fruit, fish,	
meat	MOUSSE
—of fowl, meat, etc. served in	
sauce	FRICASSEE
—of fried food	FRITURE
disinfectant	EAU DE JAVEL(LE)
dismal	MORNE
dismissal	CONGE.RENVOI
disorder	EGAREMENT
disreputable	LOUCHE
distaste	DEGOUT
distinction	ECLAT
ditty	CHANSONETTE
donkey	ANE
dormer-window	LUCARNE
dotted	CRIBLE
double meaning	
	DOUBLE ENTENDRE
downcast	ABBATTU.ALAMORT
downwards	DE HAUT EN BAS
dramatic turn of events	
	COUP DE THEATRE
drawing together	
	RAPPROCHEMENT
dream	REVE
dress	
—maker	COUTURIER(E)
—making	COUTURE
dressing	
—case	NECESSAIRE
—gown	ROBE DE CHAMBRE
drop	GOUTTE
—by drop	GOUTTE A GOUTTE
drown	NOYER
drunkenness	IVRESSE
dry	BRUT.SEC
duel	AFFAIRE D'HONNEUR
duenna	GOUVERNANTE
duke	DUC
dullness	FADEUR
dupe	BECASSE
duster	TORCHON
eagerness	EMPRESSEMENT
early fruit	PRIMEUR
earth	TERRE
east	EST
easy	DEGAGE
eat	MANGER

eccentric person		—month	TOUS-LES-MOIS
	MONSTRE SACRE	exacting	EXIGEANT(E)
educational centre of		exaggerated	OUTRE
Paris	LATIN QUARTER	example	EXEMPLE
elder	AINE(E)	exotic	RECHERCHE
elegance	CHIC	experiment	COUP D'ESSAI
elegant literature		explanation	ECLAIRCISSEMENT
	BELLES-LETTRES		FIN MOT DE L'AFFAIRE
eleven	ONZE	exposed to capture	
Elysian Fields	CHAMPS ELYSEES	(chesspiece)	EN PRISE
embarrassing situation		exposing (scandal, etc.)	EXPOSE
	CONTRETEMPS	face	FACADE
embarrassment	GENE	—to-face	VIS-A-VIS
—of choice	EMBARRAS DE CHOIX	facing foward	EN FACE
—of wealth		faded	PASSE(E)
	EMBARRAS DE RICHESSES	fairy	FEE
emblem	FLEUR DE LIS	—land	FEERIE
embroidered lace	FILET	faker	TRUQUER
embroidery	PETIT POINT	faking of works of art	TRUCAGE
enamelled metalwork			TRUQUAGE
	CHAMPLEVE	fall	CHUTE
enchantment	FEERIE	—of rocks, etc.	EBOULEMENT
encounter	RENCONTRE	false	FAUX
end of		—rumour	CANARD
—an era	FIN DE SIECLE	—step	FAUX PAS
—the century	FIN DE SIECLE	family	FAMILLE
endive	ESCAROLE	—consultation	
engaged person	FIANCE(E)		CONSEIL DE FAMILLE
English Channel	LA MANCHE	famous	
enough	ASSEZ BIEN	—make	GRANDE MARQUE
entertain as at a fête	FETE	—trial	CAUSE CELEBRE
enthusiasm	ENTRAINEMENT	fancy	
entirely	TOUT (A FAIT)	—biscuit	PETIT FOUR
entrance for carriages		—cake	GATEAU
	PORTE-COCHERE	—dress ball	BAL PARE
entry	ENTREE	farewell	ADIEU.CONGE
environment	MILIEU	farmer paying rent with	
epic poem	CHANSON DE GESTE	crop	METAYER
epicure	BON VIVANT	fashionable	A LA MODE.CHIC
	BON VIVEUR.FRIAND(E)	—dressmaking	HAUTE COUTURE
epilepsy	PETIT MAL	father	PERE
equal	PAREIL	—in-law	BEAU PERE
equipment	MATERIEL	fattened goose liver	FOIE GRAS
escapade	FREDAINE	favoured fancy	MAROTTE
estate	CHATEAU	feast day	JOUR DE FETE
evening	SOIR	feat of strength or	
—party	SOIREE	skill	TOUR DE FORCE
every	TOUT	feeler	BALLON D'ESSAI
—body	TOUT LE MONDE	fellow	

—member	CONFRERE	flower	FLEUR
—ship	CAMERADERIE	fly-catcher	GOBE-MOUCHES
female		flying	A LA VOLEE
—dancer	DANSEUSE	folly	FOLIE
—friend	BELLE AMIE	fool	BECASSE
—singer	CHANTEUSE	foolish	ETOURDI(E)
fencing		footpath	TROTTOIR
—position	SECONDE	fop	PETIT MAITRE
—thrust	BOTTE	for	
festival	FETE	—both hands	A DEUX MAINS
fickle	VOLAGE	—example	PAR EXEMPLE
fierce	ACHARNE	—four hands	A QUATRE MAINS
film		—shame!	FI DONC
—director	AUTEUR	—two	A DEUX
—maker	CINEAST(E)	—want of better	
—style	NOUVELLE VAGUE		FAUTE DE MIEUX
final outcome	DENOUEMENT	forcemeat ball	QUENELLE
finally	ENFIN	Foreign Office	QAUI D'ORSAY
find (lucky) or solution		foreigner	ETRANGER(E)
	TROUVAILLE	foremast	MISAINE
fine (penalty)	AMENDE	forerunner	AVANT COURIER
—arts	BEAUX ARTS	foresail	MISAINE
—day	BEAU JOUR	forest	BOIS
—prospect	BELLE VUE	foretaste	AVANT GOUT
finishing stroke	COUP DE GRACE	forever	A JAMAIS
fipple-flute	FLUTE-A-BEC	forfeiture	DECHEANCE
fire	FEU	forget	OUBLIER
—man	POMPIER	forlorn hope	ENFANTS PERDUS
—works	FEUX D'ARTIFICE	former(ly)	CI-DEVANT
first		forming a unit	EN SUITE
—attempt	COUP D'ESSAI	forward	EN AVANT
—floor	BEL ETAGE	foundation scholar	BOURSIER
—performance	PREMIERE	foundling	ENFANT TROUVE
fish	POISSON	fountain	JET D'EAU
—soup	BOUILLABAISSE	fragment	MORCEAU
fixed		frame	MONTURE
—idea	IDEE FIXE	frankness	FRANCHISE
—price	PRIX FIXE	free	
—price meal	TABLE D'HOTE	—thinker	ESPRIT FORT
flaming torch	FLAMBEAU	—verse	VERS LIBRE
flash	BLUETTE	freedom of	
flask	CARAFE	—access	ENTREE
flat	MAISON(N)ETTE	—action	CARTE BLANCHE
—cap	BER(R)ET	freshness	FRAICHEUR
flayed	ECORCHE	friar	RELIGIEUX
fleece	TOISON	fried	
Flemish nationalist	FLAMINGANT	—bread slice	CROUTE
flighty	VOLAGE	—bread (small piece)	CROUTON
floor	ETAGE.PLANCHER	—lightly	SAUTE

—or toasted bread with topping	CANAPE
friend	AMI(E)
	(*see also* French²)
—of the people	AMI DU PEUPLE
friendly understanding	
	ENTENTE (CORDIALE)
fritter	FRITURE
frolicsome	ESPIEGLE
from	
—bad to worse	DE MAL EN PIS
—day to day	AU JOUR LE JOUR
—hand to mouth	
	AU JOUR LE JOUR
fulcrum	POINT D'APPUI
full dress	
—military	GRANDE TENUE
—ladies' evening-dress	
	GRANDE TOILETTE
fulled cloth	FOULE
fund	FONDS
—holder	RENTIER
fundamentally	AU FOND
funeral procession	CORTEGE
furious	ACHARNE
furnishing material	MOQUETTE
fury	FUREUR
future	AVENIR
gait	ALLURE
gallant	CHEVALIER
gambling game	ROULETTE
game	JEU
—of bowls	BOULES.PETANQUE
garden	JARDIN
—party	FETE CHAMPETRE
—path	ALLEE
garish	CRIANT
gauge to test gunpowder	
	EPROUVETTE
general	
—appearance	TOUT ENSEMBLE
—view	COUP D'OEIL
genius	BEL ESPRIT
gentleman	GENTILHOMME.M
	MESSIEURS.MESSRS.MM
German	BO(S)CHE
—beer	BOCK
gibe	BROCARD
giddy	ETOURDI(E).VOLAGE

gift	CADEAU
gild the pill	DORER LA PILULE
gilded youth	JEUNESSE DOREE
girdle	CEINTURE
girl	FILLETTE.(JEUNE) FILLE
given	DONNE(E)
glance	OEILLADE
glass	VERRE
—window	VITRAGE.VITRE
glazed chestnuts	
	MARRONS GLACES
gloomy	MORNE
glory	GLOIRE
glue	COLLE-FORTE
God	DIEU
—and my right	
	DIEU ET MON DROIT
—with us	DIEU AVEC NOUS
godfather	COMPERE
godsend	AUBAINE
gold	OR
golden fleece	TOISON D'OR
good	BEAU.BELLE.BON(NE)
—appearance	BONNE MINE
—bargain	NON MARCHE
—breeding	SAVOIR-VIVRE
—Christian	BON CHRETIEN
—company	COMPAGNIE
	AGREABLE
—comrade	BON CAMARADE
—day/morning	BON JOUR
—deportment	BEL AIR
—evening	BON SOIR
—faith	BONNE FOI
—for-nothing	VAURIEN
—friend	BON AMI
—grace	BONNE GRACE
—journey	BON VOYAGE
—luck	BONNE CHANCE
—man	HOMME DE BIEN
—nature	BONHOM(M)IE
—natured fellow	BON DIABLE
—reception	BON ACCEUIL
—taste	BON GOUT
—times	BEAU JOUR
goodbye	A BIENTOT.ADIEU
	AU REVOIR
goose liver	FOIE GRAS
—paté	PATE DE FOIE GRAS

governess	GOUVERNANTE	—of hair	CHEVELURE
	MADEMOISELLE	—to-tail	TETE-BECHE
government		—waiter	MAITRE D'HOTEL
—monopoly	REGIE	headlong	A CORPS PERDU
—securities	RENTE	hearsay	ON-DIT
gown	MANTEAU	heartbreak	CREVE-COEUR
grace (your)	MONSEIGNEUR	heartfelt appeal	CRI DE COEUR
gracious gesture	BEAU GESTE	heartland	LANDE
grand love affair		heavenly voice	VOIX CELESTE
	GRANDE PASSION	heedless	ETOURDI(E)
grant	OCTROYER	height of fashion	BON TON
gravy	JUS	helmet	HEAUME
great	GRAND(E)	help!	AU SECOURS
—army	GRANDE ARMEE	helpless laughter	FOU RIRE
—century	GRAND SIECLE	Her Majesty	SA MAJESTE.SM
—luxury	GRAND LUXE	herb mixture	FINES HERBES
Greek	GREQUE	here	ICI
grey gown	GRISETTE	—lies. . .	CI-GIT
grocer	EPICIER	high	HAUT(E)
gropingly	A TATONS	—fashion	HAUT TON
grossness	GROSSIERETE		HAUTE COUTURE
ground	TERRE	—relief	HAUT RELIEF
group of vineyards	CRU	—society	GRAND MONDE
guerrilla	FRANC-TIREUR		HAUT MONDE
guild of clerks	BASOCHE	high class	
gullible person	GOBE-MOUCHES	—cookery	CORDON BLEU
gully	COULOIR		HAUTE CUISINE
haberdasher	MERCIER	—prostitute	GRANDE COCOTTE
hackney-coach	FIACRE	highest military officer	MARSHAL
hair	CHEVEUX	highness	ALTESSE
—dresser	FRISEUR	His Majesty	SA MAJESTE.SM
—piece	CHIGNON	hitch	CONTRETEMPS
half	DEMI	hobby horse	CHEVAL DE
—light	DEMI-JOUR		BATAILLE
hall	SALLE	holiday	FETE
hand	MAIN	holy water font	BENITIER
—kissing	BAISEMAIN	homesickness	MAL DU PAYS
handkerchief	MOUCHOIR	honest people	GENS DE BIEN
handsome	BEAU	honour as with a fête	FETE
—man	BEAU GARCON	hopper	TREMIE
—woman	BELLE	horse	CHEVAL
hang him!	A LA LANTERNE	—race	GRAND PRIX DE PARIS
happy medium	JUSTE MILIEU	horseman in armour	GENDARME
hash	HACHIS	horsemanship	MANEGE
hat	CHAPEAU	hospital	HOTEL-DIEU.HOPITAL
haughtiness	HAUTEUR	hotel-keeper	HOTELIER
hauteur	MORGUE	house	MAISON
hazelnut	NOISETTE	—keeper	GOUVERNANTE
head	TETE	—steward	MAITRE D'HOTEL

household	MENAGE	—male dress (woman)	
—of three	MENAGE A TROIS		EN TRAVESTI
hunter	CHASSEUR	—my opinion	A MON AVIS
husband	MARI	—natural state	AU NATUREL
I	JE	—outlawry	HORS LA LOI
—adjust (chess)	J'ADOUBE	—passing	EN PASSANT
ice cream	GLACE.MOUSSE	—princely style	EN PRINCE
—dessert	BOMBE.COUP	—principle	EN PRINCIPE
iced (of liqueurs, etc.)	FRAPPE(E)	—progress	EN TRAIN
idea	IDEE	—requital	EN RETOUR
identity card	CARTE-DE-VISITE	—retirement	EN RETRAITE
idler	FAINEANT.FLANEUR	—return	EN RETOUR
idling	FLANERIE	—shelter	A L'ABRI
if you please	S'IL VOUS PLAIT	—slippers	EN PANTOUFLES
ill	MALADE	—spite of everything	

illusion of having experienced
  something before   DEJA VU

	MALGRE TOUT
—succession	EN SUITE

illustration inset separately into a
  book   HORS TEXTE

		—sympathy	EN RAPPORT
immediately	TOUT DE SUITE	—the country	A LA CAMPAGNE
immortal	IMMORTEL(LE)	—the air	EN L'AIR
impish	GAMIN(E)	—the manner of	A LA
impishness	GAMINERIE	—the meantime	EN ATTENDANT
impulsive act	ACTE GRATUIT	—the open air	A LA BELLE ETOILE
in			EN PLEIN AIR
—a body	EN MASSE	—the rear	EN ARRIERE
—abundance	A GOGO	—the way	DE TROP
—all seriousness		—town	EN VILLE
	AU GRAND SERIEUX	—truth	EN VERITE
	TRES AU SERIEUX	—tune	D'ACCORD
—any case	EN TOUT CAS	incendiary	PETROLEUR
—broad daylight	EN PLEIN JOUR	income	RENTE
—cavalier manner	EN CAVALIER	indeed	EN EFFET
—due order	EN REGLE	indefinable quality	
—emulation	A L'ENVI		JE NE SAIS QUOI
—fact	EN EFFET	indifferent to pleasure	BLASE
—festive dress or		infatuated	ENTETE(E)
surroundings	EN FETE	infatuation	ENGOU(E)MENT
—front	EN FACE	(informal) talks	POURPARLER
—full court dress		injured	HORS DE COMBAT
	EN GRANDE TENUE	inlaid work	MARQUETERIE
—fun	EN BADINANT	inn	AUBERGE
—good form	EN BON POINT	—keeper	AUBERGISTE
—hand	A LA MAIN	innocent	NAIF (NAIVE)
—harmony	EN RAPPORT	insanity	FOLIE
—line	EN QUEUE	insectivorous plant	
—lodgings with meals			GOBE-MOUCHES
provided	EN PENSION	insight	APERCU
—love	EPRISE	insipid	FADE
		instrument of execution by	

beheading	GUILLOTINE	—'s throne	LIT DE JUSTICE
international		kitchen	CUISINE
—law	DROIT DES GENS	knave	FRIPON
—motor race	GRAND PRIX	knavery	FRIPONNERIE
—permit for importing car		knick-knack	BIBELOT
	TRIPTYQUE	knight	CHEVALIER
intimate	INTIME	know	CONNAITRE.SAVOIR
iridescence	REFLET	lace	ALENCON.CLUNY
iridescent	CHATOYANT		COLBERTINE.VALENCIENNES
irresistible beauty		—frill	JABOT
	BEAUTE DU DIABLE	—with openwork design	
is it not so?	N'EST-CE PAS		TORCHON (LACE)
island	ILE	lack of taste	MAUVAIS GOUT
item	PIECE	lady	DAME
jacket	VESTE.VESTON	—'s-maid	FEMME DE CHAMBRE
—book	COUVERTURE.JAQUETTE	—'s room	BOUDOIR
janitor	CONCIERGE	lake	LAC
jargon	BARAGOUIN	lampstand	TORCHIERE
jellied sauce	CHAUDFROID	land	TERRE
jet of water	JET D'EAU	landed property	FONDS
jewel	BIJOU	landslide	EBOULEMENT
—on chain as head adornment		langour	ENNUI
	FERRON(N)IERE	language	LANGUE
jewelled pendant	LAVAL(L)IERE	—(north)	LANGUE D'OIL
jewellery	BIJOUTERIE.PARURE	—(south)	LANGUE D'OC
—setting	PAVE	last	DERNIER
joiner	MENUISIER	—resort	DERNIER RESSORT
—joint stock company		—resource	PIS ALLER
	SOCIETE ANONYME	—word	DERNIER CRI
joke collection	SOTTISIER	latest fashion	DERNIER CRI
joker	FARCEUR	Latin quarter	QUARTIER LATIN
jokingly	EN BADINANT	laundress	BLANCHISSEUSE
joust	PAS D'ARMES	lawyer	AVOCAT.AVOUE
joy of living	JOI DE VIVRE	lawyers	GENS DE LOI
judge's bench	BANC	leader of Republic	CONSUL
jugglery	LEGERDEMAIN	leading	
juggling	ESCAMOTAGE	—actress, dancer etc.	PREMIERE
	JONGLERIE	—film or theatre star	
junior	FILS		GRANDE VEDETTE
juvenile lead	JEUNE PREMIER	learned woman	FEMME SAVANTE
key	CLEF	leather	CUIR
—chain	CHATELAINE	—hardened by soaking	
kidnapped	ENLEVE	in wax	CUIR-BOUILLI
kind	SORTE	lecturer	CONFERENCIER
king	ROI.SM	leer	LORGNER
—without power	ROI FAINEANT	left	GAUCHE
—'s eldest son	DAUPHIN	leg of mutton	GIGOT
—'s eldest son's wife		legislative bill	PROJET DE LOI
	DAUPHINESSE	lending against	

—landed property CREDIT FONCIER
—moveable property CREDIT MOBILIER
let
—do LAISSER-FAIRE
LAISSEZ-FAIRE
—go LAISSER-ALLER
LAISSEZ-ALLER
—pass LAISSEZ-PASSER
—us go ALLONS.EN ROUTE
Lent CAREME
letter LETTRE
—of marque LETTRE DE MARQUE
—under royal
seal LETTRE DE CACHET
liaison AFFAIRE
light
—fitting LUMINAIRE
—dish served between
courses ENTREMETS
—infantryman CHASSEUR
VOLTIGEUR
—o'-love COCOTTE
—verse VERS DE SOCIETE
lightning FOUDRE
like a
—bachelor EN GARCON
—great lord
EN GRAND SEIGNEUR
—tail EN QUEUE
likelihood VRAISEMBLANCE
limited BORNE
—liability company SA
SOCIETE ANONYME
line LIGNE
—of support POINT D'APPUI
linen LINGE
liqueur after
coffee CHASSE(-CAFE)
POUSSE-CAFE
literally AU PIED DE LA LETTRE
little BIJOU.PETIT
—curl FRISETTE
—song CHANSONETTE
live VIVRE
liveliness ENTRAIN
lively VIF.VIVE
—dance GIGUE

liver paté PATE DE FOIE GRAS
liveried attendant CHASSEUR
living picture TABLEAU VIVANT
loafer FAINEANT.FLANEUR
lobster LANGOUSTE
long live VIVE
look well AVOIR BONNE MINE
looked upon with distaste MAL VU
looped yarn BOUCLE
loose
—overcoat PALETOT
—woman COCOTTE
loosely tied bow LAVAL(L)IERE
lost
—children ENFANTS PERDUS
—one's bearings DESORIENTE
—soul AME PERDUE
louvred screen BRISE SOLEIL
love AMOUR
—affair AFFAIRE(D'AMOUR)
AFFAIRE DE COEUR
—at first sight COUP DE FOUDRE
—letter BILLET DOUX
lover AMOUREUSE.AMOUREUX
BEAU.BELLE.BON AMI
low BAS
—cut (dress) DECOLLETE
lower middle class
PETIT BOURGEOIS(IE)
loyalty to group ESPRIT DE CORPS
lucky charm PORTE-BONHEUR
luggage van FOURGON
lunch DEJEUNER
luxurious DE LUXE
machine-gun MITRAILLEUSE
madness FOLIE
magistrate BAILLI
maid BONNE
—of honour FILLE D'HONNEUR
DAME D'HONNEUR
mail POSTE
main
— attraction CLOU
—dish of meal
PIECE DE RESISTANCE
maintain MAINTENIR
major domo MAITRE D'HOTEL
makeshift PIS ALLER
male servant GARCON

man	HOMME.M.MONSIEUR.RENE
—about town	BON VIVEUR
—at-arms	GENDARME
—in the street	
	HOMME DE LA RUE
—of fashion	HOMME DU MONDE
—of letters	HOMME DE LETTRES
—of principle	HOMME DE BIEN
—of wit	HOMME D'ESPRIT
management	MANEGE
manager of	
hotel	MAITRE D'HOTEL
manger	CRECHE
manner of dress	TENUE
many thanks	GRAND MERCI
marchioness	MARQUISE
mark	MARQUE
market-woman	
	DAME DE LA HALLE
marmoset	OUSTITI
marriageable person	PARTI
marshal	NEY
marvellous	MERVEILLEUX
masked ball	BAL MASQUE
master	MAITRE
—key	PASSE-PARTOUT
—of ceremonies	COMPERE
—piece	CHEF D'OEUVRE
—stroke	COUP DE MAITRE
material	MATERIEL
matter	CHALOIR
mattress	MATELAS
mayor	MAIRE
me	MOI
—with dishes individually	
listed and priced	A LA CARTE
meal	
—with limited choice	
at a fixed price	TABLE D'HOTE
mean	MESQUIN(E)
—minded person	AME DE BOUE
meaning of the matter	
	FIN MOT DE L'AFFAIRE
meanness	MESQUINERIE
measure	DEMARCHE
measures	
—small	MILLIMETRE
—$^1/_3$ inch	CENTIMETRE
—$3^1/_2$ inches	DECIMETRE

—39 inches	METRE
—33 feet	DECAMETRE
—2 metres	TOISE
—$^5/_8$ mile	KILOMETRE
—2.8 miles	LEAGUE
—11 square feet	CENTIARE
—12 square yards	DECIARE
—120 square yards	ARE
—1200 square yards	DECARE
—1-1$^1/_4$ acres (old)	ARPENT
—2$^1/_2$ acres	HECTARE
—cubic metre	STERE
—$^1/_{100}$ litre	CENTILITRE
—$^1/_{10}$ litre	DECILITRE
—1$^1/_4$ pints	LITRE
—heat	THERMIE
—old capacity	MUID
—old pint	CHOPIN
—pressure	CENTIBAR
medieval	
—bishop's deputy	VIDAME
—poet	TROUVERE
—tale(s)	FABLIAU(X)
medium	MILIEU
medley	MACEDOINE.MELANGE
melt	FONDRE
melted	FONDU(E)
member of	
—literary brotherhood	FELIBRE
—majority	MAJORITAIRE
memorandum	BORDEREAU
	CAHIER
men	MESSIEURS.MM
—of letters	GENS DE LETTRES
mental reservation	
	ARRIERE PENSEE
menu	CARTE (DU JOUR)
merchant	MARCHAND
mere form of	
words	FACON DE PARLER
message	DEPECHE
methodical	RAISONNE
middle	MILIEU
—class	BOURGEOISIE
—course	JUSTE MILIEU
mien	ALLURE
mild	DOUX.DOUCE
military	
—courier	ESTAFETTE

—man	HOMME D'EPEE	my	
—men	GENS DE GUERRE	—goodness!	MA FOI
—policeman	GENDARME	—lord	MONSEIGNEUR
—stratagem	RUSE DE GUERRE	nail	CLOU
mill	MOULIN	naive young woman	INGENUE
minor noble	VIDAME	naked	AU NATUREL
mischievous goblin		name	NOM
	ESPRIT FOLLET	named	DIT
misery	MISERE	Napoleon's army	GRANDE ARMEE
miss	M(D)LLE.MADEMOISELLE	narrow	ETROIT
mistake	EGAREMENT.FAUX PAS	—braid	SOUTACHE
mister	MONSIEUR	—minded	BORNE
mistress	BELLE AMIE.MAITRESSE	naturalistic painting	
—of ceremonies	COMMERE		BELLE PEINTURE
misunderstanding	MALENTENDU	nave	NEF
mitten	MOUFFLE	near	PRES
mix	MELER	nearly	A PEU PRES
mixture	MELANGE	neck	COU
—(fruit, etc.)	MACEDOINE	—tie	CRAVATE
mob	CANAILLE	necklace	COLLIER
mock serenade	CHARIVARI	—of diamonds etc.	RIVIERE
mocking	NARQUOIS	need	BESOIN
model	EXEMPLE	neglected	A L'ABANDON
—of sculpture	MAQUETTE		NEGLIGE
moderate Republican	GIRONDIN	neighbourhood	VOISINAGE
	GIRONDIST	Netherlands	LES PAYS-BAS
moistened	MOUILLE	network	RESEAU
money	ARGENT.FONDS	nevertheless	QUAND MEME
	MONNAIE	new	NOUVEAU.NOUVELLE
—changing office		—art	ART NOUVEAU
	BUREAU DE CHANGE	—Year's gift(s)	ETRENNE(S)
monk	RELIGIEUX	newly rich	NOUVEAU RICHE
monomania	IDEE FIXE	newspaper	JOURNAL
months	(see calendar above)	next	PROCHAIN
morning	MATIN	night	NUIT
morsel	MORCEAU	—club	BOITE DE NUIT
mother	MERE	—mare	CAUCHEMAR
—in-law	BELLE MERE	no	NON
mottled	CHINE	—more bets	RIEN NE VA PLUS
mountebank	BALADIN(E)	—performance	RELACHE
	CHARLATAN.JONGLEUR	nobility	NOBLESSE
mounting	MONTURE	—'s obligation to be	
mournful	FUNEBRE	honourable	NOBLESSE OBLIGE
Mrs	MADAME	noble	GRAND SEIGNEUR.VIDAME
mule litter	CACOLET	—man	GENTILHOMME
museum	MUSEE	non-interference	LAISSER-FAIRE
musketeer	MOUSQUETAIRE		LAISSEZ-FAIRE
muslin	MOUSSELINE	nonsense	FADAISE
muzzle	MUSEROLLE	noon	MIDI

nose	NEZ
nostalgia	MAL DU PAYS
not	
—at home	EN VILLE
—in cipher	EN CLAIR
—in competition	
	HORS CONCOURS
notary	GREFFIER
notice	AFFICHE
	AVIS (AU LECTEUR)
notoriety	ESCLANDRE.RECLAME
novel	
—about successive generations	
	ROMAN FLEUVE
—about real people under	
fictitious names	ROMAN A CLEF
nozzle	A(D)JUTAGE.BEC.NEZ
number	NOMBRE
—(issue) of magazine	LIVRAISON
nun	RELIGIEUSE
nursemaid	BONNE
object	OBJET
obsession	IDEE FIXE
occasional verse	
	VERS D'OCCASION
of course	BIEN ENTENDU
off the peg	PRET-A-PORTER
off with you!	ALLEZ-VOUS-EN
officer in attendance	
	AIDE DE CAMP
official	FONCTIONNAIRE
offprint	TIRAGE A PART
often repeated	SANS NOMBRE
ogle	LORGNER
old	VIEUX
—democrat	MONTAGNARD
—fashioned	ARRIERE
	VIEUX JEUX
—game or joke	VIEUX JEU
—nobility	ANCIEN NOBLESSE
—order	ANCIEN REGIME
—quilted doublet	POURPOINT
—reworked material	RECHAUFFE
—supreme court	PARLIAMENT
on	SUR
—a level with	A LA HAUTEUR DE
—a pillion	EN CROUPE
—a skewer	EN BROCHETTE
—account	A COMPTE
—equal footing	AU PAIR
—every occasion	A TOUT PROPOS
—guard!	EN GARDE
—half-pay	EN RETRAITE
—purpose	A DESSAIN
—the best of terms	AU MIEUX
—the carpet	SUR LE TAPIS
—the contrary	AU CONTRAIRE
—the first floor	AU PREMIER
—the road	EN ROUTE
—the second floor	AU SECOND
—the spot	SUR PLACE
one	UN(E)
—who avoids army	
service	EMBUSQUE
—who enjoys luxury and	
good living	BON VIVANT
	BON VIVEUR
open air	PLEIN AIR
opera with spoken	
dialogue	OPERA COMIQUE
opinion	
—held generally	IDEE RECUE
—sounding	BALLON D'ESSAI
opposite	EN FACE.VIS-A-VIS
—number	VIS-A-VIS
order	ORDONNER
ordinary	ORDINAIRE
organ	ORGUE
ornamental	
—candlestick	TORCHERE
—design in book	CUL-DE-LAMPE
our lady	NOTRE DAME
out of	HORS
—date	PASSE(E)
—fashion	DEMODE
—season	HORS SAISON
outcast	EXILE.PARIA
outcome	DENOUEMENT
outlaw	HORS LA LOI
outline	APERCU.CROQUIS
	ESQUISSE
outside	DEHORS
outstanding item (of collection	
etc.)	PIECE DE RESISTANCE
over	SUR
overthrow	BOULEVERSER
overturn	BOULEVERSER
ox	BOEUF

—blood	SANG-DE-BOEUF	pet	CHOU
pain	MAL	pewter	ESTAIN
paint	PEINDRE	picnic	FETE CHAMPETRE
painting			PIQUE-NIQUE
—in dots of colour		picture	TABLEAU
	POINTILLISM(E)	piece of music	MORCEAU
—showing figures in pastoral		pilot balloon	BALLON D'ESSAI
setting	FETE GALANTE	pithy saying	MOT
paper	PAPIER	place	
—trade	PAPETERIE	—setting	COUVERT
Parisian working-girl	MIDINETTE	—your bets!	FAITES VOS JEUX
parasol	EN TOUT CAS	plain cooking	AU NATUREL
particular		plausibility	VRAISEMBLANCE
—administrative system	REGIME	play on words	JEU DE MOTS
—aversion	BETE NOIRE	pleasant	
—district in town	QUARTIER	—looks	BONNE MINE
partition	CLOISON	—taste	BONNE BOUCHE
party (political)	PARTI	pleated	PLISSE
pass	LAISSEZ-PASSER	plebiscite	APPEL AU PEUPLE
passage	COULOIR	plume	AIGRETTE
past	PASSE(E)	pocket-book	PORTE-MONNAIE
paste	PATE	police	
pastry case	CROUSTADE	—force	GENDARMERIE
pastry(-shop)	PATISSERIE	—man	AGENT DE POLICE.FLIC
patent	BREVET D'INVENTION	—spy	MOUCHARD
patented	BREVETE	political moderate	POLITIQUE
patron saint	DENIS	poppy	COQUELICOT
patterned with dots	POINTILLE	popularisation	VULGARISATION
pavement	PAVE.TROTTOIR	porcelain	SEVRES
pear	BLANQUETTE.POIRE	porter	CONCIERGE
pen	PLUME	pout	MOUE
—name	NOM DE PLUME	poster	AFFICHE
penalty	AMENDE	pouting	BOUDERIE
people	GENS	power behind the	
—of fashion	GENS DU MONDE	scenes	EMINENCE GRISE
—of humble means	GENS DE PEU	prank	FREDAINE
—of rank	GENS DE CONDITION	prattle	BAVARDAGE
perfect	PARFAIT	praying-desk	PRIE-DIEU
perfectly	A MERVEILLE	precinct	BANLIEUE
perfume	MILLEFLEURS.PARFUM	precious	CHICHI
period of Louis		precocious child	
XIV-XVI	HAUTE EPOQUE		ENFANT TERRIBLE
permission to depart	CONGE	preconceived opinion	PARTI PRIS
permit	LAISSEZ-PASSER	preface	AVANT PROPOS
persecution of Huguenots		pregnant	ENCEINTE
	DRAGONNADE	present	CADEAU
person of independent		pretended	SOI-DISANT
means	RENTIER	pretentious	CHICHI
pert girl	GAMINE	pretty	

—well	ASSEZ BIEN
—woman	BEAUX YEUX
—young working girl	GRISETTE
priest	ABBE.CURE.PERE
primogeniture	MAJORAT
prisoner	ACCUSE(E).DETENU
private	
—conversation between two people	TETE-A-TETE
—soldier	PIOU-PIOU.POILU
—staircase	ESCALIER DEROBE
procession	CORTEGE
procurator	PROCUREUR
profession	METIER
professional male partner	GIGOLO
profligate	ROUE
prolixity	LONGUEUR
prop	POINT D'APPUI
propriety	BIENSEANCE
prostitute	FILLE DE JOIE
protected	A COUVERT
Protestant	HUGUENOT
pseudonym	NOM DE GUERRE
public	
—confession	AMENDE HONORABLE
—dancer	BALADIN(E)
—executioner	MONSIEUR DE PARIS
—house	BISTRO
—nursery	CRECHE
—prosecutor	PROCUREUR GENERAL
—room off lobby	FOYER
publicity	RECLAME
puffed out (hair style)	BOUFFANT
pulped and sieved food	PUREE
pun	JEU DE MOTS
punch	COUP DE POING
punctured like a sieve	CRIBLE
pupil	ELEVE
pure	PUR
—blood	PUR SANG
purr	CALEMBOUR
purse	PORTE-MONNAIE
queen	REINE.SA MAJESTE.SM
quick(ly)	A LA VOLEE.VITE
quickstep	PAS REDOUBLE
quite	TOUT

—at home	ENFANT DE LA MAISON
—brief(ly)	TOUT COURT
—the contrary	TOUT AU CONTRAIRE
rabbit	LAPIN
rabble	CANAILLE
race	LE MANS
ragout	BLANQUETTE
railway	CHEMIN DE FER.METRO
—station	GARE
rainbow	ARC EN CIEL
raise	LEVER
raised	LEVE(E)
—in relief	REPOUSSE
rake	ROUE
rank	ETAT.RANG.ORDRE
—imposes obligations	NOBLESSE OBLIGE
rare	RECHERCHE
rascal	FRIPON
raven	CORBEAU
ravishingly	A RAVIR
raw	BRUT
ready	A LA MAIN
—money	ARGENT COMPTANT
really	VRAIMENT
rear	ARRIERE
—part of motor car	TONNEAU
reason	RAISON
—for existence	RAISON D'ETRE
recommended dish of day	PLAT DU JOUR
red	ROUGE
—tape	PAPERASSERIE
referring	RENVOI
reflection	REFLET
refugee	EMIGRE(E).REFUGIET(E)
refusal	NON
regimen	REGIME
registrar	GREFFIER
reheated leftover food	RECHAUFFE
relating to values of end of (19th) century	FIN DE SIECLE
relaxation	DELASSEMENT
	RELACHE
—of strained relations	DETENTE
relegation	RENVOI.RENVOY

reluctantly	A CONTRE-COEUR	rocky edge	ARETE
reminder	AIDE MEMOIRE	rogue	FRIPON
remove	OTER	roguish	ESPIEGLE
renewal of friendly relations		roll	BRIOCHE.CROISSANT
	RAPPROCHEMENT	rope	CORDAGE.CORDE
reply	REPONDEZ	—ladder	ETRIER
report	COMPTE RENDU.CAHIER	—soled shoe	ESPADRILLE
representation of scene etc.		rose-coloured	COULEUR DE ROSE
by person(s) posed		rosette	CHOU
motionless	TABLEAU VIVANT	rough	
Republic		—draft	EBAUCHE
	REPUBLIQUE FRANCAISE	—sketch	CROQUIS
republican	SANSCULOTTE	royal warrant	LETTRE DE CACHET
required by etiquette or		rubble	MOELLON
fashion	DE RIGUEUR	rudeness	GROSSIERETE
resident's permit		ruin	BOULEVERSEMENT
	PERMIS DE SEJOUR	rumour	ON-DIT
respectable people	GENS DE BIEN	running	COURANT
rest	RELACHE	sailor	MATELOT
restaurant	BRASSERIE	Saint's day	(JOUR DE) FETE
reticent	BOUTONNE	salt	SEL
review	COMPTE RENDU	sauce	HOLLANDAISE
	CRITIQUE	savouries before meal	
revolutionary	SANSCULOTTE		HORS D'OEUVRE(S)
—calendar	(*see* calendar *above*))	scatterbrain	ECERVELE
—fighters	NATIONAL GUARD		TETE FOLLE
—hymn	MARSEILLAISE	scent	PARFUM
—song	CARMAGNOLE	—bottle	FLACON
rich soup from shellfish	BISK	school	ECOLE.LYCEE
	BISQUE	scored against	TOUCHE
riddled with	CRIBLE	scraper	GRATTOIR.RACLOIR
right	DROIT	scuffle	BAGARRE
—of superior		sea	MER
	DROIT DE SEIGNEUR	—man	MATELOT
—thinking	BIEN PENSANT	—sickness	MAL DE MER
—to work	DROIT AU TRAVAIL	seaport without duties	ENTREPOT
—word	MOT JUSTE	seat of member of French	
riot	BAGARRE.EMEUTE	Academy	FAUTEUIL
river	RIVIERE	second	SECONDE
rivers	GIRONDE.MEUSE	secondary school	LYCEE
	RHONE.SEINE	see	VOIR
road	CHEMIN	—you again soon	A BIENTOT
—coastal, cliff	CORNICHE	seize up	GRIPPER
—side cafe	BUVETTE	select group	CORPS D'ELITE
roasted meat shop		self	
(restaurant)	ROTISSERIE	—consciousness	
rock	ROCHE		MAUVAISE HONTE
—angle	DIEDRE	—criticism	AUTO-CRITIQUE
—peak	AIGUILLE	—esteem	AMOUR PROPRE

—possession	APLOMB	sketch	ESQUISSE
	SANG-FROID	ski trail	PISTE
—seeker	ARRIVISTE	skirmish	ESCARMOUCHE
—styled	SOI-DISANT		RENCONTRE
sending back	RENVOI.RENVOY	skirmisher	TIRAILLEUR
senior	AINE(E)		VOLTIGEUR
serial story, article	FEUILLETON	skirt-like trousers	CULOTTES
seriously	AU SERIEUX	skull cap	CALOTTE
servant	BONNE.VALET	skylight	ABAT-JOUR
served in flaming		slacker	EMBUSQUE
brandy	FLAMBE(E)	slang	ARGOT
set of jewellery	PARURE	sleeping	
setting	MILIEU.MONTURE	—berth on train	COUCHETTE
settled matter	CHOSE JUGEE	—car	WAGON-LIT
shadow	OMBRE	sleeve	MANCHE
shady	LOUCHE	—less jacket	JUPON
shaft of a column	FUT.TIGE	sleight-of-hand	LEGERDEMAIN
sharecropping	METAYAGE	slice	
sharp-shooter	TIRAILLEUR	—of bread and butter	TARTINE
sheath	ETUI	—(s) of veal, larded	
sheep	BREBIS.MOUTON		FRICANDEAU(X)
shirker	EMBUSQUE	slight amount	SOUPCON
shock troops	ENFANTS PERDUS	slipshod	EN PANTOUFLES
shooting contest	TIR	sly	RUSE
shop	BOUTIQUE	small	PETIT(E)
—keeper	BOURGEOIS	—and dainty	MIGNON(NE)
	MARCHAND(E)	—and elegant	BIJOU
short		—and private	INTIME
—and stiff (hair)	EN BROSSE	—café	ESTAMINET
—review of book, etc.		—cut of beef from	
	COMPTE RENDU	inside loin	FILET MIGNON
—story	CONTE.NOUVELLE	—dish	COCOTTE
—sword	ESTOC	—hatch in door etc.	GUICHET
Shrove Tuesday	MARDI GRAS	—house	MAISON(N)ETTE
shudder	FRISSON	—pastry	BOUCHE
shutter	JALOUSIE	—shot	MITRAILLE
sick	MALADE	smart	CHIC
sickness	MAL.MALAISE	smooth	
signal for parley		—rich white sauce	VELOUTE
or surrender	CHAMADE	—surfaced woollen	FOULE
silk	SOIE	snail	ESCARGOT
silkworm disease	PEBRINE	sniper	FRANC-TIREUR
silly	NAIF.SOT	so much	TANT
silver	ARGENT	—the better	TANT MIEUX
simpering	MINAUDERIE	—the worse	TANT PIS
simply	TOUT COURT	social activities after	
singed	FLAMBE(E)	skiing	APRES-SKI
sir	MONSIEUR	society	SOCIETE
sister	SOEUR	sofa for two, facing	TETE-A-TETE

soft	DOUX.MOU.MOLLET
—bun	BRIOCHE
—silk or rayon fabric	SURAH
soldier	POILU.SOLDAT
sombre	MORNE
something	
—composed for a special occasion	PIECE D'OCCASION
—disagreeable	DESAGREMENT
—found	OBJET TROUVE
—that deceives the eye	TROMPE L'OEIL
son	FILS
song	CHANSON
—collection	CHANSONNIER
soul	AME
sound and light	SON ET LUMIERE
sounding-board	ABBAT-VOIX
soup	POTAGE
—bowl	ECUELLE
—smooth, strained	PUREE
south of France	MIDI
spangle	PAILLETTE
spark	BLUETTE
speculator	BOURSIER
spire	FLECHE
spirit	ENTRAIN.ESPRIT
spit	ROTISSERIE
splendour	ECLAT
spoilt child	ENFANT GATE(E)
spray of jewels like plume	AIGRETTE
spring	PRINTEMPS
square	CARRE.PLACE
squinting	LOUCHE
S-shaped couch	VIS-A-VIS
stable	ECURIE
staff of army, etc.	ETAT-MAJOR
stag's trail	ABATTURE
stage	ESTRADE.SCENE.THEATRE
—coach	DILIGENCE
—setting	MISE-EN-SCENE
stained glass	VITRAIL
staircase	ESCALIER
star	ETOILE
state	ETAT
—approval	AGREMENT
—owned company	REGIE
—pawnshop	MONT-DE-PIETE

—prison	BASTILLE
statement of account	COMPTE RENDU
statesman	HOMME D'ETAT
stationery	PAPETERIE
steak cut from between ribs	ENTRECOTE
step	PAS.DEMARCHE
stew	CASSOULET
stewed beef	BOUILLI
stirrup	ETRIER
stock exchange	BOURSE
stocking	BAS
stone	PIERRE
stonecrop	ORPIN
stop thief!	AU VOLEUR
stopping place	ETAPE
storehouse	ENTREPOT.ETAPE
storey	ETAGE
stout(ness)	EMBONPOINT
straight in the face	EN FACE
strange	ETRANGE
stratagem of war	RUSE DE GUERRE
straw	PAILLE
street	RUE
—urchin	GAMIN
striking	FRAPPANT
stroking massage	EFFLEURAGE
stroller	FLANEUR
strong	FORT(E)
—broth	BOUILLON
—punishment	PEINE FORTE ET DURE
stubborn	ENTETE(E)
students' quarter in Paris	LATIN QUARTER
studied	VOULU
studio	ATELIER
stuffed	FARCI
stupid	BETE.SOT.STUPIDE
—blundering	ETOURDERIE
—person	BETE
stupidity	BETISE
style	CHIC.ELAN
—of 1795-99	DIRECTOIRE
stylish	CHIC
subdivision of department	ARRONDISSEMENT

subscription	ABONNEMENT
suburb	BANLIEUE.FAUBOURG
subway	METRO
success	SUCCES
—wild	SUCCES FOU
sudden	SOUDAIN.SUBIT
—and severe (of disease)	
	FOUDROYANT
—change (of views)	VOLTE-FACE
—descent	DEGRINGOLADE
overthrow of government	
	COUP D'ETAT
suddenly	A L'IMPROVISTE
SUBITEMENT.TOUT A COUP	
sulking	BOUDERIE
summary	ABREGE.APERCU
summer	ETE
sumptuous	DE LUXE
superfluous	DE TROP
superior	
—power	FORCE MAJEURE
—wine	VDQS
support	(POINT D')APPUI.APPUY
supporter	ADHERENT.PARTISAN
surfeited	BLASE
surprise	SURPRISE
—attack	COUP DE MAIN
swaddling-clothes	MAILLOT
sweet	DOUX.DOUCE
sweetmeat	BONBON
—box	BONBONNIERE
swim	NAGER
systematic	RAISONNE
table	TABLE
—cloth	NAPPE
—wine	VIN ORDINAIRE
tact	SAVOIR-FAIRE
tactless(ness)	GAUCHE(RIE)
take	
—leave	POUR PRENDRE CONGE
	PPC
—one's bearings	S'ORIENTER
taste	GOUT
—less	FADE
tasty morsel	BONNE BOUCHE
tavern	BISTRO
tax on salt	GABELLE
tea with dancing	THE DANSANT
team	

—in sport	EQUIPE
—of cars	ECURIE
technical college	GRANDE ECOLE
tedious passage (in	
book, etc.)	LONGUEUR
tell	DIRE.RACONTER
teller of anecdotes	RACONTEUR
tempest	TEMPETE
temporary or secondary	
lodging	PIED-A-TERRE
tenderloin	FILET
territorial division	COMMUNE
thanks to God	GRACE A DIEU
that	CE.CET.CETTE
—is all	VOILA TOUT
—is to say	C'EST A DIRE
theatre	
—box	BAIGNOIR
—stall	FAUTEUIL
theatrical piece featuring	
fairies	FEERIE
there is/are	VOILA
thick	
—foliage	BOSCAGE
—grilled steak	CHATEAUBRIAND
—soup	POTAGE
thin glassware	MOUSSELINE
thing already done and	
unalterable	FAIT ACCOMPLI
think	PENSER
third estate	TIERS ETAT
this	CE.CET.CETTE
thoroughbred	PUR SANG
thoroughly	A FOND.TOUT A FAIT
thou	TOI.TU
thoughtless	ETOURDI(E)
	INSOUCIANTE(E)
thousand	MILLE
three	TROIS
—cornered hat	CHAPEAU-BRAS
	TRICORNE
thrill	FRISSON
through	A TRAVERS
throw	JETER
ticket	BILLET.CACHET
—office (window)	GUICHET
tilt	PAS D'ARMES
tip	POURBOIRE.TRONC
tip of toe	POINTE

to		twenty	VINGT
—a certainty	A COUP SUR	—one	VINGT-ET-UN
—a nicety	A POINT	twilight	DEMI-JOUR
—arms!	AUX ARMES	twin	JUMELLE
—no purpose	EN PURE PERTE	two	DEUX
—the bitter end	A OUTRANCE	—men and two women	
—the death	A OUTRANCE		PARTIE CARREE
—the left	A GAUCHE	unaffected	NAIF.NAIVE
—the right	A DROIT	unconstraint	LAISSER-ALLER
—the very end	JUSQU'AU BOUT		LAISSEZ-ALLER
—your health!	A VOTRE SANTE	under	SOUS
today	AUJOURDHUI	—discussion	EN L'AIR
toilet-water	EAU DE COLOGNE		SUR LE TAPIS
tomorrow	DEMAIN	undercut of beef	FILET
tongue	LANGUE	underground	SOUS TERRE
too		—chamber	SOUTERRAIN
—late	APRES COUP	—railway	METRO
—much	TROP	understanding	ENTENTE
top		undertaker's parlour	
—fashion-house	GRAND ATELIER		CHAPELLE ARDENTE
—to bottom	DE HAUT EN BAS	undressed	DESHABILLE
total	PUR SANG	uneasiness	MALAISE
tourney	PAS D'ARMES	unembarrassed	DEGAGE
town	BOURG.VILLE	unexpected meeting	RENCONTRE
—hall	HOTEL DE VILLE	unexpectedly	A L'IMPROVISTE
—house	MAISON DE VILLE	unfit to fight	HORS DE COMBAT
toy	JOUET.JOUJOU	unkempt	MAL SOIGNE(E)
tradesman's stock	BOUTIQUE	unknown (person)	INCONNU(E)
traditional (art)	POMPIER	unoriginal material	DEJA VU
train	MANEGE	unpleasantness	ESCLANDRE
—of attendants	CORTEGE	unravelling of plot	DENOUEMENT
tramp	CLOCHARD	unrestrained	DEGAGE
travelling companion		unsuccessful	MANQUE
	COMPAGNON DE VOYAGE	unsuitable marriage	
treachery	TRAHISON		MESALLIANCE
treason	LESE-MAJESTE	unsweetened	BRUT
	TRAHISON	untrustworthy friend	
trench	CUNETTE.CUVETTE		AMI DE COUR
trick	ARTIFICE.TOUR	unwillingly	MALGRE
trickery	LEGERDEMAIN	up to date	A LA PAGE
triumphal arch	ARC DE TRIOMPHE	upon	SUR
truly	VRAIMENT	upper middle class	
tumble	DEGRINGOLER		HAUTE BOURGEOISIE
tun	TONNEAU	uproar	EMEUTE.TUMULTE
turmoil	TUMULTE	upstart	NOUVEAU RICHE
turned up	RETROUSSE		PARVENU
turning round	VOLTE-FACE	urchin	GAMIN
tutor	REPETITEUR	usher	HUISSIER
twaddle	FADAISE	valiant knight	PREUX CHEVALIER

varnishing	VERNISSAGE
vatful	CUVEE
Venetian blind	JALOUSIE
verisimilitude	VRAISEMBLANCE
verse	VERS
very	TRES
—best	CREME DE LA CREME
—dear	AU POIDS DE L'OR
—small amount	SOUPCON
vine	VIGNE
—grower	VIGNERON
	VITICULTEUR
—yard	CRU.VIGNOBLE
violent epilepsy	GRAND MAL
visiting card	CARTE DE VISITE
visitor's permit	CARNET
voting method	
	SCRUTIN-DE-LISTE
waif	GAMIN
waiter	GARCON
walk	MARCHER
wall	MUR
wandering minstrel	JONGLEUR
want	BESOIN
war	GUERRE
—to the death	GUERRE A MORT
	GUERRE A OUTRANCE
warbler	FAUVETTE
warden	CONCIERGE
warehouse	ENTREPOT
warhorse	CHEVAL DE BATAILLE
warmth	CHALEUR
wartime guerrilla	MAQUISARD
—band	MAQUIS
watch-chain ornament	BRELOQUE
water	EAU
—bottle	CARAFE
—sprinkler	ASPERSOIR
wave	ONDE
way of speaking	
	FACON DE PARLER
weariness	ENNUI
weight	POIDS
—1 pound (old)	LIVRE
—1 cwt	QUINTAL
—small	MG.MILLIGRAM(ME)
—10 milligrams	CENTIGRAM(ME)
	CG
—100 milligrams	DECIGRAM(ME)

	DG
—200 milligrams	
	(METRIC) CAR(R)AT
—10 grams	DECAGRAM(ME).DG
—100 grams	
	HECTOGRAM(ME).HG
—1000 grams	KG.KILOGRAM(ME)
—1000 kilograms	MILLIER.T
	TONNE.TONNEAU
well	BIEN
—done!	A LA BONNE HEURE
—groomed	SOIGNE(E)
—informed	AU COURANT
	AU FAIT
—loved	BIEN-AIME
—mannered	BIEN ELEVE
—shod	BIEN CHAUSSE
—to-do classes	CLASSES AISEES
—versed	BIEN ENTENDU
what	QUE.QUOI
—'s the good of it	A QUOI BON
whatever the consequences	
	QUAND MEME
while waiting	EN ATTENDANT
white	
—porcelain	BLANC DE CHINE
—wine	VIN BLANC
who	QUI
—goes there?	QUI VA LA
whole	TOUT
wholly yours	TOUT A VOUS
wide road	BOULEVARD
widow	VEUVE
wig	CHEVALURE.PERRUQUE
—maker	PERRUQUIER
wild laughter	FOU RIRE
William pear	BON CRETIEN
willing	BON GRE
willy-nilly	BON GRE MAL GRE
	MALGRE LUI
	MALGRE MOI
windfall	AUBAINE
wine	VIN
—bottle	CARAFE
—from good vineyards	
	GRAND CRU
	LES GRANDS VINS
—waiter	SOMMELIER
	(*see also* drink²)

wing	AILE
wink	CLIN D'OEIL.OEILLADE
winter	HIVER
wit	BEL ESPRIT
witticism	JEU D'ESPRIRT
	BON MOT
with	AVEC.PAR
—a giant stride	A PAS DE GEANT
—air of superiority	
	DE HAUT EN BAS
—both hands	A DEUX MAINS
—cheese	AU FROMAGE
—child	ENCEINTE
—closed doors	A HUIS CLOS
—good reason	A BON DROIT
—open arms	A BRAS OUVERTS
—pleasure	AVEC PLAISIR
—reference to	APROPOS
within range/reach	A PORTEE
without	SANS
—breeches	SANSCULOTTE
—care	SANS SOUCI
—ceremony	EN FAMILLE
	SANS CEREMONIE
—preface	TOUT COURT
—reality	EN L'AIR
—restraint	SANS GENE
—serifs	SANSERIF
—worry	SANS SOUCI
witty saying	(BON) MOT
woman	FEMME
—of the world	
	FEMME DU MONDE
wonder	ETONNEMENT
	SURPRISE.MERVEILLE
—ful	ETONNANT.MERVEILLEUX
—fully (well)	A MERVEILLE
wood	BOIS
—land	BOSCAGE
wooden shoe	SABOT
word	MOT
—describing something exactly	
	MOT JUSTE
work	TRAVAIL
—box	NECESSAIRE
—laid on as decoration	APPLIQUE
—of artist, etc.	OEUVRE
—shop	ATELIER
worker	OUVRIER(E)

worn out	EPUISE(E)
worry	TRACASSERIE
worse and worse	DE PIS EN PIS
worst shift	PIS ALLER
worthless	MAUVAIS(E)
—fellow	MAUVAIS SUJET
would-be	SOI-DISANT
woven	BROCHE
write	ECRIRE
writer	AUTEUR.ECRIVAIN
—of farces	FARCEUR
writing	
—book	CAHIER
—desk	E(S)CRITOIRE
written statement	
	PROCES-VERBAL
yesterday	HIER
you	TOI.TU.VOUS
young	JEUNE
—love	JEUNE AMOUR
—man kept by an older	
woman	GIGOLO
—rebel	BLOUSON NOIR
frenzied dash	SHAD
frequent	
frequency	F
frequency modulation	FM
frequently	FR
fresh	
fresh bread	BARED.BEARD.DEBAR
fresh fellow	NEWMAN
fresh spell of rain	REIGN
fresh start for boy	COY.GOY.HOY
	ROY.SOY.TOY
freshness of dawn	WAND
friar	TUCK
friar's dance	TUCKSHOP
Friday	F.FR.FRI.MAN
friend[1]	ALLY.PAL
hence	
•alternative friend	ORALLY
•boy friend	REGALLY.ROYALLY
•little boy friend	TOTALLY
•stout friend	FATALLY
•support friend	LEGALLY
and	
•girl friend	PALMARY.PALMYRA
•friend and expert	PALACE
•good friend	PIPAL

•no friend	OPAL
friend*less*	omit ALLY.omit PAL
•truly friend*less*	RE(ally)
•(pal)try, *friendless*,...	TRY

friend²

Friendly Society	OUTGOINGS
Friends of Europe	FOE
Friends of the Earth	FOE
frightful time	EMIT

fringe

fringed by *	incl in *
•motorway *fringed by* tre-es	TREMIES
fringes a...	incl A
fringes *	incl *
•tre-es *fringe* motorway	TREMIES
fringes of society	SY

Fritz

Fritz = German	
•*Fritz's* house	HAUS
•with *Fritz's*...	MIT
frolicking lionesses	NOISELESS

from¹   EX

hence

•from a pit	EXAMINE
•from shelter	EXTENT
•from the first	EXIST

from²

from *French*	DE

hence

•from *French* girl	DECLARE
•from *French* islands	DECAYS
•from *French* records	DEFILES
from *Latin*	AB

hence

•from *Latin* customs	ABUSES
•from *Latin* scholar	ABBA
•from *Latin* spoken...	ABORAL
from the *French*	DELA.DES.DU

hence

•from the *French* bird, note	DELAMINATE
•from the *French* in the East	DELAINE
•from the *French* youth	DELATED

and

•from the *French* city	DESTROY
•from the *French* couple	DESPAIR
•from the *French* I call	DESIRING
•from the *French* church	DUCE
•from the *French* scholar	DUMA
•from the *French* members	DUMPS

from³

indicates omission:

•alternative *from* the(or)y	THEY
•doctor *from* Bor(d)e(r)s	BORES
•letter *from* (m)other	OTHER

from⁴

indicates use of foreign words:

•agreement *from Moscow* (Russian)	DA
•boy *from Milan* (Italian)	RAGAZZO
•*Cairngorm*-stone (Scottish)	STANE
•children *from Germany*	KINDER
•dog *from Lyons* (French)	CHIEN
•girl *from Perth* (Australian)	SHEILA
•man *from Ayr* (Scottish)	MON
•uncle *from Pretoria* (S.African)	OOM
•woman *from Malaga* (Spanish)	SENORA

from⁵

from A-K and M-Z	NOEL
from Bir/ming/ham	MING
from East	TOW
from Mali	MAIL
from Northwest	TOSE
from point-to-point = between N.S.E.W	
•Bill King *goes from point to point*	NACRE
•goddess *goes from point to point*	EATEN
•Hal *goes from point to point*	WHALE
from south	TON
from southwest	TONE
from the beginning	AB INIT(IO)
from the queen	OFFER
from the rear rank⟨	KNAR
from West	TOE
from what we hear, he'll...	HEAL.HEEL

front

front cover	APRON
front cover	C
front of house	FACADE
front of house	H
front page	P
front runner	ADAM
front runner	R
front-runner in Derby	D

frost   DAVID.HOAR.JACK.RIME

fruit

fruit bats	BANANAS
fruit pulp	SQUASH

fuddled in bar   BAIRN.BRAIN

fugitive   EPHEMERAL

full   DRUNK.STONED.TIGHT

full-*back*⟨	DEF
full board	THOROUGHFARE
full meal	THOROUGHFARE
full moon	O
full of *	incl *
•bo-x *full of* gunners. . .	BORAX
Full Organ	FO

funeral contractors
     FIRM UNDERTAKING

fungus

edible   BLEWITS.BOLETUS
CEPE.CEPS.CHANTERELLE
JEW'S EAR.LAWYER'S WIG
OYSTER.PARASOL
PENNY BUN.PUFFBALL
STINKHORN.TRUFFLE
WOOD BLEWITS

poisonous   DEATH CAP
FLY AGARIC.PANTHER CAP

some descriptions

—black   DEAD MAN'S FINGERS

—black and brown
BACHELOR'S BUTTONS
POPE'S BUTTONS

—bluish-grey to brown
OYSTER (MUSHROOM)

—brown to brick-red   BOLETUS
CEPE.CEPS

—greyish to pale brown
BIRCH POLYPORE
RAZORSTROP FUNGUS

—orange   ORANGE CUP

—reddish brown   THE DECEIVER

—red or liver-coloured
BEEFSTEAK FUNGUS

—red with white spots
FLY AGARIC

—whitish   COMMON EARTHBALL
MUSHROOM.SLIMY BEECHCAP
STINKHORN.WOOD WITCH

—yellow
COMMON YELLOW RUSSULA
SULPHUR TUFT

funny

funny cry	SCREAM
funny idea	AIDE
funny thing	NIGHT

fur

American marten	SKUNK
Arctic marten	SABLE
coypu	NUTRIA
grey	GRIS(E)
musk-rat	MUSQUASH
polecat	FITCHEW
sable	ZIBEL(L)INE
selectively bred	MUTATION MINK
squirrel	VAIR
stoat	ERMINE
weasel	MINK

Furies   ERINYES.EUMENIDES
ALECTO.MEGAERA.TISIPHONE

furious rage	GEAR
furled sails	SILAS
furlong	FUR
furniture designer	ADAM

CHIPPENDALE.HEPPLEWHITE
KENT.SHERATON

further *round* the bend   MORSE

fuse

fused lights	SLIGHT
fusion of alloy	LOYAL
fuss	ADO

hence

•fuss about	ADORE
•fuss *about* one. . .	ADIO
•fuss *in* the Navy	RADON
fuss about. . .	U-BOAT
fussy gown in. . .	OWNING
get *fussed*	TEG
future	FUT

G

acceleration. agent. clef. four hundred. gamma. gamut. gauss. gee. George. Germany. giga. girl. good. gram. gramme. grand. gravity. guinea. gulf. key. man. note. string. suit

G-man's son	GLAD
gad	
gad*about*	GA-D
gadding about in the...	THINE
Gaelic	ERSE.GAEL
gain honour	APPRECIATE
Galatians	GAL
gallery	TATE
Gallic king	ROI.SM
gallon	GAL(L)
galloping <u>horse</u>	SHORE
Gallup poll	GP
Gambia	WAG
gambling theorist	SPECULATOR
gambolling <u>lambs</u>	BALMS
game	BRIDGE.LOO.POLO.RU
game bird	HOBBY
game couple	TWOSOME
game *over*⟨	UR
game redhead	MATCH
game reserves	POOL
gamma	G
gangster	AL
gaoled	(in) C-AGE.(in) PE-N
garbage in, garbage out	GIGO
garbled <u>words</u>	SWORD
garden	EDEN.PLOT
garden *centre*	RD
garden maker	ADAM
<u>garden</u> *maker*	DANGER
garden-party	OUTDO
gardener	ADAM
garments	
African	K(H)ANGA
anorak	CAGOUL(E)
	KAGOOL.KAGOUL(E)
baby's coat	MATINEE JACKET
ballet	
—all-over garment	LEOTARD
—skirt	TUTU
—tights	MAILLOT
baptismal robe	CHRIS(T)OM
bikini	TANGA
blouse	TUNIC

—loose	GARIBALDI
—woman's	SHIRT.SHIRTWAIST
—American	WAIST
—short	BLOUSON
blue garment	MAZARINE
bodice	
—American	WAIST
—and skirt combined	PRINCESS
—extension	BASQUE
—loose-fitting	BLOUSE
—of ballet dress	GILET
—Scottish	JIRKINET
—woman's (18th c.)	PIERROT
bonnet, small	KISS-ME-QUICK
breeches	TRUSSES
—buff-coloured	
cotton	NANKEENS.NANKINS
—closefitting	HOSE.TREWS
	TROUSE
—footman's	PLUSHES
—full (16th c.)	TRUNK BREECHES
	TRUNK HOSE
—knee	SMALL-CLOTHES
—long	TROUSERS
—loose	KNICKERBOCKERS
—baggy	PLUS FOURS
—man's (17th c.)	
	PETTICOAT-BREECHES
—wide	OXFORD BAGS.SLOPS
Burmese skirt	TAMEIN
bustle	DRESS-IMPROVER
cape	TIPPET
—Mexican	SERAPE.ZARAPE
—shoulder	TIPPET
—fur	VICTORINE
—short	MOZETTA
—worn by Pope	FAN(I)ON
—triangular	FICHU
—with hood	DOMINO
—woman's	MANTEEL.PELERINE
—knitted	SONTAG
cardigan, American	WAMUS
chemise	SHIFT.SMOCK
chest-protector	PECTORAL

child's
—bodice and skirt
  (Scottish)   POLONAISE
—coat, fur-trimmed   PELISSE
—pants and shirt
  (American)   PANTYWAIST
—outer garment   PILCH
—pinafore (American)   TIER
cloak   MANTEAU.MANTLE
                      PALL.WRAP
—coarse leather or woollen PILCH
—fur-trimmed   PELISSE
—Levantine   GREGO
—long   CAPOTE
—loose   GABARDINE
        GABERDINE.TALMA
—man's, short   ROQUELAURE
—military   PELISSE
—Roman   TOGA.TOGE
  —military   ABOLLA
  —travelling   PAENULA
—small   MANT(E)LET
—soldier's   MANTEEL
—South American   PONCHO
—with cape   INVERNESS
—woman's
  —19th c.   VISITE
  —Roman   PALLA
  —Russian   SARAFAN
  —short (Scottish) ROK(E)LAY
closefitting   JEISTIECOR
—ballet garment   LEOTARD
—breeches   HOSE.TREWS
—coat NEWMARKET.TRUSS
  —French   JUPON
—upper garment   DOUBLET
  —French   POURPOINT
—waistcoat   JERKIN
coat
—baby's   MATINEE JACKET
—belted   TUNIC
—closefitting   NEWMARKET
                    TRUSS
  —French   JUPON
—cut diagonally front
  to back   CUTAWAY
—double-breasted FROCKCOAT
  —19th c.   SURTOUT
—dress   SWALLOWTAIL

—hanging loosely
       SWAGGER.COAT
—herald's   TABARD
—Indian   ACHKAN
—knight's   TABARD
—loose   SACK-COAT
     WRAP RASCAL
—man's
—formal   TAIL-COAT
—loose   SACK-COAT
—military   BRITISH WARM
     TRENCH-COAT
—regimental   FROCK
—of duffel   DUFFEL COAT
—of twilled cotton/wool
  GABARDINE.GABERDINE
—policeman's   TUNIC
—raincoat (Japanese)   MINO
—riding   NEWMARKET
—short   JERKIN.JUMP
  SHOOTING-JACKET
—woollen   MACKINAW
—sleeveless   CAPE.JERKIN
    WAISTCOAT
—small   PETTICOAT
—soldier's   TUNIC
—waterproof   RAIN COAT
  TRENCH-COAT
—American   SLICKER
collar
—stand-up   PICCADILLY
—woman's (17th c.) WHISK
collarless undergarment
    UNDERSHIRT
cravat
—18th c.   SOUBISE
—lace   STEENKIRK
crinoline, small CRINOLETTE
denim trousers JEANS.LEVIS
dinner jacket
 (American)   TUXEDO
divided skirt   CULOTTES
  HAREM SKIRT
doublet (French) POURPOINT
drawers   HOSE
—frilled   PANTALETS
—short   PANTIES
dress FROCK.ROBE
—African K(H)ANGA

—Alpine   DIRNDL
—coat   SWALLOWTAIL
—18th-c.   TROLLOPEE
—for riding   RIDING HABIT
—full length   MOTHER HUBBARD
—Hawaiian, loose   MUU-MUU
—homespun   RUSSET
—improver   BUSTLE
—Indian   BANIAN.BANYAN
                                 SARI
—Japanese   KIMONO
—Moslem woman's   BURKHA
                              BURQA
—of brownish Indian silk   TASAR
            TUSSAH.TUSSEH
            TUSSER.TUSSORE
—of flowered muslin
            DOLLY VARDEN
—rich   ROBE
—straight   SHIRT DRESS
                SHIRTWAISTER
dressing
—gown   PEIGNOIR.ROBE
—woman's   NEGLIGEE.PEIGNOIR
—jacket   NIGHT-RAIL
ecclesiastical
—alb (Greek)   STICHARION
—bishop's vestment   CHIMER(E)
   PALLIUM.RATIONAL(E)
                       ROCHET
 —eastern   OMOPHORION
                      SAKKOS
—cape   MOZETTA
—cassock   SLOP.SOUTANE
                 SUBUCULA
—scarf or stole   TIPPET
—surplice   COTTA.EPHOD
             STOLA.STOLE
  —Scottish   SARK
—vestments   ALB.TUNICLE
                DALMATIC
—eucharistic   FANNEL(L)
   FANON.MANIPLE
—subdeacon's   TUNICLE
     (*see also* vestment *below*)
enveloping garment   BURKHA
                      BURGA
farmworker's garment
           SMOCK-FROCK

flannel
—scarf with sleeves
              NIGHTINGALE
—undervest (Scottish)
              WYLIE-COAT
foundation
—for skirt   UNDERSKIRT
—garment   PANTY-GIRDLE
frockcoat   FROCK
—19th c.   SURTOUT
gown   SLOP.STOLA.STOLE
—belted   TUNIC
—loose   MOTHER HUBBARD
—old   SLAMMAKIN
              SLAMMERKIN
—18th c.   NEGLIGE
—morning   PEIGNOIR
—preaching   GENEVA GOWN
—Roman   STOLA
—17th-18th c.   MANTEAU
     MANTO.MANTUA
greatcoat   PETERSHAM
—Afghan   POS(H)TEEN
—loose (18th c.)   WRAP RASCAL
hat trimmed with
   flowers   DOLLY VARDEN
Hawaiian dress   MUU-MUU
high
—collar (17th c.)   PICCADILL(O)
   PICCADILLY.PIKADELL
—necked garment   TURTLE NECK
hood
—old   SURTOUT
—riding   NITHSDALE
   TROT-COSEY.TROT-COZY
hooped skirt   CRINOLINE
—small   CRINOLETTE
hose, wide (16-17th c.)
              GALLIGASKINS
house gown
—informal, long   HOUSECOAT
—loose   TEA GOWN
Inquisition victim's
   garment   SANBENITO
jacket   JERKIN
—American, strong   WAM(M)US
              WAMPUS
—casual   SPORTS JACKET
—dinner (American)   TUXEDO

—hooded (Levantine)   GREGO
—indoor   SMOKING-JACKET
—loose   NORFOLK JACKET
  —American   VAREUSE
—sailor's   PEA-JACKET
—short (Basque)   BASQUE
—sleeveless (French)   JUPON
—old   SAYON
—military undress   MESS JACKET
  SHELL JACKET
—woman's
  —16th-17th c.   HALF-KIRTLE
—19th c.   POLKA
—loose (Scottish)   SHORTGOWN
—short, skirted   BASQUE
  ZOUAVE
jester's attire   MOTLEY
Jewish priest's vestment   EPHOD
kilt (Albanian or Greek)
  FUSTANELLA
knee breeches   SMALL-CLOTHES
knickerbockers, baggy
  PLUS FOURS
knitted   CARDIGAN.GUERNSEY
  JERSEY.JUMPER
  PULLOVER.SWEATER
—lace cravat   STEENKIRK
leather or quilted   GAMBESON
light, loose   CIMAR.CYMAR
loin cloth   WAISTCLOTH
made of
—corded silk   PADUASOY
—silk with wool or
  hair   FAR(R)ANDINE
  FERRANDINE
—twilled cotton   DENIMS
mantle   KIRTLE.PALL
—old   ROCHET.ROCQUET
—Roman   PALLIUM
  —woman's   PALLA
Malayan garment   SARONG
medieval body garment
  COTE HARDIE
Mexican cape   SERAPE.ZARAPE
military
—coat   BRITISH WARM
  TRENCH-COAT
  —regimental   FROCK
—cloak   PELISSE

—undress jacket   MESS JACKET
  SHELL JACKET
monastic habit (Greek)   SCHEMA
monk's garment   FROCK
  SCAPULAR
morning gown   PEIGNOIR
Moslem woman's dress
  BURK(H)A.BURQA
neckerchief, woman's (17th c.)
  WHISK
nightdress (Scottish) WYLIE-COAT
officer's overcoat
  (BRITISH) WARM
oilskin (American)   SLICKER
one-piece
—bodice and skirt   POLONAISE
—garment   LEOTARD
—swimsuit   MAILLOT
one-sleeved garment
  (Greek)   EXOMIS
outer
—garment   PALL
  —coarse linen   SMOCK-FROCK
  —loose   BLOUSE.MANTLE
  ROBE
—old   SURCOAT
—woman's   STOLE.TABARD
—petticoat   KIRTLE
—Basque   BASQUINE
overall   APRON
  JUMPER.PINAFORE
overalls   DUNGAREES
—American   COVERALLS
overcoat
—heavy   GREATCOAT
—Italian   TAGLIONI
—Levantine   GREGO
—light   ULSTERETTE
—long   REDINGOTE
—loose   CHESTERFIELD
  PALETOT.ULSTER
—officer's   (BRITISH) WARM
—old   SURTOUT
—peasant's   TABARD
—sailor's PEA-COAT.PEA-JACKET
—short   SPENCER
—with cape   INVERNESS
—with sleeves meeting
  collar   RAGLAN

overjacket, old	SURCOAT	—overcoat	PEA-COAT
overskirt	PEPLUM		PEA-JACKET
pants, woman's	KNICK(ER)S	—shore clothes	LONG-TOGS
peasant's overcoat	TABARD	—trousers	BELLBOTTOMS
penitent's robe	CILICE	shawl	WRAP
petticoat	PLACKET.UNDERSKIRT	—Scottish	MAUD
—French	JUPON	—small	TURNOVER
—Scottish	WYLIE-COAT	—triangular	FICHU
—stiffened	CRINOLINE	shepherd's plaid (Scottish)	MAUD
pinafore	OVERALL	shift	CHEMISE.SHIRT.SMOCK
—American	TIRE	—woman's	SMOCK
—dress (American)	JUMPER	shirt	
policeman's coat	TUNIC	—Indian	K(H)URTA
Polynesian garment	PAREU	—Scottish	SARK
Pope's		shore clothes (navy)	LONG-TOGS
—short cape	FAN(I)ON	shroud	WINDING SHEET
—vestment	PALLIUM	skintight garment	LEOTARD
preaching gown	GENEVA GOWN	skirt	
pullover	JERSEY	—Alpine	DIRNDL
—sleeveless	TANKTOP	—ballet	TUTU
raincoat (Japanese)	MINO	—divided	CULOTTES
ready-made clothing	SLOPS		HAREM SKIRT
restraining	STRAITJACKET	—hooped	CRINOLINE
	STRAIT-WAISTCOAT	—small	CRINOLETTE
riding		—draped (Burmese)	TAMEIN
—coat	NEWMARKET	—hung from shoulders	
—dress	RIDING-HABIT		PINAFORE DRESS
—hood, woman's (18th c.)			PINAFORE SKIRT
	NITHSDALE	—Malayan	SARONG
robe		—Polynesian	PAREU
—long	STOLE	—narrow	HOBBLE SKIRT
—long, informal	HOUSECOAT	—short, pleated	RA-RA (SKIRT)
—old	PALLIAMENT	—trouser-like	CULOTTES
	PARAMENT		DIVIDED SKIRT
—penitent's	CILICE		HAREM SKIRT
—reaching ankles	TALAR	sleeping robe	NIGHTGOWN
—Roman	STOLA	sleeved garment, short	
Roman		(Shakespeare)	SEA-GOWN
—cloak	TOGA.TOGE	sleeveless	
—gown	STOLA	—coat	CAPE.JERKIN
—mantle	PALLIUM		WAISTCOAT
—woman's	PALLA	—garment (Roman)	EXOMIS
—military cloak	ABOLLA	—jacket, short	WAISTCOAT
—robe	STOLA	—jacket (French)	JUPON
—sleeveless	EXOMIS	—old	SAYON
—travelling cloak	PAENULA	—pullover	TANKTOP
—undershirt, man's	SUBUCULA	—tabard	CHIMER(E)
sailor's		—tunic	TABARD
—jersey	FROCK	smock	SHIFT.SLOP

soldier's	
—cloak	MANTEEL
—coat	TUNIC
South American cloak	PONCHO
stand-up collar	PICCADILLY
straight dress	SHIRT DRESS
	SHIRTWAISTER
strip of tartan cloth worn	
over shoulder	PLAID
surplice	COTTA.EPHOD
	STOLA.STOLE
—Scottish	SARK
swaddling cloth	PILCH
suit	
—boy's (19th c.)	SKELETON SUIT
—cotton	SAFARI SUIT
—flashy (1940s)	ZOOT SUIT
—with long jacket	DRAPE SUIT
sweater	
—large, loose	SLOPPY JOE
—woollen	GUERNSEY
swimsuit	
—one-piece	MAILLOT
—two-piece	BIKINI.TANGA
tabard, sleeveless	CHIMER(E)
tartan trousers	TREWS
topcoat, short	COVERT COAT
triangular shaped cape	FICHU
travelling cloak	
(Roman)	PAENULA
trouser-like woman's	
garment	PANTALETS
trousers	PANTS.TREWS
—cut to resemble skirt	
CULOTTES.DIVIDED SKIRT	
HAREM SKIRT	
—denim	JEANS.LEVIS
—ending above knee	SHORTS
—ending below knee	
KNEE BREECHES.PLUS FOURS	
KNICKERBOCKERS	
—from the hips	HIP-HUGGERS
	HIPSTERS
—narrow bottomed	PEGTOPS
—narrow legged	DRAINPIPES
—tartan	TREWS
—wide, baggy	OXFORD BAGS
	SLOPS
—wide bottomed	BELLBOTTOMS

—wide legged	OXFORD BAGS
tunic	
—Indian	K(H)URTA
—sleeveless	TABARD
—small	TUNICLE
underclothes	LINGERIE.SMALLS
—woman's	UNDIES
undergarment	CIMAN.CYMAN
—collarless	UNDERSHIRT
—loose (17th c.)	CIMAR.CYMAR
—woman's	SPENCER
undershirt, man's	
(Roman)	SUBUCULA
underskirt	PETTICOAT
undertaker's	
cloak	MOURNING CLOAK
undervest (Scottish)	WYLIE-COAT
undress	
—military jacket	MESS JACKET
	SHELL JACKET
—regimental coat	FROCK
upper garment, knitted	JUMPER
	PULLOVER
veil	
—draped round head and	
shoulders	W(H)IMPLE
—short	KISS-ME
—at back of head	VOLET
vestment	
—Jewish priest's	EPHOD
—narrow	STOLE
—Pope's	PALLIUM
—shawl worn on shoulders	
HUMERAL VEIL	
—subdeacon's	TUNICLE
—surplice	COTTA.EPHOD
	STOLA.STOLE
—Scottish	SARK
—white linen	SURPLICE
(see also ecclesiastical above)	
waistcoat	GILET
—American	VEST
—closefitting	JERKIN
waterproof	
—coat	TRENCH-COAT
—light	RAINCOAT
—overgarment	MAC(K)INTOSH
weatherproof anorak	CAGOUL(E)
KAGOOL.KAGOUL(E)	

windproof	ANORAK.PARKA
	PARKEE.PARKI
woollen	
—coat, short	MACKINAW
—clothes, rough	TWEEDS
—shawl	WHITTLE
—sweater	GUERNSEY
—sleeveless	PULLOVER
	TANKTOP
wrap	HAP
—loose	NIGHT-RAIL
garrison dance	BASEBALL
gas-cooled reactor	AGR
gases	
argon	AR
(burning)	MUSTARD
carbon	
—dioxide	CO_2
—monoxide	CO
chlorine	CL
(combustible)	BUTANE
FIRE-DAMP.METHANE	
	PROPANE
fluorine	F
helium	HE
hydrogen	H
irritant	BROMINE.CS
	TEAR GAS
krypton	KR
laughing gas	NITROUS OXIDE
marsh gas	METHANE
neon	NE
nitrogen	N
oxygen	O
(poisonous)	PHOSGENE
(propellant)	FLUORINE
radon	RN
xenon	XE
gatecrasher	BATTERING RAM
Gateshead	G
gather	
gather a. . .	incl A
gather round	incl O
gather nuts	STUN.TUNS
gather *	incl *
•bo-y gathers weight	BOOZY
gathered by *	incl in *
•weight gathered by bo-y	BOOZY
gathering	DO

gauss	G
gazette(er)	GAZ
gear	FIRST.SECOND.THIRD
FOURTH.FIFTH.REVERSE.TOP	
gear change	NEW SUIT
gear change	GARE.RAGE
gearbox	SUITCASE
gee	G
Geiger(-Muller) counter	GM
gelignite	JELLY
gem weight	STONE
gems	
almandine	PURPLE GARNET
amber-coloured	AMBER.TOPAZ
aventurine	SUNSTONE
balas ruby	SPINEL
banded	AGATE.ONYX
beryllium compounds	
	ALEXANDRITE
	AQUAMARINE.BERYL
CHRYSOBERYL.CYMOPHANE	
	EMERALD.HELIDOR
	MORGANITE
black	JET.MELANITE
	SCHORL.TOURMALINE
blue	AMETHYST.AQUAMARINE
	BERYL.EMERALD
	INDICOLITE.LAPIS LAZULI
	SAPPHIRE.SPINEL.TOPAZ
	TURQUOISE.ZIRCON
blue-grey	C(H)ALCEDONY
	LABRADORITE
bloodstone	GREEN CHALCEDONY
Bohemian ruby	ROSE QUARTZ
Brazilian	
—emerald	TOURMALINE
—peridot	TOURMALINE
bronze speckled	AVENTURINE
	SUNSTONE
brown	AMBER.CELONITE
	JADEITE.JASPER
carbon	DIAMOND
carnelian	CORNELIAN.SARD
colourless	ALEXANDRITE
	DIAMOND.ROCK CRYSTAL
	TOPAZ.ZIRCON
corundum	RUBY.SAPPHIRE
emerald	SMARAGD(INE)
evening emerald	PERIDOT

fel(d)spar ADULARIA
AMAZONITE.AVENTURINE
LABRADORITE.MOONSTONE
ORTHOCLASE.SANIDINE
SUNSTONE
fossilised
—resin AMBER
—wood JET
green ALEXANDRITE
AMAZONITE.AQUAMARINE
BERYL.BLOODSTONE
CYMOPHANE.CHRYSOPRASE
DELMANTOID.GARNET
GROSSULARITE.JADE
JAD(E)ITE.MALACHITE
NEPHRITE.OLIVINE.PERIDOT
SPINEL.TOPAZ.TURQUOISE
UVAROVITE.ZIRCON
—chalcedony BLOODSTONE
—corundum ORIENTAL EMERALD
—fluorspar FALSE EMERALD
—garnet URALIAN EMERALD
—quartz MOTHER OF EMERALD
hydrated
—copper carbonate MALACHITE
—silica OPAL
jacinth GARNET.QUARTZ
TOPAZ.ZIRCON
jade JAD(E)ITE.NEPHRITE
lignite JET
lime-chrome garnet UVAROVITE
magnesia-alumina ALMANDINE
CARBUNCLE.DEMANTOID
GARNET.GROSSULARITE
MELANITE.PYROPE.TOPAZITE
magnesium-iron silicate OLIVINE
PERIDOT
Matura diamond ZIRCON
milky-white MOONSTONE.OPAL
multi-coloured AGATE
(SARD)ONYX.OPAL
orange CARNELIAN.CORNELIAN
HESSONITE.RUBICELLE.SARD
oriental
—emerald GREEN CORUNDUM
—topaz SAPPHIRE
pink MORGANITE.ROSE QUARTZ
purple ALMANDINE (SPINEL)
—garnet ALMANDINE

pyrope RED GARNET
red ALEXANDRITE
CAIRNGORM.CARBUNCLE
FIRE OPAL.GARNET.JAD(E)ITE
JASPER.RUBELLITE
RUBY.SPINEL
—garnet PYROPE
rose quartz BOHEMIAN RUBY
ruby red RUBY.SPINEL RUBY
sard CARNELIAN.CORNELIAN
silica compounds AGATE
AMETHYST
CAIRNGORM (STONE)
CARNELIAN.C(H)ALCEDONY
CHRYSOPRASE.CITRINE
CORNELIAN.JASPER
ROCK CRYSTAL.ROSE QUARTZ
SARD.(SARD)ONYX
SMOKE QUARTZ
silicate of
—aluminium, sodium JAD(E)ITE
—calcium, magnesium NEPHRITE
—fluorine, aluminium TOPAZ
sulphide of iron MARCASITE
smaragd(ine) EMERALD
smoky CAIRNGORM (STONE)
SMOKE QUARTZ
spinel BALAS RUBY
—blue SPINEL SAPPHIRE
—brown CELONITE
—crimson SPINEL RUBY
—orange RUBICELLE
—purple ALMANDINE SPINEL
—rose-red BALAS RUBY
sunstone AVENTURINE
tourmaline
—colourless ACHROITE
—black SCHORL
—blue INDICOLITE
—pink or red RUBELLITE
—violet SIBERITE
white C(H)ALCEDONY
JAD(E)ITE.OPAL
yellow AMBER.BERYL
GARNET.HELIODOR.JASPER
TOPAZ(ITE).SAPPHIRE
—quartz SCOTTISH TOPAZ
zircon
—brown MALACON

—orange	HYACINTH
	HYACYNTH
	JACINTH
—yellow	JARGO(O)N
gender	GEN
general	GEN(L).GORDON
	GRANT.LEE
hence	
•*general in* regiment	REGENT
•*general has* square. . .	GENT
•*general* name	GENEVA
General Assembly	GA
general certificate	U
General Certificate of	
Education	GCE
General Court Martial	GCM
General Electric Company	GEC
general issue	GI
General Medical Council	GMC
General Motors	GM
General Officer	
Commanding	GOC
general paralysis of the insane	GPI
General Post Office	GPO
general practitioner	GP
general-service	GS
General staff	GS
General staff officer	GSO
general stall	BOOTH
General Teaching Certificate	GTC
generate	
generate steam	MATES.MEAT
	TAMES
generation	ERA
generation of heat	HATE.THEA
genesis	(*see also* beginning)
Genesis	GEN
Genesis *I and II*	GE
genesis of life	L
genitive	GEN
genius	ID.KA
gently	P
	(*see also* quiet)
genus	GEN
Geological Society	GS
George	
Bernard Shaw	GBS
Cross	GC
Medal	GM

German[1]	BOCHE.FRITZ.GER(RY)
	HUN.JERRY.KRAUT.TEUTON
hence	
•fear of Germans, *say*	HUNDRED
•German church	HUNCH
•German youth	HUNTED
German[2]	
about	ETWA
above	UBER
aeroplane	DORNIER.HEINKEL
	MESSERSCHMITT
	STUKA.TAUBE
after	NACH
agreement	JA
air	LUFT
—force	LUFTWAFFE
—line	LUFTHANSA
alarm	STURM
amiable	GEMUTLICH
ancient tribe	ALEMANNEN
and so forth	UND SO WEITER
	USW
anxiety	ANGST
apple cake	STRUDEL
approval	JA
aristocrat	JUNKER
armed forces	WEHRMACHT
armoured corps	PANZER
army	
—reserve	LANDWEHR
—surgeon	FELDSCHER
arrangement	AUSGLEICH
art	KUNST
—school	BAUHAUS
—song	KUNSTLIED
article	DAS.DER.DIE
ass	ESEL
association	VEREIN
authentic	ECHT
bandmaster	KAPELLMEISTER
bar	BIERKELLER
baron(ess)	FREIHERR(IN)
beer	BIER.BOCK
Berlin division	WALL
biscuit rusk	ZWIEBACK
black-letter typeface	FRAKTUR
blockade position (chess)	
	ZUGZWANG
blood	BLUT

—pudding	BLUTWURST
boat	U
border-crosser	GRENZGANGER
bread studies	BROTSTUDIEN
broken	KAPUT(T)
brownie	KOBOLD
Brownshirts	STURMABTEILUNG
capital	BERLIN.BONN.G
capitalist	BERLINER
carnival	FASCHING
carp (type)	CRUCIAN.CRUSIAN
cartel	KARTELL
cast-iron (type)	SPIEGELEISEN
castle	SCHLOSS
cattle disease	RINDERPEST
cavalry	
—soldier	REITER.U(H)LAN
—captain	RITTMEISTER
Central European Time	MEZ
cheers!	PROSIT
chief	
—magistrate	BURGERMEISTER
—official	GAULEITER
child(ren)	KIND(ER)
child's play	KINDERSPIEL
civilisation	KULTUR
clamour	KATZENJAMMER
clavier	KLAVIER
climbing-boot(s)	
	KLETTERSCHUH(E)
coin	
—small	PF.PFENNIG
—100 pfennigs	DEUTSCHMARK
	DM.M.MARK
—10 marks	KRONE
—100 creutzers	FLORIN.GULDEN
—100 pfennings	GROSCHEN
—100 hellers	CROWN
—old	PFENNING.CROWN
	CREUTZER.HELLER
	KR.KREUTZER.REICHSMARK
—gold or silver	G(U)ILDER
	GULDEN
—silver	THALER
collection of essays	FESTSCHRIFT
comfortable	GEMUTLICH
commercial company	AG
	GESELLSCHAFT
co-ordination	

	GLEICHSCHALTUNG
copper	KUPFER
—ore	KUPFERSCHIEFER
cosy	GEMUTLICH
count	(LAND)GRAF.LANDGRAVE
	MARGRAVE
countess	GRAFIN.LANDGRAVINE
court	HOF
courtly love	FRAUENDIEST
crevasse	BERGSCHRUND
cross-country skiing	LANGLAUF
culture	KULTUR
—group or area	KULTURKREIS
customs union (old)	ZOLLVEREIN
dachshund	TECKEL
dance	ALLEMANDE.LANDLER
dance tune	LANDLER
day	TAG
decoration	IRON CROSS
decree	DIKTAT
defector	GRENZGANGER
defence	WEHR
Democratic Republic	DDR.GDR
dialect (type)	ALEMANNIC
diatonite	KIESELGUHR
dish	CROUT.SAUERKRAUT
district	GAU
ditch	GRABEN
dog	HUND
	(see also dog)
donkey	ESEL
don't mention it	BITTE
double(-goer)	DOPPELGANGER
dramatic presentation	SINGSPIEL
drinking vessel	POKAL
dumpling	KNODEL
earth-spirit	ERDGEIST
edition	AUFLAGE
elimination of all opposition	
	GLEICHSCHALTUNG
emergency force or	
levy	LANDSTURM
emperor	KAISER
empire	REICH
enamel	SCHMELZE
enlightenment	AUFKLARUNG
eternity	EWIGKEIT
evening	ABEND
experimental task	AUFGABE

fable(s)	MARCHEN	highway	AUTOBAHN
fake	ERSATZ	history of civilisation	
Fatherland	VATERLAND		KULTURGESCHICHTE
Federal		Hitler's bodyguard	
—armed forces	BUNDESWEHR		SCHUTZSTAFFEL.SS
—German Republic	BRD.FRG	Hitlerite	NAZI
—lower house	BUNDESTAG	homesickness	HEIMWEH
Federation of Industry	BDI	hooligan	HALBSTARKER
field		housewife	HAUSFRAU
—grey	FELDGRAU	how are you?	WIE GEHT'S
—marshal	VELT-MARESCAHL	hunter	JA(E)GER
flame-thrower	FLAMMENWERFER	hunting-horn	FLUGEL-HORN
folk			WALDHORN
—song	VOLKSLIED	I	ICH
—tales	MARCHEN	—beg your pardon	BITTE
foot	FUSS	—serve	ICH DIEN
for example	ZB.ZUM BEISPIEL	ice	EIS
foreign worker	GASTARBEITER	impact radiation	
foreigner	AUSLANDER		BREMSSTRAHLUNG
form	GESTALT	Imperial	
free thinkers (18th c.)	ILLUMINATI	—Royal	KK
freshman	PENNAL	—territory	REICHSLAND
friend	KAMERAD	industrial standard	DIN
fruit loaf	STOLLEN	infant school	KINDERGARTEN
German	HUN.TEDESCO	inspiring principle	GEIST
	TEUTON(IC)	interjection	DONNERWETTER
gentleman	HERR	is it not true?	NICHT WAHR
genuine	ECHT	is that not so?	NICHT WAHR
girl	FRAULEIN	journeymanship	WANDERJAHRE
goblet	POKAL	juvenile delinquent	
goblin	KOBOLD		HALBSTARKER
goodbye	AUF WIEDERSEHEN	kindness	GEMUTLICHKEIT
good		knight	RITTER
—health!	PROSIT	lager	PILS(E)NER
—heavens!	DONNERWETTER	lagoon	HAFF
governor	BURGRAVE	lancer	U(H)LAN
—provincial	GAULEITER	leader	FU(H)RER.G.LEITER
governess	FRAULEIN	league	BUND(E)
grand piano	FLUGEL	leather trousers	LEDERHOSEN
grease	SCHMALTZ	lightning	BLITZ
guide	FU(E)HRER	limited liability company	GMBH
gypsy	ZIGEUNER	liqueur	KIRSCH(WASSER)
hail!	HEIL		KUMMEL
hall	SAAL	long	LANG
hangover	KATZENJAMMER	lord	HERR
having music specially adapted		love	LIEB(E)
	DURCHKOMPONI(E)RT	lyric(s)	LIED(ER)
helmet	PICKELHAUBE	lyric poet	MINNESINGER
heroic warrior race	VOLSUNGS	magistrate	AM(T)MANN

man	MANN
manor	HOF
—house	SCHLOSS
many thanks	DANKE SCHON
marksman	JAEGER
master	HERR.MEISTER
—of horse	STALLMEISTER
—race	HERRENVOLK
mayor	BURGERMEISTER
medal	IRON CROSS
medieval court	FEHM(GERICHT)
mercenary	LANDSKNECHT
	LANZKNECHT.LANSQUENET
mica	GLIMMER
migrant worker	GASTARBEITER
migration	VOLKERWANDERUNG
militia	LANDWEHR
milk	MILCH
mister	HERR
mix	MISCHEN
monoplane	TAUBE
morality	SITTLICHKEIT
morning	MORGEN
—star	MORGENSTERN
motorway	AUTOBAHN
mountain	BERG
—imp	RUBESZAHL
Mrs	FRAU
musician	MEISTERSINGER
	MINNESINGER
musical instrument	KUH-HORN
	KRUM(M)HORN
National Socialist	NAZI
nettle	NESSEL
new	NEU(E)
newspaper	ZEITUNG
night	NACHT
no	NEIN
noble	EDEL.HERTZOG.JUNKER
	(LAND)GRAF.LANDGRAVE
	MARGRAVE.WALDGRAVE
—woman	GRAFIN
	LANDGRAVINE.MARGRAVINE
noodle	NUDEL
noon	MITTAG
novel of hero's	
development	BILDUNGSROMAN
	ERZIEHUNGSROMAN
now	NUN

oath	SAPPERMENT
old	ALT
one	EIN
—of United Brethren	
	HERRNHUTER
opinion	ANSCHAULING
organised	GESTALT
other	ANDER
outlook on the world	
	WELTANSCHAUUNG
over	UBER
paddle	PADDELN
palace	SCHLOSS
parliament	BUNDESTAG
	REICHSTAG
pastime	ZEITVERTREIB
pattern	GESTALT
people	HERREN
—'s car	VOLKSWAGEN.VW
philosophers	KANT.NIETZSCHE
piano	HAMMERKLAVIER
please	BITTE
pleasure in misfortune	
of others	SCHADENFREUDE
powdery deposit	BERGMEHL
power politics	MACHTPOLITIK
practical politics	REALPOLITIK
pretentious art	KITSCH
prince	ELECTOR
prisoner-of-war camp	OFFLAG
	STALAG
quick(ly)	SCHNELL
race	LAUF
rapid dance	WALTZ
reception room	KURSAAL
reconciliation	AUSGLEICH
recurring theme	LEITMOTIF
	LEITMOTIV
refusal	NEIN
relentless force	BLUT UND EISEN
religious	
—painter	NAZARENE
—reformer (17th c.)	PIETIST
revolt	PUTSCH
rifleman	JA(E)GER
rift valley	GRABEN
river	FLUSS
rivers	ELBE.RHEIN
	RHINE

rockfall	BERGFALL	—association	BURSCHENSCHAFT
room	RAUM.ZIMMER	—beerhouse	KNEIPE
—to live	LEBENSRAUM	—drinking party	KNEIPE
royal forester	WALDGRAVE	—duel	MENSUR
ruined	KAPUT(T)	—duelling sword	SCHLAGER
run	LAUF	—society	CORPS
rusk	ZWEIBACK	—songbook	KOMMERSBUCH
rye bread	PUMPERNICKEL	substitute	ERSATZ
salted biscuit	PRETZEL	superman	UBERMENSCH
scamp	EULENSPIEGEL	superstition	ABERGLAUBE
school	SCHULE	supplementary reserve	ERSATZ
—grammar or high	GYMNASIUM	swastika	HAKENKREUZ
—secondary	PROGYMNASIUM	sweet bread	STOLLEN
score (music)	PARTITUR	sword	SCHLAGER
sea	MEER	table	TISCH
secret police	GESTAPO	—wine	TAFELWEIN
sentiment	EMPFINDUNG	tank	PANZER
sentimental enthusiasm		tavern	KNEIPE
	SCHWARMEREI	teach	LEHREN
Serene Highness	DURCHLAUCHT	teacher paid in fees not	
shape	GESTALT	salary	PRIVATDOCENT
sharpshooter	JA(E)GER		PRIVATDOZENT
Shrovetide carnival	FASCHING	tendency	TENDENZ
silver	ALBATA	that is to say	DAS HEISST.DH
sir	HERR.MEINHERR	the	DAS.DER.DIE
skiing (cross country)	LANGLAUF	thing in itself	DING AN SICH
smashed	KAPUT(T)	think	MEINEN
smoked sausage	FRANKFURTER	thunder	DONNER
softly	LEISE	—storm	DONNERWETTER
soldiers	SS	timbre	KLANGFARBE
song(s)	LIED(ER)	toast	PROSIT
—without words		tone colour	KLANGFARBE
	LIED OHNE WORTE	touch wood	UNBERUFEN
spa building	KURHAUS	trash	KITSCH
spirit	GEIST	tribe	ANGLES.SAXONS
—of the times	ZEITGEIST	trombone	POSAUNE
—of the mines	KOBOLD	trooper	REITER
sprite	KOBOLD.NICKEL	under	UNTER
squire	JUNKER	union	ANSCHLUSS.VEREIN
state	REICH	—of states	ZOLLVEREIN
—bank	REICHSBANK	university	
—legislature	LANDTAG	—freshman	PENNAL
steel	STAHL	—outsider	PHILISTER.PHILISTINE
stormtroopers		upon my soul!	SAPPERMENT
	STURMABTEILUNG	upper house	OBERHAUS
street in Berlin		uproar	KATZENJAMMER
	WILHELMSTRASSE	valley	TAL
stroke	SCHLAG	veal cutlet	(WIENER)SCHNITZEL
student(s)	BURSCH(EN)	volume(s) of book	BAND(E)

war	KRIEG	get involved in war	RAW
—game	KRIEGSSPIEL	get left in. . .	incl L or LT
—of culture	KULTURKAMPF	Get lost!	TEG
water-sprite	NIX	get lost in forest	FOSTER
weight	CENTNER	get moving when I. . .	WHINE
white horse	SCHIMMEL	get on	incl ON
who is there?	WER DA	•I get on both sides	ONION
wife	FRAU	get organised	TEG
—of margrave	MARGRAVINE	get out	GE-T
—of noble	WALDGRAVINE	get out for a duck	incl O
wine	AUSLESE.KABINETT	•h-e gets out for a duck	HOE
	QUALITATSWEIN.SPATLESE	get out of a	incl A
	TAFELWEIN.WEIN	get out of a	omit A
	(see also drink[2])	get out of brea/th an/d. . .	THAN
—cask	FUDER	get out of line	incl I
wing	FLUGEL	•ma-n gets out of line	MAIN
witches' revel		get out of *	incl *
	WALPURGIS(NACHT)	•German soldier gets	
with	MIT	out of car	SCARS
	(see also with)	get out of *	omit *
woman	FRAU	•(Ch)arles gets out of	
world	WELT	church	ARLES
—philosophy		get over it⟨	TI
	WELTANSCHAUUNG	get ready	(EN)CASH
—politics	WELTPOLITIK	get rid of a. . .	omit A
—spirit	WELTGEIST	get rid of money	omit L
weariness	WELTSCHMERZ	get rid of *	omit *
yard	HOF	•the(y) get rid of unknown. . .	THE
year(s) of travelling		•get rid of odd members of	
	WANDERJAHR(E)	(p)a(r)t(i)e(s). . .	ATE
yes	JA	get right in. . .	incl R or RT
—indeed	JA WOHL	get round a. . .	incl A
young girl	BACKFISCH.FRAULEIN	get round *	incl *
your health	GESUNDHEIT	•soldier gets round it	RITE
zodiacal light	GEGENSCHEIN	get shot	SNAP.TAKE PICTURE
Germany	D.DDR.GDR.GER	get to work in car	CAIRN
germicide	TCP	get to work on time	EMIT
gerund	GER	get up(D) ↑	TEG
get		get up mad(D) ↑	DAM
get a rise(D) ↑	TEG	getting a tan	(in) SU-N
•before getting a rise	ETNA	getting firsts in Science, English	
get awkward and not. . .	DANTON	and Maths	SEAM
get drunk on ale	ALONE	getting warm	NOTICED
get cracking	DECIPHER.DECODE	getting wet	(in) RA-IN
get down	DUCK	**Ghana(ian)**	GH
get from e/vide/nce	VIDE	capital	ACCRA.G
get into *	incl in *	characters	GH
•we get into sea	MEWED	coin	
get into shape	-TION	—unit	PESEWA

—100 pesewas	CEDI
language	FANTEE.FANTI
	TSHI.TWI
leader	G
people	FANTEE.FANTI
ghost-writer	IBSEN
giant	ATLAS.TITAN
giant-killer	DAVID.JACK
Gibraltar	GIB.GBZ
giddy <u>goat</u>	TOGA
gift	GAB
gift-*wrapped*	(in) PRES-ENT
gifted father	SANTA CLAUS
giga-electron-volt	GEV
Gilbert and Sullivan	GS.GANDS
gilded	(in) O-R
gimmicky <u>means</u>	MANES
gin	
<u>gin</u> *cocktail*	IGN-.-ING.NIG
<u>gin</u> *sling*	IGN-.-ING.NIG
gin user	TRAPPER
girl[1]	DEB.G.GAL.MISS
hence	
•a royal girl	ARDEB
•girl *goes to* America	DEBUS
•girl *has* silver. . .	DEBAG
and	
•girl runner	GALLOPER
•girl *with* nothing on	GALOON
•girl *with* one lion	GALILEO
and	
•composer's girl, *say*	MISHANDLE
•girl and *French*. . .	MIS-SET
•girl-journalist	MISSED
girl[2]	
from :	
America	BROAD
Australia	ADELAIDE.ALICE
	SHEILA
France	FILLE(TTE).NANCY
Germany	FRAULEIN
Ireland	COLLEEN
Italy	FLORENCE.RAGAZZA
	SIGNORINA
Picardy	ROSE
Scotland	CUMMER
Spain	MUCHACHA.NINA
	SENORITA
Tralee	ROSE

Troy	HELEN
Wales	MEGAN
Wessex	TESS
(*see also* Appendix)	
girl[3]	
girl *and* boy	DIJON.DINED
GALLEON.MISSAL.PATRON	
girl *and* two boys	BETRAYAL
girl carrying camera	DOLLY
girl cyclist	DAISY
girl-friend	SALAMI
girl in	
—opera	AIDA.CARMEN
MIMI.NORMA.TOSCA	
—the garden	MAUD
—the shrubbery	MYRTLE
VERONICA.etc.	
—Wonderland	ALICE
girl of the soft left	MILDRED
girl who did	KATY
girlish *denial*	BOYISH
girl's best friend	DIAMOND
girls	ANN.ANNA.ANNE.DI.ENA
IDA.SAL.SUE.UNA.VERA.VI	
hence	
•girl *over*weight(D)	ANNOUNCE
•girl employees	DISTAFF
•girl's cloak	DISMANTLE
•girl *in* Lebanon	RENAL
•girl *without* energy	IDEA
•girl *with* note	SALE
•girl *going after* shirt	TUNA
•girl poses	VISITS
growing girl	DAISY.ERICA
ROSE.etc.	
(*see also* Appendix)	
give	
give a lift to diva(D) ↑	AVID
give attention to	EAR
give away a. . .	omit A
give away money	omit D.L.P
give away *	omit *
•(p)layer *gives away* pawn	LAYER
give key *to*. . .	incl A-G
give money to	incl D.L.P
give nothing *away*	omit O
give rise to <u>leer</u>	REEL
give rise to l̄eer(D) ↑	REEL
give shelter to a. . .	incl A

give shelter to *	incl *
•sh-ed *gives shelter to English*	
queen	SHEERED
given a...	incl A
given his *head*	incl H
given in hi/s pare/nts'...	SPARE
given money	incl D.L.P
given shelter by *	incl in *
•English queen *given shelter by*	
sh-ed	SHEERED
given *	incl *
•she is *given* £50	SHELL
giving her a...	HARE.HEAR
gives praise	ASPIRE
giving up drink	(on) WAGON
Gladstone	GOM
glamour	IT.SA
hence	
•glamour-queen dined	ITERATE
•glamour-girl	SAGENE.SAUNA
glass vessel	SCHOONER
gleaner	RUTH
globe	O
gnarled oaks	SOAK
go	GREEN
go *a bit* silly	GOLLY
go *away from*	omit N.S.E.W
go *back*	OG
go *back* fool⟨	PAS
go *both ways*	PEP
go crazy	DEPARTMENTAL
go *into* slide	IDLES.SIDLE
go North from	omit N
go *off* a...	omit A
go *off* *	omit *
•(br)other *goes off* rails	OTHER
go *off* meat	MATE.TAME.TEAM
go *off* with a tenor	ORNATE
go on	RIDE
go on a bender	KNEEL
go *out*	OG
go over	(*see* over)
go *over*⟨	OG
go *round*⟨	OG
go *round* the bend	incl S.U
go to the dogs	
or be...	BORE.ROBE
go *wrong*	OG
go *wrong* over an...	VERONA

goes funny	EGOS
goes out in gold...	DOLING
goes out with boys	YOBS
* *goes*	omit *
•win(k) when king *goes*	WIN
going about a...	incl A
going about *	incl *
•fish *going about* the...	GATHER
going about naked	KNEAD
* *going about*	
•saw *going about*⟨	WAS
going around slowly	SLY
going around a...	incl A
going around *	incl *
•i-s *going around* a square	ITS
going around there	ETHER
* *going around*	
•gnat *going around*⟨	TANG
going inside *	incl in *
•he, *going inside*,	
swat-s...	SWATHES
going north,	
walker...(D) ↑	RECAP
going outside a...	incl A
going outside *	incl *
•w-ere *going outside*	
house	WHERE
•go-ing *outside*-right	GORING
going rotten, a tree...	ARETE
going round a...	incl A
going round *	incl *
•c-at *going round* circle	COAT
going round on her...	HERON
* *going round*	
•bus *going round*...⟨	SUB
going through *	incl in *
•Scot *going through*	
Per-th	PERIANTH
going up step(D) ↑	PETS
going without a...	incl A
going without *	incl *
•w-e are *going without* her	WHERE
going without a...	omit A
going without *	omit *
•fat(her) *going without* her	FAT
gone bust, traders...	DARTERS
gone off meat	MATE.TAME
	TEAM
goad her...	NEEDLEWOMAN

goats

Anatolian	ANGORA
Asian	MARKHOR.SNAKE-EATER
Caucasian	ATCHI.TUR
female	CAPRA.NANNY
Himalayan	GOORAL.TAHR.TEHR
	THAR.SEROW
male	BILLY.BUTTER
Pyrenean	CHAMOIS.IBEX
	IZARD.ROCK-DOE
Tibetan	TAKIN
young	KID

gods

African	
Bushman's god	PRAYING MANTIS
—creator god	NGAI
—python god	ZOMBIE
American Indian	MANITO(U)
Assyrian	
—earth god	BEL
sky god	ANAT
—supreme or war god	AS(S)HUR
	AS(S)UR
Babylonian	BAAL.BEL
—atmosphere, clouds and	
tempest god	ADDAD
—chief god	ENKI.(H)EA.MARDUK
—earth god	BEL.ENLIL.KINGU
—sky god	ANU
—sun and harvest god	
	T(H)AMMUZ
—war god	AS(S)HUR
AS(S)HUR.MARDUK.NERGAL	
—water god	APSU.(H)EA
—wisdom god	MARDU.NABU
Buddhist	BUDDHA.GAUTAMA
	SAKYAMUNI
Celtic	
—chief god	DAGDA
—sea god	LE(I)R
Chaldean	NANNAR
Chinese	JOSS.KUANYIN
SHANGTI.SHEN-NUNG	
—Confucian supreme god	TIAN
creator of the universe	
	DEMIURGE
Egyptian	
—creator	KHNUM.PTAH
—falcon-headed god	HORUS

—ibis-headed god	THOTH
—jackal-headed god	ANUBIS
—ram-headed god	AMEN
	AM(M)ON.AMUN
—son of Osiris	HORUS
—star god	SOTHIS
—sun god	HORUS.RA.RE
—supreme god	AMEN.AM(M)ON
	AMUN.OSIRIS
—wolf god	WEPWAWET
Egyptian god of (the)	
—air	SHU
—art	THOTH
—artisans and artists	PTAH
—darkness	SET
—dead	ANUBIS.OSIRIS
—earth	GEB KEB
—learning, medicine	IMHOTEP
—life and fertility	AMEN
	AM(M)ON.AMUN
—magic	THOTH
—moon	AAH.KHONS.YAH
—Nile	HAPI
—science	THOTH
—fertility	MIN
—soul	BA
—underworld	OSIRIS.SARAPIS
SERAPIS.WEPWAWET	
—war	SEPTU
—water	NUN
—wisdom	THOTH
English war god	TIU.TIW
Etruscan	TAGES
false	BAAL.IDOL
fish god	EA
Germanic	(see Norse below)
Gnostic	ABRAXAS
greed and riches	MAMMON
Greek	
—attendant on Pan	
(inferior god)	PANISC.PANISK
—many shaped god	NEREUS
PHORCYS.PROTEUS	
—sun god	APOLLO.HELIOS
HYPERION.PHOEBUS.TITAN	
—supreme god	CRONUS
	KRONOS.ZEUS
Greek god of (the)	
—beauty	HELIOS

—dreams	MORPHEUS
—fire	HEPHAESTUS
—flocks	PAN
—healing	AESCULAPIUS
	ASCLEPIOS.ASCLEPIUS
—love	EROS
—marriage	HYMEN
—metalworking	HEPHAESTUS
—mirth	COMUS
—music	APOLLO
—north wind	BOREAS
—prophecy	APOLLO
—sailors	CASTOR.POLLUX
—sea	NEREUS.OCEANUS
	PROTEUS.POSEIDON.TRITON
—shepherds	PAN
—sky	ZEUS
—sleep	HYPNOS
—sun	HELIOS
—travellers	HERMES
—underworld	DIS.HADES.PLUTO
—universe	URANUS
—vegetation and rebirth	ADONIS
—war	ARES
—wealth	PLUTUS
—west wind	ZEPHYRUS
—winds	(A)EOLUS
—wine	BACCHUS.DIONYSUS
—wisdom	HERMES
—woods	PAN.SILENUS.SATYR
Hebrew	ELOHIM.JAH(VEH)
	JAHWEH.JEHOVAH
	YAH(VEH).YAHVIST.
	YAHWIST.YAWE(H)
Hindu	DEVA
—creator	BRAHMA
—desire	KAMA
—destroyer	S(H)IVA
—earth	KRISHNA
—elephant-headed	GANES(H)A
—fire	AGNI
—good fortune	GANES(H)A
—heavens	INDRA.VARUNA
—intoxicating spirit/plant	SOMA
—learning	GANES(H)A
—love	KAMA
—monkey god	HANUMAN
—moon	SOMA
—preserver	KRISHNA

	RAMA.VISHNU
—rain	INDRA
—reproducer	S(H)IVA
—storms	RUDRA
—sun	SURYA
—supreme	BRAHMA.INDRA
—time	KALA
—war	INDRA.KARTTIKEYA
—water	VARUNA
Japanese	KAMI
Knights Templar	BAPHOMET
Moslem	ALLAH
mysterious and awesome	
deity	DEMOGORGON
Norse	AESIR.VANIR
—earth	FREYR
—keeper of Bifrost (rainbow)	
bridge	HEIMDALL
—light	BALDUR
—mischief	LOKI
—supreme	ODIN.WODEN
	WOTAN
—thunder	THOR
—war	TYR
—wind	VAYU
Persian	(AHURA) MAZDA
	MITHRA.MITHRAS(S)
	ORMAZD.ORMUZD
Philistine	DAGON
Phoenician	BALL.BEELZEBUB
Red Indian	MANITO(U)
Roman god of (the)	
—agriculture	SATURN
—boundaries	TERMINUS
—dead	ORCUS
—good	MANES
—wicked	LARVAE.LEMRUES
—doorways	JANUS
—eloquence	MERCURY
—farming	SILVANUS
—fertility	LUPERCUS.PRIAPUS
—fire	MULCIBER
	VOLCANUS.VULCAN
—forests and woods	SILVANUS
—flocks	LUPERCUS
—founder of Rome	QUIRINUS
—gardens	PRIAPUS
	VERTUMNUS
—gateways	JANUS

—household	LAR(ES)
—larder	PENATES
—love	CUPID
—merchants	MERCURY
—metalwork	MULCIBER
	VULCAN(US)
—sea	NEPTUNE
—shepherds	FAUN(US)
—sleep	SOMNUS
—spirits of the dead	MANES
—sun	APOLLO
—supreme	JOVE.JUPITER
	MITHRAS
—theft	MERCURY
—two-faced	JANUS
—underworld	DIS.PLUTO
—war	MARS
	QUIRINUS.ROMULUS
—wine	BACCHUS.LIBER
—wisdom	MERCURY
—woods	SILVAN.SYLVANUS
—youth	JUVENTUS
Saxon	EOSTRE
Semitic	ASMODAY.ASMODEUS
	MOLECH.MOLOCH.CAB(E)IRI
Spanish love god	AMADIS
Syrian	RIMMON
West Indian snake god	ZOMBI(E)

goddesses

Australian mother	
goddess	KADJERI.KUNAPIPI
Babylonian	
—chief	ISHTAR.NANAI.NINA
—death	GULA
—dragon goddess	TIAMAT
—earth	DAMKINA
Celtic	(D)ANA.(D)ANU
—light	LUG(H)
Egyptian	
—cow goddess	HATHOR
—cobra goddess	UDOT
—creation	HEKET
—destiny	SHAIT
—fertility	ISIS
—love	HATHOR
—maternity	APET
—queen of goddesses	SATI
—sky	NUT
—truth and justice	MA(AT)

—war	NEIT(H)
Greek	
—agriculture	DEMETER
—beauty	APHRODITE
—childbirth	ARTEMIS.EILEITHYIA
	ILITHYIA
—corn	DEMETER
—dawn	EOS
—discord	ERIS
—divine justice	THEMIS
—earth	GE.GAEA.GAIA
—foretelling the future	CAMENAE
—fortune	TYCHE
—health	HYGEIA
—hearth	HESTIA
—hunting	ARTEMIS.CYNTHIA
—justice	ASTRAEA.DIKE.THEMIS
—law	THEMIS
—love	APHRODITE
—marriage	HERA
—memory	MNEMOSYNE
—mischief	ATE
—moon	ARTEMIS.SELENE
—nature	RHEA
—night	NYX
—rainbow	IRIS
—retribution	NEMESIS
—springs	CAMENAE
—underworld	PERSEPHONE
—victory	NIKE
—war	ATHENA
—wells	CAMENAE
—wisdom	ATHENA.ATHENE
	PALLAS
—witchcraft	HECATE
—youth	HEBE
Hawaiian volcano	PELE
Hindu	
—dawn	US(H)AS
—destroyer	DURGA.KALI
—divinity	DEVI
—mother-goddess	KAN.SHAKTA
—plenty	PURANDI
—rivers	SARAVATSI
—strength	DURGA.KALI
Japanese (Shinto)	AMATERASU
Norse	
—beauty	FREYJA
—dead	HEL(A)

—handmaidens, Valhalla	
	VALKYRIE
—healing	EIR
—love	FREYA
—sea	RAN
—underworld	GERD.HEL(A)
—wisdom	FRIGG(A)
Peruvian	MAMA
Roman	
—beauty	VENUS
—chastity	DIAN(A)
—childbirth	LUCINA
—corn	CERES
—crops	AN(N)ONA
—dawn	AURORA
—earth	TELLUS
—fields	BONA DEA.FAUNA
—fire	VESTA
—flowers	FLORA
—fruit	POMONA
—harvest	OPS
—hearth	HESTIA.VESTA
—horticulture	VACUNA
—horses	EPONA
—household	VESTA
—hunting	DIAN(A).LUCINA
—light	DIAN(A)
—love	VENUS
—marriage	JUNO.LUCINA
—moon	DIAN(A)
—morning	MATUTA
—orchards	POMONA
—peace	IRENE
—rumour	FAMA
—springs and wells	CAMENAE
—war	BELLONA
—wealth	OPS
—wisdom	MINERVA
Saxon	
—spring	EASTRE.EOSTRE
Semitic	
—fertility	ASTARTE.ASHTARETH
Thracian	KOTYS.KOTYTTO
godfather	CAPO.DON
going	(see go)
gold¹	AU.OR
hence	
•gold *and* potassium	AUK
•gold cross in...	AUXIN

•gold rocks, *say*	AUROCHS
•gold the *French*...	AULA
and	
•gold *and* iron	ORFE
•gold key	ORE
•gold piece	ORBIT
•gold trade	ORDEAL
and	
•gold *in* church	CORE
•gold *in* iron	FORE
•gold sh-e *took in*	SHORE
and	
•measure gold	METEOR
•old gold	PASTOR
gold²	
gold-*covered*	(in) O-R
gold-*edged*	(in) O-R
gold-*mounted*	(in) O-R
gold-*mounted*(D) ↑	RO
gold-*wrapped*	(in) O-R
•the old gold-*wrapped*...	OYER
gold *wrapped in*...	incl OR
•gold *wrapped in* pound note	
	LORD
golf	
golf suit	CLUBS
golfer's curse	ROUND OATH
golfers	PGA
gone	(*see* go)
good¹	A.AI.BON.PI
hence	
•good journey	ATRIP
•good relations	AKIN
•good team	ASIDE
and	
•good colour	AIRED
•good contest	AIR-ACE
•good fish	AILING
and	
•good figure	BOND
•good note	BONA.BOND
	BONE.BONG
•good *to us*	BONUS
and	
•good friend	PIPAL
•good laugh, *say*	PILAFF
•good value	PIRATE
good²	
good book	NT.OT

goodbye	TATA.VALE
good chap	JAKE.S.ST
good earth	FAIRGROUND
good golfer	BOGEY MAN
good man	DEAN.S.ST
hence	
•good man is not well	STILL
•good man *in* first-class. . .	ASTI
•see a good man	LOST
good number	ANAESTHETIC
	ANTHEM.HYMN
good reading	BIBLE.NT.OT
good rhyme	COULD.WOOD
good score	PAR
Good Service Pension	GSP
goodness	MY.WELL-HEAD
good³	
good-*hearted*	OO
good-*hearted*	incl OK
•good-*hearted* man	BLOKE
•good-*hearted* m-e	MOKE
goose	
domestic	BRECON BUFF
	CHINESE.EM(B)DEN
	ROMAN.TOULOUSE
wild	BARNACLE.BEAN.BRENT
	CANADA.EGYPTIAN
	GREYLAG.HAWAIIAN
	LESSER WHITE-FRONTED
	PINK-FOOTED
	RED-BREASTED.SNOW
	WHITE-FRONTED
Gort's men	BEF
Gospels	NT
got	(*see* get)
Gotham	NY
govern	
government	GOV(T)
government by. . .	(*see* power²)
government issue	GI
governor	GOV.HE
grab	
grab a. . .	incl A
grab *	incl *
•do-g *grabs* a tin	DOTING
grabbed by *	incl *
•tin *grabbed by* do-g	DOTING
Graces	CHARITIES
good cheer	THALIA

mirth	EUPHROSYNE
splendour	AGLAIA
gradually	ERIC
graduate	BA.MA
hence	
•graduate circle	BARING
•graduates are late	BASTARDY
•graduates *have a* hair-cut	
	BASS-HORN
and	
•mother *and* graduate	MAMBA
•peculiar graduate	RUMBA
•Uncle *with* graduate	SAMBA
and	
•graduate's quarrel	MASTIFF
•graduates are wise	MASSAGE
•graduates celebrate	MASSING
grain	GR
gram(me)	G.GM.GR
grammar	GR.GRAM
gran turismo	GT
Granada	WG
grand¹	G
hence	
•grand circle	GO
•grand entrance	GENTRY
•grand total	GADDING
•grand tour	GRANGE
grand²	
grand	IMPOUNDS
grand deficiency	omit G
Grand Old Man	GOM
grape	UVA
varieties	ALIGOTE.BACCHUS
	BARBERA.CABERNET
	CHARDONNAY.CHASSELAS
	CHENIN.DOLCETTO.GAMAY
	GARGANEGA.GARNACHA
	GRENACHE.HUXELREBE
	MALBEC.MALVASIA
	MARSANNE.MERLOT.MOSCATEL
	MULLER-THURGAU.ORTEGA
	MUSKAT.NEBBIOLO
	PALOMINO.PINOT.RIESLING
	SAUVIGNON.SEMILLON
	SILVANER.SYLVANER
	SYRAH.TOKAY.TRAMINER
	UGNI.ZINFANDEL
graph	(*see* write³)

graphite	KISH	Dutch rush	HORSE TAIL
grasp			SHAVE GRASS
grasped by *	incl in *	early sprouting grass	
•king *grasped by* duke	FIRST		VERNAL GRASS
grasping a. . .	incl A	eelgrass GRASSWRACK.ZOSTER	
grasping *	incl *	esparto	SPANISH GRASS
•duke *grasping* a king	FIRST		SPART
grass[1]		Falkland Islands grass	
African	PENNISETUM		TUSSAC GRASS
agave fibre	SISAL(-GRASS)		TUSSOCK GRASS
Aira	HAIRGRASS	feather grass	STIPA
Alopecurus	FOXTAIL	fescue	FESTUCA
Anthoxanthum	VERNAL GRASS	float-grass	MANNA-GRASS
anti-scorbutic	SCURVYGRASS	forage grass	RYE GRASS
aquatic grass	MANNA-GRASS	—American	GAMA GRASS
Avena	OAT	gardener's garters	
barley-type	SQUIRRELTAIL		PAINTED GRASS
basket-grass	OPLISMENUS	PHALARIS.RIBBON GRASS	
	PANICUM	Gastridium	NIT GRASS
black salsify	VIPER'S GRASS	glaucous	ELYMUS
Bouteloua	MOSQUITO GRASS	Glyceria	FLOAT(ING) GRASS
brome grass	LOP(GRASS)	gold-edged	CAREX
bulrush	CAT'S TAIL	goosegrass	CATCHWEED
butterwort	ROT-GRASS	grasswrack	EELGRASS
canary-grass	PAINTED GRASS		ZOSTER
cat's-tail	BULRUSH.PHLEUM		CLEAVERS.CLIVERS
	TIMOTHY	Holcus	SOFT-GRASS
China grass	RAMEE.RAMI(E)	horsetail	DUTCH RUSH
	RHEA	hybrid cereal	TRITICALE
coarse grass	STAR(R)	India BAJREE.DUR(R)A.JHOW	
cocksfoot	DACTYLIS	KANS.RAGI.ROOSA.RUSA	
	HARDGRASS	Juncus	RUSH
cord grass	RICEGRASS	Kentucky	BLUE GRASS
Cortaderia	PAMPASGRASS	long, dried	WINDLESTRAW
cotton grass	ERIOPHORUM	marram	MATGRASS
couch grass	DOGGRASS	MATWEED.SEA-REED	
DOGWHEAT.QUICK(EN)		meadow grass	POA
QUITCH(-GRASS)		moorland grass	MATGRASS
(S)QUITCH.TWITCH		mosquito grass	BOUTELOUA
creeping	BUFFALO-GRASS	New Zealand	TOI TOI
	CANARY-GRASS	oat	AVENA
—bent-grass	FIORIN	—type	BROME GRASS
Cynosurus	DOG'S-TAIL GRASS	Oplismenus	BASKET-GRASS
darnel	LOLIUM		PANICUM
Dactylis	COCKSFOOT	ornamental	PLUME-GRASS
Digitaria	FINGER GRASS	painted grass	CANARY GRASS
dog'stail grass	CYNOSURUS	GARDENER'S GARTERS	
dry-stalk	BEN(N)ET	Panicum	BASKET-GRASS
durra	SORGHUM		OPLISMENUS

	PANIC(-GRASS)
paper-reed	PAPYRUS
papyrus	PAPER-REED
pasture grass	DOGS'-TAIL GRASS
	RYE GRASS
	TUSSOCK GRASS
pennywort	ROT GRASS
Phalaris	GARDENER'S GARTERS
Phleum	TIMOTHY
Poa	MEADOW GRASS
	WIRE GRASS
porcupine grass	SPINIFEX
quitch grass	SQUITCH
ramee/rami(e)	CHINA GRASS
	RHEA
reed mace	CAT'S-TAIL
	ELEPHANT GRASS
rhea	RAMEE.RAMI(E).RHEA
ribbon grass	
	GARDENER'S GARTERS
rice grass	CORD-GRASS
	BUTTERWORT
	PENNYWORT
rush	JUNCUS
rye	SECALE
rye grass	DARNEL.LOLIUM
sand-binding	LYME GRASS
	MARRAM.MARRUM
scurvy grass	COCHLEARIA
sea-reed	MARRAM(-GRASS)
seaside grass	AMMOPHILA
	DOG'S-TOOTH GRASS
	MARRAM.MARRUM
Secale	RYE
sedge	CAREX
shave grass	DUTCH RUSH
sesame grass	ZAMA GRASS
smart-weed	WATERPEPPER
sorghum	DURRA.SUDAN GRASS
South American	PAMPAS GRASS
Spanish grass	ESPARTO
spartina	CORD GRASS
Stipa	FEATHER GRASS
striped canary-grass	
	RIBBON GRASS
Sudan grass	SORGHUM
sweet-smelling	HOLY GRASS
timothy	CAT'S-TAIL GRASS
	PHLEUM

Uniola	SPIKE-GRASS
variegated ribbon	
	GARDENER'S GARTERS
vernal grass	ANTHOXANTHUM
waterpepper	SMART-WEED
wheat/rye hybrid	TRITICALE
wire-grass	POA
woodland grass	MILLET GRASS
worthless	SOFT GRASS
Xyris	YELLOW-EYED GRASS
yellow-eyed grass	XYRIS
zama grass	SESAME GRASS
Zostera	EELGRASS
grass²	BETRAY.INFORM
	MARIJUANA
	SING.SQUEAL.TELL
grasser	BETRAYER.INFORMER
	SQUEALER.TELLER
grass-covered	(in) RE-ED
gratitude	TA
grave description	DEAD END
	TOMB
gravity	G
great	MEGA-.OS
Great Britain	GB
great conductor	COPPER.CU
Great Dane	HAMLET
great deal	BAGS.LOTS
great dog	DANE
great fiddle	CELLO
great flier	AUK.TIT
great flow(er) = large river	
hence	
•great flow of German. . .	RHINE
•great flower in South	
America	AMAZON
•Indian's great flower	GANGES
great fool	BF
great healer	TIME
great names	ALEXANDER
	ALFRED.CATHERINE
	(*see also* Appendix)
great physician	TIME
great sea	MEDITERRANEAN
great swimmer	WHALE
Great Universal Stores	GUS
Great Western Railway	GWR
Greater London Council	GLC
Greece	GR

Greek¹	GR
hence	
•Greek in debt	GROWER
•Greek river	GROUSE
•Greek state	GRAVER
Greek²	ARGIVE.ATTICA.GK.GR
abbot	ARCHIMANDRITE
	HEGUMEN
abode of dead	ELYSIUM
above	HYPER
—Dorian (music)	HYPERDORIAN
—Lydian (music)	HYPERLYDIAN
—Phrygian (music)	
	HYPERPHRYGIAN
account of saint's	
life	SYNAXARION
accuser	SYCOPHANT
acorn	BALANOS
additional note (music)	
	PROSLAMBANOMENOS
address by chorus	PARABASIS
admiral	NAVARCH
advocate	SYNDIC
after	META
alb	STICHARION
alcove	ZOTHECA
all	PAN
alone	MONOS
among	META
amphitheatre	ODEON.ODEUM
and	
—so forth	KTL
—the rest	KTL
angle	GONIA
annalist	LOGOGRAPHER
ant	MURMEX
antipodes	ANTICHTHON
ape	PITHEKOS
apple	MELON
arms	HOPLA
army	
—commander	TAXIARCH
—division	TAXIS
arrangement	TAXIS
art	TEKHNE
ass	ONOS
assembly	AGYRIS.ECCLESIA
Athenian	
—aristocrat	EUPATRID

—colony	CLERUCHY
—youth	EPHEBE
athletic contest	AGON
auditor	LOGOTHETE(S)
away, Satan!	APAGE SATANAS
Bacchic rout	THIASUS
back	NOTO
backward	OPISO
band of soldiers	ENOMOTY
banish	OSTRACISE
base	HEDRA
be sober	NEPHEIN
beautiful	TO KALON
—place	TEMPE
becoming	TO PREPON
bed	KLINE
bee-eater	MEROPS
behind	OPISTHEN
below	HYPO
—Aeolian (music)	HYPOAEOLIAN
—Lydian (music)	HYPOLYDIAN
—Phrygian (music)	
	HYPOPHRYGIAN
beside	META
bird	ORNIS.ORNITHOS
	STROUTHION
birth	TOKOS
bishop	EXARCH
—'s stole	EPITRACHELION
black	MELAS
bladder	KYSTIS
blade	PLATE
blind	ALAOS
blood	HAIMA
bone	OSTEON
boundary marker	HERM
boy	PAIDOS
breastplate	THORAX
bride	NYMPHE
brigand	KLEPHT
bristle	CHAITE
brother	ADELPHOS
bud	BLASTOS
bulk	ONCOS
business	ERGON.PRAGMATA
—agent	SYNDIC
cake	PIT(T)A
captain of guards	
	PROTOSPATHARIUS

capital	ATHENS.G	common informer	SYCOPHANT
case	THEKE	canonical hour	ORTHROS
cave	SPEOS	container	KYTOS
cessation	PAUSIS	contemptible Greek	GREEKLING
chamber	THALAMOS	copper	CHALKOS
champion	PROMACHOS	corn	SITOS
character	GR.PLATO	council	BOULE
	(*see also* letters *below*)	—division	PRYTANY
chariot	BIGA.TRIGA.QUADRIGA	—representing all	
cheese	AGRAFA		PANHELLENION
chest	LARNAX		PANHELLENIUM
chief magician	ARCHIMAGE	court	AREOPAGUS
child	PAIDOS	courtesan	ASPASIA.HETAIRA
choral odes	STASIMA	covering	SHEUE
chorus leader	CHORAGUS	credit	KUDOS
	CHOREGUS	crowd	OCHLOS
church stall	STASIDION	custom	NOMOS
citadel	ACROPOLIS	cut(ting)	TOME
city	POLIS	dance	ROMAIKA
—badge	EPISEMON	dawn	ORTHROS
claw	ONYX	day	HEMERA
cloak	HIMATION	deacon's stole	ORARION
cloud	NEPHELE.NEPHOS	dead (body)	NEKROS
coffin	LARNAX	decree of Athens	
coins		assembly	PSEPHISM
—small	LEPTON	defender	PROMACHOS
—100 lepta	DRACHMA	defilement	MYSOS
—1½ pence	OBOL(US)	deities	(*see* gods.goddesses)
—6 oboli	DRACHMA	delegate	SYNDIC
—2 drachmas	DIDRACHMA	—to council	AMPHICYTON
—4 drachmas	TETRADRACHM	department	NOME.NOMOS
—silver tetradrachm	STATER	diadem	STEPHANE
—100 drachmas	MINA	dialect	(A)EOLIC.ATTIC
—6000 drachmas	TALENT		DORIC.IONIC.KOINE
collection of sermons		discarded letter	SAN
	PANEGYRICON	discourse	LOGOS
colonist in		dish	MOUSSAKA
—Asia Minor	AEOLIAN	divination	MANTEIA
—Italy	ITALIOT(E)	divine voice	OMPHE
—Sicily	SICELIOT.SIKELIOT	division	DEME
colonnade	STOA.XYSTOS	—in army	TAXIS
	XYSTUS	—in verse	PERIOD
colour	CHROMA	—of people	PHYLE
commander of		Doric magistrate	EPHOR
—ten men	DECADARCH	downy hairs	PAPPUS
—thousand men	CHILIARCH	downbeat (music)	THESIS
—division	TAXIARCH	dowry	PHERNE
—subdivision	TETRARCH	dramatist	ARISTOPHANES
—trireme	TRIERARCH	dream	ONEIROS

dressing room (baths)
                    APODYTERIUM
drinking
—cup   COTYLE.CYLIX.HOLMOS
        KYLIX.RHYTON.SCYPHUS
—song   SKOLION
drug   PHARMAKON
dwarf   NANOS
ear   OTOS.OUS
eating in public   SYSSITIA
egg   OION
egotism   ITACISM
elliptical auditorium SPHENDONE
embodiment of
—justice   ARISTIDES
—self-discipline   ARISTIPPUS
epic
—poem   AENEID.ODYSSEY
—tale   ILIAD
eucharistic fan   RHIPIDION
exclude   OSTRACISE
eye   OMMA.OPHTHALMOS
fabulous robber   PROCRUSTES
fame   KUDOS
fan   RHIPIDIUM
fastening of girdle   VIRGIN KNOT
father   PAP(P)AS
fawn-skin   NEBRIS
fear   PHOBOS
festival
—(Apollo)   THARGELIA
—(Dionysius)   ANTHESTERIA
—(married women)
                    THESMOPHORIA
few   OLIGOS
fibre   MITOS
field   AGROS
fillet   MITRA
fitting   TO PREPON
flabellum   RHIPIDIUM
flask   AMPHORA.LAGENA.OLPE
flesh   KREAS
flower   ANTHEMON
fly   MYIA
folly   MORIA
fondness   PHILIA
food OPSON(ION).SITOS.TROPHE
—plant   LASER.SILPHIUM
foot   PODOS

forehead   METOPON
form   MORPHE
formation   GENESIS
fountain (Mount Helion)
                          AGANIPPE
fourth part of province
        TETRARCHATE.TETRARCHY
fracture   KLASIS
frankincense   LIBANOS
fruit   KARPOS
galley   BIREME.TRIREME
                       QUADRIREME
                     QUINQUEREME
gem   OPALLIOS
generals   DIADOCHI
generation   GENESIS
gift   DORON
gills   BRANCHIA
glade   NEMOS
globular oil-flask   ARYBALLOS
glory   KUDOS
glue   GLOIA.KOLLA
god   THEOS
        (see also gods.goddesses)
golden mean   ARISTON METRON
good genius   AGATHODAIMON
governor   EPARCH.ETHNARCH
        NOMARCH.TOPARCH
                        TAXIARCH
grandfather   PAPPUS
granule   CHONDROS
great   MEGA
Greece   HELLAS
Greek in ancient Italy ITALIOT(E)
grief   PENTHOS
ground   PEDON
group of
—verses   SYSTEM
—worshippers   THIASUS
growth   PHYSIS
gymnasium at Athens   LYCEUM
half   HEMI
head   KEPHALE
—dress   MITRE.STEPHANE
healing plant   PANAX
heavily armed soldier   HOPLITE
hero   ACHILLES.AENEAS
        AGAMEMNON.AJAX
    ALCIDES.CADMUS.HERAKLES

	HERCULES.JASON
	ODYSSEUS.PERSEUS
	PROMETHEUS.THESEUS
	ULYSSES
highest lyre string	NETE
hole	TREMA
holy meteoric stone	BAETYL
home of oracle	DELPHI
honey	MELI
hood	KALUPTRA
hook	ONKOS
hoop	TROCHUS
horn	KERAS
—shaped vessel	RHYTON
hot springs	THERMAE
house	MEGARON.OIKOS
hymns	HERMOI.HERMOS
—to Bacchus	DITHYRAMB
I have found	(H)EUREKA
imitator	MIM(IK)OS
impulse	OSMOS.OTHIMOS
incline	KLINEIN
infant	NEPIOS
infantry	
—formation	PHALANX
—man	EVZONE
inhabitant of part of	
Constantinople	FANARIOT
	PHANARIOT
inner room	THALAMOS
instalment of epic	RHAPSODY
instrument	BOUZOUKI.CITHARA
	KITHARA.PHORMINX
intestines	ENTERON
introduction to play	PROLOGUE
Ionian	TEIAN
—mode (music)	IASTIC
irregularly divided	
	ALLOIOSTROPHOS
island	NESOS
islander	NESIOTES
jar	AMPHORA.STAMNOS
jaw	GNATHOS
joint	ARTHRON
judge	DICAST.DIKAST.SYNDIC
—of games	AGNOTHETES
—'s court	DICASTERY
jug	OLPE
juice	OPOS

junior archon	THESMOTHETE
keynote	MESE
kidney	NEPHROS
kilt	FUSTANELLA
know thyself	GNOTHI SEAUTON
knowing	GNOSIS
lament	THRENE
lamp attendant	LAMPADARY
land	GAIA
—owner	EUPATRID
late	OPSE
law	NOMOS
—giver	NOMOTHETES
	THESMOTHETE
lead	MOLYBDOS
leader	G.AGOGOS
learning	MATHE
legislator	DRACO.NOMOTHETES
length	MEKOS
letter	GRAMMA
—Y	PYTHAGOREAN LETTER
	SAMIAN LETTER
letters	ALPHA.BETA.CHI.DELTA
	EPSILON.ETA.GAMMA.IOTA
	KAPPA.LA(M)BDA.MU.NU
	OMEGA.OMICRON.PHI.PI
	PSI.RHO.SIGMA.TAU.THETA
	UPSILON.XI.ZETA
	(*see also* obsolete letters *below*)
life	BIOS
—saving reward	SOSTRUM
lightly armed soldier	PELTAST
liking for	PHILIA
line (poetry)	STICHOS
liqueur	OUZO
litany	SYNAPTE
little	MIKROS.OLIGOS
lizard	SAUROS
longhand reporter	
	LOGOGRAPHER
long-jump	HALMA
lord of men	ANAK ANDRON
lowest	
—note but one	PARHYPATE
—string of lyre	HYPATE
lyre	CITHARA.KITHARA
madness	MANIA
magical meteoric stone	BAETYL
	PANTARBE

magistrate	ARCHON.EPHOR
magnet for gold	PANTARBE
main gate of Athens	DIPYLON
man	ANDROS.ANER
	ANTHROPOS
manner of life	BIOSIS
marker	STELE
market-place	AGORA
marriage	GAMOS
marrow	MYELOS
mass	ONCOS
measure(ment)	METRON
—600 feet	STADIUM
measuring cup ($^1/_{12}$ pint)	CYATHUS
medical	IATRIKOS
meeting	
—place in Athens	PNYX
—room	ANDRON
method of investigation	
	ORGANON
metre	METRON
metrical foot	
	DOCHMIOS.DOCHMIUS
metropolitan	EXARCH
middle	MESE
—course	ARISTON METRON
—string of lyre	MESE
military	
—commander	POLEMARCH
—formation	PHALANX
—ruler	DIADOCHI
mill	MYLE.MYLON
mind	NOOS
mine	METALLON
misanthrope	TIMON
mist	NEPHELE
mix	MISGEIN
modern	
—franc	DRACHM(A)
—Greek	DEMOTIC.ROMAIC
modesty	AIDOS
monastic habit	SCHEMA
monk	CALOYER.MONASTES
—'s settlement	SCETE.SKETE
monster	SPHINX
month	MEN
moon	MENE.SELENE
morning service	ARTHROS
mother-city of colony	

	METROPOLIS
mountain	OROS
mouse	MYS
mouth	STOMA
mucus	MYXA
muscle	MYS
mushroom	MYKES
music hall	ODEON.ODEUM
musical	
—concert hall	ODEON
	ODEUM
—instrument	AULOS.BARBITOS
	BOUZOUKI.CITHARA.KITHARA
	LYRE.PHORMINX.SYRINX
—interval	DITONE
—modes	AEOLIAN.IONIAN.IASTIC
	(MIXO)LYDIAN.PHRYGIAN
—separation of chords	
	DIAZEUXIS
—tempo	AGOGE
mussel	MYAX
myth	MYTHOS
nail	ONYX
name	ONOMA
narrow-necked flask	LEKYTHOS
national festival	PANATHENAEA
	PYTHIAN GAMES
native of Zante	ZANTIOT(E)
nature	PHYSIS
navel	OMPHALOS
necessity	ANANKE
nerve	NEURON
new	KAINOS.NEOS
night	NYKTOS.NYX
nobleman	EUPATRID
northern	ARKTIKOS
nose	RHINOS.RHIS
note above hypate	PARHYPATE
now	NYN
numberless	MYRIOS
numbness	NARKE
numeral	SAMPI
nursing	TROPHEIA
obsolete letters	EPISEMON
	DIGAMMA.KOPPA
	SAN.SAMPI.VAU
ode	STASIMON
office of	
—exarch	EXARCHATE

—harmost	HARMOSTY
official	POLEMARCH
on	EPI
Old Testament	SEPTUAGINT
olive tree	ELATA
one of Greek official class	
	FANARIOT
	PHANARIOT
one-sleeved garment	EXOMIS
opinion	DOXA
order of architecture	CORINTHIAN
	DORIC.IONIC
orchestra	KONISTRA
outer garment	HIMATION
over	HYPER
oyster	OSTREON
pain	ALGE.ALGOS.ODYNE
pale yellow	OCHROS
palm	PALAME
panacea	PANAX
paradise	ELYSIUM
parliament	BOULE
part	MEROS
—of Greek comedy	PARABASIS
—Of tetrachord	PYCNON
penalty	POINE
peninsula	CHERSONESE
people	DEMOS
perception	AISTHESIS
philosophers	ARISTOTLE.PLATO
	SOCRATES
pick-axe	ORYX
place of beauty	TEMPE
plant	PHYTON
poem about returning	NOSTOS
poet	(see writers below)
poetess	SAPPHO
poetic inspiration	AGANIPPE
point	AKME
political animal	
	ZOON POLITIKON
pollution	MIASMA
poor freeman	THETE
popular assembly	ECCLESIA
porch	STOA
portico	PTERON.STOA
—covered	XYSTOS.XYSTUS
—with four columns or fewer	PROSTYLE

potsherd	OSTRACON.OSTRAKON
pottery horn	RHYTON
poverty	PENIA
power	KRATOS
prayer-book	TRIODION
preliminary oblation	PROTHESIS
president of symposium	
	SYMPOSIARCH
prestige	KUDOS
priest	PAPA
—'s stole	EPITRACHELION
princess	IO
principal hall	MEGARON
professional orator	RHETOR
prophet	MANTIS
prostitute	HETAIRA
province	NOME.NOMOS
—of eparch	EPARCHATE
	EPARCHY
—of ephor	EPHORALTY
prudence	METIS
public	
—baths	THERMAE
—eating	SYSSITIA
purchase of food	OPSONIA
purple cope	CHLAMYS
push	OTHEEIN
rabble	HOI POLLOI
racecourse	DROMOS
rain-storm	OBROMOS
rational principle	LOGOS
raw	OMOS
rear-chamber in temple	OPISTHODOMOS
reason	LOGOS
renown	KUDOS
return	NOSTOS
revolving prism in theatre	PERIAKTOS
right	ORTHOS
river encircling world	OKEANOS
rostrum	BEMA
row	STICHOS
—of trees	ORCHATOS
rule	ARCHE
ruler of	
—district	TOPARCH
—people	ETHNARCH
running	DROMOS

sacred enclosure	SEKOS
sacristan	SCEUOPHYLAX
sacristy	DIACONICON.PARABEMA
	SCEUOPHYLACIUM
said only	
once	HAPAX LEGOMENON
sailor	NAUTES.NAUTILOS
—in Argo	ARGONAUT
sanctuary	SEKOS
sap	OPOS
saw	PRION
sayings of Jesus not in	
Gospels	AGRAPHA
scale	CHROMA
school of philosophy	PORCH
sea	
—nymph	NEREIS
—perch	ORPHOS
—sickness	NAUSIA
—weed	PHYKOS
secret writing	SCYTALE
sect (14th c.)	HESYCHAST
seed	SPERMA
seemly	TO PREPON
seen	OPTOS
sell	POLEEIN
senate	BOULE
serf	HELOT.PENEST.THETE
service-book	TRIODION
setting down	THESIS
seven	
—prayers	LYCHNAPSIA
—tones	HEPTACHORD
severe critic	ARISTARCH
shame	AIDOS
shape	MORPHE
sharp	OXYS
shawl	PEPLOS.PEPLUM
shell	OSTRAKON
shield	AEGIS
ship	ARGO.CAIQUE.HOLCAD
	NAUS.SAIC.SAIK.SAIQUE
—with 30 oars	TRIACONTER
—with 50 oars	PENTECOSTER
shoot	BLASTOS
short	
—anthem	ISODICON
—cloak	CHLAMYS
—hymn	CATHISMA.TROPARION

—sighted	MYOPS
shoulder	OMOS
shrew	MYGALE
shut	MYEIN
sickness	NOSOS
side	
—scene	PARASCENIUM
—wall of temple	PTEROMA
sight	OPSIS
single	MONOS
skill	TEKHNE
skin	DERMA
skull	KRANION
slave	HELOT
slime	MYXA
smallest subdivision	ENOMOTY
smell	OSME
snake	OPHIS
snout	RHUNKHOS
soda	NITRON
soft	MALAKOS
soldier	EVZONE.HOPLITE
solitary	MONACHOS
song	MELOS.OIDE
—by chorus	STROPHE.OXYS
south	NOTOS
southern hemisphere	
	ANTICHTHON
space in temple	PERIDROME
Spartan governor	HARMOST
speaking	PHRASIS
speech	LALIA
sphere	SPHAIRA
spirit	DAIMON
spirit (drink)	OUZO.RAKI
spit	OBELOS
standing	STATOS
stanza	STROPHE
stationary	STASIMON
statue	KOUROS.XOANON
step	BEMA
stink	OSME
stone	LITHOS
—at Delphi	OMPHALOS
—of the sun	PANTARBE
story	MYTHOS
straight	ORTHOS
stroke	PLEGE
strong drink	METHE

subdivision	DEME	—of worshippers	THIASUS
sun	HELIOS	trumpet	SALPINX
sweat	HIDROS	tumour	ONCOS
swelling	OIDEMA	tunic	CHITON.EXOMIUM
	ORGASMOS		EXOMIS
swimming	NEUSTOS	turn(ing)	TROPOS
talk	MYTHOS	tusk	ODOUS
teacher	PAIDEUTES	tutelary god	PROMACHOS
—of rhetoric	RHETOR	two-handled vase	DIOTA
temple	NAOS	underground water	
—of Athene	ATHENAEUM	channel	KATABOTHRON
—slave	HIERODULE		KAVAVOTHRON
—with single ring of		union	ENOSIS
columns	MONOPTERON	unit	MONAS
	MONOPTEROS	universe	KOSMOS
ten thousand	MYRIAS	unripe grape	OMPHAX
tend	KOMEEIN	upright	ORTHOS
the many	HOI POLLOI	urn	STAMNOS
—the vulgar	HOI POLLOI	vase	DIOTA.PELIKE.PITHOS
theatre	ODEON.ODEUM	veil	KALYPTRA
thick	PACHYS	vespers	LYCHNIC
third		vessel	KYTOS
—actor	TRITAGONIST	—drinking, horn-shaped	RHYTON
—string of lyre	TRITE	vestibule in front of temple	
—tone of tetrachord	TRITE		PRONAOS
thread	MITOS.NEMA	vestment	SACCOS.SAKKOS
three-branched candlestick		victory	NIKE
	TRICERION	view	HORAMA
tile	OSTRAKON	voice	OPS.PHONE
time	CHRONOS	waist-belt	ZOSTER
tone		war	
—above the mese	PARAMESE	—cry	ALALAGMOS
—below the nete	PARANETE	—dance	PYRRHIS
tongue	GLOSSA	watching	SKOPIA
tooth	ODOUS	water-vase	HYDRIA.KALPIS
torch-race	LAMPADEDROMY	wax	KEROS
	LAMPADEPHORIA	way	HODOS
town	DEME	weasel	GALEE
—hall	PRYTANEUM	weight (ancient)	DRACHMA
—ship	DEME	—3 lbs	OCQUE
toy	KLEIS.KLEIDOS	—26–38 kilograms	
	ICHNOS	(gold or silver)	TALENT
translation of Hebrew		—money	MINA
bible	SEPTUAGINT	well done!	EUGE
tree-planted walk	XYST(OS)	wheel	TROCHOS
	XYSTUS	white	LEUKOS
tribe (ancient)	PELASGI.PHYLE	—kilt for men	FUSTANELLA
troop		wild	AGRIOS
—leader of	PHYLARCH	—beast	THERION

—dance	SIKINNIS
wine	RESINATA.RETSINA
—jar	PITHOS
—throwing game	COTTABUS
	KOTTABUS
wing	PTERON
wing (theatre)	PARASCENIUM
wisdom	SOPHIA
with	META
woman	GYNE
—'s head-band	SPHENDONE
—'s robe	PEPLOS
	PEPLUM.PEPLUS
womb	DELPHYS
wood	HYLE
wooded pasture	NEMOS
wooden figure	ACROLITH
word	LEXIS
work	ERGON
world	KOSMOS
worship	LATREIA
writers	AESCHYLUS
	APOLLODORUS.APOLLONIUS
	ARISTOPHANES.EURIPIDES
	HERODOTUS.HESIOD.HOMER
	LUCIAN.PAUSANIAS.PINDAR
	SOPHOCLES.TYRTAEUS
yes	OHI
young citizen	EPHEBE
youthful	NEANIKOS
	(see also classic(al))

green   GO.NAIVE.RAW
green cotton	LAWN

Greenwich Mean Time   GMT

greet
greet icily	HAIL
greeting	AVE.HI

grey
grey suit	SLATE CLUB
greylag	GAOLBIRD

grievous
grievous bodily harm	GBH
grievous hurt	RUTH
grievously stinted	DENTIST

grim situation   STERNPOST
grimace   MOUE.MOW
grinding oats   STOA
grip
grip a...	incl A

grip *	incl *
•a v-ice *grips* a king	AVARICE
gripped by *	incl in *
•a king *gripped by* a v-ice	
	AVARICE
gripper	CLAM.VICE.VISE
groggy males	LAMES.MEALS

gross national product   GNP
ground
ground control approach	GCA
ground plan	PLOT
ground rent	FISSURE
ground rent deposit	LAVA

group   SET
hence
•group of fliers	POSSET
•group of graduates	BASSET
•group of officers	COSSET
group of workers	BEE
group in charge	CLASSIC

grouse   GR
grouse-meat	BEEF

growing
     (see also becoming.rearing)
growing attractive	BECOMING
growing division	HEDGE
growing girl	MYRTLE.ROSE
	VERONICA

     (see also Appendix)

guard
guard	SCREW
guarding a...	incl A
guarding *	incl *
•do-g *guarding* a tin	DOTING
guarded by *	incl in *
•tin *guarded by* a do-g	DOTING

Guatemala   GCA
coin	QUETZAL

Guernsey   GBG
guide dog   POINTER
guilder   GLD
guile
guile of devil	LIVED
guileful ways	SWAY.YAWS
guilefully slid	LIDS

guinea   G.GU
gules   GU
gulf   G
gullible fool   CHARLEY.CHARLIE

gum

American	BLACK GUM
	LIQUIDAMBAR
	PEPPERIDGE.SOUR GUM
	SWEET GUM. TUPELO
Asian	DAM(M)AR.DAMER
	LIQUIDAMBAR
	STORAX
fetid	SAGAPENUM
frankincense	OLIBANUM
from	
—balsam poplar	TACAMAHAC
—Cistus leaves	LA(B)DANUM
—Commiphora	MYRRH
	SWEET CICELY
—Convolvulus	SCAMMONY
—elm	ULMIN
—Ferula	GALBANUM
—starch	DEXTRIN(E)
—Styrax	STORAX
Mediterranean	LA(B)DANUM
olibanum	FRANKINCENSE
Persian	OPOPANAX
	SARCOCOLLA
purgative	JALAP.JALOP
red	DRAGON'S BLOOD.LAC
tropical	COPAL.ELEMI.KINO
	TACAMAHAC
yellow pigment	GAMBOGE

gun¹ ARM.BREN.GAT.LEWIS
MAXIM.ROD.STEN

gun-*whip*	GNU
gunmen	GRS.RA
gunner	FIREMAN.GR
gunners	FIREMEN.GRS.RA
guns	GRS.RA
Guy's revolver	
	CATHERINE WHEEL

gun²

Afghan musket	JEZAIL
air gun	WIND GUN
American	
—pistol	COLT
—rifle	WINCHESTER
anti	
—aircraft	BOFORS.OERLIKON
	POMPOM
—submarine mortar	SQUID
arquebus	HACKBUT.HAGBUT

automatic pistol	
—American	BROWNING.COLT
	SMITH AND WESSON
—British	WEBLEY
—German	LUGER.MANNLICHER
	MAUSER.WALTHER
—Italian	BERETTA
—Japanese	NAMBU
bell-mouthed	BLUNDERBUSS
big gun	BERTHA
British	
—flintlock	BROWN BESS
—rifle	LEE-ENFIELD
	MARTINI(-HENRY)
camel-mounted	ZOMBORUK
	ZUMBOORU(C)K
cannon	FALCON
—light medium	FALCON
—medium-heavy	CULVERIN
—long	LONG TOM
—old	BASILISK.SERPENTINE
—short	CARRONADE.HOWITZER
—small	CHAMBER.FALCONET
	MURDERER
	MURDERING-PIECE
	SAKER
carbine	ESCOPETTE
cavalry pistol	PETRONEL
dummy gun	QUAKER(GUN)
elephant gun	ROER
field-gun	FOUR-POUNDER
fired with spike	NEEDLE-GUN
firing stones, etc.	PADERERO
	PATERERO.PED(E)RERO
	PERRIER
flintlock	SNAPHA(U)NCE
	SNAPHAUNCH
—musket	FUSIL
for firing salutes	PADERERO
	PATERERO.PED(E)RERO
four-barrelled pistol	DUCKSFOOT
fowling-piece	SHOTGUN
French army rifle	CHASSEPOT
grenade-thrower	CO(E)HORN
handgun	IRON.PISTOL
	REVOLVER
large pistol	HORSE PISTOL
light	
—machine gun	BREN

	SUBMACHINE GUN
—musket	CALIVER.CAR(A)BINE
—shotgun	FOWLING-PIECE
machine gun	BROWNING
	GATLING.LEWIS GUN
	MAXIM.VICKERS
—French	MITRAILLEUSE
—German	SPANDAU
multi-barrelled	DUCKSFOOT
	MAXIM.ORGUE.POMPOM
	PEPPERPOT
old	
—cannon	BASILISK.SERPENTINE
—musket	BISCAYAN.CALIVER
	DRAGOON
—rifle	MUZZLE-LOADER
—smooth-bore	ARQUEBUS
	FLINTLOCK.HARQUEBUSS
	MATCHLOCK.MUSKET
	SNAPHAUNCE.WHEEL-LOCK
on pivot	SWIVEL-GUN
pistol	GAT.IRON.ROD
—(15-16th c.)	DAG
queen's-arm	MUSKET
revolver	GAT.HEATER.IRON.ROD
	ROSCOE.SHOOTING IRON
	SIX-SHOOTER
rifle	
—Afghan	JEZAIL
—African	ROER
—American	ARMALITE.GARAND
	WINCHESTER
—British	LEE-ENFIELD
	MARTINI(-HENRY)
—German	MANNLICHER
	MAUSER
—Russian	KALASHNIKOV
short	
—cannon	CARRONADE

	HOWITZER
—musket	MUSQUETOON
	MUSKETOON
—pistol	DAG
—revolver	BULLDOG
shotgun	CHOKE-BORE
	SCATTER-GUN
siege-gun	HOWITZER
small	
—bore rifle	PEA-RIFLE
—cannon	CHAMBER.FALCONET
	MURDERER
	MURDERING-PIECE.SAKER
—handgun	DERRINGER.PISTOLET
smooth-bore	MUSKET.SHOTGUN
sub-machine gun	STEN
	STERLING
—American	THOMPSON
	TOMMY GUN
—British	STEN.STERLING
—German	SCHMEISSER
—Israeli	UZI
swivel-gun	LONG TOM
used in shooting	
gallery	SALOON PISTOL
	SALOON RIFLE
wind gun	AIR GUN
gutted h(errin)g	HG
Guyana	GUY
capital	G.GEORGETOWN
gypsy	CHAL.ROM
gentleman	RYE
priest	PATERCOVE.PATRICO
woman	CH(A)I
gyrate	
gyrate <u>orb</u>	ROB
gyrating <u>top</u>	OPT.POT
gyration of <u>centre</u>	RECENT

H

bomb. complex cube root. Dirac's constant. hand. hard. heart. hecto-.
height. henry. *horse*. hospital. hot. hotel. hour. house. Hungary. husband.
hydrant. hydrogen. Planck's constant. tap. two hundred.
two hundred thousand. vitamin.

Habakkuk	HAB	*half length of* tunnel	TUN.NEL
Haggai	HAG	half-mile	MI.LE
hail	AVE	half-minute	MIN.UTE
hail Mary	AM	half-moon	MO.ON
hailing from Rome	ROAM	half-Nelson	NEL.SON
hair		half of bitter	BIT.TER
hair fasteners	LOCKS	half sister	SIS.TER
(h)air-*piece*	AIR	half the capital	LON.DON
hairdresser	COMB	half-time	TI.ME
Haiti	RH	half-volume	BO.OK
coin	GOURDE	halfway	STR.EET
leader	H	**ham**	OVERACT
half[1]	DEMI-.HF.SEMI-	**Hamlet**	
common*ly halved*	ONLY	Hamlet, *say*	DEIGN
half a score	TEN.X	Hamlet's rest	SILENCE
half alphabet	ATOM	**Hampton** *maze*	PHANTOM
half-*back*⟨	IMES	**hand**[1]	AB.H.L.MAN.R
half-century	L	hence	
half-*cut*	ALF.HAL	•hand-loom	ABLOOM
half-day	AM.PM	•hand-out	ABOUT
half-dozen	VI	•hands pamphlet...	ABSTRACT
half-*hearted*	AL	and	
half-inch	PINCH.STEAL	•hand fish...	HEEL.HID.HIDE
half-minute	MO	•hand permits...	HALLOWS
half moon	FORTNIGHT	•hand-work	HOP
half *of France*	DEMI	and	
half[2]	HF	•colour *round* hand	HUMANE
half a jiffy	SEC.OND	•hand *has* army...	MANTA
half-afraid	AFR.AID	•warning *to* hand	FOREMAN
halfback	BA.CK	and	
half-baked	COO.KED	•bird *in* hands	LEMUR
half-day	MON.FRI.SUN	•copper hands	CURL
hence		•hands *round* girl	LANNER.LEVER
•*half*-day early	MONSOON		REVEL
•*half*-day closing	FRIEND	**hand**[2]	
•*half*-day *and* night, *say*	SUNNITE	hand in...	incl H.L or R
half-days	DA.YS	•had hand *in* ma-king	MARKING
half-dead	DE.AD	*handover of* loot⟨	TOOL
half-ditch	HA	*hand over* reins	RESIN
half-dry	T	hands down	SIX-THIRTY
half-full	FU.LL	hands up	TWELVE
half-hearted bel(l)ow	BELOW	handy fitters	GLOVES
half-length	LEN	handy fruit	BANANAS

handy pair	THUMBS
handicap	EBOR
handle	
handled <u>adroitly</u>	IDOLATRY
handling <u>dogs</u>	GODS
hang	
hang over a lot(D) ↑	TOLA
hangman	JACK KETCH
happy ignorance	BLISS
harbour	
harbour a...	incl A
harbour *	incl *
•ship *harbouring* a convict	SLAGS
harboured by *	
•convict *harboured by* ship	SLAGS
hard¹	H
very hard	HH
hence	
•hard and fast	HANDFAST
•hard ground	HEARTH
•hard *to* say	HAVER
hard *for outsiders*...	H-H
•as hard *for outsiders*...	HASH
hard-*headed*	H
<u>hard</u>-*hearted*	incl H
•hard-*hearted* c-ad	CHAD
hard²	
hard bed	STRATUM
hard black	HB
hard case	SAFE.SHELL
hard drop	HAILSTONE
hard tack	WARFARE
hard time	ROUGHAGE
hard water	GLACIER.ICE.ICICLE
hardback	STERN
hard*headed*	H
<u>hard</u>*hearted*	AR
•<u>saint</u> *and* hard*hearted*...	STAR
hardly credi<u>ble</u>	TALL
Harpies	AELLO.CELAENO
	(or PODARGE).OCYPETE
harry	
Harry <u>lived</u>	DEVIL
harry the <u>deer</u>	REDE.REED
has	(*see* have)
hash of <u>meal</u>	MALE.LAME
hassle <u>players</u>	REPLAYS
hat	
hat measurement	CAPSIZE

hatless black woman(D)	
	(n)EGRESS
hate	(*see* fear)
haughty clique	UPSET
have	
has a way with	incl N.S.E.W
	incl RD.ST
•he *has a way with*...	HEN.HET
	HEW
•she *has a way with*...	SHERD
has *difficulty*	ASH
<u>has</u> made *mistakes*	ASHAMED
has no...	incl NO
has no horse	omit G
has no money	omit L
has no time	omit T
has no *	omit *
•I(r)an *has no* king	IAN
has nothing	incl O
has nothing on	end in O
has nothing on	incl OON
has on	incl ON
* *has gone off*	omit *
•clot(he)s he *has gone off*	CLOTS
has *trouble*	ASH
(h)ave *an hour off*	AVE
have an hour *off*	omit H
•Cat(h) has an hour *off*	CAT
have it *at heart*	incl IT
having¹	(*see also* bearing.having²)
having a...	incl A
having money	incl L
having *	incl *
•s-py *having* cut...	SLOPPY
having changed <u>a note</u>	ATONE
	OATEN
having²	
all	
—knowledge	OMNISCIENT
—stamens joined	
	MONADELPHOUS
backbone	VERTEBRATE(D)
bad breath	HALITOTIC
bag	UTRICULAR
base enclosing stem	PERFOLIATE
beak	
—and keel	ROSTROCARINATE
—curved downwards	
	CURVIROSTRAL

beard	BARB(ELL)ATE
belts	ZONATE(D)
bladder	UTRICULAR
blisters	BULLATE
blood	SANGUINEOUS
branchlets	RAMULOSE
	RAMULOUS
breasts	MAMMATE
	MAMMIFEROUS
bristle	STYLAR.STYLATE
broad	
—bill	LATIROSTRAL
—nose	PLATYRRHINE
—partition	LATISEPTATE
bulges	TOROSE
calyx	
—distinct from corolla	
	HETEROCHLAMYDEOUS
—not distinct from corolla	
	HOMOCHLAMYDEOUS
case	THECATE
cavities	LACUNOSE
cell	UTRICULAR
chinks	FATISCENT
claws	UNGUAL.UNGUICULATE(D)
cleft beak	FISSIROSTRAL
closed ring of	
—dissimilar atoms	
	HETEROCYCLIC
—similar atoms	HOMOCYCLIC
cloven	
—feet	BISULCATE
—tongue	FISSILINGUAL
column	SCAPIGEROUS
comb-shaped gills	
	PECTINIBRANCHIATE
conical beak	CONIROSTRAL
cracks	FATISCENT
crest	CRISTATE
crossed mandibles	
	METAGNATHOUS
crystalline structure	IDIOMORPHIC
curving	
—leaves	CURVIFOLIATE
—ribs	CURVICOSTATE
—tail	CURVICAUDATE
daily rest	MONOPHASIC
definite form	EFFIGURATE
depression	FOSSULATE

—navel-like	UMBILICATE
different	
—kinds of mycelium	
	HETEROTHALLIC
—names	DISQUIPARANT
—numbers of	
parts	HETEROCYCLIC
	HETEROMEROUS
—types of leaf	
	HETEROPHYLLOUS
—types of spores	
	HETEROSPOROUS
divided ribs	FISSICOSTATE
double	
—beak	BIROSTRATE
—nature	TWY-NATURED
—womb	DIDELPHIC
down	PLUMULATE
energy above that of thermal	
agitation	EPITHERMAL
equal power	EQUIPOLLENT
even number of	
toes	ARTIODACTYL(OUS)
extra	
—chromosomes	POLYPLOID
—day of leap year	BISSEXTILE
—syllable	PERISSOSYLLABIC
eyelike marking	OCELLATE(D)
	OCULATE(D)
eyes	OCULATE(D)
—meeting in front	HOLOPTIC
—on stalks	PODOPHTHALMUS
feathered feet	PLUMIPED
feathers	PENNATE.PINNATE(D)
feet or legs used as oars	REMIPED
few parts	OLIGOMEROUS
fine wrinkles	RUGULOSE
fins	PENNATE.PINNATE(D)
fissure	SULCATE(D)
flat nose	CAMUS
flavour	SAPOROUS
flowers	
—female and hermaphrodite	
	GYNOMONOECIOUS
—in spathe	SPADICIFLORAL
—of both sexes	MONOECIOUS
foot	PEDATE
forms from different	
declensions	HETEROCLITE

freckles	LENTIGINOSE
	LENTIGINOUS
fringe	FIMBRIATE
full power	PLENIPOTENTIARY
furrow	SULCATE(D)
fused digital	
bones	SYNDACTYL(OUS)
gaps	LACUNOSE
gills in tufts	LOPHOBRANCHIATE
glistening scales	GANOID
great variety	MULTIFARIOUS
groove	SULCATE(D)
groups of four	
spores	TETRASPORIC
	TETRASPOROUS
hair	CRINATE(D).CRINITE
	CRINOSE
hard plates, scales or	
shell	LORICATE
heather-like leaves	ERICOID
hoof divided into three or more	
parts	MULTUNGULATE
hoofs	UNGULATE
hooks	HAMATE.HAMOSE
	HAMOUS.UNCATE
—at end of structure	
	UNCINATE(D)
itch	PSOR(AT)IC
inserted day	BISSEXTILE
jaws sloping backwards	
	OPISTHOGNATHOUS
keel	CARINATE
knots	NODOSE.NODOUS
lacunae	LACUNOSE
large head	MACROCEPHALIC
	MEGA-CEPHALOUS
layers	STRATIFORM.STRATOSE
leaf-edges overlapping	INCUBOUS
leaflets in pairs	PINNATE
lips	LABIATE
little	
—feathers	PLUMULATE
—scales	SQUAMULOSE
lobes pointing	
backwards	RUNCINATE
long	
—feathers	LONGIPENNATE
—fingers	MACRODACTYLOUS
—fins	MACROPTEROUS

—nose	LEPTORRHINE
—tail	LONGICAUDATE
	MACRURAL.MACRUROUS
—toes	MACRODACTYLOUS
—wings	LONGIPENNATE
	MACROPTEROUS
lower jaw protruding	
	HYPOGNATHOUS
lungs	PULMONARY
made a will	TESTATE
mane	JUBATE
mantle	PALLIATE
many. . .	(see many)
medium-sized head	
	MESATICEPHALOUS
membrane	VELATE(D)
more than	
—one embryo	
	POLYEMBRYONATE
	POLYEMBRYONIC
—one spouse	POLYGAMOUS
—three wheels	MULTICYCLE
—three dimensions	
	MULTIDIMENSIONAL
—two names or terms	
	MULTINOMIAL
	POLYNOMIAL
—two cusps	MULTICUSPID(ATE)
—usual number of digits	
	POLYDACTYL
mouth-like opening	OSTIATE
narrow	
—bill	ANGUSTIROSTRATE
—nose	LEPTORRHINE
—leaves	ANGUSTIFOLIATE
neck	TRACHELATE
needles	SPICULATE
nipples	MAMILLATE(D)
nodes	NODOSE
nodules	NODULATED.NODULOSE
	NODULOUS
notched	
—antennae	SERRICORN
—beak	DENTIROSTRAL
nucleus	NUCLEOLATE
odd number of	
toes	PERISSODACTYL(ATE)
	PERISSODACTYLIC
	PERISSODACTYLOUS

one buttock	HEMPYGIC	same	
opening	OSTIOLATE	—basic structure	HOMOTYPIC
ossified septum	TICHORRINE	—curvature in every	
ovary		direction	SYNCLASTIC
—above other flower		—essence	HOMO(O)USIAN
parts	HYPOGYNOUS	—number of leaves	EUCYCLIC
—below other flower		—number of petals and	
parts	EPIGYNOUS	stamens	ISOSTEMONOUS
paired gills	ZYGOBRANCHIATE	—parts throughout	
palatal bones			HOMOGENEOUS
separate	SCHIZOGNATHOUS	—tone	HOMOTONOUS
panicles	PANICLED.PANICULATE	saw-bill	SERRATIROSTRAL
parts in eights	OCTAMEROUS	scales	SQUAMATE
pearl-like lustre	MARGAR(IT)IC		SQUAMOSE
perianth leaves			SQUAMOUS
free	POLYPHYLLOUS	scattered	
petals		—hairs	PILOSE
—free	POLYPETALOUS	—small holes	TEREBRATE
—fused	GAMETOPETALOUS	seal	SIGILLATE
	SYMPETALOUS	separate	
phosphorescence	NOTILUCOUS	—carpels	APOCARPOUS
pit	FOSSULATE	—digits	FISSIPED(E)
plate-like scales	PLACOID	—sepals	POLYSEPALOUS
point	COSTATE	several	
pouch	SACCATE	—alternating currents	
power to			POLYPHASE
—combine with hydrogen		—axons	MULTIPOLAR
atoms	(*see* valency *below*)	—beats	POLYCROTIC
—strike	PERCUTIENT	—broods	MULTIVOLTINE
pressure higher than		—bundles of	
normal	HYPERBARIC	stamens	POLYADELPHOUS
prickles	ECHINATE(D)	—cells	POLYTHALAMOUS
proboscis	PROMUSCULATE	—chambers	POLYTHALAMOUS
protective plates	SCUTATE	—cotyledons	
protective shell	LORICATE		POLYCOTYLEDONOUS
pupa-case	PUPIGEROUS	—hydrogen atoms	POLYACID
pupae formed within		—hydroxyl groups	POLYHYDRIC
mother	PUPIPAROUS	—mates	POLYANDROUS
rank smell	OLID	—meanings	POLYSEM(ANT)IC
reduced wings	MICROPTEROUS	—nuclei	MULTINUCLEAR
resistance to disease	KLENDUSIC		MULTINUCLEATE
rhizoids	RADICULOSE	—nucleoli	MULTINUCLEOLATE
rootlets	RADICULOSE	—origins	POLYPHYLETIC
rough scales	SQUARROSE	—phases	POLYPHASIC
rows of leaflets	PINNATE(D)	—poles	MULTIPOLAR
royal prerogatives	PALATINE	—words	POLYONYMIC
ruddy glow	RUTILANT		(*see also* many)
runners	SARMENTOSE	—young at one	
	SARMENTOUS	birth	POLYTOCOUS

shape like comb	PECTINAL	—attached near middle	
	PECTINATE(D)	of leaf	PELTATE
sharp points	MURICATE(D)	stamens	STAMINATE
shaft	SCAPIGEROUS	—in two bundles	DIADELPHOUS
sheath	THECATE	stems	
short wings	BREVIPENNATE	—visible above	
similar		ground	CAULESCENT
—essence	HOMOIOUSIAN	—without leaves	NUDICAUL(OUS)
—parts	HOM(O)EOMEROUS	straight bill	RECTIROSTRAL
	HOMOIOMEROUS	styles	STYLAR.STYLATE
single		—of different lengths	
—nucleus	MONONUCLEAR		HETEROSTYLOUS
—opening	MONOTREMATOUS	swelling in middle	VENTRICOSE
	MONOTREME		VENTRICOUS
siphon	SIPHONATE	swellings	NODOUS.TOROSE
slender		sword-like leaves	XIPHOPHYLLUS
—bill	TENUIROSTRAL	symmetrical tail fin	HOMOCERCAL
—build	LEPTOSOM(AT)IC	tail	CAUDATE(D)
—nose	LEPTORRHINE	taste	SAPOROUS
—tail	LEPTOCERCAL	teeth	DENTATE(D)
—toes	LEPTODACTYLOUS	—all of same type	HOMODONT
small		—transversely ridged	
—bladders	VESICULATE(D)		LOPHODONT
	VESICULOSE	—with paired cusps	ZYGODONT
—blisters	VESICULATE(D)	—with single V-shaped	
	VESICULOSE	ridge	ZALAMBDODONT
—bulges	TORULOSE	temperature independent of	
—compartments	LOCELLATE	environment	IDIOTHERMOUS
	LOCULATE	thick	
—fibres	FIBRILLOSE.FIBRILLOUS	—digits	PACHYDACTYL(OUS)
—head	MICROCEPHALOUS	—pericarp	PACHYCARPOUS
—holes	FORAMINATED	—skin	PACHYDERMIC
	FORAMINOUS		PACHYDERM(AT)OUS
—hooks	HAMULATE	—woolly leaves	DASYPHYLLOUS
—scattered crystals	POIKILITIC	threads	FILAR
—serrations	SERRATULATE	toes turned in opposite	
—spines	SPINULATE	directions	HETERODACTYLOUS
	SPINULIFEROUS	tongue attached at front	
	SPINULOSE.SPINULOUS		OPISTHOGLOSSAL
—swellings	TORULOSE	toothed	
smell	OLENT	—beak	RHYNCHODONT
smooth hair	LISSOTRICHOUS	—jaws	ODONTOSTOMATOUS
spaces	LACUNOSE	transverse	
spicules	SPICULATE	—bars	TRABECULATE(D)
spike	SPICATE(D)	—lamellae on edge of	
spines	SPINATE(D).SPINIFEROUS	bill	LAMELLIROSTRAL
spore-case	THECATE	triple form	TRIFORM(ED)
stalk	PEDICELLATE	tubercles	TUBERCLED
	PETIOLATE(D)	TUBERCULAR.TUBERCULATE(D)	

tuberculosis	TUBERCULOSE(D)
	TUBERCULOUS
tubers	TUBEROSE.TUBEROUS
tufts	PENICILLATE.SCOPATE
tunic	TUNICATE(D)
turrets	CASTELLATED
	TURRICULATED
twenty or more	
stamens	ICOSANDRIAN
	ICOSANDROUS
twigs	SARMENTOSE
	SARMENTOUS
uncloven hoof	SOLIDUNGULATE
	SOLIPED(OUS)
unequal convex sides	GIBBOUS
united sepals	MONOSEPALOUS
unlimited power	OMNIPOTENT
up-curved bill	RECURVIROSTRAL
valency	
—above one	MULTIVALENT
—of one	UNIVALENT
—of two	DIVALENT
—of three	TERVALENT
	TRIVALENT
—of four	QUADRIVALENT
	TETRAVALENT
—of five	PENTAVALENT
	QUINQUEVALENT
—of six	SEX(I)VALENT
valve	VALVATE.VALVULAR
variable body temperature	
	POIKILOTHERMIC
veil	VELATE(D)
veins	NERVATE.VENOSE
warts	VERRUCOSE.VERRUCOUS
waves	CRISPATE
webbed feet	PALMATE
	PALMIPED(E)
	STEGANOPODOUS
windpipe	TRACHEATE(D)
wings	ALARY
	PENNATE.PINNATE(D)
wires	FILAR
woody stem-base	SUFFRUTICOSE
woolly hair	ULOTRICHOUS
wrinkles	RUGOSE.RUGOUS
zones	ZONATE(D)
Hawaii(an)	HI
acacia	KOA

capital	H.HONOLULU
dance	HULA(-HULA)
dish	POI
dress	MUU-MUU
drink	(K)AVA
fibre	PULU
garland	LEI
goddess	PELE
goose	NENE
greeting	ALOHA
rough lava	AA
smooth lava	PAHOEHOE
wreath	LEI
Haworth residence	PARSONAGE
haymaker	YAH
hazard I ran	RAIN.RANI
Hazel's descendant	AMENT
	CATKIN
hazy idea	AIDE
he	MALE.MAN
he *abandons*. . .	omit HE
•he *abandons* (he)r	R
•he *abandons* t(he). . .	T
he *escapes from*. . .	omit HE
•he *escapes from* (h)ol(e)	OL
•he *escapes from* t(he). . .	T
he *leaves*. . .	omit HE
•he *leaves* (he)r. . .	R
•he *leaves* (h)om(e)	OM
(h)e *lost his head*	E
he makes one cross	ELECTOR
he-man	HELEN.HEROD.HERON
he painted	PINXIT.PXT
he *quits*. . .	omit HE
•he *quits* (he)ad. . .	AD
•he *quits* t(he). . .	T
he sculpted	SC.SCULP(SIT)
	SCULPT
he *turned over*⟨	EH
he will, say	HEEL.HELL
he would	HED.HEED
head¹	LOAF.NESS.PATE.RAS
hence	
•hard head	TOUGHNESS
•head *aboard*. . .	SPATES
•head *in* church	CRASH
head²	
head *away*	omit first letter
•head *away* from (S)lough	LOUGH

head not seen	omit first letter
•*head not seen* in (c)lass	LASS
head not shown	omit first letter
•*head not shown* on (s)nap	NAP

head³

head of bear	B
Head of Department	D
head off (b)ear	EAR
head teacher	T
heads I win	IW
heads of State are gathered. . .	
	SAG
heads you lose	YL
heading ball	B
heading from (W)are	ARE
heading from Ware	W
*head*land	L
headless (f)lower	LOWER
*head*long *into*	incl L
*head*master	M
headquarters of sect	SE

head⁴

head *covering*	(in) NU-T.(in) RA-S
head east	
•agent *headed* east	ESPY
•man *heading* east	MANE
head-over-heels, Eros. . .⟨	SORE
head south	
•sailor *headed* south	STAR
•sailor *heading* south	TARS
head's side	OBVERSE
head specialist	HAIRDRESSER
	TRICHOLOGIST
head-to-tail dates⟨	SATED
head-to-tail pins⟨	SNIP
head lining	BRAIN(S)
headmaster	ARNOLD
headpiece	EAR.NOSE

head⁵

boat-shaped	SCAPHOCEPHALOUS
bony-plated	STEGOCEPHALOUS
flat-headed	PLATYCEPHALOUS
having a head	CEPHALATE
	CEPHALOUS
four-headed	QUADRACEPS
QUADRICEPS.QUADRICIPTAL	
large-headed	MACROCEPHALIC
	MACROCEPHALOUS
long-headed	DILOCOCEPHALOUS

many-headed	MULTICAPITATE
	MULTICIPITAL
medium-sized head	
	MESATICEPHALIC
	MESATICEPHALOUS
	MESENCEPHALIC
	MESENCEPHALOUS
	MESOCEPHALIC
	MESOCEPHALOUS
short-headed	
	BRACHYCEPHALOUS
small-headed	MICROCEPHALIC
	MICROCEPHALOUS
three-headed	
	TRICEPHALOUS.TRICEPS
two-headed	BICEPS.BICIPITAL
	DICEPHALOUS

healer	DR
health	
health-*centre*	AL
health resort	CLINIC
heaps of soil	SILO
hear	
do we hear rain	REIN.REIGN
hear forty. . .	EXCEL.FORTE.XL
(he)ar he *left*	AR
heard a noise	ANNOYS
heard more than ever	CLEVER
	TREVOR
hearing a girl	ALAS
hearing aid	EAR
hearing test	TRIAL
hear wails	WALES.WHALES
rumour *that is hearsay*	ROOMER
heart	H
heart*broken*	EARTH.HATER
	RATHE
heartless f(emal)e	FE
heart of Fren/ch Arm/y	CHARM
heart of gold	OL
heart of Midlothian	OT
heart transplant for Begin	BEING
heartthrob	PULSE
*heart*throb	R
m/aide/n's *heart*	AIDE
* *to heart*	incl *
•captures *with* blow *to heart*	
	TRAPS
•see m-e *take* it *to heart*	MITE

heat
  heat *treatment*   HATE.THEA
  heated issue   LAVA.STEAM
heavens   COO.COR.MY.SKY
heavy
  heavy artillery   HA
  heavy blow   CYCLONE.GALE
              HURRICANE.ONER
  heavy goods vehicle   HGV
  heavyweight
    ANTON.BOXER.STONE.TON
Hebrew   HEB(R)
  acacia wood   SHITTIM(WOOD)
  agricultural settlement   KIBBUTZ
                      MOSHAVA
  airline   EL AL
  ancient incense   ONYCHA
  annual festival   PASSOVER
  armies   SABAOTH
  ascetic   ESSENE.NAZARITE
                      NAZIRITE
  assembly   SANHEDRIM
                SANHEDRIN
  —for worship   SYNAGOGUE
  avenger   GOEL
  bible   TANAKH.T(H)ORAH
  bitterness   MARAH
  book of law   TALMUD.T(H)ORAH
  bond   STARR
  bread   (C)HALLAH.MATZO
  —offering   SHEW-BREAD
  cabbalistic interpretation of
    Scriptures   GEMATRIA
  ceremonial meal   SEDER
  character   MOSES
       (*see also* letters *below*)
  Christian   EBIONITE.MARRANO
  coins   PRUTAH
  —small   GERAH
  —10 gerahs   BEKA(H)
  —12 gerahs   (GOLDEN) DADIC
  —2 bekahs   SHEKEL
  —50 shekels   MANEH.MINA
  —3000 shekels   TALENT
  —old   ZUZ
  commandment   MITZVAH
  commentaries on OT   AGADAH
    HAGGADA(H).HALACHA(H)
    HALAKAH.MIDRASHIM

  commune   KIBBUTZ
  container for Torah scrolls   ARK
  council or court   SANHEDRIM
                SANHEDRIN
  critical OT notes   MASORA(H)
               MASORETH
              MASSORAH
  dance   HORA
  deities   (*see* gods.goddesses)
  devotional offering   CORBAN
  dirge   KINNAH
  dispersion   DIASPORA.GOLAH
  divine presence   SHECHINAH
               SHEKINAH
  divorce   GET
  doctor of law   RABBI.RABIN
  dolt   GOLEM
  drum   TOPH
  early Christian Jew   NAZARENE
  Easter   PASCH
  eve of Sabbath   PARASCEVE
  evening prayer   SHEMA
  evil spirit   DYBBUK
  exposition of OT   AGADAH
             HAGGADA(H)
  HALACHA(H).HALAKAH
             MIDRASH
  expounder of law   RABBI.RABBIN
  expounders of law   SOPHERIM
  fallow year   SABBATICAL YEAR
  Feast of Lots   PURIM
  feasts   HANUKAH.ISODIA
        PASSOVER.PURIM
  YOM KIPPUR.YOM TERUAH
      YOM TOB.YOM TOV
  festival   PASSOVER
             PENTECOST
  field of blood   ACELDEMA
  fiftieth year festival   JUBILEE
  formalist   PHARISEE
  Friday   PARASCEVE
  funeral prayer   KADDISH
  garment   TALIS
  gentile   GOY
  German and Polish
    Jews   ASHKENAZIM
  giant   ANAK
  god   ELOHIM.JEHOVAH
           (*see also* gods)

good deed	MITZVAH	months		
harp	NEBEL	Civil	Ecclesiastic	
high priest's headdress	TIARA	1. Sep-Oct	7.	ETHANIM
humanoid image	GOLEM			TIS(H)RI
idol	REMPHAN	2. Oct-Nov	8.	BUL
image(s)	TERAPH(IM)			(C)HES(H)VAN
Jehovah	LORD OF HOSTS			MARCHESVAN
Jew-baiting	JUDENHETZE	3. Nov-Dec	9.	CHISLEV
land of rest	BEULAH			KISLEU.KISLEV
language	IVRIT.YIDDISH	4. Dec-Jan	10.	TEBET(H)
law	T(H)ORAH			THEBET
lawyers	SOPHERIM	5. Jan-Feb	11.	S(H)EBAT
leader	H.MOSES	6. Feb-Mar	12.	ADAR
letters	AIN.ALEPH.AYIN	7. Mar-Apr	1.	ABIB.NISAN
	BETH.CAPH.CHETH	8. Apr-May	2.	(I)YAR
DALETH.GIMEL.HE.HETH				YAVAR.ZIF
JOD.KAPH.KOPH.LAMED		9. May-Jun	3.	SIVAN
LOD.MEM.NUN.PE.RESH		10. Jun-Jul	4.	TAMMUS
SAMECH.SAMEKH.SCHIN.SHIN				THAMMUZ
TAU.TETH.TZADDI.VAU		11. Jul-Aug	5.	AB
ZADE.ZAIN.ZAYIN		12. Aug-Sep	6.	ELUL
literary collection of laws and		—intercalary		VEADAR
practices	TALMUD	morning prayer		SHEMA
lord	ADONAI.ELOHIM	Moslem		DEUNME
lost book	JASHAR.JASHER	musical instrument		ASOR
manhood ceremony			SHOFAR.SHOPHAR	
	BAR MI(T)ZVAH		TIMBREL.TOPH	
lyre	ASOR	native Israeli		SABRA
manna	GEN	non-Jewish		GENTILE.GOY
marginal note	K'RI.KTHIBH	—woman		SHIKSA
marriage		non-kosher	TEREFA(H).TREF(A)	
—broker	SHADCHEN	obligatory marriage		LEVIRATE
—custom	LEVIRATE	oil of myrrh		STACTE
measures		OT commentary		AGADAH
—18 inches	CUBIT	HAGGADA(H).HALACHA(H)		
—52 inches	REED	HALAKAH.MIDRASH		
—6 cubits	CANEH.KANEH	MASORA(H).MASSORA(H)		
—¹/₄ pint	LOG		MASORETH	
—3 pints	CAB	oracle	URIM.THUMMIM	
—12 pints	HIN	oral law	GEMARA.MISHA(H)	
—14 pints	SEAH		MISHN(AY)OTH	
—6 gallons	BATH	parchment slip with religious		
—¹/₁₀ ephah	OMER	text	PHYLACTERY	
—1 bushel	EPHA(H)	parliament	KENESET.KNES(S)ET	
—11 bushels	COR.HOMER	SANHEDRIM.SANHEDRIN		
mercy seat	PROPITIATORY	part of		
militia	HAGANAH	—Mishnah	AGADAH.HAGGAD(H)	
miraculously provided		HALACHA(H).HALAKAH		
food	GEN.MANNA	—Talmud	GEMARA.MISHNA(H)	

Passover ritual	HAGGADA.SEDER		TABERNACLE
pause (in Psalms)	SELAH	—servants	NETHINIM
Pentateuch	T(H)ORAH	thanksgiving	KADDISH
phylacteries containing sacred		theological college	YESHIVAH
texts	TEFILLIN	The Seventy	SANHEDRIM
place of			SANHEDRIN
—departed souls	SHE'OL	title	RABBONI
—torment	TOPHET	tree	SHITTAH
—worship	SYNAGOGUE	tribe	DAN.GAD.LEVITE
Portuguese Jews	SEPHARDIM	unclean	TEREFA(H)
prayer	KADDISH.SHEMA	unleavened bread	MATZA(H)
—book	MAHZOR.SIDDUR		MATZO(H)
—shawl	TALLIT(H)	veil	HUMERAL
priest	AARONITE.LEVITE.RABBI	vowel point	SCHWA.SEG(H)OL
	RABIN.SAGAN		SHEVA
—'s breastplate	PECTORAL	wafer of bread	MATZA(H)
	RATIONAL		MATZO(H)
quarter	GHETTO	weight	
received tradition	QUBALLAH	—14 grams	SHEKEL
religious symbol	STAR OF DAVID	—20 gerahs	SHEKEL
ritual food preparation	KOSHER	wise man	HAKAM
robot	GOLEM	**hectare**	HA
roll	BAGEL	**hectolitre**	HL
room at synagogue for		**hedge**	HAW
safe-keeping of documents		**height**	H
	GENIZAH	*height of* fashion(D)	F
Sabbath	SATURDAY.SHABBOS	**held**	(*see* hold)
—eve	PARAS(C)EVE	**Hell**	ABADDON.AVERNUS.DIS
sacred objects	URIM		EREBUS.PIT.HADES
sage	HAKAM		TARTARUS
Sanhedrin	SYNEDRION	hellhound	PLUTO
	THE SEVENTY	hellish boss	DEVIL.DIS
scribes	SOPHERIM	**help**	
scripture scroll	MEZUZA(H)	Help!	SOS
secret lore	CAB(B)ALA	*help get* o/ver y/our...	VERY
	KAB(B)ALA	*help* mot/her d/ust...	HERD
sect	ESSENE.HEMEROBAPTIST	help out	(in) AI-D
	KARAITE.MANDAEAN	•five help *out*	AVID
	MARONITE	*help to make* aero/plan/es	PLAN
seventh year	SABBATICAL YEAR	*help to make* <u>notes</u>	ONSET
song	HAT(T)IKVAH		STONE.TONES
Spanish Jews	SEPHARDIM	**hem**	
spice	STACTE	*hemmed in* a...	incl A
Supreme Council	SANHEDRIM	*hemmed in* *	incl *
	SANHEDRIN	•sea *hemmed* us *in*	MUSED
surplice	EPHOD	*hemmed in by* *	incl in *
synagogue	S(C)HUL	•us *hemmed in by* sea	MUSED
teacher	RABBI.RABIN	**hen**	ANDALUSIAN.BANTAM
temple	SYNAGOGUE		CUCKOO MARAN

DORKING.MARENNES	
MINORCA.LIGHT SUSSEX	
NORTH HOLLAND BLUE	
ORPINGTON.PLYMOUTH ROCK	
RHODE ISLAND RED.SPANISH	
SEBRIGHT BANTAM.SUSSEX	
WHITE LEGHORN.WYANDOTTE	

henry   H
Henry   HAL
Henry VIII   HEIGHT
her
Her (Britannic) Majesty   H(B)M
her *counterpart*   HIS
Her Exalted Highness   HEH
Her Grace   HG
Her Imperial Majesty   HIM
Her Majesty's Customs   HMC
Her Majesty's Government   HMG
Her Majesty's Inspectorate   HMI
Her Majesty's Service   HMS
Her Majesty's Ship   HMS
Her (Royal) Highness   H(R)H
Her Serene Highness   HSH
Heralds' College   HC
heraldry   BLAZONRY.HER
  about to take
    wing   RISING.ROUSANT
  added charge   AUGMENTATION
  antelope   ARGASILL
  antelope/horse   BAGWYN
  arched   ENARCHED.INVEXED
  arms of deceased   HATCHMENT
  art of describing
    arms   EMBLAZONRY
  back to back   ADDORSED
  barbed arrowhead   PHEON
  barrel-shaped metal cage   HERSE
  baton   BASTON.WARDER
  bear diagonally   QUARTER
  bearing   FLEUR-DE-LIS
     FLEUR-DE-LYS
  —arms   ARMIGEROUS
  —fruit   FRUCTED
  —like a fish-trap   WEEL
  —like a pallium   PALL
  beast's leg   GAMB.JAMB
  beasts   (*see* monsters)
  bendlets interlaced around
    a mascle   FRET

bent   FLEXED
—round to strike
  side   PERCUSSANT
bird's leg cut off at
  thigh   A LA QUISE
black   DWALE.SABLE
blue   AZURE
border
—near edge of shield   ORLE
—of shield   BORDURE
—with cotises   COT(T)IS
—with semi-circular
  indents   ENGRAIL
bowed   FLEXED
branch   SCROG
broad vertical stripe   PALE
broken   ROMPU
cadency mark of
—eldest son   LABEL
—fourth son   MARTLET
—son   MULLET
cap   CHAPEAU
centre of escutcheon
     FESSE-POINT
charge borne upon an
  ordinary   SUPERCHARGE
charged with
—flowers etc.   VERDOY
—squirrel fur   VERR(E)Y
—vair   VAIRE.VAIRY
charges used as border   ORLE
chequered   CHECKY
chief herald
     GARTER KING-OF-ARMS
—of Scotland   (LORD) LYON
circular
—shield (Scottish)   TARGE(T)
—wreath   CHAPLET.GARLAND
clover-leaf   TREFOIL
coat of arms   BLAZON
colour   TINCTURE
—black   SA.SABLE
—blood red   SANGUINE
—blue   AZURE
—flesh colour   CARNATION
—gold   OR
—green   VT.VERT
—mulberry   MU.MURREY
—orange   TENNE

—purple	PURP.PURPURE	divide into quarters	QUARTER
—scarlet	GU.GULES	divided	PARTY
—sky-blue	BLEU CELESTE	—into bends	BENDY
—tawny	TENNE	—into quarters	QUARTERLY
—yellow	OR	—into three	TIERCED.TRIPARTED
column with bifurcated capital		diving	URINANT
and base	ZULE	division of	
combine palewise	IMPALE	—coat	QUARTERING
coming forth	NAISSANT	—shield for two	
concave	CHAMPAGNE	coats	IMPALEMENT
	CHAMPAINE.INVEXED	double-bodied	BICORPORATE
—indentation	FLA(U)NCH	drapery of coat-of-arms	
conventional figure	ORDINARY		MANTLING
cormorant	LIVER BIRD	drop	GOUTTE
covered with shells	ESCALLOPED	eagle	AL(L)ERION
crest	TIMBRE	eight	
cross	QUADRATE	—leaved flower	EIGHTFOIL
—with foot sharpened to		—spoked charge (ES)CARBUNCLE	
point	FITCH(E).FITCHY	emerging from	
—with curved ends	MOLINE	—another	ISSUANT
—with floriated ends	PATONCE	—behind	ISSUANT
—with three claw-like		—middle	NAISSANT
divisions	PATTE(E)	encircled	ENVIRONED.INVOLVED
crutch-shaped	POTENT	—by sun's rays	EN SOLEIL
curved backwards	REFLEXED	end-to-end	ABOUTE
cushion tied at		entwined	ENVELOPED
corners	WOOL PACK	facing	
cut		—each other	RESPECTANT
—off cleanly	COUPE(D)	—the beholder	G(U)ARDANT
—to a point	FITCHE(E).FITCHY	—the sinister	TRAVERSED
death's head	MORTHEAD	fan of feathers	PANACHE
depict	EMBLAZON	fettered	SPANCELLED
—in heraldic terms	BLAZON	field	CHAMP
device on a shield	CHARGE	figure surmounting helmet	CREST
devouring	VORANT	fillet and pendants	LABEL
—prey	TRUSSING	fire-bucket on	
diagonal cross	SALTIRE	pole	BEACON.CRESSET
diagonally	BENDWISE	five-point star	MULLET
diamond-shaped		flame-shaped	RAYONNE
panel	HATCHMENT	fleur-de-lis	LIS
diminish	REBATE	floating in air or water	FLOTANT
diminutive of		flower with	
—bend	COT(T)IS	—four petals	QUATREFOIL
—bend sinister	SCARP	—five petals	CINQUEFOIL
—fess	TRANGLE	—eight petals	OCTOFOIL
—orle	TRESSURE	flying	
displaced	ROMPU	—horizontally	VOLANT
distinguishing arms of branch		—upwards	SOARING
from main line	DIFFERENCE	formed of crutch-heads	POTENT

full-face	CABOCHED.CABOSHED
fullness (of moon)	COMPLEMENT
fully armed	CAP-A-PIE
funeral banner	GUMPHION
fur	ERMINE(S).ERMINOIS
	PEAN.TINCTURE.VAIR
gliding	GLISSANT
goat rampant	CLIMANT
gold	OR
—circle	BESA(U)NT.BEZANT
	TALENT
—or silver as tincture	METAL
green	VERT
grenade	PETARDIER
half a quarter	ESQUIRE.GYRON
halo	GLORY
hanging	PENDENT
having	
—a pommel	POMMELE
—a square opening	
	SQUARE-PIERCED
—a tongue	LANGUED
—another crest laid	
over	SURMOUNTED
—border of convex	
curves	INVECTED
—branch stubs	RAGULY
—convex curve	NOWY
—crown or coronet about the	
neck	GORGED
—endorse each side	ENDORSED
—ends that enter mouth of	
animal	ENGOULED
—fesses	FESSE(E)-WISE
—fleurs de lis	FLEUR(ETT)Y
	FLOR(ETT)Y
—gyrons	GYRONNY
—head facing up	HAURIENT
—horns etc. a different colour	
from body	ENARMED
—inner area cut away	VOIDED
—narrow border	FIMBRIATE
—one foot raised	TRIPPANT
—overlapping	
—feathers	PLUMET(T)E
	PLUMETTY
—scales	PAPELLONE
	PAPILLONE
—part displaced	FRACTED

—points	URDE(E).URDY
—raised wings	SEGREANT
—small squares	CHECKY
—steps	GRIECED
—trellis pattern	FRETTY
—wings	
—expanded	DISPLAYED
—folded	TRUSSED
—joined	A VOL.IN LURE
—open	OVERT
—thrown back	ENDORSED
—water flowing	
through	TRANSFLUENT
head downward	URINANT
hedgehog	HERISSON.HERIZON
	URCHIN
herald	BLAZONER
Herald of Arms	
—England	ARUNDEL.CHESTER
	NORFOLK.SOMERSET
	SURREY.YORK
—Scotland	ALBANY.DINGWALL
	MARCHMONT.RICHMOND
	SNOWDOUN
hollowed with border	CLECHE
horizontal band	BAR.FESS(E)
horseman	CHEVALIER
in	
—sleeping posture	DORMANT
—the direction of	PER
—the manner of	PER
—upper part of shield	IN CHIEF
indentation in curving	
lines	ENGRAILMENT
indented	WAVED
interlaced	BRACED
inverted	
—V-shape	CHEVRON
—wedge shape	PILE
iron hat	CHAPEL-DE-FER
issuing from another	ISSUANT
King of Arms	
—England	CLARENC(I)EUX
	GARTER
	NORROY AND ULSTER
—Scotland	LYON
knight	MILES
knotted gold or silver	
cord	CORDELIERE

leaping	SALIENT
—in opposite directions	COUNTER-SALIENT
left-hand side from front	DEXTER
like	
—a dragon in hinder parts	DRAGONNE
—an arch	ENARCHED
—mill-rind	MOLINE
lily	FLEUR-DE-LIS.FLEUR-DE-LYS
line	DOUBLE
lines from edge of escutcheon to fesse-point	GIRON.GYRON
lion passant gardant	LEOPARD(ESS)
lizard	AMPHISBAEMA
long flag	STANDARD
looking backwards	REG(U)ARDANT
lower part of shield	BASE
lozenge	FUSIL
—pierced with circle	RUSTRE
—shaped bearing	MASCLE
lying down	
—head on paws	DORMANT
—head up	COUCHANT
mark	
—of dishonour	ABATEMENT
—with sign or badge	ENSIGN
mastiff	ALANT
merman	NEPTUNE
metal	ARGENT.OR.TINCTURE
monster	(see monster)
most ancient	PREMIER
narrow	
—band of colour	FIMBRIATION
—bendlet	RIBAND
negro	BLACKAMOOR
often repeated	SANS NOMBRE
one of nine fixed positions	POINT
open lozenge	MASCLE
ordinary	
—from dexter chief to sinister base	BEND
—from sinister chief to dexter base	BEND SINISTER
—horizontal	FESS(E)
—occupying fourth of shield	QUARTER
outline sketch	TRICK
overlaid	OPPRESSED
	SUPPRESSED
overlying	JESSANT
painted in	TRICKED
pair of bars	GEMMAL
parrot	POPINJAY
part of quartered shield	QUARTER
parted	PARTY
pass through	ENFILE
passing in opposite directions	COUNTER-PASSANT
personal flag on horizontal pole	GONFALLON.GONFANNON
pierced	TRANSFIXED
place bearing	
—on	CHARGE
—quarterly	QUARTER
point	
—at centre of shield	FESSE-POINT
—below centre of shield	NAVEL.NOMBRIL
—just above fesse-point	HONOUR-POINT
pointed	URDE(E).URDY
—at the foot	FITCHE(D).FITCHY
pole battle-axe	DOLOIRE
	HALBERD
potent	POTENCE
powdered	SEME(E)
pursuivant	
—English	FITZALAN
	BLUE MANTLE.PORTCULLIS
	ROUGE CROIX.ROUGE DRAGON
—Scottish	BUTE.CARRICK
	KINTYRE.MARCH.ORMONDE
rabbit	CONEY
ragged	RAGULY
raguly	RAGGED
raised on steps	MOUNTED
rampant	
—goat	CLIMANT
—griffin	SEGREANT
raven	CORBIE
rearguard	ARRIERE-GARDE
rearing	CABRE
—horse	FORCENE
red	GULES
reel of golden thread	TRUNDLE

reference book	ORDINARY
repeated throughout the field	SANS NOMBRE
represent half of	DIMIDIATE
represented as flying	VOLANT
revealing tincture of field	VOIDED
right-hand side from front	SINISTER
ring	ANNULET
rising	NAISSANT
—as a bird	ROUSANT
—fish, as if breathing	HAURIANT
	HAURIENT
—from the sea	ASSURGENT
rosette	COCKADE
roundel	
—azure	HURT
—black	GUNSTONE
	OGRESS.PELLET
—blue	H(E)UT.HEURTE
—blue/silver	FOUNTAIN
—green	POMEIS.POMEY.POMME
—gold	BEZANT
—gules	TORTEAU
—murrey	MULBERRY
—purpure	GOLP(E)
—sable	GUNSTONE
	OGRESS.PELLET
—sanguine	GUZE
—silver	PLATE
—tenne	ORANGE
row of alternating tinctures	COMPONE.COMPONY
	GOBONY
running	COURANT
St Andrew's cross	SALTIER
	SALTIRE
scattered with bearings	SEME(E)
Scottish	
—Herald	ALBANY
—King of Arms	(LORD) LYON
—pursuivant	UNICORN
scroll	ESCROL(L)
sea-horse	HIPPOCAMPUS
secondary armorial charge	SUBORDINARY
segment of circle	FLANCH
segmented cross	ARRONDEE
shackle for horse	FETTERLOCK

sheaf	GARB(E)
shedding drops of. . .	DISTILLING
shield	BUCKLER.(E)SCUTCHEON
	SCOTCHEON
ship (Scottish)	LYMPHAD
shoulder guard	AILETTE
sign of illegitimacy	BAR-SINISTER
	BATON-SINISTER
silver	ARGENT
simple figure	ORDINARY
single small shield in centre of shield	INESCUTCHEON
sitting	SEJANT
six-rayed star	ESTOIL
skull	MORTHEAD
sleeve	MANCH(E).MAUNCH
small	
—banner	BANNERET
	BANNEROLE.BANNEROLL
—bend	BENDLET
—chevron	CHEVRONEL
—fesse	TRANGLE
—lion	LIONCEL
—pale	PALLET
—pennon	PENCELL.PENSELL
	PENNONCELLE
—shield at fesse	INESCUTCHEON
smeared	TRICK
spreading out at ends	PATTE(E)
spur rowel	MOLET.MULLET
square charge	CANTON
squirrel fur	VAIR
standing	
—in profile	RAMPANT
—on all four feet	STATANT
—shield for archer	PAVISE TALLEVAS
—still	POSE
star with waved points	ESTOILE
status of branch descended from younger son	CADENCY
stepped	GRIECED
stick with branch-stubs	RAGGED STAFF
streamer	BANDEROLLE
stylised flower	PRIMROSE
subordinary	TRESSURE
surcoat	CYCLAS
surface of shield	CHAMP.FIELD

surrounded by	ENVIRONED
	ENTOURED
swallow with no feet	MARTLET
swimming horizontally	NAIANT
T-shaped mark	POTENCE
tail held between legs	COWARD
tearing at prey	RAPING
tent	PAVILION.TABERNACLE
three-lobed	TREFOIL
tinctures	(*see* colour *above*)
—reversed	COUNTER-CHANGED
triangular	
—flag	PINSEL.PINSIL
—wedge	PILE
tripping	TRIPPANT
two parallel diagonal	
lines	BEND (SINISTER)
unde	OUNDY
upright rectangle	BILLET
variation in coat of arms	BRISURE
vertical band on shield	ENDORSE
vertically	PALEWISE
visit of inspection by	
herald	VISITATION
walking	
—stag	TRIPPANT
—to right	PASSANT
warhorse	DESTRIER
wavy	NEBULE.NEBULY.UNDE(E)
waxing (of moon)	INCRESCENT
wheat-sheaf	GARBGERBE
wheel set with	
teeth	CATHERINE WHEEL
whirlpool	GORGE.GURGES
white	ARGENT
wild boar	SANGLIER
wound	GOLPE.VULN
wreath	TORSE
Y-shaped ordinary	PALL
—with fringed bottom	PALLIUM
yellow circle	BEZANT
yoke on water-bags	BOUGET
zigzag or indented line	DANCETTE
	DANCETTY.RAGULY
herb	SIMPLE
bennet	(WOOD-)AVENS
Christopher	BANEBERRY
Gerard	GOUTWEED
of-grace	RUE

of-repentance	RUE
others	AGRIMONY.ALOE
	AMARACUS.ANGELICA
	ANISE.AVENS.BALM
	BANEBERRY.BASIL.BAY
	BENNET.BERGAMOT
	BETONY.BLITE.BORAGE
	BURDOCK.CALAMINT.CAPER
	CARAWAY.CATMINT.CATNIP
	C(H)AMOMILE.CHERVIL
	CHICORY.CLARY.COMFREY
	CORIANDER.CORNEL
	COSTMARY.COVENS.CRESS
	DILL.DITTANY.ELECAMPANE
	ENDIVE.FENNEL.FENUGREEK
	FIN(N)OC(C)HIO.FINNOCHIO
	GENTIAN.GINSENG
	HAMBURG PARSLEY
	HELLEBORE.HENBANE
	HOREHOUND.HORSERADISH
	HYSSOP.ISATIS.LAD'S LOVE
	LADY'S MANTLE
	LEMON BALM
	LEMON VERBENA.LICORICE
	LIQUORICE.LOVAGE
	MARJORAM.MEDIC.MILFOIL
	MINT.MUGWORT.MUSTARD
	MYRRH.OREGANO.ORIGAN(E)
	ORIGANUM.ORPIN(E).PANICUM
	PARSLEY.PENNY ROYAL
	PEPPERMINT.PURSLANE
	PURSLAIN.QUINOA.RAMPION
	ROSEMARY.RUE.SAFFRON
	SAGE.SALAD BURNET
	SAMPHIRE.SAVORY.SEDUM
	SENNA.SESAME
	SOUTHERNWOOD.SPICKNEL
	SUCCORY.SWEET CHERVIL
	SWEET CICELY.TANSY
	TARRAGON.TORMENTIL
	THYME.VERVAIN.WAYBREAD
	WOAD.WOODRUFF
	WORMWOOD.YARROW
Paris	TRUE-LOVE
Peter	COWSLIP
Robert	STINKING CRANE'SBILL
trinity	PANSY
here	
here *in France*	ICI

here *in Rome*	HIC
here is (laid)	HS

hereafter

hereafter	HEAVEN
here*after*	
•guard here*after*	HEREWARD
•firm here*after*	COHERE

heretic ARIAN

Hero worshipper LEANDER

Hertz CS.CPS.HZ

hesitation ER.UM.UR

h-hem HEDGE

hide

hidden in h/er go/wn	ERGO
hidden in <u>forest</u>	FOSTER
hidden in *	incl in *
•fruit *hidden* by divine	DAPPLED
hide pepper	PELT
hiding a. . .	incl A
hiding in <u>field</u>	FILED
hiding *	incl *
•divine *hiding* fruit	DAPPLED

hi-fi buff STEREOTYPE

Higgins's girl ELIZA

high

high-alumina cement	HAC
high-class	A.AI.U
high-class band	CORONET.TIARA
high explosive	HE
high flier	COMET.CONDOR
	WHIZZ-KID
high frequency	HF
high honour	KING
high place	UP
high-powered firm	STRONG
high priest	AARON.ELI.LAMA
high road	FLYOVER
high-*sounding*	HIE
high-*sounding* girl	HYENA
high summer	ADDER
	(SENIOR) WRANGLER
high tension	HT
high time	NOON
high tower	UPKEEP
high water	TARN
high water mark	HWM
highball	LOB
Higher National Certificate	HCN
Higher National Diploma	HND

highest common factor	HCF
highest honour	ACE
highlight	MOON.STAR.SUN

Highland

Highland(er) = Scottish	
•*Highland* shoemaker	SOUTAR
	SOUTER.SOWTER
•*Highlander's* salutation	BECK
(*see also* Scottish)	
Highland Light Infantry	HLI

hill MT.TOR

hill-*climbing*(D) ↑	ROT
hill-dweller	ANT.TERMITE
hill-guide	TORMENTOR
hill*side*	H

Himalayan SHERPA

hinder

hinder man	DETERGENT
hindrance	LET

Hindu

adherent of Siva	S(H)AIVA
ages of the world	CALPA
	KALPA.YUG(A)
ambrosia of the	
gods	AMREETA.AMRITA
aphorism	SUTRA
ascetic	SAD(D)HU.YOGI(N)
aurora	USHAS
banker	SOUCAR
barge	BUDGERO(W)
bathing in Ganges	KUMBHA MELA
beauty spot	TIK(K)A
being	SAT
benevolent spirit	DEVA
blackmail	CHOUT
bliss	ANANDA
caste	JATI
—artisans	SOODRA
	S(H)UDRA
—merchants	VAISYAS
—mark	TI(K)KA
—priests	BRAHMANS.BRAHMINS
—untouchables	HARIJAN
—warriors	KSHATRIYAS
chant	HARE KRISHNA
circle	MANDOLA
collection of sayings	SUTRA
concentration	SAMADHI
cosmic age	YUGA

cycle of creation and
  destruction   CALPA.KALPA
dancing girl   BAYADERE
deities   (*see* gods.goddesses)
demi-god   GARUDA
demon   RAHU
desire   KAMA
devotion   BHAKTI
devotional
—offering   S(H)RADDHA
—song   BHAJAN
divine
—in self   ATMAN
—power   MAYA
doctrine   SUTRA
dramatic performance of
  Ramayana   RAMLILA
drug   BIKH
epic   BHAGAVADGITA
      MAHABHARATA.RAMAYANA
errand boy   HURKARU
European FARINGEE.FERINGHEE
                             FERINGHI
evil spirit   RAKSHAS(A)
extortion   CHOUT
female principle   S(H)AKTI
festivals   DEWALI.DI(PI)VALI
      DIWALI DURGA PUJA.HOLI
      KUMBHA MELA.NAVARATRA
      NAVARATRI.ONAM.PONGAL
first
—mortal   YAMA
—of Vedas   RIGVEDA
forehead mark   TI(K)KA
gate tower   GOPURAM
gentleman   BABOO.BABU
gesture   MUDRA
ghost   BHUT
gnome   YAKSKA
god in three forms   TRIMURTI
gold ornament   TAHLI
heaven   SVARGA.SWARGA
hero   ARJUNA.RAMA
highest glorification   AVATAR
holy
—book   VEDA
—man   SAD(D)HU
—writing   SHASTER.S(H)ASTRA
home of gods   MERU

idol   SWAMI
ignorance   AVIDYA
immortality   AMRITA(TTVA)
Indian Republic   BHARAT
incarnation   AVATAR
—of Vishnu   JAGANNATH
                          JUGGERNAUT
instrument   SIT(T)AR
interpreter   DHOBASH
knowledge   JNANA
land revenues   JAGHIRE
law of causation   KARMA
leader   H
liberation (from circle of
  rebirths)   MOKS(H)A
library   BHANDAR
life
—cycle rites   SAMSKARAS
—principle   ATMAN.JIVA
loin-cloth   DHO(O)TI
love   KAMA
lowest caste   HARIJAN
                        UNTOUCHABLE
manifestation   DARSHANA
material gain   ARTHA
medieval texts   PURANAS
merchant   BUN(N)IA
metal worker   KOFTGAR
moral order   RITA
musical pattern   RAGA
mythological era   KALIYUGA
non-violence   AHIMSA
of high caste   TWICE-BORN
paradise   SVARGA.SWARGA
period   CALPA.KALPA
philosophical text
                           UPANIS(H)AD
philosophy   NYAYA
      PURVA-MIMAMSA.SAMKYHA
      SANKHYA.VAISESIKA
      VEDANTA.YOGA
poison   BIKH
police officer   TANADAR
present age of the
  world   KALIYUGA
priest   PUJARI
priestly caste   BRAHMAN
                             BRAHMIN
Rajput prince   RANA

religious	
—commentary	VEDANGA
—instructor	GOOROO.GURU
	MAHARISHI.SWAMI
—school	ARYA SAMAJ
—society	BRAHMA SAMAJ
	BRAHMO SOMAJ
—treatise	UPANIS(H)AD
—writing	SMRITI.TANTRA.VEDA
ritual	PUJA
—texts	BRAHMANAS
ruling class	RAJPOOT.RAJPUT
rural districts	MOFUSSIL
sacred	
—books	MANTRA(M).PURANA
	SHASTER.S(H)ASTRA
—scriptures	SHRUTI
—snake	NAGA
—syllable	OM
—writings	TANTRA.VEDA
salvation	MOKSA
script	DEVANAGARI
sayings	SUTRA
serpent-king	SESHA
slave	DASI
society	SOMAJ
spring festival	HOLI
statues of gods	MURTI
store	BHANDAR
strands	GUNAS
spirit	PURUSHA
symbol of the god Siva	LINGAM
temple	MANDIR(A)
—attendant	PUJARI
title	MAHATMA.PANDIT.PUNDIT
trader	BANIAN.BANYAN
tradition	SRUTI
transmigration of soul	SAMSARA
trinity of gods	TRIMURTI
truth	SAT
twice-born	DVIJA
untouchable caste	HARIJAN
usher	SOUCAR
Veda	ATHARVAVEDA.RIGVEDA
	SAMAVEDA.THERAVEDA
	YAJURVEDA
—commentary on	VEDANGA
Vedic	
—hymn	MANTRA(M)

—philosophical text	
	UPANIS(H)AD
veil	CHAD(D)AR.CHADOR
	CHUDDAH.CHUDDAR
Vishnu's consort	S(H)AIVA
vision	DARSHANA
wealth	ARTHA
wife of Siva	S(H)AKTI
wisdom	JNANA
wise man	MAHATMA
	PANDIT.PUNDIT
woman's garment	SAREE.SARI
worship	BHAKTI.POOJA(H).PUJA
worshipper of	
—Sakti	S(H)AKTA
—Vishnu	VAISHNAVA
	(*see also* Indian[2])

his

His (Britannic) Majesty	H(B)M
His Catholic Majesty	HCM
his *characters*	-ISH
his *counterpart*	HER
His Eminence	HE
His Exalted Highness	HEH
His Excellency	HE
His Grace	HG
his *head*	H
His Imperial Highness	HIH
His Imperial Majesty	HIM
His Majesty's Customs	HMC
His Majesty's Government	HMG
His Majesty's Inspectorate	HMI
His Majesty's Service	HMS
His Majesty's Ship	HMS
his *novel*	-ISH
His (Royal) Highness	H(R)H
His Serene Highness	HSH

hiss

hiss *at*	incl S
•hiss *at* play	SPLAY
hissing sound	S

historian/history master   ACTON
                      GIBBON.MACAULAY
               PASTMASTER.TACITUS

hit

hit for six by real...	BARLEY
hit number	SCORE
hit *out*	-ITH

Hitler's bodyguard   SS

hive, *say*	BEHOLDER	Holy Writ	NT.OT
hoard		**home**[1]	IN
hoarded by *	incl in *	hence	
•it is *hoarded by* saints	SITS	•home bird	INTERN
hoarding a. . .	incl A	•home rented	INLET
hoarding *	incl *	•Home Rule	INLAW
•saints *hoarding* it	SITS		(*see also* in[2])
hogshead	HHD	**home**[2]	
hold		home club	FLATIRON.VILLA
held by lar/ge ne/w. . .	GENE	Home Counties	SE
held in banks indicates a river		home following	CARAVAN
•*held in French banks*	SEINE	Home Guard	HG.WATCHDOG
•*held in German banks*	RHINE	home team	VILLA
held in *	incl in *	**Homeric**	
•nitrogen *held in* ba-g	BANG	indicates use of Greek word or	
•nothing *held back in* ba-g	BALING	character:	
hold firm	incl CO	•*Homeric* character	
hold up	incl UP	wagered	ALPHABET
•firms *hold* up. . .	COUPS	**Hong Kong**	HK
hold up paws(D) ↑	SWAP	**honour**	CH.OBE.OM
holding			J.JACK.K.KING.Q.QUEEN
•pai/r are st/ill *holding*	RAREST	hence	
holding a. . .	incl A	•honour *among* mayors,	
holding agency	CLAMP.FIXATIVE	say	MARCHES
	GLUE.GUM.PASTE.VICE	•act *with* honour	DOOM
holding *	incl *	•honourable name	OBERON
•ba-g *holding* nitrogen	BANG	honorary	HON
holding up		Honourable	HON
•doctor *held up by* girls(D)		Honourable Artillery	
	MOLASSES	Company	HAC
•girl *holding up* a. . .(D)	AMISS	**hooded bird**	CROW.ROBIN
hole	O	**hoop**	O
holed	incl O	**hopin'**	ASPIRIN
Holland	(*see* Dutch)	**hopping** <u>mad</u>	ADM-.DAM
hollow	O	**Horace's work**	ODES
hollowed	incl O	**horizontal**	HOR
holy	PI	horizontal equivalent	HE
hence		**hormone**	AUTACOID
•holy child	PITOT	adrenaline	EPINEPHRINE
•Holy City	PILA	anti-diuretic	VASOPRESSIN
•holy man	PINED	controlling milk	
Holy City	MEDINA.MECCA	secretion	PROLACTIN
	JERUSALEM.ROME	female sex	OESTRADIOL
Holy Communion	HC		OESTROGEN.PROGESTERONE
holy man	S.ST		PROGESTOGEN
Holy Mother Mary	SMM	growth	AUXIN
holy river	GANGES	initiating labour	OXYTOCIN
Holy Roman Empire	SRI	intestines	SECRETIN
Holy Virgin	HV	kidney	ACTH.ADRENALIN(E)

	ALDOSTERONE
	CORTICOSTEROID.CORTISOL
	CORTISONE.RENIN
loosening pelvic	
ligaments	RELAXIN
male sex	ANDROGEN
	ANDROSTERONE
	TESTOSTERONE
pancreas	GLUCAGON.INSULIN
	PANCREATIN.SECRETIN
parathyroid gland	CALCITONIN
	PARATHORMONE
pineal gland	MELATONIN
pituitary gland	
	CORTICOTROP(H)IN
	GONADOTROP(H)IN
	OXYTOCIN.OXYTONE
	PITUITRIN.PROLACTIN
	VASOPRESSIN
raising blood	
pressure	VASOPRESSIN
stomach	GASTRIN
stimulating	
—pancreas	SECRETIN
—thyroid	THYROTROPHIN
synthetic oestrogen	
	STILBOESTROL
thyroid	CALCITONIN.THYROXINE

horology   HOR
horrible fate   FEAT
horse¹   ARAB.BARB.BAY.COB
                GEE.GG.H.NAG
hence
•horse is. . .   ARABIS
•horsewoman   ARABELLA
•namely, a horse   SCARAB
and
•horse one can. . .   BARBICAN
•horse devoured. . .   BARBATE
•horse measures. . .   BARBELLS
and
•horseman   BAYED
•mountain horse   TORBAY
•horse, very odd   BAY RUM
and
•horse-food   COBLOAF.COBNUT
•horse painter   COBRA
•relatives *with* horse   KINCOB
and

•ban horse   BARGEE
•horse-road   GEEST
•horse *without* new. . .   GENE
and
•horse *in* a rage   BAGGIT
•horse *without* an. . .   GANG
•Oriental horse   EGG
and
•horseman   HALF.HANDY
•horse in river   HINDEE
•horse *with* no bit   HOBIT
and
•horse collection   NAGANA
•horse *in* ship   SNAGS
•horse or. . .   NAGOR
horse²
American
—Indian   CAYUSE
—piebald   APPALOOSA.PINTO
—poor   TACKY
—riding   MORGAN
—wild   DUN.MUSTANG
Asian   PRZEWALSKI'S HORSE
ass x horse   HINNY.MULE
Australian   WALER
bay   BAYARD
black and white   PIEBALD
broken-winded horse   WHISTLER
Caligula's horse   INCITATUS
carthorse   CLYDESDALE.SHIRE
chaser   HUNTER
circus   LIBERTY HORSE
competition horse   EVENTER
cowboy's mount   BRONC(H)O
dark
—coloured horse   MOREL
—horse   BLACK BEAUTY
display horse   LIPPIZ(Z)ANA
             LIP(P)IZ(Z)ANER
docked   CURTAL
—(Shakespeare)   CUT
Don Quixote's horse ROSINANTE
             ROZINANTE
draughthorse PERCHERON.SHIRE
        SUFFOLK PUNCH
entire   STALLION
extinct breed EOHIPPUS.TARPAN
fast horse   DAISY-CUTTER
female   DAM.MARE

French	ARDENNES.PERCHERON
general-purpose	
mount	HACK(NEY)
golden coloured	PALOMINO
Himalayan pony	GOONT
Indian	TAT(TOO)
Irish	CONNEMARA
Jerusalem pony	ASS
legendary	BAYARD
loser	STUMER
male	COLT.GELDING.STALLION
	STEED.STUD
miniature	FALABELLA
mixed colour	ROAN
pacer	HOBBY
pony	GRIFEN.GRIFFON.GRIPE
	GRYPHON
poor specimen	HACK.JADE
	PLUG.NAG.RIP.ROSINANTE
	ROZINANTE.SCREW
racehorse	CHASER.PLATER
reddish-brown colour	SORREL
riding-horse	NAG.HACK(NEY)
reliable horse	STAYER
saddle horse	PALFREY
short-legged type	COB
Scottish	GALLOWAY.SHELTIE
	SHETLAND
—old	AVER.YAUD
shaft-horse	FILLHORSE
	THILLHORSE
slang name	PRAD
small horse	NAG.CANUCK
	KANUCK.GARRAN
	GARRON.HOBBY.PONY
	SHETLAND
—Spanish	JENNET.GEN(N)ET
Spanish	ANDALUCIAN
	ANDALUSIAN
stallion	ENTIRE.STONE-HORSE
—x she-ass	HINNY
swift horse	BARB.CHARGER
	COURSER
Swift horse	HOUYHNHNM
trained horse	EVENTER
Dick Turpin's horse	BLACK BESS
warhorse	DESTRIER
white and black	PIEBALD
—and another colour	SKEWBALD

wild	
—horse	BRONC(H)O
	PRZEWALSKI'S HORSE
	TARPAN
—ponies	DARTMOOR
	NEW FOREST.WELSH
workhorse	CARTHORSE.DOBBIN
	DRAYHORSE.PERCHERON
young	
—horse	FOAL
—mare	FILLY
—stallion	COLT
horse³	
dark horse	NIGHTMARE
horse-carriage	HACKNEY
horse race	HOUYHNHNM
horse-race	DERBY.NATIONAL
	OAKS.PLATE
horse-riding	(in) S-ADDLE.UP
horse sound	NEIGH.WHINNY
horse *sound*	HOARSE.MAYOR
horse's foot	TROTTER
horse*back*⟨	BOC.GAN
horse*less*	omit G
horseman	CENTAUR
horse*play*	SHORE
horseshoe	MULE
sound horse	HOARSE.MAYOR
unhealthy horse	SICK-BAY
white horse	BREAKER.WAVE
horse diseases	
African	HORSE SICKNESS
	NAGANA
Asian	SURRA
blindness	GLASS-EYE
broken wind	HEAVES
contagious disease	DOURINE
	STRANGLES
crack in hoof	SAND-CRACK
distemper	FIVES
eye diseases	MOON-EYE.PINK-EYE
fever (Scottish)	WEED.WEID
foot disease	FRUSH.SEEDY-TOE
	WIRE-HEEL
glanders	FARCY
indigestion	GRASS STAGGERS
	STOMACH STAGGERS
inflammation of	
—bones	LAMINITIS

—brain	MAD STAGGERS	•hot at church	HATCH
	SLEEPY STAGGERS	•hot oven	HOAST
—frog	FRUSH.THRUSH	hotline	EQUATOR.TROPIC
—mucous membranes	FARCY	**hour**	H.HR
	GLANDERS	**house**[1]	CO.COT.H.HO.SEMI
—scaphoid bone		hence	
	NAVICULAR DISEASE	•a royal house	ARCO
jaundice	YELLOWS	•house *in* the street	SCOT
lameness	SPRING-HALT	•houses collections	COSSETS
leg tumour	GRAPE	and	
lump on back	SITFAST	•house *and* home	HONEST
lumpy jaw	ACTINOMYCOSIS	•house in good order	HOOK
parasitic infection	DOURINE	•housework	HOOP
	NAGANA	**house**[2]	
skin		house	BINGO
—disease of hock	SALLENDERS	houseboat	HOMECRAFT
—eruption	MAL(L)ANDER	house builder	JACK
	MALLENDER	house buzzer	FLY
sore hoof	QUITTER.QUITTOR	housecoat	PLASTER.STUCCO
parasitic disease spread		House of Keys	HK
by tsetse fly	NAGANA	*housed in* de/relic/t...	RELIC
study of horse		*housed in* *	incl in *
diseases	HIPPIATRICS	•scholar *housed in* for-t	FORMAT
swelling	GALL	housemaid	WENDY
—in leg	CURB.GOURDINESS	housemaid's knee	BURSITIS
—on inside of hock	BONE-SPAVIN	*housing* a...	incl A
—on pastern	CRATCHES	(ho)using *shortage*	USING
swollen		*housing* *	incl *
—glands	VIVES	•for-t *housing* scholar	FORMAT
—hoof	QUITTER.QUITTOR	**house**[3]	HANOVER
	TWITTER(BONE)		LANCASTER.PLANTAGENET
—vein on hock	BLOOD-SPAVIN		STUART.TUDOR
	BOG-SPAVIN		WINDSOR.YORK
various diseases	STAGGERS	**how**	QM
wart	ANBURY	*how* far is a...	SAFARI
wasting of shoulder		how fast	MPH
muscles	SWEENY	**hug**	
wound in hind ankle	CREPANCE	*hug* a...	incl A
Hosea	HOS	*hug* *	incl *
hospital	H	•Pa-t *hugs* son	PAST
hence		*hugged by* *	incl in *
•hospital *has* changed	HALTERED	•son *hugged by* Pa-t	PAST
•hospital *has* no use...	HOUSE	**huge**	OS
•hospital planes	HAIRLINE		(*see also* large)
hospital sign	H	huge cost	EARTH
hospitalised	(in) W-ARD	huge *majority*	HUG
hot	H	**Hugh said...**	HEW.HUE
hence		**Hull transport**	BOTTOMRY
•hot and *nearly* ful(l)	HANDFUL	**human error**	MORTAL SIN

Humberside		NE
humming-*top*(D) ↑		H
hundred[1]		C.CENTUM.CENTURY
		IC.P.R.RHO.TON
hence		
•100 I examine		CIVET
•100 in church		CINCH
•100 girls		CLASSES
•100 to one		CAN.CI.CLONE.CONE
•100 with nothing on		COON
•a hundred		AC
•centipede		CLIMBS
•hundred pounds		CL
•one hundred		IC
hundred (county division)		
		CANTRED
		CANTREF.CENTUM
hundred and one		CI
hence		
•101 fish		CIGARS
•101 grave...		CISTERN
•101 surgeons		CIVETS
hundred and four		CIV
hence		
•104 I record		CIVILIST
•104 in charge		CIVIC
•104 with one learner		CIVIL
hundred and		
twenty		GREAT HUNDRED
		LONG HUNDRED
hundred and forty nine		CIL
hundred and fifty		CL.Y
hence		
•150 deliveries		CLOVER
•150 listeners		CLEARS
•150 to one		CLAN.CLONE
and		
•a girl in 150		CAVIL
•a graduate in 150		CABAL
•or one in 150		CORAL
150th anniversary		
		SESQUICENTENNIAL
hundred and sixty		T
hundreds		CC.CS.CHILTERN.D
hundredth		CENTI-
hundred thousand		LAC.LAKH.P
		R.RHO
hundred and fifty thousand		Y
hundred and sixty thousand		T

hundred[2]	
Old Hundred	PSALM
pounds	CENTAL
weight	CWT
years	CENTENARY
	CENTENNIAL.CENTURY
hung	(*see* hang)
Hungarian	HUNG
	TRANSLEITHAN
brigand	HAIDUK.HEYDUCK
capital	BUDAPEST.H
coin	FILLER.FORINT
dance	CSARDAS.CZARDAS
division	BAN(N)AT.BANATE
fast movement of	
csardas	FRIS(KA)
governor	BAN
gypsy	TZIGANE.TZIGANY
	ZIGAN
leader	H
people	MAGYARS
pepper	PAPRIKA
river	DANUBE
soldier	PAND(O)UR
wine	TOKAY
Hungary	H
hungry	
indicates 'nothing inside'	incl O
•*hungry* c-at	COAT
hunt	LEIGH
hunter	ACTAEON.ESAU.ORION
huntress	ARTEMIS.DIANA
huntsman's drink	CHASER
hurt pride	PRIED
husband	H.MAN
husband and wife	MATES
husbandman	CARL
hush	SH.ST
husky food	BRAN
hybrid[1]	
ass x mare	MULE
cattle x bison	CAT(T)ALO
cattle x zebu	CATTEBU
citron x orange	CITRANGE
cow x bison	BEEFALO
cow x yak	DSOBO.DSO(MO)
	(D)ZO.JOMO.Z(H)O
	ZOBO.ZOBU
lion x tiger	LIGER

stallion x she-ass	HINNY	*hybrid* tea rose	ROSEATE
tangerine x grapefruit	TANGELO	*hybridised* roses	SORES
tangerine x grapefruit x orange		**hydrant**	H
	UGLI	**hymns**	AM
tiger x lion	TIGON	**hypocrite** (Dickens)	PECKSNIFF
hybrid²		**hypothesis**	IF
hybrid animal	LAMINA.MANILA		

I

a. an. ane. ay. aye. che. dotted. electric. current. *eye. individual.* iodine. *iota.* island. Italy. *line. lunchtime. one. single. straight line.* square root of **-1.** *ten.* ten thousand. *un.* upright. *yours truly*

I¹	A.AN.ANE.AY.AYE	capital	I.REYKJAVIK
	EGO.EYE.VOWEL	coin	AURA
I *abandon...*	omit I	lignite	SURTARBAND
I am	IAM.IM		SURTURBAND
I am *in...*	incl IAM.IM	parliament	ALTHING
I *am in*	incl I	**icthyology**	ICT(H)
I am *standing*(D) ↑	MI	**ideal partner**	SOUL MATE
I caught	-IC	**identification**	ID
I (dialect)	CHE	**idle**	
I *don't appear in*	omit I	idle head	LOAF
I *escape from...*	omit I	idler	DRONE
I *get* on	-ION	**idol**	MAMMET.MAUMET
I *get out of...*	omit I		MAWMET.MOMMET
I had	ID	idolatry	MAMMETRY
I have	IVE	**if**	
I have *at heart*	incl IVE	if *old*	AN
I *have left*	omit I	if it	ANT
I *have* left	IL	**ignore**	
I *intervene*	incl I	*ignore* a...	omit A
I *leave*	omit I	ignore feast	PASSOVER
I *left*	omit I	*ignore* *	omit *
I *lost*	omit I	•(ac)tress *ignores* bill	TRESS
I note	-IA.-IC.ID.IE.IF	**i-issue**	IDEAL
	IRE.-ITE	**ill**	
I object	ME	*ill-fated* <u>ship</u>	HIPS.PISH
I *omitted...*	omit I	*ill-organised* <u>trips</u>	SPIRT
I owe you	IOU	*ill-treated* <u>animal</u>	LAMINA
I possess	-IVE	*ill-treatment of* <u>salt-mine</u>	
I *quit*	omit I		AILMENTS
I *said*	AYE.EYE.OPTIC.VOWEL	illness	FLU
I *say*	AYE.EYE		(*see also* disease)
I say nothing	EGO	**illegal army**	ETA.IRA.PLO
I see	IC.IV	*illegitimate* <u>son can...</u>	CANONS
I shall/will	ILL	**illicit diamond buying**	IDB
I *won't be there*	omit I	**illiterate signature**	X
I²		**illuminated note**	LITRE
I *am told* your...	YORE	**illustrated**	ILL
I'd *say*	EYED.IDE	illustration	ILL
I *hear* news	GNUS	**image building**	PR
I *say* you...	EWE.U.YEW	*imbecile* <u>can see...</u>	SEANCE
ice		**imbibing**	
<u>ice</u>-*breaking*	CIE	*imbibing* a...	incl A
<u>icy</u> greeting	HAIL	*imbibing* *	incl *
Iceland	IS	•he-r *imbibing* drink	HEALER

imbibed by *	incl in *
•drink *imbibed by* he-r...	HEALER
imitate tenor	TENNER
immediate success	WINNOW
immerse	
immerse a...	incl A
immerse *	incl *
•king *immersed* in study	DERN
immersed	(in) WA-TER
•one *immersed*	WAITER
immersing	incl in *
•study *immersing* king	DERN
imperative	IMP
imperfect	IMP
imperfect tense	TEENS
imperial	IMP
Imperial Service Order	ISO
impersonal	IMP
impersonate	
impersonate insect	NAT
impersonating peer	PIER
impetuous rascal	TEARAWAY
implicate	
implicate a...	incl A
implicate *	incl *
•Ro-n *implicates* master	ROMAN
implicated by *	incl in *
•master *implicated by*	
Ro-n	ROMAN
import	
import a...	incl A
import *	incl *
•ship *imports* drug	SPOTS
imported	-MENT
imported by *	incl in *
•drug *imported by* ship	SPOTS
imported, *say*	-MENT
Swe/dish ed/itor's *import*	DISHED
impose on	
indicates one word above another:	
•cat *imposed on* by a...(D)	ATOM
•he *imposes on* the	
king(D)	HETHER
imposter's real...	LEAR
imprison	
imprisoned (in) C-AGE.(in) PE-N	
imprisoned by *	incl in *
•American *imprisoned* by	
German soldiers	SUSS

imprisoning a...	incl A
imprisoning *	incl *
•German soldiers *imprisoning*	
American	SUSS
improper	
improper remark	MARKER
improperly made	DAME.EDAM
	MEAD
improperly dealt with	
much...	CHUM
improvise	
improvise tale	LATE.LEAT.TEAL
	TELA
improvising ploy	POLY-
improvisation on a set...	ATONES
in¹	
in a way	-INE
in another key	IND.-INE.-ING
in church	INCE.INCH
in *French*	EN
in *French* church	-ENCE
in G and S	-INGS
in Gates*head*	-ING
in German *capital*	-ING
in one...	INA.INI
in one quarter	-INE.INN.INS-
in *some* cas(es)	INCAS
in Spain	-INE
in *the beginning*	start with IN
•obtained in *the beginning*	INGOT
in the East	-INE
in *the end*	end with IN
•firm in *the end*	COIN
in the Orient	-INE
in*turned*⟨	NI
in²	
meaning	
accepted	
•father *accepted*	PAIN
at	
•*at* work	ATOP
at home	
•mother *at home*	MAIN
at the wicket	
•*batting* after tea, *say*	TIN
belonging to	
•*belonging to* party	INSECT
during	
•*during* autumn	INFALL

elected		in death	EN-D
•*elected* to seat	INSTALL	in debt	R-ED
esoteric		in different ways	N-S.WE-S. etc.
•*esoteric* class	INFORM.INSECT	in document	DE-ED.M-S
fashionable, etc.		in drink	AL-E
•*trendy* view	INSIGHT	in dry	T-T
favoured		in dry grass	TE-D
•*favoured* friend	INMATE	in exploit	DE-ED
governing		in exposed situation	BAR-E
•*governing* staff	RODIN	in face of	DI-AL
member of		in favour	BO-ON
•*member of* group	INSET	in fact	DE-ED
planted		in fear	AW-E
•*planted* meadow	INFIELD	in feat	DE-ED
popular		in flight	W-ING
•good man and *popular*	STAND-IN	in general	LE-E
smart		in gold	O-R
•*smart* group	INSET	in hat	LI-D
wearing		in heaven	SK-Y
•*wearing* undergarments	INVESTS	in hospital	WAR-D
well-favoured		in icy clutches	COL-D
•*well-favoured* position	INSTANCE	in large measure	ROO-D
in³		in lead	P-B
indicates inclusion:		in Lincoln	AB-E
in a rush	RE-ED	in low *surroundings*	MO-O
in a way	A-RD.AS-T.R-D.S-T	in many ways	SN-ES.N-ESE etc.
in act	AC-T.DE-ED	in *mid*week	E-E
in action	AC-T.DE-ED	in motor race	T-T
in America	U-S	in need	NE-ED
in American money	C-ENT	in Norfolk town	DIS-S
in an attempt	TRI-AL.TR-Y	in opposition	E-W.W-E.N-S.S-N
in any *case*	AN-Y	in order	OB-E.O-M
in bad *shape*	AB-D	in performance	DE-ED
in bed	B-ED.CO-T.PA-D.S-ACK	in pipe	RE-ED
in bed *in France*	LI-T	in plot	BE-D
in camera	SL-R	in prepaid container	SA-E
in car	R-R.V-W	in prison	C-AGE.GA-OL
in case		in pub	BA-R.IN-N
•a letter *in* m-y *case*	MESSY	in question	E-H
•gun *in case* of ne-ed	NEGATED	in raincoat	MA-C
in character	CAR-D	in residence	N-EST
in charge	FE-E	in retirement	B-ED
in church	C-E.C-H.INCE.INCH	in Russian	RE-D
in city	E-C.E-LY	in salt water	SE-A
in communist...	RE-D.TRO-T	in shape	CON-E
in concert	PRO-M	in ship	S-S
in conclusion	EN-D	in silks	BA-R
in credit	C-R	in silver	A-G
in crib	BE-D.CO-T	in Slough	BO-G.FE-N

in some circles	O-O
in some ways	N-ESE.W-E. etc.
in the afternoon	P-M
in the air	SK-Y
in the *back* row⟨	EN-IL
in the City	E-C.E-LY
in the clutches of *	incl in *
•I'm *in the clutches of* the French...	LIME
in the cold	I-CE.I-CY
in the desert	SAN-D
in the end	EN-D
in the face	DI-AL
in the fall	R-AIN
in the front	FOR-E
in the garden	B-ED
in the grass	RE-ED
in the grip of *	incl in *
•one *in the grip of* a ca-d	CAID
in the king's name	LEA-R
in the last month	DE-C.UL-T
in the long grass	RE-ED
in the main	DE-EP.SE-A
in the match	T-EST
in the middle	COR-E
in the money	CO-IN.C-ENT
in the nude	BAR-E
in the open	OVER-T
in the race	T-T.N-ATION
in the rain	WE-T
in the red	R-ED
in the right	THE-R
in the ship	S-S
in the street	R-D.S-T
in the vessel	S-S
in the way	N-E.N-W.S-E.S-W
in time	AG-E.DA-Y.H-R.MI-N
in two ways	L-L.L-R.R-L.R-R N-S.W-E. etc.
in wet conditions	DA-MP.MO-IST
in wintry conditions	COL-D.IC-Y
in writing	M-S
in * *environment*	incl in *
•king *in* t-ough environment	TROUGH

in⁴

implies inclusion:
•grass-covered	(in) RE-ED

similar examples in this

vocabulary are preceded by (in)	

in⁵

other uses:
in a bad way <u>after</u> <u>red</u>...	RAFTERED
in a form <u>that</u>...	TATH
in a *fury*	AIN.-IAN
in a manner of speaking, bare	BEAR
in a mess <u>for us</u>	FOURS
in a *panic*	AIN.-IAN
in a way <u>mad</u>	DAM
in accordance with	SEC
in all directions	NEWS
in ascent	STANCE
in banks indicates a river	
•*in French banks*	SEINE
•*in German banks*	RHINE
in bed indicates a flower	
•girl *in bed*	ROSE
in capacity of	QUA
in *capturing*	I-N
•i-n *capturing* firm...	ICON
in charge	IC
hence	
•duke in charge	FISTIC
•graduates in charge	BASIC
•scholar *and* saint in charge	MASTIC
in confusion <u>I ran</u>	RAIN.RANI
in connection with	ON.RE
(*see also* about⁵)	
in disarray <u>his team</u>	HAMITES
in distress <u>some lad</u>...	DAMOSEL
in foreign parts = foreign language	
•travel *in foreign parts*	VIAJE
•work *in foreign parts*	LAVORO
in form <u>player</u>	REPLAY
in full = expanded abbreviation	
•do *in full*	DITTO
•do *fully*	DITTO
•*in full* fig	FIGURE
in-house publication	HANSARD
in London = Cockney	omit H
•(h)ouse *in London*	OUSE
in opposition	V
in order to <u>play she</u>...	SHAPELY
in other words	SC

in part di/vide/d	VIDE
in place of indicates substitution:	
•lane with one *in place*	
of an. . .	LIE
in poor shape <u>I cant</u>. . .	ANTIC
in *retirement*	NI
in *retirement*, star. . .	RATS
in return⟨	NI
in ruins of <u>Rome</u>	MORE
in some parts	(*see* dialect)
in *sound*	INN
in speech, told. . .	TOLLED
in su/ch ef/fort	CHEF
in support of	(*see* support)
in the *beginning*	INT-
in the Black Watch = Scottish	
•man *in the Black Watch*	MON
in the country = dialect	
•*in the country* crowd	MONG
•wander *in the country*	STROAM
in the Foreign Legion = French	
•man *in the Foreign*	
Legion	HOMME
in the glens = Scottish	
•man *in the glens*	MON
in the last month	ULT(IMO)
in the manner of <u>a Serb</u>	BARES
	BEARS.BRAES
	SABRE
in the meantime	AD INT(ERIM)
in the nude = with	
nothing on	add O
	add -OON
•father *in the nude*	DADO
•dance *in the nude*	BALLOON
	(*see also* with²)
in the time of	TEMP(ORE)
in the saddle	UP
in the same place	IB.IBID
in the style of	ALA
in the wrong direction	
a rat. . .⟨	TARA
in the year. . .	AN.ANNO
—of	
—(human) salvation	A(H)S
—the flight	AH
—the king's reign	ARR
—the queen's reign	ARR
—the reign. . .	AR

—the world	AM
in (town) indicates foreign	
language:	
•bridge *in Paris*	PONT
•house *in Milan*	CASA
•inn *in Madrid*	POSEDA
in *turn*⟨	NI
in what manner	QM
in woman's clothes	DRAGON
inaccurate <u>report</u>	PORTER
inch	IN
incisive treatment	SURGERY
in*cite*	CIT-E
include	
included	INC
included in sho/p lea/se	PLEA
included in *	incl in *
•herb *included in* group	SHERBET
including	INC
including a. . .	incl A
including *	incl *
•group *including* herb	SHERBET
income tax return	REVENUE
incompetent	NOTABLE
incomplete	
incomplete, *say*	KNOTHOLE
incomplete boo(k)	BOO
incomplete de/liver/ies	LIVER
inconclusive	
inconclusive kin(d)	KIN
inconclusive battle	SALAMI(s)
inconsistent	
inconsistency in <u>speech</u>	CHEEPS
inconsistent <u>views</u>	WIVES
inconsistently <u>said</u>. . .	AIDS.DAIS
inconstant <u>love</u>	VOLE
incorporate	
incorporate a. . .	incl A
incorporate *	incl *
•South Africa *incorporates*	
section	SPARTA
incorporated	INC
incorporated by *	incl in *
•section *incorporated by* South	
Africa	SPARTA
incorporated in hou/se in E/rith	
	SEINE
incorrect	
incorrect	(in) R-T.(in) O-K

incorrect dates	SATED.STEAD
incorrectly laid	DIAL
increase	
increased by a...	incl A
increased by one	incl A or I
increased by 100	incl C
increased by *	incl *
•weight *increased by* king	TORN
incredible soak	STEEP
indecent picture	BLUEPRINT
indeed	DE-ED
indefinite number	N.NO
independent	IND
Independent Broadcasting Authority	IBA
Independent Labour Party	ILP
Independent Television Authority	ITV
independent worker	FREE HAND
India(n)¹	IND
hence	
•Indian *and* one man	INDIGENT
•Indian *with* no alternative	INDOOR
•Indian *with* no fast...	INDOLENT
Indian²	BHARAT.IDN
aconitine	BIKH
acrobat	NAT
adept	MAHATMA
adjutant stork	ARGALA
administrative	
—district	ZILA.ZILLAH
—service	IAS
Afghan	PATHAN
allowance	BATTA
ancient	
—alphabet	BRAHMI
—language	SANSKRIT
—throne	PEACOCK THRONE
antelope	ANTILOPE
	(*see also* antelope)
armed tribal force	LASHKAR
army officer	JAMADAR
	JEMADAR.JEMIDAR
arrangement	BANDOBAST
	BUNDOBUST
artificial speech	CHEE-CHEE
ascetic	FAKEER.FAKIR
at once	EK DUM

attorney	VAKEEL.VAKIL
aubergine	BRINJAL
authority on law, etc.	PANDIT
	PUNDIT
backgammon	PACHESI.PACHISI
bailiff	NAZIR
balsam	GURJUN
Baluchi chief	TOMUNDAR
bamboo mat	TATTY
banana	PLANTAIN
bandicoot rat	PIG-RAT
bean	MUNG.URD
bears	BALOO.BALU
	HIMALAYAN BEAR.SUN BEAR
beast fables	PANCHATANTRA
bedstead	CHARPOY
beggar	FAKEER.FAKIR
Bengal quince	BHEL
best quality	FIRST CHOP
betel (leaf)	PA(W)N
birds	AMADAVAT.AVADAVAT
	BULBUL.COUCAL
	LARK-HEELED CUCKOO
	MINIVET.PRINIA.SHAMA
bitter gourd	KARELA
black	
—bear	SLOTH-BEAR
—mail	CHOUT
—soil	REGAR.REGUR
blouse	CHOLI
board game	PACHISI
boat	BUDGERO(W).LANCHA
	PULWAR.PUTELI
book of sayings	SUTRA
bosun	SERANG
bo tree	PEEPUL.PIPAL.PIPUL
bottle	DUPPER
boycott	HARTAL.SWADESHI
brand	CHOP
brandy and water	
	BRANDY-PAWNEE
brass pot	LOTA(H)
bread	CHAPAT(T)I.CHAPATTY
	CHUPAT(T)I.NA(A)N
breakfast	(CHOTA-)HAZRI
bribe	DUSTOORY
British woman	KAISAR-I-HIND
buffalo	ARNA.ARNEE.ARNI
	BUBALUS.WATER BUFFALO

bullock-cart	BANDY.HACKERY	—3 pie	PICE
burial site (holy person)	DARGA	—4 pice	ANNA
bum(m)alo	BOMBAY DUCK	—16 annas	R.RUPEE
bustard	FLORICAN	—100 new pice	R.RUPEE
butter	GHEE.GHI	—15 rupees	MOHUR
—tree	MAHUA.MAHWA	—100,000 rupees	LAC.LAKH
	MOW(R)A	—100 lac	CRORE
calico	DUNGAREE	—gold	PAGODA
camel	OONT	—silver (Goa)	XERAFIN
camp			XERAPHIN
—of soldiers	LASHKAR	collection of fables	HITOPADESA
—servant	BILDAR	collectorate	TALUK
cane sugar	GOOR.GUR	commander	SIRDAR
canopy	SHAMIANA(H)	compliment	TASHRIF
capital	DELHI.I	cooking style	TANDOORI
captain	SUBA(H)DAR	copper pot	LOTA(H)
carpet fabric	D(H)URRIE	corporal	NAIK
carriage	BANDY.BUGGY	corruption	KHUTPUT
cart	GHARRI.G(H)ARRY	costus-root	PACHAK.PUTCHOCK
cavalry commander			PUTCHUK
	RESSALDAR.RISALDAR	cotton cloth	BEZAN.SHALLI
central shrine	VIMANA		SURAT
ceremonial robe	KELLAUT	coucal	SWAMP PHEASANT
	KHALAT.KHILAT.KILLUT	court	DURBAR
champagne	SIM(P)KIN	courthouse	CUTCHER(R)Y
charging before magistrate			KACHAHRI.KACHERI
	CHAL(L)AN	crab's-eye plant	
chief	SUDDER		INDIAN LIQUORICE
—minister of Mahrattas	PESWA	crane	SARUS
	PEISHWA(H)	cremation site	GHA(U)T
chintz	KALAMKARI	—of holy person	DARGA
civet	LINSANG.MONGOOSE	crisp bread	PAPPADOM
Civil Service	ICS		POP(P)ADUM
claret	LOLL-SHRAUB	crocodile	MAGAR.MUGGER
	LOLL-SHRUB		NUGGAR.G(H)ARIAL.GAVIAL
clerk	BABOO.BABU	crop	KHARIF
	CIRCAR.SIRCAR.SIRKAR	crown	RAJ
cloak	CHUDDAH.CHUDDAR	cuckoo	BRAIN-FEVER BIRD.KOEL
cloth	KHADDAR.KHADI	cupboard	ALMIRA(H)
cloth of gold	SONERI	cymbals	DIN-DIN
coarse		dagger	KUTTAR
—calico	DUNGAREE	dal	PIGEON PEA
—sugar	JAGGERY	dam	BAND(H).BUND
coat	ACHKAN	dance	NA(U)TCH
coconut oilcake	POONAC	—drama	KATH(A)KALI
coins		dancing girl	NA(U)TCH(-GIRL)
—$^1/_{100}$ rupee	(NAYA)PAISA	—performance	NACH.NA(U)TCH
—$^1/_{40}$ rupee	DA(W)M	development of vowel	
—$^1/_{12}$ anna	PIE		SVARABHAKTI

dhak tree	PALAS
diamond mine	GOLCONDA
dish	BIRYANI.CURRY
	KEDGEREE.KORMA
	TANDOORI
district	CIRCAR.SIRCAR.SIRKAR
division	TAHSIL
door-screen	CHI(C)K
dress	BANIAN.BANYAN
	SAREE.SARI
dried mud	CUTCHA.KACH(CH)A
	KUTCHA
drink	ARRACK.SOMA
—after sunset	SUNDOWNER
drug	BHANG.BENJ.CUBSHA
	GANJA.MAJOON.SOMA
durra	GUINEA-CORN
	JAWARI.JOWAR
dye tree	DHAK
dyeing process	KALAMKARI
edible plant	SWORD-BEAN
elephant	
—driver	MAHOUT
—enclosure	KEDDAH.KHEDDA
—goad	ANKUS
embankment	BAND(H).BUND
embroidered fabric	KINGCOB
emperor	GREAT MOGUL
	NAWAB
Englishman	QUI-HI.QUI-HYE
entertainment	TAMASHA
epic tale	MAHABHARATA
Eurasian	CHEE-CHEE
European	SAHIB.TOPI-WALLAH
—lady	MEMSAHIB.SAHIBA(H)
—(plural)	SAHIB-LOG
evil-doer	BADMASH.BUDMASH
exclamation of	
surprise	BOBBERY
extortion	CHOUT
eyeshadow	KOHL.SURMA
factor	AMILDAR.AUMIL
fan	PUNKA(H)
fasting to obtain	
justice	DHARNA
festival	POOJA(H).PUJA
fibre	CUSCUS.CUSKUS.DA
JUTE.K(H)USK(H)US.MADRAS	
OADAL.SUNN (HEMP)	

fiddle	SARANGI
fig	OPUNTIA
—tree	BANIAN.BANYAN
	OPUNTIA
figured muslin	TANJIB.TANZIB
finance minister	DEWAN.DIWAN
—office of	DEWANI.DEWANNY
financier	BANIAN.BANYAN
fine flour	SOOJEE.S(O)UJEE
fish	BOMBAY DUCK
BUM(M)ALO.DORAB.HILSAH	
MAHSEER.MAHSIR	
flowers	BASTARD SAFFRON
	SAFFLOWER
foot soldier	PEON
fly-whisk	CHOWRY
forced labourer	BEGAR
fort commander	KILLADAR
fortress	GURRY
fowl	CHITTAGONG
freebooter	PINDAR(EE).PINDARI
fruit	BAEL(-FRUIT)
	BENGAL QUINCE
—tree	DURIAN.DURION
fuss	TAMASHA
game	PACHISI
gardener class	MALLEE.MALI
gentleman	PUKKA SAHIB
gift	NUZZER
ginger	CURCUMA.ZEDOARY
good	PAKKA.PUCKA.PUKKA
governor	HAKEEM.HAKIM
	NAIK.SUBA(H)DAR
grain harvest	RABI
grass	BAJREE.DUR(R)A.JHOW
KANS.ROOSA.RAGA.RUSA	
—mat	TATTY
groom	MEHTAR.S(A)ICE.SYCE
guide	DUBASH
guitar	SAROH
Gurkha knife	KUKRI
gypsy	BAZIGAR
handkerchief	BANDAN(N)A
	ROMAL.RUMAL
hat	TOPEE.TOPI
head	
—cloth	ROMAL.RUMAL
—dress	TAJ.TURBAN
heavy stick	LATHEE.LATHI

hemp	BHANG.DAGGA
—matting	TAT
—resin	CHARAS.CHURRUS
herbs	PIA.REA.SESAME.SOLA
hermitage	ASHRAM(A)
Himalayan	
—animal	PANDA.YETI
—cedar	DEODAR
—pheasant	MONA(U)L
Hindu	BABOO.BABU.GENTOO
hired	TICCA
holy leader	MAHATMA
home rule	SWARAJ(I)
honey badger	RATEL
honorary title	NAWAB
horse from Australia	WALER
hour	GHURRY
house for travellers	
	DAK(-BUNGALOW)
household attendant	CHAPRASSI
	CHUPRASSY
hunter	SHIKAREE.SHIKARI
hunting	SHIKAR
illusion	MAYA
Indian-made	SWADESHI
infantry regiment	PULTAN
	PULTO(O)N.PULTUN
inlaid metal	KOFTGARI
	KOFTWORK
—worker	KOFTGAR
instrument	CHIKARA.SERINGHI
	SIT(T)AR.VINA
intrigue	KHUTPUT
interpreter	DOBHASH
	MOONSHEE.MUNSHI
irregular	
—soldier	SEBUNDEE.SEBUNDY
—cavalryman	SILLADAR
isolated pillar	LAT
jacket	BANIAN.BANYAN
jaggery palm	KITTUL
judge	HAKEEM.HAKIM
labourer	COOLIE.COOLY
land	
—division	PARGANA
	PERGUNNAH
—owner	ZAMINDAR
—revenue	JAG(H)IR.JAGHIRE
—holder of	JAGHIRDAR

—tenure	RAIYATWARI
	RYOTWARI
languages	CANARESE
	DRAVIDIAN.GUJARAT(H)I
	GUJERAT(H)I.GURKHALI.HINDEE
	HINDI.HINDOOSTANEE
	HINDUSTANI.KANARESE
	KANNADA.KOLARIAN
	MALAYALAM.MARATHI
	MUNDA.ORIYA.PALI.PANJABI
	PUNJABI.PUNJA(U)BEE
	TAMIL.TELEGU.URDU
—group	INDIC
—or dialect	PRAKIT
law officer	NAIB
lawyer	MOOKTAR.MUKTAR
leader	I
learned man	PANDIT.PUNDIT
lease	POTTAH
leggings	PUTTEE.PUTTIE
lentil	ARRAH
—flour	BESAN
letter	DA(W)K
light	
—breakfast	CHOTA-HAZRI
—cotton fabric	SEERSUCKER
—meal	TIFFIN
—scarf	PAGRI.PUGG(A)REE
	PUGGERY
limestone	KUNKAR.KUNKUR
liquorice	JEQUIRITY
—tree seeds	CRABS-EYES
	CRAB-STONES
	JEQUIRITY (BEANS)
litter	DHOOLIE.DHOOLY.DOOLIE
loincloth	LUNGI
loom	TANTY
low caste	PARIAH
lower chamber	
(parliament)	LOK SABHA
lunch	TIFFIN
Kashmiri	PUNCHI
magic	MAYA
magistrate	COTWAL.KOTWAL
—'s office	CUTCHERY.KACHAHRI
	KACHERI
Mahratta ruler	PE(I)SHWA(H)
mail	DA(W)K
—carrier	DAK-RUNNER

makeshift	CUTCHA.KACH(CH)A
malarial fever	TAP
mallow	URENA
manager	AMILDAR.AUMIL
margosa	NIM
measures	
—1 inch	UNGUL
—1³/₄ miles	COSS.KOS(S)
—5 miles	YOJAN(A)
—½ acre	BEEGAH.BIGHA
—1 acre	CAWNY
—24 minutes	GHURRY
—hour	GHURRY
Melia	NIM
messenger	PEON
metal ware	BIDRI
military head	SIRDAR
millet	BAJRA.BAJREE.BAJRI
	DARI.D(O)URA.D(H)URRA
	RAGGEE.RAGGY.RAGI
Miss	KUMARI
money of account	FANAM
Mongol	MOGUL
mongoose	URVU
Moslems	COSSAS
—shrine	DURGAH
mountain pass	GHA(U)T
mounted attendant	SOWAR
murder	THAGI.THUGGEE
	THUGGERY
murderer	THUG
musical	
—form	RAGA
—rhythm	TALA
musk	
—rat	SONDELI
—shrew	SONDELI
musket	GINGAL(L).JINGAL
muslin	GURRAH.JAMDANI
	MAMMODIS
native tribe	GOND
needlewoman	DIRZEE
nim tree	MELIA
ne'er-do-well	BUDZAT
no good	NO CHOP
noisy argument	BOBBERY
noodle	PHALUDA
nose flute	POOGYE
nursemaid	AMAH.AYAH

nut	ILLIPE.ILLUPI
office	
—boy	CHOKRA
—messenger	CHAPRASSI
	CHUPRASSY
official residence	STATION
one-horse carriage	EKKA
orchid	FAHAM
orderly	CHAPRASSI.CHUPRASSY
ornamental metalwork	
	BENARES WARE
ox	BHYLE.BRAHMIN-BULL
	GAUR.G(A)YAL.MITHAN
	S(E)LADANG.ZEBU
—cart	HACKERY
pagan	GENTOO
palanquin	DHOOLIE.DHOOLY
	DOOLIE.PALKEE.PALKI
palm cat	MUSANG.PALM CIVET
	PARADOXURE.TODDY CAT
panther	BAGHEERA
parade ground	MAIDAN
paradoxure	MUSANG.PALM CAT
	PALM CIVET.TODDY CAT
parcel	DA(W)K
pariah dog	PI(E) DOG.PYE DOG
parliament	
—lower chamber	LOK SABHA
—upper chamber	RAJYA SABHA
parrot	ZATI
partridge	CHIK(H)OR.CHUKAR
	CHUKOR
pass	CHAL(L)AN
passive resistance	SATYAGRAHA
paymaster	BUKSHEE.BUKSHI
pea	D(H)AL.DHOLL
peasant	KISAN.RAIYAT.RYOT
percussion instrument	TABLA
perennial grass	LEMON GRASS
pheasant	IMPEYAN
pigeon pea	D(H)AL.DHOLL
pig-rat	BANDICOOT
pilaw	BIRYANI
pith helmet	TOPEE.TOPI
plain	MAIDAN
plant extract (tannin)	CATECHU
	CUTCH
plants	AMIL.DAL.CHAY(A)
	GOA BEAN.HAT-PLANT.JUTE

	MUDAR.RAMIE.SHAYA.SOLA
	SPONGEWOOD.SPIKENARD
	TELEGRAPH-PLANT
pods (tanning)	BABLAH.BABUL
poet	RISHI
police	
—man	PEON.SEPOY.SIPAHI
—officer	JAMADAR.JEMADAR
	JEMIDAR.TANNADAR
	T(H)ANADAR
—station	TANA.TANNA(H)
	THANA(H).THANNA(H)
political prisoner	DETENU
pond	TANK
pony	TAT(TOO)
—Himalayas	GOONT
poor quality	NO CHOP
prince	NIZAM.(MAHA)RAJA(H)
princess	BEGUM.(MAHA)RANEE
	(MAHA)RANI
prison	CHOKEY
province	CIRCAR.SIRCAR
	SIRKAR.SUBAH
provinces	MOFUSSIL
purée of pulse	D(H)AL.DHOLL
quince	BHEL
races	BHIL.CANARESE
	GOORKHA.GURKHA.HINDOO
	HINDU.KANARESE.LEPCHA
	MAHRATTA.MARATHA.MUNDA
	PUNJABI.TELUGU.SIKH
raft	ZAK
rat	BANDICOOT
ratel	HONEY BADGER
ravine	KHUD.NAL(L)A.NALLAH
	NULLA(H)
red dye	CHAY(A)-ROOT
reception	DURBAR
religious hostel	DHARMS(H)ALA
reservoir	TANK
respect	TASHRIF
revenue	
—division	TAHSIL
—officer	TAHSILDAR
revolution	INQILAB
ribbed woollen cloth	SATARA
rich	
—man	NABOB
—soil	REGAR.REGUR

rivers	BRAHMAPUTRA.GANGES
robber	DACOIT.DAKOIT
robbery	DACOITAGE
	DACOITY.DAKOITI
rosewood	BITI
ruler of Baroda	GAEKWAR
	GAIKWAR.GUICOWAR
sabre	TULWAR
sacking	GUNNY
sacred	
—book	PURANA
—lotus	PADMA
saddlecloth	NUMNAH
sailor	CLASHEE.LASCAR
sash	LUNGI
scarf	PAGRI.PUGG(A)REE
	PUGGERY
scholar	INDIANIST
seal	CHOP
secretary	MOONSHEE.MUNSHI
sect	JAIN(A).GHEBER.GHEBRE
	GUEBER.GUEBRE.ORIYA
	PARSEE.PARSI.SIKH
sedan chair	JAMPAN
—bearer	JAMPANEE.JAMPANI
self-government	SWARAJ(I)
sepoy mutineer	PANDY
sergeant	HAVILDAR
servant	MEHTAR.FERASH
sesame (oil)	GINGELLY.GINGILI
	JINJILI
settlement	BANDOBAST
	BUNDOBUST.BUSTEE
shawl	CHUDDAH.CHUDDAR
	ROMAL.RUMAL
ship	PATAMAR
shooting platform	MACHAN
shot (plant)	CANNA
show	TAMASHA
silk	CABESSE.SURAH
—fabric	KINGCOB.TASH
small metal pot	LOTA(H)
soldier	JAWAN.SEPOY.SIPAHI
sovereignty	RAJ
spiritual	
—father	BAPU
—teacher	GOOROO.GURU
spoken language	BAT
spotted wildcat	LEOPARD CAT

staff officers	OMLAH
starling	MINA.MYNA(H)
steel	WOOTZ
stew	CURRY.CURRIE
stoppage	BAND(H).BUND.HARTAL
stork	ADJUTANT.ARGALA
strangler	THUG
subdivision of district	TALUK
—officer	TALUKDAR
sugar	RAAB
sunblind	CHI(C)K
supreme court	SUDDER
surf boat	MASOOLAH
	MASSOOLA.MASULA
table servant	K(H)IDMUTGAR
	K(H)ITMUTGAR
tailor	DARZI
tamarind	ABLI
tannin extract	CATECHU
tax collector	AMILDAR.AUMIL
	ZAMINDAR.ZEMINDAR
Telugu-speaker	GENTOO
temple	
—gate	VIMANA
—tower	GOPURA(M)
tent	SHAMIANA(H)
throne	GADI
timber	CALAMANDER
	CHAMPAC.CHAMPAK
	COROMANDEL.KUMBAR
	POON.ROSEWOOD
	SATINWOOD.TEAK
tip	BA(C)KSHEESH.BA(C)KSHISH
	BUCKSHISH.DUSTOORY
title of honour	BAHADUR
	HUZOOR.MIAN.S(H)RI
toll station	CHOKRY
tongue disease	AGROM
torch	MUSSAL
tract of land	TALUK
travelling box for	
clothes	PETARA
tree snake	DENDROPHIS
trees	AMLI.AMPAC.BANYAN
	BASTARD TEAK.BHEL.BO
	BUTEA.CHAMPAC.CHAMPAK
	CHAULMOOGRA.CHAULMUGRA
	COTTON-TREE.DAR.DHAK
	DITA.HYDNOCARPUS.ILLIPE

	ILLUPI.IVORY-TREE.JAMBOOL
	JAMBU(L).JAMBOLAN(A)
	JAROOL.JARUL.KHAIR.
	KOKRA.MARGOSA
	MYROBALAN.NIEPA.PALAY
	POON.SA(U)L.SIRIS.SISSOO
	TEAK.TIKUL.TOON
trellis	TATTA.TATTIE
tribe	JAT.TAMIL.TELUGU
trooper	SOWAR
tunic	K(H)URTA
turban	LUNGI.PAGRI
	PUGG(A)REE.PUGGERY
two-wheeled vehicle	TONGA
umbrella	CHATTA(H)
upper chamber (parliament)	
	RAJYA SABHA
usher	CHOBDAR
viceroy	NAWAB
village	BUSTEE
—chieftain	POLIGAR
—council	PANCHAYAT
washerman	DHOBI(E)
watchman	CHOKY.CHO(W)KIDAR
water	
—carrier	BHEESTIE.BHEESTY
	BHISTI(E)
—course	NULLA(H)
—lift	JANTU
—lily	LOTE.LOTOS.LOTUS
	PADMA
—pot	CHATTY
waybill	CHAL(L)AN
weapon	PATA
weights	
—180 grains	TOLA
—2 lbs	SEER
—3 lbs	VISHAM
—25-80 lbs	MAUND
—20 maunds	CANDIE.CANDY
	KANDY
whisky and soda	STENGAH
	STINGER
widow's suicide	SATI.SUTTEE
wild	
—cat	CIVET
—dog	DHOLE
—elephants	HATHI
wise man	MAHATMA.RISHI

woman's	
—garment	SAREE.SARI
—quarters	ZENANA
worship	POOJA(H).PUJA
young prince	UPPER ROGER
zinc alloy	TUTENAG
	(see also Hindu.Sikh)

indicate

indicated horse power	IHP
indicates where...	HEWER
indicates where	WARE.WEAR
indicative	IND

indiscriminate

indiscriminate sort...	ROTS.TORS
indiscriminately throw...	WORTH
indisposed by ill...	BILLY

individual   I

individuality	KA

Indonesian

capital	I.JAKARTA
coin	SEN
leader	I
lizard	KOMODO DRAGON
measure (1½ metres)	PAAL
ox	ANOA.SAPI-(O)UTAN
wood	KAPUR

inductance   L

indulge

indulge in *	incl in *
•lieutenant indulged in drink	BELTER

industrialist   BEE

inefficient

inefficient	A-BLE
inefficient person	CHARLEY
	CHARLIE

inexperienced footballers

	GREENBACKS

infantry   FOOT.INF

infectious disease   ID

(see also disease)

inferior	B
inferior horse	ROSINANTE.TIT
inferior novelist	UNDERWRITER

infinitive   INF

inflate

inflated = containing air	
•company after inflation	CAIRO
•inflated afterthought	PAIRS

inflow	F-LOW
inform	GRASS.SQUEAL
information office	COI
informer	GRASS.NOSE
	SQUEALER
infuriated master	STREAM

ingredient

ingredient of s/orb/et	ORB
ingredients of pie	EPI-.IPE
inharmonious airs	SAIR.SARI
inhuman	NAHUM

initial

Initial Teaching Alphabet	ITA
initially they...	T
initially they were only...	TWO
initiate scheme	S
initiative to start	S

inject

inject a...	incl A
inject *	incl *
•inject nitrogen into bo-y	BONY
* injected with	incl in *
•bo-y injected with nitrogen	BONY

injure

injured parties	PIASTRE
injuring arm	MAR.RAM
injury to horse	SHORE

ink slinger	OCTOPUS
inland	LAN-D
inmate	MEAT.TAME.TEAM
inner circle	GOLD.RED
inner tube	ENTERON
innkeeper	BONIFACE
inoffensive figures	MILD
inordinate praise	PERSIA

insane

insanity plea	LEAP.PALE.PEAL
insane despot	POSTED
insanely rages	GEARS

insect[1]

some alternative names:

ant	EMMET.PISMIRE
aphis	GREENFLY.PLANT LOUSE
	SMOTHER FLY
apple pest	APPLE SAWFLY
	CODLIN(G)-MOTH
	RED SPIDER MITE
	ROSY APPLE APHID
	TORTRIX MOTH.WINTER MOTH

Arctiidae	TIGER MOTHS	cereal pest	HESSIAN FLY
arachnids	SOLIFUGAE		WHEAT FLY.WHEAT MIDGE
bark beetles	SCOLYTUS		WHEAT MOTH
bedbug	CIMEX	Cetonia	ROSE BEETLE
bee moth	WAX MOTH		ROSE CHAFER
beetle	BUPRESTIS.CHAFER	cheese	
	CLAVICORNIA.WEEVIL	—mite	TYROGLYPHID
—with long antennae		—pest	CHEESE-HOPPER
	LONGICORN		CHEESE MITE
beetles	LAMELLIFORMES	chigoe	JIGGER.SAND FLEA
bird-eating spider	AVICULARIA		SAND HOPPER
biting midge	SANDFLY	cicada	TETTIX
black		Cicindelidae	TIGER BEETLES
—aphis	DOLPHIN FLY	click beetles	ELERATIDAE
—beetle	COCKROACH	clothes moth	TINEA
—currant pest	BIG BUD MITE	Coccidae	WAX BEETLES
blister beetle	CANTHARID	cockchafer	BUZZARD-CLOCK
	SPANISH FLY		MAY BEETLE.MAY BUG
bloodsucker	FLEA.LOUSE.TICK	coffee-tree pest	COFFEE BUG
blowfly	MEAT FLY	Collembola	SPRINGTAILS
Bombyx	SILKWORM	crane fly	(DADDY-)LONGLEGS
booklice	CORRODENTIA		TIPULA
	PSOCOPTERA	—larva	LEATHERJACKET
botfly	BREESE.BREEZE	cricket	CICADA.CICALA
	BRISE.GADFLY		GRASSHOPPER.GRIG
bristletail	THYSANURA	cuckoo fly	GOLD WASP
bumblebee	HUMBLEBEE		RUBY-TAIL
burnet moth	ZYGAENA	cutworm moth	DART-MOTH
burrowing	DIGGER WASP	daddy-longlegs	CRANE FLY
	FEN CRICKET.MOLE CRICKET		TIPULA
	SAND WASP	deathwatch beetle	ANOBIUM
—mite	ITCH MITE	destructive insect	LOCUST
burying beetle	SEXTON (-BEETLE)	devil's coach-horse	OCYPUS
butterfly	(see butterfly)		ROVE BEETLE
cabbage pest	CABBAGE APHID	dor beetle	DUNG BEETLE
	CABBAGE MOTH		SHARD BEETLE
	CABBAGE-ROOT FLY	dragonfly	DEMOISELLE
	TURNIP FLEA		ODONATA
caddis fly	MAYFLY.SEDGE FLY	drone	DOG-BEE
—flies	TRICHOPTERA	Drosophila	FRUIT FLY
cantharid	BLISTER BEETLE		POMACE FLY
	SPANISH FLY	dung beetle	COPROPHAGAN
Carabidae	GROUND BEETLES		SCARAB
carnivorous water		earwig	FORFICULA
beetle	DYTI(S)CUS	Egyptian scarab	SACRED BEETLE
carrot pest	CARROT FLY	Ephemera	DRAKE.MAYFLY
caterpillar	CUTWORM	flea	PULEX
cattle fly	GADFLY.OX-WARBLE	fleas	SIPHONAPTERA
centipede	THOUSAND-LEGS	flesh flies	SARCOPHAGA

flour mite   TYROGLYPHID   insect-eating fly   ROBBER FLY
flying beetle   COCKCHAFER   Ixodidae   WOOD-TICKS
forest   jigger   CHIGOE.SAND FLEA
—ant   WOOD ANT   SAND HOPPER
—fly   HORSEFLY   jumping spiders   SALTIGRADE
froghopper   FROTH-FLY   ladybird   LADYBUG
                       FROTH-HOPPER   LADYCOW.LADYFLY
froth-fly   FROGHOPPER   large
fruit pest   DROSOPHILA   —beetle   RHINOCEROS BEETLE
                       POMACE FLY   —centipede   SCOLOPENDRA
                       RASPBERRY BEETLE   —moths   SATURNIA.THRIPS
                       RED SPIDER MITE   leaf
                       VINEGAR FLY   —insect   PHASMID.SPECTRE
Fulgoridae   LANTERN FLIES   WALKING LEAF
gadfly   BREEZE.BREESE   —pest   LEAF-HOPPER
                       BRISE.TABANUS   RED SPIDER
gall   Lepisma SILVERFISH.SPRINGTAIL
—fly   RHODITES   like leaves   LEAF INSECT
—midge   CECIDOMYA   long-legged spider   HARVESTER
—wasp   CYNIPS   longicorn beetle   LONGHORN
garden spider   ARANEA.EPEIRA   Lucilia   GREENBOTTLE
Glossina   TSETSE   Lycosa   HUNTING SPIDER
gnat   CULEX   TARANTULA.WOLF SPIDER
gold wasp   CUCKOO FLY   Lymantriidae TUSSOCK MOTHS
                       RUBY-TAIL   magpie moth
goldeneye   LACEWING   GOOSEBERRY MOTH
gooseberry moth MAGPIE MOTH   male honeybee   DRONE
gout fly   CORN FLY   mayfly   GREEN-DRAKE
grain pest   CORN THRIP   SEDGE FLY
                       CORN WEEVIL   —flies   PLECTOPTERA
                       CORN WORM   mealworm   TENEBRIO
grass moth   VENEER MOTH   Mecoptera   SCORPION FLY
grasshopper   CRICKET.CICADA   Meloe   OIL BEETLE
                       CICALA.GRIG   metallic
greenfly   APHIS.PLANT LOUSE   —coloured insect   GOLD WASP
ground beetle   CARABUS   —fly   BLUEBOTTLE
harvestman   PHALANGID   GREENBOTTLE
hawk moth   midge   CHIRONOMID
        DEATH'S-HEAD MOTH   millipede   PILL-WORM
        HAWK.SPHINX   THOUSAND-LEGS
hive bee   HONEYBEE   mite   ACARUS.TYROGLYPHID
hop pest   HOP FLEA.HOP FLY   money spider   MONEY-SPINNER
horse   moth   EMPEROR MOTH
—fly   FOREST FLY   LACKEY MOTH.OWLET
—pest   BOTFLY.FOREST FLY   VAPOURER.PINE BEAUTY
        HORSEFLY.WARBLE FLY   PINE-CARPET.PLUME MOTH
hothouse pest   MEALY BUG   PROCESSIONARY MOTH
housefly   MUSCA   SAND-DART
hunting spider   LYCOSA   moth-like midge   SANDFLY

moths	GEOMETRIDAE
	PYRALIDAE.LASIOCAMPIDAE
	NOTODONTIDAE.TORTRICIDAE
Ocypus	DEVIL'S COACH-HORSE
oil beetle	MELOE
owlet moths	NOCTUID(AE)
parasitic	ICHNEUMON (FLY)
	MALLOPHAGA
pear pest	CODLIN(G) MOTH
	PEAR SUCKER
	PEAR-BEDSTRAW APHID
	TORTRIX MOTH
Perla	STONEFLY
phalangid	HARVESTMAN
phasmid	LEAF INSECT
	STICK INSECT.SPECTRE
pine beetle	PINE CHAFER
plant pest	APHIS.CAPSID(-BUG)
	DOLPHIN FLY.GALL MIDGE
	GALL WASP.GREENFLY
	LEAF-HOPPER
Podura	SPRINGTAIL
potato pest	CLICK BEETLE
	COLORADO BEETLE
	PEACH POTATO APHID
	WIREWORM
praying mantis	
	HOTTENTOT'S GOD
Pulex	FLEA
puss moth	SALLOW KITTEN
rat pest	RAT FLEA
red moth	CINNABAR
Rhaphidia	SNAKE FLY
Rhopalocera	BUTTERFLIES
riverside insect	ALDER FLY
rose	
—beetle	CETONIA.ROSE CHAFER
—chafer	CETONIA.ROSE BEETLE
—pest	RHODITES
rove beetle	
	DEVIL'S COACH-HORSE
ruby	
—wasp	GOLD WASP
—tail	CUCKOO FLY.GOLD WASP
sacred beetle	
	(EGYPTIAN) SCARAB
sand	
—flea	CHIGOE.JIGGER
	SAND HOPPER.SAND-SKIPPER

—wasp	BEMBEX
scarab	DUNG BEETLE
	SACRED BEETLE
Scolytus	BARK BEETLES
scorpion	
—flies	MECOPTERA
—spider	WHIP SCORPION
sea spider	PYCNOGONID
sedge fly	CADDIS FLY.MAYFLY
shard beetle	DOR BEETLE
sheep pest	SHEEP LOUSE
	SHEEP KED.SHEEP TICK
short-lived	DRAGONFLY
	EPHEMERA.MAYFLY
silverfish	LEPISMA.SPRINGTAIL
Sirex	WOOD WASP
skipjack beetle	ELATER
skipper butterfly	HESPERID
small	
—fly	GNAT.SCIARID
—gnat	GNATLING
—gnat-like fly	MIDGE
—male ant	MICRANER
—spider	MONEY-SPIDER
smother fly	APHIS
snake fly	RAPHIDIA
snow flea	SPRINGTAIL
soldier ant	WHITE ANT
Solifugae	ARACHNIDS
sow bug	WOOD LOUSE
Spanish beetle	BLISTER BEETLE
	CANTHARID
spectre	LEAF INSECT.PHASMID
	STICK INSECT.WALKING LEAF
	WALKING STICK
	WALKING STRAW
Sphinx	HAWK MOTH
spider	ARACHNID.ARANEID
	EPEIRA
springtail	SILVERFISH
	SNOW FLEA
springtails	COLLEMBOLA
	LEPISMA.PODURA
stick insect	LEAF INSECT
	PHASMID.SPECTRE
	WALKING LEAF.WALKING STICK
	WALKING STRAW
stinging insect	BEE.HORSEFLY
	MOSQUITO.WASP

stonefly	PERLA.PLECOPTERA		WATER BOATMAN
Stratiotes	WATER SOLDIER		WATER BUG.WATER FLEA
sugar pest	SUGAR MITE		WATER FLY.WATER STRIDER
swallow-tailed butterfly	PAPILIO	—beetle	GYRINUS.WHIRLIGIG
Tabanus	GADFLY	—boatman	NOTONECTA
tarantula	HUNTING SPIDER	—soldier	STRATIOTES
	LYCOSA.WOLF SPIDER	wax	
Tenebrio	MEALWORM	—insects	COCCIDAE
termite	WHITE ANT.WOOD ANT	—moth	BEE MOTH
tettix	CICADA	wheat pest	GOUTFLY
Thrips	LEAF-HOPPER	whip scorpion	SCORPION SPIDER
Thysanura	BRISTLETAILS	whirligig	GYRINUS
tick	SHEEP KED		WATER BEETLE
tiger		white	
—beetles	CICINDELIDAE	—ant	SOLDIER ANT.TERMITE
—moths	ARCTIIDAE	—moth	GHOST MOTH
tinea	CLOTHES MOTH	wingless	
Tipula	CRANE FLY	—male ant	ERGATANER
	DADDY-LONGLEGS	—parasite	LOUSE
Tortrix	MOTH	wolf spider	LYCOSA.TARANTULA
tree pest	PINE BEETLE	wood	
	PINE CHAFER	—ant	TERMITE
Tricoptera	CADDIS FLIES	—beetle	WOOD-ENGRAVER
Trombidium	HARVEST BUG	—boring insect	
	HARVEST LOUSE		DEATHWATCH BEETLE
HARVEST MITE.HARVEST TICK			FURNITURE BEETLE
tsetse	GLOSSINA		SIREX.WOOD WASP
turnip pest	CUTWORM	—eating insect	CARPENTER BEE
TURNIP FLEA.TURNIP FLY		—engraver	BEETLE
tussock moth	GIPSY MOTH.NUN	—lice	ONISCUS
—moths	LYMANTRIIDAE	—louse	MILLIPED(E).PILL BUG
two-winged	DIPTERAN		SOW BUG
Tyroglyphid	CHEESE MITE	—ticks	IXODIDAE
	FLOUR MITE	—wasp	SIREX
undeveloped female		worker ant	ERGATE(S)
ant	ERGATE(S)	yellow-fever fly	STEGOMYIA
various insects	SAWFLY	Zygaena	BURNET MOTH
vegetable pest	WHITEFLY	**insect[2]**	
veneer moth	GRASS MOTH	*insect-free*	
venomous spider	SOLPUGA	•(f)air(ly) *insect-free*	AIR
very small insect	MITE	insect *impersonator*	NAT
Vespa	WASP	insecticide	DDT
vine pest	GRAPE LOUSE	**insecure**	
VINE-FRETTER.PHYLLOXERA		*insecure* door	ROOD
vinegar fly	FRUIT FLY	*insecurely* tied	DIET.EDIT.TIDE
wasp	VESPA	*insecurity* of tenure	RETUNE
wasp-like flies	SYRPHUS	*inset*	SE-T
water		**inside**	
—insect	WATER BEETLE	*inside*	LE-G.L-T.O-N.S-IDE.R-T

inside left	L-T.POR-T
•very large *inside*-left	LOST
•ten *inside* left...	PORTENT
inside left	incl L
•footballer, *inside* left	BLACK
inside out	incl in OU-T
•bend *inside* ou-t	OUST
inside out	incl OUT
•about *inside* out	ROUTE
inside right	R-T
•holes *inside* right. ..	ROOT
inside right	incl R
•child *inside* right...	TROT
inside t/he Ar/ctic	HEAR
inside *	incl in *
•measure *inside* crate	CREMATE
is *inside*	incl IS
•old fiddle is *inside*	GUISE
insolvent	(in) R-ED
inspect	
inspection chamber	
CONSULTING ROOM	
inspector	HMI
instal(l)	
install a...	incl A
install *	incl *
•*installed* king *in* state	CARL
instalment system	HP
instead	
*in*stead	STEA-D
•me *in*stea-d	STEAMED
instinct	ID
institute/institution	
of	
Actuaries	IA
Advanced Motorists	IAM
Bankers	IB
Building	IOB
Civil Engineers	ICE
Contemporary Artists	ICA
Journalists	IOJ
Linguists	IL
Mining and Metallurgy	IMM
Municipal Engineers	IMUNE
Physics	IP
Practitioners in Advertising	IPA
instrument	
(*see* measuring instrument	
musical instrument)	

integers	Z
integral	INT
integrated circuit	IC
intellectual games	MARBLES
intelligence	MI.NI
intelligence department	ID.MI.NI
intelligence quotient	IQ
intend	
*in*tend	DENT
intended	-MENT
*in*tent	T-ENT
inter	
inter	BURY
inter alia	AL-IA
inter-*reaction*	NITRE.TRINE
inter-*state*	BERRY
inter-state	AVE-R.C-AL.SA-Y
interchangeable	
inter*changeable*	NITRE.TRINE
interchangeable indicates	
substitution:	
•mates *with interchangeable*	
ends	SATEM
interest	INT
interior	INT
interior of Am/eric/a	ERIC
interior of *	incl in *
•horse *in interior of*	
coloured...	HUGGED
interject	
interject a	incl A
interject *	incl *
•'Pla-n', I *interjected*	PLAIN
interminable journey	TRI(p)
intermittent	
intermittent signs of <u>measles</u>	MALE
intern	
intern a...	incl A
intern *	incl *
•Hu-ns *intern* mother	HUMANS
interned by *	incl in *
•mother *interned by*	
Hu-ns	HUMANS
internal	
internal combustion engine	ICE
internal to househ/old	
est/ablishment	OLDEST
internally a...	incl A
internally *	incl *

•carrier *with internal* skin	BASKING
international	INT.CAP.UN
bank	BIS
Development Association	IDA
Electrotechnical Commission	IEC
Finance Corporation	IFC
honour	CAP
Labour Organisation	ILO
Monetary Fund	IMF
Olympic Committee	IOC
organisation	UNO
Phonetic Alphabet	IPA
Publishers' Association	IPA
Publishing Corporation	IPC
Rail Transport	TIF
Road Transport	TIR
Social Services	ISS
Standards Organization	ISO
subscriber dialling	ISD
Telecommunications Union	ITU
Trade Organization	ITO
unit	IU
Vehicle Registration	IVR
interpolate	
interpolate a...	incl A
interpolate *	incl *
•doctor *interpolating* figure is...	LIMBS
interpose	
interpose a...	incl A
interpose *	incl *
•*interpose* it *in* directions	SITE
interpret	
interpret <u>Norse</u>...	NOSER
interpretation of <u>Pali</u>	PAIL
interpreter	INT
interrupt	
interrupted by a...	incl A
interrupted by *	incl *
•hundreds *interrupted by* shout	CHIC
interrupting *	incl in *
•shout *interrupting* hundreds	CHIC
<u>inter</u>section	NITRE.TRINE
intertwined <u>coil</u>	-OLIC
intervene	
intervention of a	incl A
intervention of *	incl *

•*intervention of* men in this *French*...	CEMENT
•student *intervenes in* b-est...	BLEST
interview	
interview royalty	SEEKING
interview servant	SEEPAGE
interwoven	
<u>inter</u>*woven*	NITRE.TRINE
interwoven <u>mesh</u>	HEMS.SHEM
into	
into a mess <u>I ran</u>	RAIN.RANI
into <u>town</u>	WONT
pop *into*	incl PA
•pop *into* Pole's...	SPAN
run *into*	incl R
•run *into* f-og	FROG
see *into*	incl C
•see *into*, s-oon	SCOON
turn *into*	incl GO
•turn *into* a-ny...	AGONY
intoxicated <u>by all</u>...	BALLY
intricate	
intricacy of <u>plot</u> I...	PILOT
intricate <u>design</u>	SIGNED
introduce	
introduced to *	incl in *
•man *introduced to* woman	SUEDE
introducing a...	incl A
introducing *	incl *
•girl *introducing* man	SUEDE
introductions to <u>new</u> owner	NO
intrude	
intruding into *	incl in *
•one *intruding into* party	COIN
invade	
invaded by a...	incl A
invaded by *	incl *
•ship *invaded by* lice	SLICES
invading *	incl in *
•lice *invading* ship	SLICES
invariably	EER
invent	
invented	INV
inventor	EDISON
inverted cheese(D) ↑	MADE
invest	
invest a...	incl A
invest *	incl *

•mother's *investing* £50	MALLS	
invested in *	incl in *	
•£50 *invested in*		
mother's. . .	MALLS	
invitation	CARD	
invoice	INV	
involve		
involved in sc/hem/e	HEM	
involved in *	incl in *	
•me *involved in* state	CAMEL	
involved me *in*. . .	MIEN.MINE	
involving a. . .	incl A	
involving *	incl *	
•state *involving* me	CAMEL	
*in*wards	DRAWS.SWARD	
Iran	IR	
(*see also* Persia)		
Iraq	IRQ	
capital	BAGHDAD.I	
coin	DINAR.FIL	
leader	I	
Ireland	EIRE.ERIN.EMERALD ISLE	
	GREEN ISLE.IR.IR(E)L.	
Irish	IR	
accent	BROGUE	
active person	STIR-ABOUT	
again	AGIN	
agrarian rebel		
—18th c.	WHITEBOY	
—19th c.	MOONLIGHTER	
alphabet	OG(H)AM	
ancient		
—assembly (-blies)	FEIS(EANNA)	
—soldier	FIANN.GALLO(W)GLASS	
—people	TUATH	
—territorial division	TUATH	
anti-British association	FENIAN	
basket	SKEOUGH	
blandish	SOOTHE	
blood-fine	ERIC	
boat	CURRACH.CURRAGH	
booth	BOTHAN	
boy	GORSOON.GOSSOON	
	SPALPEEN	
bridge	FORD.WATERSPLASH	
brownie	LEPRECHAUN	
	LEPRECHAWN	
cajoling talk	BLARNEY	
capital	DUBLIN.I	

carriage	BIANCONI.GINGLE	
	JAUNTING CAR.JAUNTY	
Celtic noble	TOISECH	
characters	IR	
chief's heir-elect	TANIST	
clay pipe	DUDEEN	
clotted milk	BONNY-CLABBER	
club	SHILLALY.SHILLELA(G)H	
coins		
—counterfeit halfpenny	RAP	
—old halfpenny	PATRICK	
—pound	PUNT	
compulsory billeting	SOREHON	
corn	OATS	
counterfeit coin	RAP	
creature	CRATUR	
cudgel	SHILLALY.SHILLELAGH	
currant bun	BARMBRACK	
dance	FADING.PLANXTY	
	RINKAFADDA	
Danish settlers	OSTMEN	
darling	ACUSHLA.ASTHORE	
	MAVOURNEEN	
deer (extinct)	IRISH ELK	
deputy Prime Minister	TANAISTE	
devotee	VOTEEN	
district under English		
rule	(ENGLISH) PALE	
division of		
—county	BARONY	
—tribe	SEPT	
doctor	OLLAM(H).OLLAV	
driver of carriage	JARVEY	
drunk	STOTIOUS	
Dublin society	RDS	
Elysium	TIR NA N-OG	
emblem	SHAMROCK	
enforced billeting	COIGNE	
	COSHERY	
evening social gathering	CEILIDH	
expatriate soldiers	WILD GEESE	
fairy	BANSHEE.BENSHI	
favourite	WHITE-HEADED BOY	
female fairy	BANSHEE	
festival	FEIS(EANNA)	
field	PARK	
flatter	SOOTHE	
flattery	BLARNEY	
flower	SHAMROCK	

fool	OMADHAUN	land	
foot soldier	KERN(E)	—of the young	TIR NA N-OG
fort	RATH	—reform association	
fortified island	CRANNOG		LAND LEAGUE
Free State	IFS	language	CELTIC.ERSE.GAELIC
Gael	GADHEL.GOIDEL		KELTIC
Gaelic	ERSE	lament	ULLALOO
game	HURLEY.HURLING	lane	BOREEN
	SHINTY	leader	I
girl	COLLEEN	limestone	CALP
good		lower chamber (parliament)	
—chap	BROTH OF A BOY		DAIL (EIREANN)
—health!	SLAINTE	madman	OMADHAUN
guard(s)	GARDA(I)	master	OLLAM(H).OLLAV
gypsy cant	SHELTA	measures	
head		—2 feet	BANDLE
—king	ARDRI(GH)	—2240 yards	MILE
—of family	CO(M)ARB	—7840 square yards (old)	ACRE
heath	ST DABEOC'S HEATH	member of	
hero	NAOISE	—Dail	TD.TEACHTA (DALA)
hockey	HURLEY.HURLING	—rebel peasants' gang	WHITEBOY
house	DAIL	Methodist	SWADDLER
hurt badly	KILL	mischievous chap	SPALPEEN
hut	BOTHAN	mocking ballad	LILLIBULLERO
ill fortune	BAD CESS	mud	CLABBER
illegal drinking den	BOTHAN	my child	ALANNAH
illicit		national emblem	SHAMROCK
—whiskey	POT(H)EEN	never	SORRA
—whiskey shop	SHEBEEN	nickname	PAT.TEAGUE
indeed	AROO.ARU	no!	SORRA
interjection of		not	SORRA
—emotion	ARRAH	oath	BEDAD.BEGORRA(H)
—sorrow	O(C)HONE		BEJABERS
—surprise	MUSHA	old	
invite argument		—laws	BREHON LAWS
	TRAIL ONE'S COAT	—mayor	SOVRAN
Ireland forever	ERIN GO BRAGH	—Protestants	PEEP-O'-DAY BOYS
Irishman	BOG-TROTTER.GREEK	order of hierarchy	TANISTRY
	MICK(E)Y.PADDY.PAT	outlaw	WOODKERN
Irish-speaking		parliament	OIREACHTAS
region	GAELTACHT	—lower chamber	DAIL (EIREANN)
jaunting car	INSIDE-CAR	—upper chamber	
	OUTSIDE-CAR		SEANAD (EIREANN)
—driver	JARVEY	penniless gentleman	STALKO
jocose	JOCOROUS	people	TUATH
judge	BREHON	pet	WHITE-HEADED BOY
killed	KILT	petty squire	SQUIREEN
lake	LOUGH	plunderer	RAPPAREE
—dwelling	CRANNOG	police	GARDA SIOCHANA.RUC

—man	GARDA
—men	GARDAI
political parties	FIANNA FAIL
	FINE GAEL.SINN FEIN
politician	TD.TEACHTA (DALA)
porridge	STIR-ABOUT
potato	MURPHY.PRATIE.PRATY
prime minister	TAOISEACH
protestant	SWADDLER
rascal	SPALPEEN
rebel	CROPPY
Republican	
—Army	IRA
—Brotherhood	IRB
rivers	LIFFEY.SHANNON
robber	RAPPAREE
salt marsh	CORCASS
script	OG(H)AMIC.OGMIC
shale bed	CALP
shinty	CAMANACHD
—stick	CAMAN
sorcery	PISHOGUE
sorrow	SORRA
stew	COLCANNON
story teller	SE(A)NNACHIE
	SEANNACHY.SHANACHIE
stream	STREEL
stringed instrument	TYMPAN
sub	
—let	CO(R)NACRE
—tenant	WELDER
sweetheart	GRA
television service	RTE
tenant	COTTIER
tenure	SOREHON.TANISTRY
term of derision	SORRA
—to woman	STRAP
terrorists	IRA
trail	STREEL
transport organisation	CIE
tribal law	CINEL
Trinity College	TCD
trout	GILLAROO
United Ireland	FINE GAEL
upper chamber (parliament)	
	SEANAD (EIREANN)
usurer	GOMBEEN-MAN
usury	GOMBEEN
verse	RANN

wander	STREEL
warder	CORKSCREW
water-plant	PIPEWORT
whiskey	POT(H)EEN
	THE CRATUR.USQUEBAUGH
young lad	BUCKO
iron¹	FE
hence	
•gold *and* iron	ORFE
•iron *in* loa-d	LOAFED
•iron man	FETED.FEMALE
iron²	CLUB.PRESS
iron hand	LAUNDRY WORKER
iron rations	HARD TACK
	STAPLE DIET
Ironside	EDMUND
ironside	HARDSHIP
irregular verb, English	BREVE
irreversible letter of credit	ILC
irritate	
irritate(D) ↑	BUR
irritated these...	SHEET
irritation of horse's...	SHORES
is	
is *about*	SI
is *about*	I-S
is English	-ISE
is *found in*...	incl IS
•is *found in* poem	EPISODE
* *found in*	incl *
•he *is found in* c-ap	CHEAP
is *French*	EST
is *German*	IST
is hard	-ISH
is *in France*	EST
is *in Germany*	IST
is *in Spain*	ES
is *in* time	DAISY
is no...	ISO-
is not	AINT.ANT
is not considerate	DESECRATION
is nothing	ISO-
is *removed*	omit IS
•hagg(is) is *removed*...	HAGG
* *is removed from*	omit *
•he *is removed from*	
c(he)ap...	CAP
is *Spanish*	ES
is *taking* time	-IST

Isaiah	IS(A)
Islam(ic)	(see Moslem)
island	AIT.CRETE.EYOT.I(S).INCH
	IOM.IONA.IS.MAN.MONA
island king	SOLOMON
island *retreat*⟨	ABLE
Isle of Man	GBM.IOM
Isle of Wight	IOW.IW
our islands	GB
this island	UK
Israeli	(see Hebrew)
issue	LITTER.SON
issue shares	SHEARS
it	SA.T
it appears plain	PLANE
(i)t is *short*	T
it sounds like rain	REIGN.REIN
it's *broken*	-IST.TIS
it's *free*	-IST.TIS
it's *rough*	-IST.TIS
it's *wrong*	-IST.TIS
Italian¹	IT
hence	
•Italian *and* English	
share	ITERATION
•Italian church	ITCH
•Italian letters	ITEMS
Italian²	AUSONIAN
	EYETI(E).EYTIE
afternoon	POMERIGGIO
à la carte	AL CONTO
again	ANCORA
agreement	SI
all right	VA BENE
ancient	ANTICO
—language	OSCAN.SAMNITE
—people	OSCAN.SAMNITE
applause	VIVA
approval	SI
articles	GLI.I.IL.LA.LE.LO
	UN(O).UNA
artist's studio	BOTTEGA
aside	SOTTO VOCE
at	
—first sight	A PRIMA VISTA
—most	AL PIU
bagpipes	PIFFERO.ZAMPOGNA
baked dough covered with	
tomatoes, etc.	PIZZA

bakery	PANIFICIO.PANETTERIA
balcony	BALCONE.TERRAZZO
ball	PALLA
—game	PALLONE
barge	BARCA
bas relief	BASSO-RILIEVO
beat	BATTUTA
bird	BECCAFICO
black	NERO
—pudding	SANGUINACCIO
boat	BARCA.GONDOLA
—song	BARCAROLA
borough	BORGO
bound	LEGATO
boy	RAGAZZO
brazier	SCALDINO
bread	PANE
—rolls	PANINI
brother	FRA(TELLO)
burial ground	CAMPOSANTO
by	
—fits and starts	A SALTI
capital	I.ROME
car	MACCHINA
carriage	VETTURA
—procession	CORSO
carved chest	CASSONE
cathedral	DUOMO
characters	IT
cheeses	BEL PAESE.MOZZARELLA
	RICOTTO.STRACCHINO
	(see also cheese)
chief magistrate	GONFALONIERE
child	BAMBINA.BAMBINO
circuit	CONTORNO
clerk	SCRIVANO
coins	
—unit	L.LIRA
—Florentine	FLORIN
—silver	DUCAT.SCUDO
—old	AMBROSIN.SOLDO
	TESTOON
—old Papal	PAOLO
comic opera	BURLETTA
	OPERA BUFFA
company	GIA.COMPAGNIA
confused situation	IMBROGLIO
congenial	SIMPATICO
contour	CONTORNA

contract	APPALTO
cop	SBIRRO
council meeting	CONSULTA
councillors	ANZIANI
courage!	CORAGGIO
courgettes	ZUCCHINI
course	CORSO
criminal society	COSA NOSTRA
	MAF(F)IA
cup	TAZZA
dance	BERGAMASK
	BERGOMASK.RIGOLETTO
	TARANTELLA.VOLTA
dash	BRAVURA
day	GIORNO
dear	CARA.CARO
device	IMPRESA
dictator	IL DUCE
dish	PASTA.PIZZA.RISOTTO
	(see also pasta below)
do nothing	FAR NIENTE
doctor	MEDICO
double speed	
	DOPPIO MOVIMENTO
drinking song	BRINDISI
driver of carriage	VETTURINO
duel	DUELLO
earth	TERRA
Easter cake	PASTIERA
easygoing	SCIOLTO
employer	PADRONE
enamel decoration	SMALTO
encore	ANCORA
enough	BASTA
essence	ALMA
evening	SERA
evil eye	JETTATURA
face to face	A QUATTR'OCHI
farm	FATTORIA.PODERE
father	PADRE
fencing move	IMBROCCATA
festival	FESTA
field	CAMPO
fifteenth century	
	QUATTROCENTO
firm to the teeth	AL DENTE
first	PRIMA.PRIMO
fish	
—soup	BRODETTO

—stew	BURIDDA
fixed rate	AL PASTO
fizzy	FRIZZANTE
flour	FARINA
—dough	PASTA
flowering	FIORITURA
flute	ZUF(F)OLO
folk tales	LEGGENDE POPOLARE
—collection	PENTAMERON
follows	SEGUE
fool	CAPOCCHIA
forward!	AVANTI
four hundred	QUATTROCENTO
fourteenth century	TRECENTO
fresh	FRESCO
friar	FRA(TE)
friars	FRATI
gallant	CAVALIERE SERVENTE
garden warbler	BECCAFICO
girl	RAGAZZA
good	BENE
—bye	ADDIO.A(R)RIVEDERCI
—day	BUON GIORNO
—evening	BUONA SERA
—night	BUONA NOTTE
goose	OCA
government	QUIRINALE
granite	MIAROLO
great	GRAN
gypsy man	ZINGARO
—woman	ZINGARA
hand	MANO
headman	CAPITANO
hell	INFERNO
here (it) is	ECCO (LO)
hero	GARIBALDI
high fashion	ALTA MODA
highness	ALTEZZA
holiday	FESTA
hors d'oeuvre	ANTIPASTO
house	CASA
imitation stone	SCAGLIOLA
in	
—an undertone	SOTTO VOCE
—devotional manner	RELIGIOSO
—French style	ALLA FRANCA
—fugue style	FUGATO
—German style	ALLA TEDESCA
—marching style	ALLA MARCIA

—one's mind	IN PETTO		middle	MEZZO
—strict time	A BATTUTA		miss	SIGNORINA
—the breast	IN PETTO		mister	SIGNOR
—time	A TEMPO		model sculpture	BOZETTO
—white	IN BIANCO		modernising	AGGIORNAMENTO
indifferent	POCOCURANTE		monopoly	APPALTO
informal hello or goodbye	CIAO		more	PIU
inn	ALBERGO		morning	MATTINA
—keeper	PADRONE		most illustrious	ILLUSTRISSIMO
inspiration	ESTRO		mother	MADRE
instrument	CHITARRONE		motor	
king	RE		—boat	MOTOSCAFO
lady	DONNA.SIGNORA		—way	AUTOSTRADA
lake	LAGO		motto	IMPRESA
landlord	PADRONE		mount	MONTARE
large village	BORGHETTO		mountain troops	ALPINI
leader	DUCE.I		mouth	BOCCA
leading			much	MOLTO
—dancer			mural drawing	(S)GRAFFITO
PRIMA BALLERINA (ASSOLUTA)			my lady	MADONNA
—singer			Neapolitan	
PRIMA DONNA (ASSOLUTA)			—dance	TARANTELLA
leper hospital	LAZARET(TO)		—secret society	CAMORRA
life of luxury	DOLCE VITA		night	NOTTE
limestone	SCAGLIA		noble blood	BEL SANGUE
little	POCO		nonchalant	POCOCURANTE
—by little	POCO A POCO		not so fast	MENO MOSSO
liveliness	BRIO		official prosecutor	AVVOGADORE
madman	PAZZO FURIOSO		or	O.OSSIA
mafia	COSA NOSTRA		orange	ARANCIA
magistrate (old)	PODESTA		painting technique	ALLA PRIMA
maize porridge	POLENTA		pasta dishes	CANNELLONI
male			LASAGNE.RAVIOLI	
—exhibitionist	FUSTO		SPAGHETTI (BOLOGNESE)	
—soprano	CASTRATO		TORTELLINI	
marchioness	MARCHESA		pasta types	
mark	MARCARE		—bows	FIOCHETTI
marquis	MARCHESE		—butterflies	FARFALLE
master	MAESTRO		—coin-shaped	CORZETTI
meal	PRANZO		—corkscrews	FUSILLI
measure (cubit)	BRACCIO		—curls	CASARECCI
meat			—dumplings	GNOCCHI
—balls	POLPETTE		—elbows	TUBETTI LUNGHI
—rolls	INVOLTINI		—pipes	CANNELLONI.MACARONI
medieval drama	LAUDA		—quills	PENNE
medium relief	MEZZO-RELIEVO		—ribbed tubes	RIGATONI
melancholy	PENSIEROSO		—ribbons	FETTUCINE
mercenary captain	CONDOTTIERE			TAGLIATELLE
merry fellow	L'ALLEGRO		—rings	ANELLI

—ruffled ribbons	LASAGNETTE
—sheets	LASAGNE
—shells	CONCHIGLIE
—small	BUCATINI
—butterflies	FARFALLINI
—spinsters	ZITI
—spiral	TROFIE
—stars	STELLINE
—strings	SPAGHETTI
—stuffed	PANSOTI.RAVIOLI
—thin	ANGEL'S HAIR.CAPELLINI
	VERMICELLI
—ribbons	TAGLIARINI
—twists	SPIRALE
—wheels	ROUT(IN)E
peasant	CONTADINO
pensive person	IL PENSEROSO
perpetual motion	
	MOTO PERPETUO
pie	PIZZA
pleasant indolence	
	DOLCE FAR NIENTE
please	PER FAVORE.PER PIACERE
poem	L'INFERNO
poet	DANTE.TASSO
policeman	SBIRRO.CARBINIERE
political unification	
	RISORGIMENTO
Pomeranian dog	VOLPINO
popular comedy	
	COMMEDIA DELL'ARTE
post-free	FRANCO
pottery	MAIOLICA.MAJOLICA
puppets	FANTOCCINI
quicker	PIU MOSSO
quickly!	PRESTO
race	CORSO
refusal	NON
relief	RILIEVO
relish of fish roe	BOTARGO
restaurant	PIZZERIA
	RISTORANTE.TRATTORIA
revamping of musical/literary	
work	RIFACIMENTO
revival	RISORGIMENTO
rice dish	RISOTTO
rifleman	BERSAGLIERE
rightwinger	FASCISTA
river	FIUME

rivers	ARNO.PO.TIBER
run	CORSO
sad	MESTO
saint's day	FESTA
score in music	PARTITURA
second	SECONDO
secret society	CAMORRA
	COSA NOSTRA
	COMORRA.MAF(F)IA
serious opera	OPERA SERIA
sharpshooter	BERSAGLIERE
short verse form	STORNELLO
singing style	BEL CANTO
sixteenth century	CINQUECENTO
skull cap	ZUCHETTA.ZUCHETTO
sliding	GLISSANDO
slow	LENTO
small group	GRUPETTO
social gathering	CONVERSAZIONE
soldier	BERSAGLIERE
	SOLDATURA
soul	ALMA
soup	BRODO.MINESTRONE
	MINESTRA.ZUPPA
spade	PALETTA
sparkling	FRIZZANTE
spiced sausage(s)	
	SALAME (SALAMI)
spirit	BRIO
square	PIAZZA
state pawnshop	MONTE DI PIETA
stew	OSSOBUCO
storm	BORASCO
street	CALLE.CORSO
	STRADA.VIA
stringed instrument	PANDURA
sucking pig	PORCHETTA
supreme commander	
	GENERALISSIMO
sweet dish	ZABAGLIONE
taste	GUSTO
tangle	IMBROGLIO
tear	LACRIMA.LAGRIMA
terrace	TERRAZZO
thank you	GRAZIE
there	ECCO
thick application of	
paint	IMPASTO
three strings	TRE CORDE

thrusting	ALLA STOCCATA	well	BENE
time	TEMPO	—done	BEN FATTO
tip	B(U)ONAMANA	—found	BEN TROVATO
title of rank	MONSIGNOR(E)	—known	BEN NOTO
toast	BRINDISI	what	CHE
too much	TROPPO	wine	VINO
touchstone	PARAGONE		(*see also* drink)
touring car	GRANTURISMO	—shop	BOTTEGA
trio	TERZETTO	with	CON
turn	VOLTA	—fire	CON FUOCO
under (one's) breath		—grief	CON DOLORE
	SOTTO VOCE	—love	CON AMORE
uninterested	POCOCURANTE	—movement	CON MOTO
unknown	INCOGNITO	—spirit	CON BRIO.SPIRITOSO
value	VALUTA	wood inlay	INTARSIA.INTARSIO
vermouth	IT	woodcock	BECCACCIA
verse form	TERZA RIMA	zest	GUSTO
very	MOLTO	**Italy**	I
—earnestly	CON AMORE	**item of make-up**	CHROMOSOME
vivacity	BRIO		GENE
warbler	BECCAFICO	**Ivory Coast**	CI
weight (variable)	ROTOLO	**ivy,** *say*	IV

J

curve. heat. Jack. Japan. *jay.* joule. judge. justice. *knave.* one. pen. square root of -1

Jack	J.KITTY.KNAVE	commander in chief	SHOGUN(AL)
	(*see also* sailor)		TYCOON
Jack's wedding	UNION	conifer	UMBRELLA FIR
jade	YU	court	DAIRO.DARI
jagged scar	CARS	current	KUROSHIO
jailed	(in) C-AGE.(in) PE-N	dancing girl	GEISHA
Jamaican	JA	deer	SIKA
capital	J.KINGSTON	deities	(*see* gods.goddesses)
bark	CARIBBEE BARK	demi-god	KAMI
cedar	BARBADOS CEDAR	dish	SUKIYAKI.SUSHI
drink	RUM	drama	KABUKI.NOGAKU.NO(H)
ebony	COCUS-WOOD	dwarf tree	BONSAI
leader	J	elder statesmen	GENRO
pepper	ALLSPICE	emperor	MIKADO.TENNO
plum	HOG-PLUM	enamel ware	SHIPPO
James	JAS	fan	OGI
jammed cylinder	SWISS ROLL	fastener	NETSUKE
January	JAN	female entertainer	GEISHA
Japan	J.NIPPON.VARNISH	fencing	IAIDO
Japanese	JAP	feudal code of honour	BUSHIDO
abacus	SOROBAN	fish	AYU.FUGU
aboriginal race	AINO.AINU		CARP.GOLDFISH
aeroplane	ZERO	floor mat of straw	TATAMI
airline	JAL	flower arranging	IKEBANA
alphabet	KATAKANA	flowering tree	CATALPA.CHERRY
armorial device	MON	fruit	LOQUAT.KAKI
baron	DAIMIO	game	GO
bean	ADZUKI	garment	(KI)MONO
box	INRO	gentle way	JUDO
boxing	KEMPO	gentry	SHIZOKU
Buddhist sect	SOKA GAKKAI.ZEN	girdle	OBI
calligraphy	SHODO	girl	MOUSME(E)
cane	WHANGEE	god	KAMI
capital	J.TOKYO	gold foil work	KIRIKANE
carriage	JINRICKISHA	goodbye	SAYONARA
	(JIN)RICKSHA(W)	grass	WHANGEE
cedar	SUGI	grotesque figurine	MAGOT
cherry	FUJI	guitar	S(H)AMISEN
chrysanthemum badge	KIKUMON	helmet	JINGASA
church	TERA	horseradish	WASABI
coins		image	ZO
—unit	SEN	informal feeling out	NEMAWASHI
—100 sen	Y.YEN.YN	inlay work	ZOGAN
—old gold	COPANG.KOBAN(G)	ivy	UDO
	OBANG	jelly	KANTEN

judo	
—costume	JUDOGI
—expert	JUDOKA
knife	KOZUKA
lacquer	URUSHI
—work	KANAGAI
—ware	NURIMONO
language	AINU
laurel	AUCUBA JAPONICA
leader	J
lord	KAMI
low caste	ETA.HEIMIN
martial art	AIKIDO.JUDO
	J(I)U-JITSU.JUJUTSU
	KARATE.KENDO
mat	TATAMI
measures	
—1 inch	SUN
—1 foot	SHAKU
—2 yards	KEN
—120 yards	CHO
—2½ miles	RI
—4 square yards	TSUBO
—¼ peck	SHO
—5 bushels	KOKU
—4 gallons	TO
medicine chest	INRO
medlar	LOQUAT
Mikado's palace	DAIRI
military	
—caste	SAMURAI
—ruler	SHOGUN
musical	
—drama	KABUKI
—instrument	KOTO
narrow print	HASHIRA
noble	DAIMIO.KUGE
orange	SATSUMA
ornament	NETSUKE
outcast	RONIN
palanquin	KAGO.NORIMON
paper	
—folding art	ORIGAMI
—screen	SHOJI
patina	SABI
persimmon	KAKI
pinball game	PACHINKO
plant	HOSTA.KUDZU
play	NO(H)

plum	UMEBOSHI
poem	HAIKAI.HAIKU.HOKKO
—with five lines	LINKED VERSE
	RENGA.TANKA
pottery	KYOTO
	SATSUMA WARE
province	SATSUMA
puppet theatre	BUNRAKU
quince	CYDONIA JAPONICA
	PYRUS JAPONICA
radish	DAIKON
raincoat	MINO
raspberry	WINE-BERRY
raw fish	SASHIMI
religion	BUDDHISM
	SHINTO(ISM)
rice beer	SAKE.SAKI
robe	KIMONO
root binding	NEMAWASHI
rose	KERRIA
royal badge	KIKUMON.KIRIMON
ruler	MIKADO
salmon	MASU
salutation	BANZAI
sash	OBI
script	KAKEMONO.KANA
scroll	MAKIMONO
sea bream	TAI
seaweed	KO(M)BU
ship	MARO.MARU
shrub	KERRIA
sliding partition	SHOJI
sport	SUMO
street	GINZA
sudden revelation	SATORI
suicide	HARAKARI.HARAKIRI
	SEPPUKU
—attempt	KAMIKAZE
sword	
—fighting	KENDO
—hilt	TSUBA
syllabary	KATAKANA
tea ceremony	CHANOYU
temple gateway	TORII
tidal wave	TSUNAMI
title	KAMI
tree	GINGKO.GINKGO.LOQUAT
	MAIDENHAIR TREE
	PAULOWNIA.RED-LAC.TSUGA

unarmed martial art	J(I)U-JITSU
waitress	MOUSME(E)
wall-hanging	KAKEMONO
war cry	BANZAI
warm current	KUROSHIO
warrior class	SAMURAI
weights	
—1 ounce	RIO
—1½ lbs	CATTY.KIN
—8 lbs	KWAN
wood block	YOKO
wooden shoes	GETA
wrestling	SUMO
writing system	KANA
jaunt in Wye	WINEY
Javanese	JAV
badger	STINKARD.TELEDU
capital	DJAKARTA.J
bird	JAVA SPARROW
leader	J
man	PITHECANTHROPUS
plum	JAMBOLANA
tree	ANTIAR.UPAS
weapon	TOMBO.TOMBOC
jay	J
jazz	
jazz fan	CAT
jazz figure	RIFF
jelly	
jellied	SET
jellied eel	LEE
jelly	GELIGNITE.SHAPE
Jeremiah	JER
jerky stride	DIREST
Jerry	
•for *Jerry's*. . .	FUR
•*Jerry's* house	HAUS
•with *Jerry's*. . .	MIT
Jersey	GBJ.PULLOVER
Jesus	IHC.IHS.JC.JHC
	(*see also* Christ)
jet set	AIR CREW
Jewish	(*see* Hebrew)
jilt	
jilted bride	BIDER
jilted Delia	AILED
jittery	
jittery leader	DEALER
jittery *leader*	J

j-jaguar	JOUNCE
job	
job description	PATIENT
job-finder	DEVIL.SATAN
jockey's lawyers	SILKS
Joe's double	GIGI
Joel	JO
jogging	
jogging arm	MAR.RAM
the pony is *jogging*	HYPNOTISE
John	JNO
join	
join a chief	ACID
join an orchestra	ALSO
joiner	AND.HYPHEN.SNUG
joint	DIVE.ELBOW.KNEE.REEFER
Joint Matriculation Board	JMB
jokingly ingest. . .	J-EST
jolly	
jolly	MARINE.RM
hence	
•a jolly old fellow	ARMAGEDDON
•in jolly style	ALARM
•laugh *and have* jolly. . .	HARM
jolly fellow	ROGER
jolted arm	MAR.RAM
Jonathan's bearer	APPLE TREE
Jordan	HKJ
capital	AMMAN.J
coin	DINAR.FIL
leader	J
joule	J
journalist	ED
journey	
journey after dark, *say*	NITRIDE
Journey's End	DESTINATION
journey's end	Y
journeyman	GULLIVER
	ODYSSEUS
joyful cry	IO
judge	HEAR.J
judge's chauffeur	
	MASTER OF THE ROLLS
judge's condition	SOBER
	SOBRIETY
Judges	JUD(G)
juggle plates	PALEST.PETALS
	STAPLE
July	JUL

jumble sale	ALES.SEAL
jump	
jump over	ROVE
jump up	
•dog *jumps up*(D) ↑	GOD
jumper CRICKET.FLEA.JERSEY	
KANGAROO.PULLOVER	
jumper store FLEA MARKET	
jumping bean	BANE
jumping deer⟨	REED
jumpy soldier PARA(TROOPER)	
junction	T
junction of a line	ALINE
June	JUN
June 6th	D-DAY

June 25th	LONGEST DAY
MIDSUMMER.SOLSTICE	
junior	JUN(R).JR
junior common room	JCR
junior minister	CURATE
just	
just a bit of bro/ken t/ableware	
KENT
just characters	FOUR MEN
just characters, *say*	FOREMEN
just fine	FAIR
justice	FREEZING.J
Justice's clerk	JC
Justice of the Peace	JP

K

constant. kalium. kappa. kay. *Kay*. kelvin. Khmer Republic. kilo. king.
Kirkpatrick. knight. Kochel. *monarch*. Mozart's works. potassium.
Scarlatti's works. thousand. twenty. two-hundred and fifty.
twenty thousand. vitamin

K9	CANINE	**kick**	
kale	KL	kick off	KO
kaleidoscopic lights	SLIGHT	kick *out*	HA-CK
kappa	K	**kidnapper**	PARIS
Kay	K	**kill**[1]	
keeling over, Ben...⟨	NEB	algae	ALGICIDE
keep		babies	INFANTICIDE
keep quiet	incl P or SH	bacteria	BACTERICIDE
•Ro-y *keeps* quiet	ROPY		GERMICIDE
•Mar-y *keeps* quiet	MARSHY	birds	AVICIDE
Keeper of the Privy Seal	CPS	brother	FRATRICIDE
keeping a...	incl A	children	FILICIDE.INFANTICIDE
keeping *	incl *	environment	ECOCIDE
•man *keeping* girl	MAIDAN	father	PATRICIDE
keeps mum	SAY-SO	f(o)etus	F(O)ETICIDE
kept (in) by *	incl in *	fox	VULPICIDE
•girl *kept in by* man	MAIDAN	fungus	FUNGICIDE
•girl *kept by* parents	PANORAMA	giant	GIGANTICIDE
Kelly's eye	I.ONE	god	DEICIDE
kelvin	K	humanity	PROLICIDE
kennel club	KC	insects	INSECTICIDE
Kensington district	WEIGHT	king	REGICIDE
Kent	SE	larvae	LARVICIDE
Kenya	EAK	mind (brainwashing)	MENTICIDE
	(*see* Africa(n))	mites	ACARICIDE
kept	(*see* keep)	mother	MATRICIDE
kewpie (doll)	QP	parasites	PARASITICIDE
key[1]	A.B.C.D.E.F.G	parents	PARRICIDE
hence		pest	PESTICIDE
•key hole	DO.GO	plants	HERBICIDE
•key note	ATE	poet	VATICIDE
•key points	AS.ASS.BE.BEE.EWE	prophet	VATICIDE
•key ring	DO.GO	protozoa	TRYPANOCIDE
•key-stone	COPAL	race	GENOCIDE
•key *to* room	EDEN	rats	RODENTICIDE
•two keys *with* lock	ACTRESS	reputation	FAMICIDE
key[2]		rodents	RODENTICIDE
key	CAY	seaweed	ALGICIDE
key (batsman)	OPENER	self	SUICIDE
key figures	EX.EMIL.CIVIC	sheep	OVICIDE
key personnel	SKELETON STAFF	sister	SORICIDE
key-worker	CAYMAN	tyrant	TYRANNICIDE
PIANO TUNER.TYPIST		vine	VITICIDE

319

virus	VIRICIDE	king's constitution	COLESLAW
weeds	HERBICIDE.WEEDICIDE	King's Counsel	KC
wife	UXORICIDE	king's rule	COLESLAW
worms	VERMICIDE	kingly men	REGAL.ROYAL
kill²		old king	COLE.OG
kill ruler, *say*	SLAKING	Sun King	LOUIS
killer	CAIN	**king⁴**	
kilo	K	Charles I	C
kind of <u>animal</u>	LAMINA	Charles II	H
king¹		Edward III	W
king-like	ASKING	George IV	R
slim ruler	THINKING	Henry	Y
royal yacht	KINGSHIP	**Kipling's work**	IF
king²	CR.ER.GR.HM	**Kirkpatrick**	K
	K.LEAR.R	kiss	BUSS.X
hence		kite	BUS.PLANE
•king at work	CROP	**k-kip**	KNAP
•king has...	CROWNS	**KN**	CAYENNE
•king I see	CRISPY	**knew**	
and		knew (old)	WIST
•king at home, OK	ERINYES	knew, *say*	GNU.NEW
•king goes home, *say*	ERGOSOME	**knife**	
•King-rat with a...	ERRATA	African	PANGA
and		American	BOWIE KNIFE
•king and heir	GRANDSON		TOOTH-PICK
•king with no ship	GROSS	Burmese	DA(H).DHAR
•king with one son	GRISON		DOUT.DOW
and		Cuban	MACHETE
•king-fish	KEEL	dagger	
•king in fear, *say*	KINDRED	—narrow-bladed	MISERICORD(E)
•king with nothing to...	KOTO		STILET(TO).STYLET
and		—old	BASELARD.PUNCHEON
•king is dead	LATER	—Roman	SICA
•king-bird	REGRET	—small	BODKIN.DIRK
•king in debt	ROWING		DUDGEON.PONIARD
and			WHINGER.WINIARD
•two kings dine at home	KREATIN		WINYARD
king³		Dutch	SNEE
Cockney king	PEARLIE.PEARLY	fighting knife	SNICKERSNEE
King Charles	CR	folding knife	CLASP KNIFE
King Edward	ER.LEAR.LEARNED		JACK-KNIFE
king-emperor	RI	—Scottish	JOCKTELEG
King George	GR	French	COUTEAU
king of Bashan	OG	German	MESSER
king of France	ROI.SM	Gurkha	KUKRI
King William	WR	heavy knife	DA
king's associate	ANNA	Highland	DIRK.SGIAN (DHU)
King's Bench	KB		SKEAN (DHU)
King's College	KC	Indian	KUTTAR

Italian	COLTELLO
Japanese	KOZUKA
large	CUTTO(E)
leatherworker's knife	
	MOON-KNIFE
Malay CREASE.CREESE.KRIS	
	KREESE.PARANG
midshipman's knife	DIRK
Persian	HAN(D)JAR
Philippine	BOLO
Scottish	DIRK.GULLEY
SGIAN (DHU).SKEAN(DHU)	
SKEAN (OCCLE)	
short two-edged knife AN(E)LACE	
Sikh	KIRPAN
slang	CHIV.SHIV
Spanish	CUCHILLO
Turkish ATAGHAN.YATAG(H)AN	
knight	K.KT.N.SIR
Knight Bachelor	KB
knight bachelor,	
I'm told	SURCINGLE
Knight Commander of the	
—Bath	KCB
—British Empire	KBE
Knight Grand Cross of	
—Hanover	GCH
—the Bath	GCB
—the British Empire	GBE
Knight of	
—Labour	KL
—Malta	KM
—the Bath	KB
—the Legion of Honour	KLH
—the Order of the Garter	KG
—the Thistle	KT
knitting a scarf	FRACAS
knock	
knock *back*⟨	PAR.PAT
knock back drink⟨	REGAL
knock it *back*⟨	TI
knock over pins⟨	SNIP
knock*about*	PA-T.RA-P.TA-P
knock*about*⟨	PAR.PAT
knockdown prices	PRECIS
knockout	KO
knot	KN
knotted ties	SITE
knotty timber	BETRIM.TIMBRE
knowledge	-OLOGY
(*see* study[2].write[3])	
Köchel	K
Korea	ROK
airline	KAL
capital	K.SEOUL
coin	HWAN.WON
house	WON
leader	K
martial art	HAPKIDO
TAEKWONDO.TANG SOO DO	
kreutzer	KR
krone	KR
Kuala Lumpur	KL
Kuwait	KWT

L

angle. apprentice. corner. driver. el. *elevated railway.* ell. fifty. fifty thousand. half century. hand. inductance. *Labour.* lake. lambda. lambert. Latin. latitude. league. learner. *learning.* left. length. Liberal. licentiate. *line.* libra. library. lira. lire. litre. long. lumen. luminance. Luxembourg. *many. new driver. novice. number plate. overhead railway.* port. pound. *pupil. right angle.* side. student. tyro. vitamin

£1	LI
£s	LL
label	TAB.TAG
laboratory	LAB
labour	LAB
labour leader	FOREMAN
Labour leader	ATTLEE
Labour *leader*	L
l̄abour movement	CONTRACTION
labour pains	EFFORT
Labour Party	LP
Labour's record	BOOK OF JOB
lack foresight	LOOK AFTER
lacking[1]	
lacking a...	omit A
lacking dash	MINUS
lacking finish	omit last letter
lacking nothing	omit O
lacking one	omit I
lacking sex appeal	omit IT or SA
lacking the right...	omit R or RT
lacking *	omit *
mot(her)'s *lacking* her...	MOTS
lacking[2]	NO
hence	
•*lacking* direction	NOSE
•*lacking* medicine	NODOSE
•*lacking* money	NOCENT
lacking[3]	(*see* without[2])
ladder	RUN
ladderman	JACOB
lady	DAME.EVE.LUCK
	SHE.TRAMP
Ladies' Gold Union	LGU
ladies' magazine	POWDER ROOM
lady bookmaker	AUTHORESS
	RUTH
Lady Day	LD
lady-in-waiting	
EXPECTANT MOTHER	
Lady of the Lake	CONSTANCE

lady's	HER
hence	
•lady's a...	HERA
•lady's clothes, *say*	HIRSUTE
•lady's on trains	HERONRY
lady's maid	ABIGAIL
ladybird	HEN.PEN.SALTERN
laid	
laid *back*⟨	DIAL
laid up	(in) B-ED.(in) CO-T
laid *up*(D) ↑	DIAL
laid out in the...	THINE
lake	ERIE.L.LOCH
	WATER COLOUR
lamb	
Lamb (Charles Lamb)	ELIA
lamb lover	ELIAN
lambda	L
lambert	L
Lamentations	LAM
land[1]	
land girls	WLA
Land of Hope	RURITANIA
land of rest	BEULAH
land of the wizard	OZ
landline	BR.RLY.RY
landlocked	(in) L-AND
	(in) EST-ATE
land[2]	
landing on(D) indicates one word	
written above another:	
•soft *landing on* flower(D)	PROSE
language	
language buff	POLISH
language refinement	POLISH
languish	LYDIA
Laos	LAO
coin	KIP
leader	L
lap	
lap a...	incl A

lap *	incl *
•wa-ter *lapping round*	
one...	WAITER
lapped by *	incl in *
•one *being lapped by*	
wa-ter	WAITER
large[1]	OS
hence	
•large duck	OSTEAL
•large tin	OSCAN
•large vehicle	OSCAR
large[2]	
large girl	BIGAMY
large head	BIGNESS
large letters	OS
large needle-case	HAYSTACK
large number	ARMY.D.M.NATION
large part of c/once/rt	ONCE
large part of many...	MAN.ANY
large stand	GREAT BEAR
large sum	IMPOUNDS
largely wast(ed)	WAST
last[1]	END
hence	
•last debtor	ENDOWER
•last man	ENDED
•way *to* last...	SEND.WEND
last[2]	
last characters in Aida	DA
last laugh	H
last man	N
last month	H
last of the Mohicans	S
last straw	W
last[3]	
last drink	HEMLOCK
last in, first out	LIFO
last in, last out	LILO
last letter	OMEGA.Z
last man	COBBLER.SHOEMAKER
last month	DEC.ULT(IMO)
last object	END
last offer	HOLD OUT
last of the beef	OXTAIL
last vehicle	HEARSE
last word(s)	AMEN.OBIT
	RIP.EPITAPH
late	EX
	(*see also* old[3])

late opening	POST MORTEM
late *shift*	LEAT.TAEL.TALE.TEAL
later *model*	ALTER.RATEL
later message	PS
later postscript	PPS
Latin[1]	L.LAT.ROMAN
hence	
•Latin in church	LINCH
•Latin is part...	LISSOME
•Latin poem	LODE
and	
•Latin queen	LATER
•Latin *in* the Home	
Counties	SLATE
•strong Latin...	FLAT
and	
•Latin church	ROMANCE
•Latin letter	ROMANY
Latin[2]	
abandoned suit	NOLI PROSEQUI
about	CIRCA
absolute power	IMPERIUM
abyss	BARATHRUM
acceptable person	
	PERSONA GRATA
accidentally	EX ACCIDENTI
according to	SECUNDUM
—circumstances	PRO RE NATA
—prayer	EX VOTO
—the requirements of the	
case	E(X) RE NATA
achievements	RES GESTAE
acquittance	QUIETUS
action	SUIT
—by informer	QUI TAM
actual	DE FACTO
administrative board	COLLEGIUM
adorn	ORNARE
after the manner	AD MODUM
—of our ancestors	
	MORE MAJORUM
against	CONTRA.V.VS.VERSUS
—the world	CONTRA MUNDUM
agreeable	GRATUM
all	OMNIS
—go out	EXEUNT OMNES
—that sort	HOC GENUS OMNE
alternately	ALTERNIS VICIBUS
always	SEMPER

—faithful   SEMPER FIDELIS
—prepared   SEMPER PARATUS
—the same   SEMPER IDEM
amateur musicians
               COLLEGIUM MUSICUM
amicable arrangement
                    MODUS VIVENDI
among
—other people   INTER ALIOS
—other things   INTER ALIA
—themselves   INTER SE
and   AC.ATQUE.ET
—all that sort of thing
          ET HOC GENUS OMNE
—other people   ET AL.ET ALII
—other things   ET AL.ET ALIA
—so forth   ETC.ET CETERA
—the following   ET SEQUENS
—the rest   ETC.ET CETERA
—those that
   follow   ET SEQUENTES
                 ET SEQUENTIA
anew   DE NOVO
animal that can laugh
               ANIMAL RISIBILE
annual average
          COMMUNIBUS ANNIS
any   ULLUS
appease   PLACARE
applaud   PLAUDITE
apple   MALUM
arbitary assertion   IPSE DIXIT
argument   ARGUMENTUM
—directed against a person
                 AD HOMINEM
—for the sake of it
             ARGUMENTI CAUSA
—to common sense AD JUDICIUM
—to cupidity   AD CRUMENAM
—to opponent's ignorance
             AD IGNORANTIAM
—to prejudices   AD INVIDIAM
—to the point/purpose   AD REM
around   CIRCA
artificial memory
          MEMORIA TECHNICA
arbitary order or decree   FIAT
as   QUA.UT
—a favour   EX GRATIA

—a mark of
   respect   HONORIS CAUSA
—a matter of form   PRO FORMA
—a poor man
             IN FORMA PAUPERIS
—a present   EX DONO
—a warning   IN TERROREM
—above   UT SUPRA
—below   UT INFRA
—far as   QUOAD
—far as concerns religious
   affairs   QUOAD SACRA
—far as this goes   QUOAD HOC
—from the beginning
          QUALIS AB INCEPTO
—if   QUASI
—it were   QUASI
—much as he deserved
            QUANTUM MERUIT
—much more ALTERUM TANTUM
—often as   TOTIES QUOTIES
—undivided   PRO INDIVISO
asses' bridge   PONS ASINORUM
assumed to be true
            PETITIO PRINCIPII
at
—a lucky moment
          DEXTRO TEMPORE
—first sight   PRIMA FACIE
—full length   IN EXTENSO
—hand   AD MANUM
—my own risk   MEO PERICULO
—pleasure   AD LIB(ITUM)
—random   PASSIM
—the point of death
          IN ARTICULO MORTIS
                 IN EXTREMIS
—this time   HOC TEMPORE
attendant   MINISTER
Attic salt   SAL ATTICUM
author   AUCTOR
authoritatively   EX CATHEDRA
authoritive permission   FIAT
awnless   MUTICUS
back   DORSUM
bad   MALUS
badly   MALE
baggage   IMPEDIMENTA
bankruptcy proceedings

	CESSIO BONORUM
barley	HORDEUM
bastard	FILIUS NULLIUS.NOTHUS
be	ESSE
—bent, not broken	
	FLECTI NON FRANGI
—born	NASCI
—silent	TACE
beak	ROSTRUM
before	ANTE
—noon	ANTE MERIDIEM
—the light	ANTE LUCEM
—the war	ANTE BELLUM
behold the	
—man	ECCE HOMO
—sign	ECCE SIGNUM
below	INFRA
—one's dignity	
	INFRA DIG(NITATEM)
bereaved	ORBUS
besiege	OBSIDERE
best	OPTIMUS
better	MELIOR
between themselves	INTER SE
beware	
—buyer	CAVEAT EMPTOR
—doer	CAVEAT ACTOR
—of the dog	CAVEAT CANEM
beyond	ULTRA
—authority	ULTRA VIRES
—measure	EXTRA MODUM
—the walls	EXTRA MUROS
bird	AVIS
bite	MORDERE.MORSUS
black	NIGER
blank tablet	TABULA RASA
bless you	BENEDICITE
blessed are the	
peace makers	BEATI PACIFICI
bold and cautious	
	AUDAX ET CAUTUS
bone	OS
book	LIBER
—plate	EX LIBRIS
bottom	FUNDUS
bountiful mother	ALMA MATER
boxing glove	C(A)ESTUS
brain membrane	DURA MATER
	PIA MATER

branch	RAMUS
brandy	AQUA VITAE
bravely	FORTITER
bread	PANIS
—basket	PANARIUM
breast	MAMMA.PECTUS
breathe upon	INHALARE
breathing	SPIRITUS
bride	NYMPHA
bridle	FRENUM
bright	NITIDUS
brine	MURIA
bring	FERRE
—forth	PARERE
bronze	AES
brother	FRATER
burden	ONUS
butterfly	PAPILIO
buttocks	CLUNIS
by	
—an impossibility	
	PER IMPOSSIBILE
—common consent	
	COMMUNI CONSENSU
—courage and faith	
	ANIMO ET FIDE
—divine law	JURE DIVINO
—faith	
—and fortitude	
	FIDE ET FORTUDINE
—and confidence	
	FIDE ET FIDUCIA
—and love	FIDE ET AMORE
—not arms	FIDE NON ARMIS
—gift	EX DONO
—hand	MANU
—human law	JURE HUMANO
—labour and honour	
	LABORE ET HONORE
—law	JURE
—logical conversion	
	E CONVERSO
—memory	MEMORITER
—my fault	MEA CULPA
—reason of a vow	EX VOTO
—right	DE JURE
—right of office	EX OFFICIO
—right of position	EX OFFICIO
—that name	EO NOMINE

—that very fact   IPSO FACTO
—the grace of God   DEI GRATIA
—the living voice   VIVA VOCE
—the way   OBITER
—the whole heavens
                     TOTO CAELO
—virtue of office VIRTUTE OFFICII
—way of   VIA
—way of consequence
                  EX CONSEQUENTI
—way of example   EG
                  EXEMPLI GRATIA
—what right   QUO JURE
—what warrant QUO WARRANTO
—word of mouth   VIVA VOCE
—your leave   PACE TUA
canonical hours
               HORAE CANONICAE
case
—already adjudicated
                  RES JUDICATA
—of conscience
            CASUS CONSCIENTIAE
cast   DRAMATIS PERSONAE
cattle   PECUS
cause
—of war   CASUS BELLI
—(it) to be done   FIERI FACIAS
celebration of sacrament
               OPUS OPERATUM
censor of morals
               CENSOR MORUM
certain person, thing   QUIDAM
chaff   PALEA
chamber   CAMERA
characters in play
            DRAMATIS PERSONAE
chide   JUGARE
chief good FINIS BONORUM
chin   MENTUM
circle   ORBIS
circumlocution
            CIRCUITUS VERBORUM
civil law   JUS CIVILE
clamour of the meeting
            FORENSIS STREPITUM
classical passage
            LOCUS CLASSICUS
clean   MUNDUS

—slate   TABULA RASA
cloak
—Greek   PALLIUM
—military   SAGUM
—rain   LACERNA
—travel   PAENULA
closed sea   MARE CLAUSUM
cloth (piece of)   PANNUS
cloud   NUBES
collection of
   dried plants   HORTUS SICCUS
college of cardinals   COLLEGIUM
combined with   CUM
command   IMPERIUM
commander-in-chief   IMPERATOR
common   COMMUNIS
—good   COMMUNE BONUM
—people   VULGUS
commonly   VULGO
compliance   OBSEQUIUM
conclusion   FINIS
conscript fathers
            PATRES CONSCRIPTI
consider the end   FINEM RESPICE
contract   PACTUM
contrariwise   E CONTRA
contrived solution
            DEUS EX MACHINA
conversely   E CONTRARIO
                     CONTRA
country in town   RUS IN URBE
crime   FACINUS.SCELUS
—of forgery   FALSI CRIMEN
crucial test
            EXPERIMENTUM CRUCIS
crumb   MICA
cup   POCULUM
current of popular feeling
            AURA POPULARIS
current practices of speech
            USUS LOQUENDI
cursorily   OBITER
cursory remark   OBITER DICTUM
customs   MORES
day   DIES
—of judgment   DIES IRAE
—of wrath   DIES IRAE
—on which no legal business
   is transacted

DIES NON (JURIDICUS)

days	
—of festival	DIES FERIAE
	DIES FESTI
—of law	DIES FASTI
	DIES PROFESTI
—of wrath	DIES IRAE
—when verdicts could	
—be pronounced	DIES FASTI
—not be pronounced	
	DIES NEFASTI
dead force (of pressure)	
	VIS MORTUA
death	MORS
defender of the faith	FID DEF
	FIDEI DEFENSOR
deliver formally	SERVE
deputy	LOCUM(TENENS)
destination	TERMINUS AD QUEM
devised (this)	INVENIT
discernment	SAPIENTI
disc-thrower	DISCOBOLUS
disease	MORBUS
disgusting extent	AD NAUSEAM
disinterested adviser	
	AMICUS CURIAE
disputed question	
	VEXATA QUAESTIO
distinguishing properties	
	DIFFERENTIA
divide and rule	DIVIDE ET IMPERA
divided	PARTITUS
divine right	JUS DIVINUM
divinity	NUMEN
do not touch me	
	NOLI ME TANGERE
dried dung	ALBUM GRAECUM
drink	BIBERE
drink distilled from spices and	
wine	AQUA MIRABILIS
drudge	MEDIASTINUS
drugs (medical)	MATERIA MEDICA
dry wit	SAL ATTICUM
dumb	MUTUS
during life	DURANTE VITA
duty	OFFICIUM
dwelling	MANSIO
earnestly	SERIO
earth	TERRA

easily first	FACILE PRINCEPS
egg	OVUM
eighth	OCTAVUS
either	UTER
emperor	IMPERATOR
—'s decree	NOVELLA
empirical	A POSTERIORI
encumbrances	IMPEDIMENTA
end	FINIS.TERMINUS
enjoy the pleasures of the	
moment	CARPE DIEM
enlightened	ILLUMINATI
enough	SAT.SATIS
—for the wise	SAT SAPIENTI
—of words	SATIS VERBORUM
enthusiasm	FERVOR.FUROR
entirely	IN TOTO
entities	ENTIA
entity	ENS
—actually existing	ENS REALE
—existing	
—as accident	ENS PAR SE
	ENS PER ACCIDENS
—in the mind	ENS RATIONIS
equal	PAR
equally	AEQUE
equitably	AEQUE
essential condition	
	SINE QUA NON
everywhere	PASSIM.UBIQUE
evil omen	MONSTRUM
examine orally	VIVA VOCE
example	EXEMPLUM
—of all the others	
	INSTAR OMNIUM
except	NISI
excess	LUXUS
excitement	FUROR
existing condition	STATUS QUO
extinction	QUIETUS
extortioner	BARATHRUM
extravagant	IMMODERATUS
extreme perfection	
	NE PLUS ULTRA
eye	OCULUS
eyelid	PALPEBRA
facts relevant to case	RES GESTAE
fair reward	QUANTUM MERUIT
faith	FIDES

—and justice	FIDES ET JUSTITIA		EX ABUNDANTI CAUTELA
faithful and bold		—his own impulse	
	FIDUS ET AUDAX		EX MERO MOTU
fall	CADERE	—inside	AB INTRO
father	PATER	—memory	MEMORITER
favour	MERCES	—office	AB OFFICIO
fear	METUS	—one living person	INTER VIVOS
fearful	TIMIDUS	—own resources	EX PROPRIIS
feather	PENNA	—outside	AB EXTRA
—less animal	ANIMAL IMPLUME	—the beginning	AB INITIO
field of Mars	CAMPUS MARTIUS		AB OVO
finger	DIGITUS	—the books	EX LIBRIS
first	PRIMUS	—the chair of office	
—among equals			EX CATHEDRA
	PRIMUS INTER PARES	—the circumstances	E(X) RE NATA
fix	FIGERE	—the first	AB ORIGINE
flame	FLAMMA	—the founding of the city	
flax	LINUM	(Rome)	AB URBE CONDITA
flourished	FLORUIT	—the greater	A MAJORI
fluency	VERBORUM COPIA	—the hypothesis	EX HYPOTHESI
fly	MUSCA	—the less	A MINORI
following	SECUNDUS	—the mind	EX ANIMO
food	PABULUM	—the nature of things	
foot	PES		A NATURA REI
for	PRO	—the side	A LATERE
—a memorial	PRO MEMORIA	—what has been conceded	
—a pledge	IN DEPOSITO		EX CONCESSIS
—altars and firesides			EX CONCESSO
	PRO ARIS ET FOCIS	—within	AB INTRA
—instance	EG.EXEMPLI GRATIA	gain	LUCRUM
—nothing	GRATIS	garden	HORTUS
—one's country	PRO PATRIA	gardener	HORTULANUS
—so much	PRO TANTO	—(market)	(H)OLITOR
—the public good		gem	GEMMA
	PRO BONO PUBLICO	generalisation of experience	
—the time being	PRO TEMPORE		AXIOMA MEDIUM
—this special purpose	AD HOC	genuine	BONA FIDE(S)
—this way or occasion		gift of the king	REGIUM DONUM
	PRO HAC VICE	girdle	CINGULUM
force	VIS	—of Venus	CINGULUM VENERIS
—of pressure	VIS MORTUA	give us peace	
forename	PRAENOMEN		DONA NOBIS PACEM
former	QUONDAM	glory	GLORIA
freak of nature	LUSUS NATURAE	—to God	GLORIA IN EXCELSIS
frenzy	FUROR	glove	MANICA
from	EX	glowing language	
—cause to effect	A PRIORI		ARDENTIA VERBA
—effect to cause	A POSTERIORI	go	
—excess caution		—in peace	VADE IN PACE

—out	EXEUNT	—painted (it)	PINXIT
—with me	VADE MECUM	—printed (it)	EXCUDIT
God	DEUS	—said (it)	IPSE DIXIT
—be with you	DEUS VOBISCUM	—sculpted (it)	SCULPSIT
—forbid	DEUS AVERTAT	—struck (it)	EXCUDIT
—grant	DEUS DET	head	CAPUT
—willing.	DEO VOLENTE	—of family	PATERFAMILIAS
—wills it	DEUS VULT	heavenly voice	VOX ANGELICA
goddess	DEA		VOX CAELESTIS
gold	AURUM	held by the Crown	IN CAPITE
golden	AUREUS	herbarium	HORTUS SICCUS
—mean	AUREA MEDIOCRITAS	here	
good	BONUM	—and everywhere	HIC ET UBIQUE
—faith	BONA FIDE(S)	—and there	PASSIM
—health!	BENE VOBIS	—buried	HIC SEPULTUS
—manners	BONOS MORES	—lies	HIC JACET
goose	ANSER	high mass	MISSA SOLEMNIS
grand		highest	SUMMA
—father	AVUS	his very word	IPSE DIXIT
—son	NEPOS	Holy	
gratuitously	EX GRATIA	—of Holies	
great work	MAGNUM OPUS		SANCTUM SANCTORUM
greater gods		—water vessel	ASPERSORIUM
	DI MAJORUM GENTIUM	honey	MEL
grin	RISUS	hoof	UNGULA
grip	MORSUS	horn	CORNU
grove	NEMUS	hot bath	CALDARIUM
hail and farewell		household gods	DI PENATES
	AVE ATQUE VALE		LARES ET PENATES
halo of two circles	VESICA PISCIS	humanities	
hammer	MALLEUS		LIT(T)ERAE HUMANIORES
hand	MANUS	husband	MARITUS
—book	VADE MECUM	I	
—cuff	MANICA	—am present	ADSUM
happily	FELICITER	—am the judge	ME JUDICE
harbour	PORTUS	—distinguish	DISTINGUO
harlot	MERETRIX	—give that you may give	
harvest	MESSIS		DO UT DES
have the body	HABEAS CORPUS	—have spoken	DIXI
having		if anybody (wants to know	
—held an office		etc.)	SI QUIS
	FUNCTUS OFFICIO	ignorant	NESCIUS
—legal right to act	SUI JURIS	ignoring the point	
he			IGNORATIO ELENCHI
—executed (it)	FECIT	illegal agreement	
—forged (it)	EXCUDIT		PACTUM ILLICITUM
—hammered (it)	EXCUDIT	illogical conclusion	
—has left well	BENE DECESSIT		NON SEQUITUR
—made (it)	FECIT	immediately	INSTANTER

improvise	AD LIB(ITUM)		ABSENTE REO
in		—abstract	IN ABSTRACTO
—a vacuum	IN VACUO	—beginning	IN PRINCIPIO
—absence	IN ABSENTIA	—bosom	IN GREMIO
—bad faith	MALE FIDE	—father's lifetime	VITA PATRIS
—characteristic style	MORE SUO	—first place	IMPRIMIS
—chief	IN CAPITE	—highest degree	IN EXCELSIS
—crowds	GREGATIM	—Lord	IN DOMINO
—dire straits	IN EXTREMIS	—manner	MORE
—English	ANGLICE	—matter (of)	IN RE
—equal quantities	ANA.AA.A	—meantime	AD INTERIM
—express terms		—nature of things	

—express terms
EXPRESSIS VERBIS

—nature of things
IN RERUM NATURA

—extremity	IN EXTREMIS	—open air	SUB DIVO
—fact	DE FACTO	—passage cited	LOC CIT
—former state	IN STATU QUO		LOCO CITATO
—German	GERMANICE	—same place	IB.IBID(EM)
—glass	IN VITRO	—test-tube	IN VITRO
—his own way	MORE SUO	—time of	TEMPORE
—ill appearance	MALE HABITUS	—very act	

—very act
FLAGRANTE DELICTO

—just so many words
TOTIDEM VERBIS

—living organism	IN VIVO	—work cited	OP CIT
—my opinion	ME JUDICE		OPERE CITATO
—nature	IN RERUM NATURA	—this	
—order	SECUNDUM ORDINEM	—place	HOC LOCO
—original situation	IN SITU	—year	HOC ANNO
—part	PARTIM	—transit	IN TRANSITU
—peace	IN PACE	—unfavourable manner	
—person	IN PROPRIA PERSONA		IN MALAM PARTEM
—place of parent		—wine is truth	IN VINO VERITAS

—place of parent
IN LOCO PARENTIS

—unfavourable manner
IN MALAM PARTEM

—presence of		index of	
—the king		—authors	INDEX AUCTORUM
	CORAM DOMINO REGE	—places	INDEX LOCORUM
—the people	CORAM POPULO	—things	INDEX RERUM
—us	CORAM NOBIS	—words	INDEX VERBORUM
—private session	IN CAMERA	incidentally	OBITER
—proportion	AD VALOREM	indiscriminately	PASSIM
	PRO RATA	ineffectual	BRUTUM
—respect of all		ingenuity	INGENIUM
things	QUOAD OMNIA	inhabit	COLERE
—secret	IN CAMERA	inquire	QUAERE
—self-defence	SE DEFENDENDO	inspection (accounts)	VIDIMUS
—so far	QUA	into the midst of matters	
—some respects only			IN MEDIAS RES

—some respects only
SECUNDUM QUID

—the		it is	
—absence of the defendant		—denied	NEGATUR
		—not allowed	NON LICET
		—not clear	NON LIQUET
		—silent	TACET

jar	OLLA	—us be glad	GAUDEAMUS
joy of contest		—us therefore rejoice	
GAUDIUM CERTAMINIS		GAUDEAMUS IGITUR	
journey	ITER	letter	LIT(T)ERA
judge of taste		—for letter	LIT(T)ERATIM
ARBITER ELEGANTARIUM		life	VITA
judicially	EX CATHEDRA	—like	AD VIVUM
juice of grapes	MUSTUM	light	LUX
just now	MODO	—bringer	LUCIFER
keeper of the rolls		—of the world	LUX MUNDI
CUSTOS ROTULORUM		lily	LILIUM
kind reader	LECTOR BENEVOLE	limit	TERMINUS
kiss	OSCULUM	—from which	TERMINUS A QUO
knee	GENU	—to which	TERMINUS AD QUEM
knotted	NODATUS	lion	LEO
know thyself	NOSCE TEIPSUM	list of prohibited books	
lamb of God	AGNUS DEI	INDEX EXPURGATORIUS	
land	AGER	little	PARUM
landed estate	LATIFUNDIUM	—bits	MORSUS
lantern	NOCTILUCA	—mouth	OSCULUM
large	MAGNUS	living	VIVUS
—pearl	UNIO	—force	VIS VIVA
larger	MAJOR	lobster	LOCUSTA
last argument	ULTIMA RATIO	long	LONGUS
law	JUS.LEX	—live	VIVAT
—of nations	JUS GENTIUM	love of country	AMOR PATRIAE
—of nature	JUS NATURALE	lower down the page	INFRA
—of retaliation	LEX TALIONIS	lowest species	INFIMA SPECIES
leader	DUX.L	lucky day	DIES FAUSTUS
leaf	FOLIUM	male	MASCULUS
learned men	LITERATI	man	ANIMAL BIPES.HOMO
leave		manner	MODUS
—of absence	ABSIT	manners	MORES
—the stage	EXEUNT	marble	MARMOR
—to appeal	AUDITA QUERELA	mark	NOTA
leaving certificate		—well	NB.NOTA BENE
BENE DECESSIT		marks	INDICIA
legal right	JUS	mass	MISSA.MOLES
leisure	OTIUM	master	MAGISTER
less	MINOR	—of arts	MAGISTER ARTIUM
let		measure	MENSURARE
—him go out	EXEAT	measuring rod	GROMA
—him not depart	NE EXEAT	medical matter	MATERIA MEDICA
—it be done	FIAT	medlar	MESPILUS
—it be printed	IMPRIMATUR	memory assistance	
—it flourish	FLOREAT	MEMORIA TECHNICA	
—sleeping dogs lie		men of letters	LITERATI
QUIETA NON MOVERE		mere assertion	GRATIS DICTUM
—there be light	FIAT LUX	merrymaking	GAUDEAMUS

mesh	MACULA		MUTUUS CONSENSUS
messenger	NUNTIUS	myth	MYTHUS
metal	METALLUM	naked	NUDUS
method of operating		name	NOMEN
	MODUS OPERANDI	—being changed	
middle	MEDIUS		MUTATO NOMINE
—letter	MEDIA LITTERA	namely	SC.SCILICET
—vein	MEDIA NENA		VIDELICET.VIZ
—way	VIA MEDIA	native soil	NATALE SOLUM
midwife	OBSTETRIX	natural law	JUS NATURALE
mild	MITIS	nature	NATURA
military body	MILITIA	necklace	MONILE
Milky Way	VIA LACTEA	neither	NEUTER
mill	MOLA	nest	NIDUS
mind	ANIMUS.MENS	new	DE INTEGRO.NOVUS
mine and thine	MEUM ET TUUM	—wine	MUSTUM
mint	MONETA	newsmonger	QUIDNUNC
mist	NEBULA	night	NOX
mixed	MIXTUS	nine	NOVEM
mnemonic device		ninety	NONAGINTA
	MEMORIA TECHNICA	ninth	NONUS
mob	FAEX POPULI	nitric	
modillion	MUTULUS	—acid	AQUA FORTIS
money	MONETA	—and hydrochloric	AQUA REGIA
monster	MONSTRUM	no	
month	MENSIS	—evil omen	ABSIT OMEN
moon	LUNA.NOCTILUCA	—offence	ABSIT INIDIA
more	PLUS	nobody	NEMO
mosaic decoration		non-speaking character	
	OPUS MOSIVUM		PERSONA MUTA
moss	MUSCUS	none	NULLUS
mother	MATER	nose	NASUS
—of family	MATERFAMILIAS	nostrils	NARES
—stood (Latin hymn)		not	NE.NON
	STABAT MATER	—allowed	NON LICET
mountain	MONS	—any	NULLUS
mourn	LUGERE	—clear	NON LIQUET
mouse	MUS	—obstructing	NON OBSTANTE
mouth	ORIS.OSTIUM	note	NOTARE
moveable goods	BONA MOBILIA	noteworthy maxims	NOTABILIA
much	MULTUS	nothing	NIHIL
—in few	MULTUM NON MULTA	—further	NE PLUS ULTRA
—in little	MULTUM IN PARVO	—to the point	NIHIL AD REM
mud	LUTUM	notwithstanding	NON OBSTANTE
mulberry	MORUM	now	NUNC
murmur	MUTTUM	number	NUMERUS
muscle	MUS	nut	NUX
musk	MUSCUS	nutlike	NUCALIS
mutual consent		obvious leader	FACILE PRINCEPS

occupy	OBTINERE	—the depths	DE PROFUNDIS
of		outside	EXTRA
—blessed memory		over	SUPER
	BEATAE MEMORIAE	—one's cups	INTER POCULA
—himself, herself, itself	SUI	ox	BOVIS
—his own accord	EX MERO MOTU	—tripe	OMASUM
	EX PROPRIO MOTU	oyster	OSTREA
	MOTU PROPRIO	pact	PACTUM
—his/her age	AETATIS SUAE	—without deliberation	
—its own kind	SUI GENERIS		PACTUM NUDUM
—one's own accord	SPONTE SUA	paint	PIGMENTUM
—sound mind	COMPOS MENTIS	pale	PALLIDUS
—the morning	MATUTINUS	pan	PATELLA
—the same kind		pardon	VENIA
	EJUSDEM GENERIS	partial	EX PARTE
offered up	OBLATUS	partially	PARTIM
offhand	BREVI MANU	passage	PORUS
	CURRENTE CALAMO	passive resistance	VIS INERTIAE
official sanction	FIAT	patron	PATRONUS
oil	OEUM	peace	PAX
old verse metre	SATURNIAN	—be with you	PAX VOBISCUM
olive tree	OLEASTER	pending the suit	LITE PENDENTE
on		perishable goods	
—either side	EX UTRAQUE PARTE		BONA PERITURA
—high	IN EXCELSIS	perjury	CRIMEN FALSI
—one side only	EX PARTE	perpetual motion	
—that claim	EO NOMINE		PERPETUUM MOBILE
—the contrary	E CONTRARIO	person	PERSONA
—the first view	PRIMA FACIE	—of humble birth	TERRAE FILIUS
—the heights	IN EXCELSIS	physician	MEDICUS
—the threshold	IN LIMINE	pious	PIA
one	UNUS	—fraud	FRAUS PIA.PIA FRAUS
—of low birth	FILIUS TERRAE	—regrets	PIA DESIDERIA
onion	UNIO	place	LOCUS
opaque	OPACUS	—to appear	LOCUS STANDI
open	PATERE	plant	HERBA
opportunity	OCCASIO	plate	LANX
or	AUT	pledge	PIGNUS
oral examination	VIVA (VOCE)	plummet	LIBELLA
order	ORDINARE	pocket companion	VADE MECUM
original edition		poetic	
	EDITIO PRINCEPS	—frenzy	FUROR POETICUS
other	ALTER	—licence	LICENTIA VATUM
—things being equal		polite letters	
	CETERIS PARIBUS		LIT(T)ERAE HUMANIORES
out of	EX	portent	MONSTRUM
—abundance	EX ABUNDANTIA	pot herb	(H)OLUS
—court	EX CURIA	pouch	SACCUS
—office	FUNCTUS OFFICIO	power	VIS

—of decision	ARBITRIUM
—of inertia	VIS INERTIAE
powerful	POTENS
praise	LAUS
—to God	LAUS DEO
pray	ORARE
—and work	ORA ET LABORA
—for us	ORA PRO NOBIS
prayer for the dead	REQUIESCAT
precinct	PERIBOLUS
prejudiced	EX PARTE
privately	SUB ROSA
professionally	
	SECUNDUM ARTEM
profound silence	
	ALTUM SILENTIUM
proof texts	DICTA PROBANTIA
property	BONA
Psalm 95	VENITE
Psalm 98	CANTATE
Punic faith	FIDES PUNICA
	PUNICA FIDES
public announcement	SI QUIS
pure salt	MERUM SAL
puzzle for critics	
	CRUX CRITICORUM
question is asked	QUAERITUR
quickly	CITO
quite naked	
	IN PURIS NATURALIBUS
race	GENUS
rag	PANNUS
rage	FUROR
rainwater	AQUA CAELESTIS
rare bird, person or	
item	RARA AVIS
razor	NOVACULA
reader	LECTOR
reasoning person	
	ANIMAL RATIONALE
received text	TEXTUS RECEPTUS
refuse matter	EXCREMENTA
rejoicing	GAUDEAMUS
remains (on stage)	MANET
	MANENT
reproach	PROBRUM
rest in peace	
	REQUIESCAT IN PACE
	RIP
retaliation	QUID PRO QUO
retrospective(ly)	EX POST FACTO
rib	COSTA
right	
—of husband	JUS MARITI
—side	LATUS RECTUM
—to intervene	LOCUS STANDI
rightful	DE JURE
rise	ORIRI
road	VIA
roll	VOLVERE
rotten	PUTER
rough breathing	SPIRITUS ASPER
round	ROTUNDUS
rule	NORMA
ruler	IMPERATOR
sacred	SACER
safe path	VIA TUTA
safe through being	
careful	CAVENDO TUTUS
sailor	NAUTICUS
salmon	SALMO
same	IDEM
sanctuary	DELUBRUM
sane	COMPOS MENTIS
sardonic sneer	
	RISUS SARDONICUS
satisfaction	POENA
saving the right	SALVO JURE
saw	SERRA
saying	DICTUM
scale of balance	LANX
sea	MARE
—carp	MERULA
—monster	ORCA
—nymph	NERINE
seat	SEDES
second	SECUNDUM
—to none	NULLI SECUNDUS
secular arm	
	BRACHIUM SECULARE
see	VIDE
—above	VIDE SUPRA
—below	VIDE INFRA
selections	EXCERPTA
settlement	QUIETUS
service	OFFICIUM
severe test for learners	
	PONS ASINORUM

shadow	UMBRA	—the people	FILIUS POPULI
shape	FORMA	—the soil	FILIUS TERRAE
sheep	OVIS		TERRAE FILIUS
shield	SCUTUM	soul	ANIMA
shining	NITIDUS	—of the world	ANIMA MUNDI
ship	NAVIS	sounding similar	IDEM SONANS
shore	ORA	source and origin	FONS ET ORIGO
shrine	DELUBRUM	spade	PALA
side	LATUS	spirit	SPIRITUS
siege	OBSIDIO	—of the place	GENIUS LOCI
signs	INDICIA	spit	OBELUS
silencing	QUIETUS	sport	LUSUS NATURAE
silently	EX TACITO	spot	MACULA
sin	NEFAS	spring water	AQUA FONTANA
sinew	NERVUS	stake	PALUS
skilfully	SECUNDUM ARTEM	star	STELLA
slanting	LIQUIS	starting point	TERMINUS A QUO
slave-dealer	MANGO	state in which	STATUS QUO
sleeve	MANICA	statute law	LEX SCRIPTA
slight fault	CULPA LEVIS	stem	CAULIS
slip	LAPSUS	step	PASSUS
—of the memory		—mother	NOVERCA
	LAPSUS MEMORIAE	stock quotation	
—of the pen	LAPSUS CALAMI		LOCUS CLASSICUS
—of the tongue		strong	FORTIS
	LAPSUS LINGUAE	—defence	AES TRIPLEX
slippery	LUBRICUS	—smell	NIDOR
small	MINUTUS	substance	QUID
smallest	MINIMUS	substances employed in	
smallness	MINUTIA	medicine	MATERIA MEDICA
smooth		successfully	FELICITER
—breathing	SPIRITUS LENIS	sufficient amount	
—tablet	TABULA RASA		QUANTUM SUFFICIT
snow	NIX	suicide	FELO DE SE
so	SIC	sun	SOL
—much richer	TANTO UBERIOR	superior force	VIS MAJOR
—throughout	SIC PASSIM	surveying pole	GROMA
soft	MOLLIS	sweet	DULCIS
softening	MOLLITIES	table	MENSA
soldier	MILES	tail	CAUDA
some	ULLUS	take note	NB.NOTA BENE
somebody	QUIDAM	tear	LACRIMA
something		temple	DELUBRUM
—in exchange	QUID PRO QUO	thanks to God	DEO GRATIAS
—said	DICTUM	that	
—said by the way	OBITER DICTUM	—is	ID EST.IE
—sought for	QUAESITUM	—which a thing is	QUID
son of		the	
—nobody	FILIUS NULLIUS	—Fates oppose	FATA OBSTANT

—hour flies	HORA FUGIT	—this extent	QUOAD
—King's Bench	IN BANCO REGIS	—wit	SC.SCILICET
—same	ID.IDEM		VIDELICET.VIZ
—very words	IPSISSIMA VERBA	toga-wearing	
thee therefore	TE IGITUR	nation	GENS TOGATA
there sat	SEDERUNT	together	PARI PASSU
thereby	IPSO FACTO	token of respect	HONORIS CAUSA
thin plate	LAMELLA.LAMINA		HONORIS GRATIA
thing	RES	tongue	LINGUA
things		tooth	DENS
—to be seen	VIDENDA	town	OPPIDUM
—worthy of notice	NOTABILIA	traveller	VIATOR
think	COGITARE	treacherously	MALA FIDE
third	TERTIUS	treachery	FIDES PUNICA
—person in triangle		tree	ARBOR
	TERTIUM QUID	—of life	ARBOR VITAE
this	HIC.HAEC.HOC	trifles	NUGAE
—do	HOC AGE	true value	QUAESITUM
thousand	MILLE	turned against	OBVERSUS
thread	FILUM	turnip	NAPUS
threats	MINAE	twice	BIS
throughout	A.AA.ANA	two-footed animal	ANIMAL BIPES
	PASSIM	unacceptable person	
thunderbolt	FULMEN		PERSONA NON GRATA
thus	SIC	unclaimed goods	
time			BONA VACANTIA
—flies	TEMPUS FUGIT	under	
—for penitence		—consideration	SUB JUDICE
	LOCUS PAENITENTIAE	—penalty	SUB POENA
to		—that heading	SUB VOCE
—a subtle point	AD UNGUEM	—the appearance	SUB SPECIE
—be considered further		—the rose	SUB ROSA
	AD REFERENDUM	—the sky	SUB DIVO
—each his own	SUUM CUIQUE	—this condition	HAC LEGE
—everyone	URBI ET ORBI	unexpectedly	EX IMPROVISO
—for or with God	DEO	unformed mind	TABULA RASA
—infinity	AD INFINITUM	union	UNIO
—the city and the world		university	ALMA MATER
	URBI ET ORBI	unknown country	TERRA INCOGNITA
—the clergy	AD CLERUM	matter related to two known	
—the end	AD FINEM	matters	TERTIUM QUID
—the greater	AD MAJUS	unless	NISI
—the highest point	AD SUMMUM	unlucky days	DIES INFAUSTUS
—the less	AD MINUS	unmixed	MERUS
—the man	AD HOMINEM	unowned property	RES NULLUS
—the nail	AD UNGUEM	unspeakable	NEFANDUS
—the point/purpose	AD REM	unsupported assertion	IPSE DIXIT
—the purse	AD CRUMENAM	unwritten law	LEX NON SCRIPTA
—the stars	AD ASTRA	uprightly	RECTE

urn	OLLA
urge to	
—speak	
CACOETHES LOQUENDI	
—write CACOETHES SCRIBENDI	
uttermost point NE PLUS ULTRA	
vacant see	SEDES VACANS
	SEDE VACANTE
valued possessions	
LARES ET PENATES	
various readings	
VARIAE LECTIONES	
vegetable	(H)OLUS
voice	VOX
—of God	VOX DEI
—of the people	VOX POPULI
votive (offering)	EX VOTO
wages	MERCES
wall	MURUS
war of extermination	
BELLUM INTERNECINUM	
was	ERAT
wash	LUERE
water	AQUA.LYMPHA
wave	UNDA
way	VIA
—farer	VIATOR
—of life	MODUS VIVENDI
—of the Cross	VIA DOLOROSA
we	NOS
—command	MANDAMUS
—learn by teaching	
DOCENDO DISCIMUS	
weariness of existence	
TAEDIUM VITAE	
weasel	MUSTELA
well-deserved	
BENE MERENTIBUS	
what now?	QUID NUNC
wheel	ORBIS
—track	ORBITA
where	UBI
—are you going?	QUO VADIS
which (see)	QUOD (VIDE).QV
while	
—(she is) chaste	DUM CASTA
—war rages	FLAGRANTE BELLO
whisky	AQUA VITAE
whither	QUO

—goest thou?	QUO VADIS
who	QUI
—as much?	QUI TAM
—gains?	CUI BONO
whole world	ORBIS TERRARUM
why does he hinder?	
	QUARE IMPEDIT
wickedness	NEFAS
wild animals	FERAE NATURAE
will-o'-the wisp	IGNIS FATUUS
willy-nilly	NOLENS VOLENS
window	FENESTRA
wing	PENNA
wisdom	SAPIENTI
wit (incisive)	MERUM SAL
	SAL ATTICUM
with	
—a pinch of salt	
CUM GRANUM SALIS	
—distinction	
MAXIMA CUM LAUDE	
—equal step	PARI PASSU
—full authority	PLENO JURE
—God's favour	DEO FAVENTE
—greatest distinction	
SUMMA CUM LAUDE	
—many other things	
CUM MULTIS ALIIS	
—necessary alterations	
MUTATIS MUTANDIS	
—one mind	UNO ANIMO
—one voice	UNA VOCE
—privilege	CUM PRIVILEGIO
—proper exceptions	
EXCEPTIS EXCIPIENDIS	
—quiet mind	AEQUO ANIMO
—running pen	
CURRENTE CALAMO	
—stronger reason	A FORTIORI
—this law	HAC LEGE
—thumb up	POLLICE VERSO
within	INTRA
—legal powers	INTRA VIRES
—the treaty	CASUS FOEDERIS
—the wall	INTRA MUROS
without	SINE
—a day fixed	SINE DIE
—changing any letter	LITERATIM
—doubt	SINE DUBIO

—finishing the business RE INFECTA
—issue SINE PROLE
—opposition NEM CON
—payment GRATIS
witness TESTIS
woe to the defeated VAE VICTIS
wolf LUPUS
womb MATRIX
wonder at MIRARI
wonderful MIRABILIS
—to see MIRABILE VISU
—to tell MIRABILE DICTU
wonders MIRABILIA
word for word AD VERBUM
VERBATIM
work OPUS
—is prayer
LABORARE EST ORARE
working
—arrangement MODUS VIVENDI
—method MODUS OPERANDI
works OPERA
workshop OFFICINA
world MUNDUS
worth while TANTI
worthless residue
CAPUT MORTUUM
wounded majesty
LAESA MAJESTAS
wretched MISER
wrong NEFAS
yawn OSCITARE
year ANNUS
—in the year of
—Christ ANNO CHRISTI
—foundation of city (Rome)
ANNO URBIS CONDITAE
—our Lord ANNO DOMINI
—redemption
ANNO SALUTIS
—the reign ANNO REGNI
—the world ANNO MUNDI
—of wonders ANNUS MIRABILIS
yellow LUTEUS
yoke JUGUM
you too TU QUOQUE
you're another TU QUOQUE
(*see also* classic(al).Roman)

latitude L.LAT
laundry helper DETERGENT
DOLLY.IRON
SODA.SOAP
laugh HA.HAHA.HEHE
law¹ COPS.FUZZ
law agent LA
law-*breaking* AWL
lawman BL.DA.EARP
lawmen COPS.POLICE.POSSE
VIGILANTES
lawgiver MOSES.SOLON
lawmaker DRACO.MEDE
lawyer BL.DA
lawyers BAR
lawyers indicates use of legal
term
•bar *for lawyers* ESTOP
•*lawyer's* house MESSUAGE
•*lawyers'* right LIEN
(*see also* law²)
lax laws AWLS.SLAW
law²
some legal terms:
abandoned suit NOLI PROSEQUI
abandonment of writ or
action ABATEMENT
absorption of estate MERGER
acknowledgment of
justice COGNOVIT
act in opposition RETROACT
act of annulling VACATUR
admitting no denial PEREMPTORY
against V.VS.VERSUS
annulment DEFEASANCE
answer to charge PLEA
as close as possible CY PRES
assess (land) EXTEND
assize OYER
assumption from known
fact PRESUMPTION
at first sight PRIMA FACIE
attested copy VIDIMUS
backdate an application RELATE
betray by collusion PREVARICATE
body of
—canon law
CORPUS JURIS CANONICI
—civil law CORPUS JURIS CIVILIS

breach of law	OFFENCE
call for evidence	INVOCATIO
cancel bequest	ADEEM
clearing from accusation	
	PURGATION
come into operation	ENURE
concealment of facts	
	SUBREPTION
conveyance of property	GRANT
copy of legal document	
	TRANSUMPT
court	
—hearing	OYER
—sitting (Scottish)	SEDERUNT
deceitful	
misrepresentation	SUBREPTION
decision of court	PLACITUM
declare	
—heir (Scottish)	SERVE
—invalid	OVERRULE
deed	
—held by third party	
	ESCROL(L)
	ESCROW
—under seal	SPECIALTY
defamation by spoken words	
	SLANDER
defendant's answer	REJOINDER
delay	MORA
deliver legal document	SERVE
denial of	
—part of allegation	
	SPECIAL ISSUE
—whole of allegation	
	GENERAL ISSUE
deprive of property	DISSEISE
	DISSEIZE
disallow	OVER RULE
discharge (a debt)	EXTINGUISH
discuss adverse claims	
	INTERPLEAD
dispossess	DISSEISE.DISSEIZE
dispossession	OUSTER
disputed matter	ISSUE
distraint	NA(A)M.DISTRESS
document length (words)	FOLIO
ejection	OUSTER
emancipate from paternal	
control	FORISFAMILIATE
endow	VEST
enter unlawfully	TRESPASS
essential facts of the	
offence	CORPUS DELICTI
excuse for non-appearance	
in court	ESSOIN.ESSOYNE
extract of court record	ESTREAT
forbid	ENJOIN
forgery	FALSI CRIMEN
formal document	WRIT
fraud	STELLIONATE
—by mariners	BARRATRY
free transfer of title	DONATION
from one living to	
another	INTER VIVOS
hinder	ESTOP
holding the property of	
another	DETAINER
improper joining of parties	
	MISJOINDER
illegal	
—act	MALFEASANCE
—bargain	CHAMPERTY
in	
—judge's chambers	IN CAMERA
—secret	IN CAMERA
incidental facts	RES GESTAE
information not under oath	
	SUGGESTION
instigator of suit	PLAINTIFF
intermediate	MESNE
interpose in action	INTERVENE
issue for trial by agreement	
	FEIGNED ISSUE
judgement giving right of	
recovery	RECOVERY
judge's	
—commission	DEDIMUS
—order or warrant	FIAT
keep out by force	DEFORCE
kidnapping	PLAGIUM
know	WIT
land (freehold)	REALTY
—held by corporation	
	MORTMAIN
—tenure by religious body	
in return for prayers	
	FRANKALMOIGN
lapse	RESOLVE

legal
—claim   DROIT
—document   WRIT
—usage   PRACTIC
letting out on hire   LOCATION
limitation of estate or interest TAIL
—to male heirs   TAIL MALE
litigation pending
                            PENDENTE LITE
loss of civil rights resulting from
  conviction for treason
                                ATTAINDER
magistrate's warrant   PRECEPT
malicious damage   MAYHEM
married woman   FEME COVERT
misspelt word accepted
                            IDEM SONANS
mother   VENTER
moveable goods   FUNGIBLES
negligence   LACHES
no denial   PEREMPTORY
not under protection
  of husband   DISCOVERT
note of transaction
                        MEMORANDUM
oath administered to
  witness   VOIR DIRE
obtain
—a court judgment   RECOVER
—by false information
                            OBREPTION
—other than by inheritance
                             PURCHASE
offer to make oath   WAGE
old distraint warrant DISTRINGAS
on the first view   PRIMA FACIE
one
—acting as surety   MAINPERNOR
—who actively participates
  in a crime   PRINCIPAL
—who engages another to be
  his agent   PRINCIPAL
—who gives information
                              RELATOR
—who refuses to answer
  charge   MUTE
order appointing receiver to
  manage property
                   RECEIVING ORDER

organiser of conveyance
                             GRANTER
                             GRANTOR
original document   SCRIPT
paper added to will   LABEL
partial remission   RELAXATION
penalty   SANCTION
person
—having interest   PRIVY
—sued   DEFENDANT
—to whom something is
  relinquished   ABANDONEE
personal property   CHOSE
                         PERSONALTY
—immovable property   REAL
plea(ding)   PLACITUM
—that facts do not fit
  the case   DEMURRER
possession   SASINE.SEISIN
preclude   ESTOP
privately   SUB ROSA
process   INSTANCE
procuring advantage by
—concealing facts   SUBREPTION
—false information   OBREPTION
produce for court   PROPOUND
prohibit by injunction   ENJOIN
proof of will   PROBATE
property   REALTY
—gained other than by
  inheritance   PERQUISITE
—that can be inherited
                     HEREDITAMENT
—right   APPURTENANCE
put in possession   SEISE.VEST
—of whole of father's
  land   FORISFAMILIATE
receiver of
—conveyance   GRANTEE
—wrecks   ABANDONEE
receiving rents, etc.   PERNANCY
recover possession
  of (goods)   REPLEVY
reduction of
—estate value by neglect WASTE
—legacy   ABATEMENT
reference
—of case to another court REMIT
—to past events   RETROACT

refusing to answer a		theft	LARCENY
charge	MUTE (OF MALICE)	temporary owner	TERMOR
refute	REBUT	tenure by service	SOC(C)AGE
relinquish	REMISE	transfer to new owner	ATTORN
	WAIVE		TRADITION
rendering void	DEFEASANCE	transgression	OFFENCE
reply to defendant's		true copy of court	
—rebutter	SURREBUTTER	record	ESTREAT
—rejoinder	SURREJOINDER	under	
reserving clause in		—consideration	SUB JUDICE
deed	REDDENDUM	—legal age of maturity	INFANT
return an argument	REBUT	union	JOINDER
right	DROIT.LIEN	unowned property	RES NULLIUS
—of jurisdiction of lord		unreasonable delay	LACHES
of manor	SAC	unspecified fraud	STELLIONATE
—of lord to pursue thief outside		use and profit	USUFRUCT
own jurisdiction		value (land)	EXTEND
	OUTFANGTHIEF	venue	VISNE
—of property	APPURTENANCE	void	INEPT
—of way	EASEMENT	warning	MONITION
—to cut green forest wood	VERT	warrant of imprisonment	
—to hold one's own court	SOC		MITTIMUS
—to necessaries allowed by		widow	FEME SOLE
law	ESTOVER	withdrawal of suit	NONSUIT
—to cut peat	TURBARY	without consideration	NUDE
rights held in common		witness's oath	VOIR DIRE
	PRO INDIVISO	woman	FEME
royal commission to try cases		womb	VENTER
on assize	OYER AND TERMINER	writ	NOVERINT.PRECEPT
second trial for same			PROCESS
offence	DOUBLE JEOPARDY	—commanding attendance	
secure	VEST		SUBPOENA
set aside	WAIVE	—for asserting foreign	
settle	VEST	jurisdiction	PRAEMUNIRE
single woman	FEME SOLE	—for person concealed	LATITAT
spinster	FEME SOLE	—for recovery of goods	
statement of complaint	PLAINT	unlawfully taken	REPLEVIN
submission of dispute for		—maintaining papal	
judgement	REFERENCE	jurisdiction	PRAEMUNIRE
suit	INSTANCE	—moving case to High	
—pending	PENDENTE LITE	Court	CERTIORARI
summons	MONITION	—of distraint	FIERI FACIAS
surety	MAINPRISE	—of superior court	MANDAMUS
surrender of claim	REMISE	—requiring attendance at	
take		court	SUBPOENA
—effect	ENURE	—requiring information to show	
—estate away	DIVEST	cause	SCIRE FACIAS
taking back	RECAPTION	—requiring reasons for	
—possession	ENTRY	delay	QUARE IMPEDIT

—to produce prisoner		*leading* man	M
	HABEAS CORPUS	leading seaman	FIRST HAND
—to seize property of		led *astray*	-DLE.ELD
debtor	EXTENT	*led by* a. . .	start with A
—to show by what authority		*led by* *	start with *
office is held	QUO WARRANTO	•heir *led by* me	MESON
—to stop proceedings		**leaf**	
in lower court	INHIBITION	leaf-insect	PAGEANT
written defamation	LIBEL	leaf-*mould*	FLEA
wrong (civil)	TORT	league	L
Lawn Tennis Association	LTA	league members	REDHEADS
lay		**lean**	
lay *out*	LA-Y.SE-T	lean diet	SLIM
lay up nuts(D) ↑	STUN	lean nurse	TEND
lay*about*	LA-Y.SE-T	**learn**	
lay*about*‹	TES.YAL	learn	CON
layer	E.HEN	hence	
layout of town	WONT	•I learn. . .	ICON
lazy monk	ABBEY-LUBBER	•learn only. . .	CONSOLE
lead		•learn *to* dance	CONTANGO
lead	STAR	learn *about*	CO-N.REA-D
lead-coloured figures	LIVID	learned *characters*	LEANDER
lead in(to) *	incl in *	learned man	DR.MAGUS
•*lead* a king *into* r-ing	RAKING		SAGE
	RARING	learner	L
lead off	O	hence	
lead *off*	omit first letter	•learner finished	LOVER
•*lead off* (t)he. . .	HE	•learner in study	LINDEN
•lead *off* the (c)limb	LIMB	•learner *with* spectacles	LOO
leader *dropped from* (p)arty	ARTY	learning	LORE
leader has gone	omit first letter	learner's figure	FIFTY.L
•Oriental *leader has*		**least common multiple**	LCM
gone	(e)ASTERN	**leave**	
leader of flock	BELLWETHER	he *leaves* t(he). . .	T
leader of flock	F	I *leave*. . .	omit I
leader of Marathon	M.MU	king *left*. . .	omit K or R
leader's address		*leave* it out	omit IT
	DOWNING STREET	*leave* me *out*	omit ME
leaderless (w)omen	OMEN	leave work	HOLIDAY JOB
leading	(in) VA-N.NOI	*leave room for* a. . .	incl A
leading artist	PRA	*leave room for* *	incl *
leading character	A.NOI-	•*leave room for* it *in*	
leading character in play	P	south-east	SITE
leading edges of technological		*leave out* a. . .	omit A
advance	TA	*leave out* *	omit *
leading lady	EVE.USHERETTE	•p(l)ayers *leave out*	
leading lady	L	beginner	PAYERS
leading man	ADAM.GUIDE	leave the North	LEAVEN
	STAR.USHER	leaves	TEA

leaves producer	TREE
leaves supporter	STEM
left right *out*	omit R or RT
led	(*see* lead)
left[1]	L.LT.PORT.RED
hence	
•100 left	CL
•excessively left	TOOL
•fruit left	PEARL
and	
•left in church	LINCH
•left port	LADEN
•left with no ship	LOSS
and	
•is *in* left. . .	LIST
•left *out* last word	LAMENT
•left *without* spectacles	LOOT
and	
•left end	PORTEND
•left one company	PORTICO
•left one on. . .	PORTION
and	
•left a record	RED TAPE
•left, I see	REDIVIDE
•left out	REDOUT
left *back*⟨	TL
left *behind*	last letter L
•girl left *behind*	NORMAL
left centre	LC
left *inside*	incl L
•left *inside* c-ove	CLOVE
•left *ins*-ide	SLIDE
left *outside*	(in) L-T.(in) POR-T
left turn	LU
left *turns*⟨	TL
left[2]	
left centre	C
left h̄and	H
left-h̄and	LH.VERSO.VO
left hand of G̱od	G
left hands	LABOUR
left of t̄arget	T
leftist̄	RED
left wing	RED
	(*see also* leave)
leg	
leg	LEFT.ON
leg before (wicket)	LB(W)
le̱g-*break*	GEL.-GLE

leg, *say*	ELEGY
leg *up*(D) ↑	NO
legs	ELEVEN
legal	LEG
legal argument	BARROW
legal division	DIVORCE
legal document	DEED
legal exercise	CONSTITUTIONAL
legate	HE
legend	FOOT.TOE
legislature	LEG
legislator	DRACO
lemur	(*see* monkey)
length	L
lengthy stay	LONGSTOP
Lesotho	LS
capital	L.MASERU
language	SESOTHO
less	
doe(s) *less*	DOE
less dash	MINUS
less important	B
less than al(l). . .	AL
less than tw/o-pen/ce	OPEN
less than four	THREE
less than (f)our	OUR
less than (t)he *whole*. . .	HE
less than the whole (t)own	OWN
less than their. . .	THE.HEIR
let	
let	(in) R-ENT
let down	ABSEIL
let in a. . .	incl A
let in *	incl *
•sh-e *lets in* a student	SHALE
let *loose*	-TLE
l̄et *out* a. . .	omit A
let out *	omit *
•t(he)ory he *let out*. . .	TORY
l̄et *out*	-TLE
letter	
letter *from* Sp(a)in	SPIN
letter *from* S̱tell(a), *maybe*	TELLS
letter of thanks	COLLINS
letter opener	ADDRESSEE
letter opener	L
l̄etter opening	L
l̄etter or two	BORED.DORIC
	HORSE.KORAN.LORIS

PORCH.SORRY.TORUS
WORTH
(*see also* two²)
letter *out of* li(n)e   LIE
letter *to* a policeman   COPE.COPS
COPT.COPY
letter *to* hotel   FRITZ
letters *for* father   PANDA
letters of thanks   TA
letters *from* Spa(in)   SPA
letters *from* (S)tell(a)   TELL
letters of credit   LC
letters of love   VOLE
letters *to* friends
PALSHIP.PALSIED
letterheads   CAPITALS
send *letters*   DENS.ENDS
level head   EVENNESS
levitation of new....(D) ↑   WEN
Leviticus   LEV
lexicon   LEX
liar   ANANIAS.MATILDA
Liberal   L.LIB
liberate slaves   VALSES
Liberia(n)   LB
capital   L.MONROVIA
Library Association   LA
Libya(n)¹   LAR
hence
•Libya *and* America   LARUS
•Libya *has* many...   LARD
•Libya *has* railway   LARRY
and
•Libya *without* iron   FLARE
•live *outside* Libya   BLARE
•talk *about* Libya   SALARY
and
•directions *in* Libya   LASER
•grow old *in* Libya   LAAGER
•woman *in* Libya   LASHER
and
•doctor *goes to* Libya   MOLAR
•Libya *follows* a...   ALAR
•thus Libya...   SOLAR
Libyan²
capital   L.TRIPOLI
characters   LAR
leader   L
(*see also* Arab(ic)²)

licence
licence may be...   BEAMY
licentiate   L
Licentiate
—in Dental Surgery   LDS
—in Surgery   LCH
—in Theology   LTH.THL
—of Apothecaries' Company LAC
—of College of Preceptors   LCP
—of Society of Apothecaries   LSA
lie-abed   OYSTER
Liechtenstein   FL
capital   L.VADUZ
lief   WILDLIFE
lieutenant   LOOT.LT
life symbol   ANKH
lifted ban(D) ↑   NAB
light
light   MATCH.MOON.STAR
SUN.VERY
light-emitting diode   LED
light heart   DAY CENTRE
light *heart*   G
Light Infantry   LI
light machine-gun   LMG
light spasm   ARCTIC
light symbol   FLOODMARK
lighter   FIRESHIP
lighter propellor   BARGE-POLE
SCREW
lighter stone   FLINT
lightweight   CARAT.CT.FEATHER
G.GRAM(ME).OUNCE.OZ
like¹   AS
hence
•like a bird   ASTERN
•like a buccaneer   ASPIRATE
•like a fish   ASHAKE
and
•as *in* church   CASE
•beetle-like   DORAS
(*see also* as¹)
like²   ALA
hence
•black like...   BALA
•like a marine   ALARM
•like *in* m-y...   MALAY
like³   -ISH
like a bridge   SPANISH

like a couple, *say*	PERISH	•certain *to be lined by*	
like a cryptogam	FURNISH	copper	SECURE
like a French woman, *say*	FAMISH	liner	SS
like a lake	TARNISH	lines	BR.RLY.RY
like a stamp	FRANKISH	hence	
like a vehicle	VANISH	•lines have. . .	BROWN
like a WC, *say*	LAVISH	•doctor the lines	MOTHERLY
like an embargo	BANISH	•street *with* no lines	STORY
like an equal	PARISH	lines	ODE.VERSE
like anger	IRISH	hence	
like cereal	CORNISH	•right lines	RODE
like fruit, *say*	PERISH	•study lines	CONVERSE
like motor fuel	DERVISH	lines up	DRESSES
like part of Yorkshire	MOORISH	lines *up*(D) ↑	RB
like preserved meat	HAMISH	*lining* *	incl in *

like⁴

		•copper *lining* certain. . .	SECURE
like an aristocrat	U	**link**	
like kippers	ASLEEP	link-*up*(D) ↑	EIT
like rain	RIGHT	linked characters	
like rain	REIN.REIGN		SIAMESE TWINS
like you	EWE.YEW	**Linnaean Society**	LS
like one. . . .	WON	**lion**	
like some. . .	SUM	lion-tamer	ANDROCLES.DANIEL

like⁵   (*see* love³)

		lioness	ELSA
like⁶		**liqueur**	(*see* drink²)
meaning:		**liquid**	LID
of, pertaining to,		*liquidate* a mob	BOMA.MOAB
relating to	(*see* pertaining)	liquified natural gas	LNG
lime *squash*	EMIL.MILE	liquified petroleum gas	LPG
limit		**liquor**	(*see* drink²)
limited amount of		**lira(e)**	L.LR
ca/sh I p/ut	SHIP	**lisp**	
limited are(a)	ARE	•*lisp* in song	THONG
limited a/rea m/ay. . .	REAM	•*lisping* sigh	THIGH
limited liability	LTD.PLC	•sing *lispingly*	THING
limited subscription	INITIALS	**listed building**	TOWER OF PISA
limiting a. . .	incl A	**listen**	
limiting *	incl *	for *listening to*. . .	FORE.FOUR
•s-un *limiting* power	SPUN	I see why *listeners*. . .	ICY
limited by *	incl in *	*listen* to peace. . .	TWO-PIECE
•power *limited by* s-un	SPUN	listener	AUDITOR.EAR.LUG
limits of patience	PE	**literal(ly)**	LIT
limousine	OSCAR	**literary**	
line		literary hack	ROSINANTE
line	I.L.RY	literature	LIT
line of music	CONGA	**litre**	L
line-*out*	omit I	**litter container**	STY
line-*out*	LIEN.NILE	**little¹**	WEE
lined by *	incl *	hence	

•little boy	WEENED
•little for each. . .	WEEPER
•little the *German*. . .	WEEDER

little²

indicates abbreviation:

Little Bill	AC
little bounder	ROO
Little Boy Blue	VICTORY
little brother	BRER
little brothers	BROS
little change	D.-ID.P.-IP
little chap	GENT
little coin	D.-ID.P.-IP
little couple	PR
little horse	GEE.GG
Little John	JNO
little money	D.-ID.IP.P
little mother	MA
little notice	AD
little response	ANS
little river	R
little theatre	REP
little time	D.H.HR.M.MIN
	MO.S.SEC.T
little way	RD.RY.ST

little³

little butter	KID
little by little	ERIC
little change	IP.P.PENNY
little change in shape	SHADE
little change in <u>shape</u>	HEAPS
	PHASE
little charge	ION
little difference in board. . .	BEARD
little fight	SCRAP
little fish	PIKELET
little food	SHORTBREAD
little growth	BUD.LEAFLET
little help	MINUTE HAND
little of his. . .	H
little of h̄/is le/ave	ISLE
little idiot	ASSET
little letter	SHORTEN
little lower	CALF
little man	MINUTE HAND
little Mark	SCARLET
Little Mary	STOMACH.TUM
little money	IP.P.PENNY
little mother	MINIMUM

little music	NOTE
	(*see* note)
little music	-IC
little petticoat	SHORT SLIP
little ring	SHORT CIRCUIT
little time	SHORTAGE
Little Tommy	SON OF A GUN
little workman	SHORTHAND
	(*see also* small²)

live   BE

live *broadcast*	EVIL.VILE
one *lives in*. . .	incl A or I
* *lives in*. . .	incl *
•we *live in* he-r. . .	HEWER
lived so long	AV
lively dance	CANED
lively f̄igures	VIVID
lives round. . .	ISO-
living person	INCUMBENT

lizard¹   AGAMA.AGAMID(AE)

	AMPHISBAENA
	GECKO(ES).LACERTIAN
	LACERTILIAN
African	GECKO.(I)GUANA
	MONITOR.SKINK
American	GILA MONSTER.UTA
Asian	FRILLED LIZARD.MONITOR
Australian	BLUE TONGUE
	CHLAMYDOSAURUS
	FRILLED LIZARD.GO(H)ANNA
	MOLOCH.MONITOR
	MOUNTAIN DEVIL
	PERENTIE.SPINY LIZARD
	THORN-DEVIL
colour-changing	CHAM(A)ELEON
duck-billed	HADROSAUR
fish-like	ICTHYOPTERYGIA
	ICTHYOSAURUS
Philippine	IBID.IBIT
prehistoric	ALLOSAURUS
	ANATOSAURUS
	CERATOSAURUS
	CORYTHOSAURUS
	DEINOSAUR.DINOSAUR
	ELASMOSAURUS
	GORGOSAURUS
	HYPSILOPHODONT
	KRONOSAURUS
	LABYRINTHODONT

	MOSASAURUS
	ORNITHOSUCHUS
	PACHYCEPHALOSAURUS
	PARASAUROLOPHUS
	POLACANTHUS
	TYLOSAURUS
—Cretaceous	ANKYLOSAURUS
	HADROSAURUS
	IGUANADON
	MEGALOSAURUS
	TITANOSAURUS
	TYRANNOSAURUS (REX)
—Colorado/Wyoming	
	APATOSAURUS
	ATLANTOSAURUS
	BRONTOSAURUS
—flying	ORNITHOSAURUS
	PTERODACTYL(E)
—Jurassic	CETEOSAURUS
	DIPLODOCUS
	IGUANADON
	STEGOSAURUS
—Mesozoic	PLESIOSAURUS
South American	AMPHISBAENA
	BASILISK.(I)GUANA
	TEGUEXIN
venomous	GILA MONSTER

lizard[2]

lizard *skin*	LD
l̄izard's place	CORNWALL

l-letter	LESS
loaded	RICH
local[1]	INN.PH.PUB
local employee	BARMAID
	BARMAN.BARTENDER

local[2]

indicates dialect:	
•*locally* (h)er...	ER
•*locally* worse	WUSS
(*see also* dialect)	

local[3]

Local Defence Volunteers	HG
	LDV
Local Education Authority	LEA

locate

located in *	incl in *
•I am *located in* Avon	AVION
located in t/he w/oods	HEW
Location of Offices Bureau	LOB

loch	NESS
lock	
lock	TRESS
hence	
•a lock-*up*(D) ↑	ASSERT
•the *Camptown*	
lock-*up*(D) ↑	DESSERT
lock keeper	HAIR NET
locker	KEY
locksmith	WIGMAKER
lodge	
lodged in *	incl in *
•convict *lodged in*	
vil-e...	VILLAGE
lodgings	PAD
logarithm	LOG
logical *extremes*	LL
L̄ondon	LOND.
London	
—and North-Eastern	
Railway	LNER
—County Council	LCC
—Midland and Scottish	LMS
—Missionary Society	LMS
—Philharmonic Orchestra	LPO
—School of Economics	LSE
—Symphony Orchestra	LSO
London area	SE
London magazine	ARSENAL
London-town	DERRY
long	
long-distance	
runner	AMAZON.NILE
long metre	LM
long-playing record	LP
longitude	LON(G)
look[1]	LA.LO.SEE.V.VID.VIDE
hence	
•look *almost* de(a)d	LADED
•look *at* the...	LATHE
•look under	LAUNDER
and	
•look *round*⟨	OL.AL
•look *round*	L-A.L-O.SE-E.VI-D
•look round	LOO
and	
•a look of...	ALOOF
•look *in* two directions	SLOW
•look one way	LOWEST

•look *up*	AL.OL	•(s)he *loses her head*	HE
and		lose *heart*	
•look *at* fever	VAGUE	•diplomats lose *heart*	CLOSED
•look in about. . .	VINCA	*lose* heart	
•look in square	VINT	•t(he)y *lose* heart	-TY
and		*lose* heart	EARTH.HATER
•look *about* an. . .	VIAND	*lose* his shirt	omit T
•look *round* a soft. . .	VAPID	*lose* key	omit A-G
and		*lose* money	omit L
•look no. . .	VIDEO	*lose* nothing	omit O
look²	SEE	*lose* odds and *ends*	omit OD
look *out*	SE-E	*lose* one	omit A or I
•look *out* bat	SEBATE	*lose* opener	omit first letter
•*lookout* dog	SECURE	•(M)CC *lose* opener	CC
•Look *out*, Sam!	SESAME		HUNDREDS
look *up*(D) ↑	-EES	lose *out*	SLOE.SOLE
looked *around*	SE-EN	*lose* power	omit P
looked *up*(D)	WAS	*lose* silver. . .	omit AG
look³		*lose* tail	omit last letter
look *both ways*	EYE	•do(g) *loses* tail	DO
look lively!	EYEBRIGHT	*lose* the round	omit O
look out	CAVE	*lose* time	omit T
	FORE	*losing* a. . .	omit A
look *up and down*(D)	EYE	*losing* *	omit *
lookout man	EXTRAVERT	•fa(the)r *losing* the. . .	FAR
	EXTROVERT	**loss**	(*see* without²)
looking about	REGARDING	*lost* a set	SEAT.TEAS
tots *looking up*(D) ↑	STOT	**lot**	C.D.L.M
loop	O		(*see also* many¹)
loose		lot of money	IMPOUNDS
loose ends	LE	*lot of* seats	SEA
loose ends	DENS.SEND	**loud (very loud)**	F.(FF)
loose painter	CAST OFF	hence	
loosely tied ends	DESTINED	•a loud anger	AFIRE
loosen ties	SITE	•a loud blonde	AFFAIR
loosens trousers	SLACKS	•a loud listener	AFEAR
lopping (b)ranch	RANCH	and	
lord	LD	•loud instrument	FLUTE
Lord		•loud music	FROCK
—Chief Justice	LCJ	•loud yob	FLOUT
—Justice	LJ	and	
—Provost	LP	•a very loud blow	AFFRIGHT
Lordship	LDP.LP	•a very loud listener	AFFEAR
Los Angeles	LA	•a very loud song	AFFAIR
lose		**loudspeaker**	PA
lose all. . .	omit ALL	**Louis XIV**	SUN KING
•b(all)oon *loses* all. . .	BOON	**love¹**	O.ZERO
lose half that	TH.AT	hence	
lose head	omit first letter	•love divine	ODD

•love letter O
•love letter OF.OH.ON.OR.OS
•love letters OAR etc.
•love offal OLIVER
and
•dog I love CURIO
•lady's love HERO
•time for love MAYO
and
•accountants in love CASINO
•love-*in*-a-m-ist MOIST
and
•fifty loves LOO
•loves Old English coin OORIAL
•loves speed OOMPH
•love*less* omit O

love²

love POINTLESS
lover LOTHARIO
loving son TENDERS

love³

including
addiction to
excessive love for
love of
lover of
loving
mania for
obsession with:

alcohol METHOMANIA
animals ZOOPHILIA.ZOOPHILISM ZOOPHILY
archery TOXOPHILY
ballet BALLETOMANIA
birds ORNITHOPHILY
books BIBLIOMANIA BIBLIOPHILIA
cats AIL(O)UROPHILIA
Celtic matters CELTOMANIA KELTOMANIA
children PHILOPROGENITIVENESS
China SINOPHILISM.SINOPHILY
climbing buildings STEGOPHILIA
corpses NECROPHILIA NECROPHILISM NECROPHILY
Dante DANTEAN DANTOPHILIST
decaying matter SAPROPHILIA
dogs CANOPHILIA
England/English ANGLOPHILIA
ether ETHEROMANIA
familiar places NESTOMANIA
filth COPROPHILIA
fire PYROMANIA
flowers ANTHOMANIA
food of a particular kind OPSOMANIA
foreign things XENOMANIA
France/French FRANCOPHILE GALLOMANIA.GALLOPHILE
Germany/Germans GERMANOPHIL(E)
god and man THEOPHILANTHROPY
gold CHRYSOPHILITE GOLD FEVER
gramophone records DISCOPHILE
Greece PHILHELLENIC
heat THERMOPHILE
knowledge PHILOSOPHY
learning PHILOMATHY
light PHOTOPHILY
lying MYTHOMANIA
mankind PHILANTHROPY
moisture HYGROPHILE
music MELOMANIA PHILHARMONIC
negroes NEGROPHIL(E)
new things NEOPHILIA
old people GERONTOPHILIA
one's name or writings in print TYPOMANIA
pictures ICONOPHILIA
poisons TOXICOMANIA
pulling out hair TRICHOTILLOMANIA
rain OMBROPHILE
Russia/Russians RUSSOPHILE
salt (plants) HALOPHILE
sand (insects, plants) PSAMMOPHIL(E)
self EGOMANIA
sexual
—passion EROTOMANIA
—pleasure SCOP(T)OPHILIA
shells CONCHOPHILE

snakes	OPHIOPHILIST	low frequency	LF
stamps	PHILATELY	Low German	LG
	TIMBROMANIA	low grade	E
	TIMBROPHILY	low-grade German. . .	EG
stealing	KLEPTOMANIA	low interest	BOREDOM.ENNUI
stone (insects, plants)		Low Latin	LL
	LITHOPHYTE	low note, *say*	DEEP SEA
symbolism	TYPOMANIA	low pressure	LP
tulip-growing	TULIPOMANIA	low priced	PEACH
Turkey/Turks	TURCOPHILE	low ranker	PAWN.PRIVATE
water	HYDROMANIA	low *sound*	LO
wild animals	PHILOTHERIANISM	low swinger	CHARIOT
wine	OENOMANIA.OENOPHILY	low tar	SUBMARINER
wisdom	PHILOSOPHY	low tension	LT
women	PHILOGYNY	lower case	LC
low¹	MOO	lower percentage	CUT
hence		**loyal friend**	ACHATES
·low church	MOOCH	**lumen**	L
·low Latin	MOOL	**luminance**	L
·low point	MOON	*lump of* earth	EAR
·low-*rise*(D) ↑	-OOM	**lunchtime**	ONE.I
·low stream	MOOR-ILL	**lurk**	
lower	COW	*lurking in* *	incl in *
low²		·she is *lurking in* a-n. . .	ASHEN
Low character	BLIMP	**lux**	LX
low *characters*	OWL	**Luxembourg**	L
low class, *say*	FORESEE	**lysergic acid**	LSD
low-down	GEN		

M

Bond's boss. em. emma. forty. forty thousand. Frenchman. lot. maiden. male.
Malta. man. many. mare. mark. married. masculine. mass. master.
medium. member. meridian. meso-. meta-. metre. mile. mille. milli-.
modulus. Monday. monsieur. month. moon. motorway. mu. noon. number.
roof. small square. spymaster. thousand. vitamin

Mac		**made**	(*see* make)
Mac's = Scottish		**magazine**	GLOSSY.MAG
•*Mac's* house	BIGGIN	*magical* trips	SPIRT.SPRIT
(*see also* Scottish)		**magistrate's bill**	BEAK
Maccabees	MAC	**magnetic**	MAG
machine-gun	MG	**maiden**	M.OVER
mad		maiden(D)	IO
mad dog	GOD	maiden *over*⟨	LAG
mad *French*...	FOLLE.FOU	**mail**	
mad *German*	VERRUCKT	mail *order*	LIAM.MALI
Mad Hatter	THREAT	mailboat	RMS
mad individual	BATSMAN	**main**[1]	DEEP.SEA
mad *Italian*	A MATTO	hence	
mad *Roman*		•main issue	SEASON
	NON COMPOS MENTIS	•main picture	SEASCAPE
mad *Spanish*...	LOCO	•main square	SEAT
mad strikers	BATS	**main**[2]	
maddened beast	BASTE.BEATS	main distributor	AORTA
madly beats	BASTE.BEAST	main event	REGATTA
Madagascar	MALAGASH	main force	NAVY
	MALAGASY.RM	main partner	MIGHT
bird	DRONGO-CUCKOO	main road	AI.MI
brush turkey	TALEGALLA	main support	MAST.YARD(-ARM)
capital	M.TANANARIVE	main tower	TUGBOAT
civet	FO(U)SSA	*mainly* woo(d)	WOO
climbing plant	WAX FLOWER	**maintain tower**	KEEP
flower	STEPHANOTIS	**Majesties**	MM
insectivore	TENREC	**major**	BARBARA
hedgehog	TANREC.TENREC		GROWN UP.MAJ
language	MALAGASH	*majority of* th(e)...	TH
	MALAGASY	**make**	
leader	M	made *comeback*⟨	EDAM
lemur	MONGOOSE	made it	FEC(IT).FF
plants	LATTICE LEAF	*made it up* so we...	OWES.WOES
	OUVIRANDA.WATER YAM	made man	ROBOT
poison	TANGHIN	*made of* steel	LEETS.STELE
race	HOVA	*made out* case	ACES.AESC
snake	LANGAHA	*made out of* p/latin/um	LATIN
tree	TANGHIN	made *speech*	MAID
	TRAVELLER'S-TREE	*made* to run race	RACONTEUR
wingless bird	AEPYORNIS	*made up* tales	LEATS.SLATE
madam	MDM		STALE

made worse wines	SWINE
make a dash	HYPHENATE
make a hash of it when. . .	WHITEN
make a mess of things	NIGHTS
make a song *about*	S-ING
make changes in Cremona	ROMANCE
make little difference to design	RESIGN
make notes	SING
make notes *about*	S-ING
make one	MARRY.WED
*make * heard*	
•horse *makes itself heard*	HOARSE
make people laugh	BEDROLL
make play	BRAND
make-*up*(D) ↑	OD
make up a bed	BADE.BEAD
make-up of stars	TSARS
makes cars	ARCS.SCAR
makes progress	STEPSON
makes some of t/he Be/lgians. . .	HEBE
making tarts	START
making of Mary	ARMY.MYRA
Malachi	MAL
Malagasy	(*see* Madagascar)
Malawi	MW
Malay(an)	MAL
apple	OTAHEITE
aromatic oil	CAJEPUT.CAJUPUT
badger	TELEDU
bear	BRUANG.HONEY-BEAR SUN-BEAR
betel	SIRI(H)
blowpipe	SUMPIT(AN)
boat	COROCORE.COROCORO PRA(H)U.PROA
capital	KUALA LUMPUR.M
civet	HEMIGALE.PARADOXURE
courtyard	KAMPONG
field	PADANG
fish	GORAMY.GO(U)RAMI
frenzy	AMOK
fruit	RAMBUTAN
—bat	KALONG
—tree	DURIAN.DURION
garment	SARONG
grass	(L)ALANG(ALANG)

knife	CREASE.CREESE KREESE.KRIS.PARANG
language	SAKAI
leader	M
lord	TUAN
petty officer	TINDAL
phalanger	CUSCUS
rum	TAFIA
sir	TUAN
skirt	SARONG
timber	TEAK
title of esteem	TUAN
tree	ILANG-ILANG.RAMBUTAN SAP(P)AN.TEAK.YLANG-YLANG
tribe	SAKAI
tunic	KABAYA
verse form	PANTO(U)M
village	KAMPONG
whisky and soda	STENGAH STINGER
Malaysia	MAL
male[1]	HE.HIM.M.MAN
hence	
•male sheep	HET-UP
•male students	HELL
•male *with* a fellow. . .	HEAD-ON
and	
•male *aboard*	SHIMS
•male *in* church	CHIME
and	
•male as first-class. . .	MASAI
•male in a shirt	MINT
•male tree	MACER.MASH
•male *with* nothing on	MOON
and	
•English male dined. . .	EMANATE
•male composer, *say*	MANHANDLE
•male *with* English. . .	MANE
male[2]	
male chauvinist pig	MCP
male *said*. . .	MAIL
Mali	RMM
malicious light	ARSON
Malta	M
Maltese	
leader	M
measure	CANNA.PIEDE
weight	ROTOLO
maltreated horses	SHORES

man	IOM.ISLE.M	*manipulation of* <u>bone</u>	EBON
man and		***manoeuvred*** <u>his car</u>	CHAIRS
—boy	GENTLES	**manor**	HOUSE OF LORDS
—couple	DESPAIR	**manufacture**	
—woman	EVADES.MANGAL	manufactured	MFD
	SALTED.VIAL	manufacturer(s)	MFR(S)
man doing housework	BETTY	*manufacturer of* <u>china</u>	CHAIN
man from		*manufactures* <u>tables</u>	BLEATS
—ancient Rome	VIR	**manuscript(s)**	MS.(MSS)
—Adelaide	DIGGER	**Manx**	
—Ayr	MON.RAY	cat	CA(t).PUS(s)
—Berlin	MANN	leader	M
—Glasgow	IAN.MAC.MON	man	DOUGLAS.KELLY.MA(n)
—Madrid	HOMBRE	parliament	TYNWALD
—Paris	HOMME	—lower house	HOUSE OF KEYS
—Rome	HUOMO	**many¹**	C.CL.D.DI.L.M
man in		hence	
—a tub	DIOGENES	•many long	CACHE
—the ring	THEO	•many have…	CLOWN
man of		•a lot *have* a right…	DART
—determination	WILL	•many scattered	DISOWN
—India	CLIVE	•many articles	LATHE
—might	SMITH	•fight *with* a lot…	WARM
—pride	LEO	**many²**	
—Savoy	GILBERT.SULLIVAN	ma(n)y *nameless*…	MAY
—Verona	GENTLEMAN	m(an)y *won't have* an…	MY
	VALENTINE	**many³**	MULT(I)-.POLY-
man on board	BISHOP.KING	having many:	
	KNIGHT.PAWN	amino acids	POLYPEPTIDE
man's drink	PORTER	atoms	POLYATOMIC
man's man	VALET	axes	POLYAXIAL.POLYAXON
Man's man	DOUGLAS	branches	MULTIRAMIFIED
manservant	FRIDAY.JEEVES	cells	MULTICAMERATE
	VALET		MULTICELLULAR
manage	COPE.EIGHTEEN.RUN		POLYTHALAMOUS
manage <u>horse</u>	HOSER.SHORE	centres	MULTICENTRAL
managed	RAN	chambers	MULTICAMERATE
management	ADMIN.BOARD		MULTILOCULATE
management <u>team</u>	MATE.MEAT		POLYTHALAMOUS
	TAME	coils	MULTISPIRAL
managing director	MD	colours	MULTICOLOURED
mandarin's coat	ORANGE PEEL		POLYCHROM(AT)IC
mangled <u>arm</u>	MAR.RAM	columns	POLYSTYLAR
mania	(*see* love³)		POLYSTYLE
Manila fabric	JUSSI	components	MULTIPLE
manipulate		circles	POLYCYCLIC
manipulate <u>men as</u>…	MEANS	elements	MULTIPLE
	NAMES		POLYSYNTHETIC
manipulating <u>pawns</u>	SPAWN	faces	MULTIFACED

feet	MULTIPED(E)	teeth	MULTIDENTATE
fine teeth	MULTIDENTICULATE	times basic number of	
fingers	MULTIDIGITATE	chromosomes	POLYPLOID
flowers	MULTIFLOROUS	toes	POLYDACTYLOUS
foils	MULTIFOIL	tones	POLYTONAL
forms	POLYMORPHIC	tubercles	MULTITUBERCULATE
fruiting periods	POLYCARPIC	turns	POLYCYCLIC
	POLYCARPOUS	types	POLYTYPIC
furrows	MULTISULCATE	variables	MULTIVARIATE
heads	MULTICAPITATE	voices	POLYPHONIC
	MULTICIPITAL	ways	MULTIVIOUS
husbands	POLYANDROUS	whorls	POLYCYCLIC
	POLYGAMOUS	wives	POLYGYNOUS
hydroxyl groups	POLYHYDRIC	xylem strands	POLYARCH
individuals in colony	POLYZOIC	zones or belts	POLYZONAL
joints	MULT(I)ARTICULATE	**marble** *bust*	RAMBLE
languages	MULTILINGUAL	**Maori**	(*see* New Zealand)
leaflets	MULTIFOLIOLATE	**March**	MAR
leaves	MULTIFOLIATE	**Marine**	JOLLY.RM
lines	MULTILINEAL	Marine band	CREW
	MULTILINEAR	**mark**	
lobes	MULTIFID(OUS)	mark ANTONY.DM.M.MK.SCAR	
MULTILOBATE.MULTILOBED		Mark I	MI
lobules	MULTILOBULAR	Mark II	TWAIN
	MULTILOBULATE	Mark of the Beast	MB
meanings	MULTIVOCAL	mark time	LINEAGE
names	POLYONYMOUS	marksman, *say* CHICO.GROUCHO	
pairs of leaflets	MULTIJUGOUS		HARPO.KARL
	MULTIJUGATE	**maroon thread**	STRAND
parents	POLYHYBRID	**married**	M
partitions	MULTISEPTATE	hence	
parts	MULTIPARTITE	•a married woman	AMERICA
MULTI-STAGE.POLYMEROUS		•married man	MART
pistils	POLYGYNIAN	•married woman	MALICE
	POLYGYNOUS		MANNA.MINA
rays	POLYACT(INAL)	**Marshal**	FOCH.NEY
	POLYACTINE	**martial art**	
ribs	MULTICOSTATE	Chinese	KUNG-FU
rings	POLYCYCLIC	Japanese	AIKIDO.JUDO
sepals	POLYSEPALOUS	J(I)U-JITSU.JUJUTSU	
shapes	MULTIFORM	KARATE.KEMPO.KENDO	
	POLYMORPHIC	KYOKUSHINKAI.SANKUKAI	
sides	MULTILATERAL	SHOTOKAI.SHOTOKAN	
small teeth	POLYPROTODONT	Korean HAPKIDO.SULKIDO	
sounds	MULTISONANT	TANG SOO DO.TAEKWONDO	
stems	MULTICAULINE	Okinawan	KARATE
styles	POLYGYNIAN	**martyrs**	MM
	POLYGYNOUS	**Marxist drug**	OPIUM
syllables	POLYSYLLABIC	**Marylebone Cricket Club**	MCC

masculine	M.MAS(C)
mashed peas	APSE
Masonic chief	MASTER BUILDER
masquerade as Oriental	RELATION
mass	M
Massachusetts Institute of	
Technology	MIT
master[1]	AM.DAN.M.MA
hence	
•directions *to* master	SEDAN
•master is hard	DANISH
•master *at* church	DANCE
and	
•master *and* emperor	MOTTO
•master in America	MINUS
•master *with* a girl	MALICE
and	
•master *has* one study	MAIDEN
•master-key	MAC.MAD.MAE
•masterly figure	MAC
master[2]	
master key for...	HEADLOCK
Master of Ceremonies	MC
master *switch*	STREAM
master*piece*	MAS.TER
master[3]	MR
Master of	
—Arts	MA
—Dental Surgery	MDS
—Foxhounds	MOF
—Laws	LLM
—Science	MSC
—Surgery	MCH.MS.CHM.CM
—the Rolls	MR.CHAUFFEUR
—Theology	MTH
mat *finish*	T
match	LIGHT.TEST.VESTA
match points	COMPARE
matchmaker	WOOD
mate	CHINA.PAL.WIFE
mating of pairs	PEARS
mating of bears	BARES
material	
material part	TRAP
material for book	BOKO
maths function	COS.LOG
	SINE.TAN
hence	
•function put...	COSSET

•function in charge	LOGIC
•function makes	
better	SINECURES
•function with grand...	TANG
matted fibre	BRIEF
Mauretania	RIM
Mauritius	MS
extinct bird	DODO
leader	M
maximum	MAX
may	
May 8th	V-DAY
may be sent	NETS.TENS
may become weak	WAKE
may he/she rest well	BQ
May's follower	JUNE
maybe dog	SETTER
maybe it was	WAIST
maybe setter	DOG
Mayday	SOS
Mayfair	WI
maze	
Hampton *maze*	PHANTOM
maze in garden	DANGER.RANGED
me *in France*	MOI
meal ticket	LV
mean	
mean person	AVERAGE MAN
mean sea-level	MSL
mean time	MT
meant, *say*	-MENT
meantime	PARAGE
measure	
some commonly used	
units	EL(L).EM.EN
	FT.Y(D).M
other units:	
angle	SECOND
—60 seconds	MINUTE
—60 minutes	DEGREE
—15 degrees	HOUR
—57.3 degrees	RADIAN
—90 degrees	QUADRANT
—360 degrees	CIRCLE
—⅛ circle	OCTANT
—⅙ circle	SEXTANT
—¼ circle	QUADRANT
—angular distance of	
90 degrees	QUADRATURE

—division of	
—arc	SCRUPLE
—compass	POINT
—solid	STERADIAN
area	
—272 square feet	ROD.PERCH
	POLE
—$^1/_4$ acre	ROOD
—4840 square yards	ACRE
—2.48 acres	HECTARE
—13 acres	BOVATE.OXGATE
	OXGANG
—26 acres	HUSBANDLAND
—30 acres	YARDLAND.VIRGATE
—100 acres	CARUCATE
—120 acres	HIDE
atmospheric pressure	BAR
—1000 bars	KILOBAR
—normal pressure	
STANDARD ATMOSPHERE	
—low pressure unit	TORR
capacity	
—small	MINIM
—small handful or pinch	PUGIL
—mouthful	SLUG
—16 fluid ounces (American)	
	PINT
—20 fluid ounces	PINT
—$^1/_4$ pint	GILL.NOGGIN
	QUARTERN
—$^1/_2$ gallon	STOUP
—$^1/_3$ bottle	DOP
—4 gills	PINT
—577 cubic centimetres	PINT
—2 pints	QUART
—4 pints (wine)	MAGNUM
—2 bottles	MAGNUM
—4 bottles	JEROBOAM
—6 bottles	REHOBOAM
—8 bottles	METHUSELAH
—20 bottles	NEBUCHADNEZZAR
—1, 3 or 6 quarts (liquor)	TAPPIT
—2 quarts	POTTLE
—4 quarts	GALLON
—277 cubic inches	GALLON
—2 gallons	PECK
—9 pecks (apples)	SEAM
—$4^1/_2$ gallons	PIN
—8 gallons	BUSHEL

—8 bushels	QUARTER
—8 bushels (grain)	SEAM
—9 bushels	FAT
—40 bushels (corn or salt)	WEY
—9 gallons	FIRKIN
—18 gallons	KILDERKIN
—36 gallons	BARREL
—42 gallons	TIERCE
—3 tierces	PIPE
—$^1/_8$- pipe	OCTAVE
—46 gallons (claret)	HOGSHEAD
—$52^1/_2$ gallons	HOGSHEAD
—54 gallons (beer)	HOGSHEAD
—63 gallons (wine)	HOGSHEAD
—1 hogshead	MUID
—2 hogsheads	PIPE
—70-120 gallons	PUNCHEON
—108 gallons (beer, sherry)	BUTT
—126 gallons (wine)	BUTT
—216 gallons (ale)	TUN
—252 gallons (wine)	TUN
—4 bushels	CO(O)MB.COMBE
—6 bushels	BOLL
—96 bushels	CHALDER
cloth	
—$1^1/_2$ yards	ELL
—20 hanks (linen yarn)	BUNDLE
—80 yards (worsted yarn)	LEA
—120 yards (cotton yarn)	LEA
—300 yards (linen yarn)	LEA
—180,000 yards (linen	
yarn)	BUNCH
distance	
—very small	ANGSTROM.FERMI
MICROMILLIMETRE.MICRON	
—small	BARLEYCORN
	EL.EM.EN.MM
—2.25 millimetres	LIGNE
—$^1/_{16}$ inch	LINE
—$^1/_3$ inch	BARLEYCORN
—$^3/_4$ inch	DIGIT
—$2^1/_2$ inches	NAIL
—3-4 inches	PALM
—handsbreadth	PALM
—4 inches	HAND
—8 inches	LINK
—9 inches	SPAN
—12 inches	FOOT.LAST
—18-22 inches	CUBIT(US)

—30 inches	PACE
—33 inches (approx.)	METRE
—36 inches	YARD
—37 inches	CLOTH-YARD
—45 inches	ELL
—58 inches	ROMAN PACE
—6 feet	FATHOM
—stretch of arms	FATHOM
—5$\frac{1}{2}$ yards	PERCH.POLE.ROD
—20 feet	ROPE
—22 yards	CHAIN
—600 feet	CABLE
—10 chains	FURLONG
—$\frac{5}{8}$ mile (approx.)	KILOMETRE
—8 furlongs	MILE
—1760 yards	MILE
—1976 yards	SCOTTISH MILE
—2240 yards	IRISH MILE
—1000 double paces	
	ROMAN MILE
—1.4 miles	ROMAN MILE
—6082 feet	KNOT
	NAUTICAL MILE
—2.8 miles	FRENCH LEAGUE
—3 miles	LEAGUE
—4.2 miles	SPANISH LEAGUE
—60 miles	DEGREE
—93 million miles	
	ASTRONOMICAL UNIT.AU
—6 billion miles	LIGHT YEAR
—19 billion miles	PARSEC

electrical

—1000 electron volts	KEV
—capacitance	FARAD
—charging unit	KILOWATT HOUR
—conductance	MHO.SIEMENS
—current	AMPERE
—96,500 coulombs	FARADAY
—dipole moment	DEBYE
—electromotive force	VOLT
—inductance	HENRY
—power	WATT
—ratio of currents or	
voltages	NEPER
—reciprocal induction	YRNEH
—resistance	OHM
—signalling speed	BAUD
energy, work and heat	BTU.ERG
	DYNE.JOULE.POUNDAL

—746 watts	HORSEPOWER
—1000 lbs force	KIP
—1055 joules	HEAT UNIT
—100,000 BTUs	THERM
—1,000,000 joules	MEGAJOULE
—British Thermal Unit	BT(H)U
	HEAT UNIT
—energy content (food)	CALORIE
—force	NEWTON
—kilowatt-hour	KELVIN.KWH
—large unit	MEGAWATT-DAY
—power	WATT
—pressure	PASCAL
—quantum of energy	
	PLANCK'S CONSTANT
—thermal efficiency	CARNOT
frequency	CYCLES PER SECOND
	HERTZ
—transmission rate	BAUD
herrings	
—4 herrings	WARP
—33 warps	LONG-HUNDRED
—37$\frac{1}{2}$ gallons	CRAN
—100 long hundreds	
	MAZE.MEASE
—560-630 herrings	MAZE.MEASE
information	
—binary digit	BIT
—1.44 bits	NIT
—4 bits	NIBBLE
—8 bits	BYTE
—2 bytes	WORD
—4 bytes	LONGWORD
—1024 bytes	K.KILOBYTE
—million instructions per	
second	MIPS
—transmission rate	BAUD
light	
—brightness	LAMBERT.STILB
—illumination	LUX.PHOT
	THORLAND
—low intensity	SKOT
—luminance	NIT
—energy	TALBOT
—flux	LUMEN
—luminous intensity	CANDELA
	(NEW) CANDLE
magnetic	
—field strength	OERSTED

—flux	GAUSS.MAXWELL
	TESLA.WEBER
—magneto-motive force	GILBERT

metric

—area	ARE
—capacity	LITRE
—length	METRE
—volume	STERE

—increments

—million millionth	
	MICROMICR(O)-.PICO-
—thousand millionth	NANO
—millionth	MICRO-
—thousandth	MILLI-
—hundredth	CENTI-
—tenth	DECI-
—ten	DECA-
—hundred	HECTO-
—thousand	KILO-
—million	MEGA-
—thousand million	GIGA-
—million million	TERA-

miscellaneous

—12 items	DOZEN
—12 dozen	GROSS
—24 arrows	SHEAF
—20-26 tubs (coal)	SCORE
—100 cubic feet (ship)	TON
—100 runs	TON
—100 miles per hour	TON
—250 pulls (handpress)	TOKEN
—1000 tons (explosives)	KILOTON
—area of nucleus	BARN
—bundle of hay	BOTTLE
—buyer's allowance	TRET
—dried fruit in basket	CAROTEEL
—earthquakes	RICHTER SCALE
—fourth part	FARDEL
—of circle	QUADRANT
—of hour	QUARTER
—of moon period	QUARTER
—of year	QUARTER
—gold	CAR(R)AT
—gravitational unit	SLUG
—hardness	MOH
—insulation value	U-VALUE
—of fabrics	TOG
—large numbers	
—million	(*see* million)

—1 + 100 zeroes	GOGOL
—lens power	DIOPTRE
—mass	CRITH
—metre/kilogram/second	MKS
—print measure	EL.EM.EN
—rate of flow (liquid)	CUMIN
	CUSEC
—ratio of circumference to diameter	PI
—sound	(DECI)BEL.PHON.SONE
—temperature	CELSIUS
	CENTIGRADE
	FAHRENHEIT.KELVIN
—tenth part	TITHE
—type, $^1/_{72}$ inch	POINT
—unit of meaning	SEMANTEME
—viscosity	POISE.STOKES
—watch movement	LIGNE
—water flow in 24 hours	
	MINER'S INCH
—windspeed	BEAUFORT SCALE
—wool ($^1/_2$ sack)	POCKET

paper

—4 sheets	QUIRE
—216 sheets	PRINTER'S REAM
—20 quires	REAM
—2 reams	BUNDLE
—10 reams	BALE

—leaves per sheet

—2	FOLIO
—4	QUARTO
—6	SEXTO
—8	OCTAVO
—12	DUODECIMO
—16	DECIMO-SEXTO
	SEXTODECIMO
	SIXTEENMO
—18	EIGHTEENMO
	OCTODECIMO

—sizes (inches)

—9 x 11$^1/_2$	QUARTO
—13$^1/_2$ x 17	FOOLSCAP
—15 x 19	POST
—17$^1/_2$ x 22	DEMY
—20 x 25	ROYAL
—20 x 30	DOUBLE CROWN
—22 x 30	IMPERIAL
—27 x 40	DOUBLE ELEPHANT
—30 x 53	ANTIQUARIAN

—36 x 45	SADDLEBACK
—48 x 72	EMPEROR
precious stones	POINT
—100 points	CARAT
radiation	
—dosage	BECQUEREL.RAD.REM
	RONTGEN
—radioactive decay	RD
	RUTHERFORD
timber	
—35 cubic feet	STERE
—128 cubic feet	CORD
—216 cubic feet	FATHOM
—100 square feet	
flooring	SQUARE
—round timber	
	HOPPUS (CUBIC) FOOT
time	
—Canicular year	SOTHIC YEAR
—complete cycle of	
heavens	PLATONIC YEAR
—division of time	SCRUPLE
—short period	MIN.MO.SEC.TICK
—Sothic year	CANICULAR YEAR
—very short period	MILLISECOND
	NANO-SECOND
—60 seconds	MIN(UTE)
—60 minutes	H.HOUR.HR
—24 hours	D.DAY
—7 days	WK.WEEK
—14 days	FORTNIGHT
—27.32 days	PERIODIC MONTH
	SIDEREAL MONTH
	TROPICAL MONTH
	STELLAR MONTH
—27.55 days	ANOMALISTIC
	MONTH
—29.53 days	SYNODIC MONTH
—28-31 days	M.MONTH.MTH
—354 days	LUNAR YEAR
—364 days	EMBOLISMIC YEAR
—365 days	Y.YEAR.YR
—365 days 5 hours	
	ASTRONOMICAL YEAR
—365$\frac{1}{4}$ days	JULIAN YEAR
—365 days 6 hours 13 minutes	
	ANOMALISTIC YEAR
—365 days 6 hours 9 minutes	
	SIDEREAL YEAR
—366 days	LEAP YEAR
—6585 days	SAROS
—12/13 months	HEBREW YEAR
	LUNISOLAR YEAR
—5 years	LUSTRUM
—10 years	DECADE
—100 years	CENTENARY
	CENTENNIAL
	CENTURY
—1000 years	MILLENARY
	MILLENIUM
—1460 years	SOTHIC CYCLE
	SOTHIC PERIOD
—3600 years	SAROS
volume	
—144 cubic inches	CUBIC FOOT
—27 cubic feet	CUBIC YARD
—306 cubic feet	ROD

(*for* metric measures *see* French[3])

measuring instrument
for:

air breathed	PNEUMATOMETER
angles	GONIOMETER.OCTANT
	QUADRANT.THEODOLITE
angular distance of	
sun	HELIOMETER
area	PLANIMETER
atmospheric pressure	
	BAROGRAPH
	BAROMETER
	SYMPIESOMETER
atomic weights	
	MASS SPECTROGRAPH
blood pressure	
	SPHYGMO(MANO)METER
	TONOMETER
blueness of sky	CYANOMETER
bodily organs	ONCOMETER
boiling points	EBULLISCOPE
brain waves	
	ELECTROENCEPHALOGRAPH
breathing movement	
	SPIROGRAPH
changes in pressure	TASIMETER
circuit power	WATTMETER
cloudiness of liquids	
	NEPHELOMETER
compressibility	PIEZOMETER
counting paces	PEDOMETER

current of
—fluid   RHEOMETER
—pressure   SYMPIESOMETER
curvature   SPHEROMETER
dew   DROSOMETER
distance   (H)ODOMETER
    ODOGRAPH.TACHEOMETER
    TACHYMETER.TELEMETER
    TROCHEAMETER
    TROCHOMETER
—by vehicle   (H)ODOMETER
    TACHOGRAPH
    TAXIMETER
—from size of image
    ICONOMETER
—on a cycle   CYCLOMETER
    VIAMETER
—on maps   OPISOMETER
—using light beams   MEKOMETER
—walked   PEDOMETER
drops   STACTOMETER
dust in air   KONIMETER
earthquakes   SEISMOGRAPH
    SEISMOMETER
elastic qualities of wood
    XYLOPHONE
electrical
—conductivity   DIAGOMETER
    TASIMETER
—currents   AMMETER
    ELECTRODYNAMOMETER
    ELECTROGRAPH
    VOLT(A)METER
—potential   ELECTROMETER
    POTENTIOMETER
—resistance   OHMMETER
electricity in a substance
    ELECTROSCOPE
elements in metal
    QUANTOMETER
eyes   OPHTHALMOMETER
fare due   TAXIMETER
fermentation   ZYMO(SIM)METER
field of vision   PERIMETER
fluid
—flow   FLOWMETER
—pressure   KYMOGRAPH
—pressure in eyeball
    TONOMETER

fluorescence   FLUORIMETER
    FLUOROMETER
force   DYNAMOGRAPH
    DYNAMOMETER
—of breathing PNEUMATOMETER
frequency of tones   TONOMETER
gas consumed   GAS METER
gases   EUDIOMETER
gradients   GRADIENTER
heart beats
    ELECTROCARDIOGRAPH
heat concentration of
—light   ACTINOMETER
—sun's rays   PYRHELIOMETER
height   (RADIO) ALTIMETER
above sea level   HYPSOMETER
—of Nile   NILOMETER
—of water   WATER-GAUGE
high temperatures   PYROMETER
    RESISTANCE THERMOMETER
hours   CLOCK.CHRONOMETER
    HOROLOGE.SUNDIAL
humidity   GRAVIMETER
    HYGRODEIK.HYGROGRAPH
    HYGROMETER.HYGROSCOPE
    PSYCHROMETER
intensity of
—colour SPECTROPHOTOMETER
—sunlight   HELIOGRAPH
loudness   PHON(O)METER
luminescence   PHOTOMETER
lung capacity   SPIROMETER
magnetic
—field   MAGNETOMETER
—forces   VARIOMETER
—variations   MAGNETOGRAPH
meridian passage DIPLEIDOSCOPE
metronome   RHYTHMOMETER
mileage, speed, etc.
    TACHOGRAPH
molecular weight of
  gases   EFFUSIOMETER
muscular
—contraction
    ELECTROMYOGRAPH
—work   ERGOGRAPH
    ERGOMETER
musical beat   METRONOME
    RHYTHMOMETER

nitrogen	NITROMETER	slight earthquake	
	OXIMETER	shocks	TROMOMETER
pelvis	PELVIMETER	slopes	INCLINOMETER
percolation	LYSIMETER	small	
plane surfaces	PLANOMETER	—angles	MICROMETER
plant growth	AUXANOMETER	—diameters	ERIOMETER
porosity	POROSCOPE	—distances	MICROMETER
power	DYNAMOGRAPH	—strains	EXTENSOMETER
	DYNAMOMETER	—thicknesses	PACHYMETER
pressure	PIEZOMETER	solidity of minerals	
—of current	SYMPIESOMETER		SCLEROMETER
—of fluids	MANOMETER	solids	STEREOMETER
pulse	PULSIMETER	sound vibration	
	SPHYMOGRAPH		PHONAUTOGRAPH
quantity of polarisation		specific gravity	AR(A)EOMETER
of light	POLARIMETER		HYDROMETER
radiant			PYCNOMETER
—energy	LIGHT-MILL		PYKNOMETER
	RADIOMETER	—of milk	GALACTOMETER
—heat	PYROSCOPE	—of solids	STEREOMETER
radiation	DOSIMETER	—of wood	XYLOMETER
	RADIOGRAPH	speed	SPEEDOMETER
radioactivity		—in relation to	
	GEIGER(-MULLER) COUNTER	sound	MACHMETER
	OBROMETER	—of rotation	TACHOGRAPH
	SCINTILLOMETER		TACHOMETER
radio waves	RADIO TELESCOPE	squint	STRABOMETER
rainfall	HYETOGRAPH	strains in structures	TASEOMETER
	HYETOMETER	strength of wine	OENOMETER
	HYETOMETROGRAPH	subterranean temperature	
	OBROMETER.RAIN-GAUGE		GEOTHERMOMETER
	PLUVIOMETER.UDOMETER	sugar solution	SACCHARIMETER
rate of evaporation			SACCHAROMETER
	EVAPORIMETER	surface tension	
reaction times	PSYCHOMETER		STALAGMOMETER
refractive indices		surveying	TACHEOMETER
	REFRACTOMETER		TACHYMETER.THEODOLITE
	SPECTROMETER	temperature	THERMOMETER
relations of sounds			THERMO(METRO)GRAPH
	HARMONOMETER	ticket-dispensing	PASSIMETER
relative number of particles		tides	MARIGRAPH
	MASS SPECTROMETER	time	CLOCK.CHRONOMETER
salinity of water	SALI(NO)METER		SUNDIAL
sensitivity of film	SENSITOMETER	—by sand	EGG-TIMER
sight	OPSIOMETER		HOURGLASS
	OPTOMETER	—by water	HYDROSCOPE
size derived from		transmitting measurements	
image	ICONOMETER		TELEMETER
sliding friction	TRIBOMETER	trees	DENDROMETER

vapour pressure	TONOMETER
variations in body	
size	PLETHYSMOGRAPH
vibrations	VIBROGRAPH
	VIBROMETER
viscosity	VISCOMETER
volume of	
—gas	VOLUMETER
—solid bodies	VOLUMOMETER
voting changes	SWINGOMETER
water absorption	
—by plant	POTOMETER
—in ship's hold	SOUNDING-ROD
wave	
—forms	OSCILLOSCOPE
—lengths	ETALON
	INTERFEROMETER
	SPECTROMETER
whereabouts of	
clouds	NEPHOGRAPH
	NEPHOSCOPE
X-ray	
—diffraction	DIFFRACTOMETER
—examination	FLUOROSCOPE
zenith distance	ZENITH SECTOR

Meat and Livestock
  Commission   MLC
mechanical
  mechanical engineer   ME
  mechanical transport   MT
medal   MC.MM.TD
medical
  medical condition   (*see* disease)
  <u>medical *disorder*</u>   CLAIMED
    DECIMAL.DECLAIM
  medical graduate   MB
  medical man   DR.GP.MB.MO
  Medical Officer (of
    Health)   M(O)H
  Medical Research Council   MRC
  medical social worker   MSW
  medical speciality   ENT
  <u>medical *treatment*</u>   CLAIMED
    DECIMAL.DECLAIM
medicine   MED
  medicine-man   DR.GP.MB.MO
medieval   MED
Mediterranean   MED
  artichoke   CARDOON

borage	ALKANET
buckthorn	CHRIST'S THORN
	JEW'S THORN
captain of ship	PATRON
edible gall	SAGE-APPLE
fever	BRUCELLOSIS
fish	ANCHOVY.BAND-FISH
	DENTEX.MEAGRE.MAIGRE
	PARROT-WRASSE
	PEACOCK-FISH
hen	ANCONA
	ANDALUSIAN.MINORCA
Jew(s)	SEPHARDI(M)
leader	M
lizard	STELLION.STELLIO LIZARD
mock privet	PHYLLYREA
plants	CUM(M)IN.ISATIS
	LENTIL.PLUMBAGO.RUE
	ROSEMARY.WOAD
salad-plant	ROCKET
shark	PORBEAGLE
ship	(*see* ship³)
shrub	LAVENDER-COTTON
	NABK.NEBBUK.NEBE(C)K
	ANTOLINA
spirit	RAKE.RAKI
thicket	MAQUIS
tree	ALGARROBA.CAROB
	LOCUST.NUT-PINE
	STONE-PINE.TURKEY-OAK
wind	GREGALE.LEVANT(ER)
	MISTRAL
wrasse	PEACOCK-FISH

medium   MED
medium standard frequency   MSF
medium wave   MW
medley in A Flat   FANTAIL
meeting   AGM
mega-   (*see* million)
melée <u>made</u>. . . DAME.EDAM.MEAD
melt
  melt fat   AFT
  melting point   MP
  melting <u>snow</u>   OWNS.SOWN
  molten <u>steel</u>   LEETS.STELE
member¹   ARM.LEG.M
  MEM.MP.TOE
hence
•anger *about* a member RAMPAGE

•member of Dail	EMPIRE
•one member is lying	IMPLIES
•the *French* member	LAMP
member²	
Member of	
—Congress	MC
—Council	MC
—County Council	MCC
—House of Representatives	MHR
—Institute of Journalists	MJI
—Legislative Assembly	MLA
—Legislative Council	MLC
—Order of the British	
Empire	MBE
—Parliament	MP
—Pharmaceutical Society	MPS
—Philological Society	MPS
—Royal Victorian Order	MVO
members of <u>SAS</u>	ASS
memorandum	MEM(O)
memorial service	OBIT
men (*see also* man. Appendix)	
men with guns	RA
mend <u>plate</u>	PETAL
mentioned new. . .	GNU.KNEW
merchant	
Merchant Navy	MN
Merchant of Venice	ANTONIO
	POLO
merchant vessel	MV
mercy seat	MISERERE
mere existence	POND LIFE
merry	
merry fellow	ANDREW
merry minute	TIDDLY
Merseyside	NW
mess	
in a mess it <u>ran</u>	TRAIN
make a mess of <u>things</u>	NIGHTS
messed up a <u>paper</u>. . .	APPEAR
messing about in <u>boats</u>	BOAST
messy <u>eaters</u>	TEASER
met	
Met line	ISOBAR
met *on the way back* ⟨	TEM
met *up*(D) ↑	TEM
metal¹	IRON.TIN
hence	
•iron man	IRONED

•metal in charge	IRONIC
•metal unknown	IRONY
and	
•metal cover	TIN HAT
•metal key	TINE.TING
•metal ruler	TINKING
metal²	
metal club	IRON
metal container	TIN
metal *in* s/cu/lpture	COPPER.CU
metal money	BRASS
metal oxide silicon	MOS
metal van	LEAD
metal washer	COPPER
metamorphosis of an	
insect's. . .	INCESSANT
metaphorical	MET
metaphysics	MET
meteorology	MET
mete *out*	MEET.TEEM
meter (metre)	M
metre*less*	omit M
(*see also* verse)	
Methodist Episcopal	ME
Metropolitan Police	MP
Mexican	MEX
agave	HENEQUEN
HENEQUIN.HENIQUIN	
aloe AGAVE.CENTURY PLANT	
	MAGUEY
ancient	
—language	NAHUATL
—race AZTEC.MAYA.OLMEC	
avocado	CHININ.COYO
Aztec emperor	MONTEZUMA
bean	FRIJOL(E)
bird	CHAPARRAL-COCK
	ROAD-RUNNER
blanket	SERAPE.ZARAPE
brushwood thicket	CHAPARRAL
bulbous plant	JACOBEAN LILY
cactus MESCAL.NOPAL.PEYOTE	
capital	M.MEXICO CITY
cape	SERAPE.ZARAPE
cherry	CAPULIN
coarse sugar	PANOCHA
coin	DOLLAR.PESO
corn mush	ATOLE
cross of twigs	GOD'S EYE

day labourer	PEON	spiny tree	RETAMO
dish	TAMALE.TOMALLEY	spurge(wax)	CANDELILLA
dog	CHIHUAHUA	stewed pork	CARNITAS
drinks	MESCALI.PEYOTE	stirrup-guard	TAPADERA
	PULQUE.TEQUILA		TAPADERO
drugs	JALAP.MESCALINE	street musicians	MARIACHI
	PSILOCYBIN	sugar	PANOCHA
floating garden	CHINAMPA	symbol of luck	GOD'S EYE
flowers	BELLE-DE-NUIT	tea	GOOSEFOOT
	MARVEL OF PERU	temple	TEOCALLI
	TAGETES.TIGER-FLOWER	timber	CANDLEWOOD
grass	OTATE.TEOSINTE	tortilla chip	FRITO
ground cuckoo		town	PUEBLO.TULA
	CHAPARRAL-COCK	tree	MESQUITE
hat	SOMBRERO	wild pig	PECCARY
hog	PECCARY		TAJACU
horseman's leggings		**Mexico**	MEX
	CHAPARAJOS	**mezzo**	
	CHAPAREJOS	mezza-voce	MV
Indian market	TIAGUI	mezzo-forte	MF
Indians	ZUNI	mezzo-piano	MP
language	NAHUATL	**Micah**	MIC
leader	M	**mid-**	
leaf fibre	HENEQUEN	*mid*day	A
	HENEQUIN.HENIQUIN	midday	N.NOON
lily	TUBEROSE	midday *break*	NO-ON
maize		*Mid*lands	N
—cake	TORTILLA	mid-morning	ATTEN-
—dish	TAMAL(E)	*mid*-morning	N
mushroom drug	PSILOCYBIN	*mid*night	G
musical instrument	CLARIN	*mid*off	F
peasant	PEON	midshipman	EASY
peyote cactus	MESCAL	*mid*shipman	P
pepper sauce	TABASCO	*mid*-stream	RE
persimmon	CHAPOTE	*mid*-summer	MM.THOUSANDS
plums	ZAPOTE	*mid*week	EE.EASE
pyramid temple	TEOCALLI	**middle**	
rat	TUCAN.TUZA	middle age	G
ranch	HACIENDA.RANCHO	middle America	CENTER
renegade trader	COMANCHERO	Middle English	ME
ringtail (cat)	CACOMISTLE	*Middle* English	L
	CACOMIXL	*middle of* the...	H
river	RIO GRANDE	*middle of the* road	OA
rodent	TUCAN	*Middle* School	HO
rubber plant	GUYALE	middleman	MEDAL
settlement	PUEBLO	*middle*man	A
shirt	GUYAVERA	**might**	
shrub	MESQUIT(E).JOJOBA	*might appear* that Ed...	HATTED
	POINSETTIA	*might be* a pet	PATE.PEAT

mighty man	SMITH
mild	
mild man	CLEMENT
mild temper	MODERATE
mile	M
miles per gallon	MPG
miles per hour	MPH
milestone	MS
military	MIL
military agent	TEAR GAS
Military Cross	MC
military information	RENEWS
Military Intelligence	MI
Military Medal	MM
Military Police	(R)MP
military uniform	WARDESS
miller	DUSTY
miller's corn	GRIST
milli-	
millibar	MB
milligram(me)	MG
millilitre	ML
millimetre	MM
millisecond	MS
million	M.MEGA-
million cycles per second	MPS
million electron-volts	MEV
million joules	MJ
thousand million	BILLION
	MILLIARD
million to power of	
—2	BILLION
—3	TRILLION
—4	QUADRILLION
—5	QUINTILLION
—6	SEXTILLION
—7	SEPTILLION
—8	OCTILLION
—9	NONILLION
—10	DECILLION
—100	CENTILLION
Milton	
words found in the works of:	
able to speak	SPEAKABLE
abstruse	SUTTLE
acknowledge to self	SPARE
act	
—as bishop	EPISCOPATE
—of planting	PLANTATION

adverse	PERVERSE
allow oneself	SPARE
amaurosis	DROP SERENE
archangel	HIERARCH
armour for forearm	VANTBRASS
arouse	UPRAISE
assembly	FREQUENCE
assuage	SWAGE
atmosphere	REGION
attack with noise	PEAL
await	REMAIN
awakening	WAKEFUL
battle	HOSTING
be	
—bent on	RAGE
—called	HEAR
—in excess	REDOUND
—subordinate	SUBSERVE
beat	SWINDGE
bedecked with	
flowers	FLOWERY-KIRTLED
believe to exist	THINK
beloved	LIKING
beyond description	
	INEXPRESSIVE
bishop	EPISCOPANT
blameless	UNREPROVED
blindness	DROP SERENE
bottomless	UNFOUNDED
bragging	TONGUE-DOUGHTIE
bridesmaid	PARANYMPH
bring back	
—again	RECOLLECT
—improved	RECURE
budding in spring	VERNANT
called	YCLEAP'D
canopy	STATE
cast	FUSIL(E)
cause degeneration	DEGENERATE
celebrate	REPEAT
chastise	SWINDGE
claim	EXPOSTULATE
close	STRAIT
compassionate emotion	REMORSE
complete fully	SUM
confine	IMMANACLE
confirm	STABLISH
confusion	LURRY
conjunction	INJUNCTION

constant	SAD
construct	FABRIC
contemptible person	
	RAKESHAME
contrive	PRACTISE
coy	NICE
crafty	SUTTLE
crash	RACK
crowd	FREQUENCE
cunning	SUTTLE
cure	RECURE
defeat	DISCOMFIT
delicate	SUTTLE
democracy	DEMOCRATY
determine worth	STATE
dethrone	DISENTHRONE
differentiated	DISTINCT
digression	EXTRAVAGANCE
dim-eyed	PALE-EYED
diminutive being	MINIM
direct	INFORM
discharge	DISPLODE
discomposed	INCOMPOSED
disdain	SDAINE.SDAYN
	SDEIGNE.SDEIN
disfavour	DISGUST
disgrace	DISWORSHIP
dishonour	DISWORSHIP
dispensation	DISPENSE
displeasure	DISGUST
distaste	DISGUST
distinguished	DISTINCT
distracted	DISTRACT
divest of commission	
	DISCOMMISSION
division of atmosphere	REGION
Dog-Star	SWART STAR
double blackness	DOUBLE-SHADE
dye red	ENVERMEIL
early	RATHE
earn	ERN
earth's axis	HINGE
easily rotated	VOLUBLE
elusive	SUTTLE
encircle	WHEEL
encouraging	INCENTIVE
ethereal	ETHEREOUS
even	EEV(E)N
evening	EEVNING

evil	SHREWD
exalted	HAUGHT.HAU(L)T
	HIGH-BLEST
exceed	EXCEL
excessively precise	
	OVER-EXQUISITE
excite	UPRAISE
excommunication	
	EXCOMMUNION
exhausted	FAINTED
expand	INTEND
expect	SUPPOSE
experience	TRY
explode	DISPLODE
fabricate	FANGLE
false idea	IDOLISM
fancy	FANGLE
farmyard	VILLATIC
fatigued	SWINK'T
female	FEMAL
—rowdy	TURMAGANT
fetter	IMMANACLE
fiend	FEND
fine	QUAINT.SUTTLE
fish route	SEA-PATH
flourish	SWINDGE
flow	FLOAT
flowed	FLOWN
flowering in spring	VERNANT
flowing forth	PROFLUENT
fluency	FLUENCE
flying	FLIGHTED
forbid	RESTRAIN
foreign	FORREN
form a circle	INGLOBE
friar	FRIER
frightful	GREISLY
from	ON
fulminate	FULMINE
further	FURDER
fusible	FUSIL(E)
gaping asunder	INTERRUPT
ghastly	GREISLY
give	
—red colouring	ENVERMEIL
—way	RELENT.SWERVE
glassy translucent	
exterior	HYALINE
grating	SCRANNEL

goal	GOLE	limit	MEASURE
gory	GOARY	lookout	PROSPECT
granary	GRANGE	lost	UNOWNED
great expanse	MAIN	lustful	LUSTY
grieve for	PINE.PYNE	luxuriant	LUXURIOUS
grisly	GREISLY	make	
guard	VIGILANCE	—an Elysium of	IMPARADISE
guide	LAND PILOT	—stable	STABLISH
hard-pressed	STRAIT	mark out	REMARK
haughty	HAUGHT.HAU(L)T	marked	DISTINCT
having		marry	SPOUSE
—perches	PERCHED	means of nourishment	SUSTAIN
—premonitions	DIVINE	mind	NOTION
heal	RECURE	minor politician	POLITICASTER
held back	SUSPENS.SUSPENCE	mischievous	SHREWD
hesitate	DEMUR	mix in	IMMIX
hideous	DEFORM	moisten	DIP
hold out	SUBSIST	molestation	INFESTATION
honesty	REALTIE	molten	FUSIL(E)
honeysuckle	EGLANTINE	monarch	SOVRAN
hot-tempered	HOT-LIVERED	morning song	MATIN
huddle	PESTER	motive power	PRINCIPLE
hurtful	SHREWD	moving	
idolater	IDOLIST	—at a slope	SLOPE
igniting	INCENTIVE	—slowly	LEADEN-STEPPING
ill-conditioned	SHREWD	murmuring	MUTTER
ill-natured	SHREWD	mutiny	MUTINE
immaterial	UNESSENTIAL	named	YCLEAP'D
impalpable	SUTTLE	narrow	STRAIT
impossible to		natural musical note	WOOD-NOTE
—be formed	UNCONJUNCTIVE	needy	STRAIT
—undo	UNRECALLING	nice	SUTTLE
impregnate	IMPREGN	non-Christian	PANIM
in proper time	MATURE	northern	SEPTENTRION(AL)
inciting	INCENTIVE	not	
inhabited world	INHABITATION	—discordant	UNDISCORDING
inlaid ornament	EMBLEM	—having skin	UNHIDEBOUND
innocent	OFFENCELESS	—in liquor	UNLIQUORED
inordinate	DISORDINATE	—subject to suspicion	
inseparable	INDIVIDUAL		UNSUSPECT
invisible (moon)	SILENT	—suited to marriage	
jasmine	GESSAMINE		UNCONJUGAL
kindle	TINE	—to be recalled	UNRECALLING
landing place	STRAND	object of patronage	FAVOUR
landscape	LANTSKIP	obsequy	OBSEQUIE
lash	SWINDGE	opposition	RELUCTANCE
lay low	SUPPLANT	original parts	ORIGINS
layer	LOFT	outnumber	OVERMULTITUDE
lewdness	SENSUALITY	overrefined	SUTTLE

paltry	PITEOUS	resistance	RELUCTANCE
partisan	SIDESMAN	resort	SEEK
penetrating	SUTTLE	restore	REFORM
perfect	PERFET	revoke prediction	UNPREDICT
permissible	VENIAL	rigorous	STRAIT
persevere	INSIST	rise above	TOWER
persuasion	INDUCEMENT	river Oceanus	OCEAN-STREAM
pestilence	MURREN	rotation of day and	
pick decisively	SINGLE	night	RHOMB(US)
pinion	PENNON	rough	ROBUSTIOUS
pity	REMORSE	round	GLOBY
place of rest	REPOSE	rousing	WAKEFUL
plant with magic		ruffled up	TO RUFFL'D
attributes	HAEMONY	said	SED
planting	PLANTATION	sayest	SAIST
pointing to stars	STAR-POINTING	scare	SCAR(RE)
precedent	PRESIDENT	scatter	SHATTER
preface	EPISTLE	scent	SENT
preparedness	PROCINCT	school	SCUL(L).SCULLE
prescient	DIVINE	scratchy	SCRANNEL
president	PRESIDENT	scythe	SITHE
prey	RAVEN.RAVIN(E)	second	VOUCH
prisoner paraded	TRIUMPH	seize	CEAZE.SEASE.SEAZE
private person	PRIVATE	sense	SENT
product	PRODUCEMENT	separable	DIVIDUAL
prompt	PERNICIOUS	separate after betrothal	
prune	REFORM		DISESPOUSE
punishment	PENANCE	serenade	SERENATE
purpose	MIND	set	
put		—apart	EXEMPT
—in a phial	VIOLD	—as a plume	PLUME
—in chains	IMMANACLE	—aside	REPEAL
—in paradise	IMPARADISE	—in a border	EMBORDER
—into effect	ENURE		IMBORDER
—under ban	IMBAR	—in motion	WINNOW
quash	REPEAL	—to apposite words for	
raiment	WARDROP	the tune	SMOOTH-DITTIED
rarefied	SUTTLE	—up	STABLISH
ravishment	RAPINE	shaft of light	RULE
ready	PERNICIOUS	shared in common	DIVIDUAL
rebel	MUTINE	sharpness	SHARP
rebuild	REFORM	showing fine discrimination	
reck	WRECK		SUTTLE
refusing compliance		shriek	SHREIK
	UNCONNIVING	shrink	SWERVE
remedy	RECURE	sincerity	REALTIE
render	INFER	sluice	SLUSE
—unfamiliar	DISINURE	smell	SENT
repress	REPEAL	snake	ELLOPS

snare	FRAUD	turf	TERF(E)
sober	UNLIQUORED	turquoise	TURKIS
soft	DOUGH-KNEADED	ugly	OUGHLY-HEADED
southwest wind	LIBECCHIO	unchristianise	UNCHRISTEN
sovereign	SOVRAN	undergo	TRY
span	OVERLAY	undeserving	IMMERITOUS
spareness	SPARE	undistilled	UNFUME
sparing in contributing	STRAIT	uninstructed	UNPRINCIPLED
sphere	SPHEAR(E)	unless	LESS
spot	FREAK	unlike	UNCONFORM
stand fast	SUBSIST	unnaturally	UNKINDLY
steadfast	SAD.STEDFAST	unobserved	UNSP'D
steer	STEAR(E)	unoffending	OFFENCELESS
steerage	STEARAGE	unshapely	DEFORM
steersman	STEARSMATE	upper air	REGION
stir furiously	TEMPEST	vapid	FLASHY
stolen	STOLN	variegate	FREAK
strait	STREIGHT	variegated	DISTINCT
streak	FREAK	venture	VENTER
strict	STRAIT	venturous	VENTROUS
strong	MAIN.ROBUSTIOUS	verdict	VERDIT
struggling	RELUCTANT	viewpoint	PROSPECT
stupendous	STUPENDIOUS	village	VILLATIC
stupidity	INSULSITY	voluble	VOLUBIL
subjacent	SUBJECT	vouchsafe	VOUTSAFE
subtle	SUTTLE	wardrobe	WARDROP
subtlety	SUTTLETIE	watch	VIGILANCE
suffuse	DIP	western	PONENT
superintendence	EPISCOPY	whirlpool	GURGE
superintending	PRESIDENT	wing	PENNON
support	VOUCH	with	
surging	REDUNDANT	—difficulty	SCARCE
survey	EPISCOPY	—hands joined	HANDED
suspended	SUSPENS.SUSPENCE	without	
sward	SORD	—being	UNESSENTIAL
swashbuckler		—bottom	UNFOUNDED
	SWINDGE-BUCKLER	—knowing	UNWARE
sway	SWINDGE	—light	UNLIGHTSOME
swift	DISPATCHFUL.PERNICIOUS	—origin	UNORIGINAL
tapestry	TAPSTRY	—pause	UNRESPITED
tenuous	SUTTLE	womb	SIDE
thin	SUTTLE	*mimic* **nun**	NONE
things stolen	STEALTH	*mince* <u>meat</u>	MATE.TAME.TEAM
time of closing	SHUT	**miner**	
toil-worn	SWINK'T	miners	NUM
transparent	TRANSPICIOUS	mining engineer	ME
transport	RAPINE	**mineral**[1]	
troop	TURME	mineral water	EVIAN.PERRIER
turban	TURBANT		SERPENTINE

mineralogy	MIN
mineral²	(*see also* gems)
acid	
—igneous rock	LIPARITE
	RHYOLITE
—magnesium silicate	TALC
agate	SCOTCH PEBBLE
—with layers	ONYX
Alpine	
—granite	PROTOGINE
—sandstone	FLYSCH
albite feldspar	PERICLINE
	PERISTERITE
altered	
—andesite	PORPHYRITE
	PROPYLITE
—basalt	MELAPHYRE
—biotite	RUBELLAN
—dolerite or basalt	DIABASE
—feldspar	SAUSSURITE
—mica	VERMICULITE
alum-stone	ALUNITE
alumina	ARGIL.CORUNDUM
aluminate of iron	HERCYNITE
aluminium	
—hydroxide	DIASPORE
—magnesium silicate	SAPPHIRINE
—ore	B(E)AUXITE
—phosphate	SPHAERITE
	TURQUOISE.VARISCITE
—silicate	CYANITE.FIBROLITE
	FULLER'S EARTH.HALLOYSITE
	KAOLINITE.KYANITE
—sodium silicate	NOSEAN
aluminosilicate	ZEOLITE
amorphous silica	OPAL
anatase	OCTAHEDRITE
andalusite	CHIASTOLITE
antimonite	STIBNITE
antimony oxysulphide	
	KERMES(ITE)
aquamarine	BERYL
aragonite	SATIN-SPAR
arborescent agate	DENDRACHATE
argentite	SILVER-GLANCE
argillaceous rock	MUDSTONE
arsenate of	
—cobalt	COBALT BLOOM
	ERYTHRITE
—copper	ERINITE
arsenic	
—monosulphide	REALGAR
	SANDARAC(H)
—trisulphide	ORPIMENT
arsenical pyrites	MISPICKEL
arsenide of	
—nickel	COPPER-NICKEL
	NICCOLITE
—platinum	SPERRYLITE
asphalt	UINTA(H)ITE
augite	DIALLAGE
autunite	TORBERNITE.URANITE
aventurine feldspar	SUNSTONE
banded	
—chalcedony	AGATE
—silica	CHALCEDONY
barytes with sulphur smell	
	HEPATITE
basalt	WHIN(STONE)
—lava	TOAD-STONE
—with nepheline	
	NEPHELINE-BASALT
basaltic rock	TEPHRITE
basic igneous rock	DOLERITE
beryllium	
—aluminium silicate	EUCLASE
—silicate	PHENACITE.PHENAKITE
black	
—bitumen	ALBERTITE
—copper ore	MELACONITE
	TENORITE
—diamond	CARBONADO
—garnet	MELANITE
—glassy intrusion	TACHYLITE
—jasper	BASANITE
—lead	GRAPHITE
—marble	NERO-ANTICO.TOUCH
—mica	BIOTITE.LEPIDOMELANE
—mica and plagiocite	KERSANITE
—spinel	HERCYNITE
—tourmaline	SCHORL
blackjack	ZINCBLENDE
bloodstone	HELIOTROPE
blue	
—asbestos	CROCIDOLITE
—cordierite	WATER SAPPHIRE
—corundum	SAPPHIRE
—mineral like nosean	HAUYNE

—quartz   SAPPHIRE-QUARTZ
—stone   HYACINTH
—violet quartz   AMETHYST
boric acid   SASSOLITE
bornite   HORSEFLESH ORE
                    PEACOCK ORE
botryoidal graphite   PENCIL ORE
brassy yellow   IRON PYRITE(S)
brickearth   GAULT
bright translucent mineral   SPAR
brilliant zircon   JARGO(O)N
brown
—coal   LIGNITE
—iron ore   LIMONITE
—or yellow quartz
              CAIRNGORM STONE
—tin dioxide   CASSITERITE
cadmium sulphide GREENOCKITE
Cairngorm stone
                 SMOKY QUARTZ
calc-sinter   TUFA.TUFF
calcite-coloured ultramarine
                    LAPIS LAZULI
calcium
—aluminium silicate ANORTHITE
          CHABAZITE.PREHNITE
—aluminium magnesium
                        MELILITE
—carbonate   AR(R)AGONITE
          CALCITE.CALCSPAR
                      LIMESTONE
—chloride   HYDROPHILITE
—fluoride FLUORITE.FLUORSPAR
—magnesium amphibole
                      TREMOLITE
—magnesium pyroxene DIOPSIDE
—magnesium silicate
                   MONTICELLITE
—molybdate   POWELLITE
—oxalate   WHEWELLITE
—phosphate and fluoride
                        APATITE
—potassium silicate APOPHYLLITE
—salts in peat   DOPPLERITE
—silicate and titanate TITANITE
—sodium silicate   PECTOLITE
—sulphate   GYPSUM
—tantalum, oxygen   MICROLITE
—titanium antimonate LEWISITE

—tungstate   SCHEELITE
carbon   GRAPHITE
carbonate of
—calcium, etc.   ANKERITE
—copper AZURITE.CHESSYLITE
               MOUNTAIN-BLUE
—iron   IRON-STONE
—nickel   ZARATITE
—sodium   NATRON.URAO
—strontium   STRONTIANITE
cassiterite   NEEDLE-TIN
cat's-eye   CHRYSO-BERYL
                    CYMOPHANE
cerium ore   CERITE
chalcedony   CHERT.SILICA
chalcopyrite COPPER PYRITES
chalybite   SIDERITE
chiastolite CROSS-STONE.MACLE
china clay   LITHOMARGE
chloride and phosphate of
—lead   PYROMORPHITE
—potassium   CARNALLITE
chlorite with
   quartz   CHLORITE-SCHIST
chrome with iron
   oxide   CHROMITE
cinnamon-stone   (H)ESSONITE
                      HYACINTH
clay
—and sand   LOAM
—dark blue or grey
                   OXFORD CLAY
—formed by weathering
                       LATERITE
—from Lemnos LEMNIAN EARTH
—ironstone   IRON-CLAY
             SPHAEROSIDERITE
—like kaolinite   NACRITE
—yellow   LONDON CLAY
—marble   (K)NICKER
—slate   OTTRELITE-SLATE
clayey alum ore   ALUM-SHALE
          ALUM-SLATE.HALLOYSITE
clinkstone   PHONOLITE
clinochlore   RIPIDOLITE
coal   WALLSEND
—from slimy sediment
                    SAPROPELITE
—glance   ANTHRACITE

coarse	
—oolite	PISOLITE
—grained igneous rock	
	MONZONITE
	PEGMATITE.PERIDOTITE
cobalt	
—arsenide	SKUTTERUDITE
	SMALTITE
—carbonate	SPHAEROCOBALTITE
cockscomb pyrites	MARCASITE
coloured corundum	
	ORIENTAL AMETHYST
	ORIENTAL EMERALD
	ORIENTAL TOPAZ
	ORIENTAL RUBY
colourless	
—opal	HYALITE
—quartz	ROCK CRYSTAL
common feldspar	ORTHOCLASE
compacted sand	SANDSTONE
composed of	
—pebbles	PSEPHITE
—sand-grains	PSAMMITE
concretion of silica	FLINT
containing olivine	CIMINITE
copper	
—arsenate	OLIVENITE
—carbonate	MALACHITE
—glance	REDRUTHITE
—hydrogen arsenite	
	SCHEELE'S GREEN
—lead selenite	ZORGITE
—oxide	BORNITE
—pyrites	CHALCOPYRITE
	PEACOCK-COPPER
	PEACOCK-ORE
—silicate	DIOPTASE
copperas	MELANTERITE
cordierite	DICHROITE
corundum	EMERY
cryolite	ICE-STONE
crystalline	SCHIST
—igneous rock	GABBRO
—limestone	MARBLE
—olivine	DUNITE
crystallised haematite	OLIGIST
cubic	
—carbon	DIAMOND
—zeolite	ANALCIME.ANALCITE

cupric sulphide	COVELLITE
cystallised calcite	
	NAILHEAD SPAR
dark	
—blue or grey clay	OXFORD CLAY
—fine-grained igneous rock	TRAP
—green silicates	CHLORITE
—porphyritic rock	MELAPHYRE
—tuff with crystals	PEPERINO
decomposed basalt	WACKE
devitrified igneous rock	FELSITE
diabase	OPHITE
diamond	
—matrix	KIMBERITE
—ore	BLUEGROUND
diatomite	KIESELGUHR.TRIPOLI
dioptase	EMERALD-COPPER
diorite	DIABASE
—with quartz	GRANODIORITE
dolomite	BITTERSPAR
	BROWNSPAR
—rock	MAGNESIAN LIMESTONE
dome of igneous rock	LACCOLITE
	LACCOLITH
double	
—aluminium and potassium	
sulphate	ALUM
—calcium and magnesium	
carbonate	DOLOMITE
dyke rock	ELVAN
elastic bitumen	ELATERITE
electric calamine	HEMIMORPHITE
emerald	BERYL.SMARAGD
epidote and quartz	EPIDOSITE
erubescite	HORSEFLESH ORE
exfoliating clay	PYROPHYLLITE
feldspar	ANDESINE
—from Labrador	LABRADORITE
—intermediate	BYTOWNITE
—with barium	HYALOPHONE
—with slanting	
angles	ANORTHITE
	PLAGIOCLASE
—with nepheline and	
aegirine	TINGUAITE
—with olivine	TROCTOLITE
	TROUTSTONE
feldspathic rock	PETUNTSE
	PETUNTZE

felstone	FELSITE
ferric	
—arsenite	SCORODITE
—oxide	GOTHITE.LIMONITE
ferrous	
—carbonate	CHALYBITE
	SIDERITE
—phosphate	VIVIANITE
—sulphide	TROILITE
ferruginous red	
earth	TERRA ROSSA
fibrolite	SILLIMANITE
fibrous	
—amphibole	
	MOUNTAIN LEATHER
—barytes	BOLOGNA STONE
—calcite	SATIN SPAR
—serpentine	CHRYSOTILE
	PYROPE.PYROPUS
fine-grained	
—diorite	PORPHYRITE
—igneous rock	
	SPILITE.TRACHYTE
—silicious rock	NOVACULITE
—syenitic rock	ORTHOPHYRE
fire-opal	GIRASOL(E)
fissile	
—limestone	FOREST MARBLE
—greywacke	GREYWACKE SLATE
flinty chalcedony	HORNSTONE
fluoride of yttrium, etc.	
	YTTRO-CERITE
fluorspar	BLUE JOHN
found in Cornwall	REDRUTHITE
French	
—chalk	SOAPSTONE
	SPANISH CHALK
—limestone	CAEN STONE
fuller's earth	CIMOLITE
gabbro	
—and omphacite or smaragdite	
	ECLOGITE.EKLOGITE
—of horneblende and	
magnetite	GARNET ROCK
—with pyroxene	NORITE
glassy	
—lava	PUMICE
—orthoclase	ICE SPAR
—stone	AUSTRALITE.TEKTITE

glimmer	MICA
gneissose granite	PROTOGINE
gold ore	BANKET
gooseberry stone	
	GROSSULAR(ITE)
granite	
—decomposed	CHINA STONE
—with markings resembling	
Hebrew characters	GRAPHIC
	GRANITE
granular anhydrite	VULPINITE
graphic granite	PEGMATITE
graphite	PLUMBAGO
greasy nepheline	ELAEOLITE
green	
—amphibole	ACTINOLITE
	PARGASITE.SMARAGDITE
—banded marble	CIPOLLINO
—beryl	AQUAMARINE.EMERALD
—chalcedony	CHRYSOPRASE
—chlorite	CLINOCHLORE
—chromium mica	FUCHSITE
—chrysoberyl	ALEXANDRITE
—hornblende	AUGITE
—microcline	AMAZON STONE
—nickel magnesium	
silicate	GARNIERITE
—nickel-arsenate	ANNABERGITE
—porphyry	
	ORIENTAL VERD-ANTIQUE
—potassium iron and aluminium	
silicate	GLAUCONITE
—pyroxene	AEGIRINE
	OMPHACITE
—spodumene	HIDDENITE
greenish beryllium	
	CHRYSOBERYL
Greenland spar	CRYOLITE
grey or black with	
metallic sheen	GLANCE
gypsum	ALABASTER
	PLASTER-STONE
	SATIN-SPAR.SELENITE
haematite	SPECULAR IRON
halite	ROCK SALT
halloysite	MOUNTAIN SOAP
hard	
—chlorite	OTTRELITE
—coal	ANTHRACITE

	SPLINT-COAL
—green stone	JADE
—quartz	FLINT
—sandstone	MILLSTONE GRIT
—siliceous stone	GAN(N)ISTER
—stone	RAG(G)
harmotome	CROSS-STONE
hatchettite	MOUNTAIN TALLOW
heavy spar	BARYTES
hemimorphite	
	ELECTRIC CALAMINE
hone-stone	NOVACULITE
horn-silver	CERARGYRITE
hornblende	SYNTAGMATITE
hyacinth	JACINTH
hydrogen calcium	
borate	PANDERMITE
hydrous zinc	
silicate	HEMIMORPHITE
ice-stone	CRYOLITE
idocrase	VESUVIANITE
igneous rock	AMYGDALOID
	BASALT.BASANITE
	BATHOLITE
—with feldspar	VARIOLITE
ilmenite	TITANIC IRON
impure	
—apatite	PHOSPHORITE
—talc or steatite	POTSTONE
—zinc	SPELTER
in Chinese porcelain	PETUNTSE
	PETUNTZE
iolite	DICHROITE
iron	FERRITE
—arsenic and sulphur	
ARSENO-PYRITES.MISPICKEL	
—disulphide	PYRITE(S)
—olivine	FAYALITE
—ore	BABINGTONITE
CHALYBITE.HAEMATITE	
	SIDERITE
—ore with coal	BLACKBAND
—pyrites	MUNDIC
—tantalate	TANTALITE
—titanium and oxygen	ILMENITE
jacinth	HYACINTH
jade	NEPHRITE.SPLEEN-STONE
	YU-STONE
kyanite	DISTHENE
lake deposit	SHELL-MARL
laminar lignite	PAPER COAL
laminated	
—bituminous mineral	DYSODIL
	DYSODILE.DYSODYLE
—clay	SHALE
lead	
—antimony and	
sulphur	JAMESONITE
—arsenate	MIMETITE
—chromate	CROCOISITE
—glance	GALENA
—monoxide	LITHARGE
—sulphate	ANGLESITE
—vanadate and	
chloride	VANADINITE
Lemnian earth	TERRA SIGILLATA
leucite	FEL(D)SPATHOID
lignite	COLOGNE EARTH.JET
—(Iceland)	SURTARBAND
	SURTURBAND
lime	
—alumina garnet	
	GROSSULAR(ITE)
—alumina mica	MARGARITE
—chrome garnet	UVAROVITE
—feldspar etc.	EUCRITE
—silicate	HORNFELS
—zeolite	SCOLECITE
limestone	OOLITE
—fetid	STINK-STONE
—for coffins	SARCOPHAGUS
—precipitated from	
solution	TRAVERTIN(E)
—with thread-like markings	
	LANDSCAPE MARBLE
limonite	BOG-IRON.BOG-ORE
PEA-IRON.STILPNOSIDERITE	
limy clay	MARL
liparite	RHYOLITE
lithia mica	LEPIDOLITE
loadstone	MAGNETITE
loamy deposit	LO(E)SS
lustrous metamorphic	
rock	PHYLLITE
Lydian stone	TOUCHSTONE
magnesia	PERICLASE
—alumina garnet	PYROPE
	PYROPUS

—iron spinel CEYLANITE CEYLONITE.PLEONASTE
—mica PHLOGOPITE
magnesian limestone DOLOMITE
magnesium
—aluminate SPINEL
—borate and chloride BORACITE
—carbonate DIALOGITE MAGNESITE
—hydroxide BRUCITE
—orthosilicate HUMITE
—oxide BRAUNITE
—silicate ENSTATITE SERPENTINE
—sulphate KIESERITE.KAINITE
magnetic pyrites PYRRHOTITE
manganese
—alumina garnet SPESSARTITE
—aluminium arsenate SYNADELPHITE
—dioxide PYROLUSITE
—ore WAD(D)
—oxide POLIANITE
—silicate RHODONITE
—spar RHODOCHROSITE
—sulphide ALABANDITE
marble with serpentine OPHICALCITE
marcasite COCKSCOMB PYRITES SPEAR PYRITES.WHITE PYRITES
meerschaum SEPIOLITE
melaconite TENORITE
melanterite COPPERAS
mellite HONEYSTONE
mercuric sulphate QUEEN'S YELLOW TURPETH MINERAL
mercurous chloride CALOMEL HORN MERCURY
metamorphosed
—diorite EPIDIORITE
—gabbroite EPIDIORITE
—sandstone QUARTZITE
mica GLIMMER
—and quartz MICA-SCHIST MICA-SLATE
—peridotite KIMBERITE
milky quartz or opal CACHOLONG
mineral coal STONE-COAL

—pitch MALTHA
mispickel ARSENICAL PYRITES ARSENO-PYRITES
molten rock MAGMA
molybdenum disulphide MOLYBDENITE
moss agate MOCHA STONE
mostly hypersthene HYPERSTHENITE
mountain soap HALLOYSITE
mountain tallow HATCHETTITE
muscovite granite GRANITITE
nepheline FEL(D)SPATHOID
—and pyroxene NEPHELINITE
—syenite LA(U)RDALITE
nephrite GREENSTONE.JADE
nickel arsenide COPPER NICKEL KUPFERNICKEL.NICCOLITE
niobate and titanate of
 yttrium, etc. EUXENITE
nodular rhyolite PYROMERIDE
nodule of oxide of
 iron EAGLE-STONE
novaculite TURKEY HONE TURKEY STONE
oil-shale TORBANITE
olivine CHRYSOLITE.PERIDOT(E)
—and augite LIMBURGITE MONCHIQUITE
—and iron oxides MUGEARITE
—with ferromagnesium PICRITE
—with pyroxenes LHERZOLITE
onyx with cornelian
 or sard SARDONYX
onyx marble ONYCHITE ORIENTAL ALABASTER
oolitic limestone PORTLAND STONE
opal SILICA
opalescent
—chrysoberyl CYMOPHANE
—feldspar MOONSTONE
opaque
—quartz JASPER.JASPIS
—white mineral ALBIN
orange spinel RUBICELLE
orange-red opal FIRE OPAL
orbicular diorite NAPOLEONITE
oriental alabaster ONYX MARBLE

orthoclase and biotite	MINETTE
orthorhombic pyroxene	
	HYPERSTHENE
oxide of	
—aluminium	ALUMINA
—lithium	LITHIA
—manganese	PSILOMELANE
—sodium and boron	KERNITE
—tellurium	TELLURITE
—zinc	ZINCITE
pea	
—iron	LIMONITE
—stone	PISOLITE
peacock-ore	BORNITE
pearly	
—lustred mineral	MARGARITE
—zeolite	STILBITE
peridotite	SAXONITE
philosopher's stone	
	LAPIS PHILOSOPHICUS
phospate of	
—aluminium	LAZULITE
	WAVELLITE
—copper and uranium	
	TORBERNITE
—thorium etc.	MONAZITE
—uranium and calcium	AUTUNITE
picolite	CHROME-SPINEL
pink	
—garnet	RHODOLITE
—topaz	ROSE-TOPAZ
pinkish quartz	ROSE-QUARTZ
pisolite	PEA-STONE
pissasphalt	MINERAL TAR
pitchblende	CLEVEITE.URANINITE
plagioclase	
—and augite	TESCHENITE
—and hornblende	CAMPTONITE
	DIORITE
—feldspar	ANORTHITE
—nepheline and augite	
	THERALITE
pleochroic pyroxene	AEGIRINE
plumbago	GRAPHITE
plutonic rock	SYENITE
porous rock	CALC-SINTER
	TUFA.TUFF
potash	
—feldspar	MICROCLINE

	ORTHOCLASE.SANIDINE
—mica	SERICITE
potassium chloride	SYLVINE
potstone	LAPIS OLLARIS
potter's clay	ARGIL
precious spinel	RUBY-SPINEL
	SPINEL-RUBY
purple and white	
—hard rock	PORPHYRY
—garnet	RHODOLITE
pyromeride	RHYOLITE
pyrophyllite	PENCIL-STONE
pyroxene	COCCOLITE
pyrrhotite	MAGNETIC PYRITES
quartz	SILICA
—and feldspar	HALLEFLINTA
	QUARTZ-PORPHYRY
—and mica, etc.	GREISEN
—and orthoclase	ELVAN.FELSITE
—biotite diorite	TONALITE
—crystal	BRISTOL DIAMOND
—feldspar and mica	GRANITE
	GNEISS
—feldspar, etc.	GRAYWACKE
	GREYWACKE
—feldspar with garnets	
	GRANULITE
—plagioclase	DACITE
—porphyry	GRANOPHYRE
—rock	QUARTZITE
—rough	BUHRSTONE
	BURRSTONE
—with mica	AVANTURINE
	AVENTURINE
quartzite	ITACOLUMITE
quicksand	SYRTIS
realgar	SANDARAC(H)
red	
—brown or yellow	
zircon	HYACINTH
—chalcedony	CARNELIAN
	CORNELIAN.SARD(IUS)
	SARDINE
—clay	BOLE
—corundum	RUBY
—garnet	ALABANDINE
	ALMANDINE
—ochre from Lemnos	
	LEMNIAN RUDDLE

—orthosilicate GARNET
—precious stone CARBUNCLE
—spinel BALAS(RUBY)
—tourmaline RUBELLITE
redruthite COPPER-GLANCE
repidolite CLINOCHLORE
rhodochrosite
          MANGANESE SPAR
rhodonite MANGANESE SILICATE
rhyolite LIPARITE
rock
—containing ores GANG(UE)
—crystal RHINESTONE
—from mud or clay PELITE
—forming FEL(D)SPAR.MICA
—of angular shards BRECCIA
—salt HALITE
ruby STAR-STONE
—silver PROUSTITE
          PYRARGYRITE
sandarac(h) REALGAR
sandstone HOLYSTONE
—derived from granite ARKOSE
—with glauconite GREEN SAND
sandy shale FA(I)KES
sapphire STAR-STONE
scapolite MARIALITE.MEIONITE
          MIZZONITE
schistose quartzite
          QUARTZ-SCHIST
schorl TOURMALINE
—and quartz SCHORL-ROCK
scoriaceous lava SLAG
selenite MOONSTONE.PHENGITE
sepiolite MEERSCHAUM
serpentine and
   calcite VERDE-ANTICO
          VERD-ANTIQUE
—rock OPHITE
sheet of rock NAPPE
shelly limestone
          PURBECK MARBLE
          PURBECK STONE
siderite CHALYBITE
silica CHALCEDONY.QUARTZ
—in hexagonal scales TRIDYMITE
silicate of
—aluminium ANDALUSITE
          CORDIERITE.DICHROITE

HAROMTOME.IDOCRASE
IOLITE.JADEITE.LEUCITE
MUSCOVITE.PENNINE
SCAPOLITE.SPODUMENE
STAUROLITE.TOPAZ
VESUVIANITE
—borium and calcium DATOLITE
—calcium THAUMASITE
—calcium, etc. EPIDOTE
          HORNBLENDE
—iron FAYALITE.GREEN EARTH
—iron and magnesium OLIVINE
—magnesium and
   aluminium SAPONITE
—magnesium and
   iron HYPERSTHENE
—potassium, etc. PHILLIPSITE
—sodium and iron RIEBECKITE
—sodium, etc. NEPHELINE
          NEPHELITE
—yttrium, etc. GADOLINITE
—zirconium, etc. EUDIALYTE
silicon dioxide SILICA
sillimanite FIBROLITE
silver
—and antimony DYSCRASITE
—chloride CERARGYRITE
—glance ARGENTITE
—iodide IODYRITE
—mica CAT-SILVER
—ore STEPHANITE
—ore, red PROUSTITE
silvery metal ALUMINIUM
skeleton crystal DENDRITE
slaty diabase tuff SCHALSTEIN
smaltite SPEISS-COBALT
smaragd EMERALD
smoky quartz
          CAIRNGORM (STONE)
smoothed by glaciation
          ROCHE MOUTONNEE
soapstone FRENCH CHALK
          SPANISH CHALK.STEARITE
soda
—amphibole ARFVEDSONITE
—lime feldspar OLIGOCLASE
—mica PARAGONITE
—syenite LA(U)RVIKITE
—trachyte KERATOPHYRE

sodalite   FEL(D)SPATHOID
sodium
—calcium sulphate   GLAUBERITE
—carbonates   TRONA
sodium aluminium
—silicate   ANALCIME.ANALCITE
      SODALITE.LAZURITE
—fluoride   CRYOLITE
—zeolite   GMELINITE
solid rock at surface   MANTLE
South African quartz
      CROCIDOLITE
Spanish chalk   FRENCH CHALK
      SOAPSTONE
spear pyrites   MARCASITE
specular iron   HAEMATITE
speiss-cobalt   SMALTITE
spelter   ZINC
sphalerite   ZINCBLENDE
sphene   TITANITE
spheroidal crystallite   GLOBULITE
spinel containing
   iron, etc.   PICOTITE
spleen-stone   JADE
spotted
—schist   KNOTENSCHIEFER
—slate   KNOTENSCHIEFER
stalactitic calcite   DROP-STONE
star-stone   RUBY.SAPPHIRE
staurolite   CROSS-STONE
stearite   SOAPSTONE
steatite   VENICE TALC
stibnite   ANTIMONITE
stilbite   DESMINE
stilpnosiderite   LIMONITE
stinkstone   SWINESTONE
streaks in igneous
   rock   SCHLIEREN
streaky granular rock   MYLONITE
strontium sulphate   CELESTINE
sulpharsenide of cobalt
      COBALTITE.COBALT GLANCE
sulphate of
—aluminium   ALUNITE
—iron   COQUIMBITE
—iron and potassium   JAROSITE
—magnesium, etc.   POLYHALITE
sulphide of
—arsenic   REALGAR

      ZARNEC.ZARNICH
—arsenic and silver   PROUSTITE
—copper and iron
      COPPER PYRITES
—copper, iron and
   antimony   TETRAHEDRITE
—iron   IRON PYRITES
      MARCASITE
—iron and nickel   PENTLANDITE
—lead   GALENA
—lead and antimony   ZINKENITE
—mercury   CINNABAR
—silver   ARGENTITE
—silver and antimony
      PYRARGYRITE
—zinc   ZINCBLENDE
sulphur, arsenic, etc.
      TENNANTITE
sylvine and rock salt   SYLVINITE
tachylite   HYALOMELAN(E)
talc with other
   minerals   TALC-SCHIST
tantalate of yttrium, etc.
      YTTRO-COLUMBITE
      YTTRO-TANTALITE
telluride of gold or
   silver   SYLVANITE
tennantite   FAHLERZ.FAHLORE
tenorite   MELACONITE
tetrahedrite   FAHLERZ.FAHLORE
titanic iron   ILMENITE
thorium and uranium
   ore   CHERALITE
thulite   ZOISITE
tin, copper, etc.   STANNITE
titanite   SPHENE
titanium oxide   ANATASE
      BROOKITE.RUTILE
toad-stone   BASALT LAVA.TUFF
topaz   PYCNITE
torbernite   AUTUNITE.URANITE
touchstone   LYDIAN STONE
tourmaline   SCHORL
—granite   LUXUL(L)IANITE
      LUXULYANITE
translucent opal   HYDROPHANE
transparent
—calcite   ICELAND SPAR
—feldspar   ADULARIA

—mineral	SPECULAR STONE		PERIMORPH
—stone	PHENGITE	yellow	
—zircon	JACINTH	—beryl	HELIODOR
travertine	CALC-SINTER	—clay	LONDON CLAY
	CALC-TUFF.ONYX-MARBLE	—corundum	ORIENTAL TOPAZ
tripoli	DIATOMITE	—garnet	TOPAZOLITE
trisulphide of arsenic	ORPIMENT	—rock crystal	CITRINE
troetolite	TROUTSTONE	yellowish garnet	
troutstone	TROCTOLITE		CINNAMON-STONE
tufa	CALC-SINTER.TUFF	yu(-stone)	JADE
tuff	CALC-SINTER	zerolite	CHABAZITE.HEULANDITE
	TOAD-STONE.TUFA		PHACOLITE.STILBITE
Turkey stone	TURQUOISE	zinc	SPELTER
turquoise	TURKEY STONE	—carbonate	CALAMINE
under-clay	WARRANT		HYDROZINCITE.SMITHSONITE
uraninite	PITCHBLENDE	—manganese spinel	FRANKLINITE
uranite	AUTUNITE.TORBERNITE	—silicate	HEMIMOEPHITE
uranium		—spinel	GAHNITE
—ore	COFFINITE	zirconium	
	SAMARSKITE	—dioxide	BADDELEYITE
—oxides	PITCHBLENDE	—silicate	JACINTH.JARGOON
vanadate of uranium	CORNOTITE		ZIRCON
variety of garnet, etc.	JACINTH	—sulphate	GOSLARITE
veinstone	GANG(UE)	zoisite	THULITE
Venice talc	STEATITE	**minimal**	
vesuvianite	IDOCRASE	minimal amount	D.P.ID.IP
vitreous lava	PALAGONITE	minimal change	D.P.ID.IP
volcanic		*minimal* ta(x)	TA
—dust	POZZ(U)OLANA	minimum lending rate	MLR
	PUZZOLANA	**minister**	DD
—glass	PERLITE.PITCHSTONE	minister's assistant	CURATE.PPS
—rock	ANDESITE.OBSIDIAN	ministerial box	CABINET
	PALAGONITE-TUFF	ministry	MIN
—rock, banded	EUTAXITE	Ministry of Defence	MOD
—tuff	TARRAS.TERRAS.TRASS	Ministry of Transport	MOT
Wallsend	COAL	**minor**	WEE
warrant	UNDER-CLAY	minor *disagreement*	MAJOR
water sapphire	CORDIERITE	minor railway	INFANTRY
waxy hydrocarbon	HATCHETTITE	Minority Rights Group	MRG
whin(stone)	BASALT	**mint**	
white and grey		mint money	NEW GUINEA
—chalcedony	CHALCEDONYX	*minted* coins	ICONS.SONIC
—clay	MEERSCHAUM	**minus**	
—feldspar	ALBITE	*minus* a...	omit A
—lead ore, etc.	HEDYPHANE	*minus* five	omit V
—marble	PARIAN	•se(v)en minus five	SEEN
—mica	MUSCOVITE	*minus* *	omit *
—pyrites	MARCASITE	•song *minus* all...	BAD
within another	ENDOMORPH	**minute**	M.MIN

misadventure in great. . .	TEARING	*missing* student	omit L
misanthrope	TIMON	*missing* *	omit *
misbehaving with. . .	WHIT	•th(row) *missing* tier	TH
miscast		near *miss*	EARN
miscast	CATS.SCAT	**miss²**	
miscast role	LORE	Atwell	MABEL (LUCY)
mischief		Austen	JANE
mischief done	NODE	Barrett	ELIZABETH
mischievous kids	SKIS	Bronte	ANNE.CHARLOTTE
misconstrued what. . .	THAW		EMILY.JANE.SHIRLEY
miscue		Darling	GRACE
miscued	DUCE	Doone	LORNA
miscued on red	DRONE	Durbeyfield	TESS
misdirect		Eyre	JANE
misdirected	CREDITED	Garbo	GRETA
misdirected players	PARSLEY	Gardner	AVA
misfiring car	ARC	Hayworth	RITA
misfortune to meet. . .	TEEM	Liddell	ALICE
misguided souls	SOLUS	Lind	JENNY
mishandled case	AESC	Lloyd	MARIE
mishap in game	GAMINE	Locket	LUCY
mish*mash*	SHIM	MacDonald	FLORA.JEANETTE
misinterpret false. . .	FLEAS	Monroe	MARILYN
mislaid ring	GRIN	Oberon	MERLE
mislead		Piggy	GILT
misleading clue	LUCE	Scoley	AMELIA
misled a. . .	DALE.DEAL	Spenlow	DORA
	LADE.LEAD	Tilley	VESTA
mismanage		Wickfield	AGNES
mismanaged much. . .	CHUM	Wilfer	(ISA)BELLA
mismanagement of team	MATE	Woodhouse	EMMA
misplaced letters	SETTLER	*misshapen* arm	MAR.RAM
misprinted page	GAPE	**missile**	
misquote		missile	DART.IBM.SAM.VI
misquote poem	MOPE	missiles	AMMO.DARTS
misquoting verse	SERVE	**missionaries**	CMS
misquotation from		**misspell**	
bard	BRAD.DRAB	*misspelled* words	SWORD
misrepresented a lot in. . .	TALION	*misspelt* a notice	ACONITE
miss¹		**mistake**	
miss	GAL.GIRL	*mistake* in line ten	LENIENT
miss bus	SUB	*mistaken* for the. . .	FOTHER
missed *speech*	MIST	**mister**	MR
missing	AWOL	*mistreating* cat	ACT
missing a. . .	omit A	**misuse**	
missing motorway	omit M or MI	*misuse* mails	ISLAM
missing out	omit OUT	*misused* cutlery	CRUELTY
missing out part of st(or)y	STY	**mix**	
missing start of (r)ace	ACE	*mix-up of* dates	SATED

mixed <u>sort</u>	ORTS.TORS	
mixture <u>of beer</u>	BEFORE	
m-mokes	MASSES	
mm!	EMS	
mobile		
Mobile state	ALABAMA	
mobile workers	SHIFT	
mock-*up*(D) ↑	DOC	
model	POSER.T	
model <u>cars</u>	ARCS.SCAR	
model question	POSER	
moderate	MOD	
moderations	MODS	
modern		
Modern Language		
Association	MLA	
modern miss	MS	
modern *sound*	GNU.KNEW	
modern times	AD	
modern ways	NEW(S)	
modify		
modified <u>brakes</u>	BAKERS	
	BASKER.BREAKS	
modulus	M	
mole	ADRIAN.MOL	
	PIER.SPY	
molten	(*see* melt)	
Monaco	MC	
monarch	ER.K.R	
Charles I	C	
E̅lizabeth II	L	
R̅ichard III	C	
H̅enry IV	R	
George V	G	
E̅dward VI	D	
monastic̅ custom	HABIT	
Monday	M.MON	
money	BRASS.CENT.L.P	
	SHEKELS.SUM.TIN	
hence		
•money-belt	BRASS BAND	
•money collapses		
	BRASSFOUNDERS	
•about money	RECENT	
•p-ot *with* money *in*	PLOT	
•money *has* a lot...	PLOT	
money maker	MINT	
money raised	SUM UP	
monkey	BABOON	

African		
—ape	CHIMPANZEE.GORILLA	
—baboon	CHACMA.DRILL	
	MANDRILL	
—black and white	GUEREZA	
—lemur	ANGWANTIBO	
	BUSH-BABY. GALAGO	
	NIGHT-APE.POTTO	
—long-tailed	COLOBUS	
	CERCOPITHECUS	
	DIANA MONKEY	
	GRIVET.GUENON	
	MONA.VERVET	
—guenon	TALAPOIN	
—white-eyelid	MANGAB(E)Y	
American	MARMOSET	
	SPIDER MONKEY	
Assam gibbon	HOOLOCK	
Ateles	SPIDER MONKEY	
Barbary ape	INUUS	
	MAGOT.MACAQUE	
black-tailed marmoset	MICO	
Bornean	PROBOSCIS MONKEY	
Brazilian	BELZEBUTH	
	GUARIBA.MIKRIKI	
	SAI.TAMARIN	
Burmese gibbon	HOOLOCK.LAR	
capuchin	CEBUS	
Ceylonese		
—lemur	LORIS	
—langur	WANDEROO	
Cochin-Chinese	DOUC	
dog-ape	BABOON	
dog-faced baboon		
	CYNOCEPHALUS	
East Indian		
—ape	ORANG(UTAN)	
	ORANG-OUTANG.GIBBON	
—lemur	LORIS.MALMAG	
	TARSIER	
Ethiopian baboon	GELADA	
flying lemur	COLUGO	
	CYNOCEPHALUS	
	GALEOPITHECUS	
gibbon	HYLOBATE	
Guinean baboon	SPHINX	
Indian		
—bonnet monkey	MACAQUE	
	ZATI	

—lion-tailed macaque	SILENUS
	WANDEROO
—long-tailed	HANUMAN
	LANGUR.ENTELLUS
—monkeys	BANDAR.BOONDER
	LORIS.MACAQUE.RHESUS
	TARSIER.TOGUE
Javanese gibbon	WOU-WOU
	WOW-WOW
lemur	MEERCAT.MEERKAT
Madagascan	
—lemur	AYE-AYE.BABACOOTE
	BABAKOTO.INDRI(S)
	MONGOOSE
—monkey	VARI
Malayan lemur	KUKANG
mangabey	WHITE-EYED MONKEY
marmoset	MIDAS.WISTITI
pile-driver's	RAM
Satan monkey	BLACK SAKI
South American	
—black saki	SATAN MONKEY
—broad-nosed	PLATYRRHINE
—cowled monkey	CAPUCHIN
—golden	SQUIRREL MONKEY
—grey	GRISON
—howler	MYCETES.MYCETIS
—long-tailed	SAKI.UAKARI
—marmoset	JACCHUS
—monkeys	TEE-TEE.TITI
	SAGOIN.SAG(O)UIN
—night-ape	DOUROUCOULI
	DURUKULI
—spider monkey	COAITA
	SAPAJOU
—squirrel monkey	SAIMIRI
	TAMARIN
spider monkey	ATELES
Sumatran	
—gibbon	SIAMANG.WOU-WOU
	WOW-WOW
—lemur	SIMPAI
proboscis monkey	NASALIS
tarsier	SPECTRE-LEMUR
toque	MACAQUE
tufted monkey	MUSTAC
white-eyed monkey	MANGABEY
monkshood	COWL
monseigneur	MGR

monsieur	M
monsignor	MGR
monsters	
including	
heraldic beasts	
mythical beasts:	
American	BIGFOOT
amphibious	WATER-BULL
antelope	ARGASILL.IBEX
—horse	BAGWYN
—with swivelling horns	YALE
Australian	BUNYIP
bird	ROC.ROK.RUC.RUKH
—Arabian	PHOENIX
—Persian	SIMORG.SIMURG(H)
—restless	HUMA
—rising from ashes	PHOENIX
—with lethal whistle	WHISTLER
bird/woman	HARPY
bloodsucking witch	LAMIA
bull	
—fish	BULL MARINE.SEA-BULL
—headed	BONNACON
	MINOTAUR
—horse	BON(N)ACPON
—mare	JUMART
—with flames from	
mouth	CARETYNE
camel/goat	YPOTRILL
Carroll, Lewis	BANDERSNATCH
cat with horns	CALYGREYHOUND
centaur	HIPPOCENTAUR
—with bow and	
arrow	SAGITTARIUS
	SAGITTARY
chaste wife-eater	CHICHEVACHE
cock/serpent	COCKATRICE
cockatrice/dragon	BASILISK
cow/stallion	JUMART
Cretan	MINOTAUR
cruel	OGRE
decorative Chinese	KYLIN
dog	
—fish	HOUND MARINE.SEA-DOG
—three-headed	CERBERUS
dragon	BASILISK
—fish	SEA-DRAGON
—with two legs	WIVERN.WYVERN
—with wings	GORGON

—Norse	FAFNIR	—lion/antelope	SATYRAL
eagle with horns	TRAGOPAN	—lion/scorpion	MANTICORA
female	EURYALE.GORGON		MANTICORE.MANTYGRE
	MEDUSA.STHENOA	—'s head with ears of	
firebreathing	CHIM(A)ERA	ass	MIDAS'S HEAD
	DRAGON	—wolf	WEREWOLF
fish	SCOLOPENDRA	many-headed	HYDRA
—tailed, horselike	HIPPOCAMPUS		THE PEOPLE
fox/greyhound/wolf	ENFIELD	mastiff/bloodhound	TALBOT
giraffe	CAMELOPARD	Norse	
—with horns	CAMELOPARDEL	—dragon	FAFNIR
goat/stag	HIRCOCERVUS	—serpent	MIDGARD
	TRAGALEPH	Northern	TARAND
Greek	LAMIA.TYPHOEUS	Norwegian	KRAKEN
griffin with horse's		one-eyed	CYCLOPS
body	HIPPOGRIFF	reindeer with forward curving	
	HIPPOGRYPH	horns	TROGODICE
hairy tyger	NEBEK	Rocky Mountains	BIGFOOT
Himalayan	YETI	Roman	LAMIA.TYPHON
horse		Scandinavian	TROLL
—goat	SILENUS	sea horse	HIPPOCAMPUS
—griffin	HIPPOGRIFF	—Norwegian	KRAKEN
	HIPPOGRYPH	—scaly	PHOCA
—with single horn	UNICORN	—swallower	CHARYBDIS
—with wings	PEGASUS	sea monster	ORC.LEVIATHAN
human wolf	WEREWOLF		WASSERMAN
hundred-headed	TYPHON	six-headed	SCYLLA
lion		snake-haired	EURYALE.GORGON
—dragon	OPINICUS		MEDUSA.STHENO
—eagle	BOREYNE	Spenserian	ROSMARINE
	GRIFFIN.GRIFFON		SEASATYRE.ZIFFIUS
	GRIPE.GRYPHON	stag/goat	HIRCOCERVUS
—fish	SEA-LION		TRAGLEPH
—goat	CHIM(A)ERA	star-spangled hind	PANTHEON
—leopard/serpent		three-headed	CERBERUS
	QUESTING BEAST	Tibetan	YETI
—scorpion	MANTICORE	two-headed	JANICEPS
	MANTICORA	—snake	AMPHISBAENA
—wolf	TYGER	two-tailed mermaid	MELUSINE
—with helmet	BOTRAGER	under	
lizard	AMPHISBAEMA	—Etna	TYPHOEUS
—in flames	SALAMANDER	—rock	CHARYBDIS
man		unicorn/fish	SEA-UNICORN
—ass	ONOCENTAUR	water	NICKER
—covered with green		whale-like	WHIRLPOOL
hair	WODEHOUSE	whirlpool	CHARYBDIS
—goat	SATYR	wildcat	CAT-A-MOUNTAIN
—horse	(HIPPO)CENTAUR	winged	
	SAGITTARIUS.SAGITTARY	—dragon	WIVERN.WYVERN

—serpent	PYTHON
wingless dragon	LINDWORM
with knotted tail	ALPHYN
wolf	
—cat/goat	CHATLOUP
—fish	SEA-WOLF
—fox/greyhound	ENFIELD
—with cloven feet	THEOW.THOS
woman	
—fish	MERMAID
—lioness	SPHINX
—seabird	SIREN
—vulture	HARPY
monstrous regiment	WOMEN
month	M.MO.MOON.MTH
month after sight	MS
French Revolutionary(*see* French)	
Jewish	(*see* Hebrew)
moons	
Earth	LUNA
Jupiter	CALLISTO.EUROPA
	GANYMEDE.IO
Mars	DEIMOS.PHOBOS
Neptune	NEREID.TRITON
Pluto	CHARON
Saturn	DIONE.ENCELADUS
	HYPERION.IAPETUS.JANUS
	MIMAS.PHOEBE.RHEA
	TETHYS.TITAN
Uranus	ARIEL.MIRANDA
	OBERON.TITANIA
	UMBRIEL
Moor	SARACEN
Moorish	
carpet	SOFRA.ZOFRA
dance	MORESCO
drum	ATABAL
leader	M
pirate	SALLEE-MAN.SALLY-MAN
ship	GALLIVAY.XEBEC(K)
	ZEBEC(K)
violin	REBEC(K)
mop	
mop *up*(D) ↑	POM
mop up a...	incl A
mop up <u>ink</u>	KIN
mop up *	incl *
•ra-g *mops up* French	
wine	RAVING

mopped up by *	incl in *
•*French* wine *mopped up*	
by r-ag	RAVING
Moral Rearmament	MRA
more	
more cross	PLUS
More ideal	UTOPIA
more than one	ONER.TONE
more stirring	ROME
morning	AM
morning *off*	omit AM
•entertain *with*	
morning *off*(am)	USE
•S(am) *has* morning *off*	S
Moroccan	
capital	M.RABAT
coin	DERHAM.DIRHAM.DIRHEM
leader	M
measure	
—22 inches	DRAH
—bushel	MUDD
ruler	SULTAN
tree	ARGAN.ARAR
	SANDARAC(H).THYINE
tribe	RIFF.MOOR
Morocco	MA.MOR
Morris Garage	MG
Moslem	MUSLIM
	MUS(S)ULMAN
	SARACEN
ablution	WUDU.WUZU
alluring woman	HOURI
almsgiving	ZAKAT
angel of death	AZRAEL
animal slaughter	HAL(L)AL
ascetic	DERVISH.FAKIR
	FAQUIR
ascribing partners to God	SHIRK
become Moslem	TURN TURK
Bulgarian	POMAK
caliphate	KHILIFAT
call to prayer	ADAN.AZAN
canon law	SHARIA
chapter of Koran	SURA(H)
chief	AMEER.AMIR
	DATTO.EMEER.EMIR
—magistrate	SHEREEF.SHERIF
Christian turned	
Moslem	RENEGADE.RENEGADO

cloak	(D)JIBBAH.(D)JUBBAH
college	MADRAS(S)A(H)
	MEDRESSAH
confession of faith	SHAHADA
convert (Hindu)	SHEIK(H)
court official	HAJIB
dancing fanatic	
	WHIRLING DERVISH
date (after Hegira)	AH
demon	DJINN(I).GENIE.GINN
	JANN.JINN(EE).JINNI
dervish	SADITE
—'s cap	TAJ
descendant of	
—Fatima	FATIMID
	SAID.SAY(Y)ID
—Mohammed	EMIR.SEID
	SHEREEF.SHERIF
disciple	MURID
emblem	CRESCENT
example of Mohammed	SUNNA
faith	CRESCENT
fallen angel	EBLIS.IBLIS
fanatic	ABDELS.MOOLA(H)
	MOLLA(H).MULLA(H)
fast	MOHARRAM.MUHARRAM
	MUHARREM.RAMAD(H)AN
	SAUM.SAWM
festival	BAIRAM.BAYRAM
first month of year	MOHARRAM
	MUHARRAM
	MUHARREM
flight of Mohammed	HEJ(I)RA
	HEGIRA.HIJRA
god	ALLAH
great leader	MAHDI
greeting	SALAAM
hermit	MARABOUT
holy	
—city	MECCA.MEDINA
—man	IMA(U)M
—state of pilgrim	IHRAM
—war	CRESCENTADE
	JEHAD.JIHAD
home of spirits	KAF
if God wills	INSHALLAH
in India	COSSA
infidel	GIAOUR.KAFIR
interpretation of Koran	TAFSIR

Jesus	NABI ISA
knowledge of Koran	HAFIZ
law	SHERIAT
lawyer	ALFAQUI.MOOLVEE
	MOOLVI(E).MOOLWEE
	MUFTI
leader	AG(H)A
	IMA(U)M.M.MAHDI
legal decision	FEWTA
lord	OMRAH
magistrate	CADI.KADI
member of dynasty	ABBASID(E)
mendicant	FAKIR.FAQUIR
minister	VEZIR.VISIER
	VIZI(ER).WAZIR.WIZIER
miracle-worker	FAKIR.FAQUIR
monk	DERVISH
month (1st)	MOHARRAM
	MUHARRAM.MUHARREM
mosque	MADRAS(S)A(H)
	MEDRESSEH.MASJED
	MASJID
mystic	SOFI.SUFI
niche in mosque pointing to	
Mecca	MIHRAB.QIBLA
North African	SENUSSI
nymph of paradise	HOURI
one who calls to prayer	MUEZZIN
orthodox Moslem	HANIF
	SHAFI(ITE).SUNNI
pilgrim	HADJI.HAJ(J)I
—garb	IHRAM
pilgrimage	HADJ.HAJ(J)
prayer	KHOTBAH.KHOTBEH
	KHUTBAH.SALAT
preacher	MOLLA(H)
	MOOLA(H).MULLA(H)
priest	IMA(U)M.MUEDDIN
	MUEZZIN
prince	AMEER.AMIR.EMEER
	EMIR.SHEREEF.SHERIF
princess	BEGUM
prophet	MAHDI.MAHOMET
	MOHAMMED
public procession	MOHARRAM
	MUHARRAM.MUHARREM
pulpit in mosque	MIMBAR
	MINBAR
purgatory	ARAF

religion	ISLAM	warrior	GHAZI
	MOHAMMEDANISM	what God wills	MASHALLAH
	MAMMETRY.MAUMETRY	whole Moslem world	ISLAM
	MAWMETRY.MOMMETRY	witness	SHAHADA
religious		woman's	
—leader	AYATOLLAH	—garment	BURK(H)A
—war	(see holy above)		BURQA
revealed law	SHARIA	—wrap	IZAR
rites	ABDEST.MADHAHIB	women's quarters	HARAM
ritual animal slaughter	HAL(L)AL		HAREM.HARIM
ruler	SULTAN		SERAGLIO.SERAIL
sacred		worship	SALAT
—fountain	ZEMZEM	**most**	
—stone	BLACK STONE	most *disagreeable*	LEAST
saint's shrine	DURGAH	Most Excellent	ME
schoolmaster	MOLLA(H)	*most of* all	AL.LL
	MOOLA(H).MULLA(H)	*most of* the...	TH
scriptures	ALCORAN.(AL)KORAN	*most* (p)arts	ARTS
	QORAN.QURAN	*most* w/omen s/ay	OMENS
sect	DRUSE.DRUZ(E).SHIA(H)	*mostly* fashionable	ALAMO.CHICK
	SHIITE.SOFI(I)SM.SONNA	*mostly* tall	ALL.THIGH
	SONNITE.SUFI(I)SM.SUNNI(TE)	**mother**	DAM.MA.MAM.MUM
	WAHABEE.WAH(H)ABI(ISM)	hence	
Shiite	ISMAILI	•mother *and* son	DAMSON
shrine	MARABOUT.ZIARA	•mother country	DAMNATION
slave	DURGAH	•mother *gets* older	DAMAGES
spirit	GENIE.JINNEE.(D)JINNI	and	
	GINN.DJINN	•mother in court	MAINYARD
spiritual leader	CALIF.CALIPH	•mother's double	MAMA
	KALIF(A)(H)	•mother-ship	MASS
student	SOFTA	•motherlessness	NOMA
sultan's		and	
—lady	SULTANA	•mother *and* friend	MAMMATE
—standard bearer	ALEMBDAR	•mother encountered	MAMMET
teacher	MOLLA(H).MOOLA(H)	•mother *with* Scotsman	MAMMON
	MOLLA(H).MULLA(H)	and	
temple	KAABA.MOSQUE	•little mother	MINIMUM
theologians	ULEMA	•mother *has* directions	
title of respect	SIDI	on	MU-MESON
tomb cloth	CHAD(D)AR	•mother *has* power...	MUMP
	CHADOR.CHUDDAH	and	
	CHUDDAR	•two mothers	MADAM.MAMA
towards Mecca	KEBLAH.KIBLAH		MAMMA
traditional lore	HADITH.SUNNA	*motion* of tram	MART
tribune	DIKKAH	*motley* garb	BRAG.GRAB
unbeliever	KAFIR	**motor**[1]	CAR
veil	CHAD(D)AR.CHADOR	hence	
	CHUDDAH.CHUDDAR	•bird follows motor	CARGOOSE
	YASHMAK		CAROUSEL

•motor race	CARNATION
•motor travels. . .	CARGOES
motor²	
motor fleet vessel	MFV
motor torpedo boat	MTB
motor vessel	MV
motoring	(in) CA-R
motoring organisation	AA.RAC
motorists	AA.RAC
motorway	M.MI
moulded clay	LACY
mount	
mounted	UP
mounted artillery(D) ↑	SNUG
mounted police	RCMP.MP
mounted soldiers(D) ↑	AT.ER
mounting step(D) ↑	PETS
mountain	ALP.MT.TOR
a Scandinavian *mountaineer*(D) ↑	
	APPAL
mountain-*climbing*(D) ↑	
	ANTE.PLA
mountain guide	TORMENTOR
mountain *retreat*	PLA
Mountain Standard Time	MST
mountaineer	SHERPA
mouse	MICKEY
mousey female	MINNIE
mousse made. . .	DAME.EDAM
	MEAD
mouthpiece	GUM.LIP
	TONGUE.TOOTH
move	
move *	
•clam *moves* left	CALM
•four thousand *move* right	FORUM
•*move* East *of* Leith	LITHE
•*move* south *in* scow	COWS
move * *from*	omit *
•*move* North *from*	
Bar(n)es	BARES
•*move* South *from*	
(S)lough	LOUGH
•*move* pawn *from* s(p)ot	SOT
move in	omit IN
move on	omit ON
move out	omit OUT
•*move out*, p(out)ing	PING
move out of range	ANGER

move round on. . .	NO
move right *round*⟨	TR
move to South	LEAVEN
moved camp	AFFECTED
moved it to	TITO
moved into *	incl in *
•animal *moved into* church	CRATE
movement of tide	DIET.EDIT.TIED
movie actor	CROAT
moving a. . .	omit A
moving parts	SPRAT.STRAP
moving proposal	MOTION
moving spirit	PETROL
moving *	omit *
•*moving* animal from	
c(rat)e	CE
movingly depict an. . .	PEDANTIC
Mozart's works	K
Mrs	BRIDE
Boaz	RUTH
Copperfield	DORA
de Winter	REBECCA
Dombey	EDITH
Mopp	CHAR(WOMAN)
Partlett	HEN
Punch	JUDY
mu	M
much	BAGS.LOTS
much money	IMPOUNDS
much of September	EMBER
much time	TIM
much-used	(*see* old⁴)
much-v/aunt/ed	AUNT
muddle	
muddle things. . .	NIGHT
muddled men eat a. . .	EMANATE
mug	
mug-*shot*	GUM
mug *up*(D) ↑	GUM
mulch	BEDSPREAD
mulled ales	LEAS.SALE.SEAL
multiple sclerosis	MS
multiplication stable	STUD
mum	MA.SH.ST
munching oats	STOA
Municipal Police	MP
murder	
murder victim	ABEL
murderer	CAIN

Muses	PERIDES
astronomy	URANIA
comedy	THALIA
dance	TERPSICHORE
erotic poetry	ERATO
epic song	CALLIOPE
history	CLIO
singing and sacred	
dance	POLY(HY)MNIA
lyric poetry and music	EUTERPE
tragedy	MELPOMENE
museum	MUS
mushroom	(*see* fungus)
mushy <u>peas</u>	APES.APSE
music¹	MUS
music *centre*	S
music of the Muses	NONET
music school	RAM
musical cleric	CANON
musical number	SCORE
musical party	HAIR-DO
musical season	HAIRSPRING
musical whim	CAPRICE
	CROTCHET
musician's house	FLAT
musicians	RAM.MCM
music²	
above	SOPRA
accented	FORZATO.FZ
accompaniment	OBBLIGATO
agitated	AGITATO
alteration of theme	VARIATION
alternation of two notes	SHAKE
	TRILL
alternative	OSSIA
always	SEMPRE
animatedly	ANIM(ATO)
answer in fugue	REPLY
anthem	MOTET(T)
augmented fourth	TRITONE
bagpipe composition	PIBROCH
ballad	CANTILENA
	SINGSONG
barely audible	SOTTO VOCE
bass octave	GREAT OCTAVE
becoming	
—slower	RALL(ENTANDO)
—softer	DIM(INUENDO)
boating song	BARCAROL(L)E

briskly	ALLEGRO.CON MOTO
broad and slow	LARGO
cadence from subdominant	
to tonic	PLAGAL
choral composition	CANTATA
	CANTUS.MOTET(T)
chord	ITALIAN SIXTH
	NEAPOLITAN SIXTH
—three notes	TRIAD.TRICHORD
—four notes	TETRACHORD
—five notes	PENTACHORD
—six notes	HEXACHORD
—seven notes	HEPTACHORD
—eight notes	OCTACHORD
church cantata	MOTET(T)
clef	ALTO.BASS.C.F.G
	SOPRANO.TENOR
composition	OPUS.SERENADE
	SERENATA
—18th c.	CASSATION
—for	
—one	SOLO
—two	DUET.DUO
—three	TRIO
—four	QUARTET(T)
	QUARTETTE.QUARTETTO
—five	QUINTET(T)
	QUINTETTE.QUINTETTO
—six	SESTET(T).SESTETTE
	SEXTET(T).SEXTETTE
—seven	SEPTET(T).SEPTETTE
—eight	OCTET(T).OCTETTE
—nine	NONET(TE).NONETTO
—solo and orchestra	
	CONCERTO
conclusion	CODA
confusion	IMBROGLIO
continue in like manner	SIMILE
continuous glide	PORTAMENTO
country music	PASTORALE
damped	SORDO
dance music	GAVOTTE
	HORNPIPE.PASPY.PASSEPIED
	RIGADOON.TWO-STEP
—16th-17th c.	GAILLARD
	GALLIARD.MINUET
—Argentinian	TANGO
—Bohemian	POLKA.REDOWA
—Brazilian	MAXIXE.SAMBA

—German	ALLEMANDE	—fugue	RICERCAR(E).RICERCATA
	LANDLER	embellishment	ROULADE
—Irish	PLANXTY	end	FINE
—Italian	SALTARELLO	ending	CODA
—like polka	SCHOTTISCHE	entr'acte	INTERMEZZO
—Neapolitan	TARANTELLA	evening music in the open	
—Negro	WALK-AROUND	air	SERENADE.SERENATA
—Norwegian	HALLING.SPRING	excessively	TROPPO
—Polish	CRACOVIENNE	fading away	MANCANDO
	KRAKOWIAK. MAZURKA		MANCANTE
	POLONAISE.VARSOVIENNE		SMORZANDO
—Provencal	TAMBOURIN	fantasia	TOCCATA
—Scottish	REEL.SPRING	fifth	QUINT
	STRATHSPEY	figured bass	TASTO SOLO.TS
—slow	CHACONNE.WALTZ	first or principal part	PRIMO
—Spanish	PAVANE.SEGUIDILLA	florid in	
—square	QUADRILLE	—melody	MELISMATIC
—West Indian	REGGAE	—treatment	FIGURATION
	(see also dance)	—vocal passages	COLORATURA
dawn song	AUBADE	flourish	CADENZA
death of Christ	PASSION MUSIC	fluctuation in	
decrease in volume		pitch	TREMOLO.VIBRATO
	DECRESC(ENDO)	follow the singer	COLLA VOCE
decreasing	CAL(ANDO)	forced	SF(Z).SFORZANDO
depress soft pedal	UNA CORDA		SFORZATO
	UC	forerunner of fugue	RICERCAR(E)
detached	STACCATO		RICERCATA
direction to pianist	TRE CORDE	form of first	
dissonant note	WOLF(-NOTE)	movement	SONATA FORM
distorted rhythm	RUBATO	fourth	QUART
double		—fifth or octave	
—speed	DOPPIO MOVIMENTO		PERFECT INTERVAL
—tempo	ALLA BREVE	free	SCIOLTO
dramatic oratorio		—choice of time, etc.	
	AZIONE(SACRA)		AD LIB(ITUM)
draw out slightly	TEN(UTO)	—form piece	FANTASIA
drinking song (Greek)	SKOLION	—style composition	CAPRICCIO
dying away	MANCANDO	freedom of tempo	RUBATO
	MANCANTE.MORENDO	fundamental note of chord	ROOT
	PERDENDO	Gaelic boat song	JORRAM
each note		gavotte trio	MUSETTE
—emphasised	MARC(ATO)	gently	SORDAMENTE
—shortened	STACCATO	grace note	MORDENT
early counterpoint			NACHSCHLAG.ORNAMENT
	FA(UX)BURDEN		PRALLTRILLER
easy and flowing	CANTABILE	gradually	
eighth	OCTAVE	—decreasing speed	
elaborate			RIT(ARDANDO)
—composition	ARABESQUE	—fading	SMORZ(ANDO)

—slower and softer
SMORZ(ANDO)
ground-bass OSTINATO
group of
—two notes DUOLE.DUPLET
—three notes TRIAD.TRICHORD
TRIPLET
—four notes QUADRUPLET
TETRACHORD
—five notes PENTACHORD
QUINTUPLET
—six notes HEXACHORD
SEXTOLET.SEXTUPLET
—seven notes HEPTACHORD
SEPTIMOLE
SEPTUPLET
—eight notes OCTACHORD
OCTUPLET
—nine notes NONUPLET
—ten notes DECUPLET
—eleven notes UNDECIMOLE
—twelve half-tones OCTAVE
half staccato SPICCATO
harmony in thirds and
sixths FA(UX)BURDEN
hastening the time STRINGENDO
having
—five notes PENTATONIC
—seven notes HEPTATONIC
—twelve tones DODECAPHONIC
heavy PESANTE
high elaborate
soprano COLORATURA
highest voice SOPRANO.TREBLE
hold for full value TEN(UTO)
idyllic opera PASTORALE
in
—a marked manner MARC(ATO)
—declamatory style PARLANDO
—devotional manner RELIGIOSO
—free style CAPRICCIOSO
—the manner of fugue FUGATO
—the usual manner SOLITO
increase volume CRES(CENDO)
increasing in speed
ACCEL(ERANDO)
instrumental
—composition SONATA
—melody CANTILENA

—passage in vocal
work RITORNEL(LO)
RITORNELL(E)
RITOURNELLE
—piece like a madrigal CANZONE
—prelude OVERTURE
intermediate
—movement INTERMEZZO
—part MEAN
interval of
—three tones TRITONE
—three and a half tones
PERFECT FIFTH
—fifth QUINT
—sixth SEXT
—seventh HEPTACHORD
—twelfth DUODECIMO
—twelve semitones OCTAVE
—two and a half tones
PERFECT FOURTH
introduction ENTREE
inverted mordent PRALLTRILLER
irregular RHAPSODY
is silent TACET
jazz BEBOP.BLUES.BOP
DIXIELAND.MAINSTREAM
RAGTIME.TRAD(ITIONAL)
—type of folk music SKIFFLE
key of C major PROPER CHANT
lament DUMKA
left-hand part of duet SECONDO
light
—musical drama OPERETTA
—medley QUODLIBET
little aria ARIETTA
lively SPIRITOSO.VIVACE
—dance tune GIGUE
—movement SCHERZO
—tune RANT
loud F.FORTE
—as possible FFF.FORTISSISSIMO
—then soft FORTE-PIANO.FP
low soprano MEZZO-SOPRANO
madrigal FA-LA
major third PICARDY THIRD
TIERCE DE PICARDIE
mass for dead REQUIEM
medium slow ANDANTE
ANDANTINO

melodiously	ARIOSO	—in faster time	STRETTA
melody like an aria	CAVATINA		STRETTO
moderate speed	MODERATO	pastoral melody	MUSETTE
moderately		pause	FERMATA
—loud	MEZZO-FORTE.MF	percussion	TRIANGLE
—slow	LARGHETTO	perfect	
—soft	MEZZO-PIANO.MP	—fifth	HEMIOLIA
most lively	VIVACISSIMO		SESQUIALTERA
mouth music	PORT A BEUL	—fourth	SESQUITERTIA
moving nimbly	VOLANTE	piped music	MUSAK
much	MOLTO	plain	SECCO
musical		—song	CANTO FERMO
—drama	OPERA		CANTUS FERMUS
—story (usually		plaintively	LAGRIMOSO
Biblical)	ORATORIO	playful	PIACEVOLE
mute	SORDINO.SOURDINE	playfully	SCHERZANDO
muted	SORDO	pleasant	PIACEVOLE
non-stop piece	MOTO PERPETUO	pluck the strings	PIZZ(ICATO)
not sharp or flat	NATURAL	preliminary passage	ENTREE
note	BREVE.CROCHET		PRAELUDIO
	DEMI-SEMIQUAVER.MINIM		PRAELUDIUM.PRAELUSION
	QUAVER.SEMIBREVE		PRELUDE
	SEMIQUAVER	prelude	ENTREE.RITORNEL(LO)
—non harmonic	PASSING NOTE		RITORNELL(E).RITOURNELLE
notes of chord played in quick		progression up or down of	
succession	ARPEGGIO	a part	MOTION
obsolete ornament	BACKFALL	quick	PRESTO
on the		—dance	GALLOPADE
—bridge	SUL PONTICELLO	—staccato	SALTANDO.SALTATO
—key	SUL TASTO	quicker	PIU MOSSO
one string	UNA CORDA.UC	quickly	VELOCE
operatic air	CAVATINA	quivering	TREMOLO
orchestral composition			TREMOLANDO
	SYMPHONY	rapidly	VELOCE
original tempo	TEMPO PRIMO	recapitulation of first	
ornament	ACCIACCATURA	subject	REPRISE
	APPOGGIATURA	refrain	EPISTROPHE
	GRACE NOTE.REL(L)ISH		FA(UX)BURDEN
—of four notes	TURN		RITORNEL(LO).RITORNELL(E)
out of tune	SCORDATO		RITOURNELLE
overture	TOCCATA	recitative	PARLANDO
part		regular	GIUSTO
—in parallel motion	ORGANUM	reinforced	RF(Z).RINF(ORZATO)
—of fugue	STRETTO	release soft pedal	TRE CORDE
—song	ROUND	remaking of composition	
parts consisting of separate			RIFACIMENTO
melodic lines	POLYPHONY	remove mute	SENZA SORDINO
passage		repeat	REPLICA
—for orchestra	TUTTI	repeated figure in jazz	RIFF

repetitions in higher tone	ROSALIA
retrained	RITENUTO
return to	
—pitch	LOCO
—sign	DAL SEGNO.DS
—the beginning	DA CAPO.DC
reverting to original speed	A TEM(PO)
rhythm	TEMPO
run	
—between two notes	TIRADE
—elaborate	ROULADE
sad	MESTO
sailors' song	CHANT(E)Y
	CHANTIE.SHANTY
score	PARTITUR(A)
second movement	TRIO
semitone	FLAT.LIMMA.SHARP
set of variations	PARTITA
short	
—aria	CAVATINA
—cadence	TROPE
—concerto	CONCERTINO
—fugue	FUGHETTA
—opera or oratorio	CANTATA
—rondo	RONDINO
—sonata	SONATINA
—toccata	TOCCATELLA
	TOCCATINA
silent	TACET
simple	SEMPLICE
sixth	SEXT
sliding effect	GLISSANDO
slow	ADAGIO.LENTO
—and sumptuous	LYDIAN
—beginning of trill	RIBATTUTA
—movement	DUMKA
—of csardas	LASSU
—waltz	VALETA.VELETA
slowing	LENTANDO
	RALLENTANDO.RITARDANDO
	SLARGANDO(SI)
slowly	LENTAMENTE
small interval	MICROTONE
smoothly	LEG(ATO)
soft	P.PIANO
—pedal	UNA CORDA
softly	PIANO.SORDAMENTE

—and sweetly	DOLCEMENTE
solfeggio	CANTILENA
solo narrative with music	CANTATA
sonata movement	MINUET
song	LAY
—German	LIED
—like a madrigal	CANZONE
—of	
—lamentation	THRENE
	THRENODY
—thanksgiving	P(A)EAN
—the dawn	AUBADE
—West Indian	CALYPSO
—with refrain	ROUNDELAY
soprano	TREBLE
speed	TEMPO
spirited	SPIRITOSO
square dance	QUADRILLE
strike strings with bow	COL LEGNO
strongly accented	SFORZATO-PIANO.SFP
	SF(Z).SFORZANDO
sudden slowing	RITENUTO
suddenly accented	RF(Z)
	RINF(ORZATO)
suitable	GIUSTO
suite (18th c.)	PARTITA
supplementary	RIPIENO
sustained	SOS(TENUTO).TENUTO
sweet	DOLCE
symphony	SINFONIA
temporarily out of tune	SCORDATURA
temporary key signature	ACCIDENTAL
tender	AMOROSO
tenderly	AFFETTUOSO
tenor octave	SMALL OCTAVE
test piece	ETUDE
third tone of tetrachord	TRITE
three strings	TRE CORDE
throughout	SEMPRE
time	TEMPO.VOLTA
—division	MODE
tone at octave interval from another	REPLICATE
too much	TROPPO

training piece	ETUDE
treble	SOPRANO.TRIPLE
trembling	TREMOLO
	TREMOLANDO
trifling piece	TOY
triplet	HEMIOLIA
turn	GRUPETTO.VOLTA
—over quickly	VOLTE SUBITO.VS
twelve semitones	OCTAVE
two	
—beats per bar	DUPLE
—crotchets per bar	TWO-FOUR
unaccompanied	A CAPELLA
	ALLA BREVE.SECCO
—song	MADRIGAL
under one's breath	SOTTO VOCE
using several keys	
	POLYTONAL(ITY)
very	ASSAI.MOLTO
—loud	FF.FORTISSIMO
—quick	PRESTISSIMO
—slow(ly)	LENTISSIMO
—soft	PIANISSIMO.PP
virtuoso passage	CADENZA
vocal exercise	SOLFEGGIO
weighty	PESANTE
with	
—alternating subjects	RONDO
—bouncing bow	
	(ARCO)SALTANDO
	(ARCO)SALTATO
—bow close to fingerboard	
	SUL TASTO
—bow close to bridge	
	SUL PONTICELLO
—diminishing speed	
	RITARDANDO
—each note separated	STACCATO
—fervour	ZELOSO
—fire	CON FUOCO
—full time allowed for each note	SOS(TENUTO)
—fury	FURIOSO
—great speed	VELOCE
—individual melodic lines	POLYPHONY
—majesty	MAESTOSO
—moderate volume	MEZZA VOCE
—movement	CON MOTO

—mute	CON SORDINO
—spirit	CON SPIRITO.SPIRITOSO
—strong attack	RINFORZANDO
	(S)FORZANDO
	(S)FORZATO
—syncopation	(ALLO) ZOPPO
—the bow	(COLL')ARCO
—the voice	COLLA VOCE
—the wood	COL LEGNO
without	SENZA
—a break	LEG(ATO)
—a mute	SENZA SORDINO

musical instruments

accordion	MELODEON
African	GORA(H).GOURA
	ZANZE
ancient lute	DICHORD
bagpipe (Italian)	PIFFERO
	ZAMPOGNA
bandore	PANDORA.PANDORE
bandore	PANDURA
barrel organ	SERINETTE
basic oboe	PIFFERO
bass	
—drum	TAMBOUR
—fiddle	(VIOLON)CELLO
—lute	THEORBO
—saxhorn	EUPHON(IUM)
—tuba	BOMBARDON
—viol	VIOLA DA GAMBA
	VIOLONE
bassoon	FAGOTTO
—like (medieval)	RACKET(T)
bellows	ACCORDION
	CONCERTINA.MELODEON
bells	GLOCKENSPIEL
bird	
—call	QUAIL-CALL.QUAIL-PIPE
—shaped	OCARINA
boatswain's whistle	PIPE
bombardon	BASS TUBA
brass	
—bass	BOMBARDON.SAXHORN
	SOUSAPHONE.TUBA
—reed	SARRUSOPHONE
	SAXOPHONE
—slide	BAZOOKA.TROMBONE
—valved	CLARION
	CORNET(-A-PISTONS)

	CORNOPEAN.ENGLISH HORN
	EUPHONIUM.FLUGELHORN
	FRENCH HORN.MELLOPHONE
	OPHECLEIDE.TRUMP(ET)
	(WAGNER) TUBA
—valveless	BUGLE
Bronze Age horn	LUR(E)
Burmese	TURR
Chinese	KIN.SANG
cithern	GITTERN
—Shetland	LANGSP(I)EL
clavichord	MONOCHORD
concertina	SQUEEZE-BOX
	SQUIFFER
cornet-type	ZINKE
cymbal (Oriental)	ZEL
double-bass	VIOL
double-reeded	SHALM.SHAWM
drum	TAMBOUR.TAM-TAM
	TYMPAN(UM)
	TYMPANY
dulcimer	PANTALEON
Eastern	PANDORA.PANDORE
	PANDURA
Egyptian tambourine	RIZZ
electronic	MARTENOT.MOOG
	SYNTHESIZER
Elizabethan	BANDORE
English	
—flute	RECORDER
—horn	COR ANGLAIS
	CORNO INGLESE
fife	PIFFERO
Finnish	KANTELE
fipple-flute	FLAGEOLET
	FLUTE-A-BEC
	RECORDER
flageolet	FIPPLE-FLUTE
	PENNY-WHISTLE
French	
—bagpipe	MUSETTE
—horn	CORNO
—horn without valves	
	WALDHORN
glass harmonica	EUPHON
gong	TAM-TAM
gourd rattle	MARACA
grand piano	PIANO(FORTE)
Greek	AULOS.BARBITOS

	BOUZOUKI.CITHARA
	KITHARA.LYRE.PHORMINX
	SALPINX.SYRINX
guitar	GITTERN
—Eastern	TAMBOURA
—like	MANDOLIN(E)
hand organ	HARMONICON
	HURDY-GURDY
harmonica	MOUTH-ORGAN
	MUSICAL GLASSES
—early	PHYSHARMONICA
harp-like (old)	SACKBUT
	SAMBUCA.SAMBUKE
Hebrew	ASOR.SHOFAR
	SHOPHAR.TIMBREL
	TOPH
highest-toned instrument	
	SOPRANINO
hunting horn	FLUGELHORN
	WALDHORN
hurdy-gurdy	VIELLE
Indian fiddle	SARANGI
Italian	CHITARRONE
Jew's harp	TRUMP
jukebox	NICKELODEON
kettledrum	TIMBAL.TYMBAL
	TIMPANO.TYMPANO
key-bugle	FLUGELHORN
	KENT BUGLE.OPHICLEIDE
keyboard	CALLIOPE.CELESTA
	CLAVICEMBALO.CLARICHORD
	CLAVECIN.CLAVICHORD
	CLAVICYTHERIUM.CLAVIER
	HARMONICHORD
	HARMONIPHON(E)
	HARPSICHORD.ORGAN
	PIANOFORTE.SPINET(T)
	SPINETTE.VIRGINAL
—reed	SERAPHINE.VOCALION
—wind	HARMONIUM.ORGAN
large	
—dulcimer	PANTELEON
—lute	CHITARRONE.OPHARION
	OPHEOREON
—mandoline	MANDOLA
	MANDORA
light-operated	LIGHT-ORGAN
like a lute	POLYPHONE
mechanical	PANHARMONICUM

medieval	CITOLE.ROTE
Mexican	CLARIN
mouth organ	HARMONICA
	HARMONICON
—Chinese	SANG
musical	
—box	POLYPHONE
—glasses	HARMONICA
Neapolitan	PANDURA
nickelodeon	JUKEBOX
Northumberland bagpipes	
	SMALL PIPES
old	
—fiddle	GJU.GU(E).SULTAN
—harp-like	LYRE
—Scottish	STOCK-AND-HORN
—trumpet (Scandinavian)	LUR(E)
—viola	LYREA-VIOL
—zither-like	PSALTERY
orchestral	
—horn	FRENCH HORN
—kettledrum	TIMPANO
orchestrion	HARMONICON
panharmonicon	
	ORPHEUS HARMONICA
Pan's pipes	SYRINX
percussion	CYMBAL.DRUM
	GONG.TAMBOURINE
	TRIANGLE
	TUBULAR BELLS
—drums	BASS DRUM
	KETTLE DRUM.SIDE DRUM
	SNARE DRUM.TAM-TAM
	TOMTOM
	TYMPANI
—dulcimer	CEMBALO.CYMBALO
—Eastern	GAMELAN
—Indian	TABLA
—metal bars	DULCIMER
	VIBRAHARP.VIBRAPHONE
—wooden bars	MARIMBA
	XYLOPHONE
piano	PIANOFORTE
—like barrel organ	
	PIANO-ORGAN
piccolo	OCTAVE-FLUTE
player-piano	PIANOLA
pocket violin	KIT
portable organ	REGAL

primitive	
—drum	TOM-TOM
—harmonium	REED-ORGAN
—piano	FORTEPIANO
racket(t)	SAUSAGE-BASSOON
recorder	FIPPLE-FLUTE
reed-organ	HARMONIUM
	MELODEON
Russian	BALALAIKA.DOMRA
	GUSLA.GUSLE.GUSLI
sausage-bassoon	RACKETT
shallow drum	TAMBOURINE
Shetland	GU(E).LANGSP(I)EL
small	
—bagpipe (French)	SORDELINE
—banjo	BANJULELE
—drum	TABO(U)R(IN).TABRET
—flute	FIFE.PICCOLO
—tabor	TABRET
squeeze-box	CONCERTINA
	SQUIFFER
steam organ	CALLIOPE
straight trumpet (Roman)	TUBA
stringed	BASS FIDDLE.CELLO
	CONTRABASS(O)
	COUNTERBASS
	DOUBLE BASS.GUITAR
	HARP.MANDOLIN(E)
	UKELELE.UKULELE.VIOLA
	VIOLIN.VIOLONCELLO
—early	CITHERN.GITTERN.LUTE
	PSALTERY
—Irish	TYMPAN
—medieval	ROTE
—Russian	GUSLA.GUSLE.GUSLI
—Shetland	GJU.GU(E)
—with	
—one string	MONOCHORD
	GUSLA.GUSLE.GUSLI
—three strings	TRICHORD
—four strings	TETRACHORD
—five strings	BANJO
	PENTACHORD
—six strings	GUITAR
—seven strings	HEPTACHORD
—eight strings	OCTACHORD
—ten strings	TETRACHORD
—29-42 strings	ZITHER(N)
Swiss	ALPENHORN

syrinx	PAN('S) PIPES		PIPELESS ORGAN
tambourine	TIMBREL	woodwind	BASSET HORN
tenor			BASSOON.CLARI(O)NET
—fiddle	VIOLA		CONTRABASSOON
—oboe	TENOROON		CONTRAFAGOTTO
—viol	VIOLA D'AMORE		COR ANGLAIS
	VIOLA DA BRACCIO		CORNO DI BASSETTO
	VIOLA DA SPALLA		CORNO INGLESE.FLUTE.OBOE
tin whistle	PENNY-WHISTLE		PICCOLO.RECORDER
Tirolese zither	CITHER(N)	—old	BASS HORN
	CITTERN		CHALUMEAU.CORNET(T)
toy	MUSICAL BOX		CREMONA.CREMORNE.
—reed-pipe	MIRLITON		CROMORNA.CROMORNE
tromba marina	MONOCHORD		CRUMHORN.KRUM(M)HORN
	NUN'S-FIDDLE		OBOE D'AMORE
	TRUMP MARINE		OBOE DI CACCIA.SERPENT
trumpet	CLARION	xylophone	GAMELAN.MARIMBA
—Bronze Age	LUR(E)		METALLOPHONE
—Greek	SALPINX		STICCADO.STICCATO
—Roman	TUBA	zither-type	AUTOHARP
tuning forks	DULCITONE	**Muslim**	(*see* Moslem)
upright piano	PIANO(FORTE)	*muster* <u>army</u>	MARY.MYRA
using flames	PYROPHONE	**mutate**	
viol		*mutant* <u>ape</u>	PEA
—medieval	REBEC(K)	*mutated* <u>trees</u>	RESET.STERE
—obsolete	TROMBA MARINA	*mutation of* <u>flies</u>	FILES
—tenor	QUINT(E)	**mutual friend**	COPAL
viola da gamba	GAMBA	**muzzle velocity**	MV
violin	AMATI.CREMONA.FIDDLE	**my**	
	STRAD(IVARIUS)	My, my!	OGEE
Welsh	HORNPIPE.WELSH HARP	My, *no*!	omit MY
—fiddle	CROUTH.CROWD	•Fa(m)il(y)? My, *no*!	FAIL
wind instrument		**mystery**	
—with slide	SACKBUT	*mystery of* <u>death</u>	HATED
	TROMBONE	*mysterious* <u>tribe</u>	BITER
—with loudspeaker		**mythological beasts**	(*see* monster)

Avogadro number. born. bridge player. en. fifty. fifty thousand. half an em.
indefinite number. knight. name. nano-. natural numbers. natus. nepar.
neuter. *new*. newton. ninety. ninety thousand. nitrogen. noon. north.
northern. Norway. note. noun. nu. number. unknown number. unlimited

Nahum	NAH	—Students	NUS
name[1]	N	—Teachers	NUT
name unknown	NU	University of Ireland	NUI
named	DIT	Youth Orchestra	NYO
name*less*	omit N	**national**[2]	
nameless (di)ve	VE	national extremists	ETA.IRA.PLO
namely	SC.SCIL.SCIZ.VIZ	national extremists	NL
name[2]		N̄ational *Front*	N
indicates origins:		N̄ational Hunt	
•*René's (= French)* house		jockey	OVER-RIDER
	MAISON	national roll	SWISS
•*Dante's (= Italian)* house	CASA	National runner	RED RUM
(*see also* from[4])		national runner	THAMES
nanosecond	NS	nationalists	SDP
Napoleon	NAP	**native**	ABO
nasty end	DEN	**Nativity of the Virgin Mary**	NVM
national[1]	NAT	**natural**	
Board for Prices and Incomes	PIB	nature base	E
Broadcasting Company	NBC	natural drawing	MAGNETISM
Bureau of Standards	NBS	natural order	NO
Cash Register Company	NCR	**naught**	O
Coal Board	NCB	*naughty* boys	YOBS
Enterprise Board	NEB	naughty, *say*	OE
Exhibition Centre	NEC	*naughtily* trips...	SPIRT
Farmers' Union	NFU	**Navy**	RN
Fire Service	NFS	naval	NAV
Front	NF	naval architect	WREN
Graphical Association	NGA	naval commander	CORN
Health		Naval Reserve Decoration	NRD
—Insurance	NHI	navigation	NAV
—Service	NHS	navigator	HENRY
Incomes Commission	NIC.NICKY	navy flier	BLUEBIRD
Insurance	NI	**NE,** *say*	ANY
Opinion Poll	NOP	**near**	NR
Physical Laboratory	NPL	near (old)	NIE
Portrait Gallery	NPG	near miss	OUTER
Rifle Association	NRA	nearest figure	MISER
Trust (for Scotland)	NT(S)	*nearly* al(l)	AL
Union of		*nearly all* gon(e)	GON
—Journalists	NUJ	*nearly all* skin	KIN.SKEIN
—Mineworkers	NUM		SKINK.SKINT
—Railwaymen	NUR	*nearly all* th(e)...	TH
—Seamen	NUS	*nearly* there	HERE.THER

neat	CATTLE.COW.KINE.OX
	ALTERNATE
hence	
•100 neat...	COX
•neat look	OXEYE
•neat ornament	OXBOW
neat control	STEER
neat drive	ROUND-UP
neat ending	OXTAIL
neat ending	T
neat little animals	CALVES
neat looker	OXEYE
neat *Scotch*	KY(E)
neat sound	LOWING.MOO
necessary	
necessary part of ste/am en/gine	
	AMEN
necessary to ass/emble m/any...	
	EMBLEM
neckline	TIDEMARK.V
need	
needing kicks, take...	KATE.TEAK
needing repair	
•shoe *needs repair*	HOES.HOSE
needs a set...	SATE.SEAT.TEAS
needlewoman	CLEOPATRA
	GOAD HER
negative	NEG.NONPLUS
negative principle	YIN
negotiated truce	CUTER
Nehemiah	NEH
Nelson	
Nelson's employer	WRESTLER
Nelson's ship	VICTORY
Nelson's woman	EMMA
nepar	N
Neptune	NEP
nerve-*shattering*	NEVER
Netherlands	NAL
Netherlands Antilles	NT
(*see also* Dutch)	
network	BR.RY.RLY
net*work*	ENT-.TEN
neuralgia	TIC
neuter	N
neutral	(in)L-R
never	
never-*changing*	NERVE
never-*ending*	WHENEVER

never-*ending*	R
never-ending rang(e)	RANG
new¹	N
new course of action	CATION
new development in Neath	THANE
new driver	L
new edition of Wells	SWELL
new-*fangled*	WEN
new-fangled tools	LOOTS.STOOL
*new form*master	STREAM
new form of words	SWORD
new formula oils	SILO
new lines	AD LIBS
new look	NOVELLO
new order for shoes	HOES.HOSE
New Orleans	SALERNO
new position of table	BLEAT
new production of Tosca	COATS
new regulation	
made in...	MAIDEN
new *rhyme*	GNU.KNEW
new role for director	CREDITOR
new setting for garnets	STRANGE
new shoes	HOSES
new sort of medical	CLAIMED
	DECIMAL
new *sound*	GNU.KNEW
new sound of waves	WAIVES
new spell of weather	W(H)ETHER
new start for felon	MELON
new style of shoe	HOSE
new suit	GEAR CHANGE
*New*town	WONT
new use for tool	LOOT
new way to run...	NUR.URN
new writing	NOVEL
newly wed	DEW
New²	
Church	NC
England	NE
English	
—Bible	NEB
—Dictionary	NED
Jersey	CALF.NJ
Orleans	NO
Providence	NP
Smoking Material	NSM
South Wales	NSW
Testament	NT

York	BIG APPLE.GOTHAM.NY
—City	NYC
—district	BOWERY.BRONX
	HARLEM.MANHATTAN
	QUEENS
—opera	MET
Version	NV
New Zealand	NZ
including Maori:	
abalone	PAUA.PAWA
aborigine	MAORI
animal	TAEPO.TAIPO
biological zone	ORNITHOGAEA
birds	APTERYX.BELL BIRD
	BUSH WREN.HONEY BIRD
	HUIA.KABOB.KIWI.MAKO
	MAORI HEN.NOTORNIS
	OWL PARROT.PARSON BIRD
	POAKA.RIFLE(MAN) BIRD
	TAKAHE(A).WEKA.WRYBILL
blood money	UTU
canoe	WAKA
capital	WELLINGTON.NZ
casual dock labourer	SEAGULL
cloth	PAR(R)AMATTA
club	MERE.MERI
eel	TUNA
emblem	KOWHIA
feast	KAIKAI
fish	HIKU.MORWONG
	PAGROSOMUS
	SNAPPER.TRUMPETER
flax	PHORMIUM
food	KAI(-KAI)
fort	PA(H)
fruit	CHINESE GOOSEBERRY
	KIWI FRUIT
glory pea	KOWHAI
	PARROT-BEAK.PARROT-BILL
	PARROT-JAW
good luck!	KIA-ORA
grass	TOI TOI
hedge	KARO.KOHUHU
house	WHARE
image	(HEI)TIKI
Indian corn	KANGA
laburnum	KOWHIA
language	MAORI
leaders	NZ

leaves used for tea	MANUKA
lily	PHORMIUM
lizard	HATTERIA.SPHENODON
	TUATARA.TUATERA
locust	WETA
native	MAORI
New Zealander	DIGGER.KIWI
nineteenth-century Australian	
settler	SHAGROON
owl	MOPEHAWK.MOPOKE
	MOREPORK.PEHO.RURU
owl-like parrot	KAKAPO
	STRI(N)GOPS
palm	NIKAU
parrot	KAKA(-BEAK)
	KAKA-BILL.KEA
—bill	GLORY PEA
parson bird	POE(-BIRD)
	POY(-BIRD).TUI
plants	FLAX-BUSH.FLAX-LILY
	VEGETABLE SHEEP
political union	ANZUS
requital	UTU
resin	KAURI-GUM
rugby team	ALL BLACKS
settlement	PA(H)
settler	SHAGROON
shellfish	TOHEROA
shrub	HOHERIA.KARO.KIEKIE
	KOWHAI.PLAGIANTHUS.TUTU
soldier	ANZAC
spider	KATIPO.NIGHT-STINGER
spiritual power	MANA
stockade	PA(H)
sweet potato	KUMARA
tattoo pattern	MOKO
tea	MANUKA
thrush	TURNAGRA
thylacine	TIGER-WOLF
trees	HINAU.HINO.HINOU
	KARAKA.KAURI(-PINE)
	MANUKA.MAKOMAKO
	MIRO.NGAIO.PELU
	RATA.RIMU.TAWA
	TITOKI.TOTARA.TUTU
	WINE-BERRY
war chant	HAKA
white man	PAKEHA
woman	WAHINE

newcomer	DEB
newcomer	CROME
newspaper	RAG.TIMES
newspaper column	STANDARD
newspaper boss	PRESS STUD
newspaper *leader*	N
newspaper magazine	RAGTIME
newton	N
newton	NOT
next month	PROX(IMO)
Nicaragua(n)	NIC
capital	MANAGUA.N
coin	CORDOBA
nice	
Nice chap	FRENCHMAN
nice man	KINDLES
Nice people	FRENCH
Nice surroundings	RIVIERA
Nigeria	WAN
niggard	CARL
night	
night-light	MOON.STAR
night-*shift*	THING
night watchman	CHARLEY
	CHARLIE
nigh(t) *without end*	NIGH
nightmare	BLACK BEAUTY
	DARK HORSE
nil	O
nine	IX.THETA
based	NONARY
Christmas presents	LADIES
combining form	ENNEA-.NON-
groups	ENNEAD.NON-
	NONET(TE).NONETTO
	NONUPLET.NOVENARY
dancers	MORRIS MEN
days	ENNEATIC
days'...	WONDER
days of devotion	NOVENA
eyes	LAMPREY
having nine	
—angles	ENNEAGONAL
	NONAGONAL
—columns	ENNEASTYLE
—faces	ENNEAHEDRON
—petals	ENNEAPETALOUS
—pistils	ENNEAGYNIAN
	ENNEAGYNOUS
—sides	ENNEAGONAL
	NONAGONAL
—stamens	ENNEANDRIAN
	ENNEANDROUS
—styles	ENNEAGYNIAN
	ENNEAGYNOUS
hundred	CM.SAMPI
inches	SPAN
iron	NIBLICK
letters	NEIN
letters returned	IOTA
lives of...	CAT
magistrates of Athens	ARCHON
Muses	(*see* Muses)
nil	NINETY
orders of angels	ARCHANGELS
	ANGELS.CHERUBIM
	DOMINIONS.POWERS
	PRINCIPALITIES.SERAPHIM
	THRONES.VIRTUES
pins	SKITTLES
points of...	LAW
times	ENNEATIS
worthies	ALEXANDER.ARTHUR
	CHARLEMAGNE.DAVID
	GODFREY.HECTOR.JUDAS
	JULIUS.JOSHUA
yearly	NOVENNIAL
nineteenth	
nineteenth (hole)	BAR
	CLUBHOUSE
pertaining to	
nineteen	DECENNOVAL
ninety	N.Q.XC
having ninety	
faces	ENNEACONTAHEDRAL
Nineties	NAUGHTY
ninetieth	NONAGESIMAL
ninety-nine	IC
—beautiful names	ALLAH
ninety thousand	N.Q
ninety years old	NONAGENARIAN
ninth	ENNEATIC
nipped *round*	BI-T
NME	ENEMY
no[1]	O
hence	
•no love	OO
•no share	ORATION

•no-way	ORD
and	
•company *has* no. . .	COO
•cover *with* no. . .	LIDO
•girl *with* no. . .	MAYO
and	
•no credit	LENTO
•no *support for* leg(D)	LIMBO
no²	O
no *entry*	incl O
no score	incl O
no score draw	O-O
no³	NO
hence	
•no directions	NOSE
•no good	NOOK
•no one	NOI-
no⁴	NO
n͟o *beginning*	N
n͟o date	ND
no͟ *end*	O
no͟ *entry*	incl NO
no French. . .	NON
no *going back*⟨	LIN.ON
	NG.US
no *head*	start with NO
no *heart*	incl NO
•knight *has* no *heart*	KNOT
no return⟨	LIN.ON
no *turning back*⟨	LIN.ON
no *Scotch*	NA.NAE
no⁵	
indicates opposite:	
no expert	L.LEARNER
no high-flier	LOWLANDER
no inclination	FLAT.LEVEL
no mistake	CORRECT.R.RT.RIGHT
no⁶	
indicates omission:	
no account	omit AC
•*no*-account performer	(ac)TRESS
no aspiration	omit H
no claim	omit AM, IAM or IM
no end	omit END
no end of th(e)	TH
no go	omit GO
no head	omit first letter
no heart	omit H
no heart	
•M(ar)y *has no heart*	MY
no love	omit O
no money	omit L
No, no!	omit NO
•learner? *No*, no!	(no)VICE
no mistake	omit R.RT
no novice	omit L
no one	omit I
no parking	omit P
no point *in*. . .	omit N.S.E.W
no power	omit P
no publicity	omit AD
no resistance	omit R
no right	omit R
no ring	omit O
no roof on(D)	omit first letter
no start for. . .	omit first letter
no thanks	omit TA
no time	omit AGE.T
•men(age) *has no* time. . .	MEN
•(t)hey *have no* time	HEY
no way	omit N.S.E.W
•*no* way pa(s)t	PAT
no way	omit RD.ST
•*no* way ha(rd)y	HAY
•*no* way pa(st)	PA
no⁷	
other uses:	
no bloody good	NBG
no charges	FREE FOR ALL
no commercial value	NCV
no drink	TT
no good	NG.US
no longer	(*see* old³)
no *meaning*	REFUSAL
no place of publication	NP
no proper cures	CURSE
no rain *about*	(in) DR-Y
no trumps	NT
no value declared	NVD
nob	JACK.KNAVE
nobody	POOTER
nod *off*	DON.-OND
noise	
noise and number index	NNI
noise of rain	REIGN.REIN
noiseless	QUIETER
noiseless ty(ping)	TY
noisy (very noisy)	F(FF)

hence	
•a noisy attack	AFRAID
•a noisy carnival	AFFAIR
•a noisy company	AFFIRM
and	
•a very noisy listener	AFFEAR
•a very noisy tune	AFFAIR
and	
•noisy cow	FLOWER
•noisy way	FEAST
•noisy work	FOP
(*see* loud.strong)	
noisy preacher	BOANERGES
nominal winner	VICTOR
nominative	NOM
non[1]	
non-commissioned officer	CPL
CQMS.CSM.NCO.RQMS	
RSM.SGT.SM	
non-drinker	TT
non-medal-winner	FOURTH
non-military numbers	CIVIL
non-professional	LAY
non-specific urethritis	NSU
non-striker	SCAB
non[2]	
non-extreme (m)ember(s)	EMBER
non-extreme members	NN
non-finisher	N
non-runner	ONN
non-starter	N
*non-*U	omit U
*non-*union	omit TU or U
•*non-*union (tu)tor	TOR
•*non-*union to(u)r	TOR
*non-*university...	omit U
none*theless*	omit O
nonsense	
nonsense verses	SERVES
nonsensical fellow	LEAR
noon	AMENDS
HANDS UP.M.N	
normal temperature	
and pressure	NTP
Norman French	NF
Norse	
chieftain	JARL.YARL
dragon	FAFNIR
end of world	RAGNAROK

epic poem	EDDA
NIBELUNGENLIED	
SAGA.VOLUSPA	
fates	NORNA.NORNS
first man	ASK
giant	JOTUM.MIMIR.TAROLL
YMER.YMIR	
giantess	GROA.NATT
goblin	NIS.TROLL
guardians of treasure	NIBELUNG
heaven	ASGARD.ASGARTH
VALHALLA.WALHALLA	
heroic race	VOLUSPA
house of gods	ASGARD
ASGARTH.VALHALLA	
WALHALLA	
king	ATU
land of the giants	UTGARD
leader	N
maidens	VALKYRIE.WALKYRIE
myths	EDDAS.VOLUSPAS
palace of the dead	VALHALLA
WALHALLA	
paradise	ASGARD.ASGARTH
VALHALLA.WALHALLA	
pirate	VIKING
region of the dead	NIFLHEIM
serpent	MIDGARD
—race	NIBELUNG
warrior	BERSERK(ER)
wolf	FENRIS
world tree	YG(G)DRASIL(L)
north	
north	N
North Africa	NA
hence	
•North African girl	NASAL
•North African perfume	
NASCENT	
•North African tree	NAPALM
(*see also* Africa)	
North America	NA.US.USA
(*see also* America)	
North British	NB
Northeast	NE.PREMIERE
north-northeast	NNE
north-northwest	NNW
north of the Border = Scottish	
(*see* Scottish)	

North Pole	NP	not *back*⟨	TON
northwest	NW	not *bad*	TON
northern	N	not *beginning*	start with NOT
Northern French	NF	•not *beginning* sweet	NOTICE
Northern Ireland	NI	not *beginning*	N
hence		not *central*	O
•Northern Ireland apprentice	NIL	not *coming back*⟨	TON
•Northern Ireland church	NICE	not *converted*	TON
•Northern Ireland tre(e)		not *ending*	T
is cut	NITRE	not *extremely*	-NT
Northern Territory	NT	not *finally*	T
Norway	N	not head...	N
Norwegian		not *heard*	KNOT
airline	NAL	not *lacking*	omit NOT
capital	N.OSLO	•(not)ably not *lacking*	ABLY
coins	KR.KRONE.ORE	not *long ago*	NE
country dance	HALLING	not *missing*	omit NOT
dance tune	SPRING	•not *missing* s(not)ty...	STY
dog	ELKHOUND	not *moving*	TON
forest cat	SKOGCATT	not *old*	NE
hut	SAETER	not *opening*	start with NOT
language	LANDSMA(A)L	•not *opening* sweets	NOTICES
	NORSE.NYNORSK	not *opening*	N
leader	N	not *out of place*	TON
measure (²/₃ acre)	MORGEN	not *raised*(D) ↑	TON
mountain hut	SAETER	not *Scottish*...	NA.NAE
open sandwiches	SMOR(RE)BROD	not *starting*	start with NOT
parliament	STORT(H)ING	•not *starting* directions	NOTES
—lower house	ODELST(H)ING	not *starting*	N
—upper house	LAGT(H)ING	not *up*(D) ↑ ...	TON
reindeer skin boots	FINN(E)SKO	not *very old*	NE
	FINSKO	not *without*	NO-T
sea		n(o)t *without* love	NT
—loch	FIORD.FJORD	**not²**	
—monster	KRAKEN	indicates opposite:	
toast	SKOAL	*not* a man	FEMALE.,WOMAN
upland pasture	SAETER	*not* all	APART.SOME
whirlpool	MAELSTROM	*not* at home	OUT
wooden church	STAVE CHURCH	*not* automatic	MANUAL
nose		*not* bad	FAIR.GOOD
nose of rocket	R	*not* big-*hearted*	SWEET.TWEED
nose off (f)ace	ACE	*not* bound	FREE
nosey client	PARSON	*not* bulls	INNERS
not¹		*not* clear	NL
•not any *local*...	NOTARY	*not* exactly	ROUGHLY
•not decorated	NOTICED	*not* far	NEAR
•not English	NOTE	*not* fair	DARK
•not frozen	NOTICE	*not* favouring	ANTI.CON-
•not well	NOTABLY	*not* first class	B

not for	ANTI.CON-	*not fully* (o)pen	PEN
not good	BAD.OFF	*not got* *	omit *
not grand	UPRIGHT	•mother's *not got* her. . .	MOT
not here	THERE	*not* hard	omit H
not I	CONSONANT.YOU	*not having* it	omit IT
not in	OUT	*not having* money	omit L
•saint *not* in	STOUT	*not head of* (p)arty	ARTY
•S-am *not in* credit	SCRAM	*not* in	omit IN
not in first	OUTLAST	*not* long	omit L
not in step	OUTPACE	*not long enough* for the(m)	THE
not inclined	FLAT.LEVEL	*not* male	omit M
not lacking	WITH	*not* married	omit M
not left	R.RT.RIGHT	*not* me	omit ME
not long	SHORT	*not much* t(ime)	T
not natural	FLAT.SHARP	*not* noisy	omit F
not ordained	LAY	*not* OK	omit OK
not out	IN.NO	*not* one	omit I
not partial	TOTAL	*not* quiet	omit P
not positive	NEGATIVE.NO.NAY	*not quite* 50 per cent	HAL(f)
not right	L.LEFT.LT.WRONG	*not quite* al(l)	-AL
not the main. . .	LAND	*not quite* certain	SUR(e)
not that	THIS	*not* right	omit R or RT
not those	THESE	*not so*	omit SO
not top quality	B	•*not so* (so)on	ON
not upright	GRAND	*not* soft	omit P
not 'urtful	ARMLESS	*not starting*	omit first letter

indicates omission:		•(t)rain *not starting*	RAIN
not a c(o)at	CAT	*not* the capital	omit first letter
not al(l)	-AL	•*not* the capital of (C)had	HAD
not all that. . .	THA.HAT	*not* the doctor. . .	omit DR or MO
not altogether (c)lear	LEAR	*not the first* one	omit first I
not America	omit US	•*not the first* one	
•A(us)tria *not* America	ATRIA	wa(i)ling	WALING
not approved	omit OK	*not* th(e) *whole*. . .	TH
not beginning	omit first letter	*not the whole* thin(g)	THIN
•*not beginning* (r)ace	ACE	*not* unknown	omit X or Y
not charged	omit ION	*not* upper class	omit U
•ration *not charged*	RAT	*not using* head	omit first letter
not completely done	DON.ONE	* *not seen*	omit *
not entirely (c)lear	LEAR	•king *not seen in* Dove(r)	DOVE

not entirely cle(ar)	-CLE	other uses:	
not exactly (w)hat. . .	HAT	*not all* tha/t in t/he. . .	TINT
not fifty	omit L	*not altogether* c/lear n/ow. . .	
not finally sen(t)	SEN		LEARN
not finished wit(h)	WIT	not at all	-OWAY
not finishing	omit last letter		NO-WAY
•*not finishing* of(f). . .	OF	not clear (non liquet)	NL
not full ho(use)	HO	*not complete* in/stall/ation	STALL

not dated	ND	**note[2]**	
not entirely c/lea/r	LEA	noted	COMPOSED
not exactly weak	WEEK	*noted* = in music	
not exactly weak	TEAK.WEAN	•*noted* boy	DANNY
not far (non longe)	NL	•*noted* man from Seville	BARBER
not full	STILLROOM	•*noted* waltzer	MATILDA
not full stomach	TUMMY	**note[3]**	
not full stoma(ch)	STOMA	note well	NB
not full s/tom/ach	TOM	printed notes	FIVER.TENNER
not fully a/war/e	WAR	written notes	PS.PPS
not identified	X.Y	**nothing[1]**	LOVE.NIL
not just hot	SHOT.HOTEL	hence	
not much of t/he m/oney	HEM	•nothing right	LOVER
not normally made	DAME.MEAD	•nothing's right	LOVE-STORY
not otherwise provided	NOP	and	
not out	NO	•nothing *back* in s.a.e	SALINE
not paid	AMATEUR.HON	•nothing English	NILE
not permitted (non licet)	NL	•noting *in* bishop's office	SENILE
not quite beautiful	DUTIFUL	**nothing[2]**	O
not right in the...	THINE	hence	
not specific	NS	•nothing changes	OVARIES
not the whole tru/th in/side	THIN	•nothing left	OL
not to get left in...	incl R or RT	•nothing right	OR.ORT
•f-ight *not to get* left *in*	FRIGHT	•nothing *to* America	-OUS
•ma-y *not get* left *in*	MARTY	and	
not *to get* right *into*	incl L or LT	•advanced nothing	LENTO
•f-ight *not to get* right *in*	FLIGHT	•cover *with* nothing...	LIDO
•ma-y *not get* right *in*	MALTY	•surgeon *has* nothing...	VETO
not upper class	NONU	nothing *in* it	incl O
not usual in an...	NAIN	nothing *is lacking*	omit O
not usually said	DAIS	nothing *less*	omit O
not willing	INTESTATE	nothing *on*	-O
not[5]	(*see* without[2])	hence	
Notary Public	NP	•father *with* nothing *on*	DADO
notch	V	•man *with* nothing *on*	HALO
note[1]	A.B.C.D.E.F.G.N	•sailor *with* nothing *on*	TARO
	DO.DOH.UT.RE	nothing on	-OON
	ME.MI.FA.FAH	hence	
	SO.SOH.SOL.LA	•dance *with* nothing on	BALLOON
	LAH.SI.TE.TI	•girl *with* nothing on	GALOON
hence			SALOON
•cover note	CACHED	•many *with* nothing on	MOON
•love-notes	ODD.OFF	(*see also* with[3])	
•pound notes	LADE.LEE.LEG	nothing *short*	omit O
and		**notice**	AD
•notebook	SOB	hence	
•two notes	FARE.FATE	•distant notice	FARAD
•note most...	UTMOST	•notice *in* m-e...	MADE
noted	incl A.B.etc.	•notice the mud	ADMIRE

notorious kisser	JUDAS
nought	NIL.O
	(*see also* nothing)
noun	N
Nova Scotia (n)	ACADIA.NS
capital	HALIFAX.N
island	CAPE BRETON
novel	SHE
novel place	WESTWARD HO
novel present	SERPENT
novel race	NEWSPRINT
novelist	MANN.STERNE
*novel*ist	SIT
November	NOV
novice	L
now	AD.ANON
nowadays	AD
noxious weeds	SEWED.SWEDE
n-number	NONE
NTT, say	ENTITY
nu	N
nuclear *fallout*	UNCLEAR
number[1]	C.CL.D.L.M.N.NO
hence	
•a number of coins	ACCENTS
•number one	CLONE
•number in Queen's...	DINERS
•number *in* c-are	CLARE
•number in America	MINUS
•number at church	NATCH
•number play badly	NOSTRUM
•*back* number⟨	ON
number of Romans	C.L.D.M.N
number[2]	
number chooser	ERNIE
number cruncher	COMPUTER
numbered apartment	FLATTEN
number[3]	ANAESTHETIC
back number	EPIDURAL.SPINAL
number[4]	SONG.TUNE
of Argentinians	TANGO
of Brazilians	SAMBA
of Cubans	R(H)UMBA
of Hungarians	CSARDAS
of Spaniards	PASA DOBLE
number one	ADAM.I.ME.NOI
craze	EGOMANIA
French	UN.UNE
German	EIN

Italian	UNA.UNO
man	ADAM
mother	EVE
on ship	MATE
on ship	S
returning	-ION
wife	EVE
woman	EVE
numbers	NOS.NUM(B)
numerical control	NC
nurse	EDITH (CAVELL)
	FLORENCE (NIGHTINGALE)
	TEND.SHARK.SRN.VAD
nursemaid	ALICE
nursery gardener	MARY
nursery *rhyme*	BURSARY
	CURSORY
nut[1]	CHESTNUT.WALNUT
American	PECAN
—horse chestnut	BUCK-EYE
Arachis	(*see* peanut *below*)
areca	BETEL
Asiatic	PISTACHIO
Australian	QUANDONG NUT
	QUEENSLAND-NUT
beechnuts	MAST
betel	ARECA
bonduc	MOLUCCABEAN
	NICKER BEAN
Brazilian	BRAZIL NUT.COQUILLA
	PARA NUT.SAPUCAIA
Castanea	CHESTNUT
conker	HORSE CHESTNUT
crab nut	CAROB
cream nut	BRAZIL
East Indian	KOKUM
	MARKING-NUT
earthnut	(*see* peanut *below*)
groundnut	(*see* peanut *below*)
hard-shelled	ALMOND.BRAZIL
hazel	COB.FILBERT
hickory	PECAN
Indian	ILLIPE.ILLUPI
Juglans	WALNUT
monkey nut	PEANUT
nicker	BONDUC.MOLUCCA BEAN
palm	COCONUT.COHUNE NUT
	COQUILLA.COROZO NUT
	IVORY NUT

peanut	ARACHIS.MONKEY NUT
	EARTHNUT.EARTH PEA
	PIGNUT
pecan	HICKORY
Philippine	PILI(-NUT)
tropical American	
	CASHEW(NUT)
used in game	PHILOPOENA
	PHILIPPINA.PHILIPPINE
West Indian peanut	PINDA

nut²

nut*cracker*	TUN
nuts	BANANAS.MAD

nymph(s)

apple	MAELID
Mohammedan	HOURI
mountain	EGERIA.OREAD(ES)
Nysaean	HYADES
ocean	OCEANID(ES)
river	NAIAD(ES)
Russian (water)	RUSALKA
sea	AMPHITRITE.CALYPSO
	NEREID(S).THETIS
	TETHYS
spring	ARETHUSA
water	ARETHUSA
	HYDRIAD(ES)
	ONDINE.UNDINE(S)
wood	DRYAD(S)(ES)
	HAMADRYAD

O

all-round-er. around. aught. *bald patch. ball. band. blob.* blood group.*cavity.* cipher. *circle. circuit. circular letter. dial. disc. duck. egg.* eight hundred. eight hundred thousand. eleven. eleven thousand. *empty.*examination. *full moon. globe. gulf. hole. hollow. hoop. loop.* love. naught. nil. nothing. nought. Ohio. omega. omicron. *opening.* orb. *ortho-.* ought. *oval.* oxygen. *pellet. pill. ring. rotund. round. spangle. vacancy*

Obadiah	OB(AD)	*odd characters in* play	PA
object	IT.OBJ	*odd* shape	HEAPS.PHASE
objection to prices	SPICER	odd wizard	RUMMAGE
objective	OBJ	*oddly* shaped	PHASED
objector	CO	oddfellow	OF
oblique	OBL	*odd*fellow	FLO
obliterate		*oddity of* Norse. . .	SNORE
obliterate a. . .	omit A	odds	SP
obliterate *	omit *	**of**[1]	
•uproar *eliminates* us	RUMP(us)	indicates origins:	
oblong	OBL	•half *of France*	DEMI
obscure views	WIVES	•lady *of Madrid*	SENORA
observe		•leader *of Italy*	DUCE
observation	OBS	•soldiers *of Germany*	SOLDATEN
observed in Leith	LITHE	**of**[2]	
observed in Lei/th en/tirely. . .		of *French*	DE
	THEN	hence	
obsession	(see love[3])	•of *French* fathers	DESIRES
obsolete	(see old[4])	•of *French* money	DECENT
obstreperous men are. . .	RENAME	•of *French* wine	DEPORT
obtain		of *German*	VON
obtained from lime	EMIL.MILE	hence	
obtained from li/me tre/es	METRE	•of *French and German*	DEVON
obvious disagreement	PLAINTIFF	of the *French*	DELA.DES.DU
occupy		hence	
occupied by a	incl A	•of the *French* hill	DELATOR
occupied by *	incl *	•of the *French* note	DELATE
•sh-ed *occupied by* a		•of the *French* unknown	DELAY
king	SHARED	and	
occupying *	incl in *	•of the *French* affliction	DUG-OUT
•a king *occupying* sh-ed	SHARED	•of the *French* share	DURATION
occupational therapy	OT	•of the *French* sportsman	
ocean			DUSKIER
ocean-drilling rig	MAINBRACE	and	
ocean-going junk	FLOTSAM	•of the *French* city	DESTROY
	(*see also* sea)	•of the *French* couple	DESPAIR
octavo	OCT	•of the *French* hypocrisy	
October	OCT		DESCANT
odd		of the *Italian*	DEL
odd bits of food	FO	hence	

•of the *Italian* measurement	DELFT
•of the *Italian* river	DELOUSE
•of the *Italian* sweet	DELICE
of the *Spanish*	DEL
hence	
•doctor of the *Spanish*	MODEL
•of the *Spanish* army	DELTA
•of the *Spanish* victory	DELVE

of³

meaning
   like, pertaining to, relating to
          (*see* pertaining)

of⁴

of some c/once/rn	ONCE
of th/in mate/rial	INMATE
of use in the. . .	THINE
of use in the war	WREATH
of a boy	BROTH
of a gun	SON
of the world	MAN

off	BAD.OUT.R.RT.RIGHT
*off*beat	BATE
offbeat march	CHARM
off course in a golf. . .	FOALING
off Cowes(in)	SO-LENT.INSOLENT
off-drive	DIVER
off hooks	SHOOK
off its food = taking	
nothing in	incl O
off-key	omit A-G
•*off*-key (b)ass	ASS
•*off*-key son(g)	SON
off-key note	ETON.TONE
*off*side	DIES
off the rails a train	ANITRA

offer	BID
offer *up*(D) ↑	DIB
offer up a jar(D) ↑	RAJA

office

office girl	TEMP
Office of Fair Trading	OFT
officer	LT.COL
officer-commanding	OC
officer of the crown	MAJOR
Officer of the Order of the	
British Empire	OBE
officer-in-charge	OIC
Officer Training Corps	OTC

official	OFF
Official Chaplain to the	
Forces	OCF
official purposes	REFUSES
officinal	OFF
often *reduced*	OF.TEN
ogee, *say*	OG

oh

oh(s)	O.(OO.OS)
oh, why, *say*	OY

oil

oil-*change*	OLI-
oil *rig*	OLI-
OK	ROGER

old¹

meaning
  ancient
  archaic
  at one time
  Biblical
  historical
  obsolete
  once
  stale
  vintage:

'a' as a word	A-PER-SE
a short while ago	WHILE-ERE
abandon (stolen goods)	WAIVE
abate	VAIL
abdomen	WOMB
abide	WON
ability	ENGINE.INGINE
abjure	REN(A)Y.RENEY
able to	
—be seen	VISIVE
—control fate	WEIRD
—see	VISIVE
abode	INN.MANSION.WON
abounding	ENORMOUS
about 9 a.m.	UNDERN
abrupt	SQUAB
abscess	IMPOST(H)UME
absolute	MERE
absolve	ASSOIL
abstruse	EXQUISITE
abundance	COPY
abut	CONFINE
abyss	ABYSM
accept	ALLOW

acceptable	PLAUSIBLE	adorn	BEDIGHT.BESEE
acclaim	VOICE		ILLUSTRATE
accomplice	COMPLICE.FEDDARY	adorn(ed)	DIGHT
accost	ABORD	adroit	PERT
account	ACCOMPT.NOTE	adulterate	VITIATE
—of daily business	EPHEMERIS	advance	VAUNCE
accusation	TAX	—towards	COAST
accuse	ARGUE.REPROVE	advanced	FAR
accustom	OCCASION	adventure	AUNTER.AVENTURE
ace of trumps in game of gleek	TIB	advice	REDE
ache	AKE	advise	AVISE.AVIZE.AVYZE
achievement	CHEVISANCE		REDE.VISE
acid	EAGER	—against	DISSUADE
acknowledge	AGNISE.AGNIZE	affability	FACILITY
	KNOWLEDGE	affable	FACILE
acknowledgment of		affect	AMOVE
error	JEOFAIL	—coyness	COY
acquaintance	COAST	affectedly elaborate	QUAINT
acquire possessions	PURCHASE	affection	AFFECT
acquisitiveness	COVETIVENESS	affianced	ASSURED
acquit	ACQUITE.ACQUIGHT	affinity	AFFIANCE
	ASSOIL	afflict	VISIT
across	YOND	affliction	LANGUOR
act	FACT.PRESENT		TEEN(E).TENE
—as husband	HUSBAND	affray	EFFRAY
—as paid dance partner	HOSTESS	affright	DREAD.GRISE
—carnally	CARNAL	afraid	EFFRAIDE.FEARED
—earlier than	PREVENT	afternoon	UNDERN
—foolishly	FOLLY	afterwards	EFT
—of building up	STRUCTURE	again	AGEN.EFT
—of guaranteeing	WARRANTISE	against the grain	
—of theft	MAINO(U)R.MANNER		AGAINST THE HAIR
—of touching	ATTAINT	age	ELD
—the master	MASTER	aged	WINTERED
action at law	QUARREL	aghast	AGAST
active	WIELDY	agree	FADGE.CONDESCEND
activity	FUNCTION	alas	ALS.HARO.HARROW
actor	STAGER	albeit	AL(L)BE.ALBEE
adapt	APPLY	alchemical	CHEMIC
adaptation	CONTEMPERATION	alderman	EALDORMAN
address in courteous		ale	
tone	SPEAK FAIR	—4 pence per quart	FOUR-ALE
adduce	OBJECT	—house	MUG-HOUSE
adjudge	AREAD.AREDE.ARREEDE	—with wormwood	PURL
	ARET(T)	alien	FORINSECAL
administrative		aligning	LIN(E)AGE
—assembly	MOOT	alive	QUICK
—subdivision	GOVERNMENT	alkali	KALI
admiration	WONDER	allay	ALAY

allayment	ALAIMENT	answer	RESOLVE
allegation	SURMISE	ant	EMMET
allege	ALLEDGE.PRETEND	anthropoid ape	PIGMY.PYGMY
	TRUMP		TROGLODYTE
allow to leak	LET	antic	ANTICK
allowance	SIZE	anticipate	PREVENT
—of food etc. to servants	LIVERY	antiphon	ANTHEM
—to public officers		antique	ANTICKE
	APPOINTMENT	anxiety	CARK
allure	TRAIN.TROLL	anything	
ally	COLLEAGUE	—done	FACT
almond	AMYGDAL	—hackneyed	HACK
almost	NIGHLY	—prepared to recipe	RECEIPT
—always	MOST AN END	—that whirls	RHOMB(US)
alms	DEVOTION	apartment	MANSION
aloes-wood	LIGN(-)ALOES	ape	JACKANAPES.PIGMY
along	ALONGST.ENDLONG		PYGMY.TROGLODYTE
always	ALGATE	aperture	OVERTURE
ambassador	EMBASSADOR	apology	SIR-REVERENCE
	LEAGUER.LE(I)DGER	Apostle's Creed	THE BELIEF
	LEIGER.LIEGER	apparatus	EQUIPAGE
amber	LIGURE	apparel	TIRE
ambergris	GRIS-AMBER	appeal for pity	FOR MERCY
ambush	WATCH	appearance	FAVOUR.VISIBILITY
amends	MENDS	appease	ASLAKE
ammonia	VOLATILE ALKALI	appertain	EFFEIR.EFFERE
among	EMONG(ES)	application of mind	INTENTION
amongst	EMONG(E)ST	apply decoration such as	
amorous	WANTON	embroidery	LAY DOWN
—sport	TOY	appoint	VOICE
amuse	PLAY.SPORT	apprise	ASCERTAIN
ancestor	GRANDSIRE	approach	APPROPINQUATE
ancestry	OFFSPRING		APPROPINQUE.COAST
ancient	ANTIENT	approaching	TOWARD
and	AN	approbation	WELL-LIKING
anew	OF NEW	apricot	ABRICOCK.APRICOCK
anger	GRAM(E).TEEN(E).TENE	apron	BRAT.PLACARD
Anglican bishop	MAGPIE	apt	TOWARD
angling fly	WATCHET	arbitrator	STICKLER
angry	CURST	arboretum	ARBORET
aniline	CRYSTALLINE	arch	EMBOW
animal with docked tail	CURTAL	archery target	GOAL
ankle	ANCLE	area near capital	INLAND
—boot	HIGH-SHOE	argue	WRANGLE
—high shoe	HIGH-LOW	aristocratic hoodlum	MOHOCK
announce	DENOUNCE.MELD	arithmetic	ARSMETRICK
annoy	HATTER	arm	ENARM
annul	VACUATE	armed citizens	TRAIN-BAND
anoint	ANELE	armistice	STILL-STAND

armour	WEED
—for man or horse	HARNESS
armoury	GARDEROBE
army	HOST.WAR
—clothing account	
	OFF-RECKONING
arrange	ADDRESS
arranged	ADDRESSED.ADDREST
—in form of harrow	HERSED
array	BEDIGHT.RAY
arresting officer	SERGEANT
	SERJEANT
arrive	BECOME
arrogant	STOUT.WANTON
arsenic monosulphide	
	RESALGAR.ROSAKER
art	MISTERY.MYSTERY
art of	
—engraving	ENGRAVERY
—medicine	LEECHCRAFT
—pastry-making	PASTRY
artful trick	SLIGHT
artifice	CRAFT.CROOK.REACH
as	ALS
ascribe	APPLY
—importance to	FORCE
ash of glasswort	KALI
Ash Wednesday	
	PULVER WEDNESDAY
	PULVERING DAY
ask	
—back	REPEAT
—for	BID.YEARN
—price of	CHEAPEN
—question	REQUIRE
askance	ASCONCE
aspect	RESPECT.VISOR.VIZOR
aspiring knight	DONZEL
aspire to	AFFECT
assail	INSULT
assailant	ONSETTER
assay	SAY
assayer	SAY-MASTER
assembly	GEMOT.MOOT.THING
assert	VOUCH
assess	CENSE
assign	ARET(T)
assigned place	ROOM
assistance	EASEMENT

assistant	
—clown or buffoon	ZANY
—minister	HELPER
assize	SIZE
associate in agreement	WALK
assuage	ASSWAGE.LENIFY
assure	ASCERTAIN.RESOLVE
astonish	ASTONE.ASTONY
	ASTUN
astonishment	MARVEL
asunder	ATWAIN
asylum	FRITHSOKEN.GIRTH
	GRITH
—for prostitutes	PENITENTIARY
at	
—a loss to know	SEEK
—hand	TOWARD
—home	WITHIN
—once	PRESENTLY.SWITH
	TIGHT.TIT.TITE(LY).TYTE
—present	PRESENTLY
—the door	ADOORS
—the same time that	WHILES
athletic contest	PRIZE
atone	ABY(E).ABIDE
atrocious	ENORMOUS
attached strip	LABEL
attack	ATTEMPT.BRASH
	STAND UPON
attaint	TAINT
attempt	FAND.FOND
attend	INTEND
attendant	VARLET
	WAITING-VASSAL
—servant	WAITER
attentive	ADVICEFUL.LISTFUL
	WHIST
attire	SUIT.TIRE
attired	READY
auction sale	OUTROOP
auctioneer	OUTROOPER
audacity	HARDIHEAD
augury	SOOTH
aunt	NAUNT
aurochs	URE
austere	STOOR.STOUR
	STOWRE.STURE
authorisation	WARRANTISE
autumn	HARVEST

avail	DOW.STEAD.VAIL	—of river	CONTINENT
avenge	WREAK	banker	EXCHANGER
average	MEDIUM	banquet	ENTERTAINMENT
avert	FORFEND	bar	ESTOP
avoid	VOID.WAIVE	barded	BARD
await	BIDE.EXPECT	bare	LEWD
	STAY.TARRY	—place	GALL
award	ADEEM.ARET(T)	barefoot Highlander	
aware	KNOWING TO.WARE		GILLIE-WHITE-FOOT
away from	FROWARD(S)		GILLIE-WET-FOOT
awkward	UNGAIN	barely	SCRIMP
axiom	PETITION	bargain	INDENT.PURCHASE
axle	AXIS	barred	BARD
babble	BRABBLE	barrel organ	MUSIC-BOX
back	RIDGE	barter	PERMUTATION
—board	MONITOR	base	HARLOTRY
—bone	CHINE	basin	BASON
—handed	AWKWARD	bass	BURTHEN
—of head	NODDLE	bath-house	BAGNIO
—side	BREECH	baton	BATOON
—to-back	DOS-A-DOS	—of command	WARDER
—up	SOOTHE	battalion	BATTLE
backer	STICKLER	battle	
backgammon	GAMMON.TABLES	—array	HERSE
	VERQUERE	—axe	GISARME.SPARTH(E)
bad	LEWD.LITHER.NAUGHT	—field	PLACE
—lot	NAUGHTY PACK	battlement	BARMKIN
—luck to	FOUL (BE)FALL	bauble	GAUD
badger	GRAY.GREY	bay	REACH
baffle	MATE	—of library	CLASSIS
bag	COD	be	
bagpipes	SYMPHONY	—able	DOW
bail	REPLEVY	—accustomed	WON
bailiff	HUNDREDER.REEVE	—anxious about	FEAR
baker	BAXTER	—apprehensive	DOUBT
balance	PEASE.PEAZE.PEISE	—aware of	WIT
	PEIZE.PEYSE	—claimant	PRETEND
—beam	BA(U)LK	—brief	AT A WORD
baldmoney	SPICKNEL	—commonly expressed	VOICED
ball	BOWL	—defeated	GO BY THE WORST
ballast	POISE		GO WITH THE WORST
band	FASCIA	—earlier than	PREVENT
—of musicians	MUSIC.NOISE	—equal to	FILE WITH
bandalore	QUIZ	—false to	FALSE.FALSIFY
bandy words	BA(U)LK	—fitting	LONG
—in emulation	REVIE	—foolish	DOAT.DOTE.FON
bandying about	JACTITATION	—frivolous	FLUTTER
banishment	EXPULSION	—fully extended	LIE ALONG
bank	CONTINENT.LINK	—impatient	BATE

—in	
—attendance	INTEND
—expectation of	WAIT
—motion	WALK
—the habit	USE
—intemperate	EXCEED
—like	SEMBLE
—likely	LIKE
—of consequence to	IMPORT
—off	VIA.WAG
—on watch	WAIT
—pitied	SEELY.SILLY
—prominent	TOOT
—renewed	NEW
—rife	WALK
—rumoured	VOICE
—schoolmaster	MASTER
—spent (time)	WASTE
—stupid	DOAT.DOTE
—sulky	GLOUT
—troublesome	IMPORTUNE
—whimsical	WHIM
beacon	FANAL
beadle	BEDEL(L)
bear	EAN
beat	FEEZE.PHE(E)SE
	PHEEZE.BOUNCE
—back	REBUKE
—down	FOIL
—everything	PASS
—soundly	RIB-ROAST
—to windward	LAVEER
beaten	YBET
beautiful	BRIGHT.SMICKER
	SPECIOUS
beautifully	FAIRISH.LOVELY
beauty	FEATURE.FORM
beaver	BEVER
becalm	ENCALM
because	FORWHY
—of	IN RESPECT OF
become	BESIT.PROVE.WEAR
—angry	WRATH
—feeble	FAINT
—hairless	PILL
—husband	HUSBAND
—neglectful	FOR(E)SLACK
—scant	SCANTLE
—slack	FOR(E)SLACK

—surety	STIPULATE
—unveiled	UNVAIL(E)
—weak	FAINT
—worthwhile	DOW
becoming	HANDSOME
—stone	LAPIDESCENT
bed	DOWNY
bedaub	MOIL
bedraggle	DAG
bedroom	DORMER
been	BENE
beer flavoured with ground	
ivy	GILL(ALE).GILL BEER
befall	FORTUNE
—unluckily	OSFALL
befit	SORT
befool	ASSOT.BOB.FON
	POOP.POUPE
before	OR.TOFORE
befoul	BE(W)RAY
befriend	FRIEND
beg	MAUND
began	GAN
beget	KIND
begetting	GET
beggar	MAUNDER.MUMPER
—peddling glass	GLASSMAN
—posing as wounded	
soldier	RUFFLER
begging friar	MENDICANT
begin	GIN.INCEPT.INCHOATE
beginning	ENTRANCE.PRINCIPLE
	TO-FALL
begone	AVAUNT
begrime with coal dust	COLLY
beguile	AMUSE.GLEEK
beguiling grace	VENUS
behave	USE
—lewdly	PLAY THE WANTON
—riotously or noisily	ROAR
—towards	ENTREAT
—with arrogant scorn	INSULT
behaviour	CARRIAGE
	GOVERNANCE
behead	HEAD
behove	IMPORT
belabour	SAUCE
belching	RUCTATION
beleaguer	LEAGUER

believe	GUESS.TROW.WEEN
	WIS(H).WIST
believer in medicinal use of	
mercury	MERCURIALIST
bellows of organ	WIND-BAG
belly	WEM(B).WEAMB
belong	LONG
beloved	L(I)EVE.LIEF
bend	EMBOW
benign	BENEDICT
bent	WRONG
benumb	DEAD
bereaved	ORB
bereavement	ORBITY
beset	IMPEACH.OBSESS
besiege	BESIT.OBSESS
bestow part of	IMPART
bestrew	STROW
bet	HOLD
betray	BEWRAY
betrayer	TREACHER(ER)
	TREACHOUR
betroth	ENSURE.TROTH-PLIGHT
betroth(al)	HANDFAST(ING)
—by gift of ring or	
gift	SUBARR(H)ATION
betrothed	AFFIED
bewilder(ment)	AMAZE
bewitch	BESPEAK.FASCINATE
	OVERLOOK
bicycle	BONESHAKER
	VELOCIPEDE
bid	VIE
bier	HEARSE
big, jolly woman	ROUNCEVAL
bill	NOTE
bind	WAP
bird's crest	COPPLE
birthmark	NAEVE
bishop's throne	SEE
bite	PINCH
—back	CROSSBITE
bitter	EAGER
black	
—bile	MELANCHOLY
—marble	PARAGON.TOUCH
—bird	OUSEL.OUZEL
—leg	SNOB
blame	WITE.WYTE

—for	GUILTY OF
blank stone panel	ORB
bleaching agent	CHEMIC
blended	(Y)BLENT
blending together	
	CONTEMPERATION
blessed	BENEDICT
blind	BLEND
—window	ORB
blinded	YBLENT
blindfold	MUFFLE
—person in blindman's	
bluff	HOODMAN
blinking	TWINKLING
blister	BLAD.MEASLES
blockhead	MOME
blow	BUFF.HUFF.PLAGUE
	WHERRET.WHIRRET
—into	INSPIRE
—on the neck	NECK-HERRING
—on the ribs	RIB-ROASTER
blue-grey	GRISEOUS
bluster(er)	HUFF
blustering	BULLY
board	COMMON
boast	AVAUNT.CRACK
	GLORY.YELP
boastful	THRASONICAL
—spirit	GLORY
bob	DOP.S.SHILLING
bodies	BODICE
body	BULK
—living or dead	LICH
—of forces	HEAD
—of soldiers in	
square	SQUADRON
—of vassals	MANRED
—of watchmen	WATCH
boggy	QUEACHY.QUEECHY
boiled	SODDEN
—vegetables	POTTAGE
bold	HAUGHTY
—faced person	FACER
boldness	HARDIHEAD
bombastic	GRANDILOQUOUS
bond	BAND
book	
—always in the same	
place	LEDGER.LIDGER

—of Bible readings	LEGEND
—of rules	ORDINAL
—seller	STATIONER
boorish	SWAINISH
—fellow	JACK
booty	PURCHASE
border	COAST.CONFINE
bore	BARE
born a slave	NATIVE
borne	YBORE
borough	BURGH.PORT
bosses of gold set with	
diamonds	OWCHES
bottom	GROUND
bought	BOUGHTEN
—provisions	ACATES
bound	BAND.HANDFAST
—by monastic vows	VOWED
boundary	BOURN.GOAL.LIST
	MARK
—fence	MOUND
bourdon	BURTHEN
bout	BRASH
bow	CROOK.LOUT.LOWT.MOVE
	MAKE ONE'S MANNERS
Bow Street officer	RUNNER
bowels	WOMB
box	BRUISE
boxer	PUGIL
boxing glove	MUFFLE
boy	KINCHIN-COVE.GROOM
braggart	PUCKFIST
bragging	THRASONICAL
braid	BREDE
branch	BRAUNCH.GRAFT
brandish	WAG
brandy	NANTZ
—and water	MAHOGANY
brass	ALCHEMY.ALCHYMY
bravado	BRAVERY
brave person	VALIANT
bravo	BRAVE
brawl	BRABBLE
brawler	NICKER.ROARER
	ROARING-BOY
breach of law	UNLAW
bread	LOAF
—from finest	
flour	WASTEL(-BREAD)

—soaked in gravy	BREWIS
break	
—in pieces	TO-BREAK
—up	REFORM.TO-BRUISE
breakfast	DEJEUNE
breaking waves	BREACH
breastplate	PLACARD
breath	SPIRIT
breathe into	INSPIRE
breed of sheep	HERDWICK
bribe	GIFT.GRATIFICATION
	TOUCH.VALES
	VAILS.WAGE
bridesmaid	PARANYMPH
bright	NET(T).SHEER
—red	COCCINEOUS
brilliant	SPLENDIDIOUS
bring	
—about	PURCHASE
—back	REDUCE
—forward	OBJECT
—in	INBRING.INDUCE
—success	SPEED
—to an end	DEFINE.SPEED
—to court	INBRING
—to finished state	SPEED
—to sorry condition	SPEED
—vessel close to wind	LOOF
bringing	
—back	REDUCTIVE
—intelligence	INTELLIGENT
—up	NOUR(R)ITURE
brisk	GAILLARD.GALLIARD
	YARE
briskly	TIGHTLY
British soldier	LOBSTER
broach	BROCH
broke	BRAKE
broken	INFRACT
—pottery	POTSHARD
—tree	RAMPICK.RAMPIKE
brokerage	BROKERY
bronze	BRASS
brooch	BROCH
brood	TEAM
—pheasants	EYE
broth	BREWIS
brothel	BORDEL(L)O.CORINTH
	VAULTING-HOUSE

brought from distant place	FAR-FETCHED
browned by sun	ADUST
bruise severely	TO-BRUISE
brushwood	BAVIN.RICE
bucket	SITULA.STOOP.STOUP
buffoon	ANTIC.INIQUITY
	JACK-PUDDING.MOME
build	EDIFY.TIMBER
building where salt is made	SALT-COTE
bulk	GREAT
bully	HUFF
bumper	ROUSE
bumpkin	PUT(T)
bunch of flowers	BOUGHPOT
	BOWPOT
bundle	TROUSSEAU
burden	BURTHEN
burdensome	IMPORTUNATE
	IMPORTUNE
burgess	PORTMAN
burial-place	CHARNEL
burly	BRAVE
burn	BREN(NE)
—in	INURE
burned	YBRENT
—in	INUST
burnet(-saxifrage)	PIMPERNEL
burning	UST(ULA)ION
—desire	COVETISE
—in	INUSTION
burnt	YBRENT
—up	ADUST
bury	EARTH.GRAVE.INEARTH
bus conductor	CAD
bustle	COIL
butt	PUSH
buttocks	CROUPON
buy and re-sell to raise price	REGRATE
by	FORBY
—day	ADAYS
—my faith!	PERFAY
—Our Lady(kin)	BYRLADY
	BYRLAKIN
—way of love	PARAMOUR
byword	NAY-WORD
cabbage	WORT

cake of soap	BALL
calamity	BALE.RUTH
calf	VEAL
call	CLEEP.CLEPE.ENSTYLE
	HETE.HIGHT
—back	REVOKE
—from a distance	
	WHOA-HO-HO(A)
—in question	QUAREL
—out	PROVOKE
—to arms	ALARM
—to witness	ATTEST
called	HIGHT.HOTEN.NEMPT
	YCLEPED.YCLEPT
camp	LEAGUER
campaign	JOURNEY
canal without locks	WATER-PLANE
cancerous growth	WOLF
candied fruit	SUCKET
cannon	BASILISK
—balls	GUN-STONES
canopy	PAVILION
—of state	ESTATE
canto	FIT(T).FITTE.FYTTE
cap	BIGGIN(G)
capable of	NOTABLE
—erring	ERRABLE
—living	VITAL
capitalist	MONEYER
capricious	HUMOROUS
	WANTON
captious arguing	CROCODILITE
captivity	ENDURANCE
care	CARK.FORCE.PASS
—for	KEEP.RECK
career	CARIERE
careful	CHARY
carelessness	SECURITY
carousal	ROUSE.UPSEE.UPS(E)Y
carper	MOME
carry	
—off	HENT.TRUSS
—out the duties of	WAIT (UP)ON
cart for removal of night-soil	NIGHT-CART
cartload	SEAM
carve	ENTAIL.ENTAYLE.INSCULP
—birds	DISMEMBER

casque	CASK	—Whitsun	SHROVE
cast	KEST.WARP	celestial sphere	WHEEL
—a hindrance	TRUMP	censure	TAXATION
—evil eye on	FASCINATE	centring	CENTRY
—off clothes	FRIPPERY	certain	SICCAR.SICKER
—spell on	ENCHARM	certainly	IWIS.YWIS
castor	TRUCKLE	cessation	STINT
casualty	CADUAC	chafing dish	CHAFER
catalogue	CATELOG.RAGMAN	chair of	
	RAGMENT	—sanctuary	FRITHSTOOL
catamite	GANYMEDE.INGLE	—state	ESTATE
catch	DEPREHEND.FANG	chalaza	SPERM
caterer	ACATER.ACATOUR	challenge	APPEAL.CHAMPION
	CATER		DARRAIGN(E).DARRAIN(E)
cattle	AVER.FEE.NEAT		DARRAYN.DERAIGN
—herder	HAYWARD		DEFY.PROVOKE.VIE
caught	IN BY THE WEEK	challenger	APPELLANT
—at fault	TARDY	chambermaid	BOWERY WOMAN
cause	OCCASION	champion	KEMP
—not to be	UNBE	chance	CHAUNCE.VENTURE
cause to		change	EXCHANGE.WEND
—boil with anger	EMBOIL	—colour	BRAID
—fall	FALL	—one's clothes	SHIFT
—fear	DREAD	—the course of	WIND
—feel scruples	SCRUPLE	changeable	HUMOROUS
—glance	GLANCE		VOLUBLE
—grieve	RUE	chaplet	ROSARY
—know	KEN	character	HAIR.PROPRIETY
—sin	OFFEND	charcoal burner	COLLIER
—swear	ADJURE	charge	QUARREL.TAX
causing		chariot	WAG(G)ON.WAIN
—devastation	WASTEFUL	charioteer	WAG(G)ONER
—uneasiness	IRKSOME	charm	ENCHARM.WEIRD
—wasting	WASTEFUL	chase	CHACE
cauterisation	INUSTION.USTION	chaste	HONEST
caution	CAUTEL	cheap	GOOD-CHEAP
cautious	CAUTELOUS.WARE	cheat	BAFFLE.BITE
Cavalier	MALIGNANT		CONY-CATCHER
cavalry			FOB.SLUR
—man	PLUNGER	—in return	CROSSBITE
—'s fatigue cap	WATERING-CAP	check	BAFFLE.FOIL
—officer	CORNET		REBUKE.SNEAP
—standard	CORNET	—mated	MATE
caviar	CAVIARIE	cheek	WANG
cavity		cheer	ENCHEER
—in the ground	MINE	cheerful	LUSTICK
cease	STINT	chemise	SMOCK
—from	RESPITE	chemist	APOTHECARY.CHEMIC
celebrate	MEMORISE.MEMORIZE	chemistry	CHYMISTRY

cherish	REFOCILLATE
—with heat	FOMENT
chess	
—board	CHEQUER
—piece	CHEQUER
chest	CAP-CASE
chicken	CHUCK
chided	CHOSE
chief	DUKE
—fifer	FIFE-MAJOR
—magistrate	(PORT)REEVE
—place in popular esteem	VOGUE
chignon	WATERFALL
child	WENCH
—left to be minded	MINDER
—'s cap	BIGGIN
children	CHILDER
chimney-sweeper's boy	CHUMMY
chintz	PINTADO
chloride	MURIATE
choir	QUIRE
—stall facing altar	HEADSTALL
choose	CHUSE
chorister	QUIRISTER
chough	CHEWET
christening robe	BEARING-CLOTH
Christmas game	LEVEL-COIL
church building	STEEPLE-HOUSE
churl	CARL
churlish	CARLISH
cider and water	BEVERAGE
cinnamon	CANELLA
circuitous movement	WINDLASS
circulate	TROLL.WALK
circumstanced	STATED
cite	ALLEGE
city	TROY.UR
clad	YCLAD.YCLED
—in satin	SATIN
claim	DARRAIGN(E)
	DARRAIN(E).DARRAYN
	DERAIGN.PRETEND
—as one's own	OWN
—equality	MATE
claimant	TITLER
clamour	BRABBLE
clary	ORVAL
clash	HURTLE
clasp	SPANG.TACH(E)

class	SIEGE
—of inferior persons	VULGAR
—of thief	WASTER
claw	FANG.SERE
clean	EMUNGE.NEAT.NET(T)
—cut	TERSE
cleanse	GARBLE
clear	SHEER
—away	VOID
—space	HALL
—up	SALVE
clever	ARTFUL.CONCEITED
	NOTABLE
cleverly made	SLY
climate	TEMPERAMENT
climb	STY
climbed	CLOMB
clip	DOD
—for holding up skirt	PAGE
cloak	CLOKE.PALLIATE
clock	
—face	WATCH
—weight	POISE
clod	GLEBE
cloddy	GLEBOUS.GLEBY
clog	PESTER
close	STRICT.CONSTIPATE
closed handful	NIEVEFUL
close-fitting	JUST.SUCCINCT
—breeches or drawers	HOSE
closely	NIGHLY.STRAIT
—united	CONTINUATE
cloth	
—covering Eucharist	CORPORAL
—of gold	CICLATO(U)N
—of mixed colours	MOTLEY
—pieced together	PANE
—separated by slashes	PANE
clothes	SHROUD.WEARING
clothing	WEED
clove pink	SOPS-IN-WINE
clown	ANTIC
clownish	BOR(R)EL(L).CARLISH
club	BOURDON.HETAIRIA.POLT
clumsy	UNHANDSOME
co-exist	CONSIST
coal dealer	COLLIER
coarse	
—flour/meal	CRIBBLE

—woollen fabric	RUG	compassionate	PITEOUS
cobblestone	COPPLESTONE		REMORSEFUL
coddled child	COCKNEY	compel	COMPULSE
codlin	QUODLIN	compelled	FAIN
cohabit with	OCCUPY	competition	CONCURRENCE
coin	CROSS		GOAL
	(*see also* coins)	competitor	CONCURRENT
coiner	MONEYER	compiler	UNDERTAKER
cold in the head	RHEUM	complain	PLAIN
collective body	UNIVERSITY	complaint	PLAIN.QUARREL
colonial governor	PRESIDENT	complaisance	PLEASANCE
colonist	INHABITOR	complete	COMPLEAT
comb	KEMB	complexion	BLEE
combed	KEMPT	compliment	DOUCEUR
come	VIA	comply	CONDESCEND
—about	SORT	compose	DITE.STICKLE
—forth	FORTHCOME	composition	DITE
—near	LIKE	—of drugs	CONFECTION
—to grief or ruin	SPILL	compromise	TEMPERAMENT
—near its end	GROW TO WASTE	compulsion	DISTRESS
comfit	CONFIT	conceal	VIZARD
comfort	ENCHEER	concede	CONDESCEND
coming from the eye	VISUAL	conceit	DEVICE
command	HEST.HETE.WILL	conceive	CONCEIT
commemorate	REMEMBER	concern	
commendable	WELL-FOUND	—closely	NIP
comment	GLOZE	—oneself with	MEDDLE
commercial traveller	RIDER	concerned with fate	WEIRD
commit adultery	ADULTERATE	concert of voices	CONCENT
commodities	TRAFFIC	conciliatory	COASTING
common		—words	FAIR WORDS
—kite	GLED(E)	conclusion	FINE
—land	MARK	concord	CONCENT
—man	JACK	concubine	MADAM
—topic	COMMONPLACE	condemn	CAST
commons	FOLK	condescend to	
commonwealth	(COMMON)WEAL	—allow	VOUCHSAFE.VOUTSAFE
compact	COVIN.COVYNE	—grant	VOUCH(SAFE)
	MATCH		VOUTSAFE
companion	COPESMATE	condition	CENSE.LIKING
	FE(A)RE.FEER.FIERE	condole with	MOAN
	PHEERE.MARROW	conduct	RULE
company	GING.SORT	—on a journey	TRAVEL
—taking meal at fixed price		—oneself	USE
	ORDINARY	confectioner	SUGAR-BAKER
compare	CONFER.PARAGON	confess	AGNISE.AGNIZE
	RESEMBLE	confidential	INWARD
compartment in chest	TILL	confine	STRAITEN
compass	PRACTISE	confinement	CONFINE

confirm	SOOTHE.STABLISH	control	WIND
—correctness of	RATIFY	controller	RECTOR
conflict	CAMP	convenience	COMMODITY
confound	MATE	convenient	HANDSOME.HEND
confounded	POCKY	conversation	PARLANCE
confront	CROSS	conveying no idea	UNIDEAL
confused mass	FARRAGO	convict of	REPROVE
confusion	BAFFLE	convince	RESOLVE
confute	REDARGUE.REFEL	copious	FULSOME
congratulate	GRATULATE.GREET	copiousness	COPY
congratulatory	GRATULANT	copper	AS.D.P
conjectural	STOCHASTIC	copse	SPRING
connecting ridge	HALSE	copy of legal document	

copy of legal document

TRANSUMPT

conned	YCOND	copyholder	VILLEIN
conscience	INWIT	cordial	ROSA-SOLIS
consecrate	HALLOW	cornage	HORNGELD
consecration	SACRING	corner	CANTON
consent	CONDESCEND	correct	CHASTISE.CHASTIZE
conserve	CONFITURE	—thing	CHEESE
consider	ADVISE.CAST.VISE	correspondent	RESPONSIBLE
considerable	NOTABLE	corroded	CANKERED
considered	CONSIDERATE	corrosive	CORSIVE
consort	LADY.MAKE.MATE	cosmetic	FUCUS
conspiracy	COVIN.COVYNE	coupled	ME(I)NT.MENGED
conspire	COLLEAGUE.CONJURE		MEYNT.MINGED
constable	BOW STREET RUNNER	couch	DAY-BED
	HARMAN(-BECK)	could	COUTH
—'s district	CONSTABLEWICK	council	THING
constant	UNREMOVABLE	counsel	ADVISEMENT.REDE
constrain	OBLIGATE.PERSTRINGE	count	NICK
construe	CONSTER	countable	COMPTIBLE
consume	BEZZLE	countenance	CHEER.FAVOUR
consuming	WASTEFUL	count(er)	COMPT(ER)
contact	CONTINGENCY	counter	COMPTER
containing rheum	RHEUMATIC	—balance	POISE
contend	DEBATE	—point	DESCANT
—with weapons	PLAY		FA(UX)BURDEN
content in circumstances	FAIN	counterfeit coin	SLIP
contention	TOIL	counterfeiter	FALSER
contents of wardrobe		country	
	GARDEROBE	—house	GRANGE
contest for prize	WAGER	—dweller	RURAL
continuance	DURANCE	count(ship)	COUNTY
continue	DURE.PERSEVERE	couple	MARROW.TWAIN
continuity	TENOUR	—up	MENG(E).MING
contradict	OUTFACE.UNDERSAY	courageous	WIGHT
contrary	CONTRAIR	course	LOOSE.MESS.TRADE
contrivance	ENGINE	court	MOOT.SUE.THING
contrive	ENGINE.FRAME.WORK		

—held at markets and fairs	
	COURT OF PIEPOWDERS
—messenger	BEADLE
—of guild	HALL-MOOT
—of lord of manor	HALL-MOOT
—official	CH(E)IROGRAPHER
	APPARITOR
—of the manor	LEET
courteous	HEND
courtesan	STALLION
courtesy	GENTLENESSE
cousin	COOSEN
coven	COVIN.COVYNE
cover	COUR.OVERCOME
—completely	WHELM
—dispersedly	STROW
—with earthwork	ENSCONCE
—with sconce	ENSCONCE
covering	TAPIS
covetousness	COVETISE
coward(ly)	HILDING.NITHING
cower	COURE
coxcomb	PRIG
cozen	COOSIN.POOP.POUPE
craft	MISTER(Y).MYSTERY
craftsman	ARTSMAN
crafty	SUBDOLOUS
—action	WINDLASS
cram	STOP
create	
—at some time	CONCREATE
—with	CONCREATE
creature	WIGHT
creeping or crawling	
animal	WORM
crime committed	FACT
crimp linen with	
poting-stick	POTE
crimping	PRINT
—stick for ruffs	POTING-STICK
crimson	PURPLE
crippled	HALT
crisis	ACME.FIT
critic	OVERSEER
critical	NICE
—moment	ARTICLE
crooked	CRABBED.WRONG
Cross	WOOD
cross-grained	FRAMPOLD

crown	GARLAND
cruel	FELON
crupper	CROPPER
crush	OPPRESS
crust of a raised pie	COFFIN
crutch	POTENT
crwth	CROWD
cry	
—at masque	A HALL,A HALL
—in fencing	HAY
—of impatience	CRIMINE
—of surprise	CRIMINE
—out	DISCLAIM
—up	SELL
cucking-stool	TUMBREL.TUMBRIL
cuckold	CORNUTE.CORNUTO
	ENGRAFT
—maker	HORNER
cuckoldise	GRAFT
cuckoldry	HORNWORK
cudgel	WASTER
cultivate	HUSBAND.MANURE
cultivated	SATIVE
cultivation	MANURANCE
cunning	QUAINT.SLIGHT
—rogue	GREEK
curb	REFRAIN
curd	CRUD
curdle	CRUDDLE.YEARN
cure	RECURE.REMEDY
curled	CRISP
curling	CRISP
currency	PASS
curse	BAN
cursory	CURSORARY
curt	SQUAB
curtsy	DOP
	MAKE ONE'S MANNERS
curved	WRONG
custard	FLAM(M).FLAUNE.FLAWN
custody	HANDFAST
custom	WON
customer	CHAPMAN
customs officer	WAITER
cut	ENTAIL.ENTAYLE
—short	CURTAL
—the hair of	DOD
cutting	SARMENT
—back	RECISION

—off	RESCISSION	debar	CONCLUDE
—short	SYNCOPE	debate	WRANGLE
cylindrical pleat	QUILL	debauch	DEBOSH
cymbal	SYMBOLE	decamp	SCAMPER
cypress	GOPHER	decay	FAINT.FORFAIR
dagger	BASELARD.PUNCHEON	decaying tree	RAMPICK.RAMPIKE
dainties	CATES	deceit	BARRAT.FORGERY
dais	ESTATE	deceitfulness	FALLACY
dally	TICK AND TOY		FALSEHOOD
damage	WORST.WREAK	deceive	FALSE.TRUMP
damned beforehand		—with smooth speech	GLOZE
	FORE-DAMNED	deceived husband	HODDY-DODDY
dandy	FANTASTIC.JESSAMY	deceiver	TREACHER(ER)
	MASHER.MUSCADIN		TREACHOUR
	PUSS-GENTLEMAN	December 21st	MUMPING-DAY
dangerous	PERICULOUS	deception	FALLACY.FUBBERY
Danish underking	EORL		GULLERY
dark	WAN	decide	AREAD.AREDE.ARREEDE
—brown	BURNET		DARRAIGN(E).DARRAIN(E)
—colour	PUKE		DARRAYN.DERAIGN
—coloured horse	MOREL		DISCUSS
darnel	TARE	—against	CAST
dart	LANCE	decision of council	REBOUND
dash	RASH	declare	AREAD.AREDE.ARREEDE
dastard	HILDING		MELD.VIE.VOUCH
dastardly	NITHING	—on oath	ALLEGE
daunt	AMATE.DANT.PALL.QUAIL	—to be true	SOOTHE
dawdle	DRAWL	decline	DEVALL.QUAIL.WELK
dawn	DAW.SPRING	decoration	FLOURISH.PARAMENT
day		decorum	HONESTY
—for begging	MUMPING-DAY	decoy for birds	STALE
—'s work or travel	JOURNEY	decrease	WANZE
days of makeshift meals		—in volume	WANE
	SCAMBLING-DAYS	dedicate to church use	IMMOLATE
daze	AMAZE	deduce	DEDUCT
dazzle	BLEND	deduct part of	DEFALCATE
dazzling lustre	GLARE	deed	ASSURANCE.FACT
dead tree	RAMPICK.RAMPIKE	deeds	WORKINGS
deaden	DEAD	—of valour	VASSALAGE
deaf	SURD	deep metal plate	MAZARINE
deal	ENTREAT	deer's	
—with	TRANSACT	—entrails	QUARRY
dealer	CHAPMAN.OCCUPIER	—sweetbread	INCHPIN
—in horses	HORSE-COURSER	defeat	PUT TO THE WORSE
—in second-hand goods		defeated	PROFLIGATE
	UPHOLDER	defenceless	SILLY
dealing	MERCHANDISE	defend	WARRANT
dear	L(I)EVE.LIEF	—with flankers	FLANKER
death	EXPIRATION.MORT	defender	WARRANT

defiant protestation	
	MARRY COME UP
defile	HALSE.MOIL
defilement	CONSPURCATION
	MOIL
deflect	WIND
deformed person	URCHIN
defraud	COG.LURCH
degree	GRE(E)CE.GRECIAN
	GRE(E)SE.GREE
	GREESING.GRESSING
	GRI(E)CE.GRISE.GRIZE
dejected	AMORT
delay	FRIST.LET.TARRY
	TARRIANCE
—in action	RESPITE
deleterious	PREDATORY
deliberate	CONSIDERATE
delicacy	CATE.TRINKET.JUNKET
delighting	RAPING
delineate	STELL
delirium	PHRENITIS
deliver	TAKE
—of a child	LAY
delivered of a child	LIGHTER
delivery	LIVERY
demonstrate	REMONSTRATE
demonstration	MUSTER
deny	DENAY.REN(A)Y.RENEY
depart	AVAUNT.VADE.WALK
	WEND
dependent on	
humour	HUMOROUS
depict	DEVISE.RESEMBLE
depraved	FELONIOUS
	GRACELESS
deprive	TWIN(E)
—of colour	STAIN
—of provisions	DISPURVEY
deputy to earl	VISCOUNT
derived	EXTRACT
describe	DESCRIVE.DEVISE
	SPEAK
desert	DEMERIT
deserving of	GUILTY OF
—reproach	REPROACHFUL
design	MODEL
designed for looking	
through	SPECULATORY

desirable	WISHFUL
desire	COURAGE.RECK.WILL
—strongly	EARN
desired	WISHFUL
despair	WANHOPE
despicable fellow	CULLION
despise	FORHOW
despite	DESPIGHT
destinate	DESTINE
destitute	VOID
—of	HELPLESS
destroy	FORDO.SPILL
destructive	WASTEFUL
detached	DISCREET
detailed narrative	ENARRATION
deteriorate	STARVE
determine	ASSOIL.PITCH
devalued by commonness	
	PROSTITUTE
devastate	POPULATE
devastated	WASTE
devastation	WASTENESS
deviate	PREVARICATE
deviation from right course	
	ERROR
device	ENGINE
devoid	VAIN.VOID
—of shame	FRONTLESS
dexterity	SLIGHT
dexterous	FEAT(E)OUS
	FEATUOUS.WIELDY
diagram	PLAT
diamond	ADAMANT
dice	GOURDS
dictate	DITE
diction	PARLANCE
did	COUTH.GAN
die	GO UNDER.STERVE.SWELT
—impenitent	DIE HARD
—of starvation	FAMISH
difference	DIFFERENCY.DIFFICILE
difficult	UNEASY.UNEATH
difficulty	HOBBLE
diffuse	LARGE
dig	GIRD.GRAVE
digest	ENDUE.INDUE
digest(ion)	DISGEST(ION)
dignity	WORSHIP
dilute	LOWER

dinner	DINE	disperse	SPERSE
—time	DINE.PUDDING-TIME	dispirited	SACKLESS
dip	MERGE	display	MUSTER.SPLAY
direction of attention	INTENTION	displease	MISLIKE
dirty whore	PUCELLE.PUZZLE	dispose	DISPONE
disadvantageous		disposed	DIGHT
	DISADVANTAGEABLE	disproof	REPROOF
disaffected	MALIGNANT	disprove	REFEL
disapprobation	MISLIKE	dispute	REPROVE.WRANGLE
disapprove	DISPROVE.MISLIKE	disregard	WAIVE
disband	REFORM	disreputable person	SHAKE-RAG
disbanded officer	REFORMADO	dissension	SQUARE
discard	DEFY	dissolute conduct	DISSOLUTION
discern	WIT	distillate	ALCOHOL
discharge	ASSOIL	distilled from wood	PYROXILIC
disclose	UNVAIL(E)	distinctness	DISTINCTION
discomfit	SHEND	distinguished	EGREGIOUS
discontent	MISCONTENT		EXIMIOUS
discourse	PARABLE.SPELL	distort	WRITHE
discover	BEWRAY	distortion	WRY
discreet	WITTY	distracted	BESTRAUGHT
—man	PRUD'HOMME	distraint	NA(A)M
discrete	DISCREET	distraught	BESTRAUGHT
discrimination	SKILL	distress	MISEASE
disease of trees	MEASLES	—warrant	DISTRINGAS
disgrace	SCANDAL.SHEND	distressing	UNEATH
	VILLA(I)NY	district of	
—publicly	BAFFLE	—court	SOKE
—with faint praise	INDIGNIFY	—manorial court	MANOR
disgraceful	INDIGN	—warden	WARDENRY
	OPPROBRIOUS	disturb	BRASH
	REPROACHFUL	disuse	INUSITATION
disguise	PALLIATE.VIZARD	diverge from straight line	CROOK
dish of food	MESS	divide	DEPART
—cooked in cup shape	TIMBALE	—into chapters, verses, etc	
dish used in the Eucharist	PATINE		QUOTE
dishonest	UNHONEST	divinely	HEAVENLY
dishonourable	UNHONEST	division	CANTON
dislike	DEFY.DISTASTE	—of arc	SCRUPLE
	MISLIKE	—of a song	FIT
dismal	TRIST	—of the night	WATCH
dismay	AMATE	—of time	SCRUPLE
dismayed	MATED	do	EXERT
dismiss	REFORM.VOID	—for	POOP.POUPE.SPEED
dismissed officer	REFORMADO	—homage	VAIL
disobliging	INOFFICIOUS	—one's utmost	
disorder	MISTEMPER		DO ONE'S ENDEAVOUR
disown	REPROBATE	docked	CURTAL
dispel	ASSOIL	doctrine	LORE

document with attached	
seals	RAGMAN.RAGMENT
doe	TEG(G)
doff	AVAIL(E).AVALE.VAIL
dole	DOOL(E).VALES.VAILS
doll	BABY
dolphin	MEERSWINE
dolt	MOME
domain	REAME.REIGN
domestic	DOMESTICAL
—slave	ESNE
don	ADDRESS
dormitory	DORMER.DORTER
	DORTOUR
dot	PRICK
doubt	SCRUPLE
doughty	TALL
dovecote	LOUVER.LOUVRE
downward cut in fencing	
	STRAMACON.STRAMAZON
drag	RASH
dragon	WORM
drain out	EMULGE
dram-shop	GILL-HOUSE
dramatic	
—action	SCENERY
—performance	PAGEANT
draw	LIMN
—along or on	TRAIN
—together	ENTRAIN
drawer in chest	TILL
dread	GASTINESSE
dreaded	YDRAD.YDRED
dream	SWEVEN
dress	GUISE.RAY.TIFF
—distaff with flax	DIZEN
—of puppets	PUPPETRY
—ostentatiously	PRANK
—up	DIZEN
dressed	READY
dressing	
—for the head	HEAD
—gown	NIGHT-GOWN
—jacket	NIGHT-RAIL
drink	
—copiously	
	WASH ONE'S BRAINS
—deeply	BOUSE
—hard	BEZZLE
drinking	
—party	SYMPOSIUM
—vessel	RUMKIN.STOOP.STOUP
drive	DRAVE
—off	FEEZE.PHE(E)SE.PHEEZE
—out	EXTERMINATE.WREAK
drop	DRIB.GOUT
dropped	KEST
droppings of deer, hare, etc.	
	FEWMET(S).FUMET(S)
drove	DRAVE.DRIFT
drown	DRENT
druggist	APOTHECARY.DRUGGER
drum	SYMPHONY
drunk	CONCERNED.GROGGY
	OVERSEEN
drying	AREFACTION
—room	HOT-FLUE
due	DEW.LOT
duenna	GRIFFIN.GRIFFON
	GRIPE.GRYPHON
dull	DEAD.PERSTRINGE
dumpy person	HODDY-DODDY
dunnage	FARDAGE
dupe	PLOVER
durability	DURANCE
durable	
—cloth	DURANCE
—woollen cloth	SEMPITERNUM
duration	ENDURANCE
—of existence	DATE
duty	MISTERY.MYSTERY
—of sentinel	WATCH
dwell	STALL.WON
dwelling	MANSION.WONING
dye	TINCT
each other	OTHER
eager	RATH(E)
—to	FAIN
earl	COUNTY.EORL
earliest	RATHEST
early	RARE(LY).REAR.SOON
—ripe	RARE-RIPE
—variety	RATH(E)RIPE
earn	YEARN
earnest	EAGER.FORWARD
	WISTFUL
—desire	VOTE
earth	MOULD

early evening	UNDERN
easily	
—handled	YARE
—injured	NICE
East	LEVANT
Easter	PASCH
easy	EATH.ETHE
—to roll	VOLUBLE
ecclesiastical bands	TIPPET
eclipse	DELIQUIUM
eclogue	AEGLOGUE
eddish	EADISH
editor	OVERSEER.UNDERTAKER
educate	INSTITUTE
educational	INSTITUTIONARY
efficient action	EFFICIENCE
egg	COCKNEY
—fried with bacon	COLLOP
—on	EDGE
eglantine	EGLATERE
egregious	PASSING
eightieth	FOUR-SCORTH
either	OUTHER
eject	EXPULSE
elation	RUFF(E)
eldest daughter's right of	
choice as heir	ESNECY
elect	VOICE
elevation of gun	RANDOM
elf	URCHIN
eloquence	ELOCUTION
elude	DELUDE
embalm	BALM
emblematic device	IMPRESA
embrace	CLIP.COLL.COMPRESS
embroidery frame	TENT
embryo	EMBRION
emetic	PUKE
eminence where idol	
stands	HIGH-PLACE
eminent	PASSING
emit forcibly	UTTER
emollient	LENIENT
empty	AVOID.VACUATE.VAIN
encage	INCAGE
enchant	FASCINATE
enchantment	MALEFICE
encircle	EMBAIL
enclose	EMBOWEL.ENCHASE

—for safety	WARD
—in deepest recesses	EMBOWEL
enclosed	
—hollow part	WEM(B)
	WEAMB
—space	IMPALEMENT
enclosure	HAW.TOWN
end	FINE.UPSHOT
—of existence	DATE
endearment	PEAT
	PIGSN(E)Y.PIGSNIE
endeavour	WORKING
endorse	CONCLUDE
endue	ENDEW
endure	DURE.ENDEW
enfold	PLIGHT
enforced	NECESSARY
engage in	VOUCHSAFE
	VOUTSAFE
engine	GIMMAL
—of war	TREBUCHET
engraft	ENGRAFF.IMP
engulf	ENGULPH.INGULPH
enjoy	TASTE.WIELD
enjoyable	GUSTFUL
enjoyment	PLEASANCE
	SUFFISANCE
ennoble	GENTLE
enormous	ENORM
enough	ENOW
—of that	VIA
enquire after	HEARKEN
enraged like a	
cuckold	HORN-MAD
enshrine (in verse)	ENCHASE
ensign	ANCIENT.PAVILION
ensphere	EMBOW
entangle	ENGAGE
enterprise	EMPRISE.VOYAGE
entertainment for benefit of	
needy person	FRIENDLY LEAD
entice	ATTEMPT
entire	INTIRE
entirely	MERELY
entomb	GRAVE
entrance	INFARE
entrap	CROSSBITE
entreating	ENTREATIVE
entreaty	EXORATION

entremets	ENTREMES(SE)
epic poet	EPIC
epistolatory	LITERARY
epoch	EPOCHA
equal	FE(A)RE.FEER.FIERE
	PHEERE.MAKE.MARROW
	MATE.PARAGON.PEREGAL
equip	APPAREL.BEDIGHT
	DIGHT.EQUIPAGE
equipment	ORDINANCE.TIRE
equipped	ADDRESSED.ADDREST
—for fighting	WARLIKE
ermine	ERMELIN
error in pleading	JEOFAIL
erst	EARST
escape	ESCAPADE
especially	IN SPECIAL
espial	SPIAL
espoused	HANDFAST
establish	EDIFY.STABLISH
estate	HAVING
esteem	PASS
eternal	ETERNE
eulogistic	EPAENETIC.EPAINETIC
eulogy	LAUD
euphemism for excrement	
	SIR-REVERENCE
euphony	EUPHONIA
evade	SHIFT.WAIVE
eve	E'EN.EVEN
—of Jewish Sabbath	PARASCEVE
even	EEV(E)N
evening	EEVNING
evil	BALE.NAUGHT
—being	SHREW
—deed	MALEFICE.PRANK
exact transcript	TENOUR
exactitude	PRINT
example	ENSAMPLE
—for warning	SAMPLE
exceeding the	
normal	ENORMOUS
exceedingly	EXCEEDING
	HEAVENLY.MONSTROUS
	PASSING
—great	STRANGE
excellent	EXIMIOUS.PURE
except	OUTTAKEN.WITHOUT
exceptional	STRANGE

excessive	UNEQUAL
excessively	WOUND(IL)Y
excite	URGE
—loathing in	UG
excitement	RUFF(E)
exclamation of	
astonishment	ZOUNDS
	HOOKEY WALKER
exemplar	SAMPLER
exercise	INURE
exertion of influence	LABOUR
exhaust	FORDO
exhausted	FOREDONE
	FORFAUGHTEN
exhibitable	OSTENSIBLE
exile	WRETCH
expect	HOPE.WEEN
expeditate	LAW
expeditation	LAWING
expel with force	EXPULSE
expend	DISPEND
expenditure	GOINGS-OUT.MISE
experience	GUST.PROOF.RELISH
experienced	WELL-SEEN
—naval officer	TARPAULIN(G)
experiment	CONCLUSION
	EXPERIENCE
expert	SLY
—in gems	LAPIDARY
explain	AREAD.AREDE.ARREEDE
	GLOZE.SALVE
—by hypothesis	SALVE
explanation	GLOZE
expose	DETECT
exposed	OBNOXIOUS
exposition	ENARRATION
expound	GLOZE.REDE
—scriptures	PROPHESY
express	
—desire for	YEARN
—in words	LANGUAGE
—joy at	GRATULATE
expressing	
—freely	LAXATIVE
—love	ENDEARING
expression of face	MIEN
exquisite	PINK
exterminate	EXTIRP
external appearance	GARB

extinguish hope	QUENCH	farm	
extol	ADVANCE	—worker	HIND
extract gently	SOLICIT	—yard	HOMESTALL
extraction	BROOD	farthing	FARDEN.FARDING
extremity	EXIGENT	fashion	FEIGN.ENTAIL.ENTAYLE
extricate oneself	WIND OUT	fashionable	FLASH
extrinsic	FORINSECAL	fast ship	ADVICE-BOAT
eye	LIGHT.PIGSN(E)Y.PIGSNIE	fastening	TACH(E)
eyelet	OILLET	fastidiously precise	POINT-DEVICE
eyes	EINE.EYNE		POINT-DEVISE
face	CHEER.FAVOUR	fate	EVENT.WEIRD
	VISOR.VIZOR	fatigue	FATIGATE
facetious	FACETE	fatigued	SWINKED
fade	FAINT	fatten	BATTEN
faded	BRAID.FADE	fault	DEFAULT.GALL
failing to pass assay	REPROBATE	favourable	GRACIOUS
fainting fit	SWOUND.SWOUN		TOWARD(LY)
fair where servants		favoured advocate	PEAT
were hired	HIRING	favourite	GRACIOSO
fairy	FAERIE.FAERY	fear	ADREAD.DOUBT.HOPE
fairyland	FAERIE.FAERY		REDOUBT
faith	TROTH	feat	POINT
falchion (sword)	FAULCHI(O)N	feather-like structure	PLUME
fall		features	FAVOUR
—back	RECOIL	feeble	SACKLESS
—short	FAULT	feed	BATTLE
falling of jaw	JAWFALL	—with rich food	PAMPER
false		feeding	PASTURE.RELIEF
—appearance	FALSEHOOD		CIBATION
—friend	BACK-FRIEND	feel	
—representation	SUGGESTION	—joy or sorrow because	
falsehood	FALSE	of	RESENT
falsification	ADULTERY	—vexation at	ENVY
falsifier	FALSER	feeling together	CO-SENTIENT
familiar	PRIVY	feign	DISSEMBLE.FALSIFY
—acquaintance	HABITUDE	feigned	PERSONATE
—friend	GOSSIP	fel(d)spar	FELSPATH
—to all	GENERAL	fellow	JACK.WAG
fan	FLABELLUM	—Christian	EVEN-CHRISTIAN
fanciful notion	REVERIE	—lodger	INMATE
fancy	FANTASY.PHANTASY	felsite	FELSTONE
	WEEN	female	
fang	PHANG	—camp follower	LEAGUER-LADY
fantastic creation	WHIM		LEAGUER-LASS
far		—child	MAID-CHILD
—fetched	FAR-FET	—ruler	GOUVERNANTE
—through	THROUGHLY	fence	HAY
farcical interlude or afterpiece	JIG	—in with posts	IMPALE
farcy (glanders)	FARCIN	ferment (liquid)	FRET

ferrule	VERREL	fire	
festival day	GAUDY	—engine	WATER-ENGINE
festivity	GAUD.TRIUMPH	—work	WATERLOO CRACKER
fetch	FET(T)	firm	SICCAR.SICKER
fetched	FET	—grip	HANDFAST
—from distant place		first	
	FAR-FETCHED	—experience	MAIDENHEAD
fetter	BILBOES	—use	MAIDENHEAD
feudal		—born	PRIMOGENIT
—land division	VILL	firstly	ONCE
—right to choose spouse of		fish	
vassal's heir	MARITAGE	—carrier	RIPP(I)ER
—tax	TALLAGE	—hook	ANGLE
few	WHEEN	—pond	VIVER
fictitious suit	FINE	fist	NEIF.NEIVE.NIEF.NIEVE
fiddle	GU(E)	fitness	PROPERTY
fiddler	CROWDER	fix	PITCH
fidelity	TROTH	fixed	UNREMOVABLE
field	GLEBE	—payment	FARM
—glass	PROSPECT	—quantity	RATE
fierce	STOUT	flag	ANCIENT.PAVILION
fiery	FRAMPOLD	flat	
fight	CAMP	—part	PLAT
—for	DEBATE	—thing	PLAT
—with knives	SNICKERSNEE	flatter	CLAW.GLOZE.STROKE
SNICK OR SNEE.STICK OR SNEE		flatterer	COURT-DRESSER
SNICK-A-SNEE.SNICK AND SNEE		flattery	COURT HOLY WATER
fighter	GLADIATOR	flavour	GUST
fighting spirit	GAME	flax fibre or seed	LINE
figure	IDOL	flay	UNCASE
filbert	FILBERD	flee from	ESCHEW
filch	DRIP.LURCH	fleet	FLIT(T)
fill		fleeting	FLIT(T)
—full	FULFIL	flesh-colour	CARNATION
—up a deficiency in	SUPPLY	fleur-de-lis	FLOWER-DELICE
—with people	EMPEOPLE		FLOWER-DE-LUCE
fillet	FASCIA	flight of	
filling completely	FULFILLING	—larks	EXALT
film over the eye	WEB	—steps	GRE(E)CE.GRECIAN
filth	GORE		GRE(E)SE.GREESING
final settlement	FINE		GRESSING.GRI(E)CE
find fault with	PINCH		GRISE.GRIZE.SCALE
fine	ISSUE.PURE.UNLAW	flighty girl	GIG
—cloth	SINDON	fling (oneself)	LANCE
—paid by tenant's heir	RELIEF	flintlock	SNAPHA(U)NCE
—paid on marriage of daughter			SNAPHAUNCH
	MERCHET	flirt	MASH.PICKEER
—woollen cloth	PUKE	—with	COQUETTE
finger bowl	WATER-GLASS	float	FLEET.WAVE

flogging	WHIPPING-CHEER
floor	PLANCH
flout	FRUMP
flow	RAIL
flowerpot	BOUGHPOT.BOWPOT
flue	TEWEL
fluoride	FLUATE
flush	GILD
flying about	VOLATIC
foiled	NAUGHT
fold	PLIGHT.PRAN(C)K(E)
follow	USE
—after	ENSUE
followers	SEQUEL
fondness	WELL-LIKING
fool	ANTICK.FON
	PATCH.SOT.ZANY
foolish	FOND.PEEVISH
football	CAMP
footing	TROD
footpad	SCAMP
fop	FANTASTIC.MUSCADIN
foppish	FALLAL.FANTASTIC(AL)
for	
—love's sake	PARAMOUR
—the time being	PRESENTLY
forage	PICKEER
forbid	DEFEND.DISCHARGE
	FOR(E)SAY
	FOR(E)SPEAK.WARN
force	VIOLENT
—again	RENFORCE
—back	RECOIL
—open	SPORT
forcible	VIVE
forecourt	VESTIBULE
foreign	FORINSECAL
	OUTLANDISH
—coin bearing head	POLL
forenoon	UNDERN
foreshow	FIGUE
forestall	LURCH.PREVENT
forester	WALKER
—'s rights	PU(L)TURE
foretaste	ANTEPAST
foretokening	SOOTH
forfeit	CHEAT.FOR(E)GO
forgot	FORGAT
forgotten	FORGOT

fork of the body	TWIST
form	
—a scum	MANTLE
—by carving	INSCULP
—into community	EMPEOPLE
—into knot	KNIT
former	FORE
former(ly)	WHILE-ERE.WHILOM
formidable	STOOR.STOUR
	STOWRE.STURE
forming a thicket	QUEACHY
	QUEECHY
forsake	DESTITUTE.FORLESE
	WAIVE
forsaken	LORN
forsooth	QUOTHA.MARRY
forswear	REN(A)Y.RENEY
forthwith	EFT
fortified	
—dwelling	PEEL-HOUSE
	PEEL-TOWER
—town	PLACE
fortify	INSCONCE
fortress	PLACE
fortunate	SEELY
fortune	EVENT
forty	QUADRAGESIMAL
—days of Lent	QUADRAGESIMA
fought	FOUGHTEN
foul	HARLOTRY.PAW(PAW)
foulness	SOILINESS
founder of colony	OECIST
four branches of	
mathematics	QUADRIVIUM
fourth part	FARDEL.FARTHING
frankpledge	FRITHBOHR
frantic	PHRENTICK
fraud	CONVEYANCE
fraudulent	COVINOUS
fraught	FREIGHT
freckle	FERN(I)TIC(K)LE
	FAIRNITIC(K)LE
	FERNYTIC(K)LE
free	VINDICATE.VOID
—booter	SNAPHA(U)NCE
	SNAPHAUNCH
—from hindrance	EXPEDITE
—passenger	CAD
—villager	VILLEIN

freely organised composition	RHAPSODY
freeze	FRIZE
freighted	FREIGHT
frenzical	PHRENSICAL
frenzy	PHRENITIS.PHRENSY
frequent	HABITUATE.PRACTISE
fret	VEX
—into anger or dismay	GRATE
fretful	FRAMPOLD
friar licensed to beg	LIMITER
Friday	PARASCEVE
friend	INGLE
frieze	FRIZE
frightful	UGLY
frill	CHITTERLING
fringe	GUARD
—of false hair	TOUR
frisk	FISK
frock coat	SURTOUT
frog	PADDOCK
from	FRO
—the east	EOTHEN
front of top of head	FORETOP
froth on beer	YEAST
froward	AWKWARD
fruit pip	PIPPIN
fruit preserved in syrup	SUCKET
fruits of own actions	BRINGINGS FORTH
frustration	FOIL
full	
—of moans	GROANFUL
—speed	RANDOM
fully equal	PEREGAL
funeral	
—pyre	BALE-FIRE
—undertaker	UPHOLDER
furnish	BEDIGHT.BESEE
	PREPARE
—with a loft	LOFT
furniture	TIRE
further	FURDER
fuse	COLLIQUATE
fustet	FUSTIC.FUSTOC
gabble prayers	PATTER
gad	FISK
gadfly	BRIZE
gage	WAGE

gain	ESCHEAT.THRIFT.WIELD
—anew	REPRISE
gallery	ALURE
gallop	WALLOP
gallows	GALLUS.NUB
	NUBBING-CHEAT
game	NINE MEN'S MORRIS
	PARTY
—with cherry stones	CHERRY-PIT
—with pins of wood	LOGGATS
gang	GING
garb	VESTIMENT
garden	ARBOUR
gargle	GARGARISE
	GARGARISM.GARGARIZE
garland	GIRLOND
	SHROUD.WEED
garment	VESTIMENT
garrison	STUFF
gatekeeper	WARDEN
gauge	SCANTLING
gay	BONNY.BONNIE
—fellow	GAILLARD.GALLIARD
gaze at	WAIT (UP)ON
geld	GELT
general run or sense	TENOUR
genius	ENGINE.INGINE
gentile	ETHNIC
gentle	MANSUETTE
gentleman-at-arms	PENSIONARY
gentlemanly	JA(UN)TEE
gentlemen	LORDINGS
gently	FAIRISH
genuine	ENTIRE
German	ALMAIN.DUTCH
get	FALL
—along somehow	SCAMBLE
—at	AREACH
—by heart	RECORD
—goods on credit	FINEER
—over	OVERGET
—the better of	WIN OF
—the start of	LURCH
—well	RECURE
getting	
—on	TOWARD
—out of bed	LEVEE
giant	ETEN.ETTIN.ROUNCEVAL
gibbet	POTENCE

gibe	GLEEK	—away from	VOID
gimbal	GIMMAL	—before	PREVENT
gin	MAX	—down	VAIL
—and treacle	MAHOGANY	—faster than	PREVENT
gipsy	EGYPT	—forward	PRETEND
girded up	SUCCINCT	—little by little	DRIB
girdle	WAIST	—swiftly	STRIP
girl	GILL.JILL.KINCHIN-MORT	—to law	LAW
	PIGEON	—to unfashionable part	
give	TAKE	of theatre	MOB IT
—a sharp blow to	WHERRET	—wrong	MISS
	WHIRRET	goat	GATE
—an example of	ENSAMPLE	goblin	PUG
—as a remedy	EXHIBIT	God	GOG
—birth to young	YEAN	—like	GODLILY
—distinction or honour		—save	UDS
to	ILLUSTRATE	God's	UDS
—form to	INFORM	—(eye)lid	SLID
—in	KNOCK UNDER	—heart	SHEART
—one satisfaction	DO ONE	—life	SLIFE
	REASON	—light	SLIGHT
—pleasure to	PLEASURE	—nails	SNAILS
—success	SPEED	—wounds	OONS
—up	FORBEAR.RESPITE	gold	SOL
—vogue to	VOGUE	golf	GOFF
giving		good	RUM.SEELY
—freedom	LAXATIVE	—bargain	GOOD-CHEAP
—of medicine	EXHIBITION	—condition	PLIGHT
glad	FAIN	—evening	GOOD-DEN
glance	EY(E)LIAD.TWEER.TWIRE		DEN
glassy	GLAZEN	—for nothing	NAUGHT
glazed	GLAZEN	—fortune	SPEED
gleam	SHEEN	—luck to	FAIR (BE)FALL
—of light	LEAM.LEME	—many	WHEEN
gliding	LAPSE	—morning	GOOD-MORROW
—movement in dancing	SLUR	gossip	AUNT
glint	GLENT	gourmand	GORMAND
glisten	GLISTER	government	REGENCE
glittering ornament	SPANG	governor	GREAVE.GRIEVE
gloomy	WAN		RECTOR
glorify	GLORY	—of Papal province	LEGATE
gloss over	SOOTHE	—of town or district	WARDEN
glossy	POLITE	—of Moldavia	GOSPODAR
glow	LEAM.LEME		HOSPODAR
glum	GLUMPISH	—of Wallachia	GOSPODAR
glutton	LURCHER		HOSPODAR
go	BING.TRADE	gracious	HANDSOME.HEND
	WEND.WIND	graft	GRAFF.IMP
—astray	MISGO	granary	GIRNEL

grand	
—father	GRANDSIRE
—mercy	GRAMERCY
—ship	ARGOSY
—son	NEPHEW
—thanks	GRAMERCY
grant	CONDESCEND.PAY
—of money to king	SUBSIDY
—religious liberty	INDULGE
—time	FRIST
—to ministers	REGIUM DONUM
grantor's warranty	WARRANDICE
grape	WINE-BERRY
grasp	HENT
grassy plot or seat	ARBOUR
gratification	EASEMENT.GUST
gratuity to servants or officers	
of court	GLOVE-MONEY
gravel	GRIT
grazing ground	HERDWICK
grease	ENSEAM.SMEAR
great	MUCH.STOOR.STOUR
	STOWRE.STURE
—auk	PENGUIN.PINGUIN
—quantity	MICKLE
—Roll of the Exchequer	
	PIPE ROLL
—thanks	GRAMERCY
greater part	HEFT
greenhorn	PUT(T)
greet	HALSE
grey	GRIS(E).GRISEOUS
—fur	GRIS(E)
grief	GRAM(E)
	TEEN(E).TENE
grieve	RUE.VEX
grim	GRISY
grin	SNEER
grisly	GRISY
grocer	PEPPERER
groom	COISTREL.COISTRIL
	COYSTREL.COYSTRIL
groomsman	PARANYMPH
grooved border	SWAGE
gross in language	LIBERAL
grossly fat person	FUSTILUGS
ground plan	PLATFORM
grounds	WALK
group	GLOBE.SORT

grow	
—in wealth	INCREASE
—rich	RICH
—worse	WORST
growing	
—beneath	SUBNASCENT
—under water	DEMERSED
growl	GROIN
grown	WAXEN
grudge	ENVY.MALIGN
grumble	GROIN
grunt	GROIN
guarantee	VOUCHSAFE
	VOUTSAFE.WARRANDICE
	WARRANTISE
guard	WARD
guardianship	TUITION
guardship	ARMOUR
guess	AREAD.AREDE.ARREEDE
guile	DOLE
guileless	SACKLESS
guinea fowl	TURKEY
—hen	TURKEY-HEN
gullet	WEAZAND
gullible person	CHIAUS.CHOUSE
gunner's assistant	MATROSS
gunwale	PORTLAST.PORTOISE
gush	RAIL
habit	WON
hackneyed	PROSTITUTE
hair	STRAMMEL.STRUMMEL
—on horse's hoof	CRONET
—ornament	POMPOON
—pad	TOQUE
half	
—boot	START-UP
—guinea	SMELT
—penny	MAG.MAIK.MAKE
	MAGPIE.MAIL(E).PORTCULLIS
halter	WITHE
hand	HOND
handing over	LIVERY
handkerchief	MUCKENDER
	ORARIUM
handle	HAND
—clumsily	GAUM.GORM
—of dagger	DUDGEON
handsome	FEAT(E)OUS
	FEATUOUS.FEATURELY

handy	HANDSOME	—good constitution	
hang	HONG.JUSTIFY.KILT		WELL-TEMPERED
	NUB.TRUSS	—lived through many winters	
hanger	BASELARD		WINTERED
—on	CAD	—memory	MINDFUL
hanging	TAPIS	—natural ability	INGENIOUS
hangman	NUBBING-COVE	—virtue or efficacy	VIRTUAL
—'s rope	TIPPET	hawk	
haphazard meal	SCAMBLING	—in first year	SOAR(E).SORE
happen	TIDE	—'s nostril	NARE
happening	WEIRD	—'s quarry	MARK
happy	SEELY	hawker of broadsheets	
harangue	SPEECH		SPEECH-CRIER
harass	TROUNCE	hawthorn	ALBESPINE
hard			ALBESPYNE
—drinking	CAROUSE	hazard	VENTURE.WAGE
—plight	QUANDARY	hazardous	NICE
hardihood	HARDIMENT	—undertaking	EMPRISE
hardly	UNE(A)TH.UNEATHES	head	COSTARD
	UNNETHES	—and shoulders of a ling	POLL
hardship	STRESS	—dress	HEAD.HEAD-TIRE.TIRE
hare	WAT	—with flaps	LAPPET-HEAD
harlot	PUG.WAGTAIL	—of a herring	COB
harm	BANE.WREAK	—of frankpledge or	
harmonise	ATONE.SALVE	tithing	HEADBOROUGH
harmony	CONCENT	—wind	DEAD WIND
—in thirds and		headlong	PROCLIVE
sixths	FA(UX)BURDEN	—fall	PRECIPICE
harm physically	WRONG	heal	SAIN
harrow	HERSE	health	HAIL.HEAL
harsh	ASPER.STOOR.STOUR	healthy	SANE.WELL-DISPOSED
	STOWRE.STURE	heap of battle corpses	CARNAGE
hart in third year	SPADE	hearse	HERSE
	SPAY(AD).SPAYD	hearten	HEART
hasten	URGE	heartstricken	HEART-STROOK
hateful	LO(A)TH	heat	CALORIC.FLUSTER
haughtiness	HOGEN-MOGEN	heathen	ETHNIC
haughty	SUPERB	heathenism	HEATHENDOM
haunch	HANCH		HEATHENESSE
have		heavens	REGION
—a liking for	AFFECT	heavily armed soldier	
—as essence	CONSIST-IN		GALLO(W)GLASS
—sex with	KNOW	heaving	HEFT
—an inkling	SMOKE	hedge	HAW.HAY.MOUND
—lustre	SHEEN	heel	HEALD
—traffickings	TRINKET	—over suddenly	SEEL
—underhand dealings	TRINKET	height	HIGHT(H)
having		—of exaltation	RUFF(E)
—friends	FRIENDED	heiress	FORTUNE

hele (dialect)	HELL	—in tilting	TAINT
heliotrope	GIRASOL(E)	—it off	FADGE
hellenising Jew	GREEK	hoard	HOORD.MUCKER.SPARE
helm	STERN.TIMON	hoax	FUN.GULL.SHAM
helmsman	TIMONEER	hobble for horse	PASTERN
help	STEAD.SUPPLY	hoist	HOISE
—in trouble	BEETMISTER	hoisted	HOISED.HOIST
—to success	SPEED	hold	HOLT
helped	HOLP(EN)	—a late revel	WAKE
hemp	NECK-WEED	—together	CONSIST
herb	WORT	holding of land	ROOM
herdsman	HERD-GROOM	hole in wall for light	DREAM-HOLE
hereditary	SUCCESSIVE	holiness	HALIDOM
hero	EORL		SANCTIMONY
hidden	ABSTRUSE.DE(A)RN	hollow enclosed part	WEM(B)
—implication	EMPHASIS		WEAMB
hide	PELL	holy	SANCTIMONIOUS
hideous	LOATHLY	—place or thing	HALIDOM
high		homage	MANRED
—birth	GENEROSITY	homely	RUSSET
—Churchman	HIGH-FLIER	homespun	RUSSET
	HIGH-FLYER	homestead	HOMESTALL.TOFT
—Church Tory	TANTIVY	home-thrust	HAY
—cork shoe	PANTOF(F)LE	homily	PRONE
	PANTOUFLE	honey	
—minded	GENTLE	—dew	MILDEW
—official	REEVE	—moon	HONEYMONTH
—pasture-ground	WALK	—suckle	CAPRIFOLE
—spirits	HEYDAY	hoop round	EMBAIL
—standing	WORSHIP	hoot	WHOOT
Highland chief's attendant		hornbook	BATTLEDOOR
	G(H)ILLIE		BATTLEDORE
highway		horology	HOROLOGIUM
—man	HI(GH)JACKER.SCAMP	horrible	GRISY.UGLY
—robbery	LATROCINIUM	horse	
	LATROCINY	—cloth	TRAP
hill	LOW	—covering	FOOT-CLOTH
—crest	KNAP	—doctor	HORSE-LEECH
hillock	KNAP	—fly	BRIZE
hinder	EMBAR.IMPEACH.LET	—man used for light	
hindrance	LET	work	HOBBLER
hinge	GEMMAL	—'s pack strap	WANTY
hinged window	SHOT-WINDOW	—soldier	RUTTER
hired		hospital	SPITAL.SPITTLE(-HOUSE)
—assassin	BRAVE	hospitaller	HOSTEL(L)ER
—drudge	HACKNEY	host	HARBINGER
—thug	BULLY	hostage	PLEDGE
hire for pay	WAGE	hostel	ENTRY
hit	HAY	—for travellers	HOSPITAL

hostess	LANDLADY
hostile	INFEST
hostility	ENVY
hot	WHOT
—bathing establishment	
	HOTHOUSE
hound	BRACH
hour	HOWRE
house for receipt of stolen	
goods	STALLING-KEN
household management	
	ECONOMICS
housewife	HUSSY.HUSWIFE
hover	WAVE
howsoever	HOWSO
hubbub	LEVEL-COIL
huge	HIDEOUS
humble	SILLY.PLUCK.DEMISSIVE
humbug	HOOKEY WALKER
humility	LOWLIHEAD
humorous	LUDICROUS
hunchback	URCHIN
hundredweight	QUINTAL
hung	HONG
hunter's horn call	MOT
hunting ground	WALK
hurdy-gurdy	SYMPHONY
hurricane	HURRICANO
hurt	GRIEVE.NOY.NUISANCE
hurtful	NAUGHT
husband	FEARE.FEER
	FE(E)RE.LORD.PHEERE
—man	CARL.HUSBAND
hush up	HUDDLE
hushed	WHIST
hussif	HUSSY
hypnotism	BRAIDISM
hypochondria	HIP.HYP
hysteria	MOTHER
I am ready to accompany	
you	HAVE WITH YOU
I beg your pardon	ANAN
iatrochemical	CHEMIC
idiot	NATURAL.NIDGET
idle	
—fancy	FLAM
—report	TOY
—tale	TOY
idols	HIGH-PLACE
if	AN.GIF
ignorant	INGRAM.INGRUM.LEWD
—priest	LACK-LATIN
ilk	YLKE
ill	
—advised	OVERSEEN
—conduct	MISCARRIAGE
—humour	RHEUM
—mannered fellow	JACK
—will	ENVY.MAU(L)GRE
imagination	WIT
imagine	FANTASY.PHANTASY
—falsely	FEIGN
imagined	FEIGNED
—substance	MAGNESIA
imbue	TINCT
immature	UNSIZ(E)ABLE
immediately	INCESSANTLY
immerse	DEMERSE
immoral	NAUGHT.UNHONEST
immure	ENCLOISTER
imp	URCHIN
impair	APPAIR.EMPERISH
	IMPEACH.WRONG
impart	IMPUTE
impassable	INVIOUS
impede	IMPEACH.PESTER
impending	TOWARD
imperceptibly	UNSENSIBLY
impetuous	STURDY
implement	LOOM
import	CARRIAGE
importance	ESTIMATION
importunately	INSTANTLY
impose upon	SHAM
imposter	FAITOR.FAITOUR
	PHANTASM
impoverish	EMPOVERISH.WASTE
impregnated	IMPREGNANT
impression	DINT
imprison	LUMBER
improve	BEET.BETE
impudence	BRONZE
impudent person	SAUCE
in	ON
—another way	OTHERGATES
	OTHERGUESS
—as much as	WHENAS
—company	IN FERE.YFERE

—comparison with	IN RESPECT OF
—dishabille	MOBBED
—exact order	IN PRINT
—extreme danger	PERDU(E)
—front	AFRONT
—good condition	TAUGHT
	WELL-LIKING
—great excitement	IN HIGH LEG
—hardship	UNE(A)TH.UNEATHES
	UNNETHES
—inner room	WITHIN
—order to	FOR TO
—part	PARCEL
—particular	IN SPECIAL
—practice	PRACTIC
—ruins	RUINATE
—short	AT A WORD.ONCE
—some degree	SOMEDEAL
—spite of	MALGRADO
	MAU(L)GRE
—the direction facing one	
	TOWARD
—the manner of	UPSEE.UPS(E)Y
—times past	OF YORE
—vain	IN WASTE
—want	PENURIOUS
inadequate	UNEQUAL
incapable of being	
shaped	UNFASHIONABLE
incautious	WARELESS
incidence	TO-FALL
incidental occurrence	
	OBVENTION
incite	WHET
inclined	PROCLIVE
include	CONCLUDE
incommode	DISCOMMODE
inconvenience	DISCOMMODITY
inconvenient	UNGAIN
	UNHANDSOME
increase	ENCREASE.IMPROVE
—of wealth	THRIFT
incubus	EPHIALTES
incurable	RECURELESS
indecent	UNHONEST
—matter	STUFF
indecent and opprobrious	
	SCURRIL(E)

indeed	INSOOTH.IN GOOD TIME
indeed!	MARRY
indicate	PRETEND
indict	(EN)DITE
indifferent actor	JAY
indignation	INDIGNANCE
indirect	UNGAI
—action	WINDLASS
indite	(EN)DITE
individually	IN PARTICULAR
induce	ENTREAT
industrious	NOTABLE
indwelling	INEXISTENT
inelegant	UNPOLITE
inexperienced	UNSEEN
inexpressible	INEXPRESSIVE
infamous	OPPROBRIOUS
—person	NITHING
infantile thrush	SPRUE
infantry regiment	TERCIO
infect with measles	MEASLE
inferior	
—assistant	CAD
—Flemish cloth	MOCKADO
infest	PESTER
inflict bodily injury on	GRIEVE
inflow	INFLUENCE
infold	CLIP
inform	RESOLVE
information	WIT(TING)
informed of	KNOWING TO
informer	DISCOVERER
ingenious	ARTIFICIAL.QUAINT
	WITTY
ingenuity	ENGINE
ingoing	INFARE
ingot of gold or silver	WEDGE
inhabit	HABIT
inhabitant	INHABITOR
—of garret	GARRETEER
—of hundred	HUNDREDER
inhale tobacco smoke	DRINK
inhere in	CONSIST IN
inherence	INEXISTENCE
inheritance	FEE
injure	DE(A)RE.MISDO
injury	BALE.DISGRACE
	GRIEVANCE.NUISANCE
	TEEN(E).TENE

injustice	UNREASON
ink holder	INK-HORN
inland	WITHIN LAND
inn	WATERING-HOUSE
—keeper	ALE-DRAPER
innate character	KIND
innocent	SACKLESS
innovation	NOVITY
inopportune	IMPORTUNATE
inordinately large	UNSIZ(E)ABLE
inscribed with book titles	RUBRIC
insect	
—imagined to live in fire	PYRALIS
—pupa	NYMPH
—vermin	MOTH
insert between	INTERSERT
insignificant person	DANDIPRAT
	DANDYPRAT
insolent	WANTON
inspect urine	CAST WATER
inspection	PERSPECTIVE.INSPECT
installation	INSTALLMENT
instantly	INSTANTIAL
instrument	
—drum family	TYMPAN
—for winding spring of	
firearm	SPANNER
—of punishment	TUMBREL
	TUMBRIL
—of torture	ENGINE
insult	INJURY
insure	ENSURE
insurrectionary force	HEAD
intellect	INTELLECTUAL
intensify	INTEND
intent	WISTFUL
intentness	INTENT
inter	EARTH.INEARTH
intercept	WAYLAY
intercepting	INTERCIPIENT
intercession	INTERPELLATION
intercessor	MEAN
interchange	ENTERCHAUNGE
intercourse	INTERDEAL
interest	USURY
—on money	USAGE.USE
interfere with	MAR
interjection	
—of dismissal	VIA
—of failure to understand	ANAN
—of impatience	'SDEATH
—of thanks or surprise	MERCY
—pledging health	TOPE
interlaced with streams	
	WATER-SHOT
intermediate	MIDDLING
internal administration of	
state	POLICE
interpose	STICKLE
interpret	AREAD.AREDE
	ARREEDE
interpreter	TRUCHMAN
intimate	PRIVY.STRICT
intriguer	CHAMBERER.TRINETER
invention	WIT
inverted	AWKWARD
invite	BID
inviting	COASTING
involve	WIND(UP)
invulnerable	WOUNDLESS
inward	TOWARD
iris	FLOWER-DELICE
	FLOWER-DE-LUCE
Irish	
—labourer newly	
disembarked	GRECIAN
—magistrate	
	RESIDENT MAGISTRATE
	RM
irregular	HUMOROUS
issue	PROOF
item	PARCEL
—of news	OCCURRENT
itinerant	PIEPOWDER
jack maker	JACKSMITH
jackdaw	CHOUGH.DAW-COCK
jade	SPLEEN-STONE
jargon	PARLANCE
jasmine	JESSAMY
jealousy	YELLOWNESS
jemmy	BETTY
jerk	BRAID.YERK
jerking movement	JUT
jest	BOURD.JIG.TOY
jester	PATCH
—'s garb	MOTLEY
jetsam	JETSOM.JETSON
jettison	JETSAM

Jew	SMOUCH.SMOUS(E)	kindness	CANDOUR
jewelled head		king	COLE.LUD.OFFA.PRINCE
ornament	CARCANET	—'s bodyguard	HOUSE-CARL
jibe	BOB.GIRD	—'s companion	THANE
jingle	JIG	kingdom	REAME.REIGN
Joan of Arc	PUCELLE	kinship	SIB
job	SPOT	knave	BOY.VARLET
joined timber	CONTIGNATION	—in cards	MAKER.PUR
joining together	CONNEXIVE	knell	KNOLL
joint	ARTICLE	knew	COUTH
joke	GLEEK	knife	CUTTLE
journey	VOYAGE	knob	POMMEL
jovial	WANTON	know	CAN.WIS(H).WIST.WIT.WOT
joy	LIST	knowledge	CUNNING.WITTING
judge	CENSURE.SCAN.STICKLER	known	BEKNOWN.COUTH
judicial examination by		labour	MOIL
torture	QUESTION	labours of mind	WORKINGS
jug	NEWGATE	lace	GUARD
juggle	PALTER	—head-covering	SHADE
juggler	TREGETOUR	—up	TRUSS
juggling trick	SLIGHT	laciniation	DAG
jumping jack	PANTINE	lackey	SKIP-KENNEL
jury writ	VENIRE(FACIAS)	lacking in interest	INCURIOUS
justify	DARRAIGN(E).DARRAIN(E)	ladder	SCALE
	DARRAYN.DERAIGN	lady	BURD
jut	JET	—'s cape	MANTEEL
keep	WARRANT	—'s hood	SURTOUT
—away from	REFRAIN	—'s-maid	TIRE-WOMAN
—company	ASSORT	lamb	YEANLING
—in bondage or custody		lament	PLAIN
	WITHHOLD	land	MOULD
—out of the way	BE NAUGHT	—holding	ROOM
—under observation	WAIT (UP)ON	—tax	TALLAGE
—until following year	OVERYEAR	—tenure based on military	
—watch	WAKEN	service	KNIGHT SERVICE
keeper of a warren	WARRENER	—valued at a penny a	
kettledrum	TIMBAL.TYMBAL	year	PENNYLAND
key	KAIE	languish	QUAIL
—of C major	PROPER CHANT	lapdog	PUPPY
keynote	KEY	last	YESTERN
khan	CHAGAN.CHAM	—night	TONIGHT
kick	WINCE	late	LOW
—the limbs about	SPRAWL	lately	ALATE.NOW OF LATE
kid	YEANLING	later spring	MARTLEMAS
—glove	CHEV(E)RON	lavish	WASTEFUL
kidney	REIN	law-officer's cap	BIGGIN
kill	QUELL.MISDO.MORTIFY	lawsuit	PLEA
	SPILL.STRANGLE	lay	
kindly treatment	CHEER	—aside	VOID

—blame on	WITE.WYTE	liquid measure	WINE-MEASURE
—down	SUBMIT	listen	LIST
—hold of	LATCH	listening	ATTENT
—out in trade	OCCUPY	literary composition	STYLE
—table	COVER	litter	TEAM
laziness	IDLEHOOD	little	LITE.LYTE.WHEEN
lazy	LITHER	—ball	BULLET
—fellow	LUSK	—boat	NACELLE
lead astray	BEWILDER	—boy	DANDIPRAT.DANDYPRAT
leading idea	BURTHEN	—gentleman	FRANKLIN
leap	SA(U)LT	—hut	CABINET
leather		—star	STARNIE
—doublet	PLACCATE.PLACARD	livelihood	LIVELIHEAD
—water bottle	WATER-BOUGET	liveliness	LIVELIHEAD
leave out of consideration	WAIVE	lively	VIVE
leer	TWEER.TWIRE	living	
leg armour	JAMBEAU.JAMB(I)ER	—flesh	QUICK
legging	START-UP	—form	LIVELIHEAD
legislative assembly	MOOT	load	BURTHEN
legislature	STATES	loaded	LOADEN
leisure	RESPITE	loathe	UG
lengthen out	REACH	loathsome	LOATHLY
—in utterance	PROLATE	lock	SASSE
Lent	SCAMBLING-DAYS	lock-up	ROUND-HOUSE
leopard	LIBBARD.LUBBAR	lodestone	MAGNES
leper	MEAZEL.MESEL	lodge	BESTOW.KEEP
—hospital	SPITAL	lodgings for debtors	
	SPITTLE(-HOUSE)		SPUNGING-HOUSE
lesson to be memorised	LIRIPIPE	lofty	STEEP
	LIRIPOOP	log-throwing game	LOGGAT
let down	VAIL	logic	REDECRAFT
liable to censure	OBNOXIOUS	lollipop	LULIBUB
liberal	FRANK	long	PROLIX
libration of celestial		—ago	YORE
sphere	TREPIDATION	—baby clothes	LONG-COATS
lie		—for	EARN
—about	LUSK	longer	LENGER
—in ambush	WAIT	longest	LENGEST
life	LIVELIHEAD.QUICK	look	
light		—at	VISE
—blow	BOB	—at again	REVISE
—evening meal	VOIDE	—forward to	WAIT
—meal	UNDERN	—to	BESEE
lighting up	ILLUSTRATION	lookout	SPECULATOR
lightly cooked (eggs)	RARE	—place	TOOT
like	MARROW	loom	FRAME
limit	COAST.STINT.MARK	loose	
lineage	PARAGE	—character	RIBALD
lineal descendant	NEPHEW	—cloak	GABARDINE

—gown	SLAMMAKIN	—ready	ADDRESS.PRED
	SLAMMERKIN	—safe	SAFE
—greatcoat	WRAP-RASCAL	—scant	SCANTLE
—woman	MOB.NAUGHTY PACK	—stable	POISE.STABLISH
—wrap	NIGHT-RAIL	—the sign of the cross over	SAIN
lord	SIRE	—ugly	UGLY
lose	GO BY THE WORST	—up	
	GO WITH THE WORST	—hastily	JUMP
—strength	PALL	—with cosmetics	PRIME
—vitality	DEAD	—war upon	WARRAY.WARREY
lost	BEWILDERED.LORN	—wheel-shaped	WHEEL
lot	WEIRD	—worse	WORST
louvre	LOVER	male guinea fowl	TURKEY-COCK
love	AFFECT	malice	SPLEEN
—making	SWAINING	maliciously	UNHAPPILY
lover	PARAMOUR.SWAIN	manage	MANURE
Low Churchman	LOWBOY	manageable	YARE
lowborn		manganese	MAGNESIA
—fellow	LOON		MAGNESIUM
—character	RIBALD	manner	WISE
lower	SUBMIT.VAIL	manor	VILL
luck	VENTURE	manorial holding	HUSBANDLAND
lump	LOAF	mantle	ROCHET.ROCQUET
lusty	RANK	manual	MECHANICAL
luxurious	WANTON	map of the world	MAPPEMOND
mace	MAUL	marked attention	PARTICULARITY
mad	LYMPHATIC	market	VENT
madam	MISTRESS	—town	PORT
made of	EUGHEN.EWGHEN	marriage	HYMEN
	YEWEN	married woman	
magnetic	ADAMANTINE		WOMAN OF THE WORLD
magnify	MULTIPLY	Martinmas	MARTLEMAS
maid	PUCELLE	marvel	MARL(E)
—of Orleans	PUCELLE	marvellous	WOND(E)RED
maiden	BURD	marzipan	MARCHPANE
main body	CONTINENT	mask	VIZARD
—of army	BATTALIA	masked sword-dance(r)	
make			MATACHIN
—a difference	SKILL	mass	MESS.SAL(A)MON
—a lord	LORD	—of rock or stone	QUARRY
—a mouth	MOE	master	MAISTER.MAS(S)
—angry	WRATH		MES(S).SIRE
—away with	RID	match	COPE.MARROW
—bold	BOLDEN		PARAGON.SAMPLE
—bright	ILLUSTRATE	mate	MAKE.MARROW
—clear to the mind	ILLUSTRATE	material	MASS
—famous	FAMOUS	—universe	KIND
—hairless	PILL	matter	MASS.SENTENCE.SKILL
—level with the ground	SLIGHT	—of discourse	PLACE

matters of the intellect	INTELLECTUALS	—expedition	VOYAGE
may	MOTE.MOUGHT	milk	MANSUETTE
mayor	PORTREEVE	mind	WIT
mead	MEATH(E)	mineral dug from earth	FOSSIL
meadowsweet	MEAD-SWEET	miscellany	RHAPSODY
	MEADWORT	mischief	BALE
meal	MEAT.MESS	misery	BALE
—time	MEAL-TIDE	misfortune	CHANCE
mean	MEDIUM.MENE.SOUND		DECAY.RUTH
meaning	SENTENCE	misleading	SINISTER
measure	BE METE.MEED	misshapen egg	COCKNEY
meatless days	BANIAN-DAYS	missile	MISSIVE
medal	MODEL	missiles	ARTILLERY
mediate	STICKLE	mistaken	OVERSEEN
mediator	MEAN	mistletoe	MISLETOE.MISSEL
medical	PHYSIC	mistress	WENCH
medicinal	PHYSICAL	mitigate	ASLAKE
medley	RHAPSODY	mix	(CO-)MEDDLE.MENG(E)
meet	OCCUR		MING.MOULD
—in advance	PREVENT	mixed	ME(I)NT.MENGED
—on the way	OBVIATE		MEYNT.MINGED
melt	COLLIQUATE.RELENT	mixing	CONTEMPERATION
melting	COLLIQUABLE	mixture	MIXTION
	COLLIQUANT.COLLIQUATION	—of liquids	BALDERDASH
mend	BEET.BETE	mock orange	PIPE-TREE
menial of lowest grade	RIBALD	mockery	MOCKAGE
mental		mocking ballad	JIG
—activity	WORKING	model	PRECEDENT
—speculation	PROJECT	—of fashion	MODE
mention	MIND.REMEMBER	moderate	CHASTISE
merciless	WANTON		CHASTIZE.MEAN
mercurial character	MERCURY	modest	PUDENT.PUDIC
mere	MEER	moisture	HUMOUR
merry		molar	WANG(-TOOTH)
—andrew	JACK-PUDDING	moment	PUN(C)TO
	PICKLE-HERRING	monastery	MINSTER
—mood	MERRY PIN	money	CRAP.ROWDY
metal non-malleable	SEMI-METAL	—grubber	MUCKER
metaphor	TRANSUMPTION	monkey	JACKANAPES.MEERKAT
meum (plant)	SPICKNEL	monstrosity	MONSTRUOSITY
mica	DAZE	monstrous	MONSTRUOUS
middle		monumental marble	TOUCH
—class revolutionary	MUSCADIN	mope	PEAK
—of day or night	WAIST	more	MO(E)
midwife	LUCINA	mortal	WORLDLING.WORLDLY
migraine	MEGRIM	motto	MOT.POESY
military		moulded border	SWAGE
—engine	TREBUCHET	mound	MOT(T)E.MOTE-HILL
		mount	STY

mountebank	ANTIC	narrowly	STRAIT
	SALTIMBANCO	native-born	KINDLY
mousetrap	SAMSON('S) POST	natural	KINDLY
mouth	NEB	naturally able	INGENIOUS
move	MEVE.MOOVE.QUATCH	nature	KIND
	QUETCH.QUITCH.TROLL	naval screening-cloth	
—faster	PUT ON		WAISTCLOTH
—off	WALK	nave	NEF
—on	WAG	navigation manual	
moveable			PORTOLAN(O) (CHART)
—shelter for besiegers	SOW	near	FORBY.NIE
—stage	PAGEANT	neat	FEAT(E)OUS
moving	MOTIVE		FEATUOUS.NET(T)
much	MICKLE.MUCHEL	neck	HALSE.SWIRE
muffle	MOB(B)LE	—covering	PARTLET
—the head	MOB	—tie	WATERFALL
muffler	MUFFETTEE	neckerchief	NECKATEE
mugger	SCOWRER	needle	NEELD.NEELE
mulberry tree	SYCAMINE	needy	WANTING
mule	MOYL(E)	négligé	MOB
multitude	NUMBER	negotiation	PRACTICE
mummy	ANATOMY	negotiations	INTERDEAL
municipal officer	VARLET	negro	NIGER
murder	QUELL	neighbourhood	VOISINAGE
murderer	MURTHERER	neighbouring	NEIGHBOUR
muscatel	MUSCADINE	neither Christian nor	
muscle	MOUSE	Jew	HEATHEN
musical		nevertheless	ALGATE
—composition	MUSIC	news	ADVERTISEMENT
—instrument	ORGAN	newness	NOVITY
—instruments	MUSIC	nick of time	ARTICLE
—various	SYMPHONY	niggard	PUCKFIST
musicians employed at municipal		niggardly	NITHING
ceremonies	WAITS	nigh	NY
must	MOTE	night	
mutiny	MUTINE	—cap	BIGGIN
mutual dealings	INTERDEAL	—dress	NIGHT-SHIFT
nag	ROUNCY	—mare	EPHIALTES
name	CLEEP.CLEPE.HETE	nimble	FLIPPANT.WIGHT
	HIGHT.NEMN	nimbly	YARELY
—in list or document	ENGROSS	no matter what	FALL BACK
named	BENEMPT.BYNEMPT		FALL EDGE
	YCLEPT.HIGHT.NEMPT	noble	GENEROUS.GENTLE
	YCLEPED.YCLEPT		THANE
narcissus	ROSE OF SHARON	—youth	CHILD(E).CHYLDE
narrate	RECORD	nobleman's bodyguard	
narrative	PROSE		HOUSE-CARL
narrow	STRAIT.STRICT	noise	BRUIT
narrowing	REBATEMENT	noisy	STREPENT

nominate	VOICE	obedient	BUXOM
non-Christian	SARACEN	obeisance	OBEDIENCE
noodle	DAW-COCK	object	
	HODDY-DODDY	—forfeited for pious	
normal	JUST	use	DEODAND
Norfolk strong ale	NOG	—of taunts	TAUNT
nose		—of terror	BUG
—band for horse	MUSROL	—to	QUARREL
—bleed	YARROW	objection	QUARREL
nostril	NARE	objectionable	PERT
nostrum	SECRET	obliging	OFFICIOUS
not	NE	oblique	AWKWARD
—bated	BATELESS	obscene	PAW(PAW)
—burdened	UNBURTHENED	obscure	BLEND
—customary	UNCUSTOMED	obsequious person	WAGTAIL
—described	NONDESCRIPT	observance	TRIUMPH
—discovered without		observation	SPIAL
experiment	OCCULT	observe	SMOKE.SPECULATE.USE
—easily	UNEATH	obstinate	STIFF-HEARTED
—exquisite	INCURIOUS	obstruct	WAYLAY
—facetious	INFECITE	obstructed	LET
—fastidious	INCURIOUS	obstruction	LET.TRUMP
—fitting	UNDECENT	obverse of coin	CROSS
—handsome	UNDECENT	occupation of waiter	
—helped	UNHOLPEN		WAITERHOOD.WAITERING
—improbably	LIGHTLY	occupy	MANURE
—known	UNWIST	—oneself	TRADE
—made polished	UNFASHIONED	occur to	REMEMBER
—provided with	UNPURVEYED	occurrence	OCCURRENT
—to respect	DISRESPECT	octave of festival	UTAS
—used up	INEXHAUSTED	oddness	IMPARITY
—well up	UNSEEN	oeillade	EY(E)LIAD
note	COMMON-PLACE	of	ON
—G	GAMUT	—another kind	OTHERGATES
—in written music	PRICK		OTHERGUESS
notice	MIND	—good character	WELL-THEWED
notion	NOTICE	—high social standing	WORTHY
notwithstanding	MAU(L)GRE	—no	
	NATH(E)LESS(E).NAYTHLES	—avail	UNAVAILABLE
now	PRESENTLY	—effect	IN WASTE
number of people	CONSORT	—organisms of the same	
nun	VOWESS	species	UNIVOCAL
nuptials	HYMENALS	—silver	LUNAR
nurse	NOURICE	—stone	STONERN
nurture	NOUR(R)ITURE	—whatever kind	WHATSO
oaths	SBLOOD.SBODIKINS	offence	DEFAULT.DISTASTE
	SBUDDIKINS.ZBUD		INJURY
oatmeal porridge	POTTAGE	offend	DISTASTE
obedience	OBEISANCE	offer	PREFER.PRETEND

—as a pledge WAGE
—for sale UTTER
—greetings of a third
  person PRESENT
office MISTERY.MYSTERY
—in Court of Exchequer
  PIPE OFFICE
—of Chancellor CHANCERY
—of warden WARDENRY
officer
—who rounded up stray
  pigs HOG-REEVE
  HOG-CONSTABLE
—without command
  REFORMADO
official
—in lists MARSHAL
—permit PLACARD
—who clears the way WHIFFLER
offspring SPERM.STRAIN
old
—clothes ELD.YORE
—dealer FRIPPER(ER)
—shop FRIPPERY
—trade FRIPPERY
—person ELD
—time ELD.YORE
—woman AUNT.GRANDAM
  GRANNAM
omission BA(U)LK
on AN
—account of ALONG
—approval ON LIKING
—desperate enterprise PERDU(E)
—hand TOWARD
—lost cause PERDU(E)
—near or left side TOWARD
—purpose NONCE
—table ON THE TAPIS
—wheels AWHEELS
once WHILOM
one
—acting as surety MAINPERNOR
—after the other A-ROW
—apt to be fickle CHANGELING
—born under Mercury
  MERCURIAL
—bound to keep horse for
  military service HOBBLER

—given to enjoyment of
  senses EPICURE
—granting indulgences QUESTOR
—in charge of fences HAYWARD
—living within boundaries
  CONFINER
—sent before to arrange
  lodgings HARBINGER
—with coat of arms GENTLEMAN
one of
—a pair MARROW
—low rank SNOB
—worthless character PACK
—the rabble RASCAL
one who
—bartered SCORSE
—became surety PLEDGE
—cleared the table VOIDER
—complained PLAINANT
—constructed fortifications
  ENGINEER
—constructed military
  engines ENGINEER
—deposited money at
  interest PUTTER-OUT
—deserved hanging WAGHALTER
—dwelt in imagined
  security SECURITAN
—haunted draper's
  shops SILKWORM
—led astray SEDUCTOR
—plotted ENGINEER
—practised OCCUPIER
—put on a false pretence FACER
—sold short weight LEGER
—served in war SERVITOR
—talked nonsense TWADDLE
—was disliked WARLING
—was fantastical FANTASTIC
—was tolerated for paying
  the bill SHOT-CLOG
onward rush RACE
open (A)PERT
—space between woods LAWN
—to view UNVAIL(E)
opening OVERTURE
operate PLAY
operation URE
oppress OVERSET

oppressive	FAINT
optical/optics	PERSPECTIVE
oral	LIVELY
orchard	ARBOUR.ORCHAT
order	INSTITUTE.WILL
—of battle	BATTALIA
organ bellows	WIND-BAG
organised for rapid	
action	VOLANT
ornamental rosary bead	GAUD
ostentatiously vulgar	
person	SNOB
ostrich	ESTRICH.ESTRIDGE
otter	WATER-DOG
out	
—of kindness	PARAMOUR
—of the way	GEASON
—upon it	HARO.HARROW
outcast	WRETCH
outcome	PROOF
—of toil	LABOUR
outdo	SUPERATE
outer	UTTER
—garment	SURCOAT
outermost sphere	
	PRIMUM MOBILE
outflank	OVERWING
outlast	OUTDURE
outlaw a woman	WAIVE
outlawed	BROKEN
outlay	MISE
output	GET
outrageous	ENORMOUS
outride	OVERRIDE
outstrip	COTE.STRIP
outward appearance	SPECIES
—of promise	UPCOME
outwit	CROSSBITE
over	ORE
overbearing	SUPERCILIOUS
overcoat	SURTOUT
overcome	EVINCE.FORDO
	SUPERATE
—with hunger	A(N)HUNG(E)RED
	(A)HUNGRY
overflow	SURROUND
overflowing	REDUNDANT
overgarment	BRAT
overhang	OVERWHELM

overhanging	INCUMBENT
overpower	EVINCE
overpowering lustre	GLARE
overreach	LURCH.OUTGO
overrun	OVERREN
overshoe	PANTOF(F)LE
	PANTOUFLE
overspread	OVERCOME
overtake	OVERCATCH.OVERGET
	OVERRIDE
overthrown	PROFLIGATE
owner	LORD
ownership	FEE.PROPRIETY
oxygen	VITAL AIR
pack	
—horse	SUMMER
—load	SEAM
—of cards	PAIR
packet boat	POST
pah!	PAW
pain	WO(E)
—thought to be caused by a worm	
(e.g. toothache)	WORM
painful	BALE
pains	TEEN(E).TENE
paint	LIMN.PEINCT
—for face	FUCUS
painter	BRUSH.LIMNER
pair	TWAIN
pale	PALL.WHITELY
—blue	WATCHET
—by comparison	STAIN
palisade	STACKET
palisaded enclosure	PEEL
paltry	BALD
pampered effeminate person	
	WANTON
pan	WORK
panacea	DIACATHOLICON
pancake	FLAM(M).FLAUNE
	FLAWN
pander	BROKER
panegyric	ELOGE.ELOGY
	ELOGIUM
panic	AMAZE
pansy	PA(U)NCE.PAWNCE
Papal province	LEGATION
paramour	FRANION.LEMAN
parcel	SORT

pardon	GRACE	peevish	FRAMPOLD
parentage	BROOD	pellucid	SHEER
parish	TOWNSHIP	pelt with stones	LAPIDATE
park	WALK	pen-case	PENNER
parliament	THING	penalty	UNLAW
parliamentary bill	PETITION	pendant	BOB
parsimony	PARCIMONY	penned	PEND
part	PARTY.TWIN(E)	penny	D
partake	PERTAKE	peony	PINY.PION(E)Y
partition	TRAVIS.TREVIS(S)	people	FOLK
partly	PARCEL	perchance	PERCASE
—burned tree	RAMPICK.RAMPIKE	perfect	PERFET
partner	COMPANION	perform	EXERT.JUGGLE
pass	HALSE.PACE	performance	FUNCTION
—round the table	TROLL	—of music	LESSON
—the night	LIE	perhaps	BELIKE.PERCASE
passage	ALURE.PACE	periodical	
—in a book	PLACE	—muster to check	
passionate person	FUME	weaponry	WAPINS(C)HAW
password	WATCHWORD		WEAPON-S(C)HAW
past	FORBY		WAP(P)ENS(C)HAW
pastime	PASTANCE	—payment	PENSION
patch up	JUMP	perish	FORFAIR.STARVE
patchwork	MOTLEY	perjured	MANSWORN
path	STY.TROD	perquisite	VALES.VAILS
pattern	SAMPLER.SPOT	persistent diabolical	
pause	ALLOW	attack	OBSESSION
pawn	OPPIGNERATE	person	WIGHT
	OPPIGNORATE	—used as tool	ENGINE
—broker	LUMBERER	—with a tail	TAILARD
—shop	LUMBER	personal	
pay	YIELD	—appearance	CHARACTER
—out	DISPEND	—attendant	GENTLEWOMAN
—retribution for	ABY	personate	PRESENT
—wages to	WAGE	pert	BRISK
payment		—person	SAUCE.WAGTAIL
—for wet-nurse	NOURICE-FEE	pertain	LONG
—in goods	TRUCK SYSTEM	pertaining to	
—in lieu of military		—carrying	GESTATORIAL
service	WARD-CORN		GESTATORY
pea		—eggs	OVAL
—plants	PEASON	—generation	GENIAL
—shooter	TRUNK	—letters of the	
peace	FRITH	alphabet	LITERARY
pearl-grey	GRISEOUS	—marriage	GENIAL
peas	PEASON	—sight	VISIVE
peasant	PESA(U)NT.PEZANT	—whirlpool	VORAGINOUS
	SWAIN	perturbation	DISTEMPERATURE
peep-show	PERSPECTIVE	perverse	FROWARD

pestilence	MURRAIN	pineapple	PINA.PINE-CONE
pet	PEAT	pink	POUNCE
Peter's penny	ROME-PENNY	pip	PEEP
	ROME-SCOT	pippin	PIP
petitioner	ORATOR	piratical publisher	LAND-PIRATE
petticoat	PLACARD.PLACKET	pistil	POINTEL
petty	PELTING	pitch attained by bird of	
phantom	FEATURE	prey	PLACE
philosopher's stone	TINCTURE	pitched	(Y)PIGHT
philtre from mare	HIPPOMANES	pith of plants	MARROW
photography using		pity	PIETY
fluorides	FLUOROTYPE	placcate	PLACARD
phraseology	PARLANCE	place	DO
phrenetic	PHRENTICK	—for	
physical pain	WO(E)	—hawking	RIVER
physician	LEECH.MEDIC	—performance of	
	MEDICINER	penance	PENITENTIARY
physiognomy	VISNOMIE	—in favourable position	STATE
	VISNOMY	—of	
pickpocket	FILE	—abode	LIBKEN
pie		—retirement	RETIRE
—crust	COFFIN	—underneath	SUPPOSE
—of meat and eggs	LUMBER-PIE	placed	YPLAST
piece	PEECE	placket	PLACARD
—of		plague-spot	TOKEN
—cloth	PANE	plaintiff	PLAINANT
—doggerel	JIG	plait	PLIGHT
—music	LESSON	plan	MODEL.PLAT.PLATFORM
—needlework	SPOT	plane	
—news	NOVEL	—figure or surface	PLATFORM
—plunder	CHEAT	—tree	PLANTAIN
—work	SPOT	plank	PLANCH
—together	RHAPSODISE	plant	GRAFT
	RHAPSODIZE	—resembling animal	ZOOPHYTE
pieces of old rope	JUNK	platane	PLANTAIN
pierce	ENGORE.RIVE	platter	LANX
—horse's foot with nail	ACCLOY	play	
pike	PARTISAN	—the epicure	EPICURISE
pilchard	PILCHER		EPICURIZE
piles	FIG	—the fool	FON
pile up	BALK	—trick on	GLEEK
pilfer	NIM	—with	DELUDE
pilfered	NAM.NIMMED	—fingers	PADDLE
pilgrim's staff	BOURDON	—wooden sword	WASTER
pill	PEEL	playful	FLIPPANT
pillage	PEEL	plead	PERSUADE
pillory	TUMBREL.TUMBRIL	pleasant	AMENE.LUSTY
pimp	BROKER.BULLY		MERRY
pinafore	BRAT	—behaviour	PLEASANCE

—sound	EUPHONIA	pooh!	PUGH.TUSH
—words	FAIR WORDS	poor	SEELY.WANTING
pleasantness	PLEASANCE	—author	GARRETEER
please	AGGRATE.LIKE.LIST	pope	PAPA
pleasing	LIKING.LUSTY	populous part of country	INLAND
pleasure	PLEASANCE	porpoise	MEERSWINE
—of taste	GUST	port	LARBOARD
—seeking	PLEASURABLE	portable	
pleat	PINCH.PRAN(C)K(E)	—inkwell	INK-HORN
pledge	BORROW.ENGAGE	—organ	PORTATIVE
	SECURE.WAGE.WED	portcullis	CATARACT
—oneself to	BETROTH	portent	PRODIGY
plentiful (yield)	FOISON	portion	MEED.PIECE
plight	LIKING.SECURE	—of food and drink	SIZE
plighted	YPLIGHT	portrait	POURTRAICT
plot	PLOD	portray	PORTRAIT.POURTRAY
—of ground	PLAT	portrayed	POURTRAYD
plough	EAR.ERE		PURTRAID.PURTRAYD
plucked	PLUMED	position of honour	WORSHIP
plump	WELL-LIKING	positive	POZ(Z)
plunder	ESCHEAT.PEEL	possess	WIELD
	PILL.RAPE	possession	FEE.HAVEOUR
plunge	MERGE		HAVIOUR
pocket	PLACARD	possessions	AVER.WORTH
poem	DIT(T).POESY	possibility of recovery	RECOVER
poet	MAKER	post for tilting exercises	
—laureate	ARCH-POET		QUINTAIN
poetry	POESY	postman	POST
point	PIQUE	postpone	FRIST.REFER
	POYNT.PUN(C)TO	postponed	PROTRACTED
—at whist	CORNER	postulate	PETITION
—of perfection	POINT-DEVICE	posture	GESTURE
	POINT-DEVISE	posy	POESY.TUZZI-MUZZY
—of weapon	ORD	potash	KALI
pointed bar	GAD	potsherd	POTSHARD
poise	POYSE	pottage	PORRIDGE
poison	POYSON	powder	POULDER.POULDRE
poke	POTE		POUNCE
pole	PERCH	power	DANGER
policeman	RUNNER	—of explaining	INTERPRETATION
polished	POLITE	—of seeing	VISIBILITY
political	STATIST	powerless	IMPUISSANT
poll	DOD	practic	PRACTICK.PRACTIQUE
pollard	DOD	practice	URE
polluted	CANKERED	—of pastry-making	PASTRY
pomegranate	PUNIC APPLE	—with waster (fencing)	WASTER
pomp	TRIUMPH	practise	USE
ponder	POISE	—crystal-gazing	SCRY
poniard	POI(G)NADO	—extortion on	POLL

450

practising	PRACTIC
praise	LO(O)S
praiseworthy	PLAUSIBLE
prank	ESCAPE.GAUD.REAK.REIK
pranks	REAKS.REX
pranky	FROLIC
pray	BID
—thee	PRITHEE.PRYTHEE
prayer	BEAD
preach	PROPHESY
precede	PREVENT
precious	CHARY
—stone	JASPER
—metal	PLATE
preciousness	PRICE
pre-eminence	PREHEMINENCE
pre-eminently	ONLY
preen	PROIN(E).PROYN(E)
	PROIGN.WHET
preference	PRE-ELECTION
—for	MARK ON
prefix	PREPOSITION
pregnant	GREAT.QUICK
prejudge	PREJUDICE
prejudgment	PREJUDICE
preparation	ORDINANCE
	PARASCEVE
prepare	ADDRESS.INSTRUCT
prepared	YARE.BOUND
presbytery	CLASSIS
prescription	LEECHDOM
present	PREFER
—to mind	OBJECT
preserve	
—in sugar	CONSERVE
—unhurt	SALVE
press	STRIP
—hard	OVERSET
—together	CONSTIPATE
pretext	SALVO
prevail	PERSUADE
prevent	LET.SECURE
previous	FORE
price	PURCHASE
priests	MAGI
prince	
—of Moldavia or	
Wallachia	GOSPODAR
	HOSPODAR

—'s friend	PRIVADO
printed	PRINT
prison	LUMBER.NEWGATE
—chaplain	ORDINARY
privacy	PRIVITY
private	INWARD
—apartment	PARADISE
—end	SELF-END
—friend	PRIVADO
—marriage	HANDFASTING
—parts	SHAME
—property or right	PECULIAR
—room	CONCLAVE.GARDEROBE
privy	GARDEROBE.PRIVATE
	SIEGE
prize	PURCHASE
probably	BELIKE
probationary marriage	
	HANDFASTING
probe	TENT
proceed	FAND.FOND.TRACE
proceeding from divine	
grace	GRACIOUS
proceeds	AVAIL
proclamation	PLACARD
procuress	AUNT.BROKER
procuring	BROK(ER)AGE
profession	FUNCTION.MISTER
profile	PURFLE
profit	(A)VAIL.UTILITY
profitable	BEHOVEFUL
	BEHOVELY
profitless	WASTEFUL
profusely discharging	
	COLLIQUATIVE
profusion	LAVISH.WASTE
progeny	IMP.INCREASE
prohibit	DEFEND
projectile	FIREWORK
projecting window	
	SHOT-WINDOW
projector	SCHEMATIST
prolong	PROROGUE
prominent	EGREGIOUS
promise	BANK.BEHIGHT.BEHOTE
promising	TOWARDLY
prompt	EXPEDITE
promptly	BELIVE.TIGHT(LY).TIT
	TITE(LY).TYTE.YARELY

prone	PROCLIVE
proof	PREEVE.PREIF(E)
property	FEE.PROPRIETY
propitiation	PROPITIATORY
propogate	TRADUCE
	SUPPOSAL.PROPOSE
propriety	PROPERTY
prospect-glass	PROSPECT
prosperity	THRIFT.WEALTH
prostitute	COCKATRICE
	MUTTON.PLOVER
	PUBLIC WOMAN
	PUNK.STEW
protect	WARRANT
—with earthwork	ENSCONCE
—with sconce	ENSCONCE
protective covering	BARD
Protestant	RELIGIONER
Protestantism	RELIGION
protuberance	KNAP
protuberant part	WEM(B).WEAMB
proud	STIFF-RUMPT
	STOUT.SUPERB
prove	ASCERTAIN
	DARRAIGN(E).DARRAIN(E)
	DARRAYN.DERAIGN
	PREEVE
—to be true	SOOTHE
proved/proven	PREVE
proverb	PARABLE
provide	PREPARE
—battlements	BATTLE
—for	BESEE
—in advance	PREVENT
—with husband	HUSBAND
province	REAME
provision	STUFF
—in rotation	SHIFT
provisions	BELLY-TIMBER
—of the table	ENTERTAINMENT
prowess	VASSALAGE
prowl	PROLL
prowler	PROLER
prudent	CONSIDERATIVE.WARE
prune	PROIGN.PROIN(E)
	PROIN(E).PROYN(E).PRUINE
	PREWYN.SHRED
Prussia	(S)PRUCE
pshaw!	TUSH

psychosis	DERANGEMENT
public	APERT
—report or rumour	FAME
publication of book	EDITION
publisher	STATIONER
	UNDERTAKER
puck	PUG
puddle	FLUSH
puff	
—of wind	HUFF
—up	HUFF
pulley	TRICE
pulp of plants	MARROW
pulpit	CHAIR
pun	PUNDIGRION
punctilio	PIQUE.PUN(C)TO
puncture	POUNCE
punish	JUSTIFY.SHEND.VISIT
	WREAK
punishment	PINE.PYNE
	WAR(R)ISON
	WRACK.WREAK
puny	PUISNE
puppet show(man)	
	MOTION(-MAN)
purchaser	CHAPMAN
pure	MERE.NET(T)
—Dutch	HIGH DUTCH
purely	MERELY
purgative electuary	
	DIACATHOLICON
purify	CHASTISE.CHASTIZE
purity	CANDOUR
purple	PUNIC
purplish/black	PUKE
purport	TENOUR
purpose	CAST.PRETEND
	PURPORT.SHAPE
purse	BUNG
purser	NIP-CHEESE
pursue	PERSUE
push out of sight	HUDDLE
put	DO
—an end to	WASTE
—away	WAIVE
—down	DO DOWN
—forth	EXERT
—forward	PREFER
—in difficulty	STRAIT

—in front of	OBJECT
—off	FUB
—in time	PROTRACT
—one's seal to	ENSEAL
—or keep in loft	LOFT
—out	UTTER
—of countenance	DOR
—to	
—shame	REBUKE.SHEND
—trouble	PAIN
—under embargo	EMBAR
puzzle	PUSLE
quack	SALTIMBANCO
quadrate	QUARTILE
qualify	CONDITIONATE
quality	PROPRIETY
quarrel	SQUARE
quarry	CURRIE.CURRY
quay	KAY.KEY
queen	PRINCE
—bee	KING
question	SCRUPLE
quick	EXPEDITE.RATH(E).YARE
—tempered person	FUME
quickly	BELIVE.SWITH.YARELY
quiet	HUSH
quinsy	SQUINANCY
quire	QUAIR
quit	QUITE.VOID
quiz	SMOKE
quoth	QUOD
rabbit hole	CLAPPER
rabble	RASCAILLE.RASCAL
race	GOAL.ROD
—course	HIPPODROME
rack	TOUSE.TOUZE
	TOWSE.TOWZE
rag	ROW
rail	RAYLE
railway	GWR.LMS.LNER.SR
rain	RAYNE
raise one's hat	VAIL
raised edge	LEDGE
rake	SWINGE-BUCKLER
rally	REALLY.RELY
ramble	TROLL
rampart	RAMPIRE
range	RAUNGE
rank	CENSE.GREE.SIEGE

—of captain	CAPTAINRY
—with	FILE WITH
rant	TEAR A CAT.TEAR THE CAT
rapine	RAPE
rarely	SELD
rascal	RASCAILLE
rash	HASTY-WITTED
rate	ROW
—of tax	CENSE.CESS
rather	LIEFER.LIEVER
rational	SOBER
ravages	WASTES
ravish	CONSTUPRATE
	OPPRESS.VITIATE
—with delight	RAPE
raze to ground	SLIGHT
reach	AREACH.HENT
—forward	PRETEND
reached	RAUGHT.ROUGHT
read	REDE
readily	YARELY
reading	LECTURE
ready	YARE.BOUND
—for action	PREDY
—to learn	TOWARD
—to make advances	COMING
—to take offence	MIFTY
—to wither away	MIFTY
realgar	RESALGAR.ROSAKER
realm	REAME.REIGN
rebellious	MALIGNANT
rebound	RESULT
rebuked	SHENT
rebut	ELIDE
recall	REVOKE
—from banishment	REPEAL
recapture	REPRISE
receive	ENTERTAIN.LATCH
	UNDERTAKE
—news well or ill	RESENT
—part of	PARTICIPATE
recent (dates)	LOW
receptacle	RESERVATORY
reception	
—after childbirth	UPSITTING
—of visitors while dressing	TOILET
reciter of poetic romances	JESTER
reck	KEEP.PASS.RETCH

recked	RAUGHT
reckless	RECHLESS
reckon	IMPUTE.VOGUE
reckoning	NICK
recognise	ACKNOW.WIT
—at a distance	KEN
recommend	WISH
recompense	GRATIFICATION
reconcile	ATONE
record	MEMORISE.MEMORIZE
	MIND.REMEMBER
recount	REFER
recover	RECURE
—from	OVERGET
recovery	RECOVER.RECURE
red	
—ochre	RUBRIC
—pimple	BUBUKLE
reddish-brown	SOAR(E).SORE
redoubtable	REDOUBTED
reduce	
—superfluous fat on	ENSEAM
—to poverty	STRAIT
reduction	BATEMENT
reed-grass	FLAG
refinement	EXILITY
reflect	ADVISE
reflection of self in	
another's eye	BABY
reformed person	REFORMADO
reformer	REFORMADO
refract	REFRINGE
refrain	BURTHEN
	FA(UX)BURDEN.WITHHOLD
—of song	BOB
—word	DILDO
refresh	REFOCILLATE
refreshment on journey	BAIT
refuge	SUBTERFUGE
refutation	CONVINCEMENT
	ELENCH
refute	CONVINCE.REDARGUE
	REFEL(L).REPROVE
regard with envy	MALIGN
regent	WARDEN
registrar	REGISTER
regulate a contest	STICKLE
reign	RAYNE
reinforce	RENFORCE.SUPPLY
reinforcement	RECRUIT
reject	CAST.WAIVE
rejoicing	OVATION
relate	REDE
relating to	
—passions	PATHETIC
—time	CHRONIC
—yesterday	YESTERN
relation	AFFINE.HABITUDE
release	ASSOIL
relic	RELICT
relieve	BEET.BETE
—by a pause	RESPITE
religious	
—direction	CAUTEL
—faith	LAY
—offerings	DEVOTION
relish	GUST.TASTE
relishingly	SAVOURLY
remain awake	WAKEN
remarkably	UNCOMMON
—great	VENGEABLE
remedial	WHOLESOME
remedy	LEECHDOM.REMEAD
	REMEDE.REMEID
remember	PRESENT
	RECONNOITRE
remind	MIND.REMEMBER
remorse	AYENBITE.HAD-I-WIST
remove	SUBLATE.VOID
—a veil from	UNVAIL(E)
—wrongfully	MISTAKE
rend	RENT
—in pieces	TO-REND
render as a due	YIELD
renew efforts	RENFORCE
renounce	REN(A)Y.RENEY
rent	GAVEL.YRENT
repay	AP(P)AY.QUIT.YIELD
repeat the Lord's Prayer	
mechanically	PATTER
repentance	PENANCE
reprehend sharply	NIP
represent	PRESENT.REFER
—as bad	DEPRAVE
representative of King of	
Spain	VISITOR GENERAL
reprisals	MARQUE
reproach	SHEND

—with	EXPROBATE
reproduce	REFER
reproof	CORREPTION
republic	STATE
repulse	FOIL.REFEL
repulsive	LO(A)TH
reputation	LO(O)S.VOICE
	WORSHIP
repute	SAVOUR.VOGUE
request	REQUIRE
require	WILL
requite	REQUIT
reservation	SALVO
reservoir	RESERVATORY
resident	LE(I)DGER.LEIGER
	LIEGER
resign	WAIVE
resist	GAINSTRIVE
resolution	POINT
resort	FREQUENCY.USE
respect	WORSHIP
respectful	RESPECTIVE
respite	FRIST
rest	REQUIEM
resting place	GITE
—on journey	MANSION
restive	RESTIFF.HOT-MOUTHED
restless	DISQUIET
restrain	CHASTISE.CHASTIZE
	REBUKE.REFRAIN
	STINT.CONCLUDE
restrict	STINT
resulting incidentally	
	OCCASIONAL
retain in service	ENTERTAIN
retreat	RECOIL.RETIRE
	RETRAI(C)T.RETRAITE
retrograde	REGREDE
return	RETIRE.REVOLVE
reveal	BEWRAY.UNVAIL(E)
reveller	ROARER.ROARING-BOY
reversal of 'God' in oaths	DOG
reverse of coin	PILE
revert	RECOIL.RESORT
revile	MISSAY
revolving easily	VOLUBLE
reward	MEED.WAR(R)ISON
	YIELD
rhetorical figure	SCHEME

rhinoceros	RHINOCEROT(E)
rhyme	RHIME.RHYTHM.RYTHME
ribaldry	RIBAUDRY
rich	
—cloth	PALL
—decoration	PARAMENT
rid	QUIT
riddle	CRIBBLE
ridge	BA(U)LK
ridicule	SMOKE
riding horse	ROUNCY
right	
—moment	PUDDING-TIME
—to cut wood	HAY-BOTE
	HEDGE-BOTE
—to hold court	LEET
—to hunt game	WARREN
—to keep game	WARREN
rigorously	STRAIT
rim	RYMME
rime	RHIME
ring-dance	CAROL
rioter	SWINGE-BUCKLER
rise	STY
risk	PLIGHT
risque	RISK
rival	MATE.PARAGON
rive	RYVE
riven	YRIVD
river mouth	OSTIUM
roast	ROST
roasting	USTULATION
robbed	RAFT
robe	PARAMENT
robustness	HARDIHEAD
rock dug from earth	FOSSIL
rod	GAD
rode	RID
rogue	LIMMER
roguish	ROGUY
—child or animal	WANTON
roll	TROLL.WALK
—back	REVOLVE
—in blood	WELTER
—in the grass	GREEN GOWN
—of parchment	PELL
rolling	VOLUTATION
—gait	WALLOW
Roman	ROMISH

romance	ROMAUNT
room	ROUM
—beside stage for musicians	MUSIC-ROOM
—mate	CHAMBER-FELLOW
root	WROOT
rote	ROATE
rotten	PROMISCUOUS
rough	ASPER.CRABBED
	ROW.STURDY
round	ROWND
rout	HURRICANE
row of	
—stakes	ORGUE
—trees trained on stakes	ESPALIER
royal	REAL
—stables	EQUERRY
Royalist	MALIGNANT
royalty	REALTY
rub	FEEZE.PHE(E)SE.PHEEZE
ruff	PARTLET
ruffle	ROUSE
—feathers	FRILL
ruin	FORDO.HEAP
ruined	NAUGHT.RUINATE
ruinous	WASTE
rule	WIELD
—over	OVERRULE
ruler	RECTOR
rum	RUMBULLION
rumour	NOISE.SPEECH
	TOY.VOICE
rump of horse	CROUPON
run	COURSE.RACE
—about	TROLL
—aground	GRAVEL
rush	LANCE.LOOSE
	RANDOM.RASH
rustic	BOR(R)EL(L).RUSSET
	SWAIN.UPLANDISH
	WOOLLEN
sack	BUDGET
—contents	BUDGET
sacrifice	SCARIFY
—of animal's shoulder	HEAVE-SHOULDER
sacrificial victim	HOST
sad	WO(E)
sadden	ATTRIST.CONTRIST
saddle	
—bow	ARSON
—cloth	PANEL
saddler	HORSE-MILLINER
sailor	SHIPMAN
saint	HALLOW
St Thomas's Day	MUMPING-DAY
salad	SALLAD.SALLET
sale	VENT
salt	IODURET
—of uric acid	LITHATE
salutation when drinking health	WASSAIL
salute	HALSE
	MAKE ONE'S MANNERS
	MOVE.SALUE
—by raising hat	HAT
sanctuary	FRITH(SOKEN)
	GIRTH.GRITH
sane	SOBER
sarcasm	GIRD
sat	SATE
Satan	LEVIATHAN
satisfaction	CONTENTATION
	SUFFISANCE
satisfied	PAID
satisfy	AP(P)AY.PAY
—in advance	PREVENT
saucepan	CHAFER
savage	SALVAGE
save	SA.SPARE
—from objection	SALVE
—your-reverence	SIR-REVERENCE
savings	THRIFT
savour	RESENT
savourless	WEARISH
savoury	GUSTFUL
say	
—in answer	UNDERSAY
—wrongly	MISSAY
saying	SPEECH
says	SAITH
scabbiness	SCALL
scantily	SCARCELY
scanty	PENURIOUS
scarcely	UNE(A)TH.UNEATHES
	UNNETHES

scarlet pimpernel	WINCOPIPE
scatter	STROW
scattered	BESPRENT
scent out	SMOKE
scheme	PLAT
scholar	ARTSMAN
schoolteacher	SCHOOL-DOCTOR
scimitar	SEMITA(U)R.SYMITAR(E)
scion	IMP
scoff	DOR.GLEEK
scorched	ADUST
score	LAW
—for keeping reckoning	NICK
Scottish	SCOTIAN
scout	SCURRIER
	SCURRIOUR.SPIAL
scrape	HOBBLE
scratch	SCRAT
screech	SHRITCH
screw	VICE.WREST
scribe	SCRIVENER
scrub	SHRUB
scrupulous	CURIOUS
scrupulousness	CURIOSITY
sea	
—bird	PINK
—bottom	GROUND
—monster	WASSERMAN
—serpent	ELLOPS
—wolf	SEA-ELEPHANT
seal up	ENSEAL
search	INQUEST
—out	INDIGATE
seasonable	TIDY
seasoning	SEASON
seat	ROOM.SEL(LE).SIEGE
seat of	
—authority	SEE
—dignity	SEE.SIEGE
—emotions	ENTRAILS
—sanctuary	GRITH-STOOL
seclude oneself	SEQUESTER
second	STICKLER
secondary rainbow	WATER-GALL
secret	DE(A)RN
—arrangement	PACK
secure	RUG
security	BANK.WED
sedge	SEG

seduce	JAPE
seek	ENQUIRE.INQUIRE
—again	REPEAT
—to bring about	PURCHASE
—to induce belief	PERSUADE
seeking of food	RELIEF
seem	BESEEM.SEMBLE
—likely	LIKE
segment	ARTICLE
seize	DEPREHEND.AREACH
	LATCH.REACH.SEIS
	SURPRISE
—and carry off	RAPE
—upon	FANG
seized	HENT
seizure	PRIZE.PURCHASE.RAPE
seldom	SELD
select unfairly	GARBLE
self	
—congratulatory pride	GLORY
—indulgent	WANTON
—seeking cleric	ROME-RUNNER
—willed	FROWARD
selfish end	SELF-END
seller of indulgences	PARDONER
semblance	LIKELIHOOD
send	ELOI(G)N.ESLOIN
	ESLOYNE
—away	VOID
—on a journey	TRAVEL
sense	SENTENCE
—of shame	PUDOR
senseless	SURD
sensible	WITTY
sentinel	CENTINEL(L).WAIT
	WARDEN
sentry	CENTRY
separate	DISCREET.INTERVENE
	TWIN(E)
—and remove	ESLOIN.ESLOYNE
	ELOI(G)N
—from one another	DEPART
—lodging	MANSION
serf	HELOT.VILLEIN
serge	SURGE
sermon	SPELL
serpent	WORM
servant	FEEDER
(KITCHEN-)KNAVE.SCULLION	

serve	KA(E).STEAD
—as a soldier	MILITATE
	TRAIL A PIKE
service	FEE.MISTERY.MYSTERY
	WAITERAGE
set	STEAD.TILL
—aside a veil	UNVAIL(E)
—forth	RECORD
—hand to	HAND
—in array	PITCH
—in front	PREFER
—in order	DISPONE.PRAN(C)K(E)
—of dice	BALE
—of diners served together	MESS
—on edge	SURBED
—the tongue wagging	TROLL
—up	ROUSE.STABLISH
—with stars	STELLIFY
setting	PRINT
settle	DISCUSS
—in	HABITUATE
settled	SPED
settlement of dispute	MISE
settler	INHABITOR
seven years	PROPHETIC WEEK
severally	IN PARTICULAR
sewer	(COMMON-)SHORE.SURE
sex	KIND.RACE
sexual intimacy	KNOWLEDGE
shake the feathers	ROUSE
shaken	SHAKED.SHAKT
	SHOOK
shameful	PUDENDOUS
shape	FEATURE
shaped	SHAPEN
shapely	FEAT(E)OUS.FEATUOUS
share	SNACK
—a dwelling	STALL
—of expense	LAW
—out	IMPART
sharpened	GROUNDEN
sharper	CONEY-CATCHER
shed light on	ENLIGHT(EN)
sheep	MUTTON
shelter from	WEATHER
shepherd	FEEDER
—boy	HERD-GROOM
sheriff	GREAVE.GRIEVE
	VISCOUNT

shield worn on left	
arm	GLOVE-SHIELD
shifting for oneself	PURCHASE
shine	LEAM.LEME.SHEEN
ship	ARGO.WOODEN HORSE
—'s decoration	WAISTCLOTH
shire division	WAPENTAKE
shirt	PARTLET
shock	SCANDAL
shoes	SHOON
shoot	IMP.SPRNG
—arrow short or wide	DRIB
—out	LANCE
shore	CONTINENT.RIVAGE
short	
—hasty mass	HUNTING-MASS
—burst of bird song	JERK
—musical phrase	POINT
—spear	DEMI-LANCE
—time ago	EVEN NOW
—veil at back of head	VOLET
shorten (sail)	SCANTLE
shortened	DAG
shortening in pronunciation	
	CORREPTION
shortly	AT A WORD
shot	SHOTTEN
—with many nooks and	
corners	NOOK-SHOTTEN
shoulder-cloth for	
hairdressing	TOILET
show	CON
—a (bold) face	FACADE
—forth	DETECT
—in advantageous	
light	ILLUSTRATE
—show place	VISIBILITY
showing care or	
fastidiousness	CURIOUS
showy dress	BRAVERY
shrew	SHROW
shrewish	CURST
shrewd	SHROWD
shriek	SCRIKE.SHRITCH
shrivel	WELK
shrivelled	WRITHLED
shrubbery	ARBORET
shudder	GRISE
shuffle cards (dishonestly)	PACK

shut	SHET	slander	MISSAY
—in	IMPALE	slash	CARBONADO
—the eyes	WINK	slattern	SLAMMAKIN
sickly	QUEACHY.QUEECHY		SLAMMERKIN
—smelling	FAINT	slave	NATIVE.THEOW
side	COAST.PLAT	sledge taking traitors to the	
sideboard	CREDENCE	gallows	HURDLE
siege	LEAGUER.OBSESSION	slenderness	EXILITY
—engine	WAR-WOLF	slid	SLIDED
sift	CRIBBLE.GARBLE	slide a dice	SLUR
sigh	SITHE	slighting	SLIGHT
sighed	SIGHT	slimy	LIMOUS
sight	VISIBILITY	slipper	SLIP-SHOE
signify	BEMEAN.MAGNIFY.SKILL	slippery	GLIB(BERY)
silent	HUSH.WHIST	slogan	SLUGHORN(E)
—game of dice or		slovenly woman	SLAMMAKIN
cards	MUMCHANCE		SLAMMERKIN
silly person	LIRIPIPE.LIRIPOOP	slow	LASH
silver 1½ penny piece	DANDIPRAT	sluggish	LENTOUS
	DANDYPRAT	sluggishness	LENTOR
similitude	LIKELIHOOD	sluice	SASSE
simple	SILLY	slut	PUCELLE.PUZZLE
simpleton	COKES.ROOK	small	
	WOODCOCK.DAW	—branch	RICE
simulate agreement	COLLOGUE	—bulb	CHIVE
sin	FOLLY	—freeholder	FRANKLIN
since	SIN.SITHEN	—horse	PONEY
sincerely	ENTIRE	—hunting dog	KENNET
sing	RECORD	—quantity	DRIB
—for money at Whitsun	SHROVE	—river	RIVERET
singly	ONLY	—silver coin	SILVERLING
sink	DEVALL	—Stone Age tool	MICROLITH
sip	DELIBATE	—wooden articles	TREEN
sir	LORDING	smallness	EXILITY
sit	SET	smear with blood	GILD
—well on	BESIT	smile	SMOILE.SMOYLE
sixpence	TESTER(N)	smiling	BONNIE.BONNY
skein	SKENE	smock	SHIFT
ski	SNOW-SHOE	smoker	TOBACCONIST
skilful	HEND.WELL-SEEN	smooth	GLIB.SLIGHT.TERSE
skilfulness	WISDOM	smote	SMIT
skilfully	YARELY	smother	OPPRESS
skilled workman	PRUD'HOMME	smuggle sheep or wool	OWL
skin	PELL	smuggler	OWLER
skirmish	ESCARMOUCHE	snake	ELLOPS.WORM
skirt	GORE	snap	SNIP
skulk	LUSK	snare	ENGINE
slack	LASH	snatch	REACH
slake	ASLAKE	—away	HENT

sneaking	SHEEP-BITING	soused	SOUCT
snub	FRUMP	spa	SPAW
snug	RUG	space	CANTON
soaked in blood	BEWELTERED	Spanish broom	SPART
sob	SINGULT	sparing	SCARCE
sociable	COMPANIABLE	sparkle	GLISTER
social party	HURRICANE	spawn	SPERM
sociable with all	GENERAL	speak	BESPEAK
society	HETAIRIA	—fair	PALP
sofa	DAY-BED	—of	VOICE
softening	LENIENT	—to or of	WORD
spiked barrier	TURNPIKE	—wrongly	MISSAY
soil	GLEBE	speaking	WORDING.PARLANCE
sojourn	TARRY	—freely	LAXATIVE
soldier	CENTINEL(L)	spear	GAD(E).GAID.GLAIVE
	MAN-OF-WAR		LA(U)NCEGAY(E)
	MILITARY.SOULDIER	—rest	FEUTRE.FEWTER
—'s bastard	SON OF A GUN	spectacles	GLASS EYES
—'s cloak	MANTEEL	speculation	WISDOM
sole of foot	PALM	speech	PARLANCE.PARLE.SPELL
solicitude	CARK	spell	WEIRD
solitary	DEARN	spend labour on	LABOUR
solve	ASSOIL	spew	SPUE
something		spied	SPIDE
—preparatory to	INDEX	spignel	SPICKNEL
—that surrounds	WAIST	spiked portcullis	HERSE
somewhat	SOMEDEAL	spin	TROLL
son	SONNE	spine	CHINE
song	FIT(T).FITTE.FYTTE	spinner	SPINSTER
soothe	BALM.STROKE	spinning top	NUN
soothing	LENIENT	spiritless	AMORT.HILDING
sophism	ELENCH		SPRIGHTLESS
soreness of eyes	LIPPITUDE	spiritual insight	WISDOM
sorrel	SOAR(E).SORE	spit on	BESPIT
sorrow	CONDOLEMENT.TEEN	spite	MAU(L)GRE
sorrowful	BALE.TRIST	splendent	SPLENDIDIOUS
sorry	WO(E)	splint	SPLINTER
sou	SOUS(E)	spoil	BRIBE.WRONG
sound	SANE	spoilt child	WANTON
—in health	WHOLE	spokesman	ORATOR
sounding terrifyingly		sponge	SPUNGE
	HORRISONOUS	sponsor	SUSCEPTOR
soundness	HEAL		UNDERTAKER
sour	EAGER	—at baptism	GOSSIP
source	OFFSPRING	sport	BOURD
—of hangman's rope		sportive	LUDICROUS
(hemp)	NECK-WEED	—child or animal	WANTON
—of motion	PRIMUM MOBILE	spot	GOUT.MOIL
souse	SOUCE.SOWCE.SOWS(S)E	—of iron mould	MOLE

spotted as with plague	TOKENED
spouse	COMPANION.FE(A)RE
	FEER.FIERE.PHEERE
spread	SPRED(D).SPREDDE(N)
	STROW.WALK
—a report	BRUIT
—out	POUR
spring	LENT
—trap or catch	SNAPHA(U)NCE
	SNAPHAUNCH
sprinkle	POUNCE
—with ornaments	SPANG
sprinkled	SPRENT
—over	BESPRENT
spruce	BRISK
spy	SPIAL.WAIT
squander	BEZZLE.LASH.SPORT
squire	DONZEL
staff of office	WARDER
stag's brow	RIGHTS
stage	
—machine	PAGEANT
—performance	SCENE
—producer	UNDERTAKER
stain	SMIT.SOILINESS.STAYNE
stair	STAYRE
stake	PEEL.VIE
—higher	REVIE
stalemate	STALE
stall	TRAVIS.TREVIS(S)
—keeper	STALLENGER
	STALLINGER
stalwart	PRETTY
standard bearer	ANCIENT
standing out from the rest	EXTANT
stanza	STANCE
star	ASTER.STARN.STERN
start	BRAID
starting post	GOAL
starvation	FAMISHMENT
starve	STERVE
state	ESTATE.REPUBLIC
state	
—barge	GALLEY-FOIST
—governor	PRESIDENT
—of being awake	WATCH
—of being well	WEAL
static electricity	

	VITREOUS ELECTRICITY
statue	STATUA
stay	MANSION
stayed	STAID
steadfast	STEDFAST
steady	STEDDY.STEEDY
steal	BRIBE.NIM
steer	STEAR(E)
steerage	STEARAGE
steered	STEARD
steering gear	STERN
steersman	PILOT.STEARSMATE
—'s place	STERN
step	GREE.GRE(E)CE
	GRECIAN.GRE(E)SE.GREESING
	GRESSING.GRI(E)CE
	GRISE.GRIZE
—mother	STEP-DAME
steward	REEVE
stick	GAD
stiff	STOOR.STOUR
	STOWRE.STURE
stimulate	URGE
stint	SCANTLE
stir	QUATCH.QUETCH.QUITCH
—up	AMOVE
stocks	HARMANS
stocking	NETHERSTOCK
stole	NAM.NIMMED.STALE
stolen	STOLE
—article	CHEAT
—goods	PURCHASE
—goods, abandoned	WAIF
stomach	HEART.WOMB
stoop	LOUT.LOWT
stop	EMBAR.ESTOP
	STAP.STINT
—contention	STICKLE
—for refreshment	BAIT
—up	CONSTIPATE
stout	TALL
—robber	ROBERDSMAN
	ROBERTSMAN
straddle	STRODDLE
straight	STRAIT
—on	ENDLONG
straightness	RECTITUDE
straightway	INCONTINENT
strain	FIT(T).FITTE.FYTTE

	INTEND.STREIGNE
straits	STRESS
strap for horse's load	WANTY
straw	STRAMMEL.STRUMMEL
—hat	HIVE
streaked in bands	RING-STRAKED
stream	LAKE
street	
—bully	SCOWRER
—cleaner	SCAVAGER
—refuse	SCAVAGE
—thief	BULKER
strength	HEAD
strengthen	COMFORT
stretch	REACH
stretched	INTENDED
strew	STRAW.STROW
strewed	STRAWED.STRAWN
	STROWED.STROWN
strife	BARGAIN.BARRAT
strike	
—to the heart	HEART-STRIKE
—with fear	AMAZE
string up	KILT.TRUSS
stringing together of	
poems	RHAPSODY
striped	GUARDED
strive	FORCE
—against	GAINSTRIVE
strode	STRID
stroke	BUFF.JERK.STRIKE
stroll	TROLL
strong	RANK.VALIANT
	VALID.WIGHT
—drink	BUB
—tobacco	MUNDUNGUS
strop	STRAP
struck	STRAKE.STROKE
	STROOK(E).STRICKEN
	STRO(O)KEN.STRUCKEN
structure housing taps	
at conduit	STANDARD
struggle	CAMP
strumpet	BULKER.PUNK
	WAISTCOATEER
strut	JET
strutting movement	JET
stubborn	STOUT
stumbling	OFFENCE

stun	AMAZE.STON(NE)
stung	STONG
stupendous	STUPENDIOUS
stupid	NICE
—person	WOODCOCK
sturdy beggar	ABRA(HA)M-MAN
style	ENSTYLE
subtenant	VALVASSOR
	VAVASOUR
subaqueous	DEMERSAL
subdue	DO DOWN.MATE.QUAIL
subject	
—for dissection	ANATOMY
—to authority	OBNOXIOUS
—to transmutation	TINCT
sublet	UNDERSET
submissive	SUBMISS
	SUBORDINATE
submissively	SUBMISSLY
submit	PREFER
substance	SUBJECT
substitute by fraud	SUPPOSE
subtle	SUBTIL(E)
succeed	FADGE
success	SPEED
successors	SEQUEL
sucker	GRAFT
sudden	
—heeling	SEEL
—inflow	ANCOME
—movement	BRAID
suddenly	UNWARES
sue	IMPLEAD
—for	PLEAD
suffer injustice or	
injury	HAVE WRONG
suffering	PASSIVE.PINE.PYNE
sufficiency	SUFFISANCE
sugar refiner	SUGAR-BAKER
suit	EFFEIR.EFFERE
	FADGE.HIT
suitable	HANDSOME
suite	SUIT
sulks	GLOUT.GLUMPS
sulky look	GLOUT
sullen	SOLEIN
sultan	SOLDAN
sum and substance	CONTINENT
summon	PROVOKE

summons	INTERPELLATION	—meat tray	VOIDER
sun	SONNE	sweeten	EDULCORATE
—dew	ROSA-SOLIS	sweetened spiced wine	PIMENT
—flower	GIRASOL(E)	sweetness of manner	DOUCEUR
sunk and dispirited	AMORT	swell	HUFF
supercargo	MERCHANT	swerve	WRY
supercilious(ly)	OVERLY	swift	WIGHT
superintend	INTEND	swim (head)	WHIM
superior	OVERLY	swindle	BUNCKET
supernatural being	WIGHT	swindler	LEGER
supine	BOLT UPRIGHT	swine	PORK
supplement	MEND.SUPPLY	swoon	DELIQUIUM
support	EASEMENT.SOOTHE	sword	FOX.GLADIUS.GLAIVE
suppose	GUESS	swordplay	SPADROON
supposititious	SUPPOSED	sycophant	PLACEBO
supreme		symbolic meaning	MYTHOLOGY
—chief	PENDRAGON	symbolise	BETOKEN.FIGURE
—council of Anglo-Saxon		syncopation	SYNCOPE
England	WITENAGEMOT	system of	
sure	SICCAR.SICKER	—drill	MARTINET
surety	BORROW.MAINPRISE	—principles	INSTITUTION
	UNDERTAKER	table	
—for keeping the		—implement	SUCKET-FORK
peace	FRITHBORH		SUCKET-SPOON
surgeon	CHIRURGEON	—linen	NAPERY
surgery	CHIRURGERY	—of contents	INDEX
surgical	CHIRURGICAL	tag	DAG
surliness	MELANCHOLY	tail of graduate's hood	LIRIPIPE
surpass everything	PASS		LIRIPOOP
surpassing	PASSING	take	HENT.LATCH.NIM.REACH
surplus	SUPERPLUS	—across	TRAJECT
surprising by stealth	OBREPTION	—by surprise	OPPRESS
surrender	SURRENDRY	—care of	BEWARE
surviving trace	RELICT	—comfort	CHEER
survivor	RELICT	—into stomach	ENDUE.INDUE
suspect	DOUBT.SMOKE	—little	DRIB
suspicion	AIM	—on (as servant)	ENTERTAIN
swagger	SQUARER	—out	OUTTAKE
swaggerer	BRAVADO.ROARER	—pleasure in	PLEASURE
	ROARING-BOY	—possession of	HENT
sweat-bath	POWDERING-TUB	—purses	PURSE
sweating-sickness		—steps	TAKE ORDER
	STOOP-GALLANT	taken	TANE
sweep over	ENSWEEP	taking food	CIBATION
sweet	DOUCE.SOOT(E)	tale of supernatural	WEIRD
—food	SWEETMEAT	talk	DEVISE.PARLE.SPELL
—heart	AMORET	talkative	DISCOURSIVE
	JUNKET.LEMAN	talker of nonsense	TWADDLE
—meat (marzipan)	MARCHPANE	talon	FANG

tame	MANSUETTE	—abuse	SCARAB
tapestry	TAPIS	—address to king	SIRE
—frame	TENT	—contempt	JACK.MECHANIC
tarnished	BRAID		WHIPSTER
tarragon	STARAGEN	—endearment	FOOL.MOUSE
tarry	LENG	—exultation	VIA
tarrying	TARRIANCE	—familiarity	BULLY
taste	ASSAY.GUST.RELISH	—opprobrium	HARLOT
tasteless	WEARISH	—reproach	TRUANT
taunt	GIRD	terrace	TERRAS
taut	TAUGHT	terrify	FEAR
tavern open at		terrifying word	BUGWORD
night	NIGHT-HOUSE	territory	GOVERNMENT.MARK
tax	CESS.GELD.LOT	—of lord	LORDSHIP
—farmer	UNDERTAKER	terror	BUG
—on land	HIDAGE	test	EXPERIENCE.TASTE
teach	CON.LEAR(E).LEIR.LERE	—fatness	ASSAY
teacher	DOCTOR	thane	THEGN
teaching	DOCTRINE.LORE	thank	REMERCY
team	TEME	—God	GOD-A-MERCY
tear	RASH	that which	
tearful	MAUDLIN	—comes into contact	
tease out	TOUSE.TOUZE		OCCURRENT
	TOWSE.TOWZE	—contains	CONTINENT
technical	MECHANICAL	—humbles gallants	
teeming	GREAT		STOOP-GALLANT
telescope	OPTIC TUBE	—institutes	INSTITUTION
	PROSPECT.TRUNK	—instructs	INSTITUTION
tell falsehood	FABLE	—is got	GET
temper	CONDITION.TAMPER	—is laid waste	WASTE
	TEMPERATE	—is preserved from loss in	
tempering	TEMPERAMENT	conflict	PREY
temporal	TIMELY	—is worn	WEARING
tempt	ASSAY.ATTEMPT	—softens	LENIENT
temptation	TENTATION	that with which one is	
tenant		fitted out	EQUIPAGE
—by service	SOCAGER	the	YE
	SOCMAN.SOKEMAN	—one	TONE
—farmer	GEBUR	theatre	
tend	SOUND	—dressing-room	TIRING-HOUSE
tenor	TENOUR		TIRING-ROOM
tense	TAUGHT	—seat	ROOM
tenure		them	HEM
—by service	SOC(C)AGE	thick woollen cloth	WADMA(A)L
	SOKEMANRY		WADMOL(L)
—in Kent	GAVELKIND	thicken	INCRASSATE
terce	UNDERN	thicket	QUEACH
terebinth-tree	TEIL	thief	LIMMER.WASTER
term of		—'s decoy	STALE

thieving	SHEEP-BITING
thing	RES
—stolen	MAINO(U)R.MANNER
—to lean on	LEAN
—uncertain or questioned	DOUBT
—which contains	CONTINENT
think	CENSE.GUESS.WEEN
third	TIERCE
—finger of left hand	RINGMAN
—hour	UNDERN
thirst	THRIST
thong	LATCHET.LORE
thoroughly	THROUGHLY
thought	CONCEIT
thoughtful	CONSIDERATIVE
thrash	JERK.SMOKE.SWADDLE
thread	FILE
throat	HALSE.QUAIL-PIPE
	WEAZAND
throb	QUOP
throne	SEE.STOOL
through	YOND
throw	WARP
—away	ABJECT
—in or on	INJECT
—stones at	LAPIDATE
thrust	POTE.PUT.STOP
—out	ELIMINATE
thunder	INTONATE
tie	
—the points of	TRUSS
—together	KNIT
tight	STRAIT
—gripping	HANDFAST
tighten	STRAIT(EN)
tightly	STRAIT
till	EAR
tilt	JOSTLE.JUSTLE
time	
—of currency	TENOUR
—of midday meal	UNDERNTIME
—observer	TIMIST
tinder	SPUNK
tinge	TAINT.TINCT
tinker	PRIG
tin-miner's poll tax	WHITE-RENT
tint	TAINT.TINCT
tip	GRATIFICATION.VALES.VAILS
titled person	

	PERSON OF HONOUR
to	
—a great degree	
	OUT OF MEASURE
—an inner room	WITHIN
—be brief	AT A WORD
—the point of perfection	
	POINT-DEVICE
	POINT-DEVISE
—them	HEM
—windward	ALOOF
toad	PADDOCK
—stool	PADDOCK-STOOL
toady	ZANY
toast	DRINK-HAIL.WASSAIL
tobacco pipe	
	WOODCOCK'S-HEAD
toffee	TAFFY
together	IN COMMON
	INFERE.YFERE
toil	SWINK
—worn	SWINKED
token	RECOGNISANCE
tomb	BURIAL
ton	TUN
too	
—drunk to whistle	
	WHISTLE(D)-DRUNK
—early	OVERTIMELY
—little	UNSIZ(E)ABLE
took	NAM.NIMMED
tool	LOOM
toothache	WORM
top	SUPERATE
—of anything	CROP
topic	PLACE
torch-bearer	LINKBOY.LINKMAN
tore	TARE
torment	PINE.PYNE
torture	PINE.PYNE
—with heat	FRY
torturer	TORMENTOR
Tory High Churchman	TANTIVY
toss	
—a coin	FLUTTER
—about	WALK
—the limbs about	SPRAWL
tossing about	JACTITATION
touch on	PERSTRINGE

touchwood	SPUNK
touchy	MIFTY
tournament	TOURNEY
—lists	BARRACE
tout	PLIER
township	VILL
townsman	CIT
toy	
—with	FON
—with fingers	PADDLE
—dog	PUPPY
track	TROD
trackless	BEWILDERED.INVIOUS
tractable	TOWARDLY
trade	MISTER.MISTERY
	MYSTERY.OCCUPY
—guild	MISTERY.MYSTERY
trader	PLIER
trading voyage	TRAFFIC
traitor	NITHING.TREACHER(ER)
	TREACHOUR
trample under foot	FOIL
tranquillity	LEE
transcribe officially	TRANSUME
transcription	TRANSUMPTION
transept	CROSS-AISLE
transference	TRAJECT
	TRANSUMPTION
transgression	ESCAPE
translate	TRADUCE
translator	INTERPRETER
transmission	TRAJECT
transmit	TRADUCE
transmuting element	TINCTURE
transport with delight	RAPE
trapped	IN BY THE WEEK
travail	TRAVEL
travel	TRAVAIL.VOYAGE
—on foot	WAYFARE
—with post-horses	POSTAGE
travelling	
—bag	MAIL
—case	CAP-CASE
tray for dirty dishes	VOIDER
treacherous person	TREACHER
	TREACHOUR
tread	TRADE
—a measure	TRACE
treasure ships	PLATE-FLEET
treasurer	FISCAL
treat	BESEE.ENTERTAIN
	ENTREAT
—with honour	WORSHIP
treatise on gems	LAPIDARY
treatment	ENTREATMENT
tree	BEAM.WOOD
triad	TERN
trial	EXPERIENCE
tribe	ROD
tribute	GAVEL
trick	BANTER.CROOK.FOB
	FUN.GLEEK
—out	TIFF
trickery	SLIGHT
trickle	DRIB
tried	TRIDE
trifing	FALLAL
trifle	PADDLE
trim	NET(T)
trimmed	GUARDED
trimming on gown	ROBIN
trip	SPURN
tripod	TRIPOS
triumvirate	TRIUMVIRY
trivial	BALD
—dance-tune	TOY
trouble	BARRAT.GRAM(E)
	HATTER.NOY.VISIT
—taken	LABOUR
troublesome	INCOMMODIOUS
	INFEST
trousers	TROSSERS.TROWSERS
truant	MICHER
truck	TRUNDLE
true	TREW
trump	TRIUMPH
trumpery	MOCKADO
trumpet of brass	ALCHEMY
	ALCHYMY
trundle	TROLL
truss up	KILT
trust	AFFY.LET ALONE.TROW
truth	TROTH
try	FAND.FOND.TASTE.TRIE
tub	COWL
tuberculous ulcer	WOLF
tumulus	LOW.MOT(T)E
	MOTE-HILL

tune	DUMP.NOTE
tunnel	TONNEL
turban	TULBAN.TULIPANT
tureen	TERREEN
turfy	GLEBOUS.GLEBY
turkey	GUINEA-HEN
turmoil	MOIL
turn	CHAR(E)
turn	LOT.WEND
—about	CONVERT
—aside by caprice	WHIM
—from right course	CROOK
—of mind	ENGINE
—out	FADGE.SORT
—out well	PROVE
—over	VOLVE
—round (head)	WHIM
—the leaves of	TOSS
—to stone	LAPIDIFY
turned away	FROWARD
turning	VOLUTATION
—over in the mind	REVOLUTION
turnstile	TURNPIKE
turquoise	LIGURE.TURKIS
turret	GARRET
tutelage	TUTORAGE
tutor	GOVERNOR
twig	SARMENT.TWIST
twigs	RICE
twin	GEMMEL
twisted	WRONG
two	TWAIN
—tables of the Mosaic Law	TESTIMONY
type	HAIR.SAMPLER
tyrant	TYRAN(NE)
ugly	LO(A)TH.OUGHLY.OUGLIE
umbrella	OMBRELLA.UMBRELLO
unable	UNHABLE
—to take in	INCAPABLE
—to visit	UNVISITABLE
unaccustomed	UNCUSTOMED
	UNWONT.WONTLESS
unafraid	UNFEARED
unaware	WARELESS.UNWARES
unbending	STIFF-RUMPT
unborn child	BURDEN
unburdened	UNBURTHENED
uncanny	WEIRD

unchaste	LIGHT-HEELED
uncle	EME
unconnected composition or medley	RHAPSODY
uncover	DETECT
uncreated	INCREATE
uncritical	INCURIOUS
uncultivated	INCULT
under	
—consideration	ON THE TAPIS
—constable	THIRDBOROUGH
—the control of	UNDERNEATH
—iron for minting coins	PILE
underhand	
—deal	PACK
—representation	SUGGESTION
undersong	FA(UX)BURDEN
understanding	WIT
undertake with deceitful intention of defeating	PREVARICATE
undisciplined	WANTON
undo	FOREDO.POOP.POUPE
undoing	DEFEASANCE
undress	MAKE UNREADY
unearthly	WEIRD
uneasiness	DISEASE.MISEASE
uneasy	DISQUIET
unencumbered	EXPEDITE
unexpected	INOPINATE
	UNHOPED
unexpectedly	UNWARES
unfamiliar	UNCOUTH
unfitting	UNDECENT
unfledged	EYAS.NYAS
unfortunate	MISFORTUNED
unfriendliness	UNFRIENDSHIP
ungodly	WORLD
ungrateful	INGRATE
unhandsome	UNDECENT
unintelligent	INCAPABLE
union for preservation of peace	FRITHGILD
unite	ME(I)NT.MENG(E)
	MEYNT.MING
unite(d) in one body	CONCORPORATE
unjust	UNEQUAL
unknown	IGNORANT.UNCOUTH
—precious stone	LIGIURE

unless	EXCEPT.WITHOUT	useful	BEHOVEFUL.BEHOVELY
unlucky days	DISMAL	useless	WASTE
unmanageable	WANTON	usual	WONTED
unmixed	MERE.NET(T)	—fare	ORDINARY
unpleasant	DISPLEASANT	utmost	
	UNGAIN	—degree	UTTERANCE
—experience	DISTASTE	—effort or violence	UTTERANCE
unpleasing	INGRATE	utter	PEREMPTORY.WIELD
unpolished	UNPOLITE	—fluently	TROLL
unprepared	UNPURVEYED	utterance	WORDING
unprepossessing	UNLIKELY	utterly damned	FORE-DAMNED
unproductive consumer		vacate	VOID.WAIVE
	CATERPILLAR	vacillate	WAVE
unpromising	UNLIKELY	vagabond	GADLING
unprovided	UNPURVEYED	vagrant	CURSITOR.TRUANT
unquiet	DISQUIET	vain	WASTE.WASTEFUL
unreasonable	FROWARD	—regret	HAD-I-WIST
unrestrained	FRANK	valiant	PROW
unruly	WANTON	valour	VIRTUE
unseemly	UNHONEST	—proved in war	WAR-PROOF
unsettled	UNDISCUSSED	value	PRICE.VALOUR
unshaken	UNREMOVABLE	vanish	FAINT
unskilful	UNHANDSOME	variable	FLUXIONARY
unskilled	UNGAIN.UNPERFECT	vault	EMBOW.VAUT(E).VAWTE
unstock	LAUNCH	vaunt	GAB
unsuitable	UNLIKELY	vegetable	WORT
—for	INCOMMODIOUS	veil	VAIL
until	WHILE	velocipede	MULTICYCLE
untimely	IMPORTUNE	veneer	FINEER
	OVERTIMELY	venery	VENUS
unwanted	INUSITATE	vengeance	WRACK.WREAK
unwarily	UNWARELY	venial error	ESCAPE
unworthiness	INDIGNITY	venture	VENTER.VENTRE
unworthy	INDIGN.WORTHLESS	venturous	VENTROUS
unyielding	STOUT	verandah	VIRANDA.VIRANDO
up to	UP-TILL	verbal message	ERRAND
upbraid	EXPROBATE	verbose	WORDISH
upholsterer	UPHOLDER	verdict	VARDY.VERDIT
upholstery cloth	PARAGON	verse of retraction	PALINODY
upper servant	PUG	versed (in)	OVERSEEN
upshot	PROOF	versify	MAKE
upside down	UP SO DOWN	vertebra	RACK
upward curve of hat brim	PINCH	very	RIGHT.UNCOMMON
urate	LITHATE	—attentive	PARTICULAR
urge on	EDGE	vessel for table	
urgency	INSTANCE	requisites	NEF
urgent	INSTANT	vestment	VESTIMENT
urus (aurochs)	URE	vexation	NOY
use	INURE.URE	vexatious	PEEVISH

viands	CATES	wages	MEED
vice	INIQUITY	waggish	UNHAPPY
view	ADVISE	waist	GIRDLESTEAD.WAST
—in a mirror	SPECULATE	wait	EXPECT
viewing	SPECULATION	—for	WATCH
vigorous	RANK	waiting	TARRIANCE
vile	VILD(E)	wakeful	WATCHFUL
vindicate	DARRAIGN(E)	waldgrave	WILDGRAVE
	DARRAIN(E).DARRAYN	walk	GO.TRACE
	DERAIGN.SALVE	—behind battlements	ALURE
vinegar	EISEL(L).ESIL(E)	—in wooden shoes	PATTEN
violate	VITIATE	walking cane	WAND
violent	RANK.STURDY	wall	
violently	HEAD AND SHOULDERS	—in	INTERMURE
—angry	WRATH	—plant	HYSSOP
violin	ROCTA	wallow in mud	MUDDLE
virgin	PUCELLE	wallowing	VOLUTATION
virginal	SYMPHONY	wander	
virginity	PUCELAGE	—from right way	ERR
virtue	VERTU(E)	—till wearied	FORWANDER
virtuous	VIRTUAL	wandering	EXTRAVAGANT
viscid	LENTOUS	—course	ERROR
viscidity	LENTOR	wane	WELK
visible form	SPECIES	want of	
vision	SPECULATION	—equity	INIQUITY
visit of herald	VISITATION	—fairness	INIQUITY
visiting card	TICKET	wanting in strength	FAINT
visual	VISIVE	wanton	GIGLET.GIGLOT
—image	SPECIES	—woman	JAY
vital	LIVELY	war	
—power	NATURE	—club	MAUL
vitality	VIVACIOUSNESS	—equipment	WAR
	VIVACITY.VIVENCY	—horse	DESTRIER
vitiate	VICIATE	ward off	FORFEND
vivid	VIVE	wardrobe	GARDEROBE
vocabulary	NOMENCLATURE	wariness	CAUTEL
voice	BREAST	warrant	WARRAN(D)
voiceless	SHARP	—safe	VOUCHSAFE.VOUTSAFE
volunteer	VOLUNTARY	warrior	EORL.WARMAN
—serving as officer	REFORMADO	wary	WARE
vomit	PARBREAK	washed	WASHEN
voracious	VORAGINOUS	waste	WAST
vouchsafe	VOUCH.VOUTSAFE	—away	WANZE
vow	BEHIGHT.BEHOTE	—place	WASTENESS
vulgar	SCURRIL(E)	wasting	COLLIQUATION
vulture	GIER-EAGLE		COLLIQUATIVE.COLLIQUABLE
wag (tongue)	WALK		COLLIQUANT
wage war	WARFARE	watch	AWAIT
wager	WAGE.WED	—dog	HOUSEKEEPER

—for	WAIT
—man	SPECULATOR
	WAIT(ER).WAKEMAN
—'s cry	WATCH
—over	WARD
—tower	GARRET.SENTRY-GO
watchful guardian	GRIFFIN
	GRIFFON.GRIPE.GRYPHON
water	
—channel	LAKE
—monster	NICKER
—fall	OVERFALL
watery	
—place	FLUSH
—looking sky	WATER-GALL
wave	FLOTE
waver	WAVE
wax	WEX(E)
—candle	TAPER
—pale	APPAL
way	TRADE.VIA.WISE
—farer	DUSTY-FOOT.PIEPOWDER
—side shrine	WEEPING-CROSS
weak	FADE
—in spirit	FAINT
weaken	ENTENDER.INTENDER
	PALL
weald	WILD
wealth	WAR(R)ISON
weapon	WELSH-HOOK.VOU(L)GE
—with several barrels	ORGUE
wear beforehand	PREOCCUPY
wearer of	
—frock	FROCK
—silk	SILKWORM
weather	WELK
—conditions	WEATHERING
weave	PLIGHT
weaver	WEBSTER
wedding feast	BRIDE-ALE
week	SENNIGHT
weigh	
—anchor	LOOSE
—down	POISE
—in the mind	POISE
weighed	WAID(E)
weight	BURTHEN.PEASE.PEAZE
	PEISE.PEIZE.PEYSE.POISE
welcome	GRATULATE

welfare	HEAL
well	
—being	WEALTH
—born	GENTLE
—disposed	TOWARD(LY)
	WELL-GIVEN
—judged munificence	
	MAGNIFICENCE
—made	FEAT(E)OUS.FEATUOUS
—mannered	WELL-THEWED
wet	MOIL
whale-like sea	
creature	WHIRLPOOL
what kind of	WHAT FOR A
whatever	WHATSO
whatsoever	WHATSO
when	WHENAS
where	WHEAR(E)
whereas	WHENAS
which	WHILK
while	THE WHILST
whim	FLAM
whimsical	
—person	WHIM
—tune or caprice	MAGGOT
whip	
—out	BRAID
—top	GIG
whisper	ROUND
whist	WHISK
white	CANDID
—and viscous	GLA(I)REOUS
whiteness	CANDOUR
whitewash	WHITE-LIME
whiting	MIRLING
whitish	WHITELY
whitlow	ANCOME
who	WHAT
whoever	WHATSO
whole body	CONTINENT
whole	GREAT
wholemeal bread	
	RAVEL(LED) BREAD
wholesale	GREAT
whore	WENCH
why	FOR WHY
wicked	FACINOROUS.FELON
	FELONIOUS.GOAT
	SCELERAT(E).WICK

—person	FELON	—counsel or resolve	REDELESS
wickedness	NAUGHT	—favour	GRACELESS
widow	RELICT	—ideas	UNIDEAL
—'s share of husband's		—mercy	GRACELESS
estate	WIDOW'S-BENCH	—modesty	FRONTLESS
wield	WELD.WILD.WIND	—self-control	IMPOTENT
wife	LADY	witty	CONCEITED
wig	MAJOR	woe	BALE
wile	ENGINE	woman	FAIR.WOMANKIND
will not	NILL	—friend present at a birth	GOSSIP
willing	VOLITIENT	—of fashion	GALLANT
willingly	L(I)EVE.LIEF	—who has taken vows	VOWESS
wind up	SPAN	—'s morning cap	MOB(-CAP)
windfall	CADUAC	—'s shift	SMOCK
winding	MEANDRIAN	—'s silk necktie	TAWDRY-LACE
—course	ERROR	won	WAN
windlass	WINDAS	wonder at	ADMIRE.MARVEL
window shutter	SHOT-WINDOW	wonderful	GEASON
windpipe	WEAZAND	woo	ADDRESS
wine		wooden	
—cup	PIECE	—framework	CONTIGNATION
—mixing bowl	CRATER	—post	STUD
wink	EY(E)LIAD	—shoe or sole	PATTEN
winter	WINTER-TIDE	—sword	WASTER
wipeout	NULL	woodlouse	MULTIPED(E)
wise	WITTY	woodruff	WOOD-ROOF
—man	WIZARD	woolsack	WOOL-PACK
wish	WISE	words	
—for	WILL	—of a villain	VILLA(I)NY
wit	WEET	—of song	DIT(T)
witch	WEIRD	wore	WARE
witchery	GLAMOUR	work	
with		—against in secret	UNDERWORK
—difficulty	UNE(A)TH	—liquid	FRET
	UNEATHES.UNNETHES	workaday	WORKY-DAY
—exactitude	POINT-DEVICE	workmanship	ARTIFICE
	POINT-DEVISE	workshop	WORKING-HOUSE
—hardship	STRAIT	world	MAPPEMOND.MOULD
—many nooks and		—of fairies	FAERIE.FAERY
corners	NOOK-SHOTTEN	worship	SERVE
—wool next to skin	WOOLWARD	worst	WORSE
withdraw	WALK	—state	PESSIMISM
—from	VOID	worth	PRICE.VALOUR
wither	BLAST	worthless	NAUGHT(Y).RACA.VOID
withheld	WITHHAULT	—beast	HILDING
within	ENTIRE	would be willing	HAD AS LIEF
without	WITHOUTEN	would-be wit	HALF-WIT
—a mate	MAKELESS	wound	ENGORE.PLAGUE
—containing flesh	MAIGRE	—by reproach	BITE

wrangle   BRANGLE.CAMPLE
wrap   WAP
wreaked   WROKE(N).WROKEN
wretched   WO(E)
wriggle   WIND
wrinkled   WRITHLED
writ
—asserting papal supremacy
    PRAEMUNIRE
—moving case to county
   court   TOLT
—to summon jury
    VENIRE (FACIAS)
write
—between   INTERSCRIBE
—in musical notation   PRICK
writhe   WIND
writing   DITE.WRIT
written   WRATE.WRIT
wrong   UNRIGHT
wrongfully   UNDULY
wrote   WRIT.WROOT
yarrow   NOSE-BLEED
yearn   EARN
yeast   YEST
yellowish-green   GAUDY-GREEN
yeoman   GOODMAN
yew   EUGH
yield   KNOCK UNDER.VAIL
young
—girl   DELL
—lady   DEMOISELLE
—man   IMP.SWAIN
—manservant   GROOM
—person   YONKER
your   THY
youth   YOUTHHOOD
—training for knighthood   PAGE
zealot   ZEAL
zealously   INSTANTLY
zedoary   CETYWALL.SETUALE
    SETWALL

old²
meaning
former state of
  affairs   EX.LATE.OLD
hence
•*former* deed   EXACT
•*late* claim   EXCLAIM

•*no longer* clear   EXPLAIN
•*once* stood   EXPOSED
•*one-time* shelter   EXTENT
•*outdated* tax   EXCESS
•*past* it   EXIT
•*previous* pamphlet   EXTRACT
•*retired* player   EXACTOR
•*stale* wine   EXPORT
•*used to be* the thing   EXIT
and
•*Old and* New Testament   LATENT
•*old* cross   LATEX
•*old* king   LATER
and
•*late* queen   OLDER
•*retired* head   OLDNESS
•*much used* letter   OLDEN

old³
meaning
  elderly
  former:
old banger   MUSKET
old boy   ALUMNUS.OB
old Dutch   WIFE
old Etonian   OE
old girl   ALUMNA.DUTCH.WIFE
old hat   DATED
old lady   (*see* old woman *below*)
old man   DAD.PA.POP
old man of Paris   PRIAM.VIEUX
old model   T
old prime minister   EDEN.PEEL
    PITT
old *Scottish*...   AULD
old scholar   ERASMUS
old style   OS
Old Testament   OT
old woman   BETTER HALF.DUTCH
    GRAN.HAG.MA.WIFE

old⁴   PAST
hence
•*old* gold   PASTOR
•*old, old* use   PASTURE
•*old* one, German   PASTE-IN

old⁵
other uses:
old age pension(er)   OAP
old coppers   PENNYFARTHING
Old English   OE

old-*fashioned*	DOL.LOD	•pass *above*	COLON
old-fashioned medium		acting	
	STEAM RADIO	•*acting* group	ONSET
old-*fiddler*	DOL.LOD	advanced	
old fiddler	COLE.NERO	•John's *more advanced*	JACKSON
Old French	OF(R)	ahead	
old *French*	VIEILLE.VIEUX	•he is right *ahead*	RON
old *leader*	O	appearing	
Old Irish	OIR	•Greek letter *appearing*	MUON
old *Irish*	AULD	attached	
old king	COLE.LUD.OG	•orb *with* ring *attached*	BALLON
old master	CHIPS.PAINTER	available	
Old Measurement	OM	•cricketer *available*	BATON
Old Norse	ON	bowling	
old player	HARPSICHORD.SPINET	•bat *before bowling*	BATON
old players	BANDAGED	charged to	
old queen	BESS	•*charged to* group	ONSET
old sloth	MEGATHERIUM	continue	
Old Style	OS	•*continue to* signal	FLAGON
Old Testament	OT	forward	
-ology	(*see* study²)	•haul *forward*	DRAGON
Olympic *finalists*	IC	functioning	
omega	Z	•officer *functioning*	COLON
omelette of eggs or...	GORGES	further	
omicron	O	•weaken *further*	WILTON
on¹		further forward	
on board	(in)LIN-ER.(in)S-S	•bed-time *further*	
on *ending*	end in ON	*forward*	COTTON
on *ending*	N	in	
on *entering*	incl ON	•*in* the reeds	ONRUSHES
•on *entering* ship	SONS	operational	
on *finishing*	end in ON	•100 *operational* types	CONSORTS
on *finishing*	N	over	
on *leaving*	omit ON	•*over*price	ONCOST
on/*off*	omit ON	performing	
•on/*off* bat(on)	BAT	•*performing* one on...	ONION
•on/*off* butt(on)	BUTT	playing	
on *opening*	start with ON	•*playing* before church	ONCE
•on *opening* hospital		re	
wing	ONWARDS	•*re* Advent	ONCOMING
on *opening*	O	running	
on *starting*	O	•go *running*	GOON
on *the inside*	incl ON	supported by	
•painter on *the inside*	LONELY	•vehicle *supported by*...	CARTON
on²		worn by	
meaning		•hat *worn by*...	CAPON
aboard		**on³**	
•islander *aboard*	MINOR CANON	indicating addition:	
above		•company *on* the way	CORD.COST

•look *on board*	LOSS
•put *on* about...	CAPUT

on⁴

implying addition:

•farming	(on) LAND

similar examples in this
vocabulary are preceded by (on)

on⁵

indicates origins:

on Clydeside = Scottish

•man *on Clydeside*	MON

on Fujiyama = in Japan

•temple gateway *on* Fujiyama	TORII

on Mont Blanc = French

•man *on Mont Blanc*	HOMME

on the Rhine = German

•man *on the Rhine*	MANN

on the Tiber = Italian

•bridge *on the Tiber*	PONTE

on⁶

other uses:

on a ramble in the	THINE
on account of	OA
on active service	OAS
on board	(in) LIN-ER.(in) S-S
* on board	incl *
•king *on board* galle-y	GALLERY
on horseback	UP
on it	ONT
on purpose	-MENT
on side	L.LEG.LT.LEFT
on top(D)	
•parking sign *on top*	RAMP
•parking *on top of* sign...	PRAM
on the conservative side	RIGHT
on the Continent	(*see* abroad)
on the go nurse...	NURSE
on the loose in Greek...	REEKING
on the prowl animal...	LAMINA
on the rampage Huns...	SHUN
on the run in Glos	LOSING
on the ship	(in) S-S
on the way	incl N.S.E.W
•he's *on the way*	HEN.HEW
•it *is on* the way	NIT.SIT.WIT
•stop *on* the way	BAR.BARN
•*on the way North*, walker...(D) ↑	RECAP

on the wing	UP
once	(*see* old¹)

one¹　　LUNCH-TIME.MONAD
　　　　　　SINGULAR.SOLO

and a half	SESQUI-
and one	ELEVEN
and two	TWELVE
by one	ELEVEN
Christmas present	PARTRIDGE
	PEAR-TREE
combining form	MON(O)-.UNI-
each	PER
expert	ACE
French	UN.UNE
hence	
•one *French* prison	UNCAGE
•North *with* one *French*...	NUN
•king *with* one *French*...	RUNE
German	EIN

group　MONAD.SINGLETON.UNIT

having one

—adductor muscle

　　　　　　MONOMYARIAN

—amino group	MONOAMINE

—ancestral group

　　　　　　MONOPHYLETIC

—atom	MONATOMIC
—axis	MONAXIAL

　　MONAXON(I(C).UNIAXIAL

—brood per annum	UNIVOLTINE

—bundle of stamens

　　　　　　MONODELPHOUS

—carpel	MONOCARPELLARY
—case	MONOTHECAL
—cavity	UNILOCULAR
—cell	MONOTHALAMOUS

　　UNICAMERAL.UNICELLULAR

　　　　　　UNILOCULAR

—centre	UNICENTRAL
—chamber	MONOTHALAMOUS

　　　　　　UNICAMERAL

—colour	MONOCHRO(MAT)IC

　　　　　　UNICOLORATE

　　UNICOLOROUS.UNICOLOUR

—column	MONOSTYLAR

—cotyledon

　　　　　　MONOCOTYLEDONOUS

—degree of freedom	UNIVARIANT
—ear	MONAURAL.MONOPHONIC

—eye	MONOCULAR
—finger	MONODACTYLOUS
—flower	UNIFLOROUS
—foot	MONOPODE
	MONOPOD(IAL).UNIPED
—fruiting period	MONOCARPIC
	MONOTOCOUS
—god	MONOTHEISTIC
—heart	MONOCARDIAN
—horn	MONOCEROUS
	UNICORN
—husband	MONOGAMIC
	MONOGAMOUS
—hydrogen atom	MONOACID
	MONOBASIC
—hydroxyl group	MONOHYDRIC
—key	MONOTONAL
—leg	MONOPODE
	MONOPOD(IAL).UNIPOD
—language	MONOGLOT
	MONOLINGUAL.UNILINGUAL
—leaf	UNIFOLIATE
—letter	UNILITERAL
—line	MONOSTICHOUS
—lip	UNILABIATE
—lobe	MONOTHECAL
	UNILOBAR.UNILOBED
—lobule	UNILOBULAR
—loculus	MONOTHECAL
	UNILOCULAR
—marriage	MONOGAMOUS
—meaning	UNIVOCAL
—measure	MONOMETER
—metal	MONOMETALLIC
—nostril	MONORHINE
	MONORHINAL
—nucleus	MONONUCLEAR
	UNINUCLEAR
	UNINUCLEATE
—offspring at a birth	
	MONOTOCOUS
	UNIPAROUS
—ovary	MONOCARPIC
	MONOCARPOUS
—oxygen atom	MONOXIDE
—part	UNIPARTITE
—perianth whorl	
	MONOCHALMYDEOUS
—person ruling	DICTATORSHIP

	DESPOTISM.MONARCHY
—petal	MONOPETALOUS
—phase	MONOPHASE
	MONOPHASIC
—plane of symmetry	
	MONOSYMMETRIC(AL)
—pole	UNIPOLAR
—rail	MONORAIL
—ray	MONACT(INAL)
	MONACTINE
—rib	UNICOSTATE
—ring	MONOCYCLIC
—ring of columns	MONOPTERAL
—row	MONOSERIAL
	MONOSTICHOUS
	UNISERIAL.UNISERIATE
—ruler	MONARCHY
—sac	MONOTHECAL
—sepal	MONOSEPALOUS
—series	MONOSERIAL
—serrated edge	
	MONOPRIONIDIAN
—set of teeth	MONOPHYDONT
—sex	MONOECIOUS
	UNISEX(UAL)
—sheath	MONOTHECAL
—side	UNILATERAL
—stamen	MONANDROUS
—term	MONOMIAL
—thread	UNIFILAR
—toe	MONODACTYLOUS
—tone	MONOTONAL
—turn	MONOCYCLIC.UNICYCLIC
—tusk	MONODONT
—type of mycelium	
	HOMOTHALLIC
—valency	MONATOMIC
	MONOVALENT.UNIVALENT
—valve	UNIVALVE
	UNIVALVULAR
—variant quantity	UNIVARIATE
—wavelength	MONOCHROMATIC
—wheel	MONOCYCLE.UNICYCLE
—whorl	MONOCYCLIC
—whorled perianth	
	MONOCHLAMYDEOUS
—wife	MONOGAMIC
	MONOGAMOUS.MONOGYNIAN
	MONOGYNOUS

—wing   MONOPLANE
—word   MONOMIAL
—xylem strand   MONARCH
—yearly occurrence   ANNUAL
in
—a quarter   NUMERATOR
—bingo   KELLY'S EYE
—eight   OAR.STROKE
—ten   NEXT TO NOTHING
—the pack   ACE
Italian   UNA.UNO
letter   SINGLET
local   UN
nil   TEN
not identified   X.Y
number one   FIRST MATE
    LIEUTENANT
of nine   MUSE
of 27   BOOK
of 39   BOOK.STEP
of us   ME.YOU
old   J
Scotsman   SOLOMON
Scottish. . .   AE.ANE
short of team   TEN
sided   BIAS(S)ED
spell   THEN
spot   ACE
thousand   IM.LAC
—pounds   GRAND
time   (*see* old¹)
under par   BIRDIE
up   RIDER
way and another   STANDARD
one²   A.ACE.AN.UN.UNIT
    EA.EACH.EVERBODY
hence
•one-fifteen   ASIDE
•one in Poplar, *perhaps*   AINTREE
•one *in* a tree, *perhaps*   FAIR
and
•one flower   ACEROSE
•one king   ACER
•one twitch   ACETIC
and
•one I mus(t) *almost.* . .   ANIMUS
•one *in* the *French.* . .   LANE
•one man   ANDES
and

•one *local* local   UNBAR
•one *locally* bred   UNBORN
•one *rustic* hat   UNCAP
one³   A.I
one about. . .   -IC
one *and* one   AI.-IA.-IAN.II
one answer   -IANS
one *by* one   AI.-IA.-IAN.II
one cold. . .   -IC
one-eyed   incl one I
•*one-eyed* painter   TITAN
•*one-eyed* man   MAIN
one-fifty   AL.IL
one-five   IV
one head   -INESS
one hundred   -IC
one *in* a hundred   -TION
one in 100,000   LAIC
one *inside*   incl I
one *leaving*   omit I
one *less (than)*   omit A or I
one man   IRON
one measure   -ICT.-IFT.ILB
one member   IMP-
one mile   IM-
one *missing*   omit I
one-nil   IO
one on   -ION
one *performing*   -ION
one quarter   IE.IN.IS
one right   IR
one thousand   IM
one thousand *and* two   IMPAIR
one thousand pounds   IMPOUNDS
one *with* a. . .   AI.-IA
one's   AS.IS
ones   ELEVEN
one⁴
(o)ne *loses* nothing   NE
one *might say*   WON
one might say we've. . .   WEAVE
only
only daughter   SOLED
only East   NOW
only NW   NOSE
only SW   NONE
onset of <u>winter</u>   W
o-ort   OBIT
open   OVERT

hence	
•open parliament	OVERTRUMP
•open vessel	OVERTURN
•open works	OVERTOPS
open	FRANK
open = start with	
•ally *opens with* spades	SALLY
•man *to open* road	HERD
open <u>arms</u>	MARS.RAMS
open <u>house</u>	NEST
open jar	OVERTURN
open plain	TRANSPARENT
open season	FREE FALL
Open University	OU
open up <u>crate</u>	CATER.TRACE
opener	KEY
opening	O
opening gambit	PLOY
opening gambit	G
opening of <u>Parliament</u>	P
opening out <u>ends</u>	DENS.SEND
opening pair	HINGES
opening pair	P
Opening <u>Today!</u>	T
opening *up*(D) ↑	ROOD
opening word	SESAME
opera	OP
opera girl	AIDA.CARMEN
	MIMI.NORMA.TOSCA
opera house	MET
operatic part	ACT.SCENA
operate	
operating	ON
operating <u>on her</u>	HERON
operation(s)	OP(S)
operation of levers	REVELS
operational research	OR
Operations Officer	OPS
Operations Room	OPS
oppose	
opponents	(*see also* bridge)
opponents of them	US
opponents of us	THEM
opposed	CON.OPP.V
opposing us	THEM
opposite	OP(P)
opposite directions	EW.NS.SN.WE
opposite of new	OLD
opposite of new‹	WEN

opposite prompt	OP
opposition to tall. . .	SHORT
oppress (D)	
indicates one word written above	
another:	
•man *oppressed* by	
weight. . . (D)	TONAL
optative	OPT
optical	
optical character reading	OCR
optical character recognition	OCR
optical learner	PUPIL
opus	OP
or	(*see also* alternative.gold)
or nearest offer	ONO
orally I'd. . .	EYED.IDE
orange	
<u>orange</u> *peel*	OE
<u>orange</u> spot	JAFFA.SEVILLE
<u>orange</u> *squash*	ONAGER
orb	O
orchestra	LSO
ordained	ORD
order	CH.OBE.OM.ORD
order alteration	ANAGRAM
order <u>form</u>	FROM
ordered <u>wines</u>	SINEW.SWINE
orderly-<u>room</u>	MOOR
Order of	
—British Empire	OBE
—Merit	OM
—St Augustine	OSA
—St Benedict	OSB
—St Francis	OSF
ordinary	ORD
Ordinary National	
—Certificate	ONC
—Diploma	OND
ordinary seaman	OS
ordnance	ORD
ordnance datum	OD
Ordnance Survey	OS
organ	
<u>organ</u>-*grinding*	GROAN
organists	RCO
organ stops¹	COLONS.EAR PLUGS
	HEART ATTACKS
organ stops²	CLARABELLA
	CORNET.CORNO DI BASSETTO

CROMORNA.CROMORNE
DOLCE.DULCIANA.FLUTE
KRUM(M)HORN
MUTATION-STOP.NASARD
OCTAVE.PICCOLO.PRINCIPAL
PYRAMIDON.QUINT.SALICET
SALICIONAL.SESQUIALTERA
SEXT.TRUMPET.TUBA
VOIX CELESTE.VOX HUMANA
WALDFLUTE.WALDHORN

organisation

Organization of African
Unity   OAU
Organization of American
States   OAS
organisation of women
is. . .   WINSOME
organised demo   MODE
orient   E
oriental[1]   E.INE.SHAN
hence
•Oriental network   -ERY
•Oriental right. . .   INERT
•swindle Oriental   CONINE
oriental[2]   MALAY
bosun   SERANG
coin   DERHAM.DIRHAM.DIRHEM
commission   SQUEEZE
fruit   SHADDOCK
javelin   JEREED.JERID
leader   O
plant   TURBITH.TURPETH
prison   BAGNIO
sailor   LASCAR
shrub   HENNA
weight DERHAM.DIRHAM.DIRHEM
(*see also* eastern[2])
origami figure   PAPER-BOY
original
original manuscript AUTOGRAPH
MS.SIGNATURE
original plot   EDEN
original plot   POLT
originally lived. . .   DEVIL
originally seen in Newark   SIN
originally seen in Ne/war/k   WAR
origins of the Universe   TE
originates from A/sia M/inor SIAM
originator of plan   P

oscillate
oscillating wires   SWIRE
oscillograph   CRO
other
other people's   OPS
other ranks   OR
other times   ITEMS.MITES.SMITE
otherwise   OR
otherwise it was. . .   WAIST
otorhinolaryngology   ENT
ought   O
ounce   CAT.OZ.SNOW LEOPARD
our
our leader   ER
our time/era   AD
indicates a word written in front
of 'our'   OUR
•officer is our leader   COLOUR
our *leader*   O
our man   HE
oust
ousts a. . .   omit A
ousts *   omit *
•s(imp)ly *ousts* the
little devil   SLY
ousted leader   omit first letter
•(p)arty *ousted* leader   ARTY
ousted leader   DEALER
out[1]
meaning
abroad
•girl *abroad*   MISS OUT
asleep
•king *asleep*   ROUT
away
•*start* scratching *away*   SCOUT
bowled
•Guiana *opener bowled*   GOUT
caught
•learner *caught*   LOUT
considering verdict
•*considering verdict*
suitable. . .   OUTFIT
dismissed
•Black *dismissed*   BOUT
exceeding
•*exceeding* the call   OUTCRY
fielding
•*fielding* players   OUTCAST

fired	
•quietly *fired*	POUT
in error	
•*in error with* offer	OUTBID
in the field	
•run *in the field*	ROUT
not acceptable	
•odds *not acceptable*	SPOUT
not allowed	
•Rod *not allowed*. . .	STICK OUT
not in	
•out of key	NOTING
old hat	
•*old-hat* group	OUTSET
square	
•T-*square*	TOUT
strike	
•*strike* actors	OUTCAST
•*striking* clothes	OUTWEAR
unacceptable	
•*unacceptable* timber	OUTBOARD
unconscious	
•150 *unconscious*. . .	CLOUT
unfashionable	
•*unfashionable* fashion	OUTRAGE

out²

indicates inclusion:

day *out*	DA-Y
dry *out*	DR-Y
last *out*	LAS-T
out-date	D-ATE
out East	incl E
•f-ast *out* East	FEAST
out West	incl W
•ha-s *out* West	HAWS
out West	W-EST
•is *out* W-est	WISEST
sit *out*	SI-T
time *out*	A-GE
tire *out*	T-IRE
way *out*	WA-Y
wear *out*	WEA-R

out³

indicates omission:

out East	omit E
•fin(e) *out* East	FIN
out West	omit W
•(w)omen *out* West	OMEN
outline	omit I

•ma(i)n *out*line	MAN

out⁴

other uses:

out and about

•he's *out* and *about* in. . .	SHINE
out in the. . .	THINE
out west	-INE
take *out*	KATE.TEAK

out of¹   EX-

hence

•out of beer	EXPORTER
•out of money	EXPOUNDS
•out of sight, *say*	EXCITE

out of²

indicates inclusion:

out of line	incl I
out of money	incl L
out of the way	incl N.S.E.W
•ge-t *out of* the way	GENT
•*out-of*-the-way h-at	HEAT
out of time	incl T
out of the race	incl TT
out of turn	incl U
out of work	incl OP

out of³

indicates omission:

•I am *out of* ra(i)n	RAN
•I'm *out of* sl(im)y. . .	SLY
•Jack *out of* (j)ob	OB-
•one *out of* m(one)y	MY
•ran *out of* cur(ran)t. . .	CURT
•run *out of* (ru)i(n)ous. . .	-IOUS
out of *	omit *

out of⁴

other uses:

out of breath	BATHER.BERTHA
out of control I ran. . .	RAIN.RANI
out of date	(*see* old⁴)
out of form player	REPLAY
out of line steps. . .	PESTS
out of or/der at E/nglish..	DERATE
out of order today	TOADY
out of place when I. . .	WHINE
out of print	OP
out of step	PEST.PETS
out of the way town	WONT
out of time	EMIT
out of turn he is. . .	HIES
out of tune in song	NOSING

outbreak	
out*break*	TOU
*out*break	BAKER.BRAKE
outbreak of herpes	SPHERE
outbreak of herpes	H
***outburst** in ni̲g̲h̲t*	HINTING
outcast	LEPER.ISHMAEL
	PARIAH
outcome of a̲ ̲n̲e̲w̲...	WANE.WEAN
*out*cry	C-RY
outdated	(*see* old[3])
*out*do	D-O
outdoor	
out d̲o̲o̲r̲	ROOD
out̲d̲o̲o̲r̲ seat	SHOOTING STICK
*out*lawed	WALED.WEALD
*out*lay	LA-Y
outline	
outline	LIEN.NILE
out̲l̲i̲n̲e̲ a...	incl A
outline *	incl *
•r-ed *outlining* ear	REARED
outlined in *	incl in *
•ear *outlined* in r-ed	REARED
***outlying parts of* t̲o̲w̲n̲**	TN
***output of* m̲e̲n̲ ̲s̲h̲e̲...**	ENMESH
outrace	
*out*race	incl TT
out̲r̲a̲c̲e̲	ACER.ACRE
outrage	
outrage in I̲r̲a̲n̲	RAIN.RANI
outraged m̲o̲t̲h̲e̲r̲	THERMO-
outrageous p̲l̲o̲t̲ ̲o̲n̲ ̲a̲...	PLATOON
outré g̲a̲r̲b̲	BRAG
outright	
*out*right	incl R or RT
•pa-y *out*right...	DIRTY
•*out*right li-e	LIRE
*out*right	incl in R-T
•I have *out*right...	RIVET
*out*right	omit R or RT
•*out*right fa(r)ce	FACE
•*out*right pa(rt)y...	PAY
outset	
out̲s̲e̲t̲	-EST
*out*set	SE-T
outside	PEEL.SKIN
is *outside*	I-S
•member is *outside*	IMPS
*out*side	DIES.IDES
out̲s̲i̲d̲e̲ *broadcast*	TEDIOUS
out̲s̲i̲d̲e̲ a...	incl A
outside right	incl R.RT
•*outside* right ha-d...	HARD
•*outside* right ma-y...	MARTY
outside T̲o̲r̲b̲a̲y̲	TAY
outside *	incl *
•fa-r *outside* the...	FATHER
outsides of h̲o̲u̲s̲e̲	HE
rank *outsid̲e̲r̲s̲*	RK
outsize	OS
***outskirts* of c̲i̲t̲y̲**	CY
outstanding	
outstanding	OS
outstanding item	PARTICULAR
outstanding message	SIGNAL
outstanding vocalist	
	CAROL SINGER
outstanding *	incl in *
•th-e *outstanding* queen	THERE
outward	
hard, *outwardly* nic-e	NICHE
outwardly n̲i̲c̲e̲	NE
outwardly n̲-̲i̲c̲e̲	NOTICE
oval	EGG.O
over[1]	
meaning	
about, anent	
concerning	
in connection with	
on, regarding	RE
	(*see also* about[2])
over[2]	
meaning	
above	
on	ON.SUPRA
	(*see also* on[1])
over[3]	
meaning	
completed	
done	
ended	
finished	OVER
hence	
•fifty completed	LOVER
•done *to a* turn	OVERTURN
•ended *with* highest...	OVERTOP
•doctor finished...	DROVER

over⁴

indicates a word written above
  another(D):

•engineers with one *over*due	RESIDUE
•fifty *over*charge	LION
•girl *over*age	TESSERA
•he is *over*bearing	HEN.HEW
•in lieu of *over*time	FORAGE.FORT
•large *over*head	BIGNESS
•live *over*night	BENIGHT
•no *over*charge	ORATE
•numbers *over*see	TENSELY
•she is *over*bearing	SHEW
•skill is *over*t	ARTIST

over⁵

over ten	ELEVEN
over ten	TENT
over ten⟨	NET
over <u>ten</u>	ENT-.NET
overcast **but. . .**⟨	TUB
overcharge	OC
overcoat	BENJAMIN
	(*see also* garment)

overcome

indicates word written above
  another (D):

•boy *overcomes* the *French*	LADLE
•I *overcome* Bible queen	INTER
•man *overcomes* a deacon	HEAVEN
•we *overcome* the backs	WESTERNS
•woman *overcomes* 500	SHED
overdrawn	(in) R-ED

overhaul

overhaul <u>car</u>	ARC
overhaul <u>dray</u>⟨	YARD

overhead

*over*head	O
*over*head⟨	POT
*over*head	(*see* over⁴)
overhead lines	AIRWAYS
overheads	ANTLERS.HATS
	HORNS
*over*heads	HADES.SHADE

overnight

over<u>night</u>	THING
overnight trip, *say*	NITRIDE

overrun

overrun	EXTRA
*over*run⟨	NUR
over<u>run</u>	NUR.URN
over<u>run</u> a. . .	incl A
*over*run *	incl *
•soldiers *overrun* Georgia	MEGAN
overrun by *	incl in *
•Georgia *overrun by* soldiers	MEGAN
overseas	(*see* abroad)

overthrow

overthrow <u>emir</u>	MIRE.RIME
overthrow <u>emir</u>⟨	RIME

overtime

*over*time⟨	EMIT
*over*time	EMIT.MITE
over<u>time</u>	(*see* over⁴)
overtime, *say*	NITRATE

overturn

<u>over</u>*turning*	ROVE
<u>over</u>*turning* tram⟨	MART
overweight ladies	FATHERS

overwhelm

overwhelm a. . .	incl A
overwhelm *	incl *
•weight *overwhelms* a student	TALON
overwhelmed by *	incl in *
•a student *overwhelmed by* weight	TALON
overworked rhymes	BURKED
	IRKED.LURKED
	PERKED.SHIRKED

owe

owe(s)	O.(OO.OS)
owing	-IOUS.(in) DEB-T
owing money	(in) R-ED
	(in) DEB-T

own

own goal	OG
own *Scottish*. . .	AIN
owned by *	incl in *
•company *owned by* drunkard	SCOOT
owned by com/pan/y	PAN
owner	CONFESSOR
owning a. . .	incl A

owning *	incl *	European	BISON.AUROCHS
•drunkard *owning*			URUS
company	SCOOT	Himalayan	DSOMO.DSOBO
ox	KINE.NEAT		JOMO.ZOBO.ZOBU
African	CAPE BUFFALO		Z(H)O.ZHOMO
	CONGO BUFFALO	Indian	BHYLE.BRAHMIN BULL
	ZAMOUSE		G(A)YAL.GAUR.MITHAN
American	BISON.BUFFALO		S(E)LADANG.ZEBU
bison	BONAS(S)US	Indonesian	DWARF BUFFALO
buffalo	BUBALUS	musk-ox	OVIBOS
cattle/bison hybrid	CAT(T)ALO	Tibetan	SARLAC.SARLAK.YAK
cattle/zebu hybrid	CATTABU	wild ox	BUGLE.OWRE
Celebes	ANOA	**Oxford**	OXF.SHOE
	SAPI-(O)UTAN	Oxford dreamer	SPIRE
East Indian	BANTENG.BANTING	Oxford English Dictionary	OED
	TAMAROU	Oxford Street	BROAD.HIGH

P

Celt. *copper*. eighty. eighty thousand. four hundred. four hundred thousand.
Kelt. page. park. parking. participle. pawn pedal. *pea. pee. peg*. penny.
peta-. phosphorous. pi. piano. pico-. poise. Portugal. power. president.
pressure. prince. quiet. rho. soft. vitamin

Pacific Standard Time	PST
pacifist	CO.DOVE
pacifist conclusion	DOVETAIL
pack	
pack of hounds	CRY
packaged crate	TRACE
packed with *	incl in *
•ship *packed with* relatives	SKINS
packing a...	incl A
packing *	incl *
•relatives *packing* ship	SKINS
packing extra...	TAXER
paddy	
Paddy's = Irish	
•*Paddy's* accent	BROGUE
page(s)	P.(PP)
page(s) *missing*	omit P.(PP)
paid	PD
pain *in France*	BREAD
paint	
paint distributor	ARTIST.BRUSH
paint *mixing*	INAPT.PINTA
painted	PXT
painter	ARA.PRA.RA.ROPE
	TURNER
	(*see also* artist)
pair	OO.PR
pair of	
—clubs	CC
—diamonds	DD
—hearts	HH
—spades	SS
pair of ducks	OO
pair of students	LL
	(*see also* two².two³)
Pakistan	PAK
Pakistan airline	PIA
Palestine	PAL
Palestine Liberation	
Organization	PLO
palm	EUTERPE
African	DATE-PALM.DOOM PALM

	D(O)UM PALM.PALMYRA
Asian	DATE-PALM.TALIPAT
	TALIPOT.TALIPUT.PALMYRA
betel nut	ARECA
Borassus	WINE-PALM
Brazilian	ATTALEA.BABASSU
	CARNA(H)UBA
	CHIQUICHIQUI.COQUILLA
	INAJA.LEOPOLDINIA
	PIASSABA.PIASSAVA
	PAXIUBA
bussu	TROELIE.TROELY.TROOLIE
Californian	WASHINGTONIA
cane	CALAMUS
Ceylonese	CORYPHA
	JAGGERY PALM.KITTUL
	TALIPAT.TALIPOT.TALIPUT
Chilean	COQUITO
Chusan palm	TRACHYCARPUS
climbing	RAT(T)AN
Cordyline	GRASS PALM
corn palm	DRACAENA
cycad	ZAMIA
Dracaena	CORN PALM
East Indian	AT(T)AP.NIPA
Elaeus	OIL PALM
European	CHAMAEROPS
	PALMETTO
fan palm	TALIPAT.TALIPOT
	TALIPUT.WASHINGTONIA
grass palm	CORDYLINE
Indian	JAGGERY PALM.KITTUL
Leopoldinia	PIASSABA
	PIASSAVA
Malagasy	RAPHIA
Mexican	WASHINGTONIA
miriti	ITA.MORICHE
New Zealand	NIKAU
oil palm	ELAEUS
palmetto	FAN PALM
	HEMP PALM.SABAL
Philippine	NIPA

piassava	CHIQUICHIQUI	**parcel**	LOT
raphia	JUPATI.RAFFIA	*parcel* post	OPTS.POTS
	WINE PALM		STOP.TOPS.
royal palm	CABBAGE PALM	**Parent-Teachers Association**	PTA
sago palm	EJOO.GOMUTI	**parish priest**	PP
	GOMUTO	**park(ing)**	P
South American	ACCROCOMIA	hence	
	ASSAI.BURITI.BUSSO	•park at ten	PATIO.PATTEN
	COHUNE.COROZO	•park in a street	PINARD
	GROO-GROO.GRU-GRU	•park in New York	PINNY
	JUPATI.MACAHUBA	**parliament**	DIET
	MACAW TREE.MACOYA	Denmark	FOLKETING.RIGSDAG
MIRITI.PEACH-PALM.PUPUNHA		Germany	BUNDESTAG
	TUCUM.WAX PALM		REICHSTAG
tropical shore	COCO PALM	—upper house	BUNDESRAT
COCO TREE.COCONUT PALM			REICHSRAT(H)
Trachycarpus	CHUSAN PALM	Iceland	ALTHING
wine palm	BORASSUS.RAPHIA	India	
palm oil	BRIBE(RY)	—lower house	LOK SABHA
pamphlet	PAM	—upper house	RAJYA SABHA
Panama(nian)	PA(N)	Ireland	
capital	P.PANAMA CITY	—lower house	DAIL (EIREANN)
coin	BALBOA	—upper	SEANAD (EIREANN)
leader	P	Isle of Man	TYNWALD (COURT)
Pan's pipes	SYRINX	—lower house	HOUSE OF KEYS
panic		Israel	KENESET.KNES(S)ET
panic over	ROVE	Norway	STORT(H)ING
panicky fear	FARE	—lower house	ODELST(H)ING
paper(s) MS.(MSS).RAG.TIMES		—upper house	LAGT(H)ING
paper-boy	COMICAL	Persia	MAJLIS.MEJLIS
paper carrier	BRIEF CASE	Portugal	CORTES
paper cupboard	PRESS	Russia	D(O)UMA
paper flower	SUNBURN	Spain	CORTES
paper headgear	FOOLSCAP	Sweden	RIKSDAG
paper maker	EDITOR	United States	CONGRESS
(*see also* measures)		—lower house	
parade		HOUSE OF REPRESENTATIVES	
parade ground	DRILLING SITE	—upper house	SENATE
parade time	EASTER	**Parliamentary**	
paradise	EDEN	Labour Party	PLP
paragon	S.SAINT.ST	Private Secretary	PPS
paragraph	PAR(A)	**part**	PT
Paraguay(an)	PY	part company	PLATOON
capital	ASUNCION.P	*part* company	CO.PAN.ANY
coin	GUARANI	part company	DIVORCE
leader	P	part of. . .	incl in *
tea	YERBA.YERBA(DE)MATE	•it *is part of* m-e	MITE
parallel	PAR	*part of* bird	B
parasite	(in) H-OST	part of b̄ird	BITTERN

part of bird	PARSON'S NOSE		*pass round* a...	incl A
part of collar	S.ESS		*passed round* *	incl *
part of collar	COL.LAR		•prince *passed round* beer	PALER
part of col/lar ge/ts...	LARGE		*passed round by* *	incl in *
part of county	HUNDRED.RIDING		•beer *passed round by*	
part of Oxford	SOLE.UPPER		prince	PALER
part of the...	T		passed staff college	PSC
partial s̄/hade s/should...	HADES		passes fish	HANDSHAKE
partly Ic/eland/ic	ELAND		**passionfruit drink**	CRUSH
partly mad(e)	MAD		**past**[1]	EX
partly grown snake	AS(p)		hence	
parts of coffee table	FEEBLE		•past alteration	EXCHANGE
parts of cof/fee t/able	FEET		•past terrorists with it	EXPLOIT
parts of police force	CANDID		•past wrong	EXTORT
parts of <u>speech</u>	CHEEPS			(*see also* old[3])
Parts 1 & 3 of *t*hesaurus	TE		**past**[2]	PA
partaking of fo̅/od in/side...	ODIN		past Grandmaster	PGM
participate			past Master	PM
participants in the mat/ch I			pastmaster	HISTORIAN
p/layed	CHIP			HISTORY TEACHER
participate in t/he re/vels	HERE		past participle	P(A)P
participate in *	incl in *		past president	PP
•me *participating in* a-n...	AMEN		past tense	PAT
participle	P		**pasta**	(*see* Italian[2])
participial adjective	PA		**paste**	
partnership	EW.NS.SN.US.WE		paste diamond	SHAMROCK
party	CON.DO.FACTION		paste table	PLASTERBOARD
	LAB.LIB.TORY		**pat**	
party-goer	MAD HATTER		Pat's = Irish	
party *leader*	P		•*Pat's old* doctor	OLLA(H)M
party *piece*	P		*patch* over an...	VERONA
part(y) *piece*	PART		**patent agent**	CPA
p/art/y *piece*	ART		**pathetic meeting**	TOUCHING
party *pieces*	PRY		**patient**	CASE
pascal	PA		patient attention	NURSING
pass[1]	COL			TREATMENT
hence			patient helper	DOCTOR.NURSE
•pass 500	COLD		patient man	JOB
•pass our...	COLOUR		patient woman	GRISELDA
•Passover	COLON		**pawn**	P
and			pawnbroker's daughter	NIECE
•find artist *in* pass	CORAL		pawnee	UNCLE
•find nothing *in* pass	COOL		**pay**	
pass[2]			pay *back*⟨	YAP
pass *muster*	ASPS.SAPS		pay on delivery	POD
pass *out*	CO-L.PAS-S		pay *out*	PA-Y
•gunners pass *out*	CORAL		paying guest	PG
•Hill's pass-out	PASTORS		paymaster	PMR
pass *out*	ASPS.SAPS		Paymaster General	PMG

pea(s)	P.(PP.PS)
<u>pea</u> *soup*	APE
	(*see also* pulses)
peace	
peacekeepers	UN
peacemakers	ACAS
peak	BEN.TOR
peak of <u>R</u>ockies(D)	R
Pearl's mother	NACRE
peavy, *say*	PV
peck	GREG(ORY)
peculiar <u>ways</u>	SWAY.YAWS
pedal	P
pedestrian	FOOTMAN.PED
pee(s)	P.(PP.PS)
peel	
peeled (o)rang(e)	RANG
peeler	BOBBY.POLICEMAN
	ROBERT
peeper	TOM
peg	P.T.TEE.TOT
pellet(s)	O.(OO)
pen	
pen-name	PENAL
pen-pusher	SWAN-HERD
penman	PENAL
penal *settlement*	NEPAL.PANEL
	PLANE
penetrate log	ENTER
peninsula	PEN
penny	D.P
hence	
•penny a go	DAGO
•penny fine	DWELL
•penny paper	DRAG
and	
•penny and a. . .	PANDA
•penny fine	POKE
•pennyweight	POUNCE
penn*iless*	omit D or P
penny *off*	omit D.P
pennyweight	DWT.PWT
Pentateuch	T(H)ORAH
penultimate	
penultimate letter	Y
penultimate letter	E
people	MEN.NATION.RACE
per	PR
per annum	PA
percentage of **t/urn/over**	URN
perch on (D)	
indicates one word written over	
another	
•bird perching on an. . .	TITAN
perfect	
perfect(ion)	NOVICES
perfect letter	T
perfect weapon	SPEARMINT
perform	
performing	(in) A-CT
	(in) DE-ED.ON
performing <u>bear</u>	BARE.BRAE
perhaps	
soldier, *perhaps*	PRIVATE
perhaps private. . .	SOLDIER
great fiddle, *perhaps*	CELLO
perhaps <u>not</u>	TON
period	AD.AGE.BC
	EPOCH.ERA.PER
period drama	TIMEPIECE
period *piece*	PER
pe/rio/d *piece*	RIO
period *piece*	ER(a)
periodical	MAG
permissive missive	LETTER
perpetuating <u>evil</u>	LIVE.VILE
perplexed <u>by</u> a. . .	BAY
Persian	PERS
ancient people	ELAMITES.MEDES
bravo!	SHABASH
bosun	SERANG
canopy	SHAMIANA(H)
capital	TEHERAN.P
carpet	KALI
chintz	KALAMKARI
coins	
—copper	KRAN.SHAHI
—gold	DINAR.MOHUR
—old gold or silver	DARIC
—10,000 dinars	TOMA(U)N
dagger	HAN(D)JAR
decree	FIRMAN
deities	(*see* gods.goddesses)
demi-god	YIMA
dog	SALUKI
drink	BOSA.SHIRAZ
dulcimer	SANTIR.SANTO(U)R
dyeing operation	KALAMKARI

evil spirit	AHRIMAN.DEEV.DIV
excise duty	ABKARI
fabulous bird	SIMORG
	SIMURG(H)
fairy	PERI
gateway	DAR
good principle	ORMAZD.ORMUZD
gum	OPOPANAX.SARCOCOLLA
governor	CHAGAN.CHAM
	KHAN.SATRAP
headdress	TIARA
headscarf	ROMAL.RUMAL
hookah	KALIAN.NARG(H)ILE
	NARGILEH.NARG(H)IL(L)Y
inn	CARAVANSARAI
	CARAVANSARY
	CARAVANSERAI.KHAN.SERAI
lady	KHANUM
language	FARSI.IRANIAN
	PAHLAVI.PARSEE.PARSI
	PEHLEVI.ZEND
leader	P
loincloth	LUNGI
lynx	CARACAL
king	CYRUS.SHAH.XERXES
magician	MAGE.MAGUS
measure (4 miles)	FARSANG
	PARASANG
mineral	TURQUOISE
Moslem fanatics	ABDALS
nightingale	BULBUL
parliament	MAJLIS.MEJLIS
paymaster	BUCKSHEE.BUKSHI
philosophy	MAGISM.MAGIANISM
pickles	ACHAR
pleasure park	PARADISE
prayer book	YASHT
priest	MAGE.MAGUS
prince	MIRZA
province	KHANATE.SATRAPY
religion	BAB(I)ISM.BABEEISM
	BAHAI(M).PARS(I)ISM
	PARSEEISM
robe	CAFTAN.KAFTAN
rug	HAMADAN.ISFAHN.KALI
	NAMMAD.SENNA
ruler	CALIF.CALIPH.K(H)ALIF
	SASSANID.SHAH.SOPHI.SOPHY
sailor	LASCAR

sash	LUNGI
scriptures	(ZEND)-AVESTA
shah	PADISHA(H)
shawl	ROMAL.RUMAL
sovereign's seat	
	PEACOCK THRONE
tent	SHAMIANA(H)
throne	MUSNUD
title	MIRZA
—of respect	(K)HODJA.KHOJA
tribe	KURD
tobacco	TUMBUK
torture	SCAPHISM
turban	LUNGI
verse	G(H)AZAL.GHAZEL
water	
—bag	MASHAQ
—pipe	HOOKA(H).KALIAN
—wheel	NORIA.SAKIA.SAKI(Y)EH
whip	CHABOUK
women's quarters	ZENANA
writing-case	KALAMDAN
person	BOD.BLOKE.CHAP
	MAN.ONE.PER(S)
person of note	COMPOSER
	VERDI et al
personal assistant	PA
personal donation	BLOOD
personal hint	INTIMATE
personal letters	INITIALS
	SIGNATURE
personnel carrier	(SEDAN-)CHAIR
	STRETCHER

pertaining

meaning	
concerning	
like	
of	
of the nature of	
pertaining to	
relating to:	
abdomen	COELIAC
action	PRACTIC
—of heated	
water	HYDROTHERMAL
adjectives	EPITHETIC
adolescence	NEANIC
adult period	EPHEBIC
agents	INSTITORIAL

agriculture	GEOPONIC.GEORGIC	bears	ARCTOID.URSINE
air	PNEUMATIC	beasts	THERIOMORPHOUS
albumen	ALBUMINOID		THEROID
algae	CONFERVOID	beer	CERVISIAL
all-heal	VALERIANACEOUS	bees	APIAN
almonds	AMYGDALOID	beetles	SCARABOID
almsgiving	ELEEMOSYNARY	belly	ALVINE.C(O)ELIAC
amber	SUCCINIC	biological rhythms	CIRCADIAN
angels	HIERARCHAL	birds	AVIAN.AVINE.ORNITHIC
	HIERARCHIC		ORNITHOID.VOLUCRINE
animal		—of prey	RAP(TA)TORIAL
—behaviour	EPIMELETIC	birth	NATAL
	ETEPIMELETIC	birthdays	GENETHLIAC
—diseases	VETERINARY		NATALITIAL
animals	ZOIC	birthmarks	NAEVOID
—that live on surface of other		bishops	PONTIFIC(AL)
animals	EPIZOOTIC	bite	MORSAL
ankle	TARSAL	black tourmaline	
antelopes	ANTILOPINE		SCHORLACEOUS
anthrax	ANTHRACOID	bladder	UTRICULAR.VESICAL
antimony	ANTIMONIAL.STIBIAL	bladderwracks	FUCOID(AL)
ants	FORMICATE.MYRMECOID	blisters	VESICAL.VESIC(ULAR)
apes	PITHECOID.SIMIAL	blood	HAEM(AT)IC.HAEMATOID
	SIMIAN.SIMIOUS		SANGUINEOUS
apples	POMACEOUS	—vessels	ANGIOID.VASCULAR
arch	FORNICATE	body	CORPOREAL.SOMATIC
argument	ELENCTIC	bones	OSSEOUS.OSTEAL
arm	BRACHIAL		OSTEOID
armies	MILITARY	—of forearm	RADIAL.ULNAR
armpit	AXILLAR(Y)	bosom	GREMIAL
arrows	SAGITTAL	bottom of tongue	RANINE
artisans	BANAUSIC	boundaries	PERIMETRIC
asbestos	ASBESTIFORM	bracelets	ARMILLARY
	ASBESTOUS	bracts	BRACTEAL
ashes	CINERARY		GLUMACEOUS
ass/zebra hybrid	ZEBRINE	brain	CEREBRAL
	ZEBROID		CEREBRIC
athletic exercises	GYMNASTIC	bran	FURFURACEOUS.PITYROID
atmospheric situation	EPEDAPHIC	branches	RAM(E)AL.RAM(E)OUS
authors	AUCTORIAL		RAMULAR
back	DORSAL.LUMBAR	brass	ORICHALCEOUS
—consonant	VELARIC	bread	PANARY
—of knee	POPLITEAL	breams	SPAROID
—sides	PYGAL	breast	MAM(M)ILLAR(Y)
badgers	MELINE.MUSTELINE		MAMMARY
bags	UTRICULAR		MASTOID.PECTORAL
ball of thumb	THENAR	—bone	STERNAL
bathing/baths	BALNEAL	breathing orifices	
beans	FABACEOUS		SPIRACULAR.SPIRACULATE

bristles	STRIGATE.STRIGOSE
	STRIGOUS.STYLOID
bullheads	COTTOID
bulls	BOVINE.TAURIC
	TAURINE
bunches of grapes	BOTRYOID
	RACEMOSE
	STAPHYLINE
butter	BUTYRACEOUS
butterflies	PAPILIONACEOUS
	RHOPALOCERAL
	RHOPALOCEROUS
buttock	NATAL
calculations	LOGISTIC(AL)
calf	VITULAR.VITULINE
—of leg	SURAL
callings	VOCATIVE
calving	VITULAR
calyx	CALYCINAL.CALYCINE
	CALYCOIDEOUS
camels	CAMELOID
camps	CASTRAL
camphor	CAMPHORACEOUS
	CAMPHORIC
canals	CANALICULAR.MEATAL
cane	BACULINE
	FERRULACEOUS
cantons	CANTONAL
carbuncles	CARBUNCULAR
carp	CYPRINE.CYPRINOID
cartilage	CHONDROID
carvings	GLYPTIC
case of association	GENITIVE
cases	THECAL
castor oil	RICINOLEIC
cats	FELINE
catfishes	SILUROID
catechism	CATECHISMAL
	CATECHISTICAL
caterpillars	ERUCTIFORM
cattle	BOVINE.BUCOLIC
cave dwellers	TROGLODYTIC(AL)
caves	SPELEOLOGICAL
cavities	LACUNARY.LACUNATE
cells	CYTOID.UTRICULAR
centre of gravity	BARYCENTRIC
cereals	FARINACEOUS
chaff	PALEOUS
chains	CATENARY.CATENATE

chalk	CRETACEOUS
charity	ELEEMOSYNARY
chased relief	TOREUTIC
cheeks	BUCCAL.MALAR
cheese	CASEOUS
chest	PECTORAL.THORACIC
chickenpox	VARICELLAR
	VARICELLOID
chief	
—clerks of court	
	PROT(H)ONOTARIAL
—priests	PRELATIC
child	
—birth	PUERPERAL
—talk	HYPOCORISTIC(AL)
children	INFANTILE.PUERILE
—'s teeth	PAEDODONTIC
chin	GENIAL
China	SINAEAN.SINIC
choliamb	SCAZONTIC
Christian Church as a	
whole	ECUMENIC
chrysalises	PUPAL
circles	CYCLOID
circulating vessels	VASCULAR
cirrus	CIRRATE
cities	URBAN(E)
civets	VIVERRINE
civil matters	SECULAR
clauses	CLAUSULAR
claustrums	CLAUSTRAL
claws	UNGUAL
clay	ARGILLACEOUS
clergy	PRELATIC
clothes	HABILATORY.SARTORIAL
	VESTIARY
clouds	NUBIFORM
clypeus	CLYPEAL
coasts	ORARIAN
cobbling	SUTORIAL.SUTORIAN
cobras	COBRIFORM
cobwebs	ARACHNOID.ARANEOSE
	ARANEOUS
coccyx	COCCYGEAL.COCCYGIAN
cochlea	COCHLEAR
cod	GADOID
coins	NUMISMATIC
	NUMM(UL)ARY
colleges	COLLEGIATE

colours	CHROMATIC
columns	COLUMNAL.COLUMNAR
combs	PECTIN(E)AL
common	
—people	PLEBEIAN.VULGAR
—ranks	GREGARIAN
communities	CIVIL
companionship	CONTUBERNAL
condyles	CONDYLAR.CONDYLOID
cones	CONOID(AL)
conjunctions	SYZYGIAL
consent	CONSENSUAL
contractions	STENOTIC
controversy	ERISTIC
cooking	CULINARY
copper rust	AERUGINOUS
coral	CORALLACEOUS
cords	RESTIFORM
cork	PHELLOID.SUBEROSE
	SUBEROUS
corn	FRUMENTARIOUS
councils	CONCILIAR(Y)
	CONSISTORIAL
	CONSITORIAN
country	RURAL
counties	COMITAL
crabs	CANCRINE.CANCROID
cretins	CRETINOID
crosses	CRUCIAL
cross	
—examination	ELENCTIC
—roads	COMPITAL
crow's beak	CORONOID
crowns	CORONAL.CORONARY
crows	CORVINE
crustacean larvae	NAUPLOID
crypts	CRYPTAL
crystals	CRYSTALLOID
cultivation	MANURIAL
curves in rays of light	DIACAUSTIC
cushions	PULVILLAR.PULVINAR
	PULVINATE
customs of city	CUSTUMAL
cutting edges	MORSAL
cyanogen	CYANIC
dancing	TERPSICHOREAN
dauphins	DELPHIN
dawn	AURORAL.AUROREAN
days	DIURNAL.EOAN

decrees	DECRETAL
deep sea	BATHYAL
deer	CERVINE.DAMINE
descents	PHYLETIC
deserts	EREMIC
desires	EPITHYMETIC
development in	
womb	GESTATORY
devil	LUCIFER(I)AN.LUCIFERINE
dew	RORAL.RORIC
	RORID.ROSCID
dialects	DIALECTIC
diaphragm	PHRENIC
dinner	PRANDIAL
discourses	DIALECTIC
diseases of animals	VETERINARY
disintegration of red	
blood cells	HAEMOLYTIC
dispensation of justice	JURIDICAL
dissections	PROSECTORIAL
divination	MANTIC
docks (weeds)	POLYGONACEOUS
dogs	CANICULAR.CANINE
donkeys	ASININE
double wombs	DIDELPHIC
doves	COLUMBINE
down	PAPPOSE.PAPPOUS
dragons	DRACONIC
dreams	ON(E)IRIC
dressing	HABILATORY
dropsy	(O)EDEMATOUS
dross	SCORIAC(EOUS)
drugs or medicines	
	PHARMAEUTIC(AL)
drums	TYMPANIC
dryness of skin	XERODERM(AT)IC
	XERODERMATOUS
dukes	DUCAL
dung	STERCORACEOUS
	STERCORAL
dyeing	TINCTORIAL
eagles	AQUILINE
ear	AURAL.AURICULAR.OTIC
—drum	TYMPANIC
earls	COMITAL
earliest state	PRISTINE
earth	CHTHONIAN.TELLURAL
	TELLURIAN.TELLURIC
	TERRENE.TERRESTRIAL

earthquakes	SEISMAL.SEISMIC	feathered limbs	BRACCATE
	TERREMOTIVE	feathers	PENNACEOUS
edentates	EDENTAL		PLUMOSE.PLUMOUS
eels	ANGUILLIFORM	federated states	STATAL
egg yolks	VITELLARY	feet	PODAL(IC)
eggs (obsolete)	OVAL	felony	FELONIOUS
Egyptian		felt	PANNOSE
—kings	PHARAONIC	fermentation	ZYMOTIC
—writing	HIERATIC	ferns	CRYPTOGAMIAN
eight	OCTAL		CRYPTOGAMIC
electricity and heat			CRYPTOGAMOUS
	ELECTROTHERMIC	ferrets	MUSTELINE.VIVERRINE
elegies	EPICEDIAL.EPICEDIAN	fibrin	FIBRINOID
elephants	ELEPHANTINE		FIBRINOUS
	ELEPHANTOID	fibrous structures	FIBRILLAR(Y)
elves	ELFIN.ELFISH.ELVAN		FIBRILLATE(D)
	ELVISH	fibula	PERONEAL
ellipses	ELLIPTIC(AL)	field of vision	PERIMETRIC
elms	ULMACEOUS	fields	AGRESTIC.CAMPESTRAL
embossing	EMPAESTIC		CAMPESTRIAN
embryonic stage	NEPIONIC	fifth degree	QUINTIC
emeralds	SMARAGDINE	fifty	QUINQUAGESIMAL
emotional drives		filaments	FILAMENTARY
	PSYCHODYNAMIC	finches	FRINGILLACEOUS
emperors/empires	IMPERIAL		FRINGILLINE
endosmosis	ENDOSMOTIC	first	
enlarged veins	VARICOSE	—ages	PRIM(A)EVAL
episodes	EPISODICAL	—born	PRIMOGENITAL
equinoxes	EQUINOCTIAL		PRIMOGENITARY
erotic dreams	ON(E)IROTIC		PRIMOGENITIVE
exchanges	CATALLACTIC	—fruits	PRIMITIAL
excrement	EXCREMENTITIOUS	fish	PISCINE
expenses	SUMPTUARY	fishing	HALIEUTIC.PISCATORIAL
experiments	PEIRASTIC		PISCATORY
eye		fissures	SULCAL
—brows	SUPERCILIARY	flesh	CARNEOUS.CARNOSE
—lids	PALPEBRAL	flour	FARINACEOUS
—like spots	OCELLAR	flowers	FLORAL
eyes	OCULAR.OPHTHALMIC	foam	SPUMOUS.SPUMY
face	FACIAL	f(o)etal envelope	CHOR(I)OID
factors	INSTITORIAL	f(o)etus	F(O)ETAL
fairs	NUNDINAL	foliage	FOLIACEOUS.FOLIAR
Fallopian tubes	SALPINGIAN		FOLIOSE
fat	ADIPOSE.LIPOID	foot	PEDAL.PEDATE
	SEBACEOUS	—of two syllables	PYRRHIC
fathers	PATERNAL	formation of earth	GEOGONIC
fathers of Church	PATRISTIC(AL)	fowl	GALLINACEOUS
fatty tumours	STEATOMATOUS	foxes	ALOPECOID.VULPINE
feasts	FESTAL	Franks	SALIAN

frogs	BATRACHIAN.RANARIAN		HIERARCHIC.HIEROCRATIC
	RANIFORM	governors	GUBERNATORIAL
froth	SPUMOUS.SPUMY	grain	CEREAL
funerals	FERAL.FUNERARY	grandfathers	AVITAL
	FUNEREAL.FUNEBR(I)AL	grandparents	AVAL
fungi	FUNGOUS	granite	GRANITIFORM
furrows	SULCAL	graphite	PLUMBAGINOUS
gabbro	GABBROID	grass	GRAMIN(AC)EOUS
gall nuts	ELLAGIC	gravel	GLAREOUS
gallows	PATIBULARY	Greece	ACHEAN.ACHIAN
gaps	LACUNARY.LACUNATE		HELLENIC
garrisons	PRESIDIAL	gripes	TORMINAL.TORMINOUS
gas	PNEUMATIC	grit	SABULOUS
geese	ANSERINE	groin	INGUINAL
gem carving	GLYPTIC	grooves	SULCAL
generation	GENITIVE	groves	NEMORAL
Gentiles	ETHNIC	gulls	LAROID
Germans	ALEMANNIC	gullet	OESOPHAGEAL
germ plasm	BLASTOGENIC	gum	MUCILAGINOUS
giant fennel	FERRULACEOUS	gums	GINGIVAL
giants	CYCLOPEAN.CYCLOPIAN	guts	ENTERAL.ENTERIC
	CYCLOPIC		SPLANCHNIC
gills	BRANCHIAL.BRANCHIATE	hair	CAPILLACEOUS
ginger	ZINGIBERACEOUS		CRINAL.TRICHOID
	ZINZIBERACEOUS	—cutting	TONSORIAL
glands	GLANDULAR	halls	AULARIAN
	GLANDULOUS	hand	CH(E)IRAL.MANUAL
glass	HYALINE.VITREOUS	handles	MANUBRIAL
	VITRIFORM	hares	LEPORINE
glumes	GLUMACEOUS	hawks	ACCIPITRINE
gnats	CULICIFORM.CULICINE	head	(EN)CEPHALIC
gneiss	GNEISS(IT)IC.GNEISSOID	—of comet	COMAL.COMATE
	GNEISSOSE		COMOSE.COMOUS
goats	CAPRIC.CAPRIFORM	healing	AESCULAPIAN
	CAPRINE.HIRCINE	heart	CARDIAC(AL)
god	MERCURIAL	—and blood	
—of war	MARTIAL.MARTIAN	vessels	CARDIOVASCULAR
goitre	STRUMATIC.STRUMOSE	—sac	PERICARDIAC
	STRUMOUS		PERICARDIAL.PERICARDIAN
gold	AURAL.AURIC	heat of the earth	GEOTHERMAL
goldcrests	REGULINE		GEOTHERMIC
good digestion	EUPEPTIC	heath	ERICACEOUS
gorillas	GORILLINE	heathens	ETHNIC
gourds	CUCURBITACEOUS	heavens	URANIAN
	CUCURBITAL	hedgehogs	ECHINATE(D)
gout	PODAGRAL.PODAGRIC(AL)	hemp	CANABIC
	PODAGROUS	hens	GALLINACEOUS
government	POLITIC	herald(ry)	HERALDIC
—by priests	HIERARCHAL	herbs	HERBACEOUS.HERBY

high	
—atmospheric	
pressure	HYPERBARIC
—priests	PONTIFIC(AL)
highest heavens	EMPYREAL
	EMPYREAN
holidays	FERIAL.FESTAL
horses	CABALLINE.EQUINAL
	EQUINE.HIPPIC
horsemanship	EQUESTRIAN
hospitality	XENIAL
hospitals	NOSOCOMIAL
hours	HORAL.HORARY
houses	DOMAL.DOMESTIC
hunting	CYNEGETIC
	VENATIC(AL)
husbands	MARITAL
hyacinths	HYACINTHINE
hyoid bone and lower	
jaw	MYLOHYOID
hypersthenia	HYPERSTHENIC
iambic trimeters	SCAZONTIC
ideas	NOTIONAL
ideologies	IDEOLOGIC
idylls	IDYLLIAN.IDYLLIC
ileum	ILEAC.ILIAC
ill-health	VALETUDINARIAN
	VALETUDINARY
inches	UNCIAL
infants	INFANTILE
infectious diseases	ZYMOTIC
insects	INSECTIFORM.INSECTILE
interior of the ear	ENTOTIC
internal organs	SPLANCHNIC
intestines	ENTERAL.ENTERIC
	SPLANCHNIC
introductions	PROEMIAL
	ROLEGOMENARY
	PROLEGOMENOUS
—to speech	EXORDIAL
introductory text	PRODROMAL
	PRODROMIC
iris	IRID(I)AL.IRIDIAN.IRIDIC
iron	FERREOUS
itching	PRURITIC
ivory	EBURNEAN
ivy	HEDERAL
jaundice	ICTERAL.ICTERIC
jaw	MAXILLARY

jellyfish	MEDUSIFORM
	MEDUSOID
judgements	JUDICIARY
judges	JUDICIAL.JURIDICAL
kidney	NEPHRIC.NEPHRI)IC(AL)
	RENAL
kissing	OSCULAR.OSCULATORY
kitchen	CULINARY
knee	GENUAL
kneecap	PATELLAR
knot grass	POLYGONACEOUS
labour	FABRILE
labyrinths	LABYRINTHAL
	LABYRINTHINE
	LABYRINTHIAN
lacunae	LACUNARY.LACUNATE
ladders	SCALAR(IFORM)
lakes	LACUSTRINE
land	PR(A)EDIAL
—and water	TERRAQUEOUS
—register	CADASTRAL
languages	LINGUISTIC(AL)
lap	GREMIAL
larch	LARCHEN
laughter	GELASTIC
law	EDICTAL.LEGAL
lay matters	SECULAR
lead	PLUMBAGINOUS
leaflets	FOLIOLATE.FOLIOLOSE
leather	CORI(ACE)OUS
leaves	FOLIACEOUS.FOLIAR
	FOLIOSE.FRONDESCENT
	FRONDOSE
legal investigations	FORENSIC
legislation or	
legislators	LEGISLATORIAL
leg	CRURAL
lemurs	LIMURIAN.LIMURINE
	LIMUROID.TARSIOID
lenses	LENTOID
lentil seeds	LENTICELLATE
letters of alphabet	LITERAL
	LITERARY
libido	LIBIDINAL
lice	PEDICULAR
life	ZOETIC
light	PHOTIC
lightning	FULGURAL
	FULGUROUS

lilies	ARACEOUS.AROID
	LILIACEOUS
limbs	MEMBRAL
lime	CALCAREOUS
lines of poetry	STICHIC
lithium	LITHIC
little	
—feathers	PLUMULACEOUS
	PLUMULAR
—stars	STELLULAR
	STELLULATE
—valves	VALVULAR
liver	HEPATIC
liverworts	HEPATIC
living in aquatic	
sludge	SAPROPELIC
lizards	AGAMOID.LACERT(IL)IAN
	LACERTINE
lobes	LOBAR
loins	ILIAC.LUMBAR
loss of hair	PSILOTIC
love	AMATORY
—of children	PHILOPROGENITIVE
low clouds	STRATOUS
lower leg	PERONEAL
lunch	CENAL
lungs	PNEUMONIC.PULMONARY
	PULMONIC
—and stomach	
	PNEUMO-GASTRIC
lymphs	LYMPHATIC
lymph vessels	ANGIOID
lynx	LYNCEAN
lyres	LYRICAL
mackerel	SCOMBROID
magistrates	MAGISTERIAL
maigre (fish)	SCIAENOID
mail service	POSTAL
mammals	THERIOMORPHOUS
	THEROID
man	ANTHROPOID
manors	MANORIAL
mantles	PALLIAL
many arts	POLYTECHNIC(AL)
marble	MARMOREAL
markets	NUNDINAL
marks	STIGMATIC
marriage	CONNUBIAL
	CONJUGAL

	HYMENAL.JUGAL
	MARITAL.MATRIMONIAL
	NUPTIAL.SPONSAL.SPOUSAL
—of unequals	MORGANATIC
marrow	MYELOID
Mars	MARTIAL.MARTIAN
marshes	PALUD(IN)AL.PALUDINE
	PALUDINOUS.PALUDOSE
	PALUDOUS.PALUSTRAL
	PALUSTRIAN.PALUSTRINE
martens	MELINE.MUSTELINE
master artists	MAGISTERIAL
meal	FARINACEOUS
meanings	SEMANTIC
measles	MORBILLIFORM
	MORBILLOUS
measurement	MENSURAL
	METRICAL
—by weight	GRAVIMETRIC
—of gas	GASOMETRIC
—of time	HOROMETRICAL
medical treatment of	
children	PAEDIATRIC
medicine	IATRIC(AL).PHYSICKY
medium water supply	MESIC
melody	CHROMATIC
membranes	
	MEMBRAN(AC)(E)OUS
meninx/meninges	MENINGEAL
mental forces	PSYCHODYNAMIC
merchants	MERCANTILE
messengers	INTERNUNCIAL
metalloids	METALLOIDAL
metals	METALLIC.METALLINE
metonymy	METALEPTIC(AL)
mice	MURINE
midbrain	MESENCEPHALIC
midday	MERIDIAN
midlines	MEDIAL
midwifery	OBSTETRIC
milk	LACTEAL.LACTIC
millers	MOLENDINAR
millet seed	MILIARY
millions	MILLIONARY
mills	MOLENDINAR
mimicry	MIMETIC(AL)
mind	INTELLECTUAL
ministers/ministry	MINISTERIAL
miraculous intervention	

	THEURGIC(AL)
mirrors	SPECULAR
mites	ACAROID
mitres	MITRAL
monads	MONADIC(AL)
	MONADIFORM
monasteries	MONASTERIAL
	MONASTIC
money	NUMISMATIC
	PECUNIARY
mongooses	HERPESTINE
monks	MONASTERIAL
	MONASTIC
months	MENSAL
moon	LUNAR.SELENIAN
—and sun	LUNISOLAR
morning	MATUTINAL.MATUTINE
mosses	SPHAGNOUS
mother-of-pearl	NACREOUS
mothers	MATERNAL
motion of electric	
current	ELECTROMOTIVE
mountain formation	
	OROGEN(ET)IC
mice	MURINE
mouth	BUCCAL.ORAL.OSTIAL
—and stomach	
	STOMATOGASTRIC
mucus	MUCULENT.PITUITARY
multiple origins	POLYPHYLETIC
muscles	MYOID
muses	AONIAN
mysteries	TELESTIC
names	ONOMASTIC
nasal	
—and frontal	
bone	NASOFRONTAL
—partition	VOMERINE
—and cavity	VOMERONASAL
nations	ETHNIC
native land	PATRIAL
natural right	JURAL
navel	OMPHALOID.UMBILICATE
neck	CERVICAL.JUGULAR
nectar	NECTAREAL.NECTAREAN
	NECTAR(E)OUS
—glands	NECTARIAL
needles	SPICULAR
Negroes	NEGROID(AL)

Nero	NEROTIC
nerves	NERVAL.NEURAL
nests	NIDAL
nets	RETIARY.RETICULAR
	RETICULATE(D)
nettles	URTICACEOUS
networks	RETIAL
newly born	NEONATAL
night-wandering	NOCTIVAGANT
Nile	NILOTIC
nine	NOVENARY
nineteen	DECENNOVAL
nipples	MASTOID
nodes	NODICAL.NODULAR
nonmilitary life	CIVIL
nonprotein component	
	PROSTHETIC
north	SEPTENTRIONAL
—wind	BOREAL
nose and tears	NASOLACRYMAL
nostrils	NARIAL.NARINE
nuns	MONASTERIAL
	MONASTIC
nymphs	NYMPHAL
oak	QUERCINE
oats	AVENACEOUS
oblivion	LETHEAN
oceans	PELAGIC
octaves	OCTAVAL
odes of lamentation	THRENODIAL
	THRENODIC.THRENETIC(AL)
old age	GERIATRIC
omens	OMINOUS
once in an age or	
century	SECULAR
one	
—division of	
primates	CATAR(R)HINE
—eye	MONOCULAR
—person	PRIVY
opals	OPALINE
opposites	SYZYGIAL
oracles	ORACULAR
orders	ORDINAL
organic remains in soil	HUMIC
	HUMOUS
origin	GENETIC
origins	FONTAL
orioles, etc.	ICTERIC

ostriches	STROUTHOUS
otters	LUTRINE.MUSTELINE
ounces	UNCIAL
ovary	OVARIAN
ovules	OVULAR
owls	STRIGIFORM.STRIGINE
oxide of yttrium	YTTRIC
	YTTRIOUS
oysters	OSTRACEAN
	OSTRACEOUS
painters	PICTORIAL
palate	PALATINE
palm	PALMAR.THENAR
—trees	PALMACEOUS
paper	CARTACEOUS
	PAPYRACEOUS
parabolas	PARABOLIC
parasitic diseases	TRICHINOTIC
	TRICHINOUS
parchment	PERGAMENEOUS
particular locality	LOCAL
parishes	PAROCHIAL
parrots	PSITTACINE
partition	SEPTIFORM
parturition	PARTURIENT
passages	MEATAL
pastors	PASTORAL
pastures	PASTORAL
peacocks	PAVONIAN.PAVONINE
pellagra	PELLAGROUS
penances	PENITENTIARY
people	DEMOTIC.LAY
	POPULAR
perch	PERCIFORM.PERCINE
	PERCOID
perching birds	PASSERINE
perineum	PERINEAL
phalanxes	PHALANG(E)AL
Pharisees	PHARISAIC(AL)
pharmacy	PHARMACEUTICAL
pharynx	PHARYNG(E)AL
phloxes	POLEMONIACEOUS
physicians	IATRIC(AL)
pictures	PICTORIAL.PICTURAL
	PICTURESQUE
pigeons	PERISTERONIC
pigs	PORCINE.SUIDAN
	SUILLINE
pile	VILLOSE.VILLOUS

pillars	STYLAR
pimples	PAPULOSE.PAPULOUS
pineal gland	CONARIAL
pineapples	BROMELIACEOUS
pitch	PICEOUS
plane trees	PLATANACEOUS
planets	MARTIAL.MARTIAN
	MERCURIAL.PLANETARY
	PLUTONIAN.SATURNIAN
	VENUSIAN
plantains	PLANTAGINACEOUS
plants	BOTANICAL
	HERBACEOUS
plates	PLACOID
plea(ding)s	PLACITORY
pleasure	APOLAUSTIC
ploughed land	ARVAL
plums	PLUMY
plunder	PREDATORY
policies	POLITIC
pollen	POLLINIC
—baskets	CORBICULATE
polypi	POLYPOID
polyps	POLYPOUS
polyzoa	POLYZOOID
poorest classes	LUMPEN
Pope	PONTIFIC(AL)
—'s representative	
	INTERNUNCIAL
poppies	PAPAVEROUS
pores	POROSE
porphyry	PORPHYRITC
posterior	PYGAL
pot herbs	OLERACEOUS
potassium	POTASSIC
pouches	MARSUPIAL.SACCATE
	SACCIFORM.SACCULAR
practices	PRACTIC
preaching	HOMILETIC
predetermined variations	
	ORTHOGENETIC
prefaces	PREFATORY.PROEMIAL
prelates	PRELATIC
preliminary reflection	
	PROBOULEUTIC
preludes	PRELUDIAL
	PRELUDIOUS
	PRELUSIVE
	PROEMIAL

premonitions	PRODROMAL
	PRODROMIC
presence of moisture	HYDRIC
present	
—day	HODIERNAL
—world	SECULAR
presidents	PRESIDIAL
presidios	PRESIDIAL
priests	HIERATIC.SACERDOTAL
—of Mars	SALIAN
prisms	PRISMATIC(AL)
probability of recurrence of a	
particular state	ERGODIC
proboscis	PROMUSCULATE
producing	GENITIVE
prophecies	VATIC
prostitution	MERETRICIOUS
prudence	PRUDENTIAL
pubic bones	PECTINEAL
public	
—revenues	FISCAL
—treasuries	FISCAL
pulse	SPHYGMOID
punishment	PENAL
pyrites	PYRITC(AL).PYRITOUS
quartz	QUARTOSE
quartzite	QUARTZITIC
questioning	PYSMATIC
rabbis	RABBINIC(AL)
race	ETHNIC
—courses	CURSAL
—improvement	EUGENIC
racemes	RACEMOSE
radicles	RADICULAR
rain	HYETAL.PLUVIAL
—bows	IRID(I)AL.IRIDIAN
rattlesnakes	CROTALINE
ravens	CORVINE
reasoning	LOGISTIC(AL)
red deer	ELAPHINE
reeds	FERRULACEOUS
	ARUNDINACEOUS
reflected light	CATOPTRIC
reflection and	
refraction	CATADIOPTRIC
refraction of sound	DIACOUSTIC
refutation	ELENCTIC
regions beyond the	
moon	TRANSLUNAR

registers	MATRICULAR
registrars of court	
	PROT(H)ONOTARIAL
regular patterns	QUOTIDIAN
religious art	HIERATIC
reports	REPORTORIAL
reproduction	GENITAL
—in larval state	PAEDOGENETIC
reptiles	HERPETINE.HERPETOID
rhombuses	RHOMBIC
	RHOMBOID(AL)
ribbons	TAENIATE.TAENIOID
ribs	COSTATE
river banks	RIPARIAN
rivers	FLUVIAL.FLUVIATIC
	FLUVIATILE.POTAMIC
rock masses	GEOTECTONIC
rodents	GLIRINEAL
rods	RHABDOID
Roman	
—dances	TRIPUDIARY
—heralds	FECIAL.FETIAL
—mile	MILIARY
roofs	TECTIFORM
rootlets	RADICULAR
roots	RADICAL.RADICIFORM
	RHIZOIDAL.RHIZOMATOUS
roses	ROSACEOUS.ROSEAL
	ROSEATE
rotary motion	TROCHILIC
royal palaces	BASILICAN
rubies	RUBINEOUS
runners	SARMENTACEOUS
running	CURSORIAL
rural deans or	
deaneries	RURIDECANAL
sable	ZIBEL(L)INE
sacs	THECAL
sacred writings	
	HIEROGRAPHIC(AL)
sacrum	SACRAL
saliva	SIALOID
saltworts	SALSOLACEOUS
salvation	SOTERIAL
same sex	HOMOSEXUAL
sand	SABULOUS
sandalwood	SANTALACEOUS
sapphires	SAPPHIRINE
Satan	LUCIFERAN

Saturday	SABBATINE
Saturn	SATURNIAN
scad	CARNGOID
scales	FURFURACEOUS
	SQUAMOSE
	SQUAMOUS
scallops	PECTINACEOUS
scapula	SCAPULAR
scarabs	SCARABOID
scazons	SCAZONTIC
scissors	FORFICULATE
screws	HELICOID(AL)
scurf	FURFURACEOUS
scurvy	SCORBUTIC(AL)
sea	MARINE.MARITIME
	PELAGIC.THALASSIC
—shore	LITTORAL
—trade	MARITIME
—urchins	ECHINOID
—weeds	ALGOID.FUCOID
seals	
—mammals	PHOCID.PHOCINE
—signets	SIGILLARY
	SPHRAGISTIC
second	
—skin	HYPODERMIC
—year students	
	SOPHOMORIC(AL)
sedges	CYPERACEOUS
seeds	SEMINAL
senescence	GERONTIC
sense of smell	OLFACTORY
septum	SEPTIFORM.VOMERINE
servants	MENIAL.SERVILE
servile work	MENIAL
seven	SEPTIMAL
seventy	SEPTUAGENARY
sewers	CLOACAL
sex organs	GENITAL
sexual	
—attraction to opposite	
sex	HETEROSEXUAL
—love	EROTIC
sheaths	THECAL
sheep	OVIFORM.OVINE
shells	CONCHOIDAL
shepherds	PASTORAL
sheriffs	SHRIEVAL
shops	OFFICINAL

shoulder	HUMERAL
—blade	SCAPULAR
—and hyoid	OMOHYOID
side of cranium	TEMPORAL
sides	LATERAL
sieges	OBSIDIONAL
sieves	CRIBRATE.CRIBRIFORM
	CRIBROSE.ETHMOID(AL)
sight	VISIVE.VISUAL
signatures	ONOMASTIC
signets	SPHRAGISTIC
silica	SILICEOUS.SILICIOUS
silk	SERIC(EOUS)
silver	ARGENTINE
simultaneous transmission of	
messages on one wire	DIPLEX
sixty	SEXAGESIMAL
skin	CUTANEOUS.DERMATOID
skinks	SCINCOID
skull	CRANIAL
skunks	MUSTELINE
slag	SCORIAC(EOUS)
slaves	SERVILE
sleep	HYPNIC.HYPNOID(AL)
slugs	LIMACEOUS
small	
—bladder	VESICULAR
—blisters	VESICULAR
—fibres	FIBRILLAR(Y).FIBRILLATE
	FIBRILLOUS
—hooks	HAMULAR
—matter	ATOMIC
—passage	POROSE
—worlds	MICROCOSMIC
smallpox	VARIOLOUS
smells	OLFACTORY
snakes	ANGUINE.COLUBRIFORM
	COLUBRINE.HERPETINE
	HERPETOID.OPHIDIAN
	OPHIURAN.OPHIUR(O)ID
	SERPENTINE
snow	NIVEOUS
soap	SAPONACEOUS
soda	SODAIC
soft hair	VILLOSE.VILLOUS
soil	EDAPHIC
soldiers	MILITARY
sole (foot)	PLANTAR.THENAR
sons	FILIAL

songbirds	OSC(IN)INE
sorcerers	MAGIAN
space	LACUNARY
	LACUNATE.SPATIAL
spars	SPATHIC.SPATHOSE
spicules	SPICULAR
spinach	SPINACEOUS
spindles	CLOSTRIDIAL
spinsters	SPINSTERIAL
	SPINSTERIAN
spirits	ETHEREAL.ETHERIAL
spleen	LIENAL
sponges	SPONGIFORM
	SPONGOID
spore cases	THECAL
spores	SPORIDIAL
spring	VERNAL
squints	STRABISMAL
	STRABISMIC(AL)
stalactites	STALATITAL
	STALACTITIC(AL)
	STALACTIFORM
	STALACTITIOUS
stalagmites	STALAGMITIC
stalks	PEDUNCULAR.PETIOLAR
standing water	LENTIC
starlings	STURNINE.STURNOID
stars	ASTEROID.ASTRAL
	SIDEREAL.STELLAR
statues	STATUESQUE
stems	CAULINE.CAULINARY
stepmothers	NOVERCAL
sticks	BACULINE
stimuli from movement	
	PROPRIOCEPTIVE
stomach	GASTRIC
stone fruits	DRUPACEOUS
stones	LAPIDARY.PETROSAL
storms	ORAGIOUS
straps	LIGULATE.LORATE
straw	STRAMINEOUS
striking a surface	PERCUTIENT
styles/styluses	STYLOID
suffragan bishops	
	CHOREPISCOPAL
sugar	SACCHARINE
summer	AESTIVAL
sun	HELIAC.SOLAR
surrounding areas	PERIPHERAL

	PERIPHERIC
swallows	HIRUNDINE
sweat	HIDROTIC.SUDATORY
swimming	NATATORIAL
	NATATORY
swine	PORCINE
—herds	SYBOTIC
symptoms	SEM(E)IOTIC
tables	MENSAL
tailless amphibia	BATRACHIAN
tails	CAUDAL.CERCAL
tapeworms	CESTOID
	SCOLECIFORM
	TAENIATE.TAENIOID
taste	GUSTATIVE.GUSTATORY
taxation	FISCAL
teachers	MAGISTERIAL
tears	LAC(H)RYMAL
	LAC(H)RYMARY
	LAC(H)RYMATORY.LACRIMAL
	LACRIMA(TO)RY
teeth	DENTAL.ODONTOID
—with paired cusps	ZYGODONT
tempered steel	CHALYBEOUS
temples	TEMPORAL
temporal bone	PETROSAL
tendon sheaths	SYNOVIAL
tendrils	CAPREOLATE
testing minerals by	
heat	PYROGNOSTIC
thigh (bone)	FEMORAL
thin plates	LAMELLAR
	LAMELLATE.LAMELLIFORM
	LAMELLOID.LAMELLOSE
	LAMINAR(Y)
things	
—similar in form	
	HOM(O)EOMORPHIC
—not spiritual	SECULAR
thorns	SPINIFORM
thought	DIANOETIC
thread	FILOSE
three	TERNAL
—parties	TRIPARTITE
—vowel sounds	TRIPHTHONGAL
throat	GUTTURAL
thunder and lightning	
	FULMIN(E)OUS
tigers	TIGERY.TIGRINE.TIGROID

tin	STANNOUS	valves	VALVAL.VALVAR.VALVATE
tissues in region of a		varied knowledge	POLYHISTORIC
tooth	PERIODONTAL		POLYMATHIC
titles	TITULAR	veal	VITULINE
toads	BATRACHIAN	vegetable substance	VEGANIC
	SALIENTIAN	vegetables	OLITORY
tombs	SEPULCHRAL	veins	VENOUS
tongue	GLOTTAL.GLOTTIC	verbs	RHEMATIC
	LINGUAL	verdigris	AERUGINOUS
tonsils	TONSILLAR	vervain	VERBENACEOUS
top	CACUMINAL	vessels	VASCULAR
touch	HAPTIC	vintage	VINDEMIAL
trachea	TRACHEAL	viscera	SPLANCHNIC
trade	MERCANTILE	visibility of objects within	
treatment of		the eye	ENTOPTIC
—disturbed children		vision	OCULAR
	ORTHOGENIC	vital impulses	LIBIDINAL
—horse diseases	HIPPIATRIC	voice	PHONAL.PHONIC
trees	ARBOREAL.ARBOREOUS	—training	VOCICULTURAL
trunks	TRUNCAL	vultures	VULTURINE.VULTURISH
tubers	TUBERACEOUS		VULTUROUS
tumours of		wading birds	GRALLATORIAL
teeth	ODONTOMATOUS	walking	PEDESTRIAN
turf	C(A)ESPITOSE	walls	PARIETAL
twelve	DUODENARY	walruses	PHOCINE
twenty	ICOSIAN	war	MARTIAL
twigs	SARMENTACEOUS	—dances	PYRRHIC
twilight	CREPUSCULAR	—fare	MILITARY
	CREPUSCULOUS	warts	VERRUCIFORM
two equal gods	DITHEISTIC(AL)	water	
tympanum	TYMPANIC	—ferns	SALVINIACEOUS
	TYMPANAL	—rails	RALLINE
typhoid	TYPHOIDAL	waves/waving	UNDULATORY
typhus	TYPHOID.TYPHOUS	weasels	MUSTELINE
ulcers	HELCOID	weddings	MATRIMONIAL
unborn baby	F(O)ETAL	week	HEBDOMADAL
uncles	AVUNCULAR	west wind	FAVONIAN
underground water below		wheels	TROCHAL.TROCHOID
water table	PHREATIC	wheat	TRITICEOUS
underworld	CHTHONIAN	whetstone	COTICULAR
undifferentiated plant		whirlpools	VORAGINOUS
bodies	THALLINE.THALLOID	whirlwinds	TYPHONIC
upper		whole world	MONDIAL
—alimentary tract		wives	UXORIAL
	STOMATOGASTRIC	wild beasts	FERINE
—stomach	CARDIAC(AL)	wills	TESTAMENTAL
urine	URETIC.URINARY.URINOUS		TESTAMENTARY
used in a particular		winds	AEOLIAN
country	ENCHORIAL	wine	VINOUS

wings	PENNATE.PINNATE(D)
	PTERYGOID
winter	BRUMAL.BRUMOUS
	HIBERNAL.HIEMAL
wolf	LUPINE
womb	UTERINE
women who have had more than	
one child	MULTIPAROUS
wood	LINEOUS.NEMORAL
	XYLOID
woodcocks	SCOLOPACEOUS
woodpeckers	PICARIAN
woods	SILVAN.SILVATIC
	SILVESTRIAN
wool	LANATE
words	RHEMATIC
workers	ERGATOID
working classes	PROLETARIAN
	PROLETARY
world	MONDIAL
worms	LUMBRICAL.VERMICULAR
wrasses	LABROID
wrist	CARPAL
writing	LITERARY
—desks	ESCRITORIAL
wrongful injuries	NOXAL
wrongs	TORTIOUS
yesterday	HESTERNAL.PRIDIAN
yolk of eggs	VITELLARY
zeolite	ZEOLITIC.ZEOLITIFORM
zones	ZONOID
perturbed by a	BAY
Peru	PE

Peruvian

bark	CALISAYA.CINCHONA
bird	YUTA.YUTU
capital	LIMA.P
coins	LIBRA.SOL
counting device	QUIPO.QUIPU
dance	CUECA
dried beef	CHARQUI
emperor	INCA
fever	VERRUGA
fruit	CHERIMOYA.CHERIMOYER
	CHIRIMOYA
Indian	QUECHUA.QUICHUA.INCA
king	INCA
knotted cord	QUIPO.QUIPU
language	ATMARA.QUECHUA

	QUECHIA
leader	P
pepper	MATICO
plant	INDIAN CRESS
shrub	COCA.MATICO.RATANY
skunk	ATOC.ATOK

perverse

act *perversely*	CAT
perverse boy⟨	YOB
perverted love	VOLE
pet name	CATCALL
petrol engine	ICE
Petty Officer	PO
pewter toy	TRIFLE
Pharmaceutical Society	PS
Pharmacopoeia Britannica	PR

Philippines

aborigines	AT(T)A.ITA.TAGAL
barge	CASCO
braised stew	ADOBO
candle-nut tree	LUMBANG
capital	MANILA.P
coin	PESO
fibre (Manila hemp)	ABACA
knife	BOLO
language	AT(T)A.BIKOL.MORO
	TAGAL(OG).TINO
leader	P
lizard	IBID.IBIT
measure	APATAN.CHUPA.GANTA
native	FILIPINO
nut	PILI(-NUT)
parrot	ABACAY.CAGIT
	CALANGAY
peasant	TAO
plantain	ABACA
	MANILA HEMP
plum	DUHAT.LANSEH
race	TAGALOG
rice beer	PANGASI
servant	ALILA
silk	HUSI
straw	BAKU
tree	DITA.ILANG-ILANG
	KALUMPIT.LIGAS
	MABOLA.YLANG-YLANG
white man	CACHIL
Philological Society	PS
philosopher	ARISTOTLE.AYER

	BACON.ERASMUS.HUME	**pig**[1]	
	LOCKE.PHB.PHD.PLATO	pig feed	MAST
	RUSSELL	pig*headed*	P
philosopher-king	LOCKER	pig*tail*	G
Philosophy, Politics and		**pig**[2]	
Economics	PPE	British	ESSEX
phobia	THING		GLOUCESTER OLD SPOT
	(*see also* fear)		HAMPSHIRE.LARGE BLACK
phone			LARGE WHITE
phone *about*	R-ING		LONG WHITE LOP-EARED
phoney tale	TAIL		SADDLEBACK.WELSH
phoney tale	LATE.LEAT.TEAL		WESSEX
photo-electric cell	PEC	Belgian	PIETRAIN
phrase	PHR	Swedish	LANDRACE
physic		**pigeon**	
physical education	PE	including dove:	
physical training	PT	domestic	AFRICAN OWL
physician	DR.GP.LUKE		AMERICAN DOMESTIC FLIGHT
	MB.MD.MO		ARCHANGEL.BARRED STARLING
physicians	RCP		BRUNETTE FRILL.CARRIER
physiotherapists	CSP		CHECKERED ICE
pi	P		CRESTED HELMET
piano	GRAND.P.UPRIGHT		DUN-FACED BLONDINETTE
hence			ENGLISH POUTER.FANTAIL
•piano scholar	GRANDMA		FRANCONIAN.FRILLBACK
and			FLYING POUTER.GAZZI
•girl *at* piano	PALMA		GERMAN TOY.GIANT HOMER
•piano keys	PEA.PEACE.PEG		GIANT RUNT.GIMPEL.HELMET
•piano music	PAIR		HIGHFLIER.ICE PIGEON
pianissimo	PP		LARK.LAHORE.MAGPIE
pianoforte	PF		MALTESE.MODENA
pick-up	PU		NORWICH CROPPER
pick-up notes(D) ↑	SETON		ORIENTAL FRILL
picnic	OUTDO		ORIENTAL ROLLER.OWL PIGEON
picture	SHOT.SNAP		PARLOUR TUMBLER
picture of...	(*see* write[3])		PEKIN NASAL-TUFTED
picture only	SOUND OFF		PIGMY POUTER.RACING HOMER
picture postcard	PPC		ROLLER.SATINETTE FRILL
pie is hot	HOIST		SCANDAROON.SCHIETTI
piece			SCHOENEBERG TUMBLER
piece (chess)	MAN.PAWN		SHIELD.SHOW HOMER
piece of bread	B		SHOW TIPPLER
piece of p/arch/ment	ARCH		SHORT-FACED TUMBLER
piece of toast	CHEER(s)		SILVERETTE FRILL.STARLING
pieces of stone	NOTES.ONSET		SWALLOW.SWING POUTER
	TONES		TIPPLER.TRUMPETER.TUMBLER
pieces of stone	ST.ONE		VELVET-SHIELD.WHITE DANZIG
piecemeal way	YAW	wild	BARBARY DOVE
piecework	MOSAIC		COLLARED DOVE

FERAL PIGEON.ROCK DOVE
STOCK DOVE.TURTLE DOVE
WOOD PIGEON

pigeon-perch STOOL
pile NAP
pile-*up*(D) ↑ PAN
pile up <u>earth</u> HATER.RATHE
pile up <u>maps</u>(D) ↑ SPAM
pilgrim's token ABBEY-COUNTER
ABBEY-PIECE
pill O
pilot GEORGE
Pilot Officer PO
pinch
pinch a... incl A
pinch * incl *
•bo-y *pinches* books BOOTY
pinched by * incl in *
•books *pinched by* bo-y BOOTY
pines *away* SNIPE.SPINE
ping's other half PONG
pink jumper SALMON
pin-*up*(D) ↑ -LIAN.NIP
pint P.PT
piper's child TOM
pirate BLACKBEARD.CORSAIR
MORGAN.PRIVATEER.SILVER
pirate flag (JOLLY) ROGER
pirate treasure SILVER
pirate's place PENZANCE
pirouetting dancer CRANED
pit
pit men NUM
pit workers NUM
pit*head* P
pit-stop MINEFIELD
pity, *say* PT
place
place for blow-out ETNA
VOLCANO
placed in * incl in *
•silver *placed* in r-ing RAGING
placed round * incl *
•r-ing *placed round* silver RAGING
placeholder LIEUTENANT
plain
plain chant EVENSONG
plain speaking PLANE
Plan Position Indicator PPI

Planck's constant H
plane SMOOTHER
accident to <u>plane</u> PANEL
<u>plane</u> *crash* PANEL
<u>plane</u> *disaster* PANEL
planets
major EARTH.JUPITER.LUCIFER
MARS.MERCURY.NEPTUNE
PLUTO.SATURN.URANUS
VENUS
minor CERES.PALLAS.VESTA
ruling at birth HYLEG
Venus as
—evening star HESPERUS
VESPER
—morning star LUCIFER
plant[1]
some alternative names and
descriptions:
Abrus INDIAN LIQUORICE
LIQUORICE-VINE
Acalypha CHENILLE PLANT
RED-HOT CATSTAIL
acanthus BEAR'S-BREACH
BRANKURSINE.RUELLIA
Acacia MIMOSA
Aceras MAN ORCHIS
Achillea MILFOIL.YARROW
Achimenes CUPID'S BOWER
HOT WATER PLANT
Acidanthera ETHIOPIAN
GLADIOLUS
aconite MONK'S-HOOD
WOLFSBANE
Acorus SWEET FLAG
Adam's
—flannel MULLEIN
—needle CASSAVA.YUC(C)A
adder's-tongue OPHIOGLOSSUM
adderweed BISTORT
Adoxa MOSCHATEL
Aechmea URN PLANT.VASE
PLANT
Aeschynanthus LIPSTICK VINE
African
—corn lily IXIA
—lily AGAPANTHUS
—marigold TAGETES
—rue HARMALA.HARMEL

—violet	SAINTPAULIA	anise	PIMPINELLA
Agapanthus	AFRICAN LILY	Antennaria	
	LILY OF THE NILE		EVERLASTING (FLOWER)
agave	SILK-GRASS	Anthurium	FLAMINGO FLOWER
Alchemilla	LADY'S MANTLE	Anthyllis	KIDNEY VETCH
ale-cost	COSTMARY	antirrhinum	FROG'S MOUTH
Alisma	WATER PLANTAIN		SNAPDRAGON
allheal	VALERIAN	aquatic plant	FONTINALIS
Allium	GARLIC.ESCHALOT		FROG-BIT
	GOLDEN GARLIC	Aphelandra	ZEBRA PLANT
	LEEK.SHAL(L)OT	Aquilegia	COLUMBINE
Alpine		Arabis	ROCK-CRESS
—flower	EDELWEISS.GENTIAN		WALL-CRESS
—herb	CORNEL	Aralia	CASTOR-OIL PLANT
—rose	RHODODENDRON		FATSIA.PANAX
alsike	CLOVER	Ardisia	CORAL BERRY
Alstroemeria	AMARYLLIS	Arenaria	SANDWORT
	HERB LILY	Aristolochia	DUTCHMAN'S PIPE
Althaea	HOLLYHOCK		GOOSE FLOWER.SNAKEROOT
	MARSH MALLOW	Armeria	SEA PINK.THRIFT
aluminium plant	PILEA	Arnoseris	SWINE'S SUCCORY
Alyssum	GOLD DUST	aromatic plant	HYSSOP
	MADWORT		PEPPERMINT
Amaracus	MARJORAM		SPEARMINT.SPIKENARD
Amarant(h)us	LONDON PRIDE	arrow	
	LOVE-LIES-BLEEDING	—head	SAGITTARIA
	PIGWEED.PRINCE'S FEATHER	—root	MARANTHA
Amaryllis	ALSTROEMERIA	—vine	SYNGONIUM
	HIPPEASTRUM.LILY	Artemisia	WORM-SEED
	POLIANTHES		WORMWOOD
Amaracus	MARJORAM	artillery plant	PILEA
ammoniac	OSHAC	arum	ACORUS.COLOCASIA
Ampelopsis	VIRGINIA CREEPER		ZANTEDESCHIA
Anacharis		Asclepias	MILK-WEED
	CANADIAN PONDWEED	asparagus	ASPIDISTRA
	WATER WEED	Asperugo	MADWORT
Anagallis	BOG PIMPERNEL	Asplenium	SPLEEN WORT
Anana(s)	PINEAPPLE	aster	ALYCOMPAINE
	PAINTER'S PALETTE		ELECAMPANE.STARWORT
Anatolian convolvulus			STITCHWORT
	SCAMMONY	Astilbe	GOAT'S BEARD.SPIRAEA
Andiantum	MAIDENHAIR FERN	Astragalus	GOAT'S THORN
anemone	CORONARIA		LIQUORICE-VETCH
	PASCHAL FLOWER		MILK VETCH
	PASQUE FLOWER	Astrantia	MASTERWORT
	WIND FLOWER	astrophel	PENTHIA.STARLIGHT
Angelica	AIT-SKEITER	Aubrietia	BLUE ROCK CRESS
	OAT-SHOOTER	auricula	BEAR'S-EAR
angel's wings	CALADIUM		DUSTY-MILLER

autumn crocus
    MEADOW SAFFRON
avens   GEUM.HERB BENNET
baby's tears   HELXINE
bacon and eggs   LINARIA
    TOADFLAX
baldmoney   MEUM.SPIGNEL
    SPICKNEL
balloon vine   HEARTPEA
    HEARTSEED
Ballota   BLACK HOREHOUND
    STINKING HOREHOUND
balsam   IMPATIENS
    NOLI-ME-TANGERE
    TOUCH-ME-NOT
baneberry BUGBANE.BUGWORT
    HERB CHRISTOPHER
Barbarea   WINTER-CRESS
    YELLOW ROCKET
barley   HORDEUM
bastard
—pimpernel   CENTUNCULUS
—saffron   SAFFLOWER
bayberry   CANDLEBERRY
bead plant   NERTERA
beans, peas, etc.   PULSE
bearberry FOXBERRY.UVA-URSI
bearded tongue   PENSTEMON
bedwort   CROSSWORT
beefsteak plant   IRESINE
beet   GOOSEFOOT
begonia   ANGEL'S WINGS
    ELEPHANT'S EARS
—vine   CISSUS
bellflower   CAMPANULA
    RAMPION
Beloperone   SHRIMP PLANT
Bengal fig   FICUS
Bergamot   MONARDA
bilberry   BLAEBERRY
    WHORTLEBERRY
bindweed BEARBINE.BELLBIND
    CONVOLVULUS
bird-of-paradise
  flower   STRELITZIA
bird's
—foot trefoil LOTE.LOTOS.LOTUS
—nest   MONOTROPA
—nest bromeliad   NIDULARIUM

birthwort   ASARABACCA
bishop's
—cap   SAXIFRAGE
—weed GOUTWEED.GOUTWORT
—wort   BETONY.STACHYS
bistort   ADDER('S) WORT
    (PATIENCE-)DOCK
    SNAKEROOT.SNAKEWEED
bitter
—herb   GERMANDER
—sweet   DULCAMARA
    SOLANUM
    WOODY NIGHTSHADE
—vetch   ERS
black
—cummin   FITCH
—currant QUINSY-BERRY.RIBES
—eyed Susan   THUNBERGIA
—hellebore   BEAR'S-FOOT
—medick   SHAMROCK
—salsify   SCORZONERA
    VIPER'S GRASS
—saltwort   GLAUX
bladder
—campion   CATCHFLY
    WHITE-BOTTLE
—senna   COLUTEA
—wort LENTIBULARIACEAE
    UTRICULARIA
blanket flower   GAILLARDIA
bleeding
—heart DICENTRA.DIELYTRA
—vine   CLERODENDRUM
blood
—leaf   IRESINE
—lily   HAEMANTHUS
—root   POPPY
blue
—alpine flower   GENTIAN
—bell SCILLA.WILD HYACINTH
    WOOD HYACINTH
—bottle   CORNFLOWER
—rocket   LARKSPUR
    MONK'S HOOD
—veronica
    GERMANDER SPEEDWELL
boat lily   RHOEO
Bocconia   MACLEAYA
    PLUME POPPY

bog
—myrtle MYRICA.SWEETGALE
　　　　　　　SWEET-WILLOW
—pimpernel ANAGALLIS
—plant BOG ASPHODEL
　　　　DROSERA.SUN-DEW
　　　　WATER PURSLANE
borage BUGLOSS
　　　　COOL-TANKARD
　　　　COMFREY.HELIOTOPE
　　　　HOUND'S-TONGUE
LITHOSPERMUM.LUNGWORT
　　　　SYMPHYTUM
bottlebrush POTERIUM
—plant CALLISTEMON
Bougainvillea PAPER FLOWER
Bouteloua MOSQUITO GRASS
Bouvardia JASMINE PLANT
bowstring hemp SANSEVIERIA
bramble LAWYER.RUBUS
brassica CABBAGE.KALE.TURNIP
brassock FIELD MUSTARD
brier LAWYER
brookweed WATER PIMPERNEL
broom CYSTISUS.HAG-WEED
—parasite BROOM-RAPE
—rape OROBRANCHE
Browallia BUSH VIOLET
brown spiderwort SIDERASIS
Brunella SELF-HEAL
Brunnera FORGET-ME-NOT
buck's-horn plantain
　　　　STAR-OF-THE-EARTH
buck
—bean BOGBEAN
—thorn RHAMNUS.RHINEBERRY
—wheat SARRASIN.SARRAZIN
Buddhist pine PODOCARPUS
bugle AJUGA
bugloss BORAGE
bur
—marigold XANTHIUM
—reed SPARGANIUM
—thistle SPEAR THISTLE
—weed BURDOCK.BUR-REED
burdock CLOTBUR.XANTHIUM
burnet PIMPERNEL.PROTERIUM
—rose SCOTCH ROSE
—saxifrage PIMPINELLA

burning bush
　　　　EUONYMUS.WAHOO
bush violet BROWALLIA
busy Lizzie IMPATIENS
butcher's broom JEW'S MYRTLE
　　　KNEE-HOLLY.RUSCUS
　　　SHEPHERD'S MYRTLE
Butomus FLOWERING RUSH
buttercup BACHELOR'S BUTTONS
　　　GIL(T)CUP.HELLEBORE
　　　KINGCUP.RANUNCULUS
—type MEADOW-RUE
butterfly flower SCHIZANTHUS
butterwort LENTIBULARIACEAE
　　　　PINGUICULA
cabbage BRASSICA.COLE(-WORT)
　　　COLLARD.KALE
—rose PROVINCIAL ROSE
—tree CORDYLINE
cactus (see cacti)
Cakile SEA ROCKET
Caladium ANGEL'S WINGS
calamint BASIL-THYME
calceolaria SLIPPER FLOWER
　　　　SLIPPERWORT
Calendula MARIGOLD
Californian poppy
　　　　ESCHSCHOLTZIA
calla lily ZANTEDESCHIA
Callistemon
　　　BOTTLEBRUSH PLANT
Callistriche WATER-STARWORT
Calluna HEATH(ER)
Caltha KINGCUP
Camelina GOLD-OF-PLEASURE
camomile ANTHEMIS.FEVERFEW
Campanula BELLWORT
　　　CANTERBURY BELL
　　　(GIANT) BELLFLOWER
　NETTLE-LEAVED BELLFLOWER
　　　STAR OF BETHLEHEM
　　　THROATWORT
campion CATCHFLY.LICHNIS
　FLOWER OF JOVE.LYCHNIS
　　　RAGGED ROBIN
Canada rice ZIZANIA
Canadian pondweed ANACHARIS
　　　WATER THYME
candytuft IBERIS

Cannabis	HEMP
Canterbury bell	CAMPANULA
	THROATWORT
Cape	
—cowslip	LACHENALIA
—gooseberry	GROUND-CHERRY
	PHYSALIS
—grape	RHOICISSUS
—ivy	SENECIO
—jasmine	GARDENIA
—primrose	STREPTOCARPUS
Capsella	SHEPHERD'S PURSE
caraway	AJ(O)WAN
Cardamine	CORALROOT
	TOOTHWORT
carduus	MUSK THISTLE
Carex	SEDGE
carnation	DIANTHUS
Carolina	
—jasmine	GELSEMIUM
—pink	SPIGELIA
carrion flower	STAPELIA
cassava	ADAM'S NEEDLE
	YUC(C)A
Cassia	SENNA
Castilleja	PAINTED CUP
castor-oil plant	ARALIA.FATSIA
	PANAX.RICINUS
cat's	
—ear	GROUND IVY
	MOUNTAIN EVERLASTING
—foot	GROUND IVY
	MOUNTAIN EVERLASTING
—tail	REEDMACE
catmint	CATNEP.CATNIP
	NEP(ETA)
Ceanothus	RED-ROOT
celery type	ALEXANDERS
Celosia	COCKSCOMB
	PLUME FLOWER
Centaurea	STAR THISTLE
Centranthus	RED VALERIAN
	SPUR VALERIAN
Centunculus	
	BASTARD PIMPERNEL
Cerastium	
	MOUSE-EAR CHICKWEED
Cereus	CACTUS.TORCH-THISTLE
Cestrum	NIGHT JESSAMINE

cetywall	SETUALE.SETWALL
	VALERIAN
chalk plant	GYPSOPHILA
Chamaenerion	WILLOWHERB
charlock	WILD MUSTARD
Cheiranthus/Cheirinia	
	WALL (GILLY)FLOWER
chenille plant	ACALYPHA
Chenopodium	WORM-SEED
chervil	CICELY.COW CHERVIL
	COW PARSLEY
	COW WEED
chestnut vine	TETRASTIGMA
chicken gizzard	IRESINE
chickpea	CHICH
	CHICKLING VETCH
	EGYPTIAN PEA.GRAM
chickweed	STELLARIA
	STITCHWORT
—wintergreen	TRIENTALIS
chicory	ENDIVE.SUCCORY
	WITLOOF
Chimaphila	WINTERGREEN
Chincherinchee	ORNITHOGALUM
Chinese	
—balloon flower	PLATYCODON
—lantern	PHYSALIS
Chionodoxa	
	GLORY OF THE SNOW
Chlorophytum	
	ST BERNARD'S LILY
	SPIDER PLANT
Christmas	
—pepper	CAPSICUM
—rose	BLACK HELLEBORE
cibol	WELSH ONION
Cicuta	WATER-HEMLOCK
cigar plant	CUPHEA
cinnamon	CANELLA
cinquefoil	FIVEFINGERS
	MARSH-LOCKS
	MINIATURE GRAPE IVY
	POTENTILLA
Cirsium	CNICUS.SPEAR THISTLE
Cissus	BEGONIA VINE
	KANGAROO VINE
	MINIATURE GRAPE IVY
clary	ORVAL.SAGE
Claytonia	SPRING BEAUTY

cleavers	GOOSEGRASS
clematis	TRAVELLER'S JOY
	VIRGIN'S-BOWER
Clerodendrum	
	BLEEDING HEART VINE
	GLORY BOWER
Clianthus	GLORY PEA
climbing	NASTURTIUM
	PHILODENDRON
	WISTARIA.WISTERIA
—evergreen	IVY
—gourd	BRYONY
Clivia	KAFFIR LILY
clog plant	HYPOCYRTA
clotbur	SEA-BURDOCK
	XANTHIUM
cloudberry	MOUNTAIN BRAMBLE
clove	EUGENIA
—pink	SOPS-IN-WINE
clover	ALSIKE
	HARE'S-FOOT (TREFOIL)
	TRIFOLIUM
club	
—moss	STAGHORN MOSS
—rush	BULRUSH.SCIRPUS
Cnicus	CIRSIUM
	(SPEAR) THISTLE
coarse weed	HEMP-NETTLE
Cobaea	CUP AND SAUCER VINE
cocklebur	CLOTBUR
cockscomb	CELOSIA
	YELLOW RATTLE
Codiaeum	CROTON
	JOSEPH'S COAT
Colchicum	MEADOW SAFFRON
coleseed	NAVEW
Coleus	FLAME NETTLE
coltsfoot	HORSE-FOOT
columbine	AQUILEGIA
Columnea	GOLDFISH PLANT
Colutea	BLADDER SENNA
comfrey	BORAGE.SYMPHYTUM
common	
—arum	CUCKOOPINT
	LORDS AND LADIES
—burnet	SALAD BURNET
—daisy	DOG DAISY
—polypody	POLYPODIUM
—ragwort	YELLOW-WEED

condiment	DILL
coneflower	RUDBECKIA
Convallaria	LILY OF THE VALLEY
coral	
—berry	AECHMEA.ARDISIA
—root	CARDAMINE
	TOOTHWORT
Cordatum	PHILODENDRON
Cordyline	CABBAGE TREE
	FLAMING DRAGON TREE
	GRASS PALM.TI PLANT
corn	
—bluebottle	BLAWORT.BLEWORT
—cockle	AGROSTEMMA
—feverfew	MAYWEED
—flower	BLUEBOTTLE
—marigold	OX-EYE
—salad	LAMB'S LETTUCE
—spurrey	YARR
cornfield	
—plant	POPPY
—weed	KNAWEL
Coronaria	ANEMONE
Coronopus	SENEBIERA
	SWINE'S CRESS
Corrigiola	STRAPWORT
Cortaderia	PAMPAS GRASS
cotton thistle	SCOTCH THISTLE
cough remedy	HOARHOUND
	WHITE HOREHOUND
cow	
—bane	CICUTA
—berry	VACCINIUM
—parsley	KECK(S).KECKSY(E).KEX
—parsnip	PIGWEED
—pea	CHERRY-BEAN
—slip	CULVER-KEY
	HERBPETER.PA(I)GLE
—x primrose	POLYANTHUS
cranberry	FEN-BERRY
	VACCINIUM
cranesbill	DOVE'S FOOT
	GERANIUM
Crassula	ROCHEA
creeping	
—Jenny	LOOSESTRIFE
	MONEYWORT.PILEA
—moss	SELAGINELLA
Crepis	HAWKSBEARD

cress   CARDAMINE.CORAL ROOT
Crithmum   SAMP(H)IRE
crocus   SAFFRON
Crossandra
            FIRECRACKER FLOWER
Croton   CODIAEUM
                        JOSEPH'S COAT
crow
—berry   CRAKEBERRY
—foot   ANEMONE
crown of thorns   EUPHORBIA
Cryptanthus   EARTH STAR
                        PHEASANT LEAF
                        RAINBOW STAR
                        STARFISH PLANT
cuckoo
—flower   CARDAMINE
                        LADY'S SMOCK
—pint   ARUM.WAKE-ROBIN
cucumber   COLOCYNTH
                        COLOQUINTIDA
Cucurbita   GOURD.SQUASH
cudweed   COTTONWEED
cup and saucer vine   COBAEA
Cuphea   CIGAR PLANT
Cupid's bower   ACHIMENES
Cyanotis   TEDDY BEAR VINE
cyclamen   SOW-BREAD
Cynanchum   SWALLOW-WORT
Cyperus   UMBRELLA PLANT
daffodil   NARCISSUS
daisy   BELLIS
dame violet   HESPERIS.ROCKET
dandelion   TARAXACUM
Dane's blood   DANEWORT
            DWARF ELDER.WALLWORT
darnel   TARE
Datura   THORN-APPLE
day lily   FUNKIA.HEMEROCALLIS
dead nettle   ARCHANGEL
                        DAY-NETTLE
deadly nightshade   ATROPA
            BELLADONNA.DWALE
deep-blue gentian   GENTIANELLA
Delphinium   LARKSPUR
desert privet   PEPEROMIA
devil's ivy   SCINDAPSUS
devil-in-a-bush   NIGELLA
(Devon and Cornwall)

                              ILLECEBRUM
Dianthus   (CHEDDAR-)PINK
                        SWEET WILLIAM
Dicentra
            DUTCHMAN'S BREECHES
Dieffenbachia   DUMB CANE
                        LEOPARD LILY
Digitalis   FOXGLOVE
dill   ANISE.FENNEL
dinner-plate Aralia   POLYSCIAS
Dipladenia   PINK ALLAMANDA
Dionaea   VENUS'S FLYTRAP
Diplotaxis   WALL-MUSTARD
                        WALL-ROCKET
dittander   PEPPERWORT
dittany   BURNING BUSH
                        SWEET HORSEMINT
Dizygotheca   FINGER ARALIA
dock   POLYGONUM.RUMEX
                                SORREL
dog
—bane   APOCYNUM.FLYTRAP
—'s mercury   MERCURIALIS
—tooth violet   ERYTHRONIUM
—violet   VIOLA CANINA
—wood   HOUNDS-BERRY
Doronicum   LEOPARD'S BANE
Dracaena
    (MADAGASCAR) DRAGON TREE
                        RIBBON PLANT
dragon   DRACONTIUM
—'s head   DRACOCEPHALUM
—tree   DRACAENA
Drosera   SUNDEW
Dryopteris   MALE FERN
Duchesnea
            INDIAN STRAWBERRY
duckweed   DUCK'S-MEAT
                                LEMNA
dumb cane   DIEFFENBACHIA
Dutch rush   SCOURING RUSH
Dutchman's
—breeches   DICENTRA
—pipe   ARISTOLOCHIA
dwarf
—elder   DANE'S BLOOD
            DANEWORT.WALLWORT
—marguerite   SHASTA DAISY
—poppy   ICELAND POPPY

dyer's rocket	MIGNONETTE
	WELD
earth star	CRYPTANTHUS
Echinops	GLOBE-THISTLE
Echium	VIPER'S BUGLOSS
edible root	BEETROOT
	MANGEL(-WURZEL)
MANGOLD(-WURZEL).PARSNEP	
PARSNIP.SWEDE.TURNIP	
eggplant	BRINJAL
	BROWN JOLLY
Egyptian star cluster	PENTAS
Eichhornia	WATER HYACINTH
Eleagnus	OLEASTER
elecampane	GOLDEN SAMPHIRE
elephant's	
—ear	PHILODENDRON
—foot	TORTOISE-PLANT
enchanter's nightshade	CIRCAEA
endive	ESCAROLE
Ephedra	SEA-GRAPE
Epilobium	WILLOWHERB
Epipactis	HELLEBORINE
Episcia	FLAME VIOLET
	LACE FLOWER
Eranthis	WINTER ACONITE
Erica	HEATH.HEATHER
Erigeron	FLEABANE
Erodium	STORK'S BILL
eryngo	SEA HOLLY
Erysimum	TREACLE MUSTARD
	TREACLE WORM-SEED
Erythronium	
	DOG'S-TOOTH VIOLET
eschalot	ALLIUM.SHAL(L)OT
Ethiopian gladiolus	
	ACIDANTHERA
Eupatorium	HEMP-AGRIMONY
Euphorbia	(SUN)SPURGE
euphrasy	EYEBRIGHT
evening primrose	CLARKIA
ENCHANTER'S NIGHTSHADE	
FUCHSIA.GODETIA	
OENOTHERA	
evergreen cherry	
	CHERRY-LAUREL
everlasting flower	IMMORTELLE
everlastings	XERANTHEMUM
evil-smelling	FETID IRIS.

	ROAST-BEEF PLANT
	SKUNK-CABBAGE
	SYMPLOCARPUS
Exacum	PERSIAN VIOLET
eyebright	EUPHRASY
fat-headed Lizzie	FATSHEDERA
Fatshedera	FAT-HEADED LIZZIE
	IVY TREE
Fatsia	ARALIA
	CASTOR-OIL PLANT
fennelflower	LOVE-IN-A-MIST
ferns	FILICES
	(*see also* ferns)
Ferraria	TIGRIDIA
Ferula	GIANT FENNEL
	LASERWORT
fetid iris	ROAST-BEEF PLANT
feverfew	BACHELOR'S BUTTONS
	PELLITORY.PYRETHRUM
Ficus	BENGAL FIG
	FIDDLE LEAF FIG
	MISTLETOE FIG
	RUBBER PLANT.WEEPING FIG
fiddle	
—leaf	PHILODENDRON
—fig	FICUS
field mustard	BRASSOCK
figwort	ACANTHUS.MIMULUS
	NEMESIA.SCROPHULARIA
finger	
—aralia	DIZYGOTHECA
—nail plant	
	BLUSHING BROMELIAD
	NEOREGELIA
firecracker	
—flower	CROSSANDRA
—plant	MANETTIA
fire	
—thorn	PYRACANTH(A)
—weed	ROSEBAY(WILLOWHERB)
Fittonia	NERVE PLANT
	MOSAIC PLANT
	PAINTED NET LEAF
	SILVER NET LEAF
	SNAKESKIN PLANT
five-leaved clover	CINQUEFOIL
flagflower	IRIS
flame	
—nettle	COLEUS

—of the woods   IXORA
—violet   EPISCIA
flaming
—dragon tree   CORDYLINE
—Katy   KALANCHOE
—sword   VRIESIA
flamingo flower   ANTHURIUM
flax   LINUM
fleabane   ERIGERON
fleur-de-lis   IRIS
floating plant   BLADDERWORT
                       UTRICULARIA
Florentine iris   ORRIS
flowering rush   BUTOMUS
flowerless plant   CRYPTOGAM
                       PTERIDOPHYTE
fodder-plant   SAIN(T)FOIN
fool's parsley   DOG-PARSLEY
forest lily   VELTHEIMIA
forget-me-not   BRUNNERA
               MOUSE-EAR.MYOSOTIS
               SCORPION GRASS
four-leaved clover
               TRUE-LOVE GRASS
foxglove   DEADMEN'S BELLS
                       DIGITALIS
               WITCHES' THIMBLE
Fragaria   STRAWBERRY
Frankenia   SEA-HEATH
frankincense   LASER(WORT)
freckle face   HYPOESTES
French bean   HARICOT
friendship plant   PILEA
fritillary   CROWN-IMPERIAL
                       SNAKE'S-HEAD
frogbit   HYDROCHARIS
fumitory   FUMARIA
Funkia   HOSTA.PLANTAIN LILY
furze   WHIN
Gaillardia   BLANKET FLOWER
Galanthus   SNOWDROP
Galucium   HORNED POPPY
garden
—cress   LEPIDIUM
—daisy   HEN-AND-CHICKENS
gardener's garters   PHILARIS
garlic   ALLIUM
—mustard   JACK-BY-THE-HEDGE
—like plant   ROCOMBOLE

Gaultheria   WINTERGREEN
gay feather   LIATRIS
genista   DYER'S BROOM
                 DYER'S-GREENWEED
          GREENWEED.PETTY WHIN
gentian   BALDMONEY.FELWORT
                 YELLOW CENTAURY
                 YELLOW WORT
geranium   PELARGONIUM
geum   AVENS
giant
—bellflower   CAMPANULA
                       THROATWORT
—fennel   FERULA
gigantic mare's tail   GUNNERA
gillyflower CLOVE-GILLYFLOWER
               STOCK-GILLYFLOWER
                       WALLFLOWER
gipsywort   WATER HOREHOUND
giving yellow dye   XANTHIUM
gladiolus   CORNFLAG
glasswort KALI.MARSH SAMPHIRE
                       SALICORNIA
Glaux   SEA MILKWORT
globe thistle   ECHINOPS
Gloriosa   GLORY LILY
glory
—bower   CLERODENDRUM
—lily   GLORIOSA
—of the snow   CHIONODOXA
—pea   CLIANTHUS
Gloxinia   SINNINGIA
goat's
—beard   ASTILBE
          JACK-GO-TO-BED-AT-NOON
                       SALSIFY
—weed   BISHOP('S) WEED
          GOUTWEED.GOUTWORT
Godetia   EVENING PRIMROSE
gold dust   ALYSSUM
golden
—garlic   ALLIUM
—Pothos   SCINDAPSUS
—rod   AARON'S ROD
—samphire   ELECAMPANE
—seal   YELLOW ROOT
goldfish plant   COLUMNEA
goose
—flower   PELICAN-FLOWER

—foot plant	BLITE	hedge	
GOOD-KING-HENRY.ORACH(E)		—hyssop	GRATIOLA
PIGWEED.SYNGONIUM		—mustard	FLIXWEED
gorse	ULEX	—plant	GARLIC MUSTARD
gourd	CUCURBITA.SQUASH	Hedera	IVY
goutweed	BISHOP('S) WEED	Helenium	SNEEZEWEED
	GOATWEED	Helianthemum	ROCK-ROSE
grape			SUN ROSE
—hyacinth	MUSCARI	Helianthus	SUNFLOWER
STARCH-HYACINTH		Helichrysum	
—ivy	RHOICISSUS	EVERLASTING (FLOWER)	
—vine	VITIS	Heliocharis	SPIKE-RUSH
Gratiola	HEDGE-HYSSOP	Heliotrope	CHERRY-PIE
great mullein	HAG-TAPER	hellebore	CHRISTMAS FLOWER
SHEPHERD'S CLUB			CHRISTMAS ROSE
greater		Helxine	BABY'S TEARS
—celandine	SWALLOW-WORT	MIND YOUR OWN BUSINESS	
—knapweed	MAFELON	Hemerocallis	DAY-LILY
Greek valerian	JACOB'S LADDER	Hemigraphis	RED IVY
green		hemp agrimony	EUPATORIUM
—dragon	DRACUNCULUS	henbane	HYOSCYAMUS
—flowered orchid	LISTERA	Hepaticae	LIVERWORT
TWAY-BLADE		Heptapleurum	PARASOL PLANT
—weed	GENISTA	herb	(see herbs)
Grevillea	SILK OAK	herb lily	ALSTROMERIA
gromwell	SALFERN	Herniaria	RUPTUREWORT
groundsel	SENECIO	herringbone plant	MARANTA
Guernsey lily	NERINE	Hesperis	DAME VIOLET.ROCKET
Gypsophila	SOAP-ROOT	Hieracium	HAWKWEED
Haemanthus	BLOOD LILY	high taper	MULLEIN
hag		Hippeastrum	AMARYLLIS
—taper	(GREAT) MULLEIN	hogweed	COW PARSNIP
—weed	BROOM	hollyhock	ALTHAEA.MALVA
hair-capped mosses	POLYTRICUM		ROSE-MALLOW
harebell	BLAWORT.BLEWORT	hop trefoil	SHAMROCK
BLUEBELL.CAMPANULA		horsetail	BOTTLEBRUSH
HAIRBELL.HEATH BELL		DUTCH RUSH.EQUISETINAE	
hare's ear	BUPLEVER		EQUISETALES
harlequin flower	SPARAXIS		MARE'S TAIL
hawksbeard	CREPIS	Hortensia	HYDRANGEA
hawkweed	HIERACIUM	hosta	FUNKIA.PLANTAIN LILY
hazelwort	ASARABACCA	hot-water plant	ACHIMENES
healing plant	PANACEA	Hottonia	WATER VIOLET
heart's ease	PANSY	house	
heath	ANDROMEDA	—leek	JUPITER'S BEARD
BELL HEATHER			SENGREEN
ERICA.GAULTHERIA		—lime	SPARMANNIA
heather	CALLUNA.ERICA	Hoya	WAX PLANT
—bell	HEATH BELL	Humulus	HOP

husk tomato	GROUND-CHERRY
hybrid rose	NOISETTE
hydrangea	HORTENSIA
Hydrophyllum	WATER-LEAF
Hyoscyamus	HENBANE
Hypericum	AARON'S BEARD
	ROSE OF SHARON
	ST JOHN'S WORT
	ST PETER'S WORT
Hypocyrta	CLOG PLANT
Hypoestes	FRECKLE FACE
	POLKA DOT PLANT
Iberis	CANDYTUFT
ice-plant	MESEMBRIANTHEMUM
Impatiens	BALSAM
	BUSY LIZZIE.JEWEL-WEED
	NOLI-ME-TANGERE
	PATIENT LUCY
	TOUCH-ME-NOT
Indian	
—corn	MAIZE.ZEA
—cress	LARK'S-HEEL
	TROPAEOLIUM
—pink	SPIGELIA
—pipe	MONATROPA
—poke	AMERICAN HELLEBORE
—rice	ZIZANIA
—strawberry	DUCHESNEA
indoor oak	NICODEMIA
insectivorous	BUTTERWORT
	DARLINGTONIA.DROSERA
	NEPENTHES.PITCHER-PLANT
	SARRACENIA.SUNDEW
	VENUS FLYTRAP
Ipomoea	JALAP
	MORNING GLORY
Iresine	BEEFSTEAK PLANT
	BLOOD LEAF
	CHICKEN GIZZARD
iris	GLADIOLE.GLADIOLUS
Irish heath	ST DABEOC'S HEATH
Isatis	WOAD
Ismene	PERUVIAN DAFFODIL
Isoetes	QUILLWORT
itchweed	FALSE HELLEBORE
	WHITE HELLEBORE
ivy	ARALIA.HEDERA
—bush	TOD
—leaved speedwell	HENBIT

—tree	FATSHEDERA
Ixia	AFRICAN CORN LILY
Ixora	FLAME OF THE WOODS
Jacob's ladder	GREEK VALERIAN
	POLEMONIUM
Jacobinia	KING'S CROWN
jalap	IPOMOEA
Japanese sedge	CAREX
jasmine	JESSAMINE
—plant	BOUVARDIA
Jasione	SHEEP'S BIT
	(SHEEP'S BIT) SCABIOUS
	SHEEP'S SCABIOUS
Jerusalem	
—artichoke	SUNFLOWER
—sage	PHLOMIS
jewel-weed	IMPATIENS
John-go-to-bed-at-noon	
	GOAT'S-BEARD
Joseph's coat	CODIAEUM
	CROTON
Juncus	TOAD GRASS
	TOAD RUSH
jute	CORCHORUS
Kaffir lily	CLIVIA.SCHIZOSTYLIS
Kalanchoe	FLAMING KATY
kale	BORECOLE
kalmia	MOUNTAIN LAUREL
Karatus	SILKGRASS
kidney	
—bean	FLAGEOLET
	FRENCH BEAN.HARICOT
	(SCARLET-)RUNNER
—vetch	ANTHYLLIS.CENTAUREA
	LADY'S FINGER(S)
kingcup	CALTHA
	MARSH MARIGOLD
king's crown	JACOBINIA
knapweed	CENTAURY
	HARDHEAD
	ST BARNABY'S THISTLE
knawel	SCLERANTHUS
Kniphofia	RED-HOT POKER
	TORCH-LILY
knotgrass	PERSICARIA
	POLYGONUM
knotted	
—pearlwort	SAGINA
—spurrey	SAGINA

Labrador tea	LEDUM
lace flower	EPISCIA
Lachenalia	CAPE COWSLIP
lady's	
—mantle	PARSLEY P(I)ERT
—pincushion	THRIFT
—slipper	CYPRIPEDIUM
	MOCCASIN-FLOWER.ORCHID
—thistle	MILK THISTLE
lake margin plants	LITORELLA
	SHORE-WEED
lamb's ear	STACHYS
larkspur	BLUE-ROCKET
	DELPHINIUM.LARK'S-HEEL
	MONK'S HOOD.STAVESACRE
Lathraea	TOOTHWORT
Lathyrus	SWEET PEA
	VETCHLING
laurel	LAURUS.SWEETBAY
Lavatera	TREE MALLOW
lavender	ASPIC.LAVANDULA
leafless parasite	DODDER
legume	GUAR
lentils	PULSE
Leontodon	HAWKBIT
Leonurus	MOTHERWORT
leopard lily	DIEFFENBACHIA
Lepidium	PEPPER-GRASS
lesser yellow trefoil	SHAMROCK
Leucojum	SNOWFLAKE
levantine madder	ALIZARI
Liatris	GAY FEATHER
Ligusticum	LOVAGE
Ligustrum	PRIVET
like clover	MELILOT
lily	AMARYLLIS
	ASPHODEL.FRITILLARY
—of the Nile	AGAPANTHUS
—of the valley	CONVALLARIA
—turf	OPHIOPOGON
—type	HYACINTH
Lima bean	SUGAR-BEAN
Limosella	MUDWORT
Linaria	BACON AND EGGS
	TOADFLAX
Linum	FLAX
lipstick vine	AESCHYNANTHUS
Listera	TWAYBLADE
Lithospermum	GROMWELL
Litorella	SHORE-WEED
liverwort	AGRIMONY.HEPATIC(A)
	RICCIA.MARCHANTIA
lollipop plant	PACHYSTACHYS
Lomeria	HARD FERN
London pride	NANCY-PRETTY
	NONE-SO-PRETTY
	ST PATRICK'S CABBAGE
	SAXIFRAGA
Lonicera	HONEYSUCKLE
loosestrife	MONEYWORT
lousewort	PEDICULARIS
love	
—apple	TOMATO
—in-a-mist	DEVIL-IN-A-BUSH
	NIGELLA
—lies-bleeding	AMARANT(H)US
lucerne	ALFALFA
lucky clover	OXALIS
Lunaria	HONESTY
Luzula	WOOD-RUSH
Lychnis	ROSE-CAMPION
Lycopus	GIPSYWORT
Lysimachia	LOOSESTRIFE
Lythrum	PURPLE LOOSETRIFE
Macleaya	BOCCONIA
	PLUME POPPY
Madagascar	
—dragon tree	DRACAENA
—jasmine	STEPHANOTIS
madder	GARDENIA.RUBIA
maidenhair fern	ADIANTUM
maize	INDIAN CORN
	SWEET-CORN.ZEA
Malcomia	VIRGINIA STOCK
mallow	ABUTILON.LAVATERA
	MALVA
mandrake	MANDRAGORA
	SPRINGWORT
Manettia	FIRECRACKER PLANT
Maranta	HERRINGBONE PLANT
	NEVER NEVER PLANT
	PEACOCK PLANT
	PRAYER PLANT
	RABBIT TRACKS
	RATTLESNAKE PLANT
	ZEBRA PLANT
mare's tail	BOTTLEBRUSH
	HIPPURIS

marigold   CALENDULA
marjoram AMARACUS.OREGANO
              ORIGAN(E).ORIGANUM
marsh
—gentian   BUCKBEAN
—grass   REED
—lily   CALLA
—lousewort   RED-RATTLE
—mallow   ALTHAEA
—marigold   KINGCUP
—plant   MARE'STAIL
      PENNYWORT.WATER-FERN
—samphire   GLASSWORT
                            SALICORNIA
martagon lily   TURK'S CAP
marvel of Peru   FOUR O'CLOCK
                              MIRABILIS
masterwort   ASTRANTIA
Matricaria   FEVERFEW
Matthiola   STOCK
matweed   NARD
mayweed   DOG'S FENNEL
meadow
—rue   THALICTRUM
—saffron   COLCHICUM
                           NAKED LADY
—sweet
      QUEEN-OF-THE-MEADOW(S)
                              SPIRAEA
Meconopsis   POPPY
medicinal plant   BETONY
      BIRTHWORT.CAR(R)AWAY
medick   MEDICAGO.SNAIL
melitot   FENUGREEK
Mentha   MINT.PENNYROYAL
      PEPPERMINT.SPEARMINT
Mercurialis   (DOG'S) MERCURY
mermaid vine   RHOICISSUS
Mertensia   OYSTER-PLANT
Mesembrianthemum   ICE-PLANT
Meum   BALDMONEY
                    SPIGNEL.SPICKNEL
Michaelmas daisy   ASTER
mignonette   DYER'S ROCKET
                         RESEDA.WELD
milfoil   ACHILLEA.YARROW
milk
—root   POLYGAEA
—thistle   LADY'S THISTLE

—vetch   ASTRAGALUS
                       WILD LIQUORICE
—weed   ASCLEPIAS
—wort   POLYGALA.SNAKEROOT
Mimosa   TOUCH-ME-NOT
Mimulus   MONKEY FLOWER
                        MUSK PLANT
mind your own business HELXINE
Ming Aralia   POLYSCIAS
miniature grape ivy   CISSUS
mint   CALAMINT.PENNYROYAL
Mirabilis   MARVEL OF PERU
mistletoe   VISCUM
—fig   FICUS
mock privet   PHILLYREA
Monarda   BERGAMOT
moneywort   CREEPING JENNY
monk's
—hood   ACONITE.BLUE-ROCKET
                            LARKSPUR
—rhubarb   PATIENCE DOCK
monkey-flower   MIMULUS
Monstera
      SPLIT LEAF PHILODENDRON
      SWISS CHEESE PLANT
Montbretia   TRITONIA
moonseed   MENISPERMUM
moorland plant
      GRASS OF PARNASSUS
morning glory   IPOMOEA.JALAP
mosaic plant   FITTONIA
moschatel   ADOXA
Moses in the cradle   RHOEO
moss   ACROGEN.CRYPTOGAM
mossy saxifrage LADY'S CUSHION
mother
—in-law's tongue   SANSEVIERIA
—of thousands
      STRAWBERRY GERANIUM
mountain
—bramble   CLOUDBERRY
—laurel   KALMIA
—sorrel OXYRIA.ROMAN SORREL
mourning-bride
                    SWEET SCABIOUS
mouse
—ear chickweed   CERASTIUM
                    SNOW-IN-SUMMER
—tail   MYOSURUS

mudwort	LIMOSELLA
mugwort	WORMWOOD
mulberry	MORUS
mullein	AARON'S ROD
	ADAM'S FLANNEL
	HAG-TAPER, HIGH TAPER
	SHEPHERD'S CLUB
	VERBASCUM
Muscari	GRAPE HYACINTH
	STARCH HYACINTH
musk	MIMULUS
—scented	MIMULUS
	MUSK MALLOW
—thistle	CARDUUS
mustard	SENVY
Myosotis	FORGET-ME-NOT
Myosurus	MOUSETAIL
Myriophyllum	WATER-MILFOIL
Myrrhis	MYRTLE.SWEET CICELY
myrtle	MYRRHIS.SWEET CICELY
naked lady	MEADOW SAFFRON
Nancy-pretty	LONDON PRIDE
narcissus	JONQUIL
	PHEASANT'S EYE
nasturtium	INDIAN CRESS
	LARK'S-HEEL.TROPAEOLUM
Natal plum	CARISSA
navelwort	PENNYWORT
Neapolitan violet	PARMA VIOLET
needle-furze	PETTY WHIN
Nelumbium	LOTE.LOTOS.LOTUS
Nemesia	FIGWORT
nenuphar	WATER-LILY
Neoregelia	
	BLUSHING BROMELIAD
	FINGERNAIL PLANT
Nepenthe	PITCHER PLANT
Nepeta	CATMINT.GROUND IVY
Nephthytis	SYNGONIUM
Nerine	GUERNSEY LILY
Nertera	BEAD PLANT
nerve plant	FITTONIA
nettle	URTICA
—type	PELLITORY
—leaved bellflower	CAMPANULA
	THROATWORT
—with female flowers	
	ROMAN NETTLE
never-never plant	MARANTA

New Zealand flax	PHORMIUM
Nicodemia	INDOOR OAK
Nicotiana	TOBACCO PLANT
Nidularium	
	BIRD'S NEST BROMELIAD
Nigella	DEVIL-IN-A-BUSH
	FENNELFLOWER
	FITCH.LOVE-IN-A-MIST
	RAGGED LADY
night	
—jessamine	CESTRUM
—shade	HENBANE.MOREL
	SOLANUM
none-so-pretty	LONDON PRIDE
northern fern	HARD FERN
nose-bleed	YARROW
Nuphar	WATER-LILY
Nymphaea	LOTE.LOTOS.LOTUS
	WATER-LILY
oat-shooter	ANGELICA
	AIT-SKEITER
Oenanthe	WATER-DROPWORT
	WATER-HEMLOCK
Oenothera	EVENING PRIMROSE
offensive smelling	
plants	DANE'S BLOOD
	DANEWORT.DWARF
	ELDER.WALLWORT
oil-producing plant	RAPE
old-fashioned rose	MOSS-ROSE
oleander	NERIUM.RHODDAPHNE
	ROSE-BAY(LAUREL)
	ROSE-LAUREL
oleaster	ELEAGNUS
olive	OLEA
Ononis	REST-HARROW
Ophiopogon	LILY TURF
Opuntia	PRICKLY PEAR
orange-flowered lily	TIGER LILY
orchid	CORAL-ROOT.FLY ORCHIS
	LADY'S SLIPPER
Ornithogalum	CHINCHERINCHEE
	STAR-OF-BETHLEHEM
orpine	LIVELONG
orval	CLARY
oshac	AMMONIAC
ox	
—eye daisy	MARGUERITE
—lip	FIVEFINGERS

—tongue	PIERIS
Oxalis	WOOD-SORREL
Oxyria	MOUNTAIN SORREL
oyster plant	GROMWELL
	MERTENSIA.SALSIFY
Pachystachys	LOLLIPOP PLANT
padma	SACRED LOTUS
painted	
—cup	CASTILLEJA
	PAINTED LADY
—lady	PAINTED CUP
—net leaf	FITTONIA
—tongue	SALPIGLOSSIS
painter's palette	ANTHURIUM
pampas grass	CORTADERIA
Panamiga	PILEA
Panax	ARALIA
pansy	HERB-TRINITY
	LOVE-IN-IDLENESS.VIOLA
Papaver	POPPY
paper	
—flower	BOUGAINVILLEA
—reed	PAPYRUS
parasol plant	HEPTAPLEURUM
parasitic plant	
	MISTLETOE.VISCUM
Paris quadrifolia	HERB PARIS
parkleaves	ST JOHN'S WORT
	TUTSAN
Paronychia	WHITLOW-GRASS
	WHITLOW-WORT
parsley fern	ROCK-BRAKE
parsnip-type	MASTERWORT
parti-coloured	PAINTED LADY
paschal flower	ANEMONE
	PULSATILLA
pasque flower	ANEMONE
	PULSATILLA
Passiflora	PASSION FLOWER
LOVE-IN-A-MIST.PASSIFLORA	
	WATER-LEMON
patience-dock	MONK'S RHUBARB
patient Lucy	IMPATIENS
peace lily	SPATHIPHYLLUM
peacock	
—fern	SELAGINELLA
—plant	MARANTA
pearlwort	SAGINA
Pedicularis	LOUSEWORT

Pelargonium	GERANIUM
	STORK'S BILL
pelican-flower	GOOSE-FLOWER
pellitory	FEVERFEW.YARROW
	WALL-WORT
pennywort	NAVELWORT
Penstemon	BEARDED TONGUE
Pentas	EGYPTIAN STAR CLUSTER
penthia	ASTROPHEL.STARLIGHT
pepper	
—grass	LEPIDIUM
—wort	DITTANDER
	SPANISH CRESS
perennial	
—herb	LASERPICIUM
—saxifrage	LONDON PRIDE
—weed	WILD(-)OAT
periwinkle	APOCYNUM
	STROPHANTHUS.VINCA
Persian violet	EXACUM
persicaria	KNOTGRASS
Peruvian daffodil	ISMENE
petty whin	GENISTA
	NEEDLE-FURZE
Phalaris	GARDENER'S GARTERS
pheasant leaf	CRYPTANTHUS
pheasant's eye	ADONIS
	NARCISSUS
Phillyrea	MOCK PRIVET
Philodendron	CORDATUM
ELEPHANT'S EAR.FIDDLE LEAF	
	SWEETHEART PLANT
phlox	POLEMONIUM
Phormium	NEW ZEALAND FLAX
Physalis	CAPE GOOSEBERRY
	CHINESE LANTERN
	GROUND-CHERRY
	WINTER-CHERRY
Phytolacca	POKEWEED
pickling cabbage	RED CABBAGE
Pieris	OX-TONGUE
piggyback plant	TOLMIEA
pigweed	ARAMANTH
	GOOSEFOOT
	COW PARSNIP
Pilea	ALUMINIUM PLANT
	ARTILLERY PLANT
	CREEPING JENNY
	FRIENDSHIP PLANT

PANAMIGA
pilewort   CELANDINE.FIGWORT
pillwort   PILULARIA
Pilularia   PILLWORT
Pimpinella   ANISE
BURNET-SAXIFRAGE
pincushion flower   SCABIOUS
pineapple ANANA(S).BROMELIA
—weed   (RAYLESS) MAYWEED
Pinguicula   BUTTERWORT
pink   CLOVE-GILLYFLOWER
CLOVE PINK.DIANTHUS
—Allamanda   DIPLADENIA
—root   WORM-GRASS
pipewort   ERIOCAULON
pitcher plant   NEPENTHE
Plantago RIBWORT(-PLAINTAIN)
plantain RIBGRASS.WAYBREAD
—lily   FUNKIA.HOSTA
Platycerium   STAGHORN-FERN
Platycodon
CHINESE BALLOON FLOWER
Plectranthus   SWEDISH IVY
pleurisy root BUTTERFLY WEED
Plumbago   SEA-LAVENDER
SEA-PINK
plume
—flower   CELOSIA
—poppy BOCCONIA.MACLEAYA
Podocarpus   BUDDHIST PINE
poisonous plants
FOOL'S PARSLEY
NIGHTSHADE
pokeweed   PHYTOLACCA
Polemonium   PHLOX
Polianthes   AMARYLLIS
TUBEROSE
polka-dot plant   HYPOESTES
Polyanthus   PRIMULA
Polygala   MILKWORT
Polygonatum SOLOMON'S SEAL
Polygonum   KNOTGRASS
KNOTWEED
PURPLE LOOSESTRIFE
WILLOW-WEED
Polypodium
COMMON POLYPODY
Polyscias DINNER-PLATE ARALIA
MING ARALIA

pomegranate   PUNICA
pond plant   ACORUS
SWEET-FLAG
pondweed   EELGRASS
FROG'SLETTUCE
GRASSWRACK
HYDROCHARITACEAE
PICKEREL-WEED
POTOMOGETON.ZOSTER
poor man's
—orchid   SCHIZANTHUS
—weatherglass   PIMPERNEL
poppy MECONOPSIS.PAPAVER
Portulaca   PURSLANE
pot-herb PURSLANE.PURSLAIN
potato   SOLANUM
Potentilla   CINQUEFOIL
SEPT-FOIL.TORMENTIL
WILD STRAWBERRY
BARREN STRAWBERRY
SILVERWEED
Poterium   BOTTLE-BRUSH
prayer plant   MARANTA
prickly
—pear   INDIAN FIG.OPUNTIA
—poppy   ARGEMONE
—saltwort   KALI
—samphire   SALTWORT
primrose BIRD'S EYE.PRIMULA
Primula   OXLIP.PRIMROSE
prince's feathers AMARANTHUS
LONDON PRIDE
privet   LIGUSTRUM
producing red dye   MADDER
provincial rose CABBAGE ROSE
Prunella   SELF-HEAL
Pulicaria   FLEABANE
Pulmonaria   LUNGWORT
Pulsaltilla PASQUE FLOWER
pulse CALAVANCE.CARAVANCE
Punica   POMEGRANATE
purple
—loosestrife   KNOTWEED
WILLOW-WEED
LONG-PURPLES.LYTHRUM
—heart   SETCREASEA
—medick   LUCERN(E)
—orchis   LONG-PURPLES
—passion vine   VYNURA

purslane	PORTULACA
Puschkinia	STRIPED SQUILL
pyracanth(a)	FIRETHORN
Pyrethrum	FEVERFEW
Pyrola	WINTERGREEN
queen-of-the-meadow(s)	
	MEADOWSWEET
quillwort	ISOETES
quinsy-berry	BLACKCURRANT
rabbit tracks	MARANTA
radish	RAPHANUS
ragged	
—lady	NIGELLA
—robin	CAMPION
	CUCKOO FLOWER
	WILD-WILLIAMS
rag	
—weed	AMBROSIA
	RAGWORT.SENECIO
—wort	AMROSIA.RAGWEED
	SENECIO.TANSY
rainbow star	CRYPTANTHUS
rampion	BELL-FLOWER
ramsons	WILD GARLIC
Ranunculus	BUTTERCUP
	SPEARWORT
Rapa	SUGAR-BEET
rape	NAVEW
Raphanus	RADISH
rattlesnake plant	MARANTA
rayless mayweed	
	PINEAPPLE-WEED
reate	WATER-CROWFOOT
Rechsteineria	CARDINAL FLOWER
red	
—currant	RIBES
—hot cat's-tail	ACALYPHA
—hot poker	KNIPHOFIA
	TORCH-LILY.TRITOMA
—ivy	HEMIGRAPHIS
—rattle	MARSH LOUSEWORT
—root	CEANOTHUS
—valerian	CENTRANTHUS
	SPUR VALERIAN
reedmace	BULRUSH
	CAT'S-TAIL.TYPHA
Reseda	DYER'S-ROCKET
	DYER'S-WELD
	DYER'S YELLOW-WEED

	MIGNONETTE
resinous plant	STYRAX
restharrow	LICORICE.LIQUORICE
Resurrection plant	
	ROSE OF JERICHO
Retama	SPANISH BROOM
Rhamnus	BUCKTHORN
rhapontic	RHUBARB
Rheinberry/Rhineberry	
	BUCKTHORN
Rheum	RHUBARB
rhododaphne	OLEANDER
rhododendron	ALPINE ROSE
	AZALEA.ROSEBAY
Rhoeo	BOAT LILY
	MOSES IN THE CRADLE
Rhoicissus	CAPE GRAPE
	GRAPE IVY.MERMAID VINE
rhubarb	RHAPONTIC.RHEUM
Rhus	SUMACH
ribbon plant	DRACAENA
Ribes	BLACK CURRANT
	GOOSEBERRY.RED CURRANT
ribgrass	PLANTAIN
ribwort(-plaintain)	PLANTAGO
Riccia	LIVERWORT
Richardia	LILY OF THE NILE
Ricinus	CASTOR-OIL PLANT
roadside weed	HEDGE MUSTARD
	HEDGE PARSLEY.SILVERWEED
roast-beef plant	FETID IRIS
Rochea	CRASSULA
rock	
—brake	PARSLEY FERN
—cress	ARABIS.AUBRIETIA
	WALL-CRESS
—rose	CISTUS.HELIANTHEMUM
rocket	DAME'S VIOLET.HESPERIS
roe-blackberry	ROEBUCK-BERRY
	STONE-BRAMBLE
roebuck-berry	ROE-BLACKBERRY
	STONE-BRAMBLE
rose	
—campion	LYCHNIS
—laurel	OLEANDER
—mallow	HIBISCUS.HOLLYHOCK
—of Jericho	
	RESURRECTION PLANT
—of Sharon	HYPERICUM

—root	STONECROP	saligot	WATER-CHESTNUT
rosebay (laurel)	OLEANDER	sallow-thorn	SEA-BUCKTHORN
	RHODODENDRON	Salpiglossis	PAINTED TONGUE
—willow herb	SLINKWEED	salsify	GOAT'S BEARD
Rubia	MADDER		OYSTER PLANT
rubber plant	FICUS	Salsola	GLASSWORT.SALTWORT
Rudbeckia	CONEFLOWER	salt	
rue	HERB-(OF)-GRACE	—marsh plant	SEA-BLITE
	HERB-OF-REPENTANCE		SEA-LAVENDER.STATICE
Ruellia	ACANTHUS.MANY-ROOT	—wort	PRICKLY SAMPHIRE
Rumex	DOCK.SORREL		SALICORNIA.SALSOLA
runner bean	FRENCH BEAN	salvia	SAGE
	HARICOT.KIDNEY BEAN	Salvadora	MUSTARD-TREE
	SCARLET RUNNER	Salvinia	WATER-FERN
rupturewort	HERNIARIA	samp(h)ire	CRITHMUM
Ruscus	BUTCHER'S BROOM	sand	
rutabaga	SWEDISH TURNIP	—wort	ARENARIA
Saccharum	SUGAR-CANE		SEA PURSLANE
sacred lotus	NELUMBIUM	—spurrey	SPERGULARIA
	NELUMBO.PADMA	sansevieria	BOWSTRING HEMP
safflower	BASTARD SAFFRON		MOTHER-IN-LAW'S TONGUE
saffron	CROCUS		SNAKE PLANT
sage	CLARY.SALVIA	Santolina	LAVENDER-COTTON
Sagina	KNOTTED PEARLWORT	Sapindus	SOAP-BERRY
	KNOTTED SPURREY	Sapium	TALLOW-TREE
	PEARLWORT	Saponaria	SOAP-ROOT
Sagittaria	ARROW-HEAD		SOAPWORT
sainfoin	COCKSCOMB	Sarcostemma	SOMA
St Barbara's cress		Sarracenia	SIDE-SADDLE FLOWER
	YELLOW ROCKET	sarrasin	BUCKWHEAT
St Barnaby's thistle	KNAPWEED	Saussurea	SAW-WORT
St Bernard's lily	CHLOROPHYTUM	Savoy	WINTER CABBAGE
	SPIDER PLANT	saw-wort	SAUSSUREA
St John's wort	AARON'S BEARD		SERRATULA
	HYPERICUM.PARKLEAVES	saxifrage	AARON'S BEARD
	TUTSAN		BISHOP'S CAP.STONE-BREAK
St Patrick's cabbage		scabious	DEVIL'S-BIT
	LONDON PRIDE		PINCUSHION FLOWER
Saintpaulia	AFRICAN VIOLET	scammony	
St Peter's wort	HYPERICUM		ANATOLIAN CONVOLVULUS
salad		Scandix	SHEPHERD'S NEEDLE
—herb	PURSLANE.PURSLAIN		VENUS'S COMB
—plants	CUCUMBER.LETTUCE	Scarborough lily	VALLOTA
	LOVAGE.RADISH.ROCKET	scarlet	
	WATERCRESS	—pimpernel	SHEPHERD'S GLASS
salfern	GROMWELL		WINK-O-PEEP
Salicornia	GLASSWORT	—runner	KIDNEY-BEAN
	MARSH SAMPHIRE	scentless mignonette	
	SALTWORT		DYER'S-ROCKET.WELD

Schefflera	UMBRELLA TREE	—type	XYRIS
Schizanthus	BUTTERFLY FLOWER	Sedum	STONECROP
	POOR MAN'S ORCHID		WALL-PEPPER
Schizostylis	KAFFIR LILY	selfheal	BRUNELLA.PRUNELLA
Scilla	BLUEBELL	Selaginella	CREEPING MOSS
	WOOD-HYACINTH.SQUILL		PEACOCK FERN
Scindapsus	DEVIL'S IVY	Sempervivum	HOUSE-LEEK
	GOLDEN POTHOS	Senebiera	CORONOPUS
	SILVER VINE		SWINE'S-CRESS
Scirpus	CLUB-RUSH	Senecio	CAPE IVY.CINERARIA
scorpion grass	FORGET-ME-NOT		GROUNDSEL.RAGWEED
scorzonera	BLACK SALSIFY		RAGWORT
Scotch		sengreen	HOUSE-LEEK
—bluebell	HAREBELL	senna	CASSIA
—rose	BURNET-ROSE	senvy	MUSTARD
—thistle	COTTON THISTLE	sept-foil	POTENTILLA
scouring rush	DUTCH RUSH		TORMENTIL
Scrophularia	FIGWORT	Serratula	SAW-WORT
scurvy grass	HORSE-RADISH	sesame	TEEL.TIL
Scutellaria	SKULLCAP	Seseli	MEADOW SAXIFRAGE
sea		Setcreasea	PURPLE HEART
—buckthorn	SALLOW-THORN	setterwort	STINKING HELLEBORE
—burdock	CLOTBUR.XANTHIUM	setwall	CETYWALL.SETUALE
—gilliflower	THRIFT		VALERIAN
—grape	EPHEDRA.GLASSWORT	shadbush	AMELANCHIER
	GULFWEED	shal(l)ot	ALLIUM.ESCHALOT
—heath	FRANKENIA	shamrock	
—holly	ERINGO.ERYNGO		LESSER YELLOW TREFOIL
—lavender	PLUMBAGO.STATICE	Shasta daisy	
—milkwort	GLAUX		(DWARF) MARGUERITE
—pink	ARMERIA	sheep's-bit	JASIONE
	LADY'S PINCUSHION		SHEEP'S SCABIOUS
	PLUMBAGO.THRIFT	—scabious	JASIONE
—purslane	SANDWORT	shepherd's	
—rocket	CAKILE	—club	HAG-TAPER
seaside			(GREAT) MULLEIN
—plants	CORRIGIOLA	—cress	TEESDALIA
	ENTEROMORPHA	—glass	SCARLET PIMPERNEL
	FRANKENIA.GLASSWRACK	—myrtle	BUTCHER'S BROOM
	MARRAM-GRASS	—needle	SCANDIX
	SEA-COLEWORT.SEA-HEATH		VENUS'S COMB
	SEA-GILLIFLOWER	—purse	CAPSELLA
	SEA-GRASS.SEA-KALE	—rod	SMALL TEASEL
	SEA-ORACH(E).SEA-REED	Sherardia	FIELD MADDER
	STRAPWORT.THRIFT	shield fern	ASPIDIUM
—shrubs	SEA-BUCKTHORN	shoreweed	LITORELLA
	TAMARISK	showy flowers	SILENE
sedge	CAREX.CLUB-RUSH		STRELITZIA
	SPIKE-RUSH	shrimp plant	BELOPERONE

shrub	(see shrubs)	—flake	LEUCOJUM
shrubby plant	HYDRANGEA	—in-summer	
side-saddle flower	SARRACENIA		MOUSE-EAR CHICKWEED
Siderasis	BROWN SPIDERWORT	soap	
silk		—berry	SAPINDUS
—grass	AGAVE.KARATUS.YUCCA	—root	GYPSOPHILA.SAPONARIA
—oak	GREVILLEA	—wort	SAPONARIA
silver		Solanum	BITTERSWEET.POTATO
—net leaf	FITTONIA		(WOODY) NIGHTSHADE
—vine	SCINDAPSUS		WINTER CHERRY
—weed	GOOSE-GRASS	Solidago	GOLDENROD
	POTENTILLA.TANSY	Solomon's seal	POLYGONATUM
single chrysanthemum		soma	SARCOSTEMMA
	MARGUERITE	Sonchus	SOW-THISTLE
Sinningia	GLOXINIA	sops-in-wine	CLOVE-PINK
Sison	STONEWORT	sorrel	DOCK.RUMEX
Sium	SKIRRET.WATER-PARSNIP	southernwood	BOY'S LOVE
skirret	SIUM.WATER-PARSNIP	sow	
skullcap	SCUTELLARIA	—bread	CYCLAMEN
skunk cabbage	SYMPLOCARPUS	—thistle	SONCHUS
slinkweed		Spanish	
	ROSEBAY WILLOWHERB	—bayonet	YUCCA
slipper		—broom	RETAMA.SPART(IUM)
—flower	CALCEOLARIA	—cress	PEPPERWORT
—wort	CALCEOLARIA	Sparaxis	HARLEQUIN FLOWER
sloe	BULLACE	Sparganium	BUR-REED
small teasel	SHEPHERD'S ROD	Sparmannia	HOUSE LIME
smallage	WILD CELERY	spart(ium)	SPANISH BROOM
smart-weed	WATERPEPPER	Spathiphyllum	PEACE LILY
Smithiantha	TEMPLE BELLS	spear	
snail	MEDICK	—thistle	BUR-THISTLE
snake			CIRSIUM.CNICUS
—plant	SANSEVIERIA	—wort	RANUNCULUS
—root	ARISTOLOCHIA.BISTORT	Specularia	
	MILKWORT		VENUS'S LOOKING GLASS
—'s-head	FRITILLARY	speedwell	BIRD'S EYE
—skin plant	FITTONIA		FLUELLIN.VERONICA
—weed	ADDER('S) WORT	Spergula	SPURREY
	BISTORT	Spergularia	
snapdragon	ANTIRRHINUM		SANDWORT-SPURREY
	FROG'S-MOUTH	sphagnum	BOG-MOSS
sneeze		spider	
—weed	HELENIUM	—plant	CHLOROPHYTUM
—wort	WHITE HELLEBORE		ST BERNARD'S LILY
	YARROW	—wort	TRADESCANTIA
snow		Spigelia	CAROLINA PINK
—ball tree	GUELDER-ROSE		INDIAN PINK
—berry	SYMPHORICARPUS	spignel	BALDMONEY
—drop	GALANTHUS		MEUM.SPICKNEL

spike-rush	HELIOCHARIS	
spikenard	NARD	
spinach	SPINAGE	
spinage	SPINACH	
spineless thistle	KNAPWEED	
spiny-leaved fern	HOLLY-FERN	
Spiraea	DROP-WORT	
	MEADOWSWEET	
spleenwort	ASPLENIUM	
	MAIDENHAIR.WALL-RUE	
split leaf Philodendron		
	MONSTERA	
spotted orchis	WAKE-ROBIN	
spring		
—beauty	CLAYTONIA	
—start flower	TRITELIA	
—wort	MANDRAKE	
spur valerian	CENTRANTHUS	
	RED VALERIAN	
spurge	ALEURITES.EUPHORBIA	
	POINSETTIA.WARTWEED	
—laurel	DAPHNE	
spurrey	SPERGULA	
squash	CUCURBITA.GOURD	
squill	SCILLA	
squinancy-wort	QUINSY-WORT	
Stachys	BETONY	
	BISHOP'S WORT.LAMB'S EAR	
staghorn		
—fern	PLATYCERIUM	
—moss	CLUB-MOSS	
Stapelia	CARRION-FLOWER	
star		
—fish plant	CRYPTANTHUS	
—light	ASTROPHEL.PENTHIA	
—wort	ASTER.STITCHWORT	
—of Bethlehem	CAMPANULA	
	ORNITHOGALUM	
—of-the-earth		
	BUCK'S HORN PLANTAIN	
—thistle	CENTAUREA	
starch hyacinth		
	GRAPE HYACINTH.MUSCARI	
Statice	SEA-LAVENDER	
stavesacre	DELPHINIUM	
	LARKSPUR	
Stellaria	CHICKWEED	
Stephanotis		
	MADAGASCAR JASMINE	

stinking		
—hellebore	SETTERWORT	
—camomile	MAYWEED	
—cranes bill	HERB ROBERT	
stitchwort	ASTER.CHICKWEED	
	STARWORT	
stock	MATTHIOLA	
Stoke's aster	STOKESIA	
stone		
—bramble	ROEBUCK-BERRY	
	ROE-BLACKBERRY	
—break	SAXIFRAGE	
—crop	ORPIN(E).ROSE-ROOT	
	SEDUM.WALL-PEPPER	
	WALL-WORT.WORM-GRASS	
—wort	SISON	
stork's bill	ERODIUM	
	PELARGONIUM	
strapwort	CORRIGIOLA	
Stratiotes	WATER-SOLDIER	
strawberry	FRAGARIA	
—geranium		
	MOTHER OF THOUSANDS	
—tomato	BLADDER-CHERRY	
Strelitzia	BIRD OF PARADISE	
Streptocarpus	CAPE PRIMROSE	
striped squill	PUSCHKINIA	
Strophanthus	PERIWINKLE	
sub-Alpine	SPIGNEL	
succory	CHICORY	
sugar		
—bean	LIMA BEAN	
—beet	RAPA	
—cane	SACCHARUM	
—grass	SWEET SORGHUM	
sumach	RHUS	
sun		
—dew	DROSERA	
—facing plant	TURNSOLE	
—flower	HELIANTHUS	
—flower type	RUDBECKIA	
—rose	HELIANTHEMUM	
—spurge	EUPHORBIA	
swallow-wort	ASCLEPIAS	
	CELANDINE.CYNANCHUM	
	GREATER CELANDINE	
Swedish		
—ivy	PLECTRANTHUS	
—turnip	RUTABAGA.SWEDE	

sweet	
—bay	LAUREL.LAURUS
—briar	EGLANTINE
—cicely	CHERIL.MYRRHIS
	MYRTLE
—corn	MAIZE
—flag	ACORUS.CALAMUS
—gale	BOG MYRTLE
	SWEET WILLOW.MYRICA
—heart plant	PHILODENDRON
—pea	LATHYRUS.VETCHLING
—scabious	MOURNING-BRIDE
—sorghum	SUGAR-GRASS
—William	DIANTHUS
—willow	BOG MYRTLE
	SWEET GALE
swine's	
—cress	CORONOPUS.SENEBIERA
	WART-CRESS
—succory	ARNOSERIS
Swiss cheese plant	MONSTERA
Symphoricarpus	SNOW BERRY
Symphytum	BORAGE.COMFREY
Symplocarpus	SKUNK-CABBAGE
Syngonium	ARROWHEAD VINE
	GOOSEFOOT PLANT
	NEPHTHYTIS
Syrian rue	HARMALA.HARMEL
Tagetes	AFRICAN MARIGOLD
	FRENCH MARIGOLD
tallow-tree	SAPIUM
Tanacetum	TANSY
tansy	RAGWORT.SILVERWEED
	TANACETUM.YARROW
Taraxacum	DANDELION
tare	DARNEL.VETCH
taro	COLOCASIA
tarragon	STARAGEN
teasels	DIPSACUS
teddy bear vine	CYANOTIS
teel	SESAME.TIL
Teesdalia	SHEPHERD'S CRESS
telegraph-plant	DESMODIUM
temple bells	SMITHIANTHA
Tetrastigma	CHESTNUT VINE
Thalictrum	MEADOW-RUE
Thapsia	LASERWORT
thistle	CARLINA.CNICUS
thorn-apple	DATURA

thrift	ARMERIA
	SEA-GILLIFLOWER
	SEA PINK
Throatwort	CAMPANULA
Thunbergia	BLACK-EYED SUSAN
thyme	CALAMINT.THYMUS
Ti plant	CORDYLINE
tiger-flower	TIGRIDIA
Tigridia	FERRARIA
til	SESAME.TEEL
toad	
—flax	AARON'S BEARD
	BACON AND EGGS
	FLUELLIN.LINARIA
	MOTHER OF MILLIONS
—grass	JUNCUS.TOAD-RUSH
tobacco	NICOTIANA
Tolmiea	PIGGYBACK PLANT
tomato	LOVE-APPLE
	WOLF'S PEACH
toothwort	CARDAMINE
	CORAL-ROOT
	DENTARIA.LATHRAEA
torch	
—lily	KNIPHOFIA
	RED-HOT POKER.TRITOMA
—thistle	CACTUS.CEREUS
tormentil	POTENTILLA.SEPT-FOIL
tortoise plant	ELEPHANT'S FOOT
touch-me-not	BALSAM.MIMOSA
Tradescantia	INCH PLANT
	SPIDERWORT
	WANDERING JEW
tragacanth	ASTRAGALUS
traveller's joy	CLEMATIS
	OLD MAN'S BEARD
	VIRGIN'S BOWER
treacle mustard	ERYSIMUM
tree	(see trees)
tree	
—mallow	LAVATERA
	VELVET-LEAF
—peony	MOUTAN
Treucrium	WOOD-GERMANDER
Trifolium	CLOVER
Trigonella	FENUGREEK
Tritelia	SPRING STAR FLOWERS
Triticum	WHEAT
Tritoma	KNIPHOFIA

	RED-HOT POKER
	TORCH-LILY
Tritonia	MONTBRETIA
Trollius	GLOBE-FLOWER
Tropaeolum	NASTURTIUM
truelove	HERB PARIS
trumpet flower	INCARVILLEA
tuberose	POLIANTHES
Turk's cap	MARTAGON LILY
tutsan	PARKLEAVES
	ST JOHN'S WORT
twayblade	LISTERA
two-flowered daffodil	
	PRIMROSE PEERLESS
Typha	REED MACE
Ulex	GORSE
umbrella	
—plant	CYPERUS
—tree	SCHEFFLERA
urn plant	AECHMEA
Urtica	NETTLE
Utricularia	BLADDERWORT
uva-ursi	BEARBERRY
Vaccinium	COWBERRY
	CRANBERRY
	WHORTLEBERRY
valerian	ALLHEAL
	CENTRANTHUS.CETYWALL
	SETUALE.SETWALL
Vallota	SCARBOROUGH LILY
variegated grass	
	GARDENER'S GARTERS
vase plant	AECHMEA
Veltheimia	FOREST LILY
velvet plant	VYNURA
Venus's	
—comb	SCANDIX
	SHEPHERD'S NEEDLE
—flytrap	DIONAEA
—looking glass	SPECULARIA
Veratrum	WHITE HELLEBORE
Verbascum	MULLEIN
Verbena	VERVAIN
Veronica	SPEEDWELL
vervain	LANTANA.VERBENA
vetch	FITCH.TARE.VICIA
vetchling	LATHYRUS.SWEET PEA
Viburnum	GUELDER-ROSE
Vicia	VETCH

Vinca	PERIWINKLE
Viola	PANSY.VIOLET
violet	VIOLA
viper's	
—bugloss	BLUE WEED
	BLUE THISTLE.ECHIUM
—grass	BLACK SALSIFY
Virginia	
—creeper	AMPELOPSIS
	WOODBIND.WOODBINE
—stock	MALCOMIA
virgin's-bower	CLEMATIS
	TRAVELLER'S JOY
Viscum	MISTLETOE
Vitis	GRAPE-VINE
Vreisia	FLAMING SWORD
Vynura	PURPLE PASSION VINE
	VELVET PLANT
wahoo	BURNING BUSH
wake-robin	ARUM.CUCKOO PINT
	SPOTTED ORCHIS
	FRIAR'S COWL
wall	
—cress	ARABIS.ROCK-CRESS
—flower	CHEIRANTHUS
	CHEIRINIA.GILLYFLOWER
	JILLYFLOWER
—mustard	DIPLOTAXIS
	WALL-ROCKET
—pepper	SEDUM.STONECROP
	WALL-WORT
—plant	THALE-CRESS
—rocket	DIPLOTAXIS
	WALL-MUSTARD
—rue	SPLEENWORT
—wort	DANE'S BLOOD
	DANEWORT.DWARF ELDER
	PELLITORY.STONECROP
	WALL-PEPPER
wandering Jew	TRADESCANTIA
	ZEBRINA
wart	
—cress	SWINE'S-CRESS
—weed	LICHEN.SPURGE
	WARTWORT
water	
—grass	REED
—chestnut	HORNNUT.SALIGOT
—crowfoot	REATE

—dropwort	OENANTHE
—fern	PILLWORT.SALVINIA
—flag	YELLOW IRIS
—hemlock	CICUTA.COWBANE
	OENANTHE
—hyacinth	EICHHORNIA
—leaf	HYDROPHYLLUM
—lemon	PASSION FLOWER
—lily	CANDOCK.NELUMBIUM
	NELUMBO.NENUPHAR
	NUPHAR.NYMPHAEA
—milfoil	MIRIOPHYLLUM
—parsnip	SIUM.SKIRRET
—pepper	SMART-WEED
—pimpernel	BROOKWEED
—plant	ANACHARIS
	HORNWORT.HYDROPHYTE
	MYRIOPHYLLUM.PIPEWORT
—plantain	ALISMA
—rice	ZIZANIA
—side plant	
	PURPLE LOOSESTRIFE
—soldier	STRATIOTES
—speedwell	BROOKLIME
—starwort	CALLITRICHE
—thyme	CANADIAN PONDWEED
—violet	HOTTONIA
—weed	ANACHARIS
wax	
—myrtle	CANDLE-BERRY
—plant	HOYA
waybread	PLANTAIN
weeping fig	FICUS
weld	DYER'S ROCKET
	MIGNONETTE
Welsh onion	CIBOL
wheat	TRITICUM
whin	GORSE
white	
—bottle	BLADDER CAMPION
—bryony	MANDRAKE
—clover	DUTCH CLOVER
	SHAMROCK
—hellebore	SNEEZEWORT
	VERATRUM
—lily	MADONNA LILY
whitlow-grass	PARONYCHIA
	WHITLOW-WORT
whortleberry	BILBERRY

	COWBERRY.HUCKLEBERRY
	HURTLEBERRY.VACCINIUM
wild	
—aster	MICHAELMAS DAISY
—celery	MARSHWORT
	SMALLAGE
—chrysanthemum	
	CORN-MARIGOLD.OX-EYE
—crab apple	WILDING
—fig	CAPRIFIG.GOAT-FIG
—flax	LINUM.PURGING FLAX
—garlic	RAMSONS
—geranium	CRANESBILL
—hyacinth	CULVER-KEY
—marjoram	ORIGAN(E)
—mint	HORSEMINT
—mustard	CHARLOCK
—olive	OLEASTER
—pansy	KISS-ME
—pink	MAIDEN PINK
—rice	ZIZANIA
—rose	DOG ROSE.SWEETBRIAR
	SWEETBRIER
—strawberry	POTENTILLA
—Swedish turnip	NAVEW
—Williams	RAGGED ROBIN
willow	
—herb	CHAMAENERION
	EPILOBIUM.FIRE-WEED
	ROSEBAY
—weed	KNOTWEED
	PURPLE LOOSESTRIFE
windflower	(WOOD-)ANEMONE
wink-o-peep	
	SCARLET PIMPERNEL
winter	
—aconite	ERANTHIS
	WINTER HELLEBORE
—cabbage	SAVOY
—cherry	
	CHINESE LANTERN PLANT
	PHYSALIS.SOLANUM
—cress	BARBAREA
	YELLOW ROCKET
—green	CHIMAPHILA
	GAULTHERIA.MONOTROPA
	PYROLA
witches' thimble	FOXGLOVE
with long spikes	LUPIN(E)

with ribbed leaves	HOSTA
	PLANTAIN
witloof	CHICORY
woad	ISATIS
wolf's	
—bane	ACONITE.FRIAR'S CAP
	MONKSHOOD
—peach	TOMATO
wood	
—anemone	WINDFLOWER
—bind/woodbine	HONEYSUCKLE
	VIRGINIA CREEPER
—hyacinth	BLUEBELL.SCILLA
—germander	TREUCRIUM
—land plant	SANICLE
—loosestrife	YELLOW PIMPERNEL
—rush	LUZULA
—ruff	QUINSY-WORT
	SQUINANCY-WORT
—sorrel	OXALIS
woody nightshade	BITTERSWEET
	SOLANUM
worm-grass	PINKROOT
	STONECROP
wormwood	ARTEMESIA
MUGWORT.SOUTHERNWOOD	
Xanthium	CLOTBUR
	SEA-BURDOCK
Xeranthemum	EVERLASTINGS
yarr	CORN SPURREY
yarrow	ACHILLEA.MILFOIL
NOSE-BLEED.PELLITORY	
SNEEZEWORT.TANSY	
yellow	
—centaury	GENTIAN
	YELLOW WORT
—clover	HOP-TREFOIL
—flowered narcissus	DAFFODIL
—iris	WATER-FLAG
—jasmine	GELSEMIUM
—loosestrife	LYSIMACHIA
—pimpernel	
	(WOOD) LOOSESTRIFE
—poppy	WELSH POPPY
—rattle	COCKSCOMB
—rocket	BARBAREA
	ST BARBARA'S CRESS
	WINTER-CRESS
—root	GOLDEN-SEAL

—weed	COMMON RAGWORT
	GROUNDSEL
—wort	GENTIAN
	YELLOW CENTAURY
yuc(c)a	ADAM'S NEEDLE
CASSAVA.SILK-GRASS	
SPANISH BAYONET	
SPANISH DAGGER	
Zantedeschia	ARUM LILY
CALLA LILY.LILY OF THE NILE	
Zea	INDIAN CORN.MAIZE
zebra plant	AECHMEA
APHELANDRA.MARANTA	
Zebrina	INCH PLANT
	WANDERING JEW
Zizania	CANADA RICE
	INDIAN RICE
plant²	INTER-
planted *	incl *
•the *Spanish planted in*	
row-s	ROWELS
planted round a...	incl A
planted round *	incl *
•row-s *planted round* the	
Spanish...	ROWELS
planter's dog	SETTER
planting period	BEDTIME
plasma injection	BLOODSHOT
plastered niche	CHINE
plastic bag	GAB
plate	L
play	TOY
parts *in play*	STRAP
play (Japanese)	NO(H)
play *around*	PLA-Y.TO-Y
play-boy	TOYED.WINSLOW
play of T.S. Eliot	LITOTES
play-school	
	RADA.RUGBY.SCANDAL
play-time	TEMPO
players	CAST.SIDE.STRINGS
playhouse	CAPULET.MONTAGUE
playing	IN.ON
playing about with Alf	HALFWIT
playing role	LORE
pleasant	
pleasant *at first*	P
pleasant Sunday afternoon	PSA
please turn over	PTO

pledge taker	UNCLE
plenty of scope	A-Z
plough	
plough <u>field</u>	FILED
ploughed up <u>earth</u>	HATER.RATHE
ploughman	SHAREHOLDER
plucky	
plucky attempt	PIZZICATO
plucky player	HARPIST
plumbers' association	
	SOUNDING BOARD
plump man	FATAL
plural	PLU
Pluto	DIS
Plymouth Brethren	PB
PM's address	TEN.X
pocket	
pocket a. . .	incl A
pocket *	incl *
•Ma-e *pockets* a penny	MADE
pocketed by *	incl in *
•penny *pocketed by* Ma-e	MADE
Poe's *characters*	POSE
poet	AE.DANTE.DONNE
	ELIOT.EZRA.HOOD.LEAR
	NOYES.POUND
poet laureate	PL
poets	PEN
poetic¹	
indicates old words used by	
various poets by phrases such as:	
•*according to Spenser*,	
bent	CORBE
	(*see* Spenser)
•*as the poet said* again	AGEN
•*often used in poetry*	OFT
•*Shakespeare's* child	COLLOP
	(*see* Shakespeare)
•*the old poet's* cottage	COT
	(*see* Burns)
(*see also* Browning.Milton.Scott)	
poetic²	
terms:	
act	
—as a fugleman would	FUGLE
—noisily	OBSTREPERATE
active	SPRINGE
accomplished	ARCH
adorn	BEDIGHT

again	AGEN
against	GAINST
alabaster	ALABLASTER
any day other than one's	
birthday	UNBIRTHDAY
appeal	PROVOKE
archaic term for poetry	POESY
are	ART
array	BEDIGHT
art of painting	PEINTURE
assembly	DIVAN
attack from behind	REAR
attentive	INTENTIVE.LISTFUL
auxiliary power	UNDER-POWER
avalanche	LAUWINE
avowed lover	PROTESTANT
bank	RIVAGE
base	GROUNDLING
be	
—flooded	FLOAT
—languorous	SWOON
—non-existent	UNBE
—soaked in gore	WELTER
beautiful	SHEEN
beneath	NEATH
bestially	BEASTILY
betray	CONFESS
bird song	VALENTINE
bittern	BITTO(U)R.BITTUR
black	SABLE
—tincture	BUFO
blushing girl	BLUSHET
board	BO(O)RD.BORDE
body of water	WAVE
boorish	SWAINISH
border	MARGENT
born under ill-fated	
star	EVIL-STARRED
bowstring	NERVE
brainy	INTELLECTED
bright	SHEEN
chariot	CAR
cicada	BALM-CRICKET
city urchin	TOWNSKIP
close-fitting	SUCCINCT
clothed in purple	PORPORATE
clumsy	UNHEPPEN
compelled	FAIN
complaining	MUTTERATION

contrary of wealth or wellbeing	ILLTH	flourished	ARCH
corpse	CORSE	flow in again	REINFUND
cottage	COT	flushed	HECTIC
council	DIVAN	foaming	SPOOMING
current	TIDE	follow	UPFOLLOW
daffodil	DAFFADOWNDILLY	forehead	FRONT
	DAFFODILLY	forgetfulness	OBLIVION
dash	VIRETOT	fortify	MUNITE
dead-leaf colour	PHILOMOT	fount(ain)	FONT
decoration of flowers		fragment	FRUST
	GARLANDAGE	fray	FRIDGE
desolate	WASTEFUL	free from restraint	DISYOKE
—region	WILD	frisky	WANTON
despondency	DESPOND	full of springs	FOUNTFUL
detached	UNDIVESTED	furnish	BEDIGHT
did	GAN	gad	VIRETOT
discomfit	SHEND	gay	WANTON
disfavour	DISGUST	girded up	SUCCINCT
disgrace	SHEND	glad	FAIN
disorderly	RAGMATICAL	glance	ASPECT
disorganise	UNMECHANISE	gloomy	DARKSOME
displeasure	DISGUST		DOWN-LOOKED
distaste	DISGUST	go native	GO FANTI
divulge	UNCONFINE	good news	EVANGEL
domain	BOURN(E)	green woodpecker	YAFFINGALE
double limerick	TWINER	greet	DOLE
downcast	DOWN-LOOKED	grotto	GROT
dreamy	DREAMFUL	ground	MARL
drummer	DRAKE	growing abundantly	WANTON
dullness	YAWN	guardianship	WARDENRY
dwelling	BOWER	halloo	HALLALOO
eager to	FAIN	having	
elicit	SWEEP	—intellect	INTELLECTED
embroidered	SET-STITCH'D	—the form of a tent	TENTING
emulate	EMULE	heaven	SWERGA
enchanted	FATED	heavenly spirit	GLENDOVEER
enjoyment	PLEASANCE	heed	HEARKEN
equip	BEDIGHT	idleness	IDLESSE
even	EEN	illimitable	EXTERMINABLE
evening	EVE.EVEN	illumine	ILLUME
excellent	LUMMY	imaginary beast	WHANGAM
excessive formality	WIGGERY	immaterial	UNESSENTIAL
face bravely	BIDE	impair	EMPERISH
fainting fit	SOUND.SWOUN	impatient of	RESTLESS
fancy	FANGLE	imperfectly formed	
feathery	FLEDGY		UNDERSHAPEN
field of battle	PLAIN	in	
fiery gem	PYROPUS	—another way	ANOTHERGUESS
		—strong words	IRON-WORDED

—the dark	DARKLINGS	—burdensome	UNIMPOSING
India	IND	—held back	UNWITHHOLDEN
industrious	WORKSOME	—in agreement	
inferior	UNDERRATE		UNCONSENTANEOUS
—demon	PUG	—known	UNWIST
innkeeper	INNHOLDER	—made noisy	UNBEDINNED
inquiry	INQUIRATION	obviate	MEET WITH
intensify	INTENSATE	ocean swell	WALLOW
interpretation	REDE	of	
interregnum	INTERREIGN	—another kind	ANOTHERGUESS
it seems to me	MESEEMS	—the eye	VISUAL
it's	TIS	open	OPE
joyful	FAIN	—country	WEALD
joyous	FRABJOUS	overcome by sleepiness	
kindle	TEEND		O'ER-DROWSED
knot	GORDIAN	owl	GLIMMER-GOWK
last	DURE	owlishness	OWLERY
late mint	LATTER-MINT	palmist	CH(E)IROGRAPHIST
level	STROW	pamper	POMPEY
light	ILLUME	paradise	SWERGA
like prison	PRISONOUS	pass time wearily	WEAR
listen	LIST	pay	SOLDE
—to	HEARKEN	—attention to	HEARKEN
little god	GODLING	peak	PIQUE
look	ASPECT	peasant	SWAIN
lose colour	UNFLUSH	perched above	UP-PERCHED
lovemaking	SWAINING	period of night	WATCH
lover	SWAIN	piercing	PERCEANT
lower sky	UNDERSKY	place one visits	VISIT
make		please	ARRIDE
—manifest	CONFESS	pleasantness	PLEASANCE
—purring sound	CURR	pleasure	PLEASANCE
manufacturer of idols	GOD-SMITH	poet	MINSTREL
margin	MARGENT	ponder previously	
meadow	MEAD		PREPONDERATE
medical	MEDIC	portray in pavement	IMPAVE
melting away	DELIQUIM	postpone	WITHHOLD
Milky Way	MILKEN-WAY	power of subduing	QUELL
moving		prayer	BENE
—capriciously	WANTON	pre-eminence	SOVRANTY
—freely	WANTON	previous king	FOREKING
mumbling speech	MUMBLEMENT	prodigal	PROFUSER
music	NOTE	providing redress	REDRESSIVE
musical instrument	SLUGHORN(E)	prow	PRORE
named	NEMPT	punish	SHEND
necessity	NEEDYHOOD	pure	UNDROSSY
nimble	SPRINGE	put	
north country	NORLAN(D)	—in tune	STRING
not		—to shame	SHEND

rapacity	VULTURISM	stomach	LITTLE MARY
reformed person	REFORMADO	strengthen	MUNITE
reformer	REFORMADO	study of artillery	PYROBALLOGY
remark following		subconscious thirst	UNDERTHIRST
another	SUBJOINDER	subside	SWOON
remuneration	SOLDE	supporter	UNDERSTANDER
reprisal	REPRISE	surpassing	FRABJOUS
reproach	SHEND	swarm	SWERVE
retrogression	REGREDIENCE	sword	VORPAL
reveal	CONFESS	swung	SWANG
rich cake	ROUT-CAKE	tear	RANCH
rind	RINE	tears	RHEUM
ring	CIRQUE	that	YON
riotous	RAGMATICAL	thoroughgoing	UNENDING
riven	RAFT	those	YON
river(-water)	TIDE	tie up	GORDIAN
roll like the sea	WELTER	tuft	TUZZ
romantic setting	PLAIN	turqoise	TURKIS
rub	FRIDGE	unaccustomed	UNWONT
rue	REW	undertaken	UNDERTA'EN
rush	VIRETOT	undutiful	UNDUTEOUS
rustic	SWAIN	unfortunate	EVIL-STARRED
sail	SHEET	unfrequented	WASTEFUL
savage	SALVAGE	unfriendly	INIMICITIOUS
sceptred	SCEPTRY	unhomelike	UNDOMESTIC
Scotland	SCOTIA	uninhabited	WASTEFUL
scramble	SWERVE	unrestrained	UNWITHHOLDEN
sea	FOAM.WAVE	unwary	UNAWARE
—serpent	ELLOPS	upriseth	UPRIST
separate	UNCOMBINE	using archaic language	TUSHERY
serenade	WAKE	venturous	VENTROUS
sewing	SEAMSTRESSY	village	VILL
shady retreat	HERBAR	visitor's book	VISITING BOOK
sharp-edged	VORPAL	wagon	WAIN
shining	SHEEN	winded	WIN'T
shiny-pated	GLASSYHEADED	windlass for crossbow	
ship	PRORE		WINDAC.WINDAS
shore	RIVAGE	window	WINDORE
—crab	OCHIDORE	without being	UNESSENTIAL
sly trick	UNDER-CRAFT	wood sorrel	SHAMROCK
smooth	SOOTH	wooded land	WEALD
smote	SMIT	write pompously	FUSTIANISE
soft	SOOTH	yesterday evening	YESTREEN
spend time	WEAR	yonder	YON
spendthrift	PROFUSER	young man	SWAIN
spiritual	AERIE.AERY	zealot	ZE(A)LANT
state of floating	FLOAT		(*see also* old[1])
stately building	DOME	**poetry**	(*see* verse)
steep	STEEPY	**point**[1]	HEAD.NESS.N.S.E.W

	PT.TOR
hence	
•game point	NAPE
•point *to* point	EN.WE
•point to point	ETON.STOW
and	
•he points *out*	SHEW
•points out	SNOUT
•points *out* a woman	SEVEN
pointed	incl N.S.E.W
hence	
•*pointed* ears	NEARS.SEARS
	SWEARS.WEARS
•*pointed* gun *to* South	WARMS
•*pointed* heels	SCADS
pointless	omit N.S.E.W
•*pointless* li(e)	LI
•*pointless* (s)ort...	ORT
point²	(*see* type)
poise	P
poison	BANE.TOXIN.VENOM
bacterial	EXOTOXIN.PTOMAINE
castor-oil bean	RICIN(E)
conium	HEMLOCK
dogbane	OUABAIN.WABAIN
element	ARSENIC.STRONTIUM
deadly nightshade	ATROPINE
fly agaric	MUSCARINE
fungus	PHALLOIDIN
hellebore	VERATRIN
hemlock	CONIA.CONI(I)NE
hydrocyanic acid	PRUSSIC ACID
Java	UPAS
laburnum	CYSTISINE
Madagascar	TANGHIN
monkshood	ACONITE.ACONITUM
mushroom	MUSCARINE.PHALLIN
nux vomica	STRYCHNINE
opium	THEBAINE
periwinkle	STROPHANTHIN
poppies	PAPAVERINE
putrefying flesh	NERINE
quick-acting	CYANIDE
	PRUSSIC ACID
rye	ERGOT
snake	ECHIDNINE
South American	CURARA
	CURARE.CURARI
thorn apple	DATURINE

wolfsbane	ACONITE.ACONITUM
Poland	PL
pole¹	N.NP.PO.ROD.S.SP
hence	
•he *is leading* Poles	HENS
•pointer *between* poles	NARROWS
•Poles *in* characteristic...	
	TRANSIT
pole²	
Pole Star	POLARIS
Pole-star gazer	COPERNICUS
police	
police	CID.FORCE.MET
hence	
•managed police	RANCID
•police *with* queen	CIDER
•port authority police	PLACID
and	
•police have English...	METE
•police in charge	METIC
•policeman	METAL.METED
police artist	CONSTABLE
police constable	BOBBY.PC
Police Corps	RMP
police district	MANOR
police power	FORCE
policeman	BOG(E)Y.COP.MP.PC
hence	
•policeman *standing in front of*	
queen	COPER
•policemen *with* one lot	CO-PILOT
•policeman *with* unknown	
animal	COPYCAT
polish¹	RUB.SHINE
polish picture	RUBICON
polish statue	RUBICON
Polish²	POL
capital	P.WARSAW
carriage	BRITSKA.BRITZ(S)KA
coins	GROSZY.ZLOTY
dance	CRACOVIENNE
	KRAKOWIAK.MAZURKA
	POLONAISE
Jews	ASHKENAZIM
leader	P
noble	SAROSTA
officer	HETMAN
reverse notation	RPN
politic	

Political and Economic
  Planning — PEP
politician — CON.LIB.LAB.MP.TORY
politician's claim — AMATORY

Polynesian
apple — KEVI
arrowroot — PIA
assembly — HUI
burial place — AHU
chestnut — RATA
cloth — TAP(P)A
dance — HULA(-HULA).SIVA
demigod — AITU.MAUI
drink — (K)AVA
fern — TARA
garment — MALO.PAREU
leader — P
pepper — (K)AVA
race — KANAKA
skirt — LAVA-LAVA
sky — LANGI
tree — BELAH.TO(O)A.TI.TAMANU

pond — ATLANTIC (OCEAN)
pontifical — AARONIC
poor — STONY
poor horse — JADE.ROSINANTE.TIT
poor horse... — SHORE
poorly — ILL.SICK
poorly made — DAME.MEAD
poorly made table — BLEAT.BLATE
pop — FATHER.PA
pop *back* ⟨ — AP
pop *back again* — DAD
pop *into* — incl PA
•pop *into* a-rt... — APART
pop *up*(D) ↑ — AP
pop *up again*(D) ↑ — DAD
pop up again(D) ↑ — ER
pope — CLEMENT.GREGORY
        PAUL.SSD
popular — IN.LAIC.LAY.POP
population — POP
porcelain — (*see* china[1])
pornographic writer — BLUE PENCIL
port — ADEN.L.LT.LEFT
        ORAN.RIO.WINE
port authority — PLA
hence
•PLA building — PLASHED

•PLA *has* fish — PLAID
•PLA leader — PLACID
port wine — BORDEAUX.MALAGA
portable lamp — LIGHT
portion
portion of cake — CA.KE
portion of lobster — CLAW
portion of h/is sue/t... — ISSUE
portly porter — STOUT
Portugal — LUSITANIA.P
Portuguese — PORT
capital — LISBON.P
coins
—unit — CENTAVO
—100 centavos — ESC.ESCUDO
—100 escudos — CONTO
—old — PORTAGUE.PORTIGUE
  REE.REAL.REI(S).TESTOON
—1000 reis — ESCUDO.MILREIS
—gold — CRUSADO
  JO(H)ANNES.MOIDORE
country house — QUINTA
dance — FADO
epic poem — LUSIAD(S)
folk song — FADO
gentleman — FIDALGO
Jews — SEPHARDIM
lady — DONA
leader — P
liquor — AGUARDIENTE
man — DOM
measure — MEIO.MOIO.PIPA
mountain range — SERRA
no — NAO
parliament — CORTES
plant — SERRADELLA.SERRADILLA
prince — INFANTE
princess — INFANTA
punishment of heretics
        AUTO DA FE
river — TAGUS
ship — LORCHA.MULETTE
sir — DOM
title — DOM
weight (25lbs) — ARROBA
wine — VINHO
    (*see also* drink[2])
posh
posh — U

hence
- •posh fur — USABLE
- •posh party — UDO
- •posh knight, *say* — USER
- posh car — RR

positive
- positive negative — NEVER
- positive principle — YANG

possible
- *possibly* an erg — RANGE
- *possibility of* rain — IRAN
- race starter, *possibly* — ADAM
- Rover, *possibly* — SCOUT
- scout, *possibly* — ROVER

post¹
- postcard — PC
- post chaise — MAIL COACH
- post office — PO
- hence
- •post office advanced
  a... — POLENTA
- •post office is over... — POISON
- •post office work — POOP
- post-office order — POO
- post town — PT
- postal order — PO
- postman, *say* — MAIL
- postmaster — PM
- Postmaster-General — PMG

post²
- postgraduate — BA.MA
- postscript — PS

poster — BILL

pot   (*see also* drug.trophy)
- potter's art — ONE-UPMANSHIP
- potter's ball — BLACK
- pottery — (*see* china¹)

potato — MURPHY.SPUD
               TATER.TAT(T)IE
- potato king — EDWARD
- potato *peel* — PO

potentially a choir
   man — HARMONICA

pound¹ — L.LB
- hence
- •each one pound — PERIL
- •fifty pounds — LL
- •one pound — AL.ALB.IL.ILB.L.LB
- •pound note LA.LB.LC.LD.LE.LF.LG

- •pound notes — LAC.LAD.LAG
                              LED.LEE.LEG

pound²
- five hundred pounds — MONKEY
- pound for poet — EZRA
- pound notes — STRUM
- *pounded* table — BLEAT.BLATE
- twenty-five pounds — PONY

pour
- *poured into* * — incl in *
- •drink *poured into* jug-s — JUGGINS
- *poured out* gins — -INGS.SING

power¹ — HP.P.VIS
- power bloc — E.W
- powerboat — STEAMSHIP
- powerful dives — PLUTOCRAT

power²
   meaning
   authority of
   government by
   rule by
   power of:
- absolute power — AUTARCHY
- all of the people — PANTISOCRACY
- beggars — PTOCHOCRACHY
- cotton industry — COTTONOCRACY
- demons — DEMONOCRACY
- divine rulers — THEARCHY
                      THEOCRACY
- eight persons — OCTARCHY
- élites — MERITOCRACY
- exclusive classes — OLIGARCHY
- five persons — PENTARCHY
- four persons — QUADRUMVIRATE
- holy persons — HAGIARCHY
                      HAGIOCRACY
- joint sovereignty — SYNARCHY
- landowners — SQUATTOCRACY
                      SQUIR(E)ARCHY
- law — NOMOCRACY
- many — POLYARCHY
- military despots — STRATOCRACY
- mill owners — MILLOCRACY
- mob — MOBOCRACY
                      OCHLOCRACY
- money — DOLLAROCRACY
- mothers — MATRIARCHY
- natural order — PHYSIOCRACY
- old people — GERONTOCRACY

one person	AUTOCRACY
	DESPOTISM.DICTATORSHIP
	MONARCHY.MONOCRACY
paupers	PTOCHOCRACY
paternal right	PATRIARCHY
people	DEMOCRACY
	ETHNARCHY
priests	HIERARCHY.HIEROCRACY
prominent people	MERITOCRACY
property owners	TIMOCRACY
rich	PLUTOCRACY
	PLUTO-DEMOCRACY
saints	HAGIARCHY
	HAGIOCRACY
self-government	AUTONOMY
seven persons	HEPTARCHY
	SEPTARCHY
six persons	HEXARCHY
slaves	D(O)ULOCRACY
small groups	OLIGARCHY
sovereignty of the	
seas	THALASSOCRACY
	THALATTOCRACY
squires	SQUATTOCRACY
	SQUIR(E)ARCHY
teachers	PEDANTOCRACY
technical experts	TECHNOCRACY
ten persons	DECADARCHY
	DEKADARCHY
three persons	TRIARCHY
	TRIUMVIRATE
two persons	DIARCHY
	DUUMVIRATE
wealthy	PLUTOCRACY
	PLUTO-DEMOCRACY
Whigs	WHIGGARCHY
women	GYN(AEC)OCRACY
	MATRIARCHY
workers	ERGATOCRACY
world ruler	COSMOCRAT
worst	KAKISTOCRACY
worthy	MERITOCRACY
p-pole	PROD
p-piece	PARTICLE
practice	-ISM
practice costume	HABIT
preacher	VDM
preceding MP	LO
preceptors	CP

precious stones (*see* gems.minerals)	
preferred girl	BLONDE
***premature end to* tri(p)**	TRI-
premium	PM
pre-*packed*	(in) PR-E
prepare	
preparation of <u>team</u>	
and...	MANDATE
prepare <u>meal</u>	LAME.MALE
prepare for execution	ENGROSS
prepared	ALA
prepared letter	SAE
prepared <u>tea</u>	ATE.EAT
present	AD.PR
present day	AD.BIRTHDAY
	CHRISTMAS
hence	
•people *in the present day*	AMEND
•*present day* clothes	ADDRESSES
•to the *present day*	TOAD
present pupil	PP
present time	AD.BIRTHDAY
	CHRISTMAS
preserve	
preserve jam	PICKLE
preservationists	NT
preserved	(in) CA-N.(in) TI-N
president	ABE.CHAIR.IKE
	P.PR.PRES
press	
press agent	IRON.STEAM ROLLER
Press Association	PA
press gang	CROWD
pretty	DISHY
pretty clever	CUTE
pretty *conclusive*	TY
pretty girl	BELLE.CUTIE.DISH
	DOLLY.PEACH.STUNNER
previous[1]	
previous address indicates title	
preceding name:	
ambassador	EXCELLENCY.HE
archdeacon	VEN
earl	LORD
king	MAJESTY
knight	SIR
vicar	REV
pope	EMINENCE
previous[2]	EX

hence
- •previous wrong   EXTORT
- •previously first   EXIST
- •previously played   EXACTED
  (*see also* old[1])

price   PR
Prices and Incomes Board   PIB
price-earnings ration   PE
price index   CPI.RPI
price maintenance   RPM

priest
French priest   ABBE.CURE
priest   AARON.ELI.ENOCH
    PR.REV(D)
hence
- •priest dead, *say*   ELIDED
- •priest married   ELIMATED
- •priest quoted   ELICITED
and
- •priest *and* philosopher   PRAYER
- •priest *has* no dossier   PROFILE
- •priest *with* order   PROBE
and
- •priest *by* lake   REVERIE
- •priest is fine   REVOKE
- •priest is Irish   REVERSE
priestess   HERO.PYTHIA

primary
primary school   S
primarily about the. . .   AT

prime
prime material   GUNPOWDER
Prime Minister   PM
prime piece = first letter
- *prime piece of* beef   B

primitive
primitive   UR
primitive instinct   ID
Primrose League   PL
prince   P.PR.RAS
Prince Edward Island   PEI
princess   ANNE.DI.IDA
    INA.REGAN

principal
Principal Clerk of Sessions   PCS
principal directors   STARBOARD
Principal Medical Officer   PMO
principal spinner   TOP

print
print supplier   FINGER(TIP)
printed material   BATIK
printer's measure   EL.EM.EN
    (*see also* measures.type)
prison   BIRD,CAN.CLINK.COOLER
    HOCK.JUG.NICK.QUAD.STIR
prison camp   OFFLAG.STALAG
prison-camp child, *say*
    STALAGMITE
prison food   PORRIDGE
prisoner   BIRDMAN
prisoner of war   POW

private
private   GI
hence
- •private member   GIMP
- •private road   GIST
- •private transport   GIBUS
private automatic exchange   PAX
private branch exchange   PBX
private soldier   PTE
private transport   TROOPSHIP
Privy Councillor   PC

prize
prize animal   MEDALLION
prize-ring   PR
probationary   PRO
problem   SUM
problem putter   POSER
problem solved is. . .   DISSOLVE
problematical the gain   HEATING
process
process of law   AWL
processed peas   APSE
processing past. . .   PATS.TAPS
processor   CPU
Procurator Fiscal   PF
produce
produce notes   SING
produced by goats   MOHAIR
produced by goats   TOGAS
producing   (*see* bearing[3]
    beginning[2])
producing notes   ONSET.STONE
    TONES
product I sent   INSET.TINES
product of Iran   RAIN.RANI
production of stage. . .   GATES

profess

professional	ACE.PRO
hence	
•professional *has* 500. . .	PROD
•professional suitable. . .	PROFIT
•professional tries. . .	PROTESTS
Professional Golfers' Association	PGA
Professor of Theology	STP
	(*see also* expert)

prohibitionist placard   BANNER

project

projecting place	CINEMA
projection	EAR

prominence   TOR

promise

promises to pay	-IOUS
promissory note	IOU.PN

prompt service   AUTOCUE

pronounce

pronounce complete	UTTER
pronounced gait	GATE
pronouncement is not. . .	KNOT

prop up **bar (D)** ↑   REVEL

proper

proper place	REALLOCATION
properly built <u>theatre</u>	THEREAT

property   PTY

Property Services Agency   PSA

prophet   AMOS.ELI.ELISHA
HOSEA.JEREMIAH.MOSES

prophet's grandmother	MOSES
prophetess	CASSANDRA
	DEBORAH

proportional representation   PR

proprietary   PTY

prosperous

prosperous part	SE
pros/per/ous *part*	PER

prostitute   PRO

protect

protected by *	incl in *
•king *protected* by ca-t	CARAT
protecting a. . .	incl A
protecting *	incl *
•ca-t *protecting* a king	CARAT
Protector	CROMWELL.NOLL

protein

affecting cells	INTERLEUKIN
basic protein forming	HISTONE
—fibrin	FIBRINOGEN
—gelatine	COLLAGEN
from	
—almonds	AMANDINE
—barley	HORDEIN
—blood	FIBRIN(OGEN).GLOBULIN HAEMOGLOBIN
—cereal	GLUTELIN
—egg yolk	VITELLIN
—fibrous tissue	COLLAGEN ELASTIN
—gluten	GLIADIN.PROLAMINE
—hair	KERATIN
—horn	KERATIN
—Indian corn	ZEIN
—milk	CASEIN
—mucus	MUCIN
—nails	KERATIN
—muscle	ACTOMYOSIN MYOGLOBIN
—saliva	MUCIN
—seeds	ALEURONE
—silk	FIBROIN
—skin	KERATIN
insoluble	FIBRIN
producing luminescence	LUCIFERIN
soluble in	
—alcohol	PROLAMIN(E)
—salt	GLOBULIN
—water	ALBUMIN

Protestant Episcopal   PE

prove of use <u>in the</u>. . .   THINE

Provencal   PR

proverbially

bald	COOT
bent	CORKSCREW
black	COAL.DEVIL.INK.NIGHT SOOT.THUNDER
blind	BAT
blue	SEA.SKY
brave	LION
bright	BUTTON
brown	BERRY
clean	WHISTLE
clear	BELL
cold	CHARITY.FISH.ICE

cool	CUCUMBER
cunning	FOX
damp	SQUIB
daft	BRUSH
dead	DODO.DOORNAIL
	DUCK.MUTTON
deaf	POST
deep	OCEAN.STILL WATERS
dull	DITCHWATER
euphoric	CLOUD NINE
fat	LARD.PIG
fast	LIGHTNING
flat	PANCAKE
fresh	PAINT
greased	LIGHTNING
green	GRASS
happy	LARK.SANDBOY
high	KITE.SKY
hot	FIRE.HELL
lanky	BEANPOLE
mad	HATTER.MARCH HARE
miserable	SIN
moaning	MINNIE
near	MAKES NO DIFFERENCE
nice	PIE
old	HILLS
patient	SAINT
plain	PIKESTAFF
pretty	PICTURE
pure	(DRIVEN) SNOW.LILY
quick	FLASH.LIGHTNING
red	BLOOD
right	NINEPENCE.RAIN.TRIVET
rough	BADGER
saved	BACON
sick	DOG.PARROT
silly	GOOSE
slow	SNAIL.TORTOISE
sly	FOX
smooth	SILK
snug	BUG (IN A RUG)
soft	PUTTY.SILK
strong	BULL.LION
sweet	HONEY.SUGAR
thick	(TWO) PLANK(S).THIEVES
thin	LATH.RAKE
tight	DRUM
twisted	CORKSCREW
ugly	DEVIL.SIN

weak	KITTEN.SISTER.WATER
wet	FISH
white	GHOST.LILY.SHEET.SNOW
wide	BARN DOOR

provide

provide a seat	ELECT
provide material for a new	
	WANE.WEAN
provide refuge for a. . .	incl A
provide refuge for *	incl *
•*provide refuge for* sheep *in* time	
	HEWER
provide shelter for a. . .	incl A
provide shelter for *	incl *
•w-e *provide shelter for* an. . .	
	WANE
provided	IF.LENT.SO
providing	IF
providing arms	MARS.RAMS

province (Canada)

Alberta	ALBA.ALTA
British Columbia	BC
Manitoba	MAN
New Brunswick	NB
Newfoundland	NF(D)
Northwest Territories	NWT
Nova Scotia	NS
Ontario	ONT
Quebec	PQ.Q.QUE
Saskatchewan	SASK
Yukon Territory	YT

provisional accommodation

	DEEP FREEZE
	FREEZER.FRIDGE.LARDER
	PANTRY.REFRIGERATOR

Provost Marshal	PM
prowling lion	LINO
Prudential	P
Prussian cavalryman	UHLAN

psalm

Psalm(s)	PS(A)
psalmist	DAVID
psychokinesis	PK
psychotic state	DT

public

public	OVERT
hence	
•many public. . .	COVERT
•public ballot box	OVERTURN

•public works	OVERTOPS
public address (system)	PA
public good	PB
pub(lic house)	INN.LOCAL.PH
public lending right	PLR
public library	PL
Public Record Office	PRO
public relations (officer)	PR(O)
public sector borrowing	
requirement	PSBR
public service vehicle	PSV
public services authority	PSA
publicise	AIR
publicity	AD.PR.PUFF
Puerto Rico	PR
capital	P.SAN JUAN
puff	AD
puff oxygen	GUSTO
puffy nose	SNOUT
pull	
pull out stops	SPOTS
pull punch	CLOUT
pull *up*(D) ↑	GARD.GUL.WARD
pull *up round* bend(D) ↑	GUARD
pulse code modulation	PCM
pulses	
Asian	SOYA BEANS
black-eyed beans	COWPEAS
butter beans	LIMA BEANS
chickpeas	EGYPTIAN PEA
	GARBANZO PEA
Chinese	MUNG
cowpeas	BLACK-EYED BEANS
dry peas	MARROWFAT PEAS
Egyptian pea	CHICKPEA
	GARBANZO PEA
French bean	HARICOT
Garbanzo pea	CHICKPEA
	EGYPTIAN PEA
great northern bean	HARICOT
haricot	FLAGEOLET
	NAVY BEANS.PINTO
Indian	MUNG.URD
Japan	ADZUKI
kidney beans	CANELLINI
Mexican	CHILLI
Middle Eastern	FUL MESDAMES
navy beans	HARICOT
other beans	BORLOTTI

	BROAD BEANS
	BUTTER BEANS
	FIELD BEANS
red kidney bean	CHILLI BEAN
	MEXICAN BEAN
pulverise	
pulverise bran	BARN
pulverise, pulverise	REPULSIVE
pulverised ash	HAS
pulverisation of oats	STOA
punch	
punch drunk	WALLOP
punch *up*(D) ↑	MAL.PAR
pupil	L
pupil teacher	PT
pupil's cover	EYELID
purchase tax	PT
pure	
pure *chaos*	PUER
pure lake	MERE
puree of leeks	KEELS
purloin painting	ABSTRACT
pursue	
indicates word after or below	
another:	
•award *pursued by*	
VIP	MEDALLION
•mother *pursues* the	
French(D)	LAMA
push	
push in a. . .	incl A
push in *	incl *
•fish *pushed in* the. . .	GATHER
push in *	incl in *
•*push* penny *into* s-lit	SPLIT
push lighter	BARGE
push up part. . .(D) ↑	TRAP
pussyfoot	(CAT'S) PAW
put	
put an end to	
•Con/stable/ *puts an*	
end. . .	STABLE
•*put an end to* man	MANY
•time *puts an end to*	
man	MANAGE
put away	EAT
put *back*⟨	TUP
put back part⟨	TRAP
put 'em *up*(D) ↑	ME

put in a. . .	incl A	*put round* a. . .	incl A
put in *	incl *	*put round* *	incl *
•Greek *put in* cha-ins	CHAGRINS	•cha-ins *put round*	
put into <u>gear</u>	RAGE	Greek. . .	CHAGRINS
put it *back*⟨	TI	put together	
put it *up*(D) ↑	TI	•the *French* can *put*	
put off <u>eating</u>	INGATE	together	LATIN
<u>put</u> *out*	TUP	*put through* *	incl in *
<u>put out</u> <u>fire</u>	RIFE	•tyro put through p-aces	PLACES
put out a. . .	omit A	**puzzle**	
put out *	omit *	*puzzle* <u>set in</u>. . .	INSET
•s(cat)ty to *put out* cat	STY	*puzzled* <u>by all</u>. . .	BALLY
put up nets(D) ↑ . . .	STEN	*puzzling* <u>clue</u>	LUCE

Q

boat. Celt. cue. electricity charge. farthing. five hundred.
five hundred thousand. Kelt. koppa. ninety. ninety-thousand. quadrans.
quality. Quebec. queen. Queensland. query. question. *queue.* quintal.
rational numbers

Q8	KUWAIT
QE	ER
Quaker City	PHILADELPHIA
quail	COLIN
qualified	BA.MA
quality	Q
quantity of gold	GO
quart	QT.QU(AR)
quarter[1]	N.S.E.W.NE.NW.SE.SW
hence	
•quarter *to* one	EA.NA.SA.WA
	EI.NI.SI.WI
	NAN.SAN.WAN.NONE
•quarter *to* five	EV.VE
•quarter *to* six	EVI-.VIE.VIN.VIS
•quarter *to* nine	SIX
•quarter *to* ten	EX-
•quarterly	ELY.SLY
quarter[2]	FRACTION.MERCY
	QR.QU(AR)
Jew's quarter	GHETTO
Jew's *quarter*	J.E.W.S
quarter-deck	D.E.C.K
quartermaster(-general)	QM(G)
quartermaster(-sergeant	QM(S)
quarter *of* loaf	L.O.A.F
quarter-sessions	QS
quartet	IV
quarto	QTO
quash <u>riots</u>	TIROS.TRIOS
quasi-stellar object	QSO.QUASAR
Quebec	Q.QUE
inhabitant	QUEBECOIS
leader	Q
measure (c. 1¼ acres)	ARPENT
	(*see also* Canadian)
queen[1]	ER
hence	
•queen's circle	ERRING
•queen in charge	ERIC
•Queen Street	ERST
and	

•composer *to* Queen	HOLSTER
•kneel *to* Queen	BENDER
•me and the Queen	MEANDER
•Queen's hotel	INNER
queen[2]	BESS.HM.MAB
	PEARLIE.PEARLY
	Q.QU.R
Queen Anne	AR
Queen Anne's Bounty	QAB
queen city	CINCINNATI
Queen Elizabeth	ER.ORIANA
Queen Elizabeth Hall	QEH
Queen Mary	MR
Queen of	
—Carthage	DIDO
—France	REINE
—Germany	KONIGIN
—heaven	ASHTORETH
—Italy	REGINA
—Navarre	MARGUERITE
—Sheba	AZIZ.BALKIS
—spades	BASTA
—Spain	REINA
—the dead	HEL
—the fairies	MAB.TITANIA.UNA
—the Nile	CLEO(PATRA)
Queen Victoria	VIR.VR(I)
Queen's Bench	QB
queen's carriage	VICTORIA
Queen's College	QC
Queen's Counsel	QC
queen's head-dress	CROWN
Queensland	Q
Queer **Street**	RETEST.TESTER
query	EH
question	
question	EH.Q
•pictures *in* question	EARTH
question cook	GRILL
question of identity	WHO
question of motive	WHY
question of place	WHERE

question of time	WHEN	•little quiet. . .	WEEP
questionnaire	FORM	•motor quietly	CARP
queue	CUE.Q	and	
quick		•quiet listener	SHEAR
quick cleaner	NAIL FILE	•quiet person	SHONE
quick trim	SMART	•quiet stream	SHRILL
quickest way	BEELINE	and	
quiet		•I *am in* quiet *surroundings*	SHIP
fairly quiet	MP	(*see also* soft)	
quiet	EASE.P.QT.SH	quietener	KO.SH
hence		quieter road	TAMERLANE
•many quiet. . .	LEASE.MEASE	quietly *converse*	LOUDLY
•quiet, quiet. . .	PEASE	very quiet	PP
•quiet sovereign	EASEL	hence	
and		•a very quiet conclusion	APPEND
•a quiet bit..	APORT	•a very quiet fish	APPROACH
•a quiet expert	APACE	•a very quiet man	APPAL
•a quiet square	APT		APPLES
and		**quintal**	Q
•quiet drink	PALE	**quite**	
•quiet road	PLANE	quite *wrong*	QUIET
•quiet woman	PROSE	*quite wrongly* wrote. . .	TOWER
and		**quintet**	V
•insect *has* quiet. . .	BEEP	**quip**	SALLY

R

are. arithmetic. canine letter. castle. eighty. eighty thousand. hand. *king*. *monarch*. month. queen. radius. *rain*. rand. *reading*. real numbers. Réaumur. received. recipe. regina. registered trademark. Republican. resistance. rex. rho. right. *road. Roger*. Romania. röntgen unit. rook. *rotund character. royal*. run. rupee. side. take. *writing*

rabbit[1]	BRER.POOR GOLFER	**radical**	RAD.RED
rabbit[2]	ALASKA.ANGORA	**radio**	
	ARGENTE.ASTREX	radio frequency	RF
BEAVER KING.BELGIUM HARE		radio receiver	ELECTRIC FENCE
BEVEREN.BLANC DE BUSCOT		radio telephone	RT
BLANC DE HOTOT.BRITISH GIANT		radiological safety officer	RSO
CALIFORNIAN.CASTOR (REX)		**radius**	R.RAD
CHINCHILLA (GIGANTA)		*ragged* edges	SEDGE
CHINESE SACRIFICIAL.DUTCH		*raging* gale	GAEL
ENGLISH LOP.FLEMISH.FOX		**railway**[1]	BR.MET.RLY.RY
FRENCH DWARF.HARLEQUIN		hence	
HAVANA.HIMALAYAN.LILAC		•railway in Greece	BRING
LINCOLNSHIRE SPRIG		•railway not working	BRIDLE
MARTEN SABLE		•railway points	BREW
NETHERLAND DWARF		and	
NEW ZEALAND.POLISH.REX		•company railway	COMET
RHINELANDER.SATIN		•put railway *round* a. . .	MEAT
SIAMESE SABLE.SIBERIAN		•railwayman	METAL.METED
SILVER SPRIG.SMOKED PEARL		and	
TAN.THURINGER		•lay railway *round* east. . .	RELY
race[1]	NATION.TT.DERBY	•mother *on* the railway	MARLY
LEGER.NATIONAL.OAKS		•railway *without* record. . .	REPLY
hence		and	
•change race	ALTERNATION	•and *in* railway. . .	RANDY
•motor race	CARNATION	•put railway *round* a. . .	RAY
•race *with* friend	NATIONALLY	•spoil railway. . .	MARRY
and		(*see also* transport)	
•race *in* circles	OTTO	**railway**[2]	
•race *round* circuits	TOOT	railway region	GWR.LMS.LNER.SR
•race *round* Westminster	TWIT	railway sorting office	RSO
•road race	MITT	railway sub-office	RSO
race[2]		railway *terminal*	Y
race broadcast	RELAY	Railway Traffic Officer	RTO
race commentator		railwayman	(in) B-R
ETHNOGRAPHER		railwaymen	NUR.RUNABOUT
race leader	ADAM	**rain**	R
race *leader*	R	rain*fall*	IRAN.RANI
race starter	ADAM	rain indicator	SHOWER
race *starter*	R	rain *squall*	IRAN.RANI
races	HEATS	**raise**	
radian	RAD	*raise* boy(D) ↑	YOB
radiation protection adviser	RPA	*raise* capital(D) ↑	-IA

raise money(D) ↑	NEY.NIT
raise mug(D) ↑	GUM
rake	LOTHARIO
rallying ground	TENNIS COURT
rambling <u>roses</u>	SORES
ran¹	
ran *around*	RA-N
ran *out*	RA-N
<u>ran</u> *out*	ARN
<u>ran</u> *riot*	ARN
<u>ran riot</u> <u>thereat</u>	THEATRE
ran *round*	RA-N
	(*see also* run)
ran²	SMUGGLED
hence	
•many smuggled...	CRAN
•smuggled diamonds	RAND
•smuggled king *and* queen...	
	RANKER
rand	R
random	
random <u>shot</u>	HOST
randomly <u>cast</u>...	CATS
range	
free <u>range</u>	ANGER
range <u>free</u>	REEF
Rangers	QPR
ranging <u>in on a</u>...	ANION
rank	
rank and file	OR.PBI
rank *outsiders*	RK
ransacked <u>room</u>	MOOR
rapid eye movement	REM
rare	
rare bird	RARA AVIS
rare bird	DRIB
rarely <u>read</u>	DARE.DEAR
rash	
rash investigation	SPOT CHECK
rash <u>step</u>	PEST.PETS
rasher	BACON
rate	MPH
rate highly	SPEEDWELL
rate increase	ACCELERATION
rating	AB
	(*see also* sailor)
rational numbers	Q
rattled <u>dice</u>	ICED
ravaged <u>by a</u>...	BAY

raw	
<u>raw</u> *beginner*	R
<u>raw</u>, *raw*	WAR
ray	X
razor-man	OCCAM
react	
react fast	REDOLENT
reactionary wets⟨	STEW
read	
read aloud	ALLOWED
read in T/he St/rand	HEST
read out banns	BANS
reads *novel*	DARES.DEARS
readjust	
readjust <u>ladies'</u>...	SAILED
readjustment of <u>centre</u>	RECENT
ready	CASH
real	
real numbers	R
<u>real</u> *potential*	EARL.LEAR
re(ally) *friendless*	RE
realign	
realign <u>stream</u>	MASTER.REMAST
realigning <u>rail</u>	LIRA
realignment of <u>lane</u>	LEAN
reappearance of <u>players</u>	REPLAYS
reapplied <u>his</u>...	-ISH
rear	
Rear Admiral	RA
rear of ship	STERN
rear of <u>ship</u>	P
rearing	
including cultivation:	
animals	ZOOCULTURE
bees	APICULTURE
birds	AVICULTURE
fish	PISCICULTURE
flowers	FLORICULTURE
fruit	POMICULTURE
hair (growth)	CRINICULTURE
one type of crop	MONOCULTURE
oysters	OSTREICULTURE
plants	HORTICULTURE
—stimulated by electricity	
	ELECTROCULTURE
silk worms	SERICULTURE
trees	ARBORICULTURE
vines	VINICULTURE.VITICULTURE
voice training	VOCICULTURE

woods	SILVICULTURE
re-arrange	
re-arrange diary	DAIRY
re-arrange kingpin	PINKING
reassemble warders	DRAWERS
	REWARDS
Réaumur scale	R
rebel	CADE.TYLER
rebellious race	ACRE.ACER.CARE
rebels	ETA.IRA.PLO
rebuffed moderates⟨	STEW
rebuild	
rebuild town	WONT
rebuild most of town	WON.NOT
	TON
rebuttal of large...	SMALL
recall time⟨	ARE.EMIT
recast lure	RULE
receding gums⟨	SMUG
receipts	-IOUS
receive	
receive approval	incl OK
•w-e *receive* approval	WOKE
received by *	incl in *
•car received by Ma-y	MARRY
receiver of wreck	ABANDONEE
receives a...	incl A
receives *	incl *
•Ma-y *receives* car	MARRY
receptive to a...	incl A
receptive to *	incl *
•w-e *receptive* to an...	WANE
recent	
recent delivery	NEW YORKER
recent *disturbance*	CENTRE
Rechabite	TT
recipe	R.REC
recipe book	RB
recipe for stew	WETS
reciprocate	
reciprocal action	DEED
reciprocate Ben's...⟨	SNEB
reciprocating sound	TOOT
recitation of ode	OWED
recklessly throw	WORTH
reclaimed lost...	LOTS
recollected tale	LATE.LEAT.TAEL
	TELA
recommended retail price	RRP

recondition	
recondition frayed...	DEFRAY
reconditioned or new...	OWNER
reconditioning of furs	SURF
reconstitite	
reconstitute meat	MATE.TAME
	TEAM
reconstituted soup	OPUS
reconstitution of side	DIES.IDES
reconstructed dome	MODE
record¹	DIARY.DISC.ENTER
	ENTRY.EP.FORTY-FIVE.LOG
	LP.MONO.SEVENTY-EIGHT
	STEREO.TAPE.THIRTY-THREE
record book	ALBUM.DIARY
	JOURNAL
record-*breaking*	incl EP.LP.LOG
•record-*breaking* ste-le	STEEPLE
•a-s record-*breaking*...	ALPS
•record-*breaking* gas...	CLOGS
record-*breaking*	incl in LP.LOG
•each *in* record-*breaking*...	LEAP
•win *in* record-*breaking*...	
	LOWING
record call	TAPERING
record-holder	ALBUM.SLEEVE
record-*holder*	incl EP or LP
•she is hot record-*holder*	
	SHEEPISH
•one in first is record-*holder*	
	ALPINIST
record-maker	EMI.STYLUS
record-player	DISC JOCKEY
	NEEDLE.STYLUS
	TURNTABLE
record rebellion	FORTY-FIVE
recording band	TRACK
recording head	ARCHANGEL
record²	(*see* write³)
recover	
recovered by *	incl RE
•*recovered by* th-e...	THREE
recovering *	incl in R-E
•*recovering* fish	RIDE
recovery ship	ARGO
rectify slip	LIPS
rector	REV(D)
recurrent	
recurrent moan I...⟨	NAOMI

recurrent note⟨   ETON
recycled rags in...   GRAINS
red¹
meaning:
angry
•angry *carrying* silver...   RAGED
communist, left, etc.
•anarchist deed   REDACT
•communist landlord   RED LETTER
•left study   REDDEN
•Russian sailor   RED ADMIRAL
flushed
•flushed *in* company   CREDO
Inner Circle
•like sanctimonious Inner Circle
                 ASPIRED
owing, etc.   (in) R-ED
•dismissed, owing...   ROUTED
•rower in debt   ROARED
radical
•radical water transport   REDRAFT
stop
•bet *on* red   BACK-STOP
•stop English scheme   REDEPLOY
red²
red cover   (in) R-ED
Red Cross   RC
red flower   DON.VOLGA
Red Norseman   ERIC
red setter   SUN
red suit   D.H
red*cap*   R
red*head*   GINGERNUT.POPPY
redhead(D)   R
Red Indian   COPPERSKIN
       MOUNDBUILDER
bark canoe   WOOD-SKIN
beads from shells
       WAMPUM(PEAG)
belt of shell beads
       WAMPUM-BELT
birch-bark box or basket
           MOCOCK
blanket   MACKINAW
brave   SANNOP.SANNUP
chief   MUGWUMP.SACHEM
         SAGAMORE
child   PAPOOSE
communal dwelling LONG HOUSE

confederacy of tribes
  FIVE NATIONS.SIX NATIONS
confer   POWWOW
conference   PAWAW.POWWOW
deified spirit MANITO(U).MANITU
dish of sweet corn and beans
        SUCCOTASH
drag   TRAVAIL.TRAVOIS
dried meat   PEM(M)ICAN
dwellings   HOGAN.HUT.LODGE
  TEEPEE.TENT.WICKIUP
        WIGWAM
feast   PAWAW.POWWOW
interjection   WAUGH
lavish ceremonial   POTLATCH
leaders   RI
litter   TRAVAIL.TRAVOIS
liquor   HOO(T)CH
medicine man   POWWON
paradise
  HAPPY HUNTING-GROUND
peace pipe   CALUMET
poetry   HIAWATHA
pole used in house-building
        LODGE-POLE
pony   CAYUSE
porridge from maize   SAMP
       SUP(P)AWN
religious dance   CANTICO(Y)
       KANTIKOY
shaman   PAWAW.POWWOW
shell money   PEAG.PEAK
       WAMPUM(PEAG)
shoe   MOCCASIN.MOCASSIN
sled   TRAVAIL.TRAVOIS
smoking mixture   KINNIKINICK
snakebite medicine   SENEGA
tent   TE(E)PEE.WIGWAM
tribes   ALGONQUI(A)N
  ALGONKI(A)N.APACHE
  ARAPAHO.BLACKFOOT
  BLOOD.CHEROKEE
  CHEYENNE.CHINOOK
  CHIPPEWAY.CHOCKTAW
  COMANCHE.CREE
  CREEK.CROW.DAKOTA.HOPI
  HURON.IROQUOIS
  MOHAVE.MOHAWK.MOHEGAN
  MOHICAN.MOHOCK.MUSKOGE

NAVAHO.NAVAJO.OJIBWA(Y)	
OSAGE.PAIUTE.PAWNEE	
SENECA.SEMINOLE.SHAWNEE	
SHOSHONE.SHOSHONI	
SIOUN.SIOUX.SIWASH	
UTE.WINNEBAGO	
utensil used in war ceremony	
	WAR-KETTLE
vegetable stew	SUCCOTASH
war axe	TOMAHAWK
war cry	WHOOP
white man with Red	
Indian wife	SQUAW-MAN
wife	SQUAW

redecorate *room*   MOOR

redevelop

redevelop town   WONT

redeveloping skill   KILLS

redevelopment of region   IGNORE

redhead   R

redistribute wares   SWEAR.WEARS

redraft letters   SETTLER

redrawn plans Tim. . .   IMPLANTS

reduce

reduce by a quarter   omit N.S.E.W

reduced price   RP

reduced (p)rice   RICE

reduced responsibility   (o)NUS

reduced ta(x)   TA

reduced t/o the r/ranks   OTHER

reducing velocity   V

reduction of

—height   H.HT

—power   P

—weight   WT

reduction of (h)eight   EIGHT

reduction of rat(es)   RAT

         (*see also* small²)

redundant

a *redundant*   omit A

•a *redundant* man(a)ger   MANGER

redundant *   omit *

•peas(ant), *redundant* worker

                     PEAS

re-edited Verne   NEVER

reeling in a line   ANILINE

refashion bust   BUTS.STUB

refer

refer to drawer   RD

referee   REF

reference   REF

refine

refined oils   SILO.SOIL

refinement of taste   STATE.TEATS

refitted tyre   TREY

reflected Don's. . .⟨   SNOD

reform

reform railmen   MINERAL

Reformation artist   TRAITS

reformulating recipe   PIERCE

reformulation of rules   LURES

refuge

* *is refuge for*   incl in *

•church is *refuge for* prince CRASH

refuse

refuse to declare   BATON

refuse to *return*⟨   ON

refusing *to rise*(D) ↑   ON

regarding   ON.OVER.RE

            (*see* about²)

regiment   R(E)GT

Regimental Court-Martial   RCM

Regimental Sergeant-Major   RSM

regina   R

regional   (*see* dialect terms)

Regional Seat of Government

                     RSG

Registered General Nurse   RGN

regrouping in there   NEITHER

regulating credit   TRICED

rehabilitated slum   LUMS

rehearsal   SHOW-TRIAL

reinstated master   STREAM

reject

reject a. . .   omit A

reject the article   omit A.AN.IT.THE

reject *   omit *

•fat(her) *rejects* her. . .   FAT

rejected evil⟨   LIVE

rejoin Marines   SEMINAR

relate

relating   REL

relating to   (*see* pertaining)

relation   SIB

relative   BRER.BRO.REL.SIS

relative atomic mass   RAM

relatively favourable   NEPOTIC

relatively *small*   BRER.BRO

	REL.SIS
relevant stuff	MATERIAL
relaxed rules	LURES
relief work	CAMEO.CARVING
	EMBOSSING
religion	(*see also* belief)
religious	PI
hence	
•religious character	PICARD
•religious code	PILAW
•religious group	PILOT
religious point	SPIRE.STEEPLE
remains	ASH
remains silent	SAY-SO
remarkable	TALL
remarkable man	COMMENTATOR
remarkable pearl	PALER
remarkably paler	PEARL
remodel gown in...	OWNING
remote	
remote part of China	A
remote *parts*	METEOR.-OMETER
remove	
I'd *removed*...	omit ID
•I'd *removed from* state	FLORA
remove a...	omit A
remove leader of (g)roup	ROUP
remove stain	SAINT
remove wrinkles	DECREASE
remove tail of kit(e)	KIT
•(bar)ely *remove* obstruction	ELY
remove * *from*	omit *
•*remove* child *from* class	
	LES(son)S
removed van I...	IVAN.VAIN
remuster cadres	SACRED
render	
render almost secur(e)	CURSE
rendering dues	SUED
rendition of song	NOGS.SNOG
René	
René's = French	
•*René's* house	MAISON
•with *René's*...	AVEC
renewed fears	FARES.SAFER
renounce	
renounce *	omit *
•ri(sin)g to *renounce* sin	RIG
renovate sofa	OAFS

rent	
rent-a-party	TORNADO
rent reduction	TEARDROP
ren(t) *reduction*	REN
reorganise stores	SOREST
repacked for trips..	SPIRT.STRIP
repair shoe	HOES.HOSE
repeated	(*see* double.two)
repel	
repel a...	omit A
repel one...	omit A.I.
repel king	omit K.R
repel queen	omit ER.Q.R
repel *	omit *
•wh(it)en *to repel* it	WHEN
repelling Satan⟨	LIVED
replace	
drink *replaces* one *in* th(i)s...	
	THRUMS
replace old Rover	OVERLORD
replace contents of c(as)k	CORK
replace New Deal	OLD HAND
replace R with A	WRAITH
t(r)y to *replace* R with A	TAY
replan estate	TEA SET
reply	ANS
report	POP.REP(T)
reported	DIT
reported you're...	URE
reportedly knew	GNU.NEW
reporter	REP
repose	
reposing in *	incl in *
•a king *reposing in* b-ed	BARED
reposition lamps	PALMS
represent	
represented in art	RAT.TAR
represented in art	INTRA-.TRAIN
representing Neath	THANE
representative	MP
of England	LION.ROSE
of Ireland	SHAMROCK
of Scotland	THISTLE
of Wales	DRAGON.DAFFODIL
	LEEK
reproduction	(*see* beginning[2])
republic	REP
requires me to...	MOTE.TOME
rescue ship	(NOAH'S) ARK

resemble
resembles Gerald	HERALD
resembles parents	PASTERN

reserve
Reserve Decoration	RD
reserve seat	BOOKSTALL
reserves	TA
hence	
•reserve member	TAMP
•reserve navy	TARN
•reserve team	TAXI
(*see also* army)	

reset field in. . .	INFIDEL

resettle
resettle a tribe	BAITER
resettled in Paris	PAIRS
reshuffle cards as. . .	CSARDAS

resident
Resident Medical Officer	RMO
Resident Surgical Officer	RSO
resident magistrate	RM

resin	(*see* gum)
resistance	R

resolve
resolution of tough. . .	OUGHT
resolved to send	STONED

resort	SPA
resort to a. . .	OAT

responsible for	-IC

rest
rest *centre*	ES
rest in peace	RIP
resting	(in) B-ED.(in) CO-T
resting place	BED.COT.DEN
	DORM.LAIR
restaurant bill	MENU

restore
restore law. . .	AWL
restoring much. . .	CHUM
restoration of garden	DANGER

restrict
restrict (i)t	T
restricted road	RD
restricted (s)cope	COPE
restricting a. . .	incl a
restricting *	incl *
•p-ay *restricting* learner	PLAY
restricted by *	incl in *
•learner *restricted by* p-ay	PLAY

restricting vie(w)	VIE
restyled acts	CATS.SCAT

result
result of foresight	GIFT HORSE
resulting from state. . .	TASTE

retail
retail price	RP
retail price index	RPI
retail price maintenance	RPM

retain
retained by *	incl in *
•agent *retained by* men	
	MALEFACTORS
retaining a. . .	incl A
retaining *	incl *
•men *retaining* agent	
	MALEFACTORS

retire
retire to. . .⟨	OT
retired	(in) B-ED.(in) C-OT
retired	EX.RETD
	(*see also* old³)
retired head	omit first letter
retired leader	omit first letter
retired nurse⟨	DAV
retiring at ten⟨	NETTA
retiring premier⟨	MP
retirement of sailor⟨	RAT

retreat
retreated tidily	EBBED
retreating object⟨	TI
retreating waters⟨	SLOOP
retrograde step⟨	PETS

return
return from work	INCOME
	PROFIT
return game⟨	FLOG
return to. . .	OT
returned	RETD
Returned Letter Office	RLO
returning learners⟨	SLIP-UP
returning missile	BOOMERANG
returning missile⟨	TRAD
returning nomad⟨	DAMON

rev
rev counter	ALTAR
rev *up*(D) ↑	VER
revamped room	MOOR

reveal

revealed by Fren/ch art/tist   CHART
revealing hand is. . .   DANISH
reveals a new. . .   WANE.WEAN
Revelations   REV
reverberate
reverberates tin. . .   INT-.NIT
reverberating clang I. . .   LACING
reverberation of steel. . .   LEETS
                          STELE
Reverend   REV(D)
reverse
reverse gear⟨   BRAG
reverse mail chain   ARMOUR
                CHAIN-MAIL
reverse tide⟨   EDIT
reversible notices   SEES
reversible parts⟨   STRAP
reversible revolver   ROTOR
review
review all the. . .   LETHAL
review of army   MARY.MYRA
revise
revised   REV
revised ice act   ACETIC
Revised (Standard) Version R(S)V
revision of chapter   PATCHER
revival of play   PALY
revolve
revolution   REV
revolution in art   TRAIN
revolution in art   RAT.TAR
revolutionary   CHE.RED
hence
•about *revolutionary*. . .   CARED
•*revolutionary* action   REDACT
•*revolutionary* movement
                RED SHIFT
and
•artist *and* revolutionary. . .
                RACHE
•revolutionary directions CHEESE
•revolutionary English radical
                CHEERED
revolutionary command   ABOUT
                FACE
           ABOUT TURN
revolutionary design   SIGNED
revolutionary movement   ABOUT
                FACE

          ABOUT TURN
revolutionary painter   TURNER
revolutionary part⟨   TRAP
revolutionary piece of equipment
                LATHE
revolutionise all the. . .   LETHAL
revolutions per minute   RPM
revolving door⟨   ROOD
revolving fast   FATS
rewrite
rewrite section   NOTICES
rewritten page   GAPE
rewriting note   ETON.TONE
rhetoric
including
grammar
poetry
speech
words:
accepted principle or proposition
         AXIOM.MAXIM
adaptation of word form
  according
  to meaning not grammar
              SYNESIS
addition
—of sound/syllable to end of
  word   EPITHESIS.PARAGOGE
—of words to give further
  explanation   EPEXEGESIS
adjective or verb applied to two
  nouns, appropriate to only one
     SYLLEPSIS.ZEUGMA
affected speech or writing style
           EUPHUISM
analyse   PARSE
anticipation of objections
           PROLEPSIS
apposition   PARATHESIS
arguments brought to one point
  after discussion from many
          DIALLAGE
avoiding repetition of word at
  beginning of successive clauses
          ANAPHORA
beginning successive clauses with
  the same word (rhetoric)
      (EP)ANAPHORA
bombastic style of speech or

writing   EUPHUISM
breach of grammatical
  construction   SOLECISM
break in pronunciation of
  adjacent vowel sounds   HIATUS
breaking off in mid-sentence
                                        APOSIOPESIS
change
—from one point to another
                                        METASTISIS
—of letter in words for comic
  effect   PARAGRAM
—of relation of two words in
  sentence   HYPALLAGE
—to pronunciation of an r sound
            RHOTACISE.RHOTACIZE
clauses without conjunctions
  connecting them   PARATAXIS
commentary or annotation
                                        SCHOLIUM
conditional clause   PROTASIS
concise
—saying   EPIGRAM
—style   BRACHYLOGY
                              LACON(IC)ISM
confusion of meaning
                                        SYNCHYSIS
conjunction of contradictory
  terms   OXYMORON
containing figures of
  speech   FIGURATIVE
contraction of two vowels into
—diphthong   SYN(A)ERESIS
—single syllable without
  diphthongisation   SYNIZESIS
coupling of opposites
  (rhetorical)   SYNOECIOSIS
departure from main discourse
                                        APOSTROPHE
device of mentioning subject by
  denying its mention APOPHASIS
diacritical mark over letter
  n   TILDE
dī(a)eresis   TREMA
digression APOSTROPHE.ECBOLE
elision   ECTHLIPSIS
—of final vowel of one word with
  initial vowel of the next
                              SYNAL(O)EPHA

euphemism   HYPOCORISM
exaggeration   HYPERBOLE
exclamation   ECPHONESIS
                                        EPIPHONEMA
figurative
—application of name or quality
  to comparable person or thing
                                        METAPHOR
—language   TROPOLOGY
—resemblance of one thing to
  another   SIMILE
—use of words   TROPE
grammatical arrangement of
  words in sentences   SYNTAX
having
—acute accent
—on penultimate syllable
  (Greek)   PAROXYTONE
—on third last syllable (Greek)
                              PROPAROXYTONE
—additional syllable
                              PERISSOSYLLABIC
—circumflex accent on the
  —last syllable (Greek)
                                        PERISPOMENON
—penultimate syllable (Greek)
                              PROPERISPOMENON
—full number of syllables
  (of verse)   ACATALECTIC
—one more syllable in cases other
  than nominative
                              IMPARISYLLABIC
humorous or sarcastic expression
  conveying opposite meaning
                                        IRONY
idiomatic expression   IDIOTISM
imitation of sound
                              ONOMATOPOEIA
                              ONOMATOPO(I)ESIS
immediate
—replacement of word(s)
                              EPANORTHOSIS
—reptition of word(s) EPIZEUXIS
incorrect use of words
                                        CATACHRESIS
inoffensive word substituted for
  offensive   EUPHEMISM
insertion of
—vowel or consonant into word

to aid pronunciation
EPENTHESIS
—of word or phrase for
explanation or qualifying
PARENTHESIS
inversion   ANASTROPHE
HYSTERON-PROTERON
—of antithesis ANTIMETATHESIS
—of meaning, often ironic
ANTIPHRASIS
lack of grammatical sequence
ANACOLUTHIA.ANACOLUTHON
last but one syllable PENULT(IMA)
lengthening of short syllable
ECTASIS
letter with more than one
phonetic value   POLYPHONE
litotes   M(E)IOSIS
logical deduction from general
to particular   SYLLOGISM
mark over second of two vowels,
indicating separate
pronunciation   DI(A)ERESIS
TREMA
m(e)iosis   LITOTES
metaphorical   FIGURATIVE
mixture of vernacular words with
Latin or Latinised words
MACARONIC
modification of word sound
caused by adjacent word SANDHI
name composed of more than
two words   POLYONYM
narration of facts   DIEGESIS
nonce word HAPAX LEGOMENON
omission of
—article before noun
ANARTHROUS
—conjunctions   ASYNDETON
—first letter or syllable
APH(A)ERESIS
—last sound or syllable APOCOPE
—unstressed vowel at beginning
of word   APHESIS
—vowel or syllable at beginning
or end of word   ELISION
palatalised (sound)   MOUILLE
pithy saying APHORISM.GNOME
LACON(IC)ISM

play on words   PARAGRAM
PARONOMASIA.PUN
pleasing sound in speech
EUPHONY
pretended neglect of idea as too
obvious to discuss
PARAL(E)IPSIS
prolixity   VERBOSITY
pronouncing r as l   LALLATION
proverb   ADAGE
repetition
—at beginning and end of
successive clauses   SYMPLOCE
—in reverse order
ANTIMETABOLE
—of connectives POLYSYNDETON
—of word   PALILLOGY
—at beginning and end of
sentence   EPANADIPLOSIS
—at beginning of successive
clauses   (EP)ANAPHORA
—at end of successive clauses
EPISTROPHE
—of word or clause after
subordinate or parenthetic text
EPANALEPSIS
—of words or phrases at end of
one clause and beginning of next
ANADIPOLOSIS
—useless
BATTOLOGY.TAUTOLOGY
return to main discourse
HYPOSTROPHE
reversal in second of two parallel
phrases   CHIASMUS
rhetorical question   EROTEMA
EROTEME.EROTESIS
round-about expression
PERIPHRASE.PERIPHRASIS
self-evident truth   TRUISM
separation of parts of compound
word by other word(s) TMESIS
series of interconnecting
syllogisms   POLYSYLLOGISM
setting down as premiss in
argument   THESIS
short cryptic saying containing
accepted truth APO(PH)THEGM
shortening of syllable   SYSTOLE

speech dealing with single theme   TIRADE
study of poetic metre and
   versification   PROSODY
superfluous use of words
       PLEONASM.VERBIAGE
substitution of attribute for
   thing meant   METONOMY
summing up   EPANODOS
three
—letters representing one sound
       TRIGRAPH
—vowel sounds in one syllable
       TRIPHTHONG
time category of verb (present,
   past, future)   TENSE
transposition of
—initial consonants
       SPOONERISM
—normal word order
       HYPERBATON
—sounds or letters   METATHESIS
trema   DI(A)ERESIS
trite statement   TRUISM
two
—letters representing one
   sound   DIGRAPH
—notions connected by
   conjunction   HENDIADYS
—person speaking-role
       DUOLOGUE
—vowel sounds in one syllable
       DIPHTHONG
understatement by using negation
   instead of antonym
       LITOTES.M(E)IOSIS
ungrammatical   ASYNTACTIC
unintentional misuse of
   words   MALAPROP(ISM)
unnecessary repetition
       TAUTOLOGY
use of
—part for whole or whole for part
       SYNECDOCHE
—proper name for quality or idea
       ANTONOMASIA
—redundant words   MACROLOGY
used in three cases   TRIPTOTE
valediction   APOPEMPTIC

verbosity   VERBIAGE
vocabulary of a dialect IDIOTICON
vowel
—gradation   ABLAUT
—pronunciation mark
       DI(A)ERESIS.UMLAUT
—pure   MONOPHTHONG
word
—expressing whole sentence or
   phrase   HOLOPHRASE
—coined for only one occasion
     HAPAX LEGOMENON
       NONCE WORD
—having
—one syllable   MONOSYLLABLE
—two syllables   DISYLLABLE
—three syllables   TRISYLLABLE
—four syllables
       QUADRISYLLABLE
       TETRASYLLABLE
—five syllables PENTASYLLABLE
—six syllables   HEXASYLLABLE
—seven syllables
       HEPTASYLLABLE
—eight syllables OCTOSYLLABLE
—ten syllables   DECASYLLABLE
—eleven syllables
       HENDECASYLLABLE
—twelve syllables
       DODECASYLLABLE
—many syllablesPOLYSYLLABLE
—more than one meaning
       POLYSEME
—more than three letters in root
       PLURILITERAL
—same meaning   SYNONYM
—same sound, different
meaning   HOMONYM
       HOMOPHONE
—same spelling, different
meaning   HETERONYM
       HOMOGRAPH
—two syntactical functions in
   single sentence   SYLLEPSIS
—puzzle   LOGOGRIPH
—reading the same backwards as
   forwards   PALINDROME
—represented by single sign
       GRAMMALOGUE

rhino horns	BRASS	off	
rho	R	•again to off	RETORT
Rhodesia	RSR	OK, oke	
rhyme	(*see* verse)	•OK *behind* the Post Office	PORT
ribonucleic acid	RNA	lien	
rice	ARCHIE	•*has* a lien *on* first. . .	ARTIST
rich man	DIVES.MIDAS	title	
ride		•right attendant	TITLE PAGE
rider	GILPIN.REVERE	Tory	
riding	UP	•born Tory	BRIGHT
hence		**right³**	
•riding engagement	UPDATE	right angle	L
•*riding* school	UPSET	*right half of* road	AD
•*riding* well	UPRIGHT	right-hand	RECTO.RH.RO
riding (in) S-ADDLE.(on) HORSE		right name	TITLE
riding	(*see* astride)	right of way	ROW
riding master	RM	*right of* way	Y
ridiculous idea	AIDE	Right Reverend	RR
rifle		*right side of* road	AD.D
Rifle Brigade	RB	right sign	TICK
rifle fire	SACK	Right Worthy	RW
rift in lute or. . .	ELUTOR	right *wrong*	GIRTH
rig		**ring¹**	DISC.O
rig up a net	PEANUT	hence	
rigged race	ACRE.CARE	•ring Mark. . .	OSCAR
rig-*out*	GIR.GRI	•ring twice	OO
right¹		•Ringway	ORD.OST
right	R.RT	and	
hence		•dress ring	GARBO
•right in Kent	RINSE	•key-ring	BO.GO.SOHO.SOLO
•right lines	-RRY	•smoke-ring	RE-ECHO
•right time	RAGE.RT	•tree-ring	MAYO
and		•vice-ring	SINO-
•about right	CART	ring *in*	incl O
•one *in the* right	RAT	•ring *in* bo-th. . .	BOOTH
•right *round* an. . .	RANT	ring *from*. . .	omit O
right *at the end*. . . end with R.RT		•ring *from* bo(o)th	BOTH
right *away*	omit R.RT	ring *out*	omit O
right *back*⟨	TR	ringleader	start with O
right *from the start*	omit initial R	•mark ringleader	OSCAR
•(r)ash, right *from the start*	ASH	**ring²**	
right *inside*	incl R.RT	ring-*leader*	R
right *on*	ROVER	ring-*side*	G
right *out of it*	omit R.RT	ring round bull	INNER
right *outside*	(in) R-T	*ring* a. . .	incl A
right turn	RU	*ring* *	incl *
right *turn*⟨	TR	•m-e *ringing* at. . .	MATE
right²		**riot**	
meaning		*riot of* slaves	VALSES

rioting tribe	TIBER	•road directions	MEWS
riotous ways	SWAY.YAWS	•road in America	MINUS
riots	GORDON.REBECCA	•road *with* no directions	MOSES
rip vest	VETS	and	
rise		•road *leading to* another	MIST
rising man	INSURGENT.REBEL	•road-race	MITT
	RIOTER	•road vehicle	MISLED
rising star(D) ↑	AVON.RATS	and	
river		•road *back* to ⟨	ROT
river	R	•road in the Home Counties	RINSE
hence		•road is quiet	RISP
•East River	ER	and	
•river currents	RAMPS	•directions *on* a road	SWARD
•river fish	REEL.RID.RIDE	•nothing *in* the road	ROD
•walk *by* river	RAMBLE	•road *round* an...	RAND
some commonly used names		and	
	AIRE.ALPH.CAM	•nothing *in* the road	SOT
	DEE.EXE.FAL.ISIS	•private road	GIST
	OUSE.PO.TAY.TEES.URE	•road *round* his...	SHIST
hence		road-*builder*	DORA
•river valley	AIREDALE	Road Haulage Association	RHA
•river-*side* tower	CAMSHAFT	roadside *verges*	RE
•river Dee	DEED	*Roman* road	VIA
•river *has* attractive...	EXECUTE	**roam**	
•one *in* river	FAIL	*roaming about* in gown	OWNING
•river is *twice*...	ISIS	*roaming* free	REEF
•river-*side* bird	OUSEL	**roast goat**	BUTTER DISH
•river-fleas	POLICE	**robin's home**	SHERWOOD
•learners *fall in* river	TALLY		(FOREST)
•rain *swells* river	TRAINEES	**robots**	RUR
•quiet river	PURE	**rock**	GIB
river authority	DARTBOARD	rock-*climbing*(D) ↑	BIG
river bed	DOVECOT.UNDERWEAR	*rock* garden	GANDER.RANGED
River Don	WEAR	rock music	SWING
•river-goddess	DONATE	rock-music	CRADLE SONG
•riverman	DON	*rocking*-horse	SHORE
river in Hell	ACHERON	*rocky* shore	HORSE
River Test	INDUSTRIAL	Rocky Mountain area	BC
	INDUSTRY	**rocket**	ARIANE.BLUE STREAK
River Wear	DON		SATURN.VI
	(*see also* flower²)	rocket designer	STEPHENSON
RKII	ARCHAISE	**röentgen unit**	R
road		**rogue**	
road	AVE.M.MI.R.RD.ST	*rogue* male	LAME.MEAL
hence		roguish chief	ARCH
•hard road	HAVE	**role**	HAMLET.LEAR.PART
•road *and* river	AVER	**roll**	
•road *to the* right	AVERT	rolled umbrella	BROLLY
and		rolling ruler	PLUTOCRAT

Roman	ROM
acquisition by occupation	
	USUCAP(T)ION
actor	
—in dumb show	PANTOMINE
—'s mask	PERSONA
administrator	PROCURATOR
amphitheatre	COLISEUM
	COLOSSEUM
amulet in round box worn	
round neck	BULLA
ancient kingdom	PONTUS
apartment building	INSULA
aristocrat	PATRICIAN
aristocratic family	GENS
assemblies	
—for laws	COMITIA
—of centuries	
	COMITIA CENTURIATA
—of patricians	COMITIA CURITA
—of tribes	COMITIA TRIBUTA
assembly	FORUM
auxiliary soldier	FOEDERATUS
awning	VELARIUM
barracks	CAN(N)ABA
boring engine	TEREBRA
boundary	LIMES
brickwork	OPUS LATERICUM
bridge builder	PONTIFEX
building (block)	INSULA
bundle of rods	FASCES
calendar	FASTI
camp gate	PR(A)ETORIAN GATE
cap of free slave	PHRYGIAN CAP
capital	R.ROME
catapult	BAL(L)ISTA
Catholic	RC
centurion's badge	VINE ROD
chariot	BIGA.QUADRIGA
chief	
—magistrate	CONSUL
—secretary of chancery	
	PROT(H)ONOTARY
church	
—basin	CANTHARUS
—office	NONES
citizens	QUIRITES
cloak	TOGA.TOGE
—for travelling	PAENULA

—military	ABOLLA
—of manhood	TOGA VIRILIS
—woman's	PALLA
coins	
—copper	AS.SEMUNCIA
—$1/6$ as	SEXTANS
—$1/4$ as	QUADRANS
—$1\frac{1}{2}$ as	SEMIS
—$2\frac{1}{2}$-4 asses	SESTERCE
—10 asses (silver)	DENARIUS
—2 denarii	ANTONINIANUS
—12 denarii (silver)	SOLIDUS
—1000 sesterces	SESTERTIUM
—old	DUPONDIUS
—gold	
	AUREUS.BEZANT.SOLIDUS
college of heralds	FETIALES
commander of ten cavalrymen	
	DECURION
common people	PLEBS
company of foot soldiers	
	MANIPLE
complete body of laws	PANDECT
conquered ally	FOEDERATUS
conspirator	CATILINE
cooling room	FRIGIDARIUM
couches in threes round dining	
table	TRICLINIUM
councillor	DECURION
court	CURIA
—official attending magistrate	
	LICTOR
court(yard)	ATRIUM.AULA
cross	TEN.X
curved tile	IMBREX
cushioned seat	PULVINAR
dance	TRIPUDIUM
dates	
—1st of each month	CALENDS
—9th before ides	NONES
—13th or 15th	IDES
days when business was	
—legal	FASTI
—not legal	NEFASTI
decree of senate	SC
	SENATUS CONSULT(UM)
deities	(*see* gods. goddesses)
descendant of original Roman	
family	PATRICIAN

dining room	TRICLINIUM
ditch round amphitheatre arena	
	EURIPUS
diviner by bird observance	
	AUGUR
division of tribe	CURIA
divorce	DIFFAR(R)EATION
drinking cup	CANTHARUS
dual coequal magistrates	
	DUUMVIRES
early empire	PRINCIPATE
earthenware jar	DOLIUM
earthwork forming rampart	
	AGGER
election canvasser who named	
candidates	NOMENCLATOR
emperor's	
—bodyguard	PR(A)ETORIAN
	GUARD
—decree	INDICTION.NOVELLA
engine of war	TORMENTUM
entrance hall	ATRIUM
epic poem	AENEID
fastening of woman's sash	
	VIRGIN KNOT
felt cap	PILEUS
female monster	LAMIA
festival of	
—boundaries	TERMINALIA
—crops	AMBARVALIA
—(the) dead	LEMURIA
—flocks and shepherds	PALILIA
—Vulcan	VULCANALIA
—wine	VINALIA
fifteen-year fiscal period	
	INDICTION
financial agent	PROCURATOR
flask	AMPHORA.AMPHYULLA
flat dish	PATERA
food fish	MUR(A)ENA
forename	PRAENOMEN
former master of freedman	
	PATRON
forming friendship by dividing	
stone	CONTESSERATION
galley	BIREME.TRIREME
QUADRIREME.QUINQUEREME	
games	SECULAR GAMES
general's	

—cloak	PALUDAMENT(UM)
—quarters	PRINCIPIUM
—tent	PR(A)ETORIUM
ghost of dead	LEMUR
gift to the people	CONGIARY
gladiator	SAMNITE
—armed with net and trident	
	RETIARIUS
god	DEUS
—'s headdress	MODIUS
governor	
—of senatorial province	
	PROCONSUL
residence	PR(A)ETORIUM
grappling hook	CORVUS
hall	ATRIUM.AULA
headband	VITTA
headquarters	PR(A)ETORIUM
herald	FETIAL
Hermes's rod	CADUCEUS
hot springs	THERMAE
imperial standard	LABARUM
internal quadrangle	
	COMPLUVIUM
jar	AMPHORA.OLLA
javelin	PILE.PILUM
judge	CENTUMVIR
knight	EQUES
lapsing (law)	CADUCOUS
law	LEX
leader	DUX.R
legal transfer	MANCIPATION
low-class citizen	PROLETARIUS
magistrate	(A)EDILE
(PRO)PR(A)ETOR.PRO-CONSUL	
QU(A)ESTOR.TRIBUNE	
—'s attendant	LICTOR
—'s chair	CURULE
—'s symbol of authority	FASCES
—without forefathers in office	
	NOVUS HOMO
man	VIR
—'s undergarment	SUBUCULA
mantle	PALLIUM
market	
—day	NUNDINE
—place	FORUM
material used for vases	MURRA
	MURRHINE

mausoleum	MOLE
measures	
—58 inches	PACE
—1000 double paces	MILE
—1.4 miles	LEAGUE
—1 gallon	CONGIUS
—1 peck	MODIUS
milestone	MILIARY
military	
—cloak	ABOLLA.SAGUM
—standard	LABARUM
—unit	COHORT.LEGION
missile-thrower	TORMENTUM
monarch	CAESAR
monster	LAMIA.TYPHON
moray	MUR(A)ENA
name	NOMEN
oak wreath	CIVIC CROWN
officer	
—in charge of ten men	DECURION
—in charge of one hundred men	
	CENTURION
—'s cloak	PALUDAMENT(UM)
official scrivener	TABELLION
one of	
—seven hills of Roma	QUIRINAL
—two groups of Roman people	
	PLEBS
one of ruling council	
—two men	DUUMVIR
—three men	TRIUMVIR
—four men	QUADRUMVIR
—five men	QUINQUEVIR
—six men	SEXTUMVIR
—seven men	SEPTEMVIR
—ten men	DECEMVIR
passageway to amphitheatre exit	
	VOMITORIUM
patrician	PATRON
—form of marriage	
	CONFARREATION
—virgin	VESTA
perpetual right in	
land	EMPHYTEUSIS
pickaxe	DOLABRA
platter	LANX
pledge	SACRAMENT
poet	(*see* writers *below*)
porridge	PULS

pound	LIBRA
precluding debate	PEREMPTORY
priest	FLAMEN.PONTIFEX
—of corn deity	ARVAL BRETHREN
privy council (chamber)	
	CONSISTORY
prize to first to mount wall of	
besieged city	MURAL CROWN
procession to Capitoline Hill in	
honour of victorious general	
	TRIUMPH
property tax	INDICTION
prosecutor	QU(A)ESTOR
province	PONTUS
provincial	
—administrator	PROCURATOR
—governor	PROPRAETOR
public baths	THERMAE
purification ceremony	LUSTRE
	LUSTRUM
rain-water receptacle	IMPLUVIUM
rampart	VALLUM
ramps	ASCENSI
register	ALBUM
religious	
—dance	TRIPUDIUM
—feast	LECTISTERNIUM
—festival of expiation	
	LUPERCAL(IA)
	QUIRINAL(IA)
—offerings to spirits of the dead	
	INFERIAE
—headband	INFULA
repository for Penates	
	SACRARIUM
richest booty	SPOLIA OPTIMA
road	VIA
Roman people	PR
ruler	CAESAR
rural deity	FAUN
sacrifice	INFERIAE
—of animals	SUOVETAURALIA
satirist	JUVENAL(IS)
score	DOUBLECROSS
scroll	STEMMA
sea fight	NAUMACHIA
	NAUMACHY
second name	NOMEN
senate (house)	CURIA

senators	CONSCRIPT FATHERS
	PATRES CONSCRIPTI
shallow dish	PATINA
shield	SCUTUM
—fallen from heaven	ANCILE
sleeveless garment	EXOMIS
soldier's oath	SACRAMENT
soldiers	
—company of	VEXILLATION
—lightly armed	VELITES
—one hundred	CENTURY
—squad of ten	DECURIA.DECURY
—tenth of legion	COHORT
soothsayer	AUGUR.AUSPEX
sorceress	LAMIA
spirits of the dead	MANES
staircases	ASCENSI
standard	LABARUM.VEXILLUM
—bearer	VEXILLARY
stool	CURULE
straight trumpet	TUBA
stripe on senator's tunic	
	LATICLAVE
surplice	STOLA
surveying instrument	GROMA
swimming pool	PISCINA
symbol of authority	FASCES
tax collector	PUBLICAN
temple of	
—all gods	PANTHEON
—Jupiter	CAPITOL
tenth part of	
—legion	COHORT
—tribe	CURIA
third (family) name	COGNOMEN
tile	TEGULA
training ground	
	CAMPUS MARTIUS
travelling cloak	PAENULA
tribe	GENS
trumpet	BUCCINA
two-handled bottle	AMPULLA
underfloor space for heating	
system	HYPOCAUST
undergarment	SUBUCULA.TUNIC
valuation of property	INDICTION
vampire	LAMIA
veteran	VEXILLARY
warm room in baths	TEPIDARIUM

weights	
—1½ ounce	SEMUNCIA
—12 ounces	AS
—pound	AS.LIBRA
white tablet for recording	ALBUM
wine festival	VINALIA
woman's	
—mantle	PALLA
—robe	STOLA
writers	APULEIUS.CATULLUS
	HORACE.OVID
	TERENCE.VIRGIL
	(*see also* classic(al).Latin)
Romania	R
capital	BUCHAREST.R
coins	BANI.LEU
leader	R
Romans	ROM
roof of house(D) ↑	H
rook	R
room	DEN
root	RAD
root-mean-square	RMS
root of evil	L
Rossetti's group	PRB
rotten tread	RATED.TRADE
rotund	O
rotund character	O
rough	
rough-*sounding*	RUFF
rough terrain	RETRAIN.TRAINER
roughed up a bit	BAIT
roughly	C.CA.CIRC.CIRCA
	(*see* about¹)
roughly ten	ENT.NET
roughly treated cats	ACTS.SCAT
round¹	LAP.O
hence	
•round*about*⟨	PAL
	(*see also* roundabout)
and	
•bread round	ROLLO
•whip-round	CATO
and	
•round America	-OUS
•round enclosure	OPEN
•round tree	OPINE
round²	
round a...	incl A

round a nut⟨	TUNA	Australian Navy	RAN
round about	incl C.CA.RE	Automobile Club	RAC
•particle *round* about. . .	ICON	Arch Charter	RAC
•se-nt *round* about. . .	SECANT	Armoured Corps	RAC
•si-n *round* about. . .	SIREN	Asiatic Society	RAS
round *about*	RO-UND	Astronomical Society	RAS
•ro-und *about* to. . .	ROTUND	Canadian Academy	RCA
round table	BLEAT	College of	
round the bend	MAD	—Art	RC.RCA
round the bend	incl U	—Music	RCM
round the ring	incl O	—Organists	RCO
round up(D) ↑		—Physicians	RCP
•doctor *rounded up* ducks	BOOM	—Preceptors	RCP
	ROOD	—Science	RCS
round-up⟨	PU	—Sculptors	RCS
round up⟨ father	PUPA	Corps of	
round-up of cows	SCOW	—Signals	RCS
round up lost. . .	LOTS.SLOT	—Transport	RCT
round up rats(D) ↑	STAR	Dublin Society	RDS
round *	incl *	Engineers	RE
•wat-er *round* church	WATCHER	Exchange	RE
with * *round*	incl in *	Flying Corps	RFC
•church with wat-er *round*		Geographical Society	RGS
	WATCHER	Grenadier Guards	RGG
roundabout		Highness	RH
roundabout	OC.OCA.ORE	Horse Artillery	RHA
round*about*	RO-UND	Hibernian Academy	RHA
*round*about	incl C.CA.RE	Highland	
•hi-s *round*about	HIRES	—Fusiliers	RHF
•lan-e *round*about	LANCE	—Show	RHS
•poles' *round*about	SCAN	Historical Society	RHS
*round*about⟨	AC.ER	Horse Guards	RHG
roundabout route	OUTER	Horticultural Society	RHS
rout army	MARY.MYRA	Humane Society	RHS
row	ADO.TIER	Institute	RI
row *about*	PULLOVER	—of Chemistry	RIC
row about	LIN-E.RO-W.TI-ER	Institution of Painters	RI
rowing boat	EIGHT.FOUR	Irish	
rowing expert	MASTERSTROKE	—Academy	RIA
royal¹	R	—Constabulary	RIC
hence		Mail	RM
•royal assent	RAY	—Steamer	RMS
•royal bird	REGRET	Marines	RM
•royal worker	RANT	Microscopical Society	RMS
Royal²		Military	
Academician/Academy	RA	—Academy	RMA
Academy of Music	RAM	—Police	RMP
Air Force	RAF	Naval Reserve	RNR
Artillery	RA	Navy	RN

Observer Corps	ROC	mother's ruin	GIN
Order of Victoria and Albert	VA	*mother's ruin*	SMOTHER
Philharmonic Orchestra	RPO	*ruin* meal	LAME.MALE
Photographic Society	RPS	*ruined* life	FILE.LIEF
Radar Establishment	RRE	*ruination of* much. . .	CHUM
School of Music	RSM	**rule**	(see power²)
Scottish		**ruler**	ER
—Academician/Academy	RSA	*rum* affair	RAFFIA
—Water Colour Society	RSW	**run**	BYE.CRESTA.EXTRA
Society of			R.SINGLE
—Antiquaries	RSA	run *about*	RU-N
—Arts	RSA	run *away*	omit R
—British Artists	RBA	run *back*⟨	TORT
—British Sculptors	RBS	run *into*	incl R
—Edinburgh	RSE	run *out*	NUR.URN
—Etchers and Engravers	RE	run *over*(D)	start with R
—Literature	RSL	•run *over* a pretty girl(D)	RADISH
—Medicine	RSM	run *over*⟨	NUR
—Painters in Water Colours	RWS	*run* rings *round*	O-O
—Portrait Painters	RP	run *the wrong way*⟨	
Statistical Society	RSS		NUR.RAILWAYMEN
Ulster Constabulary	RUC	run twice	DOUBLE
Yacht Squadron	RYS	* *run into*	incl *
Yachting Association	RYA	•everyone *runs into* good fortune	
Zoological Society	RZS		BALLOON
royal³		run*about*	RU-N
royal badge/insignia	ER	run*about*⟨	NUR.RAILWAYMEN
royal governess	ANNA	*run*about	U-BOAT
royal yacht	BRITANNIA	*run*about	NUR.URN
	COURTSHIP.KINGSHIP	*runabout* can go. . .	CONGA
royalty	ER	runaway	DISH.SPOON
	(*see also* king)	*runaway* trains	STRAIN
r-rower	ROAR	runner	BEAN.COE.EMU
rub		MANAGER.RILL.RIVER.STREAM	
rub out a. . .	omit A		(*see also* river)
rub out *	omit *	runner-*up*(D) ↑	RECAP.UME
•gang(st)er *rubs out* good man		*runner-up* in race	A
	GANGER	running	ADMIN
rub *up the wrong way*(D) ↑	BUR	*running amok*, IRA men. . .	
rubber	TOWEL.ULE		MARINE
rubber bands	TYRES	*running* race	ACER.ACRE.CARE
rude		running water	EA
rude Roman	MANOR.NORMA	*running wild in* Penarth	PANTHER
rudely shaped	PHASED	*runny* nose	NOES.ONES
rudimentary	ABCEDARIAN		(*see also* ran)
ruffled lake	KALE.LEAK	**runt**	ANTHONY.TANTONY
rugby	RU	**rupee(s)**	R(S)
Rugby Football Club	RFC	**rupture**	
ruin		*ruptured by* a. . .	incl A

ruptured by *	incl *	—unit	COPEC(K).KOPEC(K)
•g-ut *ruptured by* duck	GOUT		KOPEK
rupturing *	incl in *	—100 kopeks	R(O)UBLE
•duck *rupturing* g-ut	GOUT	collective farm	KOLKHOZ

rural

rural automatic exchange	RAX	Committee for State Security	KGB
Rural Dean	RD	Communist party machine	
Rural District Council	RDC		APPARAT
rural sub-office	RSO	comrade	TOVARI(S)CH

rush

rush *around*	(in) RE-ED	concierge	DVORNIK
rush job	THATCHING	coniferous forests	TAIGA
rushing <u>stream</u>	MASTER	Cossack	

Russia SU.USSR   —elected leader

Russian¹ BEAR.IVAN.RED   ATAMAN.HETMAN

RUSS.SERGE   —troop   SOTNIA

hence		council	D(O)UMA.SOVIET
•Russian dead, *say*	BEARDED	country house	DACHA
•many Russian. . .	DIVAN	croquette of minced meat/fish	
•Russian family	REDSKIN	wrapped in bacon	KROMESKY
•Rusian alien	RUSSET	dance	GOPAK.KOLO.ZIGANKA
•Russian worker	SERGEANT	dandelion	KOK-SAGYZ

Russian²

aeroplane	MIG	Decembrist	DEKABRIST
agreement	DA	department store	GUM
airline	AEROFLOT	desert	TUNDRA
approval	DA	dish	PELMENY
aristocrat	BOYAR	dissident	RASKOLNIK.REFUSENIK
art museum	HERMITAGE	district council	ZEMSTVO
beetroot soup	BORSCH(T)	doctor's assistant	FELDSCHAR
	BORTSCH(T)		FELDS(C)HER
bleached soil of coniferous		drink	KVASS.QUASS.VODKA
regions	PODSOL	dogs	BORZOI.SAMOYED(E)
	PODZOL		WOLFHOUND
blizzard	BURAN	Easter cake	KULICH
bureaucrat	APPARATCHIK	edict of the Tsar	UKASE
	CHINOVNIK	efficient worker	STAKHANOVITE
cabbage soup	SHCHI.SHTCHI	emperor	CZAR.TSAR.TZAR
capital	MOSCOW.R	—'s daughter	CZAREVNA
capitalist	MUSCOVITE		TSAREVNA
card game	VINT	—'s eldest son	CESAREVI(T)CH
carriage	DROS(H)KY.TROIKA		CESAREWI(T)CH
cart	TELEGA		TSESAREVI(T)CH
cathedral	SOBOR	—'s son	CZAREVI(T)CH
cavalry	COSSACKS		TSAREVI(T)CH
Christian	UNIAT	—'s wife	CZARINA.CZARITSA
citadel	KREMLIN		TSARITSA
cloth	SERGE	exploiter	KULAK
coins		extinct horse	TARPAN
		extreme Socialist	BOLSHEVIK
		farmer	KULAK
		fermented milk	KOUMIS

	K(O)UMISS.KOUMYSS
fertile black soil	CHERNOZEM
fish (Lake Baikal)	GOLOMYNKA
fox	KARAGAN
government department	
head	COMMISSAR
grandmother	BABUSHKA
ground squirrel	S(O)USLIK
gypsy woman	TSYGANKA
headscarf	BABUSHKA
hemp	RHYNE
hood	BASHLYK
hors d'oeuvres	ZAK(O)USKI
house	DACHA.ISBA.IZBA
hut	ISBA.IZBA
illicit vodka	SAMOGON
information bureau	COMINFORM
	KOMINFORM
insectivore	DESMAN
international Communist	
organisation	COMINTERN
	KOMINTERN
isinglass	CARLOCK
Jewish area	JEWISH PALE
leader	R
leather	YUFT
legislature	SUPREME SOVIET
local council	ZEMSTVO
marshy forest	URMAN
massacre	POGROM
measures	
—28 inches	ARSHEEN.ARSHIN(E)
—7 feet	SAGENE.SAJEN(E)
	SAZHEN
—²/₃ mile	VERST
—2.7 acres	DESSIATINE
	DESSYATIN(E)
—quart	S(H)TOFF
—3 gallons	VEDRO
minister	COMMISSAR
mink	KOLINSKY
moderate	
—liberal	OCTOBRIST
—socialist	MENSHEVIK
mole-like amphibious mammal	
	DESMAN
mountains	URALS
Muscovite guard	STRELITZ
musical instruments	BALALAIKA

	DOMRA.GUSLA.GUSLE.GUSLI
news	
—agency	TASS
—paper	ISVESTIA.PRAVDA
oil fuel	ASTATKI
openness	GLASNOST
parliament	D(O)UMA
party executive and policy-	
making committee	
	POLITBUREAU.POLITBURO
peasant	M(O)UJIK.MUZHIK
—cloak	SARAFAN
plain	STEPPE
poem	BYLINA
polecat	KOLINKSY
poor soil	PODSOL.PODZOL
porter	DVORNIK
principality	MUSCOVY
Protestant	STUNDIST
provincial council	ZEMSTVO
race	COSSACK.SAMOYED(E)
reconstruction	PERESTROIKA
refusal	NIET.NYET
religious dissenter	RASKOLNIK
revolutionary	BOLSHEVIK
rich peasant	KULAK
river	DON.VOLGA
rural Soviet	VOLOST
rye beer	KVASS.QUASS
sable	SOBOL
sandpiper	TEREK
satellite	SPUTNIK
secret	
—police	GRU.KGB.OGPU
	(T)CHEKA
—printing	SAMIZDAT
sect of Christians	
	D(O)UKHOBORS
security service	GRU.KGB
sledge	KIBITKA
snow ridge on plains	SASTRUGA
	ZASTRUGA
soldier	STRELITZ
soup	BORSCH(T).BORTSCH(T)
spermophile	S(O)USLIK
spider	KARAKUT
spirit	VODKA
standing committee	
	PR(A)ESIDIUM

state		weight	ZOLOTNIK
—farm	SOVKHOZ	—1 lb	FUNT
—store	GUM	—36 lbs	POOD.PO(U)D
sturgeon	BELUGA	wheat meal	SASHA
system of raising production by		whip	KNOUT
rewarding efficiency		wild ass	K(O)ULAN
	STAKHANOVISM	wind storm	BURAN
tea urn	SAMOVAR	woman's cloak	SARAFAN
team of three horses	TROIKA	—workers' cooperative	
tomb	KURGAN	organisation	ARTEL
travelling companion	SPUTNIK	youth organisation	
triumvirate	TROIKA		COMSOMOL.KOMSOMOL
underground printing of banned		**rustic**	HIND.HOB
literature	SAMIZDAT	rustic accommodation	
vehicle	DROS(H)KY		HINDQUARTERS
	TARANTAS(S).TROIKA	rustic skill	HOBART
village headman	STAROSTA	**rutherford**	RD
wagon	AR(A)BA.KIBITKA	**Rwanda**	RWA
water nymph	RUSALKA		

S

as. Bach's works. *bend. bob.* bridge player. dollar. es. ess. God's. has. *hiss.*
his. is. largesse. Old Bob. paragon. part of collar. Sabbath. saint. Saturday.
Schmieder. second. seven. seventy. seventy thousand. shilling. side. siemens.
sigma. *sister. snow.* society. *son. soprano.* south. southern. spade. square.
stokes. sulphur. sun. Sweden. two hundred. two hundred thousand. us

Sabbath	S	•sailor *has* a bird	OSTEAL
sabotage plane	PANEL	•sailor is able. . .	OSCAN
sack race	GOTHS.JUTES	and	
	VANDALS.VIKINGS	•sailor-boy, *say*	SALTPETRE
sacred		•sailor, English Navy	SALTERN
flower	LOTUS	•sailor is not Labour	SALTATORY
fountain	ZEMZEM	and	
language	PALI	•sailor Brown	TARTAN
mountain	OMEI	•sailor's daughter	POP-EYED
person	SHAMAN	•sailor's double	TARTAR
river	ALPH	sailor's hat	BOATER
scriptures	SHRUTI	sailor's *return*⟨	RAT
snakes	NAGA	sailor-boy	SEASON
stone	BLACK STONE	sailors	CREW.NUS.RN.TARTAR
texts	AVESTA	**saint(s)**	S.ST.(SS.STS)
tree	BO.BODHI	hence	
verse	MANTRA	•saint can. . .	STABLE
word	OM	•saint getting old	STAGED
sadly spoke	POKES		STAGING
safe	PETER	•saint not in	STOUT
safe-blower	PETER PIPER	saintly	NOVICE
said	(*see* say)	**St Lucia**	WL
sail		**St Vincent**	WV
sailed	SLD	*salad of* green and. . .	ENDANGER
sailing	(on) SHIP	**salesman**	REP
•master *sailing*	HEADSHIP	**saloon body**	CARCASE
sailing	(on) SS	**salt**	
•scholar *sailing*	MASS	salt	AB
sailing along	LOGAN	hence	
sailor	AB.HAND.JACK.HEARTY	•salt mark	ABSTAIN
	MATELOT.MATLO(W)	•salt on road	ABROAD
	OS.SALT.TAR	•salt solution	ABSOLUTION
hence			(*see also* sailor)
•ordinary sailor	ABNORMAL	salt *in it*	incl AB or TAR
•sailor-boy	ABED.ABLEN	•M-el *puts* salt *in.* . .	MABEL
•sailors in the. . .	ABSINTHE	•street *has* salt *in it*	START
and		salt container	SEA.OCEAN
•sailor *has* a few. . .	HANDSOME	**Salvation Army**	SA
•sailor hits. . .	HANDCUFFS	**same**	
•sailor's drink	HAND-SALE	same	DO.ID.IDEM
and		hence	
•Henry the sailor	HALOS	•same entrance	DOGATE

•same little vessel	DOMINICAN	*said to be* you	EWE.YEW
•same money and	DOCENT	*said* we ten...	WHEATEN
		say no	KNOW
•dress the same	RIGID	say nothing	EGO
•same fish	IDLING	*say* Sir	NIGHT
•same island	IDIOM	*saying* aloud	ALLOWED
same place	IB	**scalene triangle**	ALONGSIDE
sanctimonious	PI	**Scandinavian**	SCAND
sanctimonious people	PILOT	ancient	NORSE
sanctimonious queen	PIER	frost giant	YMIR
sanctimonious scoundrel		hors d'oeuvres	SMORGASBORD
	PIROGUE	leader	S
sandalwood	SHOE TREE	magistrate	AMMAN.AMTMAN
Sandhurst	RMA	old coin	SKILLING
Sanskrit	SANS	parliament	THING
law	DHARMA	pirate	VIKING
leader	S	spirit	AKVAVIT.AQUAVIT
righteousness	DHARMA	toast	SKO(A)L
sacred text	PURANA		(*see also* Norse)
script	NAGARI	**Scarface**	AL
unrighteousness	ADHARMA	**Scarlatti's works**	K
sap	TRENCH	**scatter**	
sapper	RE	*scatter*brain	BAIRN.BRIAN
sat		*scattered* remains	MARINES
sat *out*	SA-T		SEMINAR
sat out	ATS.TAS	*scattered around* seaport	
Satan	(*see* devil)		ESPARTO
satellite	(*see* moon)	**scenes**	ACT
Saturday	S.SAT	**Schmieder**	S
sauce	CHEEK.LIP	**scholar**	BA.MA
sauce is hot	HOIST	hence	
savaged lambs	BALMS	•scholar and Marine	BARM
save		•scholar in charge	BASIC
save a...	omit A	•scholar's quickly...	BASSOON
save *	omit *	and	
•(k)night *saves* king	NIGHT	•scholar in court	MAIN-YARD
say[1]		•scholars deceive	MASCON
say	SPEAK.UTTER	•tidier *after* scholar...	
hence			MAN-EATER
•Bishop says	BUTTERS		(*see also* graduate)
•many say	MUTTER	**school**[1]	
•say *after* President...	PUTTER	school　ETON.GAM.SCH.STOWE	
said *in France*...	DIT	hence	
say *French*...	DIT	•British school	BRETON
says nothing	SAY-SO	•master in charge *around* school	
say[2]			METONIC
Persian, *say*	CAT	•school *returns*⟨	NOTE
cat, *say*	PERSIAN	and	
nose, *say*	KNOWS	•school book	GAMB

•school *has* scholar	GAMBA
	GAMMA
•school, see	GAMELY
and	
•nothing in British school	BORSCH
•school in America	SCHINUS
•school not in	SCHOUT

school²

school <u>horses</u>	SHORES
school member	FISH.PORPOISE
	WHALE
School Mathematics Project	SMP
school teachers	NUT
school transport	TRAIN
Schubert's works	D

science

science	-OLOGY
	(*see* study².write³)
science centre	LAB
science *centre*	E
science fiction	SCIFI.SF
science institution	RS
Science Research Council	SRC
scope, plenty of	A-Z

score

score	TWENTY.XX
score *fast*	PRESTO
score *slowly*	LENTO
scoreless draw	O-O
scorer	COMPOSER
Scot/Scotsman	HAMISH.IAN
	JOCK.MAC.MON
hence	
•equal with Scot	PARIAN
•South-western Scot	DEVONIAN
•well-mannered Scot	CIVILIAN
and	
•Scot in front	MACLED
•Scot with a firm...	MACACO
and	
•Scotsman looked...	MONEYED
•Scotsman that is dead	MONIED
•Scotsman's battle	MONS

Scott

words found in the writings of:

ace of trumps	TIB
arrogance	SURQUEDY
astute	ASTUCIOUS
backgammon	VERQUIRE

bad luck	WANION
bagpiping	SACK-DOUDLING
banknotes	SNUFF(-PAPER)
blood relative	SIBB
brandish	WAMPISH
brisket	BREASKIT
brown bread roll	SOUTER'S CLOD
byelawman	BIRLIEMAN
cajole	BEFLUM
club	TRUNNION
commotion	STEERY
coward	VILLAGIO
cross-grained	FRAMPAL
cudgel	SOUPLE
curse	WANION
cut out	SNECK
dash	VIRETOT
dilapidated house	
	HURLEY-HOUSE
dry branch	ROUGHIE
eldin	YEALDON
enchanter	REIM-KENNAR
endearment	YARTO
falcon	TERCEL-GENTLE
favouritism	PEATSHIP
fierce warrior	WAR-WOLF
fiery	FRAMPAL
fish roe	RAUN.RAWN
flighty	WEATHER-HEADED
flourish	WAMPISH
fool	BEFLUM
fortified site	KAME.KAIM
fuel	YEALDON
gad	VIRETOT
grandiloquent literary style	
	BOW-WOW
half guinea	SMELT
hawk's turn	CANCELEER
	CANCELIER
heart	YARTO
help in need	BEETMASTER
horn blast	PRYSE
hypochrondriac	PHRENESIAC
infantry regiment	TERTIA
inflamed by moon	MOON-RAISED
inform	WHISTLE
irascible	TOUSTIE
kinship	SIBB
knob	NOOP

law	LAUCH	tern	PICTARNIE
loop	LOUP	tip of elbow	NOOP
low collar	RABATINE	tithes	PARSONAGE
Lowlander	SASSENACH	trinket	TRANKUM
make a show	PROPALE	trouserless	BARE-BREACHED
moon	MACFARLANE'S BOAT	twist about	WELK
nick	SNECK	unchallengeable	SACLESS
not		underground prison	MASSYMORE
—damaged	UNBRIZZED	unguarded	LIPPEN
—to be harmed	SACLESS	unsaluted	UNHALSED
note of assault	WAR(R)ISON	vengeance	WANION
old card game	PENNEECH	vessels	VASSAIL.VESSAIL
	PENNEECK	wave about	WAMPISH
overbearing	OUTRECUIDANCE	wench	GOUGE
pardoner	QUAESTIONARY	wheelbarrow	MONOTROCH
pear	QUEEZ-MADDAM	worn out	OVERSCUTCHED
peaty	TURBINACIOUS	young gull	SCOURIE.SCOWRIE
pedlar	PEDDER-COFFE	**Scottish**	SCOT
peevish	FRAMPAL	some Scottish terms:	
pigment	PIMENT	a	ANE
pinnacle	PINNET	abandon	FORHOO(IE).FORHOW
plate	VASSAIL.VESSAIL	abandon proceedings	
private	SINGLE SOLDIER		DESERT THE DIET
probationer	STIBBLER	abate	FAIK
prophetess	VOLUSPA	ablaze	ALOW(E)
pursuit of rievers	HOT TROD	able	FERE
rabble	RASCAILLE	above	ABUNE
racked	RECKAN	absconding from the	
rascal	RASCAILLE	law	FUGITATION
rascally	HOUNDS-FOOT	absolve	ASSOILZIE
ransack	RANSHA(C)KLE	abundance	FOUTH.FOWTH
ricked	RECKAN	ROUTH.ROWTH.SONCE.SONSE	
riding hood	TROT-COSEY	STOUTH AND ROUTH	
	TROT-COZY	abundant	ROUTHIE.ROWTHIE
rush	VIRETOT	abuse	SNASH
scree	SCRAE	accumulation	HARL
search	RANSHA(C)KLE	accusation	THREAP.THREEP
sibyl	VOLUSPA	accused person(s)	PANEL
slash	SCORCH	accustom oneself	USE
snick	SNECK	acquisition	CONQUEST
snip	SNECK	acrobat	SPEELER
spiced wine	PIGMENT	across	YONT
stay as guest	GUESTEN	action to	
state official	BARON-OFFICER	—declare false or	
steal	CONDIDDLE.MAG	forged	IMPROBATION
stick	TRUNNION	—prove bias	REPROBATOR
sulky	GUMPLE-FOISTED	active BIRKIE.YA(U)LD.YANKING	
sun-dried	TILED	—fellow	SWANK(E)Y
talon	TALENT	addition	EIK

adept	DEACON	amiable	COUTHIE
adjust	SORT	ample	WAL(L)Y
advancing	ONCOMING	amuse	PLAY
adze	EATCHE	amusing	
affair	EFFEIR.EFFERE	—person or thing	DIVERT
affected person		—story	BA(U)R.BAWR
	PRICK-ME-DAINTY	an	ANE
afflicted	WAESOME	ancestor	FOR(E)BEAR
afoot	AGAIT	ancient	AULD-WARLD
afraid	FEARED.RAD	—castle	BROCH.BR(O)UGH
afternoon refreshment		—race	PICTS
	FOUR-HOURS	ankle	COOT.CUIT.CUTE.QUEET
afterwards	SYNE	annat	ANN
against	ANENT	annoy(ance)	FASH
aggressively direct	RANDIE	annual fee under feu	FEU-DUTY
	RANDY	annul	REDUCE
agile	SWANK	any	ARY
agitation	CARFUFFLE.CERFUFFLE	anything	
	KEFUFFLE	—beaked	KIP(P)
—of water	JABBLE	—built	BIGGIN
ago	SYNE	—eaten as relish	KITCHEN
agree	GREE.SORT	—frightful	WIRRICOW
agreement	AYE		WORRICOW.WORRYCOW
ague	EXIES	—small	PINK
aim	ETTLE.MINT	—stunted	SCRUNT
	VISIE.VIZY.VIZZIE	apiece	THE PIECE
air	LIFT	apology	OFFCOME
ajar	AGEE.AJEE.JEE	apothecary	POTTINGAR
akin	SIB	apparatus	GRAITH
alarm	GLIFF.GLIFT	apparition	TAIS(C)H
alas	EWHOW.WAESUCKS.WALY	appeal	RECLAIM
alderman	BAIL(L)IE	appear	CAST UP
ale	YILL	—above ground	BRAIRD.BREER
—brewing	BUMMOCK	—and disappear	COOK.KOOK
—house	CHANGE-HOUSE	—ignorant	MISKEN
alert	GLEG	—in court	COMPEAR
alive	TO THE FORE	appearance	EFFEIR.EFFERE.SHAW
alley	VENNEL	appendage	POFFLE
allodial	UDAL	appetising	GUSTY
allowance of meal to mill		applaud/applause	RUFF
servants	SEQUEL	appointed deputy	DEPUTE
alms	ALMOUS.AWMOUS	apprentice	SERVITOR
alone	HIMSELF.HIS LANE	approach(ing)	ONCOMING
	MY LANE	April Fool	GOUK.GOWK
along	ENDLANG	apt	GLEG
aloof	ABEIGH.SKEIGH	arbiter	BYRLAWMAN.ODDSMAN
also	ALS	arch	COOM
alternately	TIME ABOUT	area of operation	SUCKEN
amber	LAMMER	armpit	OXTER

argue snappishly	NYAFF
arranged	RED(D)ED
array	EFFEIR.EFFERE
arts student	MAGISTRAND
as soon as	WHENE(V)ER
ascent	UPGANG
ash bucket	BACKET
ashes	AIZLE.EASLE
ask	SPEER.SPEIR
askew	AGLEE.AGLEY.SKIVIE
aslant	ASKLENT
aspire	ETTLE.MINT
assault	STOUND.STOWND
—in own house	HAMESUCKEN
assertion	THREAP.THREEP
assess	MODIFY
assess(ment)	STENT
assistant	SERVITOR
assuage	MEASE
assume	HECHT
assuming	UPSETTING
astir	AGAIT
astray	WILL.WULL
astride	STRIDE-LEGS
	STRIDE-LEGGED
at	
—a loss	WILL.WULL
—all	AVA.OUGHTLINGS
—present	PRESENTLY
—the manor	UPBY(E)
—times	WHILES
attack	ONFALL
attempt	MINT
attend to	SORT.TENT
attercop	ETHERCAP.ETTERCAP
auction	ROUP
avail	DOW
availed	DOCHT.DOUGHT
avaricious	GRIPPY
awake	WAKEN
award	MODIFY
away	AWA
awkward	BLATE
—person	BUCKIE
awl	BROG.ELS(H)IN.STOB
awnless	HUMBLE.HUMMEL
awry	AGLEE.AGLEY
back	
—of knee-joint	HOUGH

—of shoulder	BACK-SPAUL(D)
—passage of building	DUNNY
backward and	
forward	BUT AND BEN
bad luck	WANION
bag	POCK
—pudding	POCK-PUDDING
bagged	BAGGIT
bagpipe music	PIBROCH
bail	CAUTION
bailiff	FOUD
—'s jurisdiction	FOUDRIE
baker's grater	RISP
balk	HEN
ball	BA
ballad	BALLA(N)T.BALLET
bamboozle	BUMBAZE
bank	BINK.SUNK
bankrupt(cy)	DYVOUR(Y)
bankruptcy	SEQUESTRATION
—process	CESSIO BONORUM
banter	TROCK.TROKE
bar	RANCE.SPAR
—in chimney	RANDLE-TREE
RANDLE-BALK.RANDLE-PERCH	
RANNEL-TREE.RANNLE-TREE	
	RANTLE-TREE
—of grate	RIB
barefoot Highlander	
	GILLIE-WHITE-FOOT
	GILLIE-WET-FOOT
bargain	WANWORTH
barge	GABBARD.GABBART
bark like a dog	YAFF
barley	BERE.BIGG
barrel projection	LAGGEN
	LAGGIN
barren	HI(R)STIE.YELD
barrister	ADVOCATE
barter	COUP.NIFFER
	TROCK.TROKE
basement	DUNNY
bashful	BLATE
basket	MURLA(I)N.MURLIN
bathe	DOOK
baulk	REEST.REIST
bawdy talk	SCULDUDD(E)RY
	SKULDUDDERY
bay	VOE

be	
—able	CAN.DOW
—active or excited	STEER
—frightened	FLAY.FLEY
—gaudy	SKYRE
—half asleep	DOVE
—hanged	STRING
	WALLOP IN A TOW
	WALLOP IN A TETHER
—ignorant	MISKEN
—in training	BREED
—lost	TINE.TYNE
—out of bed	STEER
—perverse	THRAW
—quiet!	WHEESHT
—restive	FLISK
—smoke-dried	REAST.REEST
	REIST
—stupefied	DOVE
—submissive	SNOOL
—undecided	SWITHER
—vexed	FASHED
beacon-fire	BALE-FIRE
beam	TREST
beam of scales	WEIGH-BANK
bear	BERE.BIGG.DREE
beat	DUNT.FIRK.LOUNDER
	PHEASE.TOUK
beating	LOUNDERING.PAIK
—the bounds	COMMON RIDING
beautiful	WALY
become	SET
bed	
—of mussels	MUSSEL-SCAUP
—valance	PAND
bedaub	SLAISTER
bedraggle	TRAUCHLE
bee's hive	BINK
beetle	CLOCK
befit	SET
befool	BEGUNK
before bedtime	FORENIGHT
beg	FLEECH.THIG
beggar('s pouch)	GABERLUNZIE
begged	THIGGIT
begging	FLEECHING
	FLEECHMENT
—for eggs	PACE-EGGING
begin to move	STEER

behave riotously	GIL(L)RAVAGE
GIL(L)RAVITCH.GALRAVAGE	
	GALRAVITCH
behaviour	HAVING
behind	AHIND.AHINT
being facile	FACILITY
bell rope	TOW
bellow	BULLER
belly	KITE.KYTE.WAME
beloved one	JO(E)
bench	BINK
beneath	ANEATH
benefit society	MENAGE
bent double	TWAFALD
bequeath to charity	MORTIFY
bequest	MORTIFICATION
beside	ASIDE
besides	BY.FORBY
besom	COW.KOW
bespatter	JAUP
best	WALE
bewildered	MOIDERT.WILL.WULL
bewitch	FOR(E)SPEAK
beyond	AYONT.OUTWITH
—the bounds of	FURTH OF
bid	BODE
big knife	GULL(E)Y
bilberry	BLAEBERRY
birch	BIRK
biscuit	BAKE
bishop	PRIMUS
biting	TOOTHY
bittern	BULL-OF-THE-BOG
	MOSSBLUITER
black	
—clothes	BLACKS
—eye	KEEKER
blackberry	BRAMBLE
blackheaded gull	PICKMAW
blackish	BLAE
blacksmith	BURN-THE-WIND
blame	WITE.WYTE
blast	SCAITH.SKAITH.WAP
blaze	LOW(E).LUNT
bleak	BLAE
blemish	TASH
blight	SCOUTHER.SCOWDER
block	DIT
block of tenements	LAND

blockhead	BAMPOT.TUMPHY	—of chastity	SCULDUDD(E)RY
blood	BLUDE.BLUID		SKULDUDDERY
bloody nose	JEELY NOSE	bread	LOAF
blow	CLA(U)TLOUNDER.PAIK	breakfast	DISJUNE
	STRAIK.WHAMPLE.YANK	—roll	BAP
—on the head	CRUNT	breeches	BREEKS
—received in trying to		brewing	BROWST
stop fight	REDDIN(G) STRAIK	bridesmaid	BESTMAID
blue	BLAE	bridge	BRIG
—gown	GABERLUNZIE	—centring	COOM
bluebell	HAREBELL	bridle	BRANKS
board	BROD	brigand	CATERAN
bob	HOD	brimming	REAMING
bobbin	PIRN	bringing misery	WAESOME
bodice	JIRKINET	brisk	CANT
body	BOUK.BUIK.BUKE	bristle	BIRSE
—of vassals	MANRENT	bristly	BIRSY
bog	MOSS	brittle	BRICKLE.BRUCKLE.FRUSH
boggy		broad	BRAID
—place	SLACK	—valley	STRATH
—stream	LATCH	broil	BRU(I)LZIE.STRAMASH
boisterous	GOUSTROUS	broken branch	SCROG
—young person	GILP(E)Y	brood	CLOCK.CLECKING
boldly	CROUSE	—of children	BAIRN-TEAM
booth	CRAME		BAIRN-TIME
booty	CREACH.CREAGH	brooding hen	CLOCKER
border	ROON	brook	BURN
borough	BROGH.BURGH	—lime	WATER-PURPIE
botch	CLATCH	brother	BILLIE.BILLY
—up	CLAMPER	—in-law	GUDE-BROTHER
bother	FASH	brow	BROO
bought	COFT	browse	MOOP
bounce	STOT(TER)	brushwood	HAG(G)
bound	SCOUP.SCOWP	budge	JEE
	SPANG.STEN(D)	buffet	YANK
—along	SKELP	build	BIG
boundary	MEITH	building site	STANCE
—mark	DOOL	bulk	BOUK.BUIK.BUKE
—stone	HARE-STANE	bumblebee	BUMBEE
bow	JOUK	bump	CLOUR.DUNCH.DUNSH
box	BUIST	bun	COOKIE
boy	LOON(IE)	bunch of twigs	COW.KOW
brains	HARNS	bundle	DORLACH
brand	BUIST	bung	DOOK
—new	SPLIT-NEW	bungle	BAUCHLE.BLUNK
brat	GYTE		MIS(H)GUGGLE
brawl	FLITE.FLYTE	burial fee	GR(O)UND MAIL
	TUILYE.TUILZIE	burly	BUIRDLY
breach	SLAP	burn	SCOUTHER.SCOWDER

burrow	HOWE.HOWK
burst	LOUPEN.LOUPIT.LOWP
—of temper	FUFF
bushy place	SCROG
busy	EIDENT
butt	DUNCH.DUNSH
buttermilk and water	BLAND
buttocks	DOUP.FUD.HINDER-END
	HINDERLAN(D)S.HURDIES
buxom	GAUCY.GAWSY.SONCIE
	SONCY.SONSIE.SONSY
buy	COFF
by	
—my faith	HAITH
—stealth	STOW(N)LINS
—the time of	GIN
cabbage	KALE.KAIL
—broth	KALE.KAIL
—patch	PLANTIE-CRUIVE
—seller	KAILWIFE
—stock	CASTOCK.CUSTOCK
cackle	KECKLE
cajole	CUITTLE
cake	BUTTER-BAKE.FARL(E)
	FARTHEL
—(Shrove Tuesday)	CARCAKE
call	CA
—slanderously	MISCA(LL)
—to cows	PROO.PRUH
—to horse	HIE.HIGH
calm	LOUN(D).LOWN(D)
cannot	CANNA
—be interested	DOWNA
cap	KILMARNOCK
—Highland Regiment	
	HUMMEL BONNET
capacity	BIND
caper	SCOUP.SCOWP
—about	FLISK
capital	AULD REEKIE
	EDINBURGH.S
caraway	CARVY
card	FLAUGHT
care	K(I)AUGH.SUSSY
careful look	VISIE.VIZY.VIZZIE
carefully	HOOLY
careless	UNTENTY
carouse	BIRL(E)
carriage	HURLY-HACKET

carrion	KET
—crow	HOODIE
case law	PRACTIC
casual	ORRA
casual(ly)	OVERLY
cat	BAUDRONS
catch	CLAUGHT.KEP.TACK
—fish with seine net	TRAWL
catchword	O'ERWORD
catechism	CARRITCH
catgut	THAIRM
cattle	BESTIAL.KY(E).KYLOES
	NOUT.NOWT
—disease	MOOR-ILL
—farm	STORE-FARM
—lifting	SPREAGHERY
	SPRECHERY
—theft	HERSHIP
caught	KEPPIT
cause to	
—bounce	STOT(TER)
—flee	FLAY.FLEY
cause(d)	GAR(T)
cease	DEVALL
Celt	GADHEL
certain	SICCAR.SICKER
certainly	CERTES.CERTIE.CERTY
cesspool	JAWHOLE
chaffinch	SNABBY
chairman	PR(A)ESES
challenge	HEN(NER)
change one's	
—abode	FLIT
—mind	TAKE THE RUE
charge	DITTAY
charlock	RUNCH
charm	WEIRD
chat	CRACK
chatter	CHITTER.CLASH
	GABNASH.NASHGAB.YATTER
cheat	JINK
cheerful	CANT(Y)
cheerfully	
—complacent	JOCO
—confident	CROUSE
cheese	CABOC.KEBBOCK
	KEBBUCK
chemise	SARK
chest	BUNK.KIST

—for storing oatmeal	MEAL ARK	cleft	CLOFF
chide	QUARREL	—between hills	SLACK
chief		—in rock	RIVA
—herald	(LORD) LYON	clerical office	DIET
—city councillor	LORD PROVOST	clever	GLEG.SOUPLE
—'s galley	BIRLINN	cleverness	CLEVERALITY
—'s heir elect	TANIST	cliff	CRAIG
—town councillor	PROVOST	climb	SCLIM.SKLIM.SPEEL
child	BAIRN.CHIEL(D)	climbing-iron	SPEELER
	GAIT.GEITA.GYTE	clock	KNOCK
	LITTLEANE.LITTLIN.SMOUT	clockwise	DEASIL
	SMOWT.WEAN	clods	MOOLS.MOULS
—beginning to walk	GANGREL	clog	CLAG
—'s garment	POLONAISE	close	
children's		—fitting garment	JEISTIECOR
—entitlement	BAIRN'S-PART	—look	VISIE.VIZY.VIZZIE
	LEGITIM	closed	LUCKEN
—game	NIEVIE-NICK-NACK	clot	LAPPER
chill	OORIE.OURIE.OWRIE	—of dirt or colour	SPLATCH
chilling	CAULD-RIFE	clothes	CLAES.TROGGS
chimney	LUM	—horse	SCREEN
—cap	OLD WIFE	cloud drift	CARRY
—corner	LUG	cloven hoof	CLOOT
—top	LUM(-HEAD)	club moss	BURR
chip	SPALE	cluck	CLOCK
choice	WALE	clumsy	
choke	WORRY	—girl	TAUPIE.TAWPIE
choose/choosing	WALE	—person	BAUCHLE
chore	TROCK.TROKE	clutch	CLAUCHT.CLAUGHT
church	KIRK		GLAUM
—court	KIRK SESSION	coal	
—government system		—bin	BUNK
	PRESBYTERIANISM	—bucket	BACKET
—of Scotland	AULD KIRK	coalfish	SAITH(E).SILLOCK
—officer	BEADLE.BED(E)RAL		STENLOCK
—yard	KIRKYA(I)RD	coaly fireclay	TUMPHY
churl	BODACH	coarse	RUDAS
cibol	SYBOE.SYBO(W)	—cloth	KELT
cite	SIST	—file	RISP
city tough	KEELIE	—grained	CURN(E)Y
claim	CRAVE	coax	CUITTLE.FLEECH
clamber	SPRAICKLE.SPRAUCHLE	coaxing	FLEECHING
clasp-knife	JOCKTELEG		FLEECHMENT
clatter	HOTTER	cobbler	SOUTAR.SOUTER
clause in charter specifying			SOWTER
vassal's service	REDDENDO	cock	
claw	CLA(U)T	—crow	SKREIGH OF DAY
clear up	RED(D)	cocker	CUITER
cleavage	SLOT	codfish	KEELING

coffin	KIST
coiffure	COCKERNONY
coil	FANK
coins	
—small copper (old)	PLACK
—farthing (old)	BODDLE.TURNER
—halfpenny	BAUBEE.BAWBEE
—3d bit (old)	BAUBEE.BAWBEE
—2p (old)	QUADRUPLE
—13/4d	MERK
—18/-	UNICORN
—£1	PISTOLE
—74/-	LION
—£12 (old)	PISTOLE
—eighth of mark	URE
—gold (old)	BONNET-PIECE
—silver (old)	SWORD-DOLLAR
cold	FRAIM.FREMD.FREMIT
	WEED.WEID
colic	BATTS
collarbone	HAUSE-BANE
collect	UPLIFT
collection	
—of little objects	SMYT(E)RIE
—plate	BROD
colt	STAIG
comb	KAME.KAIM.RED(D)
come	
—across	MEET IN WI(TH)
—to light	SPUNK OUT
comely	SONSIE.SONSY
comfortable	BEIN.BIEN.CANNY
	COUTHIE.TOSH
—looking	SONSIE.SONSY
coming on	ONCOME
common sense	RUMGUMPTION
	RUM(M)EL-GUMPTION
	RUM(M)LE-GUMPTION
	RUMBLE-GUMPTION
commotion	CARFUFFLE
	CURFUFFLE.HOTTER
	KEFUFFLE.TIRRIVEE
	TIRRIVIE
communion service	OCCASION
companion-in-arms	BILLIE.BILLY
compel	GAR
compel(led)	GAR(T)
complain whingingly	GIRN
	WHEENGE.WHINGE

complete	
—set	STAND
—sum	SOLIDUM
completely	STOOP AND ROOP
comply with	OBTEMPER
concerning	
—fate	WEIRD
—some matter	THEREANENT
concurrence	CONCOURSE
condition	FID.PLISKIE.PLY
conduct	WEAR
conductor of festival	SCUDDALER
	SCUDLER.SKUDLER
confidential	PACK
confound	BUMBAZE
confuse	MOIDER
confused	
—broil	BRU(I)LZIE
—jumble	MIXTER-MAXTER
	MIXTIE-MAXTIE
	MIX(T)Y-MAX(T)Y
confute	REDARGUE
connecting ridge	HAUSE.HAWSE
connivance with partner at	
adultery	LENOCINIUM
considerable	GAY.GEY
—number	HANTLE
considerably	GAY.GEY
contemptible man	SMAIK
contend with	PINGLE
contention	STURT
continue to wait	WAIT ON
contradict	THREAP.THREEP
contrary to normal	
course	WID(D)ERSHINS
	WITHERSHINS
conundrum	GUESS
cool	CALLER
cormorant	SCART(H).SKART(H)
corn	OATS
—dolly	KIRN-BABY.KIRN-DOLLIE
—maiden	MAIDEN
corpse	LIKE
cosy	COSH
cottage	BOTHIE.BOTHY
—room	END
cottager	MAILER
cottars	COT-FOLK
—house	COT-HOUSE

cotton grass	CANNA(CH)
	MOSS-CROP
cough convulsively	KINK
counter for casting lots	CAVEL
country	
—dance	PETRONELLA
—lass	JENNY
—talk	CLASH
court	
—judgement	DECREET
—official	DEMPSTER.DOOMSTER
—sitting	SEDERUNT
—woman	WINCH
Covenanter	WHIGGAMORE
Covenanters	HILLFOLK.HILLMEN
cover	
—by drifting (snow)	WREATH
—of pot	PAT-LID
cow	
—dung	SHA(I)RN
—house	BYRE
—man	BYREMAN.NOWT-HERD
—fattened for slaughter	MART
—'s yield	MELTITH
coward	FUGIE
cower down	CROODLE
cows	KY(E).NOUT.NOWT
coy	SKEIGH
crab	PARTAN
—apple	SCROG
crafty	LOOPY
—person	SNECK-DRAWER
—twist	W(H)IMPLE
crag	HEUCH.HEUGH
cram	CRAP.PANG.STAP
crammed	PANG
crane fly	JENNY-LONG-LEGS
cranky	FIFISH
crash	FRUSH
cravat	OVERLAY
crazy	DOILED.DOILT.DOTTLE(D)
	GYTE.WOWF
cream	REAM
crease	LIRK
creature	CRATUR
credit	MENSE
creek	GEO.GIO.VOE
creep (of the flesh)	GREW.GRUE
crested	TAPPIT

criminal purpose	DOLE
cringe	SNOOL
cripple	LAMETER.LAMITER
crisp	CRUMP
crooked	CAMSHO(CH)
	CAMSHEUGH.THRAWARD
	THRAWART
crop	CRAP.STOW
cross	THRAW
—examine	TARGE
—grained	ILL-HAIRED.THRAWN
—question	BACKSPEER
	BACKSPEIR
crow steps	CORBIE-STEPS
crowd of children	SMYRTIE
crowded	PANG
crown of head of person or	
animal	CANTLE
crumb	NIRL
crumble	MURL
crupper	CURPEL
crush	CHACK.CHECK
cry	GLEET.GOWL.SPRAICH
cuckoo	GOUK.GOWK
cudgel	KEBBIE
cuff	GOWF
cunning mischief	PAWK
cup	QUAICH.QUAIGH.TASSIE
cur	MESSAN
curdle	LAPPER
—(of blood)	GREW.GRUE
curdled milk	LAPPER(ED)-MILK
cure with smoke	REAST.REEST
	REIST
curlew	(GREAT)WHAUP
curse	WEARY.WINZE
—of Scotland	
	QUEEN OF DIAMONDS
curtailed	CUTTY
cushion	COD
cut	
—and dry peat	CAST
—on something	INSCULP
—turf	FLAUGHTER
cutter on plough	CO(U)LTER
cutting of last sheaf	KERN.KIRN
dabble hands or feet	
in liquid	PLOTTER
	PLOUTER.PLOWTER

dagger	DIRK.SKEAN.SKENE
	WHINGER.WHINIARD
	WHINYARD
dainty	GENTY.SUNKET
dally	PINGLE
dam	STANK
—in stream	CAULD
damage	SCAITH.SKAITH
damson	PLUMDAMAS
dance	BOB.HIGHLAND FLING
	LOWP.PETRONELLA.REEL
	STRATHSPEY
—tune	SPRING
dandle	DOODLE
dangerous	MISCHANCY
	NO'CANNY.UNCHANCY
	WANCHANCIE
	WANCHANCY
dapple-grey	LIART.LYART
dare	DAUR
dash	JABBLE.SPANG
—of pen	SCART
daub	CLATCH.SLAKE
daunt	DANTON
daybreak	SKREIGH OF DAY
day's work	DARG
days of New Year	
festivity	DAFT DAYS
dazzling	GLAIK
dead	DEED.DEID
deafen	DEAVE
dealer	COUPER
dealings	TROCK.TROKE
dean's warrant	JEDGE
death	DEID
—throe	DEID-THRAW
deceive	MISLIPPEN
decent	WISE-LIKE
decisive point	UPCOME
deck out	DAIKER
declare	
—heir	SERVE
—to be a simpleton	COGNOSCE
decline in health	TRAIK
decorous	MENSEFUL
decree	DECERN.MODIFY
deed of qualification	BACK BOND
deep	
—draught	WILLIEWAUGHT

—sea fishing ground	HAAF
defamation	SLANDER
defeat	WA(U)RST
defile	FILE.HAUSE.HAWSE
deformed	ILL-FAURD
delay	SIST
delicate	DORTY
dell	DARGLE.HOWE
demure	MIM(-MOU'D).PRIMSIE
departing	WAY-GOING
depend	LIPPEN
dependent interest	
	RIDING-INTEREST
deplorable	WAESOME
deprive	TWIN(E)
deranged	SKIVIE
derisive gesture	GECK
derived	EXTRACT
desert	FORHOO(IE).FORHOW
desolate	GOUSTY
despicable person	FOOTRA
	FOUTRA
destine	WEIRD
devastated site	WASTAGE
Development	
—Agency	SDA
—Department	SDD
device for winding yarn	WINNLE
devil	AULD MIS(C)HANTER
	CLOOT(IE).CLOOTS.DEIL
	HORNIE.NICKIE-BEN
	(OLD) SCRATCH.WIRRICOW
	WORRICOW.WORRYCOW
devour greedily	WORRY
dib-stones	CHUCKIE STANES
	CHUCKS
die	DEE
died	DEED
difference	DIFFER
dig	HOWK
diligent	EIDENT
din	REEL.STOUND.STOWND
dingy	OORIE.OURIE.OWRIE
dinner	KALE.KAIL
dip and scald in hot water	PLOT
direction	AIRT
dirge	CORANACH.CORONACH
dirt	GUTTERS
disappoint	MISLIPPEN

disarray	TASH	door	YETT
disaster	MIS(C)HANTER	—catch	SNECK
disciplinarian in University		—knocker	RISP
HEBDOMADAR.HEBDOMADER		dotard	DOTTLE
disease with no obvious cause		double	
	INCOME	—feu-duty	DUPLICAND
disentangle	RED(D)	—handful	GOWPEN
disfigure	BLA(U)D.TASH	dove	DOO
disgust	SCOMFISH.SCUNNER	—cote	DOOCOT.DOOKET
dish	ASHET.BRO(U)GH.HAGGIS	dower	TOCHER
HOWTOWDIE.(PEASE-)BROSE		down	
dismal	DOWIE	—and out	FORFAIRN
dismiss	SHANK	—at-heel	SHAUCHLE
disorder	CARFUFFLE.CURFUFFLE	dowry	TOCHER
	KEFUFFLE	doze	DOVER
disperse	SCALE.SCAIL.SKAIL	drag	
dispirited	SACKLESS	—along ground	HARL
displacement	JEE	—oneself	HARL
dispute	THREAP.THREEP	draggle	TRACHLE.TROLLOP
disputed	THREAPIT.THREEPIT	drain	POUR.SHEUCH.SHEUGH
distort	THRAW		SIVER.SYVER
distorted	THRAWN	draining board	BUNK
distrain	POIND	dram	TIFT
distraint	POINDER.POINDING	drank	DRUCKEN
distress	PUT ABOUT	draught	WAUCHT.WAUGHT
distressed	ILL	—board	DAMBOARD.DAMBROD
district bonded to mill	SUCKEN	—man	DAM
distrust	MISLIPPEN	draw money	UPLIFT
disturb	JEE.STEER	dreary	DREICH.GOUSTY
disturbance	COLLIESHANGIE		OORIE.OURIE.OWRIE
STRAMASH.STURT		drench	DROOK.DROUK
disturbed	MISTRYSTED	drenched	DROOKIT.DROUKIT
ditch	SHEUCH.SHEUGH	dress	BOUN.GRAITH
	SIKE.STANK	—neatly	DINK
divination	TAGHAIRM	dresser	AUMRIE.AWMRY
divine	SPAE	dried	
diviner	SPAER.SPAEMAN	—heath	ROUGHIE
	SPAEWIFE	—meat	VIFDA.VIVDA
division of county	WARD	drink	HEATHER ALE.TIFT
dizziness	MIRLIGOES	—in large draughts	WAUCHT
do	DIV		WAUGHT
document exhibited in		drinking	
court	PRODUCTION	—bout	BEND
dodge	JINK.JOUK	—cup	QUAICH.QUAIGH
doggerel	RAT-RHYME	drive	CA
dolphin	CA(A)ING-WHALE	driver of ploughing	
dominate	O'ERGANG	horses	GADSMAN
donkey	CUDDIE.CUDDY	drizzle	SCOUTHER.SCOWDER
doom	WEIRD		SMIR(R).SMUR

drizzling mist	DROW
drooping	OORIE.OURIE.OWRIE
drub(bing)	PAIK
drudge	SCOGIE
drudgery	SLAISTERY
drunk	FOU.STOTIOUS
drunkard	SAND-BED
drunken	FOU.WAT
drunken(ness)	DRUCKEN(NESS)
dry	EILD.HI(R)STIE
	REEST.REIST
—in the sun	RIZZAR.RIZZER
	RIZZOR
—in the wind	WIN
—with smoke	REAST.REEST
	REIST
dryly witty	PAWKY
drystone wall	DRYSTANE DIKE
—waller	COWAN
duck	JOOK.JOUK
dull	DOWF.DOWIE
—witted	DONNERD.DONNERED
	DONNERT.FOZY
dunce	SUMPH
dunderhead	GOMERAL.GOMERIL
dung-fork	GRAIP
dust	STOOR.STOUR.STOWRE
dusty	STOURY
dwarf	DROICH
dwell	STAY
each	ILK(A)
—other	OTHER
eager	FRACK.FRECK
ear of corn	ICKER
Earl Marshal	EARL MARISCHAL
early dram	MORNING
earnest	ARLES.ARLE(S) PENNY
earth	(Y)EARD.YERD.YIRD
—house	PICTS' HOUSE
—hunger	(Y)EARD)-HUNGER
YERD-HUNGER.YIRD-HUNGER	
earthenware	PIG
Easter egg	PACE EGG
easterly	EASSEL(GATE)
	EASSIL(GATE)
	EASTLIN(G)
eastwards	EASSEL.EASSIL
eat with	
—a spoon	SUP

—feeble appetite	PINGLE
eatables	VIVERS.VIVRES
eccentric	SHKITE.SKTE
ecclesiastical office	DIET
ecstasy	EXIES
edible	
—crab	PARTAN
—seaweed	BADDERLOCK
Education	
—Certificate	SCE
—Department	SED
Educational Institute	EIS
effeminate man	JENNY.JESSIE
efficacy	FECK
eke	ECHE.EIK
elder	PRESBYTER
elderly woman	LUCKIE.LUCKY
elder tree	BOUNTREE.BOURTREE
elegant	JIMP(Y).JINTY
elude	JINK
emaciated	WANTHRIVEN
emblem	THISTLE
embrace	HAUSE.HAWSE
emerge	CAST UP
empty	BOSS.GOUSTY.TOOM
enclosure	HAINING
ends of ribbon	FATTERELS
endearment	BURD(IE).LEEZE ME
endure	DREE.THOLE.WEAR
English	SOUTHRO(U)N
—man	POCK-PUDDING
	SASSENACH
enough	ENOW.SAIRING
entail	TAILLIE.TAILYE.TAILZIE
entangle	FANKLE.TAIGLE
entreat	PRIG
equipment	GRAITH
escapade	SPLORE
established church of	
Scotland	AULD KIRK
estranged	FRAIM.FREMD.FREMIT
Evangelical	HIGH-FLIER
	HIGH-FLYER
even if	SUPPOSE
evening	FORENIGHT
—party	ROCKING
everything	HALE HYPOTHEC
ewe	YOW(E)
—after lambing	KEB

examine	COGNOSCE
exclamation	TOOTS.TUTS
excavation	HEUCH.HEUGH
excel	WA(U)RST
excellent	WAL(L)Y.GEY
excessive	NIMIOUS
exchange	EXCAMB.NIFFER
	SCORSE.TROCK.TROKE
—of goods	TROCK.TROKE
—of lands	ESCAMBIUM
	EXCAMBION
excuse	FAIK
exempt	EXEEM.EXEME
exert oneself	PINGLE
exhausted	FORFAIRN
	FORFEUCHEN.FORFOUGHEN
—from travelling	WAYGONE
expect	LIPPEN
expenses for arresting	
criminals	ROGUE MONEY
experience sudden	
emotion	STOUND.STOWND
experienced	USED
expert	SKEELY.SKILLY.USED
expiry	ISH
explain significance of	
communion	FENCE THE TABLES
extinguish	SLO(C)KEN
extract	HOWK
extraordinary	BY-ORDINAR
	BYOUS
eye	EE.KEEKER
—brow	BREE
eyes	EEN.EYNE
face	GIZZ
fail	MISGIVE
—in health	DWALM.DWAUM
—to keep appointment	MISTRYST
—to recognise	MISKEN
faint	DWAMY.SWERVE
fairly	GAY.GEY
faithful	AEFA(U)LD.AFA(W)LD
fall	FA
—of snow	STORM
familiar situation	HEICH-HOW
famous	NAMELY
fantastic	
—elaboration	WHIGMALEERIE
	WHIGMALERY

—ornament	CURLIEWURLIE
farm	
—cottage	BOTHIE.BOTHY
—in joint tenancy	TOWNSHIP
—overseer	GRIEVE
—small	CROFT
—song	CORN-KISTER
—stead	FARM-TOUN.ONSTEAD
	TOWN
—worker	HIND
fasten	STEEK
fastened	SNECKED
fat	FOZY
fate	WEIRD
fated to die	FAY.FEY.FIE
father-in-law	GUDE FATHER
faulty condition	VICIOSITY
	VITIOSITY
favoured	FA'ARD.FAURD
fearless	RAUCLE
fearsome	UNCO
feathered legs	COOTIE
feeble	FIZZENLESS
	FUSHIONLESS.SACKLESS
	SHILPIT.SOBER.WERSH
—person or animal	WALLYDRAG
	WALLYDRAIGLE
feed with corn	CORN
female	
—auctioneer	ROUPING-WIFE
—fish	RAUN.RAWN
—outworker	BONDAGER
ferrule	VIRL
feudal service	ARRIAGE
few	WHEEN
fibre	TAIT.TATE
fiddle	GJO.GJU.GU(E)
	GOU.ITCH
fidget	FIDGE.FIKE.FYKE
field	PAIRK
fierce	WUD
fiery person	SPUNKIE
fight	TUILYE.TUILZIE.WAP
—in heat of the moment	
	CHAUD-MELLE
fight(er)	FECHT(ER)
filled full	PANGFU(LL)
find by skill	EXPISCATE
fine	GRASSUM.UNLAW

—misty rain SMIR(R).SMUR
finely dressed BRAW
finger hole of wind
  instrument LILL
finical PERJINK(ETY).PREJINK
fire screen HALLAN
fireside debate KILFUD-YOKING
firm SICCAR.SICKER.STEEVE
  STIEVE
—place in bog HAG(G)
first
—attendance of councillor after
  election KIRKIN(G)
—church attendance
  after marriage KIRKIN(G)
—furrow FEERING
—shoots of crop BRAIRD.BREER
fish
—roe RAUN.RAWN
—spawn REDD
—trap CRU(I)VE
—with the hands GUDDLE.GUMP
fit
—of hysterics EXIES
—of passion TIRRIVEE.TIRRIVIE
—of stubbornness REEST.REIST
—of sullenness TOUT.TOWT
—time FID
fitting WISE-LIKE
flagstones PLAINSTANES
flake FLAUGHT
flame LOW(E)
flannel underwear WYLIE-COAT
flap FLACK.FLAFF(ER).WAP
—about WALLOP
flapping FLAUGHT
—rag WALLOP
flash FLAUGHT.GLAIK
flat
—bonnet BALMORAL
—fish CRAIGFLUKE
—moist land FLOW
flatter FLEECH.PHRASE
flattering FLEECHING
  FLEECHMENT
flaunt SKYRE
flax seed LINT SEED
fled LOUPEN.LOUPIT
flee LOWP

fleece KET.PLOT
flicker FLAUGHTER
flight FLAUGHT
flighty HELLICAT
  LOUP-THE-DYKE
flock of sheep HIRSEL
flourish WAMPISH
fluff OOS.OOZE
fluffy PLUFFY
flurry SWITHER
flutter FLAUGHTER.FLICHTER
—of wings FLAFF
fold LIRK
—back FLIPE
food BROSE.SCAFF.VIVERS
  VIVRES
—scraps BROCK
fool DOTTLE.GOUK.GOWK
foolish DOILED.DOILT.DOTTLE(D)
  FOOL.GLAIKIT
—fellow GOMERAL.GOMERIL
—person HAVEREL
—talk HAVER(ING)S
foot-stamping RUFF
football game BA'ING.BA'SPIEL
footballers SFA
footless coarse stocking HOGGER
  MOGGAN
for ON
—the express
  purpose ONCE ERRAND
  ANCE ERRAND.YINCE ERRAND
foray CREACH.CREAGH.SPREAGH
forcible VIVE
ford LIRK.RACK
foreign FRAIM.FREMD.FREMIT
foreman TOPSMAN
forenoon FOREDAY
foretell SPAE
forewarn WEIRD
form of Scottish
  language LALLAN(S)
formerly UMQUHILE
forth FURTH
fortified
—house BASTEL-HOUSE
—island CRANNOG
forward FORRIT.THRAWARD
  THRAWART

—girl	YIP	fussy	FIKISH.FIKY.FYKISH.FYKY
foster child	DA(U)LT	—talk	PHRASE
found	FAND	gable	GAVEL
fourth part	FORPET.FORPIT	gad	TRAIK
fowl	BRISSEL-COCK	Gael	GAHDEL.GOIDEL
fox	LOWRIE(-TOD)	Gaelic-speaking	
	TOD-LOWRIE.TOD	regions	GAIDHEALTACHD
fragment	BLA(U)D	gag	BRANKS
freckle	FAIRNYTIC(K)LE	gaiter	COOTIKIN.CU(I)TIKIN
free			QUEET
—of claim	ASSOILZIE	gallows	DULE-TREE.WOODIE
—range	SCOUTH.SCOWTH	game	SHINNY.SHINTY
Free Church of		gamekeeper	GILLY.G(H)ILLIE
Scotland	WEE FREES	gap in wall	SLAP
freebooter	CATERAN	garb	THRATCH
freehold estate	BARONY	garish	ROARIE.ROARY
freeholder	UDALLER	garret	ROOST
frequency	COMMONALTY	gate	YATE.YET(T)
fresh	CALLER	—crash	SORN
—man	BAJAN(T).BEJAN(T)	gave	GAE.GIED
friable	CRUMP	generous	MENSEFUL
fried oatmeal and		gentle	CANNY
onions	SKIRL-IN-THE-PAN	get	
friendly	COUTHIE.TOSH	—by begging	THIG
fright	FLEG.GLIFF.GLIFT	—by groping	POWTER
frighten	FLEG.FLAY.FLAY.RICHT	—lost	TRAIK
	SCAUR	—over	OVERCAST
frivolous excuse		ghastliness	GASHLINESS
	WHITTIE-WHATTIE	ghastly	GASH(FUL).GASHLY
frog	PADDOCK	ghost	CHAPPIE.WAFF
—spawn	REDD	giddy	GLAIKIT
frolic	SPLORE	—headed	HELLICAT
from	FRAE.THRAE	gift	PROPINE
froth	REAM	—of goods obtained	
fuddled	TA(I)VERT	by deceit	SUBREPTION
fuel	EILDING	—on New Year's	
fulfilment	IMPLEMENT	Eve	HOGMANAY
full	FOU.SKELPING	gig	HURLY-HACKET
funeral banner	GUMPHION	girdle	GRIDDLE
furious	WUD	girl	CUMMER.CUTTY.KIMMER
furnace cinders	DANDER		LASSIE.QUEAN.QUEYN(IE)
furnish	PLENISH		QUIN(I)E
furniture	INSIGHT.PLENISHING	give	GIE
	STOUTH(E)RIE	—and take	GIFF-GAFF
furrow	FUR(R).SHEUCH.SHEUGH	—judgement on	COGNOSCE
further		—suretyship	CAUTIONRY
—ahead	UPBY(E)	—up an action	DESERT THE DIET
—in	INBY(E)	given	GIEN
fuss	FIKERY.FYKERY	giving possession	SASINE

glance	GLEY
glancing blow	SKITE.SKYTE
gleam	SHEEN
—of sunshine	SUN-BLINK
glen	HOWE
glide	SCRIEVE.SKITE.SKYTE
glimmer	STIME.STYME
glimpse	GLEDGE.GLIFF.GLIFT
	GLIM.GLISK.GLIST
	STIME.STYME.WAFF
globe flower	LUCKENGOWAN
gloom	DOOL
gloomy	DRUMLY
glower	GLAUR
gluttonous	GUTSY
go	GAE.GANG
—about or forth	STEER
—arm-in-arm	CLEEK
—counter	THRAW
—easy	CA'CANNY
—on crutches	STILP
—slowly	WEAR
—to sleep	FALL OVER
—wearily	TRAIK
go-by	GANG-BY
goal	DOOL
—in games	HAIL
gob	GAB
goblin	BODACH.BROWNIE
	RED-CAP.RED-COWL
godmother	CUMMER.KIMMER
going	GAUN
gold	GOOL.GULE.GOWD
goldfinch	GOUDIE.GOWDIE
	GOWDSPINK
golf	GOWF
—ball	GOWF-BA
gone	GANE
good	GUID.GUDE
—condition	PLY
—deal	HANTLE
—for-nothing	NE'ER-DO-WEEL
—fortune	SEIL
—health!	SLAINTE
—looking	WEEL-FAIRED
	WEEL-FA(U)R'D
	WEEL-FA(U)RT
—luck	SONCE.SONSE
—manners	HAVING
—many	HANTLE
—turn	CAST
—natured	SONCIE.SONCY
	SONSIE.SONSY
goodly	FAIR-FARAND
goodness!	MY CONSCIENCE
gooseberry	GROSER(T).GROSET
	GROSSART
gore	GAIR
gossip	CLASH.CLATTER.CLAVER
	CLISH-CLASH.CLISHMACLAVER
	CUMMER.JAUNDER.KIMMER
got	GOTTEN
—off lightly	CHEAP OF
grace	MENSE
graceful	GENTY
graceless	MENSELESS
gracious	MENSEFUL
grain	CURN
—chest	CORN-KIST
—crops before or after	
harvesting	VICTUAL
—due to miller's	
servant	KNAVESHIP
—measure	WECHT
—of corn	PICKLE
granary	GIRNEL
grand	
—child	OE.OY(E)
—father	GUDESIRE.GUTCHER
	LUCKIE-DAD
—mother	GUDE-DAME
granular	CURN(E)Y
grasp	CLA(U)T.GLAUM
grass field	PARK
grate	CHIRK.RISP
grating over drain	SIVER.SYVER
gratuity	MAG(G)S
grave	GRAFF
—digger	BEADLE.BED(E)RAL
gravel	CHANNEL
graze	SKIFF
grease	CREESH
great	FELL.UNCO
—stride	STEN(D)
greedy	GARE
gridiron	BRANDER
grief	VEX
grim	DOUR.GURLY

grimace	MURGEON		REDDING-KAME
grin	GIRN	—piece	COCKERNONY
grocers	SGF	—powder	M(O)UST.MUIST
groove in stone or wood	RAGGLE	halberd	LOCHABER-AXE
grope	GRAPE.RIPE	hale	FRACK.FRECK.RAUCLE
gross amount	SLUMP	half	HALFLIN(G)S
ground	GRUND	—a silver penny	HALFLIN(G)
—floor house	MAINDOOR	—grown person	HALFLIN(G)
—for family burial plot	LAIR	hall	HA
—rent	GROUND ANNUAL	ham	HOUGH
grounds of estate	POLICIES	handful	GOWPEN
group of		handful	LOOFFUL.RIP(P)
—cot-houses	COT TOWN	handkerchief	NAPKIN
—houses	TOWN	handsome	BRAW
growl	GURL	hang	STRAP
gruel	BROCHAN.CROWDY	hanging clock	WAG-AT-THE-WALL
grumble	GIRN		WAG-BY-THE-WALL
grunt	GRUMPH	hangman	LOCKMAN
guarantee	WARRANDICE	—'s rope	TOW
guarantor	OBLIGANT	happening	WEIRD
guard	WEAR	happiness	SEIL
guardian of minor	TUTOR	harass	PINGLE
guess	ETTLE	harbour	RESET
guide	W(E)ISE	—due	SHORE-DUE
	WEIZE	harbour criminal	RESET
guild membership	GUILDRY	hard blow	DEV(V)EL
guileless	SACKLESS	hardened clay	BLAE
guillemot	LUNGIE	hardly	JIMPLY
guillotine	MAIDEN	hare	BAUDRONS.MALKIN
gull	SCAURY.SCOURIE.SCOWRIE		MAWKIN
	SEA-MAW	—'s tail	FUD
gully	GEO.GIO	harebell	BLAWORT
gunsight	VISIE.VIZY.VIZZIE	harm	SCAITH
gurgle	BULLER.RUCKLE	—physically	WRONG
gurgling sound	GOLLAR	harmless	CANNY
gust	FLAUGHT	harry	HERRY
gutsiness	GREEDINESS	harvest	HAIRST
gutter	STRAND.STRAUN	—field	HAIRST-RIG
guttural roar	GOLLER	—home	KERN.KIRN
gypsy	CAIRD.TINK(LER)	hasp	HESP
habitual expression	O'ERWORD	hatch eggs	CLECK
	OWREWORD	haughty	PAUGHTY
habituate	USE	haul	RUG
hack	HAG	haunch	HAINCH
haddock	HADDIE.SPELD(R)IN(G)	haunt	HOUFF.HOWFF
hag	RUDAS	have	HAE
haggle	NIFFER.PRIG	—a holiday	PLAY
hair	HAR	—dealings	INTROMIT
—comb	REDDING-COMB	—done	BE THROUGH

—lustre	SHEEN
hawk	KEELIE
hawker	YAGGER
hazard	NIFFER
hazy	URY
head	POW
—of hair	POW
—to foot	HEADS AND THRAWS
head of field	HEAD-RIG
headlong	RAMSTAM
health	HEAL
heard	HARD
heart	JARTA.YARTA
heave up	HEEZE
heavens	LIFT
heavy	DOWF
—blow	LOUNDER
—impact	DUSH
heed	TENT
heifer	QUEY
held	HADDEN.HUDDEN
helmet	KNAPSCAL
	KNAPSCULL.KNAPSKULL
hemp nettle	DAE-NETTLE
	DAY-NETTLE
herald	UNICORN
hesitate	TARROW
hew	HAG
hide	FLAUGHT
hideous	GASH(FUL).GASHLY
hideousness	GASHLINESS
hiding place	HIDLING(S).HIDLINS
	HIDY-HOLE
higgledy-piggledy	
	THROUGH-OTHER
high tea	TOUSY TEA
Highland	HIELAND
—dancer's shout	HOOCH
—dagger	DIRK
—festival	MOD
—gentleman of secondary	
rank	DUN(N)I(E)WASSAL
—whisky	PEAT-REEK
Highlander	NAINSEL(L)
	PLAIDMAN
—'s cap	GLENGARRY
hill	LAW.BRAE
—pass	SLAP
hinder	TAIGLE
hint	MINT
hire	FEE
hired mourner	SALLIE.SALUIE
	SAULIE
hitch	HOTCH
hive of bees/wasps	BIKE.BYKE
hoar frost	CRANREUCH
hoarse	ROOPIT.ROOPY.ROUPIT
hoarseness	ROOP.ROUP
hoax	GEGG
hobble	HILCH
hobgoblin	WIRRICOW
	WORRICOW.WORRYCOW
hobnail	TACKET
hock	HOUGH
hoe	CLA(U)T
hog's lard	SAIM
hoist	HEEZE
hold	CLAUCHT.CLAUGHT.HAD
	HAU(L)D
holder of	
—document	HAVER
—land under feu	FEUAR
—small feu	PORTIONER
—underlease	SUBTACKSMAN
holding	HADDIN
holiday	PLAYING
hollow	BOSS.CORRIE.HOWE
—of both hands	GOWPEN
homage	MANRENT
home	HAME
—farm	MAINS
—made firework	PEEOY.PIOY(E)
—spun	RAPLOCH
homewards	HAMEWITH
honey	HINNY
—with oatmeal	ATHOLE BROSE
hoof	CLOOT
hoop	GIRD.GIRR
hooped dish	LUGGIE
hopscotch	PEEVERS
horizontal tombstone	
	THROUGH-STANE
hornless	
—cow	DODDY.HUMLIE
—stag	HUMBLE.HUMMEL
horse	GALLOWAY
—collar	BRECHAM
—dealer	HORSE-COUPER

—disease	WEED.WEID		ETTERCAP
—fever	WEED.WEID	—omened	UNCHANCY
—old	AVER.YAUD	—tempered	GIRNIE
—shoe	PANTON-SHOE	—treat	DEMEAN.MISGUIDE
—'s backband	RIGWIDDIE	illegal pub	BOTHAN
	RIGWOODIE	impervious clay	TILL
horsefly	CLEG	impetuosity	BIRR
hot	HET	importune	PRIG
—pursuit	HOT-TROD	impound	POIND
—water bottle	PIP	improvised trough or	
house	BIGGIN	sledge	HURLY-HACKET
—agent	HOUSE-FACTOR	impudent	BARDY
—of turf	BLACKHOUSE	in	INTIL
—one room deep	SINGLE HOUSE	—arrear	BACK-GANGING
—the harvest	LEAD IN	—being	TO THE FORE
—warming	INFARE	—confusion	HIRDY-GIRDY
household goods	INSIGHT	—contrary direction	
hovel	CRU(I)VE		WID(D)ERSHINS
howl	GOWL		WITHERSHINS
huff	STRUNT	—dotage	DOITED.DOITIT
hug	OXTER	—mixed-up manner	
hum quietly	SOWF(F).SOWTH		THROUGH-OTHER
hungry	YAUP	—the country	LANDWARD(S)
hurl	BUM	—turns	TIME ABOUT
hurry off	WHIRRY	into	INTIL
hurt	MIS(C)HANTER.SCAITH	incline to think	DOUBT
	SKAITH	inclined to	
hush!	WHEESHT	—avarice	GRIPPY
hussy	LIMMER	—shiver or shudder	OORIE.OURIE
hut	BOTHAN.BOTHIE.BOTHY		OWRIE
	SHEAL(ING).SHEEL(ING)	increase in periodical	
	SHEIL(ING).SHIEL(ING)	payment	AUGMENTATION
	SKEO.SKIO	indecision	SWITHER
hysterics	EXIES	indeed	ATWEEL.DEED
I shall	ISE	indictment	DITTAY
ice cream wafer	SLIDER	indoors	THEREIN
idiot	TUMPSHIEHEID	indulge	PETTLE
idle		inert	THOWLESS
—about	DAIDLE	infield	INTOWN
—talk	CLAVER	infuse	MASK
if	GIF.GIN	inhabitant	RESIDENTER
ignorant of	UNACQUAINT	injure	SCAITH.SKAITH
ignore	MISKEN	injury	MIS(C)HANTER.SCAITH
ill			SKAITH
—conditioned	MISLEARED	innkeeper	STABLER
—favoured	ILL-FAURD	inner room	BEN.SPENCE
—grown	WANTHRIVEN	innocent	SACKLESS
—looking	ILL-FAURD	inquire	SPEER.SPEIR
—natured person	ETHERCAP	insignificant person	SCOOTER

insist	THREAP.THREEP	join	OOP.OUP
insisted	THREAPIT.THREEPIT	joint	
insolence	SNASH	—heiress	HEIR-PORTIONER
insolent	BARDY	—on hind leg	HOUGH
inspector of coal	KEEKER	jollification	SPLORE
inspiration	TAGHAIRM	jolly	GAUCIE.GAUCY
instalment selling	MENAGE		GAWCY.GAWSY
instrumental tune	PORT	jolt	HOTTER
intent	ETTLE	jostle	HOG-SHOUTHER
intercourse	TROCK.TROKE	joust	GIOUST
interdict	INJUNCTION	judge	DECERN
interfere	INTROMIT	—of Court of Session	LAW LORD
interjection	OCH	—private consideration of	
—deploring	AICH WOW		AVISANDUM
	(EH) WHOW.EWHOW		AVIZANDUM
—of		—'s decree	INTERLOCUTION
—concession	OU.OW	judicious	WISE-LIKE
—irritation	HOOT	jumble	JABBLE
	HOOT(S)-TOOT(S)	jurisdiction	FOUDRIE.SUCKEN
	HOUT.HOUT(S)-TOUT(S)	jury	ASSIZE
—lamentation	O(C)HONE	keen	GLEG.SNELL
—surprise	HECH	keep in subjection	SNOOL
interpose	INTERPONE	kestrel	KEELIE
intestine	THAIRM	kill in fit of passion	CHAUD-MELLE
intimate	CHIEF.PACK.TOSH	kilt	FILABEG.FIL(L)IBEG
—friend	FAR BEN		PHIL(L)ABEG.PHIL(L)IBEG
intractable	KITTLE	kind	ROUTHIE
intricate	TIRLIE-WIRLIE	kindle	LUNT
invest with legal		kindly	COUTHIE
possession	INFEFT	kine	KY(E)
inwards	INBY(E)	King's evil	CRUEL(L)S.CREWELS
iron	AIRN	kiss	PREE
—mould	IRON-MAIL	kitchen	BUT
irregular soldiers	WATCH	—boy	GALOPIN
island	INCH	—garden	KAILYARD
issue	ISH		PLANTIE-CRUIVE
jabber	YAB.YATTER	knave	JOCK
Jack	JOCK	knick-knack	WHIGMALEERIE
jackdaw	KA(E)		WHIGMALERY
jade	LIMMER	knife	GULLEY
jaded	DISJASKIT	knob of hair	TOORIE
jam sandwich	JEELY PIECE	knock	CA.CLOUR.DAUD.DAWD
jape	BEGUNK	—at door	CHAP
jaw	CHAFT	—down	DING DOUN
jelly	JEELY	—off work	LOWSE
jest	BA(U)R.BAWR	knotty	NIRLIE.NIRLY
Jew's harp	TRUMP	know	KEN
jog	DUNCH.DUNSH.HOD.HOTCH	—not	KENNO
—along	WHIG	knowing	CANNY

lace	PEARLIN(G)
lack of spirit	FOZINESS
lacking freshness	FOZY
lad	CALLANT
ladder to loft	TRAP
laid aside for future use	PAST
lake	LOCH
—dwelling	CRANNOG
lament	GLEET
lamp	CRU(I)SIE.CRUSY
—lighter	LEERIE
land	
—paying feu duty	URE
—tenure	RUNDALE.RUNRIG
landholder	F(E)UAR
landmark	MEITH
landowner	LAIRD
—liable to parish burdens	HERITOR
lane	LOAN(ING).VENNEL.WYND
language	GADHELIC.GAELIC
languid	DWAMY
lank	SCRANKY
lantern	BOWAT.BOWET.BUAT
lapdog	MESSAN
lapwing	PEASEWEEP.PEESWEEP PEEWEE.TEUCHAT
large	
—beetle	CLOCKER
—cravat	O'ERLAY
—draught	WAUCHT.WAUGHT
—hook	CLEEK
last	
—clause of deed	TESTING CLAUSE
—day of year	HOGMANAY
—night	YESTREEN
—of cow's milk	JIBBINGS
—of family	BIRD-ALANE BURD-ALANE
—three days of March	BORROWING DAYS
latch	SNECK
latched	SNECKED
late	UMQUHILE
later	SYNE
Latin prose	VERSION
latter end	HINDER-END
laugh	LAUCH
laughed	LEUCH(EN).LEUGH(EN)
laughing stock	OUTSPECKLE
lavatory	CLUDGIE
lawsuit	PLEA
lawyer's clerk	SERVITOR
lay	
—blame on	WITE.WYTE
—eggs away from usual nest	LAY AWA
—out (corpse)	STRAUCHT STRAUGHT.STREEK.STREAK
lazy	SWEER.SWEIR
lead pencil	KEELIVINE.KEELYVINE
leader	S
leaky	GIZZEN
leap	LOWP
—over	OWERLOUP
leaped/leapt	LAP.LOUPEN LOUPIT.LUPPEN
learning	LEAR(E).LEIR.LERE
lease	SET.TACK
leased tenement	TACK
ledge	SCARCEMENT
left	
—handed	FISTY
—over	ORRA
legal	
—practitioner	WRITER
—ratification	HOMOLOGATION
—restriction	BURDEN
—usage	PRACTIC
lengthwise	ENDLANG
lessee	TACKSMAN
let	LITTEN.LOOT(EN) LUIT(EN).LUTTEN
letters in the sovereign's name demanding action	LETTERS OF HORNING
levity	GLAIKITNESS
levy	STENT
liar	LEEAR
licensed beggar	BEAD(S)MAN BEDE(S)MAN
lichen (red dye)	CORKIR.KORKIR
lick	SLAKE
lie	LEE.WHID.YANKER
lifeless	CAULD-RIFE
lift	HEEZE.HEEZIE
light	LICHT

—and soft	FUFFY	loiter	TAIGLE
limb	SPALL.SPAUL.SPA(U)LD	lone	LANE
limp	HILCH	long	DEE.GREEN.GREIN.LANG
limping walk	HIRPLE	—ago	(AULD) LANG SYNE
line	LING	—drawn out	DREICH
linen	LIARN	—for	WEARY
linger	TAIGLE	—frost	STORM
linnet	LINTIE.LINTWHITE	—handled spade	PATTLE.PETTLE
liquor	SKINK	—since	LANG SYNE
—from boiling	BROO	look warily	GLEDGE
liquorice	SUGAR-ALLY	looking glass	KEEKING-GLASS
list	ROON.RUND	loose	LOWSE
—of		—pile	RICKLE
—candidates	LEET	—young female	GILLET.JILLET
—court cases	SUMMAR ROLL	loosed	LOWSIT
—nobles sworn to		lord	LOSH
Edward I	RAGMAN ROLLS	lore	LAIR
—persons for		lose	TINE.TYNE
trial	PORTEOUS ROLL	—courage	HEN
—poor litigants	POOR'S-ROLL	loss	TINSEL
listless	THOWLESS.UPSITTING	lost	AMISSING.TINT
	WAFF	lot	CAVEL.KAVEL.WEIRD
listlessness	UPSITTING	loth	LAITH.SWEER(ED).SWEERT
little			SWEIR(T)
—amount	CURN	loud rattling	REEL
—auk	DOVEKIE	lounge	DA(C)KER.DAIKER
—bit	BITTOCK.KENNING	lout	COOF.CUIF.GOMERIL.KEELIE
—drop	DRAPPIE.DRAPPY	love	LEAR(E).LEIR.LERE.LO'E.LOO
—finger	PINKIE.PINKY	lover	LAD
—hat	HATTOCK	low	LAW
—lamb	LAMBIE	—born person	GUTTERBLOOD
—star	STARNIE	—lying land	LAIGH
—way over	O(W)ERBY	—lying meadow	INCH
live on alms	THIG	—price	WANWORTH
lively	CANT(Y).CROUSE.VIVE	—spirited	DOWIE
livid	BLAE	lowering	GURLY
load	LADE.LAID	lowland	LALLAN.LAWLAND
loaf made in pan or tin	PAN LOAF	luck	SONCE.SONSE
loan	LEN(D)	—bringing	SONSIE.SONSY
loathing	SCUNNER	lucky	CANNY.SONCIE.SONCY
loathly	LAIDLY		SONSIE.SONSY
local jurisprudence	BOURLAW	lumbering object	CLATCH
	BYRLAW	lump	CLA(U)T.NIRL.SLUMP
lock of hair	TAIT.TATE	—sum paid on lease	GRASSUM
lodging	UP-PUTTING	lumpsucker	PADDLE.PA(I)DLE
loft	ROOST	—female	HEN-PAIDLE
—ladder	TRAP	—male	COCK-PAIDLE
lofty	BRENT	lunch	DISJUNE.TIFT
loin	LUNGIE.LUNYIE	lurch	STOIT

lurk	SNOWK	matted	TATTY.TAUTIT.TAWTIE
lusty	FRACK.SKELPING	—wool	KET
mad	DOILED.DOILT	matter	MAKE
	GYTE.WOWF.WUD	May 28th	REMOVAL TERM
magician	WARLOCK	meal	MELTITH
magpie	PIET.PYAT.PYET.PYOT	—and honey	ATHOLE BROSE
maidservant	LASS	—and water	DRAMMACH
maintain(ed) insistently			DRUMMOCK.DRUMMOCK
	THREAP(IT).THREEP(IT)		WATER-BROSE
make	MA(C)K.MAIK	—chest	GIRNEL
—grating sound	RISP	—time	MELTITH
—groove in stonework	RAGGLE	—sponger	SCAMBLER
—long drawn-out cry	WHEEPLE	means of	
—low sound	CHIRL	—compelling	COMPULSITOR
—hoarse sound	ROOP	—ignition	LUNT
—scratchy sound	SCRAICH	measures	
	SCRAIGH	—37 inches	ELL
—squawk	SCRAUCH.SCRAUGH	—1976 yards	MILE
—afraid	FRICHT	—6150 square yards (old)	ACRE
—faces at	MURGEON	—variable land	
—known	KITHE.KYTHE	area	PLOUGHGATE
—one's way softly		—$^{1}/_{4}$ pint (Scottish)	MUTCHKIN
	SLIP ONE'S WAYS	—$^{3}/_{4}$ pint (imperial)	MUTCHKIN
—over to another	DISPONE	—1 quart	CHOPIN
—palatable	KITCHEN	—3 pints	(SCOTTISH) PINT
—ready	GRAITH	—1$^{1}/_{2}$ gallons	LIPPIE.LIPPY
—tidy	RED(D)	—$^{1}/_{4}$ peck	LIPPIE.LIPPY
—to last	KITCHEN	—1 bushel	FOU
—trial of	PREE	—$^{1}/_{4}$ boll	FIRLOT
—void	IRRITATE	—2-6 bushels	BOLL
maker	WRIGHT	—16 bolls	CHALDER
man	CHIEL(D).MAN-BODY.MON	—40 bottles of hay or	
manner of acting	GATE	straw	KEMPLE
many	MONY	meat	
mar	MIS(H)GUGGLE	—plate	ASHET
marble	BOWL	—turnover	BRIDIE
mare	YAUD	meatless broth	MUSLIN-KALE
market	MERCAT	meeting	
—for hiring farm		—place	HOUFF.HOWFF
workers	FEEING MARKET	—in front of house	COVIN-TREE
—place	TRON(E)	mentally weak	FACILE
marriage settlement		merry	VOGIE
	DOWN-SITTING	messenger	SEND
marry	WAD	—returning late or	
marshal	MARISCHAL	never	CORBIE-MESSENGER
Martinmas	REMOVAL TERM	metal knitting needle	WIRE
master	MAISTER	mettle	SMEDDUM
—of company	DEACON	mettlesome	METTLE
mat	TAUT.TAWT	—person	SPUNKIE

mickle	MUCKLE	MODIWORT.MOULDWARP	
midday drink	MERIDIAN	moment	GLIFF(ING).GLIFT
midwife	HOWDIE.HOWDY	money	SILLER
	WISE WOMAN	—box	PENNY-PIG
mighty	FELL	mongrel	MESSIN
mild bang	PLUFF	monkey	PUGGY
milk		mood	FID
—can	PITCHER	moor	MUIR
—cheese	CROWDIE	morass	FLOW
—closely	JIB	more	MAE
—strainer	MILSEY	morning	FORENOON
milking pail	LEGLAN.LEGLEN	mortgage	HERITABLE SECURITY
	LEGLIN.SKEEL		WADSET(T)
mill		mortgagee	WADSETTER
—district	SUCKEN	moss	FOG
—race or tailrace	MILLDAM	mostly	FECKLY
—stream	LADE	mother-in-law	GUDE MOTHER
miller	MULLER	mouldy	MOOL.MOUL
minced meat	MINCED COLLOPS	mountain over 3000 feet	MUNRO
mine own	MINE AIN	mountaineers	SMC
minimum of vision	STIME.STYME	mounting-stone	
minister	PRESBYTER		LOUPING-ON-STANE
—'s house	MANSE	mouth	GAM.MOU
—with no parish		—music	PORT A BEUL
	STICKIT MINISTER	move	STEER
mire	GLAUR.LAIR.LATCH	—along briskly	SKELP
mirror	KEEKING-GLASS	—around or to activity	STEER
mischievous	ILL-DEEDY.SCATHY	—nimbly	LINK
—boy	NICKUM	—quickly	WHID.WHIRRY
—girl/woman	CUTTY	—slowly	WEAR
—trick	PLISKIE	much	MUCKLE
miser	SCRUNT	mud	DUBS.GUTTERS
miserly	GARE.HOODOCK	muddle	FANKLE
misfortune	MIS(C)HANTER	muddled	MOIDERT.TA(I)VERT
mishap	MIS(C)HANTER	muddy	DRUMLY.SLASHY
missing	AWANTING	mule	MUIL
mistaught	MISLEARED	multitude	HIRSEL
mistress of house	HERSELF	multure	MOUTER
mitigate	MEASE	mummer	GUISER
mixed		—'s leader	SKUDLER.SCUDDALER
—confusedly	THROUGH-OTHER		SCUDLER
—grain	MASHLIN.MASHLOCH	musical	
	MASHLUM.MASHLAM	—instrument	STOCK-AND-HORN
	MASHLIM	—string	THAIRM
mixture of foods	POWSOWDIE	musk	M(O)UST.MUIST
	POWSOWDY	must	MAUN
moisten	SLO(C)KEN	—not	MAUNNA
mole	MOUDI(E)WART	mutter	WHITTIE-WHATTIE
	MOUDI(E)WORT	mythical dwarf	PICT

nag	YAFF
named	HECHT
nap	OOZE
narrow	
—alley	WYND
—strait	KYLE
national	
—emblem	THISTLE
—Orchestra	SNO
—Party	SNP
native of the town	TOWN'S BAIRN
natural death	STRAE-DEATH
nauseate	SCOMFISH.SCUNNER
ne'er-do-well	SKELLUM
near	EWEST.INBY(E)
—the farmhouse	INTOWN
—the house	INBY(E)
nearly	FECKLY.NEAR-HAND
neat	DINK.DONSIE.GENTY
	JIMP(Y).NOUT.SNOD.TOSH
necessity	MISTER
neck	CRAIG.HAUSE.HAWSE
—ring	JOUGS
need	MISTER
neglect	MISLIPPEN
neglected	WAIF
neigh	NICHER.NICKER
neither one thing nor the other	
	NEITHER HUP NOR WIND
nevertheless	STILL AND ON
new	
—ale	SWATS
—pupil in Edinburgh	GAIT
	GEIT.GYTE
New Year	
—gift	NE'ERDAY
—'s Day	NE'ERDAY
news	SPEERINGS.SPEIRINGS
next	STANCHEL.SYNE
nibble	MOOP
nicety	PERJINKITY
nickname for man	SAWN(E)Y
niggard	CARL
niggardly	NEAR-(BE)GAUN
	NIRLIE.NIRLY
nightcap	KILMARNOCK COWL
	PIRNIE
nightdress	WYLIE-COAT
nimble	SWACK.YA(U)LD

no	NA(E)
—laughing matter	NAE MOWS
nobody	NAEBODY
noisy	ROARIE.ROARY
—frolic	GALRAVAGE
	GALRAVITCH.GIL(L)RAVAGE
	GIL(L)RAVITCH.RANT
—musician	RANTER
—quarrel	BRULYIE.BRULZIE
—wrangling	COLLIESHANGIE
none	NAE
nonsense	CLAMJAMFRY
	CLAMJAMPHRIE
	CLANJAMFRAY.HAVER
noonday meal	TWALHOURS
noose	FANK
Norse dialect	NORN
north country	NORLAN(D)
not	NA.NO
—akin	FRAIM.FREMD.FREMIT
—altogether	
absurd	NO SAE HIELANT
—dangerous	CANNY
—frosty	FRESH
—giving milk	YELD
—matched	ORRA
—of gentle birth	SEMPLE
—so bad as might	
be	NO SAE HIELANT
—to mention	LET BE
—yielding milk	EILD
notch edges of	LIP.MUSH
nothing	NAETHING
notice	TENT
notorious	NOTOUR
—rumour about clergyman	
	FAMA CLAMOSA
November 28th	REMOVAL TERM
now	PRESENTLY
nozzle	STROUP
nudge	DUNCH.DUNSH
number	FECK
O yes	OCH AYE.OU AY
oak	AIK
oat	AIT
—cake	BANNOCK.FARLE
—meal	GRITS
—and honey	ATHOLE BROSE
—dish	BROWSE.CROWDIE

FLUMMERY.SOWANS.SOWENS

object of	
—loathing	SCUNNER
—scorn	GECK
obligation to entertain	WATTLE
observant	TENTIE
obstinate	DOUR.THRAWART
obtrude oneself	SORN
occasional	DAIMEN.ORRA
odd	ORRA
—job man	ORRA-MAN
—looking	ODD-LIKE
odour	WAFF
of good fortune	CANNY
offer	BODE.PROPINE.SHORE
—and acceptance	MISSIVES
offspring	BURD
old	AULD
—fashioned	AULD-FARAND
—horse	AVER.YAUD
—man	BODACH
—rusty sword	SHABBLE
—woman	CAILL(E)ACH
	CAILLIACH.CARLINE.LUCKIE
—world	AULD-WARLD
omen	FREET.FREIT
on one's feet	UPSTANDING
once	ANCE.ENE.YINCE
one	AE.ANE.YIN
—in nervous state	
	HEN ON A HOT GIRDLE
—licensed to preach	
	PROBATIONER
—of a pair	NEIGHBOUR
—sent to bring a bride	SEND
—to whom feu is	
paid	SUPERIOR
—who	
—cuts corn left by reaper	
	STIBBLER
—lets go	LETTER-GAE
—lifts the latch	
	SNECK-DRAWER
—presents graduates	
	PROMOTOR
—submits meekly to	
injustice	SNOOL
—talks nonsense	
	BLETHER(AN)SKATE

one-roomed	
dwelling	SINGLE-END
onion	FOUAT.FOUET.INGAN
only	ANERLY
onset of disease	ONCOME
	ONFA(LL)
onslaught	ONFA(LL)
onward rush	RACE
ooze	GLEET
open	
—stitching	OPEN-STEEK
—weather	FRESH
opportune moment	SEIL
opportunity to read	READ
opposite to	FORNENT
ordinary	ORDINAR
—plain bread	LOAF-BREAD
organ	KIST O' WHISTLES
ornament	MENSE
ounce	UNCE
out of doors	OUTBY(E)
	THEREOUT
outdoor possessions	OUTSIGHT
outlaw	BROKEN-MAN.HORN
—proclaimed	
	PUT TO THE HORN
outside	FURTH OF
—of	FURTH.OUTWITH
—stair	FORE-STAIR
outwards	OUTWITH
oven	OON
over	O'ER.OUT-OWRE
	OWER.OWRE
—bearing	
assumption	UPSETTING
—precise	PRICK-ME-DAINTY
—flow	REAM
—hanging bank	HAG(G)
—heat	SCOUTHER.SCOWDER
—look	MISLIPPEN
—plus	O'ERCOME
—turn	COUP.COWP
own	AIN.NAIN
—self	NAINSEL(L)
owner	
—of estate	HERSELF
—'s mark	BUIST
ox-eye daisy	(HORSE-)GOWAN
oxen	OWSEN

pact	PACTION
pad	SUNK
paddle	PLOTTER.PLOUTER
	PLOWTER
paddock	PARK
pains	FASH
pair of scales	WEIGH-BANKS
pale	WHITELY
palm of hand	LOOF
paltry	WAESOME.WAFF
pamper	CUITER
panel	BOX
pang	STOUND.STOWND.THRAW
pant	FLACK.FLAFF.PECH.PEGH
pantry	AWMRIE.AWMRY
parched grain	GRADDAN
pare	FLAUGHT
paring of turf	FLAUGHTER
parish	PARISCHAN(E)
	PARISHEN.PAROCHIN(E)
—minister	MAS(S)-JOHN
	MES(S)-JOHN
park	PAIRK
parlour	SPENCE
paroxysm	THRAW
part	TWIN(E)
—of beef carcase	SEY
—of flail	SOUPLE
—the hair	SHADE
partially	HALFLIN(G)S
particle	CURN
parting cup	DEOCH-AN-DORUIS
partition	HALLAN
partridge	PAITRICK
Pasch	PACE
pass	HAUSE.HAWSE
—judgement	DECERN
passage	
—for animals through	
fields	LOAN(ING)
—in salmon cruive	SLAP
Passover	PACE
pasture for one cow	SOUM
	SOWM
pat	CLAP
path	GATE
patron	STOOP.STOUP
—saint	ANDREW
paunch	KITE.KYTE

pavement	PLAINSTANES
pawky	CANNY
pawn	WADSET(T)
pay penalty	PAY THE CAIN
payment	MAIL
—in goods	TROCK.TROKE
peacable	DOUCE
peacock	PAWN.POW(I)N
peasant	BLUEBONNET
	COTTAR.COTTER
peat	VAG
—hole	HAG(G)
—spade	TUSKAR.TUSKER
	TWISCAR
peaty soil	YARFA.YARPHA
pedlar	PEDDER.PETHER.YAGGER
peep	COOK.KEEK.KOOK.PEEK
peewit	PEASEWEEP
	PEESWEEP.PEEWEE
peg top	PEERIE
pellicle of ice	GREW.GRUE
pen	CRU(I)VE
penalty	UNLAW
—drink	KELTIE.KELTY
pendant	POFFLE
pendicle	POFFLE
penny (English)	TWALPENNY
peppermint sweet	PAN DROP
perhaps	A(I)BLINS.YIBBLES
periodical review to check	
weaponry	WAP(P)ENS(C)HAW
	WAPINS(C)HAW
	WEAPON-S(C)HAW
peroration	PIRLICUE.PURLICUE
perplex	FICKLE
persevere	STICK IN
person	WYE
—first named as heir	INSTITUTE
—in disguise	GUISARD.GUISER
—sued or accused	DEFENDER
pert	CROUSE
—chatterer	GABNASH.NASHGAB
—girl	YIP
pertaining to	
—a sucken	INSUCKEN
—will	TESTAMENTAR
perverse	CAMSTAIRY
	CAMSTEARY.CAMSTEERIE
	DONSIE.THRAWN

pet	DAUT(IE).DAWT(IE).MAKE OF PETTLE.TOUT.TOWT
petticoat	WYLIE-COAT
pettish	DORTY
petty stolen goods	SPREAGHERY SPRECHERY
petulant	TOUTIE
pick	WALE
Pict	PECH(T).PEGH(T)
philosopher	HUME
piece of	
—news	UNCO
—property	SUBJECT
—slate	SCLATE-STANE
pierce	SLAP.STEEK
pigswill	BROCK
pile up	BIG
pilfering	PICKERY
pillory	JOUGS
pillow	COD
pin	PREEN
—of door latch	TIRLING-PIN
pinch	CHACK.POOK.POUK TATE.TAIT
—of snuff	SNEESH(AN) SNEESHIN(G)
—with cold	NIRL
pinched	POOKIT.POUKIT
pink	CLOW-GILLIEFLOWER
pinnacle	PINNET
pipeclay	CA(L)M.CAUM
pit in a bog	MOSS-HAG(G)
pitch dark	PIT MIRK
pithless	THOWLESS
pitiful	WAEFU(L).WAESOME
place	
—for milking cows	LOAN(ING)
—of punishment	TRON(E)
plaid	MAUD
plain needlework	WHITE-SEAM
plaintiff	PURSUER
plant	
—refuse	ROSS
—temporarily	SHEUCH.SHEUGH
plantation	PLANTING
plaster	CLATCH.PLAISTER
plate rack	BINK
play	
—fool	DAFF
—marbles	BOWL
—truant	KIP
playing card	CARTE
pleaded	PLED
pledge	WAD
—in drinking	PROPINE
plentiful	FOUTH.FOWTH ROUTH.ROWTH
plenty	SCOUTH.SCOWTH STOUTH AND ROUTH
pliant	SWACK.SWANK
plight	PLISKIE
plough	PLEUCH.PLEUGH
—cleaning tool	PATTLE.PETTLE
—up	RIVE
pluck	POOK.POUK
plucked	POOKIT.POUKIT
plug of tobacco	DOTTLE
plump	BONNIE.BONNY.SONCIE SONCY.SONSIE.SONSY
plunder	HERSHIP.REAVE.REIVE SPREAGH(ERY).SPRECHERY SPU(I)LZIE.SPULY(I)E
pochard	SCAUP-DUCK
pocket or flap in plaid	PLAID-NEUK
poet	MAKAR
pointed hill	KIP(P)
poke	POCK.POWTER
pole	CABER.KENT
poll	POW
pollack	LYTHE
polled cow	HUMLIE
pollute	FILE
pond	LOCHAN.POUND
pool	STANK
—of foul water	DUB
—or hole in bog	HAG(G)
poor	PUIR.SOBER
—thin beer	SWANK(E)Y
popgun	BOURTREE-GUN
—made of quill	PEN-GUN
porpoise	PELLACH.PELLACK PELLOCK
porridge	BROCHAN.CROWDIE PARRITCH
—stick	SPURTLE
portly	GAUCIE.GAUCY.GAWCY GAWSY

portmanteau	POCKMANKY
	POCKMANTIE
possession	SASINE
post	STELL
posthumous stipend	ANN.ANNAT
potato	TATTIE
—fork	GRAIP
—stalk and leaves	TATTIE-SHAW
—soup	TATTIE-CLAW
potatoes served in skins	PEEL-AND-EAT
potsherd	PIG
potter	DA(C)KER.DAIDLE.DAIKER
	PLOTTER.PLOUTER.PLOWTER
pouch	SPORRAN
poult	POOT.POUT
pour	TOUT.TOWT
—out	BIRL(E)
—unsteadily	JIRBLE
powder	M(O)UST.MUIST
	.POUTHER
—puff	PLUFF
powerlessness	DOWNA-DO
praise	ROOSE
prank	GLAIK
prattle	GABNASH.NASHGAB
precentor	LETTER-GAE
precise	PRECEESE
precocious	AULD-FARAND
prejudice	SCUNNER
preliminary interviewing of witnesses	PRECOGNITION
premature birth of lamb	KEB
premium	GRASSUM
prepare	BOUN
Presbyterian	WHIG(AMORE)
—transgressor	DIKE-LOUPER
present	PROPINE
presently	ENOW
preserve	HAIN
president	PR(A)ESES
presiding bishop	PRIMUS
presumption	UPSETTING
pretentious display	PARAF(F)LE
preternatural	NO'CANNY
pretext	OFFCOME
pretty	BONNIE.BONNY
prey	SPREAGH
price of grain	FIARS

prick	BROG.JAG
prim	MIM(-MOU'D).PERJINK(ETY)
	PREJINK.PRIMSIE
prime a pump	FANG
private agreement among creditors	SUPERSEDERE
proceedings in criminal libel	DIET
proclaim banns	CRY
procure	SORT
prodigality	WAST(E)RY
progeny	BURD
projection of wall or building	OUTSHOT
promise	HECHT
promontory	MULL
prompt	FRACK
promptly	BELIVE
proof	PRIEF(E)
prop	RANCE
propel	CA
property	
—given as dowry	TOCHER-GOOD
—which is heritable	DEAD-PART
propose	PROPONE
propound	PROPONE
propriety	MENSE
prosecute	PURSUE
prosecuting solicitor	CROWN AGENT
prosecutor	(PROCURATOR-)FISCAL
prosperous	WELL-TO-LIVE
protection	BEELD.BIELD
Protestant sect	BEREAN
Protestor	REMONSTRANT
prove	PREE.PRIEF(E)
proved/proven	PREE
provide	PLENISH.SORT
provision	STOUTH(E)RIE
prowl about	SNOWK
pshaw!	OCH
public	
—house	HOUFF.HOWFF
—knowledge	HABIT AND REPUTE
—notice	PROGRAMME
—weighing-machine	TRON(E)
puddle	DUB
puff	FLAFF.FUFF.PLUFF.SKIFF
puffed up	PLUFFY

puffin	TAMMIE NORIE
puffy	PLUFFY
pull forcibly	RUG
punch	KNEVELL.NEVEL
pungency	NIPPING
pungent	FELL
punting staff	KENT
purblind person	STIMIE.STIMY
	STYMIE
purport	FECK
purpose	ETTLE.MINT
purse	SPLEUCHAN
purslane	PURPIE.PURPY
pursue	TRAIK AFTER
pursuer's reply	TRIPLY
put	PAT.PIT.PITTEN.PUTTEN
—before a court	PROPONE
—forward	PROPONE
—in order	RED(D)
—into goal	HAIL
—out	MISTRYSTED.SMORE
—of humour	MISSET
—of shape	SHAUCHLE
—to flight	FLEME
—to rights	SORT
puzzle	FICKLE.KITTLE
—game	GLAIK
quaint	AULD-FARAND
quantity of liquid	JABBLE
quarrel	CAST OUT.OUTCAST
	WAP.WHID
quarry face	HEUCH.HEUGH
quarter	AIRT
—days	BELTANE.CANDLEMAS
	HALLOWMAS.LAMMAS
—evil	SPAULD-ILL
—of round oatcake	FARL(E)
	FARTHEL
queer	FIFISH
—person	SKITE.SKYTE
quench	SLO(C)KEN
quick turn	JINK
quickly	BELIVE
quiet	LOUN(D).LOWN(D)
	SACKLESS
quite	REAL
—alone	LEE(SOME)-LANE
quiver	DIRL.TIRL
quoth	CO.QUO

rabbit's tail	FUD
rabble	CLAMJAMPHRIE
CLAMJAMPHRY.CLANJAMFRAY	
race at country wedding	BROOSE
	BROUZE
rail	SPAR
rain suddenly	PLUMP
rainy	SODDEN
—blast	BLATTER
raise a bump	CLOUR
rake	CLA(U)T
rampage	RAMPAUGE
ramshackle and	
disintegrating	RICKLE
range	
—over	SCUR.SKER
	SKIRR.SQUIRR
—of pasturage	GANG
ransack	RIPE
rap	YANKER
rapid quiet movement	WHID
rascal	SMAIK
rasp	RISP
rather	GAY.GEY.LOOR
ratification of	
executor	CONFIRMATION
rattle	TIRL
—in throat	RUCKLE
raucous screech	SCRAUCH
	SCRAUGH
rave	TA(I)VER
ravine	CLEUCH.CLOUGH.HEUCH
	HEUGH
raw (weather)	WERSH
rawhide shoe	RULLION
ray	STIME.STYME
reach	RAX.RYKE
—out	RAX
real property	
	HERITABLE PROPERTY
really	RAEL.RALE.REAL
reap with sickle	SHEAR
reaping contest	KEMP
rear premises	BACKSIDE
rebound	STOT(TER)
rebuke	THREAP.THREEP
rebuked	THREAPIT.THREEPIT
receive knowing to be	
stolen	RESET

receptacle	LOOM
recess	BOLE
—in wall of room	OUTSHOT
reckless	RAMSTAM
reclaimed wilderness	NOVALIA
Records Office	REGISTER HOUSE
recover	OVERCAST
red	
—currant	RIZZAR(D)
	RIZZART.RIZZER
—ochre	KEEL
rede	RED(D)
redeem	LOWZE
redeemed	LOWSIT
reel	PIRN
refrain	O'ERCOME.O'ERWORD
refusal	NAE.REEST.REIST
refuse	RED(D)
—to move (horse)	REEST.REIST
—to recognise	MISKEN
refute	REDARGUE
rehabilitate	REPONE
reign	RING
reinstatement	REPOSITION
relapse	WEED.WEID
relating to Argyll	ARGATHELIAN
relative	FRIEND
—by common descent	SIB
—on mother's side	COGNATE
release	EXEEM.EXEME
—from outlawry	RELAXATION
religion	PRESBYTERIANISM
relish	SA(I)R
reluct	TARROW
reluctant	SWEER.SWEIR
rely	LIPPEN
remainder	LAVE
remarkably	UNCO
remedy	REMEAD.REMEDE
	REMEID
remember	MIND
remind	MIND
rendering null and void	IRRITANT
rent	MAIL(ING)
—in kind	CAIN.KAIN
—in money	PENNY MAIL
rented farm	MAILING
repentance fine	BUTTOCK-MAIL
replication	REPLY

reprimand	TARGE
reproach	UPCAST
reproof	SLOAN
residence	HADDIN
resist law officer	DEFORCE
resourceful	FENDY
respectable	MENSEFUL
restive	FLISKY
restless	WANRESTFUL
restlessness	FIKE.FYKE
restore to office or previous	
rights	REPONE
restrain	COMPESCE.HEFT
resume in conclusion	PIRLICUE
	PURLICUE
retain (milk or urine)	HEFT
return	RETOUR
—of the feu	RECOGNISANCE
revival of a legal	
action	WAKENING
Reynard (the fox)	TOD-LOWRIE
riddle	GUESS
ridge of land for oats	CORN-RIG
riding hood	TROTCOSY
	TROTCOZY
right	
—opposite	FOREANENT
	FORNEN(S)T
—to cut turf	FEAL AND DIVOT
—to use for life	LIFERENT
rigmarole	RAGMAN.RAGMENT
rill	SIKE
rim	ROON
ring	JOW
—dove	CUSHAT
ringing in	JOWING IN
rinse	SIND.SYND
riotous merriment	GALRAVAGE
	GALRAVITCH.GIL(L)RAVAGE
	GIL(L)RAVITCH
rippling	JABBLE
rise	PLUFF
rived	RAVE
river	CLYDE.FORTH.TAY.TWEED
—horse	KELPIE.KELPY
	WATER-HORSE
riverside	
—meadow or flat	HAUGH
—plain	CARSE

rivulet	STRAND	—wild	LAMP
road	RAID	runaway	FUGIE.LOUP-THE-DYKE
—junction	TOLL	rush	RASH.THRESH
rob	REAVE.REIVE.RUB	rustle	FISSLE
robbed	RUBBET.RUBBIT	rusty sword	SHABBLE
	RAFT.REFT	sackless	SAIKLESS
robber	CATERAN.REAVER	sad	DOWIE
	REIVER	sadness	WAENESS
rock	JOW	safe	AWMRIE.AWMRY
rode	RADE.RAID	sagacious	AULD-FARAND
Rogation Days	GANG DAYS	sailor	TARRY-BREEKS
rogue	HEMPY	saint	SAUNT
roguery	JOOKERY.JOUKERY	sale by auction	ROUP
	JOUKERY-PAWKERY	salmon-curing	
roll	ROW	house	CORF-HOUSE
—the eyes	WAUL.WAWL	salmon spear	LEISTER.WASTER
rolling Easter eggs	PACE-EGGING	salt	SAUT
roof		salutation	BECK
—gutter	ROAN.R(H)ONE	salute by raising hat	HAT
—of loft or garret	ROOST	salve	SAW
rope	TOW	same	AE.SAMEN
rose	RA(I)SE	sample	SWATCH
rosin	ROSET.ROSIT.ROZET.ROZIT	sandlark	SANDY-LAVEROCK
rough	GURLY.RAMGUNSHOCH	sandstone	KINGLE
	RAUCLE	sated	STAWED
—justice	JEDDART JUSTICE	satisfy	SAIR
roughcast	HARL	saucepan	GOBLET.KAIL-PAT
roughened bar	RISP	saucy	NEBBY
round		saunter	DA(C)KER.DAIKER
—flat stone	PENNY-STANE		DA(U)NDAR.DAUNER
—hillock	KNOWE		DAWNER
rounded hilltop	DOD	save	HAIN
rouse	FIRK.STEER	savour	SAIR
routine	HEICH-HOW	savoury	GUSTY
row	SPLORE	Saxon	SASSENACH
rowan	RODDIN	say	
royal steward	MAORMAR	—be quiet!	WHEESHT
rubbish	BROCK.CLAMJAMPHRIE	—nothing of	LET BE
	RED(D).TROCK.TROKE	scald	SCAUD
	CLAMJAMPHRY	—and pluck	PLOT
	CLANJAMFRAY	scales	WEIGHT
—tip	COUP.TOOM	scallop edges	MUSH
rude	GOUSTROUS	scalp	SCAUP
rugby union	SRU	scamp	SKELLUM
rummage	POWTER	scamper	LAMP.SCAUP
rump	RUMPLE		SCOUP.SCOWP
run	RACE.RIN.SCOUP	scant	JIMP(Y).JINTY
—as if lame	HIRPLE	scare	GLIFF.GLIFT
—jauntily	LAMP		SCAR(RE).SCAUR

scarecrow	TATTIE-BOGLE	security	CAUTION.WAD
scatter	SCALE.SCAIL.SKAIL	—on goods	HYPOTHEC
scavenger	SCAFFIE	sedate	DOUCE
scholarship	BURSARY	seed time	VOAR
school fight	BICKER	seek	SIK
schoolmaster	DOMINIE	seer	SPAEMAN.SPAER
scold	FLITE.FLYTE.RAGE.YAFF		SPAEWIFE
scolding	DIRDUM.DURDUM	seethe	BULLER
	THROUGH-GAUN	seisin	SASINE
—woman	KAILWIFE.SCAUD	select list of candidates	
—match	FLYTE.FLYTING		SHORT LEET
scold's bridle	BRANKS	selection of verse	BLA(U)D
scope	SCOUTH.SCOWTH	self	SEL(L)
—of choice	WALE	—righteously moral	UNCO GUID
scorch	BIRSLE.SCOUTHER	selvage	ROON.RUND
	SCOWDER	sensible	WISE-LIKE
score	RIT(T)	sensitive	KITTLY
—(goal)	HAIL	sentimental-fiction school	
scorn	GECK.SCOUTHER	of writers	KAILYARD SCHOOL
scour	SCUR.SKER.SKIRR.SQUIRR	separate	RED(D).TWIN(E)
scowl	GLOOM	separation of churches	
scramble	SPRATTLE		DISRUPTION
scrap	GLIM	serve	SAIR
scrape	SCART.SNAPPER.SPLORE	—as relish	KITCHEN
scratch	CLA(U)T.RIT(T).SCART	serving dish	ASHET
screech	SCRAICH.SCRAIGH	session	DOWN-SITTING
	SCREICH.SCREIGH	set	STELL
	SKRIECH.SKREIGH	—in motion	STEER
screen	HALLAN	—in order	SNOD
scrofula	CRUEL(L)S.CREWELS	—off	MENSE
scruff	CUFF	—on one side	JEE
scuff	CUFF	—things in order	RED(D)
scuffle	TUILYE.TUILZIE	—to work	YOKE
sea basin or sound	FLOW.VOE	setting in order	REDDING UP
seahorse	TANGIE	severe	ILL.SNELL
seal	SEALCH.SEALGH	shabby	OORIE.OURIE.OWRIE
search	RIPE.SCUR.SKER	shadow	SCO(O)G.SCOUG
	SKIRR.SQUIRR	shake	WAP
—for stolen goods	RANCEL	shaky	COGGLY
	RANSEL.RANZEL	shallow ford	RACK
season	SEIL	shamble	BAUCHLE
seaweed	WARE	share	RUG
second		sharp	GLEG.SNELL
—reply in law case	DUPLY	shavings	RISPINGS
—sight	TAIS(C)H	sheaf	DORLACH
—year student	SEMI-BAJAN	shed	SKEO.SKIO
secrecy	HIDLING(S).HIDLINS	sheep	
secret	HIDLING(S).HIDLINS	—disease	BRAXY.LOUPING-ILL
—hoard	POSE	—fold	FANK

—shelter	SHEAL(ING).SHEIL(ING)
	STELL
shelf	BINK
shellfish	BUCKIE
shelter	BEELD.BIELD.SCO(O)G
	SCOUG.SHEAL(ING)
	SHIEL(ING)
sheltered	LOUN(D).LOWN(D)
shepherd's	
—crook	KEBBIE
—own sheep	PACK
—plaid	MAUD
sheriff	SHIRRA
—'s messenger	SHELLYCOAT
shilling	TWALPENNY
shilly-shally	WHITTIE-WHATTIE
shinbone soup	SKINK
shine	SHEEN.SKYRE
shinty stick	CAMAN
ship	LYMPHAD
shirt	SARK
shiver	CHITTER.GREW.GRUE
shock	STOUND.STOWND
shoemaker	SOUTAR
	SOUTER.SOWTER
—'s thread	LINGEL.LINGLE
shoot	PLUFF
—like a pang	STOUND.STOWND
shore	RANCE
short	CUTTY
—clay pipe	CUTTY
—connecting tube	HOGGER
—distance	WEE
—dumpy girl	CUTTY
—shift	CUTTY SARK
—time	WEE
—winded	PURFLED
shot	PLUFF
shoulder	SHOUTHER.SPALL
	SPAUL.SPA(U)LD
	SPEAL.SPULE
—blade	SPULEBANE
—of hill	DOD
shovel	SHOOL
show	EFFEIR.EFFERE.SHAW
—perturbation	
	JEE ONE'S GINGER
	JOW ONE'S GINGER
shower	SCOWTHER

showy	BRANKY.BRAW
shred	TA(I)VER
shrewd	CANNY
shriek	SCRAICH.SCREICH
	SCREIGH.SKIRL.SKREICH
	SKREIGH.SKRIECH.SKRIEGH
	SPRAICH
shrill lament	SKIRL(ING)
shrink	CRINE.NIRL
—from dryness	GIZZEN
shrivel	NIRL
shrivelled	GIZZEN
Shrove Tuesday	
	BROSE AND BANNOCK DAY
	FASTE(R)N('S)-E'EN
shudder	GREW.GRUE
shuffle	SHAUCHLE
shut	STEEK
shy	BLATE.SKEIGH
	WILLYARD.WILLYART
sickly	DONSIE.DWAMY.WERSH
—looking	SHILPIT
side	
—by side	HEADS AND THRAWS
—glance	GLEDGE
sieve	SILE.SYLE
sift	SEARCE
signal	WAFF
silence!	WHEESHT
silly person	DOTTLE
silver	SILLER
simple	AFA(W)LD.AEFA(U)LD
	SACKLESS.SEMPLE
simpleton	GOMERAL.GOMERIL
since	SIN(E).SYN(E)
—that time	SINSYNE
sing shrilly	SKIRL
singe	SCOUTHER.SCOWDER
single	AFA(W)LD.AEFA(U)LD
sink	JAWBOX
sinner	DIKE-LOUPER
sip	SOWP.TIFT
sir	STIR
sirloin	(BACK-)SEY
sirrah	STIRRA(H)
sister	TITTY
—in-law	GUDE-SISTER
sit	CLOCK
sitting	DOWN-SITTING

six	SAX
sketch	SKIFF
skilful	CANNY.SKEELY
skilled	SKEELY.SKILLY
skim	REAM.SKIFF
skimming	SKIFF
skin	FLAUGHT
skip about	FLISK
skittish	SKEIGH
—young woman	GILLET.JILLET
skua	BONXIE
skull	HARN-PAN
sky	LIFT
slabbery daub	SLAKE
slake	SLO(C)KEN
slant	SKLENT
slap	CLATCH.SCUD.SKELP
slate	SCLATE.SKLATE
—pencil	CA(L)M.CAUM
slatternly female	BESOM
sledging	HURLY-HACKET
sleek	SNOD
sleepy	SLEEP(E)RY
slender	JIMP(Y).JINTY.SWANK
slice of	
—beef	RUNNER
—bread	SHIVE
slid	SLADE.SLAID
slide	HIRSLE
slight	LICHTLY
—attack of illness	BRASH
—fit of ill humour	DOD
—shower	SCOUTHER.SCOWDER
—slap	SCLAFF
—touch	SKIFF
slip	SKITE.SKYTE
—in conduct	SNAPPER
—suddenly	SCOOT
slipper	MUIL.PANTON
slippery	GLID(DERY)
slit	RIT(T)
sloe	SLAE
sloping-ceilinged	COOMCEILED
sloppy	
—drink	SWANK(E)Y
—thing	CLATCH
slops	CLATS.SLAISTERY
slothful	SWEER(ED).SWEERT
	SWEIR(T)

sloven	HACHEL
slovenly	
—person	WALLYDRAG
	WALLYDRAIGLE
—work	SLAISTER
slow	
—match	LUNT
—moving stream	POW
sluggish stream	LANE
slush	LAPPER
slut	CLATCH
sly	CANNY.SLEE
—person	TOD
slyly	PAWKILY
smacking	SKELPING
small	PINKIE.PINKY
—amount of bread	PIECE
—cake	NABKET
—creek	POW
—cup	TASSIE
—drawer	SHOTTLE.SHUTTLE
—drink	SOWP
—drop	DRAPPIE.DRAPPY
—goods	TROCK.TROKE
—heap	TOORIE
—inn	CHANGE-HOUSE
—job	TROCK.TROKE
—landowner	BONNET LAIRD
—person	NYAFF.SMOUT.SMOWT
—portion	KENNING.TATE.TAIT
—quantity	CURN.HARL
	PICKLE.WHEEN
—thing	NYAFF
—tree	SCROG
—wage	PENNY-FEE
—wares	TROCK.TROKE
smash	STRAMASH
smear	SLAKE
smell	SNOWK
smelt	SPARLING.SPIRLING
smithy	SMIDDY
smoke	SMEEK.SMEIK
	SMEKE.SMOOR
—tobacco	LUNT
smoky	REEKIE
smolt	SMOUT.SMOWT
smooth	BRENT.SLEEKIT.SNOD
—tongued	SLEEKIT
smother	SMORE

smothered snigger	SNIRT
snack	CHACK
snap	CHACK.SNACK
—at	HANCH
snare	GIRN
snarl	GIRN
snatch	CLAUCHT.CLAUGHT
snicker	SNIRTLE
snigger	SNICHER.SNICKER
snipe	HEATHER-BLEAT(ER)
	HEATHER-BLUITER
	HEATHER-BLUTTER
sniveller	SNOOL
snob	SNAB
snooze	DOVER
snub	SLOAN.SNIB.SNOOL
snuff	NABKET.SNEESH(AN)
	SNEESHIN(G)
—about	SNOWK
—box	MILL.MULL
	SNEESHIN-MULL
snug	COSH.COUTHIE.SNOD
snuggle	CROODLE
so	SAE
soap suds	SAPPLES
sob	SAB
sober	DOUCE
sock	HUSHION
sod	FAIL
—for roofing	DIVOT
softly	HOOLY
softness	FOZINESS
soil	TASH
solely	ALLENARLY
solicitor	LAW AGENT
somehow	SOMEGATE
something	
—of little importance	
	SHEEPSHANK
—pledged	WADSET(T)
somewhere	SOMEGATE
son of	MAC
song	SANG
soon	BLIVE.ENOW
sore	SAIR
sorrel	SOUROCK
sorrow	DOOL.TEAN
sorrowful	WAE(SOME)
soul	SAUL

sound	FERE
—of liquid from bottle or of cork	
drawn	CLUNK.GLUNK
—of slap	SCLAFF
soundness	HEAL
soup	COCKALEEKIE
	COCKIELEEKIE
	COCKILEEKY
—ladle	DIVIDER
sour liquor	TIFT
southern	SOUTHRO(U)N
southernwood	APPLERINGIE
sow	SAW
sowens	FLUMMERY
space	
—before kiln fire	LOGIE
—in front of kiln	KILLOGIE
spare	HAIN
spark	FLAUGHT.SPUNK
sparrow	SPRUG
spasm	THRAW
spatter	JA(U)P
spawning site	REDD
specify	CONDESCEND
specious	FAIR-FARAND
spectacle	OUTSPECKLE
speech impediment	HALT
spell	TACK.WEIRD
spend	BIRL.MOIDER.WARE
—thriftlessly	WASTER
spiced hot drink	PLOTTIE.PLOTTY
spider	ETHERCAP.ETTERCAP
spill	SCALE.SCAIL.SKAIL
spin	BIRL
spinning party	ROCKING
spirit	SMEDDUM
spiritless(ness)	DOWF(NESS)
spirituous drink	STRUNT
spitting of cat	FUFF
splash	BLASH.JABBLE.JA(U)P
—of dirt or colour	SPLATCH
splashing sound	CLATCH
splinter	FRUSH.SPALE
split	
—and dried fish	SPELD(R)IN(G)
—and lay open	SPELD(ER)
splotch	SPLATCH
spoil	BAUCHLE.BLUNK
	SPUILZIE.SPULYE

spoliation	HERRIMENT
	HERRYMENT.REIF
	SPU(I)LZIE.SPULY(I)E
spongy	FOZY
spool	PIRN
spoonful	SOWP
spot (of iron oxide)	MAIL
spout	STROUP
sprain	STAVE.WREST
sprat	GARVIE.GARVOCK
spread apart	SPELD(ER)
spree	SKITE.SKYTE.SPLORE
spring	
—in a marsh	WELL-HEAD
—time	WARE
sprinkle	STRINKLE
—of snow	SCOUTHERING
	SCOWDERING
sprout	BREER.BRERE
spruce	SPRUSH
spur-leather	SPUR-WHANG
squall	DROW
squat	SQUATTLE
squint	GLEDGE.GLEE.GLEY
	SKELLY
—eyed	GLEED.GLEYED
squirt	SCOOT
stablekeeper	STABLER
stagger	DAIDLE.WINTLE.STOITER
	WINTLE
stake	STOB
stale liquor	TIFT
stallion	COOSER.CU(I)SER.STAIG
stalwart	BUIRDLY.PRETTY
stamp	STRAMP
stanchion	STANCHEL.STANCHER
standing	
—place	STANCE
—stone	HARE-STANE
star	STARN.STERN
starched cap	COCKERNONY
stark mad	RED-WOOD.RED-WUD
start with fear	STURT
state	
—of excitement or anger	KIPPAGE
—the object	CONCLUDE
statement of	
case	CONDESCENDENCE
station	STANCE

stay	STAW.SIST
—as guest	GUESTAN.GUESTEN
steelyard	BISMAR
steep	BRENT.MASK.STEY
steep-sided valley	HEUCH.HEUGH
stew	STOVE
stewardship	STEWARTRY
stewed potatoes and	
onions	STOVIES
sticky and filthy	CLARTY
stiff	STEEVE.STIEVE
—clay	TILL
stiffly	STEEVELY
stifle	SCOMFISH
still	ALWAY
stingy	CANNY
stir	JEE.STEER
stirrup cup	DEOCH-AN-DORUIS
stitch	STEEK
stock	PLENISH
—and goods in lease	STEELBOW
—farm	STORE-FORM
stocking-shaped net	HOSE-NET
stoke	TOUK
stole	STAW.STEALED.STEALT
stolen	STOWN.STEALED.STEALT
stomach	GEBBIE
stone hammer	
	KNAPPING-HAMMER
stood	STOODEN.STUDDEN
stool	BUFFET.SUNKIE.TREST
—of repentance	CREEPIE
	CUTTY-STOOL
stop	DEVALL.DIT.SIST
storm	WAP
storyteller	SEANNACHIE
	SEANNACHY.SENNACHIE
	SHANACHIE
stout	STUFFY
straight	STRAICHT.STRAUCHT
	STRAUGHT
—on	ENDLANG
—staircase	SCALE-STAIR(CASE)
strain	RAX.SEIL.SILE.SYLE
strainer	SEIL.SILE(R)
strait	KYLE
strange/stranger	FRAIM.FREMD
	FREMIT.UNCO
strangle	THRAPPLE

strap	TAWS(E)
straw	STRAE
stray	TRAIK.WAFF
streaked	HAWKIT
stream	BURN
streamer	PINNET
street	GATE
—fight	BICKER
—leading to water	WATER-GATE
—sweepings	POLICE-MANURE
—swindler	MAGSMAN
strength	FIZZEN.FUSHION
strenuous competition	PINGLE
stress (pronunciation)	BIRR
stretch	RAX.STRAUCHT
	STRAUGHT
strict examination	EXPISCATION
stride	
—along	LAMP
—vigorously	STEN(D)
strife	BICKER
strike	BLA(U)D.GOWF
—(clock)	CHAP
—heavily against	DUSH
striking part of flail	SUPPLE
string to secure trousers	
below knees	NICKIE-TAM
strip	JIB.TIRL.TIRR
—of thread or cloth	ROON.RUND
—off	TIRR
—worn over shoulder	PLAID
striped	PIRNIE.PIRNIT
—woollen nightcap	PIRNIE
strive	BARGAIN.PINGLE
stroke	STOUND.STOWND
	STRAIK
—of bell	JOW
—of pen	SCART
stroll	DA(U)NDER.DAUNER
	DAWNER
strolling beggar	GABERLUNZIE
strong	YA(U)LD
struck	STRA(C)K
struggle	TUILYE.TUILZIE
—with difficulties	PINGLE
strut	STRUNT
stub	STOB
stubble	STIBBLE
stubborn	RIGWIDDIE.RIGWOODIE

—insistence	THREAP.THREEP
stuck	STACK.STICKIT
stuff	CRAP.PANG.STAP
stuffed	PANG
—haddock's head	CRAPPIT-HEAD
	CRAPPIT-HEID
stumble	SNAPPER.STOIT
stump	STOB
—and rump	STOOP AND ROOP
stumpy	NIRLIE.NIRLY
stun by hitting	DEV(V)EL
stunned	DONNERD.DONNERT
stunt	NIRL
stunted	WANTHRIVEN
—bush	SCROG(-BUSS)
—child	URF
—person	NIRL
—tree	SCRUNT
stupefy	DOZEN
stupid	TA(I)VERT
—fellow	HASH.SUMPH
—person	CUDDIE.CUDDY
sturdy	STEEVE.STIEVE.STUFFY
—beggar	HALLAN-SHAKER
stutter	HABBLE
sty	CRU(I)VE
subdue	DANTON
submerge	TAKE
substance	FECK
substitution of legal	
obligation	INNOVATION
subterfuge	OFF-COME
subterranean habitation	WEEM
such	SICCAN
sudden	
—blow	SPANG.WHAMPLE
—fall of rain	PLUMP
—flame	LUNT
—illness	TOUT.TOWT
	WEED.WEID
—movement	SPANG
—sickness	DWALM.DWAUM
—storm	ONCOME.ONFALL
suddenness	SUDDENTY
sue	PURSUE
—for	PLEAD
suffer pangs	THRAW
suffocate	SMORE
suit of clothes or armour	STAND

sulk	DORT
sulks	DORTS.STRUNTS
sulky	STUNKARD
sullen	DOUR.STUNKARD
—look	GLOOM
summary	SUMMAR
summer pasture	SHEALING
	SHIELING
summon	SIST
sunken	LAIGH
sunrise	DEASI(U)L.DEASOIL
	DEIS(H)EAL
supernumary	ORRA
superstition	FREET.FRIET
superstitious	FREETY.FREITY
supervise strictly	TARGE
supplement	EIK
support under arm	OXTER
supporter	STOOP.STOUP
sure	SICCAR.SICKER
surety	CAUTIONER.VADIUM
surfeit	STAW
surge of liquid	JAW
surly	GURLY
surpass	DING
surplice	SARK
suspect	J(E)ALOUSE.MISLIPPEN
swaggerer	BIRKIE
swarm	BIKE.BYKE.HOTTER
swarming	HOTTER
sway	SWEE.THRAW
sweated	SWAT
sweep	SOOP
sweetheart	JO(E)
swell	HOVE
swelling	CLOUR
swig of drink	SCOUR
swim	SOOM
swine	GRUMPHIE
swing	SWEE
swingle	SUPPLE
swipple	SOUPLE.SUPPLE
swoon	DWALM.DWAUM
sword	CLAYMORE
	SPURTLE(-BLADE)
—blade	ANDREA FERRARA
	ANDREW FERRARA
	ANDRO FERRARA
—rusty	SHABBLE

symbolical action	INFEFTMENT
system of	
—succession	TANISTRY
—weights	TRON(E)
table linen	NAPERY
tailor	PRICK-(THE-)LOUSE
take	TA(C)K
—a dislike to	SCUNNER
—copy of	EXTRACT
—heed	TENT
—pains	FASH
—trouble	FASH
—under the arm	OXTER
—up for burial	LIFT
—no problem	
	NEVER FASH YOUR THUMB
taking of evidence in	
court	PROOF
tale of fate	WEIRD
talk	
—frivolously	NYAFF
—impudently	SNASH
—nonsense	BLETHER.HAVER
talkative	GASH
talker of rubbish	
	BLETHER(AN)SKATE
tall hat	LUM(-HAT)
tangle	FANK(LE).TAUT.TAWT
tangled	TATTY.TAUTIT.TAWTIE
tantrum	TIRRIVEE.TIRRIVIE
tap	TOUK
tar barrel	CLAVIE
task	DARG
taste	PREE
tasteless	SAURLESS.WERSH
tattle	GASH
tavern bill	LAW
tax	STENT.WATTLE
—assessor	STENTO(U)R
	STENTMASTER
tea urn	KITCHEN
teach	LEAR(E).LEIR.LERE
tear	TIRR
tease	TEAN
tedious	DREICH.EDI(OU)SOME
television	STV
tell tales	CLIPE.CLYPE
temples	HAFFET.HAFFIT
tenant	SUCKENER

—bound by thirlage	SUCKENER
—of crown	THANE
—of same family as landlord or owning land in succession	KINDLY TENANT
tenure	FEU.HOLDING.TACK
—watching	BURGAGE
term day (11th November)	MARTINMAS
territorial jurisdiction	REGALITY
Text Society	STS
than	BY.NOR
thank God!	BE THANKIT BETHANKIT
thatch	THACK.THEEK
thaw	FRESH
—bulk	FECK
—one	TA(N)E
—sulks	THE DODS
theft	STOUTH(E)(RIE)
—with violence	STOUTHRIEF
them	THAIM
then	SIN(E).SYN(E)
theological college	DIVINITY HALL
these	THIR
thick	
—bawl	GOLLAR
—witted Highlander	TEUCHTER
—woollen	WA(AD)MAL WADMOL(L)
thin	SKINKING
—broth	MUSLIN-KALE
—liquor	TIFT
—porridge	WATER-BROSE
third reply in law case	TRIPLY
thistle	THRISSEL.THRISTLE
thorn	STUG
thorough-going	THROUGH-GANGING
those	THAE
thrash	TARGE
thrashing	LICKS
threaten	SHORE
—by movement	MINT
—rain or snow	SCOUTHER SCOWDER
threatening	SHORE
—gesture	MINT
thrifty	FENDY

thrill	DINDLE.DINNLE.DIRL
throat	CRAIG.HAUSE.HAWSE THRAPPLE
throe	THRAW
throng	THRANG
thropple	THRAPPLE
throttle	THRAPPLE
through	YONT
—passage	TRANCE.TRANSE
throw	CLOD.THRAW
—down	DING DOUN.DUSH
—into a lump	SLUMP
thrown	THRAWN
thrust	STAP
—onward	STAVE
thump	DAUD.DAWD.DUNT LOUNDER.PAIK
thwart	THRAW
tickle	KITTLE
—trout	GUDDLE
ticklish	KITTLE
tidal race	ROOST.SWELCHIE
tidied	REDDED
tidy up	RED(D)
tight	ANG
timber mover	JANKER
time	STOUND.STOWND
—long past	LANG SYNE
—of day	SEIL
—of trial	HOUR OF CAUSE
—of trouble	STOUND.STOWND
timid	BLATE
tingle	DINDLE.DINGLE DIRL.TIRL
tingling after being struck	DIRL
tinker	CAIRD.TINK(LER)
tiny	WEE
tip	MAG(G)S.PROPINE
—up	COUP.COWP
tired out	FORJASKIT.FORJESKIT
tiresome	DREICH
—chatter	YATTER
tirl	RISP
tithe	TEIND
titlark	MOSS-CHEEPER
to	ON.TAE
toad	PADDOCK
—stool	PADDOCK-STOOL
toast	BIRSLE

—slightly	SCOUTHER.SCOWDER
tobacco	
—pipe stem	PIPE-STAPPLE
	PIPE-STOPPLE
—pouch	SPLEUCHAN
toe	TAE
together	THEGITHER
toil	MOIDER
told	TAULD.TELD.TELL'D.TELT
toll	JOW
tomboy	GILP(E)Y
tomorrow	THE MORN
—morning	THE MORN'S MORN
—night	THE MORN'S NICHT
too	TAE
—bright	ROARIE.ROARY
tooth	GAM
top	TAP
—of chimney	LUM-HEAD
toper	SAND-BED
topsyturvy	REEL-RALL
	TAPSALTEERIE.TAPSIETEERIE
torrent of speech	BLATTER
toss	BUM
—coin	BIRL
totter	HOTTER
tough	TEUCH.TEUGH
towards	ANENT
—the inside	INBY(E)
town (burgh)	BURROWSTOWN
tractable	TAWIE
trade	TREAD
traditional	
—belief	THREAP.THREEP
—dish	HAGGIS
trample	STRAMP
tranquil	LOWN
transient experience	GLIFF.GLIFT
transmitter of family	
tradition	SEANNACHIE
	SEANNACHY.SENNACHIE
	SHANACHIE
trash	TRASHTRIE
tread	TRAMP
—clothes in tub	TRAMP
treason	PURDELLION
treat in restitution	ARCHILOWE
tree trunk	CABER
tremble	HOTTER

trench	SHEUCH.SHEUGH
trews	SKILTS
trial	
—at instigation of Lord	
Advocate	INDICTMENT
—without jury	PROOF
tribute	CAIN.KAIN
trick	BEGUNK.CANTRIP.GEGG
	GLAIK.SHAVIE.PAWK
	SKITE.SKYTE
trickery	JOCKERY.JOUKERY
	JOUKERY-PAWKERY
trifle	DAIDLE.PINGLE
trim	DINK.DONSIE.SNOD.TOSH
trinket	WHIGMALEERIE
	WHIGMALERY
troll for fish	DROW.HARL.TROW
troth	TROGGS
trouble	FASH.K(I)AUGH.STURT
troublesome	BRICKLE.FASHIOUS
trouser braces	GALLUSES
trousers	BREEKS.TREWS
truce	BARLEY
truck	TROCK.TROKE
trudge	TAIGLE
truss	DORLACH
trust	LIPPEN
try to barter	PRIG DOWN
tub	SKEEL
tuft	TATE.TAIT
—on a bonnet	TOORIE
tug	RUG.TIT
tumult	HIRDY-GIRDY.STRAMASH
turbid	DRUMLY
turbulence in water	BULLER
turf	FAIL.FLAUGHT
—seat	SUNK
—wall	FAIL-DIKE
turkey cock	BUBBLY-JOCK
turn	THRAW.TIRI
—down a bed	MAKE DOWN
—edge of	LIP
—to left	HIE.HIGH
—up	CAST UP
turnip	TUMPSHIE.NEEP
turnstile	TIRL
tusk	GAM
tut	OCH.TOOT(S).TUTS
tutor	DOMINIE

twelve	TWAL	unpleasantly strict	UNCANNY
—month	TOWMON(D)	unproductive	YELD
	TOWMONT	unqualified mason	COWAN
twill	TWEEL	unruly CAMSTEARY.CAMSTEERIE	
twirl(ed)	TIRLIE-WIRLIE		CAMSTAIRY
twist	THRAW.TWISTLE	unsafe	UNCANNY
twisted	THRAWN	unsalted	WERSH
twitch	TIT.TWIRK	unstable	BRUCKLE
two	TWA(E).TWA(Y)	untilled farmland to placate	
—fold	TWAFALD	Devil	GOODMAN'S CROFT
—roomed house	A BUT AND BEN	unto	INTIL
—some	TWASOME	unusual	UNCO
—storied	TWA-LOFTED	unworthy	WANWORDY
—wheeled barrow	HURLY	unyoke (horses)	LOWSE
—year old animal	TWINTER	unyoked	LOWSIT
—years old	TWINTER	up	
ugly	ILL-FAURD	—the way	UPBY(E)
umpire	BYRLAWMAN	—there	UPBY(E)
	ODDSMAN.OVERSMAN	—to	UPTILL
unacquainted	UNACQUAINT	uphold	UPHAUD
uncanny	ELDRITCH	upright beam	STANCHEL
	WANCHANCIE		STANCHER
	WANCHANCY.WEIRD	uproar	COLLIESHANGIE
uncared for	UNTENTED		DIRDUM.DURDUM
uncivil	MENSELESS	upset	UPCAST.WHEMMLE
uncommon	UNCO	—plans	COUP (THE CRAN)
under a liability	PASSIVE		COWP
undergo one's fate		upside down	HEELS O'ER GOWDY
	DREE ONE'S WEIRD	urchin	HURCHEON
underground		urge(d)	THREAP(IT).THREEP(IT)
—dweller	PICT	—forward	WHIG
—dwelling	WEEM	use	
underlease	SUBTACK	—sparingly	KITCHEN.TAPE
undershirt	SEMMIT	—thriftlessly	WASTER
unearthly	WEIRD	useful	WAKERIFE
unevenly wrought	PIRNIE	useless person	BAUCHLE
unfriendly FRAIM.FREMD.FREMIT		usher in court	MACER
ungainly person	CLATCH	utter loquaciously	BLATTER
unheeded	UNTENTED	vacated	RED(D)
unite closely	WAD	vagabond	RINTHEROUT.WAIF
unlucky	DONSIE.MISCHANCY	vagrant	CAIRD.RINABOUT
UNCHANCY.WANCHANCIE		GANGREL.GANG-THERE-OUT	
	WANCHANCY	RINTHEROUT.TINK(LER)	
—chance	MIS(C)HANTER	vague speech	WHITTIE-WHATTIE
unmanageable		vain	VOGIE
	NEITHER HUP NOR WIND	valance	PAND
unmannerly	MISLEARED	valise	DORLACH.WALISE
unmusical	TIMBER	valley CLEUCH.CLOUGH.CORRIE	
unnecessary fuss	HUMDUDGEON		GLEN.STRATH

valuation	STENT
value	APPRIZE
variegated	BROCKED.BROCKIT
vault	COOM
vaulted passage	PEND
venture	MINT
veritably	REAL
very	AE.GEY(AN).UNCO
—big	SKELPING
—hard rock	KINGLE
—much	FELL
vessel with spout	POURIE
vex	FASH.TEAN
vexatious	FASHIOUS
—detail in work	FIKE.FYKE
vibrate	DIRL.TIRL.HOTTER
vibration	DIRL.HOTTER
victuals	VIVERS
vigilant	WAKERIFE
vigorous	RAUCLE
village	CLACHAN
—with parish church	KIRKTO(W)N
violent push	BIRR
violin	GJO.GJU
	GU(E).GOU
virago	RUDAS
viscera	HARIGAL(D)S
vitality	FIZZEN.FUSHION
vivid	VIVE
voice of one doomed	TAIS(CH)
voracious	
hunger	(Y)EARD-HUNGER
	YERD-HUNGER
	YIRD-HUNGER
vow	HECHT
waddle	DAIDLE
wag	LICK
wainscot	BOX
wait	BIDE
—at appointed place	BIDE TRYST
wakeful	WAKERIFE
waking	WAKEN
walk lamely	HIRPLE
walker	GANGER
wall	DIKE.WA
—opening	BOLE
—plug	DOOK
wander	STRAVAIG.TRAIK
	TA(I)VER

wandering	WAFF
wanting	AMISSING
wanton girl	GILLFLIRT.JILLFLIRT
warble	CHIRL
ward off	WEAR
warn	SHORE
warning cry	GARDYLOO
	JORDELOO
warrant to	
—arrest debtor	CAPTION
—produce witnesses,	
etc.	DILIGENCE
was able	DOCHT.DOUGHT
washy	SHILPIT
wasps' nest	BINK
waste away	DWINE
wasteful	WASTERIFE
wasteland	REESK
watch over dead	LIKEWAKE
	LIKEWALK.LYKEWAKE
water	
—bailiff	WATER-BAILIE
—goblin	SHELLYCOAT
—plant	PIPEWORT
—spirit	TANGIE
—sprite	KELPIE.KELPY
	RIVER HORSE
watery	SKINKING
—bog	MOSS-FLOW
—stuff	BLASH
wave	WAFF
waxed thread	LINGEL.LINGLE
way	GATE
wayward	LOUP-THE-DYKE
weak	BRICKLE.FIZZENLESS
	FUSHIONLESS
wean	SPANE.SPAIN.SPEAN
wearer of	
—kilt	KILTIE.KILTY
—short shirt	CUTTY SARK
weary with menial	
work	TRAUCHLE
weasel	WHIT(T)RET
	WHITTERICK
weathered stone	HARE-STANE
weaver	WABSTER
wed	WAD
week	OU(L)K
—day	ILKADAY

weep	GLEET.GREET	whit	HAET.HAIT
weighing machine	TRON	white	
weir	CAULD	—faced	HAWKIT
weird	ELDRITCH	—pudding	WHITE-HASS
weld	WALD		WHITE-HAWSE
welfare	HEAL	whitening stone	CAMSTA(U)NE
well	A(T)WEEL.WEEL		CAMSTONE
—favoured	WEEL-FA(U)R'D	whitish	WHITELY
—known	NOTOUR	Whitsuntide	REMOVAL TERM
—off	BEIN.BIEN.WELL-TO-LIVE	whiz	WHIDDER
—wishing	GOOD-WILLY	whole	HALE
went	GAED	—affair	HALE HYPOTHEC
wept	GRAT.GRUTTEN	wholesome	HEALSOME
western	WESTLIN	whooping cough	KINK-H(O)AST
wet	WAT	whortleberry	BLAEBERRY
—sloppy work	SLAISTER	why yes	OU AY
wether	DINMONT	wicked person or	
what!	SICCAN	animal	HELLICAT
what		widow's right to a third	TERCE
—does it signify?	WHAT RECK	wig	GIZZ.JIZ
—manner of?	WHATEN	wild	
	WHATNA	—daisy	GOWAN
wheedle	CUITER.PHRASE	—radish	RUNCH
wheel	HURL	wilful	WILLYARD.WILLYART
—barrow	HURL-BARROW	will not	WINNA
wheeze	WHAISLE.WHAIZLE	will-o'-the-wisp	SPUNKIE
where	WHAUR	willow	SAUCH.SAUGH
which	QUHILK.WHILK	wind (clock)	ROLL
whilom	UMQUHILE	winding stair	TURNPIKE(STAIR)
whim	FLISK.WHIGMALEERIE	window	WINDOCK.WINNOCK
	WHIGMALERY	—seat	BUNK
whimbrel	LITTLE WHAUP	windpipe	THRAPPLE
whimper	PEENGE	winnowing device	WECHT
whine	PEENGE.WHEENGE	winter sport	CURLING
	WHINGE	wipe	DICHT
whinstone	WHUNSTANE	wish	WISS
whip	FIRK	witch	CARLINE.GYRE-CARLIN
whirl	BIRL.TIRL		WEIRD
whirlpool	SWELCHIE	—'s spell	CANTRIP
whirring noise	BIRR	wither	GIZZEN.SCAITH
whisk	WHID		SKAITH
whisky	AULD KIRK.THE CRATUR	within	BEN.INWITH
	USQUEBAUGH	without	
—bottle	AULD KIRK	—dowry	UNTOCHERED
whisper	HARK.WHEESHT	—feudal superior	UDAL
	WHITTIE-WHATTIE	—injury	SCAITHLESS
whistle	FISSLE.SOWTH		SKAITHLESS
—feebly	WHEEPLE	—intermission	EVEN ON
—softly	SOWF(F).SOWTH	—scratches	SCART-FREE

woe	DOOL(E).DULE.WAE
woeful	DOLENT.WAEFU(L)
	WAESOME
woman	CUTTY.CUMMER
	KIMMER.WOMAN-BODY
—(contemptuous)	GIMMER
—keeping ale house	LUCKIE
	LUCKY
—practising	
witchcraft	WITCH-WIFE
—who buys at	
auction	ROUPING-WIFE
—'s cap	MUTCH
—'s cap with side flaps	TOY
—'s loose jacket	SHORTGOWN
—'s short cloak	ROCKLAY
	ROKELAY
womanish man	JENNY.JESSIE
wonder	FERLY
wood	WUD
wooden	
—bowl	COG.COG(G)IE
—drinking cup	CA(U)P
—in tone	TIMBER
—leg	PIN-LEG
—peg-top	PEERIE.PEERY
—vessel	COG(UE)
wool	OO
—of sheep's neck	HAUSE-LOCK
word	WHID
—of reproach	RIGWIDDIE
	RIGWOODIE
work	WARK
—contest	KEMP
—ineffectually	PINGLE
—into miry matter	CLATCH
—house	POOR'S-HOUSE
	PUIR'S-HOOSE
worker's allowance	MAG(G)S
worn out	DISJASKIT.FORFAIRN
	TRAIKIT
—shoe	BAUCHLE
worry	DEAVE.FASH
	PHEESE.PINGLE
worse	WAR(RE).WAUR
worst	WA(U)RST
worthless	ORRA.WAFF
	WANWORDY
—fellow	FOOTRA.FOUTRA
—person	NYAFF.WALLYDRAG
	WALLYDRAIGLE
—thing	NYAFF
wot	WAT
wound	DUNT
wrack and ruin	
	PIGS AND WHISTLES
wrap	HAP
wreck	STRAMASH
wrench	THRAW.TWISTLE
wrest	THRAW
wrestle	WARSLE
wretched	WAESOME
wriggle	HIRSLE
wring	THRAW
wrinkle	LIRK
writ requiring security against	
acting violently	LAW-BURROWS
writhe	THRAW.WINTLE
written	WRATE
—assertion	TESTIFICATE
wrong way	WID(D)ERSHINS
	WITHERSHINS
wry	THRAWN
yap	NYAFF
yarn-winding appliance	WINNLE
yawn	GA(U)NT
yearn	GREEN.GREIN
yell	SKELLOCH.YELLOCH
yelp	NYAFF
yeoman	COCKLAIRD
yesterday evening	YESTREEN
yon(der)	THON(DER)
young	YOUTHY
—animal	BURD
—bird	BURD
—coalfish	PODLEY
—ewe	GIMMER
—hen	EIRACK
—onion	SYBOE.SYBO(W)
youngest of family	WALLYDRAG
	WALLYDRAIGLE
youth	HALFLIN(G)
scrambling nets	STEN
scrap paper as...	APPEARS
scratched record	PALIMPSEST
screecher	SWIFT
screen *production*	CENSER
screw steamer	SS

scrimmage near the. . .	EARTHEN
scripture	
Scripture Union	SU
scriptures	NT.OT
scruffy nurse	RUNES
scrummage for the. . .	FOTHER
scruple	SCR
sculptured	SC.SCULP(SIT)
sculptured bust	STUB
scuttle	
scuttled ship	HIPS.PISH
scuttling along	LOGAN.LONGA
sea¹	
sea	DEEP.MAIN.MED
hence	
•sea-bed	DEEP LITTER
•sea directions	DEEPENS
•sea-ice	DEEP FREEZER
and	
•shirt *in* sea	MATIN
•the same sea	DOMAIN
•the sea remains. . .	MAINSTAYS
and	
•sea, I see	MEDIC
•sea touching America	MEDUSA
•seaman	MEDAL
sea *of France*	MER
hence	
•sea-lines	MERRY
•sea-song	MERCHANT
•the sea I hold back	MERISTEM
sea²	
sea(s)	C.(CC.CS)
sea air	SHANTY
sea bird	WREN
sea *change*	ASE
sea-dog	OCEAN GREYHOUND
sea-green	WATER COLOUR
sea room	CABIN
sea-*storm*	ASE
sea-*trip*	ASE
Seabee (American)	CB
seafront	PROM(ENADE)
sea*front*	S
seaman	(see sailor)
seamen	NUS
seaport	SPT
sea*sick*	ASE
seamstress	MIMI

season	FALL
season well	SPRING
seasoned pair	SALTED
season food	SPRINGBOARD
seat	
seat material	SATIN
seat of Empire	OTTOMAN
seaweed	ALGA.(BLADDER)WRACK
	OARWEED.ORE(WEED)
	SEA TANG(LE).SEA WARE
	TANGLE
Ascophyllum	SEA WHISTLE
bladderwrack	FUCUS
	ROCKWEED.SEA BOTTLE
blue-green	NOSTOC
brown	KELP.KILP.LAMINARIA
	PHAEOPHYCEAE
	SEA FURBELOW.WRACK
carrag(h)een	SEA MOSS
cast ashore	WRACK
Channel Islands	VRAIC
Chorda(ria)	WHIPCORD
coarse	TANG(LE)
coralline	NULLIPORE
dialect	ORE.WARE
edible	DULSE.LAMINARIA.LAVER
	PORPHYRA.TANGLE
Fucaceae	WRACK
grasswrack	EELGRASS
	EELWRACK
green	CHLOROPHYCEAE
	ENTEROMORPHA
	ISOKONT
growing in tidal zone	WRACK
gulfweed	SARGASSO
	SARGASSUM
	SEA GRAPE.SEA LENTIL
kelp	VAREC(H)
Laminaria	SEA GIRDLE.TANGLE
laver	PORPHYRA
olive-brown	GULF-WEED
pink	CORALLINE
Porphyra	(PURPLE) LAVER
purple	CARRAG(H)EEN
	IRISH MOSS.LAVER
red	CHONDRUS.FLORIDEAE
	LAVER.PORPHYRA
	RHODOPHYCEAE
	RHODYMENIA

ribbonweed	SUGARWRACK		second mover	BLACK
rockweed	BLADDERWRACK		second person	EVE.YOU
Sargassum	GULFWEED		second-rate	B
	SEA GRAPE		Second Test	RETRIAL
sea			**secondary**	B
—girdle	LAMINARIA.TANGLE		hence	
—grape	GULFWEED		•company *has* secondary. . .	COB
	SARGASSUM		•secondary road	BROAD
—lentil	GULFWEED		•secondary school	BETON
—lettuce	GREEN LAVER.ULVA		**secret**	
—moss	CARRAG(H)EEN		secret drinkers	AA
—whistle	ASCOPHYLLUM		Secret Intelligence Service	SIS
sugarwrack	RIBBONWEED		secret service	CIA
tangle	LAMINARIA.SEA GIRDLE		secret service *leaders*	SS
translucent	BLADDERWRACK		**secretary**	
	SEA BOTTLE		secretaries	CIS
Ulva	GREEN LAVER		secretary	SECY.TEMP
	SEA LETTUCE		**secrete**	
varec(h)	KELP.WRACK		*secreting* a. . .	incl A
whipcord	CHORDA.CHORDARIA		*secreting* *	incl *
wrack	FUCACEAE.VAREC(H)		•ma-n *secreting* one. . .	MAIN
secant	SEC		*secreted by* *	incl in *
second[1]	B.MO.S.SEC		•one *secreted by* ma-n	MAIN
hence			**section**	
•second row	BRANK		inter*section*	NITRE.TRINE
•second man	MORON		*section of* the. . .	T.H.E
•Second Avenue	SMALL		*section of* th/e lates/t	ELATES
•second best	SCREAM		**secure**	
•second eleven	STEAM		secure post	CHAIN MAIL
•second beer	SECALE		*secured by* *	incl in *
second[2]			•organ *secured by* sh-ed	
Charles *II*	H			SHEARED
second character in play	L		*secured in* stron/g room/s	GROOM
second class	L		*securing* a. . .	incl A
second eleven	L		*securing* *	incl *
second half of game	ME		•sh-ed *securing* an organ	SHEARED
second-hand	A		**see**[1]	LO.V.VID.VIDE
*second-in-*command	O		hence	
second of August	U		•see fruit	LOP-EAR
second rate	A		•see fur	LOSABLE
Second Test	E		•see nothing	LOO
second wind	I		and	
second[3]			•see flowers	VLEI
second character	B.EVE		•see no married. . .	VOWED
second child	ABEL		•see one vehicle	VICAR
second class	B		and	
second-hand	SL.SR.STAR.USED		•see last one	VIDENDA
second-hand *addition*	PAWPAW		•see nothing	VIDEO
second helping	DOUBLE TAKE		**see**[2]	C

hence
•see girl	CLASS
•see one	CONE
•see one rear. . .	CISTERN

and

•see *into* far-e	FARCE
•see why, *say*	CY
•see you, *say*	COPPER.CU
see³	ELY
see *about*	E-LY.SE-E
<u>see</u> *differently*	-ESE
<u>seen</u> *around*	-ENSE.-NESE
seen in <u>China</u>	CHAIN
seen in <u>Phi/lad/elphia</u>	LAD
seen in *	incl in *
•German *seen in* ship	SHUNS
seedy, say	CD
seem	
seems like new. . .	GNU.KNEW
seems right	WRITE
seems to be fur	FIR
seer	EYE.OPTIC
seize	
seized by *	incl in *
•king *seized by* b-east	BREAST
seizing a. . .	incl A
seizing *	incl *
•b-east *seizing* king	BREAST
select	
select fish	PICKLING
selected from t/he be/st. . .	HEBE
selection <u>panel</u>	PLANE
Selective Employment Tax	SET
self	
self-banking aircraft	AUTOGIRO
self-*centred*	EL
<u>self</u>-confessed	AM.IAM.IM

hence

•self-confessed essayist	AMELIA
•self-confessed fool	AMASS
•self-confessed Scotsman	AMMON

and

•self-confessed adult	IMMATURE
•self-confessed pretender	
	IMPOSER
(*see also* admitting)	
self-contained	SC
self-description	AM.IAM.IM
self help	DIY

self-*starter*	S
<u>se</u>ller's option	SO
seminary	SEM
semi-	
<u>semi</u>-*molten*	-IMES
semi-tone	TO.NE
semitone	FLAT.SHARP
senator	SEN
send	
send greetings	SD
send *letters*	DENS.ENDS
send notes to. . .	SERENADE
send *off*	DENS.ENDS
send to bed	SCUTTLE.SINK
Senegal	SN
senior	SENR.SR
senior common room	SCR
Senior Deacon	SD
Senior Medical Officer	SMO
senseless	omit -NOUS
separate	
separate parts of house	HUE
separate way	SEVERE
separated by a. . .	incl A
separated by *	incl *
•Poles *separated by* father	SPAN
separating *	incl in *
•father *separating* Poles	SPAN
September	SEPT
Serbian	
dance	KOLO
leader	S
sergeant	NCO.SERG(T).SGT
sergeant-at-law	SL
sergeant-major	SM
sergeant's *mess*	GREATNESS
series	SER
sermon	SER
serve	
served up in. . .(D) ↑	NI
service	ACE.LET.MASS.RAF.RN
	SORB
service-charge	COURT MARTIAL
service vehicles	MASS MEDIA
serviceman	AIRMAN.GI.PRIEST
	SAILOR.SOLDIER.WAITER
servicewoman	ATS.WAITRESS
serving girl	ATS.AIRWOMAN
	WAITRESS.WREN

serving man	AIRMAN.GI.SAILOR
	SOLDIER.WAITER

set

set a test	TASTE
set *about*	SE-T
set *about*...⟨	TES
set about a	incl A
set *about* it⟨	TI
set about *	incl *
•w-e *set about* her	WHERE
set free slave	LAVES.VALES
set of books	NT.OT
set *off*	-EST.STE.TES
set *off* quietly	first letter P
•I led *and set off* quietly	PILED
set off with a...	first letter A
set off with king	first letter K or R
set off with student	first letter L
set in *...	incl in *
•one *set in* he-r...	HEAR
set *out*	SE-T
•se-t *out* new...	SENT
set *out*	EST.TES.STE
set out in bedroom	BOREDOM
set out in pla/in ter/ms	INTER
se-t *outside* a...	SEAT
set up pins(D) ↑	SNIP
setback⟨	DIAL.TES
setback for Cupid⟨	SORE
setback ten...	NET
set*off*	EST.STE.TES
setter	DOG.PECTIN
setting for a...	incl A
setting for *	incl *
•h-e *provides setting for* queen	HERE
setting sun is...	MINUS
set*up*(D) ↑	TES

settle

settle on(D)	
•bird *settles on* the *French*	TITLE
settle score	COMPOSE
settlement of case	ACES.AESC

seven   VII.S

against Thebes	ADRASTUS
	AMPHIARAUS
CAPANEUS.HIPPOMEDON	
PARTHENOPAEUS	
POLYNICES.TYDEUS	

based	SEPTENARY.SEPTIMAL
books of OT	HEPTATEUCH
champions	ST ANDREW
	ST ANTHONY
	ST DAVID.ST DENIS
ST GEORGE.ST.JAMES	
	ST PATRICK
Christmas presents	SWANS
cleft	SEPTEMFID
combining forms	HEPTA-.SEPT(I)-
	SEPTEM-
groups	HEBDOMAD.HEP.HEPTAD
SEPTENARY.SEPTET(T	
SEPTETTE.SEPTUOR	
creations	ANIMALS.EARTH.FIRE
HUMANS.PLANTS	
SKY.WATER	
daughters of Atlas	PLEIADES
days	HEBDOMAD.WEEK
deadly sins	ANGER
COVETOUSNESS	
ENVY.GLUTTONY.LUST	
PRIDE.SLOTH	
Dwarfs	BASHFUL.DOC.DOPEY
GRUMPY.HAPPY	
SLEEPY.SNEEZY	
fold	SEPTIFORM.SEPTUPLE
having seven	
—angles	HEPTAGONAL
	SEPTANGULAR
—cusps	SEPT-FOIL
—faces	HEPTAHEDRONAL
—feet	HEPTAPODIC
SEPTEMPEDAL.SEPTIPEDAL	
—languages	HEPTAGLOT
—leaflets	SEPTEMFOLIATE
—measures	HEPTAMETER
—parts	HEPTAMEROUS
SEPTEMPARTITE	
—sides	HEPTAGONAL
SEPTILATERAL	
—stamens	HEPTANDRIAN
HEPTANDROUS	
—styles	HEPTAGYNIAN
HEPTAGYNOUS	
—syllables	HEPTASYLLABIC
Heptateuch	Pentateuch
	(*see* five) plus
	JOSHUA.JUDGES

Hills of Rome	AVENTINE
	CAELIAN.CAPITOLINE
	ESQUILINE.PALATINE
	QUIRINAL.VIMINAL
hundred	PSI
hundredth anniversary	
	SEPTINGENTENARY
hundred thousand	PSI
in government	HEPTARCHY
	SEPTEMVIRATE
letters	EVENS
Magnificent	FILM
nil	SEVENTY
notes	SEPTIMOLE.SEPTUPLET
one of seven men	SEPTEMVIR
one of seven offspring at one	
birth	SEPTUPLET
sages	BIAS.CHILON.CLEOBOLUS
	PERIANDER.PITTACUS
	SOLON.THALES
seas	ANTARCTIC.ARCTIC
	N. & S. ATLANTIC.INDIAN
	N. & S. PACIFIC
senses	(see five) plus SPEECH
	UNDERSTANDING
sevens	RUGBY
Sisters	ROCKS
sleepers	CHRISTIAN YOUTHS
Stars (of Pleiades)	GREAT BEAR
	PLOUGH.SEPTENTRION(ES)
stories told in seven	
days	HEPTAMERON
thousand	Z
times original bet added to	
stake	SEPTLEVA
tones	HEPTACHORD
virtues	CHARITY.FAITH
	FORTITUDE.HOPE.JUSTICE
	PRUDENCE.TEMPERANCE
Wonders of the	
World	COLOSSUS
	HANGING GARDENS
	MAUSOLEUM.PHAROS
	PYRAMIDS.STATUE OF ZEUS
	TEMPLE OF ARTEMIS
works	SPIRITUAL MERCY
year...	ITCH
years	PROPHETIC WEEK
	SEPTENATE.SEPTENNIUM

seventy	O.OMICRON.S
miles per hour	LIMIT
per cent of hall	AUDITOR(ium)
seventy-eight	DISC.RECORD
The Seventy	JEWISH COUNCIL
	SANHEDRIN
thousand	O.OMICRON.S
year old	SEPTUAGENARIAN
years	LIFESPAN
several	VI.V.VI.TEN.X
	(see also some)
sewer cover	THIMBLE
sex	
sex appeal	IT.SA
sex-*change*	EXS
sextet	VI
Seychelles	SY
capital	S.VICTORIA
coin	RUPEE
shake	
no great *shakes*	ETON RAG
shake dice	ICED
shake up bolster	LOBSTER
shaken by a...	BAY
shaking rattle	TATLER
shaky notes	QUAVERS
shaky notes	SETON.STONE
	TONES
Shakespeare	
words found in the works of:	
abate	PLUCK OFF
abhorred	HELL-HATED
abide	REMAIN
able to work wonders	
	WOND(E)RED
abode	BEING.REMAIN
abominable	EXSUFFLICATE
abounding in rooks	ROOKY
about	SOON AT
abreast	AFRONT
absence	REMOVE
—of restraint	LET-ALONE
abstain from	REFRAIN
abundance	TALLENT
abusive language	ROPE-TRICKS
acceptance	ADMITTANCE
accident	UPCAST
accompanied by a	
woman	WOMAN'D

accompany	ASSOCIATE.ASSIST
	SERVE
accomplice	FEDAR(AR)IE
	FEDDARY.FEDERARY
	FOEDAIRE.FOEDARIE
accomplishment	COMPLIMENT
	EXERCISE
accord	CONGREE
accost	ASSAY.BOARD
account	RENDER
accountant	ONEYER
accruing	GROWING
accumulation	ENGROSSMENT
accusation	CAUSE
accuse	APPEACH.APPEAL
	DETECT.PEACH
accustomed	TAME
acid	AYGRE.EAGER
acquit	UNCHARGE
act	ISSUE
—according to one's	
nature	DO ONE'S KIND
—as a boy	BOY
—as regent for	PROTECT
—bumblingly	DRUMBLE
—of	
—aiming	LEVEL
—devising	FRAME
—extending	EXTENT
—seizing	PREY
—standing	STATION
—up	EVEN
—upon	SALUTE
actions	EFFECTS
active	FACTIOUS.QUIVER
—youth	LEAPING-TIME
actor's profession	QUALITY
actual	BODILY
adopt measures	ORDER
add up	PARCEL
addicted to gazing in mirror	
	GLASS-GAZING
addition	VANTAGE
additional title	SURADDITION
address	BOARD.SUPERSCRIPT
addicted	FREQUENT
admonition	ADVERTISEMENT
adorn as with a brooch	BROOCH
adorned	CROWNED

adroit	QUAINTLY
adulterate	CARD
—wine with lime	LIME
adulterer	BED-SWERVER
advantage	COMMODITY
	EMINENCE
	PRISE.PROCEEDING
—yielded	PRIVILEGE
advent	INCOME
adventurous	DAREFUL
adverse	AWKWARD
advisement	VIZAMENT
affair	CAUSE
affect	SALUTE
affectation	AFFECTION
affirmed before	FOREVOUCHED
affright	GHAST
afraid	AF(F)EARD
against proper feeling	UNKINDLY
aggressive person	SQUARER
agitate	BETOSS.JUMP
agree	ATONE.CONGRUE
	COVENT.GREE.HIT
—to	CONGREE.UNDERWRITE
agreement	COMART
alarm	TIRRIT
alas!	WELLANEAR
alchemist's elixir	TINCT
alembic	LIMBEC(K)
Algiers	ARGIER
all	
—destroying	NONE-SPARING
—night drinkers	
	CANDLE-WASTERS
—round	FULL-FRAUGHT
allege	LEGE
allot	SORT
allotment	DOLE.LOTTERY
allow	BETEEM(E)
alloy like brass	LATTEN
allusion	POLLUTION
amazed	AGAZED
Amazon	PENTHESILEA
ambitious	EMULATE
amorous	LOVELY
amount	SUBSTANCE
amulet	PERIAPT
ancient	FANS
anger	INCENSEMENT

animal
—entrails CHAWDRON
—'s bed CABINET
animated AUDACIOUS
—by lust LUST-BREATHED
annoyance NOYANCE
annul UNDO
—with a kiss UNKISS
anoint BALM
answer REIN
antagonism OPPUGNANCY
anticipating FOREHAND
antipodes UNDER-GENERATION
any odds LOTS TO BLANKS
anything
—calculated to arouse
feelings HUNT'S-UP
—engraved SCULPTURE
—human CIVIL
—of value WORTHY
—protuberant and baggy WALLET
—showy FLAUNT
—that dashes
feelings COOLING-CARD
—very small HALFPENNY
anyway ALL-THING
apparently true TRUE-SEEMING
apparitor PARITOR
appear EYE.LOOK OUT
appearance OSTENT.PORT
—of life LIVELIHOOD
appendages ASSIGNS
appendix to bill SCHEDULE
apple LEATHER-COAT
POMEWATER.SWEETING
apply mouths MOUTH
appoint LIMIT.SCEDULE
—a time for SET DOWN
—by writing PAPER
appointment MATCH
apposite PREGNANT
appraisal PRISE
appraise PRAISE
approach COST(E)
approaching the sky SKYISH
approbation ALLOWANCE
APPROOF
appropriate PROPERTY
apt to learn SPACKT.SPRAG

arbitration COMPROMISE
ardour WRATH
arithmetician COUNTER-CASTER
armour for arm BRACE
army BATTLE
aromatic herb NOSE-HERB
arrange SCEDULE
arrest REST
arrogance OPINION
arrow BIRD-BOLT
—for level shot FOREHAND
art of fencing DEFENCE
artful ARTIFICIAL.CAUTELOUS
FINE
as it may happen HEREBY
ashamed SHENT
ask for writ delivering lands to
heir SUE ONE'S LIVERY
askance ASCONCE
aspire to SPEAK TO
ass ASNICO.ASSINEGO
assail ASSAY
—with rattling RATTLE
—with words TONGUE
assailant OFFERING
assault ASSAY
assay SAY
assayer SAY-MASTER
assemble CONDUCE
assembled DREW
assembly DISSEMBLY
assert repeatedly VIE
assign SORT
—to one side SIDE
—value to PRAISE
assistant tapster UNDERSKINKER
associate COMPETITOR
COMPLICE
assume UNDERTAKE
assurance SURANCE
assure PASS.SECURE
assured THOUGHTEN
assuredly PARDIE.PARDY
PERDIE.PERDY
astonishment ADMIRATION
astride COLOSSUS-WISE
at
—an end EXPIATE
—any rate AT ANY HAND

—night	ANIGHT	banker	ONEYER
—peace	WHIST	bankrupt	TRADE-FALNE
—the beginning	AT HAND	bar	MAKE
—the present time	THE WHILE	bargain	COMPOSITION
—this very time	INSTANTLY	barrel	BOMBARD.BUMBARD
—variance	ODD	bartailed godwit	SCAMEL
atmosphere	REGION	base	CULLIONLY
atone	ABIDE.ABY(E)	—tyke	HUNT-COUNTER
atrociously villainous		basket	MAUND
	FACINERIOUS	baste	ENLARD
attack	BOARD.EXTENT	bathed	BALKED
attend	TEND	batter by violence of	
—as servant	STAY	weather	OVERWEATHER
—to	RECK	battle	WAGE
attendant who cleared way for		baubles with fool's head	
procession	WHIFFLER		FOOL'S ZANIES
attendants	TENDANCE	bawd	GREEK
attention	OBSERVANCE	bawl	GAPE
attentive	ADVERTISING	be	BIN
attraction	FAVOUR	—a	
auburn	ABRAM	—guest	HOST
augment	ECH(E).EECH.ICH	—pattern for	PATTERN
auspicious	FAIR-BODING	—widow	WIDOW
avarice	MISERY	—wooer	SUE
avaricious	CHUFF	—amends for	PURCHASE
avenge	VENGE	—an accessory	BE OF CONSENT
avenging	REVENGE	—conciliatory	
averse to discussion			MAKE FAIR WEATHER
	UNQUESTIONABLE	—consistent	ADHERE
avoid	EVITATE	—daunted	DISMAY
avowed	BARE-FACED	—dilatory	FORESLOW
awry	CAM.KAM(ME)	—distasteful	DISTASTE
back up	VERIFY	—to	RESIST
backbiting	BACK-WOUNDING	—equal in value	WAGE
backward fall	TAILOR	—equivalent to	REANSWER
bad luck	WANION	—heir	INHERIT
badly tempered	ILL-TEMPERED	—imprisoned	LIE
bailiff	BUM-BAYLIE	—in	
	SHOULDER-CLAPPER	—fashion	WEAR
bait	STALE	—service	DEPEND
balance	PEASE.PEAZE.PEISE	—waiting	TEND
	PEIZE.PEYSE	—inconstant	BLENCH
—evenly	WEIGH	—intent	TIRE
—of an account	REMAINDER	—interspersed	LARDED
ball of thread	BOTTOM	—lodged	LIE AT HOST
balsamic liquor	MUMMY	—married	GO TO THE WORLD
baneful	BATEFUL	—over-punctilious	
banish	ABANDON		STRAIN COURTESY
bank of river	RIVAGE.WHARF	—perverse	BE OPPOSITE WITH

—security for	SURETY
—silent	PEACE
—sluggish	DRUMBLE
—suitable	CONVENT
—surety for	UNDERTAKE
—the better	AVAIL
—transacted	PROCEED
bear	
—in mind	REMEMBER
—like a crest	UNDERCREST
beard	EXCREMENT
beardless	UNRUFFE
bearing	CONCERNANCY
	PORTANCE
beast of the chase	VENISON
beat	COMB.FIRK.PAY.PRAT
	SWINDGE.SWITS
beater	SWITS
beauty	FAIR
because	THAT
beckoning	WAFTURE
become	BESORT
—an informer	PEACH
—lank	LANK
—mouldy	HOAR
bedcover	COUNTERPOINT
bedraggle	BEMOIL
been	BIN
befall	BEFORTUNE
befit	BESORT
before	TOFORE
beforehand	FORMER
beggar	BEZONIAN
begging bowl	CLACK-DISH
begone	AROINT.AROYNT
behaviour	GESTURE.PORTANCE
beholden	BEHOLDING
belated	LATED
beldame	TROT
believe	WIS(T)
belladonna	INSANE ROOT
beloved	TENDER
belt	CENTER
bend	COMPASS.CURB
—one's course	SWAY
beneficiary	BENEFIT
bent	CRIPS
—upon prey	PREYFUL
benumb	PROROGUE

beset	LAY
beshrew	SHREW
best	DEAR.WHIP
bestially drunk	SWINE-DRUNK
bet	LAY
bethink	REMEMBER
betide	BETIME
betray	PEACH
betroth	ASSURE.TROTH
betrothal	ASSURANCE
betrothed	COMBINATE
	TROTH-PLIGHT
bewitchment	TAKING
beyond	
—description	UNEXPRESSIVE
—reckoning	OUT OF ALL NICK
bias	PARTIALIZE
Bible	TEXT
biliousness	CHOLER
bind	COMBINE
—in fetters	ENFETTER
—in gratitude	ENDEAR
bindweed	WOODBIND
	WOODBINE
bird	
—of ill omen	NIGHT-CROW
—'s nest	CABINET
bitter	AYGRE.EAGER
—end	UTTERANCE
black	COLLIED.ROOKY
—as hell	HELL-BLACK
—bird	WOOSEL(L)
—jack	BOMBARD
blandishment	SOOTH
blast	STRIKE.TAKE
—by lightning	THUNDER-STROKE
blasted	DEROGATED
bleacher	WHITSTER
bleaching-time	WHITING-TIME
blight	BLASTMENT.STRIKE
blind	BEESOME.BISSON
	C(O)URB.WINKING
—fold	W(H)IMPLE
—man's buff	HOODMAN-BLIND
blinding	SEELING
blinking	PINK
blockhead	CLOTPOLL.SNIPE
bloodhound	LYM
blooming	PRIMY

blow	PASH
—in fencing	MONTANTO
blunt	DISEDGE
blunt arrow	BIRD-BOLT
blusterer	RUDESBY.SWASHER
boarded	PLANCHED
boasting	MAGNIFICENT
—of	REPUTING
bodge	BUDGE
bodily	
—constitution	COMPLEXION
—pain	GRIEF
—quality	THEW
body	
—of people in realm	SUBJECT
—servant	GENTLEMAN
boggled	BODGED
boiling pot	STEW
boisterous	ROISTING.ROYSTING
boldness	DARE
book-mate	INKHORN-MATE
bootlicker	PLEASEMAN
born	
—in dung	SHARD-BORNE
—to a procuress	BAWD-BORN
bosom friend	CATER-COUSIN
botcher	COSIER.COZIER
bout	VENEW
bowl-beating	BOLD-BEATING
bowsprit	BEAK
boy	CRACK.JACK-A-LENT.KNAVE
brabble	PRABBLE
brain	PIA MATER
—sick	BRAINISH
brand	WIPE
—with infamy	INFAMONISE
bravery	HARDIMENT
bravest	BEST
brawl	BRABBLE.PRAWLE
breach of harmony	FRACTION
break	FRACT.FRUSH
brevity	FEWNESS
bright red	WAX-RED
brimming with	
tears	WATER-STANDING
bring	PROCURE
—back to normal state	RECURE
—forth young	EAN.KINDLE
—into plot	PACK

—on	INFER
—safely	SAFE
—to an end	FINE
—to me	DUCDAME
broach	STRIKE
broad linen tape	INKLE
broken by care	CARE-CRAZED
brood	KINDLE
—in nest	AERIE.AERY.AYRIE
	EYRIE.EIRY
brothel	HOTHOUSE
	LEAPING-HOUSE
brother-in-law	GOOD-BROTHER
brown stained	UMBERED
brought from a depth	DEEP-FET
bruise	FRUSH
bruised	PASHED
bubonic plague	RED-MURRAIN
	RED-PLAGUE
buck of fourth year	SOAR(E)
	SORE
bucket	STO(O)PE
budge	BOUGE
bully	CUTTLE
bullying	SWASHING
bumblebee	DRUMBLEDOR
burden	CARRIAGE
—of a song	FADING.HOLDING
	WHEEL
burdensome	CHARGEFUL
burdock	HARDOKE.HORDOCK
bury	INHEARSE.INHERCE
but slightly	SMALL
buy too expensively	OVERBUY
buzzard	PUTTOCK
by	
—all means	OF ALL LOVES
—common report	REPORTINGLY
—God!	BEGAD.BEGAR
—scent of the foot	DRY-FOOT
—starts	STARTINGLY
—word of mouth	VERBATIM
bystander	STANDER-BY
byword	AYWORD
Caesar	KEISAR
cake	BAKE
calamity	BALE
call	
—a whore	BEWHORE

—to account | TAKE UP
calling
—for haste | RASH
—in question | IMPEACH
camp follower | BOY
candlestick | CANSTICK
cane | SWITS
cannot
—be wounded | INTRENCHANT
—cloy | CLOYLESS
canon | SQUIER.SQUIRE
canto | CANTON
cap for Sundays | STATUTE-CAP
capable | DELIGHTED
—of taking oath | OATHABLE
capacious | CAPTIOUS.WOMBY
caparisoned in armour | BARBED
captiousness | CURIOSITY
card | TOAZE
care | TENDER
careful of | OBSEQUIOUS
carefully chosen | CHOICE-DRAWN
caress | COY
carousal | ROUSE
carpenter's square | SQUIER
| SQUIRE
carriage | PORTANCE
carried by itself | SELF-BORNE
carry
—a false appearance | FACE
—away with joy or in spirit | RAP
—off | TRANSPORT
carted | SCUTCHED
carve(d) | INSCULP(T)
case | SHALE
cast
—a light | REFLECT
—a spell | TAKE
—down | DEJECT
—off | CASTED
castrate | GLIB
casually dropped | SCATTERED
cataract | PIN AND WEB
| WEB AND PIN
catch | FANG.GYVE.PHANG
—in the act | WATCH
—of the voice | SNATCH
catch phrase | NAYWORD
catgut string | CATLING

cause to
—act | COMMAND
—be remembered | MEMORIZE
| MEMORISE
—contract or shrivel | WARP
—mourn | YEARN
—start | FIT
—tremble | QUAKE
—numbness | NUMB
cautious | ADVISED
—in speech | CLOSE-TONGUED
—person | ACHITOPHEL
| AHITHOPHEL
cave | ANTAR
censure | APPEACH
centre | CENTRY
certain | PERFECT
cesspool | DRAUGHT
chaffering | BARGAIN
chain | CARKANET
challenge | ASSAY
chamber | LONDON
—pot | JORDAN
chance | UPCAST
change to a worse
state | DISSTATE
changeable | MOTLEY-MINDED
changed person
| TRANSFORMATION
changeover | SWITS
character | COMPOSURE.OPINION
—of fox | FOXSHIP
charm worn round neck | PERIAPT
chaste | GRACED
chastise | FIRK.SWINDGE
chastity | HONESTY
chatterer | CHEWET
cheat | BOB.COLT.CONY-CATCH
| GULL-CATCHER.HARLOT
check | TRASH
cheese rind | CHEESE-PARING
cherub | CHERUBIN
chided | ACOLD
chief | ARCH
child | BA(I)RN.COLLOP.CRACK
| EYAS-MUSKET.KIND
—'s nature | CHILDNESS
children | IMAGES
children's game | PUSH-PIN

chin	SHINNE	combat	OPPOSITION
chlorosis	WHITE DEATH	combination	QUILL
chop logic	BA(U)LK	combustible	COMBUSTIOUS
church service	MASS	come	
churl	CARLOT	—down the scale	PLUCK OFF
cincture	CENTER	—to a head	HEADED
circle	OE.RONDURE.ROUNDER	—to an end	DETERMINE
circlet	RIGOL(L)	—with me	DUCDAME
cite	CONVENT	comedy	COMMONTY
civilised	INLAND	coming	
clad in armour	IRON	—close upon	THICK-COMING
claim	PLEA	—in	INCOME
clamour	UTIS	command	CHECH.IMPOSE
clandestine activity	TRUNK-WORK	commit adultery	ADULTERATE
clasp	TASSEL	common	MODERN.UNPROPER
claw	CLOYE	—sewer	FILTH
clever	QUAINTLY	—woman	CUSTOMER
close	SEAM	commonalty	COMMON
—connection	IMMEDIACY	commonness	COMMUNITY
—covering	MODEL	commonplace	MODERN
—in approach	UPON	commotion	GARBOILS.ROMAGE
closed	WINKING	communicative	INTELLIGENT
closely interwoven		companion	COMATE
	THICK-PLEACHED		COPES-MATE.SKAIN(E)S MATE
—cloth made in Wales	FRIZE	—devil	YOKE-DEVIL
clothed	SUITED	—in study	BOOK-MATE
clothes-washing			INKHORN-MATE
implement	BATLER.BATLET	companionable	FELLOWLY
cloths hung round ship to conceal		company	HAUNT.HEAP
men from the enemy	FIGHTS	—arriving	ARRIVANCY
clotted with blood		compare	LIKE
	BLOOD-BOLTERED	compartment	SQUARE
clouded	NIGHTED	compassionate	PASSIONATE
clover stalk	HONEY-STALK	—feeling	REMORSE
clown	CARL.LOWT	complain	MEAN(E).MEIN.MENE
	NORTHERN MAN	complaint	PLAINING
club	BAT	complaisance	GENTRY
coarse	UNBOLTED	complete	PARCEL.REPLENISHED
—beef	BULL-BEEVES	completely	HOME
coated with bitumen	BITUMED	—contented	PERFECT
cobbler	COSIER.COZIER	complexion	HAIR.LEER
cockboat	COCK	complimentary	BREATHING
cockchafer	DRUMBLEDOR	composition	COMPOSTURE
coign	COIN	compost	COMPOSTURE
coin	G(U)ILDER.STAMP	compound	TAKE UP
collar of boot	RUFF	compounded	CREATE
colliding	HURTLING	comprehensive	CAPABLE
colour	LEER	compulsory	COMPULSATIVE
comb	PHEEZE	conceal	OVERGREEN

conceit	OPINION	constant	STILL
conceive	ENWOMB	consume	CONFOUND
—of	BRAIN	consummate	MADE UP
conceived in heat of			REPLENISHED
passion	MAD-BRED	contemplation	BEHOLDING
conception	HENT	contemptible	EXSUFFLICATE
concern	CERNE.TENDER		PELTING
concerted music	BROKEN MUSIC	—person	SNIPE
conclude	CROWN.INCLUDE	contemptuous expression	
concordancy	COMPOSITION		FICO.FIGO
concupiscence	CONCUPY	contend	WAGE
condescend	YIELD	contention	BATE
—to take	DEIGN	contents	ARGUMENT
conduce	SHAPE	—of bag or satchel	SCRIPPAGE
conduct	GOVERNMENT	continuously	AN-END
	ORDER.PASS	contradict	TAKE-UP
—itself	CONDUCE		FORESPEAK
confederate	COMPETITOR	contrariety	ADVERSITY
	FEDAR(AR)IE.FEDARARY	contrary	RETROGRADE
	FOEDAIRE.FOEDARIE	control	CHECK.DANGER
	QUALITY	controller of provisions	
confession	EXERCISE.RENDER		PANT(L)ER
	SUBMISSION	controversy	DEBATEMENT
confessional	SHRIFT	convene	CONVENT
confidence	INWARDNESS	convent	COVENT
confine	BALE	conversation	ENTREATMENT
—as in hoop	INHOOP		QUESTION
confinement	PRISONMENT	converse	DIALOGUE.PROPOSE
confirm	AFFEAR.AFFEER		QUESTION.REASON
	COMPACT.STABLISH.TIE	conveyance	ASSURANCE
confirmation	APPROBATION		TRANSPORTANCE
confirmed	AFFEARD	convict	
—possession	STABLISHMENT		APPROVE.CONVINCE.INDITE
confoundedly	PLAUGUY	convinced	PERFECT
confused sound	WHOOBUB	cool	KEEL.RESPECTIVE
confutation	REPROOF	cope with	TAKE UP
confute	CONTROL.PUT DOWN	copy	TAKE OUT
conjecture	CONJECT	corner	COIGNE
	ESTIMATION	—stone	COIN
conjoin	COJOIN	corollary	COLLECTION
connectedness	DEPENDENCY	coroner	CROWNER
connecting link	COMMA	corporal	NYM
conquer	HARROW	corpulent	GORBELLIED
conscious of	WITTOL	corrected	ATTASKED.ATTASKT
consciousness	CONSCIENCE		CORRIGIBLE
consent	GRANT	corroded	CORROBORATE
consequence	COLLECTION	corrupt	CORROBORATE
considerate	RESPECTIVE		DISTASTE
consideration	CONSIDERANCE	Cotswold	COTSALE

cough	TISICK	crust of a pie	CUSTARD-COFFIN
countenance	PATRONAGE	cuckold-maker	HORN-MAKER
counterpane	COUNTERPOINT	cudgel	BALLOW.BAT(TERO)
course	STERNAGE	cunning	FOXSHIP.SKILL
—of events	OCCASION		SUBTILE-WITTED
courtesan	BONA-ROBA	Cupid	BOW-BOY
	GUINEA-HEN	cur	TYKE
courtesy	GENTRY	—with tail docked	CURTAL
cover		curdle	POSSET
—for sinister purpose	STALE	cure	RECURE
—ground	RID WAY	curry	PHEEZE
—up	HOODWINK	curse	VENGEANCE.WANION
—with red colour	OVERRED	cursory	CURSELARIE
covered with			CURSENARY
—high growth	HIGH-GROWN	curtail	ABATE
—wickerwork	TWIGGEN	curtains	CHAMBER-HANGINGS
cow	ROTHER(-BEAST)	curve	COMPASS
—dung	SHARD	cut	SLISH
coward	MEACOCK.VILIACO	—notches in	NICK
	VILLIAGO	—slightly	SCOTCH
—cock	COSTREL.CONSTRIL	—to pieces	MAMMOCK
	COYSTRIL	cutpurse	BUNG
cowardice	COWARDSHIP	cutting	SECT
cowardly	COWISH.MEACOCK	cynic	CRITIC
	MILK-LIVERED	dabchick	DIVE-DAPPER
coxcomb	PRINCOX	daily	JOURNAL
coyness	NICETY	dairymaid	DAY-WOMAN
crabbed	CURST	dance	CINQUE-PACE
crack	WHIP		SINK(E)-A-PACE
cradle	LULLABY	—tune	LIGHT-O'-LOVE
craft	CAUTEL	—with much leaping	LAVOLT(A)
crafty	BRAID(E)	Dane	DANSHER
craftiness	FOXSHIP	dark	
cram	FRANK	—as night	NIGHTLY
crazy	WOOD	—complexioned	
creative	FORGETIVE	person	WOOSEL(L)
creep on knees	KNEE	—spot on horse's face	CLOUD
crewel	INKLE	darken	COLLY
crime	MALEFACTION	darkened	NIGHTED
critic	CARREN	—room for confinement of	
crone	TROT	madmen	DARK-HOUSE
crooked	CAM.KAM(E)	darling	SWEETING
crowd	VARLETRY	dart in	ENDART
crowfoot	CROW-FLOWER	dash	PASH
crown	PALE	daubing	DAWBRY
crude	CRUDY	Dauphin	DOLPHIN
—artful device	DAWBRY	day for settlement of	
cruelly holy	HOLY-CRUEL	disputes	LOVE-DAY
crush	PASH	daze	ASTONISH.DARE

dead	
—body	GHOST
—dog	DITCH-DOG
deaden	PROROGUE
dealing	MERCHANDISE
dear	CHARITABLE
—to the heart	HEART-DEAR
dearest	LIEFEST
death	DEFUNCTION
	FUNERAL.LETHE
debtors' prison	HELL
decay	BRUSH
decease	CEASE
deceitful	BRAID(E).DECEPTIOUS
	PROPER-FALSE
deceive	BLEAR.MISUSE
decency of	
conduct	GOVERNMENT
decide	MAKE UP.PASS
—by evidence	TESTIMONY
—to go to a place	RESOLVE ON
decipher	CIPHER.CYPHER
decisive	EFFECTUAL
deck	DUE
declare	DISCUSS
decorations	FURNITURE
deed	ISSUE
deer	VENISON
—out of condition	RASCAL
defame	INFAMONISE
defect	DECIPHER
defence	PROPUGNATION
defend	ENGUARD
—by bars	SPERR(E)
—from the	
weather	WEATHER-FEND
defer	REJOURN
deficient (horse bit)	HALF
	-CHEEK'D
defile	ENSEAM.FILE.RAY
deformed	STIGMATIC
deft	FEAT
deftest	EFTEST
degenerate	DEROGATE.RECOIL
degraded	DEROGATE
deify	GOD
deign	DAINE
delay	FOR(E)SLOW.FORSLOE
	INDURANCE

delegation	SUBSTITUTION
delicacies	CATES
delicate	INCONIE.INCONY.KONY
delightful	DELIGHTED
delineated	STEELD
deliver back	RELIVER
demeaned	BORE
demolish	RUINATE
demure	PRENZIE
den	ANTRE
dentist	TOOTH-DRAWER
departed from the world	
in peace	PEACE-PARTED
departure	DEPART
depict	IMPAINT
depravity	FOLLY
depress	ABATE
deprive of	UNPROVIDE
—a horse	UNCOLT
—all chance	LURCH
—beauty	UNFAIR
—edge	DISEDGE
—life	UNLIVE
—possession	DISPROPERTY
—state or dignity	UNSTATE
—wits	UNWIT
deprived of sphere	DISORBED
deputation	ATTORNEY
deranged	BRAIN-SICKLY
description	ADDITION
	DEFINEMENT
design	INTENDMENT
	PRETENCE.SKILL
desire	AFFECTION.BOSOM
—strongly	EARN
despatch	EXPEDIENCE
destination	LIST
destitute of feeling	KINDLESS
destroy	CONFOUND
LANDDAMNE.QUELL.RUINATE	
SPOIL.STROY.UNLACE	
destruction	DEFEAT
detachment	DISTRACTION
detail	SEVERAL
determine	DETERMINATE
determined	FAST
—person	RESOLUBLE
detractor	SUBTRACTOR
detrition	BRUSH

device	IMPRESS.PLATFORM		disdainful	DISDAINED
	PRETENCE			ORGILLOUS.ORGULOUS
devil	GOODYEAR.SETEBOS		disfigure	DEFEAT
devolve	SUCCEED		disfigurement	DEFEATURE
devotion	DEVOTEMENT		disgrace	REPROOF
devouring	MOUSING		disguise	DAUB.IMMASK
dexterously	FEATLY		disguised	SELF-COVERED
diadem	CIRCUIT		dishearten	UNHEART
dice game	NOVUM.TRAY-TRIP		dishonest	LOZEL(L)
die	CEASE.GO OFF		—practice	INDIRECTION
difficulty	STRAIN		dislodge	DISHABIT
dignified	CROWNED		dismal	TRISTFUL
dilate	DELATE		dismiss	CAST.DAFF
dilatory	PROLIXIOUS		dismissal	AVAUNT
dim-sighted	THICK-SIGHTED		disorder	DEFUSE.GARBOIL(S)
diminutive figure	AGLET BABIE		—at night	NIGHT-RULE
	AGLET BABY		disordered	BETUMBLED
din	UTIS		disparage	DISVALUE
direct	REFLEX		dispel	RESOLVE
—one's course	INTEND		dispersal	SEGREGATION
direction			dispirited	PALE-HEARTED
—by gesture	ACTION		display to view	IMBARE
—of the eye	BEND		dispose	SORT
dirty	RAY		disposition	AFFECTION
—drab	PUSSEL			INTENDMENT
—woman	MALKIN.MAWKIN		disposed	PREGNANT
disavow	DISVOUCH		disregard	OMIT
disarmed of			dissembling	BRAIDE
faculties	UNQUALIFIED		disseminate	SCALE
disburse	DISPURSE		dissolution	CRACK
discandying	DISCANDERING		dissolve	RESOLVE
discharge			—from candy	DISCANDIE
—from a sponge	DISPUNGE			DISCANDY
—from nose	SALT-RHEUM		distant sighting	DESCRY
—shatteringly	RIVE		distempered	ILL-TEMPERED
disclosure	OVERTURE		distinction	DISTINGUISHMENT
discoloured by smoke	RE(E)CHIE		distinguishable	DIVIDANT
	REECHY		distress at sea	SEA-SORROW
discontent	DISEASE		disturbance	GARBOILS
discourse	PROPOSE.REASON		diurnal	JOURNAL
discourteousness	KILL-COURTESY		divert	SWITS
discover	SMOKE		divided	DIVIDABLE
discovery	DENOTEMENT		dividing	MEER'ED
discuss	EXPOSTULATE		division of atmosphere	REGION
	QUESTION		do	
discussion	QUESTION		—battle	DARRAIGN(E)
discussed too				DARRAIN(E)
much	OVERHANDLED			DARRAYN.DERAIGN
disdain	COY		—homage	VAIL

—it	DICH
—up	DUP
—without	MISS
doctor	BODY-CURER
dog	LYM.SHOUGH.SHOWGHE
	TYKE
—rose	CANKER
doing	OCCASION
domestics	MEINIE.MEIN(E)Y
dominion	EMPERY
done	SPED
dotard	DOTANT
doubt	STRAIN
—to the smallest detail	TO POINT
down	
—on a feather	DOWL(E)
down(y)	DOWLNE(Y)
dragged by the	
head	HEAD-LUGGED
draw	
—advantage	AVAIL
—in	INSHELL
—out	EXHALE.TOAZE
drawn	
—by doves	DOVE-DRAWN
—justly from	
scabbard	RIGHT-DRAWN
—out of bogs	FEN-SUCKED
dread	GASTNESS(E)
—of evil to come	MISDREAD
dreadful	DE(A)RN
—event	STRATAGEM
dreamy fellow	JOHN-A-DREAMS
dress	TRICKING
—of new-born child	SWATH
dressed	SUITED
dressing trendily	
	FASHION-MONGING
drift	HULL.RACK
drinking	
—between meals	BY-DRINKING
—cry	RIVO
—vessel	STO(O)PE
drive	RACK
—away	OVERBLOW
—by fits	FIT
—mad	MAD
—out of roost	UNROOST
droop	LOB

—in spirit	PEAK
drown the voice of	OUTVOICE
drowsy	YAWNING
drub without drawing	
blood	DRYBEAT
drudge	DRUG
drunk	FAP.PAID
drunken fellow	COYSTRIL
dry up	ENSEAR
due	FITMENT
—performance	PROPERTY
dull	BARREN.BLUNT-WITTED
	DISEDGE.FAT.MULL
	ILLUSTRIOUS
dutiful	OFFICIOUS
dwarfish person	AGATE
dwell	REMAIN
dying young	TENDER-DYING
eager	AYGRE.PRONE.WATERY
—to rival	EMULATE
earnest	DEAR
earnestly	WISTLY
easily	LIGHTLY
easy work	BEDWORK
eat one's words	EAT THE LEEK
echo	CHIDE.REPLICATION
	RESPEAK.REWORD
edict	PROCESS
efface	DISLIMN
effeminate	MEACOCK
—person	CARPET-MONGER
effusion	EFFUSE
eggs	PULLET-SPERM
eke out	ECH(E).EECH.ICH
elicit	TOAZE
emanate	VANISH
emasculated	NICKED
embark	INSHIP
embassy	EMBASSADE
embed in sand or mud	DOCK
emblem	IMPRESS(E)
embrace	CHAIN.EMBRASURE
	INCLIP
emotion	GIRO
empire	EMPERY
empiricutic	EMPIRICK QUTIQUE
employ	EXECUTE
employment	ENTERTAINMENT
—of exercise	EXECUTION

empty	CAST
enactment	ENACT
encamp	SET DOWN
encamped	FIELDED
encircle	ENWHEEL.PALE
enclose	EMBOSS.EMBOUND.RIB
	WOMB
—as in hearse	INHEARSE
	INHERCE
enclosing wall	EMURE
encounter	CLOSE.COPE
encouragement	AIM
encroach	JET
end	LOOSE.SPOIL.UTMOST
—of all	EXIGENT
endanger	DANGER
endearing	CHARITABLE
endless	FINELESS
endow with widow's	
rights	WIDOW
endowed	FULL-FRAUGHT
—with grace	GRACED
—with parts	PARTED
endowments	BELONGINGS
endue	DUE
endurable	PORTABLE
endure	ABROOKE.PERDURE
enduring	UNDERGOING
enema syringe	CLYSTER-PIPE
enfold	INCLIP
engage in fight	MEDDLE
engineer	ENGENER
engraving	SCULPTURE
enigma	EGMA
enjoy carnally	TASTE
enjoyment	SUFFIGANCE
enormously wicked	HIGH-VICED
enough	BASTA
enrich	RICH
enriched	MADE
enseam	INSEEM
enshelled	ENSHIELD
entangle	ENROOT
—hair	ELF
enter upon terms	ARTICULATE
entered into	
manhood	MAN-ENTERED
enterprise	DESIGNMENT
	EXPEDIENCE

entertain in kitchen	KITCHEN
entertainment	ENTERTAIN
entice(ment)	TICE
entire	MEERED
entrails	CHAUDRON
entrance	INDUCTION
entreaty	BESEECH.TREATY
entry on probation	APPROBATION
epithet(on)	APATHATON
equal	COMPEER.EGAL
—rank	RIVALTY
equality	RIVALITY
equipment	FURNITURE.TIRE
equipped	FULL-FRAUGHT
erect	STRAIGHT-PIGHT
ergo	ARGAL
escort	TEND
essential quality	PROPERTY
establish	APPROVE.STABLISH
estimated amount or value	RATE
estimation	RATE
evade by trick or lie	FUB OFF
evening just past	OVERNIGHT
evenness of	
temper	GOVERNMENT
evens	MEET
event	LOOSE.SPEED
—foretold	OMEN
events	OCCASION
everlasting	PERDURABLE
everyday	MODERN
evidence	ARGUMENT.AVOUCH
	INSTANCE
evident	PREGNANT
evil	SHREWD
—usage or behaviour	MISUSE
exact	COMMAND
exactly	JUMP
exaggerate	RACK
exalted	HAUGHT.HAU(L)T
examine	QUOTE
—on oath	DEPOSE
example for imitation	SAMPLE
exceed in	
—clamour	OUTVOICE
—cunning	OUTCRAFTY
—estimation	OUTPRIZE
—poisonousness	OUTVENOM
—value	OUTWORTH

—villainy	OUTVILLAIN	extracted	EXTRAUGHT
exceedingly	VENGEANCE	extractor of teeth	
excel	OUTPEER		TOOTH-DRAWER
—in		extravagant	DIFFUSED
—beauty	OUTBRAG		FANATICAL
—boldness	OUTBRAVE	extremely	VENGEANCE
—splendour	OUTBRAG	—dim-sighted	
	OUTBRAVE		HIGH-GRAVEL-BLIND
excellence	WORTHY	extremity	UTTERANCE
excelling	PASSED	exultant	TRIUMPHANT
except	ABATE	eye disease	PIN AND WEB
excess	VANTAGE		WEB AND PIN
excessively	OUT OF ALL CESSE	eyelids	WINDOWS
exchange	COUNTERCHANGE	eyes	CHRYSTALS
excite	ACCITE.SOLICIT.TARRE	face	PROPOSE
execute	OVERSEE	—down	OUTLOOK
executioner	EXECUTOR	—in profile	HALF-CHEEK
exercise		fade	VADE
—of power	FACULTY	fail to check	UNCHECK
—office over	O'REOFFICE	faint	SWELT
—one's craft	CRAFT	fair	PROPER-FALSE
exhale	VANISH	fairy	OUPH(E)
exhausted	EMBOWELLED	—ring	ORB
exhibited in articles	ARTICULATED	faith	FAY
exhilaration preceding death		faithful	HOLY
	LIGHTENING	falcon	TASSEL-GENTLE
exhortation	EXERCISE	falconer	ASTRINGER
existent	ESSENTIAL	fall	
expectation	EXPECT.SUPPOSE	—headlong	PRECIPITATE
expediency	COMMODITY	—short of	SHORT
expeditious	EXPEDIENT	falling	CADENT
expend	CONFOUND	fallow deer, second year	PRICKET
expensive	CHARGEFUL	false	
experience	ASSAY	—friend	MOUTH-FRIEND
expired	EXPIATE	—in religion	IRRELIGIOUS
explain	UNBOLT	—pretence	DAWBRY
exploit	TOUCH	—step	MISTREADING
express		falsehood	DAUBERY.DAWBRY
—in writing	PRINT	falsify	COG
—purpose	NONCE	falsifying	FALSING
expressing deep feeling		familiarity	INWARDNESS
	PASSIONING	fancy	LOVE.TOY
expression	EXPRESSURE	fanfare	SENNET
exquisite	PICK	fang	PHANG
exterminate	EXTERMINE.EXTIRP	fantastic	FANTASTICO
	KILL-UP	—head-dress	TIRE-VALIANT
external appearance	OUTWALL	—person	PHANTASIM(E)
	OUTWARD	far-fetched	EXQUISITE
extinguished	EXTINCTED	farcin, farcy	FASHIONS

fashion	FEAT
fasten	LATCH
—by rein	REIN
—talons on	TIRE
fastening	TASSEL
fastidious	CHARY
fat	GORBELLIED
—in lump for candle-making	
	TALLOW KEECH
fat-bellied	GOR-BELLIED
father	MALE
fatigued	WAPPEND
fatten	ENGROSS.FRANK
faucet-seller	FOSSET-SELLER
favour done	LOVE
favoured	GRACED
favouring	SECOND
fawn on	SPANIEL
fawned on	SMOOTHED
—as by spaniel	PANELLED
feast together	CONVIVE
feather	DOWLE
feature	LEER.TOUCHE
features	FAVOUR
feeble old man	PANTALOON
feed	REPAST
—greedily	TIRE
—one's desires or thoughts	TIRE
—on false hopes	EAT THE AIR
feel tenderness for	TENDER
feign	TAKE UPON ONESELF
feigned	SUPPOSED
fellow	COMPANION.COMPETITOR
	RIVAL.SEMBLABLE
felt	APPROVED
female	
—child	MAID-CHILD
—fox	FIXEN
—infant	CHILD
—messenger	WOMAN-POST
—offender	OFFENDRESS
feminine	EFFEMINATE
fencer	SCRIMER.SCRIMURE
fencing term	HAY
—thrust	PASSADO.STUCK
ferry	TRANECT
fervent	PRONE
festivity	
	CARPET-CONSIDERATION

few	PAUCAS
—words	FEWNESS
fickle-person	CHANGING-PIECE
fickleness	CHANGE
fiend	OBIDICUT
fierce	WALL-EYED.WOOD
fig	FICO.FIGO.FOOTRA.FOUTRA
fight	STRIKE
—against	REPUGN
fighting person	SQUARER
figure and rank	SORT AND SUIT
fill with	
—horror	ABHOR
—lies	BELIE
filthy	SCALD
final throw at bowls	UPCAST
fine	INCONIE.INCONY.KONY
—collector	CHEATER
—fellow	BAWCOCK
—filament	SLEAVE
—velvet	THREE-PILE
finger	
—as keys of a virginal	VIRGINAL
—hole	VENTIGE
—nails	TEN COMMANDMENTS
finical	NEAT
—delicacy	CURIOSITY
fire for trying, proving	TRIAL-FIRE
firm in belief	THOUGHTEN
firmly	FASTLY
firmness	FIXTURE
first	
—taste of blood	FLESHMENT
—part	VAUNT
fish on land	LAND-FISH
fist	NEAF(F)E
fit	FADGE.RAPTURE
—of lunacy	LUNE
—to be shaved	RAZORABLE
fits of temper	LINES
fitting	LIABLE
five-spotted	CINQUE-SPOTTED
fix firmly	CONFIX
fixed	PIGHT.STEELED
flake	FLAW
flap wings impatiently	BATE
flash	FLAKE
flat	
—buttock	QUATCH-BUTTOCK

—pancake	FLAPJACK	—from		OUTFACE
flatter	MAKE FAIR WEATHER	forefront		VAWARD
	WORD	forehead		FRONTIER
fleece	FETCH OFF	foreign		STRANGE
flesh-eating	CARNAL	foremost		FORMER
fleshing	FLESHMENT	forenamed		PRENOMINATE
flew	FLEWED	forerunner		PRECURRER
flexible twig	SWITS	forfend		SHIELD
float	HULL	form of particulars		SCEDULE
flock bed	QUILT	formed		FEATED
flood	RAGE	—into ridges		ENRIDGED
florid	TAFFETA(S).TAFFETY	—into stars		STEELED
flourish	SWINDGE	formulate		PROPOSE
—of trumpet music	TUCKET	forsaken		
flout	LOUT	—by mistress		LASS-LORN
flow	RECOURSE	—person		FORLORN
flowed	FLOWN	fortune		HAVING
fluke	UPCAST	foul		REEKY
flushed	ROSED	found		STAY
flutter	BEAT	four		
—like a hawk	BATE	—inches wide		FOUR-INCHED
fly		—people at banquet		MESS
—off	BLENCH	fowl		BIDDY
—over	OREPEARCH	fragment	FLAW.QUANTITY	
—up and perch on	OREPEARCH	frail		UNTIMBERED
flying cloud	RACK	frame of mind		TEMPERALITIE
foam on water	YEAST	frantic		WOOD
fodder	STOVER	free		LARGE
fold	PLEACH	—from		
follow like a spaniel	SPANIEL	—deafness		UNDEAF
follower	SEQUENT	—domestic cares	UNHOUSED	
food	REPASTURE	free school	CHARGE-HOUSE	
fool	ASNICO.ASSINEGO.	freedom		LET-ALONE
	CHIPOCHIA.COLT	frenzy		LUNES
	GECK.LACK-BRAIN	frequent		OLD
	PIED NINNY.SNIPE	frequenter of theatre		
—'s word	IMPETICOS	pit		GROUNDLING
foolhardy	DARING-HARDY	freshness		YOUTH
foolish person	BAUBLE	friend		LOVER
foolishly	SHALLOWLY	friendliness		FRIENDING
footing	FEET	fright		TIRRIT
footpad	FOOT-LAND-RAKER	frighten	DARE.GALLOW	
	STRIKER			GAST
fop	BARBER-MONGER	frightened at		
foppish	FANGLED	oneself	SELF-AFFRIGHTED	
—megalomaniac	MONARCHO	fringed with hair		VALANCED
for any sake	OF ALL LOVES	from		ON
force		—time to time	STILL AND END	
—back against current	RESTEM	front	FOREWARD.VAWARD	

fruitful	CHILDING.CONCEPTIOUS	—with dice	TRAY-TRIP
	INCREASEFUL	gamester	CHEATER
fruiting	CHILDING	gaming	DIE
fuddled	FAP	gaoler	ADAM
fulfil in place of another		gap in fence	MUSIT
	STEED UP	gape in astonishment	YAWN
fulfilment	ENACTURE	garment worn at sea	SEA-GOWN
full		garter-tape	CADDIS.CADDYSS
—of		gash	SCOTCH
—daring	DAREFUL	gay fellow	CAVALERO
—faults or crimes	FAULTFUL	gelded	UNPAVED
—honest zeal	TRUE-DEVOTED	gelding	CUT
—impediments	BARFUL	genuflection	KNEE
—obstructions	BARREFUL	get married	GO INTO THE WORLD
—small openings	LOOPED	ghostly	SPRIGHTLY
—speed	RANDON	gibberish	LINSEY-WOOLSEY
—to the brim	TOPFULL	gibe	GLEEK.GLIKE
—with acorns	FULL-ACORNED	gift of no value	NOTHING-GIFT
fully	BY WEIGHT.IN WEIGHT	gild	ENGILD
	WITH WEIGHT	gillyflower	GILLYVOR
—charged	FULL-FRAUGHT	gimmal	GIMMOR
—completed	EXPIATE	gimmalled	JYMOLD
fumitory	FEMETARY.FEMITER	ginger root	RACE
	FENITAR.FUMITER	give	BETEEM(E)
funeral garland	CRANTS	—a share of	PARTAKE
funnel	TUN-DISH	—away	LEAVE
furious	BRAINISH.WOOD	—freedom to	ENFREEDOM
furnish	STUFF	—new life to	REQUICKEN
—supper for	SUP	—place	BACCARE.BACKARE
furniture	TIRE	—up by signing	SUBSCRIBE
gain		given due consideration	
—advantage			WELL-RESPECTED
over	RECOVER (THE WIND)	giving	
—money	COIN	—attention	ATTENT
gallant	CHAMBERER	—no help	HELPLESS
gallantry	GAME	—offence	OFFENCE-FUL
gallants	GALLANTRY	glade	LAUND
gallery of theatre	SCAFFOL(D)AGE	glance	ELIAD.ILLIAD.OEILIAD
galligaskins	GASKINS	glaring	WALL-EYED
gallows	GALLOWSES	glittering	CLINQUANT
gallows-bird	CRACK-HEMP	glory	GARLAND
	HEMP-SEED.CRACK-ROPE	glorying	MAGNIFICENT
	CRACK-HALTER	glutted with prey	RAVINED
game		go	PATH
—killed in hunt	HUNT	—hang	SNECK UP.SNICK UP
—like bagatelle	TROLL-MY-DAME	—on	CONDUCE
	TROU-MADAME	—over to enemy	FALL OVER
—running figure-of-eight		—to the deuce	GO WHISTLE
	QUAINT-MAZES	go-between	RING-CARRIER

—in romantic affairs	LOVE-BROKER
goblin	OUPH
God's	
—foot	'SFOOT
—pity	OD'S-PIT(T)IKINS
gold thread made in Venice	VENICE GOLD
golden	
—money	GILD
—russet	LEATHER-COAT
—tresses	TALLENT
gone by	BY-PAST
good	
—manners	GENTRY
—sense	MATTER
gorged	RAVIN'D
gorgeously variegated	PROUD-PIED
gorging	MOUSING
gorse	GOSSE
grace	DUE.FAVOUR
graduation on a dial	PRICK
grant	BETEEM(E)
granted three suits a year	THREE-SUITED
grasping	LARGE-HANDED
grassy place	LAUND
gratification	SUPPLIANCE
gratifying	GRATULATE
gratuity	GRATILLITY
grave	CICIL
—digger	GRAVE-MAKER
—import	STATE
grease	ENLARD.SEAM(E)
greasy	RE(E)CHIE.REECHY
great	
—event	STRATEGEM
—expanse	MAIN
—gun	CHAMBER
greet	
—again	REGREET
—one another	CONGREET
greeting	COMMEN
greetings	REGREET
grieve	CONDOLE.TAKE THOUGHT
grieving	HEART-SORE
grievous	DEAR(E).DERE
grimace	MOE.MOP

grip	FANG.VICE
gross	SALT-BUTTER
grossly	GREASILY
—covered	MABLED.MOBLED
grotesque pageant	ANTIC
group of fish	SCUL(L).SCULLE
grow cold	QUENCH
guarantee legal possession	VOUCH
guard	ENGUARD.FORTRESS
guess	AIM
guilt	FACT
guilty	GUILTY-LIKE
guinea(-hen)	GYNN(E)Y
gull	ZANY
gun (30lbs)	DEMI-CANNON
gypsy	TURLEYGOOD TURLUPIN
habit of frequenting	HAUNT
hale	EXHALE
half	
—gallon drinking pot	POTTLE-POT
—wolf	DEMI-WOLF
halloo	SO-HO
handkerchief	HANDKERCHER
handsome	GOOD-FACED
—and deceitful	PROPER-FALSE
hanging	
—in rags	TOTT'RING
—like fetters	DOWN-GYVED
hangman's noose	HEMPEN CAUDLE
hamstring	HOX
hands	PICKERS
happen	PROCEED
—to	BEFORTUNE
harden by cold	BAKE
hardhearted	FLINT-HEART(ED)
hardship	DISGRACE
hare	BAUD
harlot	HIREN
harm	VENGEANCE
harsh	AYGRE.EAGER
haste	EXPEDIENCE.POST
hasty	FESTINATE
hat fringed with tassels	THRUMMED-HAT
hatch	DISCLOSE

haughty	HAUGHT.HAU(L)T.SURLY
haul out	EXHALE
haunt	SPRIGHT
have	
—a holiday	PLAY
—engagement	BE PROMISED
—done	BE THROUGH
—ill will towards	BEAR HARD
—in the womb	ENWOMB
—value	WEIGH
having	
—a child	CHILDED
—a lover	LOVERED
—abilities	PARTED
—curly hair	CURLED-PATE
—dislocated shoulder	
	SHOULDER-SHOTTEN
—fewer customers	
	CUSTOM-SHRUNK
—fiery eyes	FIRE-EYED
—literary knowledge	
	LITERATURED
—mind of a	
puppy	PUPPY-HEADED
—nailed soles	CLOUTED
—power to do many	
things	MULTIPOTENT
—right to	CAPABLE
—skin eruptions	TETTEROUS
—the chaps of a hound	FLEWED
—weals	WHELKED
hawk-keeper	ASTRINGER
hawklike	HAWKING
hazard	JUMP
head	COCKSCOMB.MAZ(Z)ARD
	NOLE.NOWL.PASH
—dress shaped like soup dish	
	PORRENGER.PORRINGER
heal	RECURE
health-giving	VIRTUOUS
healthy	LUSTICK.LUSTIQUE
	WHOLESOME
heap up	UPHOORD
hear	
—in turn	OVERHEAR
—over again	OVERHEAR
hearken	TEND
heart	BOWER
—'s desire	BOSOM

heartily	AGOOD
hearty eater	TRENCHER-MAN
heaving	HEFT
heavy galley	GALLEASS
Hecate	HECAT
hedged in by poles	POLE-CLIPT
height	BROW
—of mockery	ARCH-MOCK
heir	
—apparent	APPARENT
—to much wealth	RICH-LEFT
held	HILD
—in no awe	AWELESS
hell	TARTAR
helm	STERN
helpful	SECOND
hemlock	INSANE ROOT
henbane	INSANE ROOT
	HEBENON.HEBONA
hen-pecked	WOMAN-TIRED
hesitate	MAMMER
hiccough	WAXEN.YEXEN
hide	ENCAVE.HOODWINK
high-crowned	COPATAINE
highly accomplished	ABSOLUTE
hill where grain is winnowed	
by wind	SHEALING-HILL
SHEELING-HILL.SHIELING-HILL	
	SHILLING-HILL
hinged	JYMOLD
hiss	HIZZ
hist	PEACE
hit	PAY
—in fencing	VENEWE.VENEY
ho!	WHOOP
hoard	UPHOORD
hold	
—aloof	STAND OFF
—up as example	PARAGON
holding power of destiny	FATED
holiday	PLAYING
hollow	COVERED.WOMBY
holy-water vessel	STO(O)PE
homely	FOUL
homicidal (malapropism)	
	HON(E)Y-SUCKLE
homicide (malapropism)	
	HON(E)Y-SEED
honest fellow	TRUEPENNY

hook for hose or breeches	POINT
hope	ESPERANCE
horn call to rally	
hounds	RECH(E)ATE.RECHEAT
horned	FORKED
horoscope	FIGURE
horse	CUT
—disease	FIVES
—poor	JADE
—'s canine tooth	TUSH
horseback journey	RODE
hot	
—and transient, like	
summer	SUMMER-SEEMING
—headed	BRAINISH
	WASPISH-HEADED
—spiced gingerbread	
	PEPPER-GINGERBREAD
how does it happen	
that . . .	HOW CHANCE
howl at	BEHOWL
hubbub	WHOOBUB
human	
—creature	CIVIL
—feet	PETTITOES
humbled	PLUME-PLUCKT
humid	HUMOROUS
humorous	CAPRICIOUS
humour	COMPLEXION
hunchback	CROOKBACK
hungry	HUNGERLY.SHARP
hungrily	HUNGERLY
hunt wrong scent	HUNT COUNTER
hurried	FESTINATE
hurry away	WHIR(R)
hurtful	SHREWD
husk	SHALE.SHEAL
	SHEEL.SHIEL.SHILL
husky	CORKY
hyena	HYEN
hypocrisy	COUNTENANCE
I	CHE
—tell fortunes	DUCDAME
idle chatter	BIBBLE-BABBLE
ignoble	UNNOBLE
ignominy	IGNOMY
ignorant	UNCONFIRMED
ill	
—conditioned	SHREWD

—mannered fellow	TYKE
—mixed	ILL-TEMPERED
—natured	SHREWD
—regulated	INCORRECT
illegitimate	MISBEGOTTEN
illumine	OVERSHINE
image	MODULE.SHRINE
imaginary	AIR-DRAWN
imagination	AFFECTION
imaginative	FORGETIVE
imagine	PROPOSE
—expectantly	WEEN
imbued with a	
property	PROPERTIED
immature	PUPPY-HEADED
—peascod	SQUASH
immoderately	OUT OF ALL CESSE
immodest woman	TOMBOY
immortal	EVER-LIVING
immure	EMURE
impact	POISE
impart	PARTAKE
impatient of	
question	UNQUESTIONABLE
impeach	APPEACH
impede	RUB
impending evil	IMMINENCE
importunacy	IMPORTANCE
importunate	IMPORTANT
importunity	IMPORTANCE
imposition	DAUBERY.DAWBRY
impossible to	
undo	UNRECALLING
imprecation	GOODYEAR
impresa	IMPRESS(E)
impression	CHARACTERY
	CICATRICE
	(IM)PRESSURE
imprint	SET
imprisonment	PRISONMENT
improve	PROFIT
imprudent fellow	JACK SAUCE
in	
—a	
—body	IN SORT.IN THE QUILL
—derogatory manner	
	DEROGATELY
—moment	UPON A THOUGHT
	WITH A THOUGHT

—any case	IN ANY HAND	indifferent to	WIDE OF
—concert	IN THE QUILL	indignation	MOTIONS
—consequence of		indirect course	INDIRECTION
that	THEREUPON	individual person	SEVERAL
—custody	FORTHCOMING	individuality	PROPERTY
—full bloom	FLUSH		PROPRIETY
—full extent	HOME	indivisible	INDIVIDABLE
—good earnest	A-GOOD		INTRENCHANT
—like manner	SEMBLABLY	induce to come	PROCURE
—my name	IN MY VOICE	indulge	ALLOW
—one's prime	PRIMY	—oneself	CARVE
—one's right mind		indulged in	EMBRACED
	WELL-ADVISED	ineffective	UNPREGNANT
—rapid motion	RACKING	inevitable	UNSHUN'D
—readiness	ALL POINTS		UNAVOIDED
—state of just proportion		inexorable	INEXECRABLE
	WEAL-BALANCED	inexperienced	PUNY
—succession	SUCCESSANTLY		UNEXPERIENT
—the		inexpressible	TERMLESS
—field of battle	FIELDED	infection	ATTAINT
—least	IN THE SMALLEST	inference	COLLECTION
—meantime	THE WHILE	inferior	IMPAIR
—night	ANIGHT	infested by thieves	THIEVISH
inattentive	UNRESPECTIVE	infix strongly	CHARACTER
incapable of containing		inflammable	COMBUSTIOUS
	INTENIBLE	—as tinder	TINDER-LIKE
incite to fight	TARRE	inflated	BOMBAST
inclination	CARE	—as with pride	HIGH-BLOWN
incline	PROPEND	inflict pain on	SUFFER
incomprehensible		inform	RECOMMEND.YIELD
	UNCOMPREHENSIVE	—against	PEACH
inconsiderable	EASY.PELTING	ingoing	ENTER
	WEAK	inhabitant	CONFINER
inconsiderate	UNWEIGHING	initiated	WELL-ENTERED
inconsistent		initiating excitement	FLESHMENT
medley	GALLIMAUFRY	initiation	ELEMENT
inconstant	GIGLET.GIGLOT	injunction	IMPOSE
incontinent	UNSTANCHED	inmost thought	CONSCIENCE
incorporate	INCORPSE	inquiry	ENQUIRE.INQUIRE
—one's own share	PIECE UP	insanity	INFAMIE.INSANIE
increasing	CRESSIVE	inscrutable	INVIS'D
incredible	INCREDULOUS	insensible	BLUNT.IRON-WITTED
incurable	UNRECURING	—to shame	SHAME-PROOF
incursion	RODE	insert in a schedule	ENSCHEDULE
indebted	DEBTED	inshelled	COCKLED.ENSHIELD
indecent	UNACCUSTOMED	inside	INWARD
indeed	GOOD-DEED	insidious	CAUTELOUS
indicate	DESIGN	—purpose	CAUTEL
indication	DENOTEMENT	insignificant	PICKING.PUISNY

insincere	MOUTH-MADE
insincerity	MOUTH-HONOUR
insinuate	SUGGEST
insist	CONSIST
—upon	STRAIN
insisting	UNSISTING
inspection	OVERVIEW
inspired	BREATHED
instigator	PUTTER-ON
instruct	STUDY
—in Gospel	GOSPEL
instructed	WELL-ENTERED
insult	FIG.INSULTMENT
—by gesture	FIG
intangible	UNFELT
intensity	INTENTION
intention	DESIGNMENT.HENT
	INTENDMENT.REGARD
—of going	PURPOSE
interchange	CONVERSE
interjection	CAESE.CEAS(E)
HANDY-DANDY.SESE(Y).SESSA	
—boisterous	HOO
—of	
—impatience	TILLY-FALLY
	TILLY-VALLY
—surprise	GEMINI.GEMINY
	GEMONY.JIMINY
—imitating arrow sound	HEWGH
—to call a person	WHY
interest	MEANS.USANCE.USE
interested	INTEREST
interpret	SCAN
intertwine	IMPLEACH
interval	BETWEEN
interwoven	ENTERTISSUED
intimacy	INWARDNESS
intimate friend	INWARD
intoxication	DISTEMPER
intricate	INTRINCE.INTRINSE
	INTRINSICATE
introduction	INDEX
inventive	FORGETIVE
inventory	SCEDULE
invigoration by resting	REST
invisible	SIGHTLESS
invite	INDITE
inviting	COASTING
invoke	SWEAR

involved	PLIGHTED
involving trust	TRUSTY
irregular	DIFFUSED
irresistible	OPPOSELESS
irretentive	INTENIBLE
irritable	WASP-STUNG
	WASP-TONGUE
irritated	RAG'D.RAGDE
irritating person	WATER-FLY
is of no importance	SKILLS NOT
jack	
—at bowls	MISTRESS
—in-office	JACK GUARDANT
jade	NAG
jagged	RAG'D.RAGDE
jaunt	JAUNCE.JAUNSE
jealous of higher	
authority	EMULOUS
jerk	PECKE.SWITS
jest	GLEEK.GLIKE
jester	MOTLEY.PIED NINNY
jilt	HUSWIFE
jog-trot	RANKE
join	INJOINT.SPLINTER
—as partner	PARTNER
—together	INTERJOIN
joined as by sinews	INSINEW
joining again	REIOYNDURE
joint	
—bargain	CO-MART
—in mechanism	GIMMOR
jointed	JYMOLD
jolly	
—cock	BAWCOCK
—companion	EPHESIAN
journey	GEST
Jove	THUNDER-BEARER
	THUNDER-DARTER
	THUNDER-MASTER
judgement	DIRECTION
juicy	MOIST
just	JUMP.TRUE-DISPOSING
justify	APPROVE
keen	HAWKING.PARLOUS
keenly	SHREWD
keep	
—a hawk from sleep	WATCH
—busy with scruples	TASK
—from exertion	PROROGUE

—good watch or
  order   KEEP GOOD QUARTER
—head to wind   TRY
—in suspense   PEIZE
—off   EXPEL.OVERBLOW
keeping
—back knowledge   IGNORANT
—off the sun   SUN-EXPELLING
kept pace with   FILED
kestrel   STALLION.STANYEL
kettledrum   KETTLE
key of musical instrument   CHIP
kindness   LOVE
kindred   KINDLY
kite   PUTTOCK
knack   QUIRK
knave   COISTREL.COISTRIL
       COYSTREL.COYSTRIL
knavery PATCHERY.ROPE-TRICK
kneel   KNEE
knight's stall   INSTALLMENT
know   WEET(E).WIS(T).WOT
—how to behave UNDERSTAND
knowing ACKNOWNE.WITTOL
knowledge   KNOW
known by heart
     RECOLLECTED TERMS
knurled   GNARLED
lace tag   AGLET BABIE
laden   FRAUGHT
ladykin   LAKIN
laid
—by the wind   LODGED
—waste   BARE
lame   MAIN
lament MEAN(E).MEIN.MENE
large   WIDE-STRETCHED
lark song   TIRRA-LIRRA
           TIRRA-LYRA
lascivious CAPRICIOUS.SAUCY
lash   SWINDGE.SWITS
—made of wire   WIRE
last   LATTER
—night   TONIGHT
—purpose   CROWNET
—strait   EXIGENT
latrine   BENCH-HOLE
latter
—end   LAG-END

—part   POSTERIOR
laugh   LOFFE
laughing-stock of the company
  at table   TABLE-SPORT
lawless   IRREGULOUS
lawn   LAUND
lay
—bare   SCALE
—claim to   SPEAK TO
—man   TERRESTRIAL
—open   IMBARE
—under water   ENSTEEP
lazy fellow BED PRESSER
league   COMPACT
leaky   UNSTANCHED
lean person BARE-BONE
learned   AUTHENTIC
        LITERATURED
leave AVOID.LET.PART
—off   OMIT
lecherous   CODDING
lecture   EXERCISE
led by divisions WING-LED
left   BESTOWED
legend   LEGION
legitimate   LOYAL
lending at interest USANCE
lens of the eye EYE-GLASS
leprosy MEAZEL.MESEL
leopard   LUBBARD
let
—go   OMIT
—me understand
    TAKE ME WITH YOU
—slip   DELAY
letter   CAPON
levy   TAKE-UP
lewd
—person   GAMESTER
—woman CALLET.MALKIN
       MAWKIN
liable to corporal
  punishment BREECHING
licentious IRREGULOUS
    LARGE.LIBERAL
    UNMASTERED
lick over LATCH.LETCH
lie   COG
—to   TRY

life of pleasure	PRIMROSE PATH	loose	
	PRIMROSE WAY	—and frivolous	
lifeblood	LETHEE	person	HOBBY-HORSE
lift up	DUP.RELIEVE	—and vicious person	PAGAN
light		—part of a coat	FORESKIRT
—giver	TORCHER	loosen	TOAZE
—on a beacon	CREDIT	lose	LEESE
like	SEMBLABLE	lost	LORE.LORN
—a		lot	SORT
—contented cuckold	WITTOLLY	love	FANCY
—procurer	PANDERLY	—of oneself	SELF-CHARITY
—surgeon	CHIRURGEONLY	—of youthful	
—vault	VAULTY	pursuits	COLT'S TOOTH
—the sky	SKYISH	lovelock	LOCK
liken	LIKE	lover of malted	
limb by limb	LIMBMEAL	liquor	MALT-WORM
lime trees	LINE-GROVE	lovesick	FANCY-SICK
limit of capacity	BENT		SICK-THOUGHTED
lineage	DESCENDING	loving	BELOVING.LOVELY
liquor jug	BOMBARD	low-born	
list	FILE.SCEDULE	—fellow	LOWNE
—of actors and parts	SCRIPT	—prostitute	STALE
litigious	ACTION-TAKING	—wretch	VASSAL
litter	KINDLE	luck	ISSUE
little	PRETTY	lug out	EXHALE
—by little	BY SMALL AND SMALL	lump of	
—gentleman	FRANKLIN	—fat	KEECH
—heart	HEARTIKIN	—tallow	TALLOW-CATCH
—smile	SMILET	lunacy	LUNES
lively		lurking thief	MICHER
—child	EYAS-MUSKET	lustful	LUXURIOUS.RANK
—dance	UPSPRING	lustreless	PALE-DEAD
living under dung	SHARDED	lusty	LUSTICK.LUSTIGUE
load	BALLAST	lute-string of catgut	CATLING
loading	FRAUTAGE	mad	FOOLBEGGED.WOOD
lodge	HOST	—house	DARK-HOUSE
lofty	HIGH-STOMACHED.SKYISH	made	
loiter	FORESLOW	—a fool of	POUPT
lonely	DEARN	—neat	FEATED
long	LONGLY.SIDE	—of	
—continued	PERDURABLE	—boards	PLANCHED
—for	EARN	—ropes	TACKLED
—distance arrow	FLIGHT	—straw	SHEAVED
longingly	WISTLY	—thread	THREADEN
look	(*see* glance *above*)	—wickerwork	TWIGGEN
—demurely	DEMURE	—yew	EUGHEN.EWGHEN
—of one fated to hang	GALLOWS	—pensive	PENSIV'D
looking upwards	HIGH-SIGHTED	—up of	COMPACT
loop in sword-belt	CARRIAGE	madness	ECSTASY

magpie	MAG(G)OT-PIE	malignant	
maim	MAIN	—composition	HELL-BROTH
maintain	ESCOT	—influence	TAKING
maintenance	KEEPING	Malvolio	BIDDY
make		man	
—a fool of	BOB(B)	—of the world	TERRESTRIAL
—a pattern	PATTERN	—who busies himself with	
—a whore of	BEWHORE	housekeeping	COT-QUEAN
—aghast	GAST	—killer	MAN-QUELLER
—an agreement	CLAP HANDS	—like	MANKIND
—away with	FETCH OFF	mandragora	MANDRAKE
—believe	TAKE UPON ONESELF	mangle	MAMMOCK
—cheating arrangement		mangy	ROYNISH
with	PACK CARDS WITH	manner	QUALITY
—childless	UNCHILD	—of meeting	ENCOUNTER
—clear	SCALE	many	MUCH
—common cause	PARTAKE	mark	CICATRICE
—difficulties	MAKE IT STRANGE	marked for death	
—drunk	CUP		DEATH-PRACTISED
—faces	MOO	marriage contract	CONTRACTION
—fair	FLOURISH	marzipan	MARCHPANE
—feat	FEAT	mask	CARACT.IMMASK
—grotesque	ANTIC	mast-head	HIGH-TOP
—happy	HAPPY	match	BESORT.MEET.PATTERN
—haste	DESPATCH.DISPATCH	matchmaker	BROKER
—head	CAPITLUATE	mate	COMATE
—heir	INHERIT	matted hair	ELFLOCKS
—hoary	HOAR	matter	CAUSE
—known	DISCUSS	—of conscience	REMORSE
—much of	MAKE ON	—of responsibility	OCCASION
—neat	FEAT	mature	FLUSH
—pay dear	SAUCE	may it	
—plain	PLAIN	—do	DICH
—progress	PROFIT.RID WAY	—profit you	PROFACE
—rents in	WINDOW	meal of fish	FISH-MEAL
—secret arrangement	PACK	mean	CULLIONLY.FOXSHIP
—stable	STABLISH		ROYNISH.SCALL
—terms	DISPOSE	—fellow	COYSTRIL
—to		meanest person	LAG
—fail	SHORT	meaning	INTELLECT
—pass quickly	FLEET		INTENDMENT
—unlike	DISLIKEN	meanly	COSTER-MONGER
—up into total	PARCEL	—pretty	MODERN
maker of sport	GAMESTER	means	MEASURE
making		measure	CESS.HOOP
—maps	MAPPERY		WHOOPING
—no exception	EXCEPTLESS	—half gallon	STOUP
male puppet	MOTION GENERATIVE	—of corn	MOY
malicious person	SHEEP-BITER	measured by sand	SANDY

mechanic	MECHANICAL	modesty	PUDENCY
meddle	TEMPER	moist	HUMOROUS
medicinal virtue	FACULTY	moisten	BEWET.LATCH.MOIST
meditation	COMMENT	moment	POIZE
meek	SOFTLY SPRIGHTED	momentum	SWAY
meet	COPE	money	CHINKS.GILT
melancholy	ALLICHOLY	Moorish pike	MORRIS-PIKE
	ALLYCHOLY.THOUGHT	moral	L'ENVOY
memoranda	TABLES	more	MOE
mercenary	COSTER-MONGER	—execrable	INEXECRABLE
merchant	MARCATANT	—fish than man	LAND-FISH
	MERCATANTE	—quickly	RATHER
mermaid	SEA-MAID	—serious	SLOWER
merry		—than enough	OLD
—festival	UTIS	morning	MATIN
—meeting	ALE	most	
messenger	MISSIVE	—beloved	ALDER-LIEFEST
middle age	MID-AGE	—efficacious part	VIRTUE
mien	MINE	—rascally	RASCALLIEST
mighty	MIGHTFUL	—valuable part	HEART
mild	SARCENET.SARS(E)NET	motion of	
military trench-digger	PIONER	—a horse	CAREIRES
	PYONER	—contempt	FICO.FIGO
milksop	COCKNEY.MEACOCK	motionless	STONE-STILL
mind	MINE.NOTION	motto	IMPRESS(E)
mine	MINERAL	mould	MODEL
—uncle	NUNCLE	mournful tune or strain	DUMP
minute's time	MINUTE-WHILE	moustache	EXCREMENT
mirror	STONE	movable rail	SWITS
misanthrope	MISANTHROPOS	move in zigzag manner	INDENT
miscellaneous gathering		movement of planets	MOTION
	GALLIMAUFRY	moving part of body	MOTIVE
mischief	MALICHO.MALLECHO	much sought	
	VENGEANCE	after	WELL-ADMIRED
mischievous	SHREWD	muffled	MOBLED
misdeed	MISTREADING	murderer	MAN-QUELLER
misfortune	WROATH.WROTH	murderous	CARNAL
misgiving	GAINGIVING	murky	COLLIED.ROOKY
mistake	MISTAKING	muscle	THEW
mistaken	VICIOUS	music	NOISE
mistress	DOXY	musket	CALIVER
mitigation	REMORSE	muster-roll	MUSTER-FILE
mix	CARD	mutation	REVOLUTION
mixed	BLENT	mutineer	MUTINE
—badly	MISTEMPERED	mutiny	MUTINE
mixture	COMPOSTURE	my lady	MADONNA
moan	MEAN(E).MEIN.MENE	name	
model	MODULE	—before	FORE-RECITED
moderation	MODESTY	—beforehand	PRENOMINATE

nameless	TITLELESS	—received sacrament	
narration	RECOUNTMENT		UNHOUSLED
narrative	PROCESS		UNHOUZZLED
native		—in common use	UNTRACED
—born	SELF-BORNE	—one's own	UNPROPER
—goodness	SELF-BOUNTY	—pinked	UNPINKT
—of Denmark	DANSKER	—rustic	INLAND
natural	UNCOYNED	—swung	UNSWAI'D
—spirit	SELF-METTLE	—to be blunted	BATELESS
navel	NAVE	—to be recalled	UNRECALLING
neat(ly)	FEAT(LY)	—ventured upon	UNTRIDE
necessarily	NEEDLY	—wielded	UNSWAI'D
necessary	NEEDY	—willed	UNWILLING
necklace	CARKANET	—yet born	UNBRED
negative side	NAYWARD	notify	FRUTIFY
negligence	NEGLECTION	notion	PROJECT.SUPPOSAL
negotiate	BROKE	nourished by lust	LUST-DIETED
Negro	THICK-LIPS	number of people	POLL
neighbouring	SISTERING	nun	CLOISTRESS
neither one thing nor		nursing	NURSERY.SICK-SERVICE
another	ODD-EVEN	oaf	OUPH(E)
newborn lamb	EANLING	oath	BY COCK AND PIE
newly		oath on the Bible	BOOK-OATH
—introduced	UPSTRING	obedient	BUXOM
—baptised child	CHRISOM-CHILD	object of mockery	
nibble all over	OVEREAT		FLOUTINGSTOCK
nightmare	CACOD(A)EMON	obliged	DEBTED
	MARE	obliterate	DISLIMN
nimble	QUIVER	obsequious	
—witted	VOLABLE	—bowing	FLEXURE
nipping	SNEAPING	—attendant	OBSERVANT
no alternative	NO REASON BUT	observed	COTED
noisy	BLUSTROUS.SWASHING	observer	SPECULATION
north	SEPTENTRION	obstinacy	OPINION
—wind	AQUILON	obstinate	HIGH-STOMACHED
Norwegian	NORWEYAN		OBSTACLE
not		obtain on credit	TAKE UP
—blown	UNBLOWED	occupy onself	TIRE
—brought into action		occurences	CURRENTS
	UNEXECUTED	occurring once a	
—bruised or crushed	UNBRUSED	minute	MINUTELY
—contradicted	UNCHECKED	oeillade	ELIAD.ILLIAD
—crossed off as paid	UNCROSSED	of	
—dealt with	UNTRIDE	—a jovial turn	GOOD-LIFE
—decorated with holes	UNPINKT	—anticipation	FOREHAND
—despised	UNCONTEMNED	—good stock	WELL-DERIVED
—having		—great importance	
—a body	INCORPORAL		OF GREAT ARTICLE
—bloomed	UNBLOWED	—little account	BAWBLING

—necessity NO REMEDY
—no value IMMOMENT
—partiality PARTIAL
—the air REGION
offence MALEFACTION
offer PROPOSITION
office FACULTY
officer
—in the Exchequer CHEATER
—of (bishop's) court PARITOR
officious SUPERSERVICEABLE
—fellow PLEASEMAN
oil of consecration BALM
omission OMITTANCE
omit LET
on
—account LONG
—purpose NONCE
—the spur of the
moment UPON THE GAD
—what grounds WHEREUPON
one
—administering punishment
CORRECTIONER
—and the same ONE SELF
—bound by the same
vow VOW-FELLOW
—making progress PROFICIENT
—on quest QUESTANT.QUESTER
QUESTRIST
—only ONE SELF
—with pasty face TALLOW-FACE
one who
—affects wit WIT-SNAPPER
—breaks engagements
CRACK-TRYST
—can keep secrets
COUNSEL-KEEPER
—entreats IMPLORATOR
—foments argument BREED-BATE
—incurs punishment FORFEITER
—is suntanned TANLING
—is ill SICKMAN
—rides in front FORE-SPURRER
—seeks for another QUESTRIST
—settles business of PHEAZAR
—takes on another's
quarrel UNDERTAKER
—travels post POSTER

one's own utterances
SELF-BREATH
open DUP.RAZE
—mouthed WIDE-CHAPPED
—to question LITIGIOUS
opening PORTAGE
—up DISCLOSE.OVERTURE
operating suddenly RASH
opinion DEEM
opportunity HENT.VANTAGE
oppose REPUGN
opposition REPUGNANCY
oppress by bulk OVERBULK
orange seller ORANGE-WIFE
ordain FOR(E)SAY
ordaining ORDINANT
ordinary experience USE
orifice ORIFEX
original of a copy PRECEDENT
ornament FLOURISH.GARLAND
GUARD
—for the neck RABATO
—with puffs BLISTER
ostentation OSTENT
ostentatiously dressed CURLED
out of breath OUTBREATH'D
outcome ISSUE
outdo LURCH
—in number of mistresses
OUT-PARAMOUR
—in scorn OUTSCORN
outgrowth EXCREMENT
outlying sentinel PERDU(E)
outshine OUTLUSTRE
OVERSHINE
outside garb CASE
outstare ORE-STARE
outward WITHOUT-DOOR
outweigh completely
WEIGH TO THE BEAM
outwork FRONTIER
over
—dainty SUPERDAINTY
TAFFETA(S).TAFFETY
—come CONVINCE
—come by jesting OUTJEST
—power CONVINCE.THRONG
—reached O'ER-RAUGHT
ORE-RAUGHT.ORE-WROUGHT

—ridden	SUR-REYN'D	patronise	EMPATRON
—subtle	SUPERSUBT(I)LE	pattern	SPOTTE
—take	COTE	pawn	FINE
—value	OVERHOLD	pay	
—worked	SUR-REINED	—for	ESCOT
	SUR-REYNED	—of an army	ENTERTAINMENT
—worn	OVERSCHUTCH	—ready money	PITCH AND PAY
—wrested	ORE-RESTED	—up	COME OFF
own affairs	SELF-AFFAIRS	peace	
ox	ROTHER(-BEAST)	—maker	MAKE-PEACE
pace	RANK	—officer	FARBOROUGH
pain	MEAN		THARBOROUGH
painful	PANGING	peacock	PAIOCK(E).PAJOCK(E)
paint	IMPAINT	pearl	UNION
—face	GAUD.GAWD	peasant	CARLOT
painted in	TRICK	pedant	PEDASCULE
pale		peep under	UNDERPEEP
—as a young girl	MAID-PALE	peer	SQUINNY.TWEER.TWIRE
—faced	PALE-VISAGED	people	MEINIE.MEIN(E)Y
paltry	BARE.PELTING	perceive	SURVEY
—fellow	HILDING	perform	
pamper	ENGROSS	—by proxy	ATTORN
pander	GREEK	—sleight-of-hand	CONVEY
pang	THROW(E)	performance of	
paper of conditions	BOOK	promise	DEED OF SAYING
parallel	PATTERN	peril	APPERIL
paralyse	APOPLEX	perjured person	PERJURE
parasite	TRENCHER-FRIEND	perjury	OATH-BREAKING
	TRENCHER-KNIGHT	perky	PERT
parcel	COMMODITY	permit	BETEEM
paroxysm	THROW(E)	persistent	PERSISTIVE
parson	SOUL-CURER	person with a tail	TAILOR
part	SQUARE	personal	
—of an army, camp,		—identity	PROPERTY
etc.	QUARTER	—relation	PARTICULAR
—time bawd	PARCEL-BAWD	—sorrow	FEE-GRIEF
partake	PERTAKE.UNDERGO	personality	CHARACT
particular	SEVERAL	persuasion	INDUCEMENT
—nature	PROPRIETY	pert boy	CRACK
—purpose	NONCE	pertaining to death	DEFUNCTIVE
parting	DEPART	perverse	PEEVISH
partner	RIVAL	perversity	ADVERSITY
pass		pestilence	MURREN.MURRION
—by	COTE	petard	PETAR
—in succession	SUCCEED	petty	PELTING.PUISNY
—time	ENTREAT	phrase	COMMA
passionate	WASPISH-HEADED	—appropriate to	
passive	PRONE	pilgrims	WOOLWARD
patched	CLOUTED	—in combat	UTTERANCE

physician	MEDICINE
piano key	JACK
picked	RECOLLECTED TERMS
picture giving	
fantastic effect	PERSPECTIVE
piddling	PICKING
piece of	SPLINTER
—cow dung	SHARD
—fluff	DOWL(E)
—money	MOY
—needlework	SPOTTE
pigsty	FRANK
pilchard	PILCHER
pile-driver	THREE-MAN-BEETLE
pious	ZEALOUS
pip	PEEP(E)
pirate	WATER-THIEF
pish!	PUSH
pitch	PECKE.SET DOWN
pity	BOWEL.REMORSE
place	BIDING
—in order	ENRANK
—in the sky	ENSKY
—noted for brothels	
	PICKT-HATCH
—in lee	BELEE
—where pastry is made	PASTRY
placed in a window	WINDOWED
plague	GOODYEAR
—spot	DEATH-TOKEN
—spots	THE LORD'S TOKENS
plan	SCEDULE
—of action	PLATFORM
planning	MAPPERY
plants in general	PLANTAGE
plausible	PLAUSIVE.PROBALL
play	
—a part in a mask	JEST
—trick on	GLEEK.GLIKE
playful person	GAMESTER
plebeian	PLEBEAN
pleasant	LUSTICK
please	FREET
pleasing	PLAUSIVE
pleasure	LUST
—seeker	CORINTHIAN
pledge	FINE
plenty	FUL(L)NESS
plot	PRACTISE

pluck	RASE.TO(A)ZE
plume	PRANK
plump	PLUMPIE.PLUMPY
pocket	POAKE
point	
—at which progress	
stops	STICKING PLACE
—in tennis	CHASE
poison	BANE.MINERAL
poisonous substance	HEBONA
poke	POAKE
Pole/Polish	POLACK
pole for carrying	
baskets	COWL-STAFF
polished	INLAND
politeness	COMPLEMENT
pollute	FILE
poltroon	POULTROONE
pomander	POUNCET
pooh	POWWAW.PUH
poor	SCALD.SINGLE
popular	WELL-GRACED
porcupine	PORPENTINE
portent	AUGUR
portholes	PORTAGE
portion	COMMODITY.SCANTLE
position	FIXTURE
—for being observed	
	IN PROSPECT
post-horse	POST
postpone	PROLONG
	PROROGUE
	REJOURN
pot-thumping	BOLD-BEATING
potentate	POTENT
pound	PUN
pour	INFUSE
—out	BETEEM
power to overcome	PREVAILMENT
powerful	MIGHTFUL
practice arrow	BUTT-SHAFT
practised	TRADED
praise	COMMEND
—excessively	SUPERPRAISE
prance	JAUNCE.JAUNSE
precedent	PRESIDENT
precipice	PRECEPIT
precipitate	STEEP(E)-DOWN(E)
	STEEP(E)-UP

precisely	BY THE SQUIRE	prologue	INDEX
precondition	PREMISE.PREMISS	prolong	LINGER.RESPITE
preface	INDEX	prompt	PRIME
preening oneself	REPUTING	proof	ASSAY.INSTANCE
pregnant	GREAT-BELLIED	propensity	PROPENSION
premature	TIMELESS	propitious	WHOLESOME
preparation	APPOINTMENT	proportion	QUANTITY
	FITMENT.INDUCTION	prosperous	WELL TO LIVE
	PREPARE	prostitute	CUSTOMER
prepare	ADDRESS		GUINEA-HEN.LACED MUTTON
presage	ABODE		POLECAT.QUAIL.RODE
present with sixpence	TESTERN		STALE.VENTURE
preserve from decay	SEASON	protect plant from	
press		cold	WINTER-GROUND
—for	STRAIN	protract	LINGER
—hard	THRONG	proud	ORGILLOUS.ORGULOUS
pressure	OPPRESSION	—spirited	HIGH-STOMACHED
pretend	INTEND	—to the highest	
pretty	INCONIE.INCONY	degree	TOP-PROUD
prevail over	CARRY	prove	CITE
previous		—by evidence	TESTIMONY
—happening	PREMISE.PREMISS	—by testing	TRY
—practice	ELEMENT	provender	PROVAND.PROVEND
price	ESTIMATE		PROVIANT
prim	PRENZIE	proverb	SAW
primer	ABSEY BOOK	provocation	PROVOKEMENT
primogenture	PRIMOGENIT	provoke	TARRE
prince	HAMLET.POTENT	proxy	SUBSTITUTE
princely	PRENZIE		PREWYN.PROIN(E).PROYN(E)
principal	ARCH.CAP		PRUINE.SWITS
prison	CONFINE	public	GENERAL
private	REMOVED	pudding with many	
—grief	FEE-GRIEF	ingredients	HODGE-PUDDING
—person	PRIVATE	puff in scorn	BLURT
—room	BY-ROOM	puffed	
privilege	COMMODITY.PRISE	—out	EXSUFFLICATE
privy	AJAX.JAKES.DRAUGHT	—sleeve	TRUNK-SLEEVE
prize	PRICE.PRISE.REPRISAL	puffy	EMBOSSED
problem	CONCLUSION	pull	TOZE
proceed	SWAY	—by the ears	SOLE.SOWL
proclaim	PROTEST	pulse	PULSIDGE
procrastination	INDURANCE	punctilious	PICK
produced in		puny	PUISNY
heaven	HEAVEN-BRED	puppet	MOTION
profit	COMMODITY	—thrown at during Lent	
prognostication	PRECURSE		JACK-A-LENT
programme	SCEDULE	purblind	BEESOME.BISSOM
project	REFLEX	pure metal	UNCOINED
—beyond	JUTTY		UNCOYNED

purport	PURPOSE
purpose	DESIGNMENT.MIND
purposeless	SHAPELESS
put	
—an end to	PERIOD
—aside	DAFF.DOFF
—in	
—gaol	ENGAOL
—pocket	IMPETICOS
—shelter	ENSHELTER
—splint	SPLINTER
—the stocks	STOCK-PUNISHT
—into dialogue	DIALOGUE
—off	FUB OFF
—by	DAFF
—with contempt	SLIGHT OFF
—on oath	DEPOSE
—to death	TRANSPORT
putting under embargo	
	EMBARQUEMENT
pygmy	ATOMY
quadrangular area in	
palmistry	TABLE
qualify	ABLE
quality	AFFECTION.ASSAY
qualm	CALM
quarreller	QUARREL
quarrelsome	QUARRELOUS
—person	CHIDER.SQUARER
question proposed	PROPOSITION
quibble	SNATCH
quick!	YARE
quick	
—minded	BAVIN-WITS
—to understand	APPREHENSIVE
quickest	RATHEREST
quit	AVOID.PART
quite	
—alone	HIGH-LONE
—new	FRESH NEW
quits	MEET
quoin	COIN
quote	COAT(E).COTE
rabble	VARLETRY
race	RAZE
rage	VIOLENT
raged	RAG'D.RAGDE
ragged	RAG'D.RAGDE
raid	RODE

raise	ADVANCE
—from the dead	ARAISE.ARAYSE
raising of a siege	REMOVE
rally	RE-ENFORCE
rank	ORDINANCE
rarely shown	SELDSHOWN
rascal	COMPANION.FAITO(U)R
	LOZEL.SCROYLE
rashness	GUST
ravening	RAVEN.RAVIN(E)
ravished	YRAVISHED
reach	DANGER.MEASURE
read	SCAN
readiest	EFTEST
read(ing) over	SUPERVISE
readily	LIGHTLY
—inclined	PROMPT
ready	ADDRESSED.ADDREST
	FEAT.PREGNANT
	PREST.PRONE
—apprehension	RECEIVING
—at hand	AT AN INCH
—for tears	WEEPING-RIPE
—to sink	SINKING-RIPE
real	BODILY.ESSENTIAL
	UNCOINED.UNCOYNED
rear	CATASTROPHE.HAUNCH
reason	SKILL
reasonable	WHOLESOME
reassemble	RE-ENFORCE
rebel	MUTINE.REVOLT
rebuke	SAUCE
rebuked	SHENT
recall	
—from exile	REPEAL
—of pursuing force	RETREAT
recently made sad	NEW-SAD
receptacle for	
—bran	BOLTING-HATCH
—tallow	TALLOW-CATCH
recipient	CAPTIOUS
reciprocation	COUNTERCHANGE
recital	RECOUNTMENT
recite from first to last	DECLINE
recited before	FORE-RECITED
reck	WREAK(K)
reckon up	PARCEL
reckoner	COUNTER-CASTER
reckoning	NICK.WHOOPING

—in due ratio	PROPORTION	—trivial	TRIFLE
recoil	REQUOYLE	repairing	STILL-PEERING
recollect	ADVISE		STILL-PIECING
recompense	REGUERDON	repeat	REWORD
red	CAIN-COLOURED	repetition of same	
redolent of the		rhyme	RANKE
ale-house	RED LATTICE	replenishment	SUPPLYMENT
reduce to		repletion	PLURISIE.PLURISY
—poverty	RUINATE	report	NOISE.QUEST.YIELD
—subjugation	ASSUBJUGATE	—the words of	REDELIVER
re-echo	REWORD	reporting	REPORT
refer	PUT OVER	reposing	REPOSALL
refined	INLAND.PICK		REPOSURE
reflecting the feelings		reprehended	ATTASKED
of another	GLASS-FACED		ATTASKT
reflection	REGARD	represent anew	REFIGURE
refresh	REPAIR	representation	EXPRESSURE
refuse-basket	SIEVE	representative	IMAGE
regard	COTE.TENDER	reprieve	REPREEVE
regardful	RESPECTIVE	reproach	AYWORD.BRAID
region	CLIMAT(UR)E	reproachfully	INVECTIVELY
register of soldiers or		reprobation	REPROBANCE
sailors	MUSTER-BOOK	reproduce	REFIGURE
reinforcing	SUPPLIANT	reprove	TAKE UP
reject	ABHOR	reputation	ESTEEM
rejoining	REIOYNDURE		OPINION.PASS
	REJOINDURE	requital	QUITTAL
related to matter in		requited	REQUIT(TED)
hand	GERMAN(E)	resembling	SEMBLABLE
relevance	CONCERNANCY		SEMBLATIVE
relinquish	GIVE OUT	residence	BIDING.MASONRY
relish	SAY	resist	REPUGN
rely	STAY	resolved	PIGHT
remain		resort	HAUNT.TRADE
—chaste	VIRGIN	resorting to law	ACTION-TAKING
—in a certain clime	CLIMATE	resourceful	PREGNANT
remark	REASON	restlessly	DISQUIETLY
remedial	REMEDIATE	restore	REPAIR
remedy	RECURE	restrict	COMBINE
remit offence or debt	FORGIVE	retain	CONTAIN
remoteness	REMOTION	retard	TARDY
removal	REMOTION	retching	HEFT
remove covering	DISCASE	retinue	MEIN(E)Y.MEINIE
removed from its		retrace	UNTREAD
sphere	DISORBED	return	REGUERDON.REPAIR
render		reveal	DECIPHER
—destitute	DISFURNISH	revel at night	NIGHT-RULE
—dumb	DUMB	revengeful	VENGEABLE
—spiritless	CRAVEN		VINDICATIVE

reverberation	REPLICATION	ruck	ROOK
revival preceding		ruddock	RADDOCKE
death	LIGHTNING	ruin	RUINATE
revivify	REPAIR	ruined	SHENT
revocation	REVOKEMENT	rule	SQUIER.SQUIRE
revoke by calling back	UNSHOOT	rummage	ROMAGE
revolution	INNOVATION	rumour	MURMUR
revulsion	REVOLT	run over	HEAT
reward	REGUERDON	rush	RANDON
—with sixpence	TESTERN	rustic	BACON
rheum	RUME	said	FAINE.SAINE
rich	CHUFF	sailor	CANVAS-CLIMBER
riches	TAL(L)ENT	—'s private trading	
riddle	CONCLUSION	venture	PORTAGE
riddled with grief	GRIEF-SHOT	salacious	SALT
ride	RODE	salt hake	POOR JOHN
—hastily	SKIRR	salutation	REGREET
ridged	TWILLED	sanctities	SONTIES
ridiculous medley	GALLIMAUFRY	sane	FORMAL
riding whip	SWITS	sanity	WISDOM
right of sanctuary	PRIVILEGE	sapless	CORKY
riot	RUFFLE.WHOOBUB	sated	RAVIN'D
ripe	FLUSH	satiety	CLOYMENT
rising	MOUNTANT	satire	TAXATION
risk	JUMP	satyr	SALTIER
riverbank	WHARF	satisfaction	SUFFIGANCE
road	RODE	savage	SALVAGE
roam	WHEEL	—deeds	FELL-FEATS
roar	RORE	scabby	ROYNISH
robe	PALLIAMENT	—fellow	SCROYLE
rod	SWITS	scaffolding	SCAFFOLAGE
rogue	FAITOR	scapegrace	SKAIN(E)S MATE
roguery	PATCHERY	scar	WIPE
roll	FILE	scare	GALLOW.SCAR(RE)
Roman robe	PALLIAMENT	scarecrow	CROWKEEPER
rondure	CIRCLE	scattering silver	
root	RAZE		SILVER-SHEDDING
rope-torture	STRAPPADO	scheme	PLATFORM
rose tree	ROSIERE	school	CHARGE-HOUSE
rotation	SWAY		SCUL(L).SCULLE
rote	ROATE	—master	PEDANT
rotted to filth	DIRT-ROTTEN	scion	S(E)YEN.SIEN
rough		scissors	CIZERS
—apple	LEATHER-COAT	scoff	GALL
—hewn	UNSQUARED	scold	CALLAT
round	COMPASSED	Scotsman	BLUECAP
—off	PARCEL	scour	SKIRR
roundure	RONDURE	scout	DISCOVERER
rub with grease or oil	LIQUOR	scramble	MUSS(LE)

—for	SCAMBLE
scrap	QUANTITY
scrawl	MARTIAL-HAND
scribbler	INKHORN-MATE
scurry	SCUR.SKER.SKIRR.SQUIRR
scurvy	ROYNISH.SCALL
scythe	SIETH.SITHE
sea bird	SCAMEL.SEA-MELL
seal with others	COUNTERSEAL
seam	LARD
search party	SEARCH
season	BESPICE
seat	
—in church porch	
	CHURCH-BENCH
—of dignity	STATE
secret	INWARD
—council	CHAMBER-COUNCIL
—going or passing	STEALTH
—message	PRIVATE
secretary	CHANCELLOR
seeming	SEMBLATIVE
seen	SAWN
seigneur	SIGNIEUR
seize	CEAZE.EXTEND
	SEASE.SEAZE
—upon	PHANG
seizure	EXTENT.SEYSURE
self	
—confidence	OPINION
—deception	SELF-ABUSE
semblance	ASSEMBLY
senior	SIGNEUR
seniority	SIGNEURIE
sense	SENT
sensible	WHOLESOME
sensitive	COUNTABLE
sent before their time	PREMISED
sentence	CENSURE
sententious observation	REASON
sentry box	WATCH-CASE
separable	DIVIDANT
separate	DISTRACT
—body	DISTRACTION
sequence	SEQUEL
serge	SURGE
serious	OBSEQUIOUS
serpigo	SAPEGO.SUPPEAGO
serve	CONVENT

serviceable	COMMODIOUS
set	
—aside	REPEAL
—aside disdainfully	SLIGHT OFF
—astray	STRAY
—at defiance	BEARD
—before one's mind	PROJECT
—crosswise	TRAVERSED
—forth	PROJECT
—free	ENFREE
—in battle formation	
	DARRAIGN(E).DARRAIN(E)
	DARRAYN.DERRAIGN
—in delicate frame	
	TENDER-HEFTED
—of anchors	ANCHORAGE
—of four	MESS
—on	TARRE
—squatting	ROOK
—up	STABLISH
setting	VAIL
settle	TAKE UP
severe	WEIGHTY
	OVEREARNEST
sewer	COMMON-SHORE
shaft	FILL
—horse	PHILHORSE
shaggy	RAG'D.RAGDE
shame	REPROOF
shamefacedness	PUDENCY
shameless	UNBASHFUL
shape	PROJECT
shapeless	UNFASHIONABLE
share	COMMON
sharing	IMPARTMENT
sharp	AYGRE.EAGER
shaven	PIEL'D
she	
—cat	TIB-CAT
—physician	MEDICINE
sheathed	BREACHED
shed in droplets	DRIZZLE
shedding	EFFUSE
sheer fall	PRECIPITATION
shekel	SICKLE
shell	SHALE.SHEAL
	SHEEL.SHIEL.SHILL
shelter	WEATHER-FEND
sheriff's officer	YEOMAN

sherry	SHERRIS	skewer	PRICK
shine upon	OVERSHIRE	skilful	QUAINT
shoal	SCHOOLE	skill	DIRECTION.DOCTRINE
shock	SHOUGH		MISTERY.MYSTERY
—headed	RUG-HEADED	skin	
shoot	GERMAIN(E)	—disease	SAPEGO.SERPIGO
—up	SPIRT		SUPPEAGO
show	LOOK OUT	—eruption	TETTER
—reluctance	MAKE IT STRANGE	skirt for men	BASE
shower	ASPERSE	skull	MAZ(Z)ARD
showing		sky blue	WELKIN
—marks of travel		slacken	QUAIL
	TRAVEL-TAINTED	slaked	YSLAKED
—part of face	HALF-FACED	slanderous	VENOM'D-MOUTH'D
shrew	SHROW	slash	RACE.SCORCH
shrewd	SHROWD	slaughter	QUELL
shrewdly	UNHAPPILY	slice	SCANTLE
shrewish	SHREWD.WASP-STUNG	slight	EASY.SINGLE
	WASP-TONGUE	—salute	HALF-CAP
shriek	SHREEK.SHRIKE	slink about	PEAK
shrill voiced	SHRILL-GORGED	slow	
show	CITE.OSTENT.PORT	—dance	PAVAN(E).PAVEN
shower	ASPERSION		PAVIN.PADUAN
shrewd	PARLOUS	—flying	FLY-SLOW
shuffle	PALTER	—witted	UNPREGNANT
shut	MAKE	sluggish	RESTY
—pig in sty	FRANK	small	PINK.SINGLE
—up	SPERRE	—French coin	DENIER
shy	CHARY	—cannon	CHAMBER
sidesman	STICKLER	—coin	SOLIDARE
sigh	HEAVE	—freeholder	FRANKLIN
sight	BEHOLDING	—gratuity	GRATILLITY
sign	CARACT.DENOTEMENT	—herb	HERBELET
silent	LANGUAGELESS	—hole	VENTIGE
silk	SAY	—scent box	POUNCET-BOX
silver coin	PLATE	—share	MOIETY
similar	SEMBLABLE	—stream	FRESH
simple truth	PLAINSONG	—tinge of colour	EYE
simply	SHALLOWLY	—tusk	TUSH
simulative	SEMBLATIVE	smeared	TRICK
since	SITH(ENS).SITHENCE	smell	SENT
sincere	SINGLE	smile	SMOILE.SMOYLE
sincerely beloved	HEART-DEAR	snap	SNATCH
sing in chorus	CHOIR	snatch	RASE.RUFFLE
singular	UNTRACED	sneak about	PEAK
sink down	SWAGG	snort	BLURT
sixpence	TESTRIL(L)	social degrees	ORDINANCE
Sium	CYME	soft	LITHER
skeleton	ATOMY	soften	TEMPER

soldier	MILITARIST	splinter	FLAW
sole	MEER'ED	spoil taste of	DISTASTE
solicitation	INSUIT	spoilt child	PRINCOX
solicitous	CURIOUS	spoken against	FORESPOKE
solid		sport beyond the	
—mass	KEECH	limits	OUTSPORT
—thing	SOLIDITY	spots denoting	
something		plague	DEATH-TOKENS
—necessary	NEEDMENT	sprang	SPRONG
—savoury	SALAD	spray	ASPERSE.ASPERSION
—showing displeasure		spread	SCALE
	INDIGNATION	spring	WHITING-TIME
—to waste time	SUPPLIANCE	sprinkle	DISPUNGE
sometimes	SOME	sprinkling	ASPERSION
song		sprite	SPRIGHT
—set out in notation	PRICK-SONG	sprout	SPIRT
—to waken hunters	HUNT'S-UP	spume	YEAST
sooner	RATHER	spy	SURVEY
soonest	RATHEREST	square	SQUIER.SQUIRE
soothe	COY	squat down	ROOK
sorrowful	TRISTFUL	squatting position	AILOR
sound	CHIDING	squint	SQUINNY
sounding	SONUANCE	stab	BORE.YERK
sour	AYGRE.EAGER	stability	FIXTURE
sourness	RANCOUR	stage	GEST
souse	SOUCE.SOWS(S)E	—fanfare	SENNET
soused	SOUCT	stagger	REEL
sowing	SEEDNESS	stained	MEAL'D
sown	SAWN	stake	IMPONE
space under gable	BAY	stalking horse	STALE
Spanish wine	BASTARD	stamp	PRESSURE
	SHERRIS-SACK	stand	
sparrow	PHILIP	—as godfather	GOSSIP
spasm	THROW(E)	—back	BACCARE.BACKARE
speak		—erect (hair)	ROUSE
—against	FOR(E)SPEAK	—muttering	MAMMER
—ill of	MISREPORT.MISUSE	—under	UNDERSTAND
—louder than	OUTTONGUE	—upon	CONSIST
speaker	DISCOURSER	standstill	STILL-STAND
specify	FRUTIFY.LIMIT	stanza	STANZE.STANZO
speechless	LANGUAGELESS	start	
speedy	SOON	—aside	BLENCH
spermaceti	PARMACITIE	—of defence	BRACE
sphere	SPHEAR(E)	—off	BLENCH
spinner	SPINSTER	state	PORT
spirited	SPRIGHTFUL	—previously	PRENOMINATE
spite	SPIGHT	statesman	WEALSMAN
splendid phraseology		stay	REMAIN
	FESTIVAL TERM	—at a distance	OUTDWELL

stead	STEED	stunted	SCRUBBED
steep	ENSTEEP	stupefy	MULL
steerage	STERNAGE	stupid	BARRED.CLAY-BRAINED
steersman's place	STERN		CONCEITLESS
sterile	HUNGRY	sty	FRANK
stiff collar	RABATO.REBATER	subdue	ABATE.CONVINCE
	REBATO		HARROW
stigmatise	SEAR	subject	LIABLE
still in the bud	UNBLOWED	—by need	NECESSITIED
	UNBLOWN	—to whipping	BREECHING
stimulate	TARRE	submission	SUBSCRIPTION
stir	COIL.GARBOILS	submissive	COMPTIBLE
stocking	BOOT-HOSE	submissiveness	DEPENDACIE
stolen goods	EQUIPAGE	submit	SUBSCRIBE
	PURCHASE	subside in emotion	QUENCH
stoop to plead	C(O)URB	substance of a thing	MATERIAL
stop ringing noise	CLAMOUR	substitutions	SUPPOSES
store	STUFF	subtitles	QUIDDITS
story-spreader	FANCY-MONGER	suckling rabbit	RABBIT-SUCKER
stout	BONNIE.BONNY	suffer	BETEEM
stoutness	HARDIMENT	—pangs	THROW(E)
straight	STRAIGHT-PIGHT	sufficiency	SUFFIGANCE
—path	FORTHRIGHT	suffusion	EYE
strand	STROND	suggest	INCENSE
strange	MUCH	suggestion	PROMPTURE
strength	THEW	suitable	LIABLE
strengthen	FORSE	—company	BESORT
strictness	STRICTURE	summerhouse	GARDEN-HOUSE
strife	BATE	summon	CONVENT
strike	PASH	superabundance	PLURISIE
—aghast	GHAST		PLURISY
—off the roll	UNROLL	supercilious	HIGH-SIGHTED
—with rod	SWITS	superscription	SUPERSCRIPT
—with violence	PASH	superstitious	CEREMONIOUS
strip	DISFURNISH.UNCASE	supplementary	SUPPLIANT
—naked	CASE	—document	SCEDULE
strive	PURCHASE	supplementing	SUPPLYMENT
stroke of lightning		supply	IMP
	THUNDER-STROKE	supplying	SUPPLIANCE
strong	BONNIE.BONNY	support	KEEPING
—liquor	TICKLE-BRAIN		SUPPORTANCE
strumpet	BONA-ROBA.TIB	suppose	PROPOSE
stubborn	IMPERSEVERANT	suppositions	SUPPOSES
—enemy	WRANGLER	surface	BREAST
studied diction		surfeit	CLOYMENT
	RECOLLECTED TERMS	surpass	COME OVER.OUTPEER
stuffing for meat	PUDDING		PARAGON
stumble	PECKE	—in work	OUTWORK
stun	ASTONISH	surrender	SUBSCRIBE

surround	ENROUND
sustain	UNDERBEAR
swaddling clothes	
	SWATHLING-CLOTHES
swaggerer	RUDESBY.SQUARER
swallow	GULF
swashbuckler	
	SWINDGE-BUCKLER
swashing	WASHING
sway	SWINDGE
swayed	WAID(E)
sweet	HONEYED
—juicy apple	POMEWATER
—wine	CHARNECO
sweetness	SMOOTH
swell out	FARCE
swift	FLIGHTY
swindler	LEGGE
swinge	SWINDGE
swishing blow	SWITS
switch	SWITS
swollen	BOLLEN.EMBOSSED
	RANK
symbolic attributes	CEREMONIES
tablecloth	CARPET
tailor	COSIER.COZIER
take	
—by deceit	BOB
—counsel	RESOLVE
—in hand	UNDERGO
—in security	ARREST
—shape	INFORM
—to road	HACK
taken	TANE
—possession of	PROPERTIED
tale-bearer	CARRY-TALE
	MUMBLE-NEWS
talk	PROPOSE
—fondly	HONEY
talon	TALENT
tame	ENTAME
—a hawk	MAN
tame-spirited	
	SOFTLY-SPRIGHTED
tamper	TEMPER
tape	IN(C)KLE
tapestries	CHAMBER-HANGINGS
tapster	UNDER-SKINKER
tattered	TOTTERED

tax	TASK
team-mate	COACH-FELLOW
tear	
—and devour	TIRE
—away	RASE
—off	RASE
—to pieces	MAMMOCK
tears	EYE-DROPS
tease	PHEEZE
—out	TOAZE
teeming	CHILDING
temper	CO-MEDDLE
	TEMPERALITIE
temperament	COMPOSURE
tempered	
—badly	MISTEMPERED
—for evil	MISTEMPERED
tempt	SUGGEST
temptation	PROMPTURE
ten at cards	SINGLE TEN
tenderness	BOWEL
tending	
—in sickness	SICK-SERVICE
—sheep	SHEEP-WHISTLING
tenor	TENURE
tenth or tithe	DISME
tenure at fixed rent	FEE-FARM
term in	
—fencing	HAY.VENEWE.VENEY
—tennis	CHACE
term of	
—abuse	CUT.FUSTIL(L)IRIAN
	FUSTILARIAN.PILCHER
	RAMPALLION
—contempt	CASTILIANO VULGO
	COBBY.COBLOAF
	DRIBBLING.NIT.RAG
	SCALD.SPRAT.TILLY-FALLY
	TWANGLING
—contemptuous dismissal	
	AVAUNT
—disdain	MUCH
—endearment	CHUCK
—opprobrium	CASTILIAN
—reproach	BEZONIAN.GIB-CAT
	PATCH.RONYON.RUNNION
	SCALL.SKAINS-MATES
—the manège	HOLLA
terrify	GAST

test	APPROVE
—by evidence	TESTIMONY
testimony	ATTEST.REPORT
than	AND
thanks	THANKINGS
that which	
—cannot be cut	INTRENCHANT
—crowns or completes	CROWNET
—is distilled	DISTILMENT
—is loaned	LENDER
—is written	CHARACTERY
—stares fatally	MORTAL-STARING
thatch	STOVER
theft	CONVEYANCE.STEALTH
theme	COPY
thence	SITHENCE
thereafter	UPON
thickly intertwining	
branches	THICK-PLEACHED
thief	LIFTER.NUTHOOK
	PRIG.TROJAN
thieving	PUGGING
thigh armour	CUSHES
thill	FIL(L)
—horse	P(H)IL-HORSE
thin-faced	PAPER-FACED
thing	
—imported	IMPORTANCE
—seen	REGARD
think	
—ill of	MISTHINK
—with envy	GRUDGE A THOUGHT
third	TRIPLE
thistle	CARDUUS
thoughtless	UNWEIGHING
thrash	PAY
three-cornered	THREE-NOOKED
threnody	THRENOS
throat	GULF
throe	THROW(E)
throw	
—at bowls	UPCAST
—into disarray	UPROAR
—open	WIDEN
thrust	HAVE-AT-HIM.POTCH(E)
—in fencing	FOIN.STOCK
—rapidly	YERK
thunderbolt	THUNDER-STONE
tick	JAR

ticklish	SUBTLE
tight	STRAIT.STRICT
tighten	RESTRAIN
till now	HERETO
time	
—allowed for stay	GEST
—for confession	SHRIVING-TIME
—for giving rings	RING-TIME
—limit	GEST
—of beginning	SPRING
—of silence	SILENT
—server	MINUTE-JACK
	TIME-PLEASER
—table	SCEDULE
timorous	MEACOCK
tincture	SMATCH
tinge	EYE
tinselly	CLIQUANT
tiny	TINE.TYNE
tip with sixpence	TESTERN
tipple	POT
tippler	MALT-WORM
tired	WAPPEND
—as a dog	DOG-WEARY
—by day's work	DAY-WEARIED
—of life	LIFE-WEARY
title	ADDITION
to	
—too great an extent	OVERFAR
—what	WHEREUNTIL
token	PRECEDENT
tokens of respect	CEREMONIES
told before	FOREVOUCHED
tomcat	GIB-CAT
tonsured	PIEL'D
toothless	BROKEN
top	UPWARD
—of head	NOLE
toper	EPHESIAN
torch smoke used	
as blacking	LINK
torment someone	LANDDAMNE
toss	
—contemptuously	SLIGHT
—in blanket or canvas	CANVASS
toy	GAUD
trace	TRACT
track	TRACT
traffic	MART.PASSAGE

657

—in	MERCHANDISE	tutor	SCHOOLMASTER
	MERCHANDIZE	twenty paces	SCORE
transfixed	BROACHED	twin pair	GEMINY
transform	TRANSPOSE	twilight	COCKSHUT
	TRANS-SHAPE	twisted	TORTIVE
transport	TRANSPORTANCE	type of apple	BITTERSWEET
travel		typical woman's name	TIB
—stained	TRAVEL-TAINTED	ugly	FOUL
—worn	SEASICK	unadorned	UNCOINED
tread back	UNTREAD		UNCOYNED
treat		unassisting	UNSISTING
—as property	PROPERTY	unbearded	UNROUGH.UNRUFFE
—tenderly	TENDER	unbecoming	ILL-SEEMING
—with contempt	JADE.LOUT	unblunted	UNBATED
	LOWT	unbroken	CONTINUATE
—with overstretched		unconciliating	UNTEMPERING
courtesy	STRAIN COURTESY	unconsidered	UNSKAN'D
treatment by fasting in		uncontrolled	UNSWAI'D
hot tub	TUBFAST	uncustomary	UNTRADED
trenched	PIONED	under	
tress	SWITS	—butler	BREAD-CHIPPER
trick	BOBB.COLT.GLEEK.GLIKE	—command	BUXOM
	PASS.QUIRK	undermined	UNDERWROUGHT
tricky	SUBTLE	understanding	CONCEIT
tried	TOUCHED.TRIDE	undertaken	UNDERTA'EN
trifles befitting lady	LADY-TRIFLES	undervalue	DISABLE
trifling	BAUBLING	undeserving	UNMERITABLE
trim	GUARD	undiscriminating	UNRESPECTIVE
tripe-faced	TRIPE-VISAG'D	undo	DEFEAT.DUP.UNLACE
triple time	TRIPLEX	undress	DEVEST.DISCASE
trite	MODERN		UNCASE
triumph over	ORECROWE	undressed	UNREADY
triumphal	TRIUMPHANT	uneasily	DISQUIETLY
triumvirate	TRIUMPHERY	unexercised	UNBREATHED
Trojan	TROYAN	unexpected	UNWARIE
trousers	STROSSERS	unfaded	UNBRAIDED
truckle	CURB	unfavourably	UNHAPPILY
trull	CALLET	unfeeling	IRON-WITTED
tuft	TUFFE	unfledged bird	GULL
tumult	ROMAGE.RORE	unfurnish	UNPROVIDE
turban	TURBAND.TURBOND	unimaginative	UNPREGNANT
turbulent	COMBUSTIOUS	uninfluenced	UNSWAI'D
turn	INTEND.SWITS.WAFT	unintentional	UNWILLING
—aside	ASKANCE.ASKANT	unknowingly	UNWARES
	DAFF	unlawfully	FORBIDDENLY
—round	RETURN	unlikely	UNLIKE
—to stone	STONE	unlikeness	DISLIKENESS
turquoise	TURKIES	unlimited	CONFINEIESS
tusk	TUSH	unlucky	WICKED

unnatural	KINDLESS	—roughly	HARRY
unnoticed	UNTRIDE	usury	EXCESS
unowned	UNOWED	utter in ringing tones	TANG
unpolished person	HOMESPUN	vagrancy	EXTRAVAGANCY
unpractised	UNBREATHED	vagrant	VAGROM
unprepared	DISAPPOINTED	valuation	PRISE.PRIZE
unprolific	HUNGRY	value	PRAISE.PRICE
unready	REDELESS.UNDRESSED	—something	RESPECT
	UNPREGNANT	vanguard	VA(U)NT.VAWARD
unrefined	UNCOINED	varlet	VARLETTO
unregulated	INCORRECT	vast	WASTE
unreliable person	BREAK-VOW	vegetation	PLANTAGE
	BREAK-PROMISE	veiled	MABLED.MOBLED
unresisting	UNSISTING	velvet	VELURE
unresting	UNSISTING	—trimmings	VELVET-GUARDS
unrestrained	UNYOKED	vend	MART
—in movement	FREE FOOTED	vengeance	WANION
unripe pea-pod	SQUASH	venture	JUMP
unruly	RAG'D.RAGDE	verbose	VERBAL
—gang	TRIBULATION	verse	STANZE.STANZO
unsated	UNSTANCHED	versed	TRADED
unsearchable	UNTENTED	very	
unseasonable	UNSEASONED	—durable	PERDURABLE
unseeing	IMPERSEVERANT	—famous	WELL-FAMED
unseemly	UNACCUSTOMED	—rude	GIANT-RUDE
unseen	INVIS'D	—small creature	MINIMUS
unshaven	UNBARBED	vigorous	LUSTICK.LUSTIQUE
unsightly	SIGHTLESS	villages	VILLAGREE
unstable creature	MINUTE-JACK	villainy	PATCHERY
unsuccessful in		vindictive	VINDICATIVE
trade	TRADE-FALNE	violate	FRACT
unsuitable	IMPAIR	violation of	
unthinking	UNRESPECTIVE	promise	PROMISE-BREACH
until	WHILE(S)	violence	EXTENT.OUTRAGE
untilled	UNEARED	violent	ROBUSTIOUS
untrimmed	UNBARBED	virtuous	GRACED
unused in action	UNDEEDED	visor	SIGHT
upheaval	ROMAGE	vives	FIVES
uphold	ABLE	voluntarily	BY MY WILL
upper		vote	TONGUE
—air	REGION	vow	PROTEST
—hand	EMINENCE	voyage	SHIPPING
—part of shoe	OVERLEATHER	vulgar	GENERAL
uproot	SUPPLANT	—person	JACK-SLAVE
upshot	LOOSE	wager	IMPONE
upstart	START-UP	wait	STAY
urge	PERSUADE.STRAIN	wall	MORALL.MURAL.MURE
use		—in	CIRCUMMURE
—ceremony	COMPLY	wander	WHEEL

wandering	WINDRING	whisperer	BUZZER
want of		Whitsun	WHEESON
respect	NON-REGARDANCE	whoever	WHAT
wanton	GAMESTER	whole weight	SWAY
	NICE.RIGGISH	wholesome	PHYSICAL
—woman	FLIRT-GILL	whore	QUAIL
wantonness	LUXURY	—monger	FLESH MONGER
warble	REL(L)ISH	—son	HORSON
wardship	GUARDAGE	wicked	FACINERIOUS
warn	VOR		NAUGHTY.SPOTTED
warrant	WARN	wicker covering	TWIGGEN
washing-beetle	BATLER.BATLET		TWIGGING
waste time	BURN DAYLIGHT	wide-mouthed	
wasted	CONFOUNDED		STRETCH-MOUTH'D
watchful	OPEN-EYED	widow's prerogative	
water			WIDOWHOOD
—colours	WATER-WORK	wife	KICKY-WICKY
—parsnip	CYME	wild mustard	HARLOCKS
watering	WATERY	willing	WILFUL
waterspout	HURRICANO	wilt	WO(O)T
way	QUIRK	win	LURCH
—worn	JOURNEY-BATED	wind	BOTTLE
weak	FOND.MUDDY-METTLED	—driven clouds	RACK
	SINGLE	winding	WINDRING
wealth	FULLNESS.TALLENT	wing of beetle	SHARD
wear out	CONTRIVE	wink	ELIAD.ILLIAD
weight	POIZE	winter	HIEMS
weighted down	PEASE.PEAZE	wintry	HIEMAL
	PEISE.PEIZE.PEYSE	wise	WINNOWED
weird	WEY(W)ARD	—in folly, foolish in	
welcoming formula	PROFACE	wisdom	FOOLISH-WITTY
well		wish	BOSOM
—balanced	WEAL-BALANCED	—not to be	UNWISH
—fed	RUMP-FED	—to be away	UNWISH
—proportioned		wit	WEET(E)
	CLEAN-TIMBERED	witch-goddess	HECAT
wet	BEWET	with	
what		—a feeling of loss	MISSINGLY
—if	WHAT AN IF	—a slant	ASCAUNT.ASLANT
—the devil	WHAT A PLAGUE	—a sweeping win	SOOPSTAKE
—though	WHAT AN IF		SWOOP-STAKE-LIKE
—went before	VAUNT	—a vengeance	WITH A WITNESS
when times are		—eyes closed	WINKING
improving	TIME-BETTERING	—legs together	NEAR-LEGGED
whereunto	WHEREUNTIL	—success	SUCCESSFULLY
whip	FIRK	—wide wings	FULL-WINGED
whipped severely	OVERSCUTCH'D	—young	IN KINDLE
whippersnapper	WHIPSTER	without	
whisk	SWITS	—boundaries	CONFINELESS

—consequence	IMPORTLESS
—possessions	UNPOSSESSING
—reputation	REPUTELESS
—superior	TOPLESS
witness	TESTIFY
woman	PLACKET
—like a man	MANKIND
—of scolding nature	CALLAT
womaniser	MOUSE-HUNT
womanish	FEMALE
wonder	ADMIRATION
—struck	WONDER-WOUNDED
wonderful	MIRABLE
woo	SUE
wooded	BOSKY
word of	
any meaning	HUMOUR
—unknown meaning	HACK
	SCARRE
working horse	CUT
worn	CONFOUNDED
—in winter	WINTERED
—out	WAPPEND
worthy of admiration	RESPECTIVE
wound	BATTERY.BORE
—with spur	SPUR-GALL
wrench	FIT
wristband	SLEEVEHAND
write	CHARACTER.PAPER
—on scroll	INSCROLL
writing	CHARACTERY
wrongdoing	MISS
yearn	EARN
yellow	SANDED
—flower	CUCKOO-BUD
yew	EUGH
yield	COME.SUBSCRIBE
yielding	LITHER
—up life	LIFE-RENDERING
yoke	BOW
—of garment	SQUARE
Yorkshireman	TYKE
young	
—fox	KID-FOX
—giddy person	SKIPPER
—lamb	EANLING
younger	LATTER-BORN
youth	JUVENAL.LEAPING-TIME
	SALAD DAYS

youthful freshness	
	MAY-MORN(ING)
sham fabric	PETER

shape[1]

having:	
1 form	MONOMORPHIC
	MONOMORPHOUS
2 faces	DI(H)EDRAL.JANIFORM
	JANUFORM
—concave face each	
side	BICONCAVE
—convex face each	
side	BICONVEX
2 forms	DIMORPHIC
	DIMORPHOUS
2 sides	BILATERAL
2 sides equal	ISOSCELES
3 angles	TRIANGLE
3 faces	TRIGONAL.TRIHEDRAL
3 forms	TRIMORPHIC
	TRIMORPHOUS
3 radiating curves	TRISKELE
	TRISKELION
3 sides	TRIANGLE.TRIGON
	TRILATERAL
4 angles	QUADRANGLE
4 faces	PYRAMID.TETRAHEDRON
4 forms	QUADRIFORM
	TETRAMORPHIC
4 sides	DIAMOND.LOZENGE
	PARALLELOGRAM
QUADRANGLE.QUADRILATERAL	
RECTANGLE.RHOMB(US)	
SQUARE.TRAPEZIUM	
	TRAPEZOID
5 angles	PENTAGON.PENTANGLE
	QUINQUANGLE
5 faces	PYRAMID
5 points	PENTACLE.PENTAGON
PENTAGRAM.PENTALPHA	
5 sides	PENTAGON
6 angles	HEXAGON
6 faces	HEXAHEDRON
	PARALLELEPIPED
(rhombi)	RHOMBOHEDRON
6 points	HEXAGON.HEXAGRAM
6 sides	HEXAGON
7 angles	HEPTAGON.SEPTANGLE
7 faces	HEPTAHEDRON

7 ranges of six faces	HEPTAHEXAHEDRON	basin	PELVIFORM
7 sides	HEPTAGON	bell	CAMPANIFORM
	SEPTILATERAL	berry	BACCIFORM
8 angles	OCTAGON	bird	AVIFORM
8 faces	OCTAHEDRON	bladder	CYSTIFORM
8 sides	EIGHT-SQUARE.OCTAGON	boat	SCAPHOID
9 angles	ENNEAGON	bow	ARCUATE
9 faces	ENNEAHEDRON	brain	CEREBRIFORM
9 sides	ENNEAGON.NONAGON	breast	MAMMIFORM
10 angles	DECAGON	bristle	STYLIFORM
10 faces	DECAHEDRON	—tail	CAMPODEIFORM
10 sides	DECAGON	brush	PENICILLATE
11 sides	(H)ENDECAGON		PENICILLIFORM
12 faces	DODECAHEDRON	buckler	CLYPEATE.CLYPEIFORM
12 sides	DODECAGON		PELTATE.SCUTATE
18 faces	TETRAKISHEXAHEDRON		SCUTIFORM
20 faces	ICOSAHEDRON	bull	TAURIFORM
24 faces	ICOSITETRAHEDRON		TAUROMORPHOUS
	TRIAKISOCTAHEDRON	buttocks	NATIFORM
	TRISOCTAHEDRON	cake	PLACENTIFORM
90 faces	ENNEACONTAHEDRON	calyx	CALYCIFORM
full number of		cap	PILEATE(D)
faces	HOLOHEDRON	capital lambda	LAMBDOID(AL)
many faces	POLYHEDRON	caterpillar	ERUCIFORM
—like trapezoids		chisel	SCALPRIFORM
	TRAPEZOHEDRON	circular	
many forms	POLYMORPHIC	—pyramid	CONE
	POLYMORPHOUS	—rod	CYLINDER
various forms	VARIFORM	cirrus	CIRRIFORM
varying forms	VERSIFORM	claw	UNGUIFORM
many sides	POLYGON	cleaver	DOLABRIFORM

having shape like:		cloud	NUBIFORM
all shapes	OMNIFORM	club	CLAVATE.CLAVIFORM
almond	AMYGDALOID	—roughly club-shaped	
almost circular	PENANNULAR		CLAVULATE
anchor ring	TORIC.TOROID(AL)	coin	NUMMULAR
approximately		comb	CTENIFORM.CTENOID
circular	ORBICULAR	cone	CONIFORM
arch	ARCUATE.FORNICATE	coral	CORALLIFORM
arrow	SAGITTAL		CORALLOID(AL)
—head	SAGITTATE	cord	RESTIFORM
awl	SUBULATE	corolla	COROLLIFORM
axe	SECURIFORM		COROLLINE
bacillus	BACILLAR(Y)	crab	CANCRIFORM.CANCROID
	BACILLIFORM	crescent	CRESCENTIC.LUNATE(D)
bag	CYSTIFORM	crest	CRISTIFORM
ball	ORB.SPHERE	cross	CRUCIATE.CRUCIFORM
		crow's beak	CORACOID
		crustacean larva	NAUPLIFORM

cube	CUBIFORM	hand	MANIFORM.PALMATE
cumulus	CUMULIFORM	hatchet	DOLABRIFORM
	CUMULOSE	heap	CUMULIFORM
cup	CRATERIFORM.COTYLOID	heart	CARDOID.CORDATE
CYATHTIFORM.POCULIFORM			CORDIFORM
—in front	PROCOELOUS	honeycomb	FAVEOLATE.FAVOSE
curve	CURVIFORM	hood	CUCULLATE
cushion	PULVILLIFORM	hook	UNCIATE(D).UNCIFORM
cyst	CYSTIFORM	—beak	RHAMPHOID
diamond	LOZENGE	horn	CORNICULATE.CORNIFORM
disc	COTYLIFORM.DISCOID(AL)	horse-shoe	HIPPOCREPIAN
doughnut	TORIC.TOROID(AL)	hump-back	GIBBOUS
drum	TYMPANIFORM	indented	CRENELLATE(D)
ear	AURIFORM.AURICULATE	jellyfish	MEDUSIFORM
eel	ANGUILLIFORM	keel	CARINATE
egg	OBOVATE.OBOVOID.OOIDAL	kidney	NEPHROID.RENIFORM
OVATE.OVIFORM.OVOID(AL)		knife	CULTRATE.CULTRIFORM
fan	FLABELLATE.RHIPIDATE	ladder	SCALARIFORM
feather	PENNIFORM	lance	LANCIFORM
fiddle	PANDURATE(D)	lance-head	LANCEOLATE
	PANDURIFORM	larvae	LARVIFORM
finch	FRINGILLIFORM	lattice	CLATHRATE
finger	DIGITIFORM	lens	LENTICULAR.LENTIFORM
fish	PISCIFORM		PHACOID(AL)
flask	LAGENIFORM	lentil	LENTICULAR.PHACOID(AL)
flattened		letter	
—circle	ELLIPSE.OVAL	—S	SIGMATE.SIGMOID
(see also egg above)		—upsilon	HYOID
—sphere	OBLATE	—ypsilon	YPSILIFORM.YPSILOID
flower	ANTHOID.FLORIFORM	lily	CRINOID(AL)
fork	FURCATE(D).FURCULAR	limpet	PATELLATE.PATELLIFORM
funnel	INFUNDIBULAR	long spiral	TURRICULATED
	INFUNDIBULATE	lozenge	RETICULATE(D)
	INFUNDIBULIFORM		RHOMB(US)
globe	GLOBATE(D).GLOBED	lyre	LYRATE(D)
GLOBOID.GLOBOSE		mitre	MITRIFORM
GLOBOUS.GLOBULAR		mushroom	FUNGIFORM
gnat	CULICIFORM	needle	ACEROSE.ACICULAR
goat	CAPRIFORM		ACIFORM
granule	GRANULIFORM	net	RETIFORM
hair	VILLIFORM	nipple	MAMILLAR(Y)
half		MAMMILATE(D).PAPILLIFORM	
—arrowhead	SEMI-SAGITTATE	obelisk	OBELISCAL.OBELISCOID
—cylinder	SEMITERETE	olive	OLIVARY
—moon	SEMI-LUNAR	orange	OBLATE
	SEMI-LUNATE	oval	VULVIFORM
—sphere	HEMISPHEROID	palm	PALMATE(D)
halved	DIMIDIATE	partition	SEPTIFORM
hammer	MALLEIFORM	pea	PISIFORM

pear	PYRIFORM	sword	ENSATE.ENSIFORM
pine cone	PINEAL		GLADIATE.XIPHOID
pitcher	ARYT(A)ENOID	thin plate	LAMELLIFORM
pointed	ACULEATE(D)	thorn	SPINIFORM
	FASTIGIATE	tooth	DENTIFORM.DENTOID
pouch	SACCIFORM	top	STROMBULIFORM
prism	PRISMOID	trapezium	TRAPEZIFORM
pyramid	PYRAMIDAL	triangle	DELTOID.TRIANGULAR
	PYRAMIDIC(AL)	tube	TUBIFORM.TUBULAR
rectangle	QUADRATE		VASIFORM
rhombus	LOZENGE.RHOMBOID	tuber	TUBERIFORM
ring	ANNULAR.CIRCINATE	turnip	NAPIFORM
	CRICOID	umbrella	UMBRACULIFORM
rod	BACILLAR(Y).BACILLIFORM	undifferentiated into root,	
roof	TECTIFORM	stem and leaves	THALLIFORM
root	RADICIFORM	vase	VASCULIFORM
rounded teeth	CRENATE(D)	watch-glass	MENISCOID
—finely crenate	CRENULATE(D)	wedge	CUNEAL.CUNEATE
saddle	HYPERBOLIC PARABOLOID		CUNEIFORM.SPHENOID
saucer	PATELLATE.PATELLIFORM	whip	FLAGELLIFORM
scalpel	SCALPELLIFORM	worm	HELMINTHOID
scimitar	ACINACIFORM		LUMBRICIFORM
screw	HELICOID(AL)		LUMBRICOID
sesame seed	SESAMOID	**shape³**	
shell	CONCHATE.CONCHIFORM	*shape* of a...	OAF
shield	CLYPEATE.CLYPEIFORM	*shape of* vase	SAVE
	PELTATE.SCUTATE	*shaping* ends	DENS.SEND
	SCUTIFORM.THYR(E)OID	**share**	
sickle	FALC(UL)ATE.FALCIFORM	share issue	
sieve	CRIBIFORM		SOLOMON'S JUDGEMENT
sloping to point	FASTIGIATE	*share of* champ/agne s/upper	
slug	LIMACIFORM		AGNES
small fragments	LAPILLIFORM	*share of* money	ONE
snake	ANGUIFORM	*share of* profit	PR.OF.IT
	SERPENTIFORM	share*out*	HARES.HEARS.SHEAR
socket	GLENAL.GLENOID	**sharp**	UNNATURAL
solid parabola	PARABOLOID	*shattered* vase	SAVE
spear	HASTATE(D)	**Shaw**	GBS
spike	SPICATE(D)	Shaw's girl	ELIZA
spindle	CLOSTRIDIAL.FUSIFORM	**she**	
spine	SPINIFORM	She, *for one*	NOVEL
spiral	VOLUTE(D)	she will	SHELL
spoon	COCHLEAR(L)IFORM	she will, *say*	SHEAL.SHEEL.SHIEL
	COCHLEATE(D)	she would, *say*	SHED
stalactite	STALACTIFORM	**shed**	
star	STELLAR.STELLATE(D)	*shed a...*	omit A
	STELLIFORM	*shed* leaves	omit FF
stem	CAULIFORM	*shed* weight	omit TON
style	STYLIFORM	*shed* *	omit *

•ba(skin)g, *shedding* skin	BAG
shed tears	RATES.STARE.TARES

sheep

Angolan	ZUNA
Asian	AMMON.ARGALI
	CARACUL.KARAKUL
Australian	JUMBU(C)K
British	CHEVIOT.COTSWOLD
	HERDWICK.ROMNEY
	WENSLEYDALE
Corsican	MUS(I)MON
	M(O)UF(F)LON
female	EWE.KEB.TEG(G)
Himalayan	BHARAL.BLUE SHEEP
	BURREL(L).BUR(R)HEL
	NAHOOR.NAHOUR
	OORIAL.URIAL
Lake District	HERDWICK
	SWALEDALE
male	RAM.TUP.WETHER
North African	AOUDAD
	BARBARY SHEEP
second-year	TEG(G)
short-legged	ANCON
South American	ALPACA
	GUANACO.HUANACO
	LLAMA.PACO
Spanish	MERINO
Tibetan	SHAPO.SHAHPU
woolly-faced	MUG
yearling	HOG(G).HOGGEREL
	HOGGET

sheet — P

sheet *missing*	omit P

shelter

sheltering a...	incl A
sheltering king	incl R
sheltering *	incl *
•l-and *sheltering* bird	LOWLAND
sheltered by *	incl in *
•bird *sheltered by* l-and	LOWLAND

shield

shielding a...	incl A
shielding *	incl *
•metal *shielding* girl	TANNIN
shielded by *	incl in *
•girl *shielded by* metal...	TANNIN

shift

gear-*shift*	RAGE

shift soil	OILS.SILO
shift worker	FURNITURE REMOVER
shiftily take...	KATE.TEAK
shifting the car	THRACE
shifty person	NOMAD

Shiite *extremists* — SE

shilling — BOB.S

shilling *off*	omit S

Shinto

ancient texts	KOJIKI
code of moral principles	BUSHIDO
domestic shrine	KAMI-DANA
goddess	AMATERASU
gods and their powers	KAMI
holy	
—object in temple	SHINTAI
—part of temple	HONDON
outer shrine of temple	HAIDEN
ritual prayers	NORITO
underworld	YOMI
(*see also* Japanese)	

ship¹ — CRAFT.LINER.MV.SS

hence

•house-boat	HOMECRAFT
•ship *with* unknown...	CRAFTY
•which ship, I *ask*	WITCHCRAFT

and

•mother-ship	MASS
•ship *carrying* hot...	SHOTS
•the *French* ship	LESS

ship²

ship breaker	DESTROYER
ship-*breaking*	HIPS.PISH
ship *has left*	omit SS
ship launcher	HELEN
shipping company	LINE
ships orchestra	WAVEBAND
shipshape	SCAPHOID
ship*shape*	HIPS.PISH
ship*wreck*	HIPS.PISH

ship³

American	DORY.SHOWBOAT
	STERNWHEELER
Anamese	GAY-YOU
ancient	
—galleys	BIREME.TRIREME
	QUADRIREME
	QUINQUEREME

—oars and sails GALLEAS.GALLEY
Arabian　(see Egyptian *below*)
argosy　CAR(R)ACK.CARRACT
　　　　　CARRECT
Baltic
—one-masted　　　　　　　　COG
—two-masted　　　　　　　　NEF
—three-masted　　　　CHEBECK
　　　　　　　　　　　　SHEBECK
barge　　　　　　　　　WHERRY
battleship　AIRCRAFT CARRIER
　　CORVETTE.CRUISER
　DESTROYER.DREADNOUGHT
　　　FRIGATE.IRONSIDE
　　MAN-O(F)-WAR.SLOOP
British
—coal lighter　　　　　　　KEEL
—coal vessel　　　　　　　　CAT
—flat-bottomed　　　　　　KEEL
—small yacht　KNOCKABOUT
cargo　COASTER.FREIGHTER
　　　　　　　　　　　　TRAMP
—warship　CAR(R)ACK.CARRACT
　　　　　　　　　CARRECT
Chinese JUNK.SAMPAN.SANPAN
corvette　　　　　　　　SLOOP
cut-down　　　　　　　　RAZEE
dismantled　　　　　　　　HULK
Dutch　BESANT.BEZANT.KOFF
　　　　PINK(IE).PINKY
—one-masted　　　　　　　HOY
—two-masted　　　BILANDER
　BYLANDER.BUSS.DOGGER
　　HOOKER.HOWKER
—three-masted　　　　　FLUYT
—cargo　　　　　　GAL(L)IOT
—flat-bottomed lighter PRA(A)M
　SCOW.SCHUIT.SCHUTT
—privateer　　　　　　　CAPER
Eastern coaster　　　　　GRAB
Egyptian　　　　DAHABEEAH
　DAHABIYAH.DAHABIYEH
　　FELUCCA.NUGGAR
escort　　　　　　　CORVETTE
excavator　　　　　　DREDGER
European
—one-masted　BILLY-BOY.COG
　CUTTER.DANDY.SHALLOP
　　　　SLOOP.YAWL

—two-masted　　BRIG(ANTINE)
　　　　KETCH.LUGGER
　　　PINNACE.SNOW
—two-six masted　　SCHOONER
—three-masted　　　CLIPPER
　　CORVETTE.FRIGATE
—three-four masted
　　　　　BARK(ENTINE)
　　　　BARQUE(NTINE)
—four-masted　JACKASS-BARK
—trading CAR(A)VEL.CAR(R)ACK
　CARRACT.CARRECT.CRARE
　CRAYER.GALLEON.LUGGER
Flemish sloop　　　　　BOYER
fast sailer　　　CUTTER.SLOOP
　　　　　(TEA-)CLIPPER
fishing-boat　DOGGER.DRIFTER
　(HERRING-)BUSS.LUGGER
　PETER-BOAR.SMACK.TRAWLER
French carrack　　　　　　NEF
galleon　　　　　　GALLOON
galley
—beaked　　　　　　　DRAKE
—Greek　(see Greek *below*)
—old　(see ancient *above*)
—Scottish　　　　LYMPHAD
—small　　　　　GAL(L)IOT
Ganges　　PULWAR.PUTELI
Greek
—30 oars　　　TRIACONTER
—50 oars　PENTECONTER
guard-boat　　　　　VEDETTE
heavy galley　　　　GALLEAS
Indian　　　　　PATAMAR
Italian merchant　　ARGOSY
Japanese　　　MARO.MARU
Levantine ketch SAIC(K).SAIQUE
Malay　COROCORE.COROCORO
　GALLIVAT.PRA(H)U.PROA
Mediterranean SANDAL.SET(T)EE
　　　　　TARTAN(E)
—two-masted　　CAR(A)VEL
　　　　　FELUCCA
—three-masted　　CAR(A)VEL
　CHEBEC(K).SHEBEC(K)
　XEBEC(K).ZEBEC(K)
　POLACRE.POLACCA
—coaster　　　　MISTICO
—warship　　DROMON(D)

mixed rig	HERMAPHRODITE RIG
Norse merchant	KNORR
passenger	CRUISER.LINER
Portuguese	CAR(A)VEL.LORCHA
	MULETTE
prison ship	BRIG.HULK
privateer	CORSAIR.CRUISER
riverboat	PADDLEBOAT
	PADDLER.SHOWBOAT
	STERNWHEELER
Scottish	
—flat-bottomed	COB(B)LE
—galley	LYMPHAD
shallow, fast	WHERRY
small	LUGGER.PINK.PINNACE
—galley	GAL(L)IOT
Spanish	CAR(A)VEL.GALLEASS
	GALLEON.ZABRA
spectral	FLYING DUTCHMAN
state barge	GALLEY-FOIST
supply	MAILBOAT.PACKET
	TENDER
Thames fishing	BAWLEY.BORLEY
Tigris ferry	GUFA
trader	INDIAMAN
Turkish	CAIC.CAIQUE
underwater	SUBMARINE
Venetian	ARGOSY.FRIGATOON
	VAPORETTO
warship	(*see* battleship *above*)
West Indian coaster	DROG(H)ER
shirker	CUTHBERT
shirt	T
shirt-*tail*	T
shivering fits are...	FAIREST
shock	
shocking case	ACES.AESC
shocking drink	JAR
shockingly bad	DAB
shoe	
shoe tree	SANDALWOOD
shoemaker	CRISPIN
shoe*making*	HOES.HOSE
shoot	
shoot dog *up*...(D) ↑	GOD
shooting all over Wales	SWALE
shooting all over the place, we	
hit...	WHITE
shooting box	CAMERA

shooting brake	SAFETY-CATCH
shooting break	TRUCE
shooting-men	GUNNERS.RA
shot daring spy	DAYSPRING
shop laws	COUNTERACTS
short¹	
short answer	ANS
short break	HOL.WE
short contest	COMP
short course	PUD
short day	D.MON etc.
short drink	METHS
short holiday	HOL.VAC.WE
short measure	FT.IMM-.IN.MM.YD
Short Metre	SM
short notice	AD.CRIT
short publication	MAG
short regulation	REG
short time	HR.MIN.MO.SEC.T.YR
short walk	PROM
short wave	SW
shortly release	DEMOB
short²	
short-le(g)	LE
short of a bit of sugar	CUB(e)
short of space	SPA.ACE
short time	(h)OUR.TIM(e)
short wal(k)	WAL
shortage of cash	CAS.ASH
shorter (st)ride	RIDE
shorter than you(r)...	YOU
shortly I will	ILL
short³	
short measure	INCH.LOWELL
short of a...	omit A
short of a hundred...	omit C
short of funds	(in) R-ED
short of money	omit L
short of time	omit AGE.T
short of *	omit *
•b(all)et *short of* all...	BET
short race	DASH.PIGMIES
	LILLIPUTIANS
short stop	COMMA
short telephone call	RINGLET
shortfall	UNDERGROWTH
shot	(*see* shoot)
show	
show a...	incl A

show *	incl *	Buxus	BOX
•lea-rn *to show* the...	LEATHERN	Californian lilac	CEANONTHUS
show embarrassment	GORED	Calluna	HEATHER
show-girl	EVITA	Campsis	BIGNONIA
show hospitality			TRUMPET VINE
	ENTERTAINMENT	Cape jasmine	GARDENIA
show jumper	VAULTING HORSE	castor oil plant	FATSIA
s/how/-*piece*	HOW	Ceanothus	CALIFORNIAN LILAC
show-pieces	SPECIE	Ceratostigma	PLUMBAGO
show-ring	MANIFESTO	Chaenomales	CYDONIA
show-trial	REHEARSAL		FLOWERING QUINCE.JAPONICA
showing as it was	WAIST	Chilean firebush	EMBOTHRIUM
showing a/s it/ was	SIT	Chimonanthus	WINTER SWEET
showboat	STAGECRAFT	Chinese	
shown in t/heat/re	HEAT	—gooseberry	ACTINIDIA
shredded papers	SAPPER	—hawthorn	PHOTINIA
shrew	KATE.XANTIPPE	—sacred bamboo	NANDINA
shrubs		Choisya	
some alternative names:			MEXICAN ORANGE BLOSSOM
acacia	MIMOSA	Cistus	ROCK ROSE
Actinidia	CHINESE GOOSEBERRY	clammy azalea	SWAMP AZALEA
Alexandrian laurel	DANAE		WHITE HONEYSUCKLE
Aloysia	LIPPIA	Clerodendron	GLORY TREE
Ampelopsis	PARTHENOCISSUS	Clianthus	LOBSTER-CLAW PLANT
	VIRGINIA CREEPER		PARROT'S BILL
Andromeda	PIERIS	Cneorum	DAPHNE (MEZEREUM)
Aristolochia	DUTCHMAN'S PIPE		MEZEREON.WIDOW-WAIL
azalea	WINTER BLOOM	Colutea	BLADDER SENNA
barberry	BERBERIS	coral plant	BERBERIDOPSIS
	PODOPHYLLUM	Cornus	DOGWOOD
beauty bush	KOLKWITZIA	Cotinus	SMOKE TREE
Berberidopsis	CORAL PLANT	cranberry	FEN-BERRY.ACCINIUM
berberis	BARBERRY	Cydonia	CHAENOMELES
	PODOPHYLLUM	Cytisus	BROOM
Bignonia	CAMPSIS	Daboecia	IRISH HEATH
	TRUMPET VINE	daisy bush	OLEARIA
blackberry	DEWBERRY.RUBUS	Danae	ALEXANDRIAN LAUREL
—x raspberry	BOYSENBERRY	daphne	SPURGE LAUREL
	LOGANBERRY	—mezereum	CNEORUM
bladder			MEZEREON.WIDOW-WAIL
—nut	STAPHYLEA	Diervilla	WEIGELA
—senna	COLUTEA	dogwood	CORNUS
box	BUXUS	double-flowered gorse	ULEX
bramble	RUBUS	Dutchman's pipe	ARISTOLOCHIA
broom	CYTISUS.GENISTA	Easter rose	JEW'S MALLOW
Buddleia	BUTTERFLY BUSH		KERRIA
butcher's broom	RUSCUS	elder	SAMBUCUS
buttercup shrub	POTENTILLA	Embothrium	CHILEAN FIREBUSH
butterfly bush	BUDDLEIA	Erica	HEATHER

Exochorda	PEARL BUSH	lilac	SYRINGA
Fatsia	CASTOR-OIL PLANT	Lippia	ALOYSIA
firethorn	PYRACANTHA		LEMON-SCENTED VERBENA
flowering		lobster-claw plant	CLIANTHUS
—currant	RIBES		PARROT'S BILL
—nutmeg	LEYCESTERIA	Lonicera	HONEYSUCKLE
—quince	CHAENOMELES	magnolia	TULIP TREE
forsythia	GOLDEN BELL BUSH	Mahonia	
gardenia	CAPE JASMINE		HOLLY-LEAVED BERBERIS
Genista	BROOM.SPANISH GORSE	Mexican orange	
glory tree	CLERODENDRON	blossom	CHOISYA
golden bell bush	FORSYTHIA	mezereon	CNEORUM
guelder rose	GELDER('S) ROSE		DAPHNE (MEZEREUM)
	ROSE ELDER.VIBURNUM		WIDOW-WAIL
Halesia	SNOWDROP TREE	mile-a-minute vine	POLYGONUM
Hamamelis	WITCH HAZEL		SILVER LACE
heather	CALLUNA.DABOECIA	mimosa	ACACIA
	ERICA	mock orange	PHILADELPHUS
Hebe	VERONICA		SYRINGA
Hedera	IVY	Myrica	TAMARISK
Hibiscus	ROSE MALLOW	myrtle	MYRTUS
	ROSE OF CHINA	Nandina	
	TREE HOLLYHOCK		CHINESE SACRED BAMBOO
holly	ILEX	naseberry	NEESBERRY
—leafed Berberis	MAHONIA		SAPODILLA PLUM
honeysuckle	CAPRIFOLE	Nerium	OLEANDER
	LONICERA.WOODBIND	Oleander	NERIUM
	WOODBINE	Olearia	DAISY BUSH
Hypericum	ST JOHN'S WORT	Pachysandra	JAPANESE SPURGE
Ilex	HOLLY	parrot's bill	CLIANTHUS
Irish heath	DABOECIA		LOBSTER-CLAW PLANT
ivy	HEDERA	Parthenocissus	AMPELOPSIS
Japanese			VIRGINIA CREEPER
—bitter orange	PONCIRUS	pearl bush	EXOCHORDA
—spurge	PACHYSANDRA	periwinkle	VINCA
japonica	CHAENOMELES	Perovskia	RUSSIAN SAGE
Jerusalem sage	PHLOMIS	Philadelphus	MOCK ORANGE
Jew's mallow	KERRIA		SYRINGA
Kerria	EASTER ROSE	Phlomis	JERUSALEM SAGE
	JEW'S MALLOW	Photinia	CHINESE HAWTHORN
Kolkwitzia	BEAUTY BUSH	Pieris	ANDROMEDA
Lantana	SHRUB VERBENA	plumbago	CERATOSTIGMA
Laurus	SWEET BAY	Polygonum	MILE-A-MINUTE VINE
Laurustinus	VIBURNUM		SILVER LACE
lavender	LAVANDULA	Podophyllum	BARBERRY
lemon-scented verbena	LIPPIA		BERBERIS.RACCOON-BERRY
Leycesteria		pomegranate	PUNICA
	FLOWERING NUTMEG	Poncirus	
Ligustrum	PRIVET		JAPANESE BITTER ORANGE

Potentilla	BUTTERCUP SHRUB
privet	LIGUSTRUM
Punica	POMEGRANATE
Pyracantha	FIRETHORN
raccoon-berry	PODOPHYLLUM
raspberry	RUBUS
Rhus	SMOKE TREE
Ribes	FLOWERING CURRANT
rock rose	CISTUS
rose elder	GUELDER ROSE
rose of China	HIBISCUS
rosemary	ROSEMARINUS
Rubus	BLACKBERRY.BRAMBLE
	RASPBERRY
Ruscus	BUTCHER'S BROOM
Russian sage	PEROVSKIA
sage	SALVIA
St John's wort	HYPERICUM
Sambucus	ELDER
Sapodilla plum	NASEBERRY
	NEESBERRY
Scotch creeper	TROPAEOLUM
sea buckthorn	HIPPOPHAE
shrub verbena	LANTANA
shrubby germander	TEUCRIUM
silver lace	POLYGONUM
	MILE-A-MINUTE VINE
smoke tree	COTINUS.RHUS
snowball tree	VIBURNUM
	WHITSUN ROSE
snowberry	SYMPHORICARPUS
snowdrop tree	HALESIA
Spanish	
—broom	SPARTIUM
—gorse	GENISTA
Spartium	SPANISH BROOM
Staphylea	BLADDER NUT
swamp azalea	CLAMMY AZALEA
	WHITE HONEYSUCKLE
sweet bay	LAURUS
Symphoricarpus	SNOWBERRY
syringa	LILAC
	MOCK ORANGE
	PHILADELPHUS
tamarisk	MYRICA
Teucrium	
	SHRUBBY GERMANDER
Trachycarpus	CHUSAN PALM
tree hollyhock	HIBISCUS

Tropaeolum	SCOTCH CREEPER
trumpet vine	BIGNONIA
	CAMPSIS
tulip tree	MAGNOLIA
Ulex	DOUBLE-FLOWERED GORSE
veronica	HEBE
Viburnum	LAURUSTINUS
Vinca	PERIWINKLE
Virginia creeper	AMPELOPSIS
	PARTHENOCISSUS
Weigela	DIERVILLA
white honeysuckle	
	CLAMMY AZALEA
	SWAMP AZALEA
Whitsun rose	SNOWBALL TREE
	VIBURNUM
widow-wail	CNEORUM
	DAPHNE (MEZEREUM)
	MEZEREON
winter	
—bloom	AZALEA.WITCH HAZEL
—sweet	CHIMONANTHUS
witch hazel	HAMAMELIS
	WINTER BLOOM

shuffle

shuffling <u>along</u>	GOLAN
shuffling around <u>town</u>	WONT

shut

<u>shut</u> *off*	HUTS.THUS
<u>shut</u> *out*	HUTS.THUS
shut *up*(D) ↑	NEP

shutter   EYELID

shy

shy bear, *say*	COYPU
shy writer	LOBELIA

Siamese

capital	BANGKOK.S
coin	BAHT.SATANG.TICAL
language	THAI
leader	S
measure	
—1 inch	NIU
—20 inches	SAWK
—80 inches	WAH
—44 yards	SEN
—1/3 acre	RAI
weight (3 lbs)	CHANG

sick

sick <u>to</u> her...	OTHER

sickly child	PALETOT
side	L.R.XI.XV
side at sea	LARBOARD.PORT
	STARBOARD
side *at sea*	DIES.IDES
side-*splitting*	DIES.IDES
side-splitting one...	ACRE
side-splitting girl	LEVER.REVEL
sides of bacon	BN
siemens	S
Sierra Leone	WAL
sift clues I...	SLUICE
sight-screen	EYELID
sigma	S
sign	MINUS.PLUS.TICK.V
sign of summer	PLUS
sign of take-away	MINUS
sign of the times	X
signs	(*see* Zodiac)
signal	
signal frequency	SF
signal officer	SO
signature	SIG
Sikh	
fanatic	AKALI
holy	
—book	GRANTH (SAHIB)
—person	SANT
knife	KIRPAN
law of causality	KARMA
leader	S
nectar	AMRIT
organiser of worship	GRANTHI
script	GURMUKHI
sugar and water drink	AMRIT
temple	GURDWARI
	(*see also* Indian[2])
Sikorski's tomb	POLE VAULT
silent	MUM.SH.ST
silence	GAG.SQUASH
	RACKET.TACE
silent god	ODIN
silks	BAR
silly	
silly girl	ASSESS
silly part	TRAP
silly way to put...	PUTTO
silver	AG.ARGENTUM
hence	

•silver circle	AGROUND
•silver grass	AGREED
•silver notes	AGEE
and	
•British silver	BRAG
•hard silver	HAG
•royal silver	RAG
and	
•silver *in* river	DAGON
•silver *in* warehouse	STORAGE
silver-*covered*	(in) A-G
silver-*edged*	(in) A-G
silver-*lined*	incl AG
silver-*mounted*	(in) A-G
silver-*mounted*(D) ↑	GA
silver-*plated*	(in) A-G
simple	HERB
simple man	HERB.SIMON
simple song	HERBARIA
simple retailer	HERBALIST
simpleton ABDERITE.GOTHAMIST	
GOTHAMITE.JOHN.SIMON	
Singapore	SGP
sine	SIN
sing	BETRAY.CAROL.GRASS
SQUEAL.TELL.YODEL	
sings tenor	TRONE
singing well	INVOICE
single	A.I.LONE
single data converter	SDC
singular spirit	ONEGIN
singularly not crazy	BANANA
Sinhalese	SINH
(*see also* Ceylon)	
sinister	LEFT
sinister fighter	SOUTHPAW
sinister trait	LEFTHANDEDNESS
Sinn Fein	SF
sinuous snake	SNEAK
sir	KNIGHT.SR
sister	NUN.S.SIS
sit	
sit in *	incl in *
•he *sits in* s-et...	SHEET
sit *out*	-IST.ITS.TIS
sit up(D) ↑	TIS
six[1]	VI
hence	
•six die	VIPERISH

•six each	VIPER
•six *to* one	VIA
•six vehicles	VICARS
and	
•66 groups	VIVISECTS

six²

at dice	SICE.SIZE
balls	OVER
books of OT	HEXATEUCH
Christmas presents	GEESE
cleft in six	SEXFID
combining forms	HEX(A)-.SEXA-
	SEX(I)-.SEXTI-
counties of N. Ireland	ANTRIM
ARMAGH.FERMANAGH.DOWN	
(LONDON)DERRY.TYRONE	
daily	SEXTAN
day fever	SEXTAN
days of creation	HEXAEMERON
fold	SEXTUPLE(X)
	SEXTUPLICATE
footer	ANT.BEE.INSECT
groups	HEXAD.SESTET(T)
SESTETTE.SENARY	
SEXTET(T).SEXTETTE	
SEXTUOR	
having six	
—angles	HEXAGONAL
	SEXAGONAL
—columns	HEXASTYLE
—compartments	SEXLOCULAR
—feet	HEXAPODAL
—fingers	HEXADACTYLIC
	HEXADACTYLOUS
SEXIDIGITAL.SEXIDIGITATE(D)	
—languages	HEXAGLOT
—leaves	SEXFOIL
—lines	HEXASTICH(AL)
—lobes	SEXFOIL
—metrical feet	HEXAMETER
	HEXAMETRIC(AL)
—notes	HEXACHORD
—parts	HEXAMEROUS
	SEXPARTITE
—pistils	HEXAGYNIAN
	HEXAGYNOUS
—plane faces	HEXAHEDRON
—rays	HEXACT(INAL)
—sides	HEXAGONAL

—stamens	HEXANDRIAN
	HEXANDROUS
—styles	HEXAGYNIAN
	HEXAGYNOUS
—times normal number of	
chromosomes	HEXAPLOID
—toes	HEXADACTYLIC
	HEXADACTYLOUS
SEXIDIGITAL.SEXIDIGITATE(D)	
—valencies	SEX(I)VALENT
—vasacular strands	HEXARCH
—versions	HEXAPLAR(IC
	HEXAPLARIAN
headed monster	SCYLLA
hours	QUARTER-DAY
hundred	BALACLAVA.DC
	LIGHT BRIGADE.VIC
—years	SEXCENTENARY
nil	SIXTY.VIO-
notes	SEXTOLET
nymphs	HYADES
on die	CISE.SICE.SISE
one of six at birth	SEXTUPLET
pence	SICE.TANNER
yearly	SEXENNIAL
thirty	HANDS DOWN

sixteen

sixteen leaves per	
sheet	SEXTODECIMO
	SIXTEENMO
sixteenth note	SEMIQUAVER
verse of sixteen lines	SIXTEENER

sixth

sixth (music)	SEXT
sixth former	UPPER-CLASS
sixth of circle	SEXTANT
sixth sense	ESP

sixty   LX

60 per cent of <u>crude</u>	CRU
sixty grains	DRAM
sixty-six	VIVI
sixty-year old	SEXAGENARIAN
	SEXAGENARY
sixtieth	SEXAGESIMAL

skein   HANK

sketch fish   DRAWLING

skimmed (m)ilk   ILK

skin

lizard *skin*	LD

skin of his. . .	HS
skin of orange	OE
skin off (o)rang(e)	RANG
skin tight	TT
skin*head*	S
skip	
skip a. . .	omit A
skip it!	omit IT
skip *	omit *
skipping	OMITTING
skirmish in glade	LEADING
skirting Southampton	SOON
sky	LIMIT
slack ropes	PORES.SPORE
slap-happy sort	ORTS.TORS
slashed wrist	WRITS
slaughter deer	REDE.REED
slave girl	AIDA
sleep	
sleeper	EARRING
sleeping partner	BEDFELLOW
sleepyhead	NAPPER
sleepy*head*	S
slice	
slice of bre/ad I t/ook. . .	ADIT
sliced by *	incl in *
•c-ake *sliced by* essayist	
	CLAMBAKE
sliced beans	BANES
sliced loaf	OLAF
slide	
slide back door⟨	ROOD
sliding panel	PLANE
slight	
slight change of heart	HEARS
slight change of heart	EARTH
	HATER.RATHE
slight change of pace	PICE.PACT
slight change of pace	CAPE
slip	
slip into *	incl in *
•I *slip into* wa-ter	WAITER
slip-*up*(D) ↑	RRE.PILS
slip-up when *climbing*(D) ↑	
	PUPILS
slips *	omit *
•lin(net) *slips the* net	LIN
slip*knots*	LIPS.LISP.PILS
*slip*knots	STONK

slipper	EEL
slippery slope	LOPES.POLES
sloppy thing	NIGHT
sloth	AI
Slough	BOG
slovenly, untidy. . .	NUDITY
slow	
slow-*spoken*	SLOE.SLOUGH
slow *start*	S
slug killer	BULLET
sly	CHRISTOPHER
small¹	TINY.WEE
hence	
•small daughter	WEED
•small letters	WEEKS.WEEPS
•small points	WEENS
small²	
small arms ammunition	SAA
small book	B.BK.VOL
small bottle	BOT
small box	B
small business	BIZ.CO(Y)
small capitals	SC
small change	D.-ID.IP.P
small coin	D.-ID.IP.P
small firm	CO
small girl	DI.G
small house	H.HO.COT
small illustration	FIG
small man	GENT.M
small marsupial	ROO
small measure	CC.EL.EM.EN
	FT.IN.MM.YD
small number	NO
small point	PT
small quantity	CC
small relative	BRER.BRO.SIS
small research establishment	LAB
small section	DEPT
small space	EM.M
small square	EM.M
small volume	CC.VOL
small weight	CT.GR.OZ.WT
small³	
small amount of rice	R
small amount off (p)rice	RICE
small beer	HALF-PINT
small blow	COUPLET
small circle	RINGLET

small coat	MATINEE
small footballer	HALF
	THREE-QUARTER
small letter	MINIM
small loophole	EYELET
small luggage compartment	
	BOOTEE
small m	MINIM
small man	CHAPLET.MINIMAL
small mother	MINIMUM
small moustache	CHARLEY
	CHARLIE
small-time collector	GLEANER
smaller than Bat(h)	BAT
smallest pig	ANTHONY.RUNT
	TANTONY
	(*see also* little²)

smart

smart boy	CHICKEN.STING-RAY
smart(ypants)	ALEC

smash

smash-<u>hit</u>	-ITH
smash-<u>up</u> of <u>cars</u>	ARCS.SCAR
smashing <u>vases</u>	SAVES

smell	BO

smoke

smoke-ring	RE-ECHO
smoky city	HAVANA

smooth

smooth foil	IRON CROSS
smooth operator	LAUNDRYMAN
smoother	IRON.PLANE

smother

smother a	incl A
smother *	incl *
•s-ores *smother* husband	SHORES
smothered in *	incl in *
•husband *smothered*	
in s-ores	SHORES

smuggle(d)	RUN.(RAN)
hence	
•*smuggled in* ar-t. . .	ARRANT
•*smuggled in* church	CRANE
•*smuggled* wine	RANSACK

snake¹

commonly used names	ASP.BOA
	RATTLER
hence	
•angry snake	ASPIRATE

•snake *and* dog	BOAT-RACE

snake²

some alternative names:

African	BERG ADDER.COBRA
	MAMBA
—garter snake	ELAPS
	HOMORELAPS
—horned viper	CERASTES
—tree snake	BOOMSLANG
—viper	RIVER JACK
American	BLACK SNAKE
	COPPERHEAD
—coral snake	ELAPS.MICRURUS
—non-venomous	GARTER SNAKE
	GREEN SNAKE
	RING SNAKE
—rattlesnake	PIT VIPER
—viper	RATTLER.RATTLESNAKE
—venomous	MOCASSIN
	MOCCASIN
—water moccasin	
	COTTONMOUTH
Asiatic	KING COBRA
Australian	BLACK SNAKE
	CARPET SNAKE.DEATH ADDER
	TAIPAN.TIGER SNAKE
British	
—adder	VIPER
—common	GRASS SNAKE
	RING(ED) SNAKE
coach-whip snake	MASTICOPHIS
coral snake	SCYTALE
East Indian	BOIGA
Egyptian conjurer's snake	NAGA
	NAIA.NAJA
fabulous snake	AMPHISBAEMA
fer-de-lance	YELLOW VIPER
green	BOIOBI
Hydrophidae	SEA SNAKE
Indian	BONGAR.HAMADRYAD
—boa	JIBOYA
—cobra	COBRA DA CAPELLO
	NAGA.NAIA.NAJA
—rock snake	KAA.K(A)RAIT
	PYTHON
krait	ROCK SNAKE
legless lizard	GLASS SNAKE
Madagascan	LANGAHA
Masticophis	COACH-WHIP SNAKE

non-venomous	COLUBER.DIPSAS
	HOOP SNAKE
order	OPHIDIA
puff adder	CLOTHO
python	ROCK SNAKE
rattlesnake	CROTALUS
	CROTALIDAE
sea snake	HYDROPHIDAE
serpent	ASP.BOYUNA
short-tailed	SAND SNAKE
South American	
—anaconda	SUCURUJA
—bushmaster	SURUCUCU
—python	(A)BOMA.BOA
—venomous	BUSHMASTER
FER-DE-LANCE.JARARACA	
JARARAKA.LACHESIS	
SURUCUCU	
—water boa	ANACONDA
	SUCURUJU
spitting cobra	RINCHAL
tree snake	DENDROPHIS
two-headed	AMPHISBAEMA
venomous	ASP.ASPIC(K)
	KOKOB.SEPS
West Indian	FER-DE-LANCE
yellow viper	FER-DE-LANCE

snap

snap up(D) ↑	PANS
snap up caller's	LUPERCAL
snarl up nets	STEN.TENS

sneak

sneakily slid...	LIDS
sneaking past	PATS.STAP.TAPS
sneaky dealer	LEADER

snooker

snooker-ball	RED
snooker manual	POCKETBOOK
snoop *around*	PR-Y

snow

snow *clearing*	OWNS.SOWN
snow*drift*	OWNS.SOWN
snowing in the...	THINE
snowman	SHE.YETI
so[1]	AS
hence	
•so say...	ASSAY
•so sure	ASCERTAIN
•so *to* bed	ASCOT

so[2]	ERGO.SIC.THUS
so as to startle...	RATTLE
so it's said	SEW.SOUGH.SOW
so to speak	SEW.SOUGH.SOW
so to speak, a dew	ADIEU
so *upset*(D) ↑	OS
soaring notes	ONSET.SETON
	STONE.TONES

soccer

soccer blunder	OG
soccer suit	HEARTS

social

social crawler	ANT
social, domestic and pleasure	SDP
social *ends*	SL
social gathering	BEE
social worker	ANT.BEE
socialist	LAB.RED
socialist *backing*⟨	BAL.DER
socially acceptable	U

society — S.SOC

Society for Psychical Research	SPR
Society of	
—Antiquaries	SA
—Arts	SA
—Engineers	SE
—Incorporated Accountants	SAA
—Jesus	SJ
—the Holy Cross	SSC

soft (very soft) — P.(PP)

hence	
•soft drink	PALE
•soft stratum	PLAYER
•soft touch	PREACH
and	
•a soft fruit	APPEAR
•a soft one	APACE
•a soft spot	APPOINT
and	
•a very soft fish	APPROACH
•a very soft lotion	APPOINTMENT
•*learner has* a very soft...	LAPP
soft *centre*	OF
soft centre	incl P
•*soft-centred* ro-e	ROPE
soft-*hearted*	incl P
•soft-hearted fellow	MAPLE
soft maggot	GENTLE

sol(d) *short*	SOL
soldier	ANT.MAN.TOMMY
airborne soldier	PARA
American soldier	GI.JOE
hence	
•American infantry vehicle	GIBUS
•American officer	GILT
•soldier's double	GIGI
French soldiers	SOLDATS
German soldiers	SOLDATEN.SS
soldier's father	CHAPLAIN
	PADRE
soldier's *return*⟨	IG-
soldier's salute	PRESENT
soldiers	IMPI.MEN.OR
	RA.RE.SAS.TA
hence	
•soldiers one...	MENACE
•soldiers the *German*...	MENDER
•soldiers total...	MENTALLY
and	
•live *around* soldiers	BORE
•soldiers' friend	ORALLY
•value soldiers	ASSESSOR
and	
•soldiers in East End	RAINBOW
•soldiers offer	RABID
•soldiers watch	RASPY
and	
•soldiers guard, *I hear*	REGARD
•soldiers in certain...	REINSURE
•soldiers jumped	REBOUNDED
and	
•immerse soldiers	DIPSAS
•soldiers have hard...	SASH
•soldiers in the East	SASINE
soldiers in France	AEF.BEF
soldiers *in France*	SOLDATS
	(*see also* army)
sole	
sole expert	CHIROPODIST
sole impression	FOOTPRINT
sole supplier	FISHERMAN
	FISHMONGER
	FISHWIFE
sole tender	CHIROPODIST
solicitor	SOL(R)
Solicitor at Law	SL
solicitor before superior court	SSC

Solicitor General	SG
Solomon's judgement	
	SHARE ISSUE
solution	SOL
solution of weak...	WAKE
some[1]	IV.V.VI.PART.TEN.X
hence	
•some unknown	IVY
•some in square...	VINT
•some New Testament...	VINT
and	
•some allowed	PARTLET
•some unknown	PARTY
•someone	PARTI
and	
•some can...	TENABLE
•some church...	TENCH
•some workers	TENANTS
some[2]	
some ba/d apple/s	DAPPLE
some degree of hope	HOP
some *French*	DES
some idea	ID
some of the...	TH
some of the men	ME
some of t/he m/en	HEM
some quite...	QUIET
some *rhymes*	BUM.COME
	CRUMB.DRUM.DUMB.GUM
	HUM.LUM.MUM
	SUM.TUM
some say	(*see* dialect)
some *say*	SUM
some say folks will...	
	FORECASTLE
some time	TIM
somehow tried...	TIRED
somersault	
somersault done at...	ATONED
	DONATE
somersault made...⟨	EDAM
***something like a* cow**	CHOW
	COWL.SCOW
sometimes	TEMPI
somewhat	
*some*what	HAT
somewhat hackn/eye/d	EYE
son	
son	S

hence	
•son *and* parent	SMOTHER
•son in church	SINCE
•son *in* ho-t...	HOST
son of	
—a bitch	SOB
—an Englishman	FITZ
—a Scot	MAC
—a Welshman	AP
song	AIR.ARIA.LAY
Song of Solomon	SOLARIA
song-writer	SOLOMON
sophisticated	IN
soprano	S.SOP
sorceress	SIBYL
sore	
sore *back*⟨	EROS
<u>sore</u> *distress*	EROS.ROES.ROSE
sorry	
outfit	SACKCLOTH AND ASHES
sort	
sort of bone	T
sort of horse	ARAB
sort of <u>horse</u>	SHORE
sort of <u>shirt</u>	T
sort of square	T
sorted <u>letters</u>	SETTLER
sorted <u>*out*</u> main date	ANIMATED
soul mate	HEART
sound	
sound money	CACHE
sound of bird	CHEEP.TWEET
sound of bird	BURD.BURRED
Sound of Music	HEIR
sound of pain	OW
sound of pain	PANE
sound of sleep	Z
sound of the sea	C.CEE.SEE
sound pleased	PURR
sound properties	ACOUSTICS
sound *waves*	WAIVES
sound way...	WEIGH
sound wood	WOULD
sounded a chord	ACCORD
sounding-board	BORED
soundly based	BASTE
soundness of limb	LIMN
sounds as if I...	AYE.EYE
sounds like rain	REI(G)N

sounds weak	WEEK
soup	DAMPCOURSE
soup <u>made</u>...	DAME.EDAM
sour	
<u>sour</u> disposition	OURS
sourness	ACID-HEAD
source	PARENT
source of <u>stream</u>	MASTER
source of <u>stream</u>	S
south	S
southeast	SE
south-southeast	SSE
southwest	SW
south-southwest	SSW
South Africa(n)	RSA.SA.ZA
hence	
•South African climber	SAVINE
•South Africans	MENSA
•young Boer	SALAD
South African Airways	SAA
<u>South African leaders</u>	SA
	(*see also* Africa)
South America(n)[1]	SA.SUS.SUSA
hence	
•South American boy	SALAD
•South American gin	SATRAP
•South American	
shipping company	SALINE
South American[2]	
alligator	CAIMAN.CAYMAN
ant	SAUBA ANT
	UMBRELLA ANT
—bear	TAMANOIR
—eater	ARMADILLO.TAMANDUA
—thrush	ANT BIRD
armadillo	PEBA.TATOU
aromatic kernel	PICHURIM BEAN
arrow poison	CURARA.CURARE
balsam	COPAIBA.COPIAYA
bat	DESMODUS
beetle	HERCULES BEETLE
beetles	PYROPHORUS
birds	AGAMI.ANT THRUSH
	ARAPUNGA.BELL BIRD
	CAMPANERO
	COCK-OF-THE-ROCK.CONDOR
	COTINGA.CURASSOW
	HOA(C)TZIN.JABIRU
	JACAMAR.MANAKIN.

MOTMOT.MUSK DUCK.OVEN BIRD
PUFF BIRD.QUETZAL.RHEA
SERIEMA.STINK BIRD
SUN BITTERN.TAPACOLO
TAPACULO.TERU-TERO.TOPAZ
TOUCAN(ET).TROGON
TRUMPETER.TURCO
UMBRELLA BIRD.URUBU
YNAMBU.ZOPILOTE
—catching spider   TARANTULA
birthwort   ARISTOLOCHIA
brome grass   RESCUE-GRASS
burrowing armadillo PICHICIAGO
butterfly   MORPHO
butternut   S(A)OUARI(-NUT)
cactus   CHRISTMAS CACTUS
canoe   PERIAGUA.PIRAGUA
                         PIROGUE
Cape gooseberry
              STRAWBERRY TOMATO
capybara   RIVER HOG
carica   PA(W)PAW.PAPAYA
catfish   HASSAR
cattle
—farm   ESTANCIA
—farmer   ESTANCIERO
cavy   GUINEA PIG
cereal   QUINOA
chain   ANDES
climbing plant CANARY CREEPER
INDIAN CRESS.MARCGRAVIA
PASSION-FLOWER
PHILODENDRON
SARSAPARILLA.SMILAX
TIMBO.TROPAEOLUM
WAX FLOWER
cloak   PONCHO
coin   PESO
coral-flowered
  plant   EASTER CACTUS
corkwood   BALSA
cowboy   GAUCHO.VAQUERO
crab tree   CARAPA
—fruit   CARAP NUT
crested screamer   CHAUNA
CARIAMA.SERIEMA
crocodile   CAIMAN.CAYMAN
dance   PAVANE.ZAPATEO
dorado   GOLDEN SALMON

dormouse   ECHIMYD
drink   ASSAI.MATE
              YERBA (DE MATE)
drug   PAREIRA BRAVA
edentate   SLOTH
edible
—grub   GROO-GROO.GRU-GRU
—tuber   ARRACACHA.OCA
eel   CARAPO
estate   HACIENDA
establishment   HACIENDA
factory   HACIENDA
finch   TANAGER
fireflies   PYROPHORUS
fish   ANGEL FISH.ARAPAIMA
CARIBE.CHICHLID.PERAI.PIRAI
PIRANHA.PIRARUCU.PIRAYA
SWORD-TAIL
flea   CHIGGER.CHIGOE
              CHIGRE.JIGGER
flooded forest   (I)GAPO
flowers   ALSTROEMERIA
ANTHURIUM
GLOXINIA.TAGETES
fox   ZORRO
fruit   A(C)KEE.ASSAI
CASHEW APPLE
CASHEW NUT.GUAVA.LUCUMA
SOUR-SOP.SUGAR APPLE
SWEET-SOP
game bird   GUAN
garment   TAYO
golden
—breasted trumpeter   AGAMI
—salmon   DORADO
goosefoot   QUINOA
gourd   CACOON
grass   PASPALUM
gum   ANGICO
hare-lipped bat   NOCTILIO
hawk   CARACARA
hoatzin   STINK BIRD
holly   MATE
Honduras bark   CASCARA
horned screamer   PALAMEDEA
horseman   GAUCHO.LLANERO
hummingbird SWORD-BILL.SYLPH
hut   TOLDO
Indians   GUARANI.TUPI

indigo	COBRES
jacaranda	PALISANDER
kinkajou	HONEY BEAR.POTTO
landmark	SENAL
language	CARIB.GURANI.TUPI
lapwing	TERU-TERO
large eagle	(HARPY) EAGLE
laurel tree	PICHURIM
leaders	SA
leaf-carrying ant	SAUBA
leopard	JAGUAR
liquor	CHICA
lizard	AMPHISBAENA.BASILISK
	(I)GUANA.TEGUEXIN
lion	COUG(U)AR.PUMA
marmalade tree	
	MAMMEE-SAPOTA
marmoset	JACCHUS
measure (33-43 inches)	VARA
	VARE
missile	BOLAS
mortgage	CEDULA
moth	OWL MOTH
mountain sickness	PUNA
mudfish	LEPIDOSIREN
mulberry tree	CONTRAYERVA
	CRECOPIA
nest-building catfish	HASSAR
night-ape	DOUROUCOULI
	DURUKULI
non-Spaniard	GRINGO
oilbird	GUACHARO.GUACHERO
opossum	MARMOSE
orchid	ONCIDIUM
ostrich	NANDOO.NANDU.RHEA
pack animal	ALPACA.PACO
	GUANACO.HUANACO.LLAMA
palisander	JACARANDA
palms	(see palm)
papaya	CARICA.PA(W)PAW
	PAPAYA
parrot	AMAZON.MACAW
Peruvian Indian	QUECHA.QUICHA
pineapple	TILLANDSIA
Pithecolobium	RAIN TREE
plain	CAMPOS.LLANO.PAMPA(S)
	PARAMO.SAVANNA(H)
—dweller	LLANERO
plant	ARTILLERY PLANT.BIXA

	DUMB CANE.FUCHSIA
	FURCRAEA.PAREIRA.PETUNIA
—yielding	
—curare	(O)URALI.(O)URARI
	WOORALI.WOURALI
—snakebite antidote	GUACO
poison	CURARA.CURARE
pouch toad	NOTOTREMA
purgative nut	PHYSIC NUT
quail	TINAMOU
rabbit-squirrel	CHINCHA
race	CARIB
racoon	COATI(MONDI)
	COATI(MUNDI).KINKAJOU
rail	COURLAN
ranch	HACIENDA
red jasmine	FRANGIPANI
rescue grass	BROME GRASS
resin	CARANNA.CARAUNA
riding whip	QUIRT
river	AMAZON.ORINOCO
—hog	CAPYBARA
rodent	ACOUCHY.AG(O)UTI
	AG(O)UTY.BISCACHA
	CAPYBARA.CAVY
	CHINCH(ILL)A.COYP(O)U
	PACA.DILOCHOTIS.GUINEA PIG
	MARA.PATAGONIAN HARE
	TUCOTUCO.TUCUTUCO
	TUKUTUKU.
	VISCACHA.VIZCACHA
—colony	VISCACHERA
rosewood	PALISANDER
rubber substitute	BALATA
screamer	KAMICHI
settlement	PUEBLO
shrub	ESCALLONIA.JABORANDI
	PILOCARPUS.RHATANY
	SIMARUBA.TREE TOMATO
skunk	ATOC.ATOK.ZORILLO
sloth	AI.UNAU
spiny fish	DORAS
spirit	DEMERARA
tableland	MESETA.PUNA
three-toed sloth	AI
tiger cat	MARGAY
timber	LANA.LEOPARD WOOD
	LETTER WOOD.MAHOGANY
	PADDLE WOOD

	PARTRIDGE WOOD
	QUEBRACHO.ZEBRA WOOD
tinamous	PARTRIDGE
town	PUEBLO
tree	ACACIO.ACAJOU.A(C)KEE
	ANGICO.BEBEERU.BOMBAX
	CACAO.CANDLE TREE
	CANNONBALL TREE.CASHEW
	CHINA(CHINA).COW TREE
	FIDDLEWOOD.FUSTIC.FUSTOC
	GRAPETREE.GREENHEART
	GUAIACUM.GUAVA
	JACARANDA.KINA(KINA)
	LIMA WOOD.LOGWOOD
	LUCUMA.MAHOGANY
	MASSARANDUBA.MILK TREE
	MISSEL TREE.OITICICA.OMBU
	PAPAYA.QUASSIA
	QUEBRACHO.RAIN-TREE
	S(A)OUARI.SAVANNA-WATTLE
	SNAKEWOOD.SOAP-BARK
	SOUR-SOP.SUGAR APPLE
	SWEET SOP.SWEETWOOD
	TRUMPET TREE.WALLABA
	XYLOPIA
—frog	NOTOTREMA
—yielding quinine	CHINA(CHINA)
	CINCHONA.KINA(KINA)
	QUINA(QUINA).QUINQU(INA
turtle	MATAMATA
two-toed sloth	UNAU
ungulate	TAPIR
uplands	CUCHILLA
vulture	CONDOR.URUBU
walking fish	DORAS
water opossum	YAPO(C)K
weasel	GRISON.TAIRA.TAYRA
weevil	DIAMOND BEETLE
wet forest	SELVA
wild	
—cat	EYRA.JAGUAR(ONDI)
	JAGUARUNDI.MARGAY
	OCELOT.PUMA
—llama	GUANACO.HUANACO
	VICUNA
—pig	PECCARY.TAPIR
—turkey	CRAX.CURASSOW
	PENELOPE
wood sorrel	OCA

Yankee	GRINGO
South Australia	SA
South Island	SI
South Latitude	SL.SLAT
South Pole	SP
South Seas	
drink	(K)AVA
jargon	BEACH-LA-MAR
	BECHE-DE-MER
labourer	KANAKA
southern	S
Southern Railway	SR
Southern Region	SR
sovereign	L.K.KING.Q.R
Soviet	(*see also* Russian)
Soviet Union	SU.USSR
space	
space in Fleet Street	EM
space traveller	COMET
spacious ship	LARGESS(E)
spade	S
spaghetti	STRING COURSE
Spain	E
span	
span a. . .	incl A
spanning *	incl *
•boy *spanning* river	LARD
spanned by *	incl in *
•river *spanned by* boy	LARD
Spanish	HISPANO
	IBERIAN.SP
act	AUTO
agreement	SI
American half-caste	MESTIZO
apple	MANZANA
approval	SI
articles	EL.LA.LAS.LOS
barracks	CASERNA
Basque	
—ball game	PELOTA
—separatists	ETA
bayonet	YUCCA
bazaar	ALCAICERIA
black	NEGRO
—pudding	MONDONGO
blade	TOLEDO
blades	ESPARTO
blanket	MANTA
blusterer	CACAFOGO

	CACAFUEGO
boundary house	POSADO
boy	NINO
brazier	BRASERO
brother	HERMANO
—hood	HERMANDAD
bullfight	CORRIDA(DE TOROS)
bullfighter	BANDERILLERO
	MATADOR(E).PICADOR
	TORERO.TOREADOR
—'s dart	BANDERILLA
cabal	JUNTA.JUNTO
cabinet	VARGUENO
cape	CAPA.MANTILLA
capital	MADRID.S
cask	BARRICA
chalk	SOAPSTONE
champion	CAMPEADOR.CID
chaperone	DUENNA
cheer	OLE
chief	CID
—magistrate	CORREGIDOR
child	NINO
Christian	MOZARAB
cloak	CAPA.CAPOTE.MANTA
clown	GRACIOSO
code of law	FUEROA
coins	
—unit	PES.PESETA
—1/4 peseta	REAL.RIAL.RYAL
—8 reals	PIECE OF EIGHT
—5 pesetas	DURO.PESO
—dollar	PIECE OF EIGHT
—old copper	MARAVEDI.VELLON
—old silver	COB
—old gold	PISTOLE
—2 pistoles	DOUBLOON
cold soup	GAZPACHO
collection of songs	CANCIONERO
commander	ENCOMENDERO
commandery	ENCOMIENDA
conqueror	CONQUISTADOR
constitution	FUERO
council	JUNTA
—meeting	CONSULTA
country house	QUINTA
courtyard	PATIO
covered wagon	TARTANA
cress	PEPPERWORT

dagger	YUCCA
dance	BOLERO.CACHUCHA
	FANDANGO.FARRUCA
	FLAMENCO.JOTA.PASO DOBLE
	PASSACAGLIA.SARABAND
	SEGUIDILLA.ZAPATEADO
desk	VARGUENO
dish	PAELLA.SALPICON
doctor	MEDICO
donkey	BURRO
drama	AUTO
drunk	BORACHIO
fan	AFICIONADO
fascist	FALANGE.PHALANGE
father	PADRE
favoured	GRACIOSO
festival	FIESTA
few words	POCAS PALABRAS
fleet	ARMADA.FLOTA
fly	BLISTER BEETLE.CANTHARID
folk dance	SARDANA
fortress	ALCAZAR
gentleman	CABALLERO.DON
	HIDALGO
girl	NINA
glazed tile	AZULEJO
good	
—afternoon	BUENAS TARDES
—day/morning	BUENOS DIAS
—night	BUENAS NOCHES
goodbye	ADIOS
gorge	CAN(Y)ON
governor	ADELANTADO
	ALCA(I)DE.ALCAYDE
governess	DUENNA
grandee	ADELANTADO
grass	ESPARTO
gypsy	
—man	ZINCALO
—song	FLAMENCO
—woman	ZINCALA
gypsies	ZINCALI
hamlet	ALDEA
head	
—covering	MANTILLA
—of state	CAUDILLO
headman	CAPITANO
hero	(EL) CID
highness	ALTEZA

highway	CAMINO REAL	nap	SIESTA
highwayman	BANDOLERO	narrow canyon	CANADA
holiday	FIESTA	narrows	ANGOSTURA
horseman's cap	MONTERO	noble	DON.GRANDEE
hotel	POSADA	notary	ESCRIBANO
hunter	MONTERO	nothing	NADA
I kiss your		on	
hands	BESO LAS MANOS	—horseback	EN CABALLO
icing	ALCORZA	—the contrary	AL CONTRARIO
in tight dress	EN CUERPO	open area in town	PLAZA
inn	POSADA	operetta	ZARZUELA
insectivore	DESMAN	orange	NARANJA
instrument	TENORA	otter	NUTRIA
	ZAMBOMBA	palace	ALHAMBRA.ALCAZAR
intriguers	CARARILLA	parliament	CORTES
interjection	CARAMBA	penal settlement	PRESIDIO
jar	OLLA	police	RURALES
Jews	SEPHARDIM	—officer	ALGUACIL.ALGUAZIL
judge	ALCALDE	pot	OLLA
kidney bean	FRIJOL(E)	priest	CURA.PADRE
knife	CUCHILLO	prince	INFANTE
lady	DON(Y)A.HIDALGA	princess	INFANTA
lake	LAGO	proclamation	PRONUNCIAMENTO
language	BASQUE.CATALAN	province	ANDALUSIA
	CASTILIAN.LADINO	public	
large cigar	PERFECTO	—square	PLAZA
leader	CID.S	—walk	ALAMEDA
liquor	AGUARDIENTE	punishment of	
little	POCO	heretics	AUTO DA FE
madam	DONA.SENORA	race	BASQUE
man	HOMBRE.SENOR	ravine	ARROYO
manifesto	PRONUNCIAMENTO	refusal	NON
mantle	MANTILLA	reward	ALBRICIAS
matador	ESPADA	river	RIO.TAGUS
measure		robber	LADRON
—yard	METRO	rotten	PRODRIDA
—4.2 miles	LEAGUE	royal road	CAMINO REAL
—2¼ pints	LITRO	saddlebag	ALFORGA
military post	PRESIDIO	saint's day	FIESTA
miracle worker	SALUTER	sandal	ALPARGATA
miss	SENORITA	see you	
mister	DON.SENOR.SR	—later	HASTA LUEGO
mixed stew	OLLA-PODRIDA	—tomorrow	HASTA MANANA
Moslem lawyer	ALFAQUI	serenade	RONDENA
mounted bullfighter	PICADOR	shawl	MANTILLA.MANTO
muleteer	ARRIERO	sheep	MERINO
municipal council		—skin coat	ZAMARRA.ZAMARRO
	AYUNTAMIENTO	sherry	AMONTILLADO.JEREZ
naked	EN CUEROS	shrub	CNEORUM.WIDOW-WAIL

sir	DON.SENOR.SR	
sleep	SIESTA	
small		
—fumarole	HORNITO	
—room	CAMARILLA	
smoked pilchard	FUMADO	
soldier	SOLDADO	
song	CANCION	
standard bearer	ALFEREZ	
stew	OLLA-PODRIDA	
strangulation	GAR(R)OTTE	
street	CALLE.PASEO	
sun-dried brick	ADOBE	
sweetmeat	ALCORZA	
sword	BILBO.ESPADA.ESTOQUE	
—blade	TOLEDO	
tableland	MESA	
talk	PALABRA	
tavern	FONDO	
tomorrow	MANAN(Y)A	
treaty	AS(S)IENTO	
trooper	GINETE	
turkey buzzard	GALLINAZO	
until we meet		
again	HASTA LA VISTA	
urn	OLLA	
vaudeville	ZARZUELA	
vegetable soup	GAZPACHO	
vehicle	VOLANTE	
village	ALDEA	
waiter	MOZO	
walk	PASEO	
war	GUERRA	
—to the knife		
	GUERRA AL CUCHILLO	
watchtower	ATALAYA	
water cooler	ALCARRAZA	
weight		
—gram	GRAMO	
—25 lbs	ARROBA	
who knows?	QUIEN SABE	
wild marjoram	OREGANO	
window	VENTANA	
wine	VINO	
	(see also drink²)	
—shop	BODEGA	
—skin	BORACHIO	
woman	MUJER.SENORA	
word	PALABRA	

spare

spare *part*	SPAR.ARE
spare *parts*	PARES.PEARS
	RAPES.REAPS.SPEAR
sparkling girl	BERYL.RUBY
spattering drops	PRODS
speak¹	
speaker	MOUTH
speakers	LIPS
speak²	
French-speaking waiter	GARCON
German-speaking wife	FRAU
Italian-speaking girl	RAGAZZO
right *in speech*	RITE
so to speak, red	READ
Spanish-speaking	
teacher	MAESTRO
speaking to the...	TOOTHY
spoken aloud	ALLOWED
spoken rites	RIGHTS
spoken word which is...	WITCHES
special	
Special Air Service	SAS
Special Constable	SC
special drawing right(s)	SDR
special order	SO
special care	ACER.ACRE.RACE
special sort of plane	PANEL
specially shaped canoe	OCEAN
species	SP(P)
specify	
specific demand	EXACT
specific gravity	SG
specifically	AS.S
specification of stone	NOTES
	ONSET.SETON
	TONES
specifies whiter...	WRITHE
specifying older...	DROLE
spectacle	
spectacle case	FRAME
spectacles	OO
spectacular	incl OO
speculator	BEAR.STAG
speech	(see rhetoric.speak)
speed	MPH.RATE
speed of delivery	BIRTHRATE
speed of light	C
speeded *up*(D) ↑	NAR

spell

spell cast...	ACTS.SCAT
spell of cool...	LOCO
spelling	SP
spelling danger	RANGED

Spenser

words found in the works of:

abandon	ABAND
abash	QUELL
abate	APPAL.QUELL.RELENT
abiding place	GRANGE
able	HABLE
abounding	RANK
absolve	QUIGHT.QUYTE
accomplish	COMPLISH
accusation	CRIME
accuse	APPEAL
acquit	QUIGHT.QUYTE
act	
—amiss	MISDONNE
—of seizing	PREY
active	WIMBLE
adjudge	BEHIGHT.BEHOTE
adjudicator	DAYES-MAN
adjust	CONCENT
admiration	ADMIRA(U)NCE
adorn	ADORE.ATTRAP.DITE
advance	AVAUNT
—in hostility	SWAY
advancing	VAUNCING
advantage	VAUNTAGE
advise	AVISE.AVIZE.AVYSE
	REED(E)
affect	ASSAY
—disagreeably	UNSEASON
affectedly formal	QUAINT
afflict	ASSAY
affliction	TINE.TYNE
afraid	ADRAD.ADRED
aged	SHOT
ago	YGO(E)
agreed upon	COMPACT
aim	UPSHOT
air	DEMAINE.DEMAYNE
	DEMEANE
akin	SYBBE
alembic	LIMBEC(K)
alike	YLIKE
allegiance	FOY

alleviate	AL(L)EGGE
alleviation	AL(L)EGGAUNCE
allot	TEENE
allow	BETEEM(E)
almost	UNE(A)TH.UNEATHES
	UNNETHES
altogether	ALGATE
amaze	AWHAPE
ambush	AWAIT
amerced	AMERST
amice	AMIS
amount	MOUNTENA(U)NCE
anew	OF NEW
anger	TINE.TYNE
animated	EMPASSIONED
annoy	NOY
annoyance	NOYANCE
antagonist	PEER
anvil	ANDVILE
appeal	PEAL
appearance	HEW
appease	DEFRAY
approach	CO(A)ST.COST(E)
	SUCCEED
—death	FIT
arbour	HERBAR
arm	EMBATTLE
arrange	ENRAUNGE
arranged	COMPACT
array	ATTRAP.PLIGHT
arrear	AREAR.ARERE
arrogance	SURQUEDRY
arrowhead	FORKHEAD
art	FEAT
artifice	GIN
as	
—conveying an idea	PURPORT
—soon	ALSOON(E)
assail	ASSAY
assault	ASSAY.STOUND.STOWND
assay	SAY
assayer	SAY-MASTER
assembled	ACCOYLD
assembly	ASSEMBLA(U)NCE
assuredly	PARDIE.PARDY.PERDIE
	PERDY
astound	STOUND
astray	ABORD
astronomy	STAR-READ

Astrophel	PENTHIA.STARLIGHT
at a distance	WIDE
athletic contest	PRISE
atone	ATTONE
attack	BODRAG.BORDRAGING
attain	SEISE
attempted	FOND
attendance at court	COURTING
attention	ATTENT
attentive reflection	INTENDIMENT
augury	SOOTHE
avenger	VENGER
avowal	AVOURE
await	REMAIN
award	ADDOOM.ADWARD
away	AWAYES
axis	HENGE
back	CHINE
—up	ABET
bait	BAYT
balance	LAUNCE.PEASE.PEAZE
	PEISE.PEIZE.PEYSE.POUND
ban	BAND
banderol	BANNERALL
bandy	CHAFFER
banish	BAND.FOR(E)SAY
bar	SPARRE.SPERRE
barren	BLUNT
basket	FLASKET
bate	BAYT
bathe	BAY(E).EMBAY
battle	BATTIL
be	
—a guest	HOST
—abashed	BASH
—active	STIRE.STYRE
—at discord	DISACCORD
—filled	REDOUND
—flooded	FLOAT
—it however	HOWBE
—necessary	MISTER
—on guard	WAITE
—on adjacent side	SIDE
—out of bed	STIRE.STYRE
—painful	TINE.TYNE
—sorry for	FORTHINK
—spoken of	HEAR
—stopped by	STAY
beak	BECKE

bear	BIER
bearing	AMENAUNCE.DEMAINE
	DEMAYNE.DEMEANE
	DEMAINE.DEMAYNE
	DEMEANE.PORTANCE
—towards another	DEMEASNURE
beautiful and virtuous	
woman	BELLIBONE
because	BY MEANS
become faint	APPAL
becoming	BESITTING
bed	BID
bedyed	BEDIDE
befit	BEFALL
beforehand	PARAVA(U)NT
begin to move	STIRE.STYRE
begot	KYNDED
beguile	GUILE
behaviour	COMPORTANCE
	DEMEASNURE.HAVEOUR
	HAVIOUR
beheaded	TRUNKED
behest	HEAST(E)
belabour	LAY ON LOAD
believe mistakenly	MISTAKE
bellow in return	REBELLOW
beloved	BEL(L)AMOURE
bend	BOUGHT
benefit	VANTAGE
bent	CORBE
beseech	BESEEKE
beset	EMPEACH
—by	BESTAD(D)E
besides	FOREBY
besiege	ASIEGE
besprinkle	SHED
betroth	SPOUSE
between times	ATWEEN
bid	BED
bight	BOUGHT
bind	EMBRACE
bistort	POLYGONY
bit	WHAT
bite	REMORSE
bitten	GRYPT
bittern	BITT(O)UR
bitterness	FELL
black hellebore	MELAMPODE
blameless	UNREPROVED

685

blast	SCATH	bruise	INTUSE
blatant	BLATTANT	—with walking	SURBATE
blemish	BLEMISHMENT	bruised	
blockhead	MOME	—severely	TO-BRUSD
blood		—with walking	SURBATED
—relation	SYBBE		SURBET
—relationship	KINDRED	bubble	ROWNDELL
blossom	BLOOSME	budget	BOUGET
blow	PEASE.PEAZE.PEISE	bull's eye	MARK-WHITE
	PEIZE.PEYSE	burden	BEARE
blue	BLEW	burdensome	CHARGEFUL
boast	CRAKE	burn with rage	EMBOIL
body	SOYLE	burning	SEARE
boiling pot	STEW	—within	INBURNING
bolt	SPERRE	burst	BRUST.DISTRAIN
border	BOARD.FRONTIER	bush	TODDE
borrowed	STRAUNGE	busy with trade	TRADEFUL
bought provisions	ACHETES	by	FOREBY
bound up	UPBOUND(EN)	call	CLAME.ENQUERE
boundaries	OUTBOUNDS		ENQUIRE.INQUERE
boundary water	SHARD.SHERD		INQUIRE
brace	EMBRACE	called	HOTE.NEMPT
braid	EMBRAID	camlet	CHAMELOT
brandish	BLESS.HURTLE	canal superintendent	ZANJERO
breaded	BREDE	canon	SQUIER.SQUIRE
break	CESURE	canto	CANTICLE
—mail from	DISMAYL	cap	CALL
bright	SHERE	captain	CAPITAYN
bring		captive	CAITIVE
—back	RELATE.REVERSE	captivity	CAPTIVA(U)NCE
—back to better state	RECURE	career	CARIERE
—discredit on	BLAME	careful	HEEDY
—down	EMBACE	carpenter's square	SQUIER
—into being	REAR		SQUIRE
—on	INFER	carriage	PORTANCE
—reproach on	UPBRAY	carve	CARVEN.KERVE
—to an end	EXPIRE	case	STEAD
—to bear	SERVE	cast about	THROW ABOUT
—to mind	MIND	castaway	WEFT(E)
—together	COMPILE.UPKNIT	casually let go	SCATTERED
—up	NOUSELL.NOU(R)SLE	catch	CATCHEN.KETCH
	NUZZLE	caterwaul	WRAWL
—urgently	COMPEL	caught	KEIGHT
brittle	BRICKLE	caul	CALL
broken		cauldron	CAUDRON
—pottery	POTSHARE	cause	ENCHEASON.GARRE
—up	TO-BRUSD	—of grief	HEART-SORE
brother	SYBBE	—of wrongdoing	CRIME
brought down	EMBASTE	—to whirl or roll	REEL

cave	DELVE	coltsfoot	COLTSWOOD
cease	BLIN.CESSE.LIN	combatant	BATTEILANT
—to occupy	QUIGHT.QUYTE	come	
—to put forward	DISADVANCE	—forth alone	SINGLE
ceiled	SIELD	—to grief	MISWEND
ceiling	SEELING	comedown	AVALE.AVAIL(E)
certainly	SICCAR.SICKER	comer	COMMER
chafe	CHAUFE.CHAUFF	command	HEAST(E)
champion	DOUCEPERE	—a view of	SURVEW
	DOUZEPER	commit	ARRET(T)
chapiter	CHAPTER	companying	COMPANING
character of beast		comparison	PARAGON
	BEASTLY-HEAD	compassionate feeling	REMORSE
charge with great force		compel	GARRE
	SURCHARGE	competition	PARAGON
charged with	ENFOULDERED	complain	MEAN(E).MEIN.MENE
—passion	EMPASSIONED	completeness	COMPLEMENT
chariot	CHARET	compose	COMILE
chase	SCORSE	conceal	HEAL.HEEL.HELE
chastise	DISPLE.REFORM	concealing	COVERT
check	REVOKE	conceive	CONTRIVE
cheer	CHERRY	conclude	UPKNIT
chief wizard	ARCHIMAGO	condition	HOOD.STEAD
choice	TRYE	conference	EMPARLAUNCE
choicest	PRIMROSE	confound	AWHAPE
choke	ACCLOY	congratulate	GREET
circumstances	STEAD	conned	COND
cite	CONVENT	consent	AFFOORD
claim	CLAME	constant	SAD
clamour	OUTRAGE	consummateness	COMPLEMENT
clamourous	BLATTANT	contemptuous	DESPITEOUS
clear	CLEAN.NEAT	contradict	UNDERSAYE
—of blame	QUIGHT.QUYTE	contrivance	GIN
—off	QUIGHT.QUYTE	controversy	DEBATEMENT
clemency	CLEMENCE	convene	CONVENT
climb	STIE.STYE	conversation	BOARD
climbed	CLAMBE.SCAND	conversation	PURPOSE
clog	ACCLOY	converse	COMMON
close	STRAIT	convey	REPORT
—fight	GRAPLEMENT	corbel	CORBE
cloth covering	DRAPET	coronation	CARNATION
clothe	EMBOSS	could not	NOTE
—again	REVEST	counsel	AREAD.AREDE.ARREEDE
clown	PATCHC(H)OCKE		READ.REED(E)
coach	COCH	counterfeit	IDOL
coast	BOARD.COST(E)	counterplot	COUNTERCAST
coil	BOUGHT	courageous	STOMACHOUS
cold	FRENNE	course	FARE.TRACE
colour	HEW	cover	HEAL.HEEL.HELE

covered	COURD	decree	SAW
—over	OVERDIGHT	deemed	DEMPT
—with sweat	FORSWATT	defaced	DEFAST(E)
coward	COWHE(A)RD	defame	DEFACE
coward(ly)	HYLDING	defence	MUNIFIENCE
cowardice	COWARDREE	deformed	DISMAYD
coyness	NICETY	degenerate	DEGENDER
crew together	CONCREW	degrade	EMBACE
crimson	CREM(O)SIN	degraded	EMBASTE
crossbow bolt	QUAR'LE	deify	GOD
cry		delay	FOR(E)SLOW.FORSLOE
—like a cat	WRAWL	delight in	FAIN
—triumph over	OVERCRAW	dense	RANK
cuirass	CURAT.CURIET	depart	QUIGHT.QUYTE
cunning	PRACTIC	—from	QUIGHT.QUYTE
cur	KURRE	departure	DEPART.PARTURE
curdle	CRUDDLE	depression	DELVE
curdy	CRUDDY	deserving	CONDIGN
cure	RECURE	design	DESINE.DESYNE.SLEIGHT
curse upon	MA(U)LGRE	designate	INTEND
curtal axe	CURTAXE	desire	FAIN
custody	BAIL	—strongly	EARN
cut		desk	DESSE
—asunder	DISCIDE	despairing	DESPAIRFUL
—into	ENTRENCH.INTRENCH	despised	CONTEMPT
—into chines	CHYND	detention	DETAIN
—off	SHARE	determine	HIGHT
cutting	TRENCHAND	dethrone	DISTHRONIZE
daily	ADAYS	detriment	EMPEACH
dairy	DAYR-HOUSE	device	SLEIGHT
damage	EMPEACH.SCATH	devour	ENGORGE
danger	DOUBT	dew	DEAW
dare	DARRE	dewy	DEAWIE.DEWAY
dark, darken, darkly	DIRK(E)	dexterously	FEATEOUSLY
darling	DEARLING	dialect	LEDDEN
dastard	HYLDING	die	QUELL.STERVE
daunted	QUAYD	difficult to handle	UNWELDY
day of misfortune	DISMAL DAY	dig under	UNDERMINDE
daze	DARE	dilute	DELAY
dealt kindly with	MERCIFIDE	diminish	BAYT
dearth	DERTH	din	DEEN.STOUND.STOWND
death	FUNERAL	direct	AVENTRE.HIGHT
debase	EMBACE	disapprove	DISPROOVE
debased	EMBASTE	discern	SCERNE
deceit	MALENGINE	discharge	QUIGHT.QUYTE
deceiver	FALSER.TREACHETOUR	discipline	DISPLE
decline	WELKE	disclose	UNHEAL.UNHELE
decorate	EMBRAVE	disclosed	DISCLOST
decrease	DECREW	discomfit	YSHEND

discouraging attack	DISMAY
discourse	PURPOSE
discourteous	DISCOURTEISE
discover	DISCOURE.DISCURE
disdain	SDAINE.SDAYN
	SDEIGNE.SDEIN
dishearten	DISPARAGE
dishonourable	DISLEAL
disinherit	DISHERIT
disloyal	DISLEAL
dismal	GASTFULL
dispense	DISPENCE.SHED
dispersed	SPERST
displeasure	DISPLEASANCE
disposed	DISPOST.DITE
dispute	CONTROVERSE
dissemble	FEIGN
dissuade	DISCOUNSEL
distance	MOUNTENA(U)NCE
distract	FORHAILE
distracting	DIVERSE
distress	DISMAY
disturb	STIRE.STYRE
ditty	DIT
divide	DEPART.DISCIDE
do	DOEN.DONE.DONNE
—amiss	MIS
—battle	DARRAIGN(E).DARRAINE
	DARRAYN.DERRAIGN
—service	SUE
—wrongly	MISDONNE
doff	UNDIGHT
doing daring deeds	DER-DOING
domain	REAME
doom	DOME
doubtless	DREADLESS
drag	TRAYNE
draw	
—back	DISADVANCE
—over	OVERHA(I)LE
drawn	
—aside	DISTRAUGHT
—away	MISTRAYNED
dread(ed)	DRAD
dreariness	DRE(A)RE
	DRERYHOOD.DRERYMENT
dreary	GASTFULL
dress	AGUISE.AGUIZE.ATTRAP
drifter	DROVER
drive with thunderbolts	
	THUNDER-DRIVE
drove	DRIVE
drowned	DRENT.DROWNDED
drowsiness	DROWSIHE(A)D
drum	DROOME
due	DEWFULL
dye	HEW
earlier	RATHER
earn	ERNE
easily	EATH(E).EATHLY.ETHE
easy	EATH(E).ETHE
ebony	HEBON
efts	EWFTES
elegant	DAINT(Y).DAYNT
embrace	BRACE
embraced	HAULST
embraid	EMBREAD
emerald	EMERAUDE
emulate	AEMULE
emulation	PARAGON
encircle	STEMME
encircled	EMBAYLD
enclose	EMBOSS
—with border	EMPALE
encompass	BRACE
encounter	COUNTER
encourage	ACCO(U)RAGE
encouraged	UPCHEARD
encumber	ACCLOY
endeavour	ENDEAVOURMENT
endow	ENDEW
endue	ENDEW.INDEW
enduring	DUREFULL
enflame	ENFIRE
enfold	IMPLY
enlarge	ENLARGEN
enquire	ENQUERE
enrage	ENRANCKLE
enrolled	ENTROLD.INTROLD
enslave	BETHRALL
ensue	ENSEW
entangle	ENSNARL
entanglement	ENTRAIL
entertain	ACCOURT
—guest	HOST
entertainment	ENTERTAIN
entrails	ENTRALLES
entrance	INGATE

entrap	UNDERFONG	fall back	RECOYLE.RECU(I)LE
entreat	INTREAT	fallen unluckily	MISFALNE
entreating	ENTREATFULL	false	
entreaty	IMPLORE	—appearance	MISSEEMING
entrust	ARRET(T)	—religious belief	MISCREAUNCE
entwine	ENTRAIL	familiar friend	GOSSIB
enviable	ENVIOUS	familiarly	COMMONLY
enwrap	ENROL(L)	far	FAR-FORTH
equality	EQUAL	fasten	EMBRACE
equip	AGUISE.AGUIZE.DITE	—with a spar	SPERRE
equipment	PURVEYANCE	favour	GREE
erase	RACE	fear	AFFRAY
error	MESPRIZE	feign	FAIN(E).FAYNE
establish	STABLISH	fell	FELONOUS
esteem	PRISE.STEEM.WAY	female	
estranged	FRENNE	—animal	SHIDDER
everywhere	OVERALL	—dolphin	DOLPHINET
evil device	MALENGINE	—poet	POETRESSE
exalted	HAUGHT.HAU(L)T	festivity	JOYANCE
examine	APPOSE	feud	FOOD
excellently	GOODLY	fewter	ENCHASE
excess	OUTRAGE	fiat	FIAUNT
exchange	CHAFFER.SCORSE	fickle	CHOICEFUL
excite	EMMOVE.ENMOVE	fierce	BREEM.BREME.STOUT
excuse	ESSOIN.ESSOYNE	figure	AUMAIL
exile	EXUL	find	INVENT
exit	OUTGATE	fine	QUAINT
expectation	TENDANCE	first	PARAVA(U)NT
expensive	CHARGEFUL	—fruits	PRIMITIAS
experience	ENTERTAIN.EXPERT	—year's revenue	PRIMITIAS
explain	UPKNIT	fish basket	HASK
expound	COMMENT.REED(E)	fishing boat	DROVER
extended	DISTENT	fit	CONCENT.DEWFULL
extension in time	PROTENSE		DUEFUL.QUEME
exterminate	EXTIRP	—for war	WARHABLE
extolled	EXTOLD	fling	RUINATE
extort	OUTWREST.RACK	flitted	FLITT
extraction	EXTREAT	flock of birds	FLUSH
fabulous		flow	FLEET.RAILE.RAYLE
—beast	ANTELOPE	foam	FRY
—bird	WHISTLER	foes	FOEN.FONE
—fish	SCOLOPENDRA	foil	FOYLE
faced	FAST	foin	FOYNE
fail	MIS	fold	PLIGHT
failure to value	MESPRISE	food	PASTURE
	MESPRIZE.MISPRIZE	foolhardiness	FOOLHARDISE
faint	STANCK.SWELT	footing	TROAD(E).TRODE
fainting fit	SOWND.SWOUND	for	
falcon	TASSELL-GENT	—a long time	LONG SIN

—that	FORTHY
—the most part	MOSTWHAT
foray	FORRAY
force	
—away	WREST
—back	RECOYLE.RECU(I)LE
forced again	RENFORST
foreign	FRENNE.STRAUNGE
forester	FOSTER
forgery	COUNTERFEASAUNCE
form	
—anew	REALLIE
—into roll	ENROL(L)
forsaken	FORLORE
fortalice (fortress)	FORTILAGE
fortification	MUNIFIENCE
foster	NOUSELL.NOU(R)SLE
	NUZZLE
foul person	DREVILL
found	FOND
fountain basin	LAVER
free	QUIGHT.QUYTE
freedom	RANDON
frigate	FRIGOT
frighten	AFEAR.AFFEAR(E).DARE
frightful	GRIESLY.GRISELY
	GRYESLY
frisk	COLT
frosty	FRORY
frozen	FRORY
fulfil a term	EXPIRE
full of	
—air or fragrance	BREATHFUL
—devices	DEVICEFUL
—life	LIFULL.LYFULL
—moans	GRONEFUL
full speed	RANDON
fulminate	FULMINE
funeral service	HERSE
furious	YOND
—onset	AFFRET
furnish with buildings	EDIFY
furnishing	FURNIMENT
	PURVEYANCE
fury	DREAD
futility	VAINESSE
gaiety	JOYANCE
gain	EXCHEAT
—anew	REPRIZE

gained	WAN
gall	FELL
gape	GERNE
garb	VESTIMENT
garment	VESTIMENT
gate	YATE
gear	GEARE.GERE
Genoese coin	JANE
gentle	GENT
get	COMPARE
—back	RECURE
—out of	OUTWIN
—the better of	CONVINCE
ghastly	GREISLY.GRIESLY
	GRISELY.GRYESLY
gibbet	CROOK
gilded	GILDEN.GUILT.GYLDEN
—leather	CHECKLATON
gillyflower	GELLIFLOWRE
gilt	GELT.GUILT
girl	GERLE
give	
—excuses for	CAUSEN
—out as if on hire	OUTHYRE
—over	LIN.OVERGIVE
—up	FORGIVE.OVERGIVE
—vent to	DISCLOSE
—way	RELENT
given	YEVEN
giving attention	ATTENT
glad	GLADFUL
gladly	FAIN
glanced	YGLAUNST
glided	GLODE
glittering	GLITTERAND
gloom	DRE(A)RE
glory	GARLAND
go	GOE.YEAD.YEDE.YEED
—about or forth	STIRE.STYRE
—astray	MISWEND
—back	RECOURSE
—over in one's mind	RECORD
—up	AMOUNT
goat	GATE
gold	GOOLD
gondola	GONDELAY
gone	GOE.YGO(E)
good	
—and pretty maid	BON(N)IBELL

—day	GOD DAY	hacking	HEW
—for the heart	HARTIE-HALE	haggling	CHAFFER
—for-nothing	LORRELL.LOZEL	hailed	SALUED.SALVE'D
—friend	BELAMY	hair	HEARE
—health or fortune	WELL	hairy	HEARIE
—reception	BEL-ACCOYLE	hale	HAYLE
goodness	GOODLIHEAD	half	HALFEN(DEALE)
	GOODLYHEAD	halloo	BLEW
goodwill	GREE	hammer	MARTEL
gore	ENGORE	handle	STEAL(E).STEEL
got at	ARRAUGHT		STEIL.STELE
government	GOVERNALL	hang in bunches	SHAG
graced	GRASTE	happen	
graciously	GOODLY	—ill	MISHAPPEN
grant	BETEEM(E)	—to	BEHAPPEN
granted previously	FOR(E)LENT	hard-pressed	STRAIT
grapple	CRAPPLE.GRAPLE	harden	ENDURE
grasp	ENGRASP.HEND	harnessed in a team	TE(E)MED
grasping	GRIPLE	harsh	RIGOROUS
gravel	GRAILE.GRAYLE	hastened	HIDE
great knight	DOUCEPERE	haughty	HAUGHT.HAU(L)T
	DOUZEPER		STOMACHOUS
greedy	GRIPLE	have (plural)	HAN
greeted	SALUED.SALVE'D	—need	MISTER
grey	BLONCKET	—wrong opinion	MISWEEN
	GRIESIE,GRYSESY	having	
grief	TINE.TYNE.WAYMENT	—many layers	MANY-FOLDED
grieve	ENGRIEVE.WAYMENT	—power	VERTUOUS
grievous	CAREFUL.DEAR(E)	hazard	HAZARDIZE
	NOYOUS	heal	G(U)ARIS.RECURE
grin	GERNE.GIRN.GREN	healthy	HARTIE-HALE
grinned	GRIND	heap up	COMPILE.UPHOORD
griped	GRYPT	heaped	HEPT
griping	GRIPLE	heard	HARD
gripped	GRYPT	hearse	HERSE
grisly	GREISLY.GRIESLY	heart(en)	HART(EN)
ground tackle	GROUND-HOLD	heartily	HARTELY
growl	ROYNE	heartless	HARTLESSE
grudge	GRUTCH	heat	BEATH
guard	SAVEGARD	heaved	HEFT(E)
guess	DEVISE.GESSE	heed	RESPECT
	GHESSE	heedful	HEEDY
guild(hall)	GYELD	height	LOFT
guile	GUYLE	held	HILD
guise	GUYSE.PURPORT	hell	TARTAR(E).TARTARIE
gullet	WEASAND-PIPE		TARTARY
gush	RAILE.RAYLE	herd	HEARD
gypsy	GIPSEN	hest	HEAST(E)
habitation	HABITAUNCE	hide	HEAL.HEEL.HELE

hie	HYE
high	HAUGHTY.HYE
hind	HYNDE
hinder	EMPEACH
hindrance	IMPEACH
hither(ward)	HETHER(WARD)
hoar	HORE
hoard	UPHOORD
hold	
—down	SUPPRESS
—together	COMPRISE
hole	DELL.DELVE
hollow	DELVE
holly	HOLM
home	HAEME
honeysuckle	CAPRIFOIL
hood	CAPUCCIO
hooped in	EMBAYLD
hot	WHOT
hover	HO(O)VE
however	HOWBE
hue	HEW
humble	AFFLICTED.DEMISS
humbleness	HUMBLESSE
hurt	NOY.SCATH
hush	WHIST
husk	PILL
hyacinth (stone)	HYACINE
idea	CONCEIT
ignoble	UNNOBLE
ignorant person	IGNARO
ill	
—arranged	MISDIGHT
—gotten	MISGOTTEN
—shaped	MISHAPT
—tempered	GIRNIE
—treat	DEMEAN
—will	MALTATENT
illumine	ENLUMINE
imagined character	PERSONAGE
imbrue	EMBREWE
imbue	EMBAY
imp	YMP
impair	EMPA(I)RE.EMPAYRE
	EMPERISH
impairment	EMPEACH
impeach	EMPEACH
imped	YMPT
impede	EMPEACH

implant	ENRACE
improper feeding	MISDIET
in	
—a row	AREW
—averse direction	FROWARD
—complete confusion	
	UPSIDEOWNE
—front	PARAVA(U)NT
—some degree	SOMEDELE
—sorry plight	MISDIGHT
—time	TIMELY
inadvertent	UNADVISED
inasmuch	IN SORT
inattention	MISREGARD
incisive	TRENCHAND
increase	ACCREW
incursion	RODE
indecorous	SEEM(E)LESS(E)
indeed	SOOTHLICH
Ind(ia)	YND
indicate	DESIGN
indue	INDEW
ineffectual	RESTY
infamy	DEFAME
inflamed	FLAMED
inform	ENFORM.PARTAKE
infusion	INFUSE
inglorious	IRRENOWNED
ingots	INGO(W)ES
ingress	INGATE
inhabitant	INHOLDER
inhabiting woods	WOODY
inhospitable	HOSTLESSE
injure	SCATH
injured by cold	WINTER-BEATEN
injurious	NOYOUS
injury	BLAME.EMPEACH.SCATH
	TINE.TYNE.TORT
—to oneself	SELFE-DESPIGHT
inner	ENTIRE
innermost thoughts	PRIVITY
innocent	SEELY
inoperative	RESTY
inquire	ENQUERE.INQUERE
inscribe	ENDOSS
instruction	DOCUMENT
instrument of torture	GIN
insult	REPRIEFE
integument	PILL

intend	HIGHT	know	CON(NE).KON.WEET(E)
intention	ATTENDEMENT		WEETEN.WOT
intercourse	ENTERDEALE	knowest	KYDST
interest in property	STATE	ladder	STIE.STYE
interlace	ENTRAIL	laid before	FORELAY
interpretation	READ	lair	LARE
interruption	CESURE	lame	ACCLOY
intimately	COMMONLY	lament	MEAN(E).MEIN.MENE
intrigue against	UNDERMINDE		WAYMENT
inward	ENTIRE	lamentation	WAYMENT
Irish chieftaincy	CHEVERYE	lance	LAUNCE
irresistible	INSUPPORTABLE	lancing	LA(U)NCH
irrigating canal	ZANJA	language	LEDDEN
is not	NIS.NYS	lasting	DUREFUL
ivy bush	TODDE	latch	CLINK
jasper	JASP	launch	OUTLAUNCE
jaw	CHAW	lawless	RULESSE
jealous	GEALOUS	lay	
jealousy	GEALOUSY.GELOSY	—in a cradle	ENCRADLE
jeer	GEARE	—on	POUND
jellied	GELLY	lazy	LAESIE
journey	WAY.WENT	leak	LEKE
joust	GIOUST	lean	LEANY
joyousness	JOYANCE	leaped (leapt)	LEPPED.LOPE
	JOVYSAUNCE.JOUISANCE	learn	CON(NE).KON
	JOUYSAUNCE		LEAR(E).LEIR.LERE
judge wrongly	MISWEEN	lease	FARM
judged wrongly	MISDEMPT	leave off	QUIGHT.QUYTE
junket	JUNCATE	lecher	LEACHOUR
jurisdiction	BAIL	leech	LEACH
keen	BREEM.BREME	left	LORE.LORN.OTHER
keep		leg armour	GAIMBEUX
—head to wind	TRIE	leisure	LEASURE
—in subjection	UNDERKEEP	lest	LEAST
—watch	WAITE	—by chance	ENAUNTER
keeping time	TIMELY	let	
keyhole	CLINK	—go	QUIGHT.QUYTE
kick	RECOYLE.RECU(ILE)	—out for pay	WAGE
killed	KILD.KILT	letter of introduction	BENEFICIAL
kind	KYND(E)	levy	LEAVE
—look	BELGARD	liar	FALSER
kindled	TIND.TYND(E)	lie	LIG(GE).LIGGEN
kindly	GOODLY	—down	SEAT
kine	KYNE	—in folds	W(H)IMPLE
kingdom	REAME	—out of the way	BA(U)LK
kinship	SYBBE	—to	TRIE
kite	KIGHT	lift up	EXTOL
knew	KOND	light	LITE
knob	SNUBBE	like	LICH

—a centaur	HALF-HORSY	—busy	EMBUSY
—lightning	ENFOULDERED	—divine	DIVINE
likeness	LIKELINESS	—feeble	FEEBLE
limb	SPALLE	—fierce	EFFIERCE.ENFELON
limiter	LYMETER		ENFIERCE
lineage	LIGNAGE.LYNAGE	—footsore	SURBATE
linen	LYNE	—fortunate	FORTUNIZE
linger	HO(O)VE	—happy	FORTUNIZE
list(en)	LEST	—known	READ
listless	LUSTLESS	—known by ostentatious	
lithe	LYTHE	display	VAUNT
little bush	BUSKET	—little or less	MINISH
livelihood	LIVELO(O)D	—pregnant	ENWOMB
living thing	QUICK	—showy	EMBRAVE
load	TODDE	—thick	ENGROSS
loam	LOME	—uneasy	DISEASE
loathsome	LOTH(E)FULL	mannered	THEWED
lodestone	MAGNESSTONE	many-coloured	DISCOLOURED
lodge	BOWER.HOST	marked	DISTINCT
lodging	BRAME.FERM.HOSTRY	—with spots	EYE-SPOTTED
loiter	HO(O)VE	marred	MARD
loll (the tongue)	LILL	massive	TIMBERED
long	LENG.SIDELONG	master	MAISTERDOME.MAYSTER
—for	EARN	mastering	MAISTRING
longer	LENGER	match	AMATE.PRISE
longest	LENGEST	mate	PARAGON
look over	SURVEW	may	MOT(E)
loop	LOUP	meadowsweet	MEDAEWORT
loose	LOAST.LOSE(N)	mean person	HYLDING
—hair	UNDIGHT	meaning	INTENDIMENT
—robe	CAMIS.CAMUS	meantime	MEAN
—woman	FRANION	meet	ENTERTAIN
lose	LEESE	meeting place	GYELD
lost	LOAST.LOS'TE	melted	YMOLT
lout	LOORD	mention	HIGHT
lovingly	LOVELY	mercenary soldier	WAR-MONGER
lower	AVALE.AVAIL(E)	merciful	MERCIABLE
	EMBACE	mere	MEARE
lowered	EMBASTE	merriment	JOLLIMENT
lumpish	LOMPISH	merrymaking	MERIMAKE
mad	YOND	meted	MOTT
made		mews	MEAWES
—feet tired	SURBATED.SURBET	middle(most)	IDDEST
—of yew	EUGHEN.EWGHEN	might	MOUGHT
madman	GELT	military expedition	HOSTING
mail	MALE	misbecome	MISSEEM
make		misbegotten	MISGOTTEN
—a show of	COUNTENANCE	miscarry	MISWEND
—amends	DISPENSE	misconception	MISCONCEIT

misfortune	MISFARE
mishap	DISAVENTURE
	DRE(A)RE
misled	MISTRAYNED
mislike	MISLEEKE
mismade	DISMAYD
mismanagement	
	MISGOVERNAUNCE
misshaped	MISSHAPT
misshapen	DISMAYD.MISSHAPT
misused	MISUST
moan	MEAN(E).MEIN.MENE
moderate	RELENT
moiety	MOYITY
moil	MOYLE
momentum	POISE
monster	ROSMARINE
	SEASATYRE.ZIFFIUS
month	MONETH
mostly	MOSTWHAT
mount	STIE.STYE
movable front of	
helmet	VENTAILE.VENTAYLE
move	EMMOVE.ENMOVE.MIEVE
	QUICH.QUINCHE
—around or to	
activity	STIRE.STYRE
much	MOCHELL.MUCHELL
—worn	FORWORN
muscle	BOWR
must	MOT(E)
muster	HOSTING
musty	FROUGHY.FROWIE
	FROWY
mutter	ROYNE
mutual dealings	ENTERDEALE
name	BEHIGHT.BEHOTE.READ
named	HOT(E).NEMPT
narrow	STRAIT
narwhal	MONOCEROS
nathless	NETHELESS
near	FOREBY
nearer	NARRE
neatly	FEATEOUSLY
needy	STRAIT
negotiations	ENTERDEALE
never the more	NATHEMO(RE)
new thing	NEWELL
nimble	WIMBLE

nobility	NOBILESSE
noble	DOUCEPERE.DOUZEPER
	GENT
—youth	INFANT
noise	NOYES
not	
—akin	FRENNE
—braced	UNBRASTE
—challenged	UNDEFIDE
—civilised	UNCIVIL
—defied	UNDEFIDE
—dressed	UNDIGHT
—favouring	FAVOURLESS
—known	UNWIST
—lamented	UNPLAINED
—marred	UNMARD
—matching	MATCHLESS
—prayed for	UNBID
—provided with	UNPURVAIDE
—right in the head	ILL-HEDDED
—the more	NATHEMO(RE)
—to be placated	IMPACABLE
notwithstanding	HOWBE
object	
—aimed at	LEVEL
—gazed at	GAZEMENT
oblique	OBLIQUID
occasion	ENCHEASON
occupy	EMBUSY
—oneself with	ENTREAT
ochre	OAKER
of	
—a tree	TREEN
—straw	STRAWEN
—the same province	
	COMPROVINCIAL
—the time of day	TIMELY
offer up	APPEAL
omen	SOOTHSAY
one who proclaims	BLAZER
only	ONELY
onset	SALIAUNCE
open place	OVERTURE
orbit	SPHERE
ordain	BEHIGHT.BEHOTE
ore	OWRE
originate	REAR
ornament	GARLAND
ostrich	OSTRIGE

out of condition	RAW
outcry	STEVEN
outlet	OUTGATE
outward appearance	FORESIDE
	PURPORT
overcast	OVERKEST
overcome	CONVINCE
	UNDERFONG
—by wrestling	OVERWRESTLE
overflow	REDOUND
overlay	SPILL
overspread	OVERDIGHT
overtake	OVERHENT
overtaken	OVERCAUGHT
	OVERHENT
overtook	FORHENT
overworked	FORSWONCK
ownerless property	WAIFT.WEFT
ox	STEARE
painful experience	FIT
pains	TINE.TYNE
paint	DEPAINT
painted	IMPICTURED
paltry fellow	SQUIB
panacea	PANACHAEA
pang	STOUND.STOWND
	THROW(E)
pansy	PA(U)NCE.PAWNCE
parleying	EMPARLAUNCE
paroxysm	THROW(E)
partake	PERTAKE
pass	
—away	VADE
—like a fever	SWELT
passage	FARE
passion	BRAME
past	FOREBY
pasture	LARE
path	STIE.STYE.TROAD(E)
	TRODE.WENT
pattern	SLEIGHT
pay	QUIGHT.QUYTE.SOLD
—for	PRYSE
—the price of	PRICE
payment	HAN(D)SEL
peacock	PAVONE
peal	PELE
pease	POUSSE
pebble	PUMY(STONE)

peep	TOOT
—about	TOOT
peer	PEARE
pen	PENNE
penal retribution	VENGEMENT
penalty	HAN(D)SEL
penetrate	SEIZE
penny	PENI(E)
penthia	ASTROPHEL.STARLIGHT
perceive	UNDERTAKE
perch (of land)	LUG
performance	CHEVISANCE
perilous	PERLOUS
perish	QUELL.TINE.TYNE
perplex	DISTROUBLE
pestilence	MURRIN
phantom	PHANTOSME
pierce	EMP(I)ERCE.LA(U)NCH
	PEARCE.PERCE(N).PERSE
pierced	GRYPT.PEARST.PIERST
piercing	THRILLANT
pinion	PENNE
pinioned	PINNOED
pioneer work	PYONINGS
pitch	PRICK
pitched	PIGHT
pitied	MERCIFIDE
pity	REMORSE
placed	PLAST(E)
—above	OVERPLAST
plant (unspecified)	TETRA
playing games of	
chance	HAZARDRY
pleaded	PLED
please	QUEME
pleasure	LUST
pledge	BANK
plight	TAKING
pluck	RACE
plunder	BEROB.EXCHEAT
	HERRIMENT
	HERRYMENT.PREY
plundering	SPOYLEFULL
plunge	EMPLONGE.PLONG(E)
plunged	PLONGD
poetess	POETRESSE
poignant	POYNANT
point	PRICK
—out	PRESAGE

poise	PEASE.PEAZE.PEISE	proper	DEWFULL.DUEFUL
	PEIZE.PEYSE	prophesying	SOOTHE
poised	PAYSD	proportion	REASON
poisonous plant	SAMNITIS	prosper	THEE
policy	POLLICIE.POLLICY	protect	SAVEGARD
politeness	COMPLEMENT	protection	PATRONAGE
pollute	BLEND	prove	TRIE
pompous	STATE	provide	COMPARE
pool	PLESH	province	REAME
poplar	ASPINE	pry	TOOT
porpoise	PORCPISCE	puddle	PLESH
portion	WHAT	pull apart	DISTRAIN
portrait(ure)	RETRAITT	punching	POUNCING
	RETRATE	punish	YSHEND
portrayed	POURTRAHED	purified	TRYE
possessing virtue	VERTUOUS	purpose	DEVISE.PROPOUND
postpone	PROLONG	purse	CRUMENAL
pot	CREWE	purslane	PERSELINE
potsherd	POTSHARE	pursue	POURSEW.POURSUE
pour	POWRE		PURSEW
praise	HERRY.HERY(E)	pursuit	POURSUIT(T).SUIT
prance	PRAUNCE	put	
pre-eminently	PARAVA(U)NT	—at a distance	DISLOIGN
precarious	T(R)ICKLE	—down	UNDERLAY
precedent	PRESIDENT	—far apart	DISLOIGN
precepts	SCHOOLERY	—into action	SERVE
precisely	BY THE SQUIRE	—into operation	ENURE
predicted	FORESHEWED	—on	INVEST
preferred	PREFARD	—out as shoot or fruit	SPIRE
preparation	PURVEYANCE	—out of countenance	DEFACE
press	PEASE.PEAZE.PEISE.PEIZE	—to shame	YSHEND
	PEYSE.PREACE	—together	COMPILE
—down	SUPPRESS	putting to death	DEAD-DOING
pressure	STRAINT	quagmire	WAGMOIRE
pretended	COUNTERFECT	quaint	QUEINT
prey	PRAY.RAVEN	quaked	QUOOKE
	RAVIN(E).SOYLE	quality	ASSAY
price	PRISE	quarrel	QUAR'LE
prick	ACCLOY	quarrelsome	DEBATEFULL
private counsels	PRIVITY	quarter	QUART
prize	PRISE	quash	REPEAL
procedure of combat	DISCOURSE	quenched	QUEINT
proceed	YEAD.YEDE.YEED	question	APPOSE
proceeded	FOND.YOD(E)	quickly	B(Y)LIVE
profit	VANTAGE	quickness	NIMBLESSE
prognostication	PREJUDIZE	quince	QUEENE-APPLE
promise	BEHIGHT.BEHOTE	quit	QUIGHT.QUYTE
promptly	B(Y)LIVE	quite	QUIGHT
proof	ASSAY	race	RAUNCH

raced	RAST
raid	BODRAG.BORDRAGING
rail	SPARRE
raise	LEAVE
—in front	FORELIFT
rancid	FROUGHY
	FROWIE.FROWY
rang	RONG
range here and there	DISPACE
rapt	YRAPT
rapture	ENRAGEMENT
rare	GEASON.SE(E)LD
rashness	HAZARDRY
ravish	SUPPRESS
ray	RAYON
raze	RACE
reach	SEISE
read	RAD.RED(D)
ready	PREST
realm	REAME
reason	ENCHEASON
rebound	RECOYLE.RECU(I)LE
rebuild	RE-EDIFY
recapture	REPRIZE
receive	ENTERTAKE
recently weaned child or animal	WEANEL
reck	REKE.WREAK(E)
recognised character	PERSONAGE
recoil	REBUT.RECOYLE
	RECU(I)LE
reconcile	UPKNIT
reconciled	AFFRENDED
recover	RECOURE.RECOWER
	RECURE
rede	REED(E)
reduce	DEDUCT.MINISH
refund	REDISBURSE
refuse	NILL
—to agree	DISACCORD
refused	NILLED.NOULD(E)
regard as holy	HERRY.HERY(E)
region	QUART.REAME
regret	FORTHINK.RELENT
rehearsal	HERSALL
reign	RAIN(E)
—to the end of	OUTRAIGNE
reinforced	RENFORST
reinstate	RESEIZE

reinvigoration of sleep	REPAST
rejoined	RELIDE
relate	REED(E)
relax	RELENT
relaxed	UNBRASTE
release	
—from obligation	QUIGHT
	QUYTE
—on recompense by instalment	STAL'D
relied	RELIDE
remedy	RECURE
remembrance	SOVENA(U)NCE
remit	QUIGHT.QUYTE
remove	DISLOIGN
—wrongly	MISTAKE
removed	REMOUD
—from hearse	UNHERST
remuneration	SOLD
renewed efforts	RENFORST
renounce	FOR(E)SAY
rent	CUDDEEHIH
repay	QUIGHT.QUYTE
repeat from memory	RECORD
repent	RELENT
repentance	REPENT
reprehend	SPOT
represented beforehand	FORESHEWED
repress	REPEAL
reprieve	REPRIVE.REPRYVE
reproach	REPRIEFE.YSHEND
reproof	REPRIEFE
reprove	REPRIEVE
require	REQUERE
requite	QUIGHT.QUYTE
	REQUIGHT
requited	REQUIGHT.REQUIT
rescue	RESKEW
resentful	STOMACHOUS
resigned beforehand	FOR(E)LENT
resistless	IMPORTUNE
response	RESPONDENCE
rest one's weight	UPLEAN
restitution	RESTORE
restore to its position	REPAIR
restrain	ABSTAIN.BEHOLD
rethink	FORTHINK
retrace	REMEASURE

retreat	RECOYLE.RECU(I)LE
	RETRATE
return	RECOURSE.REVERSE
reveal	DESCRY.PRESAGE
reversed	RENVERST
revert	RECOYLE.RECU(I)LE
—in the mind	RECOURSE
revive	RELIVE
ribald	RIBAUD.RYBAULD
ribaldry	RYBAUDRYE
rid	QUIGHT.QUYTE
rife	RYFE
rightly	ARIGHTS
rigorous	STRAIT
rind	RINE
rise	HOVE.STIE.STYE
—one above another	REDOUND
riven	RIFTE
—fragment	RIFT
river	LEE
road	RODE
roar	ROYNE
rod (of land)	LUG
rode	RAD
role model	SAMPLE
roll about self-	
piteously	ENWALLOW
root out	OUTWEED
rounded	COMPAST
rouse	ABRAY.AMO(O)VE.STIRE
	STYRE
rove over	ENRAUNGE
ruby	RUBIN(E)
ruff	RUFFIN
ruffle	RUFF
rule	SQUIER.SQUIRE
ruleless	RULESSE
run	RENNE.RONNE
running	RONNING
runt	RONT(E)
rush	RANDON
rustic	HOBBINOLL
sacramental	HOUSLING
saddle	SEL(LE)
safeguard	SAUFGARD
sage	SAULGE
salience	SALIAUNCE
saluted	SALEWD.SALUED
sate	ACCLOY

satisfy	DEFRAY
savage	SALVAGE
save	SAFE
say	SAINE.SAYNE
—in answer	UNDERSAYE
sayest	SAIST
saying	READ
scale	SCAND
scaly sea monster	PHOCA
scamp	LORREL.LOZEL
scanned	SCAND
scarified	SCARIFIDE
scent	SENT
scheme	GIN
scimitar	CEMITARE
scion	SIENT
scorch	SCATH
scorn	MESPRISE.MESPRIZE
	MISPRIZE
screech owl	SHRIECH-OWL
	STRICH
screen	SCRIENE.SKREENE
scuffle	CUFFLE
scutcheon	SCUCHI(O)N
scythe	SITHE
sea	
—horse	HIPPODAME
—monster	ROSMARINE
	SEA-SATYRE.ZIFFIUS
secret meeting	COVERTURE
seemliness	SEEMLYHED
seize	HEND.SEASE.SEAZE.CEAZE
seized	ARRAUGHT.FORHENT
sell	CHAFFER
send downstream	POUR
sense	SENT
sentinel	CENTONEL(L)
set	PIGHT
—about by	BESTAD(D)E
—in battle display	DARRAI(G)N(E)
	DARRAYN.DERRAIGN
—in motion	STIRE.STYRE
—on fire	ENFIRE
—spear in rest	ENCHASE
	FEUTRE.FEWTER
—up	ADDRESSED.ADDREST
settle down	PEASE.PEAZE
	PEISE.PEIZE.PEYSE
shade	OVERCAST

shadow forth	SHADE	slacken (pace)	RELENT
shaft	STEAL(E).STEEL	slant	RASH
	STEIL.STELE	sleep	SWOON
shaken off	OFF-SHAKT	sleepiness	DROWSIHE(A)D
shallow pool	PLESH	slight	MESPRISE.MESPRIZE
shame	REPRIEFE.YSHEND		MISPRIZE
shank	STEAL(E).STEEL	slow down	RELENT
	STEIL.STELE	small boat	COTT
shaped	SHOPE	smeared in blood	BEGORED
share	CO-PORTION	smell	SENT
—out	EMPART	smite	SMIGHT
shared	SHARD	snag	SNUBBE
sheer	SHERE	snarl	GIRN.SNAR
shining	NEAT	snatch	RACE
—indistinctly	GLOOMING	snub	SNIB
shiver in pieces	DISSHIVER	solve	LOOSE
shock	STOUND.STOWND	something	WHAT
shoot like a pang or pain STOUND		—taught	SCHOOLERY
	STOWND	somewhat	SOMEDELE
shoulder	SPALLE	song	CANTION.CHARM
shout	CLAME	soot	SOUT
showed beforehand		soothe	ACCOY
	FORESHEWED	sorrow	REPENT
shower	POUND	sorrowful	CAREFUL
showing		souse	SOUCE.SOWS(S)E
—much white eye	WHALLY	soused	SOUCT
—through the skin	RAW	space of time	STEAD
shriek	SCRIKE.SHREEK	spared	SPARD
SHRIECH.SHRIGHT.SHRIKE		sparing in giving	STRAIT
shrine	SCRINE.SCRYNE	sparingly	NIGHLY
shrink from	RECOYLE.RECU(I)LE	spasm	THROW(E)
shrive	SHRIEVE	spawn	BLOT
shy	LOFT	speak to	BEHIGHT.BEHOTE
sic	SIKE	speech	LEDDEN
silence	WHIST	spire	SPYRE
similar	LIKELY	spirited	STOMACHOUS
simple	SEELY	spiritless	HYLDING
simplicity	SIMPLESSE	spite	SPIGHT
since	SENS.SITHENS.SITHENCE	spot (of iron-mould)	MOLD
sing in measure	MEASURE	spray of water	WATER-SPRINKLE
singe	SWINGE	spread	SPRAD
sister	SYBBE	—out below	SUBJECT
sit down	SEAT	sprite	SPRIGHT
skill	FEAT	spur	SPURNE
skilled	PRACTIC	spy	SPYAL
skirmish	SCARMOGE	squeeze	SCRUZE
skirt worn by knight	BASE	stagger back	RECOYLE.RECU(I)LE
skull	PANNIKELL	stain	STAYNE
sky blue	CAERULE	stair	STAYRE

stand	STANDEN.STOND
standing on end	UPSTART
start	
—back	RECOYLE.RECU(I)LE
—up	ASTART
startled bird	FLUSH
starvation	PINE.PYNE
starve	STERVE
stayed	STAID
stead	STED(D).STED(D)E
steadfast	SAD
steam	STEEM
steep	EMBAY
steer	STEAR(E).STIRE
steerage	STEARAGE
steered	STEARD
stir	STIRE.STYRE.QUICH
	QUINCHE
stone	PUMY(STONE)
—or earthenware vessel	STEANE
stop for	STAY
stoppage	BLIN
stoutly	STATE
straight	STREIGHT
strain	STRENE
strait	STREIGHT
strand	STROND
strange	FRENNE.SELCOUTH
	STRAUNGE
stray far	FORWANDER
strayed	
—animal	WAIFT.WEFT
—over	MISWANDRED
strengthening band	BEND
stretch forth	INTEND
—or in front	PRETEND
strict	STRAIT
strife	CONTECK
strifeful	STRYFULL
strike	AFFRAY
stripe	STAKE.STRAIK
strive	ENFORCE
stroke	STOUND.STOWND
—in return	COUNTERSTROKE
struck	
—by thunderbolt	YTHUNDERED
—with downward	
movement	OVERSTROOKE
stub	SNUBBE

stun	STOUN.STOUND
stunned	STOUND
—condition	STOUND
stupid	DOTED
stupidity	BRUTENESS
subdue	ADAW.SUBDEW
subject	CAITIVE
—to pangs	THROW(E)
submerge	EMPLONGE
subside	QUELL
successively	BY-AND-BY
such	SICH.SIKE
suddenly	UNWARELY
sue	SEW
suffer pangs	THROW(E)
suing	SEWING
suit	QUEME
sullen	SOLEIN
sum up	UPKNIT
summon	CONVENT
support	LIVELO(O)D
suppose	DEVISE
surely	SICCAR.SICKER.YKER
surge	REDOUND
surly	SYRLYE
surpass	UNDERLAY
survey	SURVEW
surview	SERUEWE.SERVEWE
suspected	MISDEMPT
swaddling band	SWEATH-BAND
sweated	SWAT
sweating illness	
	STOOPE-GALLAUNT
sweetly	SOOT(E)
sword	BRONDYRON.SWEARD
—belt	BAUDRICKE
swordfish	MONOCEROS
tabor player	TABRERE
take	
—away	REAR
—in	ENDEW.INDEW
—off	UNDIGHT
taken	TANE
tale	SCORE
talon	TALA(U)NT
tambourine	TAMBURIN
tame	AMENAGE
tar	TARRE
teamed	TE(E)MED

tear	
—away	RACE
—off	RACE
teen	TINE.TYNE
temper	DELAY
tender	FRAIL
terrace	TERRAS
terrify	AGRISE.AGRIZE
	AGRYZE
territory	RIGHT
that which humbles	
boldness	STOOPE-GALLAUNT
thatch	THETCH
theft	STEALTH
then	THO
therefore	FORTHY
thicket	GRE(A)VE
thirst	THRIST.THRUST
those	THO
thou art	THOUS
thought wrongly	MISDEMPT
thoughtful	CONCEITFUL
thread	RID
thrive	THEE
throat	WEASAND-PIPE
throe	THROW(E)
throw off	DISCUSS
thrust	AVENTURE
—into the bowels	EMBOWEL
thunder	FOULDER
ticklish	T(R)ICKLE
tied	TIDE.TIGHT.TYDE
tier of guns	TIRE
time	SITH(E).SYTHE.STOUND
	STOWND
—of trouble	STOUND.STOWND
tinged	TINCT
tingle	TICKLE
tint	HEW
tired animal	TYRELING JADE
titmouse	TITMOSE
to the smallest detail	TO POINT
together	SAM.YSAME
told	TELD
tomb	FUNERAL
took	WAN
top of head	NOULE
torch	TEAD(E)
torn	ENRIVEN

—to pieces	TO-RENT
toss	TOSSEN
tossed	YTOST
total number	SCORE
trace	TRACT
track	CHALLENGE.TRACT
	TRADE.TROAD(E).TRODE
trail	TRADE.TRAYNE
—of blood	PERSUE
train	TIRE
traitor	TREACHETOUR
transportable breviary	PORTAS
	PORTESS(E)
	PORT(E)OUS.PORTHORS
	PORTHOS.PORTHOUSE
transferred	TRANSFARD
transform	DISCLOSE
transmute	TRANSMEW
	TRANSMOVE
traverse	WEAR
treading	TRADE
treat	DEMEAN
—insultingly	INDIGNIFY
treatment	DEMAINE.DEMAYNE
	DEMEANE
tree	
—trunk	STUD
—used for carving	CARVER
trenching	PYONINGS
trick	COUNTERCAST
	COUNTERPOINT
tried	FOND.TRIDE
trod	TROAD(E).TRODE
Trojan	TROYAN
trouble greatly	DISTROUBLE
troublesome	BRICKLE
truce	TREAGUE
truly	SOOTHLICH
truncated	TRUNKED
try advantageous	
means	THROW ABOUT
turban	TURRIBANT
turn	
—aside	DIVERSE.REVERSE
—back	RETURN
—out	TRIE
twain	TWAY
twist	BOUGHT
twisting	ENTRAIL

703

twit	TWIGHT	untired	ENTIRE
ugly-faced	ILL-FASTE	untold	UNRED
umpire	DAYES-MAN	unusual	UNACQUAINTED
unaccustomed	UNWONT	unweave	UNREAVE
unbecoming	MISSEEMING	upbraid(ing)	UPBRAY
—a knight	KNIGHTLESS	upheld	UPHILD
uncommon	SE(E)LD	upper region	LOFT
uncontrolled state	RANDON	upriseth	UPRYST
uncounted	UNRED	upset	RENVERST
uncover	UNHEAL.UNHELE	upside down	UPSIDEOWNE
uncurdled	UNCRUDDED	urge earnestly	PROCURE
undergrowth	SPRING	urgent	IMPORTUNE
underlying	SUBJECT	utter in measure	MEASURE
understand	CONTRIVE	utterly	RANK
understanding	INTENDIMENT	vagrant	SCATTERLING
undertake	UNDERFONG	valuation	PRIZE
undertaken	UNDERTANE	vanity	VAINESSE
undo	UNDIGHT	variegate	AUMAIL
undoing	DEFEATURE	variegated	DISTINCT
undress	DISATTIRE	veil	VEALE.VELE
undue divergence from middle		velvet	VELLET
course	OUTRAGE	vengeance	VENGEMENT
unequal match	DISPARAGE	venturous	VENTROUS
unexpectedly	UNWARELY	verdict	VERDIT
unfledged	EYAS	vervain	VERVEN
unformed	INFORMED	vestment	VESTIMENT
unfriendly	FRENNE	vex	NOY
ungovernable	IMPOTENT	vexatious	NOYOUS
unguarded state	RANDON	view	ADVEW
unidentified plant	ASTROFELL	vile	VILD(E)
	ASTROPHEL	villeinage	VELLENAGE
unjustly held	WRONGFUL	violent	RIGOROUS
unknowing	UNWIST	violently	RANK
unlaced	UNLAST(E)	visor	UMBREL.UMBR(I)ERE
unlikly	UNLIKE		UMBRIL
unmanageable	UNWELDY	vitiate	BLEND
	WEELDLESSE	vulgar	BLATTANT
unobserved	UNSPIDE	wafted	WEFT
unpierceable	IMPERCEABLE	waif	WAIFT.WEFT(E)
unprepared	UNPURVAIDE	waist-belt	TAWDRY-LACE
unprovided	UNPURVAIDE	wait	WAITE
unread	UNRED	waived	WEFT(E)
unruliness	UNRULIMENT	walk about	SPACE
unruly	RULESSE	walleyed	WHALLY
unseemly	SEEM(E)LESS(E)	walrus	ROSMARINE
unshed	UNPARTED	wane	WELKE
unstable	UNSTAYED	want	PINE.PYNE
unsweet	UNSOOTE	wariness	WARIMENT
unthriftiness	UNTHRIFTYHE(A)D	warlike	BATALIOUS

warn	AWARN	—rules	RULESSE
was		woe	WAE
—called	HOT(E)	wooden cup	MAZER
—accustomed	DID WON	won	WAN.WOON
waste		wont	FAIN
—away	FORPINE	woo	WOW
—utterly	FORWASTE	worn out	TO-WORNE
watch	AWAIT	worse	WAR(RE)
watchful	AVIZEFULL	worthless	
waxed	WOX(EN)	—beast	HYLDING
way	TRACE	—fellow	JAVEL
—in	INGATE	—scamp	LORRELL.LOZEL
weak	BRICKLE	worthy	CONDIGN
weaken	DEDUCT.DELAY	wot not	NOTE
—gradually	UNDERMINDE	would not	NOULDE
weapon	SPARKE	wound	ENTRENCH.INTRENCH
weary out	FORWEARY	wrap	EMBOSS
weave	WIND	wreaked	(Y)WROKE.YWRAKE
weep	GREET	wreathe	WRETHE
weigh	WAY	wretch	MISER
weight of		wrinkled	WRIZLED
—blows	LOAD	wrong	TORT
—wool	TODDE	—doing	MISFARING
welfare	HAYLE	wrongful challenge	
well-knit	PIGHT		MISCHALLENGE
went	YOD(E)	yearn	EARN.ERNE
while	THROW	yet	HOWBE
whole(some)	HOLE(SOME)	yew	EUGH
wick	WEEKE	young	YOUTHLY
wicker	SALE	—female sheep	SHIDDER
wide as a basin	BASEN-WIDE	—gentleman	YOUNKER
wield	SOWND	—knight	YOUNKER
wifehood	WIVEHOOD	—male sheep	HIDDER
will	WULL	youth	SPRING.YOUNGTH
—not	NILL	youthful	YOUNGTHLY.YOUTHLY
windpipe	WEASAND-PIPE	**spice**	
wit	WEET(E).WEETEN.WOT	allspice	PIMENTO
with		Artemisia	TARRAGON
—attire unfastened	UNBRASTE	black berries	JUNIPER.PEPPER
—tension relaxed		cardamon	AMOMUM
(drum)	UNBRASTE	Carum	CARAWAY
withdraw	REVOKE	cayenne pepper	PIM(I)ENTO
wither	SCATH	coarse cinnamon	CASSIA
without		curcuma	TURMERIC
—knowing	UNWARE	from	
—luxury	BARE	—capsicum	CAYENNE PEPPER
—possibility of			CHILE.CHIL(L)I.PAPRIKA
escape	UNREDREST	—Ceylon	CINNAMON
—redress	UNREDREST		PIM(I)ENTO

—climbing orchid	VANILLA	**spoil**[1]	MAR
—crocus	SAFFRON	hence	
—East Indies	CLOVE.NUTMEG	•spoil a fight	MARABOUT
—Hungary	PAPRIKA	•spoil drink	MARGIN
—Mediterranean	CAPER	•spoil fish	MARID.MARLING
	CUM(M)IN	•spoils of war	MARS
—Mexico	VANILLA	**spoil**[2]	
—West Indies	ALLSPICE	*spoil* meal	LAME.MALE
	JAMAICAN PEPPER	*spoiled* brat	BART
	PIMENTO	*spoiling* all the. . .	LETHAL
ginger	AMOMUM.CARDAMON	**spokesman**	VOICE
	TURMERIC.ZINGIBER	**sport**[1]	FA.FL.RL.RU
Grains of Paradise		hence	
	(AFR)AMOMUM	•sport-shirt	FAT
	GUINEA GRAINS	•first-class *in* sport	FAIL
Jamaican pepper	PIM(I)ENTO	•for example, one *in* sport	REGAL
mixture	GARAM MASALA	•sports group	RUSSET
	TAMARA	**sport**[2]	
nutmeg	MACE	*sporting* a. . .	incl A
pimento	ALLSPICE	*sporting* a new. . .	WANE.WEAN
piper nigrum	PEPPER	sporting animal	LION
red pepper	CAYENNE.PAPRIKA		SPRINGBOK.WALLABY
Zanzibar	CLOVE	sporting bird	KIWI
zingiber	GINGER	sporting headgear	CAPON
spider	WEBSTER	*sporting* *	incl in *
spiderman	BRUCE	•learner *sporting* rosette	FLAVOUR
spies	CIA	sporting trophy	(*see* trophy)
spill		sports car	GT.ROD
spill gin	IGN-.-ING	*sports* car	ARC
spilling beans	BANES	sports-*centre*	OR
spilt ale on. . .	ALONE	**spot**	ACE
spin		spot marked	X
spin drier	RIDER	spotted bananas	DOTTY
spinner	JENNY	*spotted in* *	incl in *
spinning tops	POTS.SPOT.STOP	•dress *spotted in* Dis-s	DISROBES
spinning tops⟨	SPOT	spotted insect	SAWFLY
spirits	(see drink[2])	spotted *outside*	SE-EN
splashed scent	CENTS	**sprawl**	
splattered mud on. . .	MOUND	*sprawled about* on bed	BONED
splendid	BULLY	*sprawling* town	WONT
split		**spray**	
split atoms	MOATS.STOMA	*spray*-tested	DETEST
split by a. . .	incl A	*sprayed* into a. . .	-ATION
split by *	incl *	*spraying* trees	REEST
•lo-g *split by* pin	LOPING	**spread**	
splitting *	incl in *	spread container	GREEN BELT
•pin *splitting* lo-g	LOPING	*spread*-sheet	THESE
split fruit	BANANA	*spread* yarns	SNARY
Split tongue	SERBO-CROAT	*spreading* the slurs	RUTHLESS

spring	
spring	SPA
hence	
•spring-time	SPAT
•spring about	SPARE
•spring the. . .	SPATHE
spring	CEE
spring shrub	CAPER
springs from <u>trees</u>	STEER
spur road	DRIVE
spurn	
spurn a. . .	omit A
spurn *	omit *
•(O)liver *spurns* love	LIVER
spurious <u>art in</u>. . .	TRAIN
spy	AGENT.BOND.SNOOP
spymaster	M
squadron	SQN
squadron-*leader*	S
squall <u>coming</u>	GNOMIC
squandered <u>a lot</u>. . .	TOLA
square	FOUR.NINE
	SIXTEEN.S.SQ.T
square cape	TRAFALGAR
square garden	MADISON
square-root of -1	I.J
squash	
<u>orange</u> *squash*	ONAGER
<u>lemon</u> *squash*	MELON
<u>lime</u> *squash*	EMIL.MILE
squash fruit	GOURD
squash racket	SILENCE
squashes relative	STEPSON
squeeze	
squeeze in a. . .	incl A
squeeze in *	incl *
•fish *squeezed in* pres-s	PRESIDES
squeezing *	incl in *
•pres-s *squeezing* fish	PRESIDES
squiffy <u>Scot</u>	COTS
squirming <u>eel</u>	LEE
Sri Lanka	CL
	(*see* Ceylon)
s-shed	SHUT
staff	
Staff College	SC
Staff Corps	SC
staff criticism	STICK
Staff Officer	SO

stage *production*	GATES
stagger	
stagger <u>along</u>	LOGAN.LONGA
stagger *around*	RE-EL
staggered <u>into</u> a. . .	-ATION
staggering <u>feat</u>	FATE
stain remover	SAINT
stale	(*see* old[2])
stamp	FRANK
stamped addressed envelope	SAE
stampede	
stampede of <u>steers</u>	RESETS
stampeding <u>herds</u>	SHERD
stand	TEE
stand *astride*	TE-E
stand bats. . .(D) ↑	STAB
stand-in	LOCUM.REGENT
standing order	SO
standing order(D) ↑	EBO.MO
standing up(D) ↑	PU
standing up as Sam. . .(D) ↑	
	MASSA
standard[1]	FLAG.NORM.PAR
hence	
•standard European. . .	
	FLAG-POLE
and	
•standard article	NORM(AN)
•standard man	NORMAL
and	
•standard English	PARE
•standard operation	PARENT
•standard tim(e), *almost*	PARTIM
standard[2]	STD
Standard Book Number	SBN
standard deviation	SD
Standard Serial Number	SSN
standard setter	JONES
standard temperature and	
pressure	STP
Standard Wire Gauge	SWG
staple	
staple diet	IRON RATIONS
stapling machine	TACHOMETER
star[1]	
star	LEAD
star *potential*	ARTS.RATS
star-rating	MAGNITUDE
star *turn*⟨	RATS

star²	ACHERNA(R).ALDEBARAN		RIGEL
	ALGOL.ALTAIR	—Perseus	ALGOL
	ANTARES.ARGO.CANOPUS	—Plough	SEPTRION(E)S
	RIGEL		TRIONES
Dog star	SIRIUS	—Puppis	NAOS
evening star	HESPER(US)	—Scorpio	ANTARES
	VENUS.VESPER	—Taurus	ALDEBARAN.NATH
exploding star	NOVA	—Ursa major	ALIOTH.DUBHE
giant red star	RED GIANT		MERAK.MIZAR
group in Taurus	HYADES	—Virgo	SPICA
	PLEIAD(E)S	**start**	
morning star	LUCIFER	start of play	ACTI
	PHOSPHORUS.VENUS	*start of* play	P
nearest	PROXIMA CENTAURI	start of winter	FALL OVER
North star	TYRIAN CYNOSURE	*start of* winter	W
Pole star	LODESTAR.LOADSTAR	*start off* (t)he...	HE
	NORTH STAR.POLARIS	*start off* the (r)ace	ACE
seven stars	PLEIAD(E)S	*start on* Monday	M
—Plough	SEPTENTRION(E)S	*start* rising *up*(D) ↑	SIR
shooting star	METEOR(ITE)	*start* to...	T
small faint dense		*start* to rain	TRAIN
—red star	RED DWARF	*start to* rain	R
—white star	WHITE DWARF	*starting*-gate	G
star in		starting price	SP
—Aquila	ALTAIR	starts work	TITLE PAGE
—Aries	HAMAL	*starts* work	W
—Auriga	CAPELLA	**state¹**	
—Bootes	ARCTURUS.IZAR	inter-*state*	BERRY
—Cancer	ALTARF	state	AVER.SAY
—Canis major	SIRIUS	hence	
—Canis minor	PROCYON	•many state number	CAVERN
—Capricornus	ALGEDI	•Royal states	RAVERS
—Carina	CANOPUS	•state the time	AVERAGE
—Centaur	RIGIL	State Certificated Midwife	SCM
—Cetus	MIRA	State Enrolled Nurse	SEN
—Columba	PHAET	State Registered Nurse	SRN
—Corvus	ALGORAB	*state of collapse of*	
—Crater	ALKES	Red Inn	DINNER
—Cygnus	DENEB	*state of* the art	HATTER
—Delphinus	ROTANEV	state ownership	CLAIM
	SUALOCIN	state train	EXPRESS
—Draco	ETAMIN.THUBAN	*state* where...	WARE.WEAR
—Eridanus	ACHERNA	*stating* all...	AWL
—Gemini	CASTOR.POLLUX	stately home	PILE
—Leo	DENEBOLA.REGULUS	statement	AC
—Lyra(e)	VEGA	statement of identity	AM.IAM.IM
—Ophiuchus	SABIK.YED		(*see also* admit¹)
—Orion	BELATRIX.BETELGEUSE	statesman	AMERICAN.TEXAN
	BETELGEUX.BETELGEUZE		YANK

state² (USA)

Alabama	AL.ALA
Alaska	ALAS
Arizona	ARIZ
Arkansas	ARK
California	CAL
Colorado	COL(O)
Columbia (District)	DC
Connecticut	CT
Delaware	DEL
(District of Columbia)	DC
Florida	FLA
Georgia	GA
Hawaii	HI
Idaho	ID.IDA
Illinois	ILL
Indiana	IND
Iowa	IA
Kansas	KAN.KS
Kentucky	KEN.KY
Louisiana	LA
Maine	ME
Maryland	MD
Massachusetts	BAY STATE.MASS
Michigan	MICH
Minnesota	MINN
Mississippi	MI.MISS
Missouri	MO
Montana	MONT
Nebraska	NEB(R)
Nevada	NEV
New Hampshire	NH
New Jersey	NJ
New Mexico	NM(EX)
New York	NY
North Carolina	NC
North Dakota	ND(AK)
Ohio	O
Oklahoma	OKLA
Oregon	OR(E).OREG
Pennsylvania	PA.PENN
Rhode Island	RI
South Carolina	SC
South Dakota	SD.S DAK
Tennessee	TEN(N)
Texas	LONE STAR.TEX
Utah	U(T)
Vermont	VT
Virginia	VA

Washington	WASH
West Virginia	WVA
Wisconsin	WIS
Wyoming	WY(O)
•gold *in* state	CORAL
•South American state	SAGA
•state permit	VALET
•state publication	MEAD
•state railway	GARY.VARY
•state service	MASS
•state vehicle	RIMINI
station	ST
statuette	EMMY.OSCAR
staunch supporter	STEM
stay	
stay hidden	LILO
stay true	STAUNCH
stays silent	SAY-SO
steady habit	UNIFORM
steal	
she *steals some* epic. . .	SHEEP
steal money	TAKE NOTE
steal painting	ABSTRACT
stolen	HOT
steam	
steamer	STR
steaming hot so. . .	SHOOT
steamship	SS
step	
step *out*	PEST.PETS
step *out*	
•ste-p *out of* the way	STEEP
•step *out of* the way	PEACE
step-*up*(D) ↑	PETS
steradian	SR
sterling	STER.STG
stern	
stern Athenian	DRACO
stern of dinghy	Y
stern professional	GRIMACE
stern talk	BACKCHAT
stern warning	REAR-LIGHT
Stevenson	RLS
stew	
in a stew about seven	EVENS
stew	WILD WEST
stewed eels	ELSE.SEEL
stewing steak	KEATS.SKATE
	STAKE.TAKES

stick	
stick out	CAN-E.RO-D
stick *out*	TICKS
stick-*up*(D) ↑	DOR.GUM
sticker	CEMENT.GLUE.GUM
sticky *end*	Y
sticky hand	TAR
sticky wicket	PITCH
stiff	BODY.CORPSE
stiff paper	HARD TIMES
stiff suit	ARMOUR
stir	
stir soup	OPUS
stirring march	CHARM
stock	
stock taking	RUSTLING
stocked by wi/ne st/ore	NEST
stocked in *	incl in *
•silver *stocked in* shop	STORAGE
stocking *	incl *
•shop *stocking* silver	STORAGE
stoker	BRAM
stokes	S(T)
stone	OPAL.PIT.ST
stone circle	ETERNITY RING
stone figure	DIAMOND
stone worker	LAPIDARY
stony-*hearted*	O
stony-hearted girl	OLIVE.PEACH
(*see also* gem.mineral)	
stop	COLON.PT
stop *and* listen	ENDEAR
stop music	REFRAIN
stop short of tow(n)	TOW
stopped instrument. . .	ORGAN
store	
stored in *	incl in *
•one car *stored in* sh-ed	SHIRRED
storing a. . .	incl A
storing *	incl *
•sh-ed *storing* one car	SHIRRED
storm	
storm location	TEACUP
storm rages	GEARS
stormy waters	WASTER
story books	TALENT
stout	
stout leader	FATHEAD
stout man	FATAL.PLUMPED

straddle	
straddled by *	incl in *
•a horse *straddled by*	
J-ean	JACOBEAN
straddling a. . .	incl A
straddling river	incl R
straddling *	incl *
•J-ean *straddling*	
a horse	JACOBEAN
straggling conifers	FORENSIC
straight line	I
strait	ST
Strand entrance	PLYMOUTH
strange	
strange *origins*	ST
strange bird	DRIB
strange *end*	E
strange thing	NIGHT
strange way to act	CAT
strangely silent	ENLIST
stray dogs in. . .	DOINGS
stream	BANKER.FLOWER
street	ST
hence	
•street light	STRAY
•street needs repair	STRUTTED
•streetwarden	STRANGER
and	
•Meadow Street	LEAST
•Virginia Street	VAST
•West Fish Street	WIDEST
and	
•house *in* the street	SHOT
street *in Berlin*	STRASSE
street *in Madrid*	CALLE
street *in Paris*	RUE
street *in Rome*	STRADA.VIA
stretch	PORRIDGE.SENTENCE
stretcher	PROCRUSTES
strict	
strict *limitations*	ST
strict supporter	REGULAR GUY
strike	
strike off doctor	omit DR.MO
strike victim	LAMPREY
strikebreaker	RAT
string	
string course	SPAGHETTI
strings (violin)	A.D.E.G

stripper	LOCUST.SALOME
stroke leg	COUPON
strong (very strong)¹	F.(FF)
hence	
•strong arm	FARM
•strong back	FRUMP
•strong jug	FEWER
and	
•a strong anger	AFIRE
•a strong company	AFFIRM
•a strong flow	AFFLUX
and	
•a very strong light	AFFLUX
	AFFRAY
•a very strong melody	AFFAIR
•a very strong No.9	AFFIX
strong²	STR
strong-arm man	SAMSON
strong binding	STRAPPING
strong catkin	FIRMAMENT
strong current	CAMPS
strong man	SAMSON.TITAN
strong porter	STOUT
strong suit	ARMOUR.TRUMPS
strontium unit	SU
struggle	
struggle to rise	SIRE
struggled like...	KIEL
struggling up an...	PUNA
student	L
Student Christian Movement	SCM
Student of Civil Law	SCL
Student Representative	
Council	SRC
students	NUS
	(*see also* learner)
study¹	
study	CON.DEN.READ
hence	
•study dance	CONTANGO
•study music	CONSTRAIN
•study poetry	CONVERSE
and	
•study gallery	DENTATE
•study I'm...	DENIM
•study weight	DENOUNCE
and	
•study only...	READJUST
•study one journalist	READIED

•study with *German*...	READMIT
studies	COURSE
study²	
of (including science):	
action of	
—ice	GLACIOLOGY
—forces	MECHANICS
aerolites	AEROLITHOLOGY
aging	GERONTOLOGY
agricultural pests	PESTOLOGY
agriculture	GEOPONICS
airborne organisms	
	AEROBIOLOGY
alchemy	HERMETICS
algae	ALGOLOGY.PHYCOLOGY
amphibia	HERPETOLOGY
anatomy of fleshy	
parts	SARCOLOGY
ancient	
—customs	FOLKLORE
—geography	
	PALAEOGEOGRAPHY
—Italians	ETRUSCOLOGY
—man	PALAEOANTHROPOLOGY
—papyri	PAPYROLOGY
—soils	PALAEOPEDOLOGY
—weather	
	PALAEOCLIMATOLOGY
—writing	PALAEOGRAPHY
animal	
—behaviour	ETHOLOGY
—descriptions	ZOOGRAPHY
—diseases	ZOOPATHOLOGY
—pathology	ZOOPATHY
animals	ZOOLOGY
—like plants	ZOOPHYTOLOGY
ants	MYRMECOLOGY
applied sciences	TECHNOLOGY
aqueous vapour	ATMOLOGY
armour	HOPLOLOGY
arrangement of	
atoms	STEREOCHEMISTRY
artillery	PYROBALLOGY
assaying	DOCIMOLOGY
assisting memory	MNEMONICS
	MNEMOTECHNICS
astronomical measurement	
	URANOMETRY
astronomy	URANOLOGY

atmosphere	AEROLOGY	—of the body	ZOOCHEMISTRY
ballet	CHOREOLOGY	—of the earth	GEOCHEMISTRY
bathing (therapy)	BALNEOLOGY	children's	
being	METAPHYSICS	—diseases	PAEDIATRICS
bell ringing	CAMPANOLOGY	—teeth	PAEDODONTICS
biological		China	SINOLOGY
—functions related to electronic		Christ	CHRISTOLOGY
equipment	BIONICS	ciphers	CRYPTOLOGY
—rhythms	CHRONOBIOLOGY	citizenship	CIVICS
birds	ORNITHOLOGY	classification of animals	ZOOTAXY
birds'		climate	CLIMATOLOGY
—eggs	OOLOGY		METEOROLOGY
—nests	CALIOLOGY	clocks	HOROGRAPHY.HOROLOGY
blood	HAEMATOLOGY	clouds	NEPHOLOGY
bodies in motion	DYNAMICS	coins	NUMISMATICS
	KINETICS		NUMISMATOLOGY
body movement conveying		colour	CHROMATICS
information	KINESICS	—change	PHOTOCHROMICS
bones	OSTEOLOGY	comparative measurements of	
books	BIBLIOLOGY	parts of animals	ZOOMETRY
	BIBLIOGRAPHY	control systems	CYBERNETICS
botany	PHYTOLOGY	cooking	GASTROLOGY
breeding animals	ZOOTECHNICS	cosmetics	COSMET(IC)OLOGY
—domestic	THREMMATOLOGY	crime	CRIMINOLOGY
brewing	ZYMURGY	crustaceans	CARCINOLOGY
building	TECTONICS	crystals	CRYSTALLOGRAPHY
bumps on head	PHRENOLOGY	data acquired by touch	HAPTICS
casting nativities		demons	DEMONOLOGY
	GENETHLIALOGY	dentistry concerned with gum	
causation	(A)ETIOLOGY	diseases	PERIODONTICS
causes of fertilised cell			PERIODONTOLOGY
development	EPIGENETICS	derivation of words	ETYMOLOGY
caves	SPEL(A)EOLOGY	descent of families	GENEALOGY
cells	CYTOLOGY	descriptive	
—shed from internal parts		—astronomy	URANOGRAPHY
	EXFOLIATIVE CYTOLOGY	—botany	PHYTOGRAPHY
character from		development of earth's crust	
face	METOPOSCOPY		GEOLOGY
charters and diplomas		diagnosis	DIAGNOSTICS
	DIPLOMATOLOGY	dietetics	SIT(I)OLOGY
chemistry		dining	ARISTOLOGY
—applied to medical		diseases	PATHOLOGY
theory	IATROCHEMISTRY	—as effected by geographical	
—dealing with minute		environment	GEOMEDICINE
quantities	MICROCHEMISTRY	—classification	NOSOLOGY
—of radioactive		—of mind	PSYCHIATRY
elements	RADIOCHEMISTRY	distilling	ZYMORGY
—of reactions at high		distribution of	
pressure	PIEZOCHEMISTRY	—animals	ZOOGEOGRAPHY

—charged particles
     ELECTROKINETICS
dogma   DOGMATOLOGY
domestication of
  animals   ZOOTECHNY
dosage   DOSOLOGY
dreams   ONEIROLOGY
drugs   PHARMACOLOGY
dust in air   KONIOLOGY
duty   DEONTOLOGY
dynamic forces within the
  earth   GEODYNAMICS
dynamics of
  gases   AERODYNAMICS
ear   OTOLOGY
ear, nose and throat
    OTO(RHINO)LARYNGOLOGY
earth
—measurement   GEODESY
    GEODETICS
—quakes   SEISMOGRAPHY
    SEISMOLOGY
—sciences   NATURAL HISTORY
—'s surface
    PHYSICAL GEOGRAPHY
echoes   PHONOCAMPTICS
econometrics in
  history   CLIOMETRICS
effect of disease on body
  tissues   HISTOPATHOLOGY
eggs   OOLOGY
Egypt   EGYPTOLOGY
electric power   ELECTROTECHNICS
    ELECTROTECHNOLOGY
electricity
—and bodily processes
    ELECTROPHYSIOLOGY
—and chemical change
    ELECTROCHEMISTRY
—and electromagnetic radiation
    PHOTO-ELECTRONICS
—and heat   ELECTROTHERMICS
    ELECTROTHERMY
—and magnetism
    ELECTROMAGNETISM
—at rest   ELECTROSTATICS
—in motion   ELECTRODYNAMICS
electrical
—measurements   ELECTROMETRY

—phenomena in living
  beings   ELECTROBIOLOGY
electrolysis   ELECTROCHEMISTRY
electronics in aviation   AVIONICS
elections   PSEPHOLOGY
embryos   EMBRYOLOGY
emotions and motives
    PSYCHODYNAMICS
end of the world   ESCHATOLOGY
endemic diseases   ENDEMIOLOGY
endocrine glands
    ENDOCRINOLOGY
energy   ENERGETICS
environment   (O)ECOLOGY
—control   EUTHENICS
enzymes   ENZYMOLOGY
epidemic animal diseases
    EPIZOOTICS
epidemics   EPIDEMIOLOGY
ethics   DEONTOLOGY
excrement   SCATOLOGY
exercise   PHYSIOTHERAPEUTICS
extraterrestrial life
    ASTROBIOLOGY
    EXOBIOLOGY
eyes   OPHTHALMOLOGY
eyesight   OPTOLOGY
Fathers of the Church   PATRISTICS
    PATROLOGY
features of a region   TOPOGRAPHY
fermentation   ZYMOLOGY
    ZYMURGY
fevers   PYRETOLOGY
figures   GEOMETRY
final causes   TELEOLOGY
fingerprints   DACTYLOGRAPHY
fireworks   PYROTECHNICS
first principles   METAPHYSICS
fishes   ICHTHYOLOGY
fishing   HALIEUTICS
flags   VEXILLOLOGY
flight   AERONAUTICS
flow
— of fluids   FLUIDICS
—and change of shape and
  matter   RHEOLOGY
flower descriptions
    ANTHOECOLOGY
flowers   FLORISTICS

folklore	STORIOLOGY
food and nutrition	
	BROMATOLOGY.SIT(I)OLOGY
formation of earth	GEOGNOSY
fossil	
—animals	PALAEOZOOLOGY
—fish	PALAEOICTHYOLOGY
—footprints	ICHNOLOGY
—plants	PALAEOBOTANY
	PALAEOPHYTOLOGY
fossils	PALAEONTOLOGY
fruit growing	POMOLOGY
fungi	MYC(ET)OLOGY
future of mankind	FUTUROLOGY
gases	AEROMETRY.PNEUMATICS
gem engraving	GLYPTICS
genetics in relation to	
cells	CYTOGENETICS
geology	
—from air photographs	
	PHOTOGEOLOGY
—of dating events	
	GEOCHRONOLOGY
—of moon etc.	ASTROGEOLOGY
geographical phenomena	
	CHOROLOGY
gesture	CH(E)IROLOGY
ghosts	SPECTROLOGY
giants	GIGANTOLOGY
glaciers	GLACIOLOGY
good eating	GASTROLOGY
	GASTRONOMY
government	ARCHOLOGY
	POLITICAL SCIENCE
gramophone	
records	DISCOGRAPHY
grasses	AGROSTOLOGY
ground plans	ICHNOGRAPHY
growing plants in	
water	HYDROPONICS
hair	TRICHOLOGY
hand	CH(E)IROLOGY
—writing	GRAPHOLOGY
health maintenance	HYGIENICS
hearing	AUDIOLOGY
heart	CARDIOLOGY
heat	THERMOLOGY
—as mechanical	
agent	THERMODYNAMICS

—changes in chemical	
action	THERMOCHEMISTRY
heresies	HERESIOLOGY
history	HISTORIOLOGY
—of proper names	ONOMASTICS
horse diseases	HIPPIATRICS
human	
—antiquity	ARCHAEOLOGY
—body	SOMATOLOGY
—muscles	KINESIOLOGY
—settlements	EKISTICS
—society	SOCIOLOGY
hydrodynamics	HYDRAULICS
	HYDROMECHANICS
hymns	HYMNOLOGY
hypnotism	NEUR(OH)YPNOLOGY
icons	ICONOLOGY
ideas	IDEOLOGY
illness diagnosis from	
marks on the iris	IRIDOLOGY
improvement of living	
standards	EUTHENICS
influence of stars	ASTROLOGY
insects	ENTOMOLOGY
	INSECTOLOGY
instruction	PEDAGOGY
interpretation	
—of a text	EXEGETICS
—of Scripture	HERMENEUTICS
interrelationship of	
—environment and organisms	
	BIONOMICS.ECOLOGY
iris	IRIDOLOGY
kidneys	NEPHROLOGY
knowledge	EPISTEMOLOGY
	PHILOSOPHY
language	PHILOLOGY
—in relation to other aspects of	
behaviour	METALINGUISTICS
languages	LINGUISTICS
larynx	LARYNGOLOGY
law	JURISPRUDENCE
	NOMOLOGY
life	
—and careers	PROSOPOGRAPHY
—processes	PHYSIOLOGY
—without germs	GNOTOBIOLOGY
light	OPTICS
linguistics	GLOSSOLOGY

	PHILOLOGY
liver	HEPATOLOGY
liverworts	HEPATICOLOGY
living things	BIOLOGY.BIOMETRY
	BIOMETRICS
logic of reasoning	DIALECTICS
low temperatures	CRYOGENICS
	CRYOPHYSICS
lying	PSEUDOLOGY
magnetism	
—and electricity	
	ELECTROMAGNETISM
—of ancient rocks	
	PALAEOMAGNETISM
malaria	MALARIOLOGY
mammals	THEROLOGY
man	ANTHROPOLOGY
managing fermentation	
	ZYMOTECHNICS
manoeuvring	TACTICS
maps	CARTOLOGY
mathematical	
—drawing	GRAPHICS
—continuity and	
limits	TOPOLOGY
Maya people	MAYOLOGY
meaning	SIGNIFICS
—of words	LEXICOLOGY
meanings	SEMANTICS
	SEMASIOLOGY
measurement of	
—mental states	PSYCHOMETRICS
	PSYCHOMETRY
—social relationships	
	SOCIOMETRY
—time	HOROLOGY
measurements	METRICS
	METROLOGY
mechanics of electrical	
devices	ELECTROMECHANICS
medals	NUMISMATICS
	NUMISMATOLOGY
medicines	PHARMACEUTICS
mental	
—faculties by shape and size of	
skull	PHRENOLOGY
—disorders	PSYCHOPATHOLOGY
—forces	PSYCHODYNAMICS
—illness	PSYCHIATRY

meteors	METEORITICS
metrical systems	STICHOLOGY
metals	METALLURGY
	METALLOGRAPHY
metaphysics	IDEOLOGY
methods	METHODOLOGY
midwifery	OBSTETRICS
mineral springs	BALNEOLOGY
minerals	MINERALOGY
mites	ACAROLOGY
moisture content of the	
atmosphere	
	HYDROMETEOROLOGY
molluscs	CONCHOLOGY
	MALACOLOGY
monads	MONADOLOGY
monstrosities	TERATOLOGY
moon	SELENOGRAPHY
	SELENOLOGY
morals	DEONTOLOGY.ETHICS
mosses	BRYOLOGY
	MUSCOLOGY.SPHAGNOLOGY
motion	
—involving force	KINETICS
—not involving force	KINEMATICS
—of fluids	HYDRAULICS
	HYDRODYNAMICS
	HYDROKINETICS
mountains	OR(E)OLOGY
movement	
—and supply of troops	LOGISTICS
—human	KINESIOLOGY
—living creatures	BIOMECHANICS
mud	PELOLOGY
muscles	MYOLOGY
music of different	
cultures	ETHNOMUSICOLOGY
myths	MYTHOLOGY
natural	
—agents in forming the earth's	
crust	DYNAMICAL GEOLOGY
—science	PHYSICS
nature of being	ONTOLOGY
navigation	NAUTICS
nervous system	NEUROLOGY
nose	RHINOLOGY
nuclear physics	NUCLEONICS
numbers	NUMEROLOGY
numerical proportions in which	

chemical matter reacts	STOICH(E)IOMETRY
nutrition	SIT(I)OLOGY
	TROPHOLOGY
obstetrics	TOCOLOGY.TOKOLOGY
occult sciences	HERMETICS
ontology	METAPHYSICS
organised whole	GESTALT PSYCHOLOGY
organisms	BACTERIOLOGY
—as affected by climate	PH(A)ENOLOGY
—form and structure	MORPHOLOGY
—in germ-free conditions	GNOTOBIOTICS
origin of things	ARCHOLOGY
parasites	PARASITOLOGY
particular place	TOPOLOGY
pathology of nervous system	NEUROPATHOLOGY
peat mosses	SPHAGNOLOGY
pecuniary management	ECONOMICS
personal	
—life and career	PROSOPOGRAPHY
—interrelationships	SOCIOMETRY
pests	PESTOLOGY
phenomena	PHENOMENOLOGY
physical	
—condition of heavenly bodies	PHYSICAL ASTRONOMY
—properties of chemicals	PHYSICAL CHEMISTRY
physics	NATURAL PHILOSOPHY
—of living things	BIOPHYSICS
—of the earth	GEOPHYSICS
physiological basis of mental processes	PHYSIOTHERAPEUTICS
place names	TOPONYMICS
	TOPONYMY
plant	
—anatomy	PHYTOTOMY
—diseases	PHYTOPATHOLOGY
—distribution	PHYTOGEOGRAPHY
—growth and	

nutrition	AGROBIOLOGY
plants	BOTANY.FLORISTICS
poetry	PROSODY
poisons	TOXICOLOGY
political	
—economy	PLUTOLOGY
	PLUTONOMY
—geography	GEOPOLITICS
—science	ECONOMICS
pollen grains	PALYNOLOGY
population	DEMOGRAPHY
	LARITHMICS
portraits	ICONOGRAPHY
postcards	DELTIOLOGY
pottery	CERAMOGRAPHY
preaching	HOMILETICS
precious stones	GEM(M)OLOGY
prediction	HOROSCOPY
pressure of gases	AEROSTATICS
primitive traditions	AGRIOLOGY
prison management	P(O)ENOLOGY
processes leading to problem solving	SYNECTICS
production of wealth	POLITICAL ECONOMY
pronunciation	PHONETICS
	PHONOLOGY
properties of matter	PHYSICS
	SOMATOLOGY
proverbs	PAROEMIOLOGY
psychic phenomena	METAPHYSICS
psychical research	PARAPSYCHOLOGY
psychology	PSYCHICS
—of animals	ZOOPSYCHOLOGY
punishment	PENOLOGY
pure being	ONTOLOGY
purposelessness	DYSTELEOLOGY
quantities of drugs	DOSOLOGY
race	
—deterioration	CACOGENICS
	DYSGENICS
—improvement	EUGENICS
races	ETHNOGRAPHY
	ETHNOLOGY
radiation on tissues	RADIOBIOLOGY

radioactivity in medical
  treatment   RADIOLOGY
rainfall   HYETOLOGY
reasoning   LOGIC
refracted sounds   DIACOUSTICS
refraction of light   DIOPTRICS
relationship of mental to
  physical   PSYCHOPHYSICS
reptiles   HERPETOLOGY
rhythm   RHYTHMICS
rhythmic movement
    EURHYTHMICS
rings   DACTYLIOGRAPHY
    DACTYLIOLOGY
rivers   POTAMOLOGY
rock
—masses
    STRUCTURAL GEOLOGY
—strata   STRATIGRAPHY
rocks   LITHOLOGY
    PETROGRAPHY
    PETROLOGY
sacred literature   HIEROLOGY
sailing on rhumb lines
    LOXODROMICS
saints' lives   HAGIOLOGY
salvation   SOTERIOLOGY
sanitary principles   HYGIENICS
seals and signets   SPHRAGISTICS
seas   HYDROGRAPHY
    OCEANOLOGY
    THALASSOGRAPHY
seaweeds   ALGOLOGY
    PHYCOLOGY
secretions   ECCRINOLOGY
self   AUTOLOGY
—regulating systems
    AUTONOMICS
senility   GERONTOLOGY
    NOSTOLOGY
serums   SEROLOGY
sexual behaviour   SEXOLOGY
shells   CONCHOLOGY
significance of terms   SIGNIFICS
signets and seals   SPHRAGISTICS
skin   DERMATOLOGY
skulls   CRANIOLOGY
    PHRENOLOGY
significance of values   AXIOLOGY

small
—electronic
  systems   MICROELECTRONICS
—objects   MICROLOGY
—organisms   MICROBIOLOGY
—worlds MICROCOSMOGRAPHY
smell   OLFACTOLOGY
snakes   OPHIOLOGY
Socratic methods   MAIEUTICS
soil   EDAPHOLOGY.PEDOLOGY
sound   ACOUSTICS
—reflections   CATACOUSTICS
    CATAPHONICS
spectra   SPECTROSCOPY
speech
—sound in writing   GRAPHEMICS
—sounds   PHONEMICS
spiders   ARACHNOLOGY
spiritual beings PNEUMATOLOGY
sponges   SPONGOLOGY
spores   PALYNOLOGY
stamps PHILATELY.TIMBROLOGY
standing fluid   HYDROSTATICS
stars   ASTRONOMY
statics of rigid
  bodies   GEOSTATICS
statistical analysis of economic
  information   ECONOMETRICS
stomach and intestines
    GASTROENTEROLOGY
stones (in body)   LITHOLOGY
structural geology
    (GEO)TECTONICS
structure of tissues   HISTOLOGY
subatomic particles
    MICROPHYSICS
sun   HELIOLOGY
—dials   HOROGRAPHY
surfaces in contact   TRIBOLOGY
symbols   SYMBOL(OL)OGY
symptoms   SEM(E)IOTICS
    SYMPTOMATOLOGY
systems   SYSTEMATOLOGY
teaching   PEDAGOGY
teeth   ODONTOLOGY
terrestrial magnetism
    GEOMAGNETISM
time   CHRONOLOGY
—by sundial   GNOMONICS

—pieces	HOROGRAPHY	worms	HELMINTHOLOGY
	HOROLOGY	writing hymns	HYMNOGRAPHY
tissue	HISTOLOGY	X-rays and gamma	
topography of earth's		rays	ROENTGENOLOGY
crust	GEOMORPHOLOGY		(*see also* write[3])
touch (sense)	HAPTICS	**stuff**	
transmitting messages		*stuffed into* *	incl in *
	TELEGRAPHY	•fruit *stuffed into* cleric	DAPPLED
treatment and cure of		*stuffed with* a...	incl A
—diseases	THERAPEUTICS	*stuffed with* *	incl *
	THERAPY	•cleric *stuffed with* fruit	DAPPLED
—the aged		**stumble**	
	GERONTOTHERAPEUTICS	*stumbles* <u>over</u>...	ROVE
tree rings	DENDROCHRONOLOGY	*stumbles over* step	PEST.PETS
trees	DENDROLOGY	*stumbling* <u>words</u>	SWORD
triangles	TRIGONOMETRY	**stumped**	ST
tumours	ONCOLOGY	**stunner**	DISH.KO
types	TYPOLOGY	*stunted* (t)ree	REE
ultimate nature	AXIOLOGY	*stupidly* <u>dared</u>	ADDER.DREAD
unchanging properties of		**sty**	LITTER CONTAINER
geometric figures	TOPOLOGY	**style**[1]	
unclean matter	COPROLOGY	*style* <u>in art</u>	TRAIN
understanding	NOOLOGY	*stylish* <u>robe</u>	BOER.BORE.EBOR
unidentified flying		**style**[2]	
objects	UFOLOGY	indicates mode of address	
universe	COSMOLOGY		(*see* address)
urine	UR(IN)OLOGY	**sub-**	
values	AXIOLOGY	indicates one word written below	
venereal disease	SYPHILOLOGY	another (D):	
	VENEREOLOGY	•*sub*marine ruler	SEAR
versification	PROSODY	•*sub*standard colour	PARTAN
vines	VINOLOGY	•*sub*terranean gold	LANDAU
viruses	VIROLOGY	**subject**	SUB(J)
viscosity	RHEOLOGY	subject(D) indicates one word	
volcanoes	VOLCANOLOGY	written below another:	
	VULCANOLOGY	•head *subject to*	
water resources	HYDROLOGY	Russian...	REDPOLL
wealth	CHREMATISTICS	subject me...	I
weapons	HOPLOLOGY	subject them...	THEY
weather	AEROGRAPHY	subject us...	WE
	METEOROLOGY	**subjunctive**	SUB(J)
whales	CETOLOGY	**submariner**	LOW TAR.NEMO
wind	ANEMOLOGY	**submit return**	YIELD
wine-making	ZYMURGY	**subscriber trunk dialling**	STD
wines	OENOLOGY	**subtract**	
wisdom	PHILOSOPHY	*subtract* a...	omit A
with microscope	MICROGRAPHY	*subtract* *	omit *
women's diseases	GYNAECOLOGY	•*subtract* five *from* se(v)en	SEEN
wood	XYLOLOGY	**succeed**	FAREWELL

succeeded	S
successful day	VE
successor to Brand X	BRANDY
sudden stroke	SNAPSHOT
suffering	(in) PA-IN
suffering badly	BALDY
suffering breakdown	
I went...	TWINE
sufficient	QS
suffix	SUF(F)
sugar[1]	
aldehyde	ALDOSE
cane sugar	SUCROSE
compound	MALTOSE
from	
—arabin	ARABINOSE
—lactose	GALACTOSE
—various plants	DULCOSE
fruit sugar	FRUCTOSE
	L(A)EVULOSE
glucose	DEXTROSE.GLYCOSE
	GRAPE SUGAR
grape sugar	DEXTROSE
	GLUCOSE.GLYCOSE
Indian	JAGGERY
laevulose	FRUCTOSE
Mexican	PANOCHA
milk sugar	LACTOSE
ordinary sugar	SACCHAROSE
	SUCROSE
palm sugar	JAGGERY
refined in cigar	
shape	LOAF SUGAR
simple sugar	MONOSACCHARIDE
that hydrolyses into	
—two sugar molecules	
	DISACCHARIDE
—three sugar molecules	
	TRISACCHARIDE
—more than one sugar molecule	
	POLYSACCHARIDE
trisaccharide	RAFFINOSE
unrefined	MUSCOVADO
with	
—five carbon atoms	PENTOSE
	RIBOSE
—six carbon atoms	HEXOSE
wood sugar	XYLOSE
sugar[2]	

sugar beet	CUBE ROOT
sugarloaf	SWEETBREAD
suit	C.D.H.S.
suitcase	GEAR BOX
suitable for use	SUE
suitably sited	EDITS
sultanate	OMAN
sum of money	IMPOUNDS
summer	ADDER
summertime	BST
sun[1]	S
hence	
•sunbird	SCOOT.SKITE.SOWL
	STEAL.STERN
•sundance	SHOP
•sundown	SLOW.SNOWDROPS
•sundress	SWEAR
•sunfish	SEEL.SHAKE.SIDE
	SLING.SPIKE.STENCH
•sunflower	SLILY
•sunrise	SUP
sun *comes out*	omit S
sun[2]	
sun god	RA.SOL
sun king	LOUIS
sun*rise*(D) ↑	LOS.NUS
sun-*up*(D) ↑	LOS.NUS
sunbathed, *topless*	(b)ASKED
sunbather	BAKER
sunbathing	(in) SU-N
sunny chap	RAY
sun*set*	UNS-
sunshade	CLOUD
superfine	SUP
superior[1]	ARCH.OVER.U.UP
hence	
•superior head	ARCHNESS
•many superior...	COVER.LOVER
	MOVER
•superior philosopher	USAGE
•superior group	UPSET
superior[2]	
superior example	UPPER CASE
superior standing	DAIS
	PLATFORM.SOAPBOX
	STAGE
superior[3]	
indicates word written above	
another (D):	

•man *is superior to* many   HELOT
•staff *with* man *in superior*
  position   HEROD
superlative   SUP
supersonic transport   SST
supine   SUP
supplement   PS.SUP
supplied by hospi/tal c/linic   TALC
support[1]   BACK.BRA
                    LEG.PROP
hence
•boot-support   KICK-BACK
•proper support   RIGHT BACK
•support team   BACKSIDE
and
•county supporter   COBRA
•support church   BRACE.BRACH
•support-ship   BRASS
and
•support friend   LEGALLY
•support one on. . .   LEGION
•support queen   LEGER
and
•support no girls   PROPOSALS
•support queen   PROPER
•support railway   PROPEL
support[2]
support evil   BASE
support worker   SECOND-HAND
supporter   GUY.PROP
support[3]
indicates word written below
  another (D):
•child *supporting* mother   MASON
•mother *supported by*
  child   MASON
suppress
suppress a. . .   omit A
suppress *   omit *
•de(s)pot *suppresses* son   DEPOT
suppress a   incl A
suppress *   incl *
•k-ing *suppresses* sick. . .   KILLING
supra   SUP
supreme   SUP
  Supreme Court   SC
sure   BOUND
  sure-fire   CRACK SHOT
  sur(e)ly *not all*. . .   SURLY

surface
  surface-to-air missile   SAM
  surface-to-surface missile   SSM
surgeon   VET
  surgeons   RCS
surmount
indicates one word written above
  another(D):
•dog *surmounting* a
  height   CURATOR
surplus garment   OVERCOAT
surprise
surprising result   LUSTRE
surprisingly weak   WAKE
surrender
surrender a. . .   omit A
surrender king   omit R
surrender *   omit *
•bar(ely) *surrenders* city   BAR
surround
surrounding a. . .   incl A
surrounding *   incl *
•drunks *surrounding*
  house   SHOOTS
surrounded by *   incl in *
•house *surrounded by*
  drunks   SHOOTS
surveyor   LANDSEER
suspend
suspended sentence   HANGING
suspender   HANGMAN
              JACK KETCH
swagger
swaggering boaster   BOBADIL
swaggering boaster   BOATERS
swallow
swallowed up *   incl *
•it *is swallowed up in* t-he. . .TITHE
swallowing a. . .   incl A
swallowing *   incl *
•s-age *swallowing* tablet SPILLAGE
swallowed by *   incl in *
•tablet *swallowed by*
  s-age   SPILLAGE
swamp
swamp a. . .   incl A
swamp *   incl *
•wat-er *swamping* church
              WATCHER

swamped by *	incl in *	**swim**	
•church *swamped by*		swimmer	LEANDER
wat-er	WATCHER	swimmer	COD.EEL.LING
swan	COB.PEN.CYGNET	(*see also* fish)	
hence		swimming club	ASA
•swan painter	COBRA	*swimming in* Lido	IDOL
•swan-song	PENCHANT	swimming organisms	NEKTON
swap **coins**	SONIC		PLANKTON
swarming **flies**	FILES	swimming pool	LOOP.POLO
sway		**swindle**	CON.DO
swaying hips	PISH.SHIP	**swing**	
swaying around a lido	IDOLA	*swing* door	ODOR.ROOD
Sweden	S	*swing* door⟨	ROOD
Swedish	SW	swing music CRADLE SONG.ROCK	
aeroplane	SAAB	**swirl**	
airline	SAS	*swirl of* a skirt	AT RISK
capital	S.STOCKHOLM	*swirled* along	LOGAN.LONGA
characters	SW	*swirling* waters	WASTER
chief magistrate	LANDAMMAN(N)	**swish**	
clover	ALSIKE	*swish* cane	-ANCE
coin		*swishing* cane isn't. . .	INSTANCE
—unit	ORE	**Swiss**	HELVETIAN
—100 ore	KR.KRONA	alpenhorn melody	
complaints officer	OMBUDSMAN		RANZ-DES-VACHES
farm	TORP	cabin	CHALET
hors d'oeuvres	SMORGASBORD	capital	BERN(E).S
leader	S	characters	CH
manual training	SLOID.SLOYD	cheese	GRUYERE
measure ($^2/_3$ acre)	MORGEN	coin	FRANC.RAPPEN
parliament	RIKSDAG	dish	BERNERPLATTE
provincial council	LANDST(H)ING		MUESLI
toast	SKOAL	division	CANTON
turnip	RUTABAGA	herdsman's song	
wild turnip	NAVEW		RANZ-DES-VACHES
sweep	GRIMES	hero	TELL
swept-up hair styles(D) ↑	SNUB	leader	S
sweet		magistrate	AMMAN.AMTMAN
sweet Fanny Adams	SFA	measure (small)	LIGNE
sweet fool	GOOSEBERRY	sled	LUGE
sweet money	LOLLY	**switch**	
sweet store	HIVE.HONEYCOMB	*switch back*⟨	DOR
sweetbread	SUGARLOAF	*switch ends of* lever	REVEL
sweetheart	JO(E)	*switch* on light	THOLING
sweet*heart*	E	*switch* on⟨	NO
swift	SCREECHER	*switched* over	ROVE
Swift horse	HOUYHNHNM	*switched over* to. . .⟨	OT
Swift race	LAPUTAN	**Switzerland**	CH
Swift traveller	GULLIVER	hence	
swilling beer	BREE	•Egypt *and* Switzerland	ETCH

•old city *in* Switzerland's. . .   CHURCH
•Switzerland *has* no way   CHORD
(*see also* Swiss)

swivel
swivel gun   GNU
swivelling seat   SATE.TEAS

sword[1]
Arthur's sword   CALIBURN
    ESCALIBOR.EXCALIBUR
blunted sword   CURTEIN
broad-bladed
—curved   SEAX
—short   CURTAL-AX
Carroll's sword   VORPAL
cavalry sword   SABRE
Celtic   CLAYMORE
ceremonial   CURTEIN
Charlemagne's
   sword   FLAMBERGE
curved   SABRE.S(C)IMITAR
Damascene   DAMASCUS BLADE
Doge's bodyguard's
   sword   SCHIAVONE
duelling   SHARP.SMALLSWORD
fencing weapon   EPEE.FOIL
    SMALLSWORD
fighting   SPADROON
French (armé
   blanche)   WHITE ARM
German   SCHLAGER
Indian   TULWAR
long and slender   RAPIER
naval   CUTLASS
—short   HANGER
Norse myth   BALMUNG.GRAM
obsolete   FOX
old   GLAIVE
Persian   S(C)IMITAR
rapier (Shakespeare)   TUCK
rare   GLADIUS
St George's sword   ASCALON
    ASKELON
Scottish   CLAYMORE
    SPURTLE-BLADE
—rusty   SHABBLE
short   ESTOC

—curved   FALCHION
    FAULCHI(O)N
—naval   HANGER
Siegfried's sword   BALMUNG
Sigmund's sword   GRAM
    NOTHUNG
Sir Bevis's sword   MORGLAY
small   SHARP
Spanish   BILBO.ESPADA
    ESTOQUE
Turkish   SCIMITAR
two-edged   PATA
without a point   CURTANA
wooden   WASTER

sword[2]
sword bearer   SCABBARD
sword *dance*   WORDS
sword swallower   SCABBARD

swots *up*(D) ↑   STOWS
Sydney's box   CARTON
symbol   SYM
synonym   SYN
Syriac
alphabet   ESTRANG(H)ELO
bishop   ABBA
Syrian
Aramaic dialect   SYRIAC
bishop   ABBA
capital   DAMASCUS.S
chief priest (Roman)   SYRIARCH
cloth   AB(B)A.ABAYA
garment   AB(B)A.ABAYA
hyrax   DAMAN
leader   S
nomad   SARACEN
plant   ROSE OF JERICHO
pot herb   JEW'S MALLOW
rue   HARMALA.HARMEL
sect   DRUSE.DRUZ(E)
society   REMOBOTH
tobacco   LATAKIA
syrup   SYR
system
system made in. . .   MAIDEN
system for taxes   TEXAS
system of gears   RAGES
Système Internationale   SI

T

bandage. bar. *bone. cart. cloth. cross(ed).* hundred and sixty. hundred and sixty thousand. *half-dry.* it. junction. model. *perfect letter.* plate. rail. shirt. square. tau. *te. tea. tee.* temperature. tenor. tera-. tesla. Thailand. the. theta. time. to. ton(ne). tritium. Tuesday

tab	BILL	take in	COD.CON.DO
table	TIMES	*take* in	incl IN
table-*top*(D)	T	•support *takes* in. . .	BRAIN
tail		*take in* a. . .	incl A
tail *first*		*take in* *	incl *
•cat's tail *first*	SCAT	•w-e *take in* oars, *say*	WORSE
tail of queue	E	*take* it *to heart*	incl IT
Tail-end Charlie	E	take liberty	ENSLAVE
tail-*ender*	L	*take* money *from*	omit L
tail of the. . .	E	*take* nothing *in*	incl O
tail off th(e). . .	TH	take notice	NB
tailing ma(n)	MA	take off	APE.COPY
tail-less rabbi(t)	RABBI	*take off* a. . .	omit A
tails I win	IN	*take off* *	omit *
tails you lose	-UE	•fat(al) *to take off* a pound	FAT
tailored to his. . .	HOIST	*take off first* quarter	omit Q
Taiwan	RC	*take off* (first) quarter	
take	REC		omit N.S.E.W
take a count. . .	TOUCAN	•*take off* first quarter of	
take a day *off*	omit AD.D	(s)wing	WING
•*take* day *off*, (D)on	ON	•*take off* second quarter of	
•*take* a day *off*, l(ad)	L	s(w)ing	SING
take a day *off*	omit MON, etc	•*take off* third quarter of	
•*take* day *off*, (fri)end	END	swi(n)g	SWIG
take a toss riding	INGRID	*take* on	incl ON
takes	X	*take* on a. . .	end with A
•rocket *takes* measure	VIXEN	*take* on a new. . .	WANE.WEAN
•chesspiece *takes* another		*take out* a. . .	omit A
	MANXMAN	*take out* *	omit *
take about. . .	incl RE	•rat(her) *take out* her. . .	RAT
•mother *takes* about. . .	MARE	*take part of* Anto/nio be/fore. . .	
take apart	ACT		NIOBE
take away a. . .	omit A	*take part in* h/ome ga/mes	OMEGA
take away *	omit *	*take some*	
•m(ind)ing Indian *take-away*	MING	•he *takes some* artificial. . .	HEART
•the *Spanish* take-away	omit EL	*take* steps	PESTS
take-away sign	MINUS	*take* time *off*	omit AGE or T
take down	EAT	*take* to. . .	incl TO
take * *from*	omit *	•good men *take* to. . .	PIMENTO
•*take* one *from* ma(i)n. . .	MAN	*take to heart* a. . .	incl A
take heart *from* re(lat)ed. . .	REED	*take to heart* *	incl *
take heart out of c(it)y	CY	•doctors *take* boy *to heart*	MOBS
take in	EAT	*take up* golf(D) ↑	FLOG

*take * from*	omit *	teapot	BILLY
•*take* a hundred *from*		teatime	IV
account	COUNT	tea for two	CHA-CHA
taken aback, Liam...⟨	MAIL	teas	TS.TT
*taken to heart by *	incl in *	**tea²**	
•boy *taken to heart by*		black	CAPER-TEA
doctors	MOBS	Chinese	
taken from P/rover/bs	ROVER	—black	BOHEA.CAPER-TEA
*taken in by *	incl in *		CONGO(U)
•men *taken in by* editor	EMEND		LAPSANG SOUCHONG
takes blame	MABEL		KEEMUN.OOLONG
taking heart from...	AKIN		OULONG.PADRA.PEKOE
taking heart from			POUCHONG
Ge(rm)an...	GEAN	—green	HYSON.TWANKAY
*taking in *	incl *	Indian	ASSAM.DARJEELING
•editor *taking in* men	EMEND	Labrador	LEDUM
taking part in		Mexican	CHIA
nov/el even/ts	ELEVEN	Paraguayan	MATE
taking thought	ABSTRACTION	purgative	SENNA
tales	ANA	South American	
talent	NOUS		YERBA (DE MATE)
talk		**teacher**	MISS.SIR
talk of Bonn	GERMAN	teachers	NUT.STAFF
talk of Paris	FRENCH	**team**	SIDE.XI.XV
talk of rain	REI(G)N	team's quarters	ELEVENSES
talk of Sidney	STRINE	**tear**	
talk of the Costa del Sol	SPANISH	mothers *in tears*	THERMOS
talk of the East End	COCKNEY	tear *about*⟨	PIR
talking bird	BURRED	*tear* a T-shirt	ATHIRST
Tamil	TAM	*tear to pieces* in ring at...	
tangent	TAN		TRAINING
tangled roots	TORSO	tear*about*	RATE.TARE
tanner (sixpence)	VID.VIP	tear*away*	RATE.TARE
Tantulus's prisoner	DECANTER	*tearing* about	U-BOAT
Tanzania	EAT.EAZ	*tearing about*	TANGIER
taps	CH	*tore up* papers	SAPPER
tar	AB	*torn* trews	STREW
(*see also* sailor)		torn volume	RENT BOOK
tau	T	**tease**	TS.TT
tax	SCOT.VAT	*tease* listeners	RE-ENLISTS
tax-free	ORATED	**technology**	
tax inspector	SUPERCHARGER	technology school	CAT
tax *return*⟨	TAV	technology institute	MIT
te	T	**tee**	AFTER(S)
tea¹	CHA(R).T	tee *off*	omit T
tea-*blend*	ATE.EAT	tee *off*	-EET
tea *break*	ATE.EAT	teed *off*	-ETED
tea *in mess*	ATE.EAT	tee(s)	PEG.T.(TS.TT)
tea-*mixture*	ATE.EAT	**teenager**	UNDERSCORE

teepee, say	TP
teetotal	TT
telegraph	TEL
telegraph office	TO
telegram	TEL
telepathy	ESP
telephone	BLOWER.RING.TEL
hence	
•second telephone	BRING
•telephone *about* a race	RATTING
•telephone rental	RINGLET
telephone circuit	RING
teleprinter	TPR
television	TV
tempered <u>steel</u>	LEETS.STELE
temporary darn	STOP-GAP
ten¹	
ten	CHI.CROSS.IO.X
hence	
•ten about...	CHIC
•ten-ten	CHICHI
•ten quiet...	CHIP
and	
•doublecross	TWENTY
•ten above...	CROSSOVER
•ten land...	CROSS COUNTRY
and	
•spoil ten...	MARIO
•stroke ten...	PATIO
•ten reserves	IOTA
and	
•monkey *has* ten...	APEX
•ten *behind* the Post Office	POX
•ten *drunk*	AXLE
<u>ten</u> *letters*	ENT.NET
ten²	
10SE	TENNESSEE
based	DECIMAL.DENARY
cents	DIME
combining form	DECA-
dollar bill	SAWBUCK.TENSPOT
Christmas presents	LORDS
Commandments	DECALOGUE
	FINGERNAILS
Downing Street	LEADER'S
	ADDRESS
events	DECATHLON
fold	DECUPLE
gallon hat	SOMBRERO

gram(me)s	DECAGRAM(ME)
Green...	BOTTLES
groups	DECAD.DECADE.DENARY
having ten	
—arms	DECAPODAL
	DECAPODAN
	DECAPODOUS
—columns	DECASTYLE
—faces	DECAHEDRON
—feet	DECAPODAL.DECAPODAN
	DECAPODOUS
—lines (poem)	DECASTICH
—parts	DECAMEROUS
—pistils	DECAGYNIAN
	DECAGYNOUS
—sides	DECAGON
—stamens	DECANDRIAN
	DECANDROUS
—syllables	DECASYLLABLE
litres	DECALITRE
Lost Tribes	ASHER.EPHRAIM.DAN
	GAD.ISSACHAR.MANNASEH
	NAPHTALI.REUBEN
	SIMEON.ZEBULUN
men (Roman)	DECEMVIR
metres	DECAMETRE
steres	DECASTERE
ten-nil *reverse*⟨	LINNET
thousand	MYRIAD.X
years	DECADE.DECENNARY
	DECENNIUM
tenanted	ISLET
tender shark	NURSE
Tennessee Valley Authority	TVA
tenor	T.TEN
tenth	
tenth in methane series	DECANE
tenth of	
—are	DECIARE
—bel	DECIBEL
—franc	DECIME
—gram(me)	DECIGRAM(ME)
—litre	DECILITRE
—metre	DECIMETRE
—normal concentration	
	DECINORMAL
—stere	DECISTERE
tentmaker	PAUL
tenuto	TENE

terminate	
terminal	POLE
terminal illness	S
terminate lease	E
termination of tenancy	Y
termini of railway	RY
terrace	TER(R)
terrible	
terrible heat	HATE
terribly cruel	LUCRE
t(erribl)y *heartless*	TY
terriers	TA
hence	
•crossed terriers	TAX
•Terriers gave blood	TABLED
•Terriers I led	TAILED
terrifying ascent	SECANT
territorials	TA
Territorial Decoration	TD
Territorial Force (Reserve)	TF(R)
(*see also* army.reserve.terriers)	
territory	TER(R)
terrorists	ETA.IRA.PLO.PROVOS
hence	
•terrorist exercise	ETAPE
•terrorists, note	IRATE
•terrorist branch	PLOWING
tesla	T
test	ORAL.MOT
test match	CHECKMATE.TRIAL
	MARRIAGE
test playing	AUDITION
testy fellow	EXAMINER
text	MS
texturised vegetable protein	TVP
Thailand	T
(*see also* Siamese)	
thank	
thank you letter	COLLINS
thanks	TA
hence	
•thanks, man	TAMALE
•thanks members	TAMPS
•thanks the *French*...	TALE(S)
thank*less*	omit TA
that	
that *French*...	CELA
that is	IE.SC
hence	

•bog that is...	BOGIE
•that's *about* right	IRE
•that's right	-IER
and	
•that is current...	SCAMP
•that is *in* the e-ar	ESCAR
•that is torn	SCRIPT
that man	HIM
that old...	YT
that Roman...	ID
that woman	HER
that you cause to know	SCI FA
	SCIRE FACIAS
that's *been stolen*	omit IE or SC
that's *missing*	omit IE or SC
that's not right	LEFT.LARBOARD
	PORT
that's *not* right	omit R
•F(r)ee? That's *not* right!	FEE
that's right	STARBOARD
the¹	
the alien = foreign	
•the *alien*...	AL.DAS.DER.DIE.EL
	IL.LE.LA.LAS.LES.LOS
the *Arabic*...	AL
hence	
•drink *with* the *Arabic*...	TOTAL
•the *Arabic in* m-e	MALE
•the *Arabic* lily	ALARUM
the *Camptown*...	DE
hence	
•the *Camptown* drink	DECIDER
	DEPORT
•the *Camptown* money	DECENT
•the *Camptown* trail	DESCENT
the *foreign*...(*see* the alien *above*)	
the *French (style)*...	LA.LE.LES
hence	
•circle the *French*...	HOOPLA
•the *French-style* bird	LAMINA
•the *French in* F-red	FLARED
and	
•require the *French*...	NEEDLE
•the *French* gentleman	LET-OFF
•the *French in* need, *say*	KNEELED
and	
•bird *without* the	
French...	COOLEST
•hit the *French*...	COUPLES

•the *French* boy	LESSON
the *French/English*...	LATHE
	LETHE
the *German*...	DAS.DER.DIE
the *Italian*...	IL.LA.LE.LO
hence	
•the *Italian* has one bill	ILIAC
•the *Italian* street	LAST
•master the *Italian*...	MALE
•the *Italian* honour	LOOM
the *old (style)*...	YE
hence	
•the *old* people	YEMEN
•the *old* record-editor	YELPED
•the *old-style* students	YELL
the *Spanish*...	EL.LA.LAS.LOS
hence	
•drink the *Spanish*...	LAPEL
•the *Spanish* alcove	ELAPSE
•the *Spanish in* transport	RELY
and	
•firm *with* the *Spanish*...	COLA
•the *Spanish* hut	LASHED
•the *Spanish in* Cyprus	CLAY
and	
•knock out the *Spanish*...	KOLAS
•the *Spanish* in Communist Party	CLASP
•the *Spanish* vehicles	LASCARS
and	
•guns the *Spanish*...	HALOS
•the *Spanish* can...	LOSABLE
•the *Spanish in* church	CLOSE
the *Spanish/French*...	ELLA
the *Spanish/German*...	ELDER

the²

part of the...	T.TH.H.HE.E
some of the...	T.TH.H.HE.E
the *beginning*	T
the *border of*...	T
the *borders of*...	TE
the *central*...	H
the *central*...	incl THE
•use the *Central* fo-r...	FOTHER
the *centre*	H
the *climbing*...(D) ↑	EHT
the *contents*	incl THE
•wea-r the *contents*...	WEATHER
the *contents*	incl in TH-E

•about th-e *contents*...	THREE
the *course*	THEE.THEN.THEW
the *directions*	THESE.THEWS
the *end*	E
the *entrant*	incl THE
•see-s the *entrant*	SEETHES
the *entrant*	T
the *extremes*	TE
the *finish*	E
the *first*...	T
the *first slice of* apple	TAP
th(e) *footloose*(D)...	TH
the *front end*	T
(t)he *headless*...	HE
t(h)e *heartless*...	TE
hence	
•t(h)e *heartless* man	TEAL
•t(h)e *heartless* woman	TENANCY
•t(h)e *heartless* US agent	TEGMAN
the *initial*...	T
the *initiative*	T
the *last*...	E
the *leader*	T
the *mixture*	ETH.HET
t(he) *non-male*	T
the *novel*...	ETH.HET
the *outside*	TH-E
•queen *with* th-e *outside*...	THERE
the *penultimate*...	H
the *point*	T
the *second*...	H
th(e) *short*...	TH
the *summit*(D)	T
the *third*...	E
the *Twist*	ETH.HET
th(e) *Unfinished*...	TH
the *wrong*...	ETH.HET
the *wrong way*	ETH.HET

the³

the *beginning of* life	L
the *bitter end*	R
the *borders of* France	FE
the *centre of* Paris	R
the *end of* it	T
the *final* straw	W
the *finish of* play	Y
the *first* ball	B
the *first slice of* apple	AP
the *footloose* tram(p)(D)	TRAM

the initial gesture	G	**think**	
the last of winter	R	think *about*	MUS-E
the last *resort*	STEALTH	*think* right	WRITE
the leader of Russian. . .	R	**third**	C
The Lion's *Head*	L	third half	SIXTH
the⁴		third man	ABEL.LIME
the boy's	HIS	*third of* August	AU.GU.ST
the girl's	HER	*third of* August	G
the lady's. . .	HER	*third out of* four	U
the man's. . .	HIS	third-rate	C
the old	AGED	**thirteen**	BAKER'S DOZEN
the others	EM.DEM.THEM		DEVIL'S DOZEN.LONG DOZEN
the same	DITTO.DO		RL TEAM.UNLUCKY
the other's	THEIR	thirteen witches	COVEN
the subject	IT	thirteenth loaf	MAKEWEIGHT
theatre		**thirty**	
theatre company	REP	thirty	L.LA(M)BDA
hence		—days	APR.JUN.NOV.SEP
•Oriental theatre	REPINE	—requiem masses	TRENTAL
•theatre atmosphere	REPAIR	—seconds	MIN
•theatre is not. . .	REPAINT	—thousand	L.LA(M)BDA
•theatre royal	REPR-	thirty-three	DISC.LP.RECORD
theatre designer		thirty-nine	
	PLASTIC SURGEON	—Books	OT
theatre *movement*	THEREAT	—in novel	STEPS
theatre performer	SURGEON	—in religious belief	ARTICLES
theatrical part	BOX.GODS	**this**	
	PROSCENIUM	this country	UK
	STAGE.WINGS	this era	AD
their		this *foreign*. . .	CE.CET.CETTE
Their Majesties	MM	this *French*. . .	CE.CET.CETTE
Their Royal Highnesses	TRH	this *in France*	CE.CET.CETTE
theism	(*see* belief)	this *in Rome*	HIC
them	EM	th(is) is *missing*	TH
theologian	ANSELM.BD.BEDE.DD	this month	INST(ANT)
	ORIGEN	this *Roman*. . .	HIC
therapy	(*see* treat²)	this time	AD
there in France	LA	this way	SO.THUS
these		this year	HA
these *characters*	SHEET	*this way* leads	DALES
these days	AD		DEALS.SLADE
these in France	CES	**Thomas**	THO(S)
they		**T(h)orah**	PENTATEUCH
they *initially*	T	**though**	
they object	THEM	though *brief*	THO
they say no	KNOW	though, *say*	THEM.THOSE
thin		**thousand**	CHILIAD.G.K.M.X
thin tycoon	SPARE WHEEL	combining form	KILO-
thinner	ACETONE.TURPENTINE	group	CHILIAD

728

one and a half thousand	ID	—bundles of	
thousand and one	MI	stamens	TRIADELPHOUS
thousand million	BILLION	—carpels	TRICARPELLARY
	MILLARD	—cells	TRILOCULAR
thousand years	MILLENARY	—colours	TRICHRO(MAT)IC
	MILLENIUM		TRICOLOUR(ED)
thousands	MM	—consonants	TRICONSONANTAL
thousandth	MILLESIMAL	—corners	TRICORN(E)
—anniversary	MILLENARY	—cusps	TRICUSPID
	MILLENIUM		TRITUBERCULAR
three	CROWD.GAMMA	—dimensions	TRIDIMENSIONAL
Bs	BACH.BEETHOVEN.BRAHMS	—electrodes	TRIODE
blind. . .	MICE	—ethyl groups	TRIETHYL
boys	PATERNAL	—extremities	TRINACRIAN
cards	P(AI)RIAL.PAIR-ROYAL		TRINACRIFORM
choices	TRILEMMA	—faces	TRIFACIAL.TRIHEDRAL
Christmas presents	FRENCH HENS	—feet	TRIPEDAL
cleft in three	TRIFID.TRIPARTITE	—fingers	TRIDACTYLOUS
combining form	TER-.TRI-	—focal lengths	TRIFOCAL
cornered hat	TRICORN(E)	—forks	TRIFURCATE(D)
days	TRIDIUM	—forms	TRIFORM(ED)
Estates of the Realm	COMMONS		TRIMORPHIC.TRIMORPHOUS
	LORDS SPIRITUAL	—furrows	TRISULCATE
	LORDS TEMPORAL	—heads	TRICEPHALOUS.TRICEPS
Fs	FAIR RENT.FAIR SALE	—horns	TRICERATOPS
	FAIR TENURE		TRICORN(E)
Fates	(*see* Fates)	—hydrogen atoms	TRIACID
feet	YARD		TRIBASIC
figures	LID	—hydroxyl groups	TRIHYDRIC
fold	TRI(N)AL.TRIPLEX	—interlaced arcs	TRIQUETRAL
	TRIPLICATE	—languages	TRIGLOT
Furies	(*see* Furies)		TRILINGUAL
girls	VIVALDI	—leaflets	TERNATE.TRIFOLIATE
Graces	(*see* Graces)	—leaves	TRIFOLIATE
grooved tablet	TRIGLYPH		TRIPHYLLOUS
groups	P(AI)RIAL.TERN(ION)	—legs	TRIPOD(AL)
	TERZETTO.TRIAD.TRILOGY	—letters	TRILITERAL
	TRINE.TRINITY.TRIO.TRIPLE	—lines	TRIGRAMM(AT)IC
Harpies	(*see* Harpies)		TRILINEAR
handed murderer	CUTTHROAT	—lobes	TREFOILED
having three			TRILOBATE(D).TRILOBE(D)
—apses	TRIAPS(ID)AL	—marriages	TRIGAMOUS
—atoms	TRIATOMIC	—measures	TRIMETER.TRIMETRIC
—axes	TRIAXIAL.TRIAXONIC	—methyl radicals	TRIMETHYL
—beats	TRICOTIC.TRICOTOUS	—oxygen atoms	TRIOXIDE
—bodies	TRICORPORATE	—parts	TRIMEROUS.TRIPARTITE
—branches	TRICHOTOMOUS	—petals	TRIPETALOUS
	TRIFURCATE(D)	—phenyl groups	TRIPHENYL-
	TRIGEMINAL.TRISULCATE	—pistils	TRIGYNIAN.TRYGYNOUS

—points	TRICUSPID(ATE)	Jewels	RIGHT CONDUCT
	TRINACRIAN.TRINACRIFORM		RIGHT FAITH
—prongs	TRIDENT(AL)		RIGHT KNOWLEDGE
	TRIDENTATE.TRIDENTED	legged race	MANX
	TRINACRIAN.TRINACRIFORM	letter word	TRILITERAL
—rays	TRIACT(INAL).TRIACTINE	lines	TERCET.TERZETTA
	TRIRADIAL.TRIRADIATE	lobed fossil	TRILOBITE
—ribs	TRICOSTATE	man	TRIAL
—rings	TRICYCLIC	men in power	TRIUMVIRATE
—rows	TRIFARIOUS.TRISTICHOUS	monthly	TRIMONTHLY
—sides	TRILATERAL	months	TRIMESTER
—stamens	TRIANDRIAN	Musketeers	ARAMIS.ATHOS
	TRIANDROUS		PORTHOS
—strings	TRICHORD	nil	THIRTY
—styles	TRIGYNIAN.TRIGYNOUS	one of three at birth	TRIPLET
—sulphur atoms	TRISULPHIDE	people	CROWD
	TRITHIONIC		ETERNAL TRIANGLE
—teeth	TRIDENTATE.TRIDENTED	persons	
—terms	TRINOMIAL.TRIONYM	—ruling	TRIARCHY
—times normal number of		—speaking	TRIALOGUE
chromosomes	TRIPLOID	pipped card or domino	TREY
—times molecular mass	TRIMERIC	pronged spear	TRIDENT
—toes	TRIDACTYL(OUS)	quarters	-ENE.-ESE.NEW.-NSE
—tubercles	TRITUBERCULAR		SEN.SEW.WEN
—unequal axes	TRICLINIC	quarters of an hour	OUR
—valencies	TERVALENT	tablets	TRIPTYCH
	TRIATOMIC.TRIVALENT	thousand	B
—valves	TRIVALVE(D)	three of spades	SPA.DES
	TRIVALVULAR	times	TREBLE.TRIPLE
—ways	TRIFARIOUS	—a day	TID
—whorls	TRICYCLIC	tragedies	TRILOGY
—wives	TRIGAMOUS.TRIGAMY	under par	ALBATROSS
	TRIGYNIAN.TRIGYNOUS	wheeled vehicle	TRICAR
—wings	TRIPTEROUS		TRICYCLE.TRISHAW
—words	TRINOMIAL	winged aeroplane	TRIPLANE
	TRIONYM(AL)	Wise Men (Magi)	BALTHAZAR
—xylem strands	TRIARCH		GASPAR.MELCHIOR
—yearly occurrences	TRIENNIAL	yearly	TRIENNIAL
—wings	TRIPLANE.TRIPTEROUS	**thresh grain**	BEATRICE
—having use of three		**threw**	(*see* throw)
elements	TRIPHIBIOUS	**through**	PER
hulled boat	TRIMARAN	through, *say*	THREW
hundred	B	*through* *	incl in *
—years	TERCENTENARY	•run *through* exercises	PRUNE
in		through*out*	PE-R
—education	R	*through*out	OU-T
—one	TRINITY.TRIUNE	*throughout* *	incl in *
—the fountain	COINS	•sleep *thoughout* ship	SNAPS
Jerome characters	BOATMEN	through passage	VIADUCT

*through*put	PU-T	pony	TANGUN
throw		porch	TORAN
throw *around*	SH-Y	priest	LAMA
throw *around on*⟨...	NO	religious leader	DALAI LAMA
throw around <u>on her</u>...	HERON		PANCHEN LAMA
throw away a...	omit A	scarf	KATA
throw away money	omit L	sheep	SHAHPU.SHAPO
throw away *	omit *	monument	STUPA
•h(old)er *threw away* old...	HER	tribe	SHERPA
throw <u>caution</u> *to the*		wild ass	KIANG.KYANG
<u>winds</u>	AUCTION	**tidy**	
throw in a...	incl A	tidy sum	NEAT FIGURE
throw in *	incl *	*tidying* <u>a tress</u>	ASSERT
•two hundred *thrown*		**tie**	X
into o-ur...	OCCUR	tie *design*	DRAW
throw out a...	omit A	tie *design*	-ITE
throw out <u>man or</u>...	ROMAN	tie game DRAWBRIDGE.TIEPOLO	
throw out *...	omit *	tie-*up*(D) ↑	EIT.ROOM
•*throw* fool *out of* cl(ass)	CL	tied *in knots*	DIET.EDIT.TIDE
throw over <u>regime</u>	EMIGRE	*tied* <u>ropes</u>	PORES.SPORE
throw over <u>bows</u>⟨	SWOB	*tied* <u>Tory</u> *in knots*	RYOT.TROY
throw <u>rope</u>	PORE	**tierce**	TC
throw *up*(D) ↑	BOL	**till forbidden**	TF
throw up bat(D) ↑	TAB	**tilting object**	WINDMILL
throw*back*⟨	BOL	**timber**	
throwback part⟨	TRAP	timber merchant	ALDERMAN
threw <u>stones</u>	ONSETS	timber town	DEAL
thrust ahead	RAMON	**time^1** (A)EON.AGE.ENEMY.ERA	
Thursday	TH(UR)		HR.MO.SEC.T.YR
thus	SIC.SO	hence	
Tibetan		•time *in* ship	SAGES
abominable snowman	YETI	•student *has* time...	LEON
animal	(GIANT) PANDA	•time *to* celebrate	ERASING
antelope	GOA	•time *in* t-ough...	THROUGH
barley dish	TSAMBA	•time *to* marry	TOWED
Buddhist sect	GELUK PA	•worker *behind* time	SECANT
	SAKYA PA	•time *to* leave	GOT
capital	LHASA.T	•priest *in* time...	YABBER
cloth	KATA	(*see also* measure)	
dog LHASA APSO.SHIH TZU		**time^2**	
goat	TAKIN	time *of backwardness*⟨	EMIT
hybrid cattle	DSO(MO).DZO	time's *up*(D) ↑	EMIT.-RY
JOMO.Z(H)O.ZHOMO		time-server	CONVICT
ZOBO.ZOBU		time-*sharing* EM-IT.IM-TE.M-ITE	
language	PALI	time *warp*	EMIT
leader	LAMA.T	<u>tim</u>(e) *without end*	TIM
mysterious beast	YETI	times	X
ox SARLAC.SARLAK.YAK.Z(H)O		<u>times</u> *change*	EMITS.SMITE
—pannier	YAKHDAN	Times factor	NEWSAGENT

Times *leader*	T
Times Educational Supplement	TES
Times Literary Supplement	TLS
tin[1]	CAN.MONEY.SN
hence	
•tin is. . .	CANIS
•tinman	CANAL.CANED
	CANTED
•tin monkey	CANAPE
and	
•tin fish	SNIDE
•tin monkey	SNAPE
•tin mineral	SNORE
tin[2]	
tin fish	TORPEDO
tin-*opener*	T
tinned	(in) CA-N.(in) TI-N
tinker	SLY
tinker *about*	S-LY
tinker *about*⟨	REKNIT
tip	
asparagus *tip*	A
tip *backwards*⟨	PIT
*tip back*ward⟨	DRAW
tip of iceberg	I
tip over	ROVE
tip over jar⟨	RAJ
tip over vase	SAVE
tip *up*(D) ↑	PIT
tip up pots(D) ↑	STOP
tip stew⟨	WETS
tiptop	PEAK
tip*top*(D)	T
*tip*top⟨	POT
tiptop wear	(C)OVERALL
tipsy state	TASTE.TEATS
tire	
tired *out*	DETRI-
tires *worn*	RITES.TRIES
tissue of lies	SILE
Titus	TIT
to	
to a large extent th(e)	TH
to a large extent fish	HERRING
to do with	RE
	(*see* about[2])
to infinity	AD INF(INITUM)
to left	TOL.TOLT
to one side	TOWING
to right	TOR.TORT
to some extent	
go/od in/side. . .	ODIN
to take leave	PPC.TTL
to the *French*. . .	ALA.AU.AUX
hence	
•to the *French* doctor	ALAMO
•to the *French* spirit	AURUM
•to the *French* in. . .	AUXIN
to the *Italian*. . .	AL
hence	
•add lard to the *Italian*. . .	FATAL
•to the *Italian* group	ALLOT
•to the *Italian* in b-ed	BALED
to the beginning	AD INIT(IUM)
to the end	AD FINEM
to the ear, airs. . .	HEIRS
to the fore in nearly every way	
	NEW
to *turn* to⟨	OTTO
to windward	UP
toady	JENKINS
toast	CHEERS
French toast	BON SANTE
German toast	GESUNDHEIT
Irish toast	SLAINTE
Roman toast	BENE VOBIS
Scandinavian toast	SKOAL
very thin toast	MELBA
today	AD
toe[1]	LEGEND
twiddling toes	TOSE
toe[2]	
one-toed	MONDACTYLOUS
two-toed	DIDACTYLOUS
three-toed	TRIDACTYLOUS
four-toed	TETRADACTYLOUS
five-toed	PENTADACTYLOUS
six-toed	HEXADACTYLOUS
even-toed	ARTIODACTYLOUS
many-toed	POLYDACTYLOUS
together once	AT ONE TIME
Togo	TG
told	
told lies	LYSE
told *off*	DOLT
told, *say*	TOLLED
Toledo housing	SCABBARD

Tom		**torn**	(*see* tear)
Tom's tongue	CLAPPER	**torpedo-boat**	MTB.TB
Tommy	SOLDIER	torpedo-boat destroyer	TBD
Tommy's father	CHAPLAIN	*tortuous* lane	ELAN.LEAN
	PADRE	*tortured by* fire	RIFE
tome	TOM(US)	**Tory**	BLUE.C.CON
ton(ne)	T	Tory *backing*⟨	NOC
too[1]		**toss**	
too long for man	MANE.MANY	ship *tossed about*	HIPS.PISH
too much m/one/y	ONE	toss *up*(D) ↑	NIPS
too short to spa(n)	SPA	*toss up* Ben's...(D) ↑	SNEB
too small for arm(y)	ARM	*toss up* coin	ICON
too[2]		*tossed* caber	ACERB.BRACE
indicates palindrome:		*tossed about* in the...	THINE
•served *up, too*(D)	DID	*tossed out* into an...	NATION
•send *back, too*	REFER	**Tosti's song**	TATA
top	APEX	*tottering* steps	PESTS
top and bottom of the...(D)	TE	**touch**	
top and tail (t)wi(g̅)	WI	*touch of* garlic	G
top branch	HEAD OFFICE	touchingly written	TYPED
top company man	MD	**tough**	
top drawer(D)	U	tough defender	HARDBACK
top d̅rawer	U	tough joint	HARD SHOULDER
top gear	HAT	tough worker	NUTANT
top man	CO.KING	**tour**	
top man(D)	M	Tour de France	EIFFEL(TOWER)
top (m̅)an(D)	AN	*tour of* Rome	MORE
top mark	A.ALPHA	*toured by* *	incl in *
top mount	BESTRIDE	•north *toured by* bu-s	BUNS
top of head	VERTEX	touring car	GT
top of head(D)	H	*touring* car	ARC
top of t̅he...(D)	T	*touring* a...	incl A
top of t̅he chart(D)	C	*touring* *	incl *
top of the c̅hart	(TRUE) NORTH	•bu-s *touring* north	BUNS
top race	CROWN DERBY	**Tourist Trophy**	TT
top specialist	HAIRDRESSER	**tower**	CARTHORSE.SHIRE
	TRICHOLOGIST		TRACTOR
top trophy	GOLD.SCALP	tower maintenance	KEEP
top *up*(D) ↑	POT	**town**[1]	
topless (g)own	OWN	names used to represent country:	
topper	EXECUTIONER	•*Paris-style* hat	CHAPEAU
topping (p)lan	LAN		(*see also* from[4])
topple		**town**[2]	
dog *topples over*⟨	GOD	town-*centre*	OW
toppling over step⟨	PETS	Town Planning Institute	TPI
topsy-turvy reasons	SENORAS	town sub-office	TSO
tore	(see tear)		(*see also* city)
tormented animal	LAMINA	*toyed with* soup	OPUS
	MANILA	**tracked vehicle**	CAT.TANK

trade		translate		
trade name	TN	—*French* book	LIVRE	
Trade Union	TU	—*German* book	BUCH	
Trade Union Congress	TUC	—*Italian* book	LIBRO	
trader	INDIAMAN	—*Latin* book	LIBER	
	MERCHANT(MAN)	—*Spanish* book	LIBRO	
tradesmen	TU	translate		
tradesmen's *entrance*	T	—from *French*	DE	
traffic		—from *German*	VON	
traffic light	CAT'S-EYE	—from *Italian*	DA	
traffic signal	GO.STOP	—from *Latin*	AB	
tragic		—from *Spanish*	DE	
tragic <u>fate</u>	FEAT	—from the *French*	DELA.DES.DU	
tragic woman	ELECTRA.HECUBA	translate		
	NMEROPE	—into *French*	EN.ENTRE	
train	APT	—into *Italian*	DENTRO	
train fish	SCHOOL	—into *Latin*	INTRO	
train <u>seals</u>	SALES	—into *Spanish*	EN.ENTRE	
trained as <u>nurse</u>	RUNES	translate		
trainee	L	—the *French*...	LA.LE.LES	
training	PE.PT	—the *German*...	DAS.DER.DIE	
training <u>lion</u>	LINO	—the *Italian*...	GLI.IL.LA.LO.LE	
training manual	EXERCISE BOOK	—the *Spanish*...	EL.LA.LAS.LOS	
Training within Industry	TWI	*translated* <u>verse</u>	SEVER	
trains	BR.RY	translation	CRIB.TR	
tramp	HOBO.STEAMER	*translation of* <u>Norse</u>	SNORE	
tramples	STEPSON	translator	TR	
transactions	TR	*transmuted* <u>lead</u>	DALE.DEAL.LADE	
transactions <u>in grain</u>	RAINING	**transplant**		
transatlantic	US	*transplant* <u>shrub</u>	BRUSH	
(*see also* America)		*transplantation of* <u>trees</u>	RESET	
transcendental meditation	TM	*transplanted* <u>heart</u>	EARTH	
transcribe			HATER	
transcribe <u>older</u>...	DROLE	*transplanted heart*		
transcribing nearly all		*of* main...	MINA	
<u>Chines(e)</u>	INCHES	**transpose**		
transcription of <u>trio</u>	RIOT	*transpose* <u>result</u>	LUSTRE	
transform		*transpose* <u>reviled</u>...⟨	DELIVER	
transform <u>my pet</u>	EMPTY	**transport**		
transformation of <u>stage</u>...	GATES	transport	BR.BUS.CAB.CAR	
transforming into...	-TION		CART.ENTRANCE	
transgression of <u>rules</u>	LURES		RLY.RY.TRAM	
translate		hence		
translate		•transport expert	BRACE	
—*French* word	MOT	•transport school	BRETON	
—*German* word	WORT	•transport worker	BRANT	
—*Italian* word	PAROLA	and		
—*Latin* word	VERBUM	•transport army *by road*	BUSTARD	
—*Spanish* word	PALABRA	•transport chief	BUSKING	

•transport sheep	BUST-UP
and	
•transport fish	CABLING
•transport *in* front	CABLED
•transport *on* the *French*	
road	CABLE-WAY
and	
•transport *has* gone	CARAWAY
•transport quickly	CARAPACE
•transport *to* harbour	CARPORT
(*see also* motor)	
and	
•man *in* transport	RALLY
•mother *has* transport	MARLY
and	
•everybody *in* transport	RALLY
•mother *has* transport	MARY
and	
•transport a man. . .	TRAMMEL
•transport quiet in	
Greece	TRAMPING
Transport Officer	TO
Trans World Airlines	TWA
trap	GIN.MOUTH
trapped by *	incl in *
•one *trapped by* m-en	MIEN
trapping a. . .	incl A
trapping *	incl *
•m-en *trapping* one	MIEN
travel	
travel agency	CARRIAGE
travel <u>in car</u>	CAIRN
travel <u>west</u>	
•dog *travels* west⟨	GOD
traveller	REP
hence	
•traveller in the East	REPINE
•traveller isn't. . .	REPAINT
•traveller wandered	REPROVED
traveller's fare	PASSENGER
travelling bag	CARCASE
travelling <u>crane</u>	NACRE
treasury keeper	DRAGON
treat¹	
treated <u>timber</u>	TIMBRE
treating <u>flu</u>	-FUL
treatment of <u>yaws</u>	SWAY.WAYS
treat²	
treatment by/of/with:	

animals	ZOOTHERAPY
antigens	IMMUNOTHERAPY
blood serum	SEROTHERAPY
chemicals	CHEMOTHERAPY
children's diseases	PAEDIATRICS
combining chemicals	
	CHELATION THERAPY
deep X-rays etc.	DEEP THERAPY
defective eyesight	ORTHOPTICS
deformities in	
children	ORTHOP(A)EDICS
ORTHOP(A)EDY.ORTHOP(A)EDIA	
deformity or injury	
of bones	ORTHOP(A)EDICS
ORTHOP(A)EDY.ORTHOP(A)EDIA	
disturbed children	ORTHOGENICS
drug-induced sleep	
	NARCOTHERAPY
drugs having	
—opposite effects to	
disease	ALLOPATHY
—same effects as	
disease	HOM(O)EOPATHY
electric shocks	ECT
ELECTRO-CONVULSIVE THERAPY	
	SHOCK THERAPY
electricity	
	ELECTRO-THERAPEUTICS
	ELECTRO-THERAPY
essential oils	AROMATHERAPY
exercise	PHYSIOTHERAPY
extracts from animal	
organs	OPOTHERAPY
	ORGANOTHERAPY
eye muscles	ORTHOPTICS
faulty position of	
teeth	ORTHODONTICS
high body temperature	
	PYRETOTHERAPY
induced current	FARADISM
hypnosis etc.	
	PSYCHOTHERAPEUTICS
	PSYCHOTHERAPY
light	PHOTOTHERAPEUTICS
	PHOTOTHERAPY
low temperatures	CRYOTHERAPY
manipulation	OSTEOPATHY
many different	
drugs	POLYPHARMACY

massage	PHYSIOTHERAPEUTICS	American	
	PHYSIOTHERAPY	—larch	BLACK LARCH
mental illness			TAMARACK
	ORTHOPSYCHIATRY	—willow	PUSSY WILLOW
	PSYCHODRAMA	Amur cork tree	
movement	KINESIPATHY		PHELLODENDRON
	KINESITHERAPY	Antarctic beech	NOTHOFAGUS
mud baths	PELOTHERAPY	Antiar	UPAS
natural processes	NATUROPATHY	apple	PYRUS
neurosis	BEHAVIOUR THERAPY	'apple' tree	OAK
radiation	RADIOTHERAPEUTICS	Araucaria	MONKEY PUZZLE
	RADIOTHERAPY	arbor vitae	THUJA.THUYA
radium	CURIETHERAPY		TREE OF LIFE
salts of gold	CHRYSOTHERAPY	Arbutus	STRAWBERRY TREE
sun	HELIOTHERAPY	Aria	WHITEBEAM
ultraviolet rays	ACTINOTHERAPY	Arundinaria	BAMBOO
water	HYDROPATHY	ash	FRAXINUS
	HYDROTHERAPEUTICS	—sapling	GROUND ASH
	HYDROTHERAPY	aspen	ABELE.POPULUS
X-rays	RADIOTHERAPEUTICS		TREMBLING POPLAR
	RADIOTHERAPY	Aucuba	JAPANESE LAUREL

tree[1]

tree	ASH.FIR.MAY.OAK.PALM	Aucuparia	MOUNTAIN ASH
hence		balsam poplar	TACAMAHAC
•tree-god	ASHLAR	bamboo	ARUNDINARIA
•tree-ring	FIRRING.MAYO	baobab	ADANSONIA
•tree unknown	OAKY	Barbados cedar	JUNIPER
•tree in Greece	PALMING	bastard cedar	CEDRELA

tree[2]

		bay	LAUREL
Tree	ACTOR	beech	FAGUS
tree *climbing*(D) ↑	EMIL	Betula	BIRCH
tree expert	GENEALOGIST	birch	BETULA.BIRK
tree maintenance	SERVICE	bird cherry	HACKBERRY
tree worship	DENDROLATRY		HAGBERRY
	SERVICE	black	

tree[3]

some alternative names:		—larch	AMERICAN LARCH
Abele	ASPEN.POPLAR		TAMARACK
Abies	FIR	—mulberry	MORUS
acacia	WATTLE	—thorn	SLOE
acajou	CASHEW TREE	box	BUXUS
Adansonia	BAOBAB	Buxus	BOX
Aesculus	HORSE CHESTNUT	Brazil wood	SAP(P)IAN
alder	ALNUS	buckthorn	JUJUBE
almond	AMYGDALUS	Carpinus	HORNBEAM
amboyna	WALAN	cashew tree	ACAJOU
Amelanchier	JUNEBERRY	Castanea	CHESTNUT
	SHADBUSH	Casuarina	SWAMP OAK
	SNOWY MESPILUS	cedar	CEDRUS.DEODAR
		—gum	EUCALYPTUS
		Cedrela	RED CEDAR

Celtis	NETTLE TREE	horse chestnut	AESCULUS
Cercis	JUDAS TREE.REDBUD		CONKER TREE
chestnut	CASTANEA		HIPPOCANASTACEAE
Chilean pine	DRAUCARIA	hawthorn	CRATAEGUS
	MONKEY PUZZLE		THORN TREE.WHITETHORN
Chinese Dove tree	DAVIDIA	hazel	CORYLUS
cluster pine	PINASTER	hemlock	CONIUM
Conium	HEMLOCK	Himalayan cedar	DEODAR
conker tree	HORSE CHESTNUT	holly	ILEX
cornelian cherry	CORNEL	holm oak	HOLLY OAK.ILEX
	CORNUS	hop hornbeam	OSTRYA
Corylus	HAZEL	hornbeam	CARPINUS
cottonwood	POPULUS		WITCH HAZEL
cowrie pine	COWDIE.KAURI	incense cedar	LIBOCEDRUS
crab	MALUS	Japanese laurel	AUCUBA
Crataegus	HAWTHORN	Judas tree	CERCIS.REDBUD
Cydonia	QUINCE	jujube tree	ZIZYPHUS
cypress	CUPRESSUS	Juneberry	AMELANCHIER
damson	DAMASK PLUM		SHADBUSH
Davidia	CHINESE DOVE TREE	juniper	BARBADOS CEDAR
	GHOST TREE		JUNIPERUS
	HANDKERCHIEF TREE		PENCIL CEDAR.SAVIN(E)
deodar	HIMALAYAN CEDAR	Kauri pine	COWDIE.COWRIE
dogwood	CORNEL(IAN).CORNUS	laburnum	GOLDEN RAIN
Douglas fir	PSEUDOTSUGA	larch	LARIX
dragon tree	DRACAENA	Larix	LARCH
Draucaria	CHILEAN PINE	Librocedrus	INCENSE CEDAR
	MONKEY PUZZLE	lilac	SYRINGA
dwarf	BONSAI	lime	LIND(EN).TEIL.TILIA
elm	ULMUS	linden	LIME.TEIL.TILIA
eucalyptus	CEDAR GUM	liquidambar	SWEET GUM
evergreen oak	HOLM OAK	Liriodendron	TULIP TREE
exuding sugar	ALHAGI.MANNA	locust	ALGAR(R)OBA
	ASH.MANNA LARCH		ALGARROBO.CAROB
	TAMARISK		ROBINIA
false acacia	LOCUST TREE	magnolia	UMBRELLA TREE
	ROBINIA	maidenhair	GINGKO.GINKGO
fir	ABIES	Malus	CRAB
—with white marked		maple	ACER.MASTEL
needles	SILVER FIR	medlar	MESPILUS
forest tree	DRYAD	Mespilus	MEDLAR
fustet	YOUNG FUSTIC	mesquite	ALGAR(R)OBA
ghost tree	DAVIDIA		ALGARROBO
giving latex	MILKWOOD	miniature	BONSAI
golden rain	LABURNUM	monkey puzzle	CHILEAN PINE
great sallow	GOAT SALLOW		ARAUCARIA
	GOAT WILLOW	Morus	BLACK MULBERRY
gum	SAPOTA	mountain ash	QUICKEN (TREE)
handkerchief tree	DAVIDIA		QUICK BEAM.RODDIN

	ROWAN.SORB(IN).SORBUS	sacred	BO(DHI)
	WICKEN.WICKY.WITCHEN	Salix	SALLOW.WILLOW
mulberry	SYCAMINE	sallow	SALIX.WILLOW
—fig	SYCAMORE.SYCOMORE	sambuca	ELDER
nettle tree	CELTIS.HOOP ASH	Sapota	GUM
Nothofagus	ANTARCTIC BEECH	savin(e)	JUNIPER
nut pine	STONE PINE	screw pine	PANDANUS
oak	DURMAST.QUERCUS	Sequoia	MAMMOTH-TREE
—sapling	GROUND OAK		REDWOOD.WASHINGTONIA
oil palm	ELAEIS		WELLINGTONIA
osier	SALIX.SALLOW.WILLOW	service tree	SORB
	WIDDY.WITHE.WITHY	shadbush	AMELANCHIER
Ostrya	HOP HORNBEAM		JUNEBERRY
pagoda tree	SOPHORA	Siberian cedar	AROLLA
palm	(see palm)	silk-cotton tree	ERIODENDRON
palmetto	SABAL	sloe	BLACKTHORN
Pandanus	SCREW PINE	smoke tree	RHUS.SUMACH
papaw	CARICA.PAPAYA	Snowy Mespilus	AMELANCHIER
pear	PYRUS	Sophora	PAGODA TREE
Phellodendron	AMUR CORK TREE	sorbus	MOUNTAIN ASH
Picea	FIR.(NORWAY) SPRUCE		WHITEBEAM
pinaster	CLUSTER PINE	Spanish oak	ROBLE
Pinus	(SCOTCH, SCOTS) PINE	spindle tree	EUONYMUS
pitch tree	AMBOINA.KAURI PINE	spruce	PICEA
	SILVER FIR.SPRUCE	—fir	PICEA
plane	BUTTONWOOD.MAPLE	stone pine	NUT PINE
	PLATAN(E).PLATANUS	strawberry tree	ARBUTUS
poplar	ABELE.ASP(EN).POPULUS	sumach	RHUS.SMOKE BUSH
Populus	ASPEN.COTTONWOOD		SMOKE TREE
	POPLAR	swamp	
Pseudotsuga	DOUGLAS FIR	—cypress	TAXODIUM
Pterocarya	WING NUT	—oak	CASUARINA
Pyrus	APPLE.PEAR.WHITEBEAM	sweet gum	LIQUIDAMBAR
Quercus	OAK	Swiss stone pine	AROLLA
quince	CYDONIA		CEMBRA
red		sycamine	MULBERRY TREE
—cedar	CEDRELA	sycamore	ACER.PLANE
	VIRGINIAN JUNIPER		MULBERRY FIG
—gum	EUCALYPTUS	Syringa	LILAC
—pine	NORWAY PINE	tacamahac	BALSAM POPLAR
—wood	SEQUOIA	tallow tree	ALEURITES
	WELLINGTONIA		PENTADESMA.SAPIUM
Rhus	SMOKE BUSH	tamarack	BLACK LARCH
	SMOKE TREE.SUMACH		AMERICAN LARCH
Robinia	LOCUST TREE	Taxodium	SWAMP CYPRESS
	FALSE ACACIA	Taxus	YEW
rowan	SORBUS.MOUNTAIN ASH	teil	LIME.LINDEN
—like	SERVICE.SORB	terebinth	TURPENTINE TREE
Sabal	PALMETTO	thorntree	HAWTHORN

Thuja	ARBOR VITAE.THUYA
	TREE OF LIFE
Tilia	LIME.LINDEN
tree of	
—heaven	AILANTO.AILANTHUS
—life	ARBOR VITAE
	THUJA.THUYA
trembling poplar	ASPEN
tulip tree	LIRIODENDRON
Turkey oak	CERRIS
turpentine tree	TEREBINTH
ulmus	ELM
umbrella tree	ELKWOOD
	MAGNOLIA
upas	ANTIAR
Venetian sumach	FUSTET
Viburnum	WAYFARING TREE
Virginian juniper	RED CEDAR
Vitex	AGNUS CASTUS
walan	AMBOYNA
walnut	JUGLANS
Washingtonia	REDWOOD
	SEQUOIA
wattle	ACACIA
wax tree	JAPANESE SUMAC
	WAX MYRTLE
wayfaring tree	MEAL TREE
	VIBURNUM
Wellingtonia	REDWOOD
	SEQUOIA
whitebeam	ARIA.SORBUS.PYRUS
whitethorn	HAWTHORN
wild	
—apple	CRAB
—cherry	GEAN
willow	OSIER.SALIX
	SALLOW
	WIDDY.WITHE
	WITHY
wing nut	PTEROCARYA
witch hazel	HORNBEAM
	WYCH-ELM
with crown cut off	POLLARD
wych-elm	WITCH ELM.WITCHEN
	WITCH HAZEL
yew	TAXUS
Zizyphus	JUJUBE TREE
tree⁴	
tree, *say*	-TERY.-TRY

hence	
•half-standard tree	CEMETERY
•osier	BASKETRY
•twisted tree	BANDITRY
•river tree	INDUSTRY
•saucepan rack	PANTRY
•smelly tree	MUSKETRY
trembling lips	PILS.SLIP
tremulous speech	CHEEPS
trench digger	JCB.RE
trendy	IN
hence	
•ask trendy...	BEGIN
•trendy *in* ways	NINE.SINE.SINS
	WINE.WINS
•trendy people	INSET
Trent Bridge	NE
trial marriage	TEST MATCH
triangular	DELTA
tribe	DAN.GAD
tribute	CAIN
trick	
trick of fate	FEAT
tricky contest	BRIDGE.WHIST
tricky part	RAPT.TRAP
trim	
trim t/he len/gth	HELEN
trim ends	SEND
Trinidad and Tobago	TT
capital	PORT-OF-SPAIN
Trinity College	
Trinity College, Dublin	TCD
Trinity College of Music	TCL
trip over	JOURNEY'S END
trip over	ROVE
trip over step	PEST.PETS
trip over step〈	PETS
trip to Mars	STROMA
triumph	V
triumphant cry	IO
trivial sum	IP
troop	TP
trophy	
American football	SUPERBOWL
Australian football	
	PREMIERSHIP CUP
badminton	THOMAS CUP
	UBER CUP
baseball	CY YOUNG AWARD

bowling	WATERLOO CUP	JOHN PLAYER SPECIAL TROPHY
boxing	LONSDALE BELT	LANCE TODD AWARD
college football		PREMIERSHIP TROPHY
	HEISMAN TROPHY	—Australia WINFIELD CUP
coursing	WATERLOO CUP	rugby union WORLD CUP
cricket	GILLETTE CUP	—Australia/New Zealand
NATWEST TROPHY.THE ASHES		BLEDISLOE CUP
—Australia	SHEFFIELD SHIELD	—England/Scotland
—India	RANJI TROPHY	CALCUTTA CUP
—New Zealand	PLUNKET SHIELD	—New Zealand
—Pakistan		RANFURLY SHIELD
	QUAID-E-AZAM TROPHY	—South Africa CURRIE CUP
—South Africa	CURRIE SHIELD	shinty CAMANCHD CUP
	NISSAN SHIELD	show jumping
—West Indies	SHELL SHIELD	KING GEORGE V GOLD CUP
croquet	MACROBERTSON SHIELD	PRESIDENT'S CUP
	PRESIDENT'S CUP	QUEEN ELIZABETH II CUP
curling	STRATHCONA CUP	WORLD CUP
darts	BRITISH GOLD CUP	snooker EMBASSY CUP
	NATIONS CUP	POT BLACK CUP
golf	CURTIS CUP	soccer
HARRY VARDON TROPHY		FOOTBALL ASSOCIATION CUP
HOPMAN CUP.RYDER CUP		FOOTBALL LEAGUE CUP
WALKER CUP.WORLD CUP		FREIGHT ROVER CUP
greyhound racing		UEFA CUP.WORLD CUP
	SCURRY GOLD CUP	—amateur
horse racing	ASCOT GOLD CUP	FOOTBALL ASSOCIATION VASE
CHELTENHAM GOLD CUP		—South America
	CORONATION CUP	LIBERATORES CUP
	GOODWOOD CUP	table tennis CORBILLON CUP
ONE THOUSAND GUINEAS		SWAYTHLING CUP
TWO THOUSAND GUINEAS		tennis DAVIS CUP
—Australia	MELBOURNE CUP	FEDERATION CUP
ice hockey	CANADA CUP	NATIONS CUP.WIGHTMAN CUP
	HART TROPHY	WORLD CUP
JAMES NORRIS TROPHY		yachting ADMIRAL'S CUP
ROSS TROPHY.STANLEY CUP		AMERICA'S CUP
motocross	COUPE DES NATIONS	**tropic disease** CANCER
motorcycle racing		(*see also* disease)
	TOURIST TROPHY	**tropical**
polo	COWDRAY PARK GOLD CUP	American (*see* South America)
	CHAMPION CUP	bean COW(H)AGE.COWITCH
CUP OF THE AMERICAS		LABLAB
	WESTCHESTER CUP	bird DRONGO(-SHRIKE)
powerboat racing		HONEY-EATER.HUMMINGBIRD
	HARMSWORTH TROPHY	JACANA.KING-CROW
rowing	GRAND CHALLENGE CUP	KING VULTURE.SALAGANE
rugby league	CHALLENGE CUP	SUNBIRD.SWIFTLET
HARRY SUNDERLAND TROPHY		TROCHILUS.TROGON

cashew nut tree	LENTISK	—monkeypot	LECYTHIS
climber	COW(H)AGE	—Moringa	HORSERADISH TREE
	COWITCH.LIANA	—Poinciana	FLAMBOYANTE
dhal	PIGEON PEA		FLAME-LEAF
dish	DA(H)L.DHOLL		PEACOCK-FLOWER
fern	DICKSONIA.ELKHORN FERN	**trot**	
fever	(*see* disease)	*trot* past	PATS.SPAT.TAPS
fish	CHAETODON.CORAL FISH	*trotting* race	ACRE.ACRE.CARE
	SEA-SURGEON	**trouble**	ADO.AIL
fruit	ANANA	real *trouble*	LEAR
	CHINESE GOOSEBERRY	take *trouble*	KATE.TEAK
	MANGO(STAN).MANGOSTEEN	trouble (and strife)	WIFE
	TAMARIND	*trouble in* Iran	RAIN
gourd	LOOFA(H).LUFFA	trouble maker	GREMLIN
grass	SORGHUM	*troubled* times	ITEMS.MITES
gum	KINO	*trounced* team	MATE.MEAT.META-
herb	ZINGIBER	**true**	
hummingbird	RUBY-THROAT	*out of* true	-TURE
	SABRE-WING	true *to form*	TURE
	SAPPHIRE-WING	**trumpeter**	ARMSTRONG
	SWALLOW-TAILED BIRD		ELEPHANT.JAMES
leaf-climber	GLORIOSA		JOSHUA
mallow	GOSSYPIUM.URENA	**trunk service**	STD
narcotic fruit	INDIAN BERRY	**trust**	
orchid	DENDROBIUM	trusted friend	ACHATES
papyrus	CYPERUS	trustee	TR
pigeon-pea	DA(H)L.DHOLL	Trustee Savings Bank	TSB
plant	BATATA.BIGNONIA	**try**	
	CROTON.DERRIS.HIBISCUS	try-*out*	TR-Y
	FALSE PAREIRA.LAPORTEA	try-*out*	TYR
	SWEET POTATO	**TT**	DOUBLET.DRY.RACE
	VELVET-LEAF.YAM	**t-take in**	TEAT
potato	YAM	**tub**	BATH.BOAT
resin	ELEMI	tubby fellow	DIOGENES
seabird	PHAETON.TROPICBIRD	**tube**	
sedge	CYPERUS	Tube Investments	TI
shrub	CAPSICUM	tube traveller	TORPEDO
tree	CARAPA.GNETUM	**tuber**	MURPHY.POTATO.SPUD
	RAUWOLFIA.TAMARIND	**tuberculosis**	TB
—anchovy pear	LECYTHIS	**tuck**	
—Brazil nut	LECYTHIS	tuck, *say*	FRIAR
—cannonball tree	LECYTHIS	*tucked in* *	incl in *
—dragon tree	CORDYLINE	•tyro *tucked in* sacks	SLACKS
—erythrina	CORAL TREE	tucked into	ATE
—flamboyant	POINCIANA	*tucked into* *	incl in *
—flowering	COMBRETUM	•airman *tucked into*	
—Kigelia	SAUSAGE TREE	me-at	MEERKAT
—mangosteen	GARCINIA	*tucked round* a...	incl A
—mahogany	CARAPA.CEDRELA	*tucked round* *	incl *

•s-acks *tucked round* tyro	SLACKS
Tuesday	T.TU.TUES
tumble	
tumbled into Po	OPTION
tumbled over step⟨	PETS
tumbled over step	PEST.PETS
tumbledown shack	HACKS
tuned a sitar	TIARAS
Tunisia	TN
capital	TUNIS.T
coin	DINAR.MILLIME
governor	BEY
leader	T
turbulent priest	STRIPE
turf	
turf out	DIVOT
turf study	SODDEN
Turkey	TR
Turkish	TURK
administrative official	VAIVODE
	VOIVODE.WAIVODE
admiral	CAPITAN
ambassador	ELCHEE.EL(T)CHI
armed attendant	CAVASS
	KAVASS
army officer	BIMBASHI.BINBASHI
band	METHER
bath	HAMMAN.HUMM(A)UM
boat	PERMAGY
brazier	MANGAL
cap	MARTAGAN
capital	ANKARA.T
carpet	CADANE
cart	AR(A)BA
cavalryman	SPAHI
characters	TR
coins	
—small	KURUSH
—1/40 piastre	PARA
—silver	PIASTRE
—silver (obsolete)	ASPER
clotted cream	KAYMAK
commander	AG(H)A
—in-chief	SERASKIER
cymbal	CROTALO
dagger	ATAGHAN.YATAG(H)AN
decree	FIRMAN.HATTI-SHERIF
	IRADE
division	SANJAK

dog	ANATOLIAN
drink	AIRAN.BOZA.MASTIC(H)
dulcimer	SANTIR.SANT(O)UR
dynasty	OSMANLI.OTTOMAN
	SELJUK
emblem	CRESCENT
execution	GANCH
felt cap	CALPA(C)K.KALPAK
female slave	ODALISK
	ODALI(S)QUE
fermented milk	YAOURT
	YOGH(O)URT
feudal militiaman	TIMARIOT
flag	CRESCENT
governor	BASHAW.BEGLERBEG
	BEY.CAIMAC(AM).KAIMAKAM
	PASHA.PACHA.VALI.WALI
guard house	DERBEND
harem	SERAGLIO.SERAI(L)
head	
—gear	FEZ
—of division	MUTESSARIF
hors d'oeuvres	HUMMUS.MEZE
imperial government	PORTE
infidel	GIAOUR
inn	CAFENET.(CARAVAN)SERAI
	KHAN
instrument	SAZ
irregular soldier	BASHI-BAZOUK
javelin	JEREED.JERID
jurisdiction of pasha	PACHALIC
	PASHALIK
land division	SANJAK
language	OSMANLI.OTTOMAN
law	MULTOCA
leader	T
manna	TREHALA
measures	
—25 inches	ENDAZE
—30 inches	ARSHEEN.ARSHIN(E)
—2½ acres	DJERIB
—1 bushel	KILEH
meat	
—dish	CABOB.KABAB.KABOB
	KEBAB.KEBOB
—on skewer	SHISH KEBAB
men's quarters	SELAMLIK
military	
—chief	BASHAW.PACHA

	PASHA.ZAIM
—district	ZIAMET
—music	JANIZARY MUSIC
minister	WAZIR.WESIER
	VESIR.VISIER.VIZI(E)R
Moslem	SALAR
—sect	KARMATHIAN
non-Moslem	RAYAH
officer	AG(H)A
order of knighthood	MEDJIDIE
palace	SERAGLIO
—guard	BOSTANGI
pastry	KADAYIF
pavilion	KIOSK
pipe	CHIBOUK.CHIBOUQUE
policeman	CAVASS.KAVASS
	ZABTIEH.ZAPTIAH.ZAPTIEH
porter	HAM(M)AL
power	CRESCENT
prime minister	GRAND VIZIER
province	EYALET.VILAYET
reform bill	TANZIMAT
robe	CAFTAN.DOL(L)MAN
	KAFTAN
rug	KHILIM.KONIA
ruler	ATABEG.ATABEK.CALIPH
	KHAN.PADISHAH.SULTAN
sailor	GALIONGEE
servant	HAM(M)AL
ship	CAIC.CAIQUE.PATAMAR
	SAIC(K).SAIQUE
Siberian	YAKUT
smoking (hookah)	CHILLUM
soldier	JANISSARY
	JANIZAR(Y).NIZAM
standard	CRESCENT.HORSETAIL
sweetmeat	BULBUL.HAL(A)VA(H)
	LOKUM.LOUKOUM
sword bearer	SELICTAR
theologian	ULEMA
title	AG(H)A.BASHAW.BEG.BEY
	DEY.GHAZI.PACHA.PASHA
title of respect	EFFENDI
	HODJA.KHO(D)JA
Turk	OSMANLI.OTTAMITE
	OTTOMITE.SELJUK
vest	YELEK
vine	SOMA
wagon	AR(A)BA.AROBA

war minister	SERASKIER
waterpipe	CHILLUM.HOOKA(H)
	NARG(H)ILE.NARGILEH
	NARG(H)IL(L)Y
weight	
—1½ drams	MUSCAL
—2¾ lbs	OKE
—17 lbs	BATMAN
—125 lbs	CANTAR.KANTAR
	QUANTAR
—509 lbs	CHEKI
women's quarters	SERAGLIO
	SERAIL
turmoil in great...	TEARING
turn	S.U
turn about ⟨	ER.AC
turn again ⟨	ER
turn *back* ⟨	NIPS
*turn*coats ⟨	ASCOT.TOSCA
turn Communist ⟨	DER
turn *in*	incl U
turn in ⟨	NI
turn *into*...	-TION
turn *into* street	SETTER
turn it *over*	TI
turn it *up*(D) ↑	TI
turn left	BEND SINISTER
turn of phrase	SHERPA
turn on	SWITCH
turn on ⟨	NO
turn out the guard	DAUGHTER
turn over	TO
turn over a bit	BAIT
turn over a bit	ABORTIVE
turn over to...	OT
turn quickly	VS
turn red ⟨	DER
turn round but...	TUB
turn *tail*	
•Boer *turns tail*	BORE
•*turn tail of* line	LIEN
turn to... ⟨	OT
turn up ⟨	PU
turn up parts(D) ↑	STRAP
turned out fine	NIFE
turned out to be a dry...	DRAY
	YARD
turner	PAINTER.SPIT
turnover made... ⟨	EDAM

*turn*spit ⟨	TIPS
Turnberry's first	T.TEE
twelve	DOZ(EN).HANDS UP.XII
12½ cents	DIME
combining form	DODECA-
—Apostles	ANDREW
	BARTHOLOMEW.JAMES
	JAMES (brother of John)
	JOHN.JUDAS.MATTHEW
	PETER.PHILIP.SIMON
	THADDEUS.THOMAS
—base	DUODECIMAL
—Christmas presents	DRUMMERS
—EEC members	BELGIUM
	DENMARK.FRANCE
	GREAT BRITAIN.GREECE
	IRELAND.ITALY.LUXEMBOURG
	NETHERLANDS
	PORTUGAL.SPAIN
	WEST GERMANY
—fold	DUODENARY
having twelve	
—columns	DODECASTYLE
—faces	DODECAHEDRON
—leaves per sheet	DUODECIMO
—sides	DODECAGON
—stamens	DODECANDRIAN
	DODECANDROUS
—styles	DODECAGYNIAN
	DODECAGYNOUS
—syllables	DODECASYLLABIC
—tones	DODECAPHONIC
twelve-yearly	
intervals	DUODECENNIAL
hours	AM.PM
hundred	MCC
in Norse mythology	GODS
inches	FOOT
jobs	LABOURS OF HERCULES
men	JURY
peers of Charlemagne	PALADIN
signs of Zodiac	(*see* Zodiac)
Tables	ROMAN LAW
tribes	ISRAELITES
twelfth	DUODECIMAL
	DUODENARY
—Glorious Twelfth	AUGUST
twenty	DOUBLE CROSS.XX
combining form	ICOS(A)-

having	
—20 faces	ICOSAHEDRONAL
—20 stamens	ICOSANDRIAN
	ICOSANDROUS
—24 faces	
	ICOSITETRAHEDRONAL
Twentieth Century Dictionary	
	TCD
twenty-two	CATCH
twenty-four	BLACKBIRDS
twenty-five pounds	PONY
25 per cent *off* bee(f)	BEE
25 per cent price *cut*	COS(t)
twenty-six in Norse	
mythology	GODDESSES
twenty-seven Books	NT
twenty-twenty	VISION
twenty thousand	K
Twickenham game	RU.RUGBY
twiddle <u>toes</u>	TOSE
twin	CASTOR.POLLUX
	(*see also* two[3])
twining <u>arms</u>	MARS.RAMS
twirl	
twirl knob ⟨	BONK
twirling <u>stick</u>	TICKS
twisted <u>a leg</u>	GALE.GAEL
two[1]	COMPANY.II.PR
a penny	CHEAP.TRIVIAL
alternative courses	DILEMMA
bit	PALTRY
bits of <u>bread</u>	BR
books	CORINTHIANS
	CHRONICLES
	KINGS.PETER.TIMOTHY
	THESSALONIANS.SAMUEL
choices	DILEMMA
Christmas presents	
	TURTLE DOVES
—cleft in two	BIFID.BIPARTITE
combining form	BI-.DI-
companies monopolising	
trade	DUOPOLY
days	DD
eyed steak	KIPPER
faced	HYPOCRITICAL
—god	JANUS
fathoms	MARK TWAIN
fish	CODLING

fisted   CLUMSY
fold   BINAL.DOUBLE.DUAL
         DUPLEX.DUPLICATE.TWIFOLD
for his heels   JACK.KNAVE
grooved tablet   DIGLYPH
groups   BIS.BRACE.COMPANY
              COUPLE.DOUBLE.DUAD
              DUAL.DUO.PAIR.TWAIN
                        TWOSOME
having double
—refractive power   BIREFRIGENT
—serrations   BISERRATE
having two
—adductor muscles   DIMYARIAN
—amyl groups   DIAMYL
—ancestral groups   DIPHYLETIC
—at one birth   DITOKOUS
—atoms   DIATOMIC
—axes   DIAXIAL.DIAXON(IC)
—beats   DICROTIC
—beats per bar   DUPLE
—branches   BIFURCATE(D)
         BISULCATE.DICHOTOMOUS
         DIVARICATE.TWIFORKED
                    TWYFORKED
—breeding seasons
    per year   DIGONEUTIC
—bundles of
    stamens   DIDELPHOUS
—butyl groups   DIBUTYL
—carpels   DICARPELLARY
—cells   BICAMERAL.BILOCULAR
—chromium atoms BICHROMATE
                    DICHROMATE
—claws   DIDACTYL
—colours   DICHROM(AT)IC
—cotyledons DICOTYLEDONOUS
—cusps   BICUSPID
—ears   BINAURAL
—electrodes   DIODE
—ethyl groups   DIETHYL
—eyes   BINOCULAR
—faces   BIFACIAL.DIHEDRAL
—feet   BIPED(AL)
—fibres   BINERVATE
—fingers   DIDACTYLOUS
—focal lengths   BIFOCAL
—forms DIMORPHIC.TWIFORMED
                    TWYFORMED

—furrows   BISULCATE
—gills   DIBRANCHIATE
—gods   DITHEISTIC
—halves   DIMIDIATE
—hands   BIMANAL.BIMANOUS
—heads   BICEPS.BICIPITAL
                    DICEPHALOUS
—husbands   BIGAMOUS
         DIANDROUS.DIGAMOUS
—hydrogen atoms   DIACID
                        DIBASIC
—hydroxyl groups   DIHYDRIC
—independently heritable
    characteristics   DIHYBRID
—keys   BITONAL
—languages BIGLOT.BILINGUAL
                        DIGLOT
—leaflets   BIFOLIOLATE
—leaves   BIFOLIATE
—legs   BIPOD(AL)
—letters   BILITERAL
—lines   DIGRAM
—lips   BILABIAL
—lobes   BILOBAR.BILOBATE
         BILOBED.BILOBULAR
                    DITHECAL
—loculi   BILOCULAR.DITHECAL
—marriages   BIGAMOUS
                    DIGAMOUS
—measures   DIMETER
—metals   BIMETALLIC
—methyl radicals   DIMETHYL
—months' duration BIMESTRIAL
—oxygen atoms   DIOXIDE
—parts   BIPARTITE.DIMEROUS
                    DIDYMOUS
—perianth whorls
         DI(PLO)CHLAMYDEOUS
—petals   BIPETALOUS
                    DIPETALOUS
—phenyl groups   DIPHENYL
—pistils DIGYNIAN.DIGYNOUS
—planes   DIHEDRAL
—points   BICUSPID(ATE)
—poles   BIPOLAR.DIPOLAR
—prongs   BIDENTAL
                    BIDENTATE(D)
                    BIFURCATE(D)
—rays   DIACT(INAL).DIACTINE

—rings	DICYCLIC
—rows	BIFARIOUS.BISERIAL
	DISTICHOUS
—sacs	DITHECAL
—sepals	DISEPALOUS
—separate sexes	DIOECIOUS
—series	BISERIAL
—sets of teeth	DIPHYODONT
—sexes	BISEXUAL
—sides	BILATERAL
—sheaths	DITHECAL
—spore cases	DITHECAL
—stable states	BISTABLE
—stamens	DIANDROUS
—stomachs	DIGASTRIC
—styles	DIGYNIAN.DIGYNOUS
—sulphur atoms	BISULPHIDE
	DISULPHIDE
—syllables	DISYLLABLE
	DISYLLABIC
—terms	BINOMIAL
—thecae	DITHECAL
—threads	BIFILAR
—toes	DIDACTYLOUS
—valencies	BIVALENT.DIATOMIC
	DIVALENT
—valves	BIVALVE.DIVALVULAR
—variants	BIVARIATE.DIVARIATE
—ways	BIVIOUS
—wheels	BICYCLE
—whorls	DICYCLIC
	DIPLOSTEMONOUS
—wings	BIPLANE.DIPTERAL
	DIPTEROUS
—wives	BIGAMOUS.DIGAMOUS
	DIGYNIAN.DIGYNOUS
—wombs	DIDELPHIC
—words	BINOMIAL
—xylem strands	DIARCH
—yearly occurrences	BIANNUAL
—zones	BIZONAL
having use of two	
—elements	AMPHIBIAN
	AMPHIBIOUS
—hands	AMBIDEXT(E)ROUS
hulled boat	CATAMARAN
hundred	CC.H.S.SIGMA
—and fifty	E.K
—and fifty thousand	E

—thousand	H
—years	BICENTENARY
	BICENTENNIAL
hundred thousand	S.SIGMA
in song	LILYWHITE BOYS
letter word	BILITERAL
letters, one sound	DIGRAPH
men in office	DUUMVIR(RATE)
month period	BIMESTER
nil	TWENTY
notes	DUPLET
one of two at birth	TWIN
pair	SECOND FLOOR
pence	DD.PP
pence off	omit DD.PP
penny	CHEAP.WORTHLESS
performers	DUET(T).DUETTO
	DUO
persons	COMPANY.DUO
	TWOSOME
ruling	DIARCHY
rings	OO
Scots	TWA(E).TWAY
speaking	DIALOGUE.DUALOGUE
spots	DEUCE
stars	GEMINI
step	DANCE
thirds of par	PA.PANDA
thousand	MM.Z
time	CROSS.DECEIVE
times	DUPL(ICAT)E
under par	EAGLE
vowels sounded	
as one	DIPHTHONG
way principle	TENET
way transport	KAYAK
winged plane	BIPLANE
writer or two	TWAIN
two^2	
actions	SUITCASE
animals	BUCKRAM
bases	BEDEVIL
blues	ROYAL NAVY
boys	ALBERT.ALFRED
	BASILDON.DONJON
	EDWARDIAN.FRANKED
	GLENGARRY.GUYED
	HALBERT.HERBAL.JACKAL
	JACKED.MALTED.MARKED

	NICKED.NORMANDY.PATRON
	PATTED.PETERED.REGAL
	ROYAL.RUSSIAN.SAMIAN
	SIDLES.TOMBOY.TIMED
	VICTIM.VICTORIAN
boys and a girl	BETRAYAL
buildings	HUTCH
cards	TENACE
characters	(see letters)
circles	DISCO
coppers	CUD.CUP.DD.DP.PD.PP
directions	WANDS
	EN.WE.etc
drugs	TEAPOT
fish	CODLING.IDLING
friends	PALMATE
girls	GALENA.PATELLA
	PATINA.SALINA
holding hands	EN.EW.SW
	SE.etc.
journalists	CUBED
keys	BORA.CORA.DORA
	BORD.CORD.FORD
	BORE.CORE.FORE.GORE
kings	EDWARD LEAR
letters	BANDY.CANDY.DANDY
	MANDY.PANDA.RANDY
	SANDY.TANDEM
measures	ELLEN
men	CHAPMAN.GENTLES.PP
	(see also boys above)
men and a woman	BETRAYAL
	HELEN
months	DECOCT
mothers	MADAM.MAMMA
notes	DOTE.MERE.MIRE.REME
	SITE.SOLE.SOME.TIME
odd fellows	CRANKCASE
people	DAWNED.DIAL
	DIED.VIAL.VIED
pounds	LIQUID
regiments	RARE
rings	DINGO.DISCO
rivers	AIRER.DEER.RALPH
	ROUSE
roads	AVER.MIST
Scots	CAMERONIAN
seas	SEAMED
seater bicycle (tandem)	TM

spoons	NECK AND NECK
streets	STANDARD
things to eat	PEANUT
undergarments	BRAVEST
ways	EN.WE.etc.
whiskies	PAIR OF SHORTS
women	MADAM.MADONNA
	MALADY

two³

army men	GIGI
boys	WILLY-WILLY
cats	TOM-TOM
chants	SING-SING
coats	FURFUR
companies	COCO
cuts	CHOP-CHOP
days	DD
discounts	DIVI-DIVI
dogs	POMPOM
essays	GOGO
extras	BYE-BYE
fathers	PAPA
feet	PAWPAW
firms	COCO
French words	MOT-MOT
fruits, say	BERI-BERI
girls	LILLIL
graduates	BABA.MAMA
halves of mild	MIMI
hands	PAWPAW
hats	TAM-TAM
hundred	CC
Israelites, say	JU-JU
learners	LL
lots of salt	TARTAR
looks	SEESEE
mothers	MAMA
oaths, say	C(O)USC(O)US
	KHUSKHUS
parents	MAMA.PAPA
peers	SEESEE
pence	DD.PP
pieces of timber	LOGLOG
pounds	LL
prisons	CAN-CAN
quiet...	HUSH-HUSH
ravines	NULLANULLA
roads	MIMI
runs	BYE-BYE

sailors	TARTAR	11-point	SMALL PICA
seconds	SS	12-point	PICA
shillings	SS	13-point	CICERO
soldiers	GIGI	14-point	ENGLISH
sounds	HUMHUM	16-point	TWO-LINE BREVIER
teas	CHA-CHA	18-point	GREAT PRIMER
thousand	MM	20-point	PARAGON
tests	MOT-MOT	22-point	DOUBLE PICA
tree trunks	LOG-LOG	24-point	TWO-LINE PICA
tries	GOGO	28-point	TWO-LINE ENGLISH
workshops	LABLAB	36-point	
Tyneside	NE		TWO-LINE GREAT PRIMER
hence		40-point	TWO-LINE PARAGON
•about Tyneside	CANE	48-point	CANON.FOUR-LINE PICA
•arrive *in* Tyneside	NARRE	60-point	FIVE-LINE PICA
•Tyneside entrance	NEGATE	72-point	SIX-LINE PICA
type		error	TYPO
10 letters per inch	PICA	heavy-faced	CLARENDON
12 letters per inch	ELITE	large	CANON
$1/_{72}$ inch	POINT	measurement	EL.EM.EN
3$1/_2$-point	MINIKIN		PT.POINT
4-point	BRILLIANT.MINION	rounded script	RONDE
4$1/_2$-point	DIAMOND	special type	ELZEVIR
5-point	PEARL	typograph(y)	TYP(O)
5$1/_2$-point	AGATE.RUBY	without serifs	SANSERIF
6-point	NONPAREIL	wrong fount	WF
7-point	MINION	**typical traveller**	REPRESENTATIVE
8-point	BREVIER	**tyro**	L
9-point	BOURGEOIS		
10-point	LONG PRIMER	(*see also* learner)	

U

acceptable. aristocratic. bend. **boat. bolt.** *educational establishment. ewe. film. four hundred. four hundred thousand. high-class. posh. superior.* **trap. tube. turn. union. Unionist. universal. universe. university. upper-class. upsilon. uranium. Uruguay. Utah**

U-boat	SUB	**uncommon**	
Uganda	EAU	uncommon person	NOBLE
ugly		*uncommonly* silent	ENLIST
ugly mug	GUM		LISTEN
ugly sister	GORGON	**unconscious**	COLD.OUT
ugly truth	PLAIN FACTS	**uncover**	
Ulster	NI	un*cover*	incl UN
Defence Association	UDA	•un*covered by* note	TUNE
Defence Regiment	UDR	un*cover* *	U-N
Freedom Fighters	UFF	•un*covering* right...	URN
Unionists	UU	*uncovered* (c)ache(D)	ACHE
Volunteer Force	UVF	**uncouth** Huns	SHUN
ultimate		**undecorated**	NOTICED
ultimate letter	OMEGA.Z.ZED.ZEE	**under**[1]	
ultimate outcome	E	under canvas	(in) TEN-T
ultimately	(in) EN-D	under cover (in) HA-T.(in) TEN-T	
ultra		under the blankets	(in) BE-D
ultra high frequency	UHF		(in) CO-T
ultrashort wave	USW	**under**[2]	
ultrasonic waves	USW	under consideration	SUBJUDICE
ultraviolet	UV	under cover	INSURED
umbrella	MUSH	*under* forty	FOR.FORT
umpire	REF	under-secretary	US
hence		*under* (s)even	EVEN
•umpire allowed...	REFLET	under that heading	VV
•umpire has hurt his leg	REFLAME	under the rose	SUB ROSA
•umpire not well	REFILL	under the table	DRUNK
un	A.AN.I	under the word	SV
unaccompanied	ALLA BREVE	under this word	SHV
	A(LLA) CAPELLA	**under**[3]	
unaffected by reversal		indicates one word written under	
indicates use of a palindrome:		another(D):	
•boat *unaffected by*		•free *under*current	ACRID
reversal	KAYAK	•good *under*study	CONFINE
•woman *unaffected by*		•I am *under*study	DENIM
reversal	AVA.EVE	•or *under*sea...	MAINOR
	MADAM	•space *under* the	
uncertain		table	BOARD ROOM
uncertain sort	TORS	•the *French under*garment	
uncertainty as to...	OATS		GARBLE
unchanged	SIC	•*under*go an...	GOAN
uncle	PAWNBROKER.SAM.TOM	•*under*write church	PENCE
unclosed li(d)	LI	**under**cut	RUNED

749

underdone lam(b)	LAM	**unfortunate**	
undergarment	BRA	*unfortunate* end	DEN.NED
underground	METRO.SUBSOIL	*unfortunately* not her...	THRONE
	TUBE	**unfrozen**	NOTICE
underground spring	VAULT	*ungainly* stride	DIREST
underground vault	LANDGRAVE	*unhappily* wed	DEW
underlined	UL	**unhealthy horse**	SICK-BAY
underneath	(*see* under³)	**unhesitating**	
underpinned	ONE-LEGGED	unhesitating(ly)	omit ER
underscore	TEENAGER		omit UM or UR
understood	-MENT.ROGER	•moth(er) *unhesitating*...	MOTH
understood by foreigners =		•s(um)s *unhesitatingly*...	SS
foreign language:		•*unhesitating* co(ur)se	COSE
•language *understood by*		**unidentified**	NU
foreigners	LANGUE	unidentified flying object	UFO
•verse *understood by*		**unilateral**	
foreigners	STANZA	unilateral declaration of	
•word *understood by*		independence	UDI
foreigners	PALABRA	unilateralist	CND.DISARMER
undertakers' magazine		*uninhibited* when it...	WHITEN
	GRAVE NEWS	**uninspired footman**	PEDESTRIAN
underworld	ABADDON.DIS	**union**	RUSSIA.U
	EREBUS.HADES.HELL	union attendant	BEST MAN
	PIT.TARTARUS		BRIDESMAID
hence			MATRON OF HONOUR
•underworld class	DISORDER	union colleague	BRO.WELDER
•underworld character	DISCARD	union leader	SHERMAN
•underworld makes...	DISUSES	union *leader*	U
underwriter	SUBSCRIBER	union member	BRIDE.GROOM
undeveloped country	GREENLAND		HUSBAND.WIFE
undisciplined		union representative	UMP
undisciplined army	MARY.MYRA	Unionist	U
undisciplined career	WILDLIFE	**unique**	ONE.SOLE
undivided	ONE	unique *sound*	WON
undo		**unit**	A.I
I am *undone*	AIM	**united**	
undoing clasp	CLAPS	United Arab Republic	UAR
undone	NODE	United Dominions Trust	UDT
uneasy sleep	PEELS	United Free Church	UF
un-English	omit E	United Kingdom	UK
unexpected snag	NAGS	United Nations Association	UNA
unfamiliar taste	STATE.TEATS	United Nations	
unfashionable	OUT.SQUARE	(Organisation)	UN(O)
unfavourable aspect	N	United Presbyterian	UP
unfinished tas(k)	TAS	United Press	UP
unfixed latches	SATCHEL	United States	US.USA
unfold		—Army	USA
unfold a tale	ALATE	—(Army) Air Force	US(A)AF
unfolding arms	MARS.RAMS	—Navy	USN

—Ship	USS
universal	U
Universal Decimal	
Classification	UDC
universal organisation	UN
Universal Postal Union	UPU
universal set	E
Universal Time	UT
university	U.UNIV
at university	UP
University Grants	
Committee	UGC
university man	BA.MA.DON
	PROF
university press	CUP.OUP
university student	UL
university teachers	UAT
unkempt beard	BARED.BREAD
unknown	X.Y
unknown number	N
unlikely	TALL
unlikely tale	LATE.LEAT
unlimited (m)one(y)	ONE
unlock	
unlocked	BALD
unlocking	HAIRCUT
unmanned	omit MAN
•smuggled *unmanned*	
Ger(man)	RANGER
un*married*	omit M
un*named*	omit N
unnatural	FLAT.SHARP
unnatural desire	RESIDE
unopened (c)ask	ASK
unorthodox means	MANES.NAMES
unpaid account	BILLOWED
	BILLOWING
unpreferred girl	BRUNETTE
unravelled test case	CASSETTE
unreasonable fear	FARE
unrecognised danger	GANDER
	GARDEN.RANGED
unruly kids	SKID
unsettled NOMADIC.OWED.OWING	
unsettled score	CORES
unsnarled ropes	PORES.SPORE
unstable site	TIES
unsteady	
unsteady steps	PESTS

unsteadily rise	SIRE
unsuited	BARE.NAKED
	NUDE
untangled threads	HARDEST
unusual	
unusual fate	FEAT
unusual production	
of Tosca	COATS
unusually fat	AFT
untidy heaps	SHAPE
untied knots	STONK
unwound reel	LEER
unwraps parcel	PLACER
up[1]	
meaning	
riding	
•child *riding*	TOT UP
to windward	
•ship *to windward*	KETCHUP
up[2]	
up in arms	RAMPANT
up late(D)	MANET
up North indicates use of Scottish	
words	(*see* Scottish)
up the creek in an. . .	NAIN
up the mountain(D) ↑	ANTE.ROT
up with the lark	(in) S-KY
upped the ante(D) ↑	ETNA
upbringing of Eros(D) ↑	SORE
upper	
upper	AMPHETAMINE.SPEED
upper case	CAPS.CAPITALS
upper class	U
Upper House	ATTIC.GARRET
upper set	DENTURE.TEETH
upheaval in her. . .	RHINE
uphill(D) ↑	ROT
upholding	
upholding	U-P
upholding(D) ↑ indicates reversal	
and inclusion	
•l-aw *upholding* learner	WALL
uplift	
uplift spirits(D) ↑	SNIG
uplifting art (D) ↑	TRA-
upmarket (D) ↑	TRAM
upright[1]	I.PI.PIANO.POST
hence	
•upright board	IDEAL

•*upright* man	IRON
•*upright* one and	IAN
•*upright* attendant	PIPAGE
•*upright* friend	PIPAL
•*upright* girl and	PIANINA
•upright character	POSTCARD
•upright monarch	POSTER
•upright person	POSTAL
	POSTMAN
upright type	ROMAN

upright²

*up*right(D) ↑	TR
upright bat(D) ↑	TAB

uprising

some con/tinu/ous	
uprising(D) ↑	UNIT
up*rising*(D) ↑	PU
uprising at(D) ↑ . . .	TA

upriver

*up*river(D) ↑	
indicates name of river written	
backwards:	
•look *upriver*	LOOP
•*upriver with* man	MACRON
•sun unknown *up*river	SYNOD

upset

*up*set(D) ↑	TES
upset <u>master</u>	STREAM
upset no one(D) ↑	-ION
upset revel	LEVER
upset timer(D) ↑	REMIT

upside

upside down(D) ↑	
•draw *upside down*	WARD
•was *upside down*	SAW
•put *upside down*	TUP

upsilon	U
upstanding part(D) ↑	TRAP
up*start*	U
upsurge of sap(D) ↑	PAS
up*turn*	PU
Urban District Council	UDC

Uruguay(an)	U.URU
capital	MONTEVIDEO.U
US(A)	(*see* America)
use	US.UU
buil/d ark/ *using*. . .	DARK
not *used*	TON
<u>*usable as*</u> a bed	BADE.BEAD
use <u>a pen</u>	PANE.PEAN
<u>*use*</u> *guile*	SUE
used abroad = foreign language	
•cup *used abroad*	TAZZA
•hat *used abroad*	CHAPEAU
•piano *used abroad*	
	HAMMERKLAVIER
•shawl *used abroad*	MANTILLA
	(*see also* abroad)
used car dealer	AUTO-CHANGER
used in pa/in k/illers	INK
used in poetry	(*see* poetic)
used to be	EX
	(*see also* old³)
useless	US
use*less*	omit USE
•use*less* ho(use)	HO
using part of h/er go/od. . .	ERGO
using some ne/w ide/as	WIDE
using <u>tools</u>	LOOTS.STOOL

usher in

usher in a. . .	incl A
usher in *	incl *
•bu-tler *ushers in* son	BUSTLER
ushered in by *	incl in *
•son *ushered in by*	
bu-tler	BUSTLER

usually	USU
utter	
utter cry	CALLOW
utter some. . .	SUM
utterance of boy	BUOY
utterance of a girl	ALAS
uttering rhyme	RIME
uttermost ends of <u>the earth</u>	EH
uttermost parts of <u>C̄hīn̄a</u>	CA
u-upset	URILE

V

against. agent. bomb. day. electric potential difference. five. five thousand. fifty. fifty thousand. *look. neck. neckline. notch. nu. see*. sign. vanadium. Vatican. vee. velocity. verb. verse. versus. very. victory. vide. volt. volume. win

vacant	
vacancy	O
vacant	VAC
vacant = nothing in it	incl O
vacation	VAC
vaguely hears...	HARES.SHARE
vale	
vale = goodbye	
vale *in England*	
	FAREWELL.GOODBYE
vale *in France*	A BIENTOT.ADIEU
vale *in Germany*	
	AUF WIEDERSEHEN
vale *in Italy*	ADDIO.ARRIVEDERCI
vale *in Spain*	ADIOS
	HASTA LA VISTA
value	PH.RATE.VAL
Value-added Tax	VAT
vandalised parks	SPARK
vanguard **of** army	A
vapour	
vapour density	VD
vapour pressure	VP
varsity	U
vary	
variant	VAR
variations of Elgar...	GLARE
	LAGER.LARGE.REGAL
varies in shape	HEAPS.PHASE
variegated tints	STINT
varietal	VAR
variety	VAR
variety of crocus	OCCURS
various dates	VD
various years	VY
various items	SMITE.TIMES
vary rate	TARE.TEAR
vast	
vast *majority*	VAS
vastness	BIGHEAD
Vatican	V.VAT
vault	
vaulting horse	SHOW JUMPER

vaulting horse	SHORE
vee	V
vegetable(s)	VEG
vegetarian	
indicates word 'eating'	
vegetable(s):	
•vegetarian animal	APPEASE
vehicle	
vehicle entrance	TRANSPORT
vehicle for a...	incl A
vehicle for *	incl *
•rotten *vehicle for* learner	BALD
velocity	MPH.MV.V.VEL
venerable	VEN
venereal disease	VD
Venetian	OTHELLO
boat	GONDOLA.VAPORETTO
boatman	GONDOLIER
bridge	RIALTO
coin	BETSO.DUCATOON.SEQUIN
	ZECCHINE.ZECCHINO
	ZECHIN.ZEQUIN
dance	FORLANA.FURLANA
leader	V
magistrate	DOGE.PODESTA
merchant	ANTONIO.POLO
mosaic	TERRAZZO
noble	DOGE
prosecutor	AVVOGADORE
resort	LIDO
rose	SIEN(N)A
ship	ARGOSY.FRIGATOON
state barge	BUCENTAUR
sumach	FUSTET
sword	SCHIAVONE
Venezuela(n)	YV
capital	CARACAS.V
coin	BOLIVAR.LOCHO.MEDIO
leader	V
river	ORINOCO
verb	V.VB
verb intransitive	VI
verb transitive	VT

verbal reasoning quotient	VRQ
verbal refusal	KNOW
verbally made an...	MAIDEN
verbally not...	KNOT
verges of road	RD
vermouth	IT
verse	V
ancient metre	GALLIAMBIC
answering stanza	ANTISTROPHE
anthology	FLOREGIUM
apparent rhyme	EYE-RHYME
Byzantine	POLITICAL VERSE
canto	DUAN
choliamb	SCAZON
classical hexameter	
	HEROIC VERSE
closed rhyme	RIMA CHIUSA
collection of poems	DIVAN
comic verse	DOGGEREL
	FABLIAU
combining	
—mixed metres within a single	
line	LOGAOEDIC
—parallel sentences	
	REPORTED VERSES
concluding verse	EPILOGUE
contest in verse	TENSON
	TENZON
continuation of a sentence from	
one verse line to next	
	ENJAMB(E)MENT
couplet	DISTICH
dactylic hexameter	DOLICHURUS
	PYTHIAN VERSE
division of poem	DUAN
double	
—foot	DIPODY
—limerick	TWINER
—spondee	DISPONDEE
downbeat	THESIS
eight strophes	OCTASTROPHIC
English iambic	
pentameter	HEROIC VERSE
epic	EPOPEE.EPOPOEIA
	EPOS.RHAPSODY
extra syllable	HYPERCATALEXIS
final letters form a	
word	TELESTICH
free verse	VERS LIBRE

French	
—alexandrine	HEROIC VERSE
—medieval poem	PASTOURELLE
funeral	
—ode	EPICEDE.EPICEDIUM
—oration	ELOGE.ELOGIUM
	ELOGY
—song	ELEGY
group of	
—Greek verses	SYSTEM
—lines	STANZA
half	
—a line	HEMISTICH
—foot	SEMIPED
—of long syllable	MORA
having	
—each word a syllable longer	
than the previous	RHOPALIC
—feet	
—$\frac{1}{2}$	SEMIPED
—1	MONOMETER
—$1\frac{1}{2}$	SESQUIPEDAL(IAN)
—2	DIMETER.DIPODY
—2 half-feet	PENTHEMIMER
—3	TRIMETER.TRIPODY
—4	GLYCONIC.TETRAMETER
	TETRAPODY
—5	PENTAMETER
	PENTAPODY
—6	HEXAMETER.HEXAPODY
	SENARIUS.SENARY
—7	HEPTAMETER
	HEPTAPODY
	SEPTENARIUS
	SEPTENARY
—7 half-feet	HEPHTHEMIMER
—8	OCTAMETER.OCTAPODY
	OCTONARION
—lines	STICH
—$\frac{1}{2}$	HEMISTICH
—1	MONOSTICH
—2	COUPLET.DISTICH
—2 couplets	CLERIHEW
—3	TERCET.TERZETTA
	TRISTICH
—4	QUATRAIN.SAPPHIC
	TETRASTICH
—5	CINQUAIN.LIMERICK
	PENTASTICH

—6	HEXASTICH.SIXAINE
—7	RHYME-ROYAL
—8	HUITAIN.OCTASTICH
	OCTAVE.SPENSERIAN
—10	DECASTICH.DIZAIN
—13	RONDEAU.RONDEL
—14	RONDEL.SONNET
—necessary number of syllables	ACATALECTIC
—redundant syllable	HYPERMETRICAL
—same stanza form throughout	MONOSTROPHIC
—1 syllable	MONOSYLLABLE
—2 syllables	DISYLLABLE
—long:short	CHOREE
	TROCHEE
—long:long	SPONDEE
—short:long	IAMB(US)
—short:short	PYRRHIC
—3 syllables	TRISYLLABLE
—long:long:long	MOLOSSUS
—long:long:short	ANTIBACCHIUS
—long:short:long	AMPHIMACER
	CRETIC
—long:short:short	DACTYL
—short:long:long	BACCHIUS
—short:long:short	AMPHIBRACH
—short:short:long	ANAP(A)EST
—short:short:short	TRIBRACH
	TRISEME
—4 syllables	QUADRISYLLABLE
	TETRASYLLABLE
—long:long:long:short	EPITRITE
—long:long:short:short	IONIC
—long:short:short:long	CHORIAMB
—long:short:short:short	PAEON
—short:long:long:short	ANTISPAST
—short:short:long:long	IONIC
—short:short:short:short	PROCELEUSMATIC
	TETRASEME

—5 syllables	PENTASYLLABLE
—dactyl and spondee	ADONIC
—short:long:long:short:long	DOCHMIUS
—6 syllables	SEXISYLLABLE
—7 syllables	HEPTASYLLABLE
	SEPTASYLLABLE
—8 syllables	OCTASYLLABLE
—10 syllables	DECASYLLABLE
—11 syllables	HENDECASYLLABLE
—12 syllables	DODECASYLLABLE
—6 iambs	ALEXANDRINE
—14 syllables	FOURTEENER
—15 syllables	FIFTEENER
—16 syllables	SIXTEENER
heroic couplet	RIDING-RHYME
humorous	
—4 lines	CLERIHEW
—5 lines	LIMERICK
iambic trimeter	CHOLIAMB
	SCAZON
incomplete at end of line and completed on next	ROVE-OVER
initial letters reproduce first verse	PARACROSTIC
introduction	PROLOGUE
introductory syllable	ANACRUSIS
Italian stanza	OTTAVA RIMA
Japanese	HAIKAI.HAIKU
	HOKKO.LINKED VERSE
	RENGA.TANKA
lacking a syllable	CATALECTIC
last	
—part of ode	EPODE
—six lines of sonnet	SESTET(T)
	SESTETTE
Latin	LEONINE
—old	SATURNIAN
light	VERS DE SOCIETE
line of verse	STICH
—beginning and ending with same word	SERPENTINE VERSE
long instead of short	IRRATIONAL
longer line followed by shorter one	EPODE
lyrical	ODE

Malayan	PANT(O)UM	reversed dactyl	ANAP(A)EST
mark of division	SEMEION	rhyme of	
metrical tale	FABLIAU	—final syllables	MALE RHYMES
mixed language	MACARONIC	—words similar in spelling but	
modern Greek	POLITICAL VERSE	different in sound	EYE RHYME
mournful ode	MONODY	ribald verse	FABLIAU
mourning song	ELEGY	sandwich rhyme	RIMA CHIUSA
narrative poem	BALLAD	scazon	CHOLIAMB
natural metre	SPRUNG RHYTHM	series of	
nonsense	AMPHIGORY	—rhyming lines	MONORHYME
occasional	VERS D'OCCASION	—stanzas (Italian)	CANZONE
ode of lamentation	THRENE	short	
	THRENODY	—clause in Latin	
old		prose	CLAUSULA
—lyrical	SONNET	—epic	EPYLLION
—six-lined six-stanza		—form (Italian)	STORNELLO
poem	SESTINA	—lines with same	
—two-rhyme poem	VILLANELLE	ending	KYRIELLE
part of ode	STROPHE	—narrative	LAY
passionate	DITHYRAMB	—pastoral poem	ECLOGUE
pastoral poem	IDYL(L)	—pithy saying	GNOME
patchwork of quotations	CENTO	—poem	DITHYRAMB.EPIGRAM
pause		—syllable	MORA
—in verse line	C(A)ESURA	—single theme	TIRADE
—of one mora	LIMMA	specific number of	
pithy saying	GNOME	syllables	SYLLABICS
poem			SYLLABLE VERSE
—about agricultural life	GEORGIC	spondee, choriamb,	
—about return voyage	NOSTOS	iambus	ASCLEPIAD
—about people's traditions	EPOS	stanza	STROPHE
—celebrating		string of verses on one	
marriage	EPITHALAMION	rhyme	LAISSE.TIRADE
	EPITHALAMIUM	study of versification	
	PROTHALAMION	and metre	PROSODY
	PROTHALAMIUM	tetrameter (Ionic)	SOTADEAN
—in honour of victory	EPINICION		SOTADIC
	EPINIKION	three stanzas	TRIAD
—in three stanzas	BALLADE	tribrach, iamb, trochee	TRISEME
—(Italian)	TERZA-RIMA	triple rhyme	SDRUCCIOLA
—of Alcaeus	ALCAIC	trochaic dipody	DITROCHEE
—of recantation	PALINODE	two-rhymed French	
—on husbandry	GEORGIC	verse	VIRELAY
—with witty ending	EPIGRAM	unequal strophes	
quatrain	COMMON METRE		HETEROSTROPHIC
	SERVICE METRE	unit of time	SEMEION
	SHORT METRE	unsophisticated	
quatrains of eight-syllable		verse	MACARONIC
lines	LONG-METRE	upbeat	ARSIS
redundant word	CHEVILLE	vowel elision	SYNAL(O)EPHA

756

wedding ode	EPITHALAMION
	EPITHALAMIUM
	PROTHALAMION
	PROTHALAMIUM
Welsh improvised	
verse	PENNILL(ION)
writing omitting words containing	
a particular letter	LIPOGRAM

version

new *version*	WEN
version of a...	OAF
version of Tuscan's	SANCTUS
versus	V
vertical take-off (and landing)	
	VTO(L)
very	V
black	BB
French	TRES
good	VG
high frequency	VHF
large	OS
low frequency	VLF
hard	HH
little	WEE
loud	FF
much like Leeds	LEADS
musical	ASSAI.MOLTO
quiet	PP
Scottish	UNCO
short	V
soft	PP
soft *centre*	incl PP
•apple *with* very soft *centre*	PIPPIN
•co-in *with* very soft *centre*	COPPIN
sore	REDRAW
strong	FF
young	ONE OR TWO
vessel	MV.SHIP.SS.SUB
	EWER.URN.VASE.VES
veterinary	VET
verterinary surgeon	VET.VS
vicar	REV(D).VIC
Vicar Apostolic	VA
Vicar-General	VG
vicarage	VIC
vice	
Vice-Chancellor	VC
Vice-Consul	VC
Vice-President	VP

Vichy water	EAU
Victoria	
Victoria Cross	VC
Victoria Medal of Honour	VMH
victory	V.VE.VJ
vide	V
video	
video cassette recorder	VCR
video frequency	VF
video tape recorder	VTR
Vietnam	VN
capital	HANOI.V
coin	DONG
leader	V
view	SCAPE
viewer	EYE
vile	
may be vile	EVIL
vile *outsiders*	VE
village	HAMLET.VIL(L)
village drama	HAMLET
vintage poet	GRAVES
violated rules	LURES
violent push to...	UPSHOT
violin	AMATI.CREMONA
	STRAD
old violin	GJO.GJU.GU(E)
Shetland violin	GJO.GJU.GU(E)
violin strings	A.D.E.G
viscount	VIS
viscount's son	HON
visual	
visual aid	CONTACT LENS
	MICROSCOPE.MONOCLE
	SPECTACLES.TELESCOPE
visual display unit	VDU
vitamin	A.B.C.D.E.F.G.H
	K.L.M.P.X
A	AXEROPHTHOL
	CAROTENE.RETINOL
B	ADERMIN.ANEURIN.BIOTIN
	CHOLINE.COBALAMINE
	CYANOCOBALAMIN(E)
	FOLIC ACID.LACTOFLAVIN
	NIACIN.NICOTINAMIDE
	NICOTINIC ACID.PANTHENOL
	PANTOTHENIC ACID
	PTEROIC ACID.PYRIDOXIN(E)
	RIBOFLAVIN.THIAMIN(E)

C	ASCORBIC ACID	**volcanic rock**	LAVA.MOYA
	CEVITAMIC ACID	**volt**	V
D	CALCIFEROL	volt-amp	VA
	CHOLECALCIFEROL	volt-ampere-reactive	VAR
	ERGOSTEROL	**volume**	TOM.TOME
E	TOCOPHEROL		TOMUS.V.VOL
G	LACTOFLAVIN.RIBOFLAVIN	**volunteer**	VOL
H	BIOTIN	Voluntary Aid Detachment	VAD
K	MENADIONE.MENAQUINONE	Voluntary Defence Corps	VDC
	PHYLLOQUINONE	Voluntary Service Overseas	VSO
	PHYTOMENADIONE	Volunteer (Officers')	
M	FOLIC ACID	Decoration	VD
	PTEROYLGLUTAMIC ACID	Volunteer Reserve	
P	BIOFLAVONOID.CITRIN	Decoration	VRD
vivisection of rat	ART.TAR	volunteers	TA.THETA
viz	SC	(*see also* army.reserves.terrier)	
vocal		**vote**	CROSS.X
vocal turn	TERN	**voguish**	IN
vocalising all. . .	AWL	*voyaging* in the. . .	THINE
vocally rough	RUFF	**vulgar**	VUL(G)
vocative	VOC	*vulgar* (h)at	AT
voice frequency	VF	**Vulgate**	VUL(G)
volatile oils	SILO.SOIL	**v-ventilated**	VAIRY

bridge player. complex cube root. tungsten. watt. weak. Wednesday. Welsh. west. western. whole numbers. wicket. width. wife. William. wolfram. woman

W8	WEIGHT	**warm**	
wacky ideas	AIDES.ASIDE.SADIE	warm bird	HEATHEN
wader	HERON	warm coat	BLAZER
wag		warm drink	CORDIAL.TOAST
wag finger	FRINGE	warm-*hearted*	AR
*wag*tail in a. . .	ITALIAN	warming up	OFFICE
Wagner's work	RING	**warning**	AMBER.CAVE.FORE
waiters	QUEUE	warning card	CAUTION
Wales	CYMRU	*warp* into an. . .	NATION
	(*see also* Welsh²)	**Warrant Officer**	WO
walk		**Warsaw Pact**	WP
walk *about*	TREA-D	warship	SUB
walk *about*⟨	MAOR	**was**	
walk over	WO	was not loud	WASP
walk *over*⟨	MAOR	was not loud	QUIET
walker	JAY.PED	was *wrong*	SAW
walking	(on) FOOT	**wash comb**	SCOUR
•bird walking	CROWFOOT	**Washington**	DC
wall		**waste**	
wall builder	HADRIAN	waste *disposal*	SWEAT.TAWSE
wall *in France*	MUR	waste food	FRITTER
(w)all *with no opening*	ALL	waste of water	OCEAN
wall's make-up	ROUGHCAST	waste-paper basket	WPB
walled city	BERLIN	wasting away	omit *
Walloon	WAL	•b(adl)y *wasting away*	BY
walrus	MORSE	•ca(usi)ng *wasting away*	CANG
wander		**watch**	
Ezra *the wanderer*	RAZE	watchchain	ALBERT
wander about in the. . .	THINE	watches crop	TURNIPS
wandering stream	MASTER	watcher	ARGUS.EYE
want		watchful people	SPIES.SWISS
want of	(*see* without²)	watching cricket	ATTEST
wants a. . .	incl A	watchword	HUNTER.OMEGA
wants *	incl *		TURNIP
•*wants* everything *in* p-et	PALLET	**water**	ADAM'S ALE.ADAM'S WINE
wanted	(in) NE-ED		AQ.EA.H-O
wanton act	CAT	water at 0°C	JUSTICE
war		water colour	LAKE.SEA-GREEN
spoils of war	MARS	waterfall	EBB-TIDE.RAIN
war criminal	HESS	water*front*	W
War Office	WO	Waterloo	ROUT.WC
war record	LILI MARLENE	waterway	CANAL.RIVER
war*head*	W	water(way) indicates name of	
	(*see also* battle)	river:	

•free *in* waterway	DERIDE	

•free *in* waterway   DERIDE
•learner *on* water   LOUSE
•waterway *to* the East   CAME
watt   W
wave
  waver <u>a bit</u>   BAIT
  waving <u>to me</u>   MOTE
way¹   AVE.MALL.RD.RLY.RY
               ST.VIA.N.S.E.W
hence
•quiet way   PAVE
•Southern way is hard   SMALLISH
•he is *on* a way   HEARD
•fellow *has* first-class way. . .
               FAIRLY
•standard way   PARRY
and
•a way *to divide* a hen   HASTEN
•a way *to* the hill   AVIATOR
and
•do *in* many ways   ENDOWS
•way *in* t-o. . .   TWO
•ways *to* wrap. . .   ENFOLD
and
•way *back*⟨   DR.EVA.TS.YAW
     (*see also* street.transport)
way²
  the way   HOW
  way home   ROADHOUSE
  way of working   MO
  way to <u>Paris</u>   PAIRS
  way *out*   omit RD.ST
•co(rd)on the way *out*   COON
•ha(st)y way *out*   HAY
  way *out*   (in) R-D.S-T.WA-Y
•first-class way *out*   RAID
•very small way *out*   SWEET
•right way *out*   WARTY
  way *out*   omit N.S.E.W
•fi(n)d way *out*   FID
  way out   EGRESS.EXIT
  <u>way</u>-out   YAW
  way-out <u>design</u>   SIGNED
  way-out name   EGRESS.EXIT
  ways *out*   omit NE.NW.SE.SW.etc
•fi(n)d(s) ways *out*   FID
•(sw)itch ways *out*   ITCH
  ways *out*   incl in N-E etc.
•all ways *out*   WALLS

we
  we have, *say*   WEAVE
  we *hear* talk   TORQUE
  we object   US
  we, *say*   OUI.WEE
  we will, *say*   WEAL.WELL.WHEEL
  we would, *say*   WED.WEED
weak   W
weapon search   RIFLE
wear
  wearing   IN
  wearing long hair   (in) MAN-E
  wearing spots   (in) RA-SH
  wearing vest   SINGLETON
  wearing *   incl in *
•learner *wearing* a ha-t   HALT
  worn by a. . .   incl A
  worn by *   incl *
•ha-t *worn by* learner   HALT
  worn down (m)at   AT
  worn foundations   BRA(SSIERE)
     CORSETS.PANTS.VESTS
weather
  weather permitting   WP
  weather-station   STANDPOINT
  weather-*talk*   WETHER.WHETHER
weave
  weave <u>satin</u>   STAIN
  weaver   BOTTOM
  woven <u>lace if</u>. . .   FACILE
weber   WB
Wednesday   WED
weed
  weedkiller   HOE
  weeds   SACKCLOTH
week   WK
  weekend   WE
  week<u>end</u>   K
weeper   CROCODILE.NIOBE
weight¹
  weight   CT.G.GR.OZ.ST
               TON(NE).WT
  weight-*lifting*(D) ↑   NOT
  weight*less* package   CAR(ton)
  weighty harvest   STONECROP
  weighty rollers   STONES
weight²
  ¹/₁₆ ounce   DRAM.DRACHM
  16 drams   OUNCE

20 grains	SCRUPLE	well qualified	BA.MA
24 grains	DWT.PENNYWEIGHT	**welsh**[1]	LEVANT.RAT
480 grains	OUNCE	**Welsh**[2]	CAMBRIAN.CYMRIC.W
8 ounces (gold, silver)	MARK	bardic institution	GORSEDD
12 ounces Troy	POUND	beloved	BACH
16 ounces	POUND	boat	CORACLE
4 lbs (loaf)	QUARTERN	bribe to new king	MISE
4 lbs on 104 lbs allowance	TRET	burial chamber	CISTVAEN
7-10 lbs (wool or cheese)	CLOVE		KISTVAEN
14 lbs	STONE	capital	CARDIFF.W
16 lbs (cheese)	STONE	char	TORGOCH
22 lbs (hay)	STONE	dog	CORGI
24 lbs (wool)	STONE	druids' meeting	GORSEDD
25 lbs (US)	QUARTER	emblem	LEEK
28 lbs	QUARTER	fervour	HYWL
28 lbs (wool)	TOD	festival	EISTEDDFOD
36 lbs (straw)	TRUSS	fiddler	CROWDER
56 lbs (butter)	FIRKIN	fish (Lake Bala)	GWINIAD
56 lbs (old hay)	TRUSS		GWYNIAD
60 lbs (new hay)	TRUSS	flower	AFON.AVON.TAFF
100 lbs	CENTAL.QUINTAL	four-line stanza	ENGLIN
112 lbs	CWT.HUNDREDWEIGHT	giant	IDRIS
120 lbs (glass)	SEAM	girl	MEGAN
140 lbs (flour)	BOLL	hollow	CWM
240 lbs	PACK	improvised verse	PENNILL(ION)
240 lbs (wool)	WOOL-PACK	lament	PLANXTY
750-1200 lbs (tobacco)		leader	W
	HOGSHEAD	liquor	METHEGLIN
4000 lbs	LAST	literary form	TRIAD
13 stone	WEY	man	DAI.EVAN.TAFFY
2 weys	SACK	Nationalist Party	PLAID
¹/₂ cwt (hops)	HOP-POCKET		CYMRU.WNP
cwt (old)	QUINTAL	patron saint	DAVID
19¹/₂ cwts (lead)	FOTHER	people	CYMRY
25¹/₂ cwts (coal)	CHALDRON	porch	GALILEE
nylon, rayon, silk	DENIER	riots	REBECCA
silver and gold	TROY	sea	MOR
(*for metric weights see* French[3])		stanza	PENNILL
weird		valley	CWM
weird sister	WITCH	violin	CROUD.CROUTH
weird <u>sister</u>	RESIST		CROWD.CRWTH
weird <u>sisters</u>	COVEN	**Wembley game**	FA.FOOTBALL
weird <u>sisters</u>	RESISTS	*went wrong* there	ETHER
well		**Wesleyan chapel**	WC
well content	TREACLE	**west**	
well-earned money		west	W
	PETRO-DOLLARS	hence	
well-favoured	IN	•West in church	WINCE.WINCH
well-off	(SOUND) ASLEEP	•West has a very...	WAVERY

•West has no study	WODEN
West Africa	WA
	(*see also* Africa)
West Brom(wich Albion)	WBA
West Country trip	FLORAL DANCE
West *End*	T
West Indies	WI
west-northwest	WNW
west-southwest	WSW
western	W
hence	
•western aid	WHELP
•western side	WEDGE
•western art	WART
Western Australia	WA
Western Central	WC
Western European Union	WEU
Western Region	WR
Western Samoa	SS
Westminster	WI
Westminster district	SWI
West Indian	WI
allspice	JAMAICAN PEPPER
Barbados cherry	MALPHIGIA
bark	CARIBBEE BARK
	CASCARILLA
belief in snake god	ZOMBIISM
bird	GREEN SPARROW
	SOLITAIRE.TODY.TREMBLER
bobolink	BUTTER-BIRD
cake	BAMMIE
Canna	TOUS-LES-MOIS
capsicum	CHERRY-PEPPER
	PIM(I)ENTO
cassava	MANIOC.TAPIOCA
—juice	CASSAREEP.CASSARIPE
chief	CACIQUE.CAZIQUE
clay	BARBADOS EARTH
climbing plant	
	SCOTCH ATTORNEY
compressed dika seed	
	DIKA-BREAD
dance	BEGUINE.CHA-CHA(-CHA)
	LIMBO.MAMBO.R(H)UMBA
dish	PEPPER POT
drink	CURACAO.CURACOA
	EAU DE CREOLES.MOBBIE
	MOBBY.RUM.SANGAREE
	SANGRIA.TAFIA

drum	BONGO
durra	NEGRO-CORAN
edible starch	TOUS-LES-MOIS
extinct tribe	TAINO
farm	PEN
fibre	ABACA.MANIL(L)A HEMP
fish	BARRACOUTA.BARRACUDA
	COBIA.COW-PILOT.CRAB-EATER
	DAMSELFISH.DEMOISELLE
	GUPPY.MILLIONS
	SERGEANT-FISH
flea	CHIGGER.CHIGOE
	CHIGRE.JIGGER
flycatcher	SOLITAIRE
folk song	CALYPSO
freshwater tortoise	HIC(C)ATEE
fruit	A(C)KEE.ANANA(S)
	ANCHOVY PEAR
	BARBADOS CHERRY
	BARBADOS GOOSEBERRY
	BULLOCK'S HEART
	COCOPLUM.CUSTARD APPLE
	GENIPAP.GRANADILLA
	GRENADILLA.MAMMEE(-APPLE)
	PASSION FRUIT.PINGUIN
	SAPODILLA PLUM.STAR-APPLE
ghost	DUPPY.JUMBIE.JUMBY
groundnut	PINDA
gum	ANIME.COURBARIL
hog-rat	HUTIA.MUSK-CAVY
Jamaican	
—birthwort	CONTRAYERVA
—pepper	ALLSPICE
language	CARIB.TAINO
leaders	WI
lizard	GALLIWASP
locust tree	COURBARIL
magic	MYALISM.OBEAH
	OBI(A).OBY.VAUDOO
	VAUDOUX.VOODOO
	VOUDOU
manioc	CASSAVA.TAPIOCA
marmalade tree	
	MAMMEE-SAPOTA
mesquite	CASHAW
mulberry	RAMOON
music	CALYPSO.REGGAE
Negro	QUASHEE.QUASHIE
oil from dika	DIKA-BUTTER

orange dye	AN(N)ATTA
	AN(N)ATTO.ARNOTTO
passionflower	BULL-HOOF
	LOVE-IN-A-MIST
peanut	PINDA
pepper	PIM(I)ENTO
pineapple	KARATAS
pirate	BUCCANEER.BUCCANIER
	FILIBUSTER
plant	BIKA.SAVANNA FLOWER
plantation	PEN
poinciana	PEACOCK-FLOWER
potatoes	EDDOES
prickly pear	TUNA
race	CARIB
rat-like insectivore	AGOUTA
resin	ANIME
rodent	HOG-RAT.HUTIA
rock music	REGGAE
rum	TAFIA
ship	DROG(H)ER
shrub	BARBADOS PRIDE
spice	PIMENTO
spiny cactus	DILDO
spurge	MANIHOT.MANIOC
superstition	VAUDOO.VAUDOUX
	VOODOO.VOUDOU
sweet potato	BATATA
tapioca	CASSAVA.MANIOC
thrush	SOLITAIRE
thunderstorm	HOUVARI
timber	CANDLEWOOD

COCO(A)-WOOD.COCUS WOOD
JAMAICA EBONY
KOKRA-WOOD.LANCEWOOD

tortoise	HIC(C)ATEE
tree	A(C)KEE

BARBADOS CHERRY
BLACKBULLY.BOLLETRIE
BULLY-TREE.BULLET-TREE
BULLETRIE.CANELLA
COCO-PLUM.COCUS-WOOD
GAUZE-TREE.GENIPAP
GRANADILLA.GRENADILLA
HERCULES CLUB.HOG-PLUM
MALPHIGIA.LACE-TREE
LOCUST TREE.MAMMEE
PIMENTO.PRICKLY ASH.QUASSIA
SAPODILLA.SWEETWOOD

TOOTHACHE TREE
XANTHOXYLUM.YACCA

tree-nesting termite	DUCK-ANT
voodoo priestess	MAMBO
white man	BUCKRA
wild mango	DIKA
witchcraft	OBEAH.OBI(A).OBY
	MYALISM
wet suit	BATHING COSTUME
whale food	JONAH.KRILL
	PLANKTON

what

what *French*...	QUE
what *German*...	WAS
what *Italian*...	CHE
what *Spanish*...	CHE
what *did you say*	WATT.WOT

wheel

wheel round Eton⟨	NOTE
wheel spin⟨	NIPS
wheeling bats⟨	STAB

when

when *ordered*	HEWN
when speaking aloud	ALLOWED
when *speaking aloud*	WEN
when talking, Scandinavians...	
	LAPSE

where

where *in ancient Rome*	UBI
where *in France*	OU
where *in Germany*	WO
where *in Italy*	DOVE
where *in Spain*	DONDE
where the sun rises	(in) EAS-T
where the sun sets	(in) W-EST
wherein w/e lan/guish	ELAN

which

which is	QE
which see	QV
which was to be done	QEF
which was to be found	QEI
which was to be proved	QED

whichever

whichever way indicates a
  palindome:
•a lady, *whichever way*...MADAM
•grass *whichever way you*
  look   MARRAM
•*whichever way* it goes, boat...

	KAYAK
whip	
whip cream	MACER
whip *round* ⟨	TAC
whip *round*	CA-T.LA-SH
•he *has* whip-*round*	CHEAT
•six *have* whip-*round*	LAVISH
whirling dervish	SHRIVED
whisking flies	FILES
whistler	REF
white horse	BREAKER.WAVE
whittling stick	TICKS
who	
French	QUI
German	WER
Italian	CHI.CHE
Spanish	QUIENE
whole	
the whole gamut	A-Z
whole numbers	W
whole speech	HOLE
wholly sound	HOLEY
	MOTH-EATEN
why, *say*	WYE.Y
wicked sister	REGAN
wicket	W
wide shed	BROADCAST
wife	BRIDE.DUTCH.RIB.UX.W
wigmaker	LOCKSMITH
wild	
wild animal	LAMINA.MANILA
wild region	IGNORE
wild state of garden	DANGER
	GANDER.RANGED
Wild West	STEW
wildcat	ACT
wildcat strike	TRIKES
wildfowl	FLOW.WOLF
wilder than ripe...	PERIANTH
wildlife	FILE
wildlife sanctuary	NOAH'S ARK
wildly rage	GEAR
wilds of Burma	RUMBA
will	
Will's appendix	CODICIL
willing man	BARKIS
willing person	TESTATOR
willing woman	TESTATRIX
William	WM

willy-nilly into an...	NATION
wily men are...	MEANER
win	V
wind¹	
wind rag...⟨	GAR
wind up an...	PUNA
winding stream	MASTER
wind²	
48-55 knots	GALE
56-65 knots	STORM
65+ knots	HURRICANE
Australian	
—cyclone	WILLY-WILLY
—stormy	BUSTER
China Sea	TYPHOON
cold	
—Andean	PUNA
—French	BISE.MISTRAL
Cuban squall	BAYAMO
east	EURUS
—Mediterranean	LEVANT(ER)
gentle breeze	ZEPнYR
high altitude	JET STREAM
hot	
—African	BER WIND.CHILI
	HARMATTAN
—Andean	ZONDA
—Arabian	HABOOB.SAMIEL
	SHAMAL.SIMOOM.SIMOON
—Argentinan	ZONDA
—Asian	TEBBAD
—Egyptian	K(H)AMSIN
—Italian	S(C)IROCCO
—Kurdistan	RESHABAR
—mountain	FO(E)HN
—Rockies	CHINOOK
—South American	NEVADOS
—Sudanese	HABOOB
hurricane	BAGUIO
north	AQUILO(N).BOREAS
—Italian	TRAMONTANA
—Persian	SEISTAN
northeast	IMBAT.TRADE
—Adriatic	BORA
—African	HARMATTAN
—Central Asian/Siberian	BURAN
—Mediterranean	GREGALE
	MELTEMI
—Switzerland	BISE

northwest (Milton)	ARGESTES
Philippine hurricane	BAGUIO
rotating	TORNADO.TYPHOON
	WHIRLWIND
Russian windstorm	BURAN
sandstorm	HABOOD.TEBBAD
short, violent storm	SQUALL
slight breeze	MACKEREL-BREEZE
south	AUSTER.NOTUS
—African	LESTE
southeast	EURUS.TRADE
—African	CAPE DOCTOR
—Indian Ocean	MONSOON
—Spanish	SOLANO
southwest	AFER.LIBECC(H)IO
—Spanish	LEVECHE
—South American	PAMPERO
squall	BLIRT.BLORE
—Cuban	BAYAMO
—East Indian	SUMATRA
storm	GALE.HURRICANE
	TEMPEST
tempestuous	EUROCLYDON
transitory breeze	SLANT
tropical thunderstorm	TORNADO
violent gust	BLORE
west	FAVONIUS.TRADE(S)
	ZEPHYR
whirlwind	TORNADO.TYPHOON
	TOURBILLION.WHITE SQUALL
windstorm	BURAN.CYCLONE

window

window *doesn't open*	(d)ORMER
	(o)RIEL
window *opening*	W

wine

wine	ASTI.PORT.ROSE.TENT
hence	
•compere *drinks* wine	MASTIC
•run *after* wine	ASTIR
•wine *in* company	PLASTIC
and	
•drink wine	SUPPORT
•*put* wine *before* the queen	
	PORTER
•ship *carrying* wine	SPORTS
and	
•*put* nothing *in* wine	ROOSE
•soft wine	PROSE

•wine *by* rail	ROSERY
and	
•directions *about* wine	ENTENTE
•*put* wine *before* the queen	
	TENTER
•wine *without* an. . .	TENANT
wine container	SACK
	(*see also* drink²)

wing

wings	ALA
short-winged	BRACHYPTEROUS
wide *wings*	WE
wings of song	SG
wings off (r)oo(k)	OO
wing*tip*	W
winner	ACE
wire gauge	WG

wise

wise judge	DANIEL.SOLOMON
wise man	BALTHAZAR.GASPAR
	MAGUS.MELCHIOR
	SAGE.SOLON
Wise Men	MAGI
wise, *say*	YS.YY

wit

witless	omit WIT
•witless bird	T(wit)E
wit's *end*	T
Witchville	SALEM

with¹

with *French*	AVEC
with *German*	MIT
hence	
•with *German backing*⟨	TIM
•with *German* Communist	MITRED
•woman with *German*. . .	HERMIT
with *Italian*	CON
with *Latin*	CUM
with *Spanish*	CON

with²

indicates inclusion:

with a. . .	incl A
with a hole in	incl O
with a name	incl AN
with *	incl *
•*wea-r with* the. . .	WEATHER
with an overdraft	(in) RE-D
with hesitation	incl ER
with no. . .	incl O

with nothing *in*	incl O	*without* a. . .	omit A
with³		*without* a head	omit first letter
with a <u>grin</u>	RING	*without* a lead(*er*)	omit first letter
with a *loss*	omit A	•(c)how *without a lead*	HOW
with a *missing*. . .	omit A	•(p)arty *without a leader*	ARTY
with a tenant	LET	*without* a name	omit AN
with difficulty <u>masters</u>	STREAMS	*without* a penny	omit D or P
with hesitation	-ER	*without* a starter	omit first letter
with much hesitation	-ERER	*without* aspiration	omit H
with no aspiration	omit H	*without* back	omit last letter
with nothing (on)	-O	•sea(t) *without* back	SEA
hence		*without* capital	omit first letter
•father *with* nothing	DADO	*without* energy	omit E
•Prince *with* nothing	HALO	*without* eyes, *say*	omit Is or ISE
•surgeon *with* nothing	VETO	*without* hesitation	omit ER
with nothing on	-OON	*without* love	omit O
hence		*without* money	omit L
•dance *with* nothing on	BALLOON	*without* my fa(m)il(y)	FAIL
•girl *with* nothing on	GOON	*without* name	omit N
•many *with* nothing on	LOON	*without* nothing	omit O
	MOON	*without* one. . .	omit I
with praise	CL	*without* passion	omit IRE
with string	CORDON	*without* royal. . .	omit KING
with⁴		•win(king) *without* royal. . .	WIN
meaning having	(*see* having)	*without* tail	omit last letter
withdraw		•do(g) *without tail*	DO
withdraw a. . .	omit A	*without* (t)he *initiative*	HE
withdraw part. . .⟨	TRAP	*without the initiative to* (s)tart	
withdraw *	omit *		TART
•in (cr)ash, *withdraw* credit	ASH	*without* the queen	omit ER
withdrawn from du/ty ro/ster		*without* victory	omit V
	TYRO	**without²**	prefix A or AN
withhold		meaning:	
withhold a. . .	omit A	absence of/deficiency of	
withhold money	omit L	failure of/lack of	
withhold *	omit *	lacking/loss of	
•*withhold* everything from		minus/want of, etc.	
sh(all)ow	SHOW	ability	
with*holding*	W-ITH	—of heart to pump	ASYSTOLE
within		—to	
*with*in	incl IN	—communicate	APHASIA
•mother *with*in	MAIN	—manipulate objects	APRAXIA
within 24 hours	(in) DA-Y	—read	ALEXIA
within call	R-ING	—speak	ALOGIA
within the/se w/alls	SEW	—swallow	APHAGIA.APHAGY
within *	incl in *	—transmit radiant heat	
•learner *within* s-ight	SLIGHT		ATHERMANCY
without¹		—write	AGRAPHIA
indicating omission:		accent	ATONIC

an article	ANARTHROUS
angle	AGONIC
anxiety	ATARAXIA.ATARAXY
appetite	ANOREXIA.ANOREXY
arrangement	
—in belts	AZONAL
—in rows	ASTICHOUS
being	
—joined	AZYGOUS
—leavened	AZYMOUS
—straight	ATROPOUS
belief in God	ATHEISM
blood	ANAEMIA
body channel	ATRESIA
brain	ANCEPHALY
breathing	APNOEA
carbon dioxide	ACAPNIA
care (sloth)	ACEDIA
cause	ACAUSAL
central column	ASTELY
chain structure	ACYCLIC
change	AMETABOLOUS
columns	ASTYLAR
connection	ASYNARTETE
—conforming to type	ATYPICAL
comprehensibility	ACATALEPSY
conjunctions	ASYNDETON
co-ordination	ASYNERGIA
correct vision	ASTIGMATISM
death	ATHANASY
distinct joints	ANARTHROUS
disturbance	ATARAXIA.ATARAXY
disproportion in dwarfism	
	ATELEIOSIS
echo	ANECHOIC
energy	ATONY
feeling	ANAESTHESIA
feet	APODOUS
fingers	ADACTYL
fever	APYREXIA
food	ABROSIA
germs	ASEPTIC
gills	ABRANCHIATE
grammatical structure	
	ASYNTACTIC
gravity	AGRAVIC
growth	ATROPHY
hands	AMANOUS
harmony	ANHARMONIC

head	ACEPHALOUS
honour	ATIMY
hope	ANOMIE.ANOMY
horns	ACEROUS
inclination	ACLINIC
intervening vowel	ATHEMATIC
law	ANARCHY.ANOMIA
leaves	APHYLLOUS
lens (eye)	APHACIA
life	AZOIC
light	APHOTIC
limbs	AMELIA
liquid	ANEROID
literacy	ANALPHABETIC
logic	ALOGICAL
memory	AMNESIA
mental ability	AMENTIA
meeting	ASYMPTOTE
milk	AGALAXY
mitosis	AMITOSIS
morals	AMORAL
mouth	ASTOM(AT)OUS
muscular coordination	ATAXIA
	ATAXY
nerves	ANEURIN
nervous energy	ANEURIA
offspring	ATOCIA
oxygen	ANAEROBIC.ANOXIA
pain	ANALGESIA.ANODYNE
perception	AGNOSIA
perfect vision	ANASTIGMATIC
perianth	ACHLAMYDEOUS
petals	APETALOUS
point	ASTIGMATIC
placenta	APLACENTAL
political attitudes	APOLITICAL
portrayal in human or animal	
form	ANICONIC
power	ADYNAMIA.ADYNAMY
proper development	APLASIA
pulsation	ACROTISM
pulse	ASPHYXIA.ASPHYXY
rays	ABACTINAL
regular intervals	APERIODIC
secreting milk	AGALACTIA
sense of	
—smell	ANOSMIA
—taste	AGEUSIA
—touch	ANAPHIA

sepals	ASEPALOUS
septum	ASEPTATE
sex	ASEXUAL
sexual desire	ANAPHRODISIAC
shadow	ASCIAN
sight	ANOPSIA
social interest	ASOCIAL
sound	ANACOUSTIC
speech	ALALIA.APHEMIA
spherical aberration	APLANATIC
stability	ASTATIC
stem	ACAULESCENT
strength	ADYNAMIA.ADYNAMY
	ASTHENIA
strong digestion	APEPSIA
	APEPSY
symmetry	ASSYMMETRY
synchronism	ASYNCHRONOUS
syntactical sequence	
	ANACOLUTHIA
tail	AN(O)UROUS
theme (music)	ATHEMATIC
theology	ATHEOLOGY
tone	ATONIC
turning	ATROPOUS
understanding	ANOESIS
vitamins	AVITAMINOSIS
voice	ANAUDIA
	APHONIA.APHONY
water	ANHYDROUS
willpower	AB(O)ULIA
without³	EX.IN.SIN.SINE.X
meaning:	
lacking	
minus:	
a day fixed	SD.SINE DIE
albumen	EXALBUMINOUS
alteration	INVARIABLE
animation	INANIMATE
awns	MUTICOUS
beak	EROSTRATE
blame	INCULPABLE
blood	EXSANGUINOUS
body	INCORPOREAL
bracteoles	EBRACTEOLATE
bracts	EBRACTEATE
change	INVARIABLE
children	ISSUELESS
	SINE PROLE.SP

congruousness	INCONCINNOUS
consideration (law)	NUDE
date	SA
desire	INAPPETENT
distinct margin	IMMARGINATE
doubt	SINE DUBIO
effect	INSIGNIFICANT.INVALID
equality	IMPARITY
faith	NULLIFIDIAN
fault	IMPECCABLE
fear	IMPAVID
feeling	INSENSATE
flavour	INSIPID
foresight	IMPROVIDENT
form or shape	INFORM
glands	EGLANDULAR
hinges	ECARDINATE
horns	MOOLY.MUL(L)EY
importance	INDIFFERENT
indication	INDESIGNATE
interest	INSIPID
issue	SP.SINE PROLE
knowledge	NESCIENT
lid	INOPERCULATE
life	EXANIMATE.INANIMATE
male issue	SMP
means of communication	
	INCOMMUNICADO
method	IMMETHODICAL
modesty	IMPRUDENT
money	BROKE.IMPECUNIOUS
morals	IMMORAL
movement	IMMOBILE
name	INNOMINATE
nodes	ENODAL
nucleus	ENUCLEATE
operculum	INOPERCULATE
opposition	NEM CON
permanence	IMPERMANENT
personality	IMPERSONAL
placenta	IMPLACENTAL
point	MUTICOUS
power	IMPOTENT
probity	IMPROBITY
proportion	INCONCINNOUS
qualification	LAY
religion	IRRELIGIOUS
restraint	IMMODEST
ribs	ECOSTATE

sap	EXSUCCOUS
sensation	INSENSATE
settled dwelling	
	NOMADIC.VAGRANT
shame	IMPRUDENT
smell	INODOROUS
speech	OBMUTESCENT
spine	MUTICIOUS
spirit	EXANIMATE.INANIMATE
	INSIPID
stalk	SESSILE
stipules	EXSTIPULATE
surviving issue	SPS
tail	ECAUDATE
taste	INSIPID
tax	EXCESS.ORATED
teeth	EDENTATE.EDENTULOUS
thought	IMPROVIDENT
transparency	OPAQUE
validity	INVALID
water	NEAT
weight	IMPONDERABLE
will	INTESTATE
willingness	NOLITION
wisdom	INSIPIENT

without⁴
meaning:
outside
without a. . .	incl A

without a synonym
	EXTERNAL.OUTSIDE
without hesitation	incl ER.UM
without money	incl L
without *	incl *
•*w-e without* her	WHERE

without⁵
meaning:
with out
•sailor *with*out. . .	ABOUT

without⁶
other uses:
without end	ETERNAL.INFINITE
without *end*	T
without fully ap/pear/ing	PEAR
witty rhyme	BITTY.CITY
	DITTY.PITY
wizened hag sat. . .	AGHAST

wobble
wobbling chin	INCH
wobbly note	ETON.TONE
wobbly note	QUAVER

woe
woe-*begotten*	OWE
woeful expression	OH

wolf
wolf *returns*	FLOW
wolf *wild*	WILDFOWL

woman¹ EVE.F.HER.RIB.SHE.W
hence
•woman *is given* directions	EVENS
•woman *is neutral*	LEVER
•woman n(o)t *heartless*	EVENT

and
•woman is hot	FISH
•woman or man	FORM
•woman *with* one aim	FIEND

and
•strike woman	HITHER
•tie *back* woman. . .	EITHER
•woman with *German*. . .	HERMIT

and
•about a woman	CARIB
•b-e *without* a woman	BRIBE
•woman *with* good *French*	
	RIBBON

and
•woman *has* a red. . .	SHEARED
•woman *is given* directions	SHEWN
•woman *with* learners	SHELL

and
•woman *has* all. . .	WALL
•woman is queen	WISER
•woman's crew	WEIGHT

woman²
headless (w)oman	OMAN
short (w)omen	OMEN
woman *with* man	EVADES
	MANGAL.SALTED.VIAL
(w)oman *losing* her head	OMAN
woman *losing her head*	(m)ARIA
woman *losing* her *head*	BET(h)
woman's angle	NORMAL
woman's army	ATS
(w)omen *losing* their head	OMEN
women's extra	WX
Women's Institute	WI
Women's Land Army	WLA

Women's Liberal Federation WLF
Women's Rural Institute WRI
Women's Voluntary Service WVS

woman³

Australian woman ADELAIDE
SHEILA
Dutch woman FROW.VROUW
Egyptian woman BINT
French woman FEMME
German woman FRAU
Italian woman DONNA
nursemaid ALICE
Spanish woman MUJER
tragic woman ELECTRA.HECUBA
MEROPE
women (*see also* Appendix)

won't

* *won't be there* omit *
•p(r)ay king *won't be there* PAY

wood

wood ASH.DEAL.FIR
hence
•wooden measure ASHEN
•wooden saint FIRST
•wooden square DEALT
wood BOWL.JACK
wooden-faced VENEERED
wooden junk LUMBER

woolly JERSEY
woolly coat ATOC

word

word of four
letters
QUADRILITERAL.TETRAGRAM
word processor WP
word processing WP
words per minute WPM
word of mouth news GNUS

work¹ ERG.OP.OPUS
hence
•second-class work BERG
•work *in* an-y, *say* ENERGY
•work *with* no. . . ERGO
and
•quiet work SHOP
•work problems OPPOSERS
•workman OPAL.OPTED

work²
work into shape HEAPS.PHASE

wor(k) *not finished* WOR
work on road DORA
work out sums MUSS
work *over*⟨ PO
work record BOOK OF JOB
worked out in gym MINGY
working (in) HAR-NESS
working men are. . . RENAME
working models SELDOM
*work*rate TARE.TEAR

worker

worker ANT.BEE.HAND.MAN
hence
•defame worker MALIGNANT
•worker in charge ANTIC
•worker in afterthought PANTS
and
•worker at church BEECH
•worker for each. . . BEEPER
•worker on railway BEERY
Workers' Education
Association WEA
workers' group TU

world

world bank BIS
world terminal EARTH
World
—Boxing Association WBA
—Boxing Council WBC
—Championship Tennis WCT
—Council of Churches WCC
—Federation of Trade
Unions WFTU
—Health Organization WHO
—Meteorological Organization
WMO
—Wide Fund for Nature WWF
worldwide MONDIAL

worn (*see* wear)

worry

worried mien MINE
worry over ROVE
worrying sheep PHESE

worship
of:
animals THERIOLATRY
ZOOLATRY
angels ANGELOLATRY
books BIBLIOLATRY

Christ	CHRISTOLATRY
church forms and traditions	ECCLESIOLATRY
dead	NECROLATRY
devil	SATANISM
earth	GEOLATRY
fetishes	FETICHISM.FETISHISM
fire	PYROLATRY
fish	ICTHYOLATRY
idols	IDOLATRY.IDOLISM
images	ICONOLATRY
man	ANTHROPOLATRY
nature	PHYSIOLATRY
nobility	LORDOLATRY
one god	MONOLATRY
sacred things	HIEROLATRY
saints	HAGIOLATRY.HIEROLATRY
self	AUTOLATRY
Shakespeare	BARDOLATRY
snakes	OPHIOLATRY
stars	ASTROLATRY
sun	HELIOLATRY
symbols	SYMBIOLATRY
trees	DENDROLATRY
Virgin Mary	MARIOLATRY
wonders	THAUMATOLATRY
words	EPEOLATRY
world	COSMOLATRY
Worshipful	WP
worsted a Red...	DARE.DEAR.RADE.READ
would *you say*	WOOD
wound	
wound stripe	SCAR
wounded deer that's...	SHATTERED
woven	(*see* weave)
wrap	
wrapped in pa/per for m/y...	PERFORM
wrapped in *	incl in *
•is *wrapped in* hide	SISKIN
wrapping a...	incl A
wrapping *	incl A
•hide *wrapping* is...	SISKIN
wrecked ship	HIPS
wrestling ring is...	RISING
wretched life	FILE
wriggling eels	ELSE.SEEL

wrinkled skin	INKS.SINK
write¹	PEN
hence	
•write a number...	PENNINE
•write *to* Edward	PENNED
•write *to* Gotham	PENNY
write *back*⟨	NEP
write-*up*(D) ↑	NEP
•write-*up* in i-t	INEPT
•write-*up* song	NEPTUNE
•*writing* material, *say*	PENTACLE
write²	
write up notes(D) ↑	SETON
writer	NIB.PEN
	ELIA.POE.WELLS
Writer to the Signet	WS
writer's block	PAD
writing	MS
writing out the list	THISTLE
written in prose	PORES.POSER.SPORE
written in S/pan/ish	PAN
written into *	incl in *
•*outset written in* wor-ds	WORSTEDS
written about a...	incl A
written about *	incl *
•wor-ds *written about* outset	WORSTEDS
wrote off	TOWER
write³	
including	
description of	
engraving	
drawing (of)	
photograph (of)	
record (of)	
writing (about):	
atmosphere	AEROGRAPHY
bad	
—spelling	PSEUDOGRAPHY
—writing	CACOGRAPHY
bones	OSTEOGRAPHY
books	BIBLIOGRAPHY
brain X-ray	ENCEPHALOGRAPH
calculation chart	ABAC
	NOMOGRAM
	NOMOGRAPH
ciphers	STEGANOGRAPHY

colour
—analysis   CHROMATOGRAPHY
—frequencies   SPECTROGRAPH
—printing
        CHROMOLITHOGRAPHY
        CHROMOTYPOGRAPHY
        CHROMOXYLOGRAPHY
contour feathers
        PTERYLOGRAPHY
copying   MIMEOGRAPH
        PANTOGRAPHY
        XEROGRAPHY
—drawings   EIDOGRAPHY
correct writing   ORTHOGRAPHY
dancing   CHORE(O)GRAPHY
description of
—nature   PHYSIOGRAHPY
—skin   DERMATOGRAPHY
dictionaries   LEXICOGRAPHY
diseases   NOSOGRAPHY
        PATHOGRAPHY
ellipses   ELLIPSOGRAPH
engraving
—in wood   XYLOGRAPHY
—on brass or copper
        CHALCOGRAPHY
exact copy   APOGRAPH
features of Mars   AREOGRAPHY
fine writing   CALLIGRAPHY
geography   CHOROGRAPHY
        TOPOGRAPHY
geographical distribution of
  plants and animals
        BIOGEOGRAPHY
ground plans   ICHNOGRAPHY
handwriting   CH(E)IROGRAPHY
heart movements
        CARDIOGRAPHY
heat   THERMOGRAPHY
height and depth of land
  and water   BATHYOROGRAPHY
hymns   HYMNOGRAPHY
ideography   PASIGRAPHY
illustration   ICONOGRAPHY
impression (photographic) on
—wood block
        PHOTOXYLOGRAPHY
—zinc plate
        PHOTOZINCOGRAPHY

interwoven letters   MONOGRAM
laws   NOMOGRAPHY
life
—and writings BIOBIBLIOGRAPHY
—of individual   BIOGRAPHY
light image   PHOTOGRAPHY
many copies   POLYGRAPH
map making   CARTOGRAPHY
—from aerial photographs
        PHOTOGRAMMETRY
meteorological records
        AEROGRAPHY
        METEOROGAPHY
microscopic
—images PHOTOMICROGRAPHY
—objects   MICROGRAPHY
—photograph   MICROCOPY
        MICROPHOTOGRAPH
mimes   MIMOGRAPHY
miracles   THAUMATOGRAPHY
motion pictures
        CINEMATOGRAPHY
        KINEMATOGRAPHY
—through microscope
        CINEMICROGRAPHY
mountains   OR(E)OGRAPHY
muscular contractions
        MYOGRAPHY
myths   MYTHOGRAPHY
obituaries   NECROGRAPHY
omission of letters or syllables
        LIPOGRAPHY
on both sides   OPISTHOGRAPHY
on one subject   MONOGRAPH
on wax   CEROGRAPHY
opinions of Greek
  philosophers   DOXOGRAPHY
organs of animals or plants
        ORGANOGRAPHY
original manuscript AUTOGRAPH
perspective drawing
        SCENOGRAPHY
picture-writing   PICTOGRAPHY
poker work   PYROGRAPHY
printing   TYPOGRAPHY
printing from
  photographic plates
        PHOTOLITHOGRAPHY
—stone   LITHOGRAPHY

—type cast in one word   LOGOGRAPHY
private mark   IDIOGRAPH
proverbs   PAROEMIOGRAPHY
quick writing   SHORTHAND
radiography   ROENTGENOGRAPHY
reverse-image photograph   ROTOGRAPH
rocks   PETROGRAPHY
scene painting   SCENOGRAPHY
seas   OCEANOGRAPHY
shorthand   BRACHYGRAPHY
   TACHYGRAPHY
   STENOGRAPHY
signed by all parties   SYNGRAPH
silk-screen printing   SERIGRAPHY
sounds as symbols   PHONOGRAPHY
spirit-writing   PSYCHOGRAPHY
split laser photography   HOLOGRAPHY
still-life painting   RHYPAROGRAPHY
sun   CORONAGRAPHY
   CORONOGRAPHY
—photographed on particular wavelength   SPECTROHELIOGRAPH
symbol
—for phrase   PHRASEOGRAM
representing
—concept or idea   IDEOGRAM.IDEOGRAPH
teeth   ODONTOGRAPHY
three-dimensional
—image   HOLOGRAM
—picture   STEREOGRAPH
   VECTOGRAPH
time   CHRONOGRAPHY
topography   CHOROGRAPHY
trade mark   IDIOGRAPH
transmission by
—electric impulses   TELAUTOGRAPH
   TELEGRAPHY

—telegraphy   PHOTOTELEGRAPHY
unintentional repetition   DITTOGRAPHY
vibrations   VIBROGRAPH
voluminous writing   POLYGRAPHY
weather   METEOROGRAPHY
wholly by author   HOLOGRAPH
wind measurements   ANEMOGRAPHY
with stylus   STYLOGRAPHY
world   COSMOGRAPHY
wonders of nature   THAUMATOGRAPHY
woven in silk   STEVENGRAPH
written
—character   IDEOGRAM
   IDEOGRAPH
—cyphers   CRYPTOGRAPHY
wrong words   PARAGRAPHIA
X-ray   RADIOGRAM
   SKIAGRAPH
—photography   ROENTGENOGRAPHY
—xerography   XERORADIOGRAPHY
   (*see also* X-ray)

wrong
wrong again   SECOND SLIP
wrong fount   WF
wrong mark   X
wrong river   TORTOISE
wrong sign   X
wrong *parts*   GROWN
wrong parts   STRAP
wrong version of <u>song</u>   SNOG
wrong way ⟨   YAW
wrong way to VIP⟨   PIVOT
wrong way up(D) ↑   PU
wrong <u>ways</u>   SWAY.YAWS
wrongfully <u>the law</u>...   WEALTH
wrongly constructed arch   CHAR
wrought <u>iron panel</u>   NONPAREIL
w-worker   WANT
Wye, *say*   WHY.Y
Wyeville   ROSS

X

across. body. chi. Christ. chromosome. cross. draw. ex. *Exe*. film. illiterate's sign. kiss. particle. *PM's address*. ray. *sign of the times*. sixty. *sixty thousand*. *spot marked*. takes. ten. ten thousand. thousand. times. unknown. vitamin. vote. wrong sign. xi. Xmas

X-ray	CROSSBEAM	—salivary tract	SIALOGRAM
—of		—spinal cord	MYELOGRAPHY
—blood-vessels	ANGIOGRAPHY	—urinary tract	UROGRAPHY
	ARTERIOGRAPHY	**xanthium**	BURDOCK
—bones	OSTEOGRAPHY		BURMARIGOLD
—brain	ENCEPHALOGRAPHY		CLOTBUR.CLOTE
	VENTRICULOGRAPHY	**Xantippe**	SHREW
—breast	MAMMOGRAPHY	**Xeres**	SHERRY
—kidneys	PYELOGRAPHY	**XLNC**	EXCELLENCY
—layer or body	TOMOGRAPHY	**XPDNC**	EXPEDIENCY

Y

alloy. chromosome. level. moth. one hundred and fifty. one hundred and fifty thousand. track. unknown. *why*. yard. year. yen. *young*. *youth*. yttrium.

yacht			**VOSOTROS**
yacht's *bow*	Y	you *in the middle*	O
yacht's *stern*	T	*you may have* to shout	OUTSHOT
yard	CID.Y.YD	*you might say* we. . .	WEE
year	Y.YR	you *no longer*	THEE.YE
year after Hegira	AH	you *once*	THEE.YE
year of reign	AR	you queue	UQ
yearly	PA	you, *say*	EU.EWE.U.YEW
hence		*you say* no	KNOW
•yearly call	PARING	you see	UC
•yearly employment	PAUSE	you *sound*. . .	EU.EWE.U.YEW
•yearly expense	PARENTAL	you will, *say*	YULE
yearly meeting	AGM	**young**	
yellow	OR	young feller	WASHINGTON
yellow plate	CHROME	young swimmer	ELVER
yen	YN	(*see also* fish[2])	
yeomanry	YEO	younger	YR
yes	AY.AYE	youngster	MINOR
French	OUI	**your**	YR
French/German	OUIJA	your head	Y
German	JA	Your Holiness	
Italian	SI		SANCTITAS.VESTRA
Russian	DA		SV
Spanish	SI	your uncle	BOB
yew(s)	U.(US.UU)	yours truly	I.ME
Yiddish	(*see* Hebrew)	**youth**	
yield		youth	MINOR
yield from shares	SHEARS	youth leader	GUIDER
yielding oil	OLI-	youth *leader*	Y
yields much. . .	CHUM	youth *leaders*	WISE.YS
you	U	youth *leaders*	YO
you are, *say*	UR	**Yugoslavia(n)**	YU
you can *hear*	YUKON	capital	BELGRADE.Y
you can hear a noise	ANNOYS	coins	DINAR.DNR.PARA
you *in France*	TU.VOUS	leader	Y
you *in Germany*	DU.DICH.SIE	parliament	SKUPSHTINA
you *in Italy*	LEI.TU.VOI	province	BANAT
you *in Spain*	TU.USTED	**Yule log**	HOLLYWOOD

Z

Zaire	ZR	bull	TAURUS
Zambia(n)	Z	crab	CANCER
capital	LUSAKA.Z	fishes	PISCES
coin	KWA(T)CHA.NGWEE	goat	CAPRICORN(US)
leader	Z	lion	LEO
Zamenhof's language	ESPERANTO	ram	ARIES
Zantippe (Zentippe)	SHREW	scorpion	SCORPIO
zero		twins	GEMINI
zero	DUCK.LOVE.NAUGHT.NIL	virgin	VIRGO
	NO.NOTHING.NOUGHT.O	water-carrier	AQUARIUS
hence		**Zone Standard Time**	ZST
•zero hour	OH	**zoological regions**	
•zero mark	OSCAR	Arctic	ARCTOGAEA
•zero-rated	ORATED	Australasian	NOTOGAEA
zero population growth	ZPG	Neotropical	NEOGAEA
zodiac (signs)		region of the bear	ARCTOGAEA
archer	SAGITTARIUS	southern	NOTOGAEA
balance	LIBRA	tropical America	NEOGAEA

APPENDIX: NAMES

The following are largely 'compiler's definitions' of some personal names. Most names also have literal meanings (eg: Agatha = good) which can be found in standard dictionaries

MEN

AARON	AA man
	high priest
ABE	LINCOLN
ABEL	able
	ADAMSON
	third man
ACHATES	Bill doesn't like
	trusted friend
ACTAEON	cuckold
	hunter
ACTON	historian
ADAM	architect
	BEDE
	first mate
	front runner
	furniture designer
	gaoler
	leading man
	race leader
	SMITH
ADAMSON	ABEL.CAIN.SETH
ADONIS	beau.dandy
ADRIAN	MOLE
AIDAN	NADIA.DIANA
AL	CAPONE
	gangster
ALAN	*from* New Ze/alan/d
ALBERT	two boys
	watchchain
Albert's place	HALL
ALEC	smart(ypants)
ALEX	a Roman law
ALEXANDER	a Great name
ALF	*is from* S/alf/ord
ALFRED	a Great name
	almost (h)alf Communist
	cake-burner
ALGY	*in* hospit/al gy/m
	LG, *say*
ALI	boxer
	CLAY
ALVIN	anvil
AMOS	Andy's partner

	bookmaker
	OT book
ANANIAS	liar
ANDREW	Apostle
	fisherman
	may wander
	merry fellow
ANDY	Amos's partner
	CAPP
	with us *in* spirit (br/andy/)
ANSELM	bishop
	theologian
ANTHONY	ADVERSE
	smallest pig in litter
ANTON	is a heavyweight
ANTONIO	Merchant of Venice
ANTONY	MARK
ARCHIE	AA gun
	RICE
ARCHY	Mehitabel's biographer
ARISTOTLE	philosopher
ARNE	composer
ARNOLD	BENEDICT
	headmaster
	ROLAND
	RONALD
ARTHUR	lived at Camelot
ATLAS	giant
	map book
	mountains
AUTOLYCUS	plagiarist
	thief
BACON	rasher
	philosopher
BALTHAZAR	wise man
BARKER	dog
BARKIS	carrier
	is willing
BARNABY	RUDGE
BASIL	BRUSH
	herb
BEN	big man
	big timer
	HUR

	peak		niggard
BENJAMIN	gum benzoin	CARLO(S)	CAROL(S)
	overcoat	CATO	censor
	youngest son	CHARLES	Bonny Prince
BERT	*has some* li/bert/y		Chas
BERTIE	WOOSTER		LAMB
BERTRAND	RUSSELL	CHARLEY/CHARLIE	
BILL	AC		gullible fool
	account		inefficient person
	act		moustache
	ad		night watchman
	poster		small beard
	tab	CHARON	ferryman
BILLY	brother	CHRISTIAN	Bunyan's man
	BUNTER	CHRISTOPHER	KIT
	can		SLY
	companion-in-arms	CLARENCE	carriage
	goat		diligence
	teapot	CLAUD	ducal
BILLY's		CLAUDE	painter
—boy	kid	CLEMENT	mild man
—wife	nanny		Pope
BOANERGES	noisy preacher	CLIVE	man of India
	shouting orator	COLIN	quail
BOB	shilling	COLLINS	letter of thanks
	your uncle	CONSTANT	LAMBERT
BOBADIL	swaggering boaster	CRAIG	*rolls* cigar
BOBBY	PC	CRISPIN	shoemaker
	policeman	CROMWELL	NOLL
BOOTH	assassin		Protector
	jeer *at most of* th(e)...	CUTHBERT	shirker
	stall	CYRIL	*writes* lyric
BORIS	GOUDENOV	CYRUS	Persian king
	is good enough	DAI	Welshman
BOTTOM	weaver	DAMON	*returning* nomad
BROWN	capability		RUNYON
	tan	DAN	black belt man
BROWNE	SAM		Dangerous
BRUCE	ROBERT		*in some* /dan/ger
	spiderman		MCGREW
BUD	American friend	DANIEL	bookmaker
	FLANAGAN		lion-tamer
BUTLER	RAB		OT book
	RHETT		wise judge
CAIN	ADAMSON	DANTE	*made* a dent
	(first) murderer		poet
	tribute	DAVID	giant-killer
CARL	churl		his work, Psalms
	husbandman	DENIS	is *after* a room

	is snide
	the man I send
DENNIS	fell *back*
	sinned ⟨
DENRY MACHIN	card
DICKENS	BOZ
DIOGENES	tubby man
DON	assume
	dress
	Fellow
	riverman
	Spanish noble
DONALD	duck
DONNE	done, *say*
	poet
DORIAN	*makes* inroad
DOUGLAS	fir
	his pet, Manx cat
	Man's man
	Manxman
DUNCAN	ISADORA
DUSTY	MILLER
EDDY	goes in circles
	NELSON
EDGAR	*makes the* grade
	raged *wildly*
EDISON	*has* no side
	inventor
EDWARD	confessor
	potato king
EDMUND	Ironside
ELGAR compositions	glare
	lager
	large
	regal
ELI	priest
	Samuel's teacher
ELIA	LAMB
	unr/elia/ble writer
ELIAS	*in the* aisle
ELIOT	poet
	TS
ELISHA	prophet
	SHEILA
ELVIS	*changed* lives
	destroyed evils
	PRESLEY
EMIL	*makes* lime
	running mile
ENOCH	Ayli's mate
	priest
ERASMUS	masseur
	philosopher
ERIC	blood money
	cooks rice
	Central Am/eric/an
	gradually
	Red Norseman
ERNIE	bondsman
	number chooser
	WISE
	upsets IRENE
ERNEST	earnest, *say*
	HEMINGWAY
	important to be
	sounds sincere
ESAU	hunter
ETTY	artist
EVAN	Welsh John
EVELYN	diarist
EZRA	bookmaker
	OT book
	poet
	POUND
FELIX	cat
FLASHMAN	bully
FLETCHER	arrowmaker
FOX	TOD
FRANK	franc, *say*
	open
	sincere
	stamp
GABRIEL	archangel
GANYMEDE	cup-bearer
GARIBALDI	biscuit
	Italian hero
GARY	state railway
GASPAR	wise man
GENE	item of make-up
GEORGE	automatic pilot
	BOY
	ELIOT
	SAND
GERALD	*wildly* glared
GIBBON	historian
	monkey
GILBERT	composer
	WS

GILES	farmer	JACK	AB
GOLDSMITH	or mighty man		American detective
GORDON	general		breadfruit tree
	riots		card.car lifter
GREGORY	PECK		defensive coat
	pope		fellow
GRIMES	sweep		flag
GUS	large store.theatre cat		FROST
GUY	FAWKES		hearty.honour
	helps with camp upkeep		house builder
	supporter		in the box
HADRIAN	wall-builder		Jill's boy
HAL	HENRY		knave.knife.nave, *say*
	comes from /Hal/ifax		nob
HAMLET	great Dane		SPRAT
	upset THELMA		sailor.salt.tar
	village		term of contempt
HANK	skein		union.wood (bowls)
HARRY	harass		young pike
HECTOR	badger	JACK KETCH	hangman
	bully		suspender
	Trojan hero	JACOB	ladderman
HENRY	navigator	JAKE	good fellow
HENRY FORD's bunk	history	JAMES	baked sheep's head
HENRY, Sir	WOOD		bookmaker
HERB	simple		crowbar
HERMAN	*bit of a* fis/herman/		homely fellow
HERBERT	AP.APH		NT book
HIRAM	employs people		overcoat
HOMER	pigeon		WATT
	poet	JASON	Argonaut
HUGH	hew or hue, *say*		JONAS
HUME	philosopher		looks both ways
HUMPHREY	bogey.bogie	JASPER	stone
IAN	FLEMING	JAY	bird
	one and one		J, *say*
	Scot		walker
IBSEN	ghost-writer	JEEVES	manservant
INGE	dean	JENKINS	society reporter
INIGO	in I go, *say*		toady
	JONES	JEREMIAH	bookmaker
IRA	*captured by* p/ira/tes		OT book
	terrorists		prophet of doom
ISAIAH	bookmaker	JEROME	boatman
	OT book		KERN
	prophet		writer
ISHMAEL	outcast	JERRY	builder
IVOR	is from L/ivor/no		can-man
IXION	fiery revolutionary		chamber pot

	German	JULIUS	CAESAR
JIM	CROW	KELLY	Man's man.Manxman
	lucky	KINGSLEY	his friends are AMIS
JOB	bookmaker	KIT	CHRISTOPHER
	OT book		outfit
	patient one	LAMB	CHARLES
JOCK	Scot		ELIA
JOE	GI		Mary's follower
	sweetheart	LANCE	pierce
	threepenny piece		spear
	US soldier		weapon
JOEL	bookmaker	LANG	archbishop
	OT book	LAUD	archbishop
JOEY	kangaroo		praise
	roo	LAWRENCE	DH
JOHN	AUGUSTUS		ROSS
	bookmaker		TE
	BULL	LEANDER	hero-worshipper
	DOE	LEO	lion
	EVAN (Welsh)		man of pride
	GAUNT		sign of Zodiac
	IAN (Scottish)	LEON	NOEL
	lavatory	LEONARDO	top drawer
	NT book	LEWIS	CARROLL
	PEEL		gun
	PRESTER		island
	SEAN (Irish)		metal cramp
	simpleton	LIAM	mail *order*
JONATHAN	American (people)		*from* Mali
	apple	LINCOLN	ABE
	SWIFT	LIONEL	young lion
JONAH	bookmaker	LLOYD	DOLLY
	OT book		MARIE
	whale-food	LOTHARIO	lover
JONAS	JASON		rake
JONES	riding-coat	LOUIS	coin
	standard-setter	LUKE	bookmaker
JOSEPH	coloured coat man		NT book
	dreamer		physician
JOSHUA	bookmaker	LUTHER	MARTIN
	OT book	MAC	Scot
	trumpeter	MAL	degree student
JOSHUA, Sir	PRA	MARCEL	*could be* calmer
	REYNOLDS	MARCO	POLO
JUDAS	notorious kisser	MARIO	LANZA
	spyhole		March 10th
	traitor	MARK	ANTONY
JUDE	bookmaker		bookmaker
	OT book		German coin.DM

	imprint	NOAH	ARKWRIGHT
	NT book		boatbuilder
	scar	NOEL	Christmas
	TWAIN		COWARD
MARK TWAIN	two fathoms		LEON
MARTIN	bird	NORMAN	and not male
	birdman		conqueror
	LUTHER		standard article
MATTHEW	bookmaker		windlass bar
	NT book		WISDOM
MAX	makes master cross	NYE,Nicholas	ass
	maximum.most	NYM	corporal
MELCHIOR	wise man		Falstaff's henchman
MICHAEL	angel.archangel	OBERON	fairy king
MICK	Irishman		from Borneo
MICKEY	FINN		has no robe
	gets taken		honoured name
	MOUSE		is no Boer
MILES	knight	OG	King of Bashan
MILL	economist	OLAF	sliced loaf
	factory	OLD BILL	police
	fight	OLD BOB	shilling
MILLER	dusty	OLIVER	duck liver
	GLENN		or evil
	grinder		NOLL
MONTAGUE	ROMEO		orphan
MORGAN	pirate		TWIST
MOSES	lawgiver	OMAR	*comes from* Roma
	prophet		*may* roam
Mr Turner⟨	RM	ONEGIN	singular spirit
MURPHY	potato.SPUD.tuber	ORIGEN	theologian
NAT	insect impersonator		*may* ignore
	sounds fly	OSCAR	film award.statuette
NED	*half* stoned		large vehicle
NEDDY	donkey		WILDE
	economic council		zero mark
NELSON	admiral	OSWALD	assassin
	arm-lock		MOSLEY
	EDDY	OTHELLO	black lead
NERO	emperor		Moor
	fiddler		Venetian
NEWTON	ISAAC	OTTO	emperor
	force		German
	not new		perfume
	physicist		race in circles
NICK	Devil		to *turn* to⟨
	notch	PABLO	sailor in P-LO
	prison	PADDY	is Irish
	steal		rage.temper

	rice field
PARIS	kidnapper
PAT	butter
	glib
	is Irish
	light blow
PAUL	Pope
	PRY
	REVERE
	silver coin
	tentmaker
PECKSNIFF	hypocrite
PEDRO	fisherman
PEPYS	diarist
PETER	a Great name
	Bishop of Rum-ti-foo
	Blue boy
	bookmaker
	dwindle away
	fisherman
	flag
	makes sham fabric
	NT book
	PAN
	RABBIT
	safe
	some trum/peter/s
PHIL	fluter
PHILIP	fillip, *say*
	PIP
	sparrow
PICKWICK	clubman
PISTOL	ancient
PLATO	philosopher
POLO	Merchant of Venice
POOTER	nobody
PROCRUSTES	stretcher
PUNCH	tight-fisted character
RABBIE	BURNS
RALPH	imp
	sacred river (R.Alph)
RAMON	NORMA
	Roman
RAPHAEL	archangel
	artist
RAVEL	*in* t/ravel/ogue
	tangle
RAY	bright boy
	fish

	is from Ayr
	light
	sunny chap
	X
REG	man *from* O/reg/on
	short regulation
RENE	DESCARTES
	Frenchman
REYNOLDS	JOSHUA
	PRA
RHET	butler
ROBERT	BRUCE
	BURNS
	peeler
	policeman
ROBIN	ADAIR
	GOODFELLOW
	hob
	HOOD
	is sometimes round
ROGER	acknowledgment.OK
	jolly fellow
	pirate flag
	understood.well received
ROLAND	ARNOLD
	Oliver's mate
	RAT
	RONALD
ROLLO	has bread-round
RON	*something of* an ast/ron/aut
RONALD	ARNOLD
	ROLAND
RUDOLPH	reindeer
RUSSELL	AE
	BERTRAND
SAM	BROWNE
	missile
	together
	Uncle
	WELLER
SAMUEL	bookmaker
	OT book
	PEPYS
	PICKWICK
SANDY	two characters
SETH	ADAMSON
	fourth man
SILAS	*makes* sails
SILVER	AG

783

	pirate		grass
SIMON	PURE		OT book
	Saint.TEMPLAR	TITUS	bookmaker
	simple(ton)		NT book
SLY	tinker		OATES
SMITH	ADAM	TOBIAS	has some prejudice
	besieged Lady		SMOLLETT
	FE	TOBY	BELCH
	forger		jug
	mighty man		Punch's dog
SNUG	joiner	TOM	BOWLING
SOLOMON	bookmaker		(he-)cat
	OT book		fool
	song-writer		peeper
	wise man		piper's son
SOLON	wise man		THUMB
STAN	*is in the* di/stan/ce		TIDDLER
STEPHENSON	rocket designer		uncle
STEVEN	outcry		with Dick and Harry
	voice	TOM EAST	HECATE
STEVENSON	RLS	TOMMY	ATKINS
SULLIVAN	Gilbert's partner		gun
SWIFT	JONATHAN		soldier
	screecher	TONY	theatrical award
SYDNEY	CARTON	TREE	actor
TACITUS	historian	TURNER	WHITTINGTON
TAFFY	flattery	TWAIN	a twin
	is Welsh		author
	sweet		pair.two
TED	can make hay	ULYSSES	GRANT
TEDDY	bear		Greek hero
	ROOSEVELT	URIAH	HEEP
TELL	archer	VALENTINE	
	hill		gentleman of Verona
	utter		tank
TERENCE	old dramatist	VA/LEN/TINO's name	LEN
	RATTIGAN	VICTOR	HUGO
TERRY	towelling		winner
THEO	KOJAK	WALTER	bridegroom
	man in the ring		MITTY
	the love...	WALTER,Sir	SCOTT.Scot
THOMAS	AQUINAS	WAT	TYLER
	doubter	WATT	engine man
TIM	*is from* Bal/tim/ore		power unit
	is tiny		what, *say*
	tim(e) *without end*	WEBSTER	spider
TIMON	Athenian	WELLER	boots
	misanthrope		SAM
TIMOTHY	bookmaker	WHITE	chalky

paleface
part of egg

WHITTINGTON   TURNER
WILL   bard
inclination
man of determination
poet
testament
WRIGHT   early flier
right, *say*

WOMEN

ABIGAIL   has a large drink, *say*
lady's maid
takes a lot of trouble
ADELAIDE   Australian girl
city girl
state capital
AELLO   Harpy
AGATHA   CHRISTIE
crime writer
AGNES   Miss Wickfield
takes some m/agnes/ia
AIDA   opera
slave girl
AILSA   *may be* alias
ALECTO   Fury
ALICE   Australian town
Carroll's girl
CELIA
city girl
band
Miss Liddell
Wonderland girl
ALMA   dancing girl
essense.soul
mother of AL
AMELIA   claims to be Lamb
Miss Scoley
AMI   an /ami/able girl
French friend
AMY   MAY
steeped in inf/amy/
ANITA   LOOS
ANNA   coin.King's associate
royal governess
ANNE   *from* the Ch/anne/l
ANNIE   gun girl

orphan
APHRODITE   *is* atrophied
ATROPOS   Fate
AVA   Miss Gardner
AYESHA   she
BARBARA   ALLEN
Major
BEATRICE   BEA.BEE
thresh grain, *say*
BEATRIX   POTTER
BELLA   Miss Wilfer
BERTHA   bed *with* a...
big gun
falling collar
is a bather
out of breath
BERYL   gem
sparkling girl
BETTY   burglar's jemmy
man doing housework
BEULAH   land of rest
BLANCHE   white
CALLIOPE   Muse
CARMEN   opera girl
CAROL   CARLO
Christmas girl
makes coral
CAROLE   *works* the oracle
CARRIE, *say*   bear
tote
CASSANDRA   accountant's girl
prophetess
CATHARINE   *makes* a nicer hat
CATHERINE   ARAGON
fireworks girl
Great name
CATHY   *makes a* yacht
CELAENO   Harpy
CELESTE   sky-blue
soft pedal
CELIA   ALICE
CICELY   chervil
growing girl
CLARA   BUTT
makes de/clara/tion
CLARE   college girl
in the clear
CLEMENTINE's
father   Forty-niner

Appendix

lived in cavern
miner
CLEO — caught *by* lion
CLIO — Muse
CLOTHO — Fate
CONSTANCE — lady of Lake
CORAL — CAROL
CARLO
DAISY — flower girl
girl cyclist
growing girl
DAPHNE — growing girl
in a shrubbery
DELIA — has daughter by Lamb
I lead *astray*
is ideal
DELILAH — courtesan
Samson's girl
temptress
DELLA — *uses* ladle
DIANA — AIDAN
huntress
NADIA
sort of naiad
princess
DINAH — diner, *say*
might dynamite
nobody finer
DOLLY — carries a camera
easy catch
laundry aid.peg
LLOYD
PARTON
rivet-holder
truck
VARDEN
DOLORES — *has* old rose
DORA — Defence of the Realm Act
Miss Spenlow
Mrs Copperfield
road-*builder*
DORIS — some drink
EDITH — CAVELL
Mrs Dombey
nurse
EFFIE — FE,*say*
ELEANOR — queen
ELECTRA — tragic woman
ELIZA — Higgins's girl

Shaw's girl
ELIZABETH — ER
ELLEN — LN, *say*
one measure after another
TERRY
ELSA — lioness
in sale
ELSIE — ELISE
LC, *say*
EMILY — BRONTE
PANKHURST
suffragette
EMMA — HAMILTON
letter M
MA, *say*
Miss Woodhouse
Nelson's woman
EMMY — ME,*say*
TV award
ENA — is a girl *of* m/ena/ce
ENID — *taken to* dine
ERATO — Muse
ERICA — growing girl
heather
I care *about*
is from Am/erica/n stock
ling
ESTHER — bookmaker
OT book
EU/GENIE/ — girl with spirit
EUTERPE — Muse
EVE — first lady
first mate
is *half* cl/eve/r
leading lady
EVELYN — diarist
EVITA — showgirl
FAITH — trust
with Hope and Charity
FANNY — by gaslight
PRICE
FLEUR — flower girl
growing girl
FLORA — flower girl
growing girl
MACDONALD
ROBSON
FLORENCE — army nurse
city girl

	NIGHTINGALE
FREDA	fared *badly*
GEMMA	bud.growing girl
GEORGE	SAND
GIGI	Joe's double
GINA	*has some* ima/gina/tion
GINA *TURNER*	*makes* <u>gain</u>
GLENDA	*badly* <u>angled</u>
GRACE	darling girl
GRETA	*is a* <u>great</u> girl
GRISELDA	patient
HAZEL	growing girl
	is a nut case
HEATHER	erica.growing girl.ling
HECUBA	tragic woman
HEL	queen of the dead
HELEN	girl from Troy
	he-man
	ship-launcher
HERO	priestess
HOPE	with Faith and Charity
IDA	eider, *say*
	princess
	Fr/ida/y's girl
INGRID	*goes* <u>riding</u>
IO	cowgirl
IRA	*captured by* p/ira/tes
	terrorists
IRENE	*in* d/ire ne/ed
	upsets <u>Ernie</u>
IRIS	flag
	flower girl
	is *almost* Iris(h)
	growing girl
	part of eye
	rainbow
	rainbow goddess
ISABELLA	Miss Wilfer
ISADORA	dancer
	DUNCAN
IVY	climber
	growing girl
JANE	EYRE
	Genoese coin
	JEAN
	Tarzan's mate
	woman
JEAN	cloth
	JANE

	GENE,*say*
	(plural) trousers
JEANETTE	light twilled cotton
	MACDONALD
JENNY	country lass
	in-off
	LIND
	owl
	she ass = assess
	spinner
	womanish man
	wren
JESSIE	effeminate man
JEZEBEL	shameless woman
JILL	flirt
	Jack's girl
JO	sweetheart
JULIET	cap
	CAPULET
JUDY	frump
	girl
	Mrs Punch
	odd-looking woman
JUNE	May's follower
	summer girl
KATE	shrew
KATY	girl who did
	KT, *say*
KAY	after Jay
	K, *say*
KITTY	cat
	jack (bowls)
	(jack)pot
	jail
	pool (cards)
LACHESIS	Fate
LILIAN	*makes* <u>Ian</u> ill
LILITH	Adam's first wife
LILY	flower girl
	growing girl
	lote
	lotus
	of Laguna
	of the valley
LILY MARLENE	war record
LISA	*may be in* <u>sail</u>
	MONA
LOIS	*breaks* <u>soil</u>
	found in <u>silo</u>

LORNA	DOONE
LORRAINE	part of France
LUCY	Miss Locket
LYDIA	*works* daily
	languish
MAB	fairy queen
MABEL	*apportions* blame
	LUCY ATTWELL
	may amble
	MELBA
MAGDALEN(E)	asylum
	college
	hospital
	repentant prostitute
MADGE	barmaid
	magpie
MAME	took the blame
MARGARET	MEG
	peg
MARGUERITE	flower girl
	growing girl
	Queen of Navarre
MARIE	LLOYD
MARINA	*could be* airman
MARTINA	*could be* Martian
MARY	*in the* Army
	MOLL(Y)
	MYRA
	nursery gardener
	shepherdess
MARY's follower	LAMB
MATILDA	bushman's swag
	liar
	tank
	waltzer
MAUD	in the garden
	plaid
MAUD AND RUTH	truth
MAVIS	songbird
	thrush
MAY	AMY
	flower girl
	follower of April
	growing girl
MEG	bit of a nut
	MARGARET
MEGAERA	Fury
MEGAN	million to one girl
	Welsh girl

MELBA	MABEL
	takes blame
MELISSA	*is* aimless
MELPOMENE	Muse
MERLE	blackbird
	OBERON
MEROPE	tragic woman
MILDRED	of the soft left
	pinkish girl
MIMI	dual carriageway
	has very cold hand
	seamstress
MINNIE	mine
	moaner
	MOUSE
MIRIAM	right *in* Miami
MOIRA	could be Maori
MOLL	FLANDERS
	gangster's girl
MOLLY	little Mary
	milksop
MONA	island
	LISA
MOPP, Mrs	char
MYRA	*in the* Army
	MARY
MYRTLE	growing girl
	in the shrubbery
NADIA	AIDAN
	DIANA
NANCY	city girl
	effeminate male
	French city
	milksop
NAOMI	*brokenly* I moan
	is not ruthless
	Ruth's friend
NELL	a Little woman
	Charlie's girl
	knell, *say*
	orange-seller
NELLY	petrel
NETTA	*retires* at ten
NIOBE	daughter of Tantalus
	stone maiden
	weeper
NORA	is no painter
NORMA	constellation
	may be Roman

nearly norma(l)	
opera girl	
standard article	
OCYPETE	Harpy
OLGA	*in* <u>gaol</u>
	in <u>goal</u>
OLIVE	colour
	drab
	fruit
	growing girl
	in the drink
	OBE
	stony-hearted
	wood
PANSY	effeminate man
	flower girl
	growing girl
PARTLETT, Mrs	hen
PATIENCE	card game
	kind of dock
	sufferance
PEARL	can handle a gun
	gem
	gets fruit *by* the pound
	grey
	loop of lace
	may be <u>paler</u>
	purl,*say*
	type size
	WHITE
	woman of wisdom
PEG	dolly
	takes hat and coat
PEGGY	roofing slate
	warbler
	whitethroat
PHOEBE	ARTEMIS
	moon-goddess
PIGGY, Miss	gilt
PODARGE	Harpy
POLLY	parrot
	pretty girl
	repetitive type
POLYHYMNIA	Muse
PRIMROSE	flower girl
	growing girl
	League
PRUDENCE	caution
PYTHIA	priestess

RACHEL	du Maurier's cousin
REBECCA	Mrs de Winter
	Welsh rioter
REGAN	Lear's daughter.princess
	wicked sister
RENEE	born again
RITA	*found in* B/rita/in
ROSE	colour
	flower girl
	growing girl
	is from Picardy
	is from Tralee
	sprinkler
	stood up
	wine
ROSEMARY	growing girl
	in the shrubbery
	cider drinker
ROSIE	<u>osier</u> *weaver*
	tea girl
RUBY	kind of gem
	kind of type
	sparkling girl
RUTH	babe
	bookmaker
	friend of Naomi
	gleaner
	OT book
	pity
	wife of Boaz
SADIE	*changes* <u>aides</u>
	has peculiar <u>ideas</u>
SELINA	*is* <u>saline</u>
SALLY	aunt
	flight
	part of bellrope
	quip
	repartee
	sortie
	willow
	witty girl
SALOME	dancing girl
	stripper
SHEILA	Aussie girl
	ELISHA
SIBYL	prophetess
	sorceress
SOPHIA	wisdom
SUE	will prosecute

Appendix

SUSIE	*may take* issue	VESTA	goddess
SYLVIA	warbler		match
TABITHA	*has strange* habitat		planet
TERESA	Easter *break*		TILLEY
TESS	Hardy's girl	VICTORIA	carriage
	Miss Durbeyfield		city girl
	Wessex girl		plum
THATCHER, Mrs	MAGGIE.MEG		queen
THELMA	*makes* Hamlet *mad*		station
TINA	metal article		water lily
TISIPHONE	Muse	VIOLA	fiddle
UNA	*some* l/una/tic		flower girl
URANIA	Muse		growing girl
VANESSA	butterfly		pansy
	Red Admiral	VIRGINIA	creeper
VENUS	is (h)armless		growing girl
VERA	a/vera/ge girl		stock
	magnetic recorder		tobacco
VERONICA	growing girl		US state
	in shrubbery		VA
	pass in the bullring		water
	patron saint of bullring	WENDY	housemaid
	speedwell		